How to Prepare for the
PSAT/
NMSQT

Preliminary SAT*/National Merit Scholarship Qualifying Test

Ninth Edition

SAMUEL C. BROWNSTEIN

Former Chairman, Science Department
George W. Wingate High School, Brooklyn, New York

MITCHEL WEINER

Former Member, Department of English
James Madison High School, Brooklyn, New York

SHARON WEINER GREEN

Former Instructor in English
Merritt College, Oakland, California

BARRON'S

*SAT is a registered trademark of the College Entrance
Examination Board, which does not endorse this book.

All inquiries should be addressed to:
Barron's Educational Series, Inc.
250 Wireless Boulevard
Hauppauge, New York 11788

Library of Congress Catalog Card No. 96-36567

International Standard Book No. 0-8120-9639-8

Library of Congress Cataloging-in-Publication Data

Brownstein, Samuel C.
    PSAT/NMSQT : how to prepare for the Preliminary SAT/
National Merit Scholarship Qualifying Test / Samuel C.
Brownstein, Mitchel Weiner, Sharon Weiner Green.—9th ed.
        p.   cm.
    ISBN 0-8120-9639-8
    1. Preliminary SAT—Study guides.   2. National merit
scholarship qualifying test—Study guides.   I. Weiner, Mitchel.
II. Green, Sharon. III. Title.
LB2353.56.B76   1997   96-36567
378.1'662—dc20   CIP

PRINTED IN THE UNITED STATES OF AMERICA

9 8 7 6 5

Contents

Writing Skills

Mathematical Reasoning

TEST YOURSELF

Preface

Welcome to the Ninth Edition of Barron's *How to Prepare for the PSAT/NMSQT*. If you are preparing for today's new PSAT, this is the book you need.

Over the past four years our research staff has been analyzing all released versions of the PSAT and SAT I. The result of our investigations is in your hands.

This Ninth Edition represents a solid update of America's leading book focused on the PSAT. Containing the best of the time-tested features of earlier editions, today's Ninth Edition provides much, much more.

It features eleven full-length model tests based on the new PSAT in length and difficulty, eleven crucial "dress rehearsals" for the day you walk into the examination room.

It preps you for the *new* writing skills section, teaching you how to spot errors and polish rough drafts so that you can conquer today's PSAT.

It briefs you on the vocabulary-in-context and critical reading questions, giving you key tips on how to tackle these important verbal question types.

It takes you step by step through the double reading passages, showing you how to work your way through a pair of reading passages without wasting effort or time.

It introduces you to the non-multiple-choice questions in the mathematics section, teaching you shortcuts to solving problems and entering your own answers on a sample grid.

It offers you advice on how (and when) to use a calculator in dealing with both multiple-choice and "grid-in" questions.

It gives you the *newly revised* 257-word PSAT High Frequency Word List, 257 vital words that have been shown by computer analysis to occur and reoccur on actual published PSATs, plus Barron's PSAT Basic Word List, more than 1,300 words that you'll want to master as you work to build a college-level vocabulary. For quick study, there's also a section on Basic Word Parts.

No other book tells you as much about the test. No other book offers you as many questions modeled on the new PSAT.

The PSAT is your chance to get yourself set for the tests ahead—SAT I and SAT II. It's also your chance to qualify for some of the nation's most prestigious college scholarships. Go for your personal best; take the time to learn how to prepare for the PSAT.

This Ninth Edition of Barron's *How to Prepare for the PSAT/NMSQT* is a sign of Barron's ongoing commitment to make this publication America's outstanding PSAT study guide. It has benefited from the dedicated labors of the editorial staff of Barron's, in particular Max Reed, and from the critical insights of George Ehrenhaft and Lexy Green. We are greatly indebted to them.

Acknowledgments

The authors gratefully acknowledge all those sources who granted permission to use materials from their publications:

Page 8: From *Summer of '49* by David Halberstam, William Morrow & Co., Inc. ©1989, pp. 42–44.

Pages 8–9: From *Take Time for Paradise* by permission of the Estate of A. Bartlett Giamatti, published by Summit Books, a division of Simon and Schuster, New York, Copyright © 1989, pp. 40–41.

Page 29: From "Ruin" in *Dove of the East and Other Stories* by Mark Helprin, Laurel Books (Dell), New York, 1975, pp. 41–43.

Pages 30–31: From *Bury My Heart at Wounded Knee* by Dee Brown, © 1981, pp. xi–xiii. Reprinted with permission of Henry Holt & Co., Inc.

Page 41: From *The Forest* by Peter Farb, Time-Life Books, Alexandria, VA, 1980, pp. 75–76.

Page 42: From "A Modern Dancer's Primer for Action" by Martha Graham in *Dance: A Basic Educational Technique*, edited by Selma Jean Cohen, Macmillan, New York, 1941 in *Dance as a Theatre Art*, Dodd Mead, New York, 1974, pp. 135–137.

Pages 42–43: From *The Chez Panisse Menu Cookbook* by Alice Waters copyright © 1982, Reprinted with permission of Random House.

Pages 83, 84, 86, 87, and 88: From "The Odds Are You're Innumerate" by John Allen Paulos in *The New York Times Book Review*, January 1, 1989, pp. 16–17.

Page 99: From "The Birth of Massive Stars" by Michael Zelik in *Scientific American Inc.*, April 1978.

Page 102: From *The English Novel: Form and Function* by Dorothy Van Ghent copyright © 1953, 1981. Holt, Rhinehart and Winston, Inc.

Page 105: From *Rodents* by Peter W. Hanney, Taplinger Publishing Company, Inc., New York, 1975, pp. 103–104.

Page 222: From *King Solomon's Ring* by Konrad Z. Lorenz, © 1952, Harper & Row, pp. 128–129.

Pages 223–224: From *From Slavery to Freedom,* by John Hope Franklin. Copyright © 1980 by Alfred A. Knopf, Inc., pp. 325–327.

Pages 232–233: From "Renaissance to Modern Tapestries in the Metropolitan Museum of Art" by Edith Appleton Standen in *Metropolitan Museum Bulletin*, Spring 1987, pp. 4, 6.

Page 234: From "Yonder Peasant, Who Is He?" by Mary McCarthy in *Memories of a Catholic Girlhood,* copyright © 1948 and 1975, pp. 5–7. Reprinted with permission of Harcourt Brace & Co.

Pages 234–235: From *Reinventing Womanhood* by Caroline G. Heilbrun. copyright © 1979. Reprinted with permission of W.W. Norton & Company, Inc., pp. 56–57.

Page 252: From "Medicine's Home Front" in *The Economist,* June 6, 1987, p. 86.

Page 264: From *Geoffrey Chaucer* by John Livingston Lowes, Copyright © 1934, renewed 1955 by John Wilbur Lowes. With permission of Houghton Mifflin Co.

Page 282: From "So Many Female Rivals" by Christine Froula, copyright © 1988, 1989, *The New York Times Book Review,* February 7, 1988, pp. 12–13.

Pages 283–284: From *The Eyes on the Prize Civil Rights Reader* by Clayborne Carson et al. Copyright © 1991 by Blackside, Inc. used by permission of Viking Penguin, a division of Penguin Books USA Inc., pp. 54–55.

Page 294: From *Native Stranger: A Black American's Journey into the Heart of Africa* by Eddy L. Harris, with permission of Simon & Schuster, copyright © 1992, pp. 31–33.

Pages 295–296: From *The Greenpeace Book of Dolphins* edited by John May, © 1990. By permission of Greenpeace.

Pages 316–317: From *I Love Paul Revere, Whether He Rode or Not* by Richard Shenkman © 1991, HarperCollins Publishers.

Pages 317–318: From *One Writer's Beginnings* by Eudora Welty, Harvard University Press, Cambridge, 1984, pp. 3–5.

Page 329: From *The Soul of the Night* by Chet Raymo, © 1985, pp. 68–70. With permission of the author.

Pages 329–330: From "The Most Wanted Particle" by J. Madeleine Nash, *Time,* January 11, 1993, p. 41. Copyright 1993 Time Inc. Reprinted by permission.

Pages 349–350: From "Huge Conservation Effort Aims to Save Vanishing Architect of the Savanna" by William K. Stevens, copyright © 1988, 1989 *The New York Times,* February 28, 1989, pp. C1, C15.

Pages 358–359: From *Black Americans in the Roosevelt Era* by John B. Kirby, University of Tennessee Press, copyright © 1980.

Page 360: From "Let's Say You Wrote Badly This Morning" by David Huddle in *The Writing Habit,* University Press of New England, Hanover, 1994.

Pages 360–361: From "My Two One–Eyed Coaches" by George Garrett. First published in *The Virginia Quarterly Review,* 1987.

Pages 381–382: From *A Garlic Testament: Seasons on a Small New Mexico Farm* by Stanley Crawford, HarperCollins Publishers, © 1992, pp. 181–183.

Pages 391–392: From "Standards" by E. L. Doctorow. First published in *Harper's,* 1991. By permission of International Creative Management, Inc.

Page 393: From *Take Time for Paradise* by permission of the Estate of A. Bartlett Giamatti, published by Summit, © 1989, pp. 48–50.

Page 393: From *City* by William H. Whyte. By permission of Doubleday, New York, © 1989, p. 341.

Pages 413–414: From "W. E. B. Du Bois: Protagonist of the Afro-American Protest" in *Black Leaders of the Twentieth Century* edited by John Hope Franklin and August Meier, by permission of University of Illinois Press, © 1982.

Pages 423–424: From "The Subduction of the Lithosphere" by M. Nafi Toksöz in *Scientific American Inc.,* November 1975, p. 88.

Page 425: From "Introduction" in *A Treasury of Satire* edited by Edgar Johnson, S&S, New York, 1945, pp. 36–37.

Page 425: From "The Tornado" by John T. Snow in *Scientific American Inc.,* April 1984, pp. 41–42.

Pages 447–448: From *An American Childhood* by Annie Dillard, HarperCollins Publishers, Inc., © 1987, pp. 74–77.

Pages 457–458: From *The Overworked American: The Unexpected Decline of Leisure* by Juliet B. Schor. Copyright © 1991 by Basic Books, Inc. Reprinted by permission of Harper Collins Publishers Inc., pp. 10–11.

Page 459: From "Women and Fiction" in *Granite & Rainbows* by Virginia Woolf, © 1958 by Leonard Woolf and renewed by M.T. Parsons, Executor of Leonard Sidney Woolf, reprinted by permission of Harcourt Brace & Co. pp. 43–44.

Pages 459–460: From *A Literature of Their Own* by Elaine Showalter, Princeton University Press, Princeton, 1977, pp. 10–12.

Page 478: From "The Captain's Dinner" © 1982 by M.F.K. Fisher in *As They Were,* Alfred A. Knopf. Reprinted with permission.

Pages 479–480: Reprinted by permission of the publishers from *Century of Struggle: The Woman's Rights Movement in the United States* by Eleanor Flexner, Cambridge, Mass.: Harvard University Press, copyright © 1959, 1975 by Eleanor Flexner, pp. 222–223.

Pages 489–490: From *Athabasca* by Alistair MacLean © 1980, with permission of Doubleday, pp. 3–4.

Page 491: From *Our Marvelous Native Tongue,* copyright © 1983 by Robert Claiborne. Reprinted by permission of Times Books, a division of Random House, Inc. pp. 222–223, 226–227.

Pages 510–511: From *Black History and the Historical Professions* by August Meier and Elliot Rudwick, by permission of University of Illinois Press, © 1986.

Pages 511–512: From *What Mad Pursuit* by Francis Crick, M.D. Copyright © 1988 by Francis Crick, M.D. Reprinted by permission of Basic Books, a division of HarperCollins Publishers Inc., pp. 24–26.

Page 523: From "The Feeling of Flying" by Samuel Hynes. First published in *The Sewanee Review,* vol. 95, no. 1, Winter. 1987. Reprinted with permission of the editor and the author.

Pages 523–524: From "The Stunt Pilot" by Annie Dillard, © 1989, in *The Best American Essays,* Ticknor & Fields.

PSAT/NMSQT test directions, College Entrance Examination Board and Educational Testing Service, 1997. Reprinted by permission of the College Entrance Examination Board and Educational Testing Service, the copyright owners.

PSAT/NMSQT ACTUAL TEST TIME: 2 HOURS AND 10 MINUTES

Section 1
Verbal Reasoning
    sentence completion
    reading comprehension
	25 minutes	26 questions

Section 2 Mathematical Reasoning multiple choice	25 minutes	20 questions

Section 3
Writing Skills
    find-the-error
    sentence correction
    paragraph correction
	30 minutes	39 questions

	BREAK	

Section 4
Verbal Reasoning
    analogies
    reading comprehension
	25 minutes	26 questions

Section 5
Mathematical Reasoning
    quantitative comparison
    student–produced response
	25 minutes	20 questions

1

The Preliminary SAT/ National Merit Scholarship Qualifying Test

Your plan to take the PSAT/NMSQT is perhaps your first concrete step toward planning a college career. PSAT/NMSQT, SAT I—what do they mean to you? When do you take them? Where? What sort of hurdle do you face? How do these tests differ from the tests you ordinarily face in school? In this chapter we answer these basic questions so that you will be able to move on to the following chapters and concentrate on preparing yourself for this test.

SOME BASIC QUESTIONS ANSWERED

What is the PSAT/NMSQT?

The PSAT/NMSQT is a standardized test designed to measure your ability to do college work. Students sometimes are able to take it on a practice basis in junior high school. High school students get to take it "for real" early in their junior year.

The test consists of five sections, two testing verbal reasoning skills, two testing mathematical reasoning skills, and one testing writing skills. Fifty minutes is allowed for answering the verbal questions, fifty for the math questions, and thirty minutes for the writing questions.

Why is the test called the PSAT/NMSQT?

This preliminary SAT is also the qualifying test for the scholarship competitions conducted by the National Merit Scholarship Corporation (NMSC). NMSC used to offer a separate examination, but began cosponsoring this test in 1971.

What are Merit Scholarships?

Merit Scholarships are prestigious national awards that carry with them a chance for solid financial aid. Conducted by NMSC, an independent, nonprofit organization with offices at One America Plaza, Evanston, Illinois 60201, the Merit Program today is supported by grants from over 600 corporations, private foundations, colleges and universities, and other organizations. The top-scoring PSAT/NMSQT participants in every state are named Semifinalists. Those who advance to Finalist standing by meeting additional requirements compete for one-time National Merit $2000 Scholarships and renewable, four-year Merit Scholarships, which may be worth as much as $8,000 a year for four years.

What is the National Achievement Scholarship Program for Outstanding Black Students?

This is a program aimed at honoring and assisting promising black high school students throughout the country. It is also administered by NMSC. Students who enter the Merit Program by taking the PSAT/NMSQT and who are also eligible to participate in the Achievement Program mark a space on their test answer sheets asking to enter this competition as well. Top-scoring black students in each of the regions established for the competition compete for nonrenewable National Achievement $2,000 Scholarships and for four-year Achievement Scholarships supported by more than 1,775 sponsor organizations. *Note*: To be considered for this program, you *must* mark the appropriate space on your answer sheet.

How can the PSAT/NMSQT help me?

If you are a high school junior, it will help you see just how able you are to do college work. It will give you some idea of which colleges you should apply to in your senior year. It will give you access to scholarship competitions. It will definitely give you practice in an important factor.

In addition, you may choose to take advantage of the College Board's Student Search Service. This service is free for students who fill out the biographical section of the PSAT/NMSQT. If you fill out this section, you will receive mail from colleges and search programs.

How do I apply for this test?

You apply through your school. Fees, when required, are collected by your school. The test is given in October. In December the results are sent to your school and to the scholarship program that you indicated on your answer sheet in the examination room.

What makes the Preliminary SAT different from other tests?

The PSAT is trying to measure your ability to reason using facts that are part of your general knowledge or facts that are included in your test booklet. You're not required to recall great chunks of history or literature or science. You're not even required to recall most math formulas—they're printed in the test booklet.

Your score depends upon how many correct answers you get within a definite period of time. Speed is important. So is accuracy. You have to pace yourself so that you don't sacrifice speed to gain accuracy (or sacrifice accuracy to gain speed).

How is the new PSAT different from the old PSAT?

It's ten minutes longer and now tests three areas: critical reading, math problem-solving, and writing skills. The old PSAT consisted of two 30-minute verbal sections (sixty questions in all) and two 30-minute math sections (fifty questions). The new PSAT consists of five sections: two 25-minute verbal sections (fifty-two questions total), two 25-minute math sections (forty questions), and one 30-minute writing skills section (thirty-nine questions). To do well on this new test, you must demonstrate solid verbal proficiency.

How is the new PSAT different from SAT I?

The PSAT is a mini version of SAT I. For most students, it serves as a practice test. The new PSAT takes two hours and ten minutes. SAT I takes three hours. You have to answer fewer verbal and math questions on the PSAT than you do on SAT I; however, some of them are real stumpers.

The new PSAT also serves as a preview of the SAT II: Subject Test in Writing. The writing skills section of the new PSAT has the same kinds of multiple-choice questions as the SAT II: Subject Test in Writing. There are just fewer of them.

Is it smart to leave answers blank?

Probably not. But don't just make wild guesses. Wild guessing *will* lower your final score, because the test-makers subtract a fraction of your wrong answers from the number of your correct answers. Wrong answers *do* count against you on the test, so you may think that you should never guess if you aren't sure of the right answer to a question. But even if you guessed wrong four times for every time you guessed right, you would still come out even. A wrong answer costs you only ¼ of a point (⅓ on the quantitative comparison questions). On the multiple-choice questions, the best advice is to guess if you can eliminate one or two of the answer choices. You have a better chance of hitting the right answer when you make this sort of "educated" guess.

As you go through this book, try this experiment to find out what kind of guesser you are. First, take part of any test that you have not taken before. You don't have to take an entire test section, but you should take at least twenty questions (fifteen in math). Answer only those questions to which you *definitely* know the answers. See what your score is.

Next, take the same test section. Do not change any of your original answers, but whenever you can make an educated guess on one of the questions you originally skipped, do it. See what your score is now. Finally, retake the same test section, this time guessing blindly to answer all the remaining questions.

Compare your scores from the three different approaches to the test. For most people, the second score (the one with the educated guesses) will be the best one. But you may be different. Maybe you are such a poor guesser that you should never guess at all. Or maybe you are such a good guesser that you should try every question. The important thing is to know yourself.

What tactics can help me get ready for the PSAT?

1. Memorize the directions for each type of question. These are only slightly different from the exact words you'll find on the PSAT. The test time you would normally spend reading directions can be better spent answering questions.
2. Know the test. In the verbal sections, you will have reading passages with reading comprehension questions that measure critical reading skills and knowledge of vocabulary in context. There will also be questions involving analogies and sentence completion. In the math sections, you will find standard multiple choice, quantitative comparisons, and student-produced response questions. In the writing skills section, you will encounter find-the-error questions, sentence correction questions, and paragraph correction questions. The number of questions breaks down as follows:

52 Verbal Questions (2 Sections, 25 Minutes Each)
13 sentence completion questions
13 analogy questions
26 critical reading questions

40 Math Questions (2 Sections, 25 Minutes Each)
20 standard multiple-choice questions
12 quantitative comparison questions
8 student-produced response (grid-in) questions

38 Writing Skills Questions (1 Section, 30 Minutes)
19 find-the-error questions
14 sentence correction questions
6 paragraph correction questions

3. Expect easy questions at the beginning of each set of the same question type. Within each set (except for the reading comprehension questions), the questions progress from easy to difficult. In other words, the first analogy question in a set will be easier than the last analogy in that set; the first quantitative comparison question will be easier than the last quantitative comparison question.

4. Take advantage of the easy questions to boost your score. Remember, each question is worth the same number of points. Whether it was easy or difficult, whether it took you ten seconds or two minutes to answer, you get the same number of points for each question you answer correctly. Your job is to answer as many questions as you possibly can without rushing ahead so fast that you make careless errors or lose points for failing to give some questions enough thought. So take enough time to get those easy questions right!

5. *First* answer all the easy questions; *then* tackle the hard ones if you have time. You know that the questions in each segment of the test get harder as you go along (except for the reading comprehension questions). But there's no rule that says you have to answer the questions in order. You're allowed to skip. So, if the last three analogy questions are driving you crazy, move on to the reading passages right away. Likewise, don't let yourself get bogged down on a difficult quantitative comparison question when only three questions away the easy "grid" questions begin. Test-wise students know when it's time to move on.

6. Eliminate as many wrong answers as you can. Deciding between two choices is easier than deciding among five. Even if you have to guess, every answer you eliminate improves your chances of guessing correctly.

7. Change answers only if you have a reason for doing so. Don't give in to last-minute panic. It's usually better for you not to change your answers on a sudden hunch or whim.

8. Now that calculators are permitted in the test room, bring along a calculator you are comfortable using. No question on the test will *require* the use of a calculator, but if you are experienced using one, it may be helpful for some questions. Almost any standard calculator will do: four-function, scientific, and graphing calculators all are allowed. However, printer-calculators, pocket organizers, palm-top minicomputers, and lap-tops are not.

9. Be careful not to make any stray marks on your answer sheet. This test is graded by a machine, and a machine cannot tell the difference between an accidental mark and a filled-in answer. When the machine sees two marks instead of one, it calls the answer wrong.

10. Check frequently to make sure you are answering the questions in the right spots. No machine is going to notice that you made a mistake early in the test, answered question 4 in the space for question 5, and all your following answers are in the wrong place. (One way to avoid this problem is to mark your answers in your test booklet and transfer them to your answer sheet by blocks.)

11. Line up your test book with your answer sheet. Whether you choose to fill in the answers question by question or in blocks, you will do so most efficiently if you keep your test book and your answer sheet aligned.

12. Be particularly careful in marking the student-produced responses on the math grid. Before you fill in the appropriate blanks, write your answer at the top of the columns. Then go down each column, making sure you're marking only the right spaces.

13. Don't get bogged down on any one question. By the time you get to the actual PSAT, you should have a fair idea of how much time to spend on each question. If a question is taking too long, leave it and go on to the next question. This is no time to try to show the world that you can stick to a job no matter how long it takes. All the machine that grades the test will notice is that after a certain point you didn't have any correct answers.

How can I prevent PSAT anxiety from setting in?

1. The best way to prepare for any test you ever take is to get a good night's sleep before the test so that you are well rested and alert.

2. Eat breakfast for once in your life. You have a full morning ahead of you. You should have a full stomach as well.

3. Allow plenty of time for getting to the test site. Taking a test is pressure enough. You don't need the extra tension that comes from worrying about whether you will get there on time.

4. Recognize how long this is going to take. There are five sections. They will take two hours and ten minutes total. Add to that a ten-minute break midway in the test, plus thirty minutes for paper pushing. If the test starts at 9 A.M., don't make a dentist appointment for 11:30. You can't possibly get there on time, and you'll just spend the last half hour of the test worrying about it.

5. The College Board traditionally tells you to bring two sharpened No. 2 pencils to the test. Bring four. They

don't weigh much, and this might be the one day in the decade when two pencil points decide to break. And bring full-size pencils, not little stubs. They are easier to write with, and you might as well be comfortable.

6. Speaking of being comfortable, wear comfortable clothes. This is a test, not a fashion show. Aim for the layered look. Wear something light, but bring a sweater. The test room may be hot, or it may be cold. You can't change the room, but you can put on the sweater.

7. Bring an accurate watch. You need one. The room in which you take the test may not have a clock, and some proctors are not very good about posting the time on the blackboard. Don't depend on them. Each time you begin a test section, write down in your booklet the time according to your watch. That way you will always know how much time you have left.

8. The use of a calculator is permitted but not required. Bring a calculator you are comfortable using. No question on the test will *require* the use of a calculator, but if you have experience using one, it will be helpful for some questions.

9. Smuggle in some quick energy in your pocket—trail mix, raisins, a candy bar. Even if the proctors don't let you eat in the test room, you can still grab a bite en route to the rest rooms during the ten-minute break. Taking the test can leave you feeling

drained and in need of a quick pickup—bring along your favorite comfort food.

10. There will be a break midway through the test. Use this period to clear your thoughts. Take a few deep breaths. Stretch. Close your eyes and imagine yourself floating or sun-bathing. In addition to being under mental pressure, you're under physical pressure from being stuck so long in an uncomfortable seat with a No. 2 pencil clutched in your hand. Anything you can do to loosen up and get the kinks out will ease your body and help the oxygen get to your brain.

How are the results of your PSAT/NMSQT reported?

About six to eight weeks after the test, you will receive, through your school, the following:

(1) a Report of Student Answers with your scores
(2) a copy of the answers you gave
(3) a copy of the correct answers
(4) a Selection Index, which identifies those eligible for NMSC programs
(5) a copy of the original test booklet which you used in the examination room
(6) a booklet entitled "About Your PSAT/NMSQT Scores," which helps you interpret your scores and gives you advice about college planning.

ABOUT CALCULATORS

Here are some comments, along with some questions and answers that are often asked, regarding the use of a calculator.

May you bring a calculator to the examination room?

Yes. The use of the calculator on the math section of the PSAT is recommended but not required. Do not expect the solution to any problem to require the use of the calculator.

What type of calculator is permitted for use at the test room?

You may bring a *four-function*, scientific, or graphing calculator but you may not bring calculators with paper tape or printer, hand-held minicomputers, pocket organizers, or laptop computers.

Know your calculator; there are many different models on the market. Bring to the test room a model with which you are familiar. Don't buy a sophisticated calculator for the test. Some have keys that are not exactly like the ones on the model you use. The calculator will help you only if you strike the right keys. It is wise to estimate the result of making calculations. Bear in mind that adding whole numbers will result in a larger whole number and that the average

of several numbers is between the largest and the smallest numbers.

The Arithmetic Operations

The arithmetic operations of addition, subtraction, multiplication, and division are possible on all calculators; therefore, the term *four-function* is used. A manual usually accompanies your calculator; study it to become familiar with your calculator and all its functions. The use of the number keys is obvious. This is also true for the four basic operation keys: $\boxed{+}$ $\boxed{-}$ $\boxed{\times}$ $\boxed{\div}$. Bear in mind that your calculator will make an error only if *you* make an error. If you discover that you hit the wrong key, you may clear your last entry by pressing the CLEAR KEY once. This key may appear on your calculator as: $\boxed{\text{CLR}}$ $\boxed{\text{C E/C}}$ $\boxed{\text{C/CE}}$ or $\boxed{\text{ON/C}}$. The CLEAR KEY will not clear an operation symbol. If you pressed the wrong key and produced the wrong operation, you must redo the problem; however, in some models you may be able to remove the wrong symbol by pressing the CLEAR KEY twice or by pressing the ON/AC key.

Using the Percent Key

In order to compute a percent, you must put it in decimal form. The $\boxed{\%}$ key changes a percent to decimal form. For example, to find 25% of 440, enter 440, then ✕ , then 25, then % . The display will show 110. Note that it was not necessary to enter the equal = sign. On some models, to do this problem you must first enter 25, then % , then ✕ , then the = key to have 110 displayed. Know your calculator! Mathematically, 440 times 25% is the same as 25% of 440, but your calculator will accept only the first of these. (You can, however, convert the 25 to .25 and multiply times 440.)

A second type of percent problem asks you to find what percent one number is of another. To solve such problems, divide the first number by the second and use the % key to change the quotient to a percent. For example: What must you pay for a book marked $12.00 in a town where a sales tax of 8.5% is charged? Solution: $12.00 + 8.5% of $12.00 is the cost of the book. On the calculator enter 12, then press + then enter 8.5, then press % and the display will show $13.02 without the need to enter the marked price twice.

The following example demonstrates how the calculator saves time with double percentage problems. A radio marked $149.50 is on sale at a 20% discount. What is the cost of this radio during the sale in a town that has a 7% sales tax?

Solution: $149.50 less 20% plus 7% is the cost of the radio during the sale period. On the calculator enter 149.50, then press − then 20, then % . The display will show 119.60, to which the sales tax must be added. Then press the + key, then 7, then % . The display will show 127.972, which you will round out to $127.97.

Now try these: (1) What is 20% of $720? (2) What is the final cost of an import valued at $540, to which a tax of 30% is added? (3) What is the cost of an item marked $800 when a 20% discount is allowed?

Correct Answers: (1) $144, (2) $702, (3) $640.

Powers and Roots

The expression 6^3 means $6 \times 6 \times 6$. In other words, 6 is to be used as a factor 3 times. The base is 6 and the exponent is 3. If you are using a scientific calculator, you have a key that computes the value of the power; otherwise, you can compute the value of the power by using multiplication. If your calculator has an x^2 key, enter the base and then press the x^2 key. Some examples: What is the value of 22.5^2? Solution: Using the special key x^2 , enter 22.5, then press the special key x^2 and 506.25 will appear. By multiplication, enter 22.5, then press the ✕ key, then enter 22.5, and 506.25 will appear. Again, know your calculator! Some calculators do not require entering the base each time. For example, to find the value of 3.5^5, enter 3.5, then press the ✕ key, then enter the = sign four times. Remember, in the first multiplication, the base (3.5) is used as a factor twice. For that reason multiplication is performed three more times. For the value of 3.5^5 did you get 525.21875? Using the suggested method, find the value of 7^6. Did you get 117649?

Square Root

The square root of a number is one of two equal factors of a number. Your calculator has a key marked √ or $\sqrt{x}$. To find the square root of 7225 enter 7225, then press the √ key. Without pressing the = key, 85 will appear. Now try these: What is $\sqrt{5329}$? Did you get 73? Try $\sqrt{729}$. Did you get 27?

When do you use the calculator in the exam room?

Don't use the calculator more than you have to. You are expected to do simple arithmetic computations. Even if you encounter a complicated computation, don't rush to use the calculator. First decide on a strategy for solving the problem, and then decide whether the calculator will be helpful. Examine the following two examples, which can be solved with the calculator but can also be solved using methods that you may find easier.

Examples:

$$\frac{87955936}{284} \text{ equals exactly}$$

(A) 309701
(B) 309702
(C) 309703
(D) 309704
(E) 309705

Observe that the answer choices are similar except for the last integer. Note the last integer of the numerator and the last digit of the denominator. Use your eyes instead of the calculator, and you will quickly see that the last integer of the numerator (the dividend) is 6 and the last integer of the denominator (the divisor) is 4. Therefore, the quotient must have a last integer of 4 or 9. Since none of the choices end in 9, choose (D).

$$\text{If } x = \left(\frac{2}{3}\right)\left(\frac{3}{4}\right)\left(\frac{2}{5}\right), \text{ then } x =$$

Rather than use the calculator, you should cancel the common factors:

$$\frac{\left(\frac{2}{3}\right)\left(\frac{3}{4}\right)\left(\frac{2}{5}\right)}{2}$$

and come up with the answer $\frac{1}{5}$.

Here are some types of questions for which you may find the calculator useful. In each case ask yourself whether the calculator is a time-saver.

1. In quantitative comparison questions you may have to compare fractions like

    $$\frac{7}{8} \text{ and } \frac{8}{9}$$

    According to a calculator, $\frac{7}{8} = 7 \div 8 = 0.875$, and $\frac{8}{9} = 8 \div 9 = 0.888 \ldots$ Hence, $\frac{8}{9}$ is greater than $\frac{7}{8}$.

2. In applying the Pythagorean theorem, you may be dealing with squares and square roots. For example:

    In right triangle *ABC*, *AB* = 12, *BC* = 15. What is the length of base *CA?*

    Let *CA* = *x*; then

    $$x^2 + 12^2 = 15^2$$
    $$x^2 + 144 = 225$$
    $$x^2 = 81$$
    $$x = \sqrt{81} = 9$$

    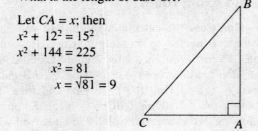

3. Some problems involve simple arithmetic. Whether you decide to use a calculator may depend on your power of observation:

    Wynn Miller has the following charges on her monthly credit card: $28.75, $75.28, $104.03. She decides to pay half the charges now. If she does so, what will her balance be?

    (A) $28.75
    (B) $75.28
    (C) $104.03
    (D) $150.56
    (E) $208.06

    You will obtain choice (C) as the answer if you find the sum of the figures with your calculator and then divide this sum by 2. You don't need the calculator if you observe that the third charge ($104.03) is equal to the sum of the first two and is therefore equal to one-half the total.

4. This question asks for several quotients that can be obtained quickly and accurately with a calculator:

Which of the following is the least expensive item?

(A) 5 for $21
(B) $21 for 6
(C) 8 for $23
(D) $42 for 12
(E) 7 for $42

The calculator gives the following results: (A) $21 \div 5 = \$4.20$ each; (B) $21 \div 6 =$ less than $4.20 each; (C) $23 \div 8 = \$2.875$ each; (D) $42 \div 12 = \$3.50$ each; (E) $42 \div 7 = \$6$ each. The correct answer is (C).

5. To find the cubes of several numbers, the calculator may save time. Try this question:

    How many numbers from 1 to 100 inclusive have cubes that do not exceed 100?

    (A) 1 (B) 2 (C) 3 (D) 4 (E) 5

    Make a chart as follows:

Number	Cube of Number		
1	$1 \times 1 \times 1$	=	1
2	$2 \times 2 \times 2$	=	8
3	$3 \times 3 \times 3$	=	27
4	$4 \times 4 \times 4$	=	64
5	$5 \times 5 \times 5$	=	125

    Reject (E) since 125 is more than 100.
    The correct choice is (D).

6. With some questions you need to decide what strategy you will use to solve the problem. The calculator can then make the compuation easier:

    Waban has an adult population of 60,000. There are, on average, 1.2 adults in each household in this town. Each household has an average of 2.1 children of school age. How many children of school age (in thousands) live in Waban?

    (A) 105
    (B) 110
    (C) 150
    (D) 151
    (E) 238

    Using a calculator, $60,000 \div 1.2 = 50,000$ households and $50,000 \times 2.1 = 105,000$ children of school age.
    The correct choice is (A).

SAMPLE PSAT QUESTIONS

The purpose of this section is to familiarize you with the kinds of questions that appear on the PSAT by presenting questions like those on recent PSATs. Knowing what to expect when you take the examination is an important step in preparing for the test and succeeding in it.

The directions that precede the various types of questions are similar to those on the PSAT. For all except the student-produced response questions, you are to choose the best answer and fill in the corresponding blank on the answer sheet.

Verbal Reasoning Sections

The verbal aptitude sections consist of fifty-two questions to be answered in fifty minutes. A typical test is made up of thirteen sentence completion questions, thirteen analogy questions, and twenty-six questions testing reading comprehension and vocabulary in context.

Sentence Completions

The sentence completion question tests your ability to use words in context and is in part a test of reading comprehension.

For each question in this section, select the best answer from among the choices given and fill in the corresponding oval on the answer sheet.

Directions

Each sentence below has one or two blanks, each blank indicating that something has been omitted. Beneath the sentence are five words or sets of words labeled A through E. Choose the word or set of words that, when inserted in the sentence, <u>best</u> fits the meaning of the sentence as a whole.

Example:

Medieval kingdoms did not become constitutional republics overnight; on the contrary, the change was ____ .

(A) unpopular   (B) unexpected
(C) advantageous   (D) sufficient
(E) gradual   Ⓐ Ⓑ Ⓒ Ⓓ ●

---

1. Folk dancing is ____ senior citizens, and it is also economical; they need neither great physical agility nor special accoutrements to enjoy participating in the dance.
   (A) bewildering to   (B) costly for   (C) foreign to
   (D) appropriate for   (E) impracticable for

2. Fame is ____ ; today's rising star is all too soon tomorrow's washed-up has-been.
   (A) rewarding   (B) gradual   (C) essential
   (D) spontaneous   (E) transitory

3. The author contended that his insights were not ____ , but had been made independently of others.
   (A) derivative   (B) esoteric   (C) fallacious
   (D) hypothetical   (E) concise

4. Suspicious of the ____ actions of others, the critic Edmund Wilson was in many ways a ____ man, unused to trusting anyone.
   (A) altruistic..cynical   (B) questionable..contrite
   (C) generous..candid   (D) hypocritical..cordial
   (E) benevolent..dauntless

5. Although Roman original contributions to government, jurisprudence, and engineering are commonly acknowledged, the artistic legacy of the Roman world continues to be judged widely as ____ the magnificent Greek traditions that preceded it.
   (A) an improvement on   (B) an echo of
   (C) a resolution of   (D) a precursor of
   (E) a consummation of

6. ____ though she appeared, her journals reveal that her outward maidenly reserve concealed a passionate nature unsuspected by her family and friends.
   (A) Effusive   (B) Suspicious   (C) Tempestuous
   (D) Domineering   (E) Reticent

7. Crabeater seal, the common name of *Lobodon carcinophagus*, is ____ , since the animal's staple diet is not crabs, but krill.
   (A) a pseudonym   (B) a misnomer   (C) an allusion
   (D) a digression   (E) a compromise

Analogies (Word Relationships)

The analogy question tests your ability to see relationships between words. These relationships may be degree of intensity, part to whole, class and member, synonyms, antonyms, or others, which are discussed fully in Chapter 4.

For each question in this section, select the best answer from among the choices given and fill in the corresponding oval on the answer sheet.

Directions

Each question below consists of a related pair of words or phrases, followed by five pairs of words or phrases labeled A through E. Select the pair that <u>best</u> expresses a relationship similar to that expressed in the original pair.

Example:

CRUMB:BREAD:: (A) ounce:unit
(B) splinter:wood   (C) water:bucket
(D) twine:rope   (E) cream:butter

                     Ⓐ ● Ⓒ Ⓓ Ⓔ

8. WOLF:PACK:: (A) horse:saddle
(B) goose:flock (C) fox:lair (D) pig:sow
(E) lion:cub

9. BRANCH:TREE:: (A) lid:eye
(B) strap:sandal (C) sand:beach
(D) frame:picture (E) wing:building

10. FOIL:SCHEME:: (A) alter:decision
(B) conceal:weapon (C) sketch:blueprint
(D) block:passage (E) lose:competition

11. FLIMSY:PRETEXT:: (A) frail:illness
(B) shaky:alibi (C) apprehensive:risk
(D) sorrowful:confession (E) final:judgment

12. EMBRACE:POSITION:: (A) disentangle:knot
(B) espouse:cause (C) propose:ceremony
(D) reverse:decision (E) enforce:law

13. EAGER:OVERZEALOUS::
(A) alluring:repulsive
(B) finicky:fussy
(C) temperate:abstemious
(D) guileless:ingenuous
(E) thrifty:parsimonious

14. QUACK:CHARLATANRY::
(A) miser:extravagance
(B) braggart:flattery
(C) insurgent:revelry
(D) ascetic:misanthropy
(E) blackguard:knavery

Reading Comprehension

Your ability to read and understand the kind of material found in college texts and the more serious magazines is tested in the reading comprehension section of the PSAT/NMSQT. Passages generally range from 400 to 850 words in length. You may be asked to find the central thought of a passage, interpret just what the author means by a specific phrase or idea, determine the meaning of individual words from their use in the text, evaluate the special techniques the author uses to achieve different kinds of effects, or analyze the author's mood and motivation. You will also be asked to answer two or three questions that compare the viewpoints of two passages on the same subject. You can expect to spend about three-quarters of your verbal testing time reading the passages and answering the twenty-six reading comprehension questions.

Directions

Each passage below is followed by questions based on its content. Answer the questions following each passage on the basis of what is <u>stated</u> or <u>implied</u> in that passage and in any introductory material that may be provided.

Questions 15–22 are based on the following passages.

The following passages are excerpted from books on America's national pastime, baseball.

PASSAGE 1

DiMaggio had size, power, and speed. McCarthy, his longtime manager, liked to say that DiMaggio might have stolen sixty bases a season if
Line he had given him the green light. Stengel, his new
5 manager, was equally impressed, and when DiMaggio was on base he would point to him as an example of the perfect base runner. "Look at him," Stengel would say as DiMaggio ran out a base hit, "he's always watching the ball. He isn't watching
10 second base. He isn't watching third base. He knows they haven't been moved. He isn't watching the ground, because he knows they haven't built a canal or a swimming pool since he was last there. He's watching the ball and the outfielder, which is
15 the one thing that is different on every play."

DiMaggio complemented his natural athletic ability with astonishing physical grace. He played the outfield, he ran the bases, and he batted not just effectively but with rare style. He would glide
20 rather than run, it seemed, always smooth, always ending up where he wanted to be just when he wanted to be there. If he appeared to play effortlessly, his teammates knew otherwise. In his first season as a Yankee, Gene Woodling, who played
25 left field, was struck by the sound of DiMaggio chasing a fly ball. He sounded like a giant truck horse on the loose, Woodling thought, his feet thudding down hard on the grass. The great, clear noises in the open space enabled Woodling to mea-
30 sure the distances between them without looking.

He was the perfect Hemingway hero, for Hemingway in his novels romanticized the man who exhibited grace under pressure, who withheld any emotion lest it soil the purer statement of his
35 deeds. DiMaggio was that kind of hero; his grace and skill were always on display, his emotions always concealed. This stoic grace was not achieved without a terrible price: DiMaggio was a man wound tight. He suffered from insomnia and
40 ulcers. When he sat and watched the game he chain-smoked and drank endless cups of coffee. He was ever conscious of his obligation to play well. Late in his career, when his legs were bothering him and the Yankees had a comfortable lead in a
45 pennant race, columnist Jimmy Cannon asked him why he played so hard—the games, after all, no longer meant so much. "Because there might be somebody out there who's never seen me play before," he answered.

PASSAGE 2

50 Athletes and actors—let actors stand for the set of performing artists—share much. They share the need to make gesture as fluid and economical as

possible, to make out of a welter of choices the single, precisely right one. They share the need for
55 thousands of hours of practice in order to train the
body to become the perfect, instinctive instrument
to express. Both athlete and actor, out of that abundance of emotion, choice, strategy, knowledge of
the terrain, mood of spectators, condition of others
60 in the ensemble, secret awareness of injury or
weakness, and as nearly an absolute *concentration*
as possible so that all externalities are integrated,
all distraction absorbed to the self, must be able to
change the self so successfully that it changes us.
65 When either athlete or actor can bring all these
skills to bear and focus them, then he or she will
achieve that state of complete intensity and complete relaxation—complete coherence or integrity
between what the performer wants to do and what
70 the performer has to do. Then, the performer is
free; for then, all that has been learned, by thousands of hours of practice and discipline and by
repetition of pattern, becomes natural. Then intellect is upgraded to the level of an instinct. The body
75 follows commands that precede thinking.
    When athlete and artist achieve such self-
knowledge that they transform the self so that we
are re-created, it is finally an exercise in power.
The individual's power to dominate, on stage or
80 field, invests the whole arena around the locus of
performance with his or her power. We draw from
the performer's energy, just as we scrutinize the
performer's vulnerabilities, and we criticize as if
we were equals (we are not) what is displayed. This
85 is why all performers dislike or resent the audience
as much as they need and enjoy it. Power flows in a
mysterious circuit from performer to spectator (I
assume a "live" performance) and back, and while
cheers or applause are the hoped-for outcome of
90 performing, silence or gasps are the most desired,
for then the moment has occurred—then domination is complete, and as the performer triumphs, a
unity rare and inspiring results.

15. In Passage 1, Stengel is most impressed by
DiMaggio's
(A) indifference to potential dangers
(B) tendency to overlook the bases in his haste
(C) ability to focus on the variables
(D) proficiency at fielding fly balls
(E) overall swiftness and stamina

16. It can be inferred from the content and tone of
Stengel's comment (lines 9–15) that he would
regard a base runner who kept his eye on second
base with
(A) trepidation
(B) approbation
(C) resignation
(D) exasperation
(E) tolerance

17. The phrase "a man wound tight" (line 39) means a
man
(A) wrapped in confining bandages
(B) living in constricted quarters
(C) under intense emotional pressure
(D) who drank alcohol to excess
(E) who could throw with great force

18. Which best describes what the author is doing in
the parenthetical comment "let the actors stand for
the set of performing artists" [lines 50–51]?
(A) Indicating that actors should rise out of respect
for the arts
(B) Defining the way in which he is using a particular term
(C) Encouraging actors to show tolerance for their
fellow artists
(D) Emphasizing that actors are superior to other
performing artists
(E) Correcting a misinterpretation of the role of
actors

19. To the author of Passage 2, freedom for performers
depends on
(A) their subjection of the audience
(B) their willingness to depart from tradition
(C) the internalization of all they have learned
(D) their ability to interpret material independently
(E) the absence of injuries or other weaknesses

20. The author's attitude toward the concept of the
equality of spectators and performers (lines 83–84)
is one of
(A) relative indifference
(B) mild skepticism
(C) explicit rejection
(D) strong embarrassment
(E) marked perplexity

21. The author of Passage 2 would most likely react to
the characterization of DiMaggio presented in lines
45–49 by pointing out that DiMaggio probably
(A) felt some resentment of the spectator whose
good opinion he supposedly sought
(B) never achieved the degree of self-knowledge
that would have transformed him
(C) was unaware that his audience was surveying
his weak points
(D) was a purely instinctive natural athlete
(E) was seldom criticized by his peers

VERBAL ANSWER KEY

1. D	*4.* A	*7.* B	*10.* D	*13.* E	*16.* D	*19.* C
2. E	*5.* B	*8.* B	*11.* B	*14.* E	*17.* C	*20.* C
3. A	*6.* E	*9.* E	*12.* B	*15.* C	*18.* B	*21.* A

VERBAL ANSWER EXPLANATIONS

1. **D** *Because* senior citizens don't need great physical agility to enjoy folk dancing, it is an *appropriate* activity for them.

2. **E** If one's fame disappears as quickly as the second part of the sentence indicates, then fame must be brief or *transitory.*

3. **A** If the author got his insights independently, then he did not get or derive them from the insights of other people. In other words, his insights were not *derivative.*

4. **A** Someone given to distrusting the motives and actions of other is by definition *cynical.* Such a person would question even the *altruistic,* unselfish deeds of other, suspecting ulterior motives for these charitable acts.

5. **B** The view of Rome's contributions to government, law, and engineering is wholly positive; these original additions to human knowledge are generally acknowledged or recognized. *In contrast,* Rome's original contributions to art are *not* recognized: they are seen as just an *echo* or imitation of the art of ancient Greece. Note that *Although* sets up the contrast here.

6. **E** Her outward appearance was one of "maidenly reserve" (self-restraint; avoidance of intimacy). Thus, she seemed to be *reticent* (reserved; disinclined to speak or act freely), even though she actually felt things passionately.

7. **B** Because these seals eat far more krill than crabs, it *misnames* them to call them crabeater seals. The term is thus a *misnomer,* a name that's wrongly applied to someone or something. Beware eye-catchers. Choice A is incorrect. A *pseudonym* isn't a mistaken name; it's a false name that an author adopts.

8. **B** A *wolf* belongs to a *pack.* A *goose* belongs to a *flock.*   (Group and Member)

9. **E** A *branch* is an offshoot from the main part of a *tree.* A *wing* is an extension from the main part of a *building.*   (Part to Whole)

10. **D** To *foil* a *scheme* is to hinder or obstruct it. To *block* a *passage* is to close or obstruct it.
                                                          (Function)

11. **B** A *flimsy pretext* (pretended reason) is by definition too weak to stand up to close examination. A *shaky alibi* (excuse to avoid blame) is likewise too weak to stand up to close examination Beware of eye-catchers. Choice A is incorrect. While illness may make someone frail, an illness can't be described as being frail.
                                        (Defining Characteristic)

12. **B** To *embrace* a *position* is to choose a particular point of view; to *espouse* a *cause* is to support a particular movement.   (Function)

13. **E** Someone *overzealous* is excessively *eager;* someone *parsimonious* (stingy) is excessively *thrifty.*   (Degree of Intensity)

14. **E** A *quack* (impostor; fraud) is noted for *charlatanry* (making fraudulent claims). A *blackguard* (scoundrel; rogue) is noted for *knavery* (behaving villainously).
                                        (Defining Characteristic)

15. **C** Stengel's concluding sentence indicates that DiMaggio watches "the one thing that is different on every play." In other words, DiMaggio *focuses on the variables,* the factors that change from play to play.

16. **D** The sarcastic tone of Stengel's comment suggest that he would be *exasperated* or irritated by a base runner who had his eye on second base when he should have been watching the ball and the outfielder.

17. **C** Look at the sentences following this phrase. They indicate that DiMaggio was a man *under intense emotional pressure,* one who felt so much stress that he developed ulcers and had problems getting to sleep.

18. **B** The author is taking a moment away from his argument to make sure the reader knows exactly who the subjects of his comparison are. He is not simply comparing athletes and actors. He is comparing athletes and *all* performing artists, "the set of performing artists," to use his words. Thus, in his side comment, he is *defining* how he intends to use the word *actors* throughout the discussion.

19. **C**   Performers are free when all they have learned becomes so natural, so internalized, that it seems instinctive. In other words, freedom depends on *the internalization* of what they have learned.

20. **C**   The author bluntly states that we spectators are not the performers' equals. Thus, his attitude toward the concept is one of *explicit rejection*.

21. **A**   Passage 1 indicates DiMaggio always played hard to live up to his reputation and to perform well for anyone in the stands who had never seen him play before. Clearly, he wanted the spectators to have a good opinion of him. Passage 2, however, presents a more complex picture of the relationship between the performer and his audience. On the one hand, the performer needs the audience, needs its good opinion and its applause. On the other hand, the performer also resents the audience, resents the way spectators freely point out his weaknesses and criticize his art. Thus, the author of Passage 2 might well point out that DiMaggio *felt some resentment* of the audience whom he hoped to impress with his skill.

Writing Skills Section

The writing skills section consists of thirty-nine questions to be answered in thirty minutes. A typical test is made up of nineteen find-the-error questions, fourteen sentence correction questions, and six paragraph correction questions.

Find-the-Error Questions

The find-the-error questions test your ability to spot faults in usage and sentence structure.

Directions: The following sentences contain problems in grammar, usage, diction (choice of words), and idiom.

        Some sentences are correct.

        No sentence contains more than one error.

You will find that the error, if there is one, is underlined and lettered. Assume that elements of the sentence that are not underlined are correct and cannot be changed. In choosing answers, follow the requirements of standard written English.

If there is an error, select the one underlined part that must be changed to make the sentence correct and blacken the corresponding space on your answer sheet.

If there is no error, blacken answer space Ⓔ.

EXAMPLE:

    The region has a climate <u>so severe that</u> plants
                            A

    <u>growing there</u> rarely <u>had been</u> more than twelve
        B   C

    inches <u>high</u>. <u>No error</u>
         D   E

SAMPLE ANSWER

Ⓐ Ⓑ ● Ⓓ Ⓔ

---

1. Despite <u>the fact that</u> <u>some states</u> have resisted, the
        A   B

   Congress <u>have passed</u> legislation <u>permitting</u>
          C   D

   highway speed limits to 65 miles per hour on rural

   Interstates. <u>No error</u>
          E

2. Mohandas Gandhi, <u>to who</u> the title "Father of
           A

   Passive Resistance" <u>may be given</u>, <u>bravely led</u> the
            B   C

   nationalist movement in India <u>against</u> British rule.
                     D

   <u>No error</u>
    E

3. Joe DiMaggio, <u>whose</u> style was one of
          A

   <u>quiet excellence</u>, was consistently the New York
       B

   Yankees' <u>outstanding player</u> <u>during</u> his thirteen
           C   D

   years on the team. <u>No error</u>
             E

4. If Ms. Rivera <u>was</u> <u>truly</u> happy, she would not
          A   B

   <u>constantly</u> complain <u>that</u> she has no purpose in
      C   D

   life. <u>No error</u>
      E

Sentence Correction Questions

The sentence correction questions test your ability to select the wording that makes the strongest sentence—the clearest, the smoothest, the most compact.

<u>Directions</u>: The following sentences test correctness and effectiveness of expression. In choosing answers, follow the requirements of standard written English; that is, pay attention to grammar, choice of words, sentence construction, and punctuation.

In each of the following sentences, part of the sentence or the entire sentence is underlined. Beneath each sentence you will find five ways of phrasing the underlined part. Choice A repeats the original; the other four are different.

Choose the answer that best expresses the meaning of the original sentence. If you think the original is better than any of the alternatives, choose it; otherwise choose one of the others. Your choice should produce the most effective sentence—clear and precise, without awkwardness or ambiguity.

EXAMPLE: SAMPLE ANSWER

Laura Ingalls Wilder published her first book   Ⓐ ● Ⓒ Ⓓ Ⓔ
<u>and she was sixty-five years old then.</u>

(A) and she was sixty-five years old then
(B) when she was sixty-five
(C) being age sixty-five years old
(D) upon reaching of sixty-five years
(E) at the time when she was sixty-five

---

5. <u>More than any animal</u>, the wolverine exemplifies the unbridled ferocity of "nature red in tooth and claw."
   (A) More than any animal
   (B) More than any other animal
   (C) More than another animal
   (D) Unlike any animal
   (E) Compared to other animals

6. The reviewer knew that Barbara Cartland had written several Gothic <u>novels, she didn't remember any of their titles.</u>
   (A) novels, she didn't remember any of their titles
   (B) novels, however she didn't remember any of their titles
   (C) novels, their titles, however, she didn't remember
   (D) novels without remembering any of their titles
   (E) novels, but she remembered none of their titles

7. I think the United States will veto the resolution imposing sanctions against Israel <u>regardless of the desires of the Arab nations</u> for strong action.
   (A) regardless of the desires of the Arab nations
   (B) irregardless of the Arab nations' desires
   (C) regardless of the Arab nations desires
   (D) irregardless of the Arab nation's desires
   (E) mindful of the desires of the Arab nations

Paragraph Correction Questions

The paragraph correction questions test your ability to improve an essay by combining sentences or manipulating sentence parts. You may need to arrange sentences to improve the essay's logical organization, or to pick evidence to strengthen the writer's argument.

Directions: The passage below is the unedited draft of a student's essay. Some of the essay needs to be rewritten to make the meaning clearer and more precise. Read the essay carefully.

The essay is followed by three questions about changes that might improve all or part of its organization, development, sentence structure, use of language, appropriateness to the audience, or its use of standard written English. Choose the answer that most clearly and effectively expresses the student's intended meaning. Indicate your choice by filling in the corresponding space on the answer sheet.

---

[1] As people grow older, quite obviously, the earth does too. [2] And with the process of the earth aging, we must learn to recycle. [3] The idea of using things over and over again to conserve our supply of natural resources is a beautiful one. [4] Those who don't see how easy it is to recycle should be criticized greatly.

[5] As we become more aware of the earth's problems, we all say "Oh, I'd like to help." [6] However, so few really do get involved. [7] Recycling is a simple, yet effective place to start. [8] Taking aluminum cans to the supermarket to be recycled is an ingenious idea. [9] It attracts those who want the money (5 cents a can), and it is also a convenient place to go to. [10] In addition, in almost every town, there is a Recycling Center. [11] I know that there are separate bins for paper, bottles, cans, etc. [12] This is a convenient service to those who recycle. [13] It is so easy to drive a few blocks to a center to drop off what needs to be recycled. [14] This is just another simple example of how easy it really is to recycle and to get involved. [15] Those who don't see its simplicity should be criticized for not doing their part to help make the world a better place.

[16] When I go to other people's houses and see aluminum cans in the garbage, I can honestly say I get enraged. [17] Often I say, "Why don't you just recycle those cans instead of throwing them out?" [18] What makes me even more angry is when they say "We have no time to recycle them." [19] Those people, I feel, should be criticized for not recycling in the past and should be taught a lesson about our earth and how recycling can conserve it.

8. Which of the following most effectively expresses the underlined portion of sentence 2 below?

   And <u>with the process of the earth aging</u>, we must learn to recycle.

   (A) with the aging process of the earth
   (B) the process of the earth's aging
   (C) as the earth ages
   (D) with the aging earth's process
   (E) as the process of the earth's aging continues

9. Considering the essay as a whole, which of the following best explains the main purpose of the second paragraph?

   (A) To explain the historical background of the topic
   (B) To provide a smooth transition between the first and third paragraphs
   (C) To define terms introduced in the first paragraph
   (D) To give an example of an idea presented in the first paragraph
   (E) To present a different point of view on the issue being discussed

10. Which of the sentences below most effectively combines sentences 10, 11, and 12?

   (A) Recycling centers offer recyclers convenience by providing separate bins for paper, bottles, and cans and by being located in almost every town.
   (B) Recycling centers, located in almost every town, serve recyclers by providing convenient bins to separate paper, bottles, and cans.
   (C) Almost every town has a recycling center with separate bins for paper, bottles, and cans, and this is a convenient service for people who want to recycle.
   (D) People who want to recycle will find recycling centers in almost every town, providing a convenient separation of paper, bottles, and cans into bins.
   (E) For the convenience of recyclers, separate bins for paper, bottles, and cans are provided by almost every town's recycling center.

WRITING SKILLS ANSWER KEY

1. **C**	*3.* **E**	*5.* **B**	*7.* **A**	*9.* **D**
2. **A**	*4.* **A**	*6.* **E**	*8.* **C**	*10.* **B**

WRITING SKILLS ANSWER EXPLANATIONS

1. **C** Error in agreement. The antecedent, *Congress,* is singular. Change *have passed* to *has passed.*

2. **A** Error in case. Change *who* to *whom.* It is the object of the preposition *to.*

3. **E** Sentence is correct.

4. **A** Error in mood. Since the past tense of the subjunctive mood expresses a condition contrary to fact, change *was* to *were.*

5. **B** Choice (B) includes the necessary word *other,* which makes the comparison correct. Choice (D) changes the meaning of the sentence by its implication that the wolverine is *not* an animal.

6. **E** Choices (A), (B), and (C) are run-on sentences. Choice (D) changes the meaning of the sentence by implying that it was Barbara Cartland who could not remember the titles.

7. **A** *Irregardless* in choices (B) and (D) is incorrect. Also, in choices (C) and (D), the case of *nations* is incorrect. The correct form of the plural possessive case of *nation* is *nations'.* Choice (E) changes the meaning of the sentence; in fact, it reverses it.

8. **C** This question asks you to find an alternative to a rather awkward group of words, composed of two phrases, *with the process* and *of the earth aging.* The second is graceless and ungrammatical. It should have read *of the earth's aging,* because in standard usage, nouns and pronouns modifying gerunds are usually written as possessives. Knowing what it should have been, however, is not much help in answering the question. You still must select from the five alternatives the one best way to express the essay writer's idea. In the context of the whole sentence, two of the choices, (B) and (D), make no sense at all. (A) also borders on incomprehensibility. Left with (C) and (E), the better choice is (C) because it is more concise and it expresses exactly what the writer intended.

9. **D** To answer this question you need to have read the whole essay. You also need to know the way individual paragraphs function in an essay—any essay. (More on that in Chapter 7 of this book.) Here, all five choices describe legitimate uses of a paragraph, but they don't all apply to this particular essay. Choices (A), (C), and (E) can be quickly discarded. Choice (B) is a possibility because in a unified essay every paragraph (except the first and last) in some sense serves as a bridge between paragraphs. Because the second paragraph is the longest in the essay, however, its main function is probably more than transitional. In fact, it develops by example an idea originating in the first paragraph—how easy it is to recycle. Therefore, (D) is the best choice.

10. **B** In a series of short sentences, every idea carries equal weight. By combining short sentences, writers may emphasize the important ideas and subordinate the others. To answer this question, then, you have to decide which idea expressed by the three sentences ought to be emphasized. Since two of the sentences (11 and 12) refer to the convenient arrangement of recycling centers, that's the point to stress. In the context of the whole essay, the other sentence (10), which pertains to the location of recycling centers, contains less vital information. Usually, the main point of a sentence is contained in the main, or independent, clause, and secondary ideas are found in subordinate, or dependent, clauses.

    With that principle in mind, read each of the choices. (A) and (C) give equal weight to the location and convenience of recycling centers. (D) stresses the location rather than the convenience. (E) subordinates properly but changes the meaning. Therefore, (B) is the correct answer. In (B), information about the location of recycling centers is contained in a subordinate clause included parenthetically inside the main clause.

Mathematical Reasoning Sections

Directions and Reference Information

In this section solve each problem, using any available space for scratchwork. Then decide which is the best of the choices given and fill in the corresponding oval on the answer sheet.

Notes:

(1) The use of a calculator is permitted. All numbers used are real numbers.

(2) Figures that accompany problems in this test are intended to provide information useful in solving the problems. They are drawn as accurately as possible EXCEPT when it is stated in a specific problem that the figure is not drawn to scale. All figures lie in a plane unless otherwise indicated.

Reference Information

$A = \pi r^2$ $A = \ell w$ $A = \frac{1}{2} bh$ $V = \ell w h$ $V = \pi r^2 h$ $c^2 = a^2 + b^2$ Special Right Triangles
$C = 2\pi r$

The number of degrees of an arc in a circle is 360.
The measure in degrees of a straight angle is 180.
The sum of the measures in degrees of the angles of a triangle is 180.

There are two sections, each allowing twenty-five minutes. You will find some questions in the mathematical section require you to apply graphic, spatial, numerical, symbolic, and logical techniques to situations already familiar to you; these may be similar to exercises in your textbooks. In other questions you are presented with novel situations and are called upon to do original thinking and to solve problems. You will not be expected to use mathematical knowledge beyond elementary algebra and geometry.

Twenty of the forty questions are Multiple Choice, twelve are Quantitative Comparison, and eight are Student-Produced Response questions.

Multiple Choice

Choose the correct answer from the choices given.

1. What is the exact quotient when 133,578 is divided by 543?
    (A) 243 (B) 244 (C) 245 (D) 246 (E) 247

2. What part of an hour elapses from 11:55 A.M. to 12:15 P.M.?

    (A) $\frac{1}{3}$ (B) $\frac{1}{4}$ (C) $\frac{1}{5}$ (D) $\frac{1}{6}$ (E) $\frac{2}{3}$

3. The enrollment at the North Shore Academy is b boys and g number of girls. What part of the academy student body is composed of girls?

(A) $\frac{b}{b+g}$ (B) $\frac{g}{b}$ (C) $\frac{b}{bg}$ (D) $\frac{g}{g+b}$ (E) b

4. In isosceles right triangle ABC, $AB = BC$ and $AC = 10$. What is the area of $\triangle ABC$?
    (A) $5\sqrt{2}$ (B) $2\sqrt{5}$ (C) 5
    (D) $\sqrt{25}$ (E) 25

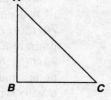

5. If the sum of the lengths of three sides of a square is r, then the perimeter of this square is
    (A) $\frac{3}{r} + 1$ (B) $\frac{r}{3} + 4$ (C) $\frac{4r}{3}$
    (D) $\frac{r}{3} + 1$ (E) $\frac{3}{r} + r$

6. When the rate for first-class postage was increased from 18¢ to 20¢, the percent of increase was
    (A) 1.1% (B) 2% (C) 9% (D) 10% (E) 11.1%

7. If the angles of a triangle are in the ratio 3:4:5, then one of these angles must have a measure in degrees of
    (A) 30 (B) 60 (C) 90 (D) 100 (E) 120

8. For which figure is the area equal to the product of two of its sides?
    (A) right triangle (B) isosceles triangle
    (C) trapezoid (D) rectangle (E) parallelogram

9. What is the average measure of the angles of a triangle?
(A) 30° (B) 45° (C) 60° (D) 90°
(E) cannot be determined from the information furnished

10. If $\dfrac{a+b}{c+2b}$ equals 1, then b equals

(A) $\dfrac{a}{c+2}$ (B) $a-c$ (C) $a+c$

(D) $\dfrac{a-c}{2}$ (E) $\dfrac{a+c}{3}$

11. If the perimeter of ΔABC is 29
meters, then the length (in meters)
of the shortest side is
(A) 3   (B) 5   (C) 7
(D) 10   (E) 12

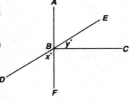

12. The length of a rectangle is 5 more than its width.
If the width is represented by x, which expression
represents the area of the rectangle?
(A) $x^2 + 5x$ (B) $x^2 + 5$ (C) $5x^2$
(D) $4x + 10$ (E) $6x^2$

13. $AB \perp BC$ and DBE is a line
segment. In terms of x, $y =$
(A) x (B) $x - 90$
(C) $90 - x$ (D) $180 - x$
(E) $x - 180$

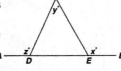

14. What is the value of z, if
$x = 100$, $y = 30$, and AB is a
line segment?
(A) 30   (B) 80   (C) 100
(D) 110   (E) 120

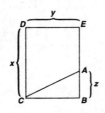

15. In rectangle $DEBC$, CA is
drawn, forming ΔABC. In
terms of x, y, and z, what is
the area of $ACDE$?
(A) $xy - yz$ (B) $yz - xy$
(C) $xy - z$ (D) $y(x - z)$
(E) $xy - \dfrac{yz}{2}$

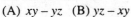

Quantitative Comparison

Another type of question you can expect to
encounter is the type known as quantitative comparison.
Questions 16–21 are examples. There are only four
choices from which to select an answer. The following
instructions are given for these questions.

Questions 16–21: Compare the quantities in
Column A and Column B. There may sometimes
be data, centered above the two columns, that concerns one or both quantities to be compared.
Consider a symbol that appears in both columns to
represent the same thing. Letters such as x, y, n,
and k represent real numbers. Compare the two
quantities and choose A if the quantity in Column
A is greater, B if the quantity in Column B is
greater, C if the two quantities are equal, or D if
the relationship cannot be determined on the basis
of the information supplied.

EXAMPLES		
Column A	Column B	Answers
E1. 2×6	$2 + 6$	● Ⓑ Ⓒ Ⓓ
E2. $p - q$	$q + p$	Ⓐ Ⓑ Ⓒ ●

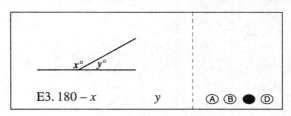

E3. $180 - x$	y	Ⓐ Ⓑ ● Ⓓ

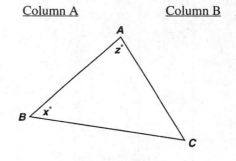

Column A	Column B

$z = 80$ and $x = 50$

	Column A	Column B
16.	AB	AC

$$xy = 16$$

	Column A	Column B
17.	x	y
18.	$\dfrac{k}{400}$	$\dfrac{k}{4}\%$
19.	$\sqrt{14.4}$	0.12

$$a = 2$$
$$b = 3$$
$$c = 4$$

	Column A	Column B
20.	$\dfrac{b^2 - a^2}{ab}$	$\dfrac{a+b}{c}$

Column A	Column B

1 kilogram = 2.2 pounds

21.   1 pound   0.33 kilogram

Questions 22 and 23: Write your answers to these two questions on the blank line that follows each. (In the model tests in this book and in the exam room, you will be entering your answers in the grids provided.)

22. Ten minutes after takeoff the plane is 40 miles from the airport. What is the average speed (in miles per hour) of this plane?

   _____

23. On a diagram of a camp site drawn to scale 1:120, the size of a building is $7\frac{1}{5}$ inches. What is the actual length (in feet) of this building?

   _____

Student-Produced Response Questions

This type of question requires you to produce an answer that is entered on a grid, which is scored mechanically. The grid looks something like this:

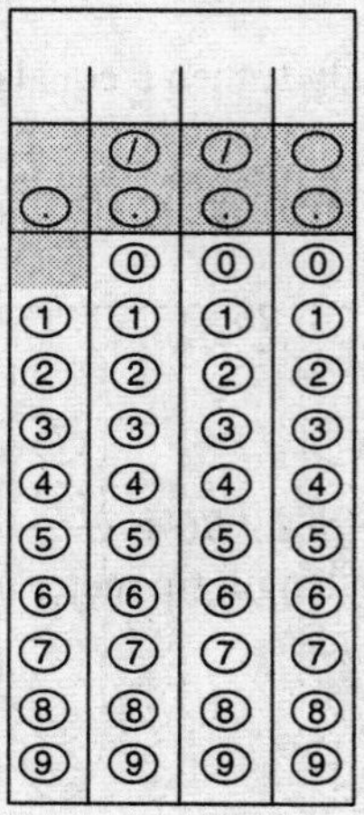

Directions: Enter the following by writing the number in the box above the columns and marking the spaces in the grid.

24.	4/13	29.	2.56	34.	.234
25.	3.5	30.	3 ½	35.	6 ¼
26.	302	31.	73/4	36.	1
27.	2/3	32.	1.49	37.	62.3
28.	.7	33.	0	38.	9 ⅛

MATHEMATICS ANSWER KEY

1. **D**	*8.* **D**	*15.* **E**	*22.* **240**	*29.* **2.56**	*36.* **1**
2. **A**	*9.* **C**	*16.* **C**	*23.* **72**	*30.* **7/2**	*37.* **62.3**
3. **D**	*10.* **B**	*17.* **D**	*24.* **4/13**	*31.* **73/4**	*38.* **73/8**
4. **E**	*11.* **C**	*18.* **C**	*25.* **3.5**	*32.* **1.49**	
5. **C**	*12.* **A**	*19.* **A**	*26.* **302**	*33.* **0**	
6. **E**	*13.* **C**	*20.* **B**	*27.* **2/3**	*34.* **.234**	
7. **B**	*14.* **D**	*21.* **A**	*28.* **.7**	*35.* **25/4**	

MATHEMATICS ANSWER EXPLANATIONS

1. D This is not an arithmetic test. Also, time does not permit using the standard method of long division. Observe that the dividend ends with the digit 8 and the divisor ends with the digit 3. The quotient must end with the digit 6.

$$\overset{\text{quotient}}{\text{divisor }\overline{)\text{dividend}}}$$

2. A Time elapsed is 20 minutes.

$\dfrac{20}{60}$ is $\dfrac{1}{3}$ of an hour.

3. D The entire student body $= b + g$.

$\dfrac{g}{b + g}$ = part of entire student body composed of girls

4. E Let $x = BC = AB$.
Using the Pythagorean Theorem,
$(x)^2 + (x)^2 = (10)^2$
or $2x^2 = 100$, or $x^2 = 50$.
Area of $\triangle ABC = \frac{1}{2}(AB)(BC)$, or $\frac{1}{2}(x)(x)$, or
$\frac{1}{2}(x)^2$, or $\frac{1}{2}(50) = 25$

5. C If the sum of the lengths of 3 sides of a square
$= r$, then each side $= \dfrac{r}{3}$ and 4 sides $= \dfrac{4r}{3}$.

6. E The increase was 2¢.

$\dfrac{\text{increase}}{\text{original}} \times 100$ = percent increase

$\dfrac{2¢}{18¢} = \dfrac{1}{9} = 11.1\%$

7. B $3x + 4x + 5x = 180°$
$12x = 180°$
$x = 15°$
∴ measure of angles = 45°, 60°, and 75°

8. D In a rectangle the length is perpendicular to the width. The area of the rectangle equals the product of the length (one of the sides) and the width (the other side).

9. C The sum of the measure of the angles of a triangle equals 180°. 180° ÷ 3 = 60°.

10. B If the value of a fraction is 1, the numerator equals (has the same value as) the denominator.
$a + b = c + 2b$
$a - c = b$

11. C $4x - 2 + 2x + 1 + x + 9 = 29$
$7x + 8 = 29$
$7x = 21$
$x = 3$
Thus, side $4x - 2 = 10$
side $x + 9 = 12$
side $2x + 1 = 7$ (answer)

12. A x = width (given)
∴ $x + 5$ = length
$x(x + 5)$ = area, or area $= x^2 + 5x$

13. C $\angle ABE = \angle DBF$ (vertical angles)
$\angle DBF = x°$ (given)
∴ $ABE = x°$
$\angle ABC = 90°$ ($AB \perp BC$)
∴ $EBC = 90° - x°$
$y° = 90° - x°$
$y = 90 - x$

14. D $\angle CED \overset{\circ}{=} 80$
$\angle CDE \overset{\circ}{=} 180 - (80 + 30)$ or 70
$z° = 180 - 70$ or 110

15. E The area of $ACDE$ = area of rectangle $BCDE$ − area of $\triangle ABC$.
Area of $BCDE = xy$
Area of $\triangle ABC = \dfrac{yz}{2}$
Area of $ACDE = xy - \dfrac{yz}{2}$

16. C $\angle ACB \overset{\circ}{=} 180 - (80 + 50)$ or 50
∴ $AB = AC$ (If 2 angles of a $\triangle$ are equal, the sides opposite those angles are equal.)

17. D x and/or y may have negative values.

18. C % means $\dfrac{1}{100}$.

$\dfrac{k}{4}\% = \left(\dfrac{k}{4}\right)\left(\dfrac{1}{100}\right)$ or $\dfrac{k}{400}$

19. A $\sqrt{14.4} = 3+$
$3+ > 0.12$

20. **B** $\dfrac{9-4}{6} = \dfrac{5}{6}$ (Column A)

$\dfrac{2+3}{4} = \dfrac{5}{4}$ (Column B)

$\dfrac{5}{4} > \dfrac{5}{6}$

21. **A** 0.33 kilogram is about $\frac{1}{3}$ of a kilogram or $\frac{1}{3}$ of 2.2 pounds, which is 0.7 pound. Column A is 1 pound.

22. **240** Ten minutes is $\frac{1}{6}$ of an hour. Because it covers 40 miles in $\frac{1}{6}$ of an hour, it will cover, on the average, 240 miles per hour.

23. **72** $(120)(7\frac{1}{5}$ inches$) = 864$ inches or 72 feet.

24. 4 / 13

25. 3 . 5

26. 302

27. 2 / 3

28. . 7

29. 2 . 56

30. 7 / 2

31. 73 / 4

32. 1 . 49

33. 0

34. . 234

35. 25 / 4

36. 1

37. 62 . 3

38. 73 / 8

After the PSAT/NMSQT

After the scores of the PSAT/NMSQT are received, you, your parents, and your guidance counselor can begin to make plans for college. Some references follow:

BARRON'S HOW TO PREPARE FOR SAT I, by Samuel C. Brownstein, Mitchel Weiner, and Sharon Weiner Green. *This classic of college entrance examinations now includes a diagnostic test as well as six complete simulated exams that enable you to practice under exact* SAT I *format and test conditions; all model tests have answer keys and answer explanations. Verbal aptitude practice includes selected and graded word lists, definitions and vocabulary tests. Mathematical aptitude practice reviews necessary math from arithmetic through high school algebra and geometry, and features the quantitative comparison questions included on* SAT I. *Testing tactics and strategies are featured.* 1996, 19th Edition.

BARRON'S NEW MATH WORKBOOK FOR SAT I, by Lawrence Leff. *All-new workbook is geared to today's test-takers' needs. Practice exercises contain hundreds of multiple-choice questions, quantitative comparisons, and grid-in questions with answers. Lesson topics include calculators, the new Student-Produced Response Question type, and a wide array of math subjects related to* SAT I. 1996.

BARRON'S VERBAL WORKBOOK FOR SAT I, by Mitchel Weiner and Sharon Weiner Green. *A companion to the Math Workbook—it provides hundreds of practice exercises and diagnostic tests for intensive review of vocabulary, sentence completion, word relationships, and reading comprehension. Suggested study plan and 1000 questions plus 10 complete model verbal aptitude tests prepare students to score high on college boards, admission, placement, and scholarship examinations where word usage and understanding are tested.* 1997, 9th Edition.

BARRON'S PROFILES OF AMERICAN COLLEGES. *Searching studies of more than 1600 regionally accredited four-year American colleges and universities that will give the prospective student a preview of his or her relationship to a particular college—based on its facilities, outstanding features and programs, admission requirements, costs, available financial aid, extracurricular activities, programs and major offerings, degrees awarded, enrollment, religious affiliation, housing facilities, social or honorary societies, religious or other regulations for student life. The comprehensive and detailed information on each college will be of tremendous help to guidance counselors, college-bound students, and their families.* 1997, 22nd Edition.

BASIC WORD LIST, by Samuel C. Brownstein, Mitchel Weiner, and Sharon Weiner Green. *This effective vocabulary builder presents more than 2,000 words that all students should know to prepare for* SAT I, ACT, *and other standardized college entrance and college level exams. Each new word is defined and placed in a model sentence. Practice vocabulary exercises and a review of word prefixes and roots.* 1997, 3rd Edition.

VOCABULARY BUILDER (A Systematic Plan for Building a Vocabulary, Testing Progress, and Applying Knowledge), by Samuel C. Brownstein and Mitchel Weiner. *This procedure will enable students to acquire the vocabulary required to comprehend high school and college texts and outside reading. Offers instruction on how to answer vocabulary sections on college admission and similar tests. Contains 3000 word entries, divided into 40 word study groups, each followed by a brief test.* 1984, 9th Edition.

DIAGNOSE YOUR PROBLEM

_____

Answer Sheet
A DIAGNOSTIC TEST

Each mark should completely fill the appropriate space, and should be as dark as all other marks. Make all erasures complete. Traces of an erasure may be read as an answer. See pages vii and 27 for explanations of timing and number of questions.

Section 1 — Verbal
30 minutes

1 Ⓐ Ⓑ Ⓒ Ⓓ Ⓔ
2 Ⓐ Ⓑ Ⓒ Ⓓ Ⓔ
3 Ⓐ Ⓑ Ⓒ Ⓓ Ⓔ
4 Ⓐ Ⓑ Ⓒ Ⓓ Ⓔ
5 Ⓐ Ⓑ Ⓒ Ⓓ Ⓔ
6 Ⓐ Ⓑ Ⓒ Ⓓ Ⓔ
7 Ⓐ Ⓑ Ⓒ Ⓓ Ⓔ
8 Ⓐ Ⓑ Ⓒ Ⓓ Ⓔ
9 Ⓐ Ⓑ Ⓒ Ⓓ Ⓔ
10 Ⓐ Ⓑ Ⓒ Ⓓ Ⓔ
11 Ⓐ Ⓑ Ⓒ Ⓓ Ⓔ
12 Ⓐ Ⓑ Ⓒ Ⓓ Ⓔ
13 Ⓐ Ⓑ Ⓒ Ⓓ Ⓔ
14 Ⓐ Ⓑ Ⓒ Ⓓ Ⓔ
15 Ⓐ Ⓑ Ⓒ Ⓓ Ⓔ
16 Ⓐ Ⓑ Ⓒ Ⓓ Ⓔ
17 Ⓐ Ⓑ Ⓒ Ⓓ Ⓔ
18 Ⓐ Ⓑ Ⓒ Ⓓ Ⓔ
19 Ⓐ Ⓑ Ⓒ Ⓓ Ⓔ
20 Ⓐ Ⓑ Ⓒ Ⓓ Ⓔ
21 Ⓐ Ⓑ Ⓒ Ⓓ Ⓔ
22 Ⓐ Ⓑ Ⓒ Ⓓ Ⓔ
23 Ⓐ Ⓑ Ⓒ Ⓓ Ⓔ
24 Ⓐ Ⓑ Ⓒ Ⓓ Ⓔ
25 Ⓐ Ⓑ Ⓒ Ⓓ Ⓔ
26 Ⓐ Ⓑ Ⓒ Ⓓ Ⓔ
27 Ⓐ Ⓑ Ⓒ Ⓓ Ⓔ
28 Ⓐ Ⓑ Ⓒ Ⓓ Ⓔ
29 Ⓐ Ⓑ Ⓒ Ⓓ Ⓔ
30 Ⓐ Ⓑ Ⓒ Ⓓ Ⓔ

Section 2 — Math
30 minutes

1 Ⓐ Ⓑ Ⓒ Ⓓ Ⓔ
2 Ⓐ Ⓑ Ⓒ Ⓓ Ⓔ
3 Ⓐ Ⓑ Ⓒ Ⓓ Ⓔ
4 Ⓐ Ⓑ Ⓒ Ⓓ Ⓔ
5 Ⓐ Ⓑ Ⓒ Ⓓ Ⓔ
6 Ⓐ Ⓑ Ⓒ Ⓓ Ⓔ
7 Ⓐ Ⓑ Ⓒ Ⓓ Ⓔ
8 Ⓐ Ⓑ Ⓒ Ⓓ Ⓔ
9 Ⓐ Ⓑ Ⓒ Ⓓ Ⓔ
10 Ⓐ Ⓑ Ⓒ Ⓓ Ⓔ
11 Ⓐ Ⓑ Ⓒ Ⓓ Ⓔ
12 Ⓐ Ⓑ Ⓒ Ⓓ Ⓔ
13 Ⓐ Ⓑ Ⓒ Ⓓ Ⓔ
14 Ⓐ Ⓑ Ⓒ Ⓓ Ⓔ
15 Ⓐ Ⓑ Ⓒ Ⓓ Ⓔ
16 Ⓐ Ⓑ Ⓒ Ⓓ Ⓔ
17 Ⓐ Ⓑ Ⓒ Ⓓ Ⓔ
18 Ⓐ Ⓑ Ⓒ Ⓓ Ⓔ
19 Ⓐ Ⓑ Ⓒ Ⓓ Ⓔ
20 Ⓐ Ⓑ Ⓒ Ⓓ Ⓔ
21 Ⓐ Ⓑ Ⓒ Ⓓ Ⓔ
22 Ⓐ Ⓑ Ⓒ Ⓓ Ⓔ
23 Ⓐ Ⓑ Ⓒ Ⓓ Ⓔ
24 Ⓐ Ⓑ Ⓒ Ⓓ Ⓔ
25 Ⓐ Ⓑ Ⓒ Ⓓ Ⓔ

Section 3 — Writing
30 minutes

1 Ⓐ Ⓑ Ⓒ Ⓓ Ⓔ
2 Ⓐ Ⓑ Ⓒ Ⓓ Ⓔ
3 Ⓐ Ⓑ Ⓒ Ⓓ Ⓔ
4 Ⓐ Ⓑ Ⓒ Ⓓ Ⓔ
5 Ⓐ Ⓑ Ⓒ Ⓓ Ⓔ
6 Ⓐ Ⓑ Ⓒ Ⓓ Ⓔ
7 Ⓐ Ⓑ Ⓒ Ⓓ Ⓔ
8 Ⓐ Ⓑ Ⓒ Ⓓ Ⓔ
9 Ⓐ Ⓑ Ⓒ Ⓓ Ⓔ
10 Ⓐ Ⓑ Ⓒ Ⓓ Ⓔ
11 Ⓐ Ⓑ Ⓒ Ⓓ Ⓔ
12 Ⓐ Ⓑ Ⓒ Ⓓ Ⓔ
13 Ⓐ Ⓑ Ⓒ Ⓓ Ⓔ
14 Ⓐ Ⓑ Ⓒ Ⓓ Ⓔ
15 Ⓐ Ⓑ Ⓒ Ⓓ Ⓔ
16 Ⓐ Ⓑ Ⓒ Ⓓ Ⓔ
17 Ⓐ Ⓑ Ⓒ Ⓓ Ⓔ
18 Ⓐ Ⓑ Ⓒ Ⓓ Ⓔ
19 Ⓐ Ⓑ Ⓒ Ⓓ Ⓔ
20 Ⓐ Ⓑ Ⓒ Ⓓ Ⓔ
21 Ⓐ Ⓑ Ⓒ Ⓓ Ⓔ
22 Ⓐ Ⓑ Ⓒ Ⓓ Ⓔ
23 Ⓐ Ⓑ Ⓒ Ⓓ Ⓔ
24 Ⓐ Ⓑ Ⓒ Ⓓ Ⓔ
25 Ⓐ Ⓑ Ⓒ Ⓓ Ⓔ
26 Ⓐ Ⓑ Ⓒ Ⓓ Ⓔ
27 Ⓐ Ⓑ Ⓒ Ⓓ Ⓔ
28 Ⓐ Ⓑ Ⓒ Ⓓ Ⓔ
29 Ⓐ Ⓑ Ⓒ Ⓓ Ⓔ
30 Ⓐ Ⓑ Ⓒ Ⓓ Ⓔ
31 Ⓐ Ⓑ Ⓒ Ⓓ Ⓔ
32 Ⓐ Ⓑ Ⓒ Ⓓ Ⓔ
33 Ⓐ Ⓑ Ⓒ Ⓓ Ⓔ
34 Ⓐ Ⓑ Ⓒ Ⓓ Ⓔ
35 Ⓐ Ⓑ Ⓒ Ⓓ Ⓔ
36 Ⓐ Ⓑ Ⓒ Ⓓ Ⓔ
37 Ⓐ Ⓑ Ⓒ Ⓓ Ⓔ
38 Ⓐ Ⓑ Ⓒ Ⓓ Ⓔ
39 Ⓐ Ⓑ Ⓒ Ⓓ Ⓔ

Section 4 — Verbal
30 minutes

31 Ⓐ Ⓑ Ⓒ Ⓓ Ⓔ
32 Ⓐ Ⓑ Ⓒ Ⓓ Ⓔ
33 Ⓐ Ⓑ Ⓒ Ⓓ Ⓔ
34 Ⓐ Ⓑ Ⓒ Ⓓ Ⓔ
35 Ⓐ Ⓑ Ⓒ Ⓓ Ⓔ
36 Ⓐ Ⓑ Ⓒ Ⓓ Ⓔ
37 Ⓐ Ⓑ Ⓒ Ⓓ Ⓔ
38 Ⓐ Ⓑ Ⓒ Ⓓ Ⓔ
39 Ⓐ Ⓑ Ⓒ Ⓓ Ⓔ
40 Ⓐ Ⓑ Ⓒ Ⓓ Ⓔ
41 Ⓐ Ⓑ Ⓒ Ⓓ Ⓔ
42 Ⓐ Ⓑ Ⓒ Ⓓ Ⓔ
43 Ⓐ Ⓑ Ⓒ Ⓓ Ⓔ
44 Ⓐ Ⓑ Ⓒ Ⓓ Ⓔ
45 Ⓐ Ⓑ Ⓒ Ⓓ Ⓔ
46 Ⓐ Ⓑ Ⓒ Ⓓ Ⓔ
47 Ⓐ Ⓑ Ⓒ Ⓓ Ⓔ
48 Ⓐ Ⓑ Ⓒ Ⓓ Ⓔ
49 Ⓐ Ⓑ Ⓒ Ⓓ Ⓔ
50 Ⓐ Ⓑ Ⓒ Ⓓ Ⓔ
51 Ⓐ Ⓑ Ⓒ Ⓓ Ⓔ
52 Ⓐ Ⓑ Ⓒ Ⓓ Ⓔ
53 Ⓐ Ⓑ Ⓒ Ⓓ Ⓔ
54 Ⓐ Ⓑ Ⓒ Ⓓ Ⓔ
55 Ⓐ Ⓑ Ⓒ Ⓓ Ⓔ
56 Ⓐ Ⓑ Ⓒ Ⓓ Ⓔ
57 Ⓐ Ⓑ Ⓒ Ⓓ Ⓔ
58 Ⓐ Ⓑ Ⓒ Ⓓ Ⓔ
59 Ⓐ Ⓑ Ⓒ Ⓓ Ⓔ
60 Ⓐ Ⓑ Ⓒ Ⓓ Ⓔ

Section 5 — Math
30 minutes

26 Ⓐ Ⓑ Ⓒ Ⓓ Ⓔ
27 Ⓐ Ⓑ Ⓒ Ⓓ Ⓔ
28 Ⓐ Ⓑ Ⓒ Ⓓ Ⓔ
29 Ⓐ Ⓑ Ⓒ Ⓓ Ⓔ
30 Ⓐ Ⓑ Ⓒ Ⓓ Ⓔ
31 Ⓐ Ⓑ Ⓒ Ⓓ Ⓔ
32 Ⓐ Ⓑ Ⓒ Ⓓ Ⓔ
33 Ⓐ Ⓑ Ⓒ Ⓓ Ⓔ
34 Ⓐ Ⓑ Ⓒ Ⓓ Ⓔ
35 Ⓐ Ⓑ Ⓒ Ⓓ Ⓔ
36 Ⓐ Ⓑ Ⓒ Ⓓ Ⓔ
37 Ⓐ Ⓑ Ⓒ Ⓓ Ⓔ
39 Ⓐ Ⓑ Ⓒ Ⓓ Ⓔ
39 Ⓐ Ⓑ Ⓒ Ⓓ Ⓔ
40 Ⓐ Ⓑ Ⓒ Ⓓ Ⓔ

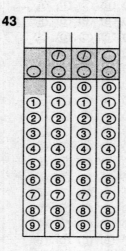

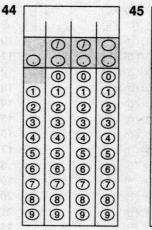

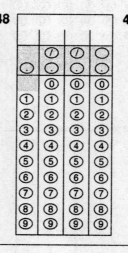

41 42 43 44 45 46 47 48 49 50

2

A Diagnostic Test

This chapter offers a simulated PSAT/NMSQT test. The purpose is to provide you with a fairly accurate evaluation of what your score would be without any special preparation. Take this test, following directions for time allowances for each of the sections. Then score your answers and evaluate the results, using the self-rating guides provided. Consult the explanations of answers for all test items that you failed to answer correctly.

You will then be in a position to approach your review program realistically and allot your time for study. You will know which topics in mathematics require your review and drill, which of your verbal skills require concentrated study, and how you should improve your writing skills.

Simulate Test Conditions   TOTAL TIME: 180 MINUTES*

Find a quiet place to work, in order to simulate examination conditions. Keep an accurate record of your time. If you complete one section before the suggested time has elapsed, check your work over rather than start the next section. Don't be worried, however, if you are not able to answer all questions in the allotted time. This may also occur on the actual test. No one is expected to know the answers to all questions on any of these tests. Read the questions carefully. Work carefully and rapidly. Do not spend too much time on questions that seem difficult for you. If time permits, go back to the ones you left out.

Except for ten questions in the mathematics section, which are student-produced response questions, the questions are of the objective type with a penalty imposed for guessing. The score is determined by the number of correct answers minus a fraction of the num-

ber of incorrectly marked answers. Omitted answers do not count. Economy of time is of utmost concern. It is best to work rapidly and carefully and not to waste time on questions that contain difficult or unfamiliar material. Whereas wild guessing is inadvisable, educated or shrewd guessing is to be encouraged. You may sometimes eliminate certain possible answers to a question because of your general knowledge, and, despite your inability to explain by good reasoning why you choose a specific answer, you may feel that it is the correct one. Such a shrewd guess may be right and you should therefore give that answer.

*The actual test will take only 130 minutes (see page vii); all of the tests in this book are a bit longer, to give you more practice.

DIAGNOSTIC TEST

For each question in this section, select the best answer from among the choices given and fill in the corresponding oval on the answer sheet.

Directions

Each sentence below has one or two blanks, each blank indicating that something has been omitted. Beneath the sentence are five words or sets of words labeled A through E. Choose the word or set of words that, when inserted in the sentence, best fits the meaning of the sentence as a whole.

Example:

Medieval kingdoms did not become constitutional republics overnight; on the contrary, the change was ____ .

(A) unpopular
(B) unexpected
(C) advantageous
(D) sufficient
(E) gradual   Ⓐ Ⓑ Ⓒ Ⓓ ●

1. Normally an individual thunderstorm lasts about 45 minutes, but under certain conditions the storm may ____ , becoming ever more severe, for as long as four hours.
   (A) wane   (B) moderate   (C) persist   (D) vacillate
   (E) disperse

2. For Miró, art became a ____ ritual: paper and pencils were holy objects to him, and he worked as though he were performing a religious rite.
   (A) superficial   (B) sacred   (C) banal
   (D) cryptic   (E) futile

3. Many Wright scholars, striving for accurate reconstructions of the architect's life, have been ____by the palpable ____ and smoke screens of Wright's autobiography.
   (A) delighted . . truths   (B) amazed . . facts
   (C) vexed . . errors   (D) confused . . precision
   (E) entertained . . omissions

4. The newest fiber-optic cables that carry telephone calls cross-country are made of glass so ____that a piece 100 miles thick is clearer than a standard windowpane.
   (A) fragile   (B) immaculate   (C) tangible
   (D) transparent   (E) iridescent

5. A certain ____ in Singer's prose always keeps one at arm's length from his protagonist's emotions.
   (A) detachment   (B) lyricism   (C) fluency
   (D) brevity   (E) rhythm

6. Her employers could not complain about her work because she was ____ in the ____ of her duties.
   (A) derelict . . performance
   (B) importunate . . observance
   (C) meticulous . . postponement
   (D) assiduous . . .execution
   (E) hidebound . . conception

7. My grandmother hated having her chairs sat in or her lawns stepped on or the water turned on in her basins; she even ____ the mailman his daily promenade up her sidewalk.
   (A) awarded   (B) grudged   (C) dispensed
   (D) mocked   (E) facilitated

8. Any numerical description of the development of the human population cannot avoid ____ , simply because there has never been a census of all the people in the world.
   (A) analysis   (B) conjecture   (C) disorientation
   (D) corroboration   (E) statistics

9. The mayfly is an ____ creature: its adult life lasts little more than a day.
   (A) elegant   (B) ephemeral   (C) idiosyncratic
   (D) impulsive   (E) omnivorous

10. Decorated in ____ style, his home contained bits and pieces of furnishings from widely divergent periods, strikingly juxtaposed to create a unique decor.
    (A) an aesthetic   (B) a lyrical   (C) a traditional
    (D) an eclectic   (E) a perfunctory

11. The books' topics are no less varied than their bindings, for their prolific author has ____ specialization as energetically as some of his colleagues have ____ it.
    (A) resisted . . pursued
    (B) admired . . supported
    (C) endorsed . . accepted
    (D) defended . . attacked
    (E) repudiated . . deliberated

12. Despite an affected ____ , which convinced casual observers that he was indifferent about his painting and enjoyed only frivolity, Warhol cared deeply about his art and labored at it ____ .
    (A) nonchalance . . diligently
    (B) empathy . . methodically
    (C) fervor . . secretly
    (D) gloom . . intermittently
    (E) hysteria . . sporadically

GO ON TO THE NEXT PAGE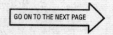

13. Equipped with mechanisms that deliberately delay sprouting, woodland seeds often seem strangely ____ to germinate.
(A) prone   (B) reluctant   (C) qualified
(D) prolific   (E) modified

14. Soap operas and situation comedies, though given to distortion, are so derivative of contemporary culture that they are inestimable ____ the attitudes and values of our society in any particular decade.
(A) contradictions of   (B) antidotes to
(C) indices of   (D) prerequisites for
(E) determinants of

15. Alec Guinness has few equals among English-speaking actors, and now in his autobiography he reveals himself to be an uncommonly ____ prose stylist as well.
(A) ambivalent   (B) infamous   (C) supercilious
(D) felicitous   (E) pedestrian

16. Although eighteenth-century English society as a whole did not encourage learning for its own sake in women, nonetheless it illogically ____ women's sad lack of education.
(A) palliated   (B) postulated   (C) decried
(D) brooked   (E) vaunted

17. Compromise is ____ to passionate natures because it seems a surrender, and to intellectual natures because it seems a ____ .
(A) odious..confusion
(B) inherent..fabrication
(C) welcome..fulfillment
(D) unsuited..submission
(E) intimidating..dichotomy

Directions

Each passage below is followed by questions based on its content. Answer the questions following each passage on the basis of what is <u>stated</u> or <u>implied</u> in that passage and in any introductory material that may be provided.

Questions 18–22 are based on the following passage.

The following passage is an excerpt from a short story entitled "Ruin."

My father was a cattle rancher in Jamaica. One day after the war he had become sick after eating a bad piece of frozen meat, and that was it. Suddenly
Line all our cane went down and men began putting up
5   fences. By himself my father took the Oracabessa launch to Cuba, went up into the mountains he said, and came back a week later with a Cuban he had known during the war in North Africa. Pappy was his name, and he had two teeth in his mouth and
10   looked thin and stupid, but knew cattle.

It was a risk for my father to take the Oracabessa launch across the straits in September. It was only ninety miles, but September in Jamaica is the time for bad storms; they come up quickly.
15   He was very daring, my mother told me, after the war, and I remember it a bit myself. All the men were a little like that. My mother said that after El Alamein my father thought he could do anything. He was impetuous, like a young boy, the war hav-
20   ing taught him both how temporary life is, and how valuable. He had been a cane grower all his life, that was what he knew, but he was willing to learn cattle. He put every penny, every quattie of what we had, into a small herd, and a prize black bull
25   that came from Corpus Christi in October and was lowered from the freighter to the dock, hung from a bright yellow sling. When the yellow sash was dropped away and we could see the bull's blackness and the rotations of green that were its eyes,
30   my father was a proud man. The bull looked up and snorted, its eyes fixed on the mountain, and Pappy said with a hideous gentle smile that it smelled the herd, and that the sea voyage had done it no good.

Our house had red tiles on the roof. They
35   glowed vermilion in the sun. We heard drums on Friday and Saturday nights; drifting up from the town, the sound was marvelous and frightening. When my father was troubled he walked down the mountain on the winding road, and stayed for a
40   long time on the wall overlooking the sea. It was terribly hot and still in the morning. Everyone wore white. I was often aware of carrion rotting unseen in some soft place.

I was quite surprised when, a week after we
45   took the bull off the ship, Pappy ran onto the terrace and turning his straw hat rapidly in his hands announced that the bull had gone wild and was killing the other animals. My father got up slowly and put down the *Gleaner*. He was in white pants
50   and a white shirt, and he was stained beautifully with colors, for he had been painting fish and fruit. I followed him to his room where I watched him load a .30-06, pushing in the dull brass cartridges one by one. He seemed to be angry and perhaps a
55   little frightened. I was frightened for him.

18. The narrator states all of the following about his father EXCEPT
(A) he was audacious and impulsive
(B) he had resented his military service
(C) he had not started out as a cattle rancher
(D) his journey to Cuba was potentially dangerous
(E) he was aware of life's impermanence

GO ON TO THE NEXT PAGE

19. The narrator most likely uses the phrase "and that was it" (line 3) to pinpoint the moment that
    (A) his father first ate frozen meat
    (B) he understood his father's weakness
    (C) his father left home for good
    (D) Pappy first entered his life
    (E) his father decided to try raising cattle

20. The narrator's father sought out Pappy
    (A) because he missed their army days in North Africa
    (B) out of pity for Pappy's poverty
    (C) to find a cure for his case of food poisoning
    (D) because he needed Pappy's cattle-ranching expertise
    (E) because Pappy knew how to navigate a launch

21. Pappy most likely turned his straw hat rapidly in his hands
    (A) to fan himself in the terrible heat
    (B) because he wished to demonstrate his dexterity
    (C) to chase away the maddened bull
    (D) because he was agitated by the news he brought
    (E) to dissipate the smell of wet paint

22. The passage suggests the narrator's interest in the incidents he recounts is prompted by his desire to
    (A) excuse his father's momentary cowardice
    (B) relive a vivid childhood adventure
    (C) praise his father's ability to take risks
    (D) come to terms with his family's financial undoing
    (E) overcome his sense of nostalgia

Questions 23–30 are based on the following passage.

The passage below is excerpted from the introduction to "Bury My Heart at Wounded Knee," written in 1970 by the Native American historian Dee Brown.

Since the exploratory journey of Lewis and Clark to the Pacific Coast early in the nineteenth century, the number of published accounts describ-
Line ing the "opening" of the American West has risen
5 into the thousands. The greatest concentration of recorded experience and observation came out of the thirty-year span between 1860 and 1890—the period covered by this book. It was an incredible era of violence, greed, audacity, sentimentality,
10 undirected exuberance, and an almost reverential attitude toward the ideal of personal freedom for those who already had it.
     During that time the culture and civilization of the American Indian was destroyed, and out of that
15 time came virtually all the great myths of the American West—tales of fur traders, mountain men, steamboat pilots, goldseekers, gamblers, gunmen, cavalrymen, cowboys, harlots, missionaries, schoolmarms, and homesteaders. Only occasionally
20 was the voice of the Indian heard, and then more often than not it was recorded by the pen of a white man. The Indian was the dark menace of the myths, and even if he had known how to write in English, where would he have found a printer or a publisher?
25   Yet they are not all lost, those Indian voices of the past. A few authentic accounts of American Western history were recorded by Indians either in pictographs or in translated English, and some managed to get published in obscure journals,
30 pamphlets, or books of small circulation. In the late nineteenth century, when the white man's curiosity about Indian survivors of the wars reached a high point, enterprising newspaper reporters frequently interviewed warriors and chiefs and gave them an
35 opportunity to express their opinions on what was happening in the West. The quality of these interviews varied greatly, depending upon the abilities of the interpreters, or upon the inclination of the Indians to speak freely. Some feared reprisals for
40 telling the truth, while others delighted in hoaxing reporters with tall tales and shaggy-dog stories. Contemporary newspaper statements by Indians must therefore be read with skepticism, although some of them are masterpieces of irony and others
45 burn with outbursts of poetic fury.
     Among the richest sources of first-person statements by Indians are the records of treaty councils and other formal meetings with civilian and military representatives of the United States govern-
50 ment. Isaac Pitman's new stenographic system was coming into vogue in the second half of the nineteenth century, and when Indians spoke in council a recording clerk sat beside the official interpreter.
     Even when the meetings were in remote parts
55 of the West, someone usually was available to write down the speeches, and because of the slowness of the translation process, much of what was said could be recorded in longhand. Interpreters quite often were half-bloods who knew spoken languages
60 but seldom could read or write. Like most oral peoples they and the Indians depended upon imagery to express their thoughts, so that the English translations were filled with graphic similes and metaphors of the natural world. If an
65 eloquent Indian had a poor interpreter, his words might be transformed to flat prose, but a good interpreter could make a poor speaker sound poetic.
     Most Indian leaders spoke freely and candidly in councils with white officials, and as they became
70 more sophisticated in such matters during the 1870s and 1880s, they demanded the right to choose their own interpreters and recorders. In this latter period, all members of the tribes were free to speak, and some of the older men chose such opportunities to
75 recount events they had witnessed in the past, or sum up the histories of their peoples. Although the

GO ON TO THE NEXT PAGE →

Indians who lived through this doom period of their civilization have vanished from the earth, millions of their words are preserved in official records.
80 Many of the more important council proceedings were published in government documents and reports.

Out of all these sources of almost forgotten oral history, I have tried to fashion a narrative of
85 the conquest of the American West as the victims experienced it, using their own words whenever possible. Americans who have always looked westward when reading about this period should read this book facing eastward.
90 This is not a cheerful book, but history has a way of intruding upon the present, and perhaps those who read it will have a clearer understanding of what the American Indian is, by knowing what he was. They may learn something about their own
95 relationship to the earth from a people who were true conservationists. The Indians knew that life was equated with the earth and its resources, that America was a paradise, and they could not comprehend why the intruders from the East were
100 determined to destroy all that was Indian as well as America itself.

23. A main concern of the author in this passage is to
(A) denounce the white man for his untrustworthiness and savagery
(B) evaluate the effectiveness of the military treaty councils
(C) argue for the improved treatment of Indians today
(D) suggest that Indian narratives of the conquest of the West are similar to white accounts
(E) introduce the background of the original source materials for his text

24. The word "concentration" in line 5 means
(A) memory   (B) attention   (C) diligence
(D) imprisonment   (E) cluster

25. According to the passage, nineteenth-century newspaper accounts of interviews with Indians may contain inaccuracies for which of the following reasons?
I. Lack of skill on the part of the translators
II. The tendency of the reporters to overstate what they were told by the Indians
III. The Indians' misgivings about possible retaliations
(A) I only   (B) III only   (C) I and II only
(D) I and III only   (E) I, II, and III

26. The author's tone in describing the Indian survivors can best be described as
(A) skeptical   (B) detached   (C) elegiac
(D) obsequious   (E) impatient

27. The author is most impressed by which aspect of the English translations of Indian speeches?
(A) Their vividness of imagery
(B) Their lack of frankness
(C) The inefficiency of the process
(D) Their absence of sophistication
(E) Their bevity of expression

28. The word "flat" in line 66 means
(A) smooth
(B) level
(C) pedestrian
(D) horizontal
(E) unequivocal

29. The author most likely suggests that Americans should read this book facing eastward
(A) in an inappropriate attempt at levity
(B) out of respect for Western superstitions
(C) in order to read by natural light
(D) because the Indians came from the East
(E) to identify with the Indians' viewpoint

30. The phrase "equated with" in line 97 means
(A) reduced to an average with
(B) necessarily tied to
(C) numerically equal to
(D) fulfilled by
(E) differentiated by

IF YOU FINISH BEFORE 30 MINUTES, YOU MAY CHECK YOUR WORK ON THIS SECTION ONLY. DO NOT TURN TO ANY OTHER SECTION IN THE TEST.

S T O P

DIAGNOSTIC TEST

SECTION **2**
Mathematical Reasoning

Time—30 minutes
25 Questions

Directions and Reference Information

In this section solve each problem, using any available space for scratchwork. Then decide which is the best of the choices given and fill in the corresponding oval on the answer sheet.

Notes:

(1) The use of a calculator is permitted. All numbers used are real numbers.

(2) Figures that accompany problems in this test are intended to provide information useful in solving the problems. They are drawn as accurately as possible EXCEPT when it is stated in a specific problem that the figure is not drawn to scale. All figures lie in a plane unless otherwise indicated.

   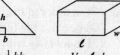

$A = \pi r^2$ $A = \ell w$ $A = \frac{1}{2}bh$ $V = \ell wh$ $V = \pi r^2 h$ $c^2 = a^2 + b^2$ Special Right Triangles
$C = 2\pi r$

The number of degrees of an arc in a circle is 360.
The measure in degrees of a straight angle is 180.
The sum of the measures in degrees of the angles of a triangle is 180.

1. 104% of 25 =
   (A) 1   (B) 26   (C) 100   (D) 260   (E) 325

2. 64 is $\frac{2}{7}$ of what number?
   (A) $18\frac{2}{7}$ (B) 48   (C) 128   (D) 224   (E) 448

3. $\frac{87955936}{284}$ equals exactly
   (A) 309701   (B) 309702   (C) 309703
   (D) 309704   (E) 309705

4. When $N = 0$ the value of $\frac{(2K)(NB)}{K+B}$ equals
   (A) 0   (B) 1   (C) $\frac{2K}{K+B}$
   (D) $K+B$ (E) $\frac{1}{K+B}$

5. How many posts are needed for a fence 144 feet long, if the posts are placed 12 feet apart?
   (A) 11   (B) 12   (C) 13   (D) 14   (E) 15

6. To get to school, a pupil must spend $\frac{1}{5}$ of an hour walking to the bus and $\frac{1}{3}$ of an hour riding in the bus, and then walk for $\frac{1}{6}$ of an hour to the school. What part of an hour does this pupil spend getting to school?
   (A) $\frac{1}{14}$ (B) $\frac{7}{30}$ (C) $\frac{7}{10}$ (D) $\frac{3}{10}$ (E) $\frac{7}{20}$

7. It took Sam 200 minutes to complete the difficult *Sunday Times* crossword puzzle. Stanley did the same puzzle in 160 minutes. By what fraction of an hour was Sam's time longer than Stanley's?
   (A) $\frac{1}{5}$ (B) $\frac{1}{4}$ (C) $\frac{2}{5}$ (D) $\frac{1}{2}$ (E) $\frac{2}{3}$

8. R and T are points on straight line PQ on which $PR = RT = TQ$. What percent of PT is PQ?
   (A) 1½%   (B) 50%   (C) 66⅔%
   (D) 33⅓%   (E) 150%

9. If 20 teachers in a faculty of 80 are transferred, what percent of the original faculty remains?
   (A) 4%   (B) 16%   (C) 25%   (D) 60%   (E) 75%

GO ON TO THE NEXT PAGE

10. The enrollment in a university is now 52,500, an increase of 5% over the enrollment last year. By how many students did the enrollment increase this year?
(A) 2500   (B) 47,500   (C) 50,000
(D) 55,000   (E) 57,750

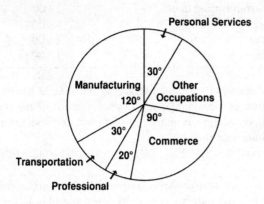

11. This circle graph expresses, in degrees, the portion of wage earners engaged in various occupations for Waban City. What percent of all the wage earners are engaged in transportation?
(A) 8.3   (B) 12   (C) 18   (D) 30   (E) 83

12. If $abc = 210$ and a, b, and c are whole numbers, which of the following CANNOT be a value of c?
(A) 1   (B) 15   (C) 21   (D) 27   (E) 35

13. When inserted in the parentheses, which of the symbols (+, –, ×, ÷ or =) will make the following a true statement?
$$12t(?)\frac{3t}{\frac{1}{4}} = \frac{4t^2}{\frac{t}{3}}$$
(A) +   (B) –   (C) ×   (D) ÷   (E) =

14. The fraction $\dfrac{t+n}{n}$ =

(A) $\dfrac{t}{n} + n$ (B) $\dfrac{t+n}{t}$ (C) $\dfrac{t}{n} + 1$

(D) $t^2 + 1$ (E) t

15. $\dfrac{a^2 - b^2}{(a-b)^2}$ is equal to

(A) $a + b$ (B) $a - b$ (C) $\dfrac{a+b}{a-b}$

(D) $\dfrac{a-b}{a+b}$ (E) 1

16. If two items cost $c¢$, how many items can be purchased for $x¢$?
(A) $\dfrac{x}{2c}$ (B) $\dfrac{2c}{x}$ (C) $\dfrac{2x}{c}$ (D) $\dfrac{cx}{2}$ (E) $2cx$

17. Circle I represents all students in a certain high school who are taking mathematics, Circle II represents all who are taking chemistry, and Circle III represents all who are taking physics. Which of the following represents all students who are taking both mathematics and chemistry but not physics?
(A) Region 4 + Region 5 – Region 6
(B) Circle I + Circle II – Circle III
(C) Region 4 + Region 8 + Region 5
(D) Region 8
(E) Circle I + Circle II – Region 10

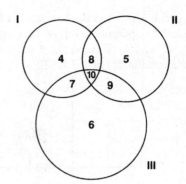

18. If the operation ϕ is defined by the equation $x \phi y = 2x + y$, what is the value of a in the equation $2 \phi a = a \phi 3$?
(A) 0   (B) –1   (C) 1   (D) 1.5   (E) –1.5

19. AB is parallel to CD. Line segment CD is divided into six equal segments.

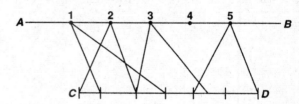

Of the triangles labeled by the numerals 1–5 on their vertices, the triangle with the greatest area is
(A) 1   (B) 2   (C) 3   (D) 4   (E) 5

20. If a and b are both positive numbers, and $a > b$, which of the following could be true?
    I. ab is greater than either a or b.
    II. ab is greater than b but less than a.
    III. ab is less than either a or b.
(A) I only   (B) II only   (C) III only
(D) I and II only   (E) I, II, and III

21. The distance between two points is correctly expressed as 720 statute miles or 630 nautical miles. Which of the following most closely approximates the value of one statute mile in terms of nautical miles?
(A) 0.88   (B) 0.89   (C) 0.90   (D) 1.14   (E) 1.25

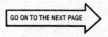

22. The average of P numbers is x and the average of N numbers is y. What is the average of all the $(P + N)$ numbers?

(A) $\dfrac{x + y}{2}$ (B) $x + y$ (C) $\dfrac{Py + Nx}{xy\,(P + N)}$

(D) $\dfrac{x + y}{P + N}$ (E) $\dfrac{Px + Ny}{P + N}$

WEIGHT DISTRIBUTION IN AVERAGE ADULT	
(Total Body Weight 70,000 Grams)	
Organ	Weight (Grams)
Muscles	30,000
Skeleton	10,000
Blood	5,000
Gastrointestinal tract	2,000
Lungs	1,000
Liver	1,700
Brain	1,500

23. In this figure K *is* the vertex of square *KLMN*, not shown. Side *KL* is parallel to either the x- or y-axis. If the area of *KLMN* is 16, each of the following could be the coordinates of L EXCEPT

(A) (2,6)
(B) (6,2)
(C) (2, −2)
(D) (−2,2)
(E) (4,4)

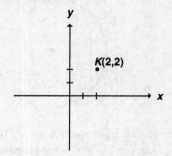

24. According to this table giving the weight distribution in the average adult, what percent of the total body weight is made up of blood and the gastrointestinal tract?

(A) 1%   (B) 2%   (C) 5%   (D) 7%   (E) 10%

25. In a jar that contains only yellow and green marbles, the ratio of yellow to green marbles is 2 : 3. What is the probability of randomly selecting a green marble?

(A) $\frac{2}{3}$ (B) $\frac{2}{5}$ (C) $\frac{3}{5}$ (D) $\frac{1}{2}$ (E) $\frac{3}{4}$

IF YOU FINISH BEFORE 30 MINUTES, YOU MAY CHECK YOUR WORK ON THIS SECTION ONLY. DO NOT TURN TO ANY OTHER SECTION IN THE TEST.

S T O P

SECTION 3
Writing Skills

Time—30 minutes
39 Questions

Directions

The following sentences contain problems in grammar, usage, diction (choice of words), and idiom.

    Some sentences are correct.

    No sentence contains more than one error.

You will find that the error, if there is one, is underlined and lettered. Assume that elements of the sentence that are not underlined are correct and cannot be changed. In choosing answers, follow the requirements of standard written English.

If there is an error, select the one underlined part that must be changed to make the sentence correct and blacken the corresponding space on your answer sheet.

If there is no error, blacken answer space Ⓔ .

Example:

    The region has a climate <u>so severe that</u> plants
                           A

    <u>growing there</u> rarely <u>had been</u> more than twelve
        B   C

    inches <u>high.</u> <u>No error</u>
          D   E

                        Ⓐ Ⓑ ● Ⓓ Ⓔ

1. <u>In order to</u> conserve valuable gasoline, motorists
     A

   <u>had ought</u> to check their speedometers <u>while</u>
      B   C

   driving along the the highways <u>since it is</u> very
                           D

   easy to exceed 55 miles per hour while driving

   on open roads. <u>No error</u>
             E

2. The book <u>must</u> be old, <u>for</u> its cover <u>is torn</u> <u>bad.</u>
         A   B   C   D

   <u>No error</u>
    E

3. <u>Not one</u> of the children <u>has ever sang</u> <u>in public</u>
    A   B   C

   <u>before.</u> <u>No error</u>
    D   E

4. Neither you nor <u>I</u> can realize the <u>affect</u> his behavior
           A   B

   <u>will have</u> on his chances <u>for</u> promotion. <u>No error</u>
     C   D   E

5. The <u>apparently</u> <u>obvious solution</u> to the problem
       A   B

   <u>was overlooked</u> by <u>many of</u> the contestants.
       C   D

   <u>No error</u>
    E

6. <u>After</u> he <u>had drank</u> the warm milk, he began
    A   B

   <u>to feel sleepy</u> and <u>finally decided</u> to go to bed.
       C   D

   <u>No error</u>
    E

7. <u>Without hardly</u> a moment's delay, the computer
       A

   began to <u>print out</u> the <u>answer to</u> the problem.
      B   C   D

   <u>No error</u>
    E

8. After <u>conferring with</u> John Brown and Mary Smith
       A

   <u>I have decided</u> that she is <u>better qualified</u> than <u>him</u>
      B   C   D

   to edit the school newspaper. <u>No error</u>
                   E

9. Of the two candidates for this newly <u>formed</u>
   <u>A</u>   B

   government position, Ms. Rivera is the

   <u>most qualified</u> <u>because</u> of her experience
      C   D

   in the field. <u>No error</u>
          E

10. Diligence and honesty <u>as well as</u> <u>being intelligent</u>
                  A   B

   are qualities which I look for <u>when</u> I interview
   C   D

   applicants. <u>No error</u>
         E

11. <u>Dashing across</u> the campus John <u>tried to</u> overtake
      A   B

   the instructor <u>who</u> <u>had forgotten</u> his briefcase.
             C   D

   <u>No error</u>
    E

GO ON TO THE NEXT PAGE

12. Neither the earthquake or the subsequent fire was

    able to destroy the spirit of the city dwellers.

    No error
    E

13. I might of passed if I had done my homework, but
       A   B   C
    I had to go to work. No error
       D   E

14. Writing a beautiful sonnet is as much an
                    A   B
    achievement as to finish a 400-page novel.
                    C   D
    No error
    E

15. The impatient customer had scarcely enough
           A   B
    money to pay the clerk at the checkout counter.
          C   D
    No error
    E

16. The principal of equal justice for all is one of
        A   B   C
    the cornerstones of our democratic way of life.
                                        D
    No error
    E

17. Neither the players nor the trainer were in the
                        A   B
    locker room when the thief broke in the door.
                    C   D
    No error
    E

18. If anyone calls while we are in conference,
    A   B
    tell them I will return the call after the meeting.
        C   D
    No error
    E

19. Either of the two boys who sing in the chorus
    A   B
    are now capable of taking the job of understudy
    C   D
    to the star. No error
                    E

20. If he was to decide to go to college, I, for one, would recommend that he plan to go to Yale.

    (A) If he was to decide to go to college
    (B) If he were to decide to go to college
    (C) Had he decided to go to college
    (D) In the event that he decides to go to college
    (E) Supposing he was to decide to go to college

21. Except for you and I, everyone brought a present to the party.

    (A) Except for you and I, everyone brought
    (B) With the exception of you and I, everyone brought
    (C) Except for you and I, everyone had brought
    (D) Except for you and me, everyone brought
    (E) Except for you and me, everyone had brought

22. Had I realized how close I was to failing, I would not have gone to the party.

    (A) Had I realized how close
    (B) If I would have realized how close
    (C) Had I had realized how close
    (D) When I realized how close
    (E) If I realized how close

GO ON TO THE NEXT PAGE

23. Being a realist, I could not accept his statement that supernatural beings had caused the disturbance.

    (A) Being a realist
    (B) Due to the fact that I am a realist
    (C) Being that I am a realist
    (D) Being as I am a realist
    (E) Realist that I am

24. Having finished the marathon in record-breaking time, the city awarded him its Citizen's Outstanding Performance Medal.

    (A) the city awarded him its Citizen's Outstanding Performance Medal
    (B) the city awarded the Citizen's Outstanding Performance Medal to him
    (C) he was awarded the Citizen's Outstanding Performance Medal by the city
    (D) the Citizen's Outstanding Performance Medal was awarded to him
    (E) he was awarded by the city the Citizen's Outstanding Performance Medal

25. The football team's winning its first game of the season excited the student body.

    (A) The football team's winning its first game of the season
    (B) The football team having won its first game of the season
    (C) Having won its first game of the season, the football team
    (D) Winning its first game of the the season, the football team
    (E) The football team winning its first game of the season

26. Anyone interested in the use of computers can learn much if you have access to a Radio Shack TRS-80 or a Pet Microcomputer.

    (A) if you have access to
    (B) if he or she has access to
    (C) if access is available to
    (D) by access to
    (E) from access to

27. I have to make dinner, wash the dishes, do my homework, and then relaxing.

    (A) to make dinner, wash the dishes, do my homework, and then relaxing
    (B) to make dinner, washing the dishes, my homework, and then relax
    (C) to make dinner, wash the dishes, doing my homework, and then relaxing
    (D) to prepare dinner, wash the dishes, do my homework, and then relaxing
    (E) to make dinner, wash the dishes, do my homework, and then relax

28. The climax occurs when he asks who's in the closet.

    (A) occurs when he asks who's
    (B) is when he asks who's
    (C) occurs when he is asking who's
    (D) is when he is asking who's
    (E) occurs when he asked who's

29. Setting up correct bookkeeping procedures is important to any new business, it helps to obtain the services of a good accountant.

    (A) is important to any new business, it helps
    (B) are important to any new business, it
    (C) is important to any new business, therefore, try
    (D) is important to any new business; it helps
    (E) are important to any new business, so try

30. The grocer hadn't hardly any of those kind of canned goods.

    (A) hadn't hardly any of those kind
    (B) hadn't hardly any of those kinds
    (C) had hardly any of those kind
    (D) had hardly any of those kinds
    (E) had scarcely any of those kind

31. Having stole the money, the police searched the thief.

    (A) Having stole the money, the police searched the thief.
    (B) Having stolen the money, the thief was searched by the police.
    (C) Having stolen the money, the police searched the thief.
    (D) Having stole the money, the thief was searched by the police.
    (E) Being that he stole the money, the police searched the thief.

32. Juan broke his hip, he has not been able to run and possibly never will be able to run the mile again.

    (A) hip, he has not been able to run and possibly never will be able to run
    (B) hip; he has not been able to run and possibly never will be able to run
    (C) hip; he has not and possibly never will be able to run
    (D) hip, he has not been and possibly never would be able to run
    (E) hip; he has not and possibly will never be able to run

33. I came late to class today; the reason being that the bus broke down.

    (A) today; the reason being that
    (B) today, the reason being that
    (C) today because
    (D) today;
    (E) today; since

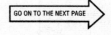GO ON TO THE NEXT PAGE

Directions

The passage below is the unedited draft of a student's essay. Some of the essay needs to be rewritten to make the meaning clearer and more precise. Read the essay carefully.

The essay is followed by six questions about changes that might improve all or part of its organization, development, sentence structure, use of language, appropriateness to the audience, or its use of standard written English. Choose the answer that most clearly and effectively expresses the student's intended meaning. Indicate your choice by filling in the corresponding space on the answer sheet.

[1] There are many reasons making it cruel to keep animals penned up in zoos for the sole purpose of letting families gawk at caged creatures. [2] There has to be a better reason to imprison animals than merely to allow visitors to drop a quarter into a food dispenser so that one can feed the monkeys or the elephant. [3] One might argue that it is educational. [4] If someone is so dumb that they don't know what a zebra looks like, they should pull out an encyclopedia and look it up. [5] Humans have no right to pull animals from their natural environment and to seal their fate forever behind a set of cold metal bars. [6] Animals need to run free and live, but by putting them in zoos we are disrupting and disturbing nature.

[7] Then there is the issue of sanitary conditions for animals at the zoo. [8] When the animals have been at the zoo for a while they adopt a particular lifestyle. [9] They lounge around all day, and they're fed at a particular time. [10] They get used to that. [11] That means that they would never again be able to be placed back in their natural environment. [12] They would never survive. [13] And if they reproduce while in captivity, the offspring are born into an artificial lifestyle. [14] After a few generations the animals become totally different from their wild and free ancestors, and visitors to the zoo see animals hardly resembling the ones living in their natural habitat.

[15] The vicious cycle should be stopped before it is too late. [16] The whole idea of a zoo is cruel. [17] If zoos are not cruel and if, as some people say, they serve a useful purpose, then why not put homo sapiens on display, too?

34. Which is the most effective revision of the underlined segment of sentence 1 below?

There are many reasons making it cruel to keep animals penned up in zoos for the sole purpose of letting families gawk at caged creatures.

(A) Many reasons exist for the cruelty of keeping animals penned up in zoos

(B) It is a cruel practice to keep animals penned up in zoos

(C) The reasons are numerous to object to the cruelty experienced by animals locked in cages

(D) There are several reasons for it being cruel toward animals to lock them up in zoos

(E) Locking up animals in zoos a cruel practice especially

35. Which revision of the underlined segment of sentence 2 below is best?

There has to be a better reason to imprison animals than merely to allow visitors to drop a quarter into a food dispenser so that one can feed the monkeys or the elephant.

(A) so that the feeding of monkeys and the elephants can take place

(B) for the feeding of the monkeys and the elephants to occur

(C) in order to buy the monkeys or the elephant food

(D) so they're buying feed for the monkeys or the elephant

(E) to buy a handful of feed for the monkeys or the elephant

36. Taking sentence 3 into account, which of the following is the most effective revision of sentence 4?

(A) Reading about animals in the encyclopedia rather than studying them first hand.

(B) In the encyclopedia you can gain more information about zebras and other animals.

(C) Viewing the animal in a zoo is clearly more informative than looking at a picture in a book.

(D) Doesn't everyone know what a zebra looks like, even little children?

(E) But if someone is so dumb that they don't know what a zebra looks like, they should look it up in an encyclopedia.

GO ON TO THE NEXT PAGE

37. Which of the following reasons most accurately describes the author's intention in the selection of words used in the underlined segment of sentence 5 below?

    Humans have no right to pull animals from their natural environment and <u>to seal their fate forever behind a set of cold metal bars</u>.

    (A) to inform the reader that animals in the zoo live in cages
    (B) to propose a solution to the plight of animals in the zoo
    (C) to arouse in the reader an emotional response to the problem
    (D) to appeal to the reader to weigh both sides of the issue
    (E) to convince the reader that animals don't enjoy being in the zoo

38. Which of the following revisions of sentence 7 is the best topic sentence for paragraph 2?

    (A) Life in captivity causes animals to change.
    (B) No one favors zoos that deliberately try to change the lifestyle of animals in captivity.
    (C) Living conditions for animals in the zoo are ordinarily harsh and cruel.
    (D) Living in the zoo, conditions for animals affect them permanently.
    (E) Life in the zoo for animals is not a bowl of cherries.

39. Which revision most effectively combines sentences 10, 11, and 12?

    (A) Because they would never be able to survive again back in their natural environment, they grow used to being fed.
    (B) Having grown used to regular feedings, the animals would be unable to survive back in their native environment.
    (C) Growing accustomed to that, placing them back in their native habitat and being unable to survive on their own.
    (D) They, having gotten used to being fed regularly, in their natural environment would never survive.
    (E) Being unable to survive back in their natural environment, the animals have grown accustomed to regular feedings.

IF YOU FINISH BEFORE 30 MINUTES, YOU MAY CHECK YOUR WORK ON THIS SECTION ONLY. DO NOT TURN TO ANY OTHER SECTION IN THE TEST.   **S T O P**

SECTION 4
Verbal Reasoning

Time—30 minutes
30 Questions

For each question in this section, select the best answer from among the choices given and fill in the corresponding oval on the answer sheet.

Directions

Each question below consists of a related pair of words or phrases, followed by five pairs of words or phrases labelled A through E. Select the pair that best expresses a relationshiop similar to that expressed in the original pair.

Example:

CRUMB:BREAD::

(A) ounce:unit
(B) splinter:wood
(C) water:bucket
(D) twine:rope
(E) cream:butter

31. MINNOW:FISH::
    (A) poodle:dog
    (B) flock:sheep
    (C) tendon:bone
    (D) snare:rabbit
    (E) fang:snake

32. TANK:OXYGEN::
    (A) automobile:gasoline
    (B) carton:milk
    (C) salt:sodium
    (D) metal:iron
    (E) molecule:atom

33. BRIDGE:GAP::
    (A) cleanse:wound
    (B) reconcile:estrangement
    (C) construct:hypothesis
    (D) enter:doorway
    (E) return:favor

34. EGGSHELL:FRAGILITY::
    (A) dewdrop:grief
    (B) peapod:variety
    (C) rainbow:mobility
    (D) barbell:weight
    (E) packrat:discrimination

35. HOSTILE:FRIENDSHIP::
    (A) inimical:opposition
    (B) traitorous:loyalty
    (C) intolerant:bias
    (D) magnificent:delicacy
    (E) bombastic:grandiloquence

36. GIRDER:SUPPORT::
    (A) stocking:mend
    (B) card:shuffle
    (C) axe:sharpen
    (D) winch:hoist
    (E) ladder:lean

37. STAMPS:PHILATELY::
    (A) paintings:museum
    (B) words:lexicon
    (C) coins:numismatics
    (D) countries:alliance
    (E) rockets:pyrotechnics

38. CIRCUMSPECT:WARINESS::
    (A) meaningful:inanity
    (B) respectful:pertinence
    (C) detrimental:misapprehension
    (D) reckless:foolhardiness
    (E) wicked:abstinence

39. PARAGON:STANDARD::
    (A) colleague:rival
    (B) painting:landscape
    (C) heredity:environment
    (D) author:publisher
    (E) imitation:copy

40. PULVERIZE:DUST::
    (A) analyze:argument
    (B) vaporize:mist
    (C) petrify:fear
    (D) permeate:odor
    (E) solidify:fluid

41. PLEAD:SUPPLIANT::
    (A) disperse:rioter
    (B) shun:outcast
    (C) revere:elder
    (D) beg:philanthropist
    (E) translate:interpreter

42. LUMINARY:ILLUSTRIOUS::
    (A) zealot:intense
    (B) miser:prodigal
    (C) atheist:radical
    (D) dignitary:conceited
    (E) celebrity:wealthy

43. APOCRYPHAL:AUTHENTICITY::
    (A) nefarious:wickedness
    (B) dogmatic:plausibility
    (C) hypocritical:integrity
    (D) perspicacious:industry
    (E) deceptive:artifice

GO ON TO THE NEXT PAGE

The passage below is followed by questions based on its content. Answer the questions following the passage on the basis of what is <u>stated</u> or <u>implied</u> in that passage and in any introductory material that may be provided.

Questions 44–49 are based on the following passage.

The world's tropical rain forests contain varieties of plant and animal life found nowhere else on earth. The following passage presents background information on the epiphytes and their relatives the strangler-trees, fascinating specimens of rain forest plant life.

The great trees furnish support for much of the other plant life of the forest. Climbers are abundant, much more so than elsewhere. Greedy for
Line light, they have various adaptations for hoisting
5 themselves to the upper canopy—some are twiners, others are equipped with tendrils, hooks, or suckers. An entire group of plants is unfitted to start low and climb high to reach the light. These are epiphytes, plants that grow on trees without
10 parasitizing them or deriving any advantage except a platform near the sun. They are extraordinarily common. However, in order to grow close to the sunlight, they have had to pay a price—they have lost their root connection with
15 the forest floor and its abundant moisture. For soil, they must often make do with the small amounts of debris that lodge in crannies in the trees, with dust from the atmosphere and organic matter and seeds deposited by ants that often nest
20 in the roots of epiphytes—a small but vital source of humus and minerals. So well have these plants managed to create their own environment that the spoonfuls of soil in which they grow do not differ significantly from normal soil in microbiological
25 processes.

Some of the epiphytes have developed remarkable adaptations for conserving water. Many are encased in a waxy layer that retards evaporation. The roots of some orchids have a spongy tissue
30 that not only soaks up water but also carries on photosynthesis. The staghorn fern accumulates water-holding humus in a sort of bucket structure at the base of its leaves. The large group of tropical plants known as bromeliads are living cis-
35 terns—their long branching leaves spring from the same place around the stem, and overlap so tightly at their bases that they can hold water, as much as four-and-a-half quarts in a large plant. These bromeliad tanks become a center of life,
40 holding breeding frogs, snails, and aquatic insects, all of which add to the supply of nutrients in the water. Hairs at the base of the leaves line the tank and perform the job of absorbing water and nutrients, making the bromeliad independent of a root
45 connection with the soil.

The problems of living in the dark rain forest, and the unusual efforts made to rise into the sun, are best symbolized by the strangler trees. They achieve their place in the sun by stealth. The
50 strangler begins life as an epiphyte, its seed germinating high up in the fork of a large tree. The seedling puts out two kinds of roots: one seizes the branch and serves as a grapple to hold the plant in place, and the other dangles like a cable,
55 growing steadily closer to the soil. Until it makes contact with the ground, the strangler grows like any other epiphyte, obtaining small quantities of water and nutrients from the debris in the tree crevice. But once the descending root reaches the
60 soil, its source of supply is increased enormously and the plant's growth quickens. It sprouts more leaves high in the canopy and grows upward toward a sunlit window between the leaves; a maze of additional feeding cables descends to the
65 soil and eventually the supporting tree is encased in a network of them. It was once thought that the strangler kills the forest giant by the simple process of enwrapping it and preventing its trunk from expanding, but it is now known that it actu-
70 ally squeezes its host to death. As the hold tightens, the strangler's roots thicken to a marked degree, preparing for the time when it will need props to stand by itself in the sunlight it has captured. The host finally expires, thoroughly
75 encased inside the "trunk" (actually the fused roots) of the strangler tree that now stands on its own pedestal as a member of the high forest canopy.

44. According to the passage, epiphytes are particularly adapted to
(A) the floor of the tropical rain forest
(B) a sunless environment
(C) the dissipation of rainwater
(D) drawing sustenance from a host
(E) the retention of liquid

45. It can be inferred from the passage that which of the following is true of epiphytes?
(A) They lack root systems.
(B) They do not require large amounts of soil for growth.
(C) They are incapable of photosynthesis.
(D) They are hard to perceive in the dense rain forest canopy.
(E) They need different nutrients than other plants do.

46. The passage can best be described as
(A) enthusiastic exhortation
(B) sophisticated analysis
(C) straightforward description
(D) indirect exposition
(E) forceful argument

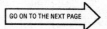
GO ON TO THE NEXT PAGE

47. The author states all of the following about the strangler tree EXCEPT

(A) It eventually becomes self-supporting.
(B) Its feeding cables ascend toward the forest canopy.
(C) Its roots extend far from its point of germination.
(D) It undergoes a rapid growth spurt.
(E) Its roots become conspicuously larger.

48. The word "marked" in line 71 means

(A) noticeable
(B) branded
(C) graded
(D) doomed
(E) unique

49. Which of the following does the passage suggest about the strangler tree?

(A) It needs only a small supply of nutrients for full growth.
(B) All its roots seek the forest floor.
(C) It outgrows its need for its host.
(D) It is killed by the forest giant that supports it.
(E) It eventually sheds its feeder cables.

The passages below are followed by questions based on their content; questions following a pair of related passages may also be based on the relationship between the paired passages. Answer the questions on the basis of what is stated or implied in the passages and in any introductory material that may be provided.

Questions 50–60 are based on the following passages.

In Passage 1, the author, the dancer-choreographer Martha Graham, draws on her experience as a dancer to generalize about her art. In Passage 2, the author, California chef Alice Waters presents her approach to cooking, as practiced at her restaurant, Chez Panisse.

PASSAGE 1

I am a dancer. My experience has been with dance as an art.

Each art has an instrument and a medium. The
Line instrument of the dance is the human body; the
5 medium is movement. The body has always been
to me a thrilling wonder, a dynamo of energy,
exciting, courageous, powerful; a delicately balanced logic and proportion. It has not been my
aim to evolve or discover a new method of dance
10 training, but rather to dance significantly. To
dance significantly means "through the medium
of discipline and by means of a sensitive, strong
instrument, to bring into focus unhackneyed
movement: a human being."
15   I did not want to be a tree, a flower, or a wave.
In a dancer's body, we as audience must see *ourselves*, not the imitated behavior of everyday
actions, not the phenomena of nature, not exotic
creatures from another planet, but something of
20 the miracle that is a human being, motivated, disciplined, concentrated.
Technique and training have never been a
substitute for that condition of awareness that is
talent, for that complete miracle of balance that is
25 genius, but it can give plasticity and tension,
freedom and discipline, balancing one against
the other. It can awaken memory of the race
through muscular memory of the body. Training
and technique are means to strength, to freedom,
30 to spontaneity.

Contrary to popular belief, spontaneity as one
sees it in dance or in theater, is not wholly dependent on emotion at that instant. It is the condition
of emotion objectified. It plays that part in theater
35 that light plays in life. It illumines. It excites.
Spontaneity is essentially dependent on energy,
upon the strength necessary to perfect timing. It is
the result of perfect timing to the Now. It is not
essentially intellectual or emotional, but is nerve
40 reaction.
To me, the acquirement of nervous, physical,
and emotional concentration is the one element
possessed to the highest degree by the truly great
dancers of the world. Its acquirement is the result
45 of discipline, of energy in the deep sense. That is
why there are so few great dancers.
A great dancer is not made by technique alone
any more than a great statesman is made by
knowledge alone. Both possess true spontaneity.
50 Spontaneity in behavior, in life, is due largely to
complete health; on the stage to a technical use—
often so ingrained by proper training as to seem
instinctive—of nervous energy. Perhaps what we
have always called intuition is merely a nervous
55 system organized by training to perceive.

PASSAGE 2

Flexibility is an essential component of good
cooking. You should never feel locked in to a
recipe or a menu unless it involves a basic principle regarding procedure or technique such as
60 those involved in breadmaking and pastry. I don't

GO ON TO THE NEXT PAGE →

ever want to write anything in this book that is so precise that the reader must invoke great powers of concentration on every last detail in order to ensure the success of a recipe or a dinner; ingredi-
65 ents are simply too variable. I want to *suggest* the expected taste; I want to *suggest* the appearance of the complete dish; I want to *suggest* the combination of ingredients; and I want to *suggest* the overall harmony and balance of the meal. Then it
70 will be up to you to determine the correct balance and composition. Perhaps the garlic is sharp and strong and you will use it sparingly in a particular presentation, or you may find the garlic to be sweet and fresh and you will want to use twice as
75 much!

    Learn to trust your own instincts. A good cook needs only to have positive feelings about food in general, and about the pleasures of eating and cooking. I have known some cooks who did not
80 seem to discover pleasure and gratification in things culinary. At the restaurant, I look for employees who are interested in working in the kitchen for reasons above and beyond those of simply needing a job, any job. This applies equal-
85 ly to the home cook: a cook who dislikes food is a bad cook. Period. Even an ambivalent cook is a bad cook. Yet, a person who responds to the cooking processes and the mound of fresh ingredients with a genuine glow of delight is likely to
90 be, or become, a very good cook indeed. Technical skills can be acquired and perfected along the way, but dislike or ambivalence toward food cannot always be overcome.

    In the early stages of my culinary pursuits, I
95 cooked as I had seen cooking done in France. I copied some of the more traditional cooks, and I stayed within the bounds they had laid out so carefully because I didn't trust my own instincts yet. Having imitated their styles, I found that with
100 time and experience, their fundamental principles had become a part of my nature and I began to understand why they had done certain things in a particular way. Then I could begin to develop a different and more personal style based on the
105 ingredients available to me here in California.

50. Graham rejects movement in dance that is
  (A) jerky
  (B) spontaneous
  (C) brief
  (D) trite
  (E) natural

51. In saying that she "did not want to be a tree, a flower, or a wave" (line 15), Graham
  (A) emphasizes that dancers must express their humanity
  (B) reveals an innate discomfort with natural phenomena
  (C) suggests a budding desire to imitate other phenomena
  (D) conveys a sense of unsatisfied longings
  (E) indicates impatience with how long such transformations take

52. The word "plasticity" in line 25 means
  (A) nervous energy
  (B) strength and endurance
  (C) mobility and pliancy
  (D) organic coherence
  (E) muscular memory

53. Graham attempts to clarify the function of spontaneity in dance or theater (lines 31–40) by means of
  (A) a digression
  (B) an analogy
  (C) a hypothesis
  (D) an anecdote
  (E) a quotation

54. In Passage 2 Waters is discussing cooking from the point of view of
  (A) a chef on the verge of opening her own restaurant
  (B) someone uninformed about traditional methods of French cuisine
  (C) an accomplished practitioner of the culinary arts
  (D) a gifted home cook and collector of recipes
  (E) a professional determined to outstrip her competitors

55. Waters uses the example of the garlic (lines 71–75) to show
  (A) the variability of ingredients
  (B) the importance of every last detail
  (C) her insistence on fresh ingredients
  (D) the need to be a flexible shopper
  (E) her preference for strong flavors

56. In writing her cookbook, Waters is trying to
  (A) anticipate any pitfalls those using her recipes might run into
  (B) provide precise measurements for her readers to follow
  (C) limit herself to basic principles and procedures
  (D) dictate the spices going into each meal
  (E) allow scope for the reader's own culinary initiative

GO ON TO THE NEXT PAGE

57. To Waters, to produce superior results, the cook must possess
(A) an excellent sense of smell
(B) first-rate technical skills
(C) the finest kitchen equipment
(D) detailed recipes to follow
(E) a love of her medium

58. In lines 81–84 Waters indicates she seeks restaurant employees who share her
(A) level of expertise
(B) classical French training
(C) enjoyment of culinary processes
(D) willingness to work long hours
(E) respect for tradition

59. In these passages, both Graham and Waters are
(A) examining their consciences
(B) presenting their artistic creeds
(C) criticizing their opponents
(D) analyzing their impact on their fields
(E) reassessing their chosen professions

60. Waters and Graham seem alike in that they both
(A) have an abundant supply of nervous energy
(B) benefitted from extensive classical training
(C) occasionally distrust their own instincts
(D) are passionately involved with their art
(E) believe in maintaining a positive attitude

IF YOU FINISH BEFORE 30 MINUTES, YOU MAY CHECK YOUR WORK ON THIS
SECTION ONLY. DO NOT TURN TO ANY OTHER SECTION IN THE TEST.   **S T O P**

DIAGNOSTIC TEST

SECTION **5** Mathematical Reasoning	Time—30 minutes 25 Questions

Directions and Sample Questions

Notes:

(1) The use of a calculator is permitted. All numbers used are real numbers.

(2) Figures that accompany problems in this test are intended to provide information useful in solving the problems. They are drawn as accurately as possible EXCEPT when it is stated in a specific problem that the figure is not drawn to scale. All figures lie in a plane unless otherwise indicated.

Questions 1–15 each consist of two quantities in boxes, one in Column A and one in Column B. You are to compare the two quantities and on the answer sheet fill in oval

A if the quantity in Column A is greater;
B if the quantity in Column B is greater;
C if the two quantities are equal;
D if the relationship cannot be determined from the information given.

Notes:

1. In some questions, information is given about one or both of the quantities to be compared. In such cases, the given information is centered above the two columns and is not boxed.
2. In a given question, a symbol that appears in both columns represents the same thing in Column A as it does in Column B.
3. Letters such as x, n, and k stand for real numbers.

EXAMPLES

	Column A	Column B	Answers
E1	5^2	20	● Ⓑ Ⓒ Ⓓ
E2	x	30	Ⓐ Ⓑ ● Ⓓ
E3	$r + 1$	$s - 1$	Ⓐ Ⓑ Ⓒ ●

E2: $150°$ $x°$

E3: r and s are integers.

PART I: QUANTITATIVE COMPARISON QUESTIONS

SUMMARY DIRECTIONS FOR QUANTITATIVE COMPARISON QUESTIONS

Answer: A if the quantity in Column A is greater;
B if the quantity in Column B is greater.

C if the two quantities are equal;
D if the relationship cannot be determined from the information given

	Column A	Column B			Column A	Column B
	In $\triangle ABC$, $\angle B \doteq 30$ and $AB = AC$				$a > 1$	
26.	The measure of $\angle A$	The measure of $\angle C$		**28.**	$(a)\left(\dfrac{1}{17}\right)(48)(6)$	$(48)\left(\dfrac{a}{17}\right)(12)$
	$a > 1$				$x \neq y$ and $x > 1$ and $y > 1$ $4x = 2y$	
27.	$(a + 1)^2$	$a(a + 2)$		**29.**	y	$2x$

GO ON TO THE NEXT PAGE

	Column A	Column B		Column A	Column B

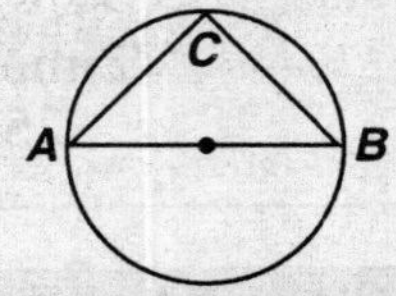

Diameter $AB = 10$
$AC = BC$

30.   Area of ABC $\sqrt{50}$

31. The area of a triangle with base $\dfrac{x}{2}$ and height y | The area of a square with side $\dfrac{\sqrt{xy}}{2}$

$x + 5 = y$
$x = \dfrac{y}{2}$

32. $2y$ 10

33. The sum of $2\frac{1}{2}$ and its reciprocal 2.5

$z < 0$

34. $2z^3$ $3z^2$

$5b = 12.5$
$3a + 2b = 12.5$

35. a b

$\dfrac{x}{6} = \dfrac{y}{4}$

36. $2x$ $3y$

$\dfrac{2}{5} + \dfrac{x}{y} = \dfrac{7}{5}$

37. x y

$3x - 2 < 0$

38. $3x$ 2

$\dfrac{3}{x} = 2$ and $\dfrac{5}{y} = 2$

39. x y

In $\triangle ABC$,
side $AB = 9$ units
and side $BC = 4$ units

40. Area of ABC 18 square units

GO ON TO THE NEXT PAGE

PART II: STUDENT-PRODUCED RESPONSE QUESTIONS

Directions for Student-Produced Response Questions

Each of the remaining ten questions (41–50) requires you to solve the problem and enter your answer by marking the ovals in the special grid, as shown in the examples below.

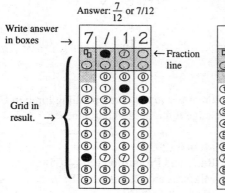

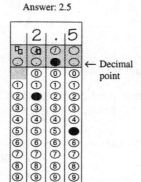

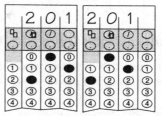

Note: You may start your answers in any column, space permitting. Columns not needed should be left blank.

- Mark no more than one oval in any column.
- Because the answer sheet will be machine-scored, **you will receive credit only if the ovals are filled in correctly.**
- Although not required, it is suggested that you write your answer in the boxes at the top of the columns to help you fill in the ovals accurately.
- Some problems may have more than one correct answer. In such cases, grid only one answer.
- No question has a negative answer.
- **Mixed numbers** such as $2\frac{1}{2}$ much be gridded as 2.5 or 5/2. (If [grid image] is gridded, it will be interpreted as $\frac{21}{2}$, not $21\frac{1}{2}$.)

- Decimal Accuracy: If you obtain a decimal answer, enter the most accurate value that the grid will accommodate. For example, if you obtain an answer such as 0.6666..., you should record the result as .666 or .667. Less accurate values such as .66 or .67 are not acceptable.

Acceptable ways to grid $\frac{2}{3}$ = .6666. . .

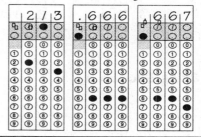

41. The average of three numbers is 67. If two of these numbers are 78 and 65 what is the third number?

42. If, on the average, 40% of the applicants are accepted to a certain college, how many of 800 applicants will be accepted?

43. The student officers voted to organize a girls' basketball team by a vote of 3 to 2. What fraction of the total vote was the affirmative vote?

44. The sum of three sides of a square is 33. What is the sum of two sides?

45. If the perimeter of a square is 16, what is the area of the square?

46. If 0.6 is the average of the following: 0.2, 0.8, 1.0 and x, what is the numerical value of x?

47. Four similar glass tumblers just fit into a cubical box. The area of the top of the circular cover of any one of the tumblers is 4π. What is the area of each side of the box?

48. $AB = AC$, $FD = FC$, and the measure of $\angle DEB$ is 120. What is the measure of angle DFC in degrees?

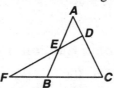

49. The area of square $EFGH$ is equal to the area of rectangle $ABCD$. GH = 6 feet, AD = 4 feet. What is the length of the perimeter (in feet)?

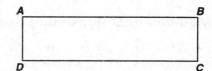

50. A damaged article is sold for $1.20, which is $\frac{2}{3}$ of its original price. What is the price (in dollars) of an undamaged article?

IF YOU FINISH BEFORE 30 MINUTES, YOU MAY CHECK YOUR WORK ON THIS SECTION ONLY. DO NOT TURN TO ANY OTHER SECTION IN THE TEST.

S T O P

ANSWER KEY

Verbal Reasoning Section 1

1. C	*6.* D	*11.* A	*16.* C	*21.* D	*26.* C
2. B	*7.* B	*12.* A	*17.* A	*22.* D	*27.* A
3. C	*8.* B	*13.* B	*18.* B	*23.* E	*28.* C
4. D	*9.* B	*14.* C	*19.* E	*24.* E	*29.* E
5. A	*10.* D	*15.* D	*20.* D	*25.* D	*30.* B

Mathematical Reasoning Section 2

Note: Each correct answer to the mathematics questions is keyed by number to the corresponding topic in Chapters 8 and 9. These numerals refer to the topics listed below, with specific page references in parentheses.

1. Basic Fundamental Operations (179–182)
2. Algebraic Operations (182–183)
3. Using Algebra (182–184, 187)
4. Exponents, Roots, and Radicals (184–185)
5. Inequalities (188–189)
6. Fractions (182, 198)
7. Decimals (200)
8. Percent (200)
9. Averages (201)
10. Motion (203)
11. Ratio and Proportion (204–205)
12. Mixtures and Solution (178)
13. Work (206–207)
14. Coordinate Geometry (194)
15. Geometry (189–193, 195)
16. Quantitative Comparisons (211–212)
17. Data Interpretation (208)

1. B (8)	*6.* C (6)	*10.* A (8)	*14.* C (2)	*18.* C (3)	*22.* E (9)
2. D (3)	*7.* E (1,7)	*11.* A (8,15)	*15.* C (2)	*19.* C (15)	*23.* E (14)
3. D (1)	*8.* E (6)	*12.* D (2)	*16.* C (11)	*20.* E (5)	*24.* E (8,17)
4. A (2)	*9.* E (8)	*13.* E (2)	*17.* D (1)	*21.* A (11)	*25.* C (11)
5. C (1)					

Writing Skills Section 3

1. A	*8.* D	*15.* E	*22.* A	*29.* D	*36.* C
2. D	*9.* C	*16.* A	*23.* A	*30.* D	*37.* C
3. B	*10.* B	*17.* B	*24.* C	*31.* B	*38.* A
4. B	*11.* E	*18.* C	*25.* A	*32.* B	*39.* B
5. E	*12.* A	*19.* C	*26.* B	*33.* C	
6. B	*13.* A	*20.* B	*27.* E	*34.* B	
7. A	*14.* C	*21.* D	*28.* A	*35.* E	

Verbal Reasoning Section 4

31. A	*36.* D	*41.* E	*46.* C	*51.* A	*56.* E
32. B	*37.* C	*42.* A	*47.* B	*52.* C	*57.* E
33. B	*38.* D	*43.* C	*48.* A	*53.* B	*58.* C
34. D	*39.* E	*44.* E	*49.* C	*54.* C	*59.* B
35. B	*40.* B	*45.* B	*50.* D	*55.* A	*60.* D

Mathematical Reasoning Section 5

26. A (15,16)	*29.* C (2,16)	*32.* A (2,16)	*35.* C (2,16)	*38.* B (2,16)
27. A (2,16)	*30.* A (15,16)	*33.* A (6,7,16)	*36.* C (2,16)	*39.* B (2,16)
28. B (6,16)	*31.* C (15,16)	*34.* B (4,16)	*37.* C (2,16)	*40.* D (15,16)

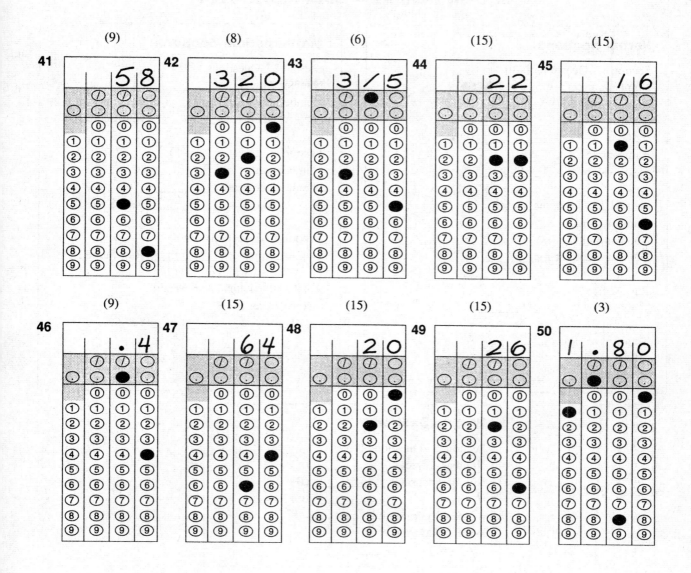

SCORING CHART — DIAGNOSTIC TEST

Verbal Sections

Section 1   Questions 1–30
Number correct _____ (A)
Number omitted _____ (B)
Number incorrect _____ (C)
$\frac{1}{4}$ (C) = _____ (D)
Raw Score:
  (A) – (D) = _____

Section 3   Questions 31–60
Number correct _____ (A)
Number omitted _____ (B)
Number incorrect _____ (C)
$\frac{1}{4}$ (C) = _____ (D)
Raw Score:
  (A) – (D) = _____

Total Verbal Raw Score:
  (Section 1 +
  Section 3) = _____

Mathematical Sections

Section 2   Questions 1–25
Number correct _____ (A)
Number incorrect _____ (B)
(A) – $\frac{1}{4}$ (B) = _____ Raw Score I

Section 4   Questions 26–40
Number correct _____ (C)
Number incorrect _____ (D)
(C) – $\frac{1}{3}$ (D) = _____ Raw Score II

Section 4   Questions 41–50
Number correct _____ Raw Score III

Total Mathematical Raw Score:
  (Raw Scores I + II
  + III) = _____

Writing Sections

Section 3   Questions 1–39
Number correct _____ (A)
Number incorrect _____ (B)
$\frac{1}{4}$ (B) = _____ (C)
(no penalty for omitted questions)
Writing Raw Score:
  (A) – (C) = _____

EVALUATION CHART

Study your score. Your raw score on the Verbal and Mathematical Reasoning Sections is an indication of your probable achievement on the PSAT/NMSQT. As a guide to the amount of work you need or want to do with this book, study the following.

Raw Score			Self-rating
Verbal	*Mathematical*	*Writing*	
55–60	41–50	37–39	Superior
44–54	25–40	31–36	Very good
39–43	20–24	25–30	Satisfactory
35–38	16–19	19–24	Average
29–34	10–15	13–18	Needs further study
20–28	7–9	6–12	Needs intensive study
0–19	0–6	0–5	Probably inadequate

The Identify Your Weaknesses chart will help you identify those areas in which you are weak and should concentrate your study efforts. After checking the Answer Key, circle the question numbers you got wrong. You will probably find that most of your errors fall under two or three topics—geometry and fractions, for example. You should then plan to spend most of your time reviewing material under that topic.

IDENTIFY YOUR WEAKNESSES

Skills	Page References	Question Numbers
Verbal Reasoning		
Sentence Completion	63–72	1–17
Analogies	73–80	31–43
Reading Comprehension	81–106	18–30, 44–60
Mathematical Reasoning		
Basic Fundamental Operations	179–182	3, 5, 7, 17
Algebraic Operations	182–183	4, 12, 13, 14, 15, 27, 29 32, 35, 37, 38, 39
Using Algebra	182–184, 187	2, 18, 50
Exponents, Roots, and Radicals	184–185	34
Inequalities	188–189	20
Fractions	182, 192	6, 8, 33, 43
Decimals	200	7
Percent	200	1, 9, 10, 11, 24, 25, 42
Averages	201	22
Ratio and Proportion	204–205	16, 21, 25
Geometry	189–195	11, 19, 23, 26, 30, 31, 40, 44, 45, 47, 48, 49
Quantitative Comparisons	211–212	26, 27, 28, 29, 30, 31, 32, 33, 34, 35, 36, 37, 38, 39, 40
Data Interpretation	208	24
Writing Skills		
Find the Error	164	1–19
Sentence Correction	165–166	21–31
Paragraph Correction	167	32–39

ANSWER EXPLANATIONS

Verbal Reasoning Section 1

1. **C** *But* signals a contrast. Normally thunderstorms last for a short time. However, sometimes they last or *persist* for a long time. Note the effect of the phrase "becoming ever more severe." If the storm keeps on getting worse, it is not *waning* (declining), *moderating* (becoming less severe), *vacillating* (wavering), or *dispersing* (being scattered).

2. **B** For Miró, art was holy or *sacred*. Note how the second clause clarifies what kind of ritual art became for Miró.

3. **C** The key term here is "smoke screen," something designed to obscure or mislead. How would accuracy-loving scholars react to an autobiography filled with misleading remarks? They would be *vexed* (annoyed) by the smoke screens and other misleading *errors*.

4. **D** Why is this 100-mile-thick piece of glass clearer than a standard windowpane? *Because* the glass is exceptionally *transparent*. The "'so . . . that" structure signals cause and effect.

5. **A** To be kept "at arm's length" from someone's emotions is to feel an emotional distance between you and that person. Singer's own quality of uninvolvement or *detachment* makes the reader feel distant from his main character.

6. **D** The *assiduous* or diligent *execution* (performance) of one's job would give one's employer no cause for complaint. Note the signal word *because* indicating the sentence's cause and effect structure.

7. **B** The grandmother disliked having others use her things. Carrying this dislike to an extreme, she *grudged* (was reluctant to allow) the mailman the right to walk on her sidewalk to deliver the mail.

8. **B** There has never been a census or numerical count of all the people in the world. *Therefore,* any attempt to describe the world's population numerically must involve guesswork or *conjecture.*

9. **B** If the mayfly's adult life lasts for such a short time, it clearly is an *ephemeral* (short-lived, fleeting) creature. Note how the second clause clarifies what the author means by *ephemeral.*

10. **D** Something *eclectic* is by definition composed of items drawn from many different sources. In this case, the style of interior decoration is eclectic.

11. **A** Break down the sentence. The prolific author has written many different books, bound in many different bindings. The books' topics vary as much as their bindings. This indicates the author has not specialized in any one topic. Instead, he has *resisted* or fought specialization as strongly as some other writers have *pursued* it.

12. **A** *Despite* signals a contrast. Although Warhol seemed *nonchalant* (coolly unconcerned; casual), he was not. Instead, he cared deeply about his art, laboring at it *diligently.*

13. **B** One expects seeds to germinate or sprout within a relatively short period of time. However, for woodland seeds, the process takes longer than normal; the seeds seem strangely *reluctant* to sprout.

14. **C** Because these shows are highly derivative of (stem from) our culture, they reflect what our culture is like. Thus, they are good *indices* (indicators or signs) of our culture's attitudes and values. *Indices* is the plural form of *index.*

15. **D** *And* is a support signal. The opening clause states something positive about Guinness. The conclusion of the sentence must support that idea: it must also say something positive about him. In this case, it says he's a good writer: an unusually *felicitous* prose stylist, one who has a special talent for finding exactly the right words.

16. **C** Given that English society didn't encourage women to get an education, you would expect it not to care that women were uneducated. However, English society was illogical: it *decried* or expressed its disapproval of women's lack of education.

17. **A** A passionate nature hates compromise (finds it *odious*) because it seems a surrender. An intellectual nature hates compromise because it seems a *confusion,* mixing together things that to the intellect are inherently distinct.

18. **B** The narrator never indicates that his father felt bitter about his army service. Choice A is incorrect. The narrator describes his father as "daring" and "impetuous." Choice C is incorrect. The narrator indicates that his father had been a sugarcane grower before he took up cattle ranching. Choice D is incorrect. Paragraph 2 stresses the riskiness of the trip during the stormy season. Choice E is incorrect. The narrator states his father had learned from the war that life was temporary.

19. **E** Look at the context of the phrase. The very next words are "Suddenly all our cane went down and men began putting up fences." Why? They are putting up fences in order to be ready to enclose the cattle the father is about to buy. The father has sensed there is a market for good, fresh, untainted meat, and has immediately decided to try his hand at raising cattle.

20. **D** Pappy "knew cattle." The father knew cane-growing, but wanted to learn cattle. This suggests that the father sought out Pappy *because he needed Pappy's cattle-ranching expertise.*

21. **D** Pappy had just had a frightening experience: he had seen the maddened bull attack the other cattle. Clearly, he would be *agitated by the news he brought.*

22. **D** In this excerpt, the narrator is taking a retrospective look at events that took place in the past. (Note the mother's comments, in lines 15–18: they make it clear that the narrator is looking back.) His father abandoned cane-growing for cattle-ranching, a new, risky venture. He put all the family's money into buying a small herd and a prize bull. That bull went mad, attacking the herd. The passage concludes with the father's loading a rifle. What does this set of events suggest? First, it suggests the father would try to kill the prize bull. Other cattle were already dead or so badly injured that they, too, would have to be killed. The father had spent all he had on cattle; he had no money left to buy a new herd. He had cut down his sugar cane. He had taken a risk and lost. As the story's title suggests, he was destined for ruin. And years later his son would look back, trying to *come to terms with his family's financial undoing.*

23. **E** Throughout the passage the author presents and comments on the nature of the original documents that form the basis for his historical narrative. Thus, it is clear that a major concern of his is to *introduce* these "sources of almost forgotten oral history" to his readers. Choice A is incorrect. The author clearly regrets the fate of the Indians. However, he does not take this occasion to denounce or condemn the white man. Choice B is incorrect. While the author discusses the various treaty councils, he does not evaluate or judge how effective they were. Choice C is incorrect. The author never touches on the current treatment of Indians. Choice D is incorrect. The author indicates no such thing.

24. **E** Of all the thousands of published descriptions of the opening of the West, the greatest concentration or *cluster* of accounts date from the period of 1860 to 1890.

25. **D** You can arrive at the correct choice by the process of elimination.
Statement I is true. The passage states that the quality of the interviews depended on the interpreters' abilities. Inaccuracies could creep in because of the translators' lack of skill. Therefore, you can eliminate Choice B.
Statement II is untrue. The passage indicates that the Indians sometimes exaggerated, telling the reporters tall tales. It does not indicate that the reporters in turn overstated what they had been told. Therefore, you can eliminate Choices C and E.
Statement III is true. The passage indicates that the Indians sometimes were disinclined to speak the whole truth because they feared reprisals (retaliation) if they did. Therefore, you can eliminate Choice A. Only Choice D is left. It is the correct answer.

26. **C** Brown speaks of the Indians who lived through the "doom period of their civilization," the victims of the conquest of the American West. In doing so, his tone can best be described as *elegiac*, expressing sadness about their fate and lamenting their vanished civilization.

27. **A** In the fifth paragraph Brown comments upon the "graphic similes and metaphors of the natural world" found in the English translations of Indian speeches. Thus, he is impressed by their *vividness of imagery.*

28. **C** Commenting about inadequate interpreters who turned eloquent Indian speeches into "flat" prose, Brown is criticizing the translations for their *pedestrian*, unimaginative quality.

29. **E** Brown has tried to create a narrative of the winning of the West from the victims' perspective. This suggests that, in asking his readers to read the book facing eastward (the way the Indians would have been looking when they first saw the whites headed west), he is asking them metaphorically to look at things from the Indians' point of view.

30. **B** In the sentence immediately preceding the one in which this phrase appears, Brown calls the Indians "true conservationists." Such conservationists know that life is *necessarily tied to* the earth and to its resources, and that by destroying these resources, by imbalancing the equation, so to speak, you destroy life itself.

Mathematical Reasoning Section 2

1. **B** 100% of 25 = 25. We are required to find an additional 4% of 25, which would make the correct answer *slightly* more than 25. Glance at the answers—a very good habit to develop. Note that only one possible answer is slightly more than 25. The more time-consuming method would be to compute (25) (104%) or (25) (1.04) to get 26.

2. **D** Algebraically, if x is the number required, then

$$\frac{2}{7}x = 64$$

$$\left(\frac{7}{2}\right)\left(\frac{2}{7}x\right) = (\overset{32}{\cancel{64}})\left(\frac{7}{2}\right)$$

$$x = 224$$

An alternate method using simple reasoning is to consider that if $\frac{2}{7}$ of the number is 64, then $\frac{1}{7}$ of the number is 32 and $\frac{7}{7}$ of the number is 224.

3. **D** This is not a test in fundamentals of arithmetic. Besides, too much time would be spent with long division. Glance at the answers given. Observe that they differ only in their last digits. Since the dividend ends with the digit 6 and the divisor with 4, then the quotient must end with the digit 4, since there is no remainder. Note the "equals exactly."

4. **A** This question should be done in seconds. Since the value of the numerator is zero, the value of the fraction is zero.

5. **C** $144 \div 12 = 12$ spaces. We must place a post where the fence begins, so that at.the first space we have 2 posts, at the end of the second space we have 3 posts . . . and at the end of the last (twelfth) space we have 13 posts.

6. **C** Since all units are in hours, do not convert to minutes, but simply add fractions. Recall that to add fractions they must all have common denominators.

$$\frac{1}{5} + \frac{1}{3} + \frac{1}{6} =$$

$$\frac{6}{30} + \frac{10}{30} + \frac{5}{30} = \frac{21}{30} = \frac{7}{10}$$

7. **E** Sam took 40 minutes longer than Stanley.
$$\frac{40}{60} = \frac{2}{3}.$$

8. **E** For problems using PART OF or PERCENT OF, the expression following OF is the denominator.

$$P \vdash\!/\!\!-\!\!+\!\!-\!\!/\!\!-\!\!+\!\!-\!\!/\!\!-\!\!/\!\!-\!\!\dashv Q$$
$$\overset{R\quad\;\; T}{}$$

$$\frac{PQ}{PT} = \frac{3 \text{ equal units}}{2 \text{ equal units}} = 1\frac{1}{2} = 150\%.$$

9. **E** We are concerned with the 60 teachers who were NOT transferred.
$$\frac{60}{80} = \frac{3}{4} = 75\%$$

10. **A** This question illustrates that often it is advisable to work back from the answers given. Bear in mind that 5% of one of the answers represents an increase that will yield 52,500. Choices (D) and (E) are unreasonable since they are each more than 52,500 and cannot express the change between the original and the present enrollment of 52,500. Choice (C) evidently gives the original enrollment, which is not asked for in this question. Choice (B) should be rejected because it represents a large increase, while we are concerned with a 5% increase. To do this algebraically, let x be the original enrollment.
$$x + .05x = 52,500$$
$$100x + 5x = 5,250,000$$
$$105x = 5,250,000$$
$$x = 50,000 \text{ (one of the incorrect choices)}$$
Since we are asked to find the *increase* in number of students,
$$52,500 - 50,000 = 2500$$

11. **A** $\dfrac{30°}{360°} = \dfrac{1}{12} = 8.3\%$

12. **D** Note the possible factors in all but choice (D)
(A) $a = 7 \quad b = 30 \quad c = 1$
(B) $a = 7 \quad b = 2 \quad c = 15$
(C) $a = 2 \quad b = 5 \quad c = 21$
(D) If $c = 27$, then $\frac{210}{27}$ or 7.77+ and a and/or b will not be whole numbers
(E) $a = 2 \quad b = 3 \quad c = 35$

13. **E** $3t \div \dfrac{1}{4} = (3t)(4) = 12t$

$$4t^2 \div \left(\frac{3}{t}\right) = (4t^2)\left(\frac{3}{t}\right) = 12t$$

14. **C** $\dfrac{t+n}{n} = \dfrac{t}{n} + \dfrac{n}{n}$ or $\dfrac{t}{n} + 1$

15. **C** Factor $\dfrac{(a+b)(a-b)}{(a-b)(a-b)} = \dfrac{a+b}{a-b}$

16. **C** Many problems involve ratio and proportion. Set up a ratio. Substitute. (Watch units!)
$$\frac{\text{number of items}}{\text{cost in } ¢} = \frac{2}{c} = \frac{?}{x}$$
$$(c)(?) = 2x$$
$$? = \frac{2x}{c}$$

17. **D** Students taking both mathematics and chemistry are represented by the regions in which Circle I and Circle II overlap, that is, Region 8 + Region 10. But Region 10 also lies in Circle III and therefore represents some who are taking physics as well. Those who are taking both mathematics and chemistry but not physics are represented by Region 8 alone.

18. **C** $2 \phi a = a \phi 3$
    $2(2) + a = 2(a) + 3$
    $4 + a = 2a + 3$
    $1 = a$

19. **C**   Since AB is parallel to CD, the altitude is the same for all five triangles. Triangle #3 is the only one that has more than 2 units as a base.

20. **E**   If a and b are both greater than 1, the product, ab, will be greater than either a or b: for example, $2 \times 3 = 6$ and $6 > 2$ or 3. If b is a fraction less than 1 and a is greater than 1, ab will be greater than b, but less than a; for example, $3 \times \frac{1}{2} = 1\frac{1}{2}$. If a and b are both positive fractions less than 1, their product, ab, will be less than either a or b: for example,
    $\frac{1}{5} \times \frac{1}{10} = \frac{1}{50}$ and $\frac{1}{50} < \frac{1}{5}$ or $\frac{1}{10}$.
    Thus, I, II, or III could each be true, depending on the values of a and b.

21. **A**   Examples of conversion of units are similar to #16.
    $$\frac{\text{nautical miles}}{\text{statute miles}} = \frac{630}{720} = \frac{x}{1}$$
    $$x = \frac{630}{720} = \frac{63}{72} = \frac{7}{8} = 0.875 \text{ or } 0.88$$

22. **E**   This example involves the combination of the averages of two different sets of numbers. They must be weighted in proportion to the numbers of members of each set. If x is the average of P numbers, then the sum of these numbers is Px. If y is the average of N numbers, the sum of these numbers is Ny: Therefore $Px + Ny$ is the sum of both sets of numbers. The average of these $(P + N)$ numbers is $\frac{Px + Ny}{P + N}$.

23. **E**   Since the area of square $KLMN$ is 16, each side must equal 4 units. Note that KL equals 4 units in all choices but (E).

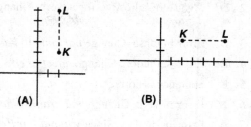

(A)   (B)

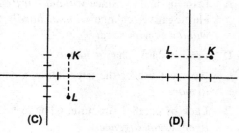

(C)   (D)

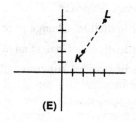

(E)

24. **E** $5000 + 2000$ or $\frac{7000}{70,000}$ (the total body weight) $= \frac{1}{10}$ or 10%.

25. **C**   Let $2x =$ the number of yellow marbles in the jar. Then $3x =$ the number of green marbles in the jar.
    $$P(\text{green}) = \frac{3x}{2x + 3x} = \frac{3x}{5x} = \frac{3}{5}$$

Writing Skills Section 3

1. **B** Error in diction. Change *had ought* to *ought*.

2. **D** Misuse of adjective for adverb. Change *bad* to *badly*.

3. **B** Error in tense. Change *has sang* to *has sung*.

4. **B** Error in diction. Change *affect* to *effect*.

5. **E** Sentence is correct.

6. **B** Error in verb. Change *had drank* to *had drunk*.

7. **A** Error in diction. Since *without hardly* is a double negative, change *without hardly* to either *without* or *with hardly*.

8 **D** Error in case. Change *him* to *he*.

9. **C** Incorrect use of the superlative. Change *most* to *more*.

10. **B** Lack of parallel structure. Change *being intelligent* to *intelligence*.

11. **E** Sentence is correct.

12. **A** Error in diction. Change *or* to *nor*.

13. **A** Error in diction. Change *might of* to *might have*.

14. **C** Lack of parallel structure. Change *to finish* to *finishing*.

15. **E** Sentence is correct.

16. **A** Error in diction. Change *principal* to *principle*.

17. **B** Error in agreement. Change *were* to *was*.

18. **C** Error in agreement. Change *them* to *him* or *her*.

19. **C** Error in agreement. Change *are* to *is*.

20. **B** This corrects the misuse of the subjunctive.

21. **D** This corrects the error in the case of the pronoun. Choice E corrects the error in case but introduces an error in tense.

22. **A** The clause is correct.

23. **A** Sentence is correct.

24. **C** This corrects the dangling participle.

25. **A** Sentence is correct.

26. **B** This corrects the unnecessary switch in the pronouns, *anyone–you*.

27. **E** This corrects the error in parallel structure.

28. **A** Sentence is correct.

29. **D** The run-on sentence is corrected by the use of a semicolon.

30. **D** This corrects the double negative *hadn't hardly* and the misuse of *those* with *kind*.

31. **B** This corrects the dangling participle and the misuse of *stole* for *stolen*.

32. **B** In Choice B, the run-on sentence is corrected by the use of a semicolon, and the omission of the past participle *been* is also corrected.

33. **C** Choice C expresses the author's meaning directly and concisely. All other choices are either indirect or ungrammatical.

34. **B** Choice A is awkwardly constructed. The phrase *for the cruelty of keeping animals* is cumbersome. Moreover, the sentence suggests that cruelty to animals can be justified—the opposite of what the writer intended to say.
Choice B states the idea clearly and economically. It is the best answer.
Choice C is wordy and awkwardly expressed.
Choice D is wordy and awkwardly expressed.
Choice E, which lacks a main verb, is a sentence fragment.

35. **E** Choice A is awkwardly constructed and illogical. It suggests that animals are fed because a machine dispenses food.
Choice B says that animals are fed because a machine dispenses food—an illogical statement. Also, the phrase *to occur* is not needed.
Choice C is awkwardly worded. The noun *food* should be closer to the verb *buy*.
Choice D contains a faulty pronoun reference. The pronoun *they* has no specific referent.
Choice E accurately and concisely expresses the intended idea. It is the best answer.

36. **C** Choice A is a sentence fragment. It lacks a main verb.
Choice B contradicts the idea that zoos can be educational.
Choice C accurately develops the idea introduced in sentence 3 that zoos can be educational. It is the best answer.
Choice D is irrelevant to the idea in sentence 3.
Choice E is written with a hostile and inappropriate tone.

37. **C** Choice A is not the best answer because most readers probably know that zoos house animals in cages. Moreover, highly charged language is not ordinarily used merely to pass along information.
Choice B is unrelated to the words in question.
Choice C is the best answer. The choice of words is meant to shock and disturb the reader.
Choice D suggest that the author is trying to be objective, but the words in question are hardly objective.
Choice E describes the purpose of the entire essay but not the particular words in question.

38. **A** Choice A introduces the main idea of the paragraph. It is the best answer.
Choice B raises an issue not mentioned in the remainder of the paragraph. Therefore, it is not a good topic sentence of the paragraph.
Choice C contains an idea not discussed in the paragraph. The paragraph focuses on how animals behave in captivity, not on living conditions at the zoo.

Choice D contains a dangling modifier. The phrase *Living in the zoo* should modify *animals* instead of *conditions*.

Choice E contains a frivolous cliché that is not consistent with the tone of the essay.

39. **B** Choice A is grammatically correct, but it reverse the cause-effect relationship stated by the original sentences.

Choice B accurately and economically conveys the ideas of the original sentences. It is the best answer.

Choice C is a sentence fragment. It lacks a main verb. The *-ing* forms of verbs (e.g., *growing, placing, being*) may not be used as the main verb without a helping verb, as in was growing, is placing, and so on.

Choice D is grammatically correct but stylistically awkward mainly because the subject *They* is too far removed from the verb *would . . . survive*.

Choice E is virtually meaningless because the cause-effect relationship has been reversed.

Verbal Reasoning Section 4

31. **A** A *minnow* is a kind of *fish*. A *poodle* is a kind of *dog*.   (Class and Member)

32. **B** *Oxygen* is stored in a *tank*. *Milk* is stored in a *carton*.   (Function)

33. **B** *Bridging a gap* spans a physical distance between two sides, making a connection between them. *Reconciling* (setting right) *an estrangement* (loss of affection, separation) spans an emotional distance between two sides, making a connection between them.   (Function)

34. **D** An *eggshell* is characterized by delicacy or *fragility*. A *barbell* is characterized by *weight*.   (Defining Characteristic)

35. **B** *Hostile* (antagonistic; unfriendly) by definition means lacking *friendship*. *Traitorous* (disloyal) by definition means lacking *loyalty*.   (Antonym Variant)

36. **D** A *girder* is used to *support* things. A *winch* is used to *hoist* or lift them.   (Function)

37. **C** *Philately*, by definition, is the study and collection of *stamps*. *Numismatics*, by definition, is the study and collection of *coins*.   (Definition)

38. **D** Someone *circumspect* (cautious) is characterized by *wariness* (carefulness). Someone *reckless* (heedless; daring) is characterized by *foolhardiness* (rashness).   (Defining Characteristic)

39. **E** *Paragon* (model of excellence) and *standard* or ideal are synonyms. Similarly, *imitation* and *copy* are synonyms.   (Synonym)

40. **B** To *pulverize* something is to convert it to powder or *dust*. To *vaporize* something is to convert it to vapor or *mist*.   (Definition)

41. **E** A *suppliant* (humble petitioner) by definition *pleads*. An *interpreter* by definition *translates*.   (Definition)

42. **A** A *luminary* (notable person) is by definition *illustrious* (renowned). A *zealot* (fanatic; extremist) is by definition *intense*.

          (Defining Characteristic)

43. **C** Something *apocryphal* (doubtful; unverified) lacks *authenticity* (genuineness). Something *hypocritical* (insincere) lacks *integrity* (honesty).

          (Antonym Variant)

44. **E** The second paragraph discusses the various methods epiphytes adopt in order to retain or conserve moisture. Choice A is incorrect. Epiphytes have lost their root connection with the forest floor. Choice B is incorrect. Epiphytes seek the sun; they are not adapted to a sunless environment. Choice C is incorrect. Epiphytes have developed ways to conserve rainwater, not to dissipate or squander it. Choice D is incorrect. Epiphytes are not parasites; they do not derive nourishment ("sustenance") from the tree trunks to which they attach themselves.

45. **B** The first paragraph states that epiphytes grow in "spoonfuls" of soil. We can infer from this that they do not need particularly large amounts of soil for growth. Choice A is incorrect. Although epiphytes have lost their root connection with the forest floor, they do possess root systems. Choice C is incorrect. The passage states that the roots of some orchids carry on photosynthesis; epiphytes clearly are not incapable of photosynthesis. Choice D is incorrect. Nothing in the passage suggests epiphytes are hard to spot. Choice E is incorrect. Epiphytes have "managed to create their own environment" so well that the soil in which they grow does not differ significantly from normal soil in microbiological processes. This does not suggest that their need for nutrients differs from that of plants that grow in normal soil.

46. **C** Epiphytes are described in a straightforward, direct manner. Choice A is incorrect. The author is not exhorting or urging anyone to do anything. Choice B is incorrect. The author is not analyzing epiphytes, that is, thoroughly studying each of the individual features that comprise these plants in order to understand their structure. He is simply saying what they are like. Choice D is incorrect. The author is being direct rather than indirect in presenting what he knows about epiphytes. Choice E is incorrect. The author is not being particularly forceful in his presentation; neither is he presenting an argument.

47. **B** The strangler tree's feeding cables do not ascend toward the canopy; they descend to the forest floor. You can double-check your answer by using the process of elimination.

The strangler tree eventually stands on its own pedestal or supports itself. You can eliminate Choice A. One set of the strangler tree's roots (the "feeding cable") extends all the way from high up in the fork of the host tree down to the forest floor. You can eliminate Choice C. When the feeder cable reaches the soil, the plant's growth quickens. You can eliminate Choice D. The strangler's roots "thicken to a marked degree" becoming conspicuously larger. You can eliminate Choice E. Only Choice B is left. It is the correct answer.

48. **A** The roots thicken to a marked or noticeable degree, eventually growing thick enough to support the strangler tree.

49. **C** The concluding sentence states that the host expires and the strangler tree stands on its own pedestal of thickened roots (its original feeding cables, now fused together). Thus, the strangler tree has *outgrown its need for its host*.

50. **D** Graham's goal is "to bring into focus unhackneyed movement." Thus, she rejects movement in dance that is hackneyed or *trite*.

51. **A** Graham insists that, in the dancer's body, the audience must see themselves, "something of the miracle that is a human being." In rejecting the idea of their imitating natural phenomena (trees, flowers, waves), she emphasizes that dancers must embody or *express their humanity*.

52. **C** Graham is pairing opposite qualities that are held in balance by training and technique. Thus, technique and training give freedom and its opposite, discipline; tension and its opposite, plasticity (*mobility and pliancy*).

53. **B** Graham draws an *analogy* or comparison between the function of spontaneity in dance or theater and that of light in life.

54. **C** Waters is an experienced cook and restauranteur, an *accomplished practitioner of the culinary arts*. You can determine the answer to this question by using the process of elimination. Waters is not a cook on the verge of opening a restaurant, or simply a gifted home cook; she has run her own restaurant for years, long enough to have developed criteria for hiring employees (lines 81–84). Therefore, you can eliminate Choices A and D. She is not uninformed about traditional methods of French cooking; she served her culinary apprenticeship in France. You can eliminate Choice B. Though she is a professional, there is nothing in the passage to suggest that she is set on outstripping her competition. You can eliminate Choice E. Only Choice C is left; it is the correct answer.

55. **A** Sometimes sharp and strong, sometimes sweet and fresh, garlic varies in quality. Waters uses the example of the garlic to show *the variability of ingredients*.

56. **E** Waters stresses that she is only making suggestions and that it is up to the reader to "determine the correct balance and composition" of the meal. Thus, she is trying to *allow scope* (room) *for the reader's own culinary initiative*.

57. **E** Waters states firmly that "a person who responds to the cooking processes and the mound of fresh ingredients with a genuine glow of delight is likely to be, or become, a very good cook indeed." Thus, to be a good cook, one who will produce superior results, one must have *a love of one's medium* (material for artistic expression; in this case, food).

58. **C** Waters is looking for employees who will take great personal satisfaction in what they are doing, people who enjoy the *culinary processes*.

59. **B** Waters and Graham are expressing their belief as artists in spontaneity, in flexibility, in energy, in joy. They are *presenting their artistic creeds*.

60. **D** Graham and Waters resemble one another in their marked enthusiasm and love for their work. Both clearly *are passionately involved with their art*.

Mathematical Reasoning Section 5

26. **A**

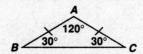

27. **A** $(a + 1)^2 = a^2 + 2a + 1$
$a(a + 2) = a^2 + 2a$

28. **B** Eliminate the terms common to both expressions:

$(8)\left(\frac{11}{17}\right)(48)\,(6) \qquad (48)\left(\frac{a}{17}\right)(12)$

29. **C** $4x = 2y$. Divide by 2 and $2x = y$.

30. **A**

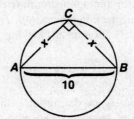

$\angle C$ inscribed in a semicircle is a right angle. Using the Pythagorean Theorem,
$x^2 + x^2 = (10)^2$
$2x^2 = 100$ and $x^2 = 50$.

Area of $\triangle ABC = \dfrac{(x)\,(x)}{2} = 25$

$25 > \sqrt{50}$ since $\sqrt{50} = 7+$

31. **C** Area of triangle =

$$\frac{bh}{2} = \frac{\left(\frac{x}{2}\right)(y)}{2} = \frac{\frac{xy}{2}}{2} = \left(\frac{xy}{2}\right)\left(\frac{1}{2}\right) = \frac{xy}{4}$$

Area of square = (side)^2 = $\left(\frac{\sqrt{xy}}{2}\right)^2 = \frac{xy}{4}$

32. **A** Substitute: $x = \frac{y}{2}$

$\frac{y}{2} + 5 = y$

$y + 10 = 2y$

$y = 10$ and $2y = 20$

33. **A** $2\frac{1}{2} = \frac{5}{2}$; Reciprocal $= \frac{2}{5}$

$\frac{5}{2} + \frac{2}{5} = \frac{25}{10} + \frac{4}{10} = \frac{29}{10} = 2.9$

$2.9 > 2.5$

34. **B** Since z is negative z^3 is negative, but z^2 is positive. Therefore $3z^2 > 2z^3$.

35. **C** $3a + 2b = 5b$ (they are each equal to 12.5)

$3a = 3b$

$a = b$

36. **C** Cross multiply: $\frac{x}{6} = \frac{y}{4}$

$4x = 6y$

Divide by 2: $2x = 3y$

37. **C** $\frac{2}{5} + \frac{x}{y} = \frac{7}{5}$ $\left(\text{subtract } \frac{2}{5}\right)$

$\frac{x}{y} = \frac{5}{5} = 1$

$x = y$

38. **B** $3x - 2 < 0$

$3x < 2$ (add 2 to each side of the inequality)

or, $2 > 3x$

39. **B** $\frac{3}{x} = 2$ $\frac{5}{y} = 2$

$2y = 3$ $2y = 5$

$x = \frac{3}{2} = 1\frac{1}{2}$ $y = \frac{5}{2} = 2\frac{1}{2}$

40. **D** We may not assume that ABC is a right triangle.

41. **58** The sum of all numbers is

67×3 or 201

$78 + 65 = 143$

$201 - 143 = 58$

42. **320** $(800)(40\%)$ or $(800)(0.4)$ equals 320.

43. **⅗** $\dfrac{\text{affirmative part}}{\text{total}} = \dfrac{3}{5}$

44. **22** Each side must be $\frac{33}{3}$ or 11. Two sides must be 22.

45. **16** If the perimeter is 16, each side of the square is 4 and the area is (4)(4) or 16.

46. **0.4** $\dfrac{\text{sum of numbers}}{\text{quantity of numbers}} = \text{average}$

$\frac{2 + x}{4} = 0.6$

$2 + x = 2.4$

$x = 0.4$

47. **64** The area of the top of each circular cover $= 4\pi$. Use the formula for the area of a circle; $\pi r^2 =$ Area. Substitute values $\pi r^2 = 4$, and divide by π: $r^2 = 4$ and $r = 2$. The length of each side of the box consists of $4r$ or 8 units. Therefore, the area of each side of the box $= 8 \times 8$ or 64.

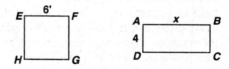

48. **20** Since $AB = AC$, m$\angle 1 =$ m$\angle 2$. Since $FD = FC$, m$\angle 3 =$ m$\angle 2$. $\therefore$ m$\angle 1 =$ m$\angle 2 =$ m$\angle 3$ The sum of the measure of the angles of $BCDE = 360°$. m$\angle 1 +$ m$\angle 2 +$ m$\angle 3 = 360° - 120°$ or $240°$, or each of these angles has a measure of $80°$. Consider $\triangle FDC$. Since $\angle 2 + \angle 3 \doteq 160$, then $\angle DFC \doteq 20$.

49. **26** Area of $EFGH = 6$ feet $\times 6$ feet $= 36$ feet^2

Area of $ABCD = 36$ feet^2

Let $x = AB$.

Area of $ABCD = 4x = 36$

$x = 9$ feet (AB)

Since $DC = AB$,

perimeter $= 9' + 9' + 4' + 4' = 26$ feet.

50. **1.80** $\frac{2}{3}x = \$1.20$ and

$x = (\$1.20)\left(\frac{3}{2}\right) = \$1.80$. Also, if $\frac{2}{3}$ is \$1.20, then $\frac{1}{3}$ is \$0.60. $\frac{2}{3} + \frac{1}{3}$ is the total original price: $\$1.20 + \$0.60 = \$1.80$.

CORRECT YOUR WEAKNESSES

Verbal Reasoning

3

The Sentence Completion Question

The sentence completion questions ask you to choose the best way to complete a sentence from which one or two words have been omitted. These questions test a combination of reading comprehension skills and vocabulary. You must be able to recognize the logic, style, and tone of the sentence so that you can choose the answer that makes sense in this context. You must also be able to recognize the way words are normally used. At some time in your schooling, you have probably had a vocabulary assignment in which you were asked to define a word and use it in a sentence of your own. In this part of the PSAT, you have to use the words in sentences that are given to you. Once you understand the implications of a sentence, you should be able to choose the answer that will make the sentence clear, logical, and stylistically consistent.

The sentences cover a wide variety of topics of the sort you have probably encountered in your general reading. However, this is not a test of your general knowledge. You may feel more comfortable if you are familiar with the topic the sentence is discussing, but you should be able to handle any of the sentences using your understanding of the English language.

TIPS FOR HANDLING SENTENCE COMPLETION QUESTIONS

1. Before you look at the answer choices, read the sentence and think of words you know that might make sense in the context. You may not come up with the exact word, but you *may* come up with a synonym.
2. Don't be hasty in picking an answer. Test each answer choice, substituting it for the missing word. That way you can satisfy yourself that you have selected the answer that best fits.
3. In double-blank sentences, eliminate answer pairs by testing their first words. Read through the entire sentence. Then insert the first word of each answer pair in the first blank of the sentence. Ask yourself whether this particular word makes sense in this blank. If the initial word of an answer pair makes no sense in the sentence, you can eliminate that answer pair.
4. If you're having vocabulary trouble, look for familiar parts—prefixes, suffixes, and roots—in unfamiliar words.

5. Watch out for negative words and words telling how long something lasts. Only a small change makes these two sentences very different in meaning:

They were not lovers.

They were not often lovers.

6. Look for words or phrases that indicate a contrast between one idea and another—words like *although, however, despite,* or *but.* In such cases an antonym or near-antonym for another word in the sentence may provide the correct answer.
7. Look for words or phrases that indicate similarities—words like *in the same way, in addition,* and *also.* In such cases, a synonym or near-synonym for another word in the sentence may provide the correct answer.
8. Look for words or phrases that indicate that one thing causes another—words like *because, since, therefore,* or *thus.*

EXAMPLE 1

See how the first tip works in dealing with the following sentence:

The psychologist set up the experiment to test the rat's ___ ; he wished to see how well the rat adjusted to the changing conditions it had to face.

Even before you look at the answer choices, you can figure out what the answer *should* be.

Look at the sentence. A psychologist is trying to test some particular quality or characteristic of a rat. What quality? How do you get the answer?

Look at the second part of the sentence, the part following the semicolon (the second clause, in technical terms). This clause defines or clarifies what the psychologist is trying to test. He is trying to see how well the rat *adjusts.* What words does this suggest to you? *Flexibility* possibly, or *adaptability* comes to mind. Either of these words could logically complete the sentence's thought.

Here are the five answer choices given:
(A) reflexes   (B) communicability   (C) stamina
(D) sociability   (E) adaptability

The best answer clearly is *adaptability,* Choice E.

EXAMPLE 2

When you're racing the clock, you feel like marking down the first correct-sounding answer you come across. *Don't.* You may be going too fast.

Because the enemy had a reputation for engaging in sneak attacks, we were ___ on the alert.
(A) frequently   (B) furtively   (C) evidently
(D) constantly   (E) occasionally

A hasty reader might be content with Choice A, *frequently,* but *frequently* is not the best fit. The best answer is Choice D, *constantly,* because "frequent" periods of alertness would not be enough to provide the necessary protection against sneak attacks that could occur at any time. "Constant" vigilance is called for: the troops would have to be always on the alert.

EXAMPLE 3

Dealing with double-blank sentences can be tricky. It helps to test the first word of each answer pair when you're narrowing things down.

The opossum is ___ the venom of snakes in the rattlesnake subfamily and thus views the reptiles not as ___ enemies but as a food source.
(A) vulnerable to . . natural   (B) indicative of . . mortal
(C) impervious to . . lethal   (D) sensitive to . . deadly
(E) defenseless against . . potential

Look at the first word of each answer pair. Do any of these words make no sense in the context? The sentence is talking about the way opossums react to rattlesnake poison. What words seem possible? Opossums could be *vulnerable* to this poison, capable of being hurt

by it. They could be *sensitive* to it, excessively affected by it. They could be *defenseless* against it, wholly unable to protect themselves from the poison. They could even be *impervious* to it, unaffected by it. But *indicative* of it? The word makes no sense. You can eliminate Choice B.

Now examine the second half of the sentence. Opossums look on rattlesnakes as a food source; they eat rattlers. What makes it possible for them to do so? They can do so *because* they're *impervious* to the poison (that is, unharmed by it). That's the reason they can treat the rattlesnake as a potential source of food and not as a *lethal* or deadly enemy. The correct answer is Choice C.

Note the cause-and-effect signal *thus.* The nature of the opossum's response to the venom explains why it can look on a dangerous snake as an easy prey.

EXAMPLE 4

After a tragedy, many people claim to have had a ___ of disaster.
(A) taste   (B) dislike   (C) presentiment   (D) context
(E) verdict

Use your knowledge of word parts to enable you to deal with unfamiliar words in sentence completion questions.

Take the unfamiliar word *presentiment.* Break it down into parts. A sentiment is *a feeling* (the root *sens* means *feel*). *Pre-* means *before.* A *presentiment* is something *you feel before* it happens, a foreboding. Your best answer is Choice C.

EXAMPLE 5

Watch out for *not:* it's easy to overlook, but it's a key word.

Madison was not ___ person and thus made few public addresses; but those he made were memorable, filled with noble phrases.
(A) a reticent   (B) a stately   (C) an inspiring
(D) an introspective   (E) a communicative

What would happen if you overlooked *not* in this question? Probably you'd wind up choosing Choice A: Madison was a *reticent* (quiet; reserved) man. *For this reason* he made few public addresses.

Unfortunately, you'd have gotten things backward. The sentence isn't telling you what Madison was like. It's telling you what he was not like. And he was not a *communicative* person; he didn't express himself freely. However, when he did get around to speaking in public, he had valuable things to say.

EXAMPLE 6

We expected him to be jubilant over his victory, but he was ___ instead.
(A) triumphant   (B) adult   (C) morose
(D) talkative   (E) culpable

Watch for words that indicate contrast: *although, however, despite,* or *but.*

But suggests that the winner's expected reaction contrasts with his actual one. Instead of being *jubilant* (extremely joyful), he is sad. The correct answer is Choice **C**, *morose.*

EXAMPLE 7

The simplest animals are those whose bodies are least complex in structure and which do the things done by all animals, such as eating, breathing, moving, and feeling, in the most ___ way.
(A) haphazard   (B) bizarre   (C) advantageous
(D) primitive   (E) unique

The transition word *and* signals you that the writer intends to develop the concept of simplicity introduced in the sentence. You should know from your knowledge of biology that *primitive* life forms were simple in structure and that the more complex forms evolved later. Choice C may seem possible. However, to secure the most *advantageous* way of conducting the activities of life, the animal would have to become specialized and complex. Thus, Choice D *(primitive)* is best, because it is the only choice that develops the idea of simplicity.

EXAMPLE 8

Because his delivery was ___ , the effect of his speech on the voters was nonexistent.
(A) halting (B) plausible (C) moving
(D) respectable (E) audible

Watch for words that show a cause-and-effect relationship: *because, since, therefore,* or *thus.*

What sort of delivery would cause a speech to have no effect? Obviously, you would not expect a moving or eloquent delivery to have such a sorry result. A *halting* or stumbling speech, however, would normally have little or no effect. Thus, Choice A is best.

The two exercises that follow will give you an indication of your ability to handle these sentence completion questions. Scoring may be interpreted as follows:

43 TO **50**—EXCELLENT
35 TO **43**—SUPERIOR
27 TO **34**—SATISFACTORY
21 TO **26**—AVERAGE
20 TO **0**—UNSATISFACTORY

SENTENCE COMPLETION EXERCISE A   TIME: 30 minutes

In the sentences below, one or two words or groups of words have been omitted. For each question, select the answer choice, labeled A through E, that best fits into the meaning of the sentence.

1. Although the play was not praised by the critics, it did not ___ thanks to favorable word-of-mouth comments.
   (A) succeed (B) translate (C) function
   (D) close (E) continue

2. Perhaps because something in us instinctively distrusts such displays of natural fluency, some readers approach John Updike's fiction with ___ .
   (A) indifference (B) suspicion (C) veneration
   (D) recklessness (E) bewilderment

3. We lost confidence in him because he never ___ the grandiose promises he had made.
   (A) forgot about (B) reneged on (C) tired of
   (D) delivered on (E) retreated from

4. Because the hawk is ___ bird, farmer try to keep it away from their chickens.
   (A) a migratory (B) an ugly (C) a predatory
   (D) a reclusive (E) a huge

5. We were amazed that a man who had been heretofore the most ___ of public speakers could, in a single speech, electrify an audience and bring them cheering to their feet.
   (A) enthralling (B) accomplished
   (C) pedestrian (D) auspicious (E) masterful

6. If you are trying to make a strong impression on your audience, you cannot do so by being understated, tentative, or ___ .
   (A) hyperbolic (B) restrained (C) argumentative
   (D) authoritative (E) passionate

7. Despite the mixture's ___ nature, we found that by lowering its temperature in the laboratory we could dramatically reduce its tendency to vaporize.
   (A) resilient (B) volatile (C) homogeneous
   (D) insipid (E) acerbic

8. No other artist rewards the viewer with more sheer pleasure than Miró: he is one of those blessed artists who combine profundity and ___ .
(A) education (B) wisdom (C) faith
(D) fun (E) depth

9. Some Central Intelligence Agency officers have ___ their previous statements denying any involvement on their part with the contra aid network and are now revising their earlier testimony.
(A) justified (B) recanted (C) repeated
(D) protracted (E) heeded

10. New concerns about growing religious tension in northern India were ___ this week after at least fifty people were killed and hundreds were injured or arrested in rioting between Hindus and Moslems.
(A) lessened (B) invalidated (C) restrained
(D) dispersed (E) fueled

11. In a happy, somewhat boisterous celebration of the origins of the United States, the major phase of the Constitution's Bicentennial got off to ___ start on Friday.
(A) a slow (B) a rousing (C) a reluctant
(D) an indifferent (E) a quiet

12. In a revolutionary development in technology, several ___ manufacturers now make biodegradable forms of plastic: some plastic six-pack rings, for example, gradually ___ when exposed to sunlight.
(A) harden (B) stagnate (C) inflate
(D) propagate (E) decompose

13. To alleviate the problem of contaminated chicken, the study panel recommends that the federal government shift its inspection emphasis from cursory bird-by-bird visual checks to a more ___ random sampling for bacterial and chemical contamination.
(A) rigorous (B) perfunctory (C) symbolic
(D) discreet (E) dubious

14. To the dismay of the student body, the class president was ___ berated by the principal at a school assembly.
(A) ignominiously (B) privately
(C) magnanimously (D) fortuitously
(E) inconspicuously

15. Although Barbara Tuchman never earned a graduate degree, she nonetheless ___ a scholarly career as a historian noted for her vivid style and ___ erudition.
(A) interrupted . . deficient
(B) relinquished . . immense
(C) abandoned . . capricious
(D) pursued . . prodigious
(E) followed . . scanty

16. When Frazer's editors at Macmillan tried to ___ his endless augmentations, he insisted on a type size so small and a page so packed as to approach illegibility; and if that proved ___ , thinner paper.
(A) protract . . unwarranted
(B) expurgate . . satisfactory
(C) reprimand . . irrelevant
(D) restrict. . insufficient
(E) revise. . idiosyncratic

17. Baldwin's brilliant *The Fire Next Time* is both so eloquent in its passion and so searching in its ___ that it is bound to ___ any reader.
(A) bitterness . . embarrass
(B) romanticism . . appall
(C) candor . . unsettle
(D) indifference . . disappoint
(E) conception . . bore

18. Unlike other examples of ___ verse, Milton's *Lycidas* does more than merely mourn for the death of Edward King; it also denounces corruption in the Church in which King was ordained.
(A) satiric (B) elegiac (C) free
(D) humorous (E) didactic

19. We now know that what constitutes practically all of matter is empty space: relatively enormous ___ in which revolve infinitesimal particles so small that they have never been seen or photographed.
(A) crescendos (B) enigmas (C) conglomerates
(D) abstractions (E) voids

20. The officers threatened to take ___ if the lives of their men were ___ by the conquered natives.
(A) liberties . . irritated
(B) measures . . enhanced
(C) pains . . destroyed
(D) reprisals . . .endangered
(E) affront . . .enervated

21. Despite his ___ appearance, he was chosen by his employer for a job that required neatness and polish.
(A) unkempt (B) impressive (C) prepossessing
(D) aloof (E) tardy

22. The ___ remarks of the speaker annoyed the audience because they were lengthy as well as meaningless.
(A) lugubrious (B) sarcastic (C) pithy
(D) inane (E) pungent

23. He was so ___ in meeting the payments on his car that the finance company threatened to seize the automobile.
(A) dilatory (B) mercenary (C) solvent
(D) diligent (E) compulsive

24. The earthquake created some damage, but the tidal wave that followed was more devastating because it ___ many villages.
(A) bypassed (B) absorbed (C) desiccated
(D) congested (E) inundated

25. The insurance company rejected his application for accident insurance because his ___ occupation made him a poor risk.
(A) desultory (B) haphazard (C) esoteric
(D) hazardous (E) peripatetic

26. Since we had been promised a definite answer to our proposal, we were ___ by his ___ reply.
(A) pleased . . equivocal (B) vexed . . negative
(C) annoyed. . noncommital
(D) delighted . . dilatory (E) baffled . . decided

27. Because she had a reputation for ___ we were surprised and pleased when she greeted us so ___ .
(A) insolence . . informally
(B) insouciance . . cordially
(C) graciousness . . amiably
(D) arrogance . . disdainfully
(E) querulousness . . affably

28. The child was so spoiled by her indulgent parents that she pouted and became ___ when she did not receive all of their attention.
(A) discreet (B) suspicious (C) elated
(D) sullen (E) tranquil

29. Just as disloyalty is the mark of the renegade, ___ is the mark of the ___ .
(A) timorousness . . hero (B) temerity . . coward
(C) avarice . . philanthropist
(D) cowardice . . craven (E) vanity . . flatterer

30. He became quite overbearing and domineering once he had become accustomed to the ___ shown to soldiers by the natives; he enjoyed his new sense of power and self-importance.
(A) disrespect (B) apathy (C) deference
(D) culpability (E) enmity

31. The ___ of time had left the castle ___ ; it towered above the village, looking much as it must have done in Richard the Lion-Hearted's time.
(A) repairs . . destroyed (B) remoteness . . alone
(C) lack . . defended (D) status . . lonely
(E) ravages . . untouched

32. One of the most ___ educators in New York's history, Dr. Shalala ignited a controversy in 1984 by calling the city public schools a "rotten barrel" in need of ___ reform.
(A) disputatious . . little (B) outspoken . . systemic
(C) caustic . . partial (D) indifferent . . pretentious
(E) sycophantic . . superficial

33. The reasoning in this editorial is so ___ that we cannot see how anyone can be deceived by it.
(A) coherent (B) astute (C) cogent
(D) specious (E) dispassionate

34. The ___ of evidence was on the side of the plaintiff since all but one witness testifed that his story was correct.
(A) paucity (B) propensity (C) accuracy
(D) brunt (E) preponderance

35. Because Inspector Morse could not contain his scorn for the police commissioner, he was imprudent enough to make ___ remarks about his superior officer.
(A) ambiguous (B) dispassionate
(C) unfathomable (D) interminable (E) scathing

36. Modern architecture has discarded ___ trimming on buildings and has concentrated on an almost Greek simplicity of line.
(A) flamboyant (B) austere (C) inconspicuous
(D) aesthetic (E) derivative

37. If you are seeking ___ that will resolve all our ailments, you are undertaking an impossible task.
(A) a precedent (B) a panacea
(C) an abstraction (D) a direction
(E) a contrivance

38. I have no ___ motive in offering this advice; I seek no personal advantage or honor.
(A) nominal (B) altruistic (C) incongruous
(D) disinterested (E) ulterior

39. This park has been preserved in all its ___ wildness so that visitors in future years may see how people lived during the eighteenth century.
(A) hedonistic (B) prospective (C) esoteric
(D) untrammeled (E) pristine

40. Though she was theoretically a friend of labor, her voting record in Congress ___ that impression.
(A) implied (B) created (C) confirmed
(D) belied (E) maintained

41. The orator was so ___ that the audience became ___ .
(A) soporific . . drowsy (B) inaudible . . elated
(C) pompous . . bombastic (D) dramatic . . affable
(E) convincing . . moribund

42. If you carry this ___ attitude to the conference, you will ___ any supporters you may have at this moment.
(A) belligerent . . delight (B) truculent. . alienate
(C) conciliatory . . defer (D) supercilious . . attract
(E) flippant . . consolidate

43. The ___ pittance the widow receives from the government cannot keep her from poverty.
   (A) magnanimous (B) indulgent (C) meticulous
   (D) munificent (E) scanty

44. Harriman, Kennan, and Acheson were part of that inner ___ of the American diplomatic establishment whose distinguished legacy ___ U.S. foreign policy to this day.
   (A) circle . . . grieves (B) sanctum . . . absorbs
   (C) core . . . dominates (D) life . . . biases
   (E) coterie . . . exacerbates

45. The young man was quickly promoted when his employers saw how ___ he was.
   (A) indigent (B) indifferent (C) assiduous
   (D) lethargic (E) cursory

46. Because it arrives so early in the season, before many other birds, the robin has been called the ___ of spring.
   (A) hostage (B) autocrat (C) compass
   (D) newcomer (E) harbinger

47. Shy and hypochondriacal, Madison was uncomfortable at public gatherings; his character made him a most ___ lawmaker and practicing politician.
   (A) conscientious (B) unlikely (C) fervent
   (D) gregarious (E) effective

48. The tapeworm is an example of ___ organism, one that lives within or on another creature, deriving some or all of its nutriment from its host.
   (A) a hospitable (B) an exemplary (C) a parasitic
   (D) an autonomous (E) a protozoan

49. In place of the more general debate about abstract principles of government that most delegates probably expected, the Constitutional Convention put ___ proposals on the table.
   (A) theoretical (B) vague (C) concrete
   (D) tentative (E) redundant

50. Overindulgence ___ character as well as physical stamina.
   (A) strengthens (B) stimulates (C) debilitates
   (D) maintains (E) provides

SENTENCE COMPLETION EXERCISE B   TIME: 30 minutes

In the sentences below, one or two words or groups of words have been omitted. For each question, select the answer choice, labeled A through E, that best fits into the meaning of the sentence.

51. The scientist maintains that any hypothesis must explain what has already been discovered and must be constantly ___ by future findings.
   (A) confirmed (B) invalidated (C) disregarded
   (D) equaled (E) reversed

52. Being cynical, he was reluctant to ___ the ___ of any kind act until he had ruled out all possible secret, uncharitable motives.
   (A) question . . benevolence
   (B) acknowledge . . wisdom
   (C) credit . . unselfishness
   (D) endure . . loss
   (E) witness . . outcome

53. In view of the interrelationships among a number of the African-American leaders treated in this anthology, there is inevitably a certain amount of ___ among some of the essays presented here.
   (A) overlapping (B) inaccuracy (C) pomposity
   (D) exaggeration (E) objectivity

54. Hellman was not an ___ woman and thus was hard to get to know; nevertheless, many made the attempt, attracted by her wit and celebrity.
   (A) enigmatic (B) eccentric (C) astute
   (D) extroverted (E) eminent

55. Most Antarctic animals ___ depend on the tiny shrimplike krill, either feeding on them directly, like the humpback whale, or consuming species that feed on them.
   (A) seldom (B) ultimately (C) preferably
   (D) immediately (E) marginally

56. Truculent in defending their rights of sovereignty under the Articles of Confederation, the newly formed states ___ constantly.
   (A) apologized (B) digressed (C) conferred
   (D) acquiesced (E) squabbled

57. If the Titanic had hit the iceberg head on, its watertight compartments might have saved it from ___ , but it swerved to avoid the iceberg, and in the collision so many compartments were opened to the sea that disaster was ___ .
   (A) foundering . . inevitable (B) sinking . . escaped
   (C) damage . . limited
   (D) buoyancy . . unavoidable
   (E) collapse . . averted

58. Written in an amiable style, the book provides a comprehensive overview of European wines that should prove inviting to both the virtual ___ and the experienced connoisseur.
(A) prodigal (B) novice (C) zealot
(D) miser (E) glutton

59. The sugar dissolved in water ___ ; finally all that remained was an almost ___ residue on the bottom of the glass.
(A) quickly . . lumpy
(B) immediately . . fragrant
(C) gradually . . imperceptible
(D) subsequently . . glassy
(E) spectacularly . . opaque

60. Traffic speed limits are set at a level that achieves some balance between the danger of ___ speed and the desire of most people to travel as quickly as possible.
(A) marginal (B) normal (C) prudent
(D) inadvertent (E) excessive

61. Although the economy suffers downturns, it also has strong ___ and self-correcting tendencies.
(A) unstable (B) recidivist (C) inauspicious
(D) recuperative (E) self-destructive

62. Since Cyrano de Bergerac did not wish to be under an obligation to any man, he refused to be a ___ of Cardinal Richelieu.
(A) skeptic (B) mentor (C) protege
(D) benefactor (E) predecessor

63. The members of the religious sect ostracized the ___ who had abandoned their faith.
(A) coward (B) suppliant (C) litigant
(D) recreant (E) proselyte

64. I am not attracted by the ___ life of the ___ , always wandering through the countryside, begging for charity.
(A) proud . . almsgiver
(B) noble . . philanthropist
(C) affluent . . mendicant
(D) natural . . philosopher
(E) peripatetic . . vagabond

65. They fired upon the enemy from behind trees, walls, and any other ___ point they could find.
(A) conspicuous (B) definitive (C) vantage
(D) exposed (E) indefensible

66. We need more men and women of culture and enlightenment; we have too many ___ among us.
(A) visionaries (B) students (C) philistines
(D) pragmatists (E) philosophers

67. It is foolish to vent your spleen on ___ object; still, you make ___ enemies that way.
(A) an inanimate . . fewer
(B) an immobile . . bitter
(C) an interesting . . curious
(D) an insipid . . dull
(E) a humane . . more

68. After the Japanese attack on Pearl Harbor on December 7, 1941, Japanese-Americans were ___ of being spies for Japan, although there was no ___ to back up this viewpoint.
(A) acquitted . . buttress (B) tired . . witness
(C) reminded . . reason (D) suspected . . evidence
(E) exonerated . . money

69. More than one friendly whale has nudged a boat with such ___ that passengers have been knocked overboard.
(A) enthusiasm (B) lethargy (C) hostility
(D) serenity (E) animosity

70. Chaotic in conception but not in ___ , Kelly's canvases are as neat as the proverbial pin.
(A) conceit (B) theory (C) execution
(D) origin (E) intent

71. After having worked in the soup kitchen feeding the hungry, the volunteer began to see her own good fortune as ___ and her difference from the ___ as chance rather than destiny.
(A) an omen . . homeless
(B) a fluke . . impoverished
(C) a threat . . destitute
(D) a reward . . indigent
(E) a lie . . affluent

72. Some students are ___ and want to take only the courses for which they see immediate value.
(A) theoretical (B) impartial (C) pragmatic
(D) idealistic (E) opinionated

73. Unlike the Shakespearean plays that lit up the English stage, the "closet dramas" of the nineteenth century were meant to be ___ rather than ___ .
(A) seen . . acted (B) read . . staged
(C) quiet . . raucous (D) sophisticated . . urbane
(E) produced . . performed

74. Japan's industrial success is ___ in part to its tradition of group effort and ___ , as opposed to the emphasis on personal achievement that is a prominent aspect of other industrial nations.
(A) responsive . . independence
(B) related . . introspection
(C) equivalent . . solidarity
(D) subordinate . . individuality
(E) attributed . . cooperation

75. I was so bored with the verbose and redundant style of Victorian novelists that I welcomed the change to the ___ style of Hemingway.
(A) prolix (B) consistent (C) terse
(D) logistical (E) florid

76. As ___ head of the organization, he attended social functions and civic meetings but had no ___ in the formulation of company policy.
(A) titular . . voice (B) hypothetical . . vote
(C) former . . pride (D) nominal . . competition
(E) actual . . say

77. Her listeners enjoyed her ___ wit but her victims often ___ at its satire.
(A) lugubrious . . suffered (B) caustic . . laughed
(C) kindly . . smarted (D) subtle . . smiled
(E) trenchant . . winced

78. It is only to the vain that all is vanity; and all is ___ only to those who have never been ___ themselves.
(A) arrogance . . proud of
(B) deception . . sincere with
(C) cowardice . . afraid for
(D) indolence . . bored by
(E) solitude . . left to

79. No act of ___ was more pronounced than his refusal of any rewards for his discovery.
(A) abeyance (B) submission (C) egoism
(D) denunciation (E) abnegation

80. The evil of class and race hatred must be eliminated while it is still in an ___ state; otherwise it may grow to dangerous proportions.
(A) amorphous (B) embryonic (C) uncultivated
(D) overt (E) independent

81. She is a pragmatist, as ___ to base her future on impractical dreams as she would be to build a castle on shifting sand.
(A) determined (B) disinclined (C) quick
(D) apt (E) diligent

82. Aimed at curbing European attempts to seize territory in the Americas, the Monroe Doctrine was a warning to ___ foreign powers.
(A) pertinacious (B) credulous (C) remote
(D) overt (E) predatory

83. Although Josephine Tey is arguably as good a mystery writer as Agatha Christie, she is clearly far less ___ than Christie, having written only six books in comparison to Christie's sixty.
(A) coherent (B) prolific (C) equivocal
(D) pretentious (E) gripping

84. The systems analyst hesitated to talk to strangers about his highly specialized work, fearing it was too ___ for people uninitiated in the computer field to understand.
(A) intriguing (B) derivative (C) frivolous
(D) esoteric (E) rudimentary

85. Through her work at the Center for the Family in Transition, Wallerstein has come to see divorce not as a single circumscribed event but as ___ of changing family relationships—as a process that begins during the failing marriage and extends over many years.
(A) a continuum (B) an episode (C) a parody
(D) a denial (E) a curtailment

86. A code of ethics governing the behavior of physicians during epidemics did not exist until 1846, when it was ___ by the American Medical Association.
(A) rescinded (B) promulgated (C) presupposed
(D) depreciated (E) implied

87. Both *China Beach* and *Tour of Duty* reflect the way dissent has become ___ in America; what were radical antiwar attitudes in the 1960s are now ___ TV attitudes.
(A) domesticated . . mainstream
(B) obsolete . . militant
(C) meaningful . . unfashionable
(D) sensationalized . . trite
(E) troublesome . . conventional

88. MacDougall's former editors remember him as a ___ man whose ___ and exhaustive reporting was worth the trouble.
(A) domineering . . . wearisome
(B) congenial . . . pretentious
(C) popular . . . supercilious
(D) fastidious . . . garbled
(E) cantankerous . . . meticulous

89. Americans have always been rightfully ___ unnecessary government coercion, feeling that the government should use its powers sparingly.
(A) disarmed by (B) chary about
(C) dependent on (D) amenable to
(E) enthusiastic about

90. Lavish in visual beauty, the film *Lawrence of Arabia* also boasts ___ of style: it knows how much can be shown in a shot, how much can be said in a few words.
(A) nonchalance (B) economy (C) autonomy
(D) frivolity (E) arrogance

91. We must try to understand his momentary ___ , for he has ___ more strain and anxiety than any among us.
    (A) outcry . . described   (B) senility . . understood
    (C) vision . . forgotten   (D) generosity . . desired
    (E) aberration . . undergone

92. He is ___ opponent; you must respect and fear him at all times.
    (A) a redoubtable   (B) a disingenuous
    (C) a pugnacious   (D) an insignificant
    (E) a craven

93. Your ___ tactics may compel me to cancel the contract as the job must be finished on time.
    (A) dilatory   (B) offensive   (C) repugnant
    (D) infamous   (E) confiscatory

94. The mind of a bigot is like the pupil of the eye: the more light you pour upon it, the more it will ___ .
    (A) blink   (B) veer   (C) stare
    (D) reflect   (E) contract

95. In the North American tribes, men were the representational artists; women, on the other hand, traditionally ___ abstract, geometrical compositions.
    (A) decried   (B) shunned   (C) devised
    (D) impaired   (E) prefigured

96. By its very nature, printmaking was judged ___ the aims of most Impressionist painters, who believed that its technical procedures ___ spontaneity and failed to render the transient appearance of nature.
    (A) antithetical to . . defeated
    (B) indicative of . . enhanced
    (C) conducive to . . increased
    (D) warranted by . . encouraged
    (E) incumbent on . . bypassed

97. Breaking with established artistic and social conventions, Dali was ___ genius whose heterodox works infuriated the traditionalists of his day.
    (A) a derivative   (B) an iconoclastic
    (C) an uncontroversial   (D) a venerated
    (E) a trite

98. Dr. Smith cautioned that the data so far are not sufficiently ___ to warrant dogmatic assertions by either side in the debate.
    (A) hypothetical   (B) tentative   (C) controversial
    (D) unequivocal   (E) imponderable

99. Mr. Wilson sets out only the broad contours of a new policy agenda, leaving it to others to ___ specific initiatives.
    (A) ignore   (B) mold   (C) apprehend
    (D) forestall   (E) regret

100. The concept of individual freedom grew from political and moral convictions that were to ___ the closed and ___ world of feudalism into a more open and dynamic society.
    (A) galvanize . . vibrant
    (B) convert . . irreverent
    (C) transform . . hierarchical
    (D) recast . . vital
    (E) merge . . unregulated

ANSWER KEY

EXERCISE A

1. D	11. B	21. A	31. E	41. A
2. B	12. E	22. D	32. B	42. B
3. D	13. A	23. A	33. D	43. E
4. C	14. A	24. E	34. E	44. C
5. C	15. D	25. D	35. E	45. C
6. B	16. D	26. C	36. A	46. E
7. B	17. C	27. E	37. B	47. B
8. D	18. B	28. D	38. E	48. C
9. B	19. E	29. D	39. E	49. C
10. E	20. D	30. C	40. D	50. C

EXERCISE B

51. A	61. D	71. B	81. B	91. E
52. C	62. C	72. C	82. E	92. A
53. A	63. D	73. B	83. B	93. A
54. D	64. E	74. E	84. D	94. E
55. B	65. C	75. C	85. A	95. C
56. E	66. D	76. A	86. B	96. A
57. A	67. A	77. E	87. A	97. B
58. B	68. D	78. B	88. E	98. D
59. C	69. A	79. E	89. B	99. B
60. E	70. C	80. B	90. B	100. C

4

The Analogy Question

In the PSAT/NMSQT, the analogy question presents a pair of words followed by five additional pairs of words. You must select the pair of words from among the five choices which best matches the relationship existing between the first two words.

These are the questions that people seem to think of most often when they think about the PSAT. Analogies may well be the most difficult kind of question on the test, but they aren't impossible, and at least some of them will be fairly easy. Questions of this kind test your understanding of the relationships among words and ideas. You are given one pair and must choose another pair that is related in the same way. Many relationships are possible. The two terms in the pair can be synonyms; one term can be a cause, the other the effect; one can be a tool, the other the user.

LONG-RANGE STRATEGY

Continue to build up your vocabulary and to study the connotations as well as the literal meanings of words. Read in a wide variety of fields. Pay particular attention to specialized technical words for things people use *(mortar, vise, blueprint)* and for natural phenomena *(foliage, chaff, eddy).* Also, be sure you know the terms for the common types of relationships that exist among people and animals *(sister* and *sibling; mare* and *foal; lion* and *pride).*

TIPS FOR HANDLING ANALOGY QUESTIONS

1. Consider the first pair in each question carefully, and try to make a clear sentence using the two terms. Then look at the other pairs. It should be possible to substitute the correct answer (and only the correct answer) into your sentence and still have the sentence make sense.
2. Do not be misled if the choices are from different fields or areas, or seem to deal with different items, from the given pair. Study the capitalized words until you see the connection between them; then search for the same relationship among the choices. BOTANIST:MICROSCOPE::CARPENTER: HAMMER, even though the two workers may have little else in common besides their use of tools.

3. If more than one answer choice fits, try making your sentence more specific. Example:

MITTEN:HAND::
(A) bracelet:wrist (B) belt:waist
(C) muffler:neck (D) ring:finger
(E) sandal:foot

You make up the sentence, "You wear a mitten on your hand." Unfortunately, *all* the answer choices will fit that sentence, so you say to yourself, "Why do you wear a mitten? You wear a mitten to keep your hand warm." Now when you try to substitute, only Choice **C** works, so you have your answer.

4. Beware of words that can have more than one meaning. A simple word like *lie* can mean either recline or fib. If you get one meaning fixed too firmly in your mind, you may miss the point of the analogy.

5. Be particularly careful of words that have different meanings when they are pronounced differently. Suppose you are given the analogy SOW:SEED. If you keep thinking of *sow* as a female pig, the analogy makes no sense. But if you change your pronunciation, you will remember that *sow* also means to plant. Try to keep flexible.

6. Be guided by what you know about parts of speech. If the capitalized words are a noun and a verb, each of your answer pairs will be a noun and a verb. If the capitalized words are an adjective and a noun, each of your answer pairs will be an adjective and a noun. Even if you don't recognize the parts of speech of the capitalized words, you can still work things out; if you can recognize the parts of speech in a single answer pair, you know the parts of speech of all the other answer pairs, and of the original pair as well. This information can help you recognize analogy types and spot the use of unfamiliar or secondary meanings of words.

7. Watch out for errors caused by eye-catchers. These are incorrect answer choices *designed* to catch your eye. Eye-catchers grab your attention because they somehow remind you of one of the capitalized words. For example, if the original pair of words is ARMOR:BODY (armor *protects* the body), a good eye-catcher would be HELMET:STEEL (a helmet *is made of* steel).

8. Eliminate answer choices whose terms are only casually linked. In your capitalized pair of words (and in your correct answer choice), the words are always clearly linked:

     Armor *protects* the body.
     A shepherd is *someone who* herds sheep.
     A chapter is *a division of* a book.

In the answer pairs, the relationship between the words can be pretty vague. There's a clear dictionary relationship between *chapter* and *book*. There's no necessary relationship between *chapter* and *pencil*.

9. Watch out for errors stemming from grammatical reversals. Ask yourself *who* is doing what to whom. FUGITIVE:FLEE is not the same as LAUGHINGSTOCK:MOCK. A fugitive is the person who flees. A laughingstock is the person who *is mocked*.

10. Remember that the test-makers usually place more difficult analogies toward the end of the analogy section. Therefore, if one of the final analogy questions in a set looks simple, *suspect a trap*.

11. Be familiar with the whole range of common analogy types. Know the usual ways in which pairs of words on the PSAT are linked.

Common Analogy Types

Synonyms
DAUNTLESS:COURAGEOUS
Dauntless (fearless) and *courageous* are synonyms.

Synonym Variant
DAUNTLESS:COURAGE
Someone *dauntless* shows *courage.*

Antonyms
DAUNTLESS:COWARDLY
Dauntless and *cowardly* are antonyms.

Antonym Variant
DAUNTLESS:COWARDICE
Someone *dauntless* does not exhibit *cowardice.*

Worker and Work Created
POET:SONNET
A *poet* creates a *sonnet.*

Worker and Tool
PAINTER:BRUSH
A *painter* uses a *brush.*

Tool and Object Worked On
SAW:WOOD
A *saw* cuts *wood.*

Function
CROWBAR:PRY
A *crowbar* is a tool used to *pry.*

Action and Its Significance
NOD:ASSENT
A *nod is* a sign of *assent* (agreement).

Manner
STAMMER:TALK
To *stammer* is to *talk* in a halting manner.

Degree of Intensity
LUKEWARM:BOILING
Lukewarm is less intense than *boiling.*

Class and Member
MAMMAL:WHALE
A *whale* is a member of the class known as *mammal.*

Defining Characteristic
TIGER:CARNIVOROUS
A *tiger* is by definition a *carnivorous* (meat-eating) animal.

Part to Whole
ISLAND:ARCHIPELAGO
An *archipelago* (chain of islands) is made up of many *islands.*

Sex
DOE:STAG
A *doe* is a female deer; a *stag,* a male deer.

Age
DEER:FAWN
A *fawn* is a young *deer.*

Symbol and Abstraction It Represents
DOVE: PEACE
A *dove* is the symbol of *peace.*

Use these tips to help you with the following examples.

EXAMPLE 1

CONSTELLATION:STARS::
(A) prison:bars (B) assembly:speaker
(C) troupe:actors (D) mountain:peak
(E) flock:shepherds

A *constellation* is made up of *stars*. A *troupe* (not *troop* but *troupe)* is made up of *actors* (and actresses, of course). Choice C is correct.

Note, by the way, the characteristics of the analogy you have just analyzed. The relationship between the words in CONSTELLATION:STARS is built-in: if you look up *constellation* in a dictionary, you will see that a constellation is a group of stars. The words are related *by definition.* The relationship is clear. You can phrase your linking sentence in several ways:

"A *constellation* is made up of *stars.*"
"A *constellation* is a group of *stars.*"
"A *constellation* is composed of *stars.*"
"The specific term for a group of *stars* is *constellation.*"

However, the essential relationship between the words is unchanged.

Your correct answer choice must have the same characteristics as the original pair. The words must have a clear relationship. They must be related by definition. If you substitute them in your linking sentence, they have got to fit—*tight.*

EXAMPLE 2

SKYCAP:AIRPORT::
(A) stenographer:office (B) cashier:box office
(C) waitress:restaurant (D) actress:theater
(E) typist:paper

If you word your sentence "A *skycap* works at an *airport,*" you will find that Choices A, B, C, and D are all good analogies. At this point, take a second look at the original relationship. A skycap works at an airport, true. What else do you know about a skycap's work? For one, he carries things for people. What's more, when he works at the airport, he relies on tips.

Refine your original sentence to include these additional facts. "A *skycap* carries bags for travelers at the *airport* in the hope of earning tips." Now test the answers. Only one answer fits: "A *waitress* carries food for patrons at a *restaurant* in the hope of earning tips." Choice C is the correct answer.

Your sentence should reflect the relationship between the two capitalized words *exactly.* If it doesn't, try, try again.

EXAMPLE 3

COMPOSER:SYMPHONY::
(A) porter:terminal (B) writer:plagiarism
(C) coach:team (D) painter:mural
(E) doctor:stethoscope

A composer creates a symphony. You therefore are looking for a relationship between a worker and a work he or she has created. You can easily eliminate Choices A and E; a porter works *at* a terminal; a doctor works *with* a stethoscope. You can also eliminate Choice C: no coach literally *creates* a team in the same way that a composer creates a symphony.

Writers and painters, however, both create works of art. Which answer is correct, B *or* D?

If you do not know the meanings of *plagiarism* and *mural,* think of a context for one (or both) of them. Someone is "accused of plagiarism." From this you can infer that *plagiarism* is a crime (passing off someone else's work as one's own), not a created work. A *mural* is a picture painted on a wall. The correct answer is Choice D.

EXAMPLE 4

EROSION:ROCKS::
(A) flatness:landscape (B) fatigue:task
(C) fasting:food (D) dissipation:character
(E) forgery:signature

The idea of a wearing away of a substance (the *erosion* of *rocks*) is repeated in Choice D. *Dissipation* implies a wasting away of energies, which results in a loss of *character.*

Note that you are dealing with a secondary meaning. *Character* is not used here as a synonym for *nature.* It is used instead with the meaning of a person's *moral constitution.*

EXAMPLE 5

CAMPAIGN:OBJECTIVE::
(A) motivation:goal (B) misdeed:consequence
(C) victory: triumph (D) talent:success
(E) voyage:destination

Just as the goal of a *campaign* is defined as its *objective,* the goal of a *voyage* is defined as its *destination* . Choice E is correct.

Note that, while a *misdeed* may have *consequences,* these consequences are not its intended goal.

ANALOGY EXERCISES

To develop your ability to handle analogy questions, work your way through the following four exercises. *Warning:* These exercises are graded in difficulty. The further you go, the harder the items get, just as on a video game. Go all the way. Even if you do less well on Exercise D than you did on Exercise A, look on every error as an opportunity to learn. Study all the analogies you found difficult. Remember these are *all* typical PSAT analogy types.

After completing each exercise, see how many questions you answered correctly. (The correct answers are given on page 79) Then *read the answer explanations*. Pay particular attention to the way the analogies are expressed in clear, concise sentences. Your job is to learn to express these relationships in sentences just as concise and clear.

The analogy questions that follow present a pair of related words or groups of words. From the five answer choices, select the pair that illustrates a relationship most similar to that of the original pair.

Example:
DANDELION:WEED::   (A) marigold:petal
(B) plant:lawn   (C) corsage:flower
(D) turnip:vegetable   (E) peanut:tree

EXERCISE A

1. MASON:WALL::
   (A) artist:easel   (B) fisherman:trout
   (C) author:book   (D) congressman:senator
   (E) sculptor:museum

2. STUDENT:KNOWLEDGE::
   (A) hypocrite:truth   (B) prospector:gold
   (C) disciple:discipline   (D) hermit:society
   (E) actor:rehearsal

3. FIRE:ASHES::
   (A) accident:delay   (B) wood:splinters
   (C) water:waves   (D) regret:melancholy
   (E) event:memories

4. GOOSE:GANDER::
   (A) duck:drake   (B) hen:chicken
   (C) sheep:flock   (D) dog:kennel
   (E) horse:bridle

5. PREDICT:FORETELL::
   (A) procrastinate:expedite   (B) lie:prevaricate
   (C) prophesy:vindicate   (D) anticipate:participate
   (E) magnify:diminish

6. CARPENTER:SAW::
   (A) stenographer:typewriter   (B) painter:brush
   (C) lawyer:brief   (D) seamstress:scissors
   (E) runner:sneakers

7. CAPTAIN:SHOALS::
   (A) lawyer:litigation   (B) pilot:radar
   (C) soldier:ambush   (D) doctor:hospital
   (E) corporal:sergeant

8. WARM:FEVERISH::
   (A) tepid:lukewarm   (B) industrious:indolent
   (C) tepid:frozen   (D) angry:irate
   (E) moist:soaked

9. RAZOR:BEARD::
   (A) scythe:time   (B) sickle:grass
   (C) carburetor:gasoline   (D) student:class
   (E) barber:hair

10. HORNS:BULL::
    (A) mane:lion   (B) wattles:turkey
    (C) antlers:stag   (D) hoofs:horse
    (E) wings:eagle

11. TIGER:ZOOLOGY::
    (A) insect:etymology   (B) tiger lily:botany
    (C) granite:biology   (D) butterfly:anthropology
    (E) essay:prosody

12. CHAIRPERSON:BOARD::
    (A) mascot:gang   (B) captain:team
    (C) wolf:pack   (D) foe:battle
    (E) politician:platform

13. FROG:AMPHIBIAN::
    (A) whale:mammalian   (B) otter:crustacean
    (C) cow:herbivorous   (D) dog:loyal
    (E) trout:reptilian

14. JUDGE:COURTHOUSE::
    (A) carpenter:bench   (B) lawyer:brief
    (C) architect:blueprint   (D) surgeon:hospital
    (E) landlord:studio

15. PAUPER:MONEY::
    (A) banker:debtors   (B) teacher:school
    (C) author:publisher   (D) pugilist:ring
    (E) moron:intelligence

EXERCISE B

1. HELMET:HEAD::
   (A) pedal:foot   (B) gun:hand
   (C) breastplate:chest   (D) pendant:neck
   (E) knapsack:back

2. GULLIBLE:DUPED::
(A) credible:cheated (B) careful:cautioned
(C) malleable:molded (D) myopic:diagnosed
(E) articulate:silenced

3. FOLLY:SENSE::
(A) insolvency:funds (B) plagiarism:books
(C) beauty:beholder (D) piety:religion
(E) anxiety:care

4. MOCK:CONTEMPT::
(A) falsify:mimicry (B) scold:disapproval
(C) imitate:respect (D) anticipate:fear
(E) atone:retribution

5. CONDIMENT:FOOD::
(A) additive:milk (B) wit:conversation
(C) tenement:building (D) prescription:patient
(E) brochure:book

6. DUNGEON:CONFINEMENT::
(A) church:chapel (B) school:truant
(C) asylum:refuge (D) hospital:mercy
(E) courthouse:remorse

7. GRIDIRON:FOOTBALL::
(A) net:tennis (B) saddle:racing
(C) round:boxing (D) puck:hockey
(E) diamond:baseball

8. HERMIT:GREGARIOUS::
(A) miser:penurious (B) ascetic:hedonistic
(C) coward:pusillanimous (D) scholar:literate
(E) crab:crustacean

9. CLANDESTINE:OVERT::
(A) thorough:complete (B) limited:unrestrained
(C) warm:feverish (D) circular:oval
(E) vacillating:tentative

10. PINE:YEARN::
(A) amaze:astonish (B) whisper:shout
(C) meander:march (D) strive:prosper
(E) collect:scatter

11. WINE:VINTNER::
(A) tobacco:smoker (B) meat:packer
(C) water:plumber (D) beer:brewer
(E) oil:masseur

12. MENDACITY:HONESTY::
(A) courage:cravenness
(B) truth:beauty
(C) strength:fortitude
(D) unsophistication:ingenuousness
(E) hirsuteness:hair

13. PREFACE: BOOK::
(A) prologue:play (B) presage:folly
(C) preamble:poem (D) appendix:text
(E) couplet:sonnet

14. LAUREL:VICTORY::
(A) black cat:defeat (B) fig leaf:license
(C) olive branch:peace (D) lantern:caution
(E) flag:triumph

15. EXPERIENCE:KNOWLEDGE::
(A) purgative:disease (B) poison:death
(C) growth:investment (D) beauty:cosmetics
(E) truth:memory

Exercise C

1. MARATHON:STAMINA::
(A) relay:independence (B) hurdle:perseverance
(C) sprint:celerity (D) jog:weariness
(E) ramble:directness

2. NAIVE:INGENUE::
(A) ordinary:genius (B) venerable:celebrity
(C) urbane:sophisticate (D) crafty:artisan
(E) modest:braggart

3. HULKING:MASSIVE::
(A) pert:polite (B) brutal:compulsive
(C) raucous:harsh (D) furtive:ironic
(E) trite:remarkable

4. DISASTER:LUGUBRIOUS::
(A) fruition:satisfied (B) success:saturnine
(C) catastrophe:fatal (D) tragedy:complacent
(E) failure:gay

5. ASSEMBLE:GATHER::
(A) dismiss:hasten (B) proclaim:confide
(C) garner:squander (D) select:collect
(E) feign:dissemble

6. RETOUCH:PHOTOGRAPH::
(A) hang:painting (B) finger:fabric
(C) retract:statement (D) compose:melody
(E) refine:style

7. HONESTY:HYPOCRISY::
(A) pacifism:belligerence
(B) treachery:duplicity
(C) pugnacity:intolerance
(D) integrity:righteousness
(E) magnanmity:greatness

8. INDIGENT:WEALTH::
   (A) contented:happiness   (B) aristocratic:stature
   (C) smug:complacency
   (D) emaciated:nourishment   (E) variegated:variety

9. SHALE:GEOLOGIST::
   (A) catacombs:entomologist
   (B) aster:botanist   (C) obelisk:fireman
   (D) love:philologist   (E) reef:astrologer

10. FLEETING:DURATION::
    (A) glancing:distance   (B) concise:length
    (C) rapid:leisure   (D) grim:manner
    (E) fragrant:smell

11. DIDACTIC:TEACH::
    (A) sophomoric:learn   (B) satiric:mock
    (C) reticent:complain   (D) chaotic:rule
    (E) apologetic:deny

12. SOPORIFIC:SLEEP::
    (A) calorific:hunger   (B) insipid:flavor
    (C) honorific:embarrassment
    (D) worrisome:anxiety   (E) obtuse:insight

13. HACKNEYED:ORIGINAL::
    (A) mature:juvenile   (B) trite:morbid
    (C) withdrawn:reserved   (D) evasive:elusive
    (E) derivative:traditional

14. AUGER:CARPENTER::
    (A) studio:sculptor   (B) awl:cobbler
    (C) seam:seamstress   (D) cement:mason
    (E) apron:chef

15. MUSTER:CREW::
    (A) convene:committee   (B) demobilize:troops
    (C) dominate:opposition   (D) cheer:team
    (E) dismiss:jury

EXERCISE D

1. DWELL:DENIZEN::
   (A) shun:outcast   (B) inherit:heir
   (C) squander:miser   (D) obey:autocrat
   (E) patronize:protege

2. HAZARDOUS:PERIL::
   (A) supercilious:modesty   (B) innovative:novelty
   (C) venerable:immaturity   (D) antagonistic:apathy
   (E) competitive:pride

3. LAUDABLE:PRAISE::
   (A) imperturbable:agitation   (B) fragile:stability
   (C) contemptible:scorn   (D) enamored:love
   (E) fastidious:taste

4. OPHTHALMOLOGIST:EYES::
   (A) podiatrist:feet   (B) cardiologist:brain
   (C) bacteriologist:atoms   (D) numismatist:nerves
   (E) pediatrician:bones

5. MEANDERING:DIRECT::
   (A) menacing:ambitious   (B) affable:permissive
   (C) digressive:concise   (D) circuitous:roundabout
   (E) aboveboard:open

6. IRON:RUST::
   (A) yeast:mold   (B) bronze:patina
   (C) cake:icing   (D) stone:gravel
   (E) coal:dust

7. EPHEMERAL:LAST::
   (A) competitive:contend
   (B) indispensable:suffice   (C) perishable:die
   (D) insignificant:matter   (E) transient:travel

8. DONOR:GIFT::
   (A) prophet:prediction   (B) zealot:detachment
   (C) advisee:counsel   (D) braggart:attention
   (E) mourner:sympathy

9. ACT:DRAMA::
   (A) chapter:essay   (B) aria:opera
   (C) platoon:company   (D) grade:course
   (E) blueprint:building

10. CEMENT:TROWEL::
    (A) lawn:rake   (B) conflagration:match
    (C) paint:brush   (D) floor:polish
    (E) wallpaper:ladder

11. PIGHEADED:YIELD::
    (A) lionhearted:retreat   (B) lilylivered:flee
    (C) dogged:pursue   (D) featherbrained:giggle
    (E) eagle-eyed:discern

12. UNCTUOUS:SINCERITY::
    (A) fatuous:ambivalence   (B) unclean:impunity
    (C) avuncular:benevolence   (D) frivolous:gravity
    (E) hypocritical:virtue

13. PIRATE:BUCCANEER::
    (A) sailor:beachcomber   (B) puritan:virtuoso
    (C) captain:admiral   (D) wanderer:nomad
    (E) cynic:flatterer

14. ALARM:TRIGGER::
    (A) prison:escape   (B) tunnel:dig
    (C) criminal:corner   (D) fright:allay
    (E) trap:spring

15. QUOTATION:QUOTATION MARKS::
    (A) remark:colon   (B) sentence:period
    (C) aside:parentheses   (D) clause:semicolon
    (E) interjection:exclamation point

ANSWER KEY

1. C	4. A	7. C	10. C	13. A
2. B	5. B	8. E	11. B	14. D
3. E	6. D	9. B	12. B	15. E

EXERCISE B

1. C	4. B	7. E	10. A	13. A
2. C	5. B	8. B	11. D	14. C
3. A	6. C	9. B	12. A	15. B

EXERCISE C

1. C	4. A	7. A	10. B	13. A
2. C	5. E	8. D	11. B	14. B
3. C	6. E	9. B	12. D	15. A

EXERCISE D

1. B	4. A	7. D	10. C	13. D
2. B	5. C	8. A	11. A	14. E
3. C	6. B	9. C	12. E	15. C

ANSWER EXPLANATIONS

EXERCISE A

1. **C** A *mason* (stoneworker) creates a *wall*. An *author* creates a *book*.

2. **B** A *student* seeks *knowledge*. A *prospector* seeks *gold*.

3. **E** A *fire* leaves behind *ashes*. An *event* leaves behind *memories*.

4. **A** A *gander* is a male *goose*. A *drake* is a male *duck*.

5. **B** Someone who can *predict* the future can be said to *foretell* it. Someone who is known to *lie* can be said to *prevaricate* or speak falsely.

6. **D** A *carpenter* uses a *saw* to cut things. A *seamstress* uses *scissors* to cut things.

7. **C** A *captain* must beware of *shoals*, shallow areas or sandbanks in the water. A *soldier* must beware of an *ambush*.

8. **E** *Warm* is less extreme in heat than *feverish*. *Moist* is less extreme in wetness than *soaked*.

9. **B** One uses a *razor* to cut a *beard*. One uses a *sickle*, a farm tool, to cut *grass* or grain.

10. **C** A *bull* has sharp *horns* on his head. A *stag* (male deer) has sharp *antlers* on his head.

11. **B** *Zoology*, the study of animals, would include a particular animal, the *tiger*. *Botany*, the study of plants, would include a particular plant, the *tiger lily*.

12. **B** The *chairperson* is the head of the *board*. The *captain* is the head of the *team*.

13. **A** The *frog* is a member of the *amphibian* class, adapted to live both on the land and in the water. The *whale* is a member of the *mammalian* class, adapted to feed its young with milk from the mother.

14. **D** A *judge* works in a *courthouse*. A *surgeon* works in a *hospital*.

15. **E** A *pauper* has very little *money*. A *moron* has very little *intelligence*.

EXERCISE B

1. **C** A *helmet* protects one's *head*. A *breastplate*, a piece of armor, protects one's *chest*.

2. **C** A person who is *gullible* is easily fooled or duped. A person who is *malleable* (impressionable) is easily influenced *or molded*.

3. **A** A person engaged in *folly* or foolishness lacks *sense*. A person in a state of *insolvency* or bankruptcy lacks *funds*.

4. **B** A person who *mocks* shows *contempt*. A person who *scolds* shows *disapproval*.

5. **B** A *condiment* enhances *food*. *Wit* enhances *conversation*.

6. **C** A *dungeon* by definition is a place of *confinement*. An *asylum* by definition is a place of *refuge*.

7. **E** People play *football* on a field called a *gridiron*. People play *baseball* on a field called a *diamond*.

8. **B** A *hermit*, who chooses to live alone, is by definition not *gregarious* (companionable and outgoing). An *ascetic*, who chooses a life of self-
denial, is by definition not *hedonistic* (devoted
to pleasure).

9. **B** An activity which is *clandestine* (secret) is not
overt or unconcealed. An activity which is *limited* (within boundaries) is not *unrestrained* or
free of restrictions.

10. **A** To *pine* (to long for or to languish) means to
yearn. To *amaze* (to astound) means to *astonish*.

11. **D** A *vintner* is a person who makes *wine*. A
brewer is a person who makes *beer*.

12. **A** *Mendacity* or untruthfulness is the opposite of
honesty. *Courage* is the opposite of *cravenness*
or cowardice.

13. **A** A *preface* is an introduction at the beginning of
a *book*. A *prologue* is an introduction at the
beginning of a *play*.

14. **C** A wreath made from the *laurel* tree symbolizes
victory. An *olive branch* symbolizes *peace*.

15. **B** *Experience* leads to *knowledge*. *Poison* leads to
death.

EXERCISE C

1. **C** A *marathon* (very long race) requires *stamina*
or endurance. *A sprint* (very short race)
requires *celerity* or speed.

2. **C** An *ingenue* or inexperienced young person is
naive (innocent, frank). A *sophisticate* or worldly person is *urbane* (suave, elegantly polite).

3. **C** *Hulking* means bulky or *massive*. *Raucous*
means grating or *harsh*.

4. **A** A person is *lugubrious* or mournful after a *disaster*. A person is *satisfied* after the *fruition* (attainment or completion) of something desired.

5. **E** To *assemble* things is to *gather* them. To *feign*
or deceive is to *dissemble*.

6. **E** To *retouch* a *photograph* is to alter its appearance, to free it from imperfections. To *refine* a
style is to free it from imperfections as well.

7. **A** *Honesty* is the opposite of *hypocrisy* (pretending to be what one isn't). *Pacifism*, a policy of
peace, is the opposite of *belligerence* (being
warlike, eager to fight).

8. **D** Someone who is *indigent* or poor lacks *wealth*.
Someone who is *emaciated* or abnormally thin
lacks *nourishment*.

9. **B** A *geologist*, who studies rocks, deals with
shale, a particular kind of rock. A *botanist*,
who studies plants, deals with the *aster*, a particular flower.

10. **B** Something *fleeting* is brief in *duration*.
Something *concise* is brief in *length*.

11. **B** *Didactic* by definition means inclined to *teach*.
Satiric by definition means inclined to *mock*.

12. **D** *Soporific* means inducing or causing *sleep*.
Worrisome means inducing or causing *anxiety*.

13. **A** *Hackneyed* (worn, trite) is the opposite of *original* or novel. *Mature* is the opposite of *juvenile*.

14. **B** An *auger* or bit is a tool used by a *carpenter*.
An *awl* (tool for piercing holes in leather) is a
tool used by a *cobbler* or shoemaker.

15. **A** To *muster* a ship's *crew* is to assemble or gather the members together. To *convene* a com-
mittee is to assemble or gather its members
together.

EXERCISE D

1. **B** A *denizen* (resident) by definition *dwells* or
resides in a region. An *heir* by definition *inherits*
or receives a legacy from someone who has died.

2. **B** Something *hazardous* (dangerous) is characterized by *peril* (danger). Something *innovative*
(new in form or design) is characterized by
novelty (newness, originality).

3. **C** *Laudable* means praiseworthy or deserving
praise. *Contemptible* means despicable or
deserving *scorn*.

4. **A** An *ophthalmologist* specializes in the care of
the *eyes*. A *podiatrist* specializes in the care of
the *feet*.

5. **C** *Meandering* (proceeding by an indirect course)
and *direct* are antonyms. *Digressive* (departing
from the main subject) and *concise* (keeping
brief and to the point) are antonyms.

6. **B** The covering of *iron* caused by oxidation is
called *rust*. The covering of *bronze* is called a
patina.

7. **D** Something *ephemeral* by definition does not
last. Something *insignificant* by definition does
not *matter*.

8. **A** A *donor* or benefactor makes a *gift*. A *prophet*
or seer makes a *prediction*.

9. **C** A *drama* or play is divided into *acts*. A military *company* is divided into *platoons*.

10. **C** *Cement* is applied with a *trowel*. *Paint* is
applied with a *brush*.

11. **A** Someone *pigheaded* or stubborn is disinclined
to *yield* (give in). Someone *lionhearted* or
brave is disinclined to *retreat*.

12. **E** An *unctuous* or excessively pious manner is
affected, having a false appearance of *sinceri-
ty*. A *hypocritical* or dissembling manner is
feigned, having a false appearance of *virtue*.

13. **D** *Pirate* and *buccaneer* are synonyms, as are
wanderer and *nomad*.

14. **E** To *trigger* an *alarm* is to release it or set it off.
To *spring* a *trap* is to release it or set it off.

15. **C** The beginning and the end of a *quotation*
(group of words repeated from a book or
speech) are indicated by *quotation marks*. The
beginning and the end of an *aside* (parenthetical remark; temporary digression from the
main subject) are indicated by *parentheses*.

5

Improving Reading Comprehension

Now more than ever, doing well on the reading comprehension questions can make the difference between success and failure on the PSAT. The last questions in each verbal section, they are also the most time-consuming and the ones most likely to bog you down. However, you can handle them, and this chapter will show you how.

LONG-RANGE STRATEGY

Read, Read, Read!

Just do it.

There is no substitute for extensive reading as a preparation for the PSAT and for college work. The only way to build up your proficiency in reading is by reading books of all kinds. As you read, you will develop speed, stamina, and the ability to comprehend the printed page. But if you want to turn yourself into the kind of reader the colleges are looking for, you must develop the habit of reading—closely and critically—every day.

Challenge yourself. Don't limit your reading to light fiction or popular biographies. Branch out a bit. Try to develop an interest in as many fields as you can. Sample some of the serious magazines: *The New Yorker, Smithsonian, Natural History, National Geographic, Newsweek, Time, The New York Review of Books, Harper's Magazine*. In these magazines you'll find articles on literature, music, science, philosophy, history, the arts—the whole range of fields touched on by the PSAT. If you take time to acquaint yourself with the contents of these magazines, you won't find the subject matter of the reading passages on the examination so strange.

TIPS FOR HANDLING READING COMPREHENSION QUESTIONS

1. Tackle passages with familiar subjects before passages with unfamiliar ones. It is hard to concentrate when you read about something wholly unfamiliar to you. Give yourself a break. In each section, first tackle the reading passage that interests you or deals with topics in which you are well grounded. Then move on to the other passage. You'll do better that way.

2. If you are stumped by a tough reading question, do not skip the other questions on that passage. The reading comprehension questions following each passage are not arranged in order of difficulty. They tend to be arranged sequentially: questions on paragraph 1 come before questions on paragraph 2. So try all the questions on the passage. That tough question may be just one question away from one that's easy for you.

3. First read the passage; then read the questions. Reading the questions before you read the passage will not save you time. It will cost you time. If you

read the questions first, when you turn to the passage you will have a number of question words and phrases dancing around in your head. You will be so involved in trying to spot the places they occur in the passage that you will not be able to concentrate on comprehending the passage as a whole.

4. Read as rapidly as you can with understanding, but do not force yourself. Do not worry about the time element. If you worry about not finishing the test, you will begin to take short cuts and miss the correct answer in your haste.

5. As you read the italicized introductory material preceding the passage and tackle the passage's opening sentences, try to anticipate what the passage will be about. Ask yourself who or what the author is talking about.

6. As you continue reading, try to identify what *kind* of writing this is, what *techniques* are being used,

who its intended *audience* may be, and what *feeling* (if any) the author has toward his subject. Try to retain names, dates, and places for quick reference later. In particular, try to remember where in the passage the author makes *major points*. Then, when you start looking for the phrase or sentence that will justify your choice of answer, you may be able to save time by going back to that section of the passage immediately without having to reread the entire selection.

7. When you tackle the questions, *go back to the passage* to verify each answer choice. Do not rely on your memory alone, and, above all, do not ignore the passage and just answer questions on the basis of other things you've read. Remember, the questions are asking you about what *this* author has to say about the subject, not about what some other author you once read said about it in another book.

8. Use the line references in the questions to be sure you've gone back to the correct spot in the passage. The reading passages on the PSAT tend to be long. Fortunately, the lines are numbered, and the questions often refer you to specific lines in the passage by number. It takes less time to locate a line number than to spot a word or phrase. Use the line numbers to orient yourself in the text.

9. When dealing with the new double passages, tackle them one at a time. The questions are organized sequentially: questions about Passage 1 come before questions about Passage 2. So, do things in order. *First* read Passage 1; then jump straight to the questions and answer all those based on Passage 1. *Next* read Passage 2; then answer all the questions based on Passage 2. *Finally*, tackle the two or three questions that refer to *both* passages. Go back to both passages as needed.

   Occasionally a couple of questions referring to *both* passages will precede the questions focusing on Passage 1. Do not let this minor hitch throw you. Use your common sense. You've just read the first passage. Skip the one or two questions on both passages, and head for those questions about Passage 1. Answer them. Then read Passage 2. Answer the questions on Passage 2. Finally, go back to those questions you skipped and answer them and any other questions at the end of the set that refer to *both* passages. Remember, however: whenever you skip from question to question, or from passage to passage, *be sure you're filling in the right ovals on your answer sheet.*

10. When the questions ask about specific information in the passage, do not expect to find it stated in exactly the same words. If the question is:

According to the passage, widgets are
(A) good   (B) bad   (C) indifferent
(D) pink   (E) purple   Ⓐ Ⓑ Ⓒ Ⓓ Ⓔ

---

do not expect to find a sentence in the passage that says, "Widgets are bad." However, you may well find a sentence that says, "Widgets are wholly undesirable and have a strongly negative influence." That is close enough to tell you that the answer must be **B**.

11. When you read, watch for key words that indicate how a passage is being developed.
    Equality or continuity of ideas (one idea is equal in importance to another, or continues a thought expressed earlier): *again, also, and, another, as well as, besides, first, furthermore, likewise, moreover, in addition*
    Contrast or change of topic: *although, despite, in spite of, instead of, notwithstanding, regardless, nevertheless, on the other hand, however*
    Conclusion: *accordingly, as a result, hence, in conclusion, in short, therefore, thus, consequently*

12. Be on the lookout for *all-inclusive words*, such as *always, at all times,* and *entirely*, and for negative or limiting words, such as *only, never, no, none, except,* and *but.*

13. Watch out for words or phrases in the question that can alert you to the kind of question being asked. Just as it will help you to know the directions for the analogy and sentence completion questions on the PSAT, it will also help you to familiarize yourself with the major types of critical reading questions on the test. If you can recognize just what a given question is asking for, you'll be better able to tell which particular reading tactic to apply.

PSAT Reading Comprehension Questions Test Your Ability to

➤ determine the meaning of individual words from their context

➤ paraphrase or interpret specific information in the text

➤ analyze or find the central thought of a passage

➤ find implications and draw inferences from the text

➤ evaluate or make judgments about the techniques, logic, and applications of the text

Determining the Meanings of Individual Words from Their Context

If you have ever looked into a dictionary, you are well aware that many words have more than one meaning: a *run* in a baseball game is not the same thing as a *run* in a nylon stocking. Now that the PSAT-makers have eliminated antonym questions from the test, they've added many of these Vocabulary in Context questions to the reading segments. Generally, the word is a common one that's being used in a specific, sometimes uncommon way; you must figure out its exact meaning as used by the author.

Read the following passage and try the vocabulary-in-context questions based upon it.

[This passage is somewhat shorter than passages you will find on the new PSAT.]

The following passage is taken from an article on mathematical and scientific illiteracy published in The New York Times *in January 1989, as Ronald and Nancy Reagan left the White House.*

The abstractness of mathematics is a great obstacle for many intelligent people. Such people may readily understand narrative particulars, but
Line strongly resist impersonal generalities. Since num-
5 bers, science, and such generalities are intimately related, this resistance can lead to an almost willful mathematical and scientific illiteracy. Numbers have appeal for many only if they're associated with them personally—hence part of the attraction
10 of astrology, biorhythms, Tarot cards and the I Ching, all individually customized "sciences."
Mathematical illiteracy and the attitudes underlying it provide in fact a fertile soil for the growth of pseudoscience. In "Pseudoscience and Society
15 in Nineteenth-Century America," Arthur Wrobel remarks that belief in phrenology, homeopathy, and hydropathy was not confined to the poor and the ignorant, but pervaded much of 19th-century literature. Such credulity is not as extensive in
20 contemporary literature, but astrology is one pseudoscience that does seem to engage a big segment of the reading public. Literary allusions to it abound, appearing in everything from Shakespeare to Don DeLillo's "Libra." A 1986
25 Gallup poll showed that 52 percent of American teenagers subscribe to it, as does at least 50 percent of the nation's departing First Couple.
Given these figures, it may not be entirely inappropriate to note here that no mechanism
30 through which the alleged zodiacal influences exert themselves has ever been specified by astrologers. Gravity certainly cannot account for these natal influences, since even the gravitational pull of the attending obstetrician is orders of mag-
35 nitude greater than that of the relevant planet or planets. Nor is there any empirical evidence; top astrologers (as determined by their peers) have failed repeatedly to associate personality profiles with astrological data at a rate higher than that of
40 chance. Neither of these fatal objections to astrology, of course, is likely to carry much weight with literate but innumerate people who don't estimate magnitudes or probabilities, or who are overimpressed by vague coincidences yet unmoved by
45 overwhelming statistical evidence.

1. The word "confined" in line 17 means
(A) enclosed
(B) jailed
(C) isolated
(D) restricted
(E) preached

ANALYSIS OF QUESTION 1

Your best bet in answering vocabulary-in-context questions is to tackle them the way you do sentence completion questions. First, read the sentence, blocking out the word in quotes. Think of words you know that might make sense in the context. Then test each answer choice, substituting it in the sentence for the word in quotes. Ask yourself whether this particular answer choice makes sense in this specific context. In question 1, for example, the original sentence states that "belief ... was not ____ to the poor and the ignorant, but pervaded much of 19th-century literature." Nonscientific belief was widespread in the 19th century; it pervaded or spread throughout the literature of the period. Therefore, it was not *restricted* or confined to poor, ignorant people, but had spread to the well-to-do, literate classes.

Note that *many* of the answer choices could be good substitutes for "confined" *in other contexts*. For example, if the sentence were "The dog catcher *confined* dozens of stray animals in the pound," Choice A, *enclosed*, would be the best word to substitute. Your job is to spot which meaning of the word works this time.

See how well you do with another vocabulary-in-context question on the same passage.

2. As used in line 21, "engage" most nearly means
(A) hire
(B) reserve
(C) attract
(D) confront
(E) interlock

ANALYSIS OF QUESTION 2

Again, look at the sentence, blocking out the key word. "Astrology ... does seem to ____ a big segment of the reading public." What word would make sense in the context? Summarize the situation here. The author is reacting to the strong hold astrology has on the reading public. Despite its being a pseudoscience, astrology has managed to *attract* or involve many members of the reading public. The correct answer is Choice C.

Try one more vocabulary-in-context question on this passage.

3. The term "subscribe to" in line 26 means
(A) sign up for
(B) agree with
(C) write about
(D) suffer from
(E) pay for

"52 percent of American teenagers _____ it, as does at least 50 percent of the nation's departing First Couple." The author has been talking about how many people have been attracted or drawn to astrology. Many of these people have been more or less won over by it: they accept it as a valid belief. Thus, the teenagers (and the Reagans) who *subscribe to* astrology *agree with* it, acquiescing to its doctrines. Once again, you've found a word that makes sense in context.

Paraphrasing or Interpreting Specific Information in the Text

In interpreting a text, you are doing what a translator does in dealing with a passage in a foreign language. Your job is to turn the original text into understandable, familiar prose. In the process, you have to do several things. You have to explain the meaning of key phrases or idioms in the passage. You have to resolve any possible ambiguities in the text, making sure that the author's meaning is absolutely clear. In other words, sentence by sentence, you have to answer the question, "Just what is this person telling me?"

Questions testing your ability to understand significant information in the text often take the following forms:

- According to the author, what is the reason for . . .
- To the author, Emily Dickinson's poetry was . . .
- The "crucial question" referred to in line 33 is the . . .

In answering these questions, you must be certain that the answer you select is in the passage. You must find a word or sentence or group of sentences that justifies your choice. You must not pick an answer just because it agrees with your personal opinions or with information on the subject that you've gotten from other sources.

The following questions based on the passage on mathematical and scientific illiteracy all require you to clarify the meaning of the text. Again, be sure to go back to the passage to verify your answer choice.

The following passage is taken from an article on mathematical and scientific illiteracy published in The New York Times *in January 1989, as Ronald and Nancy Reagan left the White House.*

The abstractness of mathematics is a great obstacle for many intelligent people. Such people may readily understand narrative particulars, but strongly resist impersonal generalities. Since num-
Line
5 bers, science, and such generalities are intimately related, this resistance can lead to an almost willful mathematical and scientific illiteracy. Numbers have appeal for many only if they're associated with them personally—hence part of the attraction

10 of astrology, biorhythms, Tarot cards and the I Ching, all individually customized "sciences."

Mathematical illiteracy and the attitudes underlying it provide in fact a fertile soil for the growth of pseudoscience. In "Pseudoscience and Society
15 in Nineteenth-Century America," Arthur Wrobel remarks that belief in phrenology, homeopathy, and hydropathy was not confined to the poor and the ignorant, but pervaded much of 19th-century literature. Such credulity is not as extensive in
20 contemporary literature, but astrology is one pseudoscience that does seem to engage a big segment of the reading public. Literary allusions to it abound, appearing in everything from Shakespeare to Don DeLillo's "Libra." A 1986
25 Gallup poll showed that 52 percent of American teenagers subscribe to it, as does at least 50 percent of the nation's departing First Couple.

Given these figures, it may not be entirely inappropriate to note here that no mechanism
30 through which the alleged zodiacal influences exert themselves has ever been specified by astrologers. Gravity certainly cannot account for these natal influences, since even the gravitational pull of the attending obstetrician is orders of mag-
35 nitude greater than that of the relevant planet or planets. Nor is there any empirical evidence; top astrologers (as determined by their peers) have failed repeatedly to associate personality profiles with astrological data at a rate higher than that of
40 chance. Neither of these fatal objections to astrology, of course, is likely to carry much weight with literate but innumerate people who don't estimate magnitudes or probabilities, or who are overimpressed by vague coincidences yet unmoved by
45 overwhelming statistical evidence.

4. Which of the following best summarizes the reason given in lines 1–7 for the extent of mathematical and scientific illiteracy today?
   (A) Many intelligent people dislike the intimacy of the connection between numbers and science.
   (B) Many otherwise intelligent people have difficulty dealing with impersonal, abstract concepts.
   (C) Intelligent people prefer speaking in generalities to narrating particular incidents.
   (D) Few people are able to appreciate the benefits of an individually customized science.
   (E) People today no longer cherish their personal associations with numbers.

In lines 1 and 2, the author states that the abstractness of mathematics is a problem for many intelligent people. People resist dealing with abstractions ("impersonal generalities"). However, to work in science or math, you must deal with abstractions: numbers, science, and abstractions are "intimately connected." *Because* many otherwise intelligent people have difficulty dealing with impersonal, abstract concepts, these people wind up mathematically and scientifically illiterate. That, according to the author, is the reason for much of the mathematical and scientific illiteracy we see today. The correct answer is Choice B.

5. According to the author, "phrenology, homeopathy, and hydropathy" (line 16) are all
(A) scholarly allusions
(B) pseudosciences
(C) branches of astrology
(D) forms of society
(E) mechanisms

ANALYSIS OF QUESTION 5

Phrenology, homeopathy, and hydropathy are three beliefs mentioned in a book entitled "Pseudoscience and Society in Nineteenth-Century America." Throughout the passage the author is being critical of various beliefs he categorizes as unscientific. He groups such beliefs together as *pseudosciences*, false sciences in which many otherwise intelligent individuals believe. Phrenology is the belief that the shape of your skull indicates your character traits and mental abilities. Homeopathy is the belief that you can cure a disease by giving someone ill minute doses of a substance that would produce in someone healthy symptoms similar to those of the disease. Hydropathy is the belief that you can cure a disease by giving someone ill huge amounts of water (both internally and externally). To the author, all three beliefs are *pseudosciences*.

Note the phrase "to the author." The question is not asking you what *you* think about phrenology, homeopathy, and hydropathy. It is asking you what *the author* thinks of these beliefs.

6. The "figures" referred to in line 28 are the
(A) pseudosciences
(B) literary references
(C) prominent political leaders
(D) numbers involved in calculating horoscopes
(E) statistics concerning believers in astrology

ANALYSIS OF QUESTION 6

The paragraph immediately preceding line 28 gives the percentage of American teenagers who go along with astrology. It also refers to the well-known fact that Nancy Reagan (half of "the nation's departing First Couple") accepts the tenets of astrology (she followed the advice of astrologers in setting up her husband's engagements during his presidency), and that her husband may possibly believe in it as well. Thus, the figures referred to are *statistics concerning believers in astrology*.

7. The term "innumerate" (line 42) is best interpreted to mean
(A) various in kind
(B) too numerous to count
(C) scientifically sophisticated
(D) unable to use mathematics
(E) indifferent to astrology

ANALYSIS OF QUESTION 7

The author contrasts the word "innumerate" with the word "literate." Since *illiterate* means unable to read, *innumerate* must mean unable to use mathematics.

You can use your knowledge of word parts to answer this question. *In-* means not; *numer-* means number. *Innumerate* means not having numbers, unable to use numbers. Watch out, however, for eye-catchers. The word *innumerable* means uncountable, too many, or too numerous to count.

Analyzing or Finding the Central Thought of a Passage

Questions that test your ability to find the central thought of a passage often take the following forms:

- Which of the following best states the theme of the passage?
- The main idea of this passage may be best expressed as . . .
- In the second paragraph of the passage, the author primarily stresses that . . .
- The passage illustrates . . .
- The author's purpose in writing this passage is . . .

When asked to find the central thought, be sure to check the opening and summary sentence of each paragraph. Authors frequently provide readers with a sentence that expresses a paragraph's main idea succinctly. Although such *topic sentences* may appear anywhere in the paragraph, readers customarily look for them in the opening or closing sentences.

Note: In PSAT reading passages, topic sentences are frequently implied rather than stated directly. If you cannot find a topic sentence, ask yourself these questions:

- Who or what is this passage about?
- What aspect of this subject is the author talking about?
- What is the author trying to get across about this aspect of the subject?

You'll be on your way to locating the passage's central thought.

Try the two questions following the passage that ask you to determine the author's main idea.

The following passage is taken from an article on mathematical and scientific illiteracy published in The New York Times *in January 1989, as Ronald and Nancy Reagan left the White House.*

The abstractness of mathematics is a great obstacle for many intelligent people. Such people may readily understand narrative particulars, but strongly resist impersonal generalities. Since numbers, science, and such generalities are intimately related, this resistance can lead to an almost willful mathematical and scientific illiteracy. Numbers have appeal for many only if they're associated with them personally—hence part of the attraction of astrology, biorhythms, Tarot cards and the I Ching, all individually customized "sciences."

Mathematical illiteracy and the attitudes underlying it provide in fact a fertile soil for the growth of pseudoscience. In "Pseudoscience and Society in Nineteenth-Century America," Arthur Wrobel remarks that belief in phrenology, homeopathy, and hydropathy was not confined to the poor and the ignorant, but pervaded much of 19th-century literature. Such credulity is not as extensive in contemporary literature, but astrology is one pseudoscience that does seem to engage a big segment of the reading public. Literary allusions to it abound, appearing in everything from Shakespeare to Don DeLillo's "Libra." A 1986 Gallup poll showed that 52 percent of American teenagers subscribe to it, as does at least 50 percent of the nation's departing First Couple.

Given these figures, it may not be entirely inappropriate to note here that no mechanism through which the alleged zodiacal influences exert themselves has ever been specified by astrologers. Gravity certainly cannot account for these natal influences, since even the gravitational pull of the attending obstetrician is orders of magnitude greater than that of the relevant planet or planets. Nor is there any empirical evidence; top astrologers (as determined by their peers) have failed repeatedly to associate personality profiles with astrological data at a rate higher than that of chance. Neither of these fatal objections to astrology, of course, is likely to carry much weight with literate but innumerate people who don't estimate magnitudes or probabilities, or who are overimpressed by vague coincidences yet unmoved by overwhelming statistical evidence.

8. In the final paragraph of the passage, the author stresses that
(A) astrologers are working to discover the mechanisms through which the zodiac affects human lives
(B) the planets are able to influence people in mysterious, imperceptible ways
(C) top astrologers strive to maintain accurate personality profiles of their clientele
(D) astrologers have been unable to corroborate their theories scientifically
(E) astrologers are more mechanically minded than mathematically literate

ANALYSIS OF QUESTION 8

The author spends the final paragraph debunking the claims of the astrologers. To their claim that the planets in the heavens at the time of one's birth influence one's destiny, he retorts that the attending physician exerts more gravitational pull on the infant than the distant planets do. To their claim that astrological data can be used to predict personality types, he retorts that no valid correlation exists between astrological predictions and the results of scientifically legitimate personality profiles. Throughout the paragraph, he stresses that the *astrologers have been unable to corroborate their theories scientifically.*

9. The author's primary purpose throughout the passage is to
(A) contrast astrology and other contemporary pseudosciences with phrenology, homeopathy, and hydropathy
(B) trace the development of the current belief in astrology to its nineteenth-century roots
(C) apologize for the rise of mathematical and scientific illiteracy in the present day
(D) relate mathematical illiteracy to the prevalence of invalid pseudoscientific beliefs today
(E) disprove the difficulty of achieving universal mathematical and scientific literacy

ANALYSIS OF QUESTION 9

Consider the opening sentences of the three paragraphs and the concluding sentence of the third paragraph. "The abstractness of mathematics is a great obstacle for many intelligent people." "Mathematical illiteracy and the attitudes underlying it provide in fact a fertile soil for the growth of pseudoscience." "Given these figures, it may not be entirely inappropriate to note here that no mechanism through which the alleged zodiacal influences exert themselves has ever been specified by astrologers." "Neither of these fatal objections to astrology, of course, is likely to carry much weight with literate but innumerate people who don't estimate magnitudes or probability, or who are overimpressed by vague coincidences yet unmoved by overwhelming statistical evidence." Throughout the passage the author is discussing mathematical illiteracy and demonstrating how it *relates to the prevalence* (widespread acceptance) of astrology and other *invalid pseudoscientific beliefs today.*

Choice A is incorrect. While the author mentions phrenology and the other pseudosciences, he never contrasts them with or differentiates them from astrology. Choice B is incorrect. While the author spends a good deal of the passage discussing astrology, his chief purpose is to use it as an example of a contemporary pseudoscientific belief, not to trace its nineteenth-century connections. Choice C is incorrect; the author is irked by the state of mathematical and scientific illiteracy today, not apologetic about it. Choice E is incorrect; it is unsupported by the passage.

Finding Implications and Drawing Inferences from the Text

Questions that ask you to draw inferences often begin in one of the following ways:

- It can be inferred from the passage that . . .
- The author implies that . . .
- The passage suggest that . . .
- It can be argued that . . .
- The author would most likely . . .
- The author probably considers . . .

Inference questions require you to use your own judgment. You are drawing a conclusion *based on what you have read in the text.* When asked to draw an inference, think about what the passage logically suggests. You must not take anything directly stated in the passage as an inference. Instead, you must look for clues in the passage that you can use in coming up with your own conclusion. Then you should choose as your answer a statement that logically develops the information the author has provided.

Turn once more to the mathematical illiteracy passage for some practice in finding the implications of an author's words.

The following passage is taken from an article on mathematical and scientific illiteracy published in The New York Times *in January 1989, as Ronald and Nancy Reagan left the White House.*

The abstractness of mathematics is a great obstacle for many intelligent people. Such people may readily understand narrative particulars, but
Line strongly resist impersonal generalities. Since num-
5 bers, science, and such generalities are intimately related, this resistance can lead to an almost willful mathematical and scientific illiteracy. Numbers have appeal for many only if they're associated with them personally—hence part of the attraction
10 of astrology, biorhythms, Tarot cards and the I Ching, all individually customized "sciences."

Mathematical illiteracy and the attitudes underlying it provide in fact a fertile soil for the growth of pseudoscience. In "Pseudoscience and Society
15 in Nineteenth-Century America," Arthur Wrobel remarks that belief in phrenology, homeopathy, and hydropathy was not confined to the poor and the ignorant, but pervaded much of 19th-century literature. Such credulity is not as extensive in
20 contemporary literature, but astrology is one pseudoscience that does seem to engage a big segment of the reading public. Literary allusions to it abound, appearing in everything from Shakespeare to Don DeLillo's "Libra." A 1986
25 Gallup poll showed that 52 percent of American teenagers subscribe to it, as does at least 50 percent of the nation's departing First Couple.

Given these figures, it may not be entirely inappropriate to note here that no mechanism
30 through which the alleged zodiacal influences exert themselves has ever been specified by astrologers. Gravity certainly cannot account for these natal influences, since even the gravitational pull of the attending obstetrician is orders of mag-
35 nitude greater than that of the relevant planet or planets. Nor is there any empirical evidence; top astrologers (as determined by their peers) have failed repeatedly to associate personality profiles with astrological data at a rate higher than that of
40 chance. Neither of these fatal objections to astrology, of course, is likely to carry much weight with literate but innumerate people who don't estimate magnitudes or probabilities, or who are overimpressed by vague coincidences yet unmoved by
45 overwhelming statistical evidence.

Here is a straightforward inference question on the passage.

10. The author most likely regards the lack of empirical evidence for astrology as
(A) an oversight on the part of the astrologers
(B) a key argument against its validity
(C) a flaw that will be corrected in time
(D) the unfortunate result of too small a sampling
(E) a major reason to keep searching for fresh data

ANALYSIS OF QUESTION 10

The final sentence of the passage characterizes these absences of empirical evidence as "fatal objections to astrology." In general, the author sees astrology as invalid, a "pseudoscience," not a real science. If he were faced with empirical experimental data supporting astrological theory, he probably would have a hard time rejecting it so sharply. Thus, he most likely regards the lack of empirical, observable evidence for astrology as *a key argument against its validity.*

Other inference questions ask you to draw conclusions about the author's attitude toward the topic, overall mood, or tone of voice. What does the author's choice of words imply about his feelings about the topic? Such inference questions often take the following forms:

- The author's attitude toward . . . is . . .
- The author regards the idea that . . . with . . .
- The author's tone in the passage . . .

Try the following two questions that ask you to interpret the author's emotional state.

11. The author's attitude toward astrology can best be described as one of
(A) grudging respect
(B) amused tolerance
(C) open disdain
(D) disguised hostility
(E) puzzled fascination

ANALYSIS OF QUESTION 11

The author states that people who believe in

astrology are the sort who are "overimpressed by vague coincidences." In his opinion, astrology as a science is fatally flawed, and he looks down on those innumerate souls who continue to believe in it. Thus, his attitude is one of *open disdain* or contempt.

12. The author's tone in referring to the nation's departing First Couple can best be described as

(A) respectful
(B) nostalgic
(C) negative
(D) mocking
(E) effusive

ANALYSIS OF QUESTION 12

In saying that *at least* 50 percent of the Reagans subscribes to a belief in astrology, the author is making a little joke. He is referring to Nancy Reagan's dependence on astrologers, and, at the same time, implying that 100 percent of the Reagans, that is, the First Lady *and* the President, may believe in a subject he considers nonsensical. Even the term *First Couple* has a mocking ring. The correct answer is Choice D.

Evaluating the Techniques, Logic, and Applications of the Text

Among the more challenging critical reading questions on the new PSAT are ones that ask you to make judgments about the techniques the author uses, to evaluate the logic of his or her argument, and to infer how what is said in this passage might apply in other situations.

Questions concerning the author's technique often have the following wording:

- Which of the following best describes the development of this passage?
- In presenting the argument, the author does all of the following EXCEPT . . .
- The relationship between the second paragraph and the first paragraph can best be described as . . .
- In the passage, the author makes the central point primarily by . . .

Questions concerning the author's logic or the applications of his or her remarks frequently are worded as follows:

- With which of the following statements would the author be in strongest agreement?
- The author's argument would be most weakened by the discovery of which of the following?
- The author's contention would be most clearly strengthened if which of the following were found to be true?

Again, look at the passage on mathematical illiteracy to answer questions on the author logic and techniques.

The following passage is taken from an article on mathematical and scientific illiteracy published in The New York Times *in January 1989, as Ronald and Nancy Reagan left the White House.*

The abstractness of mathematics is a great obstacle for many intelligent people. Such people may readily understand narrative particulars, but strongly resist impersonal generalities. Since num-
Line
5   bers, science, and such generalities are intimately related, this resistance can lead to an almost willful mathematical and scientific illiteracy. Numbers have appeal for many only if they're associated with them personally—hence part of the attraction
10 of astrology, biorhythms, Tarot cards and the I Ching, all individually customized "sciences."

Mathematical illiteracy and the attitudes underlying it provide in fact a fertile soil for the growth of pseudoscience. In "Pseudoscience and Society
15 in Nineteenth-Century America," Arthur Wrobel remarks that belief in phrenology, homeopathy, and hydropathy was not confined to the poor and the ignorant, but pervaded much of 19th-century literature. Such credulity is not as extensive in
20 contemporary literature, but astrology is one pseudoscience that does seem to engage a big segment of the reading public. Literary allusions to it abound, appearing in everything from Shakespeare to Don DeLillo's "Libra." A 1986
25 Gallup poll showed that 52 percent of American teenagers subscribe to it, as does at least 50 percent of the nation's departing First Couple.

Given these figures, it may not be entirely inappropriate to note here that no mechanism
30 through which the alleged zodiacal influences exert themselves has ever been specified by astrologers. Gravity certainly cannot account for these natal influences, since even the gravitational pull of the attending obstetrician is orders of mag-
35 nitude greater than that of the relevant planet or planets. Nor is there any empirical evidence; top astrologers (as determined by their peers) have failed repeatedly to associate personality profiles with astrological data at a rate higher than that of
40 chance. Neither of these fatal objections to astrology, of course, is likely to carry much weight with literate but innumerate people who don't estimate magnitudes or probabilities, or who are overimpressed by vague coincidences yet unmoved by
45 overwhelming statistical evidence.

13. The author's point about the popularity of astrology is made through both

(A) personal testimony and generalizations
(B) assertions and case histories
(C) comparisons and anecdotes
(D) statistics and literary references
(E) observation and analogy

ANALYSIS OF QUESTION 13

Familiarize yourself with the technical terms commonly used to describe a passage's organization: *analogies, assertions, allusions*. You need to know the meaning of these terms, and of others you'll encounter in the course of taking our model PSATs.

In this instance, the author offers as evidence of astrology's popularity both *literary references* (allusions to Don DeLillo's *Libra* and to Shakespeare) and *statistics* based on Gallup Poll figures.

14. Which of the following would most weaken the author's assumption that mathematical and scientific literacy would make people less likely to believe in a pseudoscience such as astrology?
   (A) Assertions by professional astrologers that astrology has a firm scientific basis in astronomy
   (B) Anecdotal reports that an individual astrologer has been known to use a calculator in computing horoscopes
   (C) Poll results showing that the percentage of American teenagers believing in astrology has radically decreased since 1989
   (D) Evidence that the majority of practicing astrologers have also taught mathematics or a scientific discipline
   (E) A statement by ex-President Reagan denying that he has ever believed in astrology

---

ANALYSIS OF QUESTION 14

If we assume that people who have professionally taught math or science are therefore not mathematically and scientifically illiterate, and if we also assume that practicing astrologers believe in astrology, then *evidence that the majority of practicing astrologers have also taught mathematics or a scientific discipline* would clearly weaken the author's assumption that mathematical and scientific literacy would make people less likely to believe in astrology.

15. With which of the following statements would the author be most likely to disagree?
   (A) Phrenology may be of some interest to sociologists and cultural historians, but it has no real value as a scientific discipline.
   (B) A rigorous training in mathematics would benefit young people by equipping them to estimate magnitudes and probabilities.
   (C) People were somewhat less apt to be taken in by pseudoscientific claims in the nineteenth century than they are today.
   (D) Despite the weight of the evidence against astrology, scientifically illiterate individuals will continue to believe in it.
   (E) Determining biorhythms and computing astrological horoscopes may require people to perform some mathematical calculations.

ANALYSIS OF QUESTION 15

You can answer this question by using the process of elimination.

The key word here is "disagree." Examine each statement in turn, asking yourself whether it does or does not reflect the author's point of view. Eliminate every answer choice with which the author would agree. Phrenology is one of the pseudosciences mentioned in the second paragraph; clearly, the author would agree *it has no real value as a scientific discipline* or field of study. You can eliminate Choice A.

In the concluding sentence of the passage, the author mentions the failure to estimate magnitudes and probabilities as a characteristic of innumerate, mathematically illiterate people. He wishes people to be mathematically *literate*; therefore, he would agree that *a rigorous training in mathematics* that enabled them to estimate magnitudes and probabilities *would benefit young people*. You can eliminate Choice B.

In the second paragraph, the author states that belief in various pseudosciences "pervaded much of the 19th-century literature"; it was widespread in earlier days. He then asserts that "such credulity is not as extensive in contemporary literature." In other words, the author contends that people are somewhat *less* apt to be taken in by pseudoscientific claims *today* than they were a century ago. This directly contradicts what is stated in Choice **C**, which must be the correct answer.

Double-check yourself. Test the other two answer choices.

In lines 40–45, the author states directly that the "fatal objections to astrology" he has just pointed out are unlikely to convince the innumerate, scientifically illiterate believers in astrology that the powers of the zodiac are nonexistent. Clearly, the author would agree that *scientifically illiterate individuals will continue to believe* in astrology despite the evidence. You can eliminate Choice D.

The author asserts that the only numbers that appeal to some people are ones with personal associations—numbers connected to individual biorhythms or astrological horoscopes, for example. Given this personal connection with numbers, even nonmathematically inclined individuals might wind up having *to perform mathematical computations*, though ones the author would consider of doubtful value. You can eliminate Choice E.

Only Choice C is left. As you suspected, it is the correct answer.

Dealing with the Double Passage

If the new double passage section has you worried, relax. It's not that formidable, especially if you deal with it our way.

Previews of the new PSAT indicate that the double reading passage most likely will appear in the second of the two verbal sections, where it will follow the analogies and a short, single reading passage. First you'll see a few lines in italics introducing both passages. Then will come the two passages. Their lines will be numbered as if they were one enormous passage: if PASSAGE 1 ends on line 42, PASSAGE 2 will begin on line 43. However, they are two separate passages and you should tackle them one at a time. Remember, the questions are organized sequentially: questions about PASSAGE 1 will come before questions about PASSAGE 2. Therefore, as soon as you finish reading PASSAGE 1, you should skip to the questions and try to answer the four to five questions based on PASSAGE 1. Then you should read PASSAGE 2 and answer the four to five questions based on that passage. (The line numbers in the questions will help you spot where the questions on PASSAGE 1 end and those on PASSAGE 2 begin.) At that point you'll have done everything possible to maximize your score, and will be ready to tackle the final two to three questions that ask you to evaluate both passages.

The following set of paired passages is the same set that appeared in Chapter 1. The questions following the paired passages, however, will be new to you. See how well you do in dealing with this mix of the different question types you're likely to face on the PSAT.

The following passages are excerpted from books on America's national pastime, baseball.

PASSAGE 1

DiMaggio had size, power, and speed. McCarthy, his longtime manager, liked to say that
Line DiMaggio might have stolen 60 bases a season if
5 he had given him the green light. Stengel, his new manager, was equally impressed, and when DiMaggio was on base he would point to him as an example of the perfect base runner. "Look at him," Stengel would say as DiMaggio ran out a
10 base hit, "he's always watching the ball. He isn't watching second base. He isn't watching third base. He knows they haven't been moved. He isn't watching the ground, because he knows they haven't built a canal or a swimming pool since he
15 was last there. He's watching the ball and the outfielder, which is the one thing that is different on every play."

DiMaggio complemented his natural athletic ability with astonishing physical grace. He played
20 the outfield, he ran the bases, and he batted not just effectively but with rare style. He would glide rather than run, it seemed, always smooth, always ending up where he wanted to be just when he wanted to be there. If he appeared to play effort-
25 lessly, his teammates knew otherwise. In his first season as a Yankee, Gene Woodling, who played left field, was struck by the sound of DiMaggio chasing a fly ball. He sounded like a giant truck horse on the loose, Woodling thought, his feet

30 thudding down hard on the grass. The great, clear noises in the open space enabled Woodling to measure the distances between them without looking.

He was the perfect Hemingway hero, for
35 Hemingway in his novels romanticized the man who exhibited grace under pressure, who withheld any emotion lest it soil the purer statement of his deeds. DiMaggio was that kind of hero; his grace and skill were always on display, his emotions
40 always concealed. This stoic grace was not achieved without a terrible price: DiMaggio was a man wound tight. He suffered from insomnia and ulcers. When he sat and watched the game he chain-smoked and drank endless cups of coffee.
45 He was ever conscious of his obligation to play well. Late in his career, when his legs were bothering him and the Yankees had a comfortable lead in a pennant race, columnist Jimmy Cannon asked him why he played so hard—the games, after all,
50 no longer meant so much. "Because there might be somebody out there who's never seen me play before," he answered.

PASSAGE 2

Athletes and actors—let actors stand for the set of performing artists—share much. They share the
55 need to make gesture as fluid and economical as possible, to make out of a welter of choices the single, precisely right one. They share the need for thousands of hours of practice in order to train the body to become the perfect, instinctive instru-
60 ment to express. Both athlete and actor, out of that abundance of emotion, choice, strategy, knowledge of the terrain, mood of spectators, condition of others in the ensemble, secret awareness of injury or weakness, and as nearly an absolute con-
65 centration as possible so that all externalities are integrated, all distraction absorbed to the self, must be able to change the self so successfully that it changes us.

When either athlete or actor can bring all these
70 skills to bear and focus them, then he or she will achieve that state of complete intensity and complete relaxation—complete coherence or integrity between what the performer wants to do and what the performer has to do. Then, the performer is
75 free; for then, all that has been learned, by thousands of hours of practice and discipline and by repetition of pattern, becomes natural. Then intellect is upgraded to the level of an instinct. The body follows commands that precede thinking.
80 When athlete and artist achieve such self-knowledge that they transform the self so that we are re-created, it is finally an exercise in power. The individual's power to dominate, on stage or field invests the whole arena around the locus of
85 performance with his or her power. We draw from

the performer's energy, just as we scrutinize the performer's vulnerabilities, and we criticize as if we were equals (we are not) what is displayed. This is why all performers dislike or resent the
90 audience as much as they need and enjoy it. Power flows in a mysterious circuit from performer to spectator (I assume a "live" performance) and back, and while cheers or applause are the hoped-for outcome of performing, silence
95 or gasps are the most desired, for then the moment has occurred—then domination is complete, and as the performer triumphs, a unity rare and inspiring results.

1. Stengel's comments in lines 7–16 serve chiefly to
   (A) point up the stupidity of the sort of error he condemns
   (B) suggest the inevitability of mistakes in running bases
   (C) show it is easier to spot problems than to come up with answers
   (D) answer the criticisms of DiMaggio's base-running
   (E) modify his earlier position on DiMaggio's ability

2. In line 26, the word "struck" most nearly means
   (A) halted
   (B) slapped
   (C) afflicted
   (D) enamored
   (E) impressed

3. By quoting Woodling's comment on DiMaggio's running (lines 27–29), the author most likely intends to emphasize
   (A) his teammates' envy of DiMaggio's natural gifts
   (B) how much exertion went into DiMaggio's moves
   (C) how important speed is to a baseball player
   (D) Woodling's awareness of his own slowness
   (E) how easily DiMaggio was able to cover territory

4. In the last paragraph of Passage 1, the author acknowledges which negative aspect of DiMaggio's heroic stature?
   (A) His overemphasis on physical grace
   (B) His emotional romanticism
   (C) The uniformity of his performance
   (D) The obligation to answer the questions of reporters
   (E) The burden of living up to his reputation

5. The author makes his point about DiMaggio's prowess through all the following EXCEPT
   (A) literary allusion
   (B) quotations
   (C) personal anecdotes
   (D) generalization

(E) understatement

6. The phrase "stand for" in line 52 means
   (A) tolerate
   (B) represent
   (C) advocate
   (D) withstand
   (E) surpass

7. The phrase "bring all these skills to bear" in line 68 means
   (A) come to endure
   (B) carry toward
   (C) apply directly
   (D) cause to behave
   (E) induce birth

8. Why, in lines 90–91, does the author of Passage 2 assume a "live" performance?
   (A) His argument assumes a mutual involvement between performer and spectator that can only occur when both are present.
   (B) He believes that televised and filmed images give a false impression of the performer's ability to the spectators.
   (C) He fears the use of "instant replay" and other broadcasting techniques will cause performers to resent spectators even more strongly.
   (D) His argument dismisses the possibility of combining live performances with filmed segments.
   (E) He prefers audiences not to have time to reflect about the performance they have just seen.

9. Which of the following attributes of the ideal athlete mentioned in Passage 2 is NOT illustrated by the anecdotes about DiMaggio in Passage 1?
   (A) knowledge of the terrain
   (B) secret awareness of injury or weakness
   (C) consciousness of the condition of other teammates
   (D) ability to make gestures fluid and economical
   (E) absolute powers of concentration

10. Which of the following statements is best supported by a comparison of the two excerpts?
    (A) Both excerpts focus on the development of a specific professional athlete.
    (B) The purpose of both excerpts is to compare athletes with performing artists.
    (C) The development of ideas in both excerpts is similar.
    (D) Both excerpts examine the nature of superior athletic performance.
    (E) Both excerpts discuss athletic performance primarily in abstract terms.

DOUBLE PASSAGE ANSWER KEY

1. **A**	*3.* **B**	*5.* **E**	*7.* **C**	*9.* **C**
2. **E**	*4.* **E**	*6.* **B**	*8.* **A**	*10.* **D**

ANSWER EXPLANATIONS

1. **A** Stengel's sarcastic comments about the mistakes DiMaggio *doesn't* make indicate just how dumb he thinks it is to look down at the ground when you should have your attention on the outfielder and the ball. Clearly, if one of his players made such an error, Stengel's response would be to say, "What's the matter, stupid? Are you afraid you're going to fall in a canal down there?"

2. **E** Woodling was struck or *impressed* by the sound of DiMaggio's running; he found the impact of DiMaggio's feet hitting the ground noteworthy.

3. **B** Note the context of the reference to Woodling. In the sentence immediately preceding, the author says that, if DiMaggio "appeared to play effortlessly, his teammates knew otherwise." The author then introduces a comment by Woodling, one of DiMaggio's teammates. Woodling knew a great deal of effort went into DiMaggio's playing: he describes how DiMaggio's feet pounded as he ran. Clearly, the force of DiMaggio's running is mentioned to illustrate *how much exertion went into DiMaggio's moves*.

4. **E** In the final paragraph, the author describes DiMaggio pushing himself to play hard despite his injuries. DiMaggio does so because he is trying to live up to the image his public has of him. He feels *the burden of living up to his reputation*.

5. **E** You can answer this technique question by using the process of elimination. The author makes a *literary allusion* or reference to the novels of Ernest Hemingway. He *quotes* the comments of Casey Stengel and of DiMaggio himself. He cites an *anecdote* or story about Gene Woodling's first impression of DiMaggio. He makes *generalizations*—general statements—about DiMaggio ("He was the perfect Hemingway hero . . ."). However, he always expresses himself emphatically, using strong, extremely positive words to describe his subject; he never uses any *understatements*.

6. **B** At this point, the questions on Passage 2 begin. In this brief aside, the author is defining how he intends to use a word. He wishes to use the word *actors* to stand for or *represent* all other performers. This way every time he makes his comparison between athletes and performers he won't have to list all the various sorts of performing artists (actors, dancers, singers, acrobats, clowns) who resemble athletes in their need for physical grace, extensive rehearsal, and total concentration.

7. **C** The author has been describing the wide range of skills a performer utilizes in crafting an artistic or athletic performance. It is by taking these skills and *applying them purposefully* and with concentration to the task at hand that the performer achieves his or her goal.

8. **A** While a spectator may feel powerfully involved with a filmed or televised image of a performer, the filmed image is unaffected by the spectator's feelings. Thus, for power to "flow in a mysterious circuit" from performer to spectator *and back*, the assumption is that both performer and spectator *must be present in the flesh*.

9. **C** Though DiMaggio's teammates clearly were aware of *his* condition (as the Woodling anecdote illustrates), none of the anecdotes in Passage 1 indicate or even imply that DiMaggio was specifically *conscious of his teammates' condition*. You can answer this question by using the process of elimination. In running bases, DiMaggio never lets himself be distracted by looking at the bases or down at the ground; as Stengel says, he knows where they are. Clearly, he *knows the terrain*. You can eliminate Choice A. When DiMaggio's legs are failing him late in his career, he still pushes himself to perform well for the fan in the stands who hasn't seen him play before. In doing so, he takes into account his *secret awareness* of his legs' weakness. You can eliminate Choice B. Gliding rather than running, always smooth, never wasting a glance on inessentials, DiMaggio clearly exhibits *fluidity and economy* in his movements. You can eliminate Choice D. Running bases, DiMaggio always keeps his eye on the ball and the outfielder; he *concentrates absolutely* on them. You can eliminate Choice E. Only Choice C is left. It is the correct answer.

10. **D** Though one passage presents an abstract discussion of the nature of the ideal athlete and the other describes the achievements and character of a specific superior athlete, both passages *examine the nature of superior athletic performance*.

PRACTICE EXERCISES

Many of the following passages are shorter than the actual passages you will encounter on the PSAT. Use these short passages as your opportunity to tackle a wide range of the question types that appear on the test.

On the following pages are five groups of reading exercises. The passages tend to get somewhat more difficult as you go along. You will find the correct answers at the end of the chapter.

READING EXERCISE A

The chief characteristic of art today, if we are to judge by the reactions of the common man, is its obscurity. Everybody complains about obscu-
Line rity in poetry, in painting, in music. I do not sug-
5 gest that in some cases the complaint is unjusti-
fied. But we should remember that the really original work of art in any age seems obscure to the general public. From a certain point of view it would be true to say that no great work of art
10 finds an appreciative public waiting for it. The work creates its own public, slowly and painfully. A work of art is born as an intellectual foundling. What is interesting to notice is that often the art specialists themselves are caught napping. It was
15 Andre Gide, you remember, who first saw Proust's great novel while he was working as a reader for a firm of publishers. He turned it down without hesitation. Perhaps you remember Leigh Hunt's verdict on Blake as "an unfortunate mad-
20 man whose mildness alone prevented him from being locked up." Wordsworth also thought Blake mad, and yet it was he who wrote: "Every great and original writer, in proportion as he is great and original, must himself create the taste by
25 which he is judged."

1. The passage indicates that critics often
(A) discover unknown geniuses
(B) add to obscurity in art
(C) create an audience for new works
(D) misjudge a masterpiece
(E) explain a work of art to the public

2. The phrase "are caught napping" (line 14) is best taken to mean that the art specialists
(A) are trapped in their profession
(B) are off their guard
(C) feel a need for rest
(D) find their task captivating
(E) would escape if they were able

3. The word "taste" in line 24 means
(A) detectable flavor
(B) small morsel
(C) individual artwork
(D) aesthetic attitude
(E) slight experience

4. The last four sentences in the passage (lines 14–25) provide
(A) a refutation of the contention made earlier
(B) support for the immediately preceding assertion
(C) examples of the inherent contradictions of an argument
(D) a revision of a previously held position
(E) a return to the author's original thesis

Intuition is not a quality which everyone can understand. As the unimaginative are miserable about a work of fiction until they discover what
Line flesh-and-blood individual served as the model
5 for the hero or heroine, so even many scientists doubt scientific intuition. They cannot believe that a blind person can see anything that they can-not see. They rely utterly on the celebrated induc-tive method of reasoning: the facts are to be
10 exposed, and we are to conclude from them only what we must. This is a very sound rule—for mentalities that can do no better. But it is not cer-tain that the really great steps are made in this plodding fashion. Dreams are made of quite other
15 stuff, and if there are any left in the world who do not know that dreams have remade the world, then there is little that we can teach them.

5. The primary purpose of this passage is to
(A) denounce the unimaginative snobbery of scientists
(B) correct a misconception about the nature of dreams
(C) argue against the use of inductive reasoning
(D) explain the importance of intuition in science
(E) show how challenging scientific research can be

6. The author's attitude toward those who rely solely on the inductive method of reasoning can best be described as
(A) condescending
(B) approving
(C) indignant
(D) ambivalent
(E) hypocritical

7. The word "exposed" in line 10 means
(A) bared to the elements
(B) laid open to danger
(C) held up to ridicule
(D) unmasked
(E) made known

8. The phrase "the really great steps" (line 13) most likely refers to
(A) extremely large paces
(B) vast distances
(C) grandiose fantasies
(D) major scientific advances
(E) broadly interpreted measures

Too many parents force their children into group activities. They are concerned about the child who loves to do things alone, who prefers a
Line solitary walk with a camera to a game of ball.
5 They want their sons to be "good fellows" and their daughters "social mixers." In such foolish fears lie the beginnings of the blighting of individuality, the thwarting of personality, the stealing of the wealth of one's capital for living joy-
10 ously and well in a confused world. What America needs is a new army of defense, manned by young men and women who, through guidance and confidence, encouragement and wisdom, have built up values for themselves and away from
15 crowds and companies.

9. According to the passage, too many parents push their children to be
(A) unnecessarily gregarious
(B) foolishly timorous
(C) pointlessly extravagant
(D) acutely individualistic
(E) financially dependent

10. The primary point the author wishes to make is that
(A) young people need times to themselves
(B) group activities are harmful to children
(C) parents knowingly thwart their children's personalities
(D) independent thinking is of questionable value
(E) America needs universal military training

11. The author puts quotation marks around the words "good fellows" and "social mixers" to indicate that he
(A) is using vocabulary that is unfamiliar to the reader
(B) intends to define these terms later in course of the passage
(C) can readily distinguish these terms from one another
(D) prefers not to differentiate roles by secondary factors such as gender
(E) refuses to accept the assumption that these are positive values

12. By "the wealth of one's capital for living joyously and well in a confused world" (lines 9–10), the author most likely means
(A) the financial security that one attains from one's individual professional achievements

(B) the riches that parents thrust upon children who would far prefer to be left alone to follow their own inclinations
(C) the hours spent in solitary pursuits that enable one to develop into an independent, confident adult
(D) the happy memories of childhood days spent in the company of true friends
(E) the profitable financial and personal contacts young people make when they engage in group activities

"Sticks and stones can break my bones,
But names will never harm me."
No doubt you are familiar with this childhood
Line rhyme; perhaps, when you were younger, you fre-
5 quently invoked whatever protection it could offer against unpleasant epithets. But like many popular slogans and verses, this one will not bear too close scrutiny. For names will hurt you. Sometimes you may be the victim, and find your-
10 self an object of scorn, humiliation, and hatred just because other people have called you certain names. At other times you may not be the victim, but clever speakers and writers may, through name calling, blind your judgment so that you
15 will follow them in a course of action wholly opposed to your own interests or principles. Name calling can make you gullible to propaganda which you might otherwise readily see through and reject.

13. The author's primary purpose in quoting the rhyme in lines 1–2 is to
(A) remind readers of their childhood vulnerabilities
(B) emphasize the importance of maintaining one's good name
(C) demonstrate his conviction that only physical attacks can harm us
(D) affirm his faith in the rhyme's ability to shield one from unpleasant epithets
(E) introduce the topic of speaking abusively about others

14. By "this one will not bear too close scrutiny" (lines 7–8), the author means that
(A) the statement will no longer seem valid if you examine it too closely
(B) the literary quality of the verse does not improve on closer inspection
(C) people who indulge in name-calling are embarrassed when they are in the spotlight
(D) the author cannot stand having his comments looked at critically
(E) a narrow line exists between analyzing a slogan and over-analyzing it

15. According to the passage, name calling may make you more susceptible to
    (A) poetic language
    (B) biased arguments
    (C) physical abuse
    (D) risky confrontations
    (E) offensive epithets

16. The author evidently believes that slogans and verses frequently
    (A) appeal to our better nature
    (B) are disregarded by children
    (C) are scorned by unprincipled speakers
    (D) represent the popular mood
    (E) oversimplify a problem

It takes no particular expert in foods, or even glutton, to know that no meal on the table ever is as good as the meal in the oven's roasting pan or
Line the stove's covered kettle. There is something
5   about the furtive lifting of the lid and the opening of the door that is better than all sauces and gravies. Call it the surprise appetizer. Call it, also, that one gesture which the proprietor of the kitchen hates above all others, which brings forth
10   the shortest, most succinct sentences with the word "meddling" in them. Yet it is essential a friendly gesture, one based on good will, and not on its more general misconstruction, curiosity. It is quite proper, to state the case flatly, to say that a little
15   quiet investigation of what is cooking is simply an attempt to share the good things of life. It is possi-

ble to state that, but it will take more than a statement to convince the cook that it is not an act of interference. The kitchen has special laws.

17. The author maintains that cooks
    (A) feel proprietary about their domain
    (B) readily share the good things they create
    (C) avoid making friendly gestures to strangers
    (D) exercise care in lifting hot pan lids
    (E) tend to be unusually laconic

18. We can infer that the tone of the short sentences to which the author refers (line 10) is
    (A) admonitory
    (B) tentative
    (C) nonchalant
    (D) cordial
    (E) serious

19. The word "flatly" in line 14 means
    (A) evenly
    (B) horizontally
    (C) without animation
    (D) without qualification
    (E) lacking flavor

20. The author's tone in the concluding sentence can best be described as
    (A) bitterly resentful
    (B) mildly ironic
    (C) thoroughly respectful
    (D) openly bewildered
    (E) quietly curious

READING EXERCISE B

There are exceptions to the rule of male insects being smaller than the females, and some of these exceptions are intelligible. Size and strength
Line would be an advantage to the males which fight
5   for the possession of the females, and in these cases, as with the stag beetle (Lucanus), the males are larger than the females. There are, however, other beetles which are not known to fight together, of which the males exceed the females in size.
10   The meaning of this fact is not known, but in some of these cases, as with the huge Dynastes and Megasoma, we can at least see that there would be no necessity for the males to be smaller than the females in order to be matured before
15   them, for these beetles are not short-lived, and there would be ample time for the pairing of the sexes.

1. The paragraph preceding this one most likely
   (A) discusses a generalization about the size of insects
   (B) develops the idea that male insects do not live long after maturity
   (C) emphasizes the natural belligerence of beetles
   (D) dispels some misconceptions about insect behavior
   (E) indicates the enormous variety of species of beetle

2. According to the author, the male Lucanus is particularly
   (A) adaptable
   (B) strong
   (C) massive
   (D) belligerent
   (E) long-lived

3. According to the author, which of the following is true?
   (A) Male insects are always smaller than females.
   (B) In a given species nature provides differences between the sexes to ensure successful reproduction.
   (C) Size and strength protect females from the attacks of other females.
   (D) Longevity is characteristic of the Dynastes and Megasoma.
   (E) In the stag beetle, the females are larger than the males.

4. The word "pairing" in line 16 means
   (A) lining up together
   (B) physical resemblance
   (C) full development
   (D) comparison
   (E) mating

   All museum adepts are familiar with examples of *ostrakoi,* the oystershells used in balloting in ancient Athens. As a matter of fact, these "oyster-
Line shells" are usually shards of pottery, conveniently
5 glazed to enable the voter to express his wishes in writing. In the Agora a great number of these have come to light, bearing the thrilling name Themistocles. Into rival jars were dropped the ballots for or against his banishment. On account
10 of the huge vote taken on that memorable day, it was to be expected that many ostrakoi would be found, but the interest of this collection is that a number of these ballots are inscribed in an *identical* handwriting. There is nothing mysterious
15 about it! The Boss was on the job, then as now. He prepared these ballots and voters cast them— no doubt for the consideration of an obol or two. *The ballot box was stuffed.*
   How the glory of the American boss is dimin-
20 ished! A vile imitation, he. His methods as old as Time!

5. The author evidently assumes that the reader
   (A) would have voted in favor of Themistocles' banishment
   (B) is familiar with the story of Themistocles
   (C) knows that the ostrakoi were usually made of clay
   (D) approves of the methods used by the Boss
   (E) prefers Greek customs to American ones

6. We can infer from lines 15–18 that the Boss most likely was
   (A) a leader facing banishment
   (B) a corrupt politician
   (C) an Athenian voter
   (D) a counter of ballots
   (E) an American employer

7. What additional information would undermine the author's conclusion that the ballot box was stuffed?
   (A) Educated people in ancient Greece cultivated a highly individualistic style of penmanship.
   (B) A public scribe was assigned to write Themistocles' name on the ballots of illiterate voters.
   (C) Women, children, and slaves traditionally were denied the right to vote.
   (D) More than two jars were used for the historic vote on Themistocles' banishment.
   (E) Far fewer ostrakoi have been found than museum-goers would generally expect.

8. The author's attitude toward the alleged ballot-stuffing can best be described as
   (A) detached
   (B) indignant
   (C) approving
   (D) defensive
   (E) cynical

   Good American English is simply good English, English that differs little in pronunciation, vocabulary, and occasionally in idiom from
Line English as spoken in London or South Africa, but
5 which differs no more than our physical surround-ings, our political and social institutions, and other circumstances that are reflected in language. It rests upon the same basis as that which the stan-dard speech of England rests upon—the usage of
10 reputable speakers and writers throughout the country. No American student of language is so provincial as to hope, or wish, that the American standard may some day be adopted in England. Nor does he or she share the views of such in
15 England as think that we would do well to take our standard ready-made from them. The American student will be content with the opinion of Henry Bradley that "the wiser sort among us will not dis-pute that Americans have acquired the right to
20 frame their own standards of correct English on the usage of their best writers and speakers."

9. The word "rests" in line 8 means
   (A) reposes
   (B) remains
   (C) is present
   (D) is based
   (E) lingers

10. The author considers a good American English to be
   (A) appropriate for use in America
   (B) superior to the English spoken in South Africa
   (C) inferior to the English in use in England
   (D) too idiomatic to find general acceptance
   (E) suitable as a standard for all English-speaking countries

11. According to the author, correctness in language is determined by
    (A) the will of the majority of those who speak that language
    (B) the dominant social and political structures
    (C) those who wish to standardize the language
    (D) the practice of the most respected communicators
    (E) unique geographical considerations

12. The word "frame" in line 20 means
    (A) devise
    (B) border
    (C) incriminate
    (D) line up visually
    (E) enunciate distinctly

It takes no calendar to tell root and stem that the calm days of mid-summer are here. Last spring's sprouted seed comes to fruit. None of
Line these things depends on a calendar of the days and
5 months. They are their own calendar, marks on the span of time that reaches far back into the shadows of time. The mark is there for all to see, in every field and meadow and treetop, as it was last year and ten years ago and when the centuries
10 were young.

The time is here. This is that point in the great continuity when these things happen, and will continue to happen year after year. Any summer arrives at this point, only to lead on to the next
15 and the next, and so to summer again. These things we can count on; these things will happen again and again, so long as the earth turns.

13. By "It takes no calendar to tell root and stem that the calm days of mid-summer are here" (lines 1–2), the author means that
    (A) plants respond to the changing seasons naturally
    (B) no calendar can exactly pinpoint the summer solstice
    (C) trees sink their roots deeply into the soil in mid-summer
    (D) the tranquillity of mid-summer seems timeless
    (E) calendars are more useful during the fall harvest season

14. We can infer from the passage that the author
    (A) does not possess a calendar
    (B) is a very elderly person
    (C) is writing in mid-summer
    (D) dislikes urban life
    (E) welcomes breaks in continuity

15. The author's mood can best be described as one of
    (A) keen frustration
    (B) fear of the forces of nature
    (C) regret at the rapid passage of time
    (D) moderate pessimism
    (E) serene confidence

16. The word "count" in line 16 means
    (A) include
    (B) depend
    (C) represent
    (D) check over
    (E) have merit

Most people do not think of fishes and other marine animals as having voices, and of those who are aware of the fact that many of them can
Line "speak," few understand that these "conversa-
5 tions" have significance. Actually, their talk may be as meaningful as much of our own. For example, some sea animals use their "voices" to locate their food in the ocean expanses; others, to let their fellows know of their whereabouts; and still
10 others, as a means of obtaining mates. Sometimes, "speaking" may mean the difference between life and death to a marine animal. It appears in some cases that when a predator approaches, the prey depends on no more than the
15 sounds it makes to escape.

Fish sounds are important to human beings also. By listening to them we can learn a great deal about the habits of the creatures that make them, the size of the schools they form, the pat-
20 terns of their migrations, and the nature of the environments in which they live. We can also apply this information to the more effective utilization of the listening posts we have set up to detect enemy submarines. A knowledge of fish
25 sounds can avoid confusion and unneeded effort when a "new" sound is picked up and the sound sentry must decide whether or not to call an alert.

17. The author's primary purpose in the passage is to
    (A) define a technical term
    (B) describe a natural process
    (C) explain the usefulness of a phenomenon
    (D) indicate the adaptations marine animals make
    (E) record the results of an experiment

18. Which of the following sentences is *best* supported by the information given?
    (A) Noises produced by fish are apparently random.
    (B) Fish noises are used by fishermen to increase their catch.
    (C) Fish noises can be utilized to tell whether or not a submarine is nearby.
    (D) Fish noises can puzzle users of submarine-detection equipment.
    (E) Fish noises are inaudible under water.

19. Which of the following statements can *best* be inferred from the information given?
(A) Fish noises cannot be transmitted through air.
(B) Hearing is more acute in fishes than in people.
(C) The chief use of "fish voices" is to enable one fish to communicate with another fish.
(D) The significance of some fish voices has been studied.
(E) Fishes can be surprisingly noisier than people.

20. The phrase "picked up" in line 26 means
(A) put in good order
(B) learned by experience
(C) brought into range of reception
(D) taken into an automobile or ship
(E) obtained casually

READING EXERCISE C

For the sad state of criticism the writers must hold themselves much to blame. Literary artists, concerned solely in the creation of a book or story
Line as close to perfection as their powers will permit,
5 are generally quiet individuals, contemplative, retiring. On occasion they can be influenced to anger by some grievous social wrong that calls for desperate remedy. But mostly they are prone to sit in their towers reflecting on the absurdities
10 of a foolish world, asking only to be left alone with their labor. Never aggressive in their own interest, seeking only peace, they lay themselves open to aggression. Thus they do not see the enemy who has stolen into the shadows at the rear
15 of their retreat and is slowly scaling the walls. Such has been the course of events. While the artists have slept, the critical dwarfs have appeared. They have evolved a new language, written out a new set of definitions. Black is
20 white, and white is black. The ugly and the nauseous are beautiful; the beautiful is nightmare.

1. According to the passage, literary artists are inclined to
(A) ignore what is happening around them
(B) be perpetually aroused by social injustices
(C) slight the work involved in writing
(D) welcome the onset of aggression
(E) accept criticism gladly

2. Which best captures the meaning of the word "powers" in line 4?
(A) delegated authority
(B) physical energies
(C) written statements
(D) intellectual abilities
(E) political ascendancy

3. The word "retiring" in line 6 means
(A) departing from office
(B) tending toward fatigue
(C) withdrawing from contact
(D) receiving a pension
(E) going to bed

4. Through his comments about the critical dwarfs in lines 14–21, the author wishes to convey the impression that critics
(A) deserve praise for their linguistic originality
(B) lack the intellectual stature of those they criticize
(C) appreciate the fundamental oneness of apparent opposites
(D) are as able as writers to scale the literary heights
(E) are less hostile than the authors who look down upon them

5. According to the passage, the critics' standards of criticism are
(A) a natural outgrowth of former standards
(B) a complete reversal of accepted standards
(C) an invaluable guide to the literary artist
(D) a source of suggestions of new topics to write about
(E) the result of the artists' neglect of good writing

When there is no distance between people, the only way that anyone can keep his or her distance is by a code of etiquette that has acceptance in a
Line community. Manners are the antidote to adjust-
5 ment to the group. They make social intercourse possible without any forfeit of one's personal dignity. They are armor against invasion of privacy; they are the advance patrols that report whether one should withdraw or advance into intimacy.
10 They are the friendly but noncommittal gestures of civilized people. The manners of crowded countries are, I believe, always more formal than those of open countries (as they are, for example, in Europe and Japan), and it may be that we are
15 seeing a rising concern about American manners precisely because we encounter more people in closer quarters than we ever have before. We feel the need to find ways in which to be part of the group without selling out our privacy or our indi-
20 viduality for a mess of adjustment.

6. The title that best expresses the idea of this passage is
   (A) The Function of Politeness
   (B) Invasions of Privacy
   (C) Reasons for Social Relationships
   (D) The Need for Complete Privacy
   (E) American Manners

7. According to the author, manners serve to
   (A) facilitate relationships among people
   (B) preserve certain ceremonies
   (C) help people to make friends quickly
   (D) reveal character traits
   (E) assist in pleasing one's friends

8. By stating that manners "are armor against invasion of privacy" (line 7), the author wishes to convey that manners
   (A) protect one from physical danger
   (B) are a cold, hard barrier separating people
   (C) allow us to vent our aggressions safely
   (D) shield one from unwanted intrusions
   (E) enable us to guard our possessions

9. The author suggests that in Europe good manners are
   (A) informal
   (B) excessive
   (C) essential
   (D) ignored
   (E) individual

10. In the course of the passage, the author does all of the following EXCEPT
    (A) state a possibility
    (B) use a metaphor
    (C) cite an example
    (D) make a parenthetical remark
    (E) pose a question

11. The primary purpose of the passage is to
    (A) demonstrate the evolution of the meaning of a term
    (B) depict the successive stages of a phenomenon
    (C) establish the pervasiveness of a process
    (D) support a theory considered outmoded
    (E) describe a static condition

12. The word "disturbed" in line 6 means
    (A) hindered
    (B) perplexed
    (C) disarranged
    (D) pestered
    (E) thickened

13. It can be inferred from the passage that the author views the information contained within it as
    (A) controversial but irrefutable
    (B) speculative and unprofitable
    (C) uncomplicated and traditional
    (D) original but obscure
    (E) sadly lacking in elaboration

14. The author provides information that answers which of the following questions?
    I. How does the small region's increasing density affect its gravitational field?
    II. What causes the disturbance that changes the cloud from its original static state?
    III. What is the end result of the gradually increasing concentration of the small region of gas?
    (A) I only
    (B) II only
    (C) I and II only
    (D) I and III only
    (E) I, II and III

15. Throughout the passage, the author's manner of presentation is
    (A) argumentative
    (B) convoluted
    (C) discursive
    (D) expository
    (E) hyperbolic

One simple physical concept lies behind the formation of the stars: gravitational instability. The concept is not new; Newton first perceived it
Line late in the seventeenth century.
5   Imagine a uniform, static cloud of gas in space. Imagine then that the gas is somehow disturbed so that one small spherical region becomes a little denser than the gas around it so that the small region's gravitational field becomes slightly
10 stronger. It now attracts more matter to it and its gravity increases further, causing it to begin to contract. As it contracts its density increases, which increases its gravity even more, so that it picks up even more matter and contracts even fur-
15 ther. The process continues until the small region of gas finally forms a gravitationally bound object.

Unlike the carefully weighed and planned compositions of Dante, Goethe's writings have always the sense of immediacy and enthusiasm.
Line He was a constant experimenter with life, with
5   ideas, and with forms of writing. For the same reason, his works seldom have the qualities of finish or formal beauty which distinguish the masterpieces of Dante and Virgil. He came to love the beauties of classicism, but these were never an
10 essential part of his make-up. Instead, the urgency of the moment, the spirit of the thing, guided his pen. As a result, nearly all his works have serious flaws of structure, of inconsistencies, of excesses and redundancies and extraneities.

15   In the large sense, Goethe represents the fullest
development of the romanticist. It has been
argued that he should not be so designated
because he so clearly matured and outgrew the
kind of romanticism exhibited by Wordsworth,
20 Shelley, and Keats. Shelley and Keats died
young; Wordsworth lived narrowly and abandoned his early attitudes. In contrast, Goethe
lived abundantly and developed his faith in the
spirit, his understanding of nature and human
25 nature, and his reliance on feelings as man's
essential motivating force. The result was an all-
encompassing vision of reality and a philosophy
of life broader and deeper than the partial visions
and attitudes of other romanticists. Yet the spirit
30 of youthfulness, the impatience with close reasoning or "logic-chopping," and the continued faith
in nature remained his to the end, together with an
occasional waywardness and impulsiveness and a
disregard of artistic or logical propriety which
35 savor strongly of romantic individualism. Since
so many twentieth-century thoughts and attitudes
are similarly based on the stimulus of the
Romantic Movement, Goethe stands as particularly the poet of the modern man as Dante stood for
40 medieval man and as Shakespeare for the man of
the Renaissance.

16. The word "close" in line 30 means
(A) nearby
(B) intimate
(C) fitting tightly
(D) strictly logical
(E) nearly even

17. A main concern of the passage is to
(A) describe the history of Romanticism until its
decline
(B) suggest that romantic literature is similar to
Shakespearean drama
(C) argue that romantic writings are more fully
developed than classical works
(D) compare Goethe with twentieth-century writers
and poets
(E) explain the ways in which Goethe embodied
the romantic spirit

18. A characteristic of romanticism NOT mentioned in
this passage is its
(A) elevation of nature
(B) preference for spontaneity
(C) modernity of ideas
(D) unconcern for artistic decorum
(E) simplicity of language

19. It can be inferred from the passage that classicism
has which of the following characteristics?
  I.   Sensitivity towards emotional promptings
  II. Emphasis on formal aesthetic standards
  III. Meticulous planning of artistic works
(A) II only
(B) III only
(C) I and II
(D) II and III
(E) I, II, and III

20. The author's attitude towards Goethe's writings is
best described as
(A) unqualified endorsement
(B) lofty indifference
(C) reluctant tolerance
(D) measured admiration
(E) undisguised contempt

READING EXERCISE D

    To keep clear of concealment, to keep clear of
the need of concealment, to do nothing which you
might not do out on the middle of Boston
Line Common at noonday—I cannot say how more
5   and more it seems to me the glory of a young person's life. It is an awful hour when the first
necessity of hiding anything comes. The whole
life is different thenceforth. When there are questions to be feared and eyes to be avoided and sub-
10 jects which must not be touched, then the bloom
of life is gone. Put off that day as long as possible. Put it off forever if you can.

1. The author regards the occasion when one first
must conceal something as
(A) anticlimactic
(B) insignificant
(C) fleeting
(D) momentous
(E) enviable

2. The author's tone throughout the passage can best
be described as
(A) hostile
(B) condescending
(C) playful
(D) serious
(E) impersonal

3. Which of the following does the author recommend to his audience?

  I. To deny the necessity of aging
  II. To act in an aboveboard manner
  III. To rationalize one's misconduct

  (A) I only
  (B) II only
  (C) I and II only
  (D) II and III only
  (E) I, II, and III

Most people want to know how things are made. They frankly admit, however, that they feel completely at sea when it comes to understanding
Line how a piece of music is made. Where a composer
5 begins, how he manages to keep going—in fact, how and where he learns his trade—all are shrouded in impenetrable darkness. The composer, in short, is a figure of mystery, and the composer's workshop an unapproachable ivory tower.
10 One of the first things lay persons want to hear about is the part inspiration plays in composing. They find it difficult to believe that composers are not much preoccupied with that question, that composing is as natural for the composer as eat-
15 ing or sleeping. Composing is something that the composer happens to have been born to do; and because of that, it loses the character of a special virtue in the composer's eyes.

The composer, therefore, does not say to him-
20 self: "Do I feel inspired?" He says to himself: "Do I feel like composing today?" And if he feels like composing, he does. It is more or less like saying to himself: "Do I feel sleepy?" If you feel sleepy, you go to sleep. If you don't feel sleepy,
25 you stay up. If the composer doesn't feel like composing, he doesn't compose. It's as simple as that.

4. The author of the passage indicates that creating music is an activity that is

  (A) difficult
  (B) rewarding
  (C) inspirational
  (D) fraught with anxiety
  (E) instinctive

5. When considering the work involved in composing music, the lay person often

  (A) exaggerates the difficulties of the composer in commencing work
  (B) minimizes the mental turmoil that the composer undergoes
  (C) is unaware that a creative process is involved
  (D) loses the ability to enjoy the composition
  (E) loses the ability to judge the work apart from the composer

6. The author's approach toward the subject is

  (A) highly emotional
  (B) casually informative
  (C) negative in tone
  (D) deeply philosophical
  (E) consciously prejudiced

John Greenleaf Whittier was the "Quaker-Puritan" scion of Massachusetts farmers. For this frail young man, however, farm life was too tough
Line an existence. His early interest in books and leg-
5 ends led him toward journalism, with poetry a pleasant side line. He became a Quaker firebrand and agitator, the politician among abolitionists, and a gadfly to New England Congressmen during the original "Great Debate." His impassioned
10 prose and poetry against slavery were often directed at a clergy whose acceptance of it he fought as a Quaker and a Christian.

Only after the Civil War, when emancipation had been at least nominally won, did the aging
15 Whittier emerge as the genial, easygoing "folkbard" remembered today. Until recently the prominence given this last phase of his literary life by scholarly circles has obscured his earlier contributions to American literature and political
20 freedom and tolerance.

7. The primary purpose of this passage is to

  (A) denounce a social injustice
  (B) evaluate a writer's poetic style
  (C) explain a nineteenth-century literary fashion
  (D) correct a misconception about an individual
  (E) argue against political involvement

8. The author's attitude toward Whittier's early career as a firebrand can best be described as one of

  (A) wary skepticism
  (B) moral censure
  (C) reluctant tolerance
  (D) objective neutrality
  (E) open approbation

9. It can be inferred from the passage that New England Congressmen during the time of the "Great Debate" most likely thought of Whittier as

  (A) a cordial teller of tales
  (B) an antiabolitionist
  (C) an annoying critic
  (D) a virtuous Quaker
  (E) a literary scholar

10. On the basis of the passage, which of the following opinions can appropriately be attributed to Whittier?
(A) The aim of literature is to entertain the reading public rather than to advocate a particular cause.
(B) Emancipation can only occur with the full cooperation of the slave owners, who thus must be won over gently.
(C) A poet must devote himself to his art, forsaking worldly claims in favor of aesthetic values.
(D) It is particularly reprehensible for Christian ministers to tolerate an institution as immoral as slavery.
(E) There is no place in the church for disharmony and strife, for the church is the temple of the Lord.

We were about a quarter mile away when quiet swept over the colony. A thousand or more heads periscoped. Two thousand eyes glared. Save for our wading, the world's business had stopped. A thousand avian personalities were concentrated on us, and the psychological force of this was terrific. Contingents of home-coming feeders, suddenly aware of four strange specks moving across the lake, would bank violently and speed away. Then the chain reaction began. Every throat in that rookery let go with a concatenation of wild, raspy, terrorized trumpet bursts. With all wings now fully spread and churning, and quadrupling the color mass, the birds began to move as one, and the sky was filled with the sound of judgment day.

11. The author's primary purpose in this passage is to
(A) explain a natural catastrophe
(B) issue a challenge
(C) denounce an expedition
(D) evoke an experience
(E) demonstrate a thesis

12. According to the passage, when they first noticed the visitors, the birds of the colony
(A) flew away
(B) churned their wings
(C) became very still
(D) set up a series of cries
(E) glared at the homecoming birds

13. The "four strange specks" (line 8) are
(A) wild birds
(B) animal predators
(C) intruding humans
(D) unusual clouds
(E) diners heading homeward

14. The word "bank" in line 9 means
(A) cover
(B) heap up
(C) count on
(D) tip laterally
(E) reserve carefully

15. The response of the visitors to the episode described in this passage was probably one of
(A) impatience
(B) fear
(C) anger
(D) sadness
(E) awe

With Meredith's *The Egoist* we enter into a critical problem that we have not yet before faced in these studies. That is the problem offered by a writer of recognizably impressive stature, whose work is informed by a muscular intelligence, whose language has splendor, whose "view of life" wins our respect, and yet for whom we are at best able to feel only a passive appreciation which amounts, practically, to indifference. We should be unjust to Meredith and to criticism if we should, giving in to the inertia of indifference, simply avoid dealing with him and thus avoid the problem along with him. He does not "speak to us," we might say; his meaning is not a "meaning for us"; he "leaves us cold." But do not the challenge and the excitement of the critical problem as such lie in that ambivalence of attitude which allows us to recognize the intelligence and even the splendor of Meredith's work, while, at the same time, we experience a lack of sympathy, a failure of any enthusiasm of response?

16. According to the passage, the work of Meredith is noteworthy for its elements of
(A) sensibility and artistic fervor
(B) ambivalence and moral ambiguity
(C) tension and sense of vitality
(D) brilliance and linguistic grandeur
(E) wit and whimsical frivolity

17. The word "informed" in line 5 means
(A) notified
(B) permeated
(C) disclosed
(D) acquainted
(E) incriminated

18. Meredith's chief flaw as a writer is that
(A) his writing fails to excite the reader
(B) his works have fallen out of fashion
(C) he retreated into ineffectual passivity
(D) he should have been a poet rather than a novelist
(E) his novels lack any genuine meaning

19. It can be inferred from the passage that the author finds the prospect of appraising Meredith's work critically to be
(A) counterproductive
(B) highly formidable
(C) somewhat tolerable
(D) markedly unpalatable
(E) clearly invigorating

20. It can be inferred from the passage that the author would be most likely to agree with which of the following statements about the role of criticism?
(A) Its chief task should be to make our enjoyment of the things that feed the mind as conscious as possible.
(B) It should be a disinterested attempt to learn and propagate the best that is known and thought in the world.
(C) It should enable us to go beyond personal prejudice to appreciate the virtues of works not to our own tastes.
(D) It should dwell upon virtues rather than imperfections, ignoring such defects as irrelevant.
(E) It should strive both to purify literature and to elevate the literary standards of the reading public.

READING EXERCISE E

For all of e.e. cummings's typographical innovations, he was an old-fashioned poet. He wrote about death and love, the graces of nature and the
Line disgraces of civilization. He implored beautiful
5 ladies for their favors and wittily thanked them afterwards. He distrusted power and satirized people in power. He adored Paris and said so in random lines as taking as any in English about that lovely city. He valued childhood and described its
10 innocence with wide-open-eyed clarity. He adored puns and practiced them like an Elizabethan.

In all this he was an old-fashioned poet. Even his typography, which seemed so modern, was
15 ancient in intention. Cummings revered Latin and Greek verse and understood that English, for all its excellences, had never achieved the concision and special effects available to the interlocking syntaxes of those inflected languages. In his
20 poems he wanted to make many things happen simultaneously. He wanted to catch action in words and yet keep it shivering. He wanted words to merge as impressions in the mind do. He wanted to reach backward and forward, pulling past
25 and future into a present instant. To do this he used punctuation like a second language. This was not an innovation so much as a thorough realization of a lost art.

1. Throughout the passage, the author's primary purpose is to
(A) emphasize cummings's revolutionary technique
(B) account for cummings's choice of subject matter
(C) contrast cummings with foreign poets
(D) provide specific examples of cummings's verse
(E) correct a misconception about cummings's poetry

2. As used in line 8, "taking" most nearly means
(A) grasping
(B) pleasing
(C) selective
(D) resounding
(E) ironic

3. It can be inferred from the passage that the Elizabethans
(A) believed in the value of practice
(B) were contemporaries of cummings
(C) employed modern typography
(D) enjoyed playing with words
(E) lacked childlike vision

4. Cummings admired classical verse for its
(A) succinctness
(B) piety
(C) lyricism
(D) euphony
(E) profundity

5. By "He wanted to catch action in words and yet keep it shivering" (lines 21–22), the author means that cummings
(A) hoped to evoke a sense of terror in the reader
(B) wished to preserve the act's excitement and vitality
(C) was shaken by the prospect of verbal criticism
(D) believed that it was simple to capture a moment poetically
(E) preferred the poetry of action to the poetry of contemplation

Rocks which have solidified directly from molten materials are called igneous rocks. Igneous rocks are commonly referred to as prima-
Line ry rocks because they are the original source of
5 material found in sedimentaries and metamor- phics. Igneous rocks compose the greater part of the earth's crust, but they are generally covered at the surface by a relatively thin layer of sedimenta- ry or metamorphic rocks. Igneous rocks are dis-
10 tinguished by the following characteristics: (1) they contain no fossils; (2) they have no regular arrangement of layers; and (3) they are nearly always made up of crystals.

Sedimentary rocks are composed largely of
15 minute fragments derived from the disintegration of existing rocks and in some instances from the remains of animals. As sediments are transported, individual fragments are assorted according to size. Distinct layers of such sediments as gravels,
20 sand, and clay build up, as they are deposited by water and occasionally wind. These sediments vary in size with the material and the power of the eroding agent. Sedimentary materials are laid down in layers called strata.

25 When sediments harden into sedimentary rocks, the names applied to them change to indi- cate the change in physical state. Thus, small stones and gravel cemented together are known as conglomerates; cemented sand becomes sand-
30 stone; and hardened clay becomes shale. In addi- tion to these, other sedimentary rocks such as limestone frequently result from the deposition of dissolved material. The ingredient parts are nor- mally precipitated by organic substances, such as
35 shells of clams or hard skeletons of other marine life.

Both igneous and sedimentary rocks may be changed by pressure, heat, solution, or cementing action. When individual grains from existing
40 rocks tend to deform and interlock, they are called metamorphic rocks. For example, granite, an igneous rock, may be metamorphosed into a gneiss or a schist. Limestone, a sedimentary rock, when subjected to heat and pressure may become
45 marble, a metamorphic rock. Shale under pressure becomes slate.

6. The primary purpose of the passage is to
(A) explain the factors that may cause rocks to change in form
(B) show how the scientific names of rocks reflect the rocks' composition
(C) present a new hypothesis about the nature of rock formation
(D) define and describe several diverse kinds of rocks
(E) explain why rocks are basic parts of the earth's structure

7. The word "state" in line 27 means
(A) mood
(B) pomp
(C) territory
(D) predicament
(E) condition

8. According to the passage, igneous rocks are charac- terized by
(A) their inability to be changed by heat or pres- sure
(B) the wealth of fossils they incorporate
(C) their granular composition
(D) their relative rarity
(E) their lack of regular strata

9. The passage contains information that would answer which of the following questions?
   I. Which elements form igneous rocks?
   II. What produces sufficient pressure to alter a rock?
   III. Why is marble called a metamorphic rock?
(A) I only
(B) III only
(C) I and II only
(D) II and III only
(E) I, II, and III

10. Which of the following methods is NOT used by the author?
(A) Precise examples
(B) Classification and discussion
(C) Specific enumeration
(D) Observation and hypothesis
(E) Cause and effect

The oldest adult human skull yet found belongs to the lowest grade of *Homo erectus*, and to the Australoid line. It is known as
Line Pithecanthropus (Ape-Man) Number 4, because it
5 was the fourth of its kind to be found. All four were unearthed in river banks in central Java. Number 4 is about 700,000 years old, and Numbers 1, 2, and 3 between 600,000 and 500,000. We know this because tektites—small,
10 glassy nodules from outer space—were found in the same beds as the first three, and the beds con- taining Number 4 lay underneath the tektite bed, along with the bones of a more ancient group of animals. These tektites have been picked up in
15 large numbers in Java, the Philippines, and Australia, where they all fell in a single celestial shower. Their age—approximately 600,000 years—has been accurately measured in several laboratories by nuclear chemical analysis, through
20 the so-called argon-potassium method.

Pithecanthropus Number 4 consists of the back part of a skull and its lower face, palate, and upper teeth. As reconstructed by Weidenreich, it is a brutal-looking skull, with heavy crests behind
25 four powerful neck muscle attachments, a large palate, and large teeth, as in apes. The brain size of this skull was about 900 cubic centimeters; modern human brains range from about 1,450 cc. The brains of apes and Australopithecines are
30 about 350 to 650 cc. So Pithecanthropus Number 4 was intermediate in brain size between apes and living men.

This fragmentary skull was not the only find made in the beds it lay in. Nearby were found the
35 cranial vault of a two-year-old baby, already different from those of living infants, and a piece of chinless adult lower jaw. Two other jaws have been discovered in the same deposits which were much larger than any in the world certainly
40 belonging to *Homo erectus*. They are called Meganthropus (Big Man) and may have belonged to a local kind of Australopithecine, but this not certain. If so, *Homo erectus* coexisted with, or overlapped, the Australopithecines in Java as well
45 as in South Africa, which implies that man did not originate in either place, but somewhere in between.

11. According to the passage, tektites are
(A) customarily found with the bones of animals
(B) undersized lumps of a glasslike substance
(C) a step in the evolutionary process
(D) equal in age to Ape-Man Number 4
(E) dissolved in a solution of argon-potassium

12. Scientists are certain that Pithecanthropus Number 4 is older than Pithecanthropus Numbers 1, 2, and 3 because
(A) it was discovered later than the others
(B) it was found in the company of tektites
(C) its age was measured by nuclear chemical analysis
(D) it was located below the tektite layer
(E) its skull is larger in cranial capacity

13. According to the passage, archaeological study of Pithecanthropus skulls involves which of the following?
I. Measurement of cranial capacity
II. Piecing together of bone fragments
III. Comparison with analogous primate skulls
(A) I only
(B) II only
(C) I and II only
(D) II and III only
(E) I, II, and III

14. The word "vault" in line 35 means
(A) a running jump
(B) a curved ceiling over a room or hall
(C) a strongbox for safeguarding valuables
(D) an arched roof of a cavity
(E) a burial chamber

15. The author does all of the following EXCEPT
(A) approximate an age
(B) define a term
(C) cite an authority
(D) describe an object
(E) make a comparison

A few species demonstrate conditions which are neither complete hibernation nor aestivation. Instead of going into a long "sleep" during the
Line most adverse season, they become torpid for a
5 few hours each day. This kind of behavior is known in other animals—bats become torpid during daytime, and hummingbirds at night. The first time I appreciated this phenomenon was while working with fat mice (*Steatomys*) in Africa.
10 These mice, incidentally, have a most appropriate name, for their bodies are so full of fat they resemble little furry balls. Fat storage as a method of survival has rebounded to some extent as far as the fat mice are concerned. They are regarded as a
15 succulent delicacy by many African tribes who hunt them with great tenacity; when captured, the mice are skewered and fried in their own fat. A captive fat mouse was once kept without food or water for thirty-six days; at the end of that time it
20 had lost a third of its weight but appeared quite healthy. During the dry season, some captives spent the day in such a deep state of torpor that they could be roughly handled without waking. The body temperature was a couple of degrees
25 above room temperature and the respiration was most irregular, several short pants being followed by a pause of up to three minutes. Just before dusk the mice woke up of their own accord and respired normally. In this case the torpid state was
30 not induced by shortage of food or abnormal temperatures. The forest dormouse of southern Asia and Europe also undergoes periods of torpidity during the day; this species has been recorded as having pauses of up to seventeen minutes between
35 breaths. There is also a record of a leaf-eared mouse of the Peruvian desert which became torpid under severe conditions.

16. The primary focus of the passage is on
(A) the inhumane treatment of laboratory specimens
(B) irregularities of respiration in mammals
(C) conditions that induce rodents to hibernate
(D) rodent species that exhibit brief periods of dormancy
(E) the similarities among rodent species

17. The word "rebounded" in line 13 means
    (A) recovered from discouragement
    (B) sprung back from ill health
    (C) had a negative impact
    (D) rapidly gained hold
    (E) been rejected

18. The tone of the passage can best be described as
    (A) apologetic
    (B) facetious
    (C) exhortatory
    (D) authoritative
    (E) ironic

19. This passage would most likely appear in which of the following types of publications?
    (A) A geographical atlas
    (B) A history of African exploration
    (C) A textbook on rodent biology
    (D) A guide to the care of laboratory animals
    (E) A general-interest periodical

20. It can be inferred that in the paragraph preceding this passage the author most likely discussed
    (A) his initial journey to Africa
    (B) the problems caused by sleep deprivation
    (C) other types of dormant states
    (D) the physical appearance of rodents
    (E) methods for measuring rodent respiration

ANSWER KEY

READING EXERCISE A

1. D	*5.* E	*9.* A	*13.* E	*17.* A
2. B	*6.* A	*10.* A	*14.* A	*18.* A
3. D	*7.* E	*11.* E	*15.* B	*19.* D
4. B	*8.* D	*12.* C	*16.* E	*20.* B

READING EXERCISE B

1. A	*5.* B	*9.* D	*13.* A	*17.* C
2. D	*6.* B	*10.* A	*14.* C	*18.* D
3. D	*7.* B	*11.* D	*15.* E	*19.* D
4. E	*8.* E	*12.* A	*16.* B	*20.* C

READING EXERCISE C

1. A	*5.* B	*9.* C	*13.* C	*17.* E
2. D	*6.* A	*10.* E	*14.* D	*18.* E
3. C	*7.* A	*11.* B	*15.* D	*19.* D
4. B	*8.* D	*12.* C	*16.* D	*20.* D

READING EXERCISE D

1. D	*5.* A	*9.* C	*13.* C	*17.* B
2. D	*6.* B	*10.* D	*14.* D	*18.* A
3. B	*7.* D	*11.* D	*15.* E	*19.* E
4. E	*8.* E	*12.* C	*16.* D	*20.* C

READING EXERCISE E

1. E	*5.* B	*9.* B	*13.* E	*17.* C
2. B	*6.* D	*10.* D	*14.* D	*18.* D
3. D	*7.* E	*11.* B	*15.* C	*19.* C
4. A	*8.* E	*12.* D	*16.* D	*20.* C

6

Building Your Vocabulary

Recognizing the meaning of words is essential to comprehending what you read. The more you stumble over unfamiliar words in a text, the more you have to take time out to look up words in your dictionary, the more likely you are to wind up losing track of what the author has to say.

To succeed in college, you must develop a college-level vocabulary. You must famil-iarize yourself with technical words in a wide variety of fields, mastering each field's special vocabulary. You must learn to use these words, and re-use them until they become second nature to you. The time you put in now learning vocabulary-building techniques for the PSAT will pay off later on, and not just on the PSAT.

LONG-RANGE STRATEGY

There is only one effective long-range strategy for vocabulary-building: READ.

Read—widely and well. Sample different fields—physics, art history, political science, geology—and different styles. Extensive reading is the one sure way to make your vocabulary grow.

As you read, however, take some time to acquaint yourself specifically with the kinds of words you must know to do well on the PSAT. No matter how little time you have before the test, you still can familiarize your-self with the sort of vocabulary you will be facing on the PSAT. First, look over the 257 words you will find on our PSAT High-Frequency Word List (page 108): each of these 257 words, ranging from everyday words such as *ample* and *heed* to less commonly known ones such as *esoteric* and *pervasive* has appeared (as answer choices or as question words) at least four times in PSATs during the 1980s and 1990s.

Next, proceed to master these High-Frequency words. First check off the words you think you know. Then *look up all 257 words and their definitions in our abridged Basic Word List* (pages 109–143). Pay particular attention to the words you thought you knew. See whether any of them are defined in an unexpected way.

If they are, make a special note of them. As you know from the preceding chapters, the PSAT often stumps students with questions based on unfamiliar meanings of familiar-looking words.

Not only will looking over the High-Frequency Word List reassure you that you *do* know some PSAT-type words; but also it may well help you on the actual day of the test. These words have turned up on recent tests; some of them may appear on the test you take.

Examine the abridged Basic Word List as well. Even before the College Board began publishing its own PSAT sample examinations, the Basic Word List was unique in its ability to reflect, and often predict, the actual vocabulary appearing on the PSAT. Today, thanks to our ongoing research and computer analysis of published PSAT materials, we believe our Basic Word List is the best in the field.

For this book, we have selected the most important 1,300 words of the master list. Most students preparing for the PSAT/NMSQT have little time in which to study and don't feel up to facing the 3,500-word SAT I list. We want you to have a tool that will be useful to you, both now and when you study for SAT I in the coming year. We hope this compact list will be the tool you need.

A PLAN FOR USING THE WORD LIST

For those of you who wish to work your way through the word list and feel the need for a plan, we recommend that you follow the procedure described below in order to use the lists and the exercises most profitably:

1. Allot a definite time each day for the study of a list.
2. Devote at least one hour to each list.
3. First go through the list looking at the short, simple-looking words (six letters at most). Mark those you don't know. In studying, pay particular attention to them.
4. Go through the list again looking at the longer words. Pay particular attention to words with more than one meaning and familiar-looking words which have unusual definitions that come as a surprise to you. Many tests make use of these secondary definitions.
5. List unusual words on index cards, which you can shuffle and review from time to time. (Study no more than five cards at a time.)
6. Use the illustrative sentences in the list as models and make up new sentences of your own.

For each word, the following is provided:

* The word (printed in heavy type)
* Its part of speech (abbreviated)
* A brief definition
* A sentence illustrating the word's use

Whenever appropriate, related words are provided, together with their parts of speech.

The thirty-five Word Lists are arranged in strict alphabetical order.

PSAT HIGH-FREQUENCY WORD LIST

absolve	candor	didactic	farce	ingrate	perpetual	scrutinize
abstract	captivate	digression	fastidious	inherent	pervasive	seclusion
accessible	caricature	discernible	feasible	initiate	pessimism	serenity
accommodate	censor	disclaimer	flippant	innate	petulant	sever
acknowledge	charlatan	disclose	forthright	innocuous	phenomena	severe
acrimony	chronicle	discord	frail	inscrutable	philanthropist	singular
adverse	circumspect	disinterested	futile	insightful	plagiarize	skeptical
aesthetic	cite	dismiss	garrulous	intangible	potency	stratagem
affable	cliché	disparage	generate	intricacy	precedent	subdued
affinity	coalesce	disparate	gluttonous	irony	predator	subversive
affluence	compliance	dispel	gratify	larceny	premise	superficial
alleviate	component	disperse	gregarious	loathe	premonition	superfluous
altruistic	compromise	dissent	hamper	malice	prey	suppress
ambiguous	condone	dissipate	heed	meek	profound	surpass
ambivalence	confirm	distinction	hindrance	meticulous	proliferation	suspend
amenable	conformity	divulge	hostility	misconception	prolific	sustain
ample	congenial	docile	hypocritical	misrepresent	prologue	symmetry
antagonism	consistency	doctrine	hypothetical	mock	prominent	synthesis
antiquated	console	dogmatic	iconoclastic	monotony	promote	taciturn
apathy	consolidation	eclipse	immutable	mutability	prophetic	tedious
apprehension	contentious	elusive	impair	naiveté	prosperity	temperament
apprenticeship	convention	embellish	impede	nocturnal	provocative	termination
appropriate	corrosion	endorse	imperceptible	nostalgia	prudent	thwart
aristocracy	curtail	enhance	implacable	notorious	random	toxic
arrogance	cynical	enigma	implement	nurture	recluse	transparent
aspire	dawdle	enumerate	implication	obnoxious	refine	trepidation
assert	defiance	erode	incongruity	obscure	refute	turbulence
assumption	degenerate	erratic	inconsistency	offensive	relinquish	urbane
attain	demean	erroneous	incorporate	opaque	repudiate	utopia
authentic	denounce	esoteric	indict	optimist	reserved	vacillate
autonomous	depict	espouse	indifferent	outmoded	resolution	versatile
aversion	deplete	esteem	induce	pacifist	resolve	vigor
beneficial	deplore	excerpt	industrious	pacify	restrain	volatile
benevolent	derision	exemplary	inept	paradox	retain	wary
benign	derivative	exploit	infallible	patronize	reticent	withhold
betray	detached	facilitate	ingenious	pedantic	reverent	
brittle	deterrent	fallacious	ingenuous	perjury	satirize	

BASIC WORD LIST

The abridged Basic Word List follows. *Do not let this list overwhelm you.* You do not need to memorize every word.

The present word list derives from our standard 3,500-word list, published in *Barron's How to Prepare for SAT I.* Ever since this list first appeared in 1954, countless students have reported that working with these words has helped them immensely in taking all kinds of college entrance and scholarship tests. The list has been used with profit by people preparing for civil service examinations, placement tests, and promotional examinations in many fields. Above all, it has been used with profit by students studying for SAT I and the PSAT.

An entry preceded by a bullet (●) is a High-Frequency Word.

WORD LIST 1   abase - adjacent

abase V. lower; humiliate. Defeated, Queen Zenobia was forced to *abase* herself before the conquering Romans, who forced her to march before the Emperor Aurelian in the procession celebrating his triumph.

abate V. subside; decrease; lessen. Rather than leaving immediately, they waited for the storm to *abate*. abatement, N.

abdicate V. renounce; give up. When Edward VIII *abdicated* the British throne to marry the woman he loved, he surprised the entire world. When the painter Gauguin *abdicated* his family responsibilities to run off to Samoa, he surprised no one at all.

aberration N. deviation from the expected or the normal; mental irregularity or disorder. Survivors of a major catastrophe are likely to exhibit *aberrations* of behavior because of the trauma they have experienced. aberrant, ADJ and N.

abet V. encourage; aid. She was accused of aiding and *abetting* the drug dealer by engaging in a money-laundering scheme to help him disguise his illegal income. abettor, N.

abeyance N. suspended action. The deal was held in *abeyance* until her arrival.

abject ADJ. hopeless and crushed; servile and spiritless; wretched. On the streets of New York the homeless live in *abject* poverty, lying huddled in doorways to find shelter from the wind.

abrade V. wear away by friction; scrape; erode. The sharp rocks *abraded* the skin on her legs, so she put iodine on her *abrasions.*

abscond V. depart secretly to avoid capture. The teller who *absconded* with the bonds was not captured until someone recognized him from his photograph on *America's Most Wanted.*

absolute ADJ. complete; totally unlimited; certain. Although the King of Siam was an *absolute* monarch, he did not want to behead his unfaithful wife without *absolute* evidence of her infidelity.

● **absolve** V. pardon (an offense); free from blame. The father confessor *absolved* him of his sins. absolution, N.

abstain V. refrain; hold oneself back voluntarily from an action or practice (especially one regarded as improper or unhealthy). After considering the effect of alcohol on his athletic performance, he decided to *abstain* from drinking while he trained for the race. abstinence, N.; abstinent or abstemious, ADJ.

● **abstract** ADJ. theoretical; not concrete; nonrepresentational. To him, hunger was an *abstract* concept; he had never missed a meal.

abstruse ADJ. obscure; profound; difficult to understand. She carries around *abstruse* works of philosophy, not because she understands them but because she wants her friends to think she does.

accelerate V. move faster. In our science class, we learn how falling bodies *accelerate.*

● **accessible** ADJ. easy to approach; obtainable. We asked our guide whether the ruins were *accessible* on foot.

accessory N. additional object; useful but not essential thing. The *accessories* she bought cost more than the dress. also ADJ.

acclaim V. applaud; announce with great approval. The NBC sportscasters *acclaimed* every American victory in the Olympics and lamented every American defeat. acclamation, acclaim, N.

accolade N. award of merit. In the world of public relations, a "Clio" is the highest *accolade* an advertising campaign can receive.

● **accommodate** V. provide lodgings. Mary asked the room clerk whether the hotel would be able to *accommodate* the tour group on such short notice. accommodations, N.

accommodate V. oblige or help someone; adjust or bring into harmony; adapt. Mitch always did everything possible to *accommodate* his elderly relatives, from driving them to medical appointments to helping them with paperwork. accommodating, ADJ. (secondary meaning)

accomplice N. partner in crime. Because he had provided the criminal with the lethal weapon, he was arrested as an *accomplice* in the murder.

● **acknowledge** V. recognize; admit. Although Ira *acknowledged* that the Beatles' tunes sounded pretty dated nowadays, he still preferred them to the punk rock songs his nephews played.

acquittal N. declaration of innocence; deliverance from a charge. His *acquittal* by the jury surprised those who had thought him guilty. acquit, V.

● **acrimony** N. bitterness of words or manner. The candidate attacked his opponent with great *acrimony*. acrimonious, ADJ.

acumen N. mental keenness. His business *acumen* helped him to succeed where others had failed.

adamant ADJ. hard; inflexible. Bronson played the part of a revenge-driven man, *adamant* in his determination to punish the criminals who had destroyed his family. adamancy, N.

adapt V. alter; modify. Some species of animals have become extinct because they could not *adapt* to a changing environment.

addiction N. compulsive, habitual need. His *addiction* to drugs caused his friends much grief.

adhere V. stick fast to. I will *adhere* to this opinion until someone comes up with solid proof that I am wrong. adhesive, ADJ.

adjacent ADJ. adjoining; neighboring; close by. Philip's best friend Jason lived only four houses away, close but not immediately *adjacent.*

admonish - ample

admonish V. warn; scold. The preacher *admonished* his listeners to change their wicked ways. admonition, N.

adroit ADJ. skillful; nimble. The juggler's admirers particularly enjoyed his *adroit* handling of difficult balancing tricks.

adulation N. flattery; admiration. The rock star relished the *adulation* she received from her groupies and yes-men.

adulterate V. make impure by adding inferior or tainted substances. It is a crime to *adulterate* foods without informing the buyer; when consumers learned that the manufacturer had *adulterated* its apple juice by mixing it with water, they protested vigorously.

adversary N. opponent. "Aha!" cried Holmes. "Watson, I suspect this delay is the work of my old *adversary* Professor Moriarty."

● **adverse** ADJ. unfavorable; hostile. The recession had a highly *adverse* effect on Father's investment portfolio: he lost so much money that he could no longer afford the butler and the upstairs maid. adversity, N.

adversity N. poverty; misfortune. We must learn to meet *adversity* gracefully.

advocate V. urge; plead for. Noted abolitionists such as Frederick Douglass and Sojourner Truth *advocated* the eradication of the Southern institution of slavery. also N.

● **aesthetic** ADJ. artistic; dealing with or capable of appreciation of the beautiful. The beauty of Tiffany's stained glass appealed to Alice's *aesthetic* sense. aesthete, N.

● **affable** ADJ. easily approachable; warmly friendly. Accustomed to cold, aloof supervisors, Nicholas was amazed by how *affable* his new employer was.

affected ADJ. artificial; pretended; assumed in order to impress. His *affected* mannerisms—his "Harvard" accent, his air of boredom, his flaunting of obscure foreign words—irritated many of us who had known him before he had gone away to school. affectation, N.

● **affinity** N. kinship; attraction to. She felt an *affinity* with all who suffered; their pains were her pains. Her brother, in contrast, had an *affinity* for political wheeling-and-dealing; he manipulated people shamelessly, not caring who got hurt.

affirmation N. positive assertion; confirmation; solemn pledge by one who refuses to take an oath. Despite Tom's *affirmations* of innocence, Aunt Polly still suspected he had eaten the pie. affirm, V.

affix V. add on; fasten; attach. First the registrar had to *affix* her signature to the license; then she had to *affix* her official seal.

● **affluence** N. wealth; prosperity; abundance. Galvanized by his sudden, unexpected *affluence*, the lottery winner dashed out to buy himself a brand new Ferrari. affluent, ADJ.

affront V. insult; offend. Accustomed to being treated with respect, Miss Challoner was *affronted* by Vidal's offensive behavior.

aggregate V. gather; accumulate. Before the Wall Street scandals, dealers in so-called junk bonds managed to *aggregate* great wealth in short periods of time. aggregation, N.

agility N. nimbleness. The acrobat's *agility* amazed and thrilled the audience. agile, A.

agitate V. stir up; disturb. Her fiery remarks further *agitated* the already angry mob.

alacrity N. cheerful promptness. Phil and Dave were raring to get off to the mountains; they packed up their ski gear and climbed into the van with *alacrity*.

alias N. an assumed name. John Smith's *alias* was Bob Jones. also ADV.

alienate V. make hostile; separate. Her attempts to *alienate* the two friends failed because they had complete faith in each other.

● **alleviate** V. relieve; lessen. This should *alleviate* the pain; if it does not, we will use stronger drugs.

alloy V. mix; make less pure; lessen or moderate. Our delight at the victory was *alloyed* by our concern for Dwight Gooden, who injured his pitching arm in the game.

allude V. refer indirectly. Try not to mention divorce in John's presence because he will think you are *alluding* to his marital problems with Jill.

allure V. entice; attract. *Allured* by the song of the sirens, the helmsman steered the ship toward the reef. also N.

allusion N. indirect reference. When Amanda said to the ticket scalper, "One hundred bucks? What do you want, a pound of flesh?," she was making an *allusion* to Shakespeare's *Merchant of Venice*.

aloft ADV. upward. The sailor climbed *aloft* into the rigging. To get into a loft bed, you have to climb *aloft*.

aloof ADJ. apart; reserved; standoffish. People thought James was a snob because he remained *aloof* while all the rest of the group conversed.

altercation N. noisy quarrel; heated dispute. In that hot-tempered household, no meal ever came to a peaceful conclusion; the inevitable *altercation* occasionally even ended in blows.

● **altruistic** ADJ. unselfishly generous; concerned for others. The star received no fee for appearing at the benefit; it was a purely *altruistic* act. altruism, N.

● **ambiguous** ADJ. unclear or doubtful in meaning. The proctor's *ambiguous* instructions thoroughly confused us; we didn't know which columns we should mark and which we should leave blank. ambiguity, N.

● **ambivalence** N. having contradictory or conflicting emotional attitudes. Torn between loving her parents one minute and hating them the next, she was confused by the *ambivalence* of her feelings. ambivalent, ADJ.

ambulatory ADJ. able to walk; not bedridden. Jonathan was a highly *ambulatory* patient; not only did he refuse to be confined to bed, but also he insisted on riding his skateboard up and down the halls.

ameliorate V. improve; make more satisfactory. Carl became a union organizer because he wanted to join the fight to *ameliorate* working conditions in the factory.

● **amenable** ADJ. readily managed; willing to give in; agreeable; submissive. A born snob, Wilbur was *amenable* to any suggestions from those he looked up to, but he resented advice from his supposed inferiors. Unfortunately, his incorrigible snobbery was not *amenable* to improvement.

amiable ADJ. agreeable; lovable; warmly friendly. In *Little Women*, Beth is the *amiable* daughter whose loving disposition endears her to all who have dealings with her.

amorous ADJ. moved by sexual love; loving. "Love them and leave them" was the motto of the *amorous* Don Juan.

amorphous ADJ. formless; lacking shape or definition. As soon as we have decided on our itinerary, we shall send you a copy; right now, our plans are still *amorphous*.

● **ample** ADJ. abundant. Bond had *ample* opportunity to escape. Why did he let us catch him?

amplify - arid

amplify V. broaden or clarify by expanding; intensify; make stronger. Charlie Brown tried to *amplify* his remarks, but he was drowned out by jeers from the audience. Lucy, however, used a loudspeaker to *amplify* her voice and drowned out all the hecklers.

anachronism N. something regarded as outmoded; something or someone misplaced in time. In today's world of personal copiers and fax machines, the old-fashioned mimeograph machine is clearly an *anachronism*; even the electric type-writer seems *anachronistic* next to a laptop PC.

analogy N. similarity; parallelism. A well-known *analogy* compares the body's immune system with an army whose defending troops are the lymphocytes or white blood cells. *Analogies* are useful, but you can't take them too far: cells, after all, are not soldiers; there is no boot camp for lymphocytes.

anarchist N. person who seeks to overturn the established government; advocate of abolishing authority. Denying she was an *anarchist,* Katya maintained she wished only to make changes in our government, not to destroy it entirely. anarchy, N.

anarchy N. absence of governing body; state of disorder. For weeks China was in a state of *anarchy*, with soldiers shooting down civilians in the streets and rumors claiming that Premier Deng was dead. Foreigners fleeing the country reported conditions were so *anarchic* that it was a miracle they escaped.

ancillary ADJ. serving as an aid or accessory; auxiliary. In an *ancillary* capacity Doctor Watson was helpful; however, Holmes could not trust the good doctor to solve a perplexing case on his own. also N.

animated ADJ. lively; spirited. Jim Carrey's facial expressions are highly *animated:* when he played Ace Ventura, he looked practically rubber-faced.

animosity N. active enmity. Mr. Fang incurred the *animosity* of the party's rulers because he advocated limitations of their power.

anomaly N. irregularity; something out of place or abnormal. A bird that cannot fly is an *anomaly*. A classical harpist in the middle of a heavy metal band is *anomalous;* she is also inaudible.

● **antagonism** N. hostility; active resistance. Barry showed his *antagonism* toward his new stepmother by ignoring her whenever she tried talking to him. antagonistic, ADJ.

antecedents N. preceding events or circumstances that influence what comes later; ancestors or early background. Susi Bechhofer's ignorance of her Jewish background had its *antecedents* in the chaos of World War II. Smuggled out of Germany and adopted by a Christian family, she knew nothing of her birth and *antecedents* until she was reunited with her family in 1989.

anticlimax N. letdown in thought or emotion. After the fine performance in the first act, the rest of the play was an *anti-climax*. anticlimactic, ADJ.

antipathy N. aversion; dislike. Tom's extreme *antipathy* for disputes keeps him from getting into arguments with his temperamental wife. Noise in any form is *antipathetic* to him. Among his particular *antipathies* are honking cars, boom boxes, and heavy metal rock.

● **antiquated** ADJ. obsolete; outdated. Accustomed to editing his papers on word processors, Philip thought typewriters were too *antiquated* for him to use.

antiseptic N. substance that prevents infection. It is advisable to apply an *antiseptic* to any wound, no matter how slight or insignificant. also ADJ.

antithesis N. contrast; direct opposite of or to. This tyranny was the *antithesis* of all that he had hoped for, and he fought it with all his strength.

● **apathy** N. lack of caring; indifference. A firm believer in democratic government, she could not understand the *apathy* of people who never bothered to vote. She wondered whether they had ever cared or whether they had always been *apathetic*.

aplomb N. poise; assurance. Gwen's *aplomb* in handling potentially embarrassing moments was legendary around the office; when one of her clients broke a piece of her best crystal, she coolly picked up her own goblet and hurled it into the fireplace.

apocryphal ADJ. untrue; made up. To impress his friends, Tom invented *apocryphal* tales of his adventures in the big city.

apostate N. one who abandons his religious faith or political beliefs. Because he switched from one party to another, his former friends shunned him as an *apostate*.

append V. attach. I shall *append* this chart to my report. When you *append* a bibliography to a text, you have just created an *appendix*.

● **apprehension** N. fear; discernment; capture. The tourist refused to drive his rental car through downtown Miami because he felt some *apprehension* that he might be carjacked.

● **apprenticeship** N. time spent as a novice learning a trade from a skilled worker. As a child, Pip had thought it would be wonderful to work as Joe's *apprentice;* now he hated his *apprenticeship* and scorned the blacksmith's trade.

● **appropriate** ADJ. fitting or suitable; pertinent. Madonna spent hours looking for a suit that would be *appropriate* to wear at a summer wedding.

appropriate V. acquire; take possession of for one's own use; set aside for a special purpose. The ranchers *appropriated* lands that had originally been intended for Indian use. In response, Congress *appropriated* additional funds for the Bureau of Indian Affairs.

arable ADJ. fit for growing crops. The first settlers wrote home glowing reports of the New World, praising its vast acres of *arable* land ready for the plow.

arbiter N. a person with power to decide a dispute; judge. As an *arbiter* in labor disputes, she is skillful: she balances the demands of both sides and hands down rulings with which everyone agrees. As an *arbiter* of style, however, she is worthless: she wears such unflattering outfits that no one in her right mind would imitate her.

arbitrary ADJ. unreasonable or capricious; randomly selected without any reason; based solely on one's unrestricted will or judgment. The coach claimed the team lost because the umpire made some *arbitrary* calls.

archipelago N. group of closely located islands. When Gauguin looked at the map and saw the *archipelagoes* in the South Seas, he longed to visit them.

arduous ADJ. hard; strenuous. Bob's *arduous* efforts had sapped his energy. Even using a chain saw, he found chopping down trees an *arduous,* time-consuming task.

aria N. operatic solo. At her Metropolitan Opera audition, Marian Anderson sang an *aria* from the opera *Norma*.

arid ADJ. dry; barren. The cactus has adapted to survive in an *arid* environment.

WORD LIST 4   **aristocracy - babble**

● **aristocracy** N. hereditary nobility; privileged class. Americans have mixed feelings about hereditary *aristocracy:* we say all men are created equal, but we describe people who bear themselves with grace and graciousness as natural *aristocrats.*

● **arrogance** N. pride; haughtiness. Convinced that Emma thought she was better than anyone else in the class, Ed rebuked her for her *arrogance.*

articulate ADJ. effective; distinct. Her *articulate* presentation of the advertising campaign impressed her employers. also, V.

ascendancy N. controlling influence. President Marcos failed to maintain his *ascendancy* over the Philippines. He was overthrown by the forces of Corazon Aquino when she *ascended* to power.

ascetic ADJ. practicing self-denial; austere. The wealthy, self-indulgent young man felt oddly drawn to the strict, *ascetic* life led by members of some monastic orders. also N.

● **aspire** V. seek to attain; long for. Because he *aspired* to a career in professional sports, Philip enrolled in a graduate program in sports management. aspiration, N.

assail V. assault. He was *assailed* with questions after his lecture.

● **assert** V. state strongly or positively; insist on or demand recognition of (rights, claims, etc.) When Jill *asserted* that nobody else in the junior class had such an early curfew, her parents *asserted* themselves, telling her that if she didn't get home by nine o'clock she would be grounded for the week. assertion, N.

assiduous ADJ. diligent. It took Rembrandt weeks of *assiduous* labor before he was satisfied with his self-portrait. assiduity, N.

assuage V. ease or lessen (pain); Jilted by Jane, Dick tried to *assuage* his heartache by indulging in ice cream.

● **assumption** N. something taken for granted; taking over or taking possession of. The young princess made the foolish *assumption* that the regent would not object to her *assumption* of power. assume, V.

assurance N. promise or pledge; certainty; self-confidence. When Guthrie gave Guinness his *assurance* rehearsals were going well, he spoke with such *assurance* that Guinness felt relieved. assure, V. assured, ADJ.

astute ADJ. wise; shrewd; keen. As tutor, she made *astute* observations about how to take multiple-choice tests. She was an *astute* observer: she noticed every tiny detail and knew exactly how important each one was.

asylum N. place of refuge; safety. Fleeing persecution, the political refugee sought *asylum* in the United States.

atrophy V. waste away. After three months in a cast, Stan's biceps had *atrophied* somewhat; however, he was sure that if he pumped iron for a while he would soon build it up.

● **attain** V. reach or accomplish; gain. It took Bolingbroke years to *attain* his goal of gaining the throne.

attentive ADJ. watching carefully; considerate; thoughtful. Spellbound, the *attentive* audience watched the final game of the match, never taking their eyes from the ball. Stan's *attentive* daughter slipped a sweater over his shoulders without distracting his attention from the game.

attribute N. essential quality. His outstanding *attribute* was his kindness.

attribute V. ascribe or credit (to a cause); regard as characteristic of a person or thing. I *attribute* Andrea's success in science to the encouragement she received from her parents.

attrition N. gradual decrease in numbers; reduction in the work force without firing employees; wearing away of opposition by means of harassment. In the 1960s urban churches suffered from *attrition* as members moved from the cities to the suburbs. Rather than fire staff members, church leaders followed a policy of *attrition,* allowing elderly workers to retire without replacing them.

audacity N. boldness. Luke could not believe his own *audacity* in addressing the princess. Where did he get the nerve?

augment V. increase. Armies *augment* their forces by calling up reinforcements; teachers *augment* their salaries by taking odd jobs. Lexy *augments* her salary by working in a record store. Her *augmentation* of wealth has not been great; however, she has *augmented* her record collection considerably.

auspicious ADJ. favoring success; fortunate. With favorable weather conditions, it was an *auspicious* moment to set sail. Prospects for trade were good: under such promising *auspices* we were bound to thrive. Thomas, however, had doubts: a paranoid, he became suspicious whenever conditions seemed *auspicious.*

austere ADJ. forbiddingly stern; severely simple and unornamented. The headmaster's *austere* demeanor tended to scare off the more timid students, who never visited his study willingly. The room reflected the man, for it was *austere* and bare, like a monk's cell, with no touches of luxury to moderate its *austerity.*

● **authentic** ADJ. genuine. The art expert was able to distinguish the *authentic* van Gogh painting from the forged copy. authenticate, V.

authoritative ADJ. having the weight of authority; overbearing and dictatorial. Impressed by the young researcher's well-documented presentation, we accepted her analysis of the experiment as *authoritative.*

● **autonomous** ADJ. self-governing. This island is a colony; however, in most matters, it is *autonomous* and receives no orders from the mother country. The islanders are an independent lot and would fight to preserve their *autonomy.*

autopsy N. examination of a dead body; postmortem. The medical examiner ordered an *autopsy* to determine the cause of death. also V.

avarice N. greediness for wealth. King Midas is a perfect example of *avarice,* for he was so greedy that he wished everything he touched would turn to gold.

averse ADJ. reluctant. The reporter was *averse* to revealing the sources of his information.

● **aversion** N. firm dislike. Bert had an *aversion* to yuppies; Alex had an *aversion* to punks. Their mutual *aversion* was so great that they refused to speak to one another.

avert V. prevent; turn aside. "Watch out!" she cried, hoping to *avert* an accident. She *averted* her eyes from the dead cat on the highway.

avid ADJ. greedy; eager for. Abner was *avid* for pleasure and partied with great *avidity.*

awe N. solemn wonder. The tourists gazed with *awe* at the tremendous expanse of the Grand Canyon.

babble V. chatter idly. The little girl *babbled* about her dolls and pets.

WORD LIST 5 badger - buoyant

badger V. pester; annoy; harass. Madge was forced to change her telephone number because she was *badgered* by obscene phone calls.

baffle V. frustrate; perplex. The new code *baffled* the enemy agents.

balk V. foil or thwart; stop short; refuse to go on. When the warden learned that several inmates were planning to escape, he took steps to *balk* their attempt. However, he *balked* at punishing them by shackling them to the walls of their cells.

banal ADJ. hackneyed; commonplace; trite; lacking originality. The hack writer's worn-out clichés made his comic sketch seem *banal.* He even resorted to the *banality* of having someone slip on a banana peel!

bane N. cause of ruin; curse. Lucy's little brother was the *bane* of her existence: his attempts to make her life miserable worked so well that she could have fed him some ratsbane for having such a *baneful* effect.

bastion N. stronghold; something seen as a source of protection. The villagers fortified the town hall, hoping this improvised *bastion* could protect them from the guerrilla raids.

begrudge V. resent. I *begrudge* every minute I have to spend attending meetings; they're a complete waste of time.

beguile V. mislead or delude; cheat; pass time. With flattery and big talk of easy money, the con men *beguiled* Kyle into betting his allowance on the shell game. Broke, Kyle *beguiled* himself during the long hours by playing solitaire.

belie V. contradict; give a false impression of. His coarse, hard-bitten exterior *belied* his underlying sensitivity.

benefactor N. gift giver; patron. In later years Scrooge became Tiny Tim's *benefactor* and gave him many gifts.

● **beneficial** ADJ. helpful; advantageous; useful. Tiny Tim's cheerful good nature had a *beneficial* influence on Scrooge's disposition.

beneficiary N. person entitled to benefits or proceeds of an insurance policy or will. In Scrooge's will, he made Tiny Tim his *beneficiary.* Everything he left would go to the benefit of young Tim.

● **benevolent** ADJ. generous; charitable. Mr. Fezziwig was a *benevolent* employer, who wished to make Christmas merrier for young Scrooge and his other employees.

● **benign** ADJ. kindly; favorable; not malignant. Though her *benign* smile and gentle bearing made Miss Marple seem a sweet little old lady, in reality she was a tough-minded, shrewd observer of human nature. benignity, N.

bestow V. confer. The president wished to *bestow* great honors upon the hero.

● **betray** V. be unfaithful; reveal (unconsciously or unwillingly). The spy *betrayed* his country by selling military secrets to the enemy. When he was taken in for questioning, the tightness of his lips *betrayed* his fear of being caught.

biased ADJ. slanted; prejudiced. Because the judge played golf regularly with the district attorney's father, we feared he might be *biased* in the prosecution's favor. bias, N.

● **bizarre** ADJ. fantastic; violently contrasting. The plot of the novel was too *bizarre* to be believed.

bland ADJ. soothing; mild; dull. Unless you want your stomach lining to be eaten away, stick to a *bland* diet. blandness, N.

blandishment N. flattery. Despite the salesperson's *blandishments,* the customer did not buy the outfit.

blare N. loud, harsh roar; screech. I don't know which is worse: the steady *blare* of a teenager's boom box deafening your ears or a sudden blaze of flashbulbs dazzling your eyes.

blasphemy N. irreverence; sacrilege; cursing. In my father's house, the Dodgers were the holiest of holies; to cheer for another team was to utter words of *blasphemy.* blasphemous, ADJ.

blatant ADJ. flagrant; conspicuously obvious; loudly offensive. To the unemployed youth from Dublin, the "No Irish Need Apply" placard in the shop window was a *blatant* mark of prejudice.

bloat V. expand or swell (with water or air); puff up with conceit. Constant flattery from his hangers-on *bloated* the heavyweight champion's already sizable ego.

bolster V. support; reinforce. The debaters amassed file boxes full of evidence to *bolster* their arguments.

boon N. blessing; benefit. The recent rains that filled our empty reservoirs were a *boon* to the whole community.

boundless ADJ. unlimited; vast. Mike's energy was *boundless:* the greater the challenge, the more vigorously he tackled the job.

bountiful ADJ. abundant; graciously generous. Thanks to the good harvest, we had a *bountiful* supply of food and we could be as *bountiful* as we liked in distributing food to the needy.

bourgeois ADJ. middle class; selfishly materialistic; dully conventional. Technically, anyone who belongs to the middle class is *bourgeois,* but, given the word's connotations, most people resent it if you can call them that.

boycott V. refrain from buying or using. In an effort to stop grape growers from using pesticides that harmed the farm workers' health, Cesar Chavez called for consumers to *boycott* grapes.

brackish ADJ. somewhat salty. Following the stream, we noticed its fresh, springlike water grew increasingly *brackish* as we drew nearer to the bay.

brandish V. wave around; flourish. Alarmed, Doctor Watson wildly *brandished* his gun until Holmes told him to put the thing away before he shot himself.

breach N. breaking of contract or duty; fissure; gap. Jill sued Jack for *breach* of promise, claiming he had broken his promise to marry her. They found a *breach* in the enemy's fortifications and penetrated their lines. also V.

brevity N. conciseness. Since you are charged for every transmitted word, *brevity* is essential when you send a telegram or cablegram.

● **brittle** ADJ. easily broken; difficult. My employer's self-control was as *brittle* as an eggshell. Her *brittle* personality made it difficult for me to get along with her.

brochure N. pamphlet. This free *brochure* on farming was issued by the Department of Agriculture.

brusque ADJ. blunt; abrupt. Jill was offended by Jack's *brusque* reply; he had no right to be so impatient with her.

bungle V. mismanage; blunder. Don't botch this assignment, Bumstead; if you *bungle* the job, you're fired!

buoyant ADJ. able to float; cheerful and optimistic. When the boat capsized, her *buoyant* life jacket kept Jody afloat. Scrambling back on board, she was still in a *buoyant* mood, certain that despite the delay she'd win the race. buoyancy, N.

WORD LIST 6 **burgeon - chronicle**

burgeon V. bloom; develop rapidly; flourish. From its start as a small Seattle coffeehouse, Starbucks seemed to *burgeon* almost overnight into a major national chain.

bustle V. move about energetically; teem. David and the children *bustled* about the house getting in each other's way as they tried to pack for the camping trip.

buttress V. support or prop up. The government is considering price supports to *buttress* the declining economy. The huge cathedral walls were supported by flying *buttresses*. also N.

cajole V. coax; wheedle. Jill tried to *cajole* Jack into buying her a fur coat, but no matter how much she coaxed him he wouldn't give in to her *cajolery*.

calligraphy N. beautiful writing; excellent penmanship. In the Middle Ages, before a novice scribe was allowed to copy an important document he had to spend years practicing *calligraphy*.

callous ADJ. hardened; unfeeling. Carl had worked in the hospital for so many years that he was *callous* to the suffering in the wards. It was as if he had a *callus* on his soul.

camaraderie N. good-fellowship. What Ginger loved best about her job was the sense of *camaraderie* she and her co-workers shared.

● **candor** N. frankness; open honesty. Jack can carry *candor* too far: when he told Jill his honest opinion of her, she nearly slapped his face. Instead of being so *candid*, try keeping your opinions to yourself.

canine ADJ. related to dogs; dog-like. Some days the *canine* population of Berkeley seems almost to outnumber the human population.

cant N. insincere, hypocritical speech; "pious" talk; jargon of thieves. Shocked by news of the minister's extramarital love affairs, the worshippers dismissed his talk about the sacredness of marriage as mere *cant*. *Cant* is a form of hypocrisy: those who can, pray; those who can't, pretend.

capricious ADJ. unpredictable; fickle. The storm was *capricious*: it changed course constantly. Jill was *capricious*, too: she changed boyfriends almost as often as she changed clothes.

caption N. title; chapter heading; text under illustration. The capricious *captions* that accompany "The Far Side" cartoons are almost as funny as the pictures. also V.

● **captivate** V. charm; fascinate. Although he was predisposed to dislike Elizabeth, Darcy found himself *captivated* by her charm and wit.

● **caricature** N. distortion; burlesque. The *caricatures* he drew always emphasized a personal weakness of the people he burlesqued. also V.

carping ADJ. finding fault. A *carping* critic is a nit-picker, someone who loves to point out flaws. carp, V.

● **castigation** V. punishment, severe criticism. Sensitive to even mild criticism, Virginia Woolf could not bear the *castigation* that she met in certain reviews. castigate, V.

casualty N. serious or fatal accident. The number of *casualties* on this holiday weekend was high.

catastrophe N. calamity; disaster. The 1906 San Francisco earthquake was a *catastrophe* that destroyed most of the city.

cede V. yield (title, territory) to; surrender formally. Eventually the descendants of England's Henry II were forced to *cede* their French territories to the King of France.

● **censor** N. inspector overseeing public morals; official who prevents publication of offensive material. Because certain passages in his novel *Ulysses* had been condemned by the *censor*, James Joyce was unable to publish the novel in England for many years.

censure V. blame; criticize. Though I don't blame Tony for leaving Tina, I do *censure* him for failing to pay child support.

cerebral ADJ. pertaining to the brain or intellect. The content of philosophical works is *cerebral* in nature and requires much thought.

cessation N. stopping. The airline workers threatened a *cessation* of all work if management failed to meet their demands. cease, V.

chafe V. warm by rubbing; make sore (by rubbing). Chilled, he *chafed* his hands before the fire. The collar of his school uniform *chafed* Tom's neck, but not as much the school's strict rules *chafed* his spirit. also N.

chaff N. husks and stems left over when grain has been threshed; worthless, left-over byproducts. When you separate the wheat from the *chaff*, be sure you throw out the *chaff*.

chagrin N. vexation (caused by humiliation or injured pride); disappointment. Embarrassed by his parents' shabby, working-class appearance, Doug felt their visit to his school would bring him nothing but *chagrin*. Someone filled with *chagrin* doesn't grin: he's too mortified.

chameleon N. lizard that changes color in different situations. Like the *chameleon*, the candidate assumed the political thinking of every group he met.

chaotic ADJ. in utter disorder. He tried to bring order into the *chaotic* state of affairs. chaos, N.

● **charlatan** N. quack; pretender to knowledge. When they realized that the Wizard didn't know how to get them back to Kansas, Dorothy and her friends were sure they'd been duped by a *charlatan*.

chary ADJ. cautious; sparing or restrained about giving. A prudent, thrifty, New Englander, DeWitt was as *chary* of investing money in junk bonds as he was *chary* of paying people unnecessary compliments.

chasm N. abyss. They could not see the bottom of the *chasm*.

chastise V. punish physically; scold verbally. "Spare the rod and spoil the child," Miss Watson said, grabbing her birch wand and proceeding to *chastise* poor Huck thoroughly.

chauvinist N. blindly devoted patriot. *Chauvinists* cannot recognize any faults in their country, no matter how flagrant they may be. Likewise, a male *chauvinist* cannot recognize how biased he is in favor of his own sex, no matter how flagrant that may be.

chicanery N. trickery; deception. Those sneaky lawyers misrepresented what occurred, made up all sorts of implausible alternative scenarios to confuse the jurors, and in general depended on *chicanery* to win the case.

choreography N. art of representing dances in written symbols; arrangement of dances. Merce Cunningham has begun to use a computer in designing *choreography*: a software program allows him to compose arrangements of possible moves and to view them immediately onscreen.

chronic ADJ. long established (as a disease). The doctors were finally able to attribute his *chronic* headaches and nausea to traces of formaldehyde gas in his apartment.

● **chronicle** V. report; record (in chronological order). The gossip columnist was paid to *chronicle* the latest escapades of the socially prominent celebrities. also N.

WORD LIST 7   circumscribe - conflagration

circumscribe V. limit; confine. Although I do not wish to *circumscribe* your activities, I must insist that you complete this assignment before you start anything else.

● **circumspect** ADJ. prudent; cautious. Investigating before acting, she tried always to be *circumspect*.

● **cite** V. quote; refer to; commend. Because Virginia could *cite* hundreds of biblical passages from memory, her pastor *cited* her for her studiousness. citation, N.

clairvoyant ADJ., N. having foresight; fortune-teller. Cassandra's *clairvoyant* warning was not heeded by the Trojans. clairvoyance, N.

clandestine ADJ. secret. After avoiding their chaperone, the lovers had a *clandestine* meeting.

clemency N. disposition to be lenient; mildness, as of the weather. The lawyer was pleased when the case was sent to Judge Smith's chambers because Smith was noted for her *clemency* toward first offenders. We decided to eat dinner in the garden to enjoy the unexpected *clemency* of the weather.

● **cliché** N. phrase dulled in meaning by repetition. High school compositions are often marred by such *clichés* as "strong as an ox."

climactic ADJ. relating to the highest point. When Jack reached the *climactic* portions of the book, he could not stop reading. climax, N.

clique N. small exclusive group. Fitzgerald wished that he belonged to the *clique* of popular athletes and big men on campus who seemed to run Princeton's social life.

● **coalesce** V. combine; fuse. The brooks *coalesced* into one large river. When minor political parties *coalesce*, their *coalescence* may create a major coalition.

coalition N. association; union. Jesse Jackson's Rainbow *Coalition* brought together people of many different races and creeds.

cogitate V. think over. *Cogitate* on this problem; the solution will come.

coincidence N. two or more things occurring at the same time by chance. Was it just a *coincidence* that John and she had chanced to meet at the market for three days running, or was he deliberately trying to seek her out? coincident, ADJ.

collaborate V. work together. Two writers *collaborated* in preparing this book.

colossal ADJ. huge. Radio City Music Hall has a *colossal* stage.

collusion N. conspiring in a fraudulent scheme. The swindlers were found guilty of *collusion*.

comely ADJ. attractive; agreeable. I would rather have a poor but *comely* wife than a rich and homely one.

commiserate V. feel or express pity or sympathy for. Her friends *commiserated* with the widow.

compact ADJ. tightly packed; firm; brief. His short, *compact* body was better suited to wrestling than to basketball.

compact N. agreement; contract. The signers of the Mayflower *Compact* were establishing a form of government.

comparable ADJ. similar. People whose jobs are *comparable* in difficulty should receive *comparable* pay.

compatible ADJ. harmonious; in harmony with. They were *compatible* neighbors, never quarreling over unimportant matters. compatibility, N.

compile V. assemble; gather; accumulate. We planned to *compile* a list of the words most frequently used on SAT I examinations. compilation, N.

complacent ADJ. self-satisfied; smug. Feeling *complacent* about his latest victories, he looked smugly at the row of trophies on his mantelpiece. complacency, N.

complement V. complete; make perfect. The waiter recommended a glass of port to *complement* the cheese. also N.

● **compliance** N. readiness to yield; conformity in fulfilling requirements. Bill was so bullheaded that we never expected his easy *compliance* to our requests. As an architect, however, Bill recognized that his design for the new school had to be in *compliance* with the local building code.

● **component** N. element; ingredient. I wish all the *components* of my stereo system were working at the same time.

compress V. close; squeeze; contract. She *compressed* the package under her arm.

● **compromise** V. adjust or settle by making mutual concessions; endanger the interests or reputation of. Sometimes the presence of a neutral third party can help adversaries *compromise* their differences. Unfortunately, your presence at the scene of the dispute *compromises* our claim to neutrality in this matter. also N.

compute V. reckon; calculate. He failed to *compute* the interest, so his bank balance was not accurate.

concerted ADJ. mutually agreed on; done together. All the Girl Scouts made a *concerted* effort to raise funds for their annual outing. When the movie star appeared, his fans let out a *concerted* sigh.

concise ADJ. brief but comprehensive. The instructions were *concise* and to the point: they included every necessary detail, and not one word more. Precision indicates exactness; *concision* indicates compactness. To achieve *conciseness*, cut out unnecessary words.

concoct V. prepare by combining; make up in concert. How did the inventive chef ever *concoct* such a strange dish? concoction, N.

concurrent ADJ. happening at the same time. In America, the colonists were resisting the demands of the mother country; at the *concurrent* moment in France, the middle class was sowing the seeds of rebellion. The two revolutionary movements took place *concurrently*.

condescend V. act conscious of descending to a lower level; patronize. Though Jill was a star softball player in college, when she played a pickup game at the local park she never *condescended* to her teammates or acted as if she thought herself superior to them. condescension. N.

condole V. express sympathetic sorrow. Bill's friends gathered to *condole* with him over his loss. Those unable to attend the funeral sent letters of *condolence*.

condone V. overlook voluntarily; forgive. Although she had excused Huck for his earlier escapades, Widow Douglas refused to *condone* his latest prank.

confine V. shut in; restrict. The terrorists had *confined* their prisoner in a small room. However, they had not chained him to the wall or done anything else to *confine* his movements further. confinement, N.

● **confirm** V. corroborate; verify; support. I have several witnesses who will *confirm* my account of what happened.

conflagration N. great fire. In the *conflagration* that followed the 1906 earthquake, much of San Francisco burned to the ground.

WORD LIST 8 conformity - culpable

● **conformity** N. agreement or compliance; actions in agreement with prevailing social customs. In *conformity* with the bylaws of the Country Dance and Song Society, I am submitting a petition nominating Susan Murrow as president of the society. Because Kate had always been a rebellious child, we were surprised by her *conformity* to the standards of behavior prevalent at her new school.

congeal V. freeze; coagulate. His blood *congealed* in his veins as he saw the dread monster rush toward him.

● **congenial** ADJ. pleasant; friendly. My father loved to go out for a meal with *congenial* companions.

connotation N. suggested or implied meaning of an expression. Foreigners frequently are unaware of the *connotations* of the words they use.

● **consistency** N. harmony of parts; dependability; uniformity; degree of thickness. Holmes judged puddings and explanations on their *consistency*: he liked his puddings without lumps and his explanations without contradictions or improbabilities. consistent, ADJ.

● **console** V. lessen sadness or disappointment; give comfort. When her father died, Marius did his best to *console* Cosette.

● **consolidation** N. unification; process of becoming firmer or stronger. The recent *consolidation* of several small airlines into one major company has left observers of the industry wondering whether room still exists for the "little guy" in aviation. consolidate, V.

conspicuous ADJ. easily seen; noticeable; striking. Janet was *conspicuous* both for her red hair and for her height.

constituent N. resident of a district represented by an elected official. The congressman received hundreds of letters from angry *constituents* after the Equal Rights Amendment failed to pass.

constraint N. compulsion; repression of feelings. There was a feeling of *constraint* in the room because no one dared to criticize the speaker. constrain, V.

contagion N. infection. Fearing *contagion*, the health authorities took great steps to prevent the spread of the disease.

contempt N. scorn; disdain. The heavyweight boxer looked on ordinary people with *contempt*, scorning them as weaklings who couldn't hurt a fly. We thought it was *contemptible* of him to be *contemptuous* of people for being weak.

contention N. claim; thesis. It is our *contention* that, if you follow our tactics, you will boost your score on the PSAT. contend, V.

● **contentious** ADJ. quarrelsome. Disagreeing violently with the referees' ruling, the coach became so *contentious* that they threw him out of the game.

context N. writings preceding and following the passage quoted. Because these lines are taken out of *context*, they do not convey the message the author intended.

contingent ADJ. dependent on; conditional. Cher's father informed her that any raise in her allowance was *contingent* on the quality of her final grades. contingency, N.

contingent N. group that makes up part of a gathering. The New York *contingent* of delegates at the Democratic National Convention was a boisterous, sometimes rowdy lot.

contortion N. twisting; distortion. Watching the *contortions* of the gymnast as he twisted and heaved his body from one side to the other of the pommel horse, we were awed by his strength and flexibility.

contrite ADJ. penitent. Her *contrite* tears did not influence the judge when he imposed sentence.

● **convention** N. social or moral custom; established practice. Flying in the face of *convention*, George Sand shocked society by taking lovers and wearing men's clothes.

converge V. approach; tend to meet; come together. African-American men from all over the United States *converged* on Washington to take part in the historic Million Man march.

convert N. one who has adopted a different religion or opinion. On his trip to Japan, though the President spoke at length about the merits of American automobiles, he made few *converts* to his beliefs. also V.

conviction N. judgment that someone is guilty of a crime; strongly held belief. Even her *conviction* for murder did not shake Peter's *conviction* that Harriet was innocent of the crime.

cordial ADJ. gracious; heartfelt. Our hosts greeted us at the airport with a *cordial* welcome and a hearty hug.

corroborate V. confirm; support. Though Huck was quite willing to *corroborate* Tom's story, Aunt Polly knew better than to believe either of them.

● **corrosion** N. destruction by chemical action. The *corrosion* of the girders supporting the bridge took place so gradually that no one suspected any danger until the bridge suddenly collapsed. corrode, V.

cosmic ADJ. pertaining to the universe; vast. *Cosmic* rays derive their name from the fact that they bombard the earth's atmosphere from outer space. cosmos, N.

cosmopolitan ADJ. sophisticated. Her years in the capital had transformed her into a *cosmopolitan* young woman highly aware of international affairs.

countenance V. approve; tolerate. He refused to *countenance* such rude behavior on their part.

covert ADJ. secret; hidden; implied. Investigations of the Central Intelligence Agency and other secret service networks reveal that such *covert* operations can get out of control.

covetous ADJ. avaricious; eagerly desirous of. The child was *covetous* by nature and wanted to take the toys belonging to his classmates. covet, V.

cower V. shrink quivering, as from fear. The frightened child *cowered* in the corner of the room.

crass ADJ. very unrefined; grossly insensible. The film critic deplored the *crass* commercialism of movie makers who abandon artistic standards in order to make a quick buck.

credibility N. believability. Because the candidate had made some pretty unbelievable promises, we began to question the *credibility* of everything she said.

credulity N. belief on slight evidence; gullibility; naivete. Con artists take advantage of the *credulity* of inexperienced investors to swindle them out of their savings. credulous, ADJ.

criterion N. standard used in judging. What *criterion* did you use when you selected this essay as the prizewinner? criteria, Pl.

cryptic ADJ. mysterious; hidden; secret. Thoroughly baffled by Holmes's *cryptic* remarks, Watson wondered whether Holmes was intentionally concealing his thoughts about the crime.

culinary ADJ. relating to cooking. Many chefs attribute their *culinary* skill to the wise use of spices.

culmination N. attainment of highest point. Her inauguration as President of the United States marked the *culmination* of her political career. culminate, V.

culpable ADJ. deserving blame. Corrupt politicians who condone the illegal activities of gamblers are equally *culpable*.

WORD LIST 9 cumbersome - depict

cumbersome ADJ. heavy; hard to manage. He was burdened down with *cumbersome* parcels.

curb V. restrain. The overly generous philanthropist had to *curb* his beneficent impulses before he gave away all his money and left himself with nothing.

cursory ADJ. casual; hastily done. Because a *cursory* examination of the ruins indicates the possibility of arson, we believe the insurance agency should undertake a more extensive investigation of the fire's cause.

● **curtail** V. shorten; reduce. When Elton asked Cher for a date, she said she was really sorry she couldn't go out with him, but her dad had ordered her to *curtail* her social life.

● **cynical** ADJ. skeptical or distrustful of human motives. *Cynical* from birth, Sidney was suspicious whenever anyone give him a gift "with no strings attached." cynic, N.

dabble V. work at in a non-serious fashion; splash around. The amateur painter *dabbled* at art, but seldom produced a finished piece. The children *dabbled* their hands in the bird bath, splashing one another gleefully.

daunt V. intimidate; frighten. "Boast all you like of your prowess. Mere words cannot *daunt* me," the *dauntless* hero answered the villain.

● **dawdle** V. loiter; waste time. At the mall, Mother grew impatient with Jo and Amy because they tended to *dawdle* as they went from store to store.

dearth N. scarcity. The *dearth* of skilled labor compelled the employers to open trade schools.

debase V. reduce in quality or value; lower in esteem; degrade. In *The King and I*, Anna refuses to kneel down and prostrate herself before the king, for she feels that to do so would *debase* her position, and she will not submit to such *debasement*.

debilitate V. weaken; enfeeble. Michael's severe bout of the flu *debilitated* him so much that he was too tired to go to work for a week.

decadence N. decay or decline, especially moral; self-indulgence. We named our best-selling ice cream flavor "chocolate *decadence*" because only truly self-indulgent people would treat themselves to something so calorific and cholesterol-laden.

decipher V. decode. I could not *decipher* the doctor's handwriting.

decorous ADJ. proper. Prudence's *decorous* behavior was praised by her teachers, who wished they had a classroom full of such polite and proper little girls. decorum, N.

decoy N. lure or bait. The wild ducks were not fooled by the *decoy*. also V.

decry V. express strong disapproval of; disparage. The founder of the Children's Defense Fund, Marian Wright Edelman, strongly *decries* the lack of financial and moral support for children in America today.

deducible ADJ. derived by reasoning. If we accept your premise, your conclusions are easily *deducible*.

deface V. mar; disfigure. If you *deface* a library book, you will have to pay a hefty fine.

defamation N. harming a person's reputation. *Defamation* of character may result in a slander suit. If rival candidates persist in *defaming* one another, the voters may conclude that all politicians are crooks.

defeatist ADJ. attitude of one who is ready to accept defeat as a natural outcome. If you maintain your *defeatist* attitude, you will never succeed. also N.

deference N. courteous regard for another's wish. In *deference* to the minister's request, please do not take photographs during the wedding service.

● **defiance** N. opposition; willingness to resist. In learning to read and write in *defiance* of his master's orders, Frederick Douglass showed exceptional courage. defy, V.

definitive ADJ. final; complete. Carl Sandburg's *Abraham Lincoln* may be regarded as the *definitive* work on the life of the Great Emancipator.

defrock V. strip a priest or minister of church authority. We knew the minister had violated church regulations, but we had not realized his offense was serious enough for people to seek to *defrock* him.

defunct ADJ. dead; no longer in use or existence. The lawyers sought to examine the books of the *defunct* corporation.

● **degenerate** V. become worse; deteriorate. As the fight dragged on, the champion's style *degenerated* until he could barely keep on his feet.

deign V. condescend; stoop. The celebrated fashion designer would not *deign* to speak to a mere seamstress; his overburdened assistant had to convey the master's wishes to the lowly workers assembling his great designs.

delete V. erase; strike out. Less is more: if you *delete* this paragraph, the composition will have more appeal.

delineate V. portray; depict; sketch. Using only a few descriptive phrases, Austen *delineates* the character of Mr. Collins so well that we can predict his every move. delineation, N.

delirium N. mental disorder marked by confusion. In his *delirium*, the drunkard saw pink panthers and talking pigs. Perhaps he wasn't *delirious*; he might just have wandered into a movie.

delusion N. false belief; hallucination. Don suffers from *delusions* of grandeur: he thinks he's a world-famous author when he's published just one paperback book.

● **demean** V. degrade; humiliate. Standing on his dignity, he refused to *demean* himself by replying to the offensive letter. If you truly believed in the dignity of labor, you would not think it would *demean* you to work as a janitor.

demeanor N. behavior; bearing. His sober *demeanor* quieted the noisy revelers.

demolish V. destroy; tear down. Before building a new hotel along the waterfront, the construction company had to *demolish* several rundown warehouses on that site. demolition, N.

demur V. object (because of doubts, scruples); hesitate. When offered a post on the board of directors, David *demurred:* he had scruples about taking on the job because he was unsure he could handle it in addition to his other responsibilities.

demure ADJ. grave; serious; coy. She was *demure* and reserved, a nice modest girl whom any young man would be proud to take home to his mother.

● **denounce** V. condemn; criticize. The reform candidate *denounced* the corrupt city officials for having betrayed the public's trust. denunciation, N.

deny V. contradict; refuse. Do you *deny* his story, or do you support what he says? How could Pat *deny* the truth of the accusation that he'd been swiping the Oreos when he'd been caught with his hand in the cookie jar? denial, N.

● **depict** V. portray. In this sensational exposé, the author *depicts* John Lennon as a drug-crazed neurotic. Do you question the accuracy of this *depiction* of Lennon?

WORD LIST 10 **deplete - disclaimer**

● **deplete** V. reduce; exhaust. We must wait until we *deplete* our present inventory before we order replacements.

● **deplore** V. regret strongly; express grief over. Although Ann Landers *deplored* the disintegration of the modern family, she recognized that not every marriage could be saved.

deprecate V. express disapproval of; protest against. A firm believer in old-fashioned courtesy, Miss Post *deprecated* the unfortunate modern tendency to address new acquaintances by their first names. deprecatory, ADJ.

depreciate V. lessen in value. If you neglect this property, it will *depreciate.*

deprivation N. loss. In prison she faced the sudden *deprivation* of rights she had taken for granted: the right to stay up late reading a book, the right to privacy, the right to make a phone call to a friend.

derelict ADJ. abandoned; negligent. The *derelict* craft was a menace to navigation. Whoever abandoned it in mid harbor was *derelict* in living up to his or her responsibilities as a boat owner. dereliction, N.

● **derision** N. ridicule; mockery. Greeting his pretentious dialogue with *derision,* the critics refused to consider his play seriously. deride, V.

● **derivative** ADJ. unoriginal; derived from another source. Although her early poetry was clearly *derivative* in nature, the critics felt she had promise and eventually would find her own voice.

desecrate V. profane; violate the sanctity of. The soldiers *desecrated* the temple, shattering the altar and trampling the holy objects underfoot.

despise V. look on with scorn; regard as worthless or distasteful. Mr. Bond, I *despise* spies; I look down on them as mean, *despicable,* honorless men, whom I would cheerfully wipe from the face of the earth.

despondent ADJ. depressed; gloomy. To the dismay of his parents, William became so seriously *despondent* after he broke up with Jan that they despaired of finding a cure for his gloom. despondency, N.

desultory ADJ. aimless; haphazard; digressing at random. In prison Malcolm X set himself the task of reading straight through the dictionary; to him, reading was purposeful, not *desultory.*

● **detached** ADJ. emotionally removed; calm and objective; indifferent. A psychoanalyst must maintain a *detached* point of view and stay uninvolved with her patients' personal lives. detachment, N. (secondary meaning)

determination N. resolve; measurement or calculation; decision. Nothing could shake his *determination* that his children would get the best education that money could buy. Thanks to my pocket calculator, my *determination* of the answer to the problem took only seconds of my time.

● **deterrent** N. something that discourages; hindrance. Does the threat of capital punishment serve as a *deterrent* to potential killers? deter, V.

detrimental ADJ. harmful; damaging. The candidate's acceptance of major financial contributions from a well-known racist ultimately proved *detrimental* to his campaign, for he lost the backing of many of his early grassroots supporters. detriment, N.

deviate V. turn away from (a principle, norm); depart; diverge. Richard never *deviated* from his daily routine: every day he set off for work at eight o'clock, had his sack lunch (peanut butter on whole wheat) at 12:15, and headed home at the stroke of five.

devious ADJ. roundabout; erratic; not straightforward. The Joker's plan was so *devious* that it was only with great difficulty we could follow its shifts and dodges.

dexterous ADJ. skillful. The magician was so *dexterous* that we could not follow him as he performed his tricks.

diagnosis N. art of identifying a disease; analysis of a condition. In medical school Margaret developed her skill at *diagnosis,* learning how to read volumes from a rapid pulse or a hacking cough. diagnose, V.; diagnostic, ADJ.

dichotomy N. split; branching into two parts (especially contradictory ones). Willie didn't know how to resolve the *dichotomy* between his ambition to go to college and his childhood longing to run away to join the circus. Then he heard about Ringling Brothers Circus College, and he knew he'd found the perfect school.

● **didactic** ADJ. teaching; instructional. Pope's lengthy poem *An Essay on Man* is too *didactic* for my taste: I dislike it when poets turn preachy and moralize.

diffuse ADJ. wordy; rambling; spread out (like a gas). If you pay authors by the word, you tempt them to produce *diffuse* manuscripts rather then brief ones. diffusion, N.

● **digression** N. wandering away from the subject. Nobody minded when Professor Renoir's lectures wandered away from their official theme; his *digressions* were always more fascinating than the topic of the day. digress, V.

dilemma N. problem; choice of two unsatisfactory alternatives. In this *dilemma,* he knew no one to whom he could turn for advice.

dilettante N. aimless follower of the arts; amateur; dabbler. He was not serious in his painting; he was rather a *dilettante.*

diligence N. steadiness of effort; persistent hard work. Her employers were greatly impressed by her *diligence* and offered her a partnership in the firm. diligent, ADJ.

dilute V. make less concentrated; reduce in strength. She preferred her coffee *diluted* with milk.

diminutive ADJ. small in size. Looking at the tiny gymnast, we were amazed that anyone so *diminutive* could perform with such power.

din N. continued loud noise. The *din* of the jackhammers outside the classroom window drowned out the lecturer's voice. also V.

dirge N. lament with music. The funeral *dirge* stirred us to tears.

disavowal N. denial; disclaiming. His *disavowal* of his part in the conspiracy was not believed by the jury. disavow, V.

● **discernible** ADJ. distinguishable; perceivable. The ships in the harbor were not *discernible* in the fog.

discerning ADJ. mentally quick and observant; having insight. Though no genius, the star was sufficiently *discerning* to tell her true friends from the countless phonies who flattered her.

● **disclaimer** N. denial of a legal claim or right; disavowal. Though reporter Joe Klein issued a *disclaimer* stating that he was *not* "Anonymous," the author of *Primary Colors,* eventually he admitted that he had written the controversial novel. disclaim, V.

WORD LIST 11 **disclose - downcast**

● **disclose** V. reveal. Although competitors offered him bribes, he refused to *disclose* any information about his company's forthcoming product. disclosure, N.

disconcert V. confuse; upset; embarrass. The lawyer was *disconcerted* by the evidence produced by her adversary.

● **discord** N. lack of harmony; conflict; Watching Tweedledum battle Tweedledee, Alice wondered what had caused this pointless *discord.*

discount V. discredit; reduce in price. Be prepared to *discount* what he has to say about his ex-wife.

discrimination ADJ. able to see differences; prejudiced. A superb interpreter of Picasso, she was sufficiently *discriminating* to judge the most complex works of modern art. (secondary meaning) discrimination, N.

discursive ADJ. digressing; rambling. As the lecturer wandered from topic to topic, we wondered what if any point there was to his *discursive* remarks.

disdain V. view with scorn or contempt. In the film *Funny Face,* the bookish heroine *disdained* fashion models for their lack of intellectual interests. also N.

disembark V. go ashore; unload cargo from a ship. Before the passengers could *disembark,* they had to pick up their passports from the ship's purser.

disgruntled ADJ. discontented; sulky and dissatisfied. The numerous delays left the passengers feeling *disgruntled.* disgruntle, V.

disheveled ADJ. untidy. Your *disheveled* appearance will hurt your chances in this interview.

● **disinterested** ADJ. unprejudiced. Given the judge's political ambitions and the lawyers' financial interest in the case, the only *disinterested* person in the courtroom may have been the court reporter.

dismay V. discourage; frighten. The huge amount of work she had left to do *dismayed* her. also N.

● **dismiss** V. put away from consideration; reject. Believing in John's love for her, she *dismissed* the notion that he might be unfaithful. (secondary meaning)

● **disparage** V. belittle. A doting mother, Emma was more likely to praise her son's crude attempts at art than to *disparage* them.

● **disparate** ADJ. basically different; unrelated. Unfortunately, Tony and Tina have *disparate* notions of marriage: Tony sees it as a carefree extended love affair, while Tina sees it as a solemn commitment to build a family and a home.

disparity N. difference; condition of inequality. Their *disparity* in rank made no difference at all to the prince and Cinderella.

dispassionate ADJ. calm; impartial. Known in the company for his cool judgment, Bill could impartially examine the causes of a problem, giving a *dispassionate* analysis of what had gone wrong, and go on to suggest how to correct the mess.

dispatch N. speediness; prompt execution; message sent with all due speed. Young Napoleon defeated the enemy with all possible *dispatch;* he then sent a *dispatch* to headquarters, informing his commander of the great victory. also V.

● **dispel** V. scatter; cause to vanish. The bright sunlight eventually *dispelled* the morning mist.

● **disperse** V. scatter. The police fired tear gas into the crowd to *disperse* the protesters.

disputatious ADJ. argumentative; fond of arguing. Convinced he knew more than his lawyers, Tom was a *disputatious* client, ready to argue about the best way to conduct the case.

dissemble V. disguise; pretend. Even though John tried to *dissemble* his motive for taking modern dance, we all knew he was there not to dance but to meet girls.

disseminate V. distribute; spread; scatter (like seeds). By their use of the Internet, propagandists have been able to *disseminate* their pet doctrines to new audiences around the globe.

● **dissent** V. disagree. In the recent Supreme Court decision, Justice O'Connor *dissented* from the majority opinion. also N.

dissertation N. formal essay. In order to earn a graduate degree from many of our universities, a candidate is frequently required to prepare a *dissertation* on some scholarly subject.

dissident ADJ. dissenting; rebellious. In the purge that followed the student demonstrations at Tiananmen Square, the government hunted down the *dissident* students and their supporters. also N.

● **dissipate** V. squander; waste; scatter. He is a fine artist, but we fear he may *dissipate* his gifts if he keeps wasting his time doodling on napkins.

dissuade V. persuade not to do; discourage. Since Tom could not *dissuade* Huck from running away from home, he decided to run away with him. dissuasion, N.

● **distinction** N. honor; contrast; discrimination. A holder of the Medal of Honor, George served with great *distinction* in World War II. He made a *distinction,* however, between World War II and Vietnam, which he considered an immoral conflict.

distort V. twist out of shape. It is difficult to believe the newspaper accounts of the riots because of the way some reports *distort* and exaggerate the actual events. distortion, N.

divergent ADJ. differing; deviating. Since graduating from medical school, the two doctors have taken *divergent* paths, the one going on to become a nationally prominent surgeon, the other dedicating himself to a small family practice in his home town. divergence, N.

diverse ADJ. differing in some characteristics; various. The professor suggested *diverse* ways of approaching the assignment and recommended that we choose one of them. diversity, N.

diversion N. act of turning aside; pastime. After studying for several hours, he needed a *diversion* from work. divert, V.

● **divulge** V. reveal. No lover of gossip, Charlotte would never *divulge* anything that a friend told her in confidence.

● **docile** ADJ. obedient; easily managed. As *docile* as he seems today, that old lion was once a ferocious, snarling beast.

● **doctrine** N. teachings, in general; particular principle (religious, legal, etc.) taught. He was so committed to the *doctrines* of his faith that he was unable to evaluate them impartially.

document V. provide written evidence. She kept all the receipts from her business trip in order to *document* her expenses for the firm. also N.

● **dogmatic** ADJ. opinionated; arbitrary; doctrinal. We tried to discourage Doug from being so *dogmatic,* but never could convince him that his opinions might be wrong.

dormant ADJ. sleeping; lethargic; latent. At fifty her long-*dormant* ambition to write flared up once more; within a year she had completed the first of her great historical novels.

downcast ADJ. disheartened; sad. Cheerful and optimistic by nature, Beth was never *downcast* despite the difficulties she faced.

draconian ADJ. extremely severe. When the principal canceled the senior prom because some seniors had been late to school that week, we thought the *draconian* punishment was far too harsh for such a minor violation of the rules.

dregs N. sediment; worthless residue. David poured the wine carefully to avoid stirring up the *dregs*.

dross N. waste matter; worthless impurities. Many methods have been devised to separate the valuable metal from the *dross*.

ductile ADJ. malleable; flexible; pliable. Copper is an extremely *ductile* material: you can stretch it into the thinnest of wires, bend it, even wind it into loops.

duplicity N. double-dealing; hypocrisy. When Tanya learned that Mark had been two-timing her, she was furious at his *duplicity*.

dwindle V. shrink; reduce. The food in the lifeboat gradually *dwindled* away to nothing.

ebb V. recede; lessen. Mrs. Dalloway sat on the beach and watched the tide *ebb*. also N.

ebullient ADJ. showing excitement; overflowing with enthusiasm. Her *ebullient* nature could not be repressed; she was always bubbling over with exuberance. ebullience, N.

eccentric ADJ. irregular; odd; whimsical; bizarre. The comet veered dangerously close to the earth in its *eccentric* orbit. eccentricity, N.

eclectic ADJ. composed of elements drawn from disparate sources. His style of interior decoration was *eclectic*: bits and pieces of furnishings from widely divergent periods, strikingly juxtaposed to create a unique decor. eclecticism, N.

● **eclipse** V. darken; extinguish; surpass. The new stock market high *eclipsed* the previous record set in 1995.

ecstasy N. rapture; joy; any overpowering emotion. When Allison received her long-hoped-for letter of acceptance from Harvard, she was in *ecstasy*. ecstatic, ADJ.

effervescence N. inner excitement or exuberance; bubbling from fermentation or carbonation. Nothing depressed Sue for long; her natural *effervescence* soon reasserted itself. Soda that loses its *effervescence* goes flat. effervescent, ADJ., effervesce, V.

egotistical ADJ. excessively self-centered; self-important; conceited. Typical *egotistical* remark: "But enough of this chit-chat about you and your little problems. Let's talk about what's really important: *Me!*"

egregious ADJ. notorious; gross; shocking. She was an *egregious* liar; we all knew better than to believe a word she said.

elated ADJ. overjoyed; in high spirits. Grinning from ear to ear, Carl Lewis was clearly *elated* by his ninth Olympic gold medal. elation, N.

elicit V. draw out (by discussion); call forth. The camp counselor's humorous remarks finally *elicited* a smile from the shy new camper.

eloquence N. expressiveness; persuasive speech. The crowds were stirred by Martin Luther King's *eloquence*. eloquent, ADJ.

elucidate V. explain; enlighten. He was called upon to *elucidate* the disputed points in his article.

● **elusive** ADJ. evasive; baffling; hard to grasp. Trying to pin down exactly when the contractors would be done remodeling the house, Nancy was frustrated by their *elusive* replies. elude, V.

emanate V. issue forth. A strong odor of sulphur *emanated* from the spring.

emancipate V. set free. At first, the attempts of the Abolitionists to *emancipate* the slaves were unpopular in New England as well as in the South.

● **embellish** V. adorn. We enjoyed my mother-in-law's stories about how she came here from Russia, in part because she *embellished* the bare facts of the journey with humorous anecdotes and vivid descriptive details.

embrace V. hug; adopt or espouse; accept readily; encircle; include. Clasping Maid Marian in his arms, Robin Hood *embraced* her lovingly. In joining the outlaws in Sherwood Forest, she had openly *embraced* their cause.

empathy N. ability to identify with another's feelings, ideas, etc. What made Ann such a fine counselor was her *empathy*, her ability to put herself in her client's place and feel his emotions as if they were her own. empathize, V.

empirical ADJ. based on experience. He distrusted hunches and intuitive flashes; he placed his reliance entirely on *empirical* data.

emulate V. imitate; rival. In a brief essay, describe a person you admire, someone whose virtues you would like to *emulate*.

encumber V. burden. Some people *encumber* themselves with too much luggage when they go for short trips.

● **endorse** V. approve; support. Everyone waited to see which one of the rival candidates for the city council the mayor would *endorse*. endorsement, N (secondary meaning).

enduring ADJ. lasting; surviving. Keats believed in the *enduring* power of great art, which would outlast its creators' brief lives. endure, V.

energize V. invigorate; make forceful and active. Rather than exhausting Maggie, dancing *energized* her.

engage V. attract; hire; pledge oneself; confront. "Your case has *engaged* my interest, my lord," said Holmes. "You may *engage* my services."

engaging ADJ. charming; attractive. Everyone liked Nancy's pleasant manners and *engaging* personality.

engender V. cause; produce. To receive praise for real accomplishments *engenders* self-confidence in a child.

engross V. occupy fully. John was so *engrossed* in his studies that he did not hear his mother call.

● **enhance** V. increase; improve. You can *enhance* your chances of being admitted to the college of your choice by learning to write well; an excellent essay can *enhance* any application.

● **enigma** N. puzzle; mystery. "What *do* women want?" asked Dr. Sigmund Freud. Their behavior was an *enigma* to him.

enterprising ADJ. ready to undertake ambitious projects. An *enterprising* young man, Matt saw business opportunities on every side and was always eager to capitalize on them.

entice V. lure; attract; tempt. She always tried to *entice* her baby brother into mischief.

● **enumerate** V. list; mention one by one. Huck hung his head in shame as Miss Watson *enumerated* his many flaws.

enunciate V. speak distinctly. Stop mumbling! How will people understand you if you do not *enunciate*?

ephemeral ADJ. short-lived; fleeting. The mayfly is an *ephemeral* creature: its adult life lasts little more than a day.

epic N. long heroic poem, novel, or similar work of art. Kurosawa's film *Seven Samurai* is an *epic* portraying the struggle of seven warriors to destroy a band of robbers. also ADJ.

epilogue N. short speech at conclusion of dramatic work. The audience was so disappointed in the play that many did not remain to hear the *epilogue*.

WORD LIST 13   equivocal - farce

equivocal ADJ. ambiguous; intentionally misleading. Rejecting the candidate's *equivocal* comments on tax reform, the reporters pressed him to state clearly where he stood on the issue. equivocate, V.

● **erode** V. eat away. The limestone was *eroded* by the dripping water until only a thin shell remained. erosion, N.

● **erratic** ADJ. odd; unpredictable. Investors become anxious when the stock market appears *erratic.*

● **erroneous** ADJ. mistaken; wrong. I thought my answer was correct, but it was *erroneous.*

eschew V. avoid. Hoping to present himself to his girlfriend as a totally reformed character, he tried to *eschew* all the vices, especially chewing tobacco and drinking bathtub gin.

● **esoteric** ADJ. hard to understand; known only to the chosen few. *New Yorker* short stories often included *esoteric* allusions to obscure people and events; the implication was, if you were in the in-crowd, you'd get the reference; if you came from Cleveland, you would not.

● **espouse** V. adopt; support. She was always ready to *espouse* a worthy cause.

● **esteem** V. respect; value; Jill *esteemed* Jack's taste in music, but she deplored his taste in clothes.

estranged ADJ. separated; alienated. The *estranged* wife sought a divorce. estrangement, N.

ethereal ADJ. light; heavenly; unusually refined. In Shakespeare's *The Tempest,* the spirit Ariel is an *ethereal* creature, too airy and unearthly for our mortal world.

euphemism N. mild expression used in place of an unpleasant one. Until recently, many Southern Americans avoided the word *bull* in polite speech, replacing it by a *euphemism,* such as *he-cow* or *male beast.*

euphonious ADJ. pleasing in sound. *Euphonious* even when spoken, the Italian language is particularly pleasing to the ear when sung. euphony, N.

evenhanded ADJ. impartial; fair. Do men and women receive *evenhanded* treatment from their teachers, or, as recent studies suggest, do teachers pay more attention to male students than to females?

evocative ADJ. tending to call up (emotions, memories). Scent can be remarkable *evocative:* the aroma of pipe tobacco *evokes* the memory of my father; a whiff of talcum powder calls up images of my daughter as a child.

exacting ADJ. extremely demanding. Cleaning the ceiling of the Sistine Chapel was an *exacting* task, one that demanded extremely meticulous care on the part of the restorers. exaction, N.

● **excerpt** N. selected passage (written or musical). The cinematic equivalent of an *excerpt* from a novel is a clip from a film.

exculpate V. clear from blame. Though Sid came up with excuse after excuse to *exculpate* himself, Samantha still blamed him for his conduct.

execute V. put into effect; carry out; put to death. The prima ballerina *executed* the pirouette so badly that the infuriated choreographer was ready to tear his hair. execution, N.

● **exemplary** ADJ. serving as a model; outstanding. At commencement the dean praised Ellen for her *exemplary* behavior as class president.

exonerate V. acquit; exculpate. The defense team feverishly sought fresh evidence that might *exonerate* their client.

expansive ADJ. outgoing and sociable; broad and extensive; able to increase in size. Mr. Fezziwig was in an *expansive* humor, cheerfully urging his guests to join in the Christmas feast. Looking down on his *expansive* paunch, he sighed: if his belly *expanded* any further, his pants would need an *expansive* waistline.

expedient ADJ. suitable to achieve a particular end; practical; politic. A pragmatic politician, he was guided by what was *expedient* rather than by what was ethical. expediency, N.

expedite V. hasten. Because we are on a tight schedule, we hope you will be able to *expedite* the delivery of our order.

explicate V. explain; interpret; clarify. Harry Levin *explicated* James Joyce's often bewildering novels with such clarity that even *Finnegan's Wake* seemed comprehensible to his students.

explicit ADJ. totally clear; definite; outspoken. Don't just hint around that you're dissatisfied: be *explicit* about what's bugging you.

exploit N. deed or action, particularly a brave deed. Raoul Wallenberg was noted for his *exploits* in rescuing Jews from Hitler's forces.

● **exploit** V. make use of, sometimes unjustly. Cesar Chavez fought attempts to *exploit* migrant farm workers in California. exploitation, N.

expunge V. wipe out; remove; destroy. If you hit the "Delete" key by mistake, you can accidentally *expunge* an entire block of text.

expurgate V. clean; remove offensive parts of a book. The editors felt that certain passages in the book had to be *expurgated* before it could be used in the classroom.

extraneous ADJ. not essential; superfluous. No wonder Ted can't think straight! His mind is so cluttered up with *extraneous* trivia, he can't concentrate on the essentials.

extrapolate V. infer; project from known data into the unknown; make a conjecture. Based on what they could *extrapolate* from the results of the primaries on Super Tuesday, the networks predicted that Bob Dole would be the Republican candidate for the presidency.

extricate V. free; disentangle. The fox could not *extricate* itself from the trap.

exuberant ADJ. joyfully enthusiastic; flamboyant; lavish; abundant. I was bowled over by Amy's *exuberant* welcome. What an enthusiastic greeting!

fabricate V. build; lie. If we *fabricate* the buildings in this project out of standardized sections, we can reduce construction cost considerably. Because of Jack's tendency to *fabricate,* Jill had trouble believing a word he said.

facile ADJ. easily accomplished; ready or fluent; superficial. Words came easily to Jonathan: he was a *facile* speaker and prided himself on being ready to make a speech at a moment's notice.

● **facilitate** V. help bring about; make less difficult. Rest and proper nourishment should *facilitate* the patient's recovery.

● **fallacious** ADJ. false; misleading. Paradoxically, *fallacious* reasoning does not always yield erroneous results: even though your logic may be faulty, the answer you get may nevertheless be correct. fallacy, N.

fallible ADJ. liable to err. I know I am *fallible,* but I feel confident that I am right this time.

farce N. broad comedy; mockery. Nothing went right; the entire interview degenerated into a *farce.* farcical, ADJ.

WORD LIST 14   fastidious - gale

- **fastidious** ADJ. difficult to please; squeamish. Bobby was such a *fastidious* eater that he would eat a sandwich only if his mother first cut off every scrap of crust.
- **feasible** ADJ. practical. Is it *feasible* to build a new stadium for the Yankees on New York's West Side? Without additional funding, the project is clearly unrealistic.

ferment N. agitation; commotion. With the breakup of the Soviet Union, much of Eastern Europe was in a state of *ferment.*

fervor N. glowing ardor; intensity of feeling. At the protest rally, the students cheered the strikers and booed the dean with equal *fervor.* fervid, ADJ.

fester V. provoke keen irritation or resentment. Joe's insult *festered* in Anne's mind for days, and made her too angry to speak to him.

fetid ADJ. having a foul, disgusting odor. Change the kitty litter in the cat box right now! No self-respecting cat would use a litter box with such a *fetid* smell.

fetter V. shackle. The prisoner was *fettered* to the wall.

fiasco N. total failure. Tanya's attempt to look sophisticated by smoking was a *fiasco:* she lit the wrong end of the cigarette, choked when she tried to inhale, and burned a hole in her boyfriend's couch.

fiery ADJ. easily provoked; passionate; burning. By reputation, redheads have *fiery* tempers; the least little thing can cause them to explode.

finite ADJ. having an end; limited. Though Bill really wanted to win the pie-eating contest, the capacity of his stomach was *finite,* and he had to call it quits after eating only seven cherry pies.

firebrand N. hothead; troublemaker. The police tried to keep track of all the local *firebrands* when the president came to town.

fissure N. crevice. The mountain climbers secured footholds in tiny *fissures* in the rock.

fitful ADJ. spasmodic; intermittent. After several *fitful* attempts, he decided to postpone the start of the project until he felt more energetic.

- **flippant** ADJ. lacking proper seriousness. When Mark told Mona he loved her, she dismissed his earnest declaration with a *flippant* "Oh, you say that to all the girls!" flippancy, N.

flout V. reject; mock. The headstrong youth *flouted* all authority; he refused to be curbed.

fluctuate V. waver; shift. The water pressure in our shower *fluctuates* wildly; you start rinsing yourself off with a trickle, and, two minutes later, a blast of water nearly knocks you down.

fluency N. smoothness of speech. He spoke French with *fluency* and ease.

foible N. weakness; slight fault. We can overlook the *foibles* of our friends; no one is perfect.

foliage N. masses of leaves. Every autumn before the leaves fell he promised himself he would drive through New England to admire the colorful fall *foliage.*

forbearance N. patience. We must use *forbearance* in dealing with him because he is still weak from his illness.

foreboding N. premonition of evil. Suspecting no conspiracies against him, Caesar gently ridiculed his wife's *forebodings* about the Ides of March.

foreshadow V. give an indication beforehand; portend; prefigure. In retrospect, political analysts realized that Yeltsin's defiance of the attempted coup *foreshadowed* his emergence as the dominant figure of the new Russian republic.

foresight N. ability to foresee future happenings; careful provision for the future. A shrewd investor, she had the *foresight* to buy land just before the current real estate boom.

forestall V. prevent by taking action in advance. By setting up a prenuptial agreement, the prospective bride and groom hoped to *forestall* any potential arguments about money in the event of a divorce.

forfeit V. lose; surrender. Convicted murderers *forfeit* the right to inherit anything from their victims; the law does not allow them to benefit financially from their crimes.

forgo V. give up; do without. Determined to lose weight over the summer, Michelle decided to *forgo* dessert until she could fit into a size eight again.

- **forthright** ADJ. outspoken; frank. Never afraid to call a spade a spade, she was perhaps too *forthright* to be a successful party politician.

fortuitous ADJ. accidental; by chance. Though he pretended their encounter was *fortuitous,* he'd actually been hanging around her usual haunts for the past two weeks, hoping she'd turn up.

foster V. rear; encourage. According to the legend, Romulus and Remus were *fostered* by a she-wolf who raised the abandoned infants as her own. also ADJ.

- **frail** ADJ. weak. The delicate child seemed too *frail* to lift the heavy carton.

franchise N. right granted by authority; right to vote; business licensed to sell a product in a particular territory. The city issued a *franchise* to the company to operate surface transit lines on the streets for 99 years. For most of American history women lacked the right to vote: not until the early twentieth century was the *franchise* granted to women. Stan owns a Carvel's ice cream *franchise* in Chinatown.

frantic ADJ. wild. At the time of the collision, many people became *frantic* with fear.

fraudulent ADJ. cheating; deceitful. The government seeks to prevent *fraudulent* and misleading advertising.

frivolous ADJ. lacking in seriousness; self-indulgently carefree; relatively unimportant. Though Nancy enjoyed Bill's *frivolous,* lighthearted companionship, she sometimes wondered whether he could ever be serious. frivolity, N.

fugitive ADJ. fleeting or transient; elusive; fleeing. How can a painter capture on canvas the *fugitive* beauty of clouds moving across the sky? also N.

fundamental V. basic; primary; essential. The committee discussed all sorts of side issues without ever getting down to addressing the *fundamental* problem.

furtive ADJ. stealthy; sneaky. Noticing the *furtive* glance the customer gave the diamond bracelet on the counter, the jeweler wondered whether he had a potential shoplifter on his hands.

fusion N. union; coalition. The opponents of the political party in power organized a *fusion* of disgruntled groups and became an important element in the election.

futile ADJ. useless; hopeless; ineffectual. It is *futile* for me to try to get any work done around here while the telephone is ringing every thirty seconds. futility, N.

gainful ADJ. profitable. After having been out of work for six months, Brenda was excited by the prospect of *gainful* employment.

gale N. windstorm; gust of wind; emotional outburst (laughter, tears). The Weather Channel warned viewers about a rising *gale,* with winds of up to 60 miles per hour.

galvanize - hostility

galvanize V. stimulate by shock; stir up; revitalize. News that the prince was almost at their door *galvanized* the ugly stepsisters into a frenzy of combing and primping.

garble V. mix up; jumble; distort. A favorite party game involves passing a whispered message from one person to another, till, by the time it reaches the last player, everyone has totally *garbled* the message.

garish ADJ. over-bright in color; gaudy. She wore a gaudy rhinestone necklace with an excessively *garish* gold lamé dress.

● **garrulous** ADJ. loquacious; wordy; talkative. My Uncle Henry can out-talk any three people I know. He is the most *garrulous* person in Cayuga County. garrulity, N.

gavel N. hammerlike tool; mallet. "Sold!" cried the auctioneer, banging her *gavel* on the table to indicate she'd accepted the final bid.

genealogy N. record of descent; lineage. He was proud of his *genealogy* and constantly referred to the achievements of his ancestors.

● **generate** V. cause; produce; create. In his first days in office, President Clinton managed to *generate* a new mood of optimism; we hoped he could *generate* a few new jobs.

generic ADJ. characteristic of an entire class or species. Sue knew so many computer programmers who spent their spare time playing fantasy games that she began to think that playing Dungeons & Dragons was a *generic* trait.

genteel ADJ. well-bred; elegant. We are looking for a man with a *genteel* appearance who can inspire confidence by his cultivated manner.

gibberish N. nonsense; babbling. "Did you hear that fool boy spouting *gibberish* about monsters from outer space? I never heard anything so nonsensical in all my . . ."

glimmer V. shine erratically; twinkle. In the darkness of the cavern, the glowworms hanging from the cavern roof *glimmered* like distant stars.

gloss over V. explain away. No matter how hard he tried to talk around the issue, President Bush could not *gloss over* the fact that he had raised taxes after all.

● **gluttonous** ADJ. greedy for food. The *gluttonous* boy ate all the cookies.

gorge N. small, steep-walled canyon. The white-water rafting guide warned us about the rapids further downstream, where the river cut through a narrow *gorge*.

gorge V. stuff oneself. The gluttonous guest *gorged* himself, cramming food into his mouth as fast as he could.

grandeur N. impressiveness; stateliness; majesty. No matter how often he hiked through the mountains, David never failed to be struck by the *grandeur* of the Sierra Nevada range.

grandiose ADJ. pretentious; high-flown; ridiculously exaggerated; impressive. The aged matinee idol still had *grandiose* notions of his supposed importance in the theatrical world.

graphic ADJ. pertaining to the art of delineating; vividly described. I was particularly impressed by the *graphic* presentation of the storm.

● **gratify** V. please. Amy's success in her new job *gratified* her parents.

gratuitous ADJ. given freely; unwarranted; uncalled for. Quit making *gratuitous* comments about my driving; no one asked you for your opinion.

● **gregarious** ADJ. sociable. Typically, party-throwers are *gregarious;* hermits are not.

guile N. deceit; duplicity; wiliness; cunning. Iago uses considerate *guile* to trick Othello into believing that Desdemona has been unfaithful.

gullible ADJ. easily deceived. Overly *gullible* people have only themselves to blame if they fall for scams repeatedly. As the saying goes, "Fool me once, shame on you. Fool me twice, shame on me."

hackneyed ADJ. commonplace; trite. When the reviewer criticized the movie for its *hackneyed* plot, we agreed; we had seen similar stories hundreds of times before.

halting ADJ. hesitant; faltering. Novice extemporaneous speakers often talk in a *halting* fashion as they grope for the right words.

● **hamper** V. obstruct. The new mother didn't realize how much the effort of caring for an infant would *hamper* her ability to keep an immaculate house.

harangue N. noisy speech. In her lengthy *harangue*, the principal berated the offenders. also V.

harass V. to annoy by repeated attacks. When he could not pay his bills as quickly as he had promised, he was *harassed* by his creditors.

harbor V. provide a refuge for; hide. The church *harbored* illegal aliens who were political refugees.

haughtiness N. pride; arrogance. When she realized that Darcy believed himself too good to dance with his inferiors, Elizabeth took great offense at his *haughtiness*.

hazardous ADJ. dangerous. Your occupation is too *hazardous* for insurance companies to consider your application.

headstrong ADJ. stubborn; willful; unyielding. Because she refused to marry the man her parents had chosen for her, everyone scolded Minna and called her a foolish *headstrong* girl.

heckle V. harass; taunt; jeer at. The home team's fans mercilessly *heckled* the visiting pitcher, taunting him whenever he let anyone get on base.

● **heed** V. pay attention to; consider. We hope you *heed* our advice and get a good night's sleep before the test. also N.

heresy N. opinion contrary to popular belief; opinion contrary to accepted religion. Galileo's assertion that the earth moved around the sun directly contradicted the religious teachings of his day; as a result, he was tried for *heresy*. heretic, N.

hermetic ADJ. sealed by fusion so as to be airtight. After you sterilize the bandages, place them in a container and seal it with a *hermetic* seal to protect them from contamination by airborne bacteria.

hiatus N. gap; pause. Except for a brief two-year *hiatus*, during which she enrolled in the Peace Corps, Ms. Clements has devoted herself to her medical career.

hibernate V. sleep throughout the winter. Bears are one of the many species of animals that *hibernate*. hibernation, N.

hierarchy N. arrangement by rank or standing; authoritarian body divided into ranks. To be low man on the totem pole is to have an inferior place in the *hierarchy*.

● **hindrance** N. block; obstacle. Stalled cars along the highway are a *hindrance* to traffic that tow trucks should remove without delay. hinder, V.

homespun ADJ. domestic; made at home. *Homespun* wit like *homespun* cloth was often coarse and plain.

● **hostility** N. unfriendliness; hatred. Children who have been the sole objects of their parents' attention often feel *hostility* toward a new baby in the family, resenting the newcomer who has taken their place.

WORD LIST 16 humane - impotent

humane ADJ. marked by kindness or consideration. It is ironic that the *Humane* Society sometimes must show its compassion toward mistreated animals by killing them to put them out of their misery.

humble ADJ. modest; not proud. He spoke with great feeling of how much he loved his *humble* home, which he would not trade for a palace. humility, N.

husband V. use sparingly; conserve; save. Marathon runners must *husband* their energy so that they can keep going for the entire distance.

hyperbole N. exaggeration; overstatement. As far as I'm concerned, Apple's claims about the new computer are pure *hyperbole:* no machine is that good!

● **hypocritical** ADJ. pretending to be virtuous; deceiving. It was *hypocritical* of Martha to say such nice things about my poetry to me and then make fun of my verses behind my back. hypocrisy, N.

● **hypothetical** ADJ. based on assumptions or hypotheses; supposed. Suppose you are accepted by Harvard, Stanford, and Brown. Which one would you choose to attend? Remember, this is only a *hypothetical* situation. hypothesis, N.

● **iconoclastic** ADJ. attacking cherished traditions. Deeply *iconoclastic*, Jean Genet deliberately set out to shock conventional theatergoers with his radical plays.

ideology N. system of ideas of a group. For people who had grown up believing in the communist *ideology*, it was hard to adjust to capitalism.

idiom N. expression whose meaning as a whole differs from the meanings of its individual words; distinctive style. The phrase "to lose one's marbles" is an *idiom:* if I say that Joe's lost his marbles, I'm not asking you to find some for him. I'm telling you *idiomatically* that he's crazy.

idiosyncrasy N. individual trait, usually odd in nature; eccentricity. One of Richard Nixon's little *idiosyncrasies* was his liking for ketchup on cottage cheese. One of Hannibal Lecter's little *idiosyncrasies* was his liking for human flesh.

ignite V. kindle; light. When Desi crooned "Baby, light my fire," literal-minded Lucy looked around for some paper to *ignite*.

ignoble ADJ. unworthy; base in nature; not noble. Sir Galahad was so pure in heart that he could never stoop to perform an *ignoble* deed.

illuminate V. brighten; clear up or make understandable; enlighten. Just as a lamp can *illuminate* a dark room, a perceptive comment can *illuminate* a knotty problem.

illusory ADJ. deceptive; not real. Unfortunately, the costs of running the lemonade stand were so high that Tom's profits proved *illusory*.

imbalance N. lack of balance or symmetry; disproportion. To correct racial *imbalance* in the schools, school boards have bussed black children into white neighborhoods and white children into black ones.

imbibe V. drink in. The dry soil *imbibed* the rain quickly.

imbue V. permeate completely; dye thoroughly; fill. The sight of her grandparents' names inscribed on the wall of Ellis Island *imbued* Sarah with a sense of her special heritage as the descendant of immigrants.

imminent ADJ.; near at hand; impending. Rosa was such a last-minute worker that she could never start writing a paper till the deadline was *imminent*.

immobilize V. make unable to move. For a moment, Peter's fear of snakes *immobilized* him; then the use of his limbs returned to him and he bolted from the room.

immune ADJ. resistant to; free or exempt from. Fortunately, Florence had contracted chicken pox as a child and was *immune* to it when her baby broke out in spots.

● **immutable** ADJ. unchangeable. All things change over time; nothing is *immutable*.

● **impair** V. injure; hurt. Drinking alcohol can *impair* your ability to drive safely; if you're going to drink, don't drive.

impart V. give or convey; communicate. A born dancer, she *imparted* her love of movement to her audience with every step she took.

impartial ADJ. not biased; fair. Knowing she could not be *impartial* about her own child, Jo refused to judge any match in which Billy was competing.

impassable ADJ. not able to be traveled or crossed. A giant redwood had fallen across the highway, blocking all four lanes: the road was *impassable*.

impasse N. predicament offering no escape; deadlock; dead end. The negotiators reported they had reached an *impasse* in their talks and had little hope of resolving the deadlock swiftly.

● **impede** v. hinder; block; delay. A series of accidents *impeded* the launching of the space shuttle.

impel V. drive or force onward. A strong feeling of urgency *impelled* her; if she failed to finish the project right then, she knew that she would never get it done.

● **imperceptible** ADJ. unnoticeable; undetectable. Fortunately, the stain on the blouse was *imperceptible* after the blouse had gone through the wash.

impertinent ADJ. insolent; rude. His neighbors' *impertinent* curiosity about his lack of dates angered Ted. It was downright rude of them to ask him such personal questions.

imperturbable ADJ. calm; placid; composed. In the midst of the battle, the Duke of Wellington remained *imperturbable* and in full command of the situation despite the hysteria and panic all around him. imperturbability, N.

impetuous ADJ. violent; hasty; rash. "Leap before you look" was the motto suggested by one particularly *impetuous* young man.

impiety N. irreverence; lack of respect for God. When members of the youth group draped the church in toilet paper one Halloween, the minister reprimanded them for their *impiety*. impious, ADJ.

● **implacable** ADJ. incapable of being pacified. Madame Defarge was the *implacable* enemy of the Evremonde family.

● **implement** V. put into effect; supply with tools. The mayor was unwilling to *implement* the plan until she was sure it had the governor's backing. also N.

implicate V. incriminate; show to be involved. Here's the deal: If you agree to take the witness stand and *implicate* your partners in crime, the prosecution will recommend that the judge go easy in sentencing you.

implication N. something hinted at or suggested. When Miss Watson said she hadn't seen her purse since the last time Jim was in the house, the *implication* was that she suspected Jim had taken it. imply, V.

implicit ADJ. understood but not stated. Jack never told Jill he adored her; he believed his love was *implicit* in his deeds.

importune V. beg persistently. Democratic and Republican phone solicitors *importuned* her for contributions so frequently that she decided to give nothing to either party.

impotent ADJ. weak; ineffective. Although he wished to break the nicotine habit, he found himself *impotent* to resist the craving for a cigarette.

WORD LIST 17 **impromptu - infinitesimal**

impromptu ADJ. without previous preparation; off the cuff; on the spur of the moment. The judges were amazed that she could make such a thorough, well-supported presentation in an *impromptu* speech.

inadvertently ADV. unintentionally; by oversight; carelessly. Judy's great fear was that she might *inadvertently* omit a question on the exam and mismark her whole answer sheet.

inane ADJ. silly; senseless. There's no point in what you're saying. Why are you bothering to make such *inane* remarks? inanity, N.

inanimate ADJ. lifeless. She was asked to identify the still and *inanimate* body.

inarticulate ADJ. speechless; producing indistinct speech. He became *inarticulate* with rage and uttered sounds without meaning.

incapacitate V. disable. During the winter, many people were *incapacitated* by respiratory ailments.

incentive N. spur; motive. Mike's strong desire to outshine his big sister was all the *incentive* he needed to do well in school.

incessant ADJ. uninterrupted; unceasing. In a famous TV commercial, the frogs' *incessant* croaking goes on and on until eventually it turns into a single word: "Bud-weis-er."

incipient ADJ. beginning; in an early stage. I will go to sleep early for I want to break an *incipient* cold.

incite V. arouse to action; goad; motivate; induce to exist. In a fiery speech, Mario *incited* his fellow students to go out on strike to protest the university's anti-affirmative-action stand.

inclusive ADJ. tending to include all. The comedian turned down the invitation to join the Players' Club, saying any club that would let him in was too *inclusive*.

● **incongruity** N. lack of harmony; absurdity. The *incongruity* of his wearing sneakers with formal attire amused the observers. incongruous, ADJ.

incoherent ADJ. unintelligible; muddled; illogical. The excited fan blushed and stammered, her words becoming almost *incoherent* in the thrill of meeting her favorite rock star face to face. incoherence, N.

inconsequential ADJ. insignificant; unimportant. Brushing off Ali's apologies for having broken the wine glass, Tamara said, "Don't worry about it; it's *inconsequential*."

● **inconsistency** N. state of being self-contradictory; lack of uniformity or steadiness. How are lawyers different from agricultural inspectors? While lawyers check *inconsistencies* in witnesses' statements, agricultural inspectors check *inconsistencies* in Grade A eggs. inconsistent, ADJ.

● **incorporate** V. introduce something into a larger whole; combine; unite. Breaking with precedent, President Truman ordered the military to *incorporate* blacks into every branch of the armed services. also ADJ.

incorrigible ADJ. uncorrectable. Though Widow Douglass hoped to reform Huck, Miss Watson pronounced him *incorrigible* and said he would come to no good end.

incredulous ADJ. unwilling or unable to believe; skeptical. When Marco claimed he hadn't eaten the jelly doughnut, Joyce took one *incredulous* look at his smeared face and laughed.

incrustation N. hard coating or crust. In dry dock, we scraped off the *incrustation* of dirt and barnacles that covered the hull of the ship.

incumbent N. officeholder. The newly elected public official received valuable advice from the previous *incumbent*. also ADJ.

indefatigable ADJ. tireless. Although the effort of taking out the garbage tired Wayne out for the entire morning, when it came to partying, he was *indefatigable*.

indelible ADJ. not able to be erased. The *indelible* ink left a permanent mark on my shirt. Young Bill Clinton's meeting with President Kennedy made an *indelible* impression on the youth.

● **indict** V. charge. The district attorney didn't want to *indict* the suspect until she was sure she had a strong enough case to convince a jury. indictment, N.

● **indifferent** ADJ. unmoved or unconcerned by; mediocre. Because Consuela felt no desire to marry, she was *indifferent* to Edward's constant proposals. Not only was she *indifferent* to him personally, but she felt that, given his general silliness, he would make an *indifferent* husband.

indigenous ADJ. native. Cigarettes are made of tobacco, a plant *indigenous* to the New World.

indisputable ADJ. too certain to be disputed. In the face of these *indisputable* statements, I withdraw my complaint.

indomitable ADJ. unconquerable; unyielding. Focusing on her final vault despite her twisted ankle, gymnastics star Kerri Strug proved she had an *indomitable* will to win.

indubitable ADJ. unable to be doubted; unquestionable. Auditioning for the chorus line, Molly was an *indubitable* hit: the director fired the leading lady and hired Molly in her place!

● **induce** V. persuade; bring about. After the quarrel, Tina said nothing could *induce* her to talk to Tony again. inducement, N.

indulgent ADJ. humoring; yielding; lenient. Jay's mom was excessively *indulgent*: she bought him every Nintendo cartridge and video game on the market. She *indulged* Jay so much, she spoiled him rotten.

● **industrious** ADJ. diligent; hard-working. Look busy when the boss walks past your desk; it never hurts to appear *industrious*. industry, N.

ineffable ADJ. unutterable; unable to be expressed in speech. Looking down at her newborn daughter, Ruth felt such *ineffable* joy that, for the first time in her adult life, she had no words to convey what was in her heart.

● **inept** ADJ. lacking skill; unsuited; incompetent. The *inept* glovemaker was all thumbs. ineptitude, ineptness, N.

inevitable ADJ. unavoidable. Though death and taxes are both supposedly *inevitable*, some people avoid paying taxes for years.

● **infallible** ADJ. unerring; faultless. Jane refused to believe the pope was *infallible*, reasoning: "All human beings are capable of error. The pope is a human being. Therefore, the pope is capable of error."

infamous ADJ. notoriously bad. Charles Manson and Jeffrey Dahmer are both *infamous* killers.

infer V. deduce; conclude. From the students' glazed looks, it was easy for me to *infer* that they were bored out of their minds. inference, N.

infernal ADJ. pertaining to hell; devilish. Batman was baffled: he could think of no way to hinder the Joker's *infernal* scheme to destroy the city.

infinitesimal ADJ. exceedingly small; so small as to be almost nonexistent. Making sure everyone was aware she was on an extremely strict diet, Melanie said she would have only an *infinitesimal* sliver of pie.

infraction - intrude

infraction N. violation (of a rule or regulation); breach. When Dennis Rodman butted heads with the referee, he committed a clear *infraction* of NBA rules.

● **ingenious** ADJ. clever; resourceful. Kit admired the *ingenious* way that her computer keyboard opened up to reveal the built-in CD-ROM below. ingenuity, N.

● **ingenuous** ADJ. naive and trusting; young; unsophisticated. The woodsman had not realized how *ingenuous* Little Red Riding Hood was until he heard that she had gone off for a walk in the woods with the Big Bad Wolf.

● **ingrate** N. ungrateful person. That *ingrate* Bob sneered at the tie I gave him.

ingratiate V. make an effort to become popular with others. In *All About Eve,* the heroine, an aspiring actress, wages a clever campaign to *ingratiate* herself with Margo Channing, an established star.

● **inherent** ADJ. firmly established by nature or habit. Katya's *inherent* love of justice caused her to champion anyone she considered treated unfairly by society.

inhibit V. restrain; retard or prevent. Only two things *inhibited* him from taking a punch at Mike Tyson: Tyson's left hook, and Tyson's right jab. The protective undercoating on my car *inhibits* the formation of rust.

● **initiate** V. begin; originate; receive into a group. The college is about to *initiate* a program in reducing math anxiety among students.

inkling N. hint. This came as a complete surprise to me as I did not have the slightest *inkling* of your plans.

inlet N. small bay; narrow passage between islands; entrance. Seeking shelter from the gale, Drake sailed the *Golden Hind* into a protected *inlet,* where he hoped to wait out the storm.

● **innate** ADJ. inborn. Mozart's parents soon recognized young Wolfgang's *innate* talent for music.

● **innocuous** ADJ. harmless. An occasional glass of wine with dinner is relatively *innocuous* and should have no ill effect on you.

innovation N. change; introduction of something new. Although Richard liked to keep up with all the latest technological *innovations,* he didn't always abandon tried and true techniques in favor of something new. innovate, V.

inopportune ADJ. untimely; poorly chosen. A punk rock concert is an *inopportune* setting for a quiet conversation.

inordinate ADJ. unrestrained; excessive. She had an *inordinate* fondness for candy, eating two or three boxes in a single day.

inquisitor N. questioner (especially harsh); investigator. Fearing being grilled ruthlessly by the secret police, Masha faced her *inquisitors* with trepidation.

insatiable ADJ. not easily satisfied; greedy. Welty's thirst for knowledge was *insatiable;* she was in the library day and night.

● **inscrutable** ADJ. impenetrable; not readily understood; mysterious. Experienced poker players try to keep their expressions *inscrutable,* hiding their reactions to the cards behind a so-called "poker face."

insidious ADJ. treacherous; stealthy; sly. The fifth column is *insidious* because it works secretly within our territory for our defeat.

● **insightful** ADJ. discerning; perceptive. Sol thought he was very *insightful* about human behavior, but he was actually clueless as to why people acted the way the did.

insipid ADJ. lacking in flavor; dull. Flat prose and flat ginger ale are equally *insipid*: both lack sparkle.

insolence N. impudent disrespect; haughtiness. How dare you treat me so rudely! The manager will hear of your *insolence.* insolent, ADJ.

insomnia N. wakefulness; inability to sleep. He refused to join us in a midnight cup of coffee because he claimed it gave him *insomnia.*

instigate V. urge; start; provoke. Rumors of police corruption led the mayor to *instigate* an investigation into the department's activities.

insubordination N. disobedience; rebelliousness. At the slightest hint of *insubordination* from the sailors of the *Bounty,* Captain Bligh had them flogged; finally, they mutinied.

insubstantial ADJ. lacking substance; insignificant; frail. His hopes for a career in acting proved *insubstantial;* no one would cast him, even in an *insubstantial* role.

insurgent ADJ. rebellious. Because the *insurgent* forces had occupied the capital and had gained control of the railway lines, several of the war correspondents covering the uprising predicted a rebel victory.

insurrection N. rebellion; uprising. In retrospect, given how badly the British treated the American colonists, the eventual *insurrection* seems inevitable.

● **intangible** ADJ. not able to be perceived by touch; vague. Though the financial benefits of his Oxford post were meager, Lewis was drawn to it by its *intangible* rewards: prestige, intellectual freedom, the fellowship of his peers.

integrity N. uprightness; wholeness. Lincoln, whose personal *integrity* has inspired millions, fought a civil war to maintain the *integrity* of the Republic, that these United States might remain undivided for all time.

interminable ADJ. endless. Although his speech lasted for only twenty minutes, it seemed *interminable* to his bored audience.

intermittent ADJ. periodic; on and off. The outdoor wedding reception had to be moved indoors to avoid the *intermittent* showers that fell on and off all afternoon.

interrogate V. question closely; cross-examine. Knowing that the Nazis would *interrogate* him about his background, the secret agent invented a cover story that would help him meet their questions.

intimidate V. frighten. I'll learn karate and then those big bullies won't be able to *intimidate* me any more.

intransigence N. refusal of any compromise; stubbornness. When I predicted that the strike would be over in a week, I didn't expect to encounter such *intransigence* from both sides. intransigent, ADJ.

● **intricacy** N. complexity; knottiness. Philip spent many hours designing mazes of such great *intricacy* that none of his classmates could solve them. intricate, ADJ.

intrigue V. fascinate; interest. Holmes's air of reserve *intrigued* Irene Adler; she wanted to know just what made the great detective tick.

intrinsic ADJ. essential; inherent; built-in. Although my grandmother's china has little *intrinsic* value, I shall always cherish it for the memories it evokes.

introspective ADJ. looking within oneself. Though young Francis of Assisi led a wild and worldly life, even he had *introspective* moments during which he examined his soul.

intrude V. trespass; enter as an uninvited person. She hesitated to *intrude* on their conversation.

WORD LIST 19 **intuition - longevity**

intuition N. immediate insight; power of knowing without reasoning. Even though Tony denied that anything was wrong, Tina trusted her *intuition* that something was bothering him. intuitive, ADJ.

inundate V. overwhelm; flood; submerge. This semester I am *inundated* with work: you should see the piles of paperwork flooding my desk. Until the great dam was build, the waters of the Nile used to *inundate* the river valley every year.

invalidate V. discredit; nullify. The relatives who received little or nothing sought to *invalidate* the will by claiming that the deceased had not been in his right mind when he had signed the document.

invective N. abuse. He had expected criticism but not the *invective* that greeted his proposal.

irascible ADJ. irritable; easily angered. Pop had what people call a hair-trigger temper; he was a hot-tempered, *irascible* guy.

irksome ADJ. annoying; tedious. The petty rules and regulations Bill had to follow at work irritated him: he found them uniformly *irksome*.

● **irony** N. hidden sarcasm or satire; use of words that seem to mean the opposite of what they actually mean. Gradually his listeners began to realize that the excessive praise he was lavishing on his opponent was actually *irony;* he was in fact ridiculing the poor fool.

irrational ADJ. illogical; lacking reason; insane. Many people have such an *irrational* fear of snakes that they panic at the sight of a harmless garter snake.

irrelevant ADJ. not applicable; unrelated. No matter how *irrelevant* the patient's mumblings may seem, they give us some indications of what he has on his mind.

isolate V. keep apart; pinpoint; quarantine. The medical researchers *isolated* themselves in a remote village. Until they could *isolate* the cause of the plague and develop an effective vaccine, they had to avoid potential carriers of the disease. Anyone infected they *isolated* immediately.

itinerant ADJ. wandering; traveling. He was an *itinerant* peddler and traveled through Pennsylvania and Virginia selling his wares. also N.

jabber V. chatter rapidly or unintelligibly. Why does the fellow insist on *jabbering* away in French when I can't understand a word he says?

jargon N. language used by a special group; technical terminology; gibberish. The computer salesmen at the store used a *jargon* of their own that we simply couldn't follow; we had no idea what they were jabbering about.

jaunty ADJ. lighthearted; animated; easy and carefree. In *Singing in the Rain*, Gene Kelly sang and danced his way through the lighthearted title number in a properly *jaunty* style.

jeopardize V. endanger; imperil; put at risk. You can't give me a D in chemistry; you'll *jeopardize* my chances of getting into M.I.T. jeopardy, N.

jocose ADJ. giving to joking. The salesman was so *jocose* that many of his customers suggested that he become a stand-up comic.

jocular ADJ. said or done in jest. Although Bill knew the boss hated jokes, he couldn't resist making one *jocular* remark.

judicious ADJ. sound in judgment; wise. At a key moment in his life, he made a *judicious* investment that was the foundation of his later wealth.

justification N. good or just reason; defense; excuse. The jury found him guilty of the more serious charge because they could see no possible *justification* for his actions.

juxtapose V. place side by side. You'll find it easier to compare the two paintings if you *juxtapose* them.

kindle V. start a fire; inspire. One of the first things Ben learned in the Boy Scouts was how to *kindle* a fire by rubbing two dry sticks together. Her teacher's praise for her poetry *kindled* a spark of hope inside Maya.

knit V. contract into wrinkles; grow together. Whenever David worries, his brow *knits* in a frown. When he broke his leg, he sat around the house all day waiting for the bones to *knit*.

laborious ADJ. demanding much work or care; tedious. In putting together his dictionary of the English language, Doctor Johnson undertook a *laborious* task.

laconic ADJ. brief and to the point. Many of the characters portrayed by Clint Eastwood are *laconic* types, rugged men of few words.

laggard ADJ. slow; sluggish. The sailor had been taught not to be *laggard* in carrying out orders. lag, N., V.

lament V. grieve; express sorrow. Even advocates of the war *lamented* the loss of so many lives in combat. lamentation, N.

lampoon V. ridicule. This hilarious article *lampoons* the pretensions of some movie moguls. also N.

● **larceny** N. theft. Because of the prisoner's long record of thefts, the district attorney refused to reduce the charge from grand *larceny* to petty *larceny*.

latent ADJ. potential but undeveloped; dormant; hidden. Polaroid pictures are popular at parties, because you can see the *latent* photographic image gradually appear before your eyes.

laud V. praise. The NFL *lauded* Boomer Esiason's efforts to raise money to combat cystic fibrosis. laudable, laudatory, ADJ.

leaven V. cause to rise or grow lighter; mix in something that transforms, alleviates, or enlivens. As bread dough is *leavened*, it puffs up, expanding in volume. also N.

lenience N. mildness; permissiveness. Considering the gravity of the offense, we were surprised by the *lenience* of the sentence. also leniency; lenient, ADJ.

lethal ADJ. deadly. It is unwise to leave *lethal* weapons where children may find them.

lethargic ADJ. drowsy; dull. The stuffy room made her *lethargic:* she felt as if she was about to nod off.

levity N. lack of seriousness; lightness. Stop giggling and wiggling around in your seats: such *levity* is improper in church.

libel N. defamatory statement; act of writing something that smears a person's character. If Batman wrote that the Joker was a dirty, rotten, mass-murdering criminal, could the Joker sue Batman for *libel?*

lilliputian ADJ. extremely small. Tiny and delicate, the model was built on a *lilliputian* scale. also N.

linger V. loiter or dawdle; continue or persist. Hoping to see Juliet pass by, Romeo *lingered* outside the Capulet house for hours. Though Mother made stuffed cabbage on Monday, the smell *lingered* around the house for days.

loath ADJ. reluctant; disinclined. Fearing for her son's safety, the overprotective mother was *loath* to let him go on the class trip.

loathe V. detest. Booing and hissing, the audience showed how much they *loathed* the wicked villain.

lofty ADJ. very high. Though Barbara Jordan's fellow students used to tease her about her *lofty* ambitions, she rose to hold one of the highest positions in the land.

longevity N. long life. When he reached 90, the old man was proud of his *longevity*.

WORD LIST 20   **loquacious - miserly**

loquacious ADJ. talkative. She is very *loquacious* and can speak on the telephone for hours.

lucid ADJ. easily understood; clear; intelligible. Her explanation was *lucid* enough for a child to grasp.

lucrative ADJ. profitable. He turned his hobby into a *lucrative* profession.

lugubrious ADJ. mournful; funereal. Gloomy Gus walked around town with a *lugubrious* expression on his face.

luminous ADJ. shining; issuing light. The sun is a *luminous* body.

lure V. entice; attract. Baiting his hook with the latest fly he had put together, Grandpa Joe swore that this new fly was so attractive that it could *lure* the wariest trout out of hiding.

lurk V. stealthily lie in waiting; slink; exist unperceived. "Who knows what evils *lurk* in the hearts of men? The Shadow knows!"

luxuriant ADJ. abundant; rich and splendid; fertile. Lady Godiva was completely covered by her *luxuriant* hair.

maelstrom N. whirlpool. The canoe was tossed about in the *maelstrom*.

magnanimous ADJ. generous. Philanthropists by definition are *magnanimous;* misers, by definition, are not. magnanimity, N.

● **malice** N. hatred; spite. Jealous of Cinderella's beauty, her wicked stepsisters expressed their *malice* by forcing her to do menial tasks.

malign V. speak evil of; bad-mouth; defame. Her hatred of her ex-husband ran so deep that she *maligned* anyone who even casually dated him.

malignant ADJ. having an evil influence; virulent. This is a *malignant* disease; we may have to use drastic measures to stop its spread.

malleable ADJ. capable of being shaped by pounding; impressionable. Gold is a *malleable* metal, easily shaped into bracelets and rings. Fagin hoped Oliver was a *malleable* lad, easily shaped into a thief.

manifest ADJ. evident; visible; obvious. Digby's embarrassment when he met Madonna was *manifest:* his ears turned bright pink, he kept scuffing one shoe in the dirt, and he couldn't look her in the eye.

marked ADJ. noticeable; targeted for vengeance. He walked with a *marked* limp, a souvenir of an old I.R.A. attack. As British ambassador, he knew he was a *marked* man.

marshal V. put in order. At a debate tournament, extemporaneous speakers have only a minute or two to *marshal* their thoughts before they address their audience.

martinet N. strict disciplinarian. Captain Bligh was a *martinet* who observed each regulation to the letter.

massive ADJ. solid or heavy; large in scope; severe. The bust of Beethoven emphasizes his high forehead and *massive* brow. The composer suffered a *massive* hearing loss that left him unable to hear the music the orchestra played.

materialism N. preoccupation with physical comforts and things. By its nature, *materialism* is opposed to idealism, for where the *materialist* emphasizes the needs of the body, the idealist emphasizes the needs of the soul. materialistic, ADJ.

maverick N. rebel; nonconformist. To the masculine literary establishment, George Sand with her insistence on wearing trousers and smoking cigars was clearly a *maverick* who fought her proper womanly role.

maxim N. proverb; a truth pithily stated. Aesop's fables illustrate moral *maxims*.

meager ADJ. scanty; inadequate. Still hungry after his *meager* serving of porridge, Oliver Twist asked for a second helping.

mealymouthed ADJ. indirect in speech; hypocritical; evasive. Rather than tell Jill directly what he disliked, Jack made a few *mealymouthed* comments and tried to change the subject.

meander V. wind or turn in its course. Needing to stay close to a source of water, he followed every twist and turn of the stream as it *meandered* through the countryside.

mediate V. settle a dispute through the services of an outsider. King Solomon was asked to *mediate* a dispute between two women, each of whom claimed to be the mother of the same child.

mediocre ADJ. ordinary; commonplace. We were disappointed because he gave a rather *mediocre* performance in this role.

meditation N. reflection; thought. She reached her decision only after much *meditation*.

● **meek** ADJ. quiet and obedient; spiritless. Can Lois Lane see through Superman's disguise and spot the superhero masquerading as the *meek,* timorous Clark Kent?

melancholy ADJ. gloomy; morose; blue. To Eugene, stuck in his small town, a train whistle was a *melancholy* sound, for it made him think of all the places he would never get to see.

mentor N. counselor; teacher. During this very trying period, she could not have had a better *mentor,* for her adviser was sympathetic and understanding.

mercantile ADJ. concerning trade. Seeking candy bars to his classmates whose parents had packed their lunch boxes with apples and carrot sticks, George clearly was destined to be a *mercantile* success.

mercenary ADJ. interested in money or gain. Andy's every act was prompted by *mercenary* motives: his first question was always "What's in it for me?"

mercurial ADJ. capricious; changing; fickle. Quick as quicksilver to change, he was *mercurial* in nature and therefore unreliable.

mesmerize V. hypnotize; fascinate. On a long stretch of road between Fresno and Los Angeles, the open highway began to *mesmerize* Richard; he pulled over to the side of the road and rested to free himself from highway hypnosis.

● **meticulous** ADJ. excessively careful; painstaking; scrupulous. Martha Stewart is a *meticulous* housekeeper, fussing about each and every detail that goes into making up her perfect home.

migratory ADJ. wandering. The return of the *migratory* birds to the northern sections of this country is a harbinger of spring.

minute ADJ. extremely small. The twins resembled one another closely; only *minute* differences set them apart.

misanthrope N. one who hates mankind. In *Gulliver's Travels,* Swift portrays an image of humanity as vile, degraded beasts; for this reason, some critics consider him a *misanthrope*.

● **misconception** N. misunderstanding; misinterpretation. I'm afraid you are suffering from a *misconception*, Mr. Collins: I do not want to marry you at all.

misconstrue v. interpret incorrectly; misjudge. She took the passage seriously rather than humorously because she *misconstrued* the author's ironic tone.

miserly ADJ. stingy; mean. The *miserly* old man greedily counted the gold coins he had hoarded over the years.

WORD LIST 21 **misnomer - notorious**

misnomer N. wrong name; incorrect designation. His tyrannical conduct proved to us all that his nickname, King Eric the Just, was a *misnomer*.

● **misrepresent** V. give a false or incorrect impression, usually intentionally. The ad "Lovely Florida building site with water view" *misrepresented* the property, which was actually ten acres of bottomless swamp.

mitigate V. appease; moderate. Nothing Jason did could *mitigate* Medea's anger; she refused to forgive him for betraying her.

mobile ADJ. movable; not fixed. The *mobile* blood bank operated by the Red Cross visited our neighborhood today. mobility, N.

● **mock** V. ridicule; imitate, often in derision. It is unkind to *mock* anyone; it is stupid to *mock* anyone significantly bigger than you. mockery, N.

mode N. prevailing style; manner; way of doing something. The rock star had to have her hair done in the latest *mode*: frizzed, with occasional moussed spikes for variety. Henry plans to adopt a simpler *mode* of life: he is going to become a mushroom hunter and live off the land.

mollify V. soothe. The airline customer service representative tried to *mollify* the angry passenger by offering her a seat in first class.

momentous ADJ. very important. When Marie and Pierre Curie discovered radium, they had no idea of the *momentous* impact their discovery would have upon society.

monarchy N. government under a single ruler. Though England today is a *monarchy*, there is some question whether it will be one in 20 years, given the present discontent at the prospect of Prince Charles as king.

monochromatic ADJ. having only one color. Most people who are color blind actually can distinguish several colors; some, however, have a truly *monochromatic* view of a world all in shades of gray.

● **monotony** N. sameness leading to boredom. What could be more deadly dull than the *monotony* of punching numbers into a computer hour after hour?

monumental ADJ. massive; immense. Writing a dictionary is a *monumental* task; so is reading one.

moratorium N. suspension of activity; authorized period of delay (of a payment, etc.). If we declare a *moratorium* and delay collecting all debts for six months, I am sure the farmers will be able to meet their bills.

morose ADJ. ill-humored; sullen; melancholy. Forced to take early retirement, Bill acted *morose* for months; then, all of a sudden, he shook off his sullen mood and was his usual cheerful self.

morsel N. small bit of food. "No, thank you, Aunt Polly," he said. "I'm so stuffed I can't eat another *morsel*."

mortify V. humiliate; punish the flesh. She was so *mortified* by her blunder that she ran to her room in tears.

muddle V. confuse; mix up. His thoughts were *muddled* and chaotic. also N.

mural N. wall painting. The walls of the Chicano Community Center are covered with *murals* painted in the style of Diego Rivera, the great Mexican artist.

murky ADJ. dark and gloomy; thick with fog; vague. The *murky* depths of the swamp were so dark that you couldn't tell the vines and branches from the snakes.

muse V. ponder. For a moment he *mused* about the beauty of the scene, but his thoughts soon changed as he recalled his own personal problems. also N.

● **mutability** N. ability to change in form; fickleness. Going from rags to riches, and then back to rags again, the bankrupt financier was a victim of the *mutability* of fortune.

muted ADJ. silent; muffled; toned down. Thanks to the thick, sound-absorbing walls of the cathedral, only *muted* traffic noise reached the worshippers within.

mutinous ADJ. unruly; rebellious. The captain had to use force to quiet his *mutinous* crew.

nadir N. lowest point. Although few people realized it, the Dow-Jones averages had reached their *nadir* and would soon begin an upward surge.

● **naivete** N. quality of being unsophisticated; simplicity; artlessness; gullibility. Touched by the *naivete* of sweet, convent-trained Cosette, Marius pledges himself to protect her innocence. naive, ADJ.

narrative ADJ. related to telling a story. A born teller of tales, Olsen used her impressive *narrative* skills to advantage in her story, "I Stand Here Ironing."

navigable ADJ. wide and deep enough to allow ships to pass through; able to be steered. So much sand had built up at the bottom of the canal that the waterway was barely *navigable*.

nebulous ADJ. vague; hazy; cloudy. After 20 years, she had only a *nebulous* memory of her grandmother's face.

negligence N. neglect; failure to take reasonable care. Tommy failed to put back the cover on the well after he fetched his pail of water; because of his *negligence*, Kitty fell in.

negligible ADJ. so small, trifling, or unimportant that it may be easily disregarded. Because the damage to his car had been *negligible*, Michael decided he wouldn't bother to report the matter to his insurance company.

neologism N. new or newly coined word or phrase. As we invent new devices and professions, we must also invent *neologisms* such as "microcomputer" and "astronaut" to describe them.

neophyte N. recent convert; beginner. This mountain slope contains slides that will challenge experts as well as *neophytes*.

● **nocturnal** ADJ. relating to, occurring, or active in the night. Mr. Jones obtained a watchdog to prevent the *nocturnal* raids on his chicken coops.

nonchalance N. indifference; lack of concern; composure. Cool, calm, and collected under fire, James Bond shows remarkable *nonchalance* in the face of danger.

nondescript ADJ. undistinctive; ordinary. The private detective was a *nondescript* fellow with no outstanding features, the sort of person one would never notice in a crowd.

nonentity N. person or thing of no importance; nonexistence. Don't dismiss John as a *nonentity*; in his quiet way, he's very important to the firm.

● **nostalgia** N. homesickness; longing for the past. My grandfather seldom spoke of life in the old country; he had little patience with *nostalgia*. nostalgic, ADJ.

notable ADJ. conspicuous; important; distinguished. Normally *notable* for his calm in the kitchen, today the head cook was shaking, for the *notable* chef Julia Child was coming to dinner.

● **notorious** ADJ. disreputable; widely known; scandalous. To the starlet, any publicity was good publicity: if she couldn't have a good reputation, she'd settle for being *notorious*. notoriety, N.

WORD LIST 22 novelty - overbearing

novelty N. something new; newness. The computer is no longer a *novelty* around the office; every office has one. novel, ADJ.

novice N. beginner. Even a *novice* at working with computers can install *Barron's Computer Study Program for the SAT* by following the easy steps outlined in the user's manual.

nullify V. to make invalid; make null or void. Once the contract was *nullified,* it no longer had any legal force.

● **nurture** V. nourish; educate; foster. The Head Start program attempts to *nurture* pre-kindergarten children so that they will do well when they enter public school. also N.

nutrient N. nourishing substance. As a budding nutritionist, Kim has learned to design diets that contain foods rich in important basic *nutrients.*

obdurate ADJ. stubborn. The manager was *obdurate* in refusing to discuss the workers' grievances.

obfuscate V. confuse; muddle; make unclear. Occasionally in talking with patients doctors seem to use medical terms to *obfuscate* them rather than to inform them about the state of their health.

objective ADJ. not influenced by emotions; fair. Even though he was her son, she tried to be *objective* about his behavior.

objective N. goal; aim. A degree in medicine was her ultimate *objective.*

obligatory ADJ. required; legally or morally binding. It is *obligatory* that books borrowed from the library be returned within two weeks.

oblique ADJ. indirect; slanting (deviating from the perpendicular or from a straight line). Casting a quick, *oblique* glance at the reviewing stand, the sergeant ordered the company to march "*Oblique* Right."

obliterate V. destroy completely. In the film *Independence Day* the explosion *obliterated* the White House, vaporizing it completely.

oblivion N. obscurity; forgetfulness. After a brief period of popularity, Hurston's works fell into *oblivion;* no one bothered to reprint them, or even to read them any more.

oblivious ADJ. inattentive or unmindful; wholly absorbed. Deep in her book, Nancy was *oblivious* of the noisy squabbles of her brother and his friends.

● **obnoxious** ADJ. offensive; objectionable. A sneak and a tattletale, Sid was an *obnoxious* little brat.

● **obscure** ADJ. dark; vague; unclear. Even after I read the poem a fourth time, its meaning was still *obscure.* obscurity, N.

● **obscure** V. darken; make unclear. At times he seemed purposely to *obscure* his meaning, preferring mystery to clarity.

obsequious ADJ. slavishly attentive; servile; fawning; sycophantic. Why are some waiters in fancy restaurants so *obsequious*? What makes them think diners want to have people fawning all over them?

obsessive ADJ. related to thinking about something constantly; preoccupying. Ballet, which had been a hobby, began to dominate her life; her love of dancing became *obsessive.*

obsolescent ADJ. going out of use. Given how quickly computer technology changes, I've had to reconcile myself to the fact that, no matter how up-to-date a system I buy, it's practically *obsolescent* as soon as I've gotten it out of its box.

obsolete ADJ. outmoded. "Hip" is an *obsolete* expression; it went out with love beads and tie-dye shirts.

obtrude V. push (oneself or one's ideas) forward or intrude; butt in; stick out or extrude. Because Fanny was reluctant to *obtrude* her opinions about child-raising upon her daughter-in-law, she kept a close watch on her tongue. obtrusive, ADJ.

● **offensive** ADJ. attacking; insulting; distasteful. Getting into street brawls is no minor matter for professional boxers, who are required by law to restrict their *offensive* impulses to the ring.

officious ADJ. meddlesome; excessively pushing in offering one's services. After her long flight, Jill just wanted to nap, but the *officious* bellboy was intent on showing her all the special features of the deluxe suite.

olfactory ADJ. concerning the sense of smell. A wine taster must have a discriminating palate and a keen *olfactory* sense, for a good wine appeals both to the taste buds and to the nose.

ominous ADJ. threatening. Those clouds are *ominous;* they suggest a severe storm is on the way.

omnivorous ADJ. eating both plant and animal food; devouring everything. Some animals, including man, are *omnivorous* and eat both meat and vegetables; others are either carnivorous or herbivorous.

● **opaque** ADJ. not transparent; impenetrable to light. The *opaque* window shade kept the sunlight out of the room. opacity, N.

opportunist N. individual who sacrifices principles for expediency by taking advantage of circumstances. Forget ethics! He's such an *opportunist* that he'll vote in favor of any deal that will give him a break.

opprobrium N. public disgrace or reproach; vilification. How did the Republicans manage to turn the once-honored name of "liberal" into a term of *opprobrium?*

● **optimist** N. person who looks on the good side. The pessimist says the glass is half-empty; the *optimist* says it is half-full.

opulence N. extreme wealth; luxuriousness; abundance. The glitter and *opulence* of the ballroom took Cinderella's breath away. opulent, ADJ.

orator N. public speaker. The abolitionist Frederick Douglass was a brilliant *orator* whose speeches brought home to his audience the evils of slavery.

ordeal N. severe trial or affliction. June was so painfully shy that it was an *ordeal* for her to speak up when the teacher called on her in class.

ornate ADJ. excessively or elaborately decorated. The furnishings of homes shown on *Lifestyles of the Rich and Famous* tend to be highly *ornate.*

ostentatious ADJ. showy; pretentious; trying to attract attention. Trump's latest casino in Atlantic City is the most *ostentatious* gambling palace in the East: it easily outglitters its competitors. ostentation, N.

outlandish ADJ. bizarre; peculiar; unconventional. The eccentric professor who engages in markedly *outlandish* behavior is a stock figure in novels with an academic setting.

● **outmoded** ADJ. no longer stylish; old-fashioned. Unconcerned about keeping in style, Lenore was perfectly happy to wear *outmoded* clothes as long as they were clean and unfrayed.

outwit V. outsmart; trick. By disguising himself as an old woman, Holmes was able to *outwit* his pursuers and escape capture.

overbearing ADJ. bossy; arrogant; decisively important. Certain of her own importance, and of the unimportance of everyone else, Lady Bracknell was intolerably *overbearing* in her manner. "In choosing a husband," she said, "good birth is of *overbearing* importance; compared to that, neither wealth nor talent signifies."

WORD LIST 23   overt - pervasive

overt ADJ. open to view. According to the United States Constitution, a person must commit an *overt* act before he or she may be tried for treason.

● **pacifist** N. one opposed to force; antimilitarist. Shooting his way through the jungle, Rambo was clearly not a *pacifist*.

● **pacify** V. soothe; make calm or quiet; subdue. Dentists criticize the practice of giving fussy children sweets to *pacify* them.

painstaking ADJ. expending or showing diligent care and great effort. The new high frequency word list is the result of *painstaking* efforts on the part of our research staff.

palatable ADJ. agreeable; pleasing to the taste. Neither Jack's underbaked opinions nor his overcooked casseroles were *palatable* to me.

pallid ADJ. pale; wan. Because his occupation required that he work at night and sleep during the day, he had an exceptionally *pallid* complexion.

panacea N. cure-all; remedy for all diseases. Some people claim that vitamin C is a *panacea* that can cure everything from cancer to the common cold.

pandemonium N. wild tumult. When the ships collided in the harbor, *pandemonium* broke out among the passengers.

parable N. short tale illustrating a moral principle. In the *parable* of the good shepherd, Jesus encourages his followers to seek those who have strayed from the flock.

● **paradox** N. something apparently contradictory in nature; statement that looks false but is actually correct. Richard presents a bit of a *paradox,* for he is a card-carrying member of both the National Rifle Association and the relatively pacifist American Civil Liberties Union.

paragon N. model of perfection. The class disliked him because the teacher was always pointing him out as a *paragon* of virtue.

paramount ADJ. foremost in importance; supreme. Proper nutrition and hygiene are of *paramount* importance in adolescent development and growth.

parched ADJ. extremely dry; very thirsty. The *parched* desert landscape seemed hostile to life.

parody N. humorous imitation; spoof; takeoff; travesty. The show *Forbidden Broadway* presents *parodies* spoofing the year's new productions playing on Broadway.

partial ADJ. incomplete; having a liking for something. In this issue we have published only a *partial* list of contributors because we lack space to acknowledge everyone. I am extremely *partial* to chocolate eclairs.

partisan ADJ. one-sided; prejudiced; committed to a party. On certain issues of principle, she refused to take a *partisan* stand, but let her conscience be her guide. also N.

partition V. divide into parts. Before their second daughter was born, Jason and Lizzie decided each child needed a room of her own, and so they *partitioned* a large bedroom into two small but separate rooms. also N.

passive ADJ. not active; acted upon. Mahatma Gandhi urged his followers to pursue a program of *passive* resistance rather then resorting to violence and acts of terrorism.

passport N. legal document identifying the bearer as a citizen of a country and allowing him or her to travel abroad. In arranging your first trip abroad, be sure to allow yourself enough time to apply for and receive your *passport*: you won't be allowed to travel without one.

● **patronize** V. support; act superior toward; be a customer of. Penniless artists hope to find some wealthy art lover who will *patronize* them. If a wine steward *patronized* me because he saw I knew nothing about fine wine, I'd refuse to *patronize* his restaurant.

paucity N. scarcity; lack. They closed the restaurant because the *paucity* of customers meant that it was a losing proposition to operate.

● **pedantic** ADJ. showing off learning; bookish. Leavening his decisions with humorous, down-to-earth anecdotes, Judge Walker was not at all the *pedantic* legal scholar. pedant, N.

pedestrian ADJ. ordinary; unimaginative. Unintentionally boring, he wrote page after page of *pedestrian* prose. (secondary meaning)

peerless ADJ. having to equal; incomparable. The reigning operatic tenor of his generation, to his admirers Luciano Pavorotti was *peerless:* no one could compare with him.

penitent ADJ. feeling regret or sorrow for one's offenses; repentant. When he realized the enormity of his crime, he became remorseful and *penitent.* also N.

perceptive ADJ. insightful; aware; wise. Although Maud was a generally *perceptive* critic, she had her blind spots: she could never see flaws in the work of her friends.

perdition N. damnation; complete ruin. Praying for salvation, young Steven feared he was damned to eternal *perdition*.

peremptory ADJ. demanding and leaving no choice. From Jack's *peremptory* knock on the door, Jill could tell he would not give up until she let him in.

perfidious ADJ. treacherous; disloyal. When Caesar realized that Brutus had betrayed him, he reproached his *perfidious* friend. perfidy, N.

perfunctory ADJ. superficial; not thorough; lacking interest, care, or enthusiasm. Giving the tabletop only a *perfunctory* swipe with her dust cloth, Betty promised herself she'd clean it more thoroughly tomorrow.

● **perjury** N. false testimony while under oath. Rather than lie under oath and perhaps be indicted for *perjury,* the witness chose to take the Fifth Amendment, refusing to answer any questions on the grounds that he might incriminate himself.

pernicious ADJ. very destructive. Crack cocaine has had a *pernicious* effect on urban society: it has destroyed families, turned children into drug dealers, and increased the spread of violent crimes.

perpetrate V. commit an offense. Only an insane person could *perpetrate* such a horrible crime.

● **perpetual** ADJ. everlasting. Ponce de Leon hoped to find the legendary fountain of *perpetual* youth. perpetuity, N.

perpetuate V. make something last; preserve from extinction. Some critics attack *The Adventures of Huckleberry Finn* because they believe Twain's book *perpetuates* a false image of blacks in this country.

peruse V. read with care. After the conflagration that burned down her house, Joan closely *perused* her home insurance policy to discover exactly what benefits her coverage provided her. perusal, N.

● **pervasive** ADJ. pervading; spread throughout every part. Despite airing them for several hours, she could not rid her clothes of the *pervasive* odor of mothballs that clung to them. pervade, V.

WORD LIST 24   **perverse - precursor**

perverse ADJ. stubbornly wrongheaded; wicked and perverted. When Jack was in a *perverse* mood, he would do the opposite of whatever Jill asked him. When Hannibal Lecter was in a *perverse* mood, he ate the flesh of his victims.

● **pessimism** N. belief that life is basically bad or evil; gloominess. Considering how well you have done in the course so far, you have no real reason for such *pessimism* about your final grade.

● **petulant** ADJ. touchy; peevish. If you'd had hardly any sleep for three nights and people kept on phoning and waking you up, you'd sound pretty *petulant,* too.

● **phenomena** N. Pl. observable facts or events. We kept careful records of the *phenomena* we noted in the course of these experiments.

● **philanthropist** N. lover of mankind; doer of good. In his role as *philanthropist* and public benefactor, John D. Rockefeller, Sr., donated millions to charity; as an individual, however, he was a tight-fisted old man.

phlegmatic ADJ. not easily excited to action or emotional displays; calm; sluggish. The nurse was a cheerful but *phlegmatic* person, untroubled by sudden emergencies.

pious ADJ. devout; religious. The challenge for church members today is how to be *pious* in the best sense, that is, to be devout without becoming hypocritical or sanctimonious. piety, N.

pique V. provoke or arouse; annoy. "I know something *you* don't know," said Lucy, trying to *pique* Ethel's interest.

pique N. irritation; resentment. She showed her *pique* at her loss by refusing to appear with the other contestants at the end of the competition.

pivotal ADJ. crucial; key; vital. The new "smart weapons" technology played a *pivotal* role in the quick resolution of the war with Iraq.

placate V. pacify; conciliate. The store manager tried to *placate* the angry customer, offering to replace the damaged merchandise or to give back her money right away.

placid ADJ. calm; peaceful. Looking at the storm-tossed waters of the lake, Bob wondered why they ever called it Lake *Placid.*

● **plagiarize** V. steal another's ideas and pass them off as one's own. The teacher could tell that the student had *plagiarized* parts of his essay; she could recognize whole paragraphs straight from *Barron's Book Notes.*

platitude N. trite remark; commonplace statement. In giving advice to his son, old Polonius expressed himself only in *platitudes;* every word out of his mouth was commonplace.

plausible ADJ. having a show of truth but open to doubt; specious. Your mother made you stay home from school because she needed you to program the VCR? I'm sorry, you'll have to come up with a more *plausible* excuse than that.

plethora N. excess; overabundance. She offered a *plethora* of excuses for her shortcomings.

pliable ADJ. flexible; yielding; adaptable. In remodeling the bathroom, we have replaced all the old, rigid lead pipes with new, *pliable* copper tubing.

plight N. condition, state (especially a bad state or condition); predicament. Loggers, unmoved by the *plight* of the spotted owl, plan to keep on logging whether or not they ruin the owl's habitat.

plunder N. loot; takings from a raid. Rubbing his hands with glee, the robber gloated over his ill-gotten *plunder.* also V.

podium N. pedestal; raised platform. The audience applauded as the conductor made his way to the *podium.*

polemical ADJ. aggressive in verbal attack; disputatious. Lexy was a master of *polemical* rhetoric; she should have worn a T-shirt with the slogan "Born to Debate."

ponderous ADJ. weighty; unwieldy. His humor lacked the light touch; his jokes were always *ponderous.*

pore V. study deeply; stare. In doing research on the SAT, we *pored* over back issues of *Scientific American* to locate articles from which reading passages had been excerpted.

porous ADJ. full of pores; like a sieve. Dancers like to wear *porous* clothing because it allows the ready passage of air.

portend V. foretell; presage. The king did not know what these omens might *portend* and asked his soothsayers to interpret them.

portly ADJ. stout; corpulent. The salesclerk diplomatically referred to the overweight customer as not fat but *portly.*

posterity N. descendants; future generations. We hope to leave a better world to *posterity.*

● **potency** N. power; effectiveness; influence. Looking at the expiration date on the cough syrup bottle, we wondered whether the medication still retained its *potency.* potent, ADJ.

potentate N. monarch; sovereign. The *potentate* spent more time at Monte Carlo than he did at home on his throne.

practical ADJ. based on experience; useful. He was a *practical* man, opposed to theory.

pragmatic ADJ. practical (as opposed to idealistic); concerned with the practical worth or impact of something. This coming trip to France should provide me with a *pragmatic* test of the value of my conversational French class.

prate V. speak foolishly; boast idly. Let us not *prate* about our qualities; rather, let our virtues speak for themselves.

prattle V. babble. Baby John *prattled* on and on about the cats and his ball and the Cookie Monster.

preamble N. introductory statement. In the *Preamble* to the Constitution, the purpose of the document is set forth.

precarious ADJ. uncertain; risky. Saying the stock would be a *precarious* investment, the broker advised her client against purchasing it.

● **precedent** N. something preceding in time that may be used as an authority or guide for future action. If I buy you a car for your sixteenth birthday, your brothers will want me to buy them cars when they turn sixteen, too; I can't afford to set such an expensive *precedent.*

precipitate ADJ. rash; premature; abrupt; hasty; sudden. Though I was angry enough to resign on the spot, I had enough sense to keep myself from quitting a job in such a *precipitate* fashion.

precipitous ADJ. steep; overhasty. This hill is difficult to climb because it is so *precipitous*; one slip, and our descent will be *precipitous* as well.

preclude V. make impossible; eliminate. Because the band was already booked to play in Hollywood on New Year's Eve, that *precluded* their accepting the New Year's Eve gig in London they were offered.

precursor N. forerunner. Though Gray and Burns share many traits with the Romantic poets who followed them, most critics consider them *precursors* of the Romantic Movement, not true Romantics.

predator - promote

● **predator** N. creature that seizes and devours another animal; person who robs or exploits others. Not just cats, but a wide variety of *predators*—owls, hawks, weasels, foxes—catch mice for dinner. A carnivore is by definition *predatory*, for it *preys* on weaker creatures.

predetermine V. predestine; settle or decide beforehand; influence markedly. Romeo and Juliet believed that Fate had *predetermined* their meeting. Bea gathered estimates from caterers, florists, and stationers so that she could *predetermine* the costs of holding a catered buffet. Philip's love of athletics *predetermined* his choice of a career in sports marketing.

predilection N. partiality; preference. Although my mother wrote all sorts of poetry over the years, she had a definite *predilection* for occasional verse.

preeminent ADJ. outstanding; superior. The king traveled to Boston because he wanted the *preeminent* surgeon in the field to perform the operation.

preempt V. head off; forestall by acting first; appropriate for oneself; supplant. Hoping to *preempt* any attempts by the opposition to make educational reform a hot political issue, the candidate set out her own plan to revitalize the public schools. preemptive, ADJ.

prelate N. church dignitary. The archbishop of Moscow and other high-ranking *prelates* visited the Russian Orthodox seminary.

● **premise** N. assumption; postulate. Based on the *premise* that there's no fool like an old fool, P. T. Barnum hired a 90-year-old clown for his circus.

● **premonition** N. forewarning. We ignored these *premonitions* of disaster because they appeared to be based on childish fears.

preposterous ADJ. absurd; ridiculous. When he tried to downplay his youthful experiments with marijuana by saying he hadn't inhaled, we all thought, "What a *preposterous* excuse!"

prescience N. ability to foretell the future. Given the current wave of Japan-bashing, it does not take *prescience* for me to foresee problems in our future trade relations with Japan.

preside V. act as president or chairman; exercise control. When the club president cannot attend a meeting, the vice-president will *preside* over that session.

prestige N. impression produced by achievements or reputation. Many students want to go to Harvard College not for the education offered but for the *prestige* of Harvard's name.

presumptuous ADJ. taking liberties; overstepping bounds; nervy. I thought it was *presumptuous* of Mort to butt into Bishop Tutu's talk with Mrs. Clinton and ask them for their autographs; I wouldn't have had the nerve.

pretentious ADJ. ostentatious; pompous; making unjustified claims; overly ambitious. None of the other prize winners are wearing their medals; isn't it a bit *pretentious* of you to wear yours?

● **prevail** V. triumph; predominate; prove superior in strength, power, or influence; be current. A radical committed to social change, Reed had no patience with the conservative views that *prevailed* in the America of his day. prevalent, ADJ., prevailing, ADJ.

prevaricate V. lie. Some people believe that to *prevaricate* in a good cause is justifiable and regard their false statement as a "white lie."

● **prey** N. target of a hunt; victim. In *Stalking the Wild Asparagus*, Euell Gibbons has as his *prey* not wild beasts but wild plants. also V.

privation N. hardship; want. In his youth, he knew hunger and *privation*.

procrastinate V. postpone; delay or put off. Looking at four years of receipts and checks he still had to sort through, Bob was truly sorry he had *procrastinated* for so long and not finished filing his taxes long ago.

prodigal ADJ. wasteful; reckless with money. Don't be so *prodigal* spending my money; when you've earned some money, you can waste it as much as you want! also N.

prodigious ADJ. marvelous; enormous. Watching the champion weight lifter heave the weighty barbell to shoulder height and then boost it overhead, we marveled at his *prodigious* strength.

prodigy N. highly gifted child; extraordinary accomplishment or event. Menuhin was a *prodigy*, performing wonders on his violin when he was barely eight years old.

profane V. violate; desecrate; treat unworthily. The members of the mysterious Far Eastern cult sought to kill the British explorer because he had *profaned* the sanctity of their holy goblet by using it as an ashtray. also ADJ.

profligate N. dissipated; wasteful; wildly immoral. Although surrounded by wild and *profligate* companions, she nevertheless managed to retain some sense of decency.

● **profound** ADJ. deep; not superficial; complete. Freud's remarkable insights into human behavior caused his fellow scientists to honor him as a *profound* thinker. profundity, N.

profusion N. overabundance; lavish expenditure; excess. Freddy was so overwhelmed by the *profusion* of choices on the menu that he knocked over his wine glass and soaked his host. He made *profuse* apologies to his host, the waiter, the bus boy, the people at the next table, and the man in the men's room giving out paper towels.

progenitor N. ancestor. The Roth family, whose *progenitors* emigrated from Germany early in the nineteenth century, settled in Peru, Illinois.

● **proliferation** N. rapid growth; spread; multiplication. Times of economic hardship inevitably encourage the *proliferation* of countless get-rich-quick schemes. proliferate, V.

● **prolific** ADJ. abundantly fruitful. My editors must assume I'm a *prolific* writer: they expect me to revise six books this year!

● **prologue** N. introduction (to a poem or play). In the *prologue* to *Romeo and Juliet*, Shakespeare introduces the audience to the feud between the Montagues and the Capulets.

prolong V. make longer; draw out; lengthen. In their determination to discover ways to *prolong* human life, doctors fail to take into account that longer lives are not always happier ones.

● **prominent** ADJ. conspicuous; notable; sticking out. Have you ever noticed that Prince Charles's *prominent* ears make him resemble the big-eared character in *Mad* comics?

promontory N. high point of land jutting out into a body of water; headland. They erected a lighthouse on the *promontory* to warn approaching ships of their nearness to the shore.

● **promote** V. help to flourish; advance in rank; publicize. Founder of the Children's Defense Fund, Marian Wright Edelman ceaselessly *promotes* the welfare of young people everywhere.

WORD LIST 26

promulgate - quip

promulgate V. proclaim a doctrine or law; make known by official publication. When Moses came down from the mountaintop all set to *promulgate* God's commandments, he freaked out on discovering his followers worshipping a golden calf.

prone ADJ. inclined to; prostrate. She was *prone* to sudden fits of anger.

propagate V. multiply; spread. Since bacteria *propagate* more quickly in unsanitary environments, it is important to keep hospital rooms clean.

propensity N. natural inclination. Convinced of his own talent, Sol has an unfortunate *propensity* to belittle the talents of others.

● **prophetic** ADJ. foretelling the future. I have no magical *prophetic* powers; when I predict what will happen, I base my predictions on common sense. prophesy, V.

proponent N. supporter; backer. In the Senate, *proponents* of the universal health care measure lobbied to gain additional support for the controversial legislation.

propriety N. fitness; correct conduct. Miss Manners counsels her readers so that they may behave with due *propriety* in any social situation and not embarrass themselves.

prosaic ADJ. dull and unimaginative; matter-of-fact; factual. Though the ad writers had come up with a wildly imaginative campaign to publicize the company's newest product, the head office rejected it for a more *prosaic,* down-to-earth approach.

● **prosperity** N. good fortune; financial success; physical well-being. Promising to stay together "for richer, for poorer," the newlyweds vowed to be true to one another in *prosperity* and hardship alike.

protagonist N. principal character; leading actor. Emma, the *protagonist* of Jane Austen's novel, is an overindulged young woman convinced of her ability as a matchmaker.

prototype N. original work used as a model by others. The National Air and Space Museum displays the Wright brothers' first plane, the *prototype* of all the American aircraft that came after.

protract V. prolong. Seeking to delay the union members' vote, the management team tried to *protract* the negotiations endlessly, but the union representatives saw through their strategy.

protrude V. stick out. His fingers *protruded* from the holes in his gloves. protrusion, N.

protuberance N. protrusion; bulge. A ganglionic cyst is a fluid-filled tumor that develops near a joint membrane or tendon sheath, and that bulges beneath the skin, forming a *protuberance.*

provident ADJ. displaying foresight; thrifty; preparing for emergencies. In his usual *provident* manner, he had insured himself against this type of loss.

provincial ADJ. pertaining to a province; limited in outlook; unsophisticated. As *provincial* governor, Sir Henry administered the Queen's law in his remote corner of Canada. Caught up in local problems, out of touch with London news, he became sadly *provincial.*

provisional ADJ. tentative. Kim's acceptance as an American Express card holder was *provisional:* before issuing her a card, American Express wanted to check her employment record and credit history.

provocative ADJ. arousing anger or interest; annoying. In a typically *provocative* act, the bully kicked sand into the weaker man's face.

proximity N. nearness. Blind people sometimes develop a compensatory ability to sense the *proximity* of objects around them.

● **prudent** ADJ. cautious; careful. A miser hoards money not because he is *prudent* but because he is greedy. prudence, N.

prune V. cut away; trim. With the help of her editor, she was able to *prune* her manuscript into publishable form.

pseudonym N. pen name. Samuel Clemens' *pseudonym* was Mark Twain.

pugnacious ADJ. combative; disposed to fight. "Put up your dukes!" he cried, making a fist to show how *pugnacious* he was.

pulverize V. crush or grind into dust. Before sprinkling the dried herbs into the stew, Michael first *pulverized* them into a fine powder.

pummel V. beat or pound with fists. Swinging wildly, Pammy *pummeled* her brother around the head and shoulders.

punctilious ADJ. laying stress on niceties of conduct or form; minutely attentive to fine points (perhaps too much so). Percy is *punctilious* about observing the rules of etiquette whenever Miss Manners invites him to stay. punctiliousness, N.

pungent ADJ. stinging; sharp in taste or smell; caustic. The *pungent* odor of ripe Limburger cheese appealed to Simone but made Stanley gag.

puny ADJ. insignificant; tiny; weak. Our *puny* efforts to stop the flood were futile.

purveyor N. furnisher of foodstuffs; caterer. As *purveyor* of rare wines and viands, he traveled through France and Italy every year in search of new products to sell.

quack N. charlatan; impostor. Do not be misled by the exorbitant claims of this *quack;* he cannot cure you.

quagmire N. soft wet boggy land; complex or dangerous situation from which it is difficult to free oneself. Up to her knees in mud, Myra wondered how on earth she was going to extricate herself from this *quagmire.*

qualified ADJ. limited; restricted. Unable to give the candidate full support, the mayor gave him only a *qualified* endorsement. (secondary meaning)

quandary N. dilemma. When both Harvard and Stanford accepted Lori, she was in a *quandary* as to which school she should attend.

quarry N. victim; object of a hunt. The police closed in on their *quarry.*

quarry V. dig into. They *quarried* blocks of marble out of the hillside. also N.

quell V. extinguish; put down; quiet. Miss Minchin's demeanor was so stern and forbidding that she could *quell* any unrest among her students with one intimidating glance.

quench V. douse or extinguish; assuage or satisfy. What's the favorite song of the Fire Department? "Baby, *Quench* My Fire!"

querulous ADJ. fretful; whining. Even the most agreeable toddlers can begin to act *querulous* if they miss their nap.

quibble N. minor objection or complaint. Aside from a few hundred teensy-weensy *quibbles* about the set, the script, the actors, the director, the costumes, the lighting, and the props, the hypercritical critic loved the play. also V.

quip N. taunt. You are unpopular because you are too free with your *quips* and sarcastic comments. also V.

WORD LIST 27 **quiver - rejoinder**

quiver V. tremble; shake. The bird dog's nose twitched and his whiskers *quivered* as he strained eagerly against the leash. also N.

quiver N. case for arrows. Robin Hood reached back and plucked one last arrow from his *quiver*. (secondary meaning)

quixotic ADJ. idealistic but impractical. Simon's head is in the clouds; he constantly comes up with *quixotic*, unworkable schemes.

rabid ADJ. like a fanatic; furious. He was a *rabid* follower of the Dodgers and watched them play whenever he could go to the ball park.

raconteur N. storyteller. My father was a gifted *raconteur* with an unlimited supply of anecdotes.

rally V. call up or summon (forces, vital powers, etc.); revive or recuperate. Washington quickly *rallied* his troops to fight off the British attack. The patient had been sinking throughout the night, but at dawn she *rallied* and made a complete recovery.

ramble V. wander aimlessly (physically or mentally). Listening to the teacher *ramble*, Shelby wondered whether he'd ever get to the point. also N.

rampant ADJ. growing in profusion; unrestrained. In the garden, the weeds were *rampant*: they killed all the flowers that had been planted in the spring. In the city, crime was *rampant*: the burglars and muggers were out of control.

ramshackle ADJ. rickety; falling apart. The boys propped up the *ramshackle* clubhouse with a couple of boards.

rancid ADJ. having the odor of stale fat. A *rancid* odor filled the ship's galley and nauseated the crew.

rancor N. bitterness; deep-seated hatred. Thirty years after the war, she could not let go of the past but still felt an implacable *rancor* against the foe.

● **random** ADJ. without definite purpose, plan, or aim; haphazard. Although the sponsor of the raffle claimed all winners were chosen at *random*, people had their suspicions when the grand prize went to the sponsor's brother-in-law.

rant V. rave; talk excitedly; scold; make a grandiloquent speech. When he heard that I'd totaled the family car, Dad began to *rant* at me like a complete madman.

raucous ADJ. harsh and shrill; disorderly and boisterous. The *raucous* crowd of New Year's Eve revelers got progressively noisier as midnight drew near.

raze V. destroy completely. Spelling is important: to raise a building is to put it up; to *raze* a building is to tear it down.

reactionary ADJ. recoiling from progress; politically ultra-conservative. Opposing the use of English in worship services, *reactionary* forces in the church fought to reinstate the mass in Latin.

rebuff V. snub; beat back. She *rebuffed* his invitation so smoothly that he did not realize he had been snubbed.

recalcitrant ADJ. obstinately stubborn. Donkeys are reputed to be the most *recalcitrant* of animals.

recant V. disclaim or disavow; retract a previous statement; openly confess error. Those who can, keep true to their faith; those who can't, *recant*.

recapitulate V. summarize. Let us *recapitulate* what has been said thus far before going ahead.

recession N. withdrawal; time of low economic activity. The slow *recession* of the flood waters created problems for the crews working to restore power to the area.

reciprocate V. repay in kind. It was kind of Donna to have us over to dinner; I'd like us to *reciprocate* in some way, if we can.

● **recluse** N. hermit; loner. Disappointed in love, Miss Emily became a *recluse;* she shut herself away in her empty mansion and refused to see another living soul. reclusive, ADJ.

reconcile V. correct inconsistencies; become friendly after a quarrel. Every time we try to *reconcile* our checkbook with the bank statement, we quarrel. However, despite these monthly lovers' quarrels, we always manage to *reconcile*.

recount V. narrate or tell; count over again. About to *recount* the latest adventure of Sherlock Holmes, Watson lost track of exactly how many cases Holmes had solved and refused to begin his tale until he'd *recounted* them one by one.

rectify V. set right; correct. You had better send a check to *rectify* your account before American Express cancels your credit card.

rectitude N. uprightness; moral virtue; correctness of judgment. The Eagle Scout was a model of *rectitude*.

recumbent ADJ. reclining; lying down completely or in part. The command "AT EASE" does not permit you to take a *recumbent* position.

recuperate V. recover. The doctors were worried because the patient did not *recuperate* as rapidly as they had expected.

recurrent ADJ. occurring again and again. These *recurrent* attacks disturbed us and we consulted a physician.

redundant ADJ. superfluous; repetitious; excessively wordy. The bottle of wine I brought to Bob's was certainly *redundant:* how was I to know Bob owned a winery? In your essay, you repeat several points unnecessarily; try to be less *redundant* in the future. redundancy, N.

● **refine** V. free from impurities; perfect. Just as you can *refine* sugar by removing bits of cane and other unwanted material, you can *refine* verse by removing awkward metaphors and polishing rough rhymes. refinement, N.

reflect V. consider or deliberate; show; mirror. Mr. Collins *reflected* on Elizabeth's rejection of his proposal. Did it *reflect* her true feelings, he wondered. Looking at his *reflection* in the mirror, he refused to believe that she could reject such a fine figure of a man.

refraction N. bending of a ray of light. Insert a stick in a glass of water and look at it carefully. It looks bent because of the *refraction* of the light by the water.

refrain V. abstain from; resist. Whenever he heard a song with a lively chorus, Sol could never *refrain* from joining in on the refrain.

refrain N. chorus. Whenever he heard a song with a lively chorus, Sol could never refrain from joining in on the *refrain*.

● **refute** V. disprove. The defense called several respectable witnesses who were able to *refute* the false testimony of the prosecution's only witness.

regress V. move backward to an earlier, generally more primitive state. Although Timmy outgrew his need for a pacifier well over a year ago, occasionally when he's tired or nervous he *regresses* and starts sucking his thumb.

reiterate V. repeat. He *reiterated* the warning to make sure that everyone understood it.

rejoinder N. retort; comeback; reply. When someone has been rude to me, I find it particularly satisfying to come up with a quick *rejoinder*.

WORD LIST 28 **rejuvenate - restraint**

rejuvenate V. make young again. The charlatan claimed that his elixir would *rejuvenate* the aged and weary.

relegate V. banish to an inferior position; delegate; assign. After Ralph dropped his second tray of drinks that week, the manager swiftly *relegated* him to a minor post cleaning up behind the bar.

relevant ADJ. pertinent; referring to the case in hand. How *relevant* Virginia Woolf's essays are to women writers today; it's as if Woolf in the 1930s foresaw our current literary struggles. relevancy, N.

relic N. surviving remnant; memento. Egypt's Department of Antiquities prohibits tourists from taking mummies and other ancient *relics* out of the country. Mike keeps his photos of his trip to Egypt in a box with other *relics* of his travels.

● **relinquish** V. give up something with reluctance; yield. Once you get used to fringe benefits like expense account meals and a company car, it's very hard to *relinquish* them.

relish V. savor; enjoy. Watching Peter enthusiastically chow down, I thought, "Now there's a man who *relishes* a good dinner!" also N.

reminiscence N. recollection. Her *reminiscences* of her experiences are so fascinating that she ought to write a book.

remiss ADJ. negligent. He was accused of being *remiss* in his duty when the prisoner escaped.

remnant N. remainder. I suggest that you wait until the store places the *remnants* of these goods on sale.

remonstrance N. protest; objection. The authorities were deaf to the pastor's *remonstrances* about the lack of police protection in the area. remonstrate, V.

remorse N. guilt; self-reproach. The murderer felt no *remorse* for his crime.

remunerative ADJ. compensating; rewarding. I find my new work so *remunerative* that I may not return to my previous employment. remuneration, N.

renegade N. deserter; traitor. Because he had abandoned his post and joined forces with the Indians, his fellow officers considered the hero of *Dances with Wolves* a *renegade*. also ADJ.

renounce V. abandon; disown; repudiate. Even though she knew she would be burned at the stake as a witch, Joan of Arc refused to *renounce* her belief that her voices came from God. renunciation, N.

renovate V. restore to good condition; renew. They claim that they can *renovate* worn shoes so that they look like new ones.

renown N. fame. For many years an unheralded researcher, Barbara McClintock gained international *renown* when she won the Nobel Prize in Physiology and Medicine.

rent N. rip; split. Kit did an excellent job of mending the *rent* in the lining in her coat. rent, V.

repeal V. revoke; annul. What would the effect on our society be if we decriminalized drug use by *repealing* the laws against the possession and sale of narcotics?

repel V. drive away; disgust. At first, the Beast's ferocious appearance *repelled* Beauty, but she came to love the tender heart hidden behind that beastly exterior.

repertoire N. list of works of music, drama, etc., a performer is prepared to present. The opera company decided to include *Madame Butterfly* in its *repertoire* for the following season.

replenish V. fill up again. Before she could take another backpacking trip, Carla had to *replenish* her stock of freeze-dried foods.

reprehensible ADJ. deserving blame. Shocked by the viciousness of the bombing, politicians of every party uniformly condemned the terrorists' *reprehensible* deed.

repress V. restrain; hold back; crush; suppress. Anne's parents tried to curb her impetuosity without *repressing* her boundless high spirits.

reprieve N. temporary stay. During the twenty-four-hour *reprieve*, the lawyers sought to make the stay of execution permanent. also V.

reprimand V. reprove severely; rebuke. Every time Ermengarde made a mistake in class, she was afraid that Miss Minchin would *reprimand* her and tell her father how badly she was doing in school. also N.

reproachful ADJ. expressing disapproval. He never could do anything wrong without imagining the *reproachful* look in his mother's eye.

reprove V. censure; rebuke. Though Aunt Bea at times would *reprove* Opie for inattention in church, she believed he was at heart a God-fearing lad.

● **repudiate** V. disown; disavow. On separating from Tony, Tina announced that she would *repudiate* all debts incurred by her soon-to-be ex-husband.

repulsion N. distaste; act of driving back. Hating bloodshed, she viewed war with *repulsion*. Even defensive battles distressed her, for the *repulsion* of enemy forces is never accomplished bloodlessly.

reputable ADJ. respectable. If you want to buy antiques, look for a *reputable* dealer; far too many dealers today pass off fakes as genuine antiques.

rescind V. cancel. Because of the public outcry against the new taxes, the senator proposed a bill to *rescind* the unpopular financial measure.

● **reserved** ADJ. self-controlled; careful in expressing oneself. They made an odd couple: she was outspoken and uninhibited; he was cautious and *reserved*. (secondary meaning)

resignation N. patient submissiveness; statement that one is quitting a job. If Bob Cratchit had not accepted Scrooge's bullying with such *resignation*, he might have gotten up the nerve to hand in his *resignation*. resigned, ADJ.

resilient ADJ. elastic; having the power of springing back. Highly *resilient*, steel makes excellent bedsprings. resilience, N.

● **resolution** N. determination. Nothing could shake his *resolution* to succeed despite all difficulties. resolved, ADJ.

● **resolve** V. decide; settle; solve. "I have *resolved*, Watson, to travel to Bohemia to *resolve* the dispute between Irene Adler and the King. In my absence, do your best to *resolve* any mysteries that arise."

resonant ADJ. echoing; resounding; deep and full in sound. The deep, *resonant* voice of the actor James Earl Jones makes him particularly effective when he appears on stage.

respiration N. breathing. The doctor found that the patient's years of smoking had adversely affected both his lung capacity and his rate of *respiration*. respire, V.

restive ADJ. restlessly impatient; obstinately resisting control. Waiting impatiently in line to see Santa Claus, even the best-behaved children grow *restive* and start to fidget.

● **restraint** N. moderation or self-control; controlling force; restriction. Control yourself, young lady! Show some *restraint*!

WORD LIST 29   **resumption - scapegoat**

resumption N. taking up again; recommencement. During summer break, Don had not realized how much he missed university life; at the *resumption* of classes, however, he felt marked excitement and pleasure. resume, V.

resurge V. rise again; flow to and fro. It was startling to see the spirit of nationalism *resurge* as the Soviet Union disintegrated into a loose federation of ethnic and national groups. resurgence, N.

● **retain** V. keep; employ. Fighting to *retain* his seat in Congress, Senator Foghorn *retained* a new manager to head his reelection campaign.

retaliation N. repayment in kind (usually for bad treatment). Because everyone knew the Princeton Band had stolen Brown's mascot, the whole Princeton student body expected some sort of *retaliation* from Brown. retaliate, V.

● **reticent** ADJ. reserved; uncommunicative; inclined to be silent. Fearing his competitors might get advance word about his plans from talkative staff members, Hughes preferred *reticent* employees to loquacious ones.

retract V. withdraw; take back. When I saw how Fred and his fraternity brothers had trashed the frat house, I decided to *retract* my offer to let them use our summer cottage for the weekend. retraction, N.

retrieve V. recover; find and bring in. The dog was intelligent and quickly learned to *retrieve* the game killed by the hunter.

retroactive ADJ. taking effect prior to its enactment (as a law) or imposition (as a tax). Because the new pension law was *retroactive* to the first of the year, even though Martha had retired in February, she was eligible for the pension.

revelry N. boisterous merrymaking. New Year's Eve is a night of *revelry*.

● **reverent** ADJ. respectful; worshipful. Though I bow my head in church and recite the prayers, sometimes I don't feel properly *reverent*. revere, V.

revoke V. cancel; retract. Repeat offenders who continue to drive under the influence of alcohol face having their driver's licenses permanently *revoked*.

revulsion N. sudden violent change of feeling; reaction. The feelings of many people in this country who admired dictatorships underwent *revulsion* when they realized what Hitler and Mussolini were trying to do.

rift N. opening made by splitting; open space; break in friendly relations. After the recent earthquake, geologists observed several fresh *rifts* in the Hayward hills. Through a *rift* in the dense clouds the pilot glimpsed a beacon light far below. Unsure how he had offended Jo, Laurie tried to think of some way to mend the *rift* in their friendship.

rigid ADJ. stiff and unyielding; strict; hard and unbending. By living with a man to whom she was not married, George Eliot broke Victorian society's most *rigid* rule of respectable behavior.

rigor N. severity. Many settlers could not stand the *rigors* of the New England winters.

rile V. vex; irritate. Red had a hair-trigger temper: he was an easy man to *rile*.

rivulet N. small stream. As the rains continued, the small trickle of water running down the hillside grew into a *rivulet* that threatened to wash away a portion of the slope.

rousing ADJ. lively; stirring. "And now, let's have a *rousing* welcome for TV's own Roseanne Barr, who'll lead us in a *rousing* rendition of 'The Star Spangled Banner.'"

ruddy ADJ. reddish; healthy-looking. Her *ruddy* cheeks indicated that she had been spending most of her days outdoors.

rue V. regret; lament; mourn. Tina *rued* the night she met Tony and wondered how she'd ever fallen for such a jerk. rueful, ADJ.

rummage V. ransack; thoroughly search. When we *rummaged* through the trunks in the attic, we found many souvenirs of our childhood days. also N.

rupture N. act of breaking; fracture; break in harmony or peaceful relations. The *rupture* of gas lines caused by the earthquake contributed greatly to the fire that ensued.

ruse N. trick; stratagem. Because they wanted to decorate the living room for their mother's surprise birthday party, the girls tried to think of some good *ruse* to lure her out of the house for a couple of hours.

ruthless ADJ. pitiless; cruel. Captain Hook was a dangerous, *ruthless* villain who would stop at nothing to destroy Peter Pan.

saboteur N. one who commits sabotage; destroyer of property. Members of the Resistance acted as *saboteurs*, blowing up train lines to prevent supplies from reaching the Nazi army.

saccharine ADJ. cloyingly sweet. She tried to ingratiate herself, speaking sweetly and smiling a *saccharine* smile.

sagacious ADJ. keen; shrewd; having insight. Holmes is far too *sagacious* to be fooled by a simple trick like that. sagacity, N.

salutary ADJ. tending to improve; beneficial; wholesome. The punishment had a *salutary* effect on the boy, for he became a model student.

sanction V. approve; ratify. Nothing will convince me to *sanction* the engagement of my daughter to such a worthless young man.

sap V. diminish; undermine. The element kryptonite has an unhealthy effect on Superman: it *saps* his strength.

sarcasm N. scornful remarks; stinging rebuke. Though Ralph tried to ignore the mocking comments of his supposed friends, their *sarcasm* wounded him deeply.

sate V. satisfy to the full; cloy. Its hunger *sated*, the lion dozed.

satiate V. satisfy fully. Having stuffed themselves until they were *satiated*, the guests were so full they were ready for a nap.

● **satirize** V. mock. Cartoonist Gary Trudeau often *satirizes* contemporary politicians; through the comments of the *Doonesbury* characters, Trudeau ridicules political corruption and folly. satirical, ADJ.

saunter V. stroll slowly. Too tired for his usual brisk walk, Stan *sauntered* through the park, taking time to enjoy the spring flowers.

savant N. learned scholar. Despite all her academic honors, Dr. Diamond refused to be classed as a *savant*: considering herself a simple researcher, she refused to describe herself in such grandiose terms.

savory ADJ. tasty; pleasing, attractive, or agreeable. Julia Child's recipes enable amateur chefs to create *savory* delicacies for their guests.

scamper V. run about playfully. Looking forward to the game of hide-and-seek, the children *scampered* off to find good spots in which to hide.

scanty ADJ. meager; insufficient. Thinking his helping of food was *scanty*, Oliver Twist asked for more.

scapegoat N. someone who bears the blame for others. After the *Challenger* disaster, NASA searched for *scapegoats* on whom they could cast the blame.

scavenge - smolder

scavenge V. hunt through discarded materials for usable items; search, especially for food. If you need parts for an old car that the dealers no longer have in stock, try *scavenging* for odd bits and pieces at the auto wreckers' yards. scavenger, N.

schism N. division; split. Let us not widen the *schism* by further bickering.

scintillate V. sparkle; flash. I enjoy her dinner parties because the food is excellent and the conversation *scintillates*.

scrupulous ADJ. conscientious; extremely thorough. Though Alfred is *scrupulous* in fulfilling his duties at work, he is less conscientious about his obligations to his family and friends.

● **scrutinize** V. examine closely and critically. Searching for flaws, the sergeant *scrutinized* every detail of the private's uniform.

scuffle V. struggle confusedly; move off in a confused hurry. The twins briefly *scuffled*, wrestling to see which of them would get the toy. When their big brother yelled, "Let go of my Gameboy!" they *scuffled* off down the hall.

seasoned ADJ. experienced. Though pleased with her new batch of rookies, the basketball coach wished she had a few more *seasoned* players on the team. (secondary meaning)

● **seclusion** N. isolation; solitude. One moment she loved crowds; the next, she sought *seclusion*.

sect N. separate religious body; faction. As university chaplain, she sought to address universal religious issues and not limit herself to concerns of any one *sect*.

secular ADJ. worldly; not pertaining to church matters. The church leaders decided not to interfere in *secular* matters.

sedate ADJ. composed; grave. The parents were worried because they felt their son was too quiet and *sedate*.

seep V. leak through; trickle. After all the times we'd tried to repair the leaky roof, we were discouraged to see the water *seep* through the ceiling once again.

sensory ADJ. pertaining to the physical senses. Blasted by sound waved, dazzled by flashing lights, jostled by crowds, a newcomer to rock concerts can suffer from *sensory* overload.

sequester V. isolate; retire from public life; segregate; seclude. Banished from his kingdom, the wizard Prospero *sequestered* himself on a desert island.

serendipity N. gift for finding valuable or desirable things by accident; accidental good fortune or luck. Many scientific discoveries are a matter of *serendipity*: Newton was not sitting there thinking about gravity when the apple dropped on his head.

● **serenity** N. calmness; placidity. The *serenity* of the sleepy town was shattered by a tremendous explosion.

servile ADJ. slavishly submissive; fawning; cringing. Constantly fawning on his employer, Uriah Heep was a *servile* creature.

servitude N. slavery; compulsory labor. Born a slave, Douglass resented his life of *servitude* and plotted to escape to the North.

● **sever** V. cut; separate. Dr. Guillotin invented a machine that could neatly *sever* an aristocratic head from its equally aristocratic body.

● **severity** N. harshness; intensity; austerity; rigidity. The *severity* of Jane's migraine attack was so great that she took to her bed for a week.

shackle V. chain; fetter. In a chain gang, convicts are *shackled* together to prevent their escape. also N.

shambles N. wreck; mess; slaughterhouse. After the hurricane, the Carolina coast was a *shambles*. After the New Year's Eve party, the apartment was a *shambles*.

shimmer V. glimmer intermittently. The moonlight *shimmered* on the water as the moon broke through the clouds for a moment. also N.

shortcomings N. failures; deficiencies. Aware of his own *shortcomings* as a public speaker, the candidate worked closely with debate coaches to prepare for the coming campaign.

shrewd ADJ. clever; astute. A *shrewd* investor, he took clever advantage of the fluctuations of the stock market.

shun V. keep away from. Cherishing his solitude, the recluse *shunned* the company of other human beings.

shyster N. lawyer using questionable methods. The respectable attorney was horrified to learn that his newly discovered half brother was nothing but a cheap *shyster*.

simile N. comparison of one thing with another, using the word like or as. "My love is like a red, red rose" is a *simile*.

simplistic ADJ. oversimplified. Though Jack's solution dealt adequately with one aspect of the problem, it was *simplistic* in failing to consider various complications that might arise.

simulate V. feign; pretend. The judge ruled that the accused racketeer had *simulated* insanity and was in fact sane enough to stand trial.

● **singular** ADJ. unique; extraordinary; odd. Though the young man tried to understand Father William's *singular* behavior, he still found it odd that the old man incessantly stood on his head. singularity, N.

sinister ADJ. evil; conveying a sense of ill omen. Aware of the Penguin's *sinister* purpose, Batman wondered how he could save Gotham City from the ravages of his evil enemy.

sinuous ADJ. winding; bending in and out; not morally honest. The snake moved in a *sinuous* manner.

● **skeptical** ADJ. doubting; suspending judgment until having examined the evidence supporting a point of view. I am *skeptical* about this project; I want some proof that it can work. skepticism, N.

skulk V. move furtively and secretly. He *skulked* through the less fashionable sections of the city in order to avoid meeting any of his former friends.

slacken V. slow up; loosen. As they passed the finish line, the runners *slackened* their pace.

slag N. residue from smelting metal; dross; waste matter. The blast furnace had a special opening at the bottom to allow the workers to remove the worthless *slag*.

slapdash ADJ. haphazard; careless; sloppy. From the number of typos and misspellings I've found in it, it's clear that Mario proofread the report in a remarkably *slapdash* fashion.

slothful ADJ. lazy. Lying idly on the sofa while others worked, Reggie denied he was *slothful:* "I just supervise better lying down."

sluggish ADJ. slow; lazy; lethargic. After two nights without sleep, she felt *sluggish* and incapable of exertion.

smelt V. melt or blend ores, changing their chemical composition. The furnaceman *smelts* tin with copper to create a special alloy used in making bells.

smolder V. burn without flame; be liable to break out at any moment. The rags *smoldered* for hours before they burst into flame.

WORD LIST 31   smuggler - stratagem

smuggler N. one who illegally moves goods across national borders. Suspecting Randy might be a *smuggler,* the customs inspector made a thorough search of his luggage but found nothing illicit.

sneer V. smile or laugh contemptuously; make an insulting comment or face. "I could paint better than that with both hands tied behind my back," *sneered* Marvin.

sobriety N. moderation (especially regarding indulgence in alcohol); seriousness. Neither falling-down drunks nor stand-up comics are noted for *sobriety.* sober, ADJ.

sodden ADJ. soaked; dull, as if from drink. He set his *sodden* overcoat near the radiator to dry.

solemnity N. seriousness; gravity. The minister was concerned that nothing should disturb the *solemnity* of the marriage service.

soliloquy N. talking to oneself. The *soliloquy* is a device used by the dramatist to reveal a character's innermost thoughts and emotions.

somber ADJ. gloomy; depressing; dark; drab. Dull brown and charcoal gray are pretty *somber* colors; can't you wear something bright?

somnolent ADJ. half asleep. The heavy meal and the overheated room made us all *somnolent* and indifferent to the speaker.

soporific ADJ. sleep-causing; marked by sleepiness. Professor Pringle's lectures were so *soporific* that even he fell asleep in class. also N.

sordid ADJ. vile; filthy; wretched; mean. Talk show hosts seem willing to discuss any topic, no matter how *sordid* and disgusting it may be.

spartan ADJ. avoiding luxury and comfort; sternly disciplined. Looking over the bare, unheated room with its hard cot, he wondered what he was doing in such *spartan* quarters. Only his *spartan* sense of duty kept him at his post.

spat N. quarrel. Desi and Lucy had many lovers' *spats*; however, in the end they always reconciled.

specious ADJ. seemingly reasonable but incorrect; misleading (often intentionally). To claim that, because houses and birds both have wings, both can fly, is extremely *specious* reasoning.

speculate V. theorize or ponder; assume a financial risk; gamble. Students of the stock market *speculate* that the seeds of the financier's downfall were planted when he *speculated* heavily in junk bonds.

spendthrift N. someone who wastes money. Easy access to credit encourages people to turn into *spendthrifts* who shop till they drop.

splendor N. magnificence; grandeur; brilliance. Awed by the glittering chandeliers and finely costumed courtiers, Cinderella was overwhelmed by the *splendor* of the ball.

spoke N. radiating bar supporting the rim of a wheel. The repair man at the bicycle shop took less than half an hour to fix the bent *spokes* on Bob's rear wheel.

spontaneity N. lack of premeditation; naturalness; freedom from constraint. When Betty and Jennifer met, Jen impulsively hugged her roommate-to-be, but Betty drew back, unprepared for such *spontaneity.* spontaneous, ADJ.

sporadic ADJ. occurring irregularly. Although you can still hear *sporadic* outbursts of laughter and singing outside, the big Halloween parade has passed; the party's over till next year.

spurious ADJ. false; counterfeit; forged; illogical. The hero of Jonathan Gash's mystery novels is an antique dealer who gives the reader advice on how to tell *spurious* antiques from the real thing.

spurt V. gush forth; squirt. Water suddenly *spurted* from the fountain and splashed Bert right in the face.

squabble N. minor quarrel; bickering. Children invariably get involved in petty *squabbles*; wise parents know when to interfere and when to let the children work things out on their own.

squalor N. filth; degradation; dirty, neglected state. With rusted, broken-down cars in its yard, trash piled up on the porch, and tar paper peeling from the roof, the shack was the picture of *squalor.*

squander V. waste. If you *squander* your allowance on candy and comic books, you won't have any money left to buy the new box of crayons you want.

stagnant ADJ. motionless; stale; dull. Mosquitoes commonly breed in ponds of *stagnant* water. Mike's career was *stagnant;* it wasn't going anywhere, and neither was he! stagnate, V.

staid ADJ. sober; sedate. Her conduct during the funeral ceremony was *staid* and solemn.

stalwart ADJ. strong and vigorous; unwaveringly dependable. We thought the congressman was a *stalwart* Democrat until he voted against President Clinton's health care plan.

stamina N. strength; staying power. I doubt that she has the *stamina* to run the full distance of the marathon race.

stanza N. division of a poem. We all know the first *stanza* of the "The Star Spangled Banner." Does anyone know the last?

static ADJ. unchanging; lacking development. Why watch chess on TV? I like watching a game with action, not something *static* where nothing seems to be going on. stasis, N.

statute N. law enacted by the legislature. The *statute* of limitations sets the limits on how long you have to take legal action in specific cases.

steadfast ADJ. loyal; unswerving. Penelope was *steadfast* in her affections, faithfully waiting for Ulysses to return from his wanderings.

stem V. check the flow. The paramedic used a tourniquet to *stem* the bleeding from the slashed artery.

stem from V. arise from. Morton's problems in school *stemmed from* his poor study habits.

stereotyped ADJ. oversimplified; lacking individuality; seen as a type. My chief objection to the book is that the characters are *stereotyped;* they don't come across as real people with individual quirks, fears, and dreams. stereotype, N.;V.

stifle V. suppress; extinguish; inhibit. Halfway through the boring lecture, Laura gave up trying to *stifle* her yawns.

stodgy ADJ. stuffy; boringly conservative. For a young person, Winston seems remarkably *stodgy*: you'd expect someone his age to show a little more life.

stoic ADJ. impassive; unmoved by joy or grief. I wasn't particularly *stoic* when I had my flu shot; I squealed like a stuck pig. also N.

stolid ADJ. dull; impassive. The earthquake shattered Stuart's usual *stolid* demeanor; trembling, he crouched on the no longer stable ground.

● **stratagem** N. deceptive scheme. Though Wellington's forces seemed to be in full retreat, in reality their withdrawal was a *stratagem* intended to lure the enemy away from its sheltered position.

strident - temperate

strident ADJ. loud and harsh; insistent. Whenever Sue became angry, she tried not to raise her voice; she had no desire to appear *strident*.

stupor N. state of apathy; daze; lack of awareness. The paramedics shook the unconscious man but could not rouse him from his drunken *stupor*.

stupefy V. make numb; stun; amaze. Disapproving of drugs in general, Laura refused to take sleeping pills or any other medicine that might *stupefy* her. stupefaction, N.

● **subdued** ADJ. less intense; quieter. Bob liked the *subdued* lighting at the restaurant because he thought it was romantic. I just thought it was dimly lit.

subjective ADJ. existing in the mind, rather than in the object itself; opposite of objective; personal. Your analysis is highly *subjective*; you have permitted your emotions and your opinions to color your thinking.

subordinate ADJ. occupying a lower rank; inferior; submissive. Bishop Proudie's wife expected all the *subordinate* clergy to behave with great deference to the wife of their superior.

subsequent ADJ. following; later. In *subsequent* lessons, we shall take up more difficult problems.

subside V. sink to a low(er) level; grow quiet, less active, or less violent. The doctor assured us that the fever would eventually *subside*.

subsidiary ADJ. supplementary; subordinate; secondary. Although this *subsidiary* evidence is relevant, it is insufficient by itself to prove your argument. also N.

substantial ADJ. ample; solid; in essentials. The scholarship represented a *substantial* sum of money.

substantiate V. establish by evidence; verify; support. These endorsements from satisfied customers *substantiate* our claim that Barron's *How to Prepare for the PSAT* is the best PSAT-prep book on the market.

subtlety N. perceptiveness; ingenuity; delicacy. Never obvious, she expressed herself with such *subtlety* that her remarks went right over the heads of most of her audience. subtle, ADJ.

● **subversive** ADJ. tending to overthrow or destroy. At first glance, the notion that styrofoam cups may actually be more ecologically sound than paper cups strikes most environmentalists as *subversive*.

succinct ADJ. brief; terse; compact. Don't bore your audience with excess verbiage: be *succinct*.

succulent ADJ. juicy; full of richness. To some people, Florida citrus fruits are more *succulent* than those from California. also N.

suffragist N. advocate of voting rights (for women). In recognition of her efforts to win the vote for women, Congress authorized coining a silver dollar honoring the *suffragist* Susan B. Anthony.

● **superficial** ADJ. trivial; shallow. Since your report gave only a *superficial* analysis of the problem, I cannot give you more than a passing grade.

● **superfluous** ADJ. excessive; unnecessary. Please try not to include so many *superfluous* details in your report; just give me the bare facts. superfluity, N.

supplant V. replace; usurp. Did the other woman actually *supplant* Princess Diana in Prince Charles's affections, or did Charles never love Diana at all?

supple ADJ. flexible; pliant. Years of yoga exercises made Grace's body *supple*.

● **suppress** V. crush; subdue; inhibit. Too polite to laugh in anyone's face, Roy did his best to *suppress* his amusement at Ed's inane remark.

surfeit V. satiate; stuff; indulge to excess in anything. Every Thanksgiving we are *surfeited* with an overabundance of holiday treats. also N.

● **surpass** V. exceed. Her PSAT scores *surpassed* our expectations.

susceptible ADJ. impressionable; easily influenced; having little resistance, as to a disease; receptive to. Said the patent medicine man to the extremely *susceptible* customer: "Buy this new miracle drug, and you will no longer be *susceptible* to the common cold."

● **suspend** V. defer or postpone; expel or eject; halt or discontinue; hang from above. When the judge *suspended* his sentence, Bill breathed a sigh of relief. When the principal *suspended* her from school, Wanda tried to look as if she didn't care. When the trapeze artist broke her arm, she had to *suspend* her activities: she no longer could be *suspended* from her trapeze.

● **sustain** V. experience; support; nourish. Stuart *sustained* such a severe injury that the doctors feared he would be unable to work to *sustain* his growing family.

swill V. drink greedily. Singing "Yo, ho, ho, and a bottle of rum," Long John Silver and his fellow pirates *swilled* their grog.

swindler N. cheat. She was gullible and trusting, an easy victim for the first *swindler* who came along.

sycophant N. servile flatterer; bootlicker. Fed up with the toadies and flatterers who made up his entourage, the star cried, "Get out, all of you! I'm sick to death of *sycophants!*"

● **symmetry** N. arrangement of parts so that balance is obtained; congruity. Something lopsided by definition lacks *symmetry*.

● **synthesis** N. combining parts into a whole. Now that we have succeeded in isolating this drug, our next problem is to plan its *synthesis* in the laboratory. synthesize, V.

● **taciturn** ADJ. habitually silent; talking little. The stereotypical cowboy is a *taciturn* soul, answering lengthy questions with a "Yep" or "Nope."

tactile ADJ. pertaining to the organs or sense of touch. His callused hands had lost their *tactile* sensitivity.

taint V. contaminate; cause to lose purity; modify with a trace of something bad. One speck of dirt on your utensils may contain enough germs to *taint* an entire batch of preserves.

tangential ADJ. peripheral; only slightly connected; digressing. Despite Clark's attempts to distract her with *tangential* remarks, Lois kept on coming back to her main question: why couldn't he come out to dinner with Superman and her?

tantalize V. tease; torture with disappointment. Tom loved to *tantalize* his younger brother with candy; he knew the boy was forbidden to have it.

tarry V. delay; dawdle. We can't *tarry* if we want to get to the airport on time.

● **tedious** ADJ. boring; tiring. The repetitive nature of work on the assembly line made Martin's job very *tedious*. tedium, N.

temper V. moderate; tone down or restrain; toughen (steel). Not even her supervisor's grumpiness could *temper* Nancy's enthusiasm for her new job.

● **temperament** N. characteristic frame of mind; disposition; emotional excess. Although the twins look alike, they differ markedly in *temperament*: Todd is calm, but Rod is excitable. Racket-throwing tennis star John McEnroe was famed for his displays of *temperament*.

temperate ADJ. restrained; self-controlled; moderate in respect to temperature. Try to be *temperate* in your eating this holiday season; if you control your appetite, you won't gain too much weight.

WORD LIST 33 **tempestuous - turbid**

tempestuous ADJ. stormy; quarreling, reconciling, and quarreling again. The unhappy couple had a *tempestuous* married life.

tenet N. doctrine; dogma. The agnostic did not accept the *tenets* of their faith.

tentative ADJ. hesitant; not fully worked out or developed; experimental; not definite or positive. Unsure of his welcome at the Christmas party, Scrooge took a *tentative* step into his nephew's drawing room.

tenuous ADJ. thin; rare; slim. The allegiance of our allies is held by rather *tenuous* ties.

● **termination** N. end. Though the time for *termination* of the project was near, we still had a lot of work to finish before we shut up shop.

terrestrial ADJ. on the earth. We have been able to explore the *terrestrial* regions much more thoroughly than the aquatic or celestial regions.

terse ADJ. concise; abrupt; pithy. There is a fine line between speech that is *terse* and to the point and speech that is too abrupt.

theocracy N. government run by religious leaders. Though some Pilgrims aboard the *Mayflower* favored the establishment of a *theocracy* in New England, many of their fellow voyagers preferred a non-religious form of government.

theoretical ADJ. not practical or applied; hypothetical. Bob was better at applied engineering and computer programming than he was at *theoretical* physics and math. While I can still think of some *theoretical* objections to your plan, you've convinced me of its basic soundness.

therapeutic ADJ. curative. Now better known for its racetrack, Saratoga Springs first gained attention for the *therapeutic* qualities of its famous "healing waters."

thrifty ADJ. careful about money; economical. A *thrifty* shopper compares prices before making major purchases.

thrive V. prosper; flourish. Despite the impact of the recession on the restaurant trade, Philip's cafe *thrived.*

● **thwart** V. baffle; frustrate. He felt that everyone was trying to *thwart* his plans and prevent his success.

tiff ADJ. minor quarrel; fit of annoyance. Whenever the Kramdens had a *tiff,* Ralph would bluster, "That's it, Alice!" and storm out of the apartment.

tiller N. handle used to move a boat's rudder (to steer). Fearing the wind might shift suddenly and capsize the skiff, Tom kept one hand on the *tiller* at all times.

timidity N. lack of self-confidence or courage. If you are to succeed as a salesman, you must first lose your *timidity* and fear of failure.

tirade N. extended scolding; denunciation; harangue. Every time the boss holds a meeting, he goes into a lengthy *tirade,* scolding us for everything from tardiness to padding our expenses.

titanic ADJ. gigantic. *Titanic* waves beat against the shore during the hurricane.

title N. right or claim to possession; mark of rank; name (of a book, film, etc.). Though the penniless Duke of Ragwort no longer had *title* to the family estate, he still retained his *title* as head of one of England's oldest families. The *title* of his autobiography was *From Riches to Rags.*

toady N. servile flatterer; yes man. Never tell the boss anything he doesn't wish to hear: he doesn't want an independent adviser, he just wants a *toady.* also V.

torpor N. lethargy; sluggishness; dormancy. Throughout the winter, nothing aroused the bear from his *torpor:* he would not emerge from hibernation until spring. torpid, ADJ.

torrent N. rushing stream; flood. Day after day of heavy rain saturated the hillside until the water ran downhill in *torrents.* torrential, ADJ.

totter V. move unsteadily; sway, as if about to fall. On unsteady feet, the drunk *tottered* down the hill to the nearest bar.

● **toxic** ADJ. poisonous. We must seek an antidote for whatever *toxic* substance he has eaten. toxicity, N.

tractable ADJ. docile; easily managed. Although Susan seemed a *tractable* young woman, she had a stubborn streak of independence that occasionally led her to defy the powers-that-be when she felt they were in the wrong.

traduce V. slander; malign. His opponents tried to *traduce* the candidate's reputation by spreading rumors about his past.

transcendent ADJ. surpassing; exceeding ordinary limits; superior. Standing on the hillside watching the sunset through the Golden Gate was a *transcendent* experience for Lise: it was so beautiful it surpassed her wildest dreams.

transcribe V. copy. It took hours for the secretary to *transcribe* his shorthand notes of the conference into a form others could read.

transgression N. violation of a law; sin. Forgive us our *transgressions;* we know not what we do. transgress, V.

transient ADJ. momentary; temporary; staying for a short time. Lexy's joy at finding the perfect Christmas gift for Phil was *transient;* she still had to find presents for Roger, Laura, Allison, and Uncle Bob. Located near the airport, this hotel caters to a largely *transient* trade.

transition N. going from one state of action to another. During the period of *transition* from oil heat to gas heat, the furnace will have to be shut off.

transitory ADJ. impermanent; fleeting. Fame is *transitory*: today's rising star is all too soon tomorrow's washed-up has-been. transitoriness, N.

translucent ADJ. partly transparent. We could not recognize the people in the next room because of the *translucent* curtains that separated us.

● **transparent** ADJ. easily detected; permitting light to pass through freely. Bobby managed to put an innocent look on his face; to his mother, however, his guilt was *transparent.*

trenchant ADJ. cutting; keen. I am afraid of his *trenchant* wit for it is so often sarcastic.

trepidation N. fear; nervous apprehension. As she entered the office of the dean of admissions, Sharon felt some *trepidation* about how she would do in her interview.

trifling ADJ. trivial; unimportant. Why bother going to see a doctor for such a *trifling,* everyday cold?

trigger V. set off. John is touchy today; say one word wrong and you'll *trigger* an explosion.

trite ADJ. hackneyed; commonplace. The *trite* and predictable situations on many television programs turn off viewers, who respond by turning off their sets.

trivial ADJ. trifling; unimportant. Too many magazines ignore newsworthy subjects and feature *trivial* gossip about celebrities.

trough N. container for feeding farm animals; lowest point (of a wave, business cycle, etc.) The hungry pigs struggled to get at the fresh swill in the *trough.* The surfer rode her board, coasting along in the *trough* between two waves.

truism N. self-evident truth. Many a *truism* is summed up in a proverb; for example, "Marry in haste, repent at leisure."

turbid ADJ. muddy; having the sediment disturbed. The water was *turbid* after the children had waded through it.

WORD LIST 34 **turbulence - venturesome**

- **turbulence** N. state of violent agitation. Warned of approaching *turbulence* in the atmosphere, the pilot told the passengers to fasten their seat belts.

turgid ADJ. swollen; distended. The *turgid* river threatened to overflow the levees and flood the countryside.

turmoil N. great commotion and confusion. Lydia running off with a soldier! Mother fainting at the news! The Bennet household was in *turmoil*.

typhoon N. tropical hurricane or cyclone. If you liked *Twister,* you'll love *Typhoon!*

tyranny N. oppression; cruel government. Frederick Douglass fought against the *tyranny* of slavery throughout his entire life. tyrant, N.

ubiquitous ADJ. being everywhere; omnipresent. That Christmas "The Little Drummer Boy" seemed *ubiquitous*: Justin heard the tune everywhere he went.

ultimate ADJ. final; not susceptible to further analysis. Scientists are searching for the *ultimate* truths.

unanimity N. complete agreement. We were surprised by the *unanimity* with which members of both parties accepted our proposals. unanimous, ADJ.

unassuming ADJ. modest. He is so *unassuming* that some people fail to realize how great a man he really is.

unbecoming ADJ. unattractive; improper. What an *unbecoming* dress Mona is wearing! That girl has no color sense. At the court martial the captain was charged with conduct *unbecoming* an officer.

undermine V. weaken; sap. The recent corruption scandals have *undermined* many people's faith in the city government.

underscore V. emphasize. Addressing the jogging class, Kim *underscored* the importance to runners of good nutrition.

undulating ADJ. moving with a wavelike motion. The Hilo Hula Festival was an *undulating* sea of grass skirts.

unequivocal ADJ. plain; obvious. My answer to your proposal is an *unequivocal* and absolute "No."

unfeasible ADJ. not practical or workable. Roy's plan to enlarge the living room by knocking down a couple of internal walls proved *unfeasible* when he discovered that those walls were holding up the roof.

ungainly ADJ. awkward; clumsy; unwieldy. "If you want to know whether Nick's an *ungainly* dancer, check out my bruised feet," said Nora. Anyone who has ever tried to carry a bass fiddle knows it's an *ungainly* instrument.

uniformity N. sameness; monotony. After a while, the *uniformity* of TV situation comedies becomes boring.

unintimidating ADJ. unfrightening. Though Phil had expected to feel overawed when he met Joe Montana, he found the world-famous quarterback friendly and *unintimidating*.

unique ADJ. without an equal; single in kind. You have the *unique* distinction of being the first student whom I have had to fail in this course.

universal ADJ. characterizing or affecting all; present everywhere. At first, no one shared Christopher's opinions; his theory that the world was round was met with *universal* disbelief.

unprecedented ADJ. novel; unparalleled. Margaret Mitchell's book *Gone with the Wind* was an *unprecedented* success.

unravel V. disentangle; solve. With equal ease Miss Marple *unraveled* tangled balls of yarn and baffling murder mysteries.

unrequited ADJ. not reciprocated. Suffering the pangs of *unrequited* love, Olivia rebukes Cesario for his hardheartedness.

unseemly ADJ. unbecoming; indecent; in poor taste. When he put whoopie cushions on all the seats in the funeral parlor, Seymour's conduct was most *unseemly*.

unsightly ADJ. unpleasant to look at; ugly. Although James was an experienced emergency room nurse, he occasionally became queasy when faced with a particularly *unsightly* injury.

unsullied ADJ. spotlessly clean; unstained. The reputation of our school is *unsullied,* young ladies; you must conduct yourself modestly and discreetly, so that you never disgrace our good name.

unwarranted ADJ. unjustified; groundless; undeserved. We could not understand Martin's *unwarranted* rudeness to his mother's guests.

upbraid V. severely scold; reprimand. Not only did Miss Minchin *upbraid* Ermengarde for her disobedience, but she hung her up by her braids from a coat rack in the classroom.

uphold V. give support; keep from sinking; lift up. Bold Sir Robin was ready to fight to the death to *uphold* the honor of his lady.

uproarious ADJ. marked by commotion; extremely funny; very noisy. The *uproarious* comedy hit *Ace Ventura: Pet Detective* starred Jim Carrey, whose comic mugging provoked gales of *uproarious* laughter from audiences coast to coast.

- **urbane** ADJ. suave; refined; elegant. The courtier was *urbane* and sophisticated. urbanity, N.

usurp V. seize another's power or rank. The revolution ended when the victorious rebel general succeeded in *usurping* the throne.

- **utopia** N. ideal place, state, or society. Fed up with this imperfect universe, Don would have liked to run off to Shangri-la or some other fictitious *utopia*. utopian, ADJ.

- **vacillate** V. waver; fluctuate. Uncertain which suitor she ought to marry, the princess *vacillated,* saying now one, now the other. vacillation, N.

vacuous ADJ. empty; lacking in ideas; stupid. The politician's *vacuous* remarks annoyed the audience, who had hoped to hear more than empty platitudes.

vagabond N. wanderer; tramp. In summer, college students wander the roads of Europe like carefree *vagabonds*. also ADJ.

validate V. confirm; ratify. I will not publish my findings until I *validate* my results.

vanguard N. advance guard of a military force; forefront of a movement. When no enemy was in sight, the Duke of Plaza Toro marched in the *vanguard* of his troops, but once the bullets flew above, he headed for the rear.

vantage N. position giving an advantage. They fired upon the enemy from behind the trees, walls and any other point of *vantage* they could find.

vapid ADJ. dull and unimaginative; insipid and flavorless. "*Bor*-ing!" said Cheryl, as she suffered through yet another *vapid* lecture about Dead White Male Poets.

vehement ADJ. forceful; intensely emotional; with marked vigor. Alfred became so *vehement* in describing what was wrong with the Internal Revenue Service that he began jumping up and down and frothing at the mouth. vehemence, N.

venerate V. revere. In Tibet today, the common people still *venerate* their traditional spiritual leader, the Dalai Lama.

venturesome ADJ. bold. A group of *venturesome* women were the first to scale Mt. Annapurna.

WORD LIST 35

veracity - zephyr

veracity N. truthfulness. Asserting his *veracity,* young George Washington proclaimed, "Father, I cannot tell a lie!"

verbose ADJ. wordy. Someone mute can't talk; someone *verbose* can hardly stop talking.

verdant ADJ. green; lush in vegetation. Monet's paintings of the *verdant* fields were symphonies in green.

● **versatile** ADJ. having many talents; capable of working in many fields. She was a *versatile* athlete, earning varsity letters in basketball, hockey, and track.

vertigo N. severe dizziness. When you test potential airplane pilots for susceptibility to spells of *vertigo,* be sure to hand out air-sick bags.

vicissitude N. change of fortune. Humbled by life's *vicissitudes,* the last emperor of China worked as a lowly gardener in the palace over which he had once ruled.

vie V. contend; compete. Politicians *vie* with one another, competing for donations and votes.

● **vigor** N. active strength. Although he was over 70 years old, Jack had the *vigor* of a man in his prime. vigorous, ADJ.

vindicate V. clear from blame; exonerate; justify or support. The lawyer's goal was to *vindicate* her client and prove him innocent on all charges. The critics' extremely favorable reviews *vindicate* my opinion that *The Madness of King George* is a brilliant movie.

vindictive ADJ. out for revenge; malicious. Divorce sometimes brings out a *vindictive* streak in people; when Tony told Tina he wanted a divorce, she poured green Jello into the aquarium and turned his tropical fish into dessert.

virtuoso N. highly skilled artist. The child prodigy Yehudi Menuhin grew into a *virtuoso* whose *virtuosity* on the violin thrilled millions.

virulent ADJ. extremely poisonous; hostile; bitter. Laid up with a *virulent* case of measles, Vera blamed her doctors because her recovery took so long. In fact, she became quite *virulent* on the subject of the quality of modern medical care.

vise N. tool for holding work in place. Before filing its edges, the keysmith took the blank key and fixed it firmly between the jaws of a *vise.*

vivacious ADJ. animated; lively. She had always been *vivacious* and sparkling.

● **volatile** ADJ. changeable; explosive; evaporating rapidly. The political climate today is extremely *volatile*: no one can predict what the electorate will do next. Maria Callas's temper was extremely *volatile*: the only thing you could predict was that she was sure to blow up. Ethyl chloride is an extremely *volatile* liquid: it evaporates instantly.

voluble ADJ. fluent; glib; talkative. Excessively *voluble* speakers suffer from logorrhea: they run off at the mouth a lot!

voluminous ADJ. extensive; bulky; large. Despite her family burdens, she kept up a *voluminous* correspondence with her friends. A caftan is a *voluminous* garment; most people wearing one look as if they're draped in a small tent.

voracious ADJ. ravenous. The wolf is a *voracious* animal, its hunger never satisfied.

vulnerable ADJ. susceptible to wounds. His opponents could not harm Achilles, who was *vulnerable* only in his heel.

waive V. give up a claim or right voluntarily; refrain from enforcing; postpone considering. Although technically prospective students had to live in Piedmont to attend high school there, occasionally the school *waived* the residence requirement in order to enroll promising athletes.

wallow V. roll in; indulge in; become helpless. The hippopotamus loves to *wallow* in pools of mud. The horror film addict loves to *wallow* in tales of blood.

wanderlust N. strong longing to go off traveling. The cowboy had a bad case of *wanderlust;* he could never settle down.

wane V. decrease in size or strength; draw gradually to an end. When lit, does a wax candle *wane?*

wanton ADJ. unrestrained; willfully malicious; unchaste. Pointing to the stack of bills, Sheldon criticized Sarah for her *wanton* expenditures. In response, Sarah accused Sheldon of making an unfounded, *wanton* attack.

warble V. sing; babble. Every morning the birds *warbled* outside her window. also N.

● **wary** ADJ. very cautious. The spies grew *wary* as they approached the sentry.

wayward ADJ. ungovernable; unpredictable; contrary. Miss Watson threatened Huck that if he didn't mend his ways she would ship him off to a school for *wayward* youths.

wheedle V. cajole; coax; deceive by flattery. She knows she can *wheedle* almost anything she wants from her father.

whet V. sharpen; stimulate. The odors from the kitchen are *whetting* my appetite; I will be ravenous by the time the meal is served.

whiff N. puff or gust (of air, scent, etc.); hint. The slightest *whiff* of Old Spice cologne brought memories of George to her mind.

whimsical N. capricious; fanciful. In *Mrs. Doubtfire,* the hero is a playful, *whimsical* man who takes a notion to dress up as a woman so that he can look after his children, who are in the custody of his ex-wife. whimsy, N.

whittle V. pare; cut off bits. As a present for Aunt Polly, Tom *whittled* some clothespins out of a chunk of wood.

willful ADJ. intentional; headstrong. Donald had planned to kill his wife for months; clearly, her death was a case of deliberate, *willful* murder, not a crime of passion committed by a hasty, *willful* youth unable to foresee the consequences of his deeds.

wily ADJ. cunning; artful. She is as *wily* as a fox in avoiding trouble.

winnow V. sift; separate good parts from bad. This test will *winnow* out the students who study from those who never open a book.

withdrawn ADJ. introverted; remote. Rebuffed by his colleagues, the initially outgoing young researcher became increasingly *withdrawn.*

wither V. shrivel; decay. Cut flowers are beautiful for a day, but all too soon they *wither.*

● **withhold** V. hold back; desist from giving; keep possession of. The tenants decided to *withhold* a portion of the rent until the landlord kept his promise to renovate the building

wry ADJ. twisted; with a humorous twist. We enjoy Dorothy Parker's verse for its *wry* wit.

zeal N. eager enthusiasm. Wang's *zeal* was contagious; soon all his fellow students were busily making posters, inspired by his ardent enthusiasm for the cause. zealous, ADJ.

zenith N. highest point; culmination. When the film star's career was at its *zenith,* she was in such great demand that producers told her to name her own price.

zephyr N. gentle breeze; west wind. When these *zephyrs* blow, it is good to be in an open boat under a full sail.

BASIC WORD PARTS

In addition to reviewing the High-Frequency Word List, what other quick vocabulary-building tactics can you follow when you face a test deadline?

One good approach is to learn how to build up (and tear apart) words. You know that words are made up of other words: the *room* in which you *store* things is the *storeroom;* the person whose job is to *keep* the *books* is the *bookkeeper.*

Just as words are made up of other words, words are also made up of word parts: prefixes, suffixes, and roots. A knowledge of these word parts and their meanings can help you determine the meanings of unfamiliar words.

Most modern English words are derived from Anglo-Saxon (Old English), Latin, and Greek. Because few students nowadays study Latin and Greek (and even fewer study Anglo-Saxon!), the majority of high school juniors and seniors lack a vital tool for unlocking the meaning of unfamiliar words.

Build your vocabulary by mastering basic word parts. Learning thirty key word parts can help you unlock the meaning of over 10,000 words. Learning fifty key word parts can help you unlock the meaning of over 100,000!

Common Prefixes

Prefixes are syllables that precede the root or stem and change or refine its meaning.

Prefix	Meaning	Illustration
ab, abs	from, away from	*abduct* lead away, kidnap *abjure* renounce *abject* degraded, cast down
ad, ac, af, ag, an, ap, as, as, at	to, forward	*adit* entrance *adjure* request earnestly *admit* allow entrance *accord* agreement, harmony *affliction* distress *aggregation* collection *annexation* add to *apparition* ghost *arraignment* indictment *assumption* arrogance, the taking for granted *attendance* presence, the persons present
ambi	both	*ambidextrous* skilled with both hands *ambiguous* of double meaning *ambivalent* having two conflicting emotions
an, a	without	*anarchy* lack of government *anemia* lack of blood *amoral* without moral sense
ante	before	*antecedent* preceding event or word *antediluvian* ancient (before the flood) *ante-nuptial* before the wedding
anti	against, opposite	*antipathy* hatred *antiseptic* against infection *antithetical* exactly opposite
arch	chief, first	*archetype* original *archbishop* chief bishop *archeology* study of first or ancient times
be	over, thoroughly	*bedaub* smear over *befuddle* confuse thoroughly *beguile* deceive, charm thoroughly

Prefix	Meaning	Illustration
bi	two	*bicameral* composed of two houses (Congress) *biennial* every two years *bicycle* two-wheeled vehicle
cata	down	*catastrophe* disaster *cataract* waterfall *catapult* hurl (throw down)
circum	around	*circumnavigate* sail around (the globe) *circumspect* cautious (looking around) *circumscribe* limit (place a circle around)
com, co, col, con, cor	with, together	*combine* merge with *commerce* trade with *communicate* correspond with *coeditor* joint editor *collateral* subordinate, connected *conference* meeting *corroborate* confirm
contra, contro	against	*contravene* conflict with *controversy* dispute
de	down, away	*debase* lower in value *decadence* deterioration *decant* pour off
demi	partly, half	*demigod* partly divine being
di	two	*dichotomy* division into two parts *dilemma* choice between two bad alternatives
dia	across	*diagonal* across a figure *diameter* distance across a circle *diagram* outline drawing
dis, dif	not, apart	*discord* lack of harmony *differ* disagree (carry apart) *disparity* condition of inequality; difference
dys	faulty, bad	*dyslexia* faulty ability to read *dyspepsia* indigestion
ex, e	out	*expel* drive out *extirpate* root out *eject* throw out
extra, extro	beyond, outside	*extracurricular* beyond the curriculum *extraterritorial* beyond a nation's bounds *extrovert* person interested chiefly in external objects and actions
hyper	above; excessively	*hyperbole* exaggeration *hyperventilate* breathe at an excessive rate
hypo	beneath; lower	*hypoglycemia* low blood sugar
in, il, im, ir	not	*inefficient* not efficient *inarticulate* not clear or distinct *illegible* not readable *impeccable* not capable of sinning; flawless *irrevocable* not able to be called back

Prefix	Meaning	Illustration
in, il, im, ir	in, on, upon	*invite* call in *illustration* something that makes clear *impression* effect upon mind or feelings *irradiate* shine upon
inter	between, among	*intervene* come between *international* between nations *interjection* a statement thrown in
intra, intro	within	*intramural* within a school *introvert* person who turns within himself
macro	large, long	*macrobiotic* tending to prolong life *macrocosm* the great world (the entire universe)
mega	great, million	*megalomania* delusions of grandeur *megaton* explosive force of a million tons of TNT
meta	involving change	*metamorphosis* change of form
micro	small	*microcosm* miniature universe *microbe* minute organism *microscopic* extremely small
mis	bad, improper	*misdemeanor* minor crime; bad conduct *mischance* unfortunate accident *misnomer* wrong name
mis	hatred	*misanthrope* person who hates mankind *misogynist* woman-hater
mono	one	*monarchy* government by one ruler *monotheism* belief in one god
multi	many	*multifarious* having many parts *multitudinous* numerous
neo	new	*neologism* newly coined word *neophyte* beginner; novice
non	not	*noncommittal* undecided *nonentity* person of no importance
ob, oc, of, op	against	*obloquy* infamy; disgrace *obtrude* push into prominence *occlude* close; block out *offend* insult *opponent* someone who struggles against; foe
olig	few	*oligarchy* government by a few
pan	all, every	*panacea* cure-all *panorama* unobstructed view in all directions
para	beyond, related	*parallel* similar *paraphrase* restate; translate

Prefix	Meaning	Illustration
per	through, completely	*permeable* allowing passage through *pervade* spread throughout
peri	around, near	*perimeter* outer boundary *periphery* edge *periphrastic* stated in a roundabout way
poly	many	*polygamist* person with several spouses *polyglot* speaking several languages
post	after	*postpone* delay *posterity* generations that follow *posthumous* after death
pre	before	*preamble* introductory statement *prefix* word part placed before a root/stem *premonition* forewarning
prim	first	*primordial* existing at the dawn of time *primogeniture* state of being the first born
pro	forward, in favor of	*propulsive* driving forward *proponent* supporter
proto	first	*prototype* first of its kind
pseudo	false	*pseudonym* pen name
re	again, back	*reiterate* repeat *reimburse* pay back
retro	backward	*retrospect* looking back *retroactive* effective as of a past date
se	away, aside	*secede* withdraw *seclude* shut away *seduce* lead astray
semi	half, partly	*semiannual* every six months *semiconscious* partly conscious
sub, suc, suf, sug, sup, sus	under, less	*subway* underground road *subjugate* bring under control *succumb* yield; cease to resist *suffuse* spread through *suggest* hint *suppress* put down by force *suspend* delay
super, sur	over, above	*supernatural* above natural things *supervise* oversee *surtax* additional tax
syn, sym, syl, sys	with, together	*synchronize* time together *synthesize* combine together *sympathize* pity; identify with *syllogism* explanation of how ideas relate *system* network

Prefix	Meaning	Illustration
tele	far	*telemetry* measurement from a distance *telegraphic* communicated over a distance
trans	across	*transport* carry across *transpose* reverse, move across
ultra	beyond, excessive	*ultramodern* excessively modern *ultracritical* exceedingly critical
un	not	*unfeigned* not pretended; real *unkempt* not combed; disheveled *unwitting* not knowing; unintentional
under	below	*undergird* strengthen underneath *underling* someone inferior
uni	one	*unison* oneness of pitch; complete accord *unicycle* one-wheeled vehicle
vice	in place of	*vicarious* acting as a substitute *viceroy* governor acting in place of a king
with	away, against	*withhold* hold back; keep *withstand* stand up against; resist

Common Roots and Stems

Roots are basic words which have been carried over into English. *Stems* are variations of roots brought about by changes in declension or conjugation.

Root or Stem	Meaning	Illustration
ac, acr	sharp	*acrimonious* bitter; caustic *acerbity* bitterness of temper *acidulate* to make somewhat acid or sour
aev, ev	age, era	*primeval* of the first age *coeval* of the same age or era *medieval or mediaeval* of the middle ages
ag, act	do	*act* deed *agent* doer
agog	leader	*demagogue* false leader of people *pedagogue* teacher (leader of children)
agri, agrari	field	*agrarian* one who works in the field *agriculture* cultivation of fields *peregrination* wandering (through fields)
ali	another	*alias* assumed (another) name *alienate* estrange (turn away from another)
alt	high	*altitude* height *altimeter* instrument for measuring height

Root or Stem	Meaning	Illustration
alter	other	*altruistic* unselfish, considering others *alter ego* a second self
am	love	*amorous* loving, especially sexually *amity* friendship *amicable* friendly
anim	mind, soul	*animadvert* cast criticism upon *unanimous* of one mind *magnanimity* greatness of mind or spirit
ann, enn	year	*annuity* yearly remittance *biennial* every two years *perennial* present all year; persisting for several years
anthrop	man	*anthropology* study of man *misanthrope* hater of mankind *philanthropy* love of mankind; charity
apt	fit	*aptitude* skill *adapt* make suitable or fit
aqua	water	*aqueduct* passageway for conducting water *aquatic* living in water *aqua fortis* nitric acid (strong water)
arch	ruler, first	*archaeology* study of antiquities (study of first things) *monarch* sole ruler *anarchy* lack of government
aster	star	*astronomy* study of the stars *asterisk* star-like type character (*) *disaster* catastrophe (contrary star)
aud, audit	hear	*audible* able to be heard *auditorium* place where people may be heard *audience* hearers
auto	self	*autocracy* rule by one person (self) *automobile* vehicle that moves by itself *autobiography* story of one's own life
belli	war	*bellicose* inclined to fight *belligerent* inclined to wage war *rebellious* resisting authority
ben, bon	good	*benefactor* one who does good deeds *benevolence* charity (wishing good) *bonus* something extra above regular pay
biblio	book	*bibliography* list of books *bibliophile* lover of books *Bible* The Book

Root or Stem	Meaning	Illustration
bio	life	*biography* writing about a person's life *biology* study of living things *biochemist* student of the chemistry of living things
breve	short	*brevity* briefness *abbreviate* shorten *breviloquent* marked by brevity of speech
cad, cas	to fall	*decadent* deteriorating *cadence* intonation, musical movement *cascade* waterfall
cap, capt, cept, cip	to take	*capture* seize *participate* take part *precept* wise saying (originally a command)
capit, capt	head	*decapitate* remove (cut off) someone's head *captain* chief
carn	flesh	*carnivorous* flesh-eating *carnage* destruction of life *carnal* fleshly
ced, cess	to yield, to go	*recede* go back, withdraw *antecedent* that which goes before *process* go forward
celer	swift	*celerity* swiftness *decelerate* reduce swiftness *accelerate* increase swiftness
cent	one hundred	*century* one hundred years *centennial* hundredth anniversary *centipede* many-footed, wingless animal
chron	time	*chronology* timetable of events *anachronism* a thing out of time sequence *chronicle* register events in order of time
cid, cis	to cut, to kill	*incision* a cut (surgical) *homicide* killing of a man *fratricide* killing of a brother
cit, citat	to call, to start	*incite* stir up, start up *excite* stir up *recitation* a recalling (or repeating) aloud
civi	citizen	*civilization* society of citizens, culture *civilian* member of community *civil* courteous
clam, clamat	to cry out	*clamorous* loud *declamation* speech *acclamation* shouted approval
claud, claus, clos, clud	to close	*claustrophobia* fear of close places *enclose* close in *conclude* finish

Root or Stem	Meaning	Illustration
cognosc, cognit	to learn	*agnostic* lacking knowledge, skeptical *incognito* traveling under assumed name *cognition* knowledge
compl	to fill	*complete* filled out *complement* that which completes something *comply* fulfill
cord	heart	*accord* agreement (from the heart) *cordial* friendly *discord* lack of harmony
corpor	body	*incorporate* organize into a body *corporeal* pertaining to the body, fleshly *corpse* dead body
cred, credit	to believe	*incredulous* not believing, skeptical *credulity* gullibility *credence* belief
cur	to care	*curator* person who has the care of something *sinecure* position without responsibility *secure* safe
curr, curs	to run	*excursion* journey *cursory* brief *precursor* forerunner
da, dat	to give	*data* facts, statistics *mandate* command *date* given time
deb, debit	to owe	*debt* something owed *indebtedness* debt *debenture* bond
dem	people	*democracy* rule of the people *demagogue* (false) leader of the people *epidemic* widespread (among the people)
derm	skin	*epidermis* skin *pachyderm* thick-skinned quadruped *dermatology* study of skin and its disorders
di, diurn	day	*diary* a daily record of activities, feelings, etc. *diurnal* pertaining to daytime
dic, dict	to say	*abdicate* renounce *diction* speech *verdict* statement of jury
doc, doct	to teach	*docile* obedient; easily taught *document* something that provides evidence *doctor* learned person (originally, teacher)
domin	to rule	*dominate* have power over *domain* land under rule *dominant* prevailing

Root or Stem	Meaning	Illustration
duc, duct	to lead	*viaduct* arched roadway *aqueduct* artificial waterway
dynam	power, strength	*dynamic* powerful *dynamite* powerful explosive *dynamo* engine making electrical power
ego	I	*egoist* person who is self-interested *egotist* selfish person *egocentric* revolving about self
erg, urg	work	*energy* power *ergatocracy* rule of the workers *metallurgy* science and technology of metals
err	to wander	*error* mistake *erratic* not reliable, wandering *knight-errant* wandering knight
eu	good, well, beautiful	*eupeptic* having good digestion *eulogize* praise *euphemism* substitution of pleasant way of saying something blunt
fac, fic, fec, fect	to make, to do	*factory* place where things are made *fiction* manufactured story *affect* cause to change
fall, fals	to deceive	*fallacious* misleading *infallible* not prone to error, perfect *falsify* lie
fer, lat	to bring, to bear	*transfer* bring from one place to another *translate* bring from one language to another *conifer* bearing cones, as pine trees
fid	belief, faith	*infidel* nonbeliever, heathen *confidence* assurance, belief
fin	end, limit	*confine* keep within limits *finite* having definite limits
flect, flex	bend	*flexible* able to bend *deflect* bend away, turn aside
fort	luck, chance	*fortuitous* accidental, occurring by chance *fortunate* lucky
fort	strong	*fortitude* strength, firmness of mind *fortification* strengthening *fortress* stronghold
frag, fract	break	*fragile* easily broken *infraction* breaking of a rule *fractious* unruly, tending to break rules
fug	flee	*fugitive* someone who flees *refuge* shelter, home for someone fleeing

Root or Stem	Meaning	Illustration
fus	pour	*effusive* gushing, pouring out *diffuse* widespread (poured in many directions)
gam	marriage	*monogamy* marriage to one person *bigamy* marriage to two people at the same time *polygamy* having many wives or husbands at the same time
gen, gener	class, race	*genus* group of animals with similar traits *generic* characteristic of a class *gender* class organized by sex
grad, gress	go, step	*digress go* astray (from the main point) *regress* go backwards *gradual* step by step, by degrees
graph, gram	writing	*epigram* pithy statement *telegram* instantaneous message over great distance *stenography* shorthand (writing narrowly)
greg	flock, herd	*gregarious* tending to group together as in a herd *aggregate* group, total *egregious* conspicuously bad; shocking
helio	sun	*heliotrope* flower that faces the sun *heliograph* instrument that uses the sun's rays to send signals
it, itiner	journey, road	*exit* way out *itinerary* plan of journey
jac, jact, jec	to throw	*projectile* missile; something thrown forward *trajectory* path taken by thrown object *ejaculatory* casting or throwing out
jur, jurat	to swear	*perjure* testify falsely *jury* group of men and women sworn to seek the truth *adjuration* solemn urging
labor, laborat	to work	*laboratory* place where work is done *collaborate* work together with others *laborious* difficult
leg, lect, lig	to choose, to read	*election* choice *legible* able to be read *eligible* able to be selected
leg	law	*legislature* law-making body *legitimate* lawful *legal* lawful
liber, libr	book	*library* collection of books *libretto* the "book" of a musical play *libel* slander (originally found in a little book)
liber	free	*liberation* the fact of setting free *liberal* generous (giving freely); tolerant

Root or Stem	Meaning	Illustration
log	word, study	*entomology* study of insects *etymology* study of word parts and derivations *monologue* speech by one person
loqu, locut	to talk	*soliloquy* speech by one individual *loquacious* talkative *elocution* speech
luc	light	*elucidate* enlighten *lucid* clear *translucent* allowing some light to pass through
magn	great	*magnify* enlarge *magnanimity* generosity, greatness of soul *magnitude* greatness, extent
mal	bad	*malevolent* wishing evil *malediction* curse *malefactor* evil-doer
man	hand	*manufacture* create (make by hand) *manuscript* written by hand *emancipate* free (let go from the hand)
mar	sea	*maritime* connected with seafaring *submarine* undersea craft *mariner* seaman
mater, matr	mother	*maternal* pertaining to motherhood *matriarch* female ruler of a family, group, or state *matrilineal* descended on the mother's side
mit, miss	to send	*missile* projectile *dismiss* send away *transmit* send across
mob, mot, mov	move	*mobilize* cause to move *motility* ability to move *immovable* not able to be moved
mon, monit	to warn	*admonish* warn *premonition* foreboding *monitor* watcher (warner)
mori, mort	to die	*mortuary* funeral parlor *moribund* dying *immortal* not dying
morph	shape, form	*amorphous* formless, lacking shape *metamorphosis* change of shape *anthropomorphic* in the shape of man
mut	change	*immutable* not able to be changed *mutate* undergo a great change *mutability* changeableness, inconstancy

Root or Stem	Meaning	Illustration
nat	born	*innate* from birth *prenatal* before birth *nativity* birth
nav	ship	*navigate* sail a ship *circumnavigate* sail around the world *naval* pertaining to ships
neg	deny	*negation* denial *renege* deny, go back on one's word *renegade* turncoat, traitor
nomen	name	*nomenclature* act of naming, terminology *nominal* in name only (as opposed to actual) *cognomen* surname, distinguishing nickname
nov	new	*novice* beginner *renovate* make new again *novelty* newness
omni	all	*omniscient* all knowing *omnipotent* all powerful *omnivorous* eating everything
oper	to work	*operate* work *cooperation* working together
pac	peace	*pacify* make peaceful *pacific* peaceful *pacifist* person opposed to war
pass	feel	*dispassionate* free of emotion *impassioned* emotion-filled *impassive* showing no feeling
pater, patr	father	*patriotism* love of one's country (fatherland) *patriarch* male ruler of a family, group, or state *paternity* fatherhood
path	disease, feeling	*pathology* study of diseased tissue *apathetic* lacking feeling; indifferent *antipathy* hostile feeling
ped, pod	foot	*impediment* stumbling-block; hindrance *tripod* three-footed stand *quadruped* four-footed animal
ped	child	*pedagogue* teacher of children *pediatrician* children's doctor
pel, puls	to drive	*compulsion* a forcing to do *repel* drive back *expel* drive out, banish
pet, petit	to seek	*petition* request *appetite* craving, desire *compete* vie with others

Root or Stem	Meaning	Illustration
phil	love	*philanthropist* benefactor, lover of humanity *Anglophile* lover of everything English *philanderer* one involved in brief love affairs
pon, posit	to place	*postpone* place after *positive* definite, unquestioned (definitely placed)
port, portat	to carry	*portable* able to be carried *transport* carry across *export* carry out (of country)
poten	able, powerful	*omnipotent* all-powerful *potentate* powerful person *impotent* powerless
psych	mind	*psychology* study of the mind *psychosis* mental disorder *psychopath* mentally ill person
put, putat	to trim, to calculate	*putative* supposed (calculated) *computation* calculation *amputate* cut off
quer, ques, quir, quis	to ask	*inquiry* investigation *inquisitive* questioning *query* question
reg, rect	rule	*regicide* murder of a ruler *regent* ruler *insurrection* rebellion; overthrow of a ruler
rid, ris	to laugh	*derision* scorn *risibility* inclination to laughter *ridiculous* deserving to be laughed at
rog, rogat	to ask	*interrogate* question *prerogative* privilege
rupt	to break	*interrupt* break into *bankrupt* insolvent *rupture* a break
sacr	holy	*sacred* holy *sacrilegious* impious, violating something holy *sacrament* religious act
sci	to know	*science* knowledge *omniscient* knowing all *conscious* aware
scop	watch, see	*periscope* device for seeing around corners *microscope* device for seeing small objects
scrib, script	to write	*transcribe* make a written copy *script* written text *circumscribe* write around, limit

Root or Stem	Meaning	Illustration
sect	cut	*dissect* cut apart *bisect* cut into two pieces
sed, sess	to sit	*sedentary* inactive (sitting) *session* meeting
sent, sens	to think, to feel	*consent* agree *resent* show indignation *sensitive* showing feeling
sequi, secut, seque	to follow	*consecutive* following in order *sequence* arrangement *sequel* that which follows *non sequitur* something that does not follow logically
solv, solut	to loosen	*absolve* free from blame *dissolute* morally lax *absolute* complete (not loosened)
somn	sleep	*insomnia* inability to sleep *somnolent* sleepy *somnambulist* sleepwalker
soph	wisdom	*philosopher* lover of wisdom *sophisticated* worldly wise
spec, spect	to look at	*spectator* observer *aspect* appearance *circumspect* cautious (looking around)
spir	breathe	*respiratory* pertaining to breathing *spirited* full of life (breath)
string, strict	bind	*stringent* strict *constrict* become tight *stricture* limit, something that restrains
stru, struct	build	*constructive* helping to build *construe* analyze (how something is built)
tang, tact, ting	to touch	*tangent* touching *contact* touching with, meeting *contingent* depending upon
tempor	time	*contemporary* at same time *extemporaneous* impromptu *temporize* delay
ten, tent	to hold	*tenable* able to be held *tenure* holding of office *retentive* holding; having a good memory
term	end	*interminable* endless *terminate* end

Root or Stem	Meaning	Illustration
terr	land	*terrestrial* pertaining to earth *subterranean* underground
therm	heat	*thermostat* instrument that regulates heat *diathermy* sending heat through body tissues
tors, tort	twist	*distort* twist out of true shape or meaning *torsion* act of twisting *tortuous* twisting
tract	drag, pull	*distract* pull (one's attention) away *intractable* stubborn, unable to be dragged *attraction* pull, drawing quality
trud, trus	push, shove	*intrude* push one's way in *protrusion* something sticking out
urb	city	*urban* pertaining to a city *urbane* polished, sophisticated (pertaining to a city dweller) *suburban* outside of a city
vac	empty	*vacuous* lacking content, empty-headed *evacuate* compel to empty an area
vad, vas	go	*invade* enter in a hostile fashion *evasive* not frank; eluding
veni, vent, ven	to come	*intervene* come between *prevent* stop *convention* meeting
ver	true	*veracious* truthful *verify* check the truth *verisimilitude* appearance of truth
verb	word	*verbose* wordy *verbiage* excessive use of words *verbatim* word for word
vers, vert	turn	*vertigo* turning dizzy *revert* turn back (to an earlier state) *diversion* something causing one to turn aside
via	way	*deviation* departure from the way *viaduct* roadway (arched) *trivial* trifling (small talk at crossroads)
vid, vis	to see	*vision* sight *evidence* things seen *vista* view
vinc, vict, vanq	to conquer	*invincible* unconquerable *victory* winning *vanquish* defeat

Root or Stem	Meaning	Illustration
viv, vit	alive	*vivisection* operating on living animals *vivacious* full of life *vitality* liveliness
voc, vocat	to call	*avocation* calling, minor occupation *provocation* calling or rousing the anger of *invocation* calling in prayer
vol	wish	*malevolent* wishing someone ill *voluntary* of one's own will
volv, volut	to roll	*revolve* roll around *evolve* roll out, develop *convolution* coiled state

Common Suffixes

Suffixes are syllables that are added to a word. Occasionally, they change the meaning of the word; more frequently, they serve to change the grammatical form of the word (noun to adjective, adjective to noun, noun to verb).

Suffix	Meaning	Illustration
able, ible	capable of (adjective suffix)	*portable* able to be carried *interminable* not able to be limited *legible* able to be read
ac, ic	like, pertaining to (adjective suffix)	*cardiac* pertaining to the heart *aquatic* pertaining to the water *dramatic* pertaining to the drama
acious, icious	full of (adjective suffix)	*audacious* full of daring *perspicacious* full of mental perception *avaricious* full of greed
al	pertaining to (adjective or noun suffix)	*maniacal* insane *final* pertaining to the end *logical* pertaining to logic
ant, ent	full of (adjective or noun suffix)	*eloquent* pertaining to fluid, effective speech *suppliant* pleader (person full of requests) *verdant* green
ary	like, connected with (adjective or noun suffix)	*dictionary* book connected with words *honorary* with honor *luminary* celestial body
ate	to make (verb suffix)	*consecrate* to make holy *enervate* to make weary *mitigate* to make less severe
ation	that which is (noun suffix)	*exasperation* irritation *irritation* annoyance
cy	state of being (noun suffix)	*democracy* government ruled by the people *obstinacy* stubbornness *accuracy* correctness

Suffix	Meaning	Illustration
eer, er, or	person who (noun suffix)	*mutineer* person who rebels *lecher* person who lusts *censor* person who deletes improper remarks
escent	becoming (adjective suffix)	*evanescent* tending to vanish *pubescent* arriving at puberty
fic	making, doing (adjective suffix)	*terrific* arousing great fear *soporific* causing sleep
fy	to make (verb suffix)	*magnify* enlarge *petrify* turn to stone *beautify* make beautiful
iferous	producing, bearing (adjective suffix)	*pestiferous* carrying disease *vociferous* bearing a loud voice
il, ile	pertaining to, capable of (adjective suffix)	*puerile* pertaining to a boy or child *ductile* capable of being hammered or drawn *civil* polite
ism	doctrine, belief (noun suffix)	*monotheism* belief in one god *fanaticism* excessive zeal; extreme belief
ist	dealer, doer (noun suffix)	*fascist* one who believes in a fascist state *realist* one who is realistic *artist* one who deals with art
ity	state of being (noun suffix)	*annuity* yearly grant *credulity* state of being unduly willing to believe *sagacity* wisdom
ive	like (adjective suffix)	*expensive* costly *quantitative* concerned with quantity *effusive* gushing
ize, ise	make (verb suffix)	*victimize* make a victim of *rationalize* make rational *harmonize* make harmonious *enfranchise* make free or set free
oid	resembling, like (adjective suffix)	*ovoid* like an egg *anthropoid* resembling man *spheroid* resembling a sphere
ose	full of (adjective suffix)	*verbose* full of words *lachrymose* full of tears
osis	condition (noun suffix)	*psychosis* diseased mental condition *neurosis* nervous condition *hypnosis* condition of induced sleep
ous	full of (adjective suffix)	*nauseous* full of nausea *ludicrous* foolish
tude	state of (noun suffix)	*fortitude* state of strength *beatitude* state of blessedness *certitude* state of sureness

Writing Skills

7

Improving Written Expression

The new writing skills section on the PSAT greatly resembles the SAT II: Subject Test in Writing most students take in their senior year. You definitely want to study hard when you prepare for the writing skills section: a good score on this section of the test may make all the difference between your becoming a National Merit finalist and your coming out a runner up.

The questions test your ability to recognize clear, correct standard written English, the kind of writing your college professors will expect on the papers you write for them. You'll be expected to know basic grammar, such as subject-verb agreement, pronoun-antecedent agreement, correct verb tense, correct sentence structure, and correct diction. You'll need to know how to recognize a dangling participle and how to spot when two parts of a sentence are not clearly connected. You'll also need to know when a paragraph is (or isn't) properly developed and organized.

There are three different kinds of questions on the writing skills section of the PSAT: find-the-error questions, sentence correction questions, and paragraph correction ones. Almost half of them, nineteen of the thirty-nine, to be exact, are find-the-error questions in which you have to identify an error in the underlined section of a sentence. You do not have to correct the sentence or explain what is wrong. Here are the directions.

In the sentence correction questions, you will have five different versions of the same sentence, and you must choose the best one. Here are the directions.

Directions

In each of the following sentences, some part or all of the sentence is underlined. Below each sentence you will find five ways of phrasing the underlined part. Select the answer that produces the most effective sentence, one that is clear and exact, without awkwardness or ambiguity, and blacken the corresponding space on your answer sheet. In choosing answers, follow the requirements of standard written English. Choose the answer that best expresses the meaning of the original sentence.

Answer (A) is always the same as the underlined part. Choose answer (A) if you think the original sentence needs no revision.

EXAMPLE:

Laura Ingalls Wilder published her first book <u>and she was sixty-five years old then</u>.

    SAMPLE ANSWER
    Ⓐ ● Ⓒ Ⓓ Ⓔ

(A) and she was sixty-five years old then
(B) when she was sixty-five years old
(C) at age sixty-five years old
(D) upon reaching sixty-five years
(E) at the time when she was sixty-five

In the paragraph correction questions, you will confront a flawed student essay followed by six questions. In some cases, you must select the answer choice that best rewrites and combines portions of two separate sentences. In others, you must decide where in the essay a sentence best fits. In still others, you must choose what sort of additional information would most strengthen the writer's argument. Here are the directions.

Directions

The passage below is the unedited draft of a student's essay. Some of the essay needs to be rewritten to make the meaning clear and more precise. Read the essay carefully.

The essay is followed by six questions about changes that might improve all or part of its organization, development, sentence structure, use of language, appropriateness to the audience, or its use of standard written English. Choose the answer that most clearly and effectively expresses the student's intended meaning. Indicate your choice by filling in the corresponding space on the answer sheet.

TIPS FOR HANDLING FIND-THE-ERROR QUESTIONS

1. Remember that the error, if there is one, must be in the underlined part of the sentence. You don't have to worry about improvements that could be made in the rest of the sentence. For example, if you have a sentence in which the subject is plural and the verb is singular, you could call either one the error. But if only the verb is underlined, the error for that sentence is the verb.

2. Use your ear for the language. Remember, you don't have to name the error, or be able to explain why it is wrong. All you have to do is recognize that something *is* wrong. On the early, easy questions in the set, if a word or phrase sounds wrong to you, it probably is, even if you don't know why.

3. Look first for the most common errors. Most of the sentences will have errors. If you are having trouble finding mistakes, check for some of the more common ones: subject-verb agreement, pronoun-antecedent problems, misuse of adjectives and

adverbs, dangling modifiers. But look for errors only in the underlined parts of the sentence.

4. Remember that not every sentence contains an error. Ten to twenty percent of the time, the sentence is correct as it stands. Do not get so caught up in hunting for errors that you start seeing errors that aren't there. If no obvious errors strike your eye and the sentence sounds natural to your ear, go with Choice E: <u>No error</u>.

EXAMPLE 1

Mr. Brown <u>is</u> one of the commuters who <u>takes</u> the 7:30
     A   B
train <u>from</u> Brooktown <u>every</u> morning. <u>No error</u>
   C   D   E

Since *who* refers to *commuters*, it is plural, and needs a plural verb. Therefore, the error is (B). If you were writing this sentence yourself, you could correct it in any number of other ways. You could say, "Mr. Brown is a commuter who takes..." or "Mr. Brown, a commuter, takes..." or "Mr. Brown, who is one of the commuters, takes..." However, the actual question doesn't offer you any of these possibilities. You have to choose from the underlined choices. Don't waste your time considering other ways to fix the sentence.

<u>EXAMPLE 2</u>

See if your ear helps you with this question.

<u>In my history class</u> I learned <u>why</u> the American colonies
      A   B
<u>opposed the British</u>, how they organized the militia, and
       C
<u>the work of the Continental Congress</u>. <u>No error</u>
         D   E

The last part of this sentence probably sounds funny to you—awkward, strange, wooden. You may not know exactly what it is, but something sounds wrong here. If you followed your instincts and chose D as the error, you would be right. The error is a lack of parallel structure. The sentence is listing three things you learned,

and they should all be in the same form. Your ear expects the pattern to be the same. Since the first two items listed are clauses, the third should be too: "In my history class I learned why the American colonies opposed the British, how they organized the militia, and how the Continental Congress worked."

<u>EXAMPLE 3</u>

Marilyn and <u>I</u> ran as <u>fast</u> as we could, but we missed our
            A   B
train, <u>which</u> made <u>us</u> late for work. <u>No error</u>
      C   D   E

Imagine that you have this sentence, and you can't see what is wrong with it. Start at the beginning and check each answer choice. *I* is part of the subject, so it is the right case: after all, you wouldn't say "Me ran fast." *Fast* can be an adverb, so it is being used correctly here. *Which* is a pronoun, and needs a noun for its antecedent. The only available noun is *train*, but that doesn't make sense (the train didn't make us late—*missing* the train made us late.) So there is your error, Choice C.

Once you have checked each answer choice, if you still can't find an error, choose E, "No error." A certain number of questions have no errors.

TIPS FOR HANDLING SENTENCE CORRECTION QUESTIONS

1. If you spot an error in the underlined section, eliminate any answer that repeats it. If something in the underlined section of a sentence correction question strikes you as an obvious error, you can immediately ignore any answer choices that repeat it. Remember, you still don't have to be able to explain what is wrong. You just need to find a correct equivalent. If the error you found in the underlined section is absent from more than one of the answer choices, look over those choices again to see if they add any new errors.

2. If you don't spot the error in the underlined section, look at the answer choices to see what is changed. Sometimes it's hard to spot what's wrong with the underlined section in a sentence correction question. When that happens, turn to the answer choices. Find the changes in the answers. The changes will tell you what kind of error is being tested.

3. Make sure that all parts of the sentence are logically connected. Not all parts of a sentence are created equal. Some parts should be subordinated to the rest, connected with subordinating conjunctions or relative pronouns, not just added on with *and*. Overuse of *and* frequently makes sentences sound babyish. Compare "We had dinner at the Hard Rock Cafe, and we went to a concert" with "After we had dinner at the Hard Rock Cafe, we went to a concert."

4. Make sure that all parts of a sentence given in a series are similar in form. If they are not, the sentence suffers from a lack of parallel structure. The sentence "I'm taking classes in algebra, history, and how to speak French" lacks parallel structure. *Algebra* and *history* are nouns, names of subjects. The third subject should also be a noun: *conversational French.*

5. Pay particular attention to the shorter answer choices. (This tactic also applies to certain paragraph correction questions.) Good prose is economical. Often the correct answer choice will be the shortest, most direct way of making a point. If you spot no grammatical errors or errors in logic in a concise answer choice, it may well be right.

<u>EXAMPLE 1</u>

<u>Being as I had studied for the test</u> with a tutor, I was confident.
(A) Being as I had studied for the test
(B) Being as I studied for the test
(C) Since I studied for the test
(D) Since I had studied for the test
(E) Because I studied for the test

Since you immediately recognize that *Being as* is not acceptable as a conjunction in standard written English, you can eliminate Choices A and B right away. But you also know that both *Since* and *Because* are perfectly acceptable conjunctions, so you have to look more closely at Choices C, D, and E. The only other changes these choices make are in the tense of the verb. Since the studying occurred before the taking of the test, the past perfect tense, *had studied*, is correct, so the answer is Choice D. Even if you hadn't known that, you could have figured it out. Since *Because* and *Since* are both acceptable conjunctions, and since Choices C and E both use the same verb, *studied,* in the simple past tense, those two choices must be wrong. Otherwise, they would both be right, and the PSAT doesn't have questions with two right answers.

EXAMPLE 2

The panel narrowed the field of applicants to the three whom it thought were best qualified for the position because of training and experience.
(A) whom it thought were
(B) of whom it thought were
(C) who it thought was
(D) whom it thought was
(E) who it thought were

You can see right away that you have to choose between *who* and *whom* and between *was* and *were*. You can immediately eliminate Choice B—any choice that turns the sentence into gibberish is the wrong answer. To decide the pronoun question, check on the way it is used in the sentence. In this sentence it is the subject of the verb *was* or *were* and therefore it must be *who*. This leaves you with Choices C and E. Now you want to know if you need a plural or singular verb. Since *who* refers to *three,* it is plural, and needs the plural verb *were*. The correct answer is E.

EXAMPLE 3

The rock star always had enthusiastic fans and they loved him.
(A) and they loved him
(B) and they loving him
(C) what loved him
(D) who loved him
(E) which loved him

The original version of this sentence doesn't have any grammatical errors, but it is a poor sentence because it doesn't connect its two clauses logically. The second clause ("and they loved him") is merely adding information about the fans, so it should be turned into an adjective clause, introduced by a relative pronoun. Choices D and E both seem to fit, but you know that *which* should never be used to refer to people, so Choice D is obviously the correct answer.

EXAMPLE 4

In this chapter we'll analyze both types of questions, suggest useful techniques for tackling them, providing some sample items for you to try.
(A) suggest useful techniques for tackling them, providing some sample items for you to try
(B) suggest useful techniques for tackling them, providing some sample items which you can try
(C) suggest useful tactics for tackling them, and provide some sample items for you to try
(D) and suggest useful techniques for tackling them by providing some sample items for you to try
(E) having suggested useful techniques for tackling them and provided some sample items for you to try

To answer questions like this correctly, you must pay particular attention to what the sentence means. You must first decide whether *analyzing, suggesting,* and *providing* are logically equal in importance here. Since they are—all are activities that "we" will do—they should be given equal emphasis. Only Choice C provides the proper parallel structure.

EXAMPLE 5

The turning point in the battle of Waterloo probably was Blucher, who was arriving in time to save the day.
(A) Blucher, who was arriving
(B) Blucher, in that he arrived
(C) Blucher's arrival
(D) when Blucher was arriving
(E) that Blucher had arrived

Which answer choice uses the fewest words? Choice C, *Blucher's arrival*. It also happens to be the right answer.

Choice C is both concise in style and correct in grammar. Look back at the original sentence. Strip it of its modifiers, and what is left? "The turning point . . . was Blucher." A turning point is not a person; it is a *thing*. The turning point in the battle was not Blucher, but Blucher's *action*, the thing he did. The correct answer is Choice C, *Blucher's arrival*. Pay particular attention to such concise answer choices. If a concise choice sounds natural when you substitute it for the original underlined phrase, it's a reasonable guess.

TIPS FOR HANDLING PARAGRAPH CORRECTION QUESTIONS

1. First read the passage; then read the questions. Whether you choose to skim the student essay quickly or to read it closely, you need to have a reasonable idea of what the student author is trying to say before you set out to correct this rough first draft.

2. First tackle the questions that ask you to improve individual sentences; then tackle the ones that ask you to strengthen the passage as a whole. In the sentence correction questions, you've just been weeding out ineffective sentences and selecting effective ones. Here you're doing more of the same. It generally takes less time to spot an effective sentence than it does to figure out a way to strengthen an argument or link up two paragraphs.

3. Consider whether the addition of signal words or phrases—transitions—would strengthen the passage or particular sentences within it. If the essay is trying to contrast two ideas, it might benefit from the addition of a contrast signal.
Contrast Signals: *although, despite, however, in contrast, nevertheless, on the contrary, on the other hand.*

If one portion of the essay is trying to support or continue a thought developed elsewhere in the passage, it might benefit from the addition of a support signal.
Support Signals: *additionally, furthermore, in addition, likewise, moreover.*

If the essay is trying to indicate that one thing causes another, it might benefit from the addition of a cause and effect signal.
Cause and Effect Signals: *accordingly, as a result of, because, consequently, hence, therefore, thus.*

Pay particular attention to answer choices that contain such signal words.

4. When you tackle the questions, *go back to the passage* to verify each answer choice. See whether your revised version of a particular sentence sounds right in its context. Ask yourself whether your choice follows naturally from the sentence before.

COMMON GRAMMAR AND USAGE ERRORS

Here are a dozen errors that appear frequently on the examination. Watch out for them when you do the practice exercises and when you take the PSAT. Not all examples will fit exactly into a specific category.

The Run-on Sentence

Mary's party was very exciting, it lasted until 2 A.M.
It is raining today, I need a raincoat.

You may also have heard this error called a comma splice. It can be corrected by making two sentences instead of one:

Mary's party was very exciting. It lasted until 2 A.M.

or by using a semicolon in place of the comma:

Mary's party was very exciting; it lasted until 2 A.M.

or by proper compounding:

Mary's party was very exciting and lasted until 2 A.M.

You can also correct this error with proper subordination. The second example above could be corrected:

Since it is raining today, I need a raincoat.
It is raining today, so I need a raincoat.

The Sentence Fragment

Since John was talking during the entire class, making it impossible for anyone to concentrate.

This is the opposite of the first error. Instead of too much in one sentence, here you have too little. Do not be misled by the length of the fragment. It must have a main clause before it can be a complete sentence. All you have in this example is the cause. You still need a result. For example, the sentence could be corrected:

Since John was talking during the entire class, making it impossible for anyone to concentrate, the teacher made him stay after school.

Error in the Case of a Noun or Pronoun

Between you and I, this test is not really very difficult.

Case problems usually involve personal pronouns, which are in the nominative case (*I, he, she, we, they, who*) when they are used as subjects or predicate nominatives, and in the objective case (*me, him, her, us, them, whom*) when they are used as direct objects, indirect objects, and objects of prepositions. In this example, if you realize that *between* is a preposition, you know that *I* should be changed to the objective *me* because it is the object of a preposition.

Error in Subject-Verb Agreement

Harvard College, along with several other Ivy League schools, are sending students to the conference.

Phrases starting with *along with* or *as well as* or *in addition to* that are placed in between the subject and the verb do not affect the verb. The subject of this sentence is *Harvard College,* so the verb should be *is sending.*

There is three bears living in that house.

Sentences that begin with *there* have the subject after the verb. The subject of this sentence is *bears,* so the verb should be *are.*

Error in Pronoun-Antecedent Agreement

Every one of the girls on the team is trying to do their best.

Every pronoun must have a specific noun or noun substitute for an antecedent, and it must agree with that antecedent in number (singular or plural). In this example, *their* refers to *one* and must be singular:

Every one of the girls on the team is trying to do her best.

Error in the Tense or Form of a Verb

After the sun set behind the mountain, a cool breeze sprang up and brought relief from the heat.

Make sure the verbs in a sentence appear in the proper sequence of tenses, so that it is clear what happened when. Since, according to the sentence, the breeze did not appear until after the sun had finished setting, the setting belongs in the past perfect tense:

After the sun had set behind the mountain, a cool breeze sprang up and brought relief from the heat.

Failure to Use the Subjunctive Mood When Needed

If I was your parent, I would ground you for a month.

The subjunctive mood is not very common in English, but it is used to indicate a condition contrary to fact. Since I am not your parent, the subjunctive is needed in this example:

If I were your parent, I would ground you for a month.

Error in Comparison

I can go to California or Florida. I wonder which is best.

When you are comparing only two things, you should use the comparative form of the adjective, not the superlative:

I wonder which is better.

Comparisons must also be complete and logical.

The rooms on the second floor are larger than the first floor.

It would be a strange building that had rooms larger than an entire floor. Logically, this sentence should be corrected to:

The rooms on the second floor are larger than those on the first floor.

Misuse of Adjectives and Adverbs

She did good on the test.
They felt badly about leaving their friends.

These are the two most common ways that adjectives and adverbs are misused. In the first example, when you are talking about how someone did, you want the adverb *well,* not the adjective *good:*

She did well on the test.

In the second example, after a linking verb like *feel* you want a predicate adjective to describe the subject:

They felt bad about leaving their friends.

Dangling Modifiers

Reaching for the book, the ladder slipped out from under him.

A participial phrase at the beginning of the sentence should describe the subject of the sentence. Since it doesn't make sense to think of a ladder reaching for a book, this participle is left dangling with nothing to modify. The sentence needs some rewriting:

When he reached for the book, the ladder slipped out from under him.

Lack of Parallel Structure

In his book on winter sports, the author discusses ice-skating, skiing, hockey, and how to fish in an ice-covered lake.

Logically, equal and similar ideas belong in similar form. This shows that they are equal. In this sentence, the author discusses four sports, and all four should be presented the same way:

In his book on winter sports, the author discusses ice skating, skiing, hockey, and fishing in an ice-covered lake.

Error in Diction or Idiom

The affects of the storm could be seen everywhere.

Your ear for the language will help you handle these errors, especially if you are accustomed to reading standard English. These questions test you on words that are frequently misused, on levels of usage (informal versus formal), and on standard English idioms. In this example, the verb *affect,* meaning "to influence," has been confused with the noun *effect,* meaning "result."

The effects of the storm could be seen everywhere.

The exercise that follows will give you practice in answering the three types of questions you'll find on the usage questions, sentence correction questions, and paragraph correction questions. When you have completed the exercise, check your answers against the answer key. Then, read the answer explanations for any questions you either answered incorrectly or omitted.

Writing Skills Exercise

Directions

The following sentences contain problems in grammar, usage, diction (choice of words), and idiom.

Some sentences are correct.

No sentence contains more than one error.

You will find that the error, if there is one, is underlined and lettered. Assume that elements of the sentence that are not underlined are correct and cannot be changed. In choosing answers, follow the requirements of standard written English.

If there is an error, select the one underlined part that must be changed to make the sentence correct and blacken the corresponding space on your answer sheet.

If there is no error, blacken answer space Ⓔ.

EXAMPLE:

The region has a climate <u>so severe that</u> plants
A

<u>growing there</u> rarely <u>had been</u> more than twelve
BC

inches <u>high.</u> <u>No error</u>
DE

SAMPLE ANSWER
Ⓐ Ⓑ ● Ⓓ Ⓔ

PRACTICE EXERCISE

1. We were <u>already</u> <u>to leave for</u> the amusement park
AB
when John's car <u>broke down</u>; we <u>were forced to</u>
CD
postpone our outing. <u>No error</u>
E

2. <u>By order of</u> the Student Council, the <u>wearing of</u>
AB
slacks by <u>we</u> girls in school <u>has been permitted.</u>
CD
<u>No error</u>
E

3. <u>Each one</u> of the dogs in the show <u>require</u> a <u>special</u>
ABC
kind of diet. <u>No error</u>
DE

4. The major difficulty <u>confronting the authorities was</u>
AB
the reluctance of the people <u>to talk</u>; they had been
C
warned not <u>to say nothing</u> to the police. <u>No error</u>
DE

5. If I were you, I would never permit him
      A   B
   to take part in such an exhausting and painful
      C   D
   activity. No error
             E

6. Stanford White, who is one of America's
                    A
   most notable architects, have designed many
        B   C
   famous buildings, among them the original
                        D
   Madison Square Garden. No error
                          E

7. The notion of allowing the institution of slavery
              A   B
   to continue to exist in a democratic society had no
      C
   appeal to either the violent followers of John Brown

   nor the peaceful disciples of Sojourner Truth.
   D
   No error
   E

8. Some students prefer watching filmstrips to
                  A
   textbooks because they feel uncomfortable with
      B   C
   the presentation of information in a non-oral
                     D
   form. No error
         E

9. There was so much conversation in back of me that
   A   B   C
   I couldn't hear the actors on the stage. No error
   D   E

10. This book is too elementary; it can help neither
                 A   B
    you nor I. No error
    C   D   E

11. In a way we may say that we have reached the
            A   B   C
    end of the Industrial Revolution. No error
    D   E

12. Although the books are altogether on the shelf,
    A   B
    they are not arranged in any kind of order.
    C   D
    No error
    E

13. The reason for my prolonged absence from class
        A   B
    was because I was ill for three weeks. No error
    C   D   E

14. According to researchers, the weapons and work
    A
    implements used by Cro-Magnon hunters appear
              B
    being actually quite "modern." No error
    C   D   E

15. Since we were caught completely unawares, the
                        A
    affect of Ms. Rivera's remarks was startling; some
    B   C
    were shocked, but others were angry. No error
                  D   E

16. The committee had intended both you and I to
                   A   B
    speak at the assembly; however, only one of us
                          C   D
    will be able to talk. No error
                         E

17. The existence of rundown "welfare hotels"

    in which homeless families reside at enormous
    A   B
    cost to the taxpayer provides a shameful
    C
    commentary of America's commitment to house
    D
    the poor. No error
              E

18. We have heard that the principal has decided
                        A
    whom the prize winners will be and will
    B   C   D
    announce the names in the assembly today.

    No error
    E

19. As soon as the sun had rose over the mountains,
       A   B   C
    the valley became unbearably hot and stifling.
                      D
    No error
    E

20. They are both excellent books, but this one is
    A   B   C
    best. No error
    D   E

21. Although the news <u>had come</u> as a surprise <u>to all</u>
                    A   B
    in the room, everyone tried to do <u>their</u> work
                                  C
    <u>as though</u> nothing had happened. <u>No error</u>
       D   E

22. <u>Even</u> well-known fashion designers have difficulty
    A
    staying on top <u>from one season to another</u>
                        B
    because of <u>changeable moods</u> and needs in the
        C   D
    marketplace. <u>No error</u>
               E

23. Arms control has been <u>under discussion</u> for
                    A
    decades with the former Soviet Union, <u>but</u>
                             B
    solutions <u>are still</u> <u>alluding</u> the major powers.
           C   D
    <u>No error</u>
      E

24. Perhaps sports enthusiasts are realizing <u>that</u>
                       A
    jogging is <u>not easy on</u> joints and tendons, for
             B
    the <u>latest</u> fad <u>is being walking</u>. <u>No error</u>
        C   D   E

25. Technological advances <u>can cause</u> factual data to
                       A
    become obsolete within a <u>short time</u>; <u>yet</u>, students
                     B   C
    should concentrate on <u>reasoning skills</u>, not facts.
                      D
    <u>No error</u>
      E

26. <u>If</u> anyone cares <u>to join</u> me in this campaign, <u>either</u>
    A   B   C
    now or in the near future, <u>they</u> will be welcomed
                             D
    gratefully. <u>No error</u>
              E

27. The poems <u>with which</u> he occasionally
               A
    desired to <u>regale</u> the fashionable world were
           B
    <u>invariably bad</u>—stereotyped, bombastic, and
         C
    <u>even ludicrous</u>. <u>No error</u>
        D   E

28. <u>Ever since</u> the <u>quality of</u> teacher education came
       A   B
    under public scrutiny, suggestions for <u>upgrading</u>
                                     C
    the profession <u>are abounding</u>. <u>No error</u>
                 D   E

29. <u>Because</u> the door was locked and bolted, the police
    A
    were forced <u>to break</u> into the apartment <u>through</u>
      B   C   D
    the bedroom window. <u>No error</u>
                    E

30. I <u>will</u> <u>always</u> remember <u>you</u> <u>standing by</u> me
      A   B   C   D
    offering me encouragement. <u>No error</u>
                       E

31. With special training, capuchin monkeys
    <u>can enable</u> quadriplegics <u>as well as</u> other
       A   B
    handicapped individuals <u>to become</u>
                        C
    increasingly independent. <u>No error</u>
             D   E

32. <u>Contrary to</u> what had previously been reported, the
    A
    conditions <u>governing</u> the truce between Libya and
            B
    Chad <u>arranged by</u> the United Nations <u>has</u> not yet
          C   D
    been revealed. <u>No error</u>
              E

33. Avid readers generally either admire <u>or</u> dislike
                           A
    Ernest Hemingway's journalistic <u>style of</u> writing;
                            B
    <u>few have</u> no opinion <u>of him</u>. <u>No error</u>
       C   D   E

34. In 1986, the nuclear disaster at Chernobyl
    <u>has aroused</u> intense speculation <u>about the</u>
       A   B
    long-term <u>effects of</u> radiation that continued
               C
    for <u>the better part</u> of a year. <u>No error</u>
           D   E

35. Howard Hughes, <u>who</u> <u>became</u> the subject of bizarre
                 A   B
    rumors <u>as a result of</u> his extreme reclusiveness,
               C
    was well-known as an aviator, industrialist, and
    <u>in producing motion pictures</u>. <u>No error</u>
                  D   E

Directions

In each of the following sentences, some part or all of the sentence is underlined. Below each sentence you will find five ways of phrasing the underlined part. Select the answer that produces the most effective sentence, one that is clear and exact, without awkwardness or ambiguity, and blacken the corresponding space on your answer sheet. In choosing answers, follow the requirements of standard written English. Choose the answer that best expresses the meaning of the original sentence.

Answer (A) is always the same as the underlined part. Choose answer (A) if you think the original sentence needs no revision.

EXAMPLE:

Laura Ingalls Wilder published her first book and she was sixty-five years old then.
(A) and she was sixty-five years old then
(B) when she was sixty-five years old
(C) at age sixty-five years old
(D) upon reaching sixty-five years
(E) at the time when she was sixty-five

SAMPLE ANSWER

Ⓐ ● Ⓒ Ⓓ Ⓔ

36. The child is neither encouraged to be critical or to examine all the evidence before forming an opinion.
    (A) neither encouraged to be critical or to examine
    (B) neither encouraged to be critical nor to examine
    (C) either encouraged to be critical or to examine
    (D) encouraged either to be critical nor to examine
    (E) not encouraged either to be critical or to examine

37. The process by which the community influence the actions of its members is known as social control.
    (A) influence the actions of its members
    (B) influences the actions of its members
    (C) had influenced the actions of its members
    (D) influences the actions of their members
    (E) will influence the actions of its members

38. Play being recognized as an important factor improving mental and physical health and thereby reducing human misery and poverty.
    (A) Play being recognized as
    (B) By recognizing play as
    (C) Their recognizing play as
    (D) Recognition of it being
    (E) Play is recognized as

39. To be sure, there would be scarcely any time left over for other things if school children would have been expected to have considered all sides of every matter, on which they hold opinions.
    (A) would have been expected to have considered
    (B) should have been expected to have considered
    (C) were expected to consider
    (D) will be expected to have considered
    (E) were expected to be considered

40. Using it wisely, leisure promoted health, efficiency and happiness.
    (A) Using it wisely
    (B) If it is used wisely
    (C) Having used it wisely
    (D) Because of its wise use
    (E) Because of usefulness

41. In giving expression to the play instincts of the human race, new vigor and effectiveness are afforded by recreation to the body and to the mind.
    (A) new vigor and effectiveness are afforded by recreation to the body and to the mind
    (B) recreation affords new vigor and effectiveness to the body and to the mind
    (C) there are afforded new vigor and effectiveness to the body and to the mind
    (D) by recreation the body and the mind are afforded new vigor and effectiveness
    (E) to the body and to the mind afford new vigor and effectiveness to themselves by recreation

42. Depending on skillful suggestion, argument is seldom used in advertising.
    (A) Depending on skillful suggestion, argument is seldom used in advertising.
    (B) Argument is seldom used in advertising, who depend instead on skillful suggestion.
    (C) Skillful suggestion is depended on by advertisers instead of argument.
    (D) Suggestion, which is more skillful, is used in place of argument by advertisers.
    (E) Instead of suggestion, depending on argument is used by skillful advertisers.

43. When this war is over, no nation will either be isolated in war or peace.
    (A) either be isolated in war or peace
    (B) be either isolated in war or peace
    (C) be isolated in neither war nor peace
    (D) be isolated either in war or in peace
    (E) be isolated neither in war or peace

44. Thanks to the prevailing westerly winds, dust blowing east from the drought-stricken plains travels halfway across the continent to fall on the cities of the East Coast.
    (A) blowing east from the drought-stricken plains
    (B) that, blowing east from the drought-stricken plains,
    (C) from the drought-stricken plains and blows east
    (D) that is from the drought-stricken plains blowing east
    (E) blowing east that is from the plains that are drought-stricken

45. Americans are learning that their concept of a research worker toiling alone in a laboratory and who discovers miraculous cures has been highly idealized and glamorized.
    (A) toiling alone in a laboratory and who discovers miraculous cures
    (B) toiling alone in a laboratory and discovers miraculous cures
    (C) toiling alone in a laboratory to discover miraculous cures
    (D) who toil alone in the laboratory and discover miraculous cures
    (E) has toiled alone hoping to discover miraculous cures

46. However many mistakes have been made in our past, the tradition of America, not only the champion of freedom but also fair play, still lives among millions who can see light and hope scarcely anywhere else.
    (A) not only the champion of freedom but also fair play
    (B) the champion of not only freedom but also of fair play
    (C) the champion not only of freedom but also of fair play
    (D) not only the champion but also freedom and fair play
    (E) not the champion of freedom only, but also fair play

47. Examining the principal movements sweeping through the world, it can be seen that they are being accelerated by the war.
    (A) Examining the principal movements sweeping through the world, it can be seen
    (B) Having examined the principal movements sweeping through the world, it can be seen
    (C) Examining the principal movements sweeping through the world can be seen
    (D) Examining the principal movements sweeping through the world, we can see
    (E) It can be seen examining the principal movements sweeping through the world

48. The FCC is broadening its view on what constitutes indecent programming, radio stations are taking a closer look at their broadcasters' materials.
    (A) The FCC is broadening its view on what constitutes indecent programming
    (B) The FCC, broadening its view on what constitutes indecent programming, has caused
    (C) The FCC is broadening its view on what constitutes indecent programming, as a result
    (D) Since the FCC is broadening its view on what constitutes indecent programming
    (E) The FCC, having broadened its view on what constitutes indecent programming

49. As district attorney, Elizabeth Holtzman not only has the responsibility of supervising a staff of dedicated young lawyers but she has the task of maintaining good relations with the police also.
    (A) but she has the task of maintaining good relations with the police also
    (B) but she also has the task of maintaining good relations with the police
    (C) but also has the task of maintaining good relations with the police
    (D) but she has the task to maintain good relations with the police also
    (E) but also she has the task to maintain good relations with the police

50. Many politicians are now trying to take uncontroversial positions on issues; the purpose being to allow them to appeal to as wide a segment of the voting population as possible.
    (A) issues; the purpose being to allow them to appeal
    (B) issues in order to appeal
    (C) issues, the purpose is to allow them to appeal
    (D) issues and the purpose is to allow them to appeal
    (E) issues; that was allowing them to appeal

Essay

[1] Throughout history, people have speculated about the future. [2] Will it be a utopia? they wondered. [3] Will injustice and poverty be eliminated? [4] Will people accept ethnic diversity, learning to live in peace? [5] Will the world be clean and unpolluted? [6] Or will technology aid us in creating a trap for ourselves we cannot escape, for example such as the world in 1984? [7] With the turn of the millennium just around the corner these questions are in the back of our minds.

[8] Science fiction often portrays the future as a technological Garden of Eden. [9] With interactive computers, TVs and robots at our command, we barely need to lift a finger to go to school, to work, to go shopping, and education is also easy and convenient. [10] Yet, the problems of the real twentieth century seem to point in another direction. [11] The environment, far from improving, keeps deteriorating. [12] Wars and other civil conflicts breakout regularly. [13] The world's population is growing out of control. [14] The

majority of people on earth live in poverty. [15] Many of them are starving. [16] Illiteracy is a problem in most poor countries. [17] Diseases and malnourishment is very common. [18] Rich countries like the U.S.A. don't have the resources to help the "have-not" countries.

[19] Instead, think instead of all the silly inventions such as tablets you put in your toilet tank to make the water blue, or electric toothbrushes. [20] More money is spent on space and defense than on education and health care. [21] Advancements in agriculture can produce enough food to feed the whole country, yet people in the U.S. are starving.

[22] Although the USSR is gone, the nuclear threat continues from small countries like Iraq. [23] Until the world puts its priorities straight, we can't look for a bright future in the twenty-first century, despite the rosy picture painted for us by the science fiction writers.

51. Considering the context of paragraph 1, which of the following is the best revision of sentence 6?
  (A) Or will technology create a trap for ourselves from which we cannot escape, for example the world in *1984*?
  (B) Or will technology aid people in creating a trap for themselves that they cannot escape; for example, the world in *1984*?
  (C) Or will technology create a trap from which there is no escape, as it did in the world in *1984*?
  (D) Or will technology trap us in an inescapable world, for example, it did so in the world of *1984*?
  (E) Perhaps technology will aid people in creating a trap for themselves from which they cannot escape, just as they did it in the world of *1984*.

52. With regard to the essay as a whole, which of the following best describes the writer's intention in paragraph 1?
  (A) To announce the purpose of the essay
  (B) To compare two ideas discussed later in the essay
  (C) To take a position on the essay's main issue
  (D) To reveal the organization of the essay
  (E) To raise questions that will be answered in the essay

53. Which of the following is the best revision of the underlined segment of sentence 9 below?

  [9] With interactive computers, TVs and robots at our command, we barely need to lift a finger to go to school, to work, to go shopping, and education is also easy and convenient.

  (A) and to go shopping, while education is also easy and convenient
  (B) to go shopping, and getting an education is also easy and convenient
  (C) to go shopping as well as educating ourselves are all easy and convenient
  (D) to shop, and an easy and convenient education
  (E) to shop, and to get an easy and convenient education

54. Which of the following is the most effective way to combine sentences 14, 15, 16, and 17?
  (A) The majority of people on earth are living in poverty and are starving, with illiteracy, and disease and being malnourished are also a common problems.
  (B) Common problems for the majority of people on earth are poverty, illiteracy, diseases, malnourishment, and many are illiterate.
  (C) The majority of people on earth are poor, starving, sick, malnourished and illiterate.
  (D) Common among the poor majority on earth is poverty, starvation, disease, malnourishment, and illiteracy.
  (E) The majority of the earth's people living in poverty with starvation, disease, malnourishment and illiteracy a constant threat.

55. Considering the sentences that precede and follow sentence 19, which of the following is the most effective revision of sentence 19?
  (A) Instead they are devoting resources on silly inventions such as tablets to make toilet tank water blue or electric toothbrushes.
  (B) Instead, they waste their resources on producing silly inventions like electric toothbrushes and tablets for bluing toilet tank water.
  (C) Think of all the silly inventions: tablets you put in your toilet tank to make the water blue and electric toothbrushes.
  (D) Instead, tablets you put in your toilet tank to make the water blue or electric toothbrushes are examples of useless products on the market today.
  (E) Instead of spending on useful things, think of all the silly inventions such as tablets you put in your toilet tank to make the water blue or electric toothbrushes.

56. Which of the following revisions would most improve the overall coherence of the essay?
  (A) Move sentence 7 to Paragraph 2
  (B) Move sentence 10 to Paragraph 1
  (C) Move sentence 22 to paragraph 2
  (D) Delete sentence 8
  (E) Delete sentence 23

ANSWER KEY

1. A	*9.* B	*17.* D	*25.* C	*33.* D	*41.* B	*49.* C
2. C	*10.* D	*18.* B	*26.* D	*34.* A	*42.* B	*50.* B
3. B	*11.* E	*19.* B	*27.* E	*35.* D	*43.* D	*51.* C
4. D	*12.* B	*20.* D	*28.* D	*36.* E	*44.* A	*52.* E
5. E	*13.* D	*21.* C	*29.* E	*37.* B	*45.* C	*53.* E
6. C	*14.* C	*22.* E	*30.* C	*38.* E	*46.* C	*54.* C
7. D	*15.* B	*23.* D	*31.* E	*39.* C	*47.* D	*55.* B
8. B	*16.* B	*24.* D	*32.* D	*40.* B	*48.* D	*56.* C

ANSWER EXPLANATIONS

1. **A** Should be *all ready. All ready* means the group is ready; *already* means prior to a given time, previously

2. **C** Should be *us*. The expression *us girls* is the object of the preposition *by*.

3. **B** Should be *requires*. Verb should agree with the subject (*each one*).

4. **D** Should be *to say anything. Not to say nothing* is a double negative.

5. **E** Sentence is correct.

6. **C** Error in agreement. Since the subject is Stanford White (singular), change *have designed* to *has designed*.

7. **D** Error in use of correlatives. Change *nor* to *or*. The correct form of the correlative pairs *either* with *or*.

8. **B** Error in parallel structure. Change *textbooks* to *reading textbooks*. To have parallel structure, the linked sentence elements must share the same grammatical form.

9. **B** Error in diction. Change *in back of* to *behind*.

10. **D** Should be *me*. Pronoun is the object of the verb *can help*.

11. **E** Sentence is correct.

12. **B** Should be *all together. All together* means in a group; *altogether* means entirely.

13. **D** Improper use of *because*. Change to *that* (*The reason . . . was that . . . .*).

14. **C** Incorrect verbal. Change the participle *being* to the infinitive *to be*.

15. **B** Error in diction. Change *affect* (a verb meaning to influence or pretend) to *effect* (a noun meaning result).

16. **B** Should be *me*. Subjects of infinitives are in the objective case.

17. **D** Error in diction. Change *commentary of* to *commentary on*.

18. **B** Should be *who*. The pronoun is the predicate complement of *will be* and is in the nominative case.

19. **B** Should be *had risen*. The past participle of the verb *to rise* is *risen*.

20. **D** Should be *better*. Do not use the superlative when comparing two things.

21. **C** Should be *his* or *her* instead of *their*. The antecedent of the pronoun is *everyone* (singular).

22. **E** Sentence is correct.

23. **D** Error in diction. Change *alluding* (meaning to refer indirectly) to *eluding* (meaning to evade).

24. **D** Confusion of verb and gerund (verbal noun). Change *is being walking* to *is walking*.

25. **C** Error in sentence connector. Change *yet* to *therefore* or another similar connector to clarify the connection between the clauses.

26. **D** Should be *he* or *she*. The antecedent of the pronoun is *anyone* (singular).

27. **E** Sentence is correct.

28. **D** Error in tense. Change *are abounding* to *have abounded*. The present perfect tense talks about an action that occurs at one time, but is seen in relation to another time.

29. **E** Sentence is correct.

30. **C** Should be *your*. The pronoun modifying a gerund (verbal noun) should be in the possessive case.

31. **E** Sentence is correct.

32. **D** Error in agreement. Since the subject is *conditions* (plural), change *has* to *have*.

33. **D** Error in pronoun. Since the sentence speaks about Hemingway's style rather than about Hemingway, the phrase should read *of it*, not *of him*.

34. **A** Error in tense. Change *has aroused* to *aroused*. The present perfect tense (*has aroused*) is used for indefinite time. In this sentence, the time is defined as *the better part of a year*.

35. **D** Lack of parallel structure. Change *in producing motion pictures* to *motion picture producer*.

36. **E** This question involves two aspects of correct English. *Neither* should be followed by *nor; either* by *or*. Choices A and D are, therefore, incorrect. The words *neither . . . nor* and *either . . . or* should be placed before the two items being discussed—*to be critical* and *to examine*. Choice E meets both requirements.

37. **B** This question tests agreement. Agreement between subject and verb and pronoun and antecedent are both involved. *Community* (singular) needs a singular verb, *influences*. Also, the pronoun that refers to *community* should be singular (*its*).

38. **E** This is an incomplete sentence or fragment. The sentence needs a verb to establish a principal clause. Choice E provides the verb (*is recognized*) and presents the only complete sentence in the group.

39. **C**   *Would have been expected* is incorrect as a verb in a clause introduced by the conjunction *if. Had been expected* or *were expected* is preferable. *To have considered* does not follow correct sequence of tense and should be changed to *to consider.*

40. **B**   One way of correcting a dangling participle is to change the participial phrase to a clause. Choices B and D substitute clauses for the phrase. However, choice D changes the meaning of the sentence. Choice B is correct.

41. **B**   As it stands, the sentence contains a dangling modifier. This is corrected by making *recreation* the subject of the sentence, in the process switching from the passive to the active voice. Choice E also provides a subject for the sentence; however, the meaning of the sentence is changed in choice E.

42. **B**   As presented, the sentence contains a dangling participle, *depending.* Choice B corrects this error. The other choices change the emphasis presented by the author.

43. **D**   *Either . . . or* should precede the two choices offered (*in war* and *in peace*).

44. **A**   Sentence is correct.

45. **C**   In the underlined phrase, you will find two modifiers of *worker-toiling* and *who discovers.* The first is a participial phrase and the second a clause. This results in an error in parallel structure. Choice B also has an error in parallel structure. Choice C corrects this by eliminating one of the modifiers of *worker.* Choice D corrects the error in parallel structure but introduces an error in agreement between subject and verb—*who* (singular) and *toil* (plural). Choice E changes the tense and also the meaning of the original sentence.

46. **C**   Parallel structure requires that *not only* and *but also* immediately precede the words they limit.

47. **D**   Choices A, B, and E are incorrect because of the dangling participle. Choice C is incoherent. Choice D correctly eliminates the dangling participle by introducing the subject *we.*

48. **D**   The punctuation in choices A and C creates a run-on sentence. Choices B and E are both ungrammatical. Choice D corrects the run-on sentence by changing the beginning clause into the adverb clause that starts with the subordinating conjunction *since.*

49. **C**   Since the words *not only* immediately precede the verb in the first half of the sentence, the words *but also* should immediately precede the verb in the second half. This error in parallel structure is corrected in choice C.

50. **B**   The punctuation in choices A, C, D, and E creates an incomplete sentence or fragment. Choice B corrects the run-on phrase by linking the elements with *in order to.*

51. **C**   Choice A is awkward and shifts the pronoun usage in the paragraph from third to first person. Choice B is awkward and contains a semicolon error. A semicolon is used to separate two independent clauses. The material after the semicolon is a sentence fragment. Choice C is succinctly and accurately expressed. It is the best answer. Choice D contains a comma splice between *world* and *for.* A comma may not be used to join two independent clauses. Choice E is awkwardly expressed and contains the pronoun *it,* which lacks a clear referent.

52. **E**   Choice A indirectly describes the purpose of paragraph 1 but does not identify the writer's main intention. Choices B, C, and D fail to describe the writer's main intention. Choice E accurately describes the writer's main intention. It is the best answer.

53. **E**   Choice A is grammatically correct but cumbersome. Choice B contains an error in parallel construction. The clause that begins *and getting* is not grammatically parallel to the previous items on the list. Choice C contains a mixed construction. The first and last parts of the sentence are grammatically unrelated. Choice D contains faulty parallel structure. Choice E is correct and accurately expressed. It is the best answer.

54. **C**   Choice A is wordy and awkwardly expressed. Choice B contains an error in parallel structure. The clause *and many are illiterate* is not grammatically parallel to the previous items on the list of problems. Choice C is concise and accurately expressed. It is the best answer. Choice D is concise, but it contains an error in subject-verb agreement. The subject is *poverty, starvation . . . etc.,* which requires a plural verb; the verb *is* is singular. Choice E is a sentence fragment; it has no main verb.

55. **B**   Choice A contains an error in idiom. The standard phrase is *devoting to,* not *devoting on.* Choice B ties sentence 19 to the previous sentence and is accurately expressed. It is the best answer. Choice C fails to improve the coherence of the paragraph. Choice D is unrelated to the context of the paragraph. Choice E is insufficiently related to the context of the paragraph.

56. **C**   Choice A should stay put because it provides a transition between the questions in paragraph 1 and the beginning of paragraph 2. Choice B is a pivotal sentence in paragraph 2 and should not be moved. Choice C fits the topics of paragraph 2, therefore, sentence 22 should be moved to paragraph 2. Choice C is the best answer. Choice D is needed as an introductory sentence in paragraph 2. It should not be deleted. Choice E provides the essay with a meaningful conclusion and should not be deleted.

Mathematical Reasoning

8

Reviewing Mathematics

This chapter reviews the principles of elementary mathematics through plane geometry, since the PSAT/NMSQT attempts to find out how well these topics have been mastered. The drill is especially important since many students have not had recent experience with some of the ideas such as percents or fractions, and others have never really mastered these topics. However, with a few hints and a bit of practice, students should be able to understand the basic concepts involved and put them to use.

Students who have just completed a course in plane geometry may find the exercises in this chapter different from the type they are used to, as these questions do more than check on knowledge. They often attempt to find out whether knowledge can be applied to new situations.

Some mathematics questions are designed to test reasoning and thinking. This chapter furnishes such problems within the framework of familiar topics as well as in special exercises such as evaluating information necessary to solve problems.

Another use of this chapter is to offer drill in a particular topic that may turn up as a weakness when the student attempts to do the sample tests in the latter part of this book.

TIPS FOR HANDLING REGULAR MATHEMATICS QUESTIONS

1. Read each question carefully to understand what the question is asking. In the multiple-choice questions, look at the answer choices to direct your attention to the purpose of the question. You may find that some of the answer choices are contrary to fact. As you eliminate those that are obviously wrong, you have fewer items from which to choose. Also, sometimes it is quicker to work back from the answers, but try the easiest choices first. Very often the test makers reward ingenuity.

2. Avoid lengthy computation. Bear in mind that the test is constructed so that the fifty math questions can be completed in sixty minutes. Should you find yourself involved in lengthy computation, you may be misreading the question or missing a shortcut. If you are dealing with a right triangle of the 3-4-5, 5-12-13, or 8-15-17 type, avoid lengthy computations involving the Pythagorean Theorem. Use your time wisely.

3. If you are answering a question that requires you to apply a formula not given to you (for example, the area or circumference of a circle or the sides of a 30°-60°-90° or 45°-45°-90° triangle), write the formula on the question paper to be sure you substitute it correctly.

4. In the multiple-choice questions, estimate your answer. Make sure you have chosen a reasonable answer. Give your answer the common-sense test.

5. Don't panic if you encounter a new type of question. It may be nothing more than a combination of familiar topics. If unusual symbols are used, replace them with the definitions that accompany them.

6. Don't expect to be able to answer all questions. Very few students do. Work carefully and accurately on the questions you can answer, and don't waste time worrying about the others.

7. If you skip a question, make sure to skip the corresponding number on the answer sheet.

8. Express your answer in the units required. In solving word problems, convert measurements to the same units. If the problem involves hours, minutes, and seconds and you observe that all the answer choices are in minutes, confine your calculations to minutes.

9. If you find that none of the answer choices resemble the answer you get, the equivalent of your answer may be there. For example, $\frac{a+b}{b} = \frac{a}{b} + 1$.

10. If a geometry problem does not provide a figure, draw one. However, don't waste time making a work of art. No one looks at your scratchwork. If a diagram is furnished, mark it up to help you solve the problem. Also, look for diagrams marked NOT DRAWN TO SCALE. Don't make unwarranted assumptions.

11. All but the student-produced response questions will ask you to choose the one right answer from five choices. In such questions, if you have spotted a choice you are sure is correct, do not waste time examining the other choices. However, a special type of question sometimes occurs in which several possibilities are presented within the question itself; these possibilities are always identified with Roman numerals I, II, and III. You are then asked to state whether I only is true, II only is true, I and II only are true, and so forth. In this type of question, you must examine *all* the possibilities since several of them (and maybe even all of them) may be correct.

12. Most questions present five possible choices, only one of which fits the requirements stated in the question. However, sometimes a special question is asked in which all *except* one of the choices fit the requirements stated in the question and you are asked to choose the one that is the exception. The examiners warn you of this reverse emphasis by printing the word EXCEPT in bold capital letters. In answering such a question, it is helpful to try to spot some common property that all but one choice share; for example, all but one may be even numbers, or all but one may be positive numbers.

13. Because most of the regular mathematics questions provide five choices, a random guess is likely to be correct only $\frac{1}{5}$ of the time. But $\frac{1}{4}$ of a point is deducted for each wrong answer in the scoring. Therefore, it is unwise to make a random guess. However, if you can definitely rule out one choice, it is not foolhardy to make a guess from the remaining four choices since your odds for picking the right choice now equal the deduction cost for a wrong answer. If you can rule out more than one choice, it is definitely advisable to guess from among the remaining ones becausee the odds for picking the correct choice are greater than the deduction cost for a wrong answer.

A SUGGESTED STUDY PROGRAM

1. BASIC MATHEMATICS—Review the definitions, important principles, and fundamental operations.

2. ALGEBRA—Review the definitions and basic algebraic operations. Study the hints on solving problems. Do the practice exercises. Study the important facts about inequalities. Do the exercises.

3. GEOMETRY—Review the principles, formulas, and definitions. Study the rules involving coordinate geometry. Do the exercises.

4. FRACTIONS—Review the principles. Study the hints on solving problems. Do the practice exercises. Check your answers.

5. PERCENT—Study the hints on solving problems. Do the practice exercises. Check your answers.

6. AVERAGE—Study the principles. Do the practice exercises. Check your answers.

7. MOTION—Review the formulas. Study the hints on solving problems. Do the exercises. Check your answers.

8. RATIO AND PROPORTION—Study the principles and hints on solving problems. Be able to differentiate between direct and inverse proportions. Study the illustrative examples. Do the practice exercises. Check your answers.

9. WORK—Study the hints on solving problems. Do the practice exercises. Check your answers.

10. DATA INTERPRETATION—Study the explanations given. Do the practice exercises. Check your answers.

11. QUANTITATIVE COMPARISON (Chapter 9)—Study the format of this type of question. Study the hints on solving problems. Do the practice exercises. Check your answers.

12. Take the Sample Tests in Chapter 10. Correct your answers. Analyze the correct answers.

BASIC MATHEMATICS

SYMBOLS USED IN MATHEMATICS

=	equals	∴	therefore
≠	not equal to	△	triangle
>	more than	⌢	arc of circle
<	less than	°	degree
≥	greater than or equal to	∠	angle
		m ∠	measure of the angle (degrees)
≤	less than or equal to	⊥	perpendicular
≅	congruent	∥	parallel
~	similar	±	plus or minus
≗	equals in degrees		

Whole Numbers

Integers The numbers 0, 1, 2, 3, 4, 5, . . . are called POSITIVE INTEGERS; $7\frac{1}{2}$ is *not* an integer. WHOLE NUMBERS are 0, 1, 2, 3, 4, 5, ...

Divisibility The number 12 divides by 4 evenly. We therefore say that 12 is divisible by 4 or that 4 is a FACTOR of 12. Besides 4, other factors of 12 are: 1, 2, 3, 6, and 12. Any whole number is divisible by itself and 1.

Prime Numbers A whole number greater than 1 that is divisible only by itself and 1 is a PRIME NUMBER; 2, 3, 5, 7, 11, and 13 are all prime. 14 is not prime since it is divisible by 2 and 7.

Odd and Even Numbers An integer that is divisible by 2 is called an EVEN NUMBER. Other integers are ODD NUMBERS.

Addition: Even + even = even; odd + odd = even; even + odd = odd.

Subtraction: Even – even = even; odd – odd = even; even – odd or odd – even = odd.

Multiplication: Even × even = even; odd × odd = odd; even × odd = even.

Division (assuming the quotient is an integer): odd ÷ odd = odd; even ÷ odd = even; even ÷ even can be even or odd [if the dividend has more factors of 2 than the divisor, the quotient is even; if the dividend has the same number of factors of 2 as the divisor, the quotient is odd: $36 \div 6 = (9 \times 2 \times 2) \div (3 \times 2) = 6$, but $36 \div 12 = (9 \times 2 \times 2) \div (3 \times 2 \times 2) = 3$].

If an odd number is divided by an even number, the quotient can never be a whole number.

Consecutive Numbers A collection of numbers is CONSECUTIVE if each number is the successor of the number that precedes it. For example, 7, 8, 9, 10 are consecutive, but 7, 8, 10, 13 are not. The following are examples of consecutive even numbers: 4, 6, 8, 10. The following are examples of consecutive primes: 7, 11, 13, 17. However, 7, 13, 19, 23 are not consecutive primes since 11 is a prime between 7 and 13.

Least Common Multiple (L.C.M.) The LEAST COMMON MULTIPLE of two numbers is the smallest number which is a common multiple of both numbers. For example, the least common multiple of 2 and 3 is 6. This is useful in adding or subtracting fractions.

Real Numbers

The REAL NUMBERS, also called SIGNED NUMBERS, are *positive numbers, negative numbers,* or *zero.* Zero is neither positive nor negative. The following are real numbers: +3, –5, +6.3, –0.2, and $+\frac{2}{3}$. If no sign precedes a number, it may be assumed to be positive. Thus 3 may be considered +3.

Real numbers can be represented on a line. On a horizontal line a point is selected as a starting point (called the *origin)* and is designated by zero. A unit length is selected, and units marked off to the right of the origin are +1, +2, +3, +4, etc.; if this length is marked off to the left of the origin, we obtain points –1, –2, –3, –4, etc. Note the location of $+1\frac{1}{2}$ and $-2\frac{1}{2}$.

Absolute Value The absolute value of a signed number is the distance of that number from the origin (zero). Thus the value of any nonzero number is *positive.* The absolute value of –3 is 3; the absolute value of +3 is also 3.

Fundamental Operations

Addition To add numbers with the *same sign,* add their absolute values and write the result with the common sign.

$$14 + 12 = 26$$
$$-8 + (-9) = -17$$

To add numbers with *opposite signs,* find their absolute values, subtract the lesser absolute value from the greater, and then write the result with the same sign as that of the number with the greater absolute value. For example, to add –36 and +14, subtract 14 from 36 to get 22 and write the result as –22 since the –36 had the greater absolute value.

$$+36 + (-14) = 22$$
$$-50 + 33 = -17$$
$$50 + (-33) = 17$$
$$16 + (-16) = 0$$

To add *three or more numbers with different signs* you can, of course, combine them in the order given but it is simpler to add all the positives and all the negatives, and then combine the results. Thus, to add –22 + 37 + 64 – 18 – 46 + 13 – 85, we add 37 + 64 + 13 = 114 and –22 – 18 – 46 – 85 = –171. Then we combine the results:

$$-171 + 114 = -57$$

Subtraction Subtraction is based on the following property: $a - b = a + (-b)$

This means that subtracting a number is the same as adding its opposite. The number being subtracted is called the *subtrahend*, so to subtract signed numbers, simply change the sign of the subtrahend and add.

$27 - (-18) = 27 + 18 = 45$

$-37 - (-29) = -37 + 29 = -8$

$-26 - 14 = -26 + (-14) = -40$

$42 - (-42) = 84$

$-18 - 15 = -33$

Multiplication Multiply signed numbers by multiplying their absolute values. If the numbers have the same sign, write your answer with a positive sign. If their signs are opposite, write the answer with a negative sign.

$(-4)(-3) = 12$

$(12)(10) = 120$

$(+8)(-7) = -56$

$(-7)(16) = -112$

Division Division follows the same rule: divide absolute values and choose a positive sign for your answer if the original signs were the same, or use a negative sign if they were opposite:

$35 \div 7 = 5$

$-36 \div (-9) = 4$

$16 \div (-4) = -4$

$-27 \div 3 = -9$

Multiplication and Division Involving Fractions

Questions on the PSAT sometimes require knowing the consequences of multiplying or dividing by fractions. If two positive numbers greater than 1 (they may be whole numbers or fractions such as $\frac{3}{2}$) are multiplied together, the product is greater than either of them. For example: $2 \times 3 = 6$

If two positive numbers are multiplied together, and one is greater than 1 and the other is a fraction less than 1, the product is greater than one number and less than the other. For example: $4 \times \frac{1}{2} = 2$

If two positive fractions, both less than 1, are multiplied together, the product is less than either of them.

For example: $\frac{1}{2} \times \frac{1}{3} \times \frac{1}{6}$

If a positive number greater than 1 is divided by a positive fraction less than 1, the quotient is greater than either of them. For example: $4 \div \frac{1}{2} = 4 \times \frac{2}{1} = 8$

If a positive fraction less than 1 is raised to a power, it becomes smaller; the higher the power, the smaller it becomes. For example:

$\left(\frac{1}{2}\right)^2 = \frac{1}{4}$ and $\left(\frac{1}{2}\right)^3 = \frac{1}{8}$

ALGEBRA

Some Important Facts

1. In algebra we use letters to represent numbers or sets of numbers. Such letters are called *variables*. When two variables, or a numeral and a variable, are written with no sign of operation between them, we mean that the numbers they represent are to be multiplied. Thus $4abc$ means $4 \times a \times b \times c$.

2. The *factors* of a product are two or more numbers or letters that when multiplied yield the product. For example, two factors of 12 are 4 and 3, and the factors of $2xy$ are 2, x, and y. The factors of $x^2 - y^2$ are $(x + y)$ and $(x - y)$.

3. The *coeffcient* is any factor of a term. Ordinarily the numerical value that is multiplied by the other terms is called the coefficient. In the term $5xy$, the coefficient is 5.

4. The *exponent*, written as a small number or letter above and to the right of another number or letter, indicates how many times the number or letter is used as a factor: $b^4 = b \times b \times b \times b$.

5. An *equation* is a mathematical sentence that states that two expressions name the same number. For example, $5x = 20$ is an equation that is true when x is 4 and false when x is anything else.

6. A *root* of an equation is a number that satisfies an equation. In the preceding example, 4 is a root.

7. A *monomial* is an expression consisting of one term, such as $14ab$, $6x$, or xy.

8. A *binomial* is the sum or difference of two monomials, such as $2x + 4y$.

9. A *trinomial* has three terms, such as $9x^2 + 9xy - 4$.

Fundamental Operations

Addition and Subtraction Most algebraic additions and subtractions are carried out with the aid of a simple pattern known as the *distributive law*:

$ab + ac = a(b + c)$

or its corollary:

$ab - ac = a(b - c)$.

When adding polynomials (more than 2 terms), arrange the like terms in vertical columns. For example, to add $3x^2 + 9x - 4$ and $-7x^2 - 4x + 8$, arrange your work as follows:

$$\begin{array}{r} 3x^2 + 9x - 4 \\ -7x^2 - 4x + 8 \\ \hline -4x^2 + 5x + 4 \end{array}$$

When two polynomials are to be subtracted, arrange them in vertical columns according to like terms and change the sign of every term in the subtrahend. For example, to subtract $9x^2 - 3x - 5$ from

$2x^2 + 3x - 8$, change the signs of the first polynomial to $-9x^2 + 3x + 5$, and then add:

$$\begin{array}{r} 2x^2 + 3x - 8 \\ -9x^2 + 3x + 5 \\ \hline -7x^2 + 6x - 3 \end{array}$$

Multiplication To multiply monomials, multiply the coefficients and add the exponents of variables with the same base. For example:

$(6x^2)(5x^4) = (6 \cdot 5)(x^2 \cdot x^4) = 30x^6$

To multiply a polynomial by a monomial, multiply each term of the polynomial by the monomial. For example:

$3x^2(5x^3 + 2x - 3y) = 15x^5 + 6x^3 - 9x^2y$

To multiply a polynomial by a polynomial, multiply each term of one polynomial by each term of the other, and combine like terms.

A special case of multiplying polynomials is worth studying separately because of its use in factoring. To multiply a binomial by a binomial, note first how the pairs of terms are named:

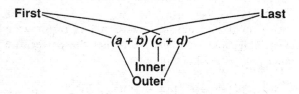

$$(x + 3)(x - 2) = x^2 - 2x + 3x - 6$$
$$= x^2 + x - 6$$

Multiply the binomials term by term in the order F, O, I, L. Frequently, the O and I terms combine to make the product a trinomial or a binomial. For example, to find the product of $3x^2 - 2x - 7$ and $2x - 4$:

$$\begin{array}{l} 3x^2 - 2x - 7 \\ \underline{\quad\quad 2x - 4} \\ 6x^3 - 4x^2 - 14x \quad \text{(Partial product when the} \\ \quad\quad\quad\quad\quad\quad\quad\quad \text{multiplier is } 2x) \\ \underline{\quad -12x^2 + 8x + 28} \quad \text{(Partial product when the} \\ \quad\quad\quad\quad\quad\quad\quad\quad\quad \text{multiplier is } -4) \\ 6x^3 - 16x^2 - 6x + 28 \end{array}$$

Removing Parentheses Parentheses are used as grouping symbols and as indicators of multiplication. Often it is necessary to remove the parentheses to simplify expressions that have grouped terms. If the parentheses are preceded by a positive sign they may be removed with no further alteration necessary.

$(x + y) + (3x - 2y) = x + y + 3x - 2y = x + 3x + y - 2y = 4x - y$

If the parentheses are preceded by a negative sign, then they may be removed only if the signs of each term inside the parentheses are changed to the opposite sign.

$(x + y) - (3x - 2y) = x + y - 3x + 2y = x - 3x + y + 2y = -2x + 3y$

$(3x^2 + 2x) - (4x^2 - 3x + 5) = 3x^2 + 2x - 4x^2 + 3x - 5 = -x^2 + 5x - 5$

If the parentheses are preceded by a multiplier, carry out the multiplication first and then use one of the rules just mentioned.

$$(x + y) - 5(x + y) = (x + y) - (5x + 5y)$$
$$= x + y - 5x + 5y = -4x - 4y$$

$$4(3x^2 + 2x) - 8(x^2 + 3x - 2)$$
$$= (12x^2 + 8x) - (8x^2 + 24x - 16)$$
$$= 12x^2 + 8x - 8x^2 - 24x + 16$$
$$= 4x^2 - 16x + 16$$

When additional grouping symbols are needed, we use brackets, [ ], and braces, { }. If grouping symbols appear within other sets, remove one set at a time starting with the innermost.

$$4x - \{2x - 3[(x + 2) - (3 - x)]\} =$$
$$4x - \{2x - 3[x + 2 - 3 + x]\} =$$
$$4x - \{2x - 3[2x - 1]\} =$$
$$4x - \{2x - 6x + 3\} = 4x - \{-4x + 3\}$$
$$= 4x + 4x - 3 = 8x - 3$$

Division To divide a monomial by a monomial, divide the coefficients algebraically and subtract exponents of factors that have the same base.

$$x^6 \div x^2 = x^{6-2} = x^4$$
$$-15x^6y^3 \div 3x^2y = \frac{-15}{3} x^{6-2}y^{3-1} = -5x^4y^2$$
$$-18x^3yz^2 \div (-6xyz) = \frac{-18}{-6} x^{3-1}y^{1-1}z^{2-1} = 3x^2 z$$

(Note that $y^\circ = 1$ as long as y is any number except 0.) To divide a polynomial by a monomial, divide each term of the dividend by the divisor.

$$(-18x^4 - 6x^3 + 2x^2) \div 2x^2 =$$
$$\frac{-18x^4 - 6x^3 + 2x^2}{2x^2} = \frac{-18x^4}{2x^2} + \frac{-6x^3}{2x^2} + \frac{2x^2}{2x^2} = -9x^2 - 3x + 1$$

Factoring

To factor an expression is to find two or more expressions whose product is the given expression. An expression or a number is *prime* if it does not have any factors except itself and one.

Type 1. To factor a polynomial that has a common monomial factor, find the largest monomial that will divide into each term of the polynomial. This is one factor. Divide the polynomial by this factor to obtain the other factor.

Factor: $4x^3y^3 - 22xy^2$
$\quad\quad\quad 2xy^2(2x^2y - 11)$

Type 2. To factor an expression that is the difference of two perfect squares, find the square root of each term. The sum of the two square roots is one factor and the difference of the two square roots is the other factor.

Factor: $x^2 - 64$
$\quad\quad\quad (x + 8)(x - 8)$

Type 3. Trinomials of the form: $ax^2 + bx + c$

The factors are two binomials where (a) the product of the first terms of both binomials equals the first term of the trinomial; (b) the product of the last terms of both binomials equals the last term of the trinomial; and (c) the algebraic sum of the cross products of these terms equals the middle term of the trinomial.

Factor: $x^2 + 8x + 12$
$(x + 6)(x + 2)$

(a)	(b)	(c)
$x + 6$	$x + 6$	$x + 6$
$x + 2$	$x + 2$	$x + 2$
x^2	$+ 12$	$+ 6x$
		$+ 2x$
		$+ 8x$

Factor: $x^2 - 6x + 8$
$(x - 4)(x - 2)$

(a)	(b)	(c)
$x - 4$	$x - 4$	$x - 4$
$x - 2$	$x - 2$	$x - 2$
x^2	$+ 8$	$- 4x$
		$- 2x$
		$- 6x$

Factor: $x^2 - 3x - 10$
$(x - 5)(x + 2)$

(a)	(b)	(c)
$x - 5$	$x - 5$	$x - 5$
$x + 2$	$x + 2$	$x + 2$
x^2	$- 10$	$- 5x$
		$+ 2x$
		$- 3x$

Roots of Numbers

Some Important Facts

1. The *square root* of a nonnegative number is one of its equal factors. The square root of 100 is +10 since $(+10)(+10) = 100$. Also, –10 is a square root of 100 since $(-10)(-10) = 100$. Thus, every positive number has two square roots.

2. The *principal square root* is its positive square root. It is indicated by writing a radical sign in front of the number. Thus $\sqrt{100} = + 10$.

3. A *negative square root* is indicated by a minus sign in front of the radical. Thus $-\sqrt{100}$ means the negative square root of 100.

4. A *radical* is an indicated root of a number or expression. The index of the root is written as a small number above the radical sign. Thus $\sqrt[3]{8}$ where the index is 3, means the cube root of 8, which is 2 since $(2)(2)(2) = 8$. Where no index is written, as in $\sqrt{100}$, the number 2 is understood. Thus $\sqrt{100}$ means $\sqrt[2]{100}$.

5. A *rational* number is a number that can be expressed as the ratio of two integers. Thus, $2\frac{1}{3}$ is a rational number since $2\frac{1}{3} = \frac{7}{3}$.

6. An *irrational* number is a number that cannot be expressed as the ratio of two integers. Thus, $\sqrt{5}$ is an irrational number.

7. To add or subtract, like radicals are combined. To add or subtract unlike radicals, change them to like radicals. To simplify a radical, separate into two factors, one of which is a perfect square. Thus, to simplify $\sqrt{98}$, write it as $\sqrt{49}\ \sqrt{2}$, which equals $7\sqrt{2}$.

EXAMPLES:

$2\sqrt{5} + 5\sqrt{5} = 7\sqrt{5}$

$6\sqrt{3} - 3\sqrt{3} = 3\sqrt{3}$

$\sqrt{50} + \sqrt{2}$ can be written as $\sqrt{25}\sqrt{2} + \sqrt{2}$, *or*
$5\sqrt{2} + \sqrt{2}$ *or* $6\sqrt{2}$

$3\sqrt{27} + \sqrt{108}$ can be written as $3\sqrt{9}\sqrt{3} + \sqrt{36}\sqrt{3}$ *or*
$(3)(3)\sqrt{3} + 6\sqrt{3}$ *or* $9\sqrt{3} + 6\sqrt{3}$ *or* $15\sqrt{3}$

$4\sqrt{32} - 6\sqrt{8}$ can be written as $4\sqrt{16}\sqrt{2} - 6\sqrt{4}\sqrt{2}$ *or*
$(4)(4)\sqrt{2} - (6)(2)\sqrt{2}$ *or* $16\sqrt{2} - 12\sqrt{2}$ *or* $4\sqrt{2}$

8. To multiply radicals, the product of the square roots of two expressions is equal to the square root of the product of the two expressions. Thus
$(\sqrt{2})(\sqrt{8}) = \sqrt{16} = 4$.

EXAMPLES:

$(\sqrt{18})(\sqrt{2}) = \sqrt{36} = 6$
$(2\sqrt{8})(3\sqrt{18}) = 6\sqrt{144} = (6)(12) = 72$
$(\frac{2}{3}\sqrt{3})(9\sqrt{27}) = (\frac{2}{3})(\frac{9}{1})(\sqrt{81}) = (\frac{2}{3})(\frac{9}{1})(\frac{9}{1}) = 54$
$(\frac{1}{3}\sqrt{8})(3\sqrt{2}) = (\frac{1}{3})(\frac{3}{1})(\sqrt{16}) = (\frac{1}{3})(\frac{3}{1})(\frac{4}{1}) = 4$
$(\frac{1}{25}\sqrt{5})(5\sqrt{5}) = (\frac{1}{25})(\frac{5}{1})(\sqrt{25}) = (\frac{1}{25})(\frac{5}{1})(\frac{5}{1}) = 1$

9. To divide radicals, the quotient of the square roots of two expressions is equal to the square root of the quotient of the two expressions. Thus
$\sqrt{32} \div \sqrt{2} = \sqrt{16} = 4$.

EXAMPLES:

$\sqrt{75} \div \sqrt{3} = \sqrt{25} = 5$
$21\sqrt{162} \div 7\sqrt{2} = 3\sqrt{81} = (3)(9) = 27$
$\frac{25\sqrt{32}}{5\sqrt{2}} = 5\sqrt{16} = (5)(4) = 20$
$24\sqrt{10} \div 3\sqrt{10} = (8)(1) = 8$
$\frac{1}{3}\sqrt{27} \div \frac{1}{3}\sqrt{3} = (\frac{1}{3})(\frac{3}{1})(\sqrt{9}) = 3$

Solving Equations

Some Important Facts

1. An *equation* is an expression of equality between two quantities. Thus $4x = 20$ is an equation because $4x$ is equal to 20 only when $x = 5$.

2. A *root* of an equation is a number that satisfies an equation. In the equation $4x = 20$, the root is 5.

3. Some equations have more than one root. In the equation, $x^2 - 7x + 12 = 0$, the roots are 4 and 3.

4. An equation is not put out of balance if an arithmetic process done to one-half of the equation is also done to the other half of the equation. We may

> add a quantity
> subtract a quantity
> multiply by a quantity
> divide by a quantity
> raise to a higher power
> extract square root, cube root, etc.,

provided the process is applied to both sides of the equation.

<u>EXAMPLES:</u>

Solve for x.
$x - 4 = 12$
Add 4 to both sides of the equation:
$x = 16$

Solve for x.
$x + 4 = 12$
Subtract 4 from both sides of the equation:
$x = 8$

Solve for x.
$4x - 5 = 3x + 2$
Add 5 to both sides of the equation:
$4x = 3x + 7$
Subtract $3x$ from both sides of the equation:
$x = 7$

Solve for x.
$\frac{x}{4} = 12$
Multiply both sides of the equation by 4:
$x = 48$

Solve for x.
$4x = 12$
Divide both sides of the equation by 4:
$x = 3$

Solve for x.
$3\sqrt{x + 2} - 3 = 4$
Add 3 to both sides of the equation:
$3\sqrt{x + 2} = 7$
Square both sides of the equation:
$9(x + 2) = 49$
Remove the parentheses:
$9x + 18 = 49$
Subtract 18 from both sides of the equation:
$9x = 31$
Divide both sides of the equation by 9:
$x = \frac{31}{9} = 3\frac{4}{9}$

Solve for x.
$\sqrt{x^2 - 4} = 4 - x$
Square both sides of the equation:
$(\sqrt{x^2 - 4})^2 = (4 - x)^2$ or
$x^2 - 4 = 16 - 8x + x^2$
Subtract x^2 from both sides of the equation:
$-4 = 16 - 8x$
Add $8x$ to both sides of the equation:
$8x - 4 = 16$
Add 4 to both sides of the equation:
$8x = 20$
Divide both sides of the equation by 8:
$x = \frac{20}{8}$ or $2\frac{1}{2}$

Solve for x.
$(\sqrt{3x - 1}) = 2$
Square both sides of the equation:
$(\sqrt{3x - 1})^2 = (2)^2$
$3x - 1 = 4$
Add 1 to both sides of the equation:
$3x = 5$
Divide both sides of the equation by 3:
$x = \frac{5}{3}$ or $1\frac{2}{3}$

Solve for x in terms of a and b.
$\sqrt{\frac{x}{b}} = a^2$
Square both sides of the equation:
$\left(\sqrt{\frac{x}{b}}\right)^2 = (a^2)^2$
$\frac{x}{b} = a^4$
Multiply both sides of the equation by b:
$x = a^4 b$

➤ PRACTICE EXERCISE

1. If $a = \frac{1}{2}$, $b = \frac{2}{3}$ and $c = \frac{3}{4}$, what is the value of

$\frac{2a + 3b}{c}$?

   (A) $\frac{1}{4}$ (B) $1\frac{1}{2}$ (C) $2\frac{1}{4}$ (D) 3 (E) 4

2. $\frac{ca^2 - cb^2}{-a - b}$ is equivalent to cb plus

   (A) ac (B) $-ca$ (C) 1 (D) –1 (E) c

3. One-half a number is 17 more than one-third of that number. What is the number?

   (A) 52 (B) 84 (C) 102 (D) 112 (E) 204

4. In which, if any, of the following can the 2's be cancelled out without changing the value of the expression?

   (A) $2x - 2m$ (B) $\dfrac{\frac{x}{2}}{\frac{2}{m}}$ (C) $\dfrac{2x - m}{2}$

   (D) $\dfrac{x^2}{m^2}$ (E) none of these

5. $-\frac{1}{7}$ and 0 are the roots of which of the following equations?

   (A) $7x^2 - 3x = 0$ (B) $7x^2 + 3 = 0$
   (C) $7x^2 - 3 = 0$ (D) $7x^2 + x = 0$
   (E) $7x + 3 = 0$

6. $\frac{y}{s - t} = \frac{s + t}{t - s}$; $y = ?$

   (A) $-s - t$ (B) $t - s$ (C) $t + s$
   (D) $s - t$ (E) $t^2 - s^2$

7. $\frac{a}{b} = c$; $b = c$. Find b in terms of a.

   (A) a (B) b (C) $\pm\sqrt{b}$
   (D) $\pm\sqrt{a}$ (E) $\pm\sqrt{ac}$

8. $2x - 4y = -10$
   $5x - 3y = 3$
   $3x - 6y = ?$

   (A) $\frac{3}{5}$ (B) $\frac{2}{3}$ (C) –7 (D) 15 (E) –15

9. $7x - 5y = 13$
   $2x - 7y = 26$
   $5x + 2y = ?$
   (A) 39 (B) –39 (C) 13 (D) –13 (E) 19.5

10. $a = \dfrac{ax}{1 - x}$
   $x = ?$

   (A) $\frac{1}{2}$ (B) 1 (C) 2 (D) a (E) $2a$

11. If $x\sqrt{.16} = 2$, then x equals
   (A) $\frac{1}{2}$ (B) 4 (C) 5 (D) 10 (E) 50

12. $\sqrt{x^2 y^2 - y^2}$ equals
   (A) $x - 1$ (B) $y\sqrt{x^2 - 1}$ (C) $y(x^2 - 1)$
   (D) $(x^2 - 1)\sqrt{y}$ (E) $xy - y$

13. $\dfrac{a + b}{a - b} \div \dfrac{b + a}{b - a} = ?$
   (A) +1 (B) –1 (C) ±1
   (D) $a^2 - b^2$ (D) $b^2 - a^2$

14. The expression a^x means that a is to be used as a factor x times. Therefore, if a^x is squared, the result is
   (A) $a^{(x 2)}$ (B) a^{2x} (C) $2a^{2x}$ (D) $2a^x$ (E) $2ax^n$

15. $\dfrac{\frac{1}{1}}{N} \div \dfrac{1}{N} = ?$
   (A) 1 (B) $\frac{1}{N^2}$ (C) $\frac{1}{N}$ (D) N (E) N^2

> Questions 16–20: These problems are not multiple choice. They are designed to give practice for the questions on the test with student-produced responses. In the typical tests in this book and in the actual test, you will be asked to enter your answers in a special grid. For the following questions, write your answer in the blank provided.

16. $\dfrac{\frac{1}{1}}{y} = \sqrt{.16}$; $y =$ _____

17. If $x^2 = 5$, then $6x^6$ equals _____

18. If $17x + 7 = 19xy$, $4xy =$ _____

19. $3x + 10 = 9x - 20$
   $(x + 5)^2 =$ _____

20. $3r - 2s = 0$; $\dfrac{9r^2}{s^2} =$ _____

Solving Problems by Equations

Many types of problems may be solved very easily by using the equation. The following five steps will be useful.

Hints on Solving Problems

1. Read the problem carefully to determine the unknown quantity. Indicate this quantity by a letter.
2. If more than one unknown quantity is obtained, express each quantity in terms of the *same* letter.
3. From the statement of the problem, determine a relationship that may be written as an equation.
4. Solve this equation.
5. Check your result by applying the answer to the original statement.

EXAMPLES:

If 4 is subtracted from one-fourth of a number, the result is 20. Find the number.

Let x = the number.

$\frac{1}{4}x - 4 = 20$ [equation]

$x - 16 = 80$ [multiplying both sides by 4]

$x = 96$ [adding 16 to both sides]

Check: $\frac{1}{4}$ of 96 = 24; 24 − 4 = 20

Find two consecutive numbers whose sum is 43.

Let x = first number.

$x + 1$ = second number

$x + x + 1 = 43$ [equation]

$2x + 1 = 43$ [combining terms]

$2x = 42$ [subtracting 1 from both sides]

$x = 21$ [dividing both sides by 2]

$x + 1 = 22$

Check: 21 + 22 = 43

A rectangular box is to be 4 feet long and 2 feet wide. How high must it be to have a volume of 24 cubic feet? Use formula: $V = lwh$

Substituting values: $24 = 4 \cdot 2 \cdot h$

$24 = 8h$

$h = 3$

The cost of a new highway was $88,000. The township agreed to pay twice as much as the state, and the county was to pay 4 times as much as the township. How much did each pay?

Let x = amount paid by state.

$2x$ = amount paid by township

$8x$ = amount paid by county

$x + 2x + 8x = 88,000$

$11x = 88,000$

$x = \$8,000$ (state)

$2x = \$16,000$ (township)

$8x = \$64,000$ (county)

Mr. Smith, who is 28 years of age, has a son who is 4 years old. In how many years will Mr. Smith be 4 times as old as his son?

Let x equal the time needed to reach the desired age ratio. At that time, the son will be $4 + x$ years old and the father will be $28 + x$ years old.

$4(4 + x) = 28 + x$ [equation]

$16 + 4x = 28 + x$ [removing parentheses]

$3x = 12$

$x = 4$

Check: In four years, Mr. Smith will be 32 years old and his son will be 8 years old. The father will be four times as old as his son.

► PRACTICE EXERCISE

1. How many cents are there in $2x - 1$ dimes?
   (A) $10x$ (B) $20x - 10$ (C) $19x$
   (D) $\frac{2x - 1}{10}$ (E) $\frac{x}{5} - 1$

2. How many nickels are there in c cents and q quarters?
   (A) $\frac{c}{5} + 5q$ (B) $5(c + q)$ (C) $5c + \frac{q}{5}$
   (D) $\frac{c + q}{5}$ (E) $c + 25q$

3. How many days are there in w weeks and w days?
   (A) $7w^2$ (B) 7   (C) $8w$ (D) $14w$ (E) $7w$

4. How many pupils can be seated in a room with s single seats and d double seats?
   (A) sd (B) $2sd$ (C) $2(s + d)$
   (D) $2d + s$ (E) $2s + d$

5. A classroom has r rows of desks with d desks in each row. On a particular day when all pupils are present 3 seats are left vacant. The number of pupils in this class is
   (A) $dr - 3$ (B) $d + r + 3$ (C) $dr + 3$
   (D) $\frac{r}{d} + 3$ (E) $\frac{d}{r} + 3$

6. A storekeeper had n loaves of bread. By noon he had s loaves left. How many loaves did he sell?
   (A) $s - n$ (B) $n - s$ (C) $n + s$
   (D) $sn - s$ (E) $\frac{n}{s}$

7. A man has d dollars and spends s cents. How many dollars has he left?
   (A) $d - s$ (B) $s - d$ (C) $100d - s$
   (D) $\frac{100d - s}{100}$ (E) $\frac{d - s}{100}$

8. How much change (in cents) would a woman receive if she purchases p pounds of sugar at c cents per pound after she gives the clerk a one-dollar bill?
   (A) $100 - p - c$ (B) $pc - 100$ (C) $100 - pc$
   (D) $100 - p + c$ (E) $pc + 100$

9. Sylvia is two years younger than Mary. If Mary is m years old, how old was Sylvia two years ago?

(A) $m + 2$ (B) $m - 2$ (C) $m - 4$

(D) $m + 4$ (E) $2m - 2$

10. A storekeeper sold n articles at $\$D$ each and thereby made a profit of r dollars. The cost to the storekeeper for each article was

(A) $Dn - r$ (B) $D(n - r)$ (C) $\dfrac{Dn - r}{n}$

(D) $\dfrac{D(n - r)}{n}$ (E) $\dfrac{Dn + r}{n}$

Inequalities

Some Important Facts

When one expression is greater than or is less than another expression, we have an inequality. The following symbols are generally used in dealing with inequalities: > for greater than, < for less than, ≠ for not equal to, ≥ for greater than or equal to, and ≤ for less than or equal to. Thus, if a number is followed by < 0, we have a negative quantity.

Rules useful in handling problems involving inequalities follow.

1. If equal quantities are added to unequal quantities, the resulting sums are unequal in the same order. If $x > y$ then $x + a > y + a$ and since $9 > 6$ then $11 > 8$.

2. If unequal quantities are added to unequal quantities of the same order, the resulting sums are unequal in the same order. Since $5 > 3$ and $9 > 6$ then $14 > 9$. If $x > y$ and $a > b$ then $x + a > y + b$.

3. If equal quantities are subtracted from unequal quantities, the results are unequal in the same order. Since $25 > 22$, then $20 > 17$. If $x > y$, then $x - a > y - a$.

4. If unequal quantities are subtracted from equal quantities, the remainders are unequal in the opposite order. Since $25 = 25$ and $5 > 3$, then $20 < 22$. If $x = y$ and $a > d$, then $x - a < y - d$.

5. If inequalities are multiplied by *positive* numbers, the order remains the same. If $x > y$ and $z > 0$, then $xz > yz$. However, if inequalities are multiplied by *negative* numbers the order is reversed. If $x > y$ and $z < 0$ then $xz < yz$.

6. If the first of three quantities is greater than the second and the second is greater than the third, then the first is greater than the third. Since $12 > 9$ and $9 > 7$, then $12 > 7$. If $a > b$ and $b > c$, then $a > c$.

7. The whole is greater than any of its parts. If point P lies on line segment AB, then $AB > AP$ and $AB > BP$.

8. A straight line is the shortest distance between two points. In a triangle, the sum of two sides of the triangle is greater than the third side. Also, a perpendicular drawn from a point to a line is the shortest distance from the point to the line.

9. An exterior angle of a triangle is greater than either remote (nonadjacent) interior angle.

10. If two angles of a triangle are unequal, the sides opposite these angles are unequal, and the greater side lies opposite the greater angle.

➤ PRACTICE EXERCISE

1. If $x = y$ and $a < b$, then

(A) $a + x = b + y$ (B) $a + x < b + y$

(C) $a + x > b + y$ (D) $a + x = b$

(E) $a + x = y$

2. If $a < b$ and $c < d$, then

(A) $ac = bd$ (B) $a = d$ (C) $b = c$

(D) $a + c > b + d$ (E) $a + c < b + d$

3. If $k < m$ and $x = y$, then

(A) $k - x > m - y$ (B) $k + x = m + y$

(C) $k - x < m - y$ (D) $k + y = m + x$

(E) $k\,x = my$

4. If $a = b$ and $x > y$, then

(A) $a - x = b - y$ (B) $a - x > b - y$

(C) $a - x < b - y$ (D) $a + x = b + y$

(E) $a + y = b + x$

5. If $x < y$, $z = \dfrac{x}{2}$, and $a = \dfrac{y}{2}$, then

(A) $z < a$ (B) $a > z$ (C) $a = z$

(D) $2a > y$ (E) $2x > 2z$

6. If $K > L$ and $x = K$, then

(A) $x = L$ (B) $x < L$ (C) $K + x < L + x$

(D) $2x < L + x$ (E) $L < x$

7. If $A < B$, $x = 2A$, and $y = 2B$, then

(A) $x = 2B$ (B) $x = A + B$ (C) $x < y$

(D) $x + y > 2A + 2B$ (E) $y = A + B$

8. If $a > b$, $b > c$, and $c > d$, then

(A) $a > d$ (B) $a < d$ (C) $a < c$

(D) $c < d$ (E) $a < b$

9. If $KL > AB$ and $LM > BC$, then

(A) $AC > KM$

(B) $KM > AC$

(C) $KL + LM < AB + BC$

(D) $KL + BC = LM + AB$

(E) $KL + AB = LM + BC$

10. If $3x - 4 > 8$, then

(A) $x = 4$ (B) $x = 0$ (C) $x = 4, 0$

(D) $x > 4$ (E) $x < 4$

11. If $x > y > 1$, then

(A) $y + x > 2x$ (B) $x^2 < xy$ (C) $x - y < 0$

(D) $x < y + 1$ (E) $x^2 > y^2$

12. If $2y > 5$, then
(A) $y > 2.5$ (B) $y < 2.5$ (C) $y = 2.5$
(D) $y = 10$ (E) $y = 5$

13. In $\triangle ABC$, K is a point on AB
and L is a point on AC, such
that $KB = LC$ and $AC > AB$.
Which of the following is
true?

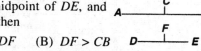

(A) $KL = \frac{1}{2}BC$ (B) $AK > AB$
(C) $AL < AK$ (D) $AL > AK$
(E) $AC < AL$

14. If C is the midpoint of AB, and
F is the midpoint of DE, and
$AC > FE$, then

(A) $AC < DF$ (B) $DF > CB$
(C) $AC = FE$ (D) $AB < DE$
(E) $AC + CB > DF + FE$

15. Which of the following is true
for $\triangle ABC$? (diagram not
drawn to scale)
(A) $AC < AB$ (B) $BC = AC$
(C) $AC > BC$ (D) $BC > AC$
(E) $AB + BC < AC$

16. LM of $\triangle KLM$ is extended to
N. All of the following are
true except
(A) $x = 120$ (B) $y + z = 120$
(C) $x = y + z$ (D) $x < y$
(E) $x > z$

17. In $\triangle ABC$ (not drawn to scale)
AD is an angle bisector, and
$AC > DC$. Which of the following is true?

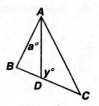

(A) $y > a$ (B) $a > y$
(C) $y + a = 90$
(D) $y = 2a$ (E) $2a = 180 - y$

18. If $AD > AC$ and $AC > AB$,
then
(A) $x = y$ (B) $x > y$
(C) $y > x$ (D) $x = 180 - y$
(E) $y = 180 - x$

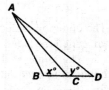

19. In the accompanying diagram
(not drawn to scale) $AB = AE$
and $BC > ED$, then
(A) $AC < BC$ (B) $BC > AE$
(C) $AC > AD$
(D) $AE + ED = AB + BC$
(E) $AC < AD$

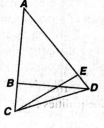

20. In $\triangle KLM$, $KM > KL$, and
MN and LO are angle bisec-
tors, then
(A) $x + y = 60$ (B) $x = 0$
(C) $x < y$ (D) $x > y$
(E) none of these is correct

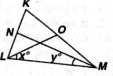

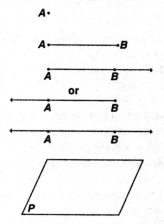

GEOMETRY

Some Important Facts

   Points, Lines, and Planes The building blocks of
geometry are points, lines, and planes. A point indicates
a position and has no length, width, or thickness. A line
is a continuous set of points which is straight, infinitely
long in two opposite directions, and has no width or
thickness. A plane is a flat surface which extends in all
directions but has no thickness. Most geometric figures
are formed by joining parts of lines—either line segments or rays. A line segment has two points of a line as
endpoints and contains all points of the line which lie
between the endpoints. A ray has one point of a line as
an endpoint and contains all of the points which lie on a
given side of the line.

In drawings, these figures appear like this:

Angles and Triangles If two different rays have the same endpoint, they form an angle.

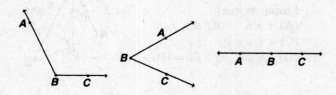

The common endpoint is called the *vertex* and the rays are called the *sides*.

The angle at the far right above has rays that are opposite to each other and is really no different from a line. Such an angle is called a *straight angle*. The measure in degrees of a straight angle is 180. Degree measures of other angles are proportional to the fractional part of a straight angle that they represent.

Two angles are *adjacent* if they have the same vertex and share a common side. Adjacent angles may not overlap. In the figure shown, there is one pair of adjacent angles, ∠ABC and ∠CBD. Note that ∠ABC and ∠ABD are not adjacent since they overlap.

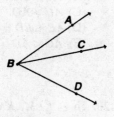

Two angles are *supplementary* if the sum of their degree measures is 180.

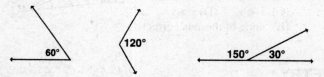

Two angles are *complementary* if the sum of their degree measures is 90.

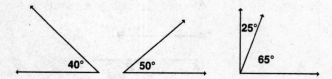

Note that two angles do not have to be adjacent to be supplementary or complementary.

An angle is a right angle if its measure is 90. Note that two adjacent right angles have sides that form a line.

If two lines intersect to form right angles the lines are *perpendicular*.

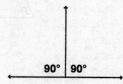

If three points of a plane do not all lie on the same line, the segments that connect these points form a triangle. The sum of the degree measures of the angles of a triangle is 180.

If a triangle has a right angle, it is called a *right triangle*. A triangle is *equilateral* if all sides have the same length. All of the angles of an equilateral triangle have the same degree measure, 60.

An *isosceles triangle* is one in which two sides have the same length. The angles opposite the sides of equal length have the same degree measure. These are called the *base angles*, and the side of the triangle which they share is called the *base* of the isosceles triangle.

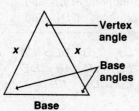

The altitude to the base of an isosceles triangle bisects the base and bisects the vertex angle.

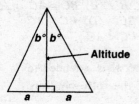

Line-Angle Relationships Two intersecting lines form two pairs of vertical angles. Note that ∠1 and ∠2 are vertical angles, and ∠a and ∠b are vertical angles.

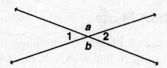

Vertical angles have the same degree measure.

If two lines that lie in the same plane do not intersect, then they are *parallel*. A line that intersects a pair of parallel lines is called a *transversal*.

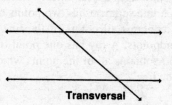

If a pair of parallel lines is intersected by a transversal, three important angle relationships exist:

(1) Alternate interior angles have the same measure:

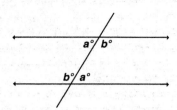

(2) Corresponding angles have the same measure:

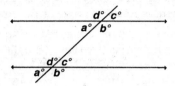

(3) Interior angles on the same side of the transversal are supplementary:

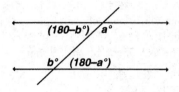

Quadrilaterals If four points lie in a plane and no three of the points lie on the same line, the segments that connect these points form a quadrilateral.

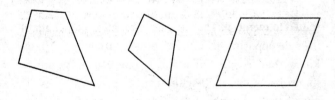

A *parallelogram* is a quadrilateral having opposite sides parallel. The opposite sides of a parallelogram are also equal in length. In the figure below, *AD is* parallel to and equal to *BC; AB is* parallel to and equal to *DC.*

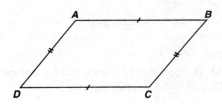

The opposite angles of a parallelogram have the same measure. ∠A has the same measure as ∠C; ∠B has the same measure as ∠D. The diagonals of a parallelogram bisect each other. In the following figure; *AE = EC* and *BE = ED.*

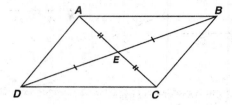

If a parallelogram has four right angles it is a *rectangle.* The diagonals of a rectangle are equal in length. *AC = BD.*

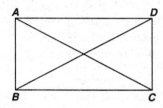

A *rhombus* is a parallelogram having all sides of the same length. *AB = BC = CD = AD.* The diagonals of a rhombus are perpendicular to each other. *AC ⊥ BD.*

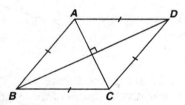

A *square* is a rectangle having all sides of the same length. Thus it has all of the properties of a parallelogram, a rectangle, and a rhombus.

A *trapezoid* is a quadrilateral having one pair of sides parallel (the *bases*) and the other pair nonparallel (the *legs*). *AD* is parallel to *BC.*

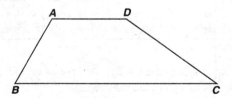

Angle-Circle Relationships
A *circle* is determined by a point and a positive number. The set of all points in a plane that are the given number of units away from the given point is a circle. The given point is its center, the given number its radius.

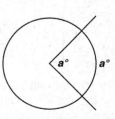

A *central angle* of a circle is an angle whose vertex is the center of the circle. The measure of the arc cut off by the central angle is the same as the measure of the angle.

An *inscribed angle* of a circle is an angle whose vertex is a point of the circle and whose sides intersect two other points of the circle. The measure of an inscribed angle is half the measure of the arc it cuts off. If an angle is inscribed in a semicircle, it must be a right angle.

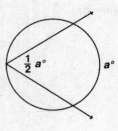

Relationships Among the Sides of Triangles

Two triangles are *similar* if all of their pairs of corresponding angles have the same measure. Roughly speaking, triangles are similar if they have the same shape but not necessarily the same size.

Corresponding sides of similar triangles are proportional.

$$\frac{AB}{A'B'} = \frac{AC}{A'C'} = \frac{BC}{B'C'}$$

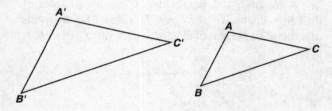

The relationship known as the Pythagorean Theorem states: In a right triangle the square of the length of the hypotenuse is equal to the sum of the squares of the lengths of the legs.

$$(\text{leg})^2 + (\text{leg})^2 = (\text{hypotenuse})^2$$

If the triangle shown above is a right triangle, then:

$$(3)^2 + (4)^2 = x^2$$
$$9 + 16 = x^2$$
$$25 = x^2$$
$$5 = x$$

3-4-5, 5-12-13, and 8-15-17 Right Triangles

The calculation above involves a special right triangle with sides of lengths 3, 4, and 5 (5 being the hypotenuse); such triangles occur frequently so that it is worth memorizing the 3-4-5 right triangle combination. Thus, if one leg of a right triangle is known to be of length 3 and the hypotenuse is known to be of length 5, it can immediately be concluded that the remaining leg is of length

4; this avoids the lengthy squaring and taking of a square root that direct application of the Pythagorean Theorem requires. More important, any multiple of the 3-4-5 lengths will also be the lengths of the sides of a right triangle, for example, 6-8-10 or 9-12-15. If the lengths of the legs of a right triangle are known to be 12 and 16, this principle can be used to immediately state the length of the hypotenuse: Since $12 = 4(3)$ and $16 = 4(4)$, the hypotenuse must be $4(5)$ or 20.

In addition to the 3-4-5 right triangle, other special right triangles are the 5-12-13 and the 8-15-17. They may be used in calculations as illustrated above for the 3-4-5 right tirangle.

One caution: The hypotenuse must always be the longest side in a right triangle. Thus, if a right triangle is given with legs of lengths 5 and 13, it is *not* a 5-12-13 right triangle and the length of its hypotenuse is *not* 12; that length can be found only by using the Pythagorean Theorem: $(5)^2 + (13)^2 = x^2$.

30°-60°-90° and 45°-45°-90° Triangles

A commonly used triangle is one whose angles are 30°, 60°, and 90°. By the use of trigonometry and the Pythagorean Theorem it can be shown that:

the length of the leg opposite the 30° angle equals one-half the length of the hypotenuse;

the length of the leg opposite the 60° angle equals one-half the length of the hypotenuse times $\sqrt{3}$.

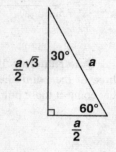

It is much easier to remember and to use these relationships if the diagram at the right is committed to memory. Thus, if we are told that the length of the side opposite 30° in a 30°-60°-90° triangle is 10, we know that $\frac{a}{2} = 10$, or $a = 20$. Therefore, we know immediately that the length of the hypotenuse, a, is 20, and that the length of the side opposite 60°, $\frac{a}{2}\sqrt{3}$ is $10\sqrt{3}$.

Another commonly used triangle is the isosceles right triangle, whose angles are 45°, 45°, and 90°. It can be shown by the use of the Pythagorean Theorem that:

the length of the hypotenuse equals the length of a leg times $\sqrt{2}$;

the length of either leg equals one-half the length of the hypotenuse times $\sqrt{2}$.

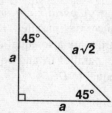

It is much easier to remember and to use these relationships if the diagram above is committed to memory. Thus, if we are told that the length of the hypotenuse of an isosceles right triangle is $6\sqrt{2}$, we know that $a\sqrt{2} = 6\sqrt{2}$, or $a = 6$. Hence each leg, a, equals 6.

Areas and Volumes The area of a rectangle is the product of the length and the width. If the length is 4 and the width is 8, the area is $4 \times 8 = 32$.

$$A = lw = 4 \times 8 = 32$$

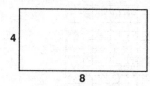

The area of a parallelogram is the product of the base and the altitude to that base. Any side can be used for the base. The altitude to the base is a segment from any point of the opposite side drawn perpendicular to the line containing the base.

$$A = bh = 4 \times 8 = 32$$

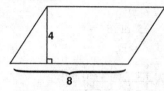

The area of a triangle is equal to one-half the product of a base and the altitude to that base. Any side may be a base. The altitude to the base is the segment from the vertex opposite to the base and perpendicular to the line containing the base.

$$A = \tfrac{1}{2} \times 4 \times 8 = 16$$

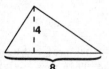 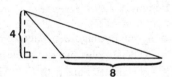

The area of a right triangle is one-half the product of the legs.

$$A = \tfrac{1}{2} \times 4 \times 8 = 16$$

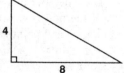

The area of a square is the square of the length of one of its sides.

$$A = 4^2 = 16$$

The area of a square is also equal to one-half the square of the length of its diagonal.

$$A = \tfrac{1}{2} \times 8^2 = 32$$

The ratio of the areas of two similar figures is equal to the square of the ratio of any two corresponding linear parts (sides, altitudes, medians, or angle bisectors).

$$\frac{\text{area } \triangle ABC}{\text{area } \triangle A'B'C'} = \left(\frac{5}{10}\right)^2 = \frac{1}{4}$$

 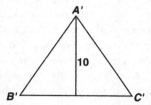

The circumference of (sometimes referred to as the "distance around") a circle is the product of the diameter and π. $C = \pi d$ or $C = 2\pi r$, if r is the radius.

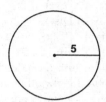

$$C = 2 \times \pi \times 5 = 10\pi$$

The area of a circle is equal to the product of π and the square of the radius. $A = \pi r^2$.

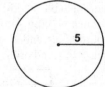

$$A = \pi \times 5^2 = 25\pi$$

A *sector* of a circle is a pie-shaped region bounded by a central angle and the arc it cuts off. Each sector of a circle represents some fractional part of the circular region. This fractional part can be found by formula.

$$\frac{\text{degree measure of central angle}}{360} = \text{fractional part of circle}$$

Hence a 60° angle cuts off a sector which represents $\frac{1}{6}$ of the circle, and a 150° angle determines a sector which is $\frac{150}{360}$ or $\frac{5}{12}$ of the circle.

To find the area of the sector, find the area of the circle and multiply by the fractional part.

$$A = \frac{1}{4} \times \pi \times 5^2 = \frac{25\pi}{4}$$

To find the arc length of a sector, find the circumference of the circle and multiply by the fractional part.

$$\text{Arc length} = \frac{1}{4} \times 2\pi \times 5 = \frac{5\pi}{2}$$

Coordinate Geometry

Coordinate geometry uses principles from algebra to solve geometric problems. In coordinate geometry two lines, called *axes,* are drawn perpendicular to each other (*XX'* and *YY'*), and their point of intersection *O* is called the *origin.* The horizontal line (*XX'*) is called the *abscissa* and is referred to as the *x*-axis, and the vertical line (*YY'*) is the *ordinate* and is referred to as the *y*-axis. These axes divide the plane into four quadrants.

Locating Points The position of point *P* is located by giving the point two coordinates, of which the first is the number of units we must move on the *x*-axis to come vertically under or above the point. (Point *P* is 4 units on the *x*-axis.) The other coordinate indicates how many units we must move up or down on the *y*-axis to become level with the point. (Point *P* is 5 units on the *y*-axis.) Distances measured to the right of the point of origin (*O*) are positive, and distances measured to the left of origin (*O*) are negative. Distances measured upward on the *y*-axis are positive, and distances measured downward on the *y*-axis are negative. The coordinates of point *Q* are (–4, –5). Points in the first quadrant have positive *x* coordinates and positive *y* coordinates. Points in the second quadrant have negative *x* coordinates and positive *y* coordinates. Points in the third quadrant have negative *x* coordinates and negative *y* coordinates. Points in the fourth quadrant have positive *x* coordinates and negative *y* coordinates. For *P*(4, 5) abscissa = 4 and ordinate = 5.

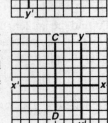

Finding the Distance Between Two Points

1. If two points have their abscissas on a line parallel to the *x*-axis, the distance is calculated by finding the difference between the abscissas.

   Length of $AB = 7 - 3 = 4$

2. If two points have their ordinates on a line parallel to the *y*-axis, the distance is calculated by finding the difference between the ordinates.

   Length of $CD = 5 - (-3) = 8$

3. According to this formula, if point P_1 has coordinates (x_1, y_1) and point P_2 is (x_2, y_2), the distance between the points is:

$$\sqrt{(x_1 - x_2)^2 + (y_1 - y_2)^2}$$

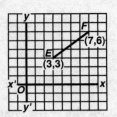

To find the distance of *EF:*

$EF = \sqrt{(7 - 3)^2 + (6 - 3)^2}$
$\quad = \sqrt{4^2 + 3^2}$ or $\sqrt{25}$ or 5

or

$EF = \sqrt{(6 - 3)^2 + (7 - 3)^2}$
$\quad = \sqrt{3^2 + 4^2}$ or $\sqrt{25}$ or 5

Draw *EA* and *FB* $\perp$ *x*-axis.

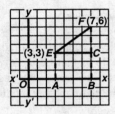

Draw *EC*.
Coordinates of *C* are (7, 3).
Length of *EC = 4;*
length of *FC = 3.*
$\therefore$ by the Pythagorean Theorem, *EF = 5.*

The simplest way to solve is to note that $\triangle ECF$ *is a* 3-4-5 right triangle with *FC = 3, EC = 4.* Therefore, the hypotenuse *EF = 5.*

Finding the Midpoint of a Line Segment The coordinates of the midpoint of a line segment are one-half the sums of the coordinates of the end points. The coordinates of the midpoints of the line segment which joins point *G*(1, 5) and point *H*(7, –1) are $\frac{1}{2}$ (1 + 7) *or* 4, and $\frac{1}{2}$ [5 + (–1)] or $\frac{1}{2}$ (4) *or* 2. Therefore *M(4, 2)* is the midpoint of *GH.*

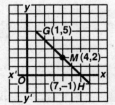

Finding the Slope of a Line The slope of a line passing through two points whose coordinates are known is the difference in the *y*-coordinates divided by the difference in the *x*-coordinates.

In the graph above, the slope of the line joining *G*(1,5) to *H*(7, –1) is

$$\frac{5 - (-1)}{1 - 7} \text{ or } \frac{5 + 1}{-6} \text{ or } \frac{6}{-6} \text{ or } -1.$$

A SUMMARY OF IMPORTANT RELATIONSHIPS IN GEOMETRY

Right Triangles

In a right triangle, $(\text{leg})^2 + (\text{leg})^2 = (\text{hypotenuse})^2$, or $a^2 + b^2 = c^2$ (Pythagorean Theorem).

Special right triangles have sides in the ratio 3-4-5, or 5-12-13, or 8-15-17, with the longest side in each case representing the hypotenuse.

In a 30°-60°-90° triangle:

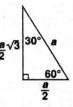

the length of the leg opposite the 30° angle equals one-half the length of the hypotenuse;

the length of the leg opposite the 60° angle equals $\frac{1}{2}$ the length of the hypotenuse times $\sqrt{3}$.

the ratio of the shorter leg to the hypotenuse is 1: 2.

The relationships can be learned and applied by memorizing the diagram:

In a 45°-45°-90° triangle:

the length of the hypotenuse equals the length of a leg times $\sqrt{2}$;

the length of the leg equals $\frac{1}{2}$ the length of the hypotenuse times $\sqrt{2}$.

The relationships can be learned and applied by memorizing the diagram:

Equilateral Triangles

Each angle of an equilateral triangle has a measure of 60°.

Each altitude of an equilateral triangle coincides with a median and an angle bisector, and its length equals $\frac{1}{2}$ the side times $\sqrt{3}$.

Areas of Polygons

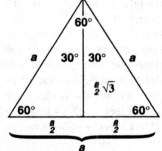

Area of a rectangle = bh.

Area of a square = s^2.

Area of a parallelogram = bh.

Area of a triangle = $\frac{1}{2} bh$.

Area of a right triangle = $\frac{1}{2}$ leg × leg.

Area of a trapezoid = $\frac{1}{2} h (b_1 + b_2)$, where h is the altitude and b_1 and b_2 are the lengths of the bases.

Area of a rhombus = $\frac{1}{2} d_1 d_2$, where d_1 and d_2 are the lengths of the diagonals.

Circles

The circumference of a circle = πD or $2\pi r$.

Length of an arc = $\dfrac{n}{360} \times 2\pi r$.

Area of a circle = πr^2.

Coordinate Geometry

Distance between two points = $\sqrt{(x_1 - x_2)^2 + (y_1 - y_2)^2}$

Coordinates of midpoint of line segment = $\left(\frac{1}{2} (x_1 - x_2), \frac{1}{2} (y_1 - y_2) \right)$

Slope of a line = $\dfrac{y_2 - y_1}{x_2 - x_1}$

PRACTICE EXERCISE

1. The perimeter of a square is p inches. The area of this square is

   (A) p^2 (B) $16p^2$ (C) $4p$ (D) $\dfrac{p^2}{16}$ (E) $4p^2$

2. $\angle 1 = \angle 5 \stackrel{\circ}{=} 30$
   $\angle 3 \stackrel{\circ}{=} ?$
   (A) 90   (B) 120
   (C) 135 (D) 150
   (E) 160

   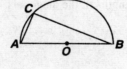

3. In $\triangle ABC$, $BD \perp AC$.
   $AB = 13$, $BC = 20$,
   $AD = 5$, $DC = ?$
   (A) 16   (B) 17   (C) 18
   (D) 19   (E) 20

   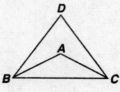

4. $AB \perp BC$, $BC \perp CD$.
   $AB = 8$, $BC = 5$, $CD = 4$
   What is the shortest
   distance from A to D?
   (A) 12   (B) 13   (C) 15
   (D) 16   (E) 17

5. One end of a ladder 13 feet long is placed 5 feet from the outer wall of a building that stands on level ground. How far up the building, to the nearest foot, will the ladder reach?
   (A) 5 feet   (B) 9 feet   (C) 12 feet
   (D) 13 feet   (E) 18 feet

6. AB is a diameter of circle O.
   $AC = 10$, $CB = 24$. What
   is the area of circle O?
   (A) 120   (B) 84.5π
   (C) 169π (D) 240
   (E) $1007\pi - 240$

7. $AB = AC$, $DB = DC$
   $\angle ABC \stackrel{\circ}{=} \frac{1}{2} \angle DBC$,
   $\angle D \stackrel{\circ}{=} 70$. What is the
   measure of $\angle A$?
   (A) 55°   (B) 70°   (C) 105°
   (D) 110°   (E) 125°

8. The diameter of a hoop is 7. How many revolutions will it make if it is rolled a distance of 182π?
   (A) 26   (B) 13π (C) 26π
   (D) 30π (E) 52π

9. A cord 200 inches long can go around a square block 10 times. The area of one side of this square is
   (A) 20 square inches   (B) 25 square inches
   (C) 100 square inches   (D) 400 square inches
   (E) 500 square inches

10. In trapezoid $ABCD$, A and B are right angles and BC is longer than AD. If $AD = 15$ and the diagonals of the trapezoid are 25 and 17, the length of AB is
    (A) 8   (B) 12   (C) 15   (D) 17   (E) 20

11. Find the area of a triangle with coordinates $(-16, 0)$, $(-6, 0)$, $(0, 8)$
    (A) 32   (B) 40   (C) 48   (D) 64   (E) 80

12. A 15-foot seesaw is balanced at its center on a base that is 3 feet high. How many feet above the ground can an end reach?
    (A) 5   (B) 6   (C) 9   (D) 10   (E) 15

13. A rectangular lot 50 feet by 100 feet is surrounded on all sides by a concrete walk 5 feet wide. Find the number of square feet in the surface of the walk.
    (A) 775   (B) 1500   (C) 1600
    (D) 5000   (E) 6600

14. Straight line MN intersects
    straight lines AB and CD as
    shown in figure. If $\angle 2 \stackrel{\circ}{=}$
    6, and $\angle 4 \stackrel{\circ}{=} 130$, then the
    measure of $\angle 7 =$
    (A) 40°   (B) 50°   (C) 60°
    (D) 90°   (E) 130°

    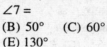
    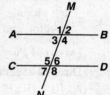

15. JK is perpendicular to KL and
    MN is perpendicular to JL. If
    JM is 6, JN is 4, and JL is 18,
    what is JK?
    (A) 4   (B) 12   (C) 18
    (D) 27   (E) none of these

    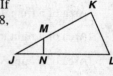

16. Straight line $SROV$ is a diameter of circle O. QRT is a 12-inch chord perpendicular to $SROV$, and RS is 3 inches. How many inches is a radius of circle O?
    (A) 4.5   (B) 6   (C) 7.5
    (D) 9   (E) 12

    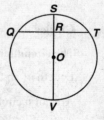

17. If the length of a rectangle is $3u + 2v$ and its perimeter is $10u + 6v$, the width is
    (A) $2u + v$ (B) $7u + 4v$ (C) $4u + 2v$
    (D) $3.5u + 2v$ (E) $2v + u$

18. In $\triangle ABC$, $AB \perp BC$, $\angle A \stackrel{\circ}{=} 45$, and $AB = 10$. $(AC)^2$ equals
    (A) 10   (B) 20   (C) 100   (D) $2\sqrt{10}$ (E) 200

19. The base of an isosceles triangle is 16 and each of the equal sides is 10. Find the area of the triangle.
    (A) 24   (B) 36   (C) 48   (D) 80   (E) 96

20. A rectangular field 100 feet long is twice as long as it is wide. The number of feet of fencing needed is
(A) 150   (B) 300   (C) 400   (D) 500   (E) 600

21. Given right triangles, I, II, III, IV, and V. The following are the lengths of the legs of each triangle: (I) 7 and 4; (I) 12 and 2; (III) 8 and 3; (IV) 6 and 4; (V) 24 and 1. Which of these have the same area?
(A) all of them   (B) none of them
(C) only I, II, III, and IV
(D) only II, III, IV, and V
(E) only I, III, IV, and V

22. Four circles each have a radius of $\frac{2}{\pi}$. The sum of the four circumferences is
(A) 4   (B) 8   (C) 16   (D) 24   (E) 32

23. What is the average measure of the angles of $\triangle ABC$?
(A) 30°   (B) 60°   (C) 90°   (D) 180°
(E) cannot be determined from the information furnished

24. Right $\triangle ABE$ shares side BE with rectangle $BCDE$. $AB = BC = 5$ and $CD = 6$. The area of $\triangle ABE$ is
(A) 10   (B) 12.5   (C) 15
(D) 30   (E) 45

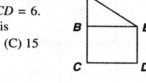

25. KL is the diameter of a circle whose circumference is 10π. If $KM = ML$, then the area of KLM is
(A) 5   (B) $5\sqrt{2}$
(C) $2\sqrt{5}$ (D) 25
(E) 50

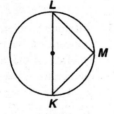

26. For right $\triangle ABC$ the coordinates of A are (3, 5) and of $C(-2, -2)$; then the coordinates of B are
(A) (−2, 3)   (B) (3, −2)   (C) (−2, −5)
(D) (−2, 8)   (E) (5, −2)

27. Side AB of square $ABCD$ is 10 units. The area of the shaded portion is
(A) $100 - 25\pi$
(B) $25\pi - 100$
(C) $100 - 100\pi$
(D) π
(E) $100 - 10\pi$

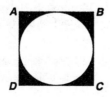

28. The area of a circle whose center is at (0, 0) is 25π. This circle passes through all of the following points EXCEPT
(A) (−5, 0)   (B) (5, 5)   (C) (0, 5)
(D) (5, 0)   (E) (0, −5)

29. Diameter AB = diameter DC =10. $AB = AD$ and $DC = BC$. The area of the shaded portion is
(A) $100 - 25\pi$
(B) $25\pi - 100$
(C) $100 - 100\pi$
(D) π
(E) $25\pi - 100$

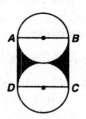

30. In rectangle $ABCD$ several triangles are drawn. All of the following triangles have identical areas EXCEPT
(A) ADC (B) EDC
(C) ACB (D) AED
(E) BCD

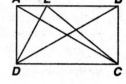

Questions 31–35: These problems are not multiple choice. They are designed to give practice for the questions on the test with student-produced responses. In the typical tests in this book and in the actual test, you will be asked to enter your answers in a special grid. For the following questions, write your answer in the blank provided.

31. Straight line AD intersects circle O at B and C. BC equals radius OD. The measure of the angle formed by drawing radii OB and OC is

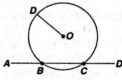

_____

32. Rectangle $ABCD$ is formed by joining the centers of equal circles, each having an area of 4π. The perimeter of $ABCD$ is

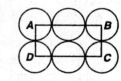

_____

33. The distance between a point with coordinates (5, 9) and another point with coordinates (2, 5) is

_____

34. The center of square $ABCD$ is located at point (3, 3) and its sides are along the x and y axes. The area of $ABCD$ is

_____

35. The vertices of rectangle $ABCD$ are the points A (0, 0), B (8, 0), C (8, k) and D (0, 5): k equals

_____

TYPICAL EXAMINATION PROBLEMS BY TOPICS

Fractions

Some Important Facts

1. A fraction is an indicated division. Thus $\frac{2}{5}$ means 2 ÷ 5. The number on top of the fraction sign is called the numerator. The number on bottom is the denominator.

2. A decimal is an indicated fraction in which the denominator is 10, 100, 1000, 10,000 . . . etc. Thus $\frac{3}{10}$ is written as 0.3 and $\frac{3}{100}$ is written as 0.03.

3. As the denominator of a fraction increases, the value of the fraction decreases. $\frac{1}{5}$ is greater than $\frac{1}{50}$. $\frac{1}{5} = 1 \div 5 = 0.2$ and $\frac{1}{50} = 1 \div 50 = 0.02$.

4. As the numerator of a fraction increases, the value of the fraction increases. $\frac{1}{5}$ is less than $\frac{10}{5}$ since $\frac{1}{5} = 0.2$ and $\frac{10}{5} = 2$.

5. The value of a fraction is not changed when the numerator and denominator are multiplied by the same number except zero. Thus $\frac{1}{3} = \frac{3}{9}$. This is useful in adding or subtracting fractions.

6. The value of a fraction is not changed when the numerator and denominator are divided by the same number except zero. Thus $\frac{4}{10} = \frac{2}{5}$. This is called "reducing a fraction to lowest terms."

Hints on Solving Problems

1. To find a number that is a fractional part of a given number, multiply the number by the fraction. The word *of* generally indicates multiplication.

   EXAMPLES:

   What is $\frac{1}{5}$ of 50? 10 (*answer*)

   How much is $\frac{1}{5}$ of $\frac{5}{12}$? $\frac{1}{12}$ (*answer*)

2. To find what fractional part one number is of another, divide the number representing the part by the number representing the whole.

   $$\frac{\text{part}}{\text{whole}} = \text{fractional part}$$

   Usually the number that follows "part of" is the *whole* and the number that follows "is" is the *part*.

   EXAMPLES:

   What part of 7 is 2? $\frac{2}{7}$ (*answer*)

3. To find a number when a fractional part of it is known, divide the given part by the fraction.

   $$\frac{\text{part}}{\text{fractional part}} = \text{whole}$$

   This type of problem can be solved algebraically.

   EXAMPLE:

   5 is $\frac{1}{4}$ of what number?

   Arithmetically: $\frac{5}{\frac{1}{4}} = 5 \div \frac{1}{4}$ or 5×4 or 20 (*answer*)

   Algebraically: Let x = the number.
   $$\frac{1}{4}x = 5$$
   $$x = 20 \ (answer)$$

4. To evaluate or compare fractions, change all fractions to same denominators and inspect numerators, or change all fractions to same numerators and inspect denominators.

   EXAMPLES:

   Which is the largest fraction: $\frac{1}{6}$, $\frac{1}{4}$, or $\frac{2}{3}$?

   $\frac{1}{6} = \frac{2}{12}$, $\frac{1}{4} = \frac{3}{12}$, and $\frac{2}{3} = \frac{8}{12}$ $\frac{2}{3}$ (*answer*)

   Which is the smallest: $\frac{4}{28}$, $\frac{2}{3}$, or $\frac{3}{9}$?

   $\frac{4}{28} = \frac{1}{7}$, $\frac{2}{3} = \frac{1}{1\frac{1}{2}}$, and $\frac{3}{9} = \frac{1}{3}$. $\frac{4}{28}$ (*answer*)

5. Mixture problems are actually applications of the concept of fractions. The denominator is the sum total of all the components or constituents, and the numerator is the part described.

   EXAMPLE:

   In a mixture of 3 parts sand and 4 parts gravel, what part of the mixture is composed of sand?

   $\frac{3}{3+4}$ or $\frac{3}{7}$ (*answer*)

6. Work problems are actually applications of the concept of fractions. The denominator is the total time required to complete a task while the numerator is the time actually worked. This fraction represents the part of the task completed.

   EXAMPLE:

   Ida has 3 hours of homework to do. What part does she complete in x hours?

   $\frac{x}{3}$ (*answer*)

➤ PRACTICE EXERCISE

1. What part of 200 is 59?
   (A) .295   (B) 2.95   (C) 9.8   (D) 29.5   (E) 98

2. How many thirds are there in $\frac{3}{4}$?
   (A) 2   (B) $2\frac{1}{4}$ (C) 3   (D) $3\frac{1}{4}$ (E) 4

3. What part of x is y?
   (A) xy (B) $\frac{x}{y}$ (C) $\frac{1}{xy}$ (D) $\frac{y}{x}$ (E) $\frac{x}{100y}$

4. Which of the following has the smallest value?
   (A) $\frac{5}{8}$ (B) $\frac{7}{12}$ (C) $\frac{8}{15}$ (D) $\frac{11}{20}$ (E) $\frac{18}{37}$

5. $\frac{1}{3}$ of $\frac{2}{9}$ equals 2 multiplied by
   (A) $\frac{1}{27}$ (B) $\frac{2}{27}$ (C) 3   (D) $13\frac{1}{2}$ (E) 27

6. Which of the following has the smallest value?
   (A) $\frac{.1}{2}$ (B) $\frac{1}{.2}$ (C) $\frac{.1}{.2}$ (D) $\frac{.2}{1}$ (E) $\frac{2}{.1}$

7. Ann, who owns $\frac{5}{6}$ of a parcel of property, sells $\frac{4}{5}$ of her share for \$48,000. At that value the entire property is worth
   (A) \$64,800   (B) \$69,200   (C) \$72,000
   (D) \$73,600   (E) \$84,000

8. A group consists of 22 girls and 18 boys. What part of the group is composed of boys?
   (A) $\frac{9}{11}$ (B) $\frac{9}{22}$ (C) $\frac{19}{28}$ (D) $\frac{9}{15}$ (E) $\frac{9}{20}$

9. In a recent civil service examination, $\frac{1}{8}$ of the candidates failed the first part of the test. Of those eligible to take the second part of the competitive examination, $\frac{2}{7}$ successfully passed. What part of the original candidates were successful in the examination?
   (A) $\frac{1}{28}$ (B) $\frac{9}{56}$ (C) $\frac{1}{5}$ (D) $\frac{1}{4}$ (E) $\frac{3}{4}$

10. Jonathan has $\frac{1}{3}$ as many green marbles as he has red marbles and $\frac{1}{6}$ as many red marbles as he has yellow marbles. What part of his collection is made up of yellow marbles?
    (A) $\frac{9}{11}$ (B) $\frac{1}{6}$ (C) $\frac{2}{11}$ (D) $\frac{3}{22}$ (E) $\frac{1}{22}$

11. If a 15-gallon gasoline tank is $\frac{3}{8}$ full, how many gallons must be added to completely fill the tank?
    (A) 5   (B) $5\frac{5}{8}$ (C) 9   (D) $9\frac{3}{8}$ (E) 10

12. Three chapters of a fraternity voted on a constitutional amendment. In Chapter A it passed with $\frac{3}{4}$ of the members in favor of it. In Chapter B only 2 out of 9 members were against it. Chapter C passed the proposition with 5 of its 36 members voting against it. Arrange the chapters in decreasing order according to the proportion in favor of the amendment.
    (A) C, B, A   (B) A, B, C   (C) A, C, B
    (D) B, A, C   (E) B, C, A

13. The annual income of a family is budgeted as follows: $\frac{1}{10}$ is for clothing, $\frac{1}{3}$ is for food and $\frac{1}{5}$ is for rent. This leaves \$11,000 for other expenses and savings. Find the annual income.
    (A) \$3000   (B) \$30,000   (C) \$33,000
    (D) \$36,000   (E) 39,000

14. J. C. Nichols department store reports that the average sales on Saturdays is twice that on Thursdays and the average sales on Thursdays is twice that on the other four days. What fraction of the weekly sales are made on Thursdays?
    (A) $\frac{1}{7}$ (B) $\frac{1}{5}$ (C) $\frac{2}{7}$ (D) $\frac{1}{3}$ (E) $\frac{2}{5}$

15. On a two-day hike, 8 campers equally share 4 loaves of bread. If there are 16 slices of bread in each loaf, how many slices of bread does each camper receive daily?
    (A) 1   (B) 2   (C) 3   (D) 4   (E) 8

Questions 16–20: These problems are not multiple choice. They are designed to give practice for the questions on the test with student-produced responses. In the typical tests in this book and in the actual test, you will be asked to enter your answers in a special grid. For the following questions, write your answer in the blank provided.

---

16. When 10 gallons are removed from a tank that is $\frac{5}{8}$ full, the tank is completely emptied. How many gallons are now needed to fill this tank?

    _____

17. The number which when increased by $\frac{1}{3}$ of itself equals 96 is

    _____

18. Joan is three years younger than Martin. How old will Joan be when she is $\frac{4}{5}$ his age?

    _____

19. A gasoline gauge registers $\frac{1}{8}$ full. After purchasing 12 gallons of gasoline it registers $\frac{7}{8}$ full. What is the capacity of the tank (in gallons)?

    _____

20. After 75 gallons of oil are removed from a cylindrical tank, its level is lowered from $\frac{1}{6}$ to $\frac{1}{7}$ of its capacity. How many gallons should now be added to the tank to fill it?

    _____

.ent

.)ME IMPORTANT FACTS

1. Percent means "hundredths."
2. A percent (%) represents a fraction with a denominator of 100. $1\% = \frac{1}{100} = .01$ and $11\% = \frac{11}{100} = .11$ and $1.1\% = \frac{1.1}{100} = .011$.

Hints on Solving Problems

1. Converting a percent to a fraction or decimal involves dropping the percent sign. Dropping the percent sign actually divides a number by 100. Example: 6% changed to 6 actually involves division by 100. Thus 6% does not equal 6 but 6% does equal $\frac{6}{100}$ or .06.

   EXAMPLE:

   Write $\frac{2}{5}$ as a percent. $\qquad \frac{2}{5} = \frac{?}{100}$ or $\frac{40}{100}$

   $\qquad$ or 40% *(answer)*

   What percent of 2 is 4?

   $\left(\frac{?}{100}\right)(2) = 4$ or 200% *(answer)*

2. Most problems require a knowledge of the meaning of percent. To find a certain percent of a number, change the percent to a decimal or fraction and multiply.

   EXAMPLE:

   What is 4% of $5?

   $(.04)(\$5) = \$.20$ *(answer)* or $\left(\frac{4}{100}\right)(\$5) = \$.20$ *(answer)*

3. Some problems can best be done algebraically. In one type you are given that one quantity is a certain percent of an unknown quantity and you are asked to find that unknown quantity. Let x = the number and solve, using the definition of percent.

   EXAMPLE:

   9 is 20% of what number?

   If x = the number, then 9 = 20% of x or $9 = \left(\frac{20}{100}\right)x$ or $9 = \frac{1}{5}x$ $\quad or \quad x = 45.$ *(answer)*

➤ PRACTICE EXERCISE

1. One-half is $\frac{1}{2}$ % of
   (A) $\frac{1}{100}$ (B) $\frac{1}{400}$ (C) 100 (D) 200 (E) 400

2. 104% of 104 equals
   (A) 0 (B) 1 (C) 4.16
   (D) 105.04 (E) 108.16

3. In a class composed of x girls and y boys what percent of the class is composed of girls?
   (A) $100xy$ (B) $\frac{x}{x+y}$ (C) $\frac{100x}{x+y}$
   (D) $\frac{y}{x+y}$ (E) $\frac{100\,y}{x+y}$

4. Seven percent of what number is 14?
   (A) 50 (B) 98 (C) 100 (D) 200 (E) 400

5. A baseball team won W games and lost L games. What percent of its games did it win?
   (A) $\frac{100W}{L}$ (B) $\frac{100W}{L+W}$ (C) $\frac{W}{L}$
   (D) $\frac{W}{L+W}$ (E) $\frac{100W}{100L+W}$

6. The enrollment in an art class was 300 when the studio opened. The present enrollment is 1200. What is the percentage in increase?
   (A) 25% (B) 40% (C) 75%
   (D) 300% (E) 400%

7. If a merchant makes a profit of 20% based on the selling price of an article, what percent profit does he make on the cost?
   (A) 20% (B) 25% (C) 30%
   (D) 40% (E) 80%

8. The ABC Company gave each employee an end-of-year bonus to be determined as follows: 15% on that part of a monthly salary that does not exceed $3000, 10% on that part of a salary over $3000 and up to and including $6000, and 5% on that part above $6000. Employee Smith received a bonus of $625. Find his basic monthly salary.
   (A) $3750 (B) $4750 (C) $5750
   (D) $6250 (E) $12,500

9. When the admission price to a movie rose from $4 to $5, the percent increase was
   (A) 1% (B) 4% (C) 20%
   (D) 25% (E) more than 25%

10. A 5-quart solution of sulfuric acid and water is 60% acid. If a gallon of water is added, what percent of the resulting solution is acid?
    (A) 3% (B) $33\frac{1}{3}$% (C) 40%
    (D) 48% (E) 50%

11. A boy finds that $57\frac{1}{2}$% of his marble collection consists of red marbles, $12\frac{1}{2}$% of his collection consists of blue marbles, and the rest are 24 multi-colored marbles. How many marbles are there in his collection?
    (A) 20 (B) 30 (C) 56 (D) 80 (E) 104

12. A man buys 2750 eggs for $100, and loses 350 of these eggs because of breakage. If he sells the remaining eggs at 70¢ a dozen, what percent of his original investment is his profit?
    (A) 20% (B) 30% (C) $33\frac{1}{3}$%
    (D) 40% (E) 60%

13. Pamela owns 37.5% of the stock of a corporation and sells $\frac{2}{3}$ of her stock at a 10% profit. What percent of this stock does she own after this transaction?
    (A) 12.5% (B) $33\frac{1}{3}$% (C) $66\frac{2}{3}$%
    (D) 72.5% (E) 90%

14. A salesperson sold a book for 105% of the marked price instead of discounting the marked price by 5%. The book was sold for $4.20. At what price should the book have been sold?
    (A) $3.00 (B) $3.80 (C) $4.00
    (D) $4.18 (E) $4.40

15. Mr. Light can pay for an article in either of two ways. He can pay the list price with a down payment of 20% and the balance in 5 installments of $16 each, or he can pay the cash price of $88. How much does Mr. Light save by paying the cash price?
    (A) $8.00 (B) $8.40 (C) $8.80
    (D) $9.60 (E) $12.00

Questions 16–20: These problems are not multiple choice. They are designed to give practice for the questions on the test with student-produced responses. In the typical tests in this book and in the actual test, you will be asked to enter your answers in a special grid. For the following questions, write your answer in the blank provided.

---

16. What percent of 12 is 3? _____

17. $66\frac{2}{3}$% of 30 is 20% of _____

18. On the average, 8% of the motorists make a right turn at a particular intersection. At that rate, out of 250 motorists, how many will most probably make this turn? _____

19. Thirty prizes were distributed to 5% of the original entrants in a contest. The number of entrants in this contest was _____

20. In June a baseball team that played 60 games had won 30% of its games played. After a phenomenal winning streak this team raised its average to 50%. How many games must the team have won in a row to attain this average? _____

Averages
SOME IMPORTANT FACTS

1. To find the average of a group of numbers, add the numbers and divide the sum by the quantity of numbers added.

   EXAMPLE:

   What is the average of 85%, 80%, and 75%? The sum is 240. The average is 240 ÷ 3 *or* 80. *(answer)*

2. When two or more averages are combined into a single average, appropriate weight must be given each average.

   EXAMPLE:

   A man buys 50 shares of stock at $30 and then buys 100 shares of this stock at $25. What is his average cost per share?
   His average is *not* $27.50 but ($30 × 50 plus $25 × 100) ÷ 150 *or* $26.67 per share. *(answer)*

Hints on Solving Problems

1. To find the average, all units must be the same.

   EXAMPLE:

   What is the average length of three strings of the following lengths: 1 inch, 1 foot, and 1 yard? Change all lengths to inches. Thus, the sum equals 1 inch, 12 inches, and 36 inches *or* 49 inches. The average equals 49 ÷ 3 *or* $16\frac{1}{3}$ inches or 1 foot and $4\frac{1}{3}$ inches. *(answer)*

2. The sum is equal to the product of the average and the quantity of numbers.

   EXAMPLE:

   What number must be added to 5, 7, 0, and 1 to attain an average of 3?
   Sum must be 3 × 5 *or* 15. Sum of four numbers given is 13. To obtain sum of 15, add 2. *(answer)*

➤ PRACTICE EXERCISE

1. A strip of linoleum 13 yards 5 feet 1 inch is to be cut into three equal parts. The length of each part will be
   (A) 4 yards 4 feet   (B) 4 yards $4\frac{1}{3}$ feet
   (C) 4 yards 2 feet $8\frac{1}{3}$ inches   (D) 4 yards 1 foot
   (E) 4 yards $5\frac{1}{3}$ feet

2. What is the average height of three boys if one boy is x inches and the other boys are each y inches tall?
   (A) $\dfrac{2xy}{3}$ (B) $\dfrac{x+2y}{3}$ (C) $\dfrac{x+y}{3}$
   (D) $x+\dfrac{y}{3}$ (E) $\dfrac{2}{3}(x+y)$

3. Three members of a track team have weights that range from 110 to 135 pounds. Which of the following *cannot* possibly be the average of the three trackmen?
   (A) 117 (B) 119 (C) 122 (D) 125 (E) 126

4. The average of the numbers represented by $z-8$ and $3z+2$ is
   (A) $11z+3$ (B) $4z-6$ (C) $\dfrac{11z+3}{2}$
   (D) $2z-3$ (E) $2z-5$

5. The average of A and another number is B. The other number is
   (A) $\dfrac{AB}{2}$ (B) $2B-A$ (C) $2A-B$
   (D) $A-B$ (E) $\dfrac{A+B}{2}$

6. The average of two numbers is XY. If one number is equal to X the other number is equal to
   (A) Y (B) $2Y$ (C) $XY-X$
   (D) $2XY-X$ (E) $XY-2X$

7. If b boys each have m marbles, and g girls each have n marbles, what is the average number of marbles per child?
   (A) $m+n$ (B) $\dfrac{m+n}{2}$ (C) $\dfrac{m+n}{b+g}$
   (D) $\dfrac{bm+gn}{m+n}$ (E) $\dfrac{bm+gn}{b+g}$

8. During a closeout sale, 30 pairs of pants are sold at $60 each. The price is then reduced to $50 and 20 pairs of pants are sold. At what price must the remaining 10 pairs be sold in order to attain an average of $55 for the entire 60 pairs of pants?
   (A) $50   (B) $52.50   (C) $55
   (D) $57.50   (E) $60

9. The average of n numbers is a. If x is subtracted from each number, the average will be
   (A) $\dfrac{ax}{n}$ (B) $\dfrac{an}{x}$ (C) $an-x$
   (D) $n-x$ (E) $a-x$

10. What fraction must be subtracted from the sum of $\frac{1}{2}+\frac{1}{3}$ in order to have an average of $\frac{1}{6}$?
    (A) $-\frac{1}{3}$ (B) $\frac{1}{3}$ (C) $\frac{1}{2}$ (D) $-\frac{1}{2}$ (E) $\frac{2}{3}$

11. Which of the following must be added to the sum of $2d$ and $4d$ in order to have an average of $3d$?
    (A) $-3d$ (B) $+3d$ (C) $9d$
    (D) $-9d$ (E) none of these

12. The average of three numbers is x. If one number is 5, then the sum of the other two numbers is
    (A) $3x$ (B) $\dfrac{3x}{2}$ (C) $3x-5$ D) 5 (E) $\dfrac{x-5}{2}$

13. A student attends Central High School for two terms and earns an average of 80%. He then attends Circle High School for five terms and earns an average of 85%. His average for the seven terms would be
    (A) 82.5%   (B) 82.6%   (C) 83.4%
    (D) 83.57%   (E) 84%

14. If 5 lbs. of nuts worth 60 cents a pound are mixed with 6 lbs. of nuts worth 50 cents a pound, the value (in cents) of each pound of mixture is
    (A) 54.5 (B) 55 (C) 55.5 (D) 56 (E) 56.5

15. The average of two numbers is V. If the smaller number is v, then the larger number is
    (A) $V-v$ (B) $v-V$ (C) $2v-V$
    (D) $2V-v$ (E) $\dfrac{V-2v}{2}$

Questions 16–20: These problems are not multiple choice. They are designed to give practice for the questions on the test with student-produced responses. In the typical tests in this book and in the actual test, you will be asked to enter your answers in a special grid. For the following questions, write your answer in the blank provided.

16. What number must be added to 8, 18, and 26 to attain an average of exactly 18?_____

17. A student who strives to attain an average of 80% has the following grades in a certain subject: 70, 74, 81, and 85. What grade must he get in the next test to achieve his goal? _____

18. What was the grade a student received on the fourth test in the Latin class if this student received grades of 80%, 90%, and 95% on the first tests, and then had an average of 75% for all four examinations?

    _____

19. If the average of the ages of three men is 44 and no one of them is younger than 42, what is the maximum age (years) of any one man? _____

20. The average closing price of the five most active stocks was $42. The average closing price of the first four stocks on the most active list was $37. The closing price of the stock that was fifth on the most active list was

    _____

Motion

Some Important Facts

1. distance = rate × time

2. rate = $\dfrac{\text{distance}}{\text{time}}$

3. time = $\dfrac{\text{distance}}{\text{rate}}$

Hints on Solving Problems

1. Use the most convenient formula of the three given.
2. Units must be similar.

   distance = rate × time

   $$\text{miles} = \frac{\text{miles}}{\text{per hour}} \times \text{hours}$$

   EXAMPLE:

   How far will a car traveling at 30 miles per hour go in 2 minutes?

   $$\text{miles} = \frac{\cancel{30} \text{ miles}}{\cancel{\text{per hour}}} \times \frac{\cancel{2}^{\,1}}{\cancel{60}_{\,2}^{\,1}} \text{ hrs. } or \text{ 1 mile } (answer)$$

3. To calculate the average rate for a trip involving two or more parts, regard the trip as a single trip, using the total distance and the total time to calculate the average rate for the whole trip.

   EXAMPLE:

   A man travels 60 miles at 40 miles per hour and then travels 40 miles at the rate of 60 miles per hour. What is his average rate for the whole trip?

   During the first part he traveled for $\frac{60}{40}$ or $1\frac{1}{2}$ hours. During the second part he traveled for $\frac{40}{60}$ or $\frac{2}{3}$ hour. He spent $1\frac{1}{2}$ plus $\frac{2}{3}$ or $2\frac{1}{6}$ hours on the entire trip. He covered a total of 100 miles. His average rate for the entire trip is $100 \div 2\frac{1}{6}$ or 46.1 miles per hour. *(answer)*

➤ PRACTICE EXERCISE

1. How many minutes will it take a motorist traveling at 40 miles an hour to reach a point $\frac{2}{5}$ of a mile away?
   (A) $\frac{4}{15}$ (B) $\frac{2}{3}$ (C) 1 (D) 4 (E) $\frac{3}{5}$

2. A man travels for 5 hours at an average rate of 40 M.P.H. He develops some motor trouble and returns to his original starting point in 10 hours. What was his average rate (in miles per hour) on the return trip?
   (A) 20 (B) 25 (C) 26.6 (D) 30 (E) 60

3. Ten minutes after a plane leaves the airport, it is reported that the plane is 80 miles away. What is the average speed of the plane, in miles per hour?
   (A) 160 (B) 240 (C) 320 (D) 400 (E) 480

4. A car travels a distance of 70 miles in $2\frac{1}{2}$ hours. How much faster on the average must it travel to make the trip in $\frac{3}{4}$ hours less time? (M. P. H.)
   (A) 12 (B) 24 (C) 28 (D) 40 (E) 51

5. How many seconds will it take an automobile to cover one mile if it is traveling at 45 miles per hour?
   (A) 27 (B) 45 (C) 60 (D) 80 (E) 90

6. How many feet will an automobile cover in one second when it travels at 45 miles per hour? (1 mile = 5280 feet)
   (A) 66 (B) 660 (C) 2138 (D) 3960 (E) 6600

7. A boy rides his bicycle ten miles at an average rate of twelve miles an hour and twelve miles at an average rate of ten miles an hour. What is the average rate for the entire trip?
   (A) 10.8 (B) 11 (C) 12 (D) 20.3 (E) 22

8. A man covers d miles in t hours. At that rate how long (in hours) will it take him to cover m miles?
   (A) dmt (B) $\dfrac{md}{t}$ (C) $\dfrac{mt}{d}$ (D) $\dfrac{dt}{m}$ (E) $\dfrac{d}{t}$

9. A motorist travels for 2 hours at 30 miles per hour and then covers the same distance in 3 hours. What was his average rate (in miles per hour) for the entire trip?
   (A) 24 (B) 25 (C) 26 (D) 27 (E) none of these

10. Martin traveled m miles at the rate of r miles per hour and arrived at his destination 1 hour late. How much time should he allow himself to make this trip again and arrive on time?
    (A) $\dfrac{m}{r} + 1$ (B) $\dfrac{m - r}{r}$ (C) $m - r$
    (D) $m - r - 1$ (E) $\dfrac{m + r}{r}$

11. As a motorist approaches the turnpike, he travels at the rate of 20 miles per hour in street traffic. For the first mile on the turnpike he travels at the rate of 30 miles per hour and then covers the next mile in one minute. What is his average rate for the first three miles of this trip?
    (A) 25 M.P.H. (B) 30 M.P.H. (C) 33 M.P.H.
    (D) $36\frac{2}{3}$ M.P.H. (E) 50 M.P.H.

12. The distance between Chicago and Cleveland is 354 miles. If a person leaves Chicago at 9:50 A.M. Central Time and arrives in Cleveland at 5:30 P.M. the same day Eastern Time, at what average speed does he travel, correct to the nearest mile? (Central Time is one hour earlier than Eastern Time).
(A) 46 M.P.H.   (B) 50 M.P.H.   (C) 53 M.P.H.
(D) 55 M.P.H.   (E) 56 M.P.H.

13. A boy travels on his bicycle at the rate of 6 miles per hour and his sister on hers at the rate of 5 miles per hour. They start at the same time and place and travel over the same road in the same direction. After traveling for 3 hours, the boy turns back. How far from the starting point has his sister traveled when they meet?
(A) 16 miles   (B) about 16.4 miles
(C) about 16.9 miles   (D) 17 miles
(E) 17.4 miles

14. Mr. B. walks for 4 hours at the rate of y miles an hour. He stops an hour for lunch and then returns to the starting point by a route that is twice as long, but he travels in an auto whose speed is five times that of his walking rate. Find the number of hours spent on the entire trip.
(A) $5\frac{3}{5}$ (B) 6   (C) $6\frac{3}{5}$ (D) 7   (E) 8

15. A train left Albany for Buffalo, a distance of 290 miles, at 10:10 A.M. The train was scheduled to reach Buffalo at 3:45 P.M. If the average rate of the train on this trip was 50 miles per hour, it arrived in Buffalo
(A) about 5 minutes ahead of schedule
(B) on time
(C) about 5 minutes late
(D) about 13 minutes late
(E) more than a quarter of an hour late

Questions 16–20: These problems are not multiple choice. They are designed to give practice for the questions on the test with student-produced responses. In the typical tests in this book and in the actual test, you will be asked to enter your answers in a special grid. For the following questions, write your answer in the blank provided.

16. At 40 miles per hour the number of minutes it will take to drive 18 miles is

_____

17. How far (in miles) can a car traveling at 30 miles per hour go in an hour and twenty minutes?

_____

18. How far (in miles) does a car travel when its average rate is 35 miles per hour and it travels for 3 hours and 24 minutes?

_____

19. An automobile party leaves at 7:55 A.M., and arrives at its destination 15 miles away at 8:15 A.M. What was the average rate on this trip (in M.P.H.)?

_____

20. Twenty minutes after a plane leaves the airport, it is reported to be 160 miles away. What is the average speed of the plane in miles per hour?

_____

Ratio and Proportion

SOME IMPORTANT FACTS

1. A ratio is an expression that compares two quantities by dividing one by the other.

EXAMPLE:

In a class with 11 girls and 12 boys the ratio of girls to boys is 11:12 *or* $\frac{11}{12}$, while the ratio of boys to girls is 12:11 *or* $\frac{12}{11}$.

2. A maximum ratio is that ratio that has the largest numerical value. To determine the maximum ratio, write the ratios in the form of fractions and evaluate. If a fraction has a value of more than 1, use the reciprocal. In the illustration above, $\frac{12}{11}$ describes the same ratio expressed as $\frac{11}{12}$.

3. A proportion is a statement of equality that exists between two ratios. For example, $\frac{1}{2} = \frac{5}{10}$ is a proportion. It consists of four terms. The first and last terms are called *extremes* (1 and 10). The second and third terms are called *means* (2 and 5).

4. In a proportion, the product of the means equals the product of the extremes. In the proportion $\frac{1}{2} = \frac{5}{10}$, 5×2 equals 1×10.

Hints on Solving Problems

1. Many verbal problems express a relationship between two variables.

   EXAMPLE:

   If 3 books costs $12, what is the cost of b books?
   In this problem as you buy more books you pay more money proportionally. Likewise, as you spend more money, you receive more books. When a problem expresses a proportion, it is necessary to determine by logical reasoning whether it is a direct proportion or an inverse proportion.

2. A *direct* proportion is one in which the two variables are so related that if one quantity is multiplied or divided by the same number, the ratio is unchanged. The example given above illustrates this type. Therefore it may be expressed as follows:

   $$\frac{3 \text{ books}}{\$12} = \frac{b \text{ books}}{\$ x}$$

   $$3x = 12b$$
   $$x = 4b$$
   $$(answer) = \$4b$$

3. A direct proportion may be expressed as $\frac{x}{y} = k$ where the value of k remains constant.

4. An *inverse* proportion is one in which an increase by multiplication in one variable results in a corresponding decrease in the other, and a decrease by division in one varible results in a corresponding increase in the other.

   EXAMPLE:

   If 6 men can do a job in 10 days, how long would it take 3 men to complete this job?
   Obviously, since the number of men working has been cut in *half*, the number of days required will be *doubled*.

5. An inverse proportion may be expressed as $xy = k$ where the value of k remains a constant. In the example above, (6 men × 10 days) equals (3 men × 20 days) equals 60 man-days. To solve a problem that is an inverse proportion, write one set of conditions as the *extremes*: $\dfrac{6 \text{ men}}{10 \text{ days}} = \underline{\quad\quad}$.

   Then add the second set of conditions, with an unknown as the *means*: $\dfrac{6 \text{ men}}{3 \text{ men}} = \dfrac{x \text{ days}}{10 \text{ days}}$

   Solve by cross multiplication, since in a proportion the product of the means equals the product of the extremes.

➤ PRACTICE EXERCISE

1. Snow is accumulating f feet per minute. How much snow will fall in h hours if it continues falling at that rate?

   (A) $60fh$ (B) fh (C) $\dfrac{60f}{h}$ (D) $\dfrac{60h}{f}$ (E) $\dfrac{f}{h}$

2. If p pencils cost x cents, how many pencils can be bought for y cents?

   (A) $\dfrac{px}{y}$ (B) $\dfrac{y}{px}$ (C) $\dfrac{xy}{p}$ (D) $\dfrac{x}{py}$ (E) $\dfrac{py}{x}$

3. If p pencils cost c cents, n pencils at the same rate will cost

   (A) $\dfrac{pc}{n}$ cents (B) npc cents (C) $\dfrac{cn}{p}$ cents

   (D) $\dfrac{np}{c}$ cents (E) $\dfrac{1}{npc}$ cents

4. A formula for infant feeding requires 13 oz. of evaporated milk and 18 oz. of water. If only 10 oz. of milk are available, how much water, to the nearest ounce, should be used?

   (A) 7 oz. (B) 14 oz. (C) 15 oz.
   (D) 16 oz. (E) 21 oz.

5. Joan can wire x radios in $\frac{3}{4}$ minute. At this rate, how many radios can she wire in $\frac{3}{4}$ of an hour?

   (A) $\dfrac{x}{60}$ (B) $\dfrac{60}{x}$ (C) $60x$ (D) 60 (E) $x+60$

6. There are 27 students in a chemistry class and 22 students in a physics class. Seven of these students take physics and chemistry. What is the ratio of the number of students taking only physics to those taking only chemistry?
   (A) 4:3 (B) 34:29 (C) 7:6
   (D) 3:4 (E) 22:27

7. The cost of 7 dozen rulers at $15.60 per gross is
   (A) $.91 (B) $1.09 (C) $1.30
   (D) $2.23 (E) $9.10

8. Three men enter a business venture. Mr. Merrill invests $40,000 while Mr. Berell invests $50,000 and Mr. Sheryll invests $60,000. When profits are divided proportionately, what part of the profits should Mr. Berell receive?

   (A) $\frac{1}{3}$ (B) $\frac{2}{5}$ (C) $\frac{1}{2}$ (D) $\frac{3}{5}$ (E) $\frac{2}{3}$

9. The direction for making a certain cereal is to use $1\frac{1}{2}$ cups of cereal with $4\frac{1}{2}$ cups of water. Mrs. Crocker finds that she has $\frac{3}{4}$ cup of cereal left. How much water should she use?

(A) 2 cups   (B) $2\frac{1}{3}$ cups   (C) $2\frac{1}{4}$ cups

(D) $2\frac{1}{2}$ cups   (E) $2\frac{3}{4}$ cups

10. In purchasing food for a party Florence spends $30, Henrietta spents $45, Joan spends half as much as Florence, and Ann spends $\frac{2}{3}$ as much as Joan. The ratio of the amount of money spent by Henrietta and Joan is

(A) 1:3   (B) 2:3   (C) 3:1   (D) 4:1   (E) 3:2

11. In a summer camp it is found that a quart of milk is consumed by four campers or three counselors. If 16 quarts of milk are brought into the dining room to feed 40 campers and 12 counselors, how many quarts of milk should be returned after the meal?

(A) 2   (B) $8\frac{4}{7}$ (C) $10\frac{2}{7}$ (D) 10   (E) 14

12. How many 3-cent stamps can be purchased for c cents?

(A) $3c$ (B) $\frac{c}{3}$ (C) $\frac{3}{c}$ (D) $300c$ (E) $\frac{3c}{100}$

13. A box of 12 tablets costs 21 cents. The same brand is packaged in bottles containing 100 tablets and sells for $1.50 per bottle. How much is saved per dozen, by purchasing the larger amount?

(A) $\frac{1}{4}$ ¢   (B) 1¢   (C) $\frac{1}{2}$ ¢   (D) $1\frac{3}{4}$ ¢   (E) 3¢

14. Samuel, Martin, and Leibow invest $5000, $7000, and $12,000 respectively in a business. If the profits are distributed proportionally, what share of a $1111 profit should Leibow receive?

(A) $231.40   (B) $264.00   (C) $333.33

(D) $370.33   (E) $555.50

15. If $5\frac{1}{2}$ yards = 1 rod and 3 feet = 1 yard, how many rods are equivalent to 1 foot?

(A) $\frac{2}{11}$ (B) $\frac{6}{11}$ (C) $\frac{2}{33}$ (D) $\frac{11}{6}$ (E) $\frac{11}{2}$

Questions 16–20: These problems are not multiple choice. They are designed to give practice for the questions on the test with student-produced responses. In the typical tests in this book and in the actual test, you will be asked to enter your answers in a special grid. For the following questions, write your answer in the blank provided.

---

16. The scale of a certain map is $\frac{3}{4}$ inch = 12 miles. Find in square miles the actual area of a part represented on the map by a square whose side is $\frac{5}{8}$ inch.

_____

17. If a light flashes every 6 seconds, how many times will it flash in $\frac{3}{4}$ of an hour?

_____

18. How many miles are there in 9.66 kilometers if there are 7 miles in 11.27 kilometers?

_____

19. If 15 cans of food are needed for 7 campers for 2 days, the number of cans needed for 4 campers for 7 days is _____

20. A diagram of a plane is drawn to the scale of 0.5 inches equals 80 feet. If the length of the diagram is 4.5 inches, the actual length in feet of the plane is

_____

Work

SOME IMPORTANT FACTS

1. Work problems apply principles involving fractions. For example if it takes a man 5 days to complete a job, in one day he does $\frac{1}{5}$ of the job, in two days $\frac{2}{5}$, in x days $\frac{x}{5}$.

2. Work problems involving many men apply the principle of *inverse proportion*. For example, if we increase the number of men on a job (assuming they perform their work at the same rate), the time required to complete the task will be decreased proportionately.

Hints on Solving Problems

1. In problems involving work by one person or by several people working at different rates or time recall:

$$\frac{\text{time actually spent working}}{\text{time required to do the entire task}} = \text{part of task done}$$

2. In problems involving people working at the same rate, apply the principle of inverse proportion and recall: $xy = k$.

► PRACTICE EXERCISE

1. It takes h hours to mow a lawn. What part of the lawn is mowed in one hour?

   (A) h (B) $\dfrac{h}{x}$ (C) hx (D) $\dfrac{1}{h}$ (E) $\dfrac{x}{h}$

2. A student has three hours of homework. He works from 8:55 P.M. to 9:15 P.M. What part of his work is left uncompleted?

   (A) $\dfrac{1}{3}$ (B) $\dfrac{2}{3}$ (C) $\dfrac{5}{6}$ (D) $\dfrac{4}{5}$ (E) $\dfrac{8}{9}$

3. Ann can type a manuscript in 10 hours. Florence can type this manuscript in 5 hours. If they both type this manuscript together, it can be completed in

   (A) 2 hrs. 30 min. (B) 3 hrs.
   (C) 3 hrs. 20 min. (D) 5 hrs.
   (E) 7 hrs. 30 min.

4. A man can paint a room in three hours. His son requires four hours to do the same job. If they both work together, the job could be done in

   (A) $1\frac{1}{2}$ hrs. (B) $1\frac{5}{7}$ hrs. (C) 2 hrs.
   (D) 3 hrs. (E) $\frac{1}{2}$ hr.

5. Joan and Ann finish the housework in 3 hours. Joan could have done it alone in 5 hours. What part of the work was done by Ann?

   (A) $\dfrac{1}{4}$ (B) $\dfrac{3}{8}$ (C) $\dfrac{2}{5}$ (D) $\dfrac{3}{5}$ (E) $\dfrac{5}{8}$

6. It was calculated that 75 men could complete a strip on a new highway in 20 days. When work was scheduled to commence, it was found necessary to send 25 men on another road project How much longer will it take to complete the strip?

   (A) 10 days (B) 20 days (C) 30 days
   (D) 40 days (E) 60 days

7. If m men take d days to complete a job. how many men will be needed to complete the job in $\frac{2}{3}$ of the time?

   (A) $\frac{2}{3}\ m$ (B) $\frac{1}{3}\ m$ (C) $1\frac{1}{2}\ m$

   (D) $\frac{2}{3}\ md$ (E) $1\frac{1}{2}\ md$

8. Marc can seal 50 letters a minute. How many minutes would it take him to seal x letters?

   (A) $50x$ (B) $\dfrac{1}{50x}$ (C) $\dfrac{50}{x}$

   (D) $\dfrac{x}{50}$ (E) $\dfrac{1}{x+50}$

9. It takes James an hour to do a job that John can do in 40 minutes. One morning they worked together for 12 minutes, then James went away and John finished the job. How long did it take him to finish?

   (A) 8 min. (B) 16 min. (C) 20 min.
   (D) 22 min. (E) 28 min.

10. If M men can complete a job in H hours, how long will it take 5 men to do this job?

    (A) $\dfrac{5M}{H}$ (B) $\dfrac{M}{5H}$ (C) $\dfrac{MH}{5}$ (D) $\dfrac{5}{MH}$ (E) $\dfrac{5H}{M}$

11. A can do a piece of work in r days and B, who works faster, can do the same work in s days. Which of the following expressions represents the number of days it would take the two of them to do the work if they worked together?

    (A) $\dfrac{r+s}{2}$ (B) $r-s$ (C) $\dfrac{1}{r}+\dfrac{1}{s}$

    (D) $\dfrac{rs}{r+s}$ (E) $\dfrac{r+s}{rs}$

12. One man can paint a house in 6 days and another man can do the same job in 2 days less. How many days will it take them if they work together?

    (A) $1\frac{1}{3}$ (B) $2\frac{2}{5}$ (C) 3 (D) $4\frac{3}{5}$ (E) 5

13. John did a piece of work in 12 hours 13 minutes. A week later he did the same job in 10 hours 5 minutes. Two weeks later he did it in 9 hours 48 minutes. What was the average amount of time spent in doing the job?

    (A) 10 hrs. 7 min. (B) 10 hrs. $8\frac{2}{3}$ min.
    (C) 10 hrs. 42 min. (D) 10 hrs. 55 min.
    (E) 32 hrs. 6 min.

14. Melinda has x minutes of homework in each of 5 subjects. What part of her homework does she do each hour?

    (A) $\dfrac{1}{5x}$ (B) $\dfrac{x}{12}$ (C) $\dfrac{12}{x}$ (D) $\dfrac{1}{12x}$ (E) $12x$

15. One printing press can print one issue of a newspaper in 4 hours. A second press can do the same job in 2 hours. How many hours would it take to print one issue with both presses working?

    (A) $\dfrac{3}{4}$ (B) $1\frac{1}{3}$ (C) $1\frac{1}{2}$ (D) $2\frac{2}{3}$ (E) 3

Questions 16–20: These problems are not multiple choice. They are designed to give practice for the questions on the test with student-produced responses. In the typical tests in this book and in the actual test, you will be asked to enter your answers in a special grid. For the following questions, write your answer in the blank provided.

---

16. Florence can do the housework in 6 hours working alone. When Joan helps her, the housework is done in 4 hours. If Joan did it alone, it would take how many more hours than Florence doing it alone?

_____

17. In $\frac{1}{3}$ of a working day a crew does $\frac{2}{3}$ of a job. If they work at that rate, what part of a day will be required to complete this job?

_____

18. In 6 days 4 men, working at uniform speed for 8 hours per day, complete a job. If these men worked at the same pace for 12 hours per day, in how many days could the job be completed?

_____

19. A boys' club decides to build a cabin. The job can be done by 3 skilled workmen in 20 days or by 5 of the boys in 30 days. How many days will it take if all work together?

_____

20. Five men can paint a house in six days. If two of the men don't work, what will be the increase of time (in days) required to complete the job?

_____

DATA INTERPRETATION

A graph is a pictorial representation of data that gives an over-all view of the facts, omitting minor details. It is generally used to make comparisons. It is a time saver, in that general conclusions can be drawn without the need for studying a mass of figures.

The line graph depicts continuity. The financial pages of our newspapers and magazines use this type of graph to show trends in business. The bar graph makes comparisons by using varying lengths of bars. In advertising, for example, the number of subscriptions to journals, or sales of various products are thus compared pictorially. The circle graph is used to show how various parts make up the whole. The government often releases for publication such graphs to show how the tax dollar is spent.

Graphs and interpretation of data are used for examination purposes because they call for calculations based on interpretations.

➤ PRACTICE EXERCISE

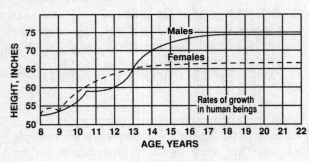

GRAPH 1

Questions 1–5 refer to Graph 1

1. How many years old is the male when he reaches the height of an eleven-year-old female?
(A) 10   (B) 11   (C) 12   (D) 12.2   (E) 12.5

2. How many years old is the male when he is one-half foot taller than the female of the same age
(A) 10.5   (B) 13   (C) 15   (D) 17   (E) 20

3. How many years old is the female when she is 4 ft. 7 in. tall?
(A) 9.2   (B) 9.5   (C) 9.6   (D) 13.3   (E) 21

4. According to this graph, how many years elapse between the occasions when males and females of the same age ar ealso of the same height?
(A) 3.8   (B) 4.1   (C) 8   (D) 9.2   (E) 13

5. How old is the male when he is 20% taller than the female is at the age of 10.5 years?
(A) 10   (B) 10.5   (C) 14   (D) 14.5   (E) 15.1

COST OF SEED PER FIFTY POUNDS

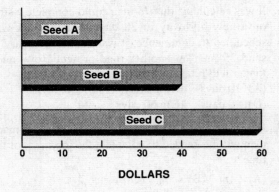

DOLLARS

GRAPH 2

Questions 6–9 refer to Graph 2.

6. What is the cost of $12\frac{1}{2}$ pounds of Seed B?
(A) \$10.   (B) \$20.   (C) \$40.
(D) \$60   (E) \$75.

7. How many pounds of Seed C would I get for \$30?
(A) $12\frac{1}{2}$ (B) 25   (C) 50   (D) 100   (E) 900

8. The price of one pound of Seed C is what percent of the price of one pound of Seed B?
(A) 20%   (B) $33\frac{1}{3}$%   (C) $66\frac{2}{3}$%
(D) 120%   (E) 150%

9. What is the ratio of the price of 20 pounds of Seed B to the price of 20 pounds of Seed A?
(A) 1:1   (B) 1:2   (C) 2:1   (D) 2:3   (E) 4:1

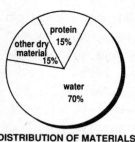 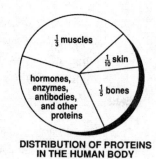

DISTRIBUTION OF MATERIALS IN THE HUMAN BODY

GRAPH 3

DISTRIBUTION OF PROTEINS IN THE HUMAN BODY

GRAPH 4

Questions 10–17 refer to Graphs 3 and 4

10. In terms of the total body weight, the distribution of materials other than water and proteins is equal to
(A) $\frac{1}{15}$ (B) $\frac{85}{100}$ (C) $\frac{1}{20}$ (D) $\frac{3}{20}$ (E) $\frac{1}{5}$

11. A person weighing 170 pounds would, according to these graphs, be composed of water weighing
(A) 17 pounds (B) 70 pounds
(C) 100 pounds (D) 119 pounds
(E) 153 pounds

12. How many degrees of the circle should be used to represent the distribution of protein?
(A) 15 (B) 45 (C) 54 (D) 60 (E) 90

13. What percent of the entire body weight is made up of skin?
(A) 0.15 (B) 1.0 (C) 1.5 (D) 10. (E) 15.0

14. If the weight of the bones of an individual is represented by x pounds, the weight of the skin of this individual is represented by
(A) $\frac{1}{x+5}$ (B) $\frac{1}{x-5}$ (C) $2x$
(D) $\frac{x}{2}$ (E) $\frac{x}{5}$

15. What part of the proteins in the body is made up of muscles and skin?
(A) $\frac{15}{1300}$ (B) $\frac{1}{130}$ (C) $\frac{1}{13}$ (D) $\frac{13}{30}$ (E) $\frac{1}{30}$

16. The ratio of the distribution of proteins in muscle to the distribution of protein in skin is
(A) 3:1 (B) 1:3 (C) 3:10
(D) $3\frac{1}{3}$:1 (E) 30:1

17. The human body, according to the data furnished by the graphs, is composed mainly of
(A) proteins
(B) hormones, enzymes, antibodies, and other proteins
(C) muscles
(D) bones
(E) water

ANSWER KEY

ALGEBRA

1. E	5. D	9. D	13. B	17. 750
2. B	6. A	10. A	14. B	18. 14
3. C	7. D	11. C	15. E	19. 100
4. E	8. E	12. B	16. 2.5	20. 4

SOLVING PROBLEMS BY EQUATIONS

1. B	3. C	5. A	7. D	9. C
2. A	4. D	6. B	8. C	10. C

INEQUALITIES

1. B	5. B	9. B	13. D	17. A
2. E	6. E	10. D	14. E	18. B
3. C	7. C	11. E	15. D	19. C
4. C	8. A	12. A	16. D	20. D

GEOMETRY

1. D	8. A	15. B	22. C	29. A
2. B	9. B	16. C	23. B	30. D
3. A	10. A	17. A	24. C	31. 60
4. B	11. B	18. E	25. D	32. 24
5. C	12. B	19. C	26. B	33. 5
6. C	13. C	20. B	27. A	34. 36
7. E	14. B	21. D	28. B	35. 5

PRACTICE EXERCISE/FRACTIONS

1. A	5. A	9. D	13. B	17. 72
2. B	6. A	10. A	14. B	18. 12
3. D	7. C	11. D	15. D	19. 16
4. E	8. E	12. A	16. 16	20. 2700

PRACTICE EXERCISE/PERCENT

1. C	5. B	9. D	13. A	17. 100
2. E	6. D	10. B	14. B	18. 20
3. C	7. B	11. D	15. E	19. 600
4. D	8. B	12. D	16. 25	20. 24

PRACTICE EXERCISE/AVERAGES

1. C	5. B	9. E	13. D	17. 90
2. B	6. D	10. B	14. A	18. 35
3. A	7. E	11. B	15. D	19. 48
4. D	8. A	12. C	16. 20	20. 62

PRACTICE EXERCISE/MOTION

1. E	5. D	9. A	13. B	17. 40
2. A	6. A	10. B	14. C	18. 119
3. E	7. A	11. B	15. D	19. 45
4. A	8. C	12. C	16. 27	20. 480

PRACTICE EXERCISE/RATIO AND PROPORTION

1. A	5. C	9. C	13. E	17. 450
2. E	6. D	10. C	14. E	18. 6
3. C	7. E	11. A	15. C	19. 30
4. B	8. A	12. B	16. 100	20. 720

PRACTICE EXERCISE/WORK

1. D	5. C	9. C	13. C	17. $1/2$
2. E	6. A	10. C	14. C	18. 4
3. C	7. C	11. D	15. B	19. 12
4. B	8. D	12. B	16. 6	20. 4

DATA INTERPRETATION

1. E	5. E	9. C	13. C	17. E
2. C	6. A	10. D	14. D	
3. A	7. B	11. D	15. D	
4. A	8. E	12. C	16. D	

9

The Quantitative Comparison Question

In the quantitative comparison questions you are given two quantities that are sometimes accompanied by information that concerns either or both quantities. Answering the question properly depends upon your ability to decide which, if either, is the greater quantity. In general, quantitative comparison questions require less time to answer, involve less reading, and require somewhat less computation than the usual multiple-choice questions. This type of question reflects the contemporary emphasis in school mathematics on inequalities; you must use the concepts of "greater than," "less than," and "equal to" to decide which choice is correct. Quantitative comparison questions will appear with the following instructions:

Compare the quantities in Column A and Column B. In some cases, there may be data centered above the two columns that concerns one or both quantities to be compared. A symbol that appears in both columns represents the same thing in both columns. Letters such as *x, y, n,* and *k* represent real numbers.

Compare the two quantities and choose
   A if the quantity in Column A is greater.
   B if the quantity in Column B is greater.
   C if the two quantities are equal.
   D if, on the basis of the information supplied, the relationship cannot be determined.

TIPS FOR HANDLING QUANTITATIVE COMPARISON QUESTIONS

1. Learn the format of the quantitative comparison questions. Remember that information relating to both columns is centered above the two quantities. Also, since there are only four choices, you do not choose answer **E**.

2. When a problem involves straightforward computation only, eliminate **D**, which cannot possibly be correct since there must be a definite answer. Even if you now have to guess, your chance of guessing correctly has improved.

3. These questions require less time, and many can be answered without lengthy computation. Some questions can be answered correctly in a few seconds.

4. When comparing expressions with variables, don't forget to try negative values, fractions, and zero. For example, $5x$ is greater than $4x$ only if x is positive; $5x$ is less than $4x$ if x is negative, and $5x = 4x$

if x is 0. Also, if $x^2 = 25$, remember that $x = +5$ or $x = -5$. Note, however, that $\sqrt{25} = 5$ only, not -5.

5. Be careful in handling multiplication of negative values. Recall that multiplying a positive number by a negative number gives you a negative, and therefore a smaller, number. If the problem does not specifically tell you that an unknown is not a negative number, it could be negative. Multiplication usually makes a number larger; but when you multiply it by a fraction less than 1 you make the number smaller, and when you divide it by a fraction less than 1 you make the number larger.

6. Eliminate from consideration any quantity that appears in both columns. Confine your thinking to the other terms or expressions.

7. If a question involves several numbers multiplied together, the product will be negative if an odd

number of them are negative, but positive if an even number of them are negative; the number that are positive does not affect the product at all. If only a single one of a group of numbers multiplied together can possibly be zero, then the entire product will be zero.

8. If a question involves powers of a variable, and the variable has a negative value, the even powers will be positive but the odd powers will be negative. If the value of a variable can be a positive fraction less than 1, the higher the power of the variable, the smaller its value.

9. If a question involves odd and even numbers, note that, if two even numbers are added, the sum is even, and if two odd numbers are added, the sum is also even. If an odd and an even number are added, the sum is odd.

   If either an even or an odd number is multiplied by an even number, the product is even. If two odd numbers are multiplied together, the product is odd.

10. If two fractions have the same numerator, the one with the larger denominator is smaller. If two fractions have the same denominator, the one with the larger numerator is larger.

11. Quantitative comparison questions provide four choices for answers. If you make a random guess, you are likely to be right only one out of four times. Since the deduction for a wrong answer on the quantitative comparison questions is $\frac{1}{3}$ of a point, it is unwise to make a purely random guess. However, if you can definitely rule out one choice as incorrect, a guess from among the remaining three is not foolhardy since the odds of its being correct equal the deduction cost for a wrong answer. If you can rule out more than one choice, it is certainly advisable to make a guess from among those remaining since the odds of getting the correct choice are better than the deduction cost of a wrong answer.

EXAMPLES:

	Column A	Column B
1.	$10 - \frac{10}{.1}$	-90

ANALYSIS

$\frac{10}{.1}$ equals $\frac{100}{1}$ or 100
$10 - 100 = -90$
The correct answer is **C**.

	Column A	Column B
2.	50%	$\frac{1}{.02}$

ANALYSIS

The value of $\frac{1}{.02} = 50$
50 is greater than 50%
The correct answer is **B**.

Column A	Column B

In J. J. High School one chemistry class had an average of 70% on a uniform city-wide test and another class had an average of 75% on this test. In K. K. High School the average mark in 2 classes for this same test was 72.5%.

	Column A	Column B
3.	School average on the chemistry test in J. J. High School	School average on the chemistry test in K. K. High School

ANALYSIS

Since we do not have the number of students involved in these various classes, we may not assign weight to the averages given. The correct answer is **D**.

In rectangle *ABCD, AB* = π and *BC* = diameter of circle *O*.

	Column A	Column B
4.	Perimeter of *ABCD*	Circumference of circle *O*

ANALYSIS

Perimeter of $ABCD = \pi + \pi + d + d$ or $2(\pi + d)$
Circumference of circle $= \pi d$
$2(\pi d) > \pi d$
The correct answer is **A**.

PRACTICE EXERCISE

DIRECTIONS: Each of the following questions consists of two quantities, one in Column A and one in Column B. Information concerning both quantities appears centered above both quantities. Diagrams need not be assumed to be drawn to scale. Letters used represent real numbers. After comparing the two quantities, choose

(A) if the quantity in Column A is greater
(B) if the quantity in Column B is greater
(C) if the two quantities are equal
(D) if the relationship between the two quantities cannot be determined from the information given.

	Column A	Column B
	$x = 0.5$	
1.	$\dfrac{\frac{3}{4}}{1+x}$	x
2.	$\dfrac{\frac{1}{4} - \frac{3}{16}}{\frac{1}{8}}$	2
3.	109 inches	3 yards 1 inch
4.	$\dfrac{7+7+7}{7-7-7}$	3
	$x = 7$	
5.	x^7	$7x^6$
	$0 < k < 32$	
	k is divisible by 3 and 9.	
6.	k	27
	$X^2 = 25$	
7.	X	5
	$\dfrac{1}{x} < 0$	
8.	1	x
	$10x^3 = y$	
	$x > 1$	
9.	y	x
	$a:b = c:d$	
10.	bc	ad

	Column A	Column B
11.	$\sqrt{\dfrac{1}{.25}}$	20%
12.	$\sqrt{1440}$	120
13.	The average of $90\%, \frac{3}{5}$, and 1.5	3
14.	$\dfrac{a}{4}$ % of 400	a
15.	$\dfrac{a-b}{-c}$	$\dfrac{b-a}{c}$

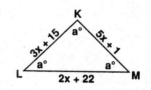

| **16.** | x | 7 |

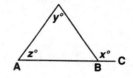

ABC is a straight line.

| **17.** | x | z |

(This diagram concerns questions 18–20.)

$z = 90$

18.	x	y
19.	$x + y$	z
20.	$z - x$	y

	$b \neq -c$	
	$\dfrac{a}{-b-c} = \dfrac{-5}{c+b}$	
21.	5	a

	Column A	Column B		Column A	Column B

22. 2 hours, 40 minutes — The elapsed time from 8:55 P.M. to 10:15 the same evening

The distance from Mark's house to the Waban school is 3 miles, while the distance from Sara's house to this school is 4 miles.

23. The distance from Mark's house to Sara's house — 5 miles

24. $(0.1)(\pi)$ — $\sqrt{.17}$

25. $\dfrac{2+2+2}{2-2-2}$ — $\dfrac{3+3+3}{3-3-3}$

26. $\sqrt{1.44}$ — 0.12

$X^2 = 100$

27. X — 10

$a > 0,\ x > 0,\ \text{and } \dfrac{a}{x} < 1$

28. a — x

$0 < a < b$

29. $\dfrac{1}{a}$ — $\dfrac{1}{b}$

30. 105% of 500 — 50% of 1000

$5x = 23 = y$

31. x — y

$X > Y \text{ and } Y > Z$

32. $2X$ — $Y + Z$

$x > 0 \text{ and } y > 0$

33. $\dfrac{1}{x+y}$ — $\dfrac{\frac{1}{xy}}{\frac{1}{x} + \frac{1}{y}}$

34. $\sqrt{\dfrac{1}{25}}$ — $\left(\dfrac{1}{5}\right)^2$

35. 15% — $\dfrac{0.3}{2}$

$0 < x < y < z$

36. $\dfrac{z}{y}$ — $\dfrac{z}{x}$

37. The percentage increase from $5 to $7 — The percentage increase from $7 to $9

38. $a + 1$ — $a - 1$

$\dfrac{1}{a} < 0$

39. zero — a

$1 \text{ kilometer} = \frac{5}{8} \text{ mile}$

40. 1.6 kilometers — 1 mile

ANSWER KEY

1. C	*9.* A	*17.* A	*25.* C	*33.* C	
2. B	*10.* C	*18.* D	*26.* A	*34.* A	
3. C	*11.* A	*19.* C	*27.* D	*35.* C	
4. B	*12.* B	*20.* C	*28.* B	*36.* B	
5. C	*13.* B	*21.* C	*29.* A	*37.* A	
6. D	*14.* C	*22.* A	*30.* A	*38.* A	
7. D	*15.* C	*23.* D	*31.* B	*39.* A	
8. A	*16.* C	*24.* B	*32.* A	*40.* C	

TEST YOURSELF

10

Ten Typical Tests

Many students, after taking the PSAT/NMSQT, report that they found the experience very exhausting. More than two hours on difficult test material may prove to be very grueling.

To alleviate this situation, the authors wish to offer two suggestions:

1. Become acquainted with the time situation before taking the actual test. Taking the ten typical tests in this chapter under timed conditions will make you familiar with the situation before you take the actual test. This familiarity should enable you to find the actual test less rigorous. Remember, too, that these tests are actually longer (two hours and thirty minutes, as opposed to the actual two hours and ten minutes) than the real test you will be taking.

2. If you recognize that the two-hour test may be physically tiring, you should recognize that you need to be physically fit. The best advice we can offer is that you stop preparation for the test several days before the scheduled date. Rest and relaxation will enable you to avoid the fatigue of a long examination and will prove to be more profitable than last-minute cramming.

Answer Sheet

TYPICAL TEST A

Each mark should completely fill the appropriate space, and should be as dark as all other marks. Make all erasures complete. Traces of an erasure may be read as an answer. See pages vii and 27 for explanations of timing and number of questions.

Section 1 — Verbal
30 minutes

1 Ⓐ Ⓑ Ⓒ Ⓓ Ⓔ
2 Ⓐ Ⓑ Ⓒ Ⓓ Ⓔ
3 Ⓐ Ⓑ Ⓒ Ⓓ Ⓔ
4 Ⓐ Ⓑ Ⓒ Ⓓ Ⓔ
5 Ⓐ Ⓑ Ⓒ Ⓓ Ⓔ
6 Ⓐ Ⓑ Ⓒ Ⓓ Ⓔ
7 Ⓐ Ⓑ Ⓒ Ⓓ Ⓔ
8 Ⓐ Ⓑ Ⓒ Ⓓ Ⓔ
9 Ⓐ Ⓑ Ⓒ Ⓓ Ⓔ
10 Ⓐ Ⓑ Ⓒ Ⓓ Ⓔ
11 Ⓐ Ⓑ Ⓒ Ⓓ Ⓔ
12 Ⓐ Ⓑ Ⓒ Ⓓ Ⓔ
13 Ⓐ Ⓑ Ⓒ Ⓓ Ⓔ
14 Ⓐ Ⓑ Ⓒ Ⓓ Ⓔ
15 Ⓐ Ⓑ Ⓒ Ⓓ Ⓔ
16 Ⓐ Ⓑ Ⓒ Ⓓ Ⓔ
17 Ⓐ Ⓑ Ⓒ Ⓓ Ⓔ
18 Ⓐ Ⓑ Ⓒ Ⓓ Ⓔ
19 Ⓐ Ⓑ Ⓒ Ⓓ Ⓔ
20 Ⓐ Ⓑ Ⓒ Ⓓ Ⓔ
21 Ⓐ Ⓑ Ⓒ Ⓓ Ⓔ
22 Ⓐ Ⓑ Ⓒ Ⓓ Ⓔ
23 Ⓐ Ⓑ Ⓒ Ⓓ Ⓔ
24 Ⓐ Ⓑ Ⓒ Ⓓ Ⓔ
25 Ⓐ Ⓑ Ⓒ Ⓓ Ⓔ
26 Ⓐ Ⓑ Ⓒ Ⓓ Ⓔ
27 Ⓐ Ⓑ Ⓒ Ⓓ Ⓔ
28 Ⓐ Ⓑ Ⓒ Ⓓ Ⓔ
29 Ⓐ Ⓑ Ⓒ Ⓓ Ⓔ
30 Ⓐ Ⓑ Ⓒ Ⓓ Ⓔ

Section 2 — Math
30 minutes

1 Ⓐ Ⓑ Ⓒ Ⓓ Ⓔ
2 Ⓐ Ⓑ Ⓒ Ⓓ Ⓔ
3 Ⓐ Ⓑ Ⓒ Ⓓ Ⓔ
4 Ⓐ Ⓑ Ⓒ Ⓓ Ⓔ
5 Ⓐ Ⓑ Ⓒ Ⓓ Ⓔ
6 Ⓐ Ⓑ Ⓒ Ⓓ Ⓔ
7 Ⓐ Ⓑ Ⓒ Ⓓ Ⓔ
8 Ⓐ Ⓑ Ⓒ Ⓓ Ⓔ
9 Ⓐ Ⓑ Ⓒ Ⓓ Ⓔ
10 Ⓐ Ⓑ Ⓒ Ⓓ Ⓔ
11 Ⓐ Ⓑ Ⓒ Ⓓ Ⓔ
12 Ⓐ Ⓑ Ⓒ Ⓓ Ⓔ
13 Ⓐ Ⓑ Ⓒ Ⓓ Ⓔ
14 Ⓐ Ⓑ Ⓒ Ⓓ Ⓔ
15 Ⓐ Ⓑ Ⓒ Ⓓ Ⓔ
16 Ⓐ Ⓑ Ⓒ Ⓓ Ⓔ
17 Ⓐ Ⓑ Ⓒ Ⓓ Ⓔ
18 Ⓐ Ⓑ Ⓒ Ⓓ Ⓔ
19 Ⓐ Ⓑ Ⓒ Ⓓ Ⓔ
20 Ⓐ Ⓑ Ⓒ Ⓓ Ⓔ
21 Ⓐ Ⓑ Ⓒ Ⓓ Ⓔ
22 Ⓐ Ⓑ Ⓒ Ⓓ Ⓔ
23 Ⓐ Ⓑ Ⓒ Ⓓ Ⓔ
24 Ⓐ Ⓑ Ⓒ Ⓓ Ⓔ
25 Ⓐ Ⓑ Ⓒ Ⓓ Ⓔ

Section 3 — Writing
30 minutes

1 Ⓐ Ⓑ Ⓒ Ⓓ Ⓔ
2 Ⓐ Ⓑ Ⓒ Ⓓ Ⓔ
3 Ⓐ Ⓑ Ⓒ Ⓓ Ⓔ
4 Ⓐ Ⓑ Ⓒ Ⓓ Ⓔ
5 Ⓐ Ⓑ Ⓒ Ⓓ Ⓔ
6 Ⓐ Ⓑ Ⓒ Ⓓ Ⓔ
7 Ⓐ Ⓑ Ⓒ Ⓓ Ⓔ
8 Ⓐ Ⓑ Ⓒ Ⓓ Ⓔ
9 Ⓐ Ⓑ Ⓒ Ⓓ Ⓔ
10 Ⓐ Ⓑ Ⓒ Ⓓ Ⓔ
11 Ⓐ Ⓑ Ⓒ Ⓓ Ⓔ
12 Ⓐ Ⓑ Ⓒ Ⓓ Ⓔ
13 Ⓐ Ⓑ Ⓒ Ⓓ Ⓔ
14 Ⓐ Ⓑ Ⓒ Ⓓ Ⓔ
15 Ⓐ Ⓑ Ⓒ Ⓓ Ⓔ
16 Ⓐ Ⓑ Ⓒ Ⓓ Ⓔ
17 Ⓐ Ⓑ Ⓒ Ⓓ Ⓔ
18 Ⓐ Ⓑ Ⓒ Ⓓ Ⓔ
19 Ⓐ Ⓑ Ⓒ Ⓓ Ⓔ
20 Ⓐ Ⓑ Ⓒ Ⓓ Ⓔ
21 Ⓐ Ⓑ Ⓒ Ⓓ Ⓔ
22 Ⓐ Ⓑ Ⓒ Ⓓ Ⓔ
23 Ⓐ Ⓑ Ⓒ Ⓓ Ⓔ
24 Ⓐ Ⓑ Ⓒ Ⓓ Ⓔ
25 Ⓐ Ⓑ Ⓒ Ⓓ Ⓔ
26 Ⓐ Ⓑ Ⓒ Ⓓ Ⓔ
27 Ⓐ Ⓑ Ⓒ Ⓓ Ⓔ
28 Ⓐ Ⓑ Ⓒ Ⓓ Ⓔ
29 Ⓐ Ⓑ Ⓒ Ⓓ Ⓔ
30 Ⓐ Ⓑ Ⓒ Ⓓ Ⓔ
31 Ⓐ Ⓑ Ⓒ Ⓓ Ⓔ
32 Ⓐ Ⓑ Ⓒ Ⓓ Ⓔ
33 Ⓐ Ⓑ Ⓒ Ⓓ Ⓔ
34 Ⓐ Ⓑ Ⓒ Ⓓ Ⓔ
35 Ⓐ Ⓑ Ⓒ Ⓓ Ⓔ
36 Ⓐ Ⓑ Ⓒ Ⓓ Ⓔ
37 Ⓐ Ⓑ Ⓒ Ⓓ Ⓔ
38 Ⓐ Ⓑ Ⓒ Ⓓ Ⓔ
39 Ⓐ Ⓑ Ⓒ Ⓓ Ⓔ

Section 4 — Verbal
30 minutes

31 Ⓐ Ⓑ Ⓒ Ⓓ Ⓔ
32 Ⓐ Ⓑ Ⓒ Ⓓ Ⓔ
33 Ⓐ Ⓑ Ⓒ Ⓓ Ⓔ
34 Ⓐ Ⓑ Ⓒ Ⓓ Ⓔ
35 Ⓐ Ⓑ Ⓒ Ⓓ Ⓔ
36 Ⓐ Ⓑ Ⓒ Ⓓ Ⓔ
37 Ⓐ Ⓑ Ⓒ Ⓓ Ⓔ
38 Ⓐ Ⓑ Ⓒ Ⓓ Ⓔ
39 Ⓐ Ⓑ Ⓒ Ⓓ Ⓔ
40 Ⓐ Ⓑ Ⓒ Ⓓ Ⓔ
41 Ⓐ Ⓑ Ⓒ Ⓓ Ⓔ
42 Ⓐ Ⓑ Ⓒ Ⓓ Ⓔ
43 Ⓐ Ⓑ Ⓒ Ⓓ Ⓔ
44 Ⓐ Ⓑ Ⓒ Ⓓ Ⓔ
45 Ⓐ Ⓑ Ⓒ Ⓓ Ⓔ
46 Ⓐ Ⓑ Ⓒ Ⓓ Ⓔ
47 Ⓐ Ⓑ Ⓒ Ⓓ Ⓔ
48 Ⓐ Ⓑ Ⓒ Ⓓ Ⓔ
49 Ⓐ Ⓑ Ⓒ Ⓓ Ⓔ
50 Ⓐ Ⓑ Ⓒ Ⓓ Ⓔ
51 Ⓐ Ⓑ Ⓒ Ⓓ Ⓔ
52 Ⓐ Ⓑ Ⓒ Ⓓ Ⓔ
53 Ⓐ Ⓑ Ⓒ Ⓓ Ⓔ
54 Ⓐ Ⓑ Ⓒ Ⓓ Ⓔ
55 Ⓐ Ⓑ Ⓒ Ⓓ Ⓔ
56 Ⓐ Ⓑ Ⓒ Ⓓ Ⓔ
57 Ⓐ Ⓑ Ⓒ Ⓓ Ⓔ
58 Ⓐ Ⓑ Ⓒ Ⓓ Ⓔ
59 Ⓐ Ⓑ Ⓒ Ⓓ Ⓔ
60 Ⓐ Ⓑ Ⓒ Ⓓ Ⓔ

Section 5 — Math
30 minutes

26 Ⓐ Ⓑ Ⓒ Ⓓ Ⓔ
27 Ⓐ Ⓑ Ⓒ Ⓓ Ⓔ
28 Ⓐ Ⓑ Ⓒ Ⓓ Ⓔ
29 Ⓐ Ⓑ Ⓒ Ⓓ Ⓔ
30 Ⓐ Ⓑ Ⓒ Ⓓ Ⓔ
31 Ⓐ Ⓑ Ⓒ Ⓓ Ⓔ
32 Ⓐ Ⓑ Ⓒ Ⓓ Ⓔ
33 Ⓐ Ⓑ Ⓒ Ⓓ Ⓔ
34 Ⓐ Ⓑ Ⓒ Ⓓ Ⓔ
35 Ⓐ Ⓑ Ⓒ Ⓓ Ⓔ
36 Ⓐ Ⓑ Ⓒ Ⓓ Ⓔ
37 Ⓐ Ⓑ Ⓒ Ⓓ Ⓔ
39 Ⓐ Ⓑ Ⓒ Ⓓ Ⓔ
39 Ⓐ Ⓑ Ⓒ Ⓓ Ⓔ
40 Ⓐ Ⓑ Ⓒ Ⓓ Ⓔ

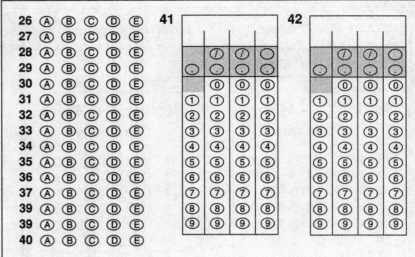

41 42 43 44 45 46 47 48 49 50

SECTION 1
Verbal Reasoning

Time—30 minutes
30 Questions

For each question in this section, select the best answer from among the choices given and fill in the corresponding oval on the answer sheet.

Directions

Each sentence below has one or two blanks, each blank indicating that something has been omitted. Beneath the sentence are five words or sets of words labeled A through E. Choose the word or set of words that, when inserted in the sentence, best fits the meaning of the sentence as a whole.

Example:

Medieval kingdoms did not become constitutional republics overnight; on the contrary, the change was ____ .

(A) unpopular
(B) unexpected
(C) advantageous
(D) sufficient
(E) gradual

Ⓐ Ⓑ Ⓒ Ⓓ ●

1. Unhappily, the psychology experiment was ____ by the subjects' awareness of the presence of observers in their midst.
(A) muted   (B) palliated   (C) marred
(D) clarified   (E) concluded

2. Nothing anyone could say was able to alter North's ____ that his attempt to lie to Congress was justified.
(A) demand   (B) conviction   (C) maxim
(D) fear   (E) ambivalence

3. Excessive use of coal and oil eventually may ____ the earth's supply of fossil fuels, leaving us in need of a new source of energy.
(A) replenish   (B) magnify   (C) merge
(D) deplete   (E) redirect

4. Until James learned to be more ____ about writing down his homework assignments, he seldom knew when any assignment was due.
(A) obstinate   (B) contrary   (C) opportunistic
(D) methodical   (E) literate

5. Despite all the advertisements singing the ____ of the new product, she remained ____ its merits, wanting to see what *Consumer Reports* had to say about its claims.
(A) virtues..an optimist about
(B) praises..a skeptic about
(C) joys..a convert to
(D) defects..a cynic about
(E) advantages..a believer in

6. Contemporary authorities have come to ____ the use of "healthy" in place of "healthful"; however, they still reject the use of "disinterested" in place of "uninterested."
(A) condone   (B) evaluate   (C) imitate
(D) disdain   (E) repudiate

7. Though Guinness was determined to make a name for himself on the stage, when he considered the uncertainties of an actor's life, his ____ wavered.
(A) resolution   (B) reverence   (C) affectation
(D) theatricality   (E) skepticism

8. After working on the project night and day for two full months, Sandy felt that she had earned a ____ .
(A) penalty   (B) scolding   (C) degree
(D) chore   (E) respite

9. In *Gulliver's Travels*, Swift's intent is ____ ; he exposes the follies of English society by ridiculing the follies of the Lilliputians.
(A) elegiac   (B) prophetic   (C) satirical
(D) questionable   (E) derivative

10. White was ____ correspondent, and the fifty boxes of his letters are addressed to a ____ array of political figures and fellow journalists.
(A) a faithful..limited
(B) an idiosyncratic..select
(C) a prolific..staggering
(D) an irregular..glittering
(E) an infrequent..vast

11. Even though the basic organization of the brain does not change after birth, details of its structure and function remain ____ for some time, particularly in the cerebral cortex.
(A) plastic   (B) immutable   (C) essential
(D) unknown   (E) static

12. Even the threat of sudden death could not ____ the intrepid pilot and explorer Beryl Markham; a true ____ , she risked her life countless times to set records for flying small planes.
(A) intimidate..patrician
(B) divert..renegade
(C) interest..dilettante
(D) daunt..daredevil
(E) survive..firebrand

13. In an attempt to ____ the severity of the sentence, the defense attorney portrayed his client as a fine young man who had been misled by false friends.
(A) aggravate   (B) impair   (C) mitigate
(D) emulate   (E) reflect

GO ON TO THE NEXT PAGE →

14. That Christmas "The Little Drummer Boy" seemed
____ ; David heard the tune everywhere he went.
(A) audible   (B) unpopular   (C) ubiquitous
(D) voluminous   (E) derivative

15. Hughes preferred ____ employees to loquacious
ones, noting that the formers' dislike of idle chatter
might ensure their ____ about his affairs.
(A) reticent..discretion
(B) taciturn..ignorance
(C) sincere..diligence
(D) industrious..curiosity
(E) skilled..silence

16. The tax investigation became so ____ petty technicalities that the Internal Revenue Service agent
could make no progress with the case.
(A) acquainted with   (B) unobstructed by
(C) removed from   (D) mired in   (E) free of

17. As an indefatigable consumer advocate, Ralph
Nader is constantly engaged in ____ the claims of
unscrupulous merchandisers and cautioning the
public to exercise a healthy ____ .
(A) asserting..autonomy
(B) deflating..prodigality
(C) debunking..skepticism
(D) affirming..indifference
(E) exaggerating..optimism

Directions

Each passage below is followed by questions based
on its content. Answer the questions following each
passage on the basis of what is <u>stated</u> or <u>implied</u> in
that passage and in any introductory material that may
be provided.

Questions 18–23 are based on the following passage.

*The following passage is from a book written by the
naturalist Konrad Lorenz and published in 1952.*

In the chimney the autumn wind sings the song
of the elements, and the old firs before my study
window wave excitedly with their arms and sing
Line   so loudly in chorus that I can hear their sighing
5   melody through the double panes. Suddenly,
from above, a dozen black, streamlined projectiles
shoot across the piece of clouded sky for which
my window forms a frame. Heavily as stones
they fall, fall to the tops of the firs where they
10   suddenly sprout wings, become birds and then
light feather rags that the storm seizes and whirls
out of my line of vision, more rapidly than they
were borne into it.

I walk to the window to watch this extraordi-
15   nary game that the jackdaws are playing with the
wind. A game? Yes, indeed, it is a game, in the
most literal sense of the word: practiced movements, indulged in and enjoyed for their own sake
and not for the achievement of a special object.
20   And rest assured, these are not merely inborn,
purely instinctive actions, but movements that
have been carefully learned. All these feats that
the birds are performing, their wonderful exploitation of the wind, their amazingly exact assessment
25   of distances and, above all, their understanding of
local wind conditions, their knowledge of all the
up-currents, air pockets and eddies—all this proficiency is no inheritance, but, for each bird, an
individually acquired accomplishment.

30   And look what they do with the wind! At first
sight, you, poor human being, think that the storm
is playing with the birds, like a cat with a mouse,
but soon you see, with astonishment, that it is the
fury of the elements that here plays the role of the
35   mouse and that the jackdaws are treating the
storm exactly as the cat its unfortunate victim.
Nearly, but only nearly, do they give the storm its
head, let it throw them high, high into the heavens, till they seem to fall upwards; then, with a
40   casual flap of a wing, they turn themselves over,
open their pinions for a fraction of a second from
below against the wind, and dive—with an accel-
eration far greater than that of a falling stone—
into the depths below. Another tiny jerk of the
45   wing and they return to their normal position and,
on close-reefed sails, shoot away with breathless
speed into the teeth of the gale, hundreds of yards
to the west: this all playfully and without effort,
just to spite the stupid wind that tries to drive
50   them towards the east. The sightless monster itself
must perform the work of propelling the birds
through the air at a rate of well over 80 miles an
hour; the jackdaws do nothing to help beyond a
few lazy adjustments of their black wings.
55   Sovereign control over the power of the elements,
intoxicating triumph of the living organism over
the pitiless strength of the inorganic!

18. The "arms" mentioned in line 3 are
(A) wings   (B) storm winds
(C) heraldic emblems   (D) branches
(E) missiles

19. According to the passage, the bird's skill in adapt-
ing to wind conditions is
(A) genetically determined
(B) limited
(C) undependable
(D) dependent on the elements
(E) gained through practice

GO ON TO THE NEXT PAGE

20. The phrase "rest assured" in line 20 most likely means
(A) sleep securely   (B) others are certain
(C) be confident   (D) remain poised
(E) in their sure leisure

21. The "sightless monster" mentioned in line 50 is
(A) an unobservant watcher
(B) a falling stone   (C) an airplane
(D) the powerful windstorm
(E) a blind predator

22. Throughout the passage, the author is most impressed by
(A) the direction-finding skills of the birds
(B) the jackdaws' superhuman strength
(C) his inability to join the jackdaws in their game
(D) the fleeting nature of his encounter with the birds
(E) the jackdaws' mastery of the forces of nature

23. The author does all of the following EXCEPT
(A) use a metaphor   (B) argue a cause
(C) clarify a term   (D) describe a behavior
(E) dismiss a notion

Questions 24–30 are based on the following passage.

The following passage is excerpted from the 40th anniversary edition of a standard work on African Americans first published in 1948.

There can be no doubt that the emergence of Negro writers in the post-war period stemmed, in part, from the fact that they were inclined to
Line exploit the opportunity to write about themselves.
5 It was more than that, however. The movement that has been variously called the Harlem Renaissance, the Black Renaissance, and the New Negro Movement was essentially a part of the growing interest of American literary circles in
10 the immediate and pressing social and economic problems facing the country. This increasing interest coincided with two developments in Negro life that fostered the growth of the New Negro Movement. The migration that began dur-
15 ing the war had thrown the destiny of blacks into their own hands more than ever before. They developed a responsibility and a self-confidence that they had not previously known. During the war they learned from their president the promise
20 of freedom, and on the battlefield black men served their country. They began to see the discrepancies between the promise of freedom and the reality of their experiences. They became defiant, bitter, and impatient.
25   In the riots and clashes that followed the war, blacks fought back with surprising audacity. By this time, moreover, they had achieved a level of

articulation that enabled them to transform their feelings into a variety of literary forms. Despite
30 their intense feelings of hate and hurt, they possessed enough restraint and objectivity to use their materials artistically. They were sufficiently in touch with the main currents of American literary thought to adapt the accepted forms of expression
35 to their own material, thus gaining a wider audience. These two factors, the keener realization of injustice and the improvement of the capacity for expression, produced a crop of black writers who constituted the Harlem Renaissance.
40   Those who contributed to the literature of the Harlem Renaissance were deeply aware of their belonging to a group that not only was a minority but also was set apart in numerous ways. If black writers accepted this separateness, they did so not
45 because they wanted to be what others wanted them to be (that is, a distinct and even exotic group in the eyes of patronizing whites), but because their experiences had given them some appreciation of their own unique cultural heritage.
50 The plantation, the slave quarters, the proscriptions even in freedom, the lynchings and the riots, the segregation and discrimination had created a body of common experiences that, in turn, helped to promote the idea of a distinct and authentic cul-
55 tural community. In the years following the First World War, this community's spokesmen protested their social and economic wrongs. They stood for full equality, but they celebrated the strength of their own integrity as a people. While they had
60 a vision of social and economic freedom, they cherished the very unhappy experiences that had drawn them closer together. They also had a vision, as Nathan Huggins has suggested, "of themselves as actors and creators of a people's
65 birth (or rebirth)...."
   The writers of the Harlem Renaissance, bitter and cynical as some of them were, were more intent on confronting American racists than on embracing the doctrines of the Socialists and
70 Communists. The editor of the *Messenger* ventured the opinion that the new Negro was the "product of the same world-wide forces that have brought into being the great liberal and radical movements that are now seizing the reins of polit-
75 ical, social, and economic power in all the civilized countries of the world." Such forces may have produced the new Negro, but the more articulate of the group did not seek to subvert American constitutional government. Indeed, the
80 writers of the Harlem Renaissance were not so much revolting against the system as they were protesting the unjust operation of the system. In this approach they proved as characteristically American as any writers of the period. Like their
85 white contemporaries, black writers were merely

GO ON TO THE NEXT PAGE

becoming more aware of America's pressing social problems, and, like the others, were willing to use their art not only to contribute to the great body of American literature but also to improve
90   the civilization of which they were a part.

All the black writers of this period cannot be described as crusaders, however, for not all of them assumed this role. Some were not immediately concerned with the injustices heaped on
95   Negroes. Some contrived their poems, novels, and songs merely for the sake of art, while others took up their pens to escape the sordid aspects of their existence. If an element of race exists in the work of these writers, it is because their material flows
100   out of their individual and group experiences reflecting the emergence of a distinct cultural community. This is not to say that such writings were ineffective as protest literature, but rather that not all the authors were conscious crusaders
105   for a better world. As a matter of fact, it was this detachment, this objectivity, that made it possible for many of the writers of the Harlem Renaissance to achieve a nobility of expression and a poignancy of feeling in their writings that
110   placed them among the great masters of recent American literature.

24. The word "stemmed" in line 2 means
(A) checked   (B) arose   (C) stripped
(D) branched   (E) restrained

25. The author is primarily concerned with
(A) arguing that the literature of the Harlem Renaissance arose from the willingness of black writers to portray their own lives
(B) depicting the part played by socially conscious black writers in a worldwide ideological and literary crusade
(C) providing examples of the injustices protested by the writers of the Harlem Renaissance
(D) describing the social and political background that led to the blossoming of the Harlem Renaissance
(E) analyzing stages in the development of the New Negro Movement into the Harlem Renaissance

26. In reference to the achievements of the Harlem Renaissance, the passage conveys primarily a sense of
(A) protest   (B) betrayal   (C) nostalgia
(D) urgency   (E) admiration

27. In analyzing the black writers' acceptance of their separateness (lines 43–49), the author
(A) condemns their willingness to be cut off from the mainstream
(B) finds a positive aspect of a largely negative experience
(C) suggests additional reasons for their desire for full integration
(D) welcomes the exoticism implicit in black culture
(E) questions the logic underlying their decision

28. The word "embracing" in line 69 means
(A) hugging   (B) accommodating
(C) espousing   (D) containing   (E) adapting

29. Which of the following is implied by the statement that the writers of the Harlem Renaissance "were not so much revolting against the system as they were protesting the unjust operation of the system" (lines 80–82)?
(A) Black writers played only a minor part in protesting the injustices of the period.
(B) Left to itself, the system was sure to operate justly.
(C) Black writers in general were not opposed to the system as such.
(D) In order for the system to operate justly, blacks must seize the reins of power in America.
(E) Black writers were too caught up in aesthetic philosophy to identify the true nature of the conflict.

30. The passage supplies information for answering which of the following questions?
(A) What factors led to the abandonment of the accepted literary forms of the day by black writers in the postwar period?
(B) Who were the leading exponents of protest literature during the Harlem Renaissance?
(C) Why were the writers of the Harlem Renaissance in rebellion against foreign ideological systems?
(D) How did black writers in the postwar period define the literary tradition to which they belonged?
(E) In what larger literary and social context did the black writers of the postwar period compose their works of protest?

SECTION **2**
Mathematical Reasoning

Time—30 minutes
25 Questions

Directions and Reference Information

In this section solve each problem, using any available space on the page for scratchwork. Then decide which is the best of the choices given and fill in the corresponding oval on the answer sheet.

Notes:

(1) The use of a calculator is permitted. All numbers used are real numbers.

(2) Figures that accompany problems in this test are intended to provide information useful in solving the problems. They are drawn as accurately as possible EXCEPT when it is stated in a specific problem that the figure is not drawn to scale. All figures lie in a plane unless otherwise indicated.

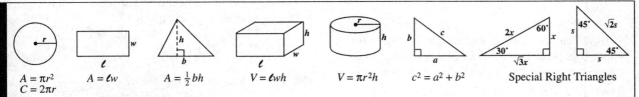

$A = \pi r^2$ $A = \ell w$ $A = \frac{1}{2}bh$ $V = \ell wh$ $V = \pi r^2 h$ $c^2 = a^2 + b^2$ Special Right Triangles
$C = 2\pi r$

The number of degrees of an arc in a circle is 360.
The measure in degrees of a straight angle is 180.
The sum of the measures in degrees of the angles of a triangle is 180.

1. If $x > 1$, which of the following expressions decrease(s) in value as x increases?

  I. $x + \dfrac{1}{x}$

  II. $x^2 - 10x$

  III. $\dfrac{1}{x+1}$

(A) I only   (B) II only   (C) III only
(D) I and II only   (E) I, II, and III

2. Which of the following has the largest numerical value?

(A) $\frac{1}{5}$ (B) $\left(\frac{1}{5}\right)^2$ (C) 0.3

(D) $\sqrt{0.16}$ (E) 0.01π

3. Which of the following is greater than $\frac{1}{4}$?

(A) $(0.25)^2$ (B) $\sqrt{\frac{1}{4}}$ (C) $\left(\frac{1}{4}\right)^4$

(D) 0.04   (E) $\frac{1}{250}$

4. The equation $x + 3y = 9$ and the equation $2x + 6y = 18$ are plotted on the same graph chart. All of the following points will lie on both graphs EXCEPT

(A) (9,0)   (B) (0,3)   (C) (6,1)
(D) (12,–1)   (E) (3,4)

5. If $ab^2c^3 > 0$ which of the following products is always positive?

(A) ab^2 (B) bc (C) b^2c^2 (D) abc (E) ac

6. What is the thickness (in inches) of a pipe that has an inner diameter of 1.25 inches and an outer diameter of 1.55 inches?

(A) 0.15   (B) 0.2   (C) 0.4   (D) 1.65   (E) 0.3

7. If $x + x + x + x = y + y + y + y$, then $4x - 3y =$

(A) 0   (B) 1   (C) x (D) y (E) $x - y$

8. The price of a shirt is \$8 more than $\frac{8}{10}$ of its price. What is the price of this shirt?

(A) \$4   (B) \$20   (C) \$40   (D) \$60   (E) \$80

9. If $(x + \frac{1}{2}) + (x - \frac{1}{2}) = 5$, then $2x =$

(A) $\frac{2}{5}$ (B) $\frac{5}{2}$ (C) $2\frac{1}{5}$ (D) 5   (E) 10

10. If two parts of molasses are mixed with three parts of sugar, what part of the mixture is molasses?

(A) $\frac{1}{3}$ (B) $\frac{2}{5}$ (C) $\frac{3}{5}$ (D) $\frac{2}{3}$ (E) $\frac{3}{2}$

11. What percent of 2 is 20% of 20?

(A) 2%   (B) 4%   (C) 20%
(D) 50%   (E) 200%

12. In a school election where 3 candidates sought election the winning candidate received $\frac{3}{5}$ of the votes. One losing candidate received $\frac{1}{4}$ of the remaining votes. What part of the total votes did the candidate with the least number of votes receive?

(A) $\frac{1}{10}$ (B) $\frac{1}{5}$ (C) $\frac{3}{10}$ (D) $\frac{2}{5}$ (E) $\frac{9}{20}$

13. If the complete contents of a fish tank $18 \times 6 \times 8$ inches is poured into a tank with a base of 36×18 inches, the height of the water (in inches) will be

(A) $\frac{1}{6}$ (B) $\frac{1}{3}$ (C) $\frac{3}{4}$ (D) $1\frac{1}{3}$ (E) $1\frac{2}{3}$

14. $r = \dfrac{rs}{1-s}$
$s^2 + 2s + 1 =$

(A) $\frac{1}{2}$ (B) $1\frac{1}{2}$ (C) $2\frac{1}{4}$ (D) 3   (E) $3\frac{1}{4}$

15. In circle O, $AO \perp OB$. The area of $\triangle AOB$ is $\frac{7}{\pi}$. The area of circle O is

(A) 7   (B) 14   (C) 7π
(D) 14π (E) 49π

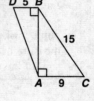

16. If the diagonal of a table with a square top is 6 feet, what is the area of the table top (in square feet)?

(A) $\sqrt{18}$ (B) 9π (C) 18   (D) $18\sqrt{2}$ (E) 36

17. In $\triangle ABC$ the measures of the three angles are represented by $(2x)°$, $(3x - 10)°$, and $(3x + 30)°$. What kind of triangle is ABC?

(A) acute   (B) isosceles   (C) oblique
(D) obtuse   (E) right

18. In the accompanying figure, points A and B are vertices of $\triangle ABC$ (not shown). The area of ABC is 12. Which of the following could be coordinates of vertex C?

(A) $(-4, -4)$
(B) $(-4, 4)$
(C) $(2, 4)$
(D) $(4, -4)$
(E) all of these

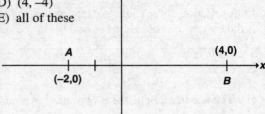

19. In the town of Toonerville there are two high schools. In one school, $16\frac{2}{3}\%$ of the 300 seniors are planning to go to college. In the other school, 90% of the 500 seniors are not planning to go to college. What percent of the seniors in both schools are planning to go to college?

(A) 12.5%   (B) 13.3%   (C) 15%
(D) 43.3%   (E) 87.5%

20. In the accompanying figure, $\angle BAC$ and $\angle DBA$ are right angles. $AC = 9$, $BC = 15$, and $DB = 5$. What is the length of AD?

(A) 17   (B) $\sqrt{74}$ (C) $5\sqrt{2}$
(D) 13   (E) 19

21. If $4^x = 8^y$, then $\dfrac{x}{y}$ equals

(A) $\frac{2}{3}$ (B) $\frac{3}{2}$ (C) $\frac{1}{2}$ (D) 2   (E) 3

22. The dial of a meter is divided into equal divisions from 0 to 60. When the needle points to 48, the meter registers 80 amperes. What is the maximum number of amperes that the meter will register?

(A) 33.5   (B) 92   (C) 100   (D) 102   (E) 120

23. On a scale drawing A is 5 inches and B is drawn 11 inches. If the actual size of B is 5 meters, then the size (in meters) of A is

(A) $2\frac{3}{11}$ (B) $4\frac{6}{11}$ (C) 5   (D) 10   (E) 11

24. $ab = 50$, $a^2 = 100$, $b^2 = 25$; $(a - b)^2 =$

(A) 5   (B) $5\sqrt{3}$ (C) 25   (D) 50   (E) 75

25. Perfume can be purchased in a 0.6-ounce bottle for $18 or in a 2-ounce bottle for $50. The difference in price per ounce is

(A) $1.50   (B) $2.50   (C) $5.00
(D) $10.00   (E) $25.00

IF YOU FINISH BEFORE 30 MINUTES, YOU MAY CHECK YOUR WORK ON THIS SECTION ONLY. DO NOT TURN TO ANY OTHER SECTION IN THE TEST.

S T O P

SECTION 3
Writing Skills

Time—30 minutes
39 Questions

Directions

The following sentences contain problems in grammar, usage, diction (choice of words), and idiom.

Some sentences are correct.
No sentence contains more than one error.

You will find that the error, if there is one, is underlined and lettered. Assume that elements of the sentence that are not underlined are correct and cannot be changed. In choosing answers, follow the requirements of standard written English.

If there is an error, select the one underlined part that must be changed to make the sentence correct and blacken the corresponding space on your answer sheet.

If there is no error, blacken answer space Ⓔ .

EXAMPLE:

The region has a climate <u>so severe that</u> plants
          A

<u>growing there</u> rarely <u>had been</u> more than twelve
          B   C

inches <u>high</u>. <u>No error</u>
          D   E

Ⓐ Ⓑ ● Ⓓ Ⓔ

1. <u>Being that</u> my car is getting <u>its</u> annual tune-up, I
        A   B

<u>will not be</u> able <u>to pick you up</u> tomorrow morning.
        C   D

<u>No error</u>
        E

2. The teacher <u>with her capable aides</u>
                        A

<u>have complete control</u> of the situation; I
        B

<u>look forward</u> to a very <u>uneventful</u> trip. <u>No error</u>
        C   D   E

3. We <u>can't hardly</u> believe that the situation is
        A

<u>so serious as to justify</u> such precautions as you
        B   C

<u>have taken</u>. <u>No error</u>
        D   E

4. No one <u>but</u> <u>he</u> knew <u>which</u> questions <u>were going</u> to
        A   B   C   D

be asked on this test. <u>No error</u>
                              E

5. You are being <u>quite</u> cynical when you say
                    A

<u>that the reason</u> <u>why</u> we have such a large turnout
        B   C

<u>is because</u> we are serving refreshments. <u>No error</u>
        D   E

6. <u>Although</u> I <u>am playing</u> golf for more <u>than</u> three
        A   B   C

years, I cannot manage <u>to break</u> 90. <u>No error</u>
                              D   E

7. I <u>have found</u> that a mild salt solution is more
        A

<u>affective</u> <u>than</u> the commercial preparations
        B   C

available in drug stores <u>in the treatment of</u> this
                                    D

ailment. <u>No error</u>
              E

8. <u>If</u> I have to make a choice <u>between</u> John, Henry
    A   B

and <u>her</u>, I think I'll select Henry because of his
        C

self-control <u>during</u> moments of stress. <u>No error</u>
                  D   E

9. This new information is <u>so important that</u> we
                                    A

must inform the authorities; <u>bring</u> this to the
                                    B

office <u>at once</u> and give <u>it</u> to Mr. Brown.
          C   D

<u>No error</u>
        E

10. <u>In order to</u> raise public consciousness concerning
        A

environmental problems, <u>everyone</u> should distribute
                                    B

leaflets, write to <u>his or her</u> Congressman,
                          C

<u>as well as signing</u> the necessary petitions. <u>No error</u>
        D   E

11. Scientists recently discovered the wreckage of

the *Titanic,* <u>which</u> sank after <u>it</u> struck an iceberg,
                    A   B

<u>furthermore</u> it was not possible for them to <u>raise</u>
        C   D

it. <u>No error</u>
        E

GO ON TO THE NEXT PAGE

12. Scientists <u>show</u> that change, <u>whether</u> good or bad,
　　　　　 A　　　　　　　　　 B
leads to stress, <u>and</u> that the <u>accumulation from</u>
　　　　　　　　　 C　　　　　　 D
stress-related changes can cause major illness.

<u>No error</u>
　 E

13. These awards, I <u>can assure</u> you, <u>will be given</u> not
　　　　　　　　　　　 A　　　　　　 B
<u>only</u> to the best player, but also to the <u>best</u> team in
　 C　　　　　　　　　　　　　　　　　 D
today's tournament. <u>No error</u>
　　　　　　　　　　 E

14. We have spent <u>all together</u> <u>too much</u> money on
　　　　　　　　　　 A　　　　　 B
this project; we have <u>exceeded</u> our budget and
　　　　　　　　　　 C
<u>can expect</u> no additional funds until the beginning
　 D
of the new year. <u>No error</u>
　　　　　　　　 E

15. <u>After</u> John broke his ankle, the teacher <u>had wanted</u>
　 A　　　　　　　　　　　　　　　　 B
<u>us all</u>—Frank, Helen, you and <u>me</u>—to visit him in
　 C　　　　　　　　　　　 D
the hospital. <u>No error</u>
　　　　　　 E

16. Between thirty <u>and</u> forty students <u>seem willing</u> to
　　　　　　　 A　　　　　　　 B
volunteer; <u>the rest</u> are not <u>planning</u> to participate
　　　　　 C　　　　　 D
in the program. <u>No error</u>
　　　　　　　 E

17. <u>Farther</u> along the road, another contestant
　 A
was <u>trying</u> to repair the tire on his <u>new shiny</u>
　　 B　　　　　　　　　　　　 C
bicycle <u>so that</u> he could win the race. <u>No error</u>
　　　 D　　　　　　　　　　　 E

18. The horse <u>that</u> won the trophies <u>differed with</u> the
　　　　　 A　　　　　　　　 B
<u>other</u> horses in <u>overall appearance</u> as well as
　 C　　　　　 D
ability. <u>No error</u>
　　　 E

19. The business executive, <u>planning</u> to attend the
conference in New Orleans, <u>could not decide</u>
whether to travel on or <u>remaining</u> at the hotel was
the <u>better</u> choice. <u>No error</u>

20. Although serfs were lucky to drink their ale from cracked wooden bowls, nobles customarily <u>drunk their wine from</u> elaborately chased drinking horns.
(A) drunk their wine from
(B) have drinked their wine from
(C) drank their wine from
(D) had drunken their wine from
(E) drinking their wine from

21. Before the search party reached the scene of the accident, the rain began to fall, making rescue efforts more difficult.
    (A) the rain began to fall
    (B) the rain had began to fall
    (C) it began to rain
    (D) the rain had begun to fall
    (E) it started to rain

22. For many students, keeping a journal during college seems satisfying their need for self-expression.
    (A) keeping a journal during college seems satisfying their need
    (B) keeping a journal during college seems to satisfy their need
    (C) keeping a journal during college seeming satisfying their need
    (D) to keep a journal during college seems satisfying their need
    (E) the keeping of a journal during college seems to satisfy their need

23. Peter Martin began to develop his own choreographic style, but he was able to free himself from the influence of Balanchine.
    (A) style, but he was able to
    (B) style; but he was able to
    (C) style only when he was able to
    (D) style only when he is able to
    (E) style: only when he was able to

24. Irregardless of the outcome of this dispute, our two nations will remain staunch allies.
    (A) Irregardless of the outcome
    (B) Regardless of how the outcome
    (C) With regard to the outcome
    (D) Regardless of the outcome
    (E) Disregarding the outcome

25. With the onset of winter the snows began to fall, we were soon forced to remain indoors most of the time.
    (A) the snows began to fall, we were soon forced to remain indoors
    (B) the snows began to fall; we were soon forced to remain indoors
    (C) the snows began to fall: we were soon forced to remain indoors
    (D) the snows began to fall, having forced us to remain indoors
    (E) the snows had begun to fall; we were soon forced to remain indoors

26. "Araby," along with several other stories from Joyce's *Dubliners,* are going to be read at Town Hall by noted Irish actress Siobhan McKenna.
    (A) are going to be read
    (B) were going to be read
    (C) are gone to be read
    (D) is going to be read
    (E) is gone to be read

27. In 1980 the Democrats lost not only the executive branch, but also their majority in the United States Senate.
    (A) lost not only the executive branch, but also their majority
    (B) lost not only the executive branch, but also its majority
    (C) not only lost the executive branch, but also their majority
    (D) lost the executive branch, but also their majority
    (E) lost not only the executive branch, but their majority also

28. Before considering an applicant for this job, he must have a degree in electrical engineering as well as three years experience in the field.
    (A) Before considering an applicant for this job, he must have
    (B) Before considering an applicant for this job, he should have
    (C) We will not consider an applicant for this job without
    (D) To consider an applicant for this job, he must have
    (E) We will not consider an applicant for this job if he does not have

29. To invest intelligently for the future, mutual funds provide an excellent opportunity for the average investor.
    (A) To invest intelligently for the future, mutual funds
    (B) As an intelligent investment for the future, mutual funds
    (C) Investing intelligently for the future, mutual funds
    (D) To invest with intelligence, mutual funds
    (E) Having invested intelligently, you must determine that mutual funds

30. She was told to give the award to whomever she thought had contributed most to the welfare of the student body.
    (A) to whomever she thought
    (B) to whoever she thought
    (C) to the senior whom she thought
    (D) to whomever
    (E) to him whom she thought

31. Since he is lying the book on the table where it does not belong.
    (A) Since he is lying the book on the table where it does not belong.
    (B) He is lying the book on the table where it does not belong.
    (C) Because he is laying the book on the table where it does not belong.
    (D) Since he is laying the book on the table where it does not belong.
    (E) He is laying the book on the table where it does not belong.

GO ON TO THE NEXT PAGE ▷

32. Mary is <u>as fast as, if not faster than, anyone</u> in her class and should be on the team.
  (A) as fast as, if not faster than, anyone
  (B) as fast, if not faster than, anyone else
  (C) as fast as, if not more fast than, anyone
  (D) as fast as, if not faster than, anyone else
  (E) as swift as, if not faster than, anyone

33. Senator D'Amato is <u>one of the legislators who are going</u> to discuss the budget with the President.
  (A) one of the legislators who are going
  (B) one of the legislators who is going
  (C) one of the legislators who has gone
  (D) the legislators who is going
  (E) the legislators who has gone

Directions

The passage below is the unedited draft of a student's essay. Some of the essay needs to be rewritten to make the meaning clearer and more precise. Read the essay carefully.

The essay is followed by six questions about changes that might improve all or part of its organization, development, sentence structure, use of language, appropriateness to the audience, or its use of standard written English. Choose the answer that most clearly and effectively expresses the student's intended meaning. Indicate your choice by filling in the corresponding space on the answer sheet.

Essay

[1] In the twentieth century, women have held a major part in influencing social change and social status. [2] In such developing countries as Saudi Arabia, restrictions on women are gradually being lifted, and they have gained the right to be in public without your head covered.

[3] In the area of social status, women have fought for better treatment and more respect. [4] An example of this is the fight for women in the workplace. [5] Not long ago most women stayed at home and took care of their families, while their husbands worked at white collar and blue collar jobs. [6] But now many women work as doctors, lawyers, and other established positions. [7] Women are finally out in the work force competing with men for the same jobs.

[8] In the area of politics and government, many women have attained high positions. [9] Hillary Rodham Clinton became a role model for many young women in this country. [10] Two women are now members of the U.S. Supreme Court. [11] Several women also are governors, senators and representatives. [12] There will never again be an all-male cabinet. [13] Ever since women's suffrage, women have won the

rights reserved for men. [14] The result was that women now have a voice in the actions of our country.

[15] In the areas of health, medicine, sciences, and the military, women have also come into their own. [16] Although the world still has a long way to go before women achieve total equality with men, the twentieth century may long be remembered as the time when the first steps were taken.

34. Considering the essay as a whole, which revision of sentence 1 would serve best as the essay's opening sentence?
  (A) The social status of women has undergone a major change during the twentieth century.
  (B) Twentieth century women will have a major influence in changing their social status.
  (C) As a major influence in the twentieth century, women have had their social status changed.
  (D) Under the influence of twentieth century women, their status has changed.
  (E) Being influenced by social change in the twentieth century, the status of women has changed.

35. Which is the most effective revision of the underlined segment of sentence 2 below?

In such developing countries as Saudi Arabia, restrictions on women are gradually being lifted, <u>*and they have gained the right to be in public without your head covered.*</u>

  (A) for example, women are gaining rights like the one to be in public bareheaded
  (B) which means that they have gained the right to be in public with their heads uncovered
  (C) and they have the right, for example, for you to go bareheaded in public
  (D) and women now have gained the right to be bareheaded in public
  (E) to the extent that women can exercise the right of going into public with their head uncovered

36. Which is the best revision of the underlined segment of sentence 6 below?

But now many women work as doctors, as lawyers, and <u>*other established positions.*</u>

  (A) in other professions
  (B) as other professionals
  (C) other established jobs
  (D) other professional positions
  (E) as other professional capacities

GO ON TO THE NEXT PAGE

37. Which revision of sentence 8 provides the best transition between the second and the third paragraphs?

(A) The competition has extended into politics and government, where many women have replaced men in high positions.

(B) Irregardless, in the field of politics and government many women have attained high positions.

(C) High positions in government and politics have been attained by women.

(D) Among the jobs that women have attained are in politics and government.

(E) The world of politics and government has changed because women have attained high positions.

38. Sentence 8 is the topic sentence of the third paragraph. Which of the following is the best revision of sentence 9?

(A) The wife of the President, Hillary Rodham Clinton, made herself a role model for many young American women.

(B) In the 1992 national election, Hillary Rodham Clinton helped her husband win the Presidency of the United States.

(C) After seven years as Prime Minister of England, Margaret Thatcher was finally defeated by a male, John Major.

(D) While she was the leader of India, Indira Ghandi was assassinated.

(E) In recent years both Margaret Thatcher of England and Indira Ghandi of India, for example, served as leaders of their countries.

39. Which sentence in the third paragraph should be revised or deleted because it contributes least to the development of the main idea of the paragraph?

(A) Sentence 10

(B) Sentence 11

(C) Sentence 12

(D) Sentence 13

(E) Sentence 14

IF YOU FINISH BEFORE 30 MINUTES, YOU MAY CHECK YOUR WORK ON THIS SECTION ONLY. DO NOT TURN TO ANY OTHER SECTION IN THE TEST.   **S T O P**

SECTION 4
Verbal Reasoning

Time—30 minutes
30 Questions

For each question in this section, select the best answer from among the choices given and fill in the corresponding oval on the answer sheet.

Directions

Each sentence below consists of a related pair of words or phrases, followed by five pairs of words or phrases labeled A through E. Select the pair that best expresses a relationship similar to that expressed in the original pair.

Example:

CRUMB:BREAD::
(A) ounce:unit
(B) splinter:wood
(C) water:bucket
(D) twine:rope
(E) cream:butter

31. FOOTBALL:GRIDIRON::
    (A) soccer:goal   (B) rugby:arena
    (C) wrestling:mat   (D) baseball:diamond
    (E) bowling:pin

32. WILT:WATER::
    (A) melt:ice   (B) starve:food
    (C) breathe:air   (D) blink:light
    (E) glow:sun

33. GOOSE:GOSLING::
    (A) sheep:flock   (B) pig:sty
    (C) bird:wing   (D) goat:kid
    (E) rooster:hen

34. LOBSTER:CRUSTACEAN::
    (A) ant:insectivore   (B) kangaroo:marsupial
    (C) larva:moth   (D) bird:aviary
    (E) salmon:roe

35. SIMPLE:ELABORATION::
    (A) practical:usefulness
    (B) foolish:consistency
    (C) thrifty:extravagance
    (D) holy:worship
    (E) distant:boundary

36. STORM:SUBSIDE::
    (A) assault:mount   (B) riot:incite
    (C) spasm:relax   (D) turbulence:disturb
    (E) attack:escalate

37. DELIRIUM:DISORIENTATION::
    (A) paralysis:immobility   (B) anorexia:pain
    (C) insomnia:apprehension
    (D) rash:vaccination   (E) malaria:relapse

38. SCURRY:MOVE::
    (A) chant:sing   (B) chatter:talk
    (C) carry:lift   (D) sleep:drowse
    (E) limp:walk

39. CORD:WOOD::
    (A) string:kite   (B) bolt:cloth
    (C) brick:wall   (D) branch:tree
    (E) ore:metal

40. EULOGY:LAUDATORY::
    (A) epigram:lengthy   (B) tirade:abusive
    (C) elegy:hyperbolic   (D) argument:offensive
    (E) apology:sincere

41. OBDURATE:FLEXIBILITY::
    (A) accurate:perception   (B) turbid:roughness
    (C) principled:fallibility
    (D) diaphanous:transparency
    (E) adamant:submissiveness

42. REPROBATE:BLAMEWORTHY::
    (A) zealot:indifferent   (B) charlatan:flagrant
    (C) adherent:vociferous   (D) braggart:venerable
    (E) traducer:slanderous

43. FEUD:ACRIMONY::
    (A) scuffle:confusion   (B) crusade:heresy
    (C) duel:brevity   (D) scrimmage:ceremony
    (E) siege:vulnerability

The passage below is followed by questions based on its content. Answer the questions following the passage on the basis of what is stated or implied in that passage and in any introductory material that may be provided.

Questions 44–49 are based on the following passage.

Tapestries are made on looms. Their distinctive weave is basically simple: the colored weft threads interface regularly with the monochrome
Line warps, as in darning or plain cloth, but as they do
5 so, they form a design by reversing their direction when a change of color is needed. The wefts are beaten down to cover the warps completely. The result is a design or picture that is the fabric itself, not one laid upon a ground like an embroidery, a
10 print, or brocading. The back and front of a tapestry show the same design. The weaver always follows a preexisting model, generally a drawing or painting, known as the cartoon, which in most cases he reproduces as exactly as he can.
15 Long training is needed to become a professional

GO ON TO THE NEXT PAGE

tapestry weaver. It can take as much as a year to produce a yard of very finely woven tapestry.

20 Tapestry-woven fabrics have been made from China to Peru and from very early times to the present day, but large wall hangings in this technique, mainly of wool, are typically Northern European. Few examples predating the late fourteenth century have survived, but from about 1400 tapestries were an essential part of aristocratic life. The prince or great nobleman sent his plate and his tapestries ahead of him to furnish his castles before his arrival as he traveled through his domains; both had the same function, to display his wealth and social position. It has frequently been suggested that tapestries helped to heat stone-walled rooms, but this is a modern idea; comfort was of minor importance in the Middle Ages. Tapestries were portable grandeur, instant splendor, taking the place, north of the Alps, of painted frescoes further south. They were hung without gaps between them, covering entire walls and often doors as well. Only very occasionally were they made as individual works of art such as altar frontals. They were usually commissioned or bought as sets, or "chambers," and constituted the most important furnishings of any grand room, except for the display of plate, throughout the Middle Ages and the sixteenth century. Later, woven silks, ornamental wood carving, stucco decoration, and painted leather gradually replaced tapestry as expensive wall coverings, until at last wallpaper was introduced in the late eighteenth century and eventually swept away almost everything else.

50 By the end of the eighteenth century, the "tapestry-room" [a room with every available wall surface covered with wall hangings] was no longer fashionable: paper had replaced wall coverings of wool and silk. Tapestries, of course, were still made, but in the nineteenth century they often seem to have been produced mainly as individual works of art that astonish by their resemblance to oil paintings, tours de force woven with a remarkably large number of wefts per inch. In England during the second half of the century, William Morris attempted to reverse this trend and to bring tapestry weaving back to its true principles, those he considered to have governed it in the Middle Ages. He imitated medieval tapestries in both style and technique, using few warps to the inch, but he did not make sets; the original function for which tapestry is so admirably suited—completely covering the walls of a room and providing sumptuous surroundings for a life of pomp and splendor—could not be

revived. Morris's example has been followed, though with less imitation of medieval style, by many weavers of the present century, whose coarsely woven cloths hang like single pictures and 75 can be admired as examples of contemporary art.

44. Tapestry weaving may be characterized as which of the following?

   I. Time-consuming
  II. Spontaneous in concept
 III. Faithful to an original

(A) I only   (B) III only   (C) I and II only
(D) I and III only   (E) II and III only

45. The word "distinctive" in line 1 means

(A) characteristic   (B) stylish
(C) discriminatory   (D) eminent   (E) articulate

46. Renaissance nobles carried tapestries with them to demonstrate their

(A) piety
(B) consequence
(C) aesthetic judgment
(D) need for privacy
(E) dislike for cold

47. The word "ground" in line 9 means

(A) terrain   (B) dust   (C) thread
(D) base   (E) pigment

48. In contrast to nineteenth century tapestries, contemporary tapestries

(A) are displayed in sets of panels
(B) echo medieval themes
(C) faithfully copy oil paintings
(D) have a less fine weave
(E) indicate the owner's social position

49. The primary purpose of the passage is to

(A) explain the process of tapestry-making
(B) contrast Eastern and Western schools of tapestry
(C) analyze the reasons for the decline in popularity of tapestries
(D) provide a historical perspective on tapestry-making
(E) advocate a return to a more colorful way of life

GO ON TO THE NEXT PAGE ⟹

The passages below are followed by questions based on their content; questions following a pair of related passages may also be based on the relationship between the paired passages. Answer the questions on the basis of what is stated or implied in the passages and in any introductory material that may be provided.

Questions 50–60 are based on the following passages.

The following passages present two portraits of grandmothers. In Passage 1 Mary McCarthy shares her memories of her Catholic grandmother, who raised McCarthy and her brother after their parents' death. In Passage 2 Caroline Heilbrun tells of her Jewish grandmother, who died when Heilbrun was 10.

PASSAGE 1

Luckily, I am writing a memoir and not a work of fiction, and therefore I do not have to account for my grandmother's unpleasing character and look for the Oedipal fixation or the traumatic Line experience that would give her that clinical
5 authenticity that is nowadays so desirable in portraiture. I do not know how my grandmother got the way she was; I assume, from family photographs and from the inflexibility of her habits,
10 that she was always the same, and it seems as idle to inquire into her childhood as to ask what was ailing Iago or look for the error in toilet-training that was responsible for Lady Macbeth. My grandmother's sexual history, bristling with infant mor-
15 tality in the usual style of her period, was robust and decisive: three tall, handsome sons grew up, and one attentive daughter. Her husband treated her kindly. She had money, many grandchildren, and religion to sustain her. White hair, glasses,
20 soft skin, wrinkles, needlework—all the paraphernalia of motherliness were hers; yet it was a cold, grudging, disputatious old woman who sat all day in her sunroom making tapestries from a pattern, scanning religious periodicals, and setting her iron
25 jaw against any infraction of her ways.

Combativeness was, I suppose, the dominant trait in my grandmother's nature. An aggressive churchgoer, she was quite without Christian feeling; the mercy of the Lord Jesus had never entered
30 her heart. Her piety was an act of war against the Protestant ascendancy. The religious magazines on her table furnished her not with food for meditation but with fresh pretexts for anger; articles attacking birth control, divorce, mixed marriages,
35 Darwin, and secular education were her favorite reading. The teachings of the Church did not interest her, except as they were a rebuke to others; "Honor thy father and thy mother," a commandment she was no longer called upon to practice,
40 was the one most frequently on her lips. The extermination of Protestantism, rather than spiritual perfection, was the boon she prayed for. Her mind was preoccupied with conversion; the capture of a soul for God much diverted her fancy—it made
45 one less Protestant in the world. Foreign missions, with their overtones of good will and social service, appealed to her less strongly; it was not a *harvest* of souls that my grandmother had in mind.

This pugnacity of my grandmother's did not
50 confine itself to sectarian enthusiasm. There was the defense of her furniture and her house against the imagined encroachments of visitors. With her, this was not the gentle and tremulous protectiveness endemic in old ladies, who fear for the
55 safety of their possessions with a truly touching anxiety, inferring the fragility of all things from the brittleness of their old bones and hearing the crash of mortality in the perilous tinkling of a teacup. My grandmother's sentiment was more
60 autocratic: she hated having her chairs sat in or her lawns stepped on or the water turned on in her basins, for no reason at all except pure officiousness; she even grudged the mailman his daily promenade up her sidewalk. Her home was a cen-
65 ter of power, and she would not allow it to be derogated by easy or democratic usage. Under her jealous eye, its social properties had atrophied, and it functioned in the family structure simply as a political headquarters. The family
70 had no friends, and entertaining was held to be a foolish and unnecessary courtesy as between blood relations. Holiday dinners fell, as a duty, on the lesser members of the organization: the daughters and daughters-in-law (converts from
75 the false religion) offered up Baked Alaska on a platter like the head of John the Baptist, while the old people sat enthroned at the table, and only their digestive processes acknowledged, with rumbling, enigmatic salvos, the festal day.

PASSAGE 2

80 My grandmother, one of Howe's sustaining women, not only ruled the household with an arm of iron, but kept a store to support them all, her blond, blue-eyed husband enjoying life rather than struggling through it. My grandmother was one of
85 those powerful women who know that they stand between their families and an outside world filled with temptations to failure and shame. I remember her as thoroughly loving. But there can be no question that she impaired her six daughters for
90 autonomy as thoroughly as if she had crippled them—more so. The way to security was marriage; the dread that stood in the way of this was sexual dalliance, above all pregnancy. The horror of pregnancy in an unmarried girl is difficult, per-
95 haps, to recapture now. For a Jewish girl not to be

GO ON TO THE NEXT PAGE

a virgin on marriage was failure. The male's rights were embodied in her lack of sexual experience, in the knowledge that he was the first, the owner.

100 All attempts at autonomy had to be frustrated. And of course, my grandmother's greatest weapon was her own vulnerability. She had worked hard, only her daughters knew how hard. She could not be comforted or repaid—as *my* mother would feel repaid—by a daughter's
105 accomplishments, only by her marriage.

50. McCarthy's attitude toward her grandmother is best described as

(A) tolerant   (B) appreciative   (C) indifferent
(D) nostalgic   (E) sardonic

51. The word "idle" in line 10 means

(A) slothful   (B) passive   (C) fallow
(D) useless   (E) unoccupied

52. According to McCarthy, a portrait of a character in a work of modern fiction must have

(A) photographic realism
(B) psychological validity
(C) sympathetic attitudes
(D) religious qualities
(E) historical accuracy

53. McCarthy's primary point in describing her grandmother's physical appearance (lines 19–20) is best summarized by which of the following axioms?

(A) Familiarity breeds contempt.
(B) You can't judge a book by its cover.
(C) One picture is worth more than ten thousand words.
(D) There's no smoke without fire.
(E) Blood is thicker than water.

54. By describing (in lines 53–63) the typical old woman's fear for the safety of her possessions, McCarthy emphasizes that

(A) her grandmother feared the approach of death
(B) old women have dangerously brittle bones
(C) her grandmother possessed considerable wealth
(D) her grandmother had different reasons for her actions
(E) visitors were unwelcome in her grandmother's home

55. The word "properties" in line 67 means

(A) belongings   (B) aspects   (C) holdings
(D) titles   (E) acreage

56. Heilbrun is critical of her grandmother primarily because

(A) she would not allow her husband to enjoy himself
(B) she could not accept her own vulnerability
(C) she fostered a sense of sexual inadequacy
(D) she discouraged her daughters' independence
(E) she physically injured her children

57. By describing the extent of the feeling against pregnancy in unmarried girls (lines 93–96), Heilbrun helps the reader understand

(A) her fear of being scorned as an unwed mother
(B) why her grandmother strove to limit her daughters' autonomy
(C) her disapproval of contemporary sexual practices
(D) her awareness of her mother's desire for happiness
(E) how unforgiving her grandmother was

58. In stating that her grandmother's greatest weapon was her own vulnerability (lines 100–101), Heilbrun implies that her grandmother got her way by exploiting her children's

(A) sense of guilt
(B) innocence of evil
(C) feeling of indifference
(D) abdication of responsibility
(E) lack of experience

59. Both passages mention which of the following as being important to the writer's grandmother?

(A) governing the actions of others
(B) contributing to religious organizations
(C) protecting her children's virtue
(D) marrying off her daughters
(E) being surrounded by a circle of friends

60. McCarthy would most likely react to the characterization of her grandmother, like Heilbrun's grandmother, as one of the "sustaining women" (line 80) by pointing out that

(A) this characterization is not in good taste
(B) the characterization fails to account for her grandmother's piety
(C) the details of the family's social life support this characterization
(D) her grandmother's actual conduct is not in keeping with this characterization
(E) this characterization slightly exaggerates her grandmother's chief virtue

---

IF YOU FINISH BEFORE 30 MINUTES, YOU MAY CHECK YOUR WORK ON THIS SECTION ONLY. DO NOT TURN TO ANY OTHER SECTION IN THE TEST.

S T O P

SECTION 5
Mathematical Reasoning

Time—30 minutes
25 Questions

Directions and Sample Questions

Notes:

(1) The use of a calculator is permitted. All numbers used are real numbers.

(2) Figures that accompany problems in this test are intended to provide information useful in solving the problems. They are drawn as accurately as possible EXCEPT when it is stated in a specific problem that the figure is not drawn to scale. All figures lie in a plane unless otherwise indicated.

Questions 1–15 each consist of two quantities in boxes, one in Column A and one in Column B. You are to compare the two quantities and on the answer sheet fill in oval

A if the quantity in Column A is greater;
B if the quantity in Column B is greater;
C if the two quantities are equal;
D if the relationship cannot be determined from the information given.

Notes:

1. In some questions, information is given about one or both of the quantities to be compared. In such cases, the given information is centered above the two columns and is not boxed.
2. In a given question, a symbol that appears in both columns represents the same thing in Column A as it does in Column B.
3. Letters such as x, n, and k stand for real numbers.

	EXAMPLES		
	Column A	Column B	Answers
E1	5^2	20	● Ⓑ Ⓒ Ⓓ
E2	x	30	Ⓐ Ⓑ ● Ⓓ
	$150°$ $x°$		
	r and s are integers.		
E3	$r + 1$	$s - 1$	Ⓐ Ⓑ Ⓒ ●

PART I: QUANTITATIVE COMPARISON QUESTIONS

SUMMARY DIRECTIONS FOR QUANTITATIVE COMPARISON QUESTIONS

Answer: A if the quantity in Column A is greater.
B if the quantity in Column B is greater.

C if the two quantities are equal.
D if the relationship cannot be determined from the information given.

	Column A	Column B
26.	x^3	x^2

The sum of a, b, and c, three consecutive integers, is 18.

	Column A	Column B
27.	abc	210

$x = 1$ and $y = -1$

	Column A	Column B
28.	$\dfrac{a(x + y)}{b}$	$\dfrac{2a(x + y)}{b}$

$$\frac{x}{-y - z} = \frac{-a}{y + z}$$

	Column A	Column B
29.	x	a

$$3x + 5y = 15 + 5y$$

	Column A	Column B
30.	$\dfrac{x}{5}$	1

GO ON TO THE NEXT PAGE ⟶

	Column A	Column B
31.	The time elapsed from 8:55 A.M. until 10:15 the same morning	2 hours, 40 minutes

Z is 4 miles from *Y*.
X is 3 miles from *Y*.

	Column A	Column B
32.	The distance from *X* to *Z*	5 miles

A bag contains 3 red marbles, 4 white marbles, and 5 green marbles. One marble is drawn without looking. At the same time a coin is tossed two times.

	Column A	Column B
33.	Probability of drawing a white marble.	Probability of tossing two heads.

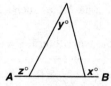

AB is a straight line and *x* = 100, *y* = 40.

	Column A	Column B
34.	*z*	*x* + *y*

	Column A	Column B

	Column A	Column B
35.	$\dfrac{BC}{AB} \cdot \dfrac{AC}{BC}$	1

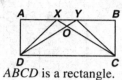

ABCD is a rectangle.

	Column A	Column B
36.	The area of △*XOD*	The area of △*YOC*

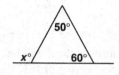

	Column A	Column B
37.	*x*	70
38.	The product of $2\frac{1}{2}$ and its reciprocal	The product of $3\frac{1}{2}$ and its reciprocal
39.	$3x$	$(-2)x$
40.	The area of a rectangle with length equal to 8 feet	The area of a square with side equal to 8 feet

GO ON TO THE NEXT PAGE

PART II: STUDENT-PRODUCED RESPONSE QUESTIONS

Directions for Student-Produced Response Questions

Each of the remaining ten questions (41–50) requires you to solve the problem and enter your answer by marking the ovals in the special grid, as shown in the examples below.

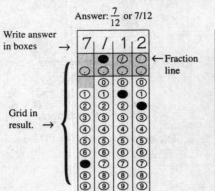

Answer: $\frac{7}{12}$ or 7/12

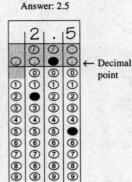

Answer: 2.5

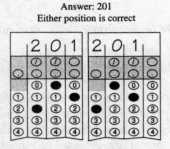

Answer: 201
Either position is correct

Note: You may start your answers in any column, space permitting. Columns not needed should be left blank.

- Mark no more than one oval in any column.

- Because the answer sheet will be machine-scored, **you will receive credit only if the ovals are filled in correctly.**

- Although not required, it is suggested that you write your answer in the boxes at the top of the columns to help you fill in the ovals accurately.

- Some problems may have more than one correct answer. In such cases, grid only one answer.

- No question has a negative answer.

- **Mixed numbers** such as $2\frac{1}{2}$ much be gridded as 2.5 or 5/2. (If [2 1 / 2] is gridded, it will be interpreted as $\frac{21}{2}$, not $\frac{21}{2}$.)

- Decimal Accuracy: If you obtain a decimal answer, enter the most accurate value that the grid will accommodate. For example, if you obtain an answer such as 0.6666..., you should record the result as .666 or .667. Less accurate values such as .66 or .67 are not acceptable.

Acceptable ways to grid $\frac{2}{3}$ = .6666. . .

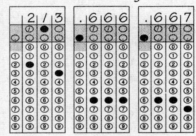

41. How many dimes must I give the postal clerk for thirty 25¢ postage stamps?

42. Twenty minutes after a car enters a turnpike it is 20 miles from the entrance gate. What was the average speed (in miles per hour)?

43. If the diameter of a circle is doubled, what will the area be multipled by?

44. $\angle B$ is formed by secant DCB and tangent AB. If the measure of $\angle B$ is 70° and $\overarc{CA}$ is 70°, how many degrees are in $\overarc{DC}$?

45. In the accompanying figure, ACE and BCD are straight lines and B and D are right angles. What is the length of AB if BC = 12, CD = 16, and DE = 12?

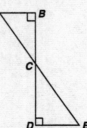

46. What is the sum of $\frac{0.3}{9}$ and $\frac{0.6}{9}$?

47. Lori can prepare 9 envelopes for mailing in 12 minutes. This task includes typing the address, assembling and enclosing the contents, and affixing the proper postage. How many envelopes can she prepare in 8 hours?

48. If $2^{x+2} = 16$, what does x equal?

49. The notation on the map reads "Scale: 1 inch = 150 miles." What is the distance (in miles) from Waban to Madison, which are $3\frac{1}{2}$ inches apart on this map?

50. A jar contains four red marbles, seven green marbles, and some blue marbles. If the probability of randomly selecting a marble that is *not* green is $\frac{2}{3}$, how many blue marbles are in the jar?

IF YOU FINISH BEFORE 30 MINUTES, YOU MAY CHECK YOUR WORK ON THIS SECTION ONLY. DO NOT TURN TO ANY OTHER SECTION IN THE TEST.

S T O P

ANSWER KEY

Verbal Reasoning Section 1

1. C	6. A	11. A	16. D	21. D	26. E
2. B	7. A	12. D	17. C	22. E	27. B
3. D	8. A	13. C	18. D	23. B	28. C
4. D	9. C	14. C	19. E	24. B	29. C
5. B	10. C	15. A	20. C	25. D	30. E

Mathematical Reasoning Section 2

Note: Each correct answer to the mathematics questions is keyed by number to the corresponding topic in Chapters 8 and 9. These numerals refer to the topics listed below, with specific page references in parentheses.

1. Basic Fundamental Operations (179–182)	10. Motion (203)
2. Algebraic Operations (182–183)	11. Ratio and Proportion (204–205)
3. Using Algebra (182–184, 187)	12. Mixtures and Solution (178)
4. Exponents, Roots, and Radicals (184–185)	13. Work (206–207)
5. Inequalities (188–189)	14. Coordinate Geometry (194)
6. Fractions (182, 198)	15. Geometry (189–193, 195)
7. Decimals (200)	16. Quantitative Comparisons (211–212)
8. Percent (200)	17. Data Interpretation (208)
9. Averages (201)	

1. C (2)	6. A (1, 7)	11. E (3, 8)	16. C (15)	21. B (4)
2. D (1, 6, 7)	7. A (2)	12. A (6)	17. E (15)	22. C (11)
3. B (4, 6, 7)	8. C (1)	13. D (15)	18. E (14, 15)	23. A (11)
4. E (3, 14)	9. D (2)	14. C (2)	19. A (8)	24. C (2)
5. E (4)	10. B (6)	15. B (15)	20. D (15)	25. C (1)

Writing Skills Section 3

1. A	8. B	15. B	22. B	29. B	36. B
2. B	9. B	16. E	23. C	30. B	37. A
3. A	10. D	17. E	24. D	31. E	38. E
4. B	11. C	18. B	25. B	32. D	39. E
5. D	12. D	19. C	26. D	33. A	
6. B	13. E	20. C	27. A	34. A	
7. B	14. A	21. A	28. E	35. D	

Verbal Reasoning Section 4

31. D	36. C	41. E	46. B	51. D	56. D
32. B	37. A	42. E	47. D	52. B	57. B
33. D	38. B	43. A	48. D	53. B	58. A
34. B	39. B	44. D	49. D	54. D	59. A
35. C	40. B	45. A	50. E	55. B	60. D

Mathematical Reasoning Section 5

26. D (4, 16)	29. C (2)	32. D (15)	35. C (15. 16)	38. C (6, 16)
27. C (1, 16)	30. C (2)	33. A (1,4)	36. C (15, 16)	39. D (2. 16)
28. C (2)	31. B (1, 8)	34. B (15, 16)	37. A (15, 16)	40. D (15, 16)

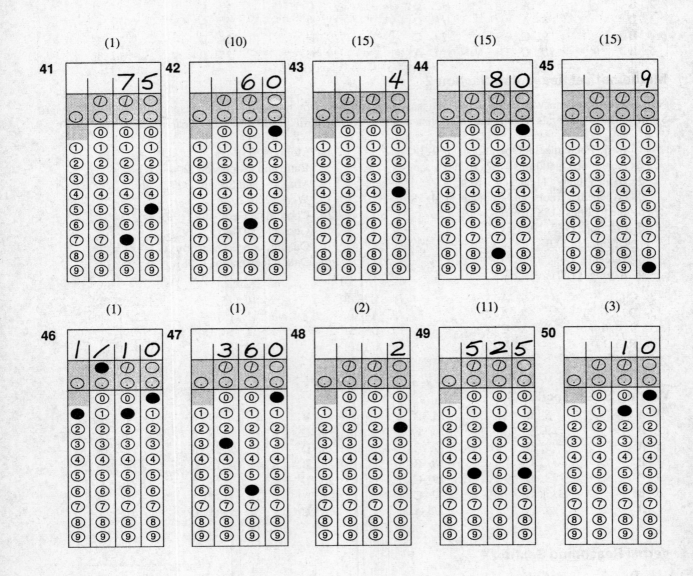

SCORING CHART — TYPICAL TEST A

Verbal Sections

Section 1   Questions 1–30
Number correct   _____ (A)
Number omitted   _____ (B)
Number incorrect   _____ (C)
$1/4$ (C) =   _____ (D)
Raw Score:
  (A) – (D) =   _____

Section 3   Questions 31–60
Number correct   _____ (A)
Number omitted   _____ (B)
Number incorrect   _____ (C)
$1/4$ (C) =   _____ (D)
Raw Score:
  (A) – (D) =   _____

Total Verbal Raw Score:
  (Section 1 +
  Section 3) =   _____

Mathematical Sections

Section 2   Questions 1–25
Number correct   _____ (A)
Number incorrect   _____ (B)
(A) – $1/4$ (B) =   _____ Raw Score I

Section 4   Questions 26–40
Number correct   _____ (C)
Number incorrect   _____ (D)
(C) – $1/3$ (D) =   _____ Raw Score II

Section 4   Questions 41–50
Number correct   _____ Raw Score III

Total Mathematical Raw Score:
  (Raw Scores I + II
  + III) =   _____

Writing Section

Section 3   Questions 1–39
Number correct   _____ (A)
Number incorrect   _____ (B)
$1/4$ (B) =   _____ (C)
(no penalty for omitted questions)
Writing Raw Score:
  (A) – (C) =   _____

EVALUATION CHART

Study your score. Your raw score on the Verbal and Mathematical Reasoning Sections is an indication of your probable achievement on the PSAT/NMSQT. As a guide to the amount of work you need or want to do with this book, study the following.

| Raw Score | | | Self-rating |
Verbal	Mathematical	Writing	
55–60	41–50	37–39	Superior
44–54	25–40	31–36	Very good
39–43	20–24	25–30	Satisfactory
35–38	16–19	19–24	Average
29–34	10–15	13–18	Needs further study
20–28	7–9	6–12	Needs intensive study
0–19	0–6	0–5	Probably inadequate

ANSWER EXPLANATIONS

Verbal Reasoning Section 1

1. **C** The use of "Unhappily" tells us that the experiment was somehow damaged or *marred* by the presence of observers.

2. **B** Remember to think of your own answer before looking at the choices. North clearly had a strong belief, since no one's words could convince him otherwise. This would guide you to choose *conviction*, one meaning of which is belief.

3. **D** If we are likely to be in need of a new source of energy, we must be about to run out of the old source of fuel. This would happen if we *deplete* or exhaust our supply. The phrase "Excessive use" is also a clue that we may be running out, through using too much.

4. **D** James didn't know when assignments were due because there was something wrong with the way he wrote them down. He was not orderly or *methodical* about it.

5. **B** The word "despite" signals a contrast. Despite the advertised *praises*, she had doubts—she remained a *skeptic about* the product. Note also that "singing the praises of" is a cliche, a customary phrase.

6. **A** The word "however" signals a contrast. The sentence says the authorities reject the use of "disinterested." Therefore, *in contrast*, they accept or *condone* the use of "healthy."

7. **A** The word "though" also signals a contrast. Although Guinness had his mind set on becoming an actor, his determination or *resolution* wavered. Note that *resolution* is not just a statement of intent; it can mean firmness of intent as well.

8. **E** Again, think of your own answer before looking at the choices. What would you need after two full months of solid work? A rest, or *respite*.

9. **C** The key word here is "ridiculing," meaning making fun of or mocking. It complements *satirical* or sarcastic and cutting.

10. **C** What sort of correspondent was White? If he produced fifty boxes of letters, he clearly was an abundantly productive or *prolific* one who wrote to an overwhelming, *staggering* number of people.

11. **A** The phrase "even though" tells us that there will be a contrast. This requires a word that is opposite in meaning to "does not change." *Plastic* can mean adaptable or pliable when used as an adjective, as it is here.

12. **D** Someone who risks his or her life frequently is a *daredevil*. Since the threat of death does not keep Markham from such activities, the first missing word must be *daunt*, meaning to frighten or lessen one's courage.

13. **C** It is the defense attorney's job to try to lessen or *mitigate* the harshness of any sentence imposed on a client.

14. **C** By definition, something found everywhere is omnipresent or *ubiquitous*. (*Ubiquitous* comes from the Latin *ubique*, meaning *everywhere*.)

15. **A** Hughes wanted employees who disliked idle chatter, people who were *not* loquacious (talkative) but were *reticent* (reserved and uncommunicative) instead. Such people would keep his secrets, maintaining their *discretion* (secrecy) about his affairs.

16. **D** The agent could make no progress. Look for a word that expresses a sense of interference with the investigation: it was stuck or *mired in* petty technicalities or minor issues.

17. **C** "Unscrupulous merchandisers" make false claims. *Debunking* means exposing falseness in something. Nader, who is an advocate or protector of the consumer, teaches people to be suspicious and to exercise *skepticism*. Note that "exercising skepticism" is a cliche, a very commonly used phrase.

18. **D** Blown about by the storm, the *branches* of the fir trees move from side to side: "the old firs...wave excitedly with their arms."

19. **E** The author states that the jackdaw's proficiency is not inherited or innate, but "an individually acquired accomplishment." In other words, it has been *gained through practice*.

20. **C** The author is stressing that you can be sure or *confident* of the truth of what he says.

21. **D** The "sightless monster" is the "stupid wind" that tries to drive the jackdaws toward the east. Note how the author personifies the wind, writing as if the wind had some degree of human intelligence and responsiveness.

22. **E** The concluding sentence of the passage celebrates the birds' "Sovereign control over the power of the elements," in other words, their *mastery of the forces of nature*. Though Choice B may seem tempting, you can rule it out: Lorenz emphasizes the storm's strength ("the pitiless strength of the inorganic"), not the strength of the birds. Choices A, C, and D are unsupported by the passage.

23. **B** The author uses several metaphors ("close-reefed sails," "the teeth of the gale," etc.) and clarifies what he means by the term game. He describes the jackdaws' behavior in detail and dismisses the notion that their behavior is purely instinctive. However, he never *argues a cause*.

24. **B** Always substitute the answer choices in the original sentence. The writers' emergence stemmed or *arose* from their willingness to take the opportunity to write about black lives.

25. D The concluding sentence of paragraph 2 states two major factors that produced the crop of black writers who made up the Harlem Renaissance. The following two paragraphs continue the discussion of these social and political factors. Choice A is incorrect. The opening sentence indicates that the willingness of black writers to portray their own lives was a factor in the Harlem Renaissance. Yet the next sentence makes it clear that this willingness was only part of what was going on. Choice B is incorrect. The author is concerned with these writers as part of an American literary movement, not a worldwide crusade. Choice C is incorrect. The author cites examples of specific injustices in passing. Choice E is incorrect. It is unsupported by the passage.

26. E The author's use of such terms as "nobility of expression" and "great masters of recent American literature" make it clear his attitude is one of *admiration*.

27. B The author casts a positive light on the writers' acceptance of their separateness, emphasizing that the sufferings of blacks "had drawn them closer together" and had given them a vision of their mission as a people.

28. C Again, substitute the answer choices in the original context. By embracing a doctrine, you adopt or *espouse* that doctrine: you come to believe in it, and defend its teachings.

29. C The writers were more involved with fighting problems in the system than with attacking the system itself. This suggests that fundamentally they *were not opposed* to the democratic system of government. Choice A is incorrect. The fact that the writers did not revolt against the system does not imply that they played only a minor part in fighting abuses of the system. Choices B, D, and E are incorrect. None is suggested by the statement.

30. E The passage discusses the growing interest of American literary circles in the social and economic problems of the country, the effects of the First World War, and the impact of the liberal and radical political movements of the period on whites and blacks alike. Choice A is unanswerable on the basis of the passage. If anything, the passage indicates that black writers did not abandon the accepted literary forms of the day. Choice B is unanswerable on the basis of the passage, which mentions no specific names. Choice C is unanswerable on the basis of the passage. While the passage indicates black writers may have been influenced by foreign ideological systems, it nowhere suggests that the writers were *in rebellion against* these systems. Choice D is unanswerable on the basis of the passage. No such information is supplied.

Mathematical Reasoning Section 2

1. C As x increases in value, the denominator $(x + 1)$ also increases and the value of the fraction $\frac{1}{x+1}$ decreases. The values of expressions I and II will both increase as the value of x increases.

2. D (A) $\frac{1}{5} = 0.2$ (B) $\left(\frac{1}{5}\right)^2 = \frac{1}{25} = 0.04$ (C) 0.3
(D) $\sqrt{0.16} = 0.4$
(E) $0.01\pi = 0.01(3.14) = 0.0314$

3. B In both (A) $(0.25)2 = \left(\frac{1}{4}\right)^2$ and C $\left(\frac{1}{4}\right)^4$, raising to a power makes the fraction smaller.
(B) $\sqrt{\frac{1}{4}} = \frac{1}{2}$ and $\frac{1}{2} > \frac{1}{4}$. (D) $0.04 = \frac{4}{100}$ and
(E) $\frac{1}{250}$ are both very small.

4. E Dividing each term of the second equation by 2 makes it $x + 3y = 9$, and therefore the two equations are equivalent. Any point that lies on one must lie on the other; their graphs are identical. Thus, it is necessary to test each point by substituting in only one of the two equations to see whether it is satisfied. Point (3,4) does not check: $3 + 3(4) \neq 9$.

5. E If $ab^2c^3 > 0$, then $(ac)(b^2c^2) > 0$. Because b^2c^2 is always positive, the factor (ac) must be positive in order that the product $(ac)(b^2c^2)$ is positive.

6. A Outside radius = 0.775 inch
Inside radius = 0.625 inch
Difference = 0.15

7. A $4x = 3y$; subtract $3y$, and then $4x - 3y = 0$.

8. C \$8 must equal the remaining $\frac{2}{10}$ of the price. Therefore $\frac{1}{10}$ is \$4, and $\frac{10}{10}$, the whole price, is \$40.

9. D $x + \frac{1}{2} + x - \frac{1}{2} = 5$
$\qquad\qquad 2x = 5$

10. B $\dfrac{\text{molasses}}{\text{molasses} + \text{sugar}} = \dfrac{2}{2+3} = \dfrac{2}{5}$

11. E 20% of 20 or $\frac{1}{5} \cdot 20 = 4$
$\% = \frac{?}{100}$
$\frac{?}{100} \cdot 2 = 4$
$\frac{(2)(?)}{100} = 4;$ $(2)(?) = 400;$ $? = 200$

12. A Winning candidate got $\frac{3}{5}$ of the votes.
One loser received $\frac{1}{4}$ of $\frac{2}{5}$ or $\frac{1}{10}$.
Since the other loser received $\frac{3}{4}$ of $\frac{2}{5}$, he must have received more votes than the one who received $\frac{1}{10}$ of the votes.

13. **D**   Let x = height of water in tank.
Volume of water in first tank = (18")(6")(8").
This volume is the same for the second tank = (36")(18")(x).

$$\overset{3}{\underset{}{}}$$
$$\overset{6}{(36)}(18)(x) = (18")(\overset{4}{6"})(8")$$
$$3x = 4$$
$$x = 1\tfrac{1}{3} \text{ inches}$$

14. **C**
$$r = \frac{rs}{1-s}$$
$$r - rs = rs$$
$$r = 2rs$$
$$\frac{r}{2r} = s$$
$$\frac{1}{2} = s$$

Substitute in $s^2 + 2s + 1$:
$$\left(\tfrac{1}{2}\right)^2 + (2)\left(\tfrac{1}{2}\right) + 1$$
$$\tfrac{1}{4} + 1 + 1 = 2\tfrac{1}{4}$$

15. **B**   Let x = radius of circle.
$OA = OB$ = radius
$$\frac{(OA)(OB)}{2} = \frac{\text{area of}}{\text{triangle}} = \frac{7}{\pi}$$
$$\frac{(x)(x)}{2} = \frac{7}{\pi}$$
$$\frac{x^2}{2} = \frac{7}{\pi}$$
$$\pi x^2 = 14 \ [\text{area of circle} = (\pi)(\text{radius})^2\ ]$$

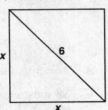

16. **B**   Let x = side of square
$$x^2 + x^2 = 36$$
[Pythagorean Theorem]
$$2x^2 = 36$$
$$x^2 = 18$$
(area of square)

17. **E**
$$2x + (3x - 10)^\circ + (3x + 30)^\circ = 180^\circ$$
$$2x + 3x - 10^\circ + 3x + 30^\circ = 180^\circ$$
$$8x = 160^\circ$$
$$x = 20^\circ$$

Therefore one angle = $2x$ or 40°
A second angle = $60^\circ - 10^\circ$ or 50°
The third angle is a right angle, since $60^\circ + 30^\circ = 90^\circ$.

18. **E**   The base of $\triangle ABC$ is 6 units. The altitude must be 4 units to attain an area of 12. All choice have altitudes of 4.

19. **A** $16\tfrac{2}{3}\%$ or $\tfrac{1}{6}$ of 300 = 50

10% or $\tfrac{1}{10}$ of 500 = 50

Total number going to college = 100

$$\frac{100}{800} = \frac{1}{8} = 12\tfrac{1}{2}\% \text{ or } 12.5\%$$

20. **D** $\triangle BAC$ is a 3-4-5 right triangle with $AC = 3(3)$ and hypotenuse $BC = 3(5)$; therefore $AB = 3(4)$ or 12.
$\triangle ABD$ is a 5-12-13 right triangle; therefore $AD = 13$.

21. **B**   Because $4^x = 8^y$, $(2^2)^x = (2^3)^y$ or $2^{2x} = 2^{3y}$.
Thus, $2x = 3y$ and $\dfrac{x}{y} = \dfrac{3}{2}$.

22. **C**   A reading of 48 corresponds to 80 amperes. Let a reading of 60 correspond to x amperes.
$$\frac{48}{80} = \frac{60}{x}$$
$$48x = 4800$$
$$x = 100$$

23. **A** $\dfrac{A}{B} = \dfrac{5"}{11"} = \dfrac{x \text{ meters}}{5 \text{ meters}}$
$$11x = 25$$
$$x = 2\tfrac{3}{11}$$

24. **C** $(a - b)^2 = a^2 - 2ab + b^2$
Substitute: $100 - 2(50) + 25$
$$100 - 100 + 25 = 25$$

25. **C**   If 0.6 ounce costs $18
$$\frac{0.6}{1.0} = \frac{\$18}{x}; \ 0.6x = 18; \ 6x = 180; \ x = \$30.$$

Since 1 ounce costs $30 and the price in the larger bottle is $25 per ounce, the difference per ounce is $5.

Writing Skills Section 3

1. **A**   Error in diction. Change *Being that* to *Since*.
2. **B**   Error in agreement between subject and verb. Change *have control* to *has control*.
3. **C**   Double negative. Change *can't* to *can*.
4. **B**   Error in case. *But,* as used in this sentence, is a preposition meaning *except*. Change *he* to *him*.
5. **D**   Change *reason . . . is because* to *reason . . . is that*.
6. **B**   Error in tense. Change *am playing* to *have been playing*.
7. **B**   Error in diction. Change *affective* to *effective*.
8. **B**   Error in diction. *Among* should be used when three or more items are being considered.
9. **B**   Error in diction. Change *bring* to *take*.
10. **D**   Lack of parallel structure. Change *as well as signing* to *and sign* in order to match the other items in the list.
11. **C**   Incorrect sentence connector. Change *furthermore* to the coordinating conjunction *but* to clarify the relationship between the clauses.
12. **D**   Error in diction. Change *accumulation from* to *accumulation of*.
13. **E**   Sentence is correct.
14. **A**   Error in diction. *Altogether* is correct.
15. **B**   Error in tense. Change *had wanted* to *wanted*.
16. **E**   Sentence is correct.

17. **E** Sentence is correct.

18. **B** Error in diction. Change *differ with* (which relates to difference of opinion) to *differ from* (which relates to difference in appearance).

19. **C** Lack of parallel structure. Change *remaining at* to the infinitive *to remain at* in order to match *to travel on.*

20. **C** Choice C uses *drank,* the correct form of the irregular verb *drink.*

21. **A** Sentence is correct as written.

22. **B** *Seems satisfying their need* is unidiomatic. *Seems to satisfy their need* is correct (Choice B).

23. **C** Choice C corrects the error in conjuction use.

24. **D** *Irregardless* is a nonstandard use of *regardless.*

25. **B** The run-on sentence is corrected in Choice B.

26. **D** The phrase *along with several other stories* is not part of the subject of the sentence. The subject is *"Araby"* (singular); the verb should be *is going to be read* (singular).

27. **A** Choice B introduces an error in agreement. Choices C, D, and E misuse the *not only . . . but also* construction.

28. **E** The dangling modifier is corrected in Choice E.

29. **B** The dangling construction is corrected in Choices B and E. However, only Choice B retains the meaning of the original sentence.

30. **B** The error in case is corrected in Choice B. *Whoever* is the subject of the verb *had contributed.*

31. **E** In this question we find two errors. Both the sentence fragment and the misuse of the intransitive verb *lie* are corrected in Choice E.

32. **D** The faulty comparison is corrected in Choice D.

33. **A** The original sentence is correct. The subject of *are going* is *legislators* (plural). Therefore, Choices B and C are incorrect. Choices D and E change the meaning of the original sentence.

34. **A** Choice A accurately describes the content of the essay. The original introductory sentence is misleading. The essay is about changes in the status of women, not about the role women played in causing the changes. It is the best answer.
Choice B is a variation of the original introductory sentence but the use of the future verb tense fails to convey the actual content of the essay.
Choice C is a confusing sentence consisting of two illogically unrelated clauses.
Choice D fails to convey the contents of the essay. It also contains the pronoun *their,* which does not have a clear antecedent.
Choice E is virtually meaningless. It also contains a dangling participle. The phrase that begins *Being influenced . . .* should modify *women,* not *status.*

35. **D** Choice A inserts a comma splice between *lifted* and *for example.* Two independent clauses should be separated by a period or semicolon.

Choice B contains the pronoun *they,* which lacks a specific referent.
Choice C improperly shifts pronouns from third person to second person.
Choice D is effectively expressed. It is the best answer.
Choice E is cumbersome and awkwardly worded. The phrase *the right of going into public* contains an idiom error. The correct phrase is *right to go into public.*

36. **B** Choice A contains faulty diction. Doctors and lawyers are not professions; they are professionals working in the fields of medicine and law.
Choice B properly revises the phrase in question. It is the best answer.
Choice C contains faulty parallelism. Words in a series should be grammatical equivalents. *Doctors* and *lawyers* are people, not jobs.
Choice D, like Choice C, contains faulty parallellism. *Doctors* and *lawyers* are people, not positions.
Choice E contains faulty idiom. The standard usage is *"in" other professional capacities.*

37. **A** Choice A provides a smooth transition by alluding to the discussion of competition in the second paragraph and introducing the main topic of the third. A is the best answer.
Choice B uses a nonstandard transitional word *irregardless,* which in the context makes no sense.
Choice C contains no specifically transitional material.
Choice D would be a decent transition were it not for its mixed construction. The first half of the sentence doesn't fit grammatically with the second half.
Choice E introduces a new idea that is unrelated to the content of the third paragraph.

38. **E** Choice A is illogical; becoming a role model is not an example of attaining a high position in politics and government.
Choice B is not a good example of attaining a high position in politics.
Choice C is irrelevant. Margaret Thatcher's defeat is not an example of an achievement inpolitics and government.
Choice D is slightly off the mark. The sentence emphasizes Indira Ghandi's assassination instead of her leadership.
Choice E gives two examples of women who have attained a high positon in politics and government. It is the best answer.

39. **E** All the sentences except sentence 14 support the idea stated in the topic sentence, that women have made gains in politics and government. Therefore, Choice E is the best answer.

Verbal Reasoning Section 4

31. **D** The playing field in *football* is called the *grid-iron*. The playing field in *baseball* is called the *diamond*.   (Defining Characteristic)

32. **B** Without *water* plants *wilt*. Without *food* animals *starve*.   (Cause and Effect)

33. **D** A *gosling* is a baby *goose*. A *kid* is a baby *goat*.   (Age)

34. **B** A *lobster* is a member of the *crustacean* class. A *kangaroo* is a member of the *marsupial* class.   (Class and Member)

35. **C** Something that is *simple* lacks *elaboration* or complex detail. Something that is *thrifty* lacks *extravagance* or excessive expense.   (Antonym Variant)

36. **C** When a *storm* ends and the weather becomes calm and quiet—that is, normal—again, the storm is said to *subside*. When a muscle which has tightened in *spasm* goes back to its normal state, it is said to *relax*.   (Function)

37. **A** *Delirium* causes *disorientation* or confusion. *Paralysis* causes *immobility* or loss of movement.   (Cause and Effect)

38. **B** To *scurry* is to *move* in a brisk and rapid manner. To *chatter* is to *talk* in a brisk and rapid manner.   (Manner)

39. **B** A measure of *wood* is a *cord*. A measure of *cloth* is a *bolt*.   (Defining Characteristic)

40. **B** A *eulogy* is a *laudatory* speech, full of praise. A *tirade* is an *abusive* speech, full of condemnation.   (Defining Characteristic)

41. **E** Someone who is *obdurate* (unyielding, inflexible) is lacking in *flexibility*. Someone who is *adamant* (unshakable in opposition) is lacking in *submissiveness*.   (Antonym Variant)

42. **E** A *reprobate* (corrupt person) is by definition *blameworthy*. A *traducer* (someone who willfully maligns or misrepresents another's conduct) is by definition *slanderous* (full of falsehood).   (Defining Characteristic)

43. **A** A *feud* or war of revenge is a fight characterized by *acrimony* or bitterness. A *scuffle* or haphazard struggle is a fight characterized by *confusion*.   (Defining Characteristic)

44. **D** Tapestry weaving is time-consuming, taking "as much as a year to produce a yard." In addition, it is faithful to the original ("The weaver always follows a preexisting model.") It is not, however, spontaneous in concept.

45. **A** The author mentions tapestry's distinctive or *characteristic* weave as something that distinguishes tapestry-woven materials from other fabrics (prints, brocades, etc.).

46. **B** By using tapestries "to display his wealth and social position," the nobleman is using them to demonstrate his *consequence* or importance.

47. **D** The "ground" upon which embroidery is laid is the cloth *base* upon which the embroiderer stitches a design.

48. **D** In comparison to the tightly-woven tapestries of the nineteenth century, present day wall-hangings are described as "coarsely woven cloths." Thus, they *have a less fine weave* than their predecessors.

49. **D** Although the passage explains the process of tapestry-making and mentions that large wall-hangings are Western rather than Eastern in origin, Choices A and B do not reflect the passage's primary purpose. This purpose is to *provide a historical perspective on tapestry-making*.

50. **E** In candidly exposing her grandmother's flaws, the author exhibits a *sardonic* or scornful and sarcastic attitude.

51. **D** McCarthy sees as little point in speculating about her grandmother's childhood as she does in wondering about the toilet-training of a fictional character like Lady Macbeth. Such speculations are, to McCarthy's mind, idle or *useless*.

52. **B** The author states (somewhat ironically) that modern fictional characters must have "clinical authenticity." In other words, they must appear to be genuine or *valid* in *psychological* terms.

53. **B** Although the grandmother's outward appearance was soft and motherly, her essential nature was hard as nails. Clearly, you cannot judge a book (person) by its cover (outward appearance).

54. **D** McCarthy is building up a portrait of her grandmother as a pugnacious, autocratic person. She describes the fear old ladies have for their belongings as a very human (and understandable) reaction: aware of their own increasing fragility (and eventual death), the old ladies identify with their fragile possessions and are protective of them. McCarthy's grandmother was also protective of her belongings, but she was not the typical "gentle and tremulous" elderly woman. She was a petty tyrant and had decidedly *different reasons for her actions*.

55. **B** Because her grandmother was more interested in maintaining her power than in being hospitable, the social properties or *aspects* of the family home had withered and decayed until no real sociability existed.

56. **D** Heilbrun's central criticism is that her grandmother "impaired her six daughters for autonomy" or independence. In other words, *she discouraged her daughters' independence*.

57. **B** Heilbrun realizes that people nowadays may have difficulty understanding what motivated her grandmother to control her daughters' lives and restrict their autonomy so thoroughly. By describing how great the horror of pregnancy in an unmarried girl was, she helps the reader understand *why her grandmother* acted as she did.

58. **A** By dwelling on how hard she had worked to support her daughters and how much she would be hurt if they failed to pay her back by making good marriages, Heilbrun's grandmother exploited their *sense of guilt.*

59. **A** The common factor in both grandmothers' lives is their need to *govern the actions of others.* McCarthy's grandmother tyrannized everyone from the mailman to her daughters and daughters-in-law; Heilbrun's grandmother "ruled the household with an arm of iron," governing her daughters' lives.

60. **D** While Heilbrun's grandmother was a "sustaining woman" who provided for her family, McCarthy's grandmother was a grudging woman, not a sustaining one. Thus, McCarthy would most likely point out that *her grandmother's actual conduct is not in keeping with this characterization.*

Mathematical Reasoning Section 5

26. **D** The value of x may be zero, positive, or negative.

27. **C** Since the sum of the consecutive integers $a + b + c = 18$, then $a = 5$, $b = 6$, and $c = 7$.
    $\therefore (a)(b)(c) = (5)(6)(7) = 210$.

28. **C** $\dfrac{a(x + y)}{b} = \dfrac{a(1 - 1)}{b} = \dfrac{a(0)}{b} = 0$

    $\dfrac{2a(x + y)}{b} = \dfrac{2a(1 - 1)}{b} = \dfrac{2a(0)}{b} = 0$

29. **C** Multiply $\dfrac{-a}{y + z}$ by $\dfrac{-1}{-1} = \dfrac{a}{-y - z}$

    $\therefore \dfrac{x}{-y - z} = \dfrac{a}{-y - z}$

    $\therefore x = a$

30. **C** $3x + 5y = 15 + 5y$
    $\quad\ \ 3x = 15$
    $\quad\ \ \ x = 5$
    $\quad\ \ \dfrac{x}{5} = 1$

31. **B** 1 hour and 20 minutes or $1\frac{1}{3}$ hours elapse from 8:55 A.M. to 10:15 A.M.

32. **D** Z could be anywhere on circumference of circle with radius = 4. X could be anywhere on circumference of circle with radius = 3.

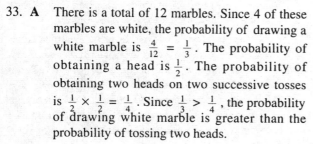

33. **A** There is a total of 12 marbles. Since 4 of these marbles are white, the probability of drawing a white marble is $\frac{4}{12} = \frac{1}{3}$. The probability of obtaining a head is $\frac{1}{2}$. The probability of obtaining two heads on two successive tosses is $\frac{1}{2} \times \frac{1}{2} = \frac{1}{4}$. Since $\frac{1}{3} > \frac{1}{4}$, the probability of drawing white marble is greater than the probability of tossing two heads.

34. **B** Since $x = 100$, $m = 180 - 100$ or 80.
    $y + m = 40 + 80$ or 120
    $z = y + m$ (exterior angle of $\triangle$)
    $z = 40 + 80$
    $z = 120$
    $x + y = 140$

35. **C** Since the base angles are equal, $AB = AC$.
    $\therefore \dfrac{BC}{AB} \cdot \dfrac{AC}{BC} = 1$

36. **C** $\triangle$s XDC and YDC share the base DC. Since $ABCD$ is a rectangle, XDC and YDC have equal altitudes. Therefore XDC and YDC are equal in area. Subtracting the area of DOC from both XDC and YDC gives YOC equal in area to XOD.

37. **A** $y = 180 - (50 + 60)$ or 70
    Or, $x = 50 + 60$, since the exterior angle of a triangle equals the sum of both remote interior (nonadjacent) angles.

38. **C** The product of any number and its reciprocal is 1. Both products are therefore 1.

39. **D** If $x = 1$, $3x = 1$ and $(-2)x = -2$
    If $x = -1$, $3x = -3$ and $(-2)(x) = +2$

40. **D** Since the width of the rectangle is not given, its area cannot be determined.

41. **75** $(30)(25\cent) = 750$ cents or 75 dimes

42. **60** Time = 20 minutes or $\frac{1}{3}$ hour
    $\dfrac{\text{distance}}{\text{time}} = \text{rate}$
    $\dfrac{20}{\frac{1}{3}} = 60$ miles per hour

43. **4** Let diameter = d.
    Then radius = $\dfrac{d}{2}$
    Area = $\dfrac{\pi d^2}{4}$
    If diameter is doubled, diameter = $2d$, then
    radius = $\dfrac{2d}{2} = d$.
    Area = πd^2, which is four times $\dfrac{\pi d^2}{4}$

44. **80** $\angle B \overset{\circ}{=} \frac{1}{2}(\overset{\frown}{DA} - \overset{\frown}{CA})$
    $70° = \frac{1}{2}(\overset{\frown}{DA} - 70°)$
    $140° = \overset{\frown}{DA} - 70°$
    $210° = \overset{\frown}{DA}$
    $\overset{\frown}{DA} + \overset{\frown}{CA} + \overset{\frown}{DC} = 360°$
    $210° + 70° + \overset{\frown}{DC} = 360°$
    $\overset{\frown}{DC} = 360° - 280°$
    $\overset{\frown}{DC} = 80°$

45. **9** $\angle ACB = \angle DCE$ (vertical angles)

The two right triangles are similar. The corresponding sides are proportional.

$$\frac{CD}{BC} = \frac{DE}{AB}$$

$$\frac{16}{12} = \frac{12}{x}$$

$$16x = 144$$
$$x = 9$$

46. $\frac{1}{10}$ **or 0.1** $\dfrac{0.3}{9} + \dfrac{0.6}{9} = \dfrac{0.9}{9} = \dfrac{9}{90} = \dfrac{1}{10}$

47. **360** 12 minutes = $\frac{1}{5}$ hour.

Let x = number of envelopes to be prepared in 8 hours.

$$\frac{9 \text{ envelopes}}{\frac{1}{5} \text{ hour}} = \frac{x}{8 \text{ hrs.}}$$

$$\frac{1}{5}x = 72$$
$$x = (72)(5) = 360$$

48. **2** Because $(2)(2)(2)(2) = 16$, then $x + 2 = 4$ and $x = 2$.

49. **525** If 1 inch = 150 miles, then $3\frac{1}{2}$ inches = $(3\frac{1}{2})(150)$ or 525 miles.

50. **10** Let x = number of blue marbles.

$P(\text{not green}) = P(\text{red or blue}) =$

$$\frac{4 + x}{4 + 7 + x} = \frac{2}{3}$$

$$3(4 + x) = 2(11 + x)$$
$$3x + 12 = 2x + 22$$
$$x = 10$$

The jar contains 10 blue marbles.

Answer Sheet
TYPICAL TEST B

Each mark should completely fill the appropriate space, and should be as dark as all other marks. Make all erasures complete. Traces of an erasure may be read as an answer. See pages vii and 27 for explanations of timing and number of questions.

Section 1 — Verbal
30 minutes

1 Ⓐ Ⓑ Ⓒ Ⓓ Ⓔ
2 Ⓐ Ⓑ Ⓒ Ⓓ Ⓔ
3 Ⓐ Ⓑ Ⓒ Ⓓ Ⓔ
4 Ⓐ Ⓑ Ⓒ Ⓓ Ⓔ
5 Ⓐ Ⓑ Ⓒ Ⓓ Ⓔ
6 Ⓐ Ⓑ Ⓒ Ⓓ Ⓔ
7 Ⓐ Ⓑ Ⓒ Ⓓ Ⓔ
8 Ⓐ Ⓑ Ⓒ Ⓓ Ⓔ
9 Ⓐ Ⓑ Ⓒ Ⓓ Ⓔ
10 Ⓐ Ⓑ Ⓒ Ⓓ Ⓔ
11 Ⓐ Ⓑ Ⓒ Ⓓ Ⓔ
12 Ⓐ Ⓑ Ⓒ Ⓓ Ⓔ
13 Ⓐ Ⓑ Ⓒ Ⓓ Ⓔ
14 Ⓐ Ⓑ Ⓒ Ⓓ Ⓔ
15 Ⓐ Ⓑ Ⓒ Ⓓ Ⓔ
16 Ⓐ Ⓑ Ⓒ Ⓓ Ⓔ
17 Ⓐ Ⓑ Ⓒ Ⓓ Ⓔ
18 Ⓐ Ⓑ Ⓒ Ⓓ Ⓔ
19 Ⓐ Ⓑ Ⓒ Ⓓ Ⓔ
20 Ⓐ Ⓑ Ⓒ Ⓓ Ⓔ
21 Ⓐ Ⓑ Ⓒ Ⓓ Ⓔ
22 Ⓐ Ⓑ Ⓒ Ⓓ Ⓔ
23 Ⓐ Ⓑ Ⓒ Ⓓ Ⓔ
24 Ⓐ Ⓑ Ⓒ Ⓓ Ⓔ
25 Ⓐ Ⓑ Ⓒ Ⓓ Ⓔ
26 Ⓐ Ⓑ Ⓒ Ⓓ Ⓔ
27 Ⓐ Ⓑ Ⓒ Ⓓ Ⓔ
28 Ⓐ Ⓑ Ⓒ Ⓓ Ⓔ
29 Ⓐ Ⓑ Ⓒ Ⓓ Ⓔ
30 Ⓐ Ⓑ Ⓒ Ⓓ Ⓔ

Section 2 — Math
30 minutes

1 Ⓐ Ⓑ Ⓒ Ⓓ Ⓔ
2 Ⓐ Ⓑ Ⓒ Ⓓ Ⓔ
3 Ⓐ Ⓑ Ⓒ Ⓓ Ⓔ
4 Ⓐ Ⓑ Ⓒ Ⓓ Ⓔ
5 Ⓐ Ⓑ Ⓒ Ⓓ Ⓔ
6 Ⓐ Ⓑ Ⓒ Ⓓ Ⓔ
7 Ⓐ Ⓑ Ⓒ Ⓓ Ⓔ
8 Ⓐ Ⓑ Ⓒ Ⓓ Ⓔ
9 Ⓐ Ⓑ Ⓒ Ⓓ Ⓔ
10 Ⓐ Ⓑ Ⓒ Ⓓ Ⓔ
11 Ⓐ Ⓑ Ⓒ Ⓓ Ⓔ
12 Ⓐ Ⓑ Ⓒ Ⓓ Ⓔ
13 Ⓐ Ⓑ Ⓒ Ⓓ Ⓔ
14 Ⓐ Ⓑ Ⓒ Ⓓ Ⓔ
15 Ⓐ Ⓑ Ⓒ Ⓓ Ⓔ
16 Ⓐ Ⓑ Ⓒ Ⓓ Ⓔ
17 Ⓐ Ⓑ Ⓒ Ⓓ Ⓔ
18 Ⓐ Ⓑ Ⓒ Ⓓ Ⓔ
19 Ⓐ Ⓑ Ⓒ Ⓓ Ⓔ
20 Ⓐ Ⓑ Ⓒ Ⓓ Ⓔ
21 Ⓐ Ⓑ Ⓒ Ⓓ Ⓔ
22 Ⓐ Ⓑ Ⓒ Ⓓ Ⓔ
23 Ⓐ Ⓑ Ⓒ Ⓓ Ⓔ
24 Ⓐ Ⓑ Ⓒ Ⓓ Ⓔ
25 Ⓐ Ⓑ Ⓒ Ⓓ Ⓔ

Section 3 — Writing
30 minutes

1 Ⓐ Ⓑ Ⓒ Ⓓ Ⓔ
2 Ⓐ Ⓑ Ⓒ Ⓓ Ⓔ
3 Ⓐ Ⓑ Ⓒ Ⓓ Ⓔ
4 Ⓐ Ⓑ Ⓒ Ⓓ Ⓔ
5 Ⓐ Ⓑ Ⓒ Ⓓ Ⓔ
6 Ⓐ Ⓑ Ⓒ Ⓓ Ⓔ
7 Ⓐ Ⓑ Ⓒ Ⓓ Ⓔ
8 Ⓐ Ⓑ Ⓒ Ⓓ Ⓔ
9 Ⓐ Ⓑ Ⓒ Ⓓ Ⓔ
10 Ⓐ Ⓑ Ⓒ Ⓓ Ⓔ
11 Ⓐ Ⓑ Ⓒ Ⓓ Ⓔ
12 Ⓐ Ⓑ Ⓒ Ⓓ Ⓔ
13 Ⓐ Ⓑ Ⓒ Ⓓ Ⓔ
14 Ⓐ Ⓑ Ⓒ Ⓓ Ⓔ
15 Ⓐ Ⓑ Ⓒ Ⓓ Ⓔ
16 Ⓐ Ⓑ Ⓒ Ⓓ Ⓔ
17 Ⓐ Ⓑ Ⓒ Ⓓ Ⓔ
18 Ⓐ Ⓑ Ⓒ Ⓓ Ⓔ
19 Ⓐ Ⓑ Ⓒ Ⓓ Ⓔ
20 Ⓐ Ⓑ Ⓒ Ⓓ Ⓔ
21 Ⓐ Ⓑ Ⓒ Ⓓ Ⓔ
22 Ⓐ Ⓑ Ⓒ Ⓓ Ⓔ
23 Ⓐ Ⓑ Ⓒ Ⓓ Ⓔ
24 Ⓐ Ⓑ Ⓒ Ⓓ Ⓔ
25 Ⓐ Ⓑ Ⓒ Ⓓ Ⓔ
26 Ⓐ Ⓑ Ⓒ Ⓓ Ⓔ
27 Ⓐ Ⓑ Ⓒ Ⓓ Ⓔ
28 Ⓐ Ⓑ Ⓒ Ⓓ Ⓔ
29 Ⓐ Ⓑ Ⓒ Ⓓ Ⓔ
30 Ⓐ Ⓑ Ⓒ Ⓓ Ⓔ
31 Ⓐ Ⓑ Ⓒ Ⓓ Ⓔ
32 Ⓐ Ⓑ Ⓒ Ⓓ Ⓔ
33 Ⓐ Ⓑ Ⓒ Ⓓ Ⓔ
34 Ⓐ Ⓑ Ⓒ Ⓓ Ⓔ
35 Ⓐ Ⓑ Ⓒ Ⓓ Ⓔ
36 Ⓐ Ⓑ Ⓒ Ⓓ Ⓔ
37 Ⓐ Ⓑ Ⓒ Ⓓ Ⓔ
38 Ⓐ Ⓑ Ⓒ Ⓓ Ⓔ
39 Ⓐ Ⓑ Ⓒ Ⓓ Ⓔ

Section 4 — Verbal
30 minutes

31 Ⓐ Ⓑ Ⓒ Ⓓ Ⓔ
32 Ⓐ Ⓑ Ⓒ Ⓓ Ⓔ
33 Ⓐ Ⓑ Ⓒ Ⓓ Ⓔ
34 Ⓐ Ⓑ Ⓒ Ⓓ Ⓔ
35 Ⓐ Ⓑ Ⓒ Ⓓ Ⓔ
36 Ⓐ Ⓑ Ⓒ Ⓓ Ⓔ
37 Ⓐ Ⓑ Ⓒ Ⓓ Ⓔ
38 Ⓐ Ⓑ Ⓒ Ⓓ Ⓔ
39 Ⓐ Ⓑ Ⓒ Ⓓ Ⓔ
40 Ⓐ Ⓑ Ⓒ Ⓓ Ⓔ
41 Ⓐ Ⓑ Ⓒ Ⓓ Ⓔ
42 Ⓐ Ⓑ Ⓒ Ⓓ Ⓔ
43 Ⓐ Ⓑ Ⓒ Ⓓ Ⓔ
44 Ⓐ Ⓑ Ⓒ Ⓓ Ⓔ
45 Ⓐ Ⓑ Ⓒ Ⓓ Ⓔ
46 Ⓐ Ⓑ Ⓒ Ⓓ Ⓔ
47 Ⓐ Ⓑ Ⓒ Ⓓ Ⓔ
48 Ⓐ Ⓑ Ⓒ Ⓓ Ⓔ
49 Ⓐ Ⓑ Ⓒ Ⓓ Ⓔ
50 Ⓐ Ⓑ Ⓒ Ⓓ Ⓔ
51 Ⓐ Ⓑ Ⓒ Ⓓ Ⓔ
52 Ⓐ Ⓑ Ⓒ Ⓓ Ⓔ
53 Ⓐ Ⓑ Ⓒ Ⓓ Ⓔ
54 Ⓐ Ⓑ Ⓒ Ⓓ Ⓔ
55 Ⓐ Ⓑ Ⓒ Ⓓ Ⓔ
56 Ⓐ Ⓑ Ⓒ Ⓓ Ⓔ
57 Ⓐ Ⓑ Ⓒ Ⓓ Ⓔ
58 Ⓐ Ⓑ Ⓒ Ⓓ Ⓔ
59 Ⓐ Ⓑ Ⓒ Ⓓ Ⓔ
60 Ⓐ Ⓑ Ⓒ Ⓓ Ⓔ

Section 5 — Math
30 minutes

26 Ⓐ Ⓑ Ⓒ Ⓓ Ⓔ
27 Ⓐ Ⓑ Ⓒ Ⓓ Ⓔ
28 Ⓐ Ⓑ Ⓒ Ⓓ Ⓔ
29 Ⓐ Ⓑ Ⓒ Ⓓ Ⓔ
30 Ⓐ Ⓑ Ⓒ Ⓓ Ⓔ
31 Ⓐ Ⓑ Ⓒ Ⓓ Ⓔ
32 Ⓐ Ⓑ Ⓒ Ⓓ Ⓔ
33 Ⓐ Ⓑ Ⓒ Ⓓ Ⓔ
34 Ⓐ Ⓑ Ⓒ Ⓓ Ⓔ
35 Ⓐ Ⓑ Ⓒ Ⓓ Ⓔ
36 Ⓐ Ⓑ Ⓒ Ⓓ Ⓔ
37 Ⓐ Ⓑ Ⓒ Ⓓ Ⓔ
39 Ⓐ Ⓑ Ⓒ Ⓓ Ⓔ
39 Ⓐ Ⓑ Ⓒ Ⓓ Ⓔ
40 Ⓐ Ⓑ Ⓒ Ⓓ Ⓔ

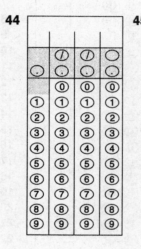

41 42 43 44 45

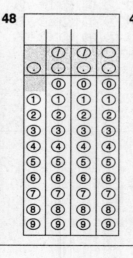

46 47 48 49 50

SECTION 1
Verbal Reasoning

Time—30 minutes
30 Questions

For each question in this section, select the best answer from among the choices given and fill in the corresponding oval on the answer sheet.

Directions

Each sentence below has one or two blanks, each blank indicating that something has been omitted. Beneath the sentence are five words or sets of words labeled A through E. Choose the word or set of words that, when inserted in the sentence, best fits the meaning of the sentence as a whole.

Example:

Medieval kingdoms did not become constitutional republics overnight; on the contrary, the change was ____ .

(A) unpopular
(B) unexpected
(C) advantageous
(D) sufficient
(E) gradual   Ⓐ Ⓑ Ⓒ Ⓓ ●

1. Because of their frequent disarray, confusion, and loss of memory, people hit by lightning while alone are sometimes ____ victims of assault.

   (A) mistaken for   (B) attracted to   (C) unaware of
   (D) avoided by   (E) useful to

2. With very few antiviral drugs at their disposal, and with only a handful of vaccines, virologists know what ____ human suffering but are relatively ____ to prevent it.

   (A) lessens..innocuous   (B) causes..helpless
   (C) creates..determined   (D) increases..concerned
   (E) comprises..hopeful

3. Because the starting quarterback had been injured in the game, the team's joy at their victory was ____ .

   (A) muted   (B) uproarious   (C) arbitrary
   (D) unanimous   (E) enhanced

4. Ms. Sutcliffe's helpful notes on her latest wine discoveries and her no-nonsense warnings to consumers about ____ wines make the present book ____ guide to the numbing array of wines of Burgundy.

   (A) excellent..a useful
   (B) overrated..an inadequate
   (C) overpriced..a trusty
   (D) unsatisfactory..a spotty
   (E) vintage..an unreliable

5. The old man's rambling conversation was like a river: it ____ along, wandering from point to point, until it trickled to a stop.

   (A) strolled   (B) swerved   (C) marched
   (D) meandered   (E) mired

6. The developing brain can be likened to a highway system that ____ use: less traveled roads may be abandoned, popular roads broadened, and new ones added where they are needed.

   (A) suffers from   (B) evolves with
   (C) detours around   (D) atrophies with
   (E) buckles under

7. ____ rather than chronologically organized, the architecture text focuses on five areas: nature, geometry, site, color, and light.

   (A) Thematically   (B) Casually
   (C) Sequentially   (D) Alphabetically
   (E) Symmetrically

8. To judge from its ____ to Singer's later autobiography, the novel describes ____ occurrences in the author's life.

   (A) similarity..imaginary
   (B) unlikeness..minor
   (C) resemblance..actual
   (D) correspondence..fictitious
   (E) importance..negligible

9. This island is a colony; however, in most matters, it is ____ and receives no orders from the mother country.

   (A) submissive   (B) amorphous   (C) distant
   (D) autonomous   (E) aloof

10. Like the best ____ fiction, Mark Helprin's *Winter's Tale* is part dream, part mad invention, and all of it hauntingly beautiful.

    (A) satiric   (B) prosaic   (C) naturalistic
    (D) documentary   (E) fantastic

11. In today's world of personal copiers and fax machines, the old-fashioned mimeograph machine is definitely an ____ .

    (A) innovation   (B) anachronism
    (C) exaggeration   (D) automaton   (E) omission

12. In the face of family and national crises that would have undone a lesser woman, Eleanor Roosevelt ____ , maintaining an air of composure and ____ dignity.

    (A) fled..unseemly   (B) cowered..spurious
    (C) persevered..unruffled   (D) triumphed..false
    (E) collapsed..hard-won

GO ON TO THE NEXT PAGE ⇨

13. In Victorian times, countless Egyptian mummies were ground up to produce dried mummy powder, hailed by quacks as a near-magical ____ able to cure a wide variety of ailments.

    (A) toxin   (B) indisposition   (C) symptom
    (D) panacea   (E) placebo

14. The orator delivered a ____ speech that was ____ by the more sophisticated in the audience who were unswayed by the pompous language.

    (A) patriotic..cheered
    (B) bombastic..ridiculed
    (C) sententious..rejected
    (D) eulogistic..derided
    (E) pretentious..acclaimed

15. A firm believer in old-fashioned courtesy, Miss Post ____ the unfortunate modern tendency to address new acquaintances by their given names.

    (A) appreciated   (B) deprecated   (C) intimated
    (D) reciprocated   (E) precipitated

16. During the middle of the eighteenth century, the ____ style in furniture and architecture, marked by scroll work and excessive decoration, flourished.

    (A) austere   (B) functional   (C) rococo
    (D) medieval   (E) abstract

17. Rather than portraying Joseph II as a radical reformer whose reign was strikingly enlightened, the play *Amadeus* depicts him as ____ thinker, too wedded to orthodox theories of musical composition to appreciate an artist of Mozart's genius.

    (A) a revolutionary   (B) an idiosyncratic
    (C) a politic   (D) a doctrinaire   (E) a lucid

Directions

Each passage below is followed by questions based on its content. Answer the questions following each passage on the basis of what is stated or implied in that passage and in any introductory material that may be provided.

Questions 18–22 are based on the following passage.

The following passage is excerpted from an article on the immune system that appeared in a popular magazine in 1987.

An oft-used, but valuable, analogy compares the immune system with an army. The defending troops are the white blood cells called lympho-
Line   cytes, born in the bone marrow, billeted in the
5   lymph nodes and spleen, and on exercise in the blood and lymph systems. A body can muster some 200,000,000 cells, making the immune system comparable in mass to the liver or brain.

10   The lymphocytes are called to action when the enemy makes itself known. They attack anything foreign. Their job is to recognize the enemy for what it is, and then destroy it. One of the key features of the immune system is its specificity.
15   Inoculation with smallpox provokes an attack on any smallpox virus, but on nothing else. This specificity of response depends on the lymphocyte's ability to identify the enemy correctly by the molecules on its surface, called antigens.

20   An antigen is an enemy uniform. It can be a protein on the surface of a cold virus, or it can be a protein on the surface of a pollen grain, in which case the immune response takes the form of an allergy. An antigen can also be a protein on the surface of a transplanted organ, in which case the
25   immune response "rejects" the transplant. Organs can therefore be transplanted only between closely related people—in whom the antigens are the same—or into people treated with a drug that suppresses the immune system, such as cyclosporin.

30   In the 1940s, an Australian immunologist, Sir Frank Macfarlane Burnet, proposed a theory that helped explain how lymphocytes recognize and are activated by specific foreign antigens. The clonal selection theory, as it was called, suggested
35   that the innate immune system was not a homogeneous mass of more or less identical lymphocytes, but rather was made up of millions of different families called clones. The members of each clone carry on their surfaces a receptor that is capable of
40   identifying and binding to just one foreign antigen (or a part of it called the determinant).

Thus, when a foreign body carrying that antigen appears, the antigen binds to the receptor of only those lymphocyte clones which are capable
45   of recognizing it. Once the antigen binds to the receptor it stimulates the lymphocyte to divide, which generates more identical copies of itself. These clone members then attack the foreign entity that carries the antigen.

50   This implies that the immune system works on a "ready-made" basis. A person's immune system inherits the knowledge of all foreign antigens to which it might be exposed. The sum of this inheritance increases as new threats are met.

18. The author's primary purpose in the passage is to do which of the following?

    (A) Demonstrate the inadequacy of an analogy.
    (B) Advocate a method to strengthen the immune system.
    (C) Compare the immune system to the brain.
    (D) Clarify the workings of the body's defense system.
    (E) Correct an outmoded view of a bodily process.

GO ON TO THE NEXT PAGE

19. The word "mass" in line 8 means

(A) bulk   (B) function   (C) company
(D) lump   (E) stack

20. The author provides information to answer which of the following questions?

(A) What is the process by which antigens are produced?
(B) What is the mechanism by which cyclosporin suppresses the immune system?
(C) What is the process that prevents closely related persons from developing dissimilar antigens?
(D) How does inoculation with smallpox wear off over a period of years?
(E) Where do the body's lymphocytes originate?

21. It can be inferred from the passage that treatment with cyclosporin might result in which of the following?

I.   An increased susceptibility to invasion by disease
II. The rejection of a transplanted organ
III. An increased effectiveness of antigens

(A) I only   (B) II only   (C) I and II only
(D) I and III only   (E) I, II and III

22. In describing the immune system, the author does all of the following EXCEPT

(A) define a term
(B) illustrate through a comparison
(C) quote an authoritative source
(D) give an approximation
(E) develop an extended metaphor

Questions 23–30 are based on the following passage.

In this adaptation of an excerpt from a short story set in Civil War times, a man is about to be hanged. The first two paragraphs set the scene; the remainder of the passage presents a flashback to an earlier, critical encounter.

A man stood upon a railroad bridge in Northern Alabama, looking down into the swift waters twenty feet below. The man's hands were
Line behind his back, the wrists bound with a cord. A
5 rope loosely encircled his neck. It was attached to a stout cross-timber above his head, and the slack fell to the level of his knees. Some loose boards laid upon the sleepers supporting the metals of the railway supplied a footing for him and his execu-
10 tioners—two private soldiers of the Federal army, directed by a sergeant, who in civil life may have been a deputy sheriff. At a short remove upon the same temporary platform was an officer in the uniform of his rank, armed. He was a captain. A

15 sentinel at each end of the bridge stood with his rifle in the position known as 'support'—a formal and unnatural position, enforcing an erect carriage of the body. It did not appear to be the duty of these two men to know what was occurring at the
20 center of the bridge; they merely blockaded the two ends of the foot plank that traversed it.

The man who was engaged in being hanged was apparently about thirty-five years of age. He was a civilian, if one might judge from his dress,
25 which was that of a planter. His features were good—a straight nose, firm mouth, broad fore-head, from which his long, dark hair was combed straight back, falling behind his ears to the collar of his well-fitting frock coat. He wore a mous-
30 tache and pointed beard, but no whiskers; his eyes were large and dark grey and had a kindly expres-sion that one would hardly have expected in one whose neck was in the hemp. Evidently this was no vulgar assassin. The liberal military code
35 makes provision for hanging many kinds of peo-ple, and gentlemen are not excluded.

Peyton Farquhar was a well-to-do planter, of an old and highly respected Alabama family. Being a slave-owner, and, like other slave-own-
40 ers, a politician, he was naturally an original secessionist and ardently devoted to the Southern cause. Circumstances had prevented him from taking service with the gallant army which had fought the disastrous campaigns ending with the
45 fall of Corinth, and he chafed under the inglorious restraint, longing for the release of his energies, the larger life of the soldier, the opportunity for distinction. That opportunity, he felt, would come, as it comes to all in war time. Meanwhile,
50 he did what he could. No service was too humble for him to perform in aid of the South, no adven-ture too perilous for him to undertake if consistent with the character of a civilian who was at heart a soldier, and who in good faith and without too
55 much qualification assented to at least a part of the frankly villainous dictum that all is fair in love and war.

One evening while Farquhar and his wife were sitting near the entrance to his grounds, a gray-
60 clad soldier rode up to the gate and asked for a drink of water. Mrs. Farquhar was only too happy to serve him with her own white hands. While she was gone to fetch the water, her husband approached the dusty horseman and inquired
65 eagerly for news from the front.

"The Yanks are repairing the railroads," said the man, "and are getting ready for another advance. They have reached the Owl Creek bridge, put it in order, and built a stockade on the
70 other bank. The commandant has issued an order, which is posted everywhere, declaring that any civilian caught interfering with the railroad, its

GO ON TO THE NEXT PAGE

bridges, tunnels, or trains, will be summarily hanged. I saw the order."

75   "How far is it to the Owl Creek bridge?" Farquhar asked.

     "About thirty miles."

     "Is there no force on this side of the creek?"

     "Only a picket post half a mile out, on the rail-
80 road, and a single sentinel at this end of the bridge."

     "Suppose a man—a civilian and a student of hanging—should elude the picket post and per-haps get the better of the sentinel," said Farquhar,
85 smiling, "what could he accomplish?"

     The soldier reflected. "I was there a month ago," he replied. "I observed that the flood of last winter had lodged a great quantity of driftwood against the wooden pier at the end of the bridge.
90 It is now dry and would burn like tow."

     The lady had now brought the water, which the soldier drank. He thanked her ceremoniously, bowed to her husband, and rode away. An hour later, after nightfall, he repassed the plantation,
95 going northward in the direction from which he had come. He was a Yankee scout.

23. The word "civil" in line 11 means

(A) polite   (B) individual   (C) legal
(D) collective   (E) nonmilitary

24. Peyton Farquhar would most likely consider which of the following a good example of how a citizen should behave in wartime?

(A) He should use even underhanded methods to support his cause.
(B) He should enlist in the army without delay.
(C) He should turn to politics as a means of enforc-ing his will.
(D) He should avoid involving himself in disas-trous campaigns.
(E) He should concentrate on his duties as a planter.

25. The word "consistent" in line 52 means

(A) unfailing   (B) agreeable   (C) dependable
(D) constant   (E) compatible

26. Farquhar's inquiry about what a man could accom-plish [lines 82–85] illustrates which aspect of his character?

(A) Morbid longing for death
(B) Weighty sense of personal responsibility
(C) Apprehension about his family's future
(D) Keenly inquisitive intellect
(E) Romantic vision of himself in a heroic role

27. It can be inferred from the fourth paragraph that Mrs. Farquhar is

(A) sympathetic to the Confederate cause
(B) uninterested in news of the war
(C) too proud to perform menial tasks
(D) reluctant to ask her slaves to fetch water
(E) inhospitable by nature

28. As used in the next-to-last paragraph, "tow" is

(A) an act of hauling something
(B) a tugboat
(C) a railroad bridge
(D) a highly combustible substance
(E) a picket post

29. From Farquhar's exchange with the soldier (line 75–90), we can infer that Farquhar most likely is going to

(A) sneak across the bridge to join the Confederate forces
(B) attempt to burn down the bridge to halt the Yankee advance
(C) remove the driftwood blocking the Con-federates' access to the bridge
(D) attack the stockade that overlooks the Owl Creek bridge
(E) undermine the pillars that support the railroad bridge

30. We may infer from the passage that

(A) the soldier has deserted from the Southern army
(B) the soldier has lost his sense of direction
(C) the scout has been tempting Farquhar into an unwise action
(D) Farquhar knew the soldier was a Yankee scout
(E) the soldier returned to the plantation unwill-ingly

IF YOU FINISH BEFORE 30 MINUTES, YOU MAY CHECK YOUR WORK ON THIS SECTION ONLY. DO NOT TURN TO ANY OTHER SECTION IN THE TEST.   **S T O P**

SECTION **2**
Mathematical Reasoning

Time—30 minutes
25 Questions

Directions and Reference Information

In this section solve each problem, using any available space for scratchwork. Then decide which is the best of the choices given and fill in the corresponding oval on the answer sheet.

Notes:

(1) The use of a calculator is permitted. All numbers used are real numbers.

(2) Figures that accompany problems in this test are intended to provide information useful in solving the problems. They are drawn as accurately as possible EXCEPT when it is stated in a specific problem that the figure is not drawn to scale. All figures lie in a plane unless otherwise indicated.

Reference Information

$A = \pi r^2$ $A = \ell w$ $A = \frac{1}{2}bh$ $V = \ell wh$ $V = \pi r^2 h$ $c^2 = a^2 + b^2$ Special Right Triangles
$C = 2\pi r$

The number of degrees of an arc in a circle is 360.
The measure in degrees of a straight angle is 180.
The sum of the measures in degrees of the angles of a triangle is 180.

---

1. $(146 \times 117) + (173 \times 146) + (146 \times 210)$ equals

(A) 69,000   (B) 70,000   (C) 71,000
(D) 72,000   (E) 73,000

2. A certain grade of eggs has a weight of 24 to 26 ounces per dozen. What is the minimum weight (in ounces) of 69 such eggs?

(A) 138   (B) 143   (C) 149   (D) 1656   (E) 1716

3. A boy has 85 cents in 12 coins consisting of nickels and dimes. How many coins are nickels?

(A) 5   (B) 6   (C) 7   (D) 8   (E) 9

4. L is east of M and west of N, J is southeast of N, M is southeast of F. Which is the farthest west?

(A) F (B) G (C) J (D) M (E) N

5. If $a - 1$ is an even integer, which of the following must be odd?

  I. $3(a - 3)$
 II. $2a + 1$
III. $a(a - 1)$

(A) I only   (B) II only   (C) III only
(D) I and III only   (E) I, II and III

6. If n is a positive integer, which of the following could be a possible value of $\dfrac{-1^n}{(-1)^n}$?

  I. 1
 II. -1
III. $\dfrac{1}{n}$

(A) I only   (B) II only   (C) III only
(D) I and III only   (E) I, II and III

GO ON TO THE NEXT PAGE

7. In this figure the lettered points are on the circumference of the circle with center O. Which letter represents the point with coordinates (5,0)?

(A) A (B) B (C) C (D) D (E) E

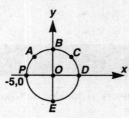

8. For what values of n and d is $\frac{n}{d} > 1$?

(A) $n = 5, d = 6$ (B) $n = 3, d = 2$
(C) $n = 1, d = 2$ (D) $n = 1, d = 1$
(E) $n = 0, d = 1$

9. The cost of sending a telegram to a certain city is 85¢ for the first 15 words and $3\frac{1}{2}$¢ for each additional word, exclusive of tax. How many words did my telegram contain if I paid $1.97, which included a tax of 70¢?

(A) 12   (B) 27   (C) 36   (D) 47   (E) 147

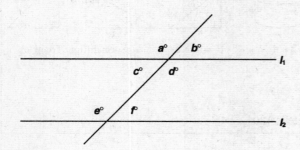

10. If $l_1 \parallel l_2$, then all of the following are true EXCEPT

(A) $d = a$ (B) $c = f$ (C) $e = a$
(D) $f = b$ (E) $c = d$

11. $\frac{2m}{3} = \frac{b}{a}, \quad \frac{2m}{b} =$

(A) $\frac{a}{b}$ (B) $\frac{3}{a}$ (C) $\frac{a}{3}$ (D) a (D) b

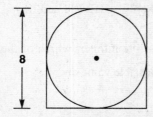

12. A dart is thrown so that it lands inside the square in the accompanying diagram. If there is an equally likely chance that the dart will land at any point in the interior of the square, what is the probability that the dart lands inside the circle?

(A) $\frac{\pi}{8}$ (B) $\frac{\pi}{6}$ (C) $\frac{\pi}{4}$ (D) $\frac{\pi}{3}$ (E) $\frac{\pi}{2}$

13. What is the value of $\dfrac{3y^2 - x^2}{\frac{1}{2}a^3}$ when $x = -2, y = 3$, and $a = -1$?

(A) $2\frac{7}{8}$ (B) -46 (C) 46   (D) -64 (E) 64

14. By selling a television set for $260 a dealer finds he is making a profit of 30% of cost. At what price must he sell it to make a profit of 40% of cost?

(A) $196.00   (B) $254.80   (C) $280.00
(D) $282.00   (E) $322.00

15. What percent of a foot is a yard?

(A) 3%   (B) $\frac{1}{3}$ %   (C) $33\frac{1}{3}$ %
(D) 300%

16. How long is the shadow of a 35-foot tree, if a 98-foot tree casts a 42-foot shadow at the same time?

(A) 14 ft.   (B) 15 ft.   (C) 16 ft.
(D) 17 ft.   (E) 18 ft.

17. This graph shows the sales (in millions) for Fine Supermarket Chain in 1992. By how many millions of dollars did the sales in the meat department exceed the sales in the dairy department?

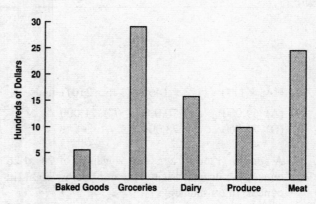

(A) 1   (B) 10   (C) 15   (D) 18   (E) 100

18. During a storewide sale many articles were reduced by 25%. To restore these articles to their original prices they must now increase their price by

(A) 25%   (B) 27.5%   (C) $33\frac{1}{3}$ %
(D) 40%   (E) 50%

GO ON TO THE NEXT PAGE

19. Of Peru's 22 million people, about 60% are mestizos (people of mixed Spanish and Indian heritage), 30% are Andean Indians, and 10% are white. Which of the following expresses the number (in millions) in each of the 3 groups?

(A) 13.2 mestizos, 6.6 Andean Indians, and 2.2 whites.

(B) 2.2 mestizos, 13.2 Andean Indians, and 6.6 whites.

(C) 6.6 mestizos, 2.2 Andean Indians, and 13.2 whites.

(D) 2.2 mestizos, 13.0 Andean Indians, and 6 whites.

(E) 13.2 mestizos, 2.2 Andean Indians, and 6.6 whites.

20. Strawberries that formerly sold for $1.20 per pint are now packaged in two-pint boxes that sell for $3.00. The ratio of the old price to the new price is

(A) 1:5   (B) 2:5   (C) 3:5
(D) 4:5   (E) 5:4

21. In right $\triangle ABC$, leg AB = leg BC. The area of the triangle is 12.5. Hypotenuse AC equals

(A) $\sqrt{5}$ (B) $\sqrt{2}$ (C) 5   (D) $4\sqrt{5}$ (E) 25

22. A point, X, is 25 feet from the center of a circle. If the diameter of the circle is 14 feet, what is the length (in feet) of a tangent from point X to the circle?

(A) $\sqrt{29}$ (B) 18   (C) $15\sqrt{2}$

(D) 24   (E) $\sqrt{673}$

23. Linda did 24 problems out of 25 correctly. In the next test she did twice as many examples correctly but received a mark only half as good. How many problems were there in the second test?

(A) 25   (B) 48   (C) 50   (D) 75   (E) 100

24. If a garage can wash 5 cars in 25 minutes, how long would it take to wash 25 cars?

(A) 2 hrs.   (B) 2 hrs. 5 min.   (C) 5 hrs.
(D) 25 hrs.   (E) none of these

25. A secondhand car dealer sold a car for Mr. Dee and, after deducting 5% commission, remitted $4750 to Mr. Dee. What was the selling price of the car?

(A) $2375   (B) $4773   (C) $5000
(D) $5500   (E) $50,000

IF YOU FINISH BEFORE 30 MINUTES, YOU MAY CHECK YOUR WORK ON THIS SECTION ONLY. DO NOT TURN TO ANY OTHER SECTION IN THE TEST.   **S T O P**

GO ON TO THE NEXT PAGE

SECTION **3**
Writing Skills

Time—30 minutes
39 Questions

Directions

The following sentences contain problems in grammar, usage, diction (choice of words), and idiom.

> Some sentences are correct.
> No sentence contains more than one error.

You will find that the error, if there is one, is underlined and lettered. Assume that elements of the sentence that are not underlined are correct and cannot be changed. In choosing answers, follow the requirements of standard written English.

If there is an error, select the <u>one underlined part</u> that must be changed to make the sentence correct and blacken the corresponding space on your answer sheet.

If there is no error, blacken answer space Ⓔ .

EXAMPLE:

The region has a climate <u>so severe that</u> plants
                                    A

<u>growing there</u> rarely <u>had been</u> more than twelve
     B   C

inches <u>high</u>. <u>No error</u>
       D   E

Ⓐ Ⓑ ● Ⓓ Ⓔ

---

1. Please help <u>me</u> decide <u>which</u> of the two activities to
              A   B

   choose—going to the theater with John <u>or</u> <u>to attend</u>
                                          C   D

   tonight's dinner-dance at the hotel. <u>No error</u>
                                        E

2. When I <u>have to decide</u> <u>which</u> of two applicants for
          A   B

   a job to hire, I find <u>myself</u> giving the positon to
                         C

   the one who uses the <u>best</u> English. <u>No error</u>
                        D   E

3. <u>Because</u> I was seated on the dais <u>just</u> <u>in back of</u>
   A   B   C

   the speaker. I could see the audience's <u>reaction to</u>
                                           D

   his vituperative remarks. <u>No error</u>
                             E

4. A complete system of checks and balances

   <u>have been incorporated</u> in <u>our</u> Constitution
          A   B

   <u>from inception</u> to protect the <u>principle of</u>
        C   D

   equality. <u>No error</u>
             E

5. Dr. Martin Luther King, <u>who</u> <u>led</u> a bus boycott
                          A   B

   to eliminate bus segregation, will be

   <u>forever remembered</u> for <u>his</u> speech, "I Have a
           C   D

   Dream." <u>No error</u>
           E

6. <u>As a result of</u> the bad weather, she is the <u>only one</u>
   A   B

   of my friends <u>who</u> <u>plan</u> to attend the graduation
                 C   D

   exercises. <u>No error</u>
              E

7. <u>When</u> the fire <u>started</u> to burn, we added kindling
   A   B

   and newspaper <u>so that</u> it would get stronger and
                 C

   <u>throw off</u> more heat. <u>No error</u>
       D   E

8. <u>During</u> the recent gasoline shortage, the <u>amount of</u>
   A   B

   accidents on our highways <u>decreased</u> <u>markedly</u>.
                             C   D

   <u>No error</u>
   E

9. <u>Having secured</u> the ball on a fumble, <u>we</u> <u>took</u>
   A   B   C

   <u>advantage of</u> our opponent's error and scored a
       D

   field goal. <u>No error</u>
               E

10. <u>Although</u> Mr. Jimenez is in this country <u>for only</u>
    A   C
                                       B

    two years, he talks <u>like</u> a native. <u>No error</u>
                        D   E

11. These cars <u>are</u> not ready for delivery as <u>they</u> come
               A   B

    <u>off of</u> the assembly line; they must be tested
    C

    before <u>being sold</u>. <u>No error</u>
           D   E

12. <u>Because</u> Charles received a <u>number of</u> free tickets
    A   B

    for the World Series, he asked whether I <u>will go</u> to
                                             C

    the game with <u>him</u>. <u>No error</u>
                  D   E

13. Your argument is no different from the last speaker
                      A   B
who also opposes this timely legislation. No error
        C   D   E

14. Every woman in the ward fervently hopes that
                            A
their child will be a normal and healthy baby.
 B   C   D
No error
 E

15. After consideration of all census polls, we realized
          A   B
that the population of California is larger
                                   C
then that of any other state in the United States.
 D
No error
 E

16. Due to the excessively high interest rate on
     A   B
installment buying, it is advisable to purchase
                    C   D
things on a cash basis. No error
                        E

17. Because of unfavorable weather, few funds, and a
     A   B
burned-out sorority house, the party had to be
                                         C
postponed indefinitely. No error
          D   E

18. Bear in mind that since words are tools, only
     A   B   C
experienced writers are permitted in taking
                    D
liberties in writing style. No error
                            E

19. The man who is laying in the aisle needs medical
          A   B   C
attention immediately. No error
          D   E

20. We are more concerned that the best possible candidate be hired than that bureaucratic affirmative action rules be followed to the letter.
   (A) than that bureaucratic affirmative action rules be followed
   (B) and not about following bureaucratic affirmative action rules
   (C) than that one should follow bureaucratic affirmative action rules
   (D) than your following bureaucratic affirmative action rules
   (E) and not in any bureaucratic affirmative action rules being followed

21. By the government failing to keep its pledges will earn the distrust of all other nations in the alliance.
   (A) By the government failing to keep its pledges
   (B) Because the government failed to keep its pledges
   (C) Since the government has failed to keep its pledges
   (D) Failing to keep its government pledges
   (E) If the government fails to keep its pledges, it

22. Although I calculate that he will be here any minute, I cannot wait much longer for him to arrive.
   (A) Although I calculate that he will be here
   (B) Although I reckon that he will be here
   (C) Because I calculate that he will be here
   (D) Although I am confident that he will be here
   (E) Because I am confident that he will be here

GO ON TO THE NEXT PAGE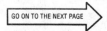

23. Bernard Malamud was a forty-year-old college professor in Oregon and his short story "The Magic Barrel" was published in *The Partisan Review*.

    (A) Oregon and his short story "The Magic Barrel"
    (B) Oregon, his short story "The Magic Barrel"
    (C) Oregon; his short story "The Magic Barrel"
    (D) Oregon when his short story "The Magic Barrel"
    (E) Oregon, furthermore, his short story "The Magic Barrel"

24. Being as how a dangerous cloud of radiation was released at the Chernobyl nuclear plant, that accident can be considered the most serious in the history of nuclear energy.

    (A) Being as how a dangerous cloud of radiation was released
    (B) Because a dangerous cloud of radiation was released
    (C) Due to the release of a dangerous cloud of radiation
    (D) In addition to a dangerous cloud of radiation being released
    (E) Releasing a dangerous cloud of radiation

25. In keeping with the hallowed Russian tradition of putting on a show to impress the visitors, the capital being painted and festooned with banners and portraits of Marx and Lenin.

    (A) the capital being painted and festooned
    (B) the capital been painted and festooned
    (C) the capital painted and being festooned
    (D) the capital's painting and festooning
    (E) the capital has been painted and festooned

26. Employers have begun to provide health club facilities for their employees because exercise build stamina, decreases tension, and absenteeism is reduced.

    (A) decreases tension, and absenteeism is reduced
    (B) tension is decreased, and absenteeism reduced
    (C) decreases tension, and reducing absenteeism
    (D) decreases tension, and reduces absenteeism
    (E) decreasing tension, and absenteeism is reduced

27. She not only was competent but also friendly in nature.

    (A) She not only was competent but also friendly
    (B) She not was only competent but friendly also
    (C) She not only was competent but friendly also
    (D) She was not only competent but also friendly
    (E) She was not only was competent but friendly also

28. The dean informed us that the applicant had not and never will be accepted by the college because of his high school record.

    (A) applicant had not and never will be accepted by the college because of his high school record
    (B) applicant had not and never would be accepted by the college because of his high school record
    (C) applicant had not been and never will be accepted by the college because of his high school record
    (D) applicant had not and never could be accepted by the college because of his high school record
    (E) applicant had not been and never would be accepted by the college because of his high school record

29. Numerous American industries have lost sales to foreign imports, in addition to which, to regain profits, some companies have merged with foreign plants.

    (A) imports, in addition to which, to regain profits
    (B) imports; to regain profits
    (C) imports; as a result, to regain profits
    (D) imports, to regain profits
    (E) imports, yet to regain profits

30. New York City hosted a four-day extravaganza for the Statue of Liberty during the July 4, 1986 weekend; the purpose being to celebrate Miss Liberty's one hundredth birthday.

    (A) weekend; the purpose being to celebrate
    (B) weekend because of celebrating
    (C) weekend, the purpose being to celebrate
    (D) weekend to celebrate
    (E) weekend; for the purpose of celebrating

31. If he were to win the medal, I for one would be disturbed.

    (A) If he were to win the medal
    (B) If he was to win the medal
    (C) If he wins the medal
    (D) If he is the winner of the medal
    (E) In the event that he wins the medal

32. The scouts were told to take an overnight hike, pitch camp, prepare dinner, and that they should be in bed by 9 P.M.

    (A) to take an overnight hike, pitch camp, prepare dinner, and that they should be in bed by 9 P.M.
    (B) to take an overnight hike, pitch camp, prepare dinner, and that they should go to bed by 9 P.M.
    (C) to take an overnight hike, pitch camp, prepare dinner, and be in bed by 9 P.M.
    (D) to take an overnight hike, pitch camp, preparing dinner, and going to bed by 9 P.M.
    (E) to engage in an overnight hike, pitch camp, prepare dinner, and that they should be in bed by 9 P.M.

33. We want the teacher to be the one who has the best rapport with the students.

    (A) We want the teacher to be the one
    (B) We want the teacher to be he
    (C) We want him to be the teacher
    (D) We desire that the teacher to be him
    (E) We anticipate that the teacher will be him

GO ON TO THE NEXT PAGE

Directions

The passage below is the unedited draft of a student's essay. Some of the essay needs to be rewritten to make the meaning clearer and more precise. Read the essay carefully.

The essay is followed by six questions about changes that might improve all or part of its organization, development, sentence structure, use of language, appropriateness to the audience, or its use of standard written English. Choose the answer that most clearly and effectively expresses the student's intended meaning. Indicate your choice by filling in the corresponding space on the answer sheet.

Essay

[1] Much of Russia lies under a cover of snow and ice for most of the year. [2] Permafrost covers the tundra. [3] Ports in northern Russia are not navigable for most of the year simply because they are frozen in. [4] In the south, the Black Sea gives Russia access to warm water ports. [5] The reason that the Black Sea is important is because it gives them the ability to export timber, furs, coal, oil, and other raw materials that are traded for food and manufactured goods. [6] The Black Sea will continue to help their economic growth.

[7] The English Channel has served as a barrier between Great Britain and the rest of Europe. [8] It has prevented attacks on Great Britain for hundreds of years. [9] Except for the Norman invasion over 900 yeas ago. [10] This allowed the nation to develop economically and remain politically stable. [11] The isolation of Great Britain allowed the industrial revolution to begin in England.

[12] Much of Egypt is covered by desert. [13] The desert is irrigated by the Nile River. [14] It is longer than any river in the world. [15] The land along the river has historically been the site of farms and other settlements. [16] For centuries, the river has deposited rich particles of soil for growing crops along its banks. [17] Since building the Aswan High Dam in 1968, the farmers downstream from the dam have been using artificial fertilizer. [18] The banks of the Nile and the river's delta are among the most productive farming areas in the world. [19] Therefore, Egypt's people depend on the Nile.

[20] Russia, Great Britain, and Egypt are only three countries that have been shaped and developed by bodies of water.

34. Which is the best revision of the underlined segment of sentence 5 below?

    The reason that the Black Sea is important is because it gives them the ability to export timber, furs, coal, oil, and other raw materials that are traded for food and manufactured goods.

    (A) that it enables Russia to export
    (B) its ability to allow exports of
    (C) the ability of Russia to export
    (D) because of exporting opportunities of
    (E) for Russian exports of

35. In the context of the second paragraph, which is the best revision of sentences 8 and 9?
    (A) The English Channel has prevented Great Britain's being attacked for hundreds of years; except for the Norman invasion in 1066.
    (B) It has prevented attacks, except for the Norman invasion of 1066, on Great Britain for hundreds of years
    (C) Except for not preventing the Norman invasion over 900 years ago, the English Channel has prevented attacks on Great Britain for hundreds of years
    (D) It has prevented attacking Great Britain for 900 years, except the Normans
    (E) For hundreds of years it has prevented attacks on Great Britain, except for the Norman invasion in 1066.

36. Which is the best way to combine sentences 12, 13, and 14?
    (A) The Nile, the longest river in the world, irrigates the desert that covers much of Egypt.
    (B) Egypt, which is covered by desert, is irrigated by the Nile, which is longer than any river in the world.
    (C) The desert, which covers much of Egypt, is irrigated by the Nile, which is longer than any river in the world.
    (D) The longest river in the world, the Nile River, irrigates the Egyptian desert, which means that the river irrigates most of the country.
    (E) Much of the desert covering much of Egypt lies alongside the Nile, the longest river in the world, and much of it is irrigated by it.

37. To improve the coherence of paragraph 3, which of the following sentences would be the best to delete?
    (A) Sentence 15
    (B) Sentence 16
    (C) Sentence 17
    (D) Sentence 18
    (E) Sentence 19

38. Which of the following sentences is most in need of further support and development?
    (A) Sentence 1
    (B) Sentence 2
    (C) Sentence 5
    (D) Sentence 11
    (E) Sentence 14

39. Considering the essay as a whole, which one of the following least accurately describes the function of paragraph 4?
    (A) It summarizes the essay's main idea.
    (B) It serves to unify the essay.
    (C) It proves the validity of the essay's main idea.
    (D) It defines the purpose of the essay.
    (E) It gives a sense of completion to the essay.

IF YOU FINISH BEFORE 30 MINUTES, YOU MAY CHECK YOUR WORK ON THIS SECTION ONLY. DO NOT TURN TO ANY OTHER SECTION IN THE TEST.

S T O P

SECTION 4
Verbal Reasoning

Time—30 minutes
30 Questions

For each question in this section, select the best answer from among the choices given and fill in the corresponding oval on the answer sheet.

Directions

Each sentence below consists of a related pair of words or phrases, followed by five pairs of words or phrases labeled A through E. Select the pair that best expresses a relationship similar to that expressed in the original pair.

Example:

CRUMB:BREAD::
(A) ounce:unit
(B) splinter:wood
(C) water:bucket
(D) twine:rope
(E) cream:butter

31. THERMOMETER:TEMPERATURE::

(A) calendar:entry   (B) barometer:distance
(C) Geiger counter:radiation
(D) pacemaker:heart   (E) weather vane:speed

32. FANS:BLEACHERS::

(A) cheerleaders:pompoms   (B) audience:seats
(C) team:goalposts   (D) conductor:podium
(E) referee:decision

33. ARCHIPELAGO:ISLAND::

(A) arbor:bower   (B) garden:path
(C) mountain:valley   (D) sand:dune
(E) constellation:star

34. GLOSSARY:WORDS::

(A) catalogue:dates   (B) atlas:maps
(C) almanac:synonyms   (D) thesaurus:rhymes
(E) lexicon:numbers

35. BUOYANT:SINK::

(A) flammable:burn   (B) waterproof:float
(C) adhesive:loosen   (D) volatile:evaporate
(E) fragile:fall

36. VINDICTIVE:MERCY::

(A) avaricious:greed   (B) insightful:hope
(C) modest:dignity   (D) skeptical:trustfulness
(E) pathetic:sympathy

37. COMET:TAIL::

(A) star:galaxy   (B) car:headlight
(C) river:bank   (D) helicopter:pad
(E) vessel:wake

38. DAMPEN:ENTHUSIASM::

(A) moisten:throat   (B) test:commitment
(C) distract:attention   (D) reverse:course
(E) mute:sound

39. BOUQUET:WINE::

(A) chaff:wheat   (B) aroma:coffee
(C) yeast:bread   (D) octane:gasoline
(E) decanter:brandy

40. OFFHAND:PREMEDITATION::

(A) upright:integrity   (B) aboveboard:guile
(C) cutthroat:competition
(D) backward:direction
(E) underlying:foundation

41. SHARD:POTTERY::

(A) handle:pitcher   (B) splinter:bone
(C) rift:rock   (D) veneer:wood
(E) vessel:clay

42. REFRACTORY:MANAGE::

(A) redoubtable:impress   (B) pedantic:convince
(C) officious:arrange   (D) lethargic:stimulate
(E) aggrieved:distress

43. CELERITY:SNAIL::

(A) indolence:sloth   (B) cunning:weasel
(C) curiosity:cat   (D) humility:peacock
(E) obstinacy:mule

The passage below is followed by questions based on its content. Answer the questions following the passage on the basis of what is <u>stated</u> or <u>implied</u> in that passage and in any introductory material that may be provided.

Questions 44–49 are based on the following passage.

The following passage on the migration of the earliest humans from the Old World to the Americas is taken from an anthropology text.

The New World was already an old world to the Indians who were in residence when Europeans took possession of it in the sixteenth century. But the life story of the human species goes back a million years, and there is no doubt that human beings came only recently to the Western Hemisphere. None of the thousands of sites of aboriginal habitation uncovered in North and South America has antiquity comparable to that of Old World sites. Human occupation of the

GO ON TO THE NEXT PAGE ▷

New World may date back several tens of thousands of years, but no one rationally argues that human life has been here even 100,000 years.

Speculation as to how human beings found their way to America was lively at the outset, and the proposed routes boxed the compass. With one or two notable exceptions, however, students of American anthropology soon settled for the plausible idea that the first immigrants came by way of a land bridge that had connected the northeast corner of Asia to the northwest corner of North America across the Bering Strait. Mariners were able to supply the reassuring information that the strait is not only narrow—it is 56 miles wide—but also shallow; a lowering of the sea level there by 100 feet or so would transform the strait into an isthmus. With little else in the way of evidence to sustain the Bering Strait land bridge, anthropologists embraced the idea that men and women walked dryshod from Asia to America.

Toward the end of the last century, however, it became apparent that the Western Hemisphere was the New World not only for human beings but also for a host of animals and plants. Zoologists and botanists showed that numerous subjects of their respective kingdoms must have originated in Asia and spread to America. (There was evidence also for some movement in the other direction.) These findings were neither astonishing nor wholly unexpected. Such spread of populations is not to be envisioned as an exodus or mass migration, even in the case of animals. It is, rather, a spilling into new territory that accompanies increase in numbers, with movement in the direction of least population pressure and most favorable ecological conditions. But the immense traffic in plant and animal forms placed a heavy burden on the Bering Strait land bridge as the anthropologists had envisioned it. Whereas purposeful human beings could make their way across a narrow bridge (in the absence of a bridge, Eskimos sometimes cross the strait in skin boats), the slow diffusion of plants and animals would require an avenue as broad as a continent and available for ages at a stretch.

44. According to the author, the movement of plants and animals from Asia to America suggests

(A) the role played by zoologists and botanists

(B) they were transported across the Bering Sea by Eskimos

(C) the continents once were connected by a large land mass

(D) the Bering Strait land bridge coped with the traffic efficiently

(E) the migration was in that one direction only

45. The author is refuting the notion that

(A) life arose in America independently of life in Europe

(B) the first settlers in America came during the sixteenth century

(C) a large continent that once existed has disappeared

(D) European archeological sites antedate American ones

(E) human life has existed in the Americas as long as it has in the Old World

46. The word "uncovered" in line 8 means

(A) exhibited   (B) unmasked   (C) unearthed

(D) undone   (E) announced

47. The word "embraced" in line 29 means

(A) readily adopted   (B) hugged tightly

(C) comprehended   (D) encompassed

(E) included

48. The author mentions all of the following reasons for the migration EXCEPT

(A) overcrowding caused by population growth

(B) the attractions of a superior environment

(C) the existence of famine in the land

(D) the existence of a land bridge

(E) natural movement toward areas of lower population density

49. We may assume that in the paragraph that follows this passage the author discusses

(A) the contributions of anthropologists

(B) the contribution of botanists and zoologists

(C) the contribution made by the American Indians

(D) the existence of a large land mass between Asia and North America

(E) the abruptness of the human exodus

GO ON TO THE NEXT PAGE

The passages below are followed by questions based on their content; questions following a pair of related passages may also be based on the relationship between the paired passages. Answer the questions on the basis of what is stated or implied in the passages and in any introductory material that may be provided.

Questions 50–60 are based on the following passages.

The following passages, written in the twentieth century, present two views of the English poet Geoffrey Chaucer. Note that in the middle paragraph of Passage 2 the writer translates a short section of Chaucer's verse, which he then repeats in the original Middle English.

PASSAGE 1

It was not until modern scholarship uncovered the secret of reading Middle English that we could understand that Chaucer, far from being a
Line rude versifier, was a perfectly accomplished tech-
5 nician, and that his verse is rich in music and ele-
gant to the highest degree. Chaucer's own urbane personality is a delight to encounter in his books. He is avowedly a bookworm, yet few poets observe nature with more freshness and delight.
10 He is a master of genial satire, but can sympathize with true piety and goodness with as much plea-
sure as he attacks the hypocritical.

It is not an uncommon estimate of Chaucer that he must be counted among the few greatest of
15 English poets. In range of interest he is surpassed only by Shakespeare. He was recognized already in the Renaissance, when it came to England, as the Father of English Poetry. He was a man of wide learning, and wrote with ease on religion,
20 philosophy, ethics, science, rhetoric. No one has more completely summed up an age than Chaucer has his, yet the people of his great poems are revealed as men and women are in all times.

Master of verse, as Chaucer was, he introduced
25 into English poetry many verse forms: the heroic couplet (in which form most of *The Canterbury Tales* is written); verse written in iambic pentameter, rhyming ababbcc (*Troilus and Criseyde*); the terza rima, three-line stanzas, rhyming aba, bcb,
30 cdc, etc. (which he imitated from Dante, in some of his minor poems); and the eight-line iambic pentameter stanza, rhyming ababbcbc (the *Monk's Tale*).

PASSAGE 2

Nothing more unlucky, I sometimes think,
35 could have befallen Chaucer than that he should have been christened "the father of English poetry." For "father" in such a context conveys to most of us, I fear, a faint suggestion of *vicarious* glory—the derivative celebrity of parents, otherwise obscure,
40 who shine, moon-like, in the reflected luster of their sons. What else than progenitors were the fathers of Plato, or Caesar, or Shakespeare, or Napoleon? And so to call Chaucer the father of English poetry is often tantamount to dismissing

45 him, not unkindly, as the estimable but archaic ancestor of a brilliant line. But Chaucer—if I may risk the paradox—is himself the very thing he begat. He is English poetry incarnate, and only two, perhaps, of all his sons outshine his fame. It is with
50 Chaucer himself, then, and not save incidentally with his ancestral eminence that we shall be concerned.

Let me begin with the very tongue that Chaucer spoke—a speech at once our own and not
55 our own. "You know," he wrote—and for the moment I rudely modernize lines as liquid in their rhythm as smooth-sliding brandy—"you know that in a thousand years there is change in the forms of speech, and words that were then judged apt and
60 choice now seem to us wondrous quaint and strange, and yet they spoke them so, and managed as well in love with them as men now do." And to us, after only half a thousand years, those very lines are an embodiment of what they state:

65   Ye knowe eek, that in forme of speche is
           chaunge
      With-inne a thousand yeer, and words tho
      That hadden prys, now wonder nyce and
           straunge
70   Us thinketh hem; and yet they spake hem
           so,
      And spedde as wel in love as men now do.

But it is not only Chaucer's speech that has undergone transformation. The change in his world
75 is greater still. And the situation that confronts us is this. In Chaucer's greatest work we have to do with *timeless creations* upon a *time-determined* stage. And it is one of the inescapable ironies of time that creations of the imagination which are at
80 once of no time and for all time must nevertheless think and speak and act in terms and in ways which are as transient as they themselves are permanent. Their world—the stage on which they play their parts, and in terms of which they think—has
85 become within a few lifetimes strange and obsolete, and must be deciphered before it can be read.

GO ON TO THE NEXT PAGE ⇒

50. The opening paragraph of Passage 1 suggests that Chaucer was underrated for a time because

(A) people looked down upon him as a mere technician
(B) he was secretive about the language in which he composed his verse
(C) people lacked the knowledge to appreciate his poetic technique
(D) readers were not drawn to the works of a bookworm
(E) his satire proved too gentle to suit the taste of the average reader

51. The word "rude" in line 4 means

(A) impertinent   (B) brusque   (C) tactless
(D) inconsiderate   (E) unpolished

52. In lines 8–9, the author's assumption is that

(A) his interest in observing nature distracted Chaucer from his proper academic pursuits
(B) Chaucer turned to the study of nature when he grew discouraged by his observations of mankind
(C) it is better to devote oneself to natural history than to become absorbed in reading dry texts
(D) it is unusual for someone so immersed in books to make original observations about nature as well
(E) Chaucer's love of poetry made him a better observer of nature than most scientists

53. According to Passage 1, Chaucer wrote on all of the following topics EXCEPT

(A) matters of faith
(B) the application of moral standards
(C) principles of literary composition
(D) the study of natural phenomena
(E) the nature of music

54. The final paragraph of Passage 1 consists of

(A) an illustrative anecdote
(B) an unproductive digression
(C) a catalog of examples
(D) an argument by analogy
(E) a detailed comparison

55. The examples of terza rima stanzas given in lines 28–30 suggest that the rhyme scheme of the 5th stanza of a poem in terza rima would be

(A) dcd   (B) ded   (C) ede   (D) efe   (E) fgf

56. The title below that best expresses the ideas of Passage 1 is

(A) Chaucer as Satirist
(B) Chaucer—Shakespeare's Superior?
(C) The Crudities of Chaucer's Poetry
(D) Chaucer's Far-Ranging Genius
(E) Inventor of the Terza Rima

57. The word "obscure" in line 39 means

(A) cryptic   (B) gloomy   (C) indefinite
(D) unrenowned   (E) dim-witted

58. A specific example of the sort of derivative celebrity referred to in lines 37–41 would be

(A) a new edition of Plutarch's life of Julius Caesar
(B) a television appearance by President Clinton's mother
(C) a review of a current revival of Shakespeare's Hamlet
(D) Plato's own account of the death of his teacher Socrates
(E) a contemporary actor's performance in the role of Napoleon

59. The author of Passage 2 uses the Middle English quotation (lines 65–72) to

(A) refute the contention that Chaucer wrote awkwardly
(B) demonstrate the idiosyncratic spelling common in Chaucer's time
(C) convey the power of reading poetry in its original form
(D) support his hypothesis about the aptness of Chaucer's choice of words
(E) illustrate the degree of linguistic change that has occurred

60. How would the author of Passage 2 respond to the way the author of Passage 1 uses the epithet "Father of English Poetry" to describe Chaucer?

(A) The term "Father of English Poetry" is an accurate assessment of an exceptionally distinguished literary figure
(B) The term implies Chaucer is important not as a great poet in his own right but as the somewhat outdated forerunner of the great poets of today.
(C) The epithet "Father of English Poetry" has been applied to so many poets that it has lost whatever meaning it originally possessed.
(D) "Father of English Poetry" is a sexist term that should be replaced by more inclusive language.
(E) It is appropriate to acknowledge the impact Chaucer had on posterity by revering him as the glorious ancestor of all English poets.

IF YOU FINISH BEFORE 30 MINUTES, YOU MAY CHECK YOUR WORK ON THIS SECTION ONLY. DO NOT TURN TO ANY OTHER SECTION IN THE TEST.   **S T O P**

SECTION 5
Mathematical Reasoning

Time—30 minutes
25 Questions

Directions and Sample Questions

Notes:

(1) The use of a calculator is permitted. All numbers used are real numbers.

(2) Figures that accompany problems in this test are intended to provide information useful in solving the problems. They are drawn as accurately as possible EXCEPT when it is stated in a specific problem that the figure is not drawn to scale. All figures lie in a plane unless otherwise indicated.

Questions 1–15 each consist of two quantities in boxes, one in Column A and one in Column B. You are to compare the two quantities and on the answer sheet fill in oval

A if the quantity in Column A is greater;
B if the quantity in Column B is greater;
C if the two quantities are equal;
D if the relationship cannot be determined from the information given.

Notes:

1. In some questions, information is given about one or both of the quantities to be compared. In such cases, the given information is centered above the two columns and is not boxed.
2. In a given question, a symbol that appears in both columns represents the same thing in Column A as it does in Column B.
3. Letters such as x, n, and k stand for real numbers.

EXAMPLES

	Column A	Column B	Answers
E1	5^2	20	● Ⓑ Ⓒ Ⓓ

$150°$ / $x°$

| E2 | x | 30 | Ⓐ Ⓑ ● Ⓓ |

r and s are integers.

| E3 | $r + 1$ | $s - 1$ | Ⓐ Ⓑ Ⓒ ● |

PART I: QUANTITATIVE COMPARISON QUESTIONS

SUMMARY DIRECTIONS FOR QUANTITATIVE COMPARISON QUESTIONS

Answer: A if the quantity in Column A is greater.
B if the quantity in Column B is greater.

C if the two quantities are equal.
D if the relationship cannot be determined from the information given.

	Column A	Column B		Column A	Column B
26.	$\dfrac{6+6+6}{6-6-6}$	$\dfrac{3+3+3}{3-3-3}$	30.	$\dfrac{1}{q}$ $0 < p < q$	$\dfrac{1}{p}$
	$x = 0.000001$			$a = 2, b = 1,$ and $c = 0$	
27.	$\sqrt{x}$	$100x$	31.	$4a + 2b + 3c^3$	10
28.	$\sqrt[3]{(\sqrt{64})}$	$\sqrt{(\sqrt[3]{64})}$	32.	105% of 500	50% of 1000
	$x^2 = 25$			$2x + y = 16$	
29.	x	5	33.	x	y

GO ON TO THE NEXT PAGE

	Column A	Column B		Column A	Column B

34. The average of the measure of the angles of quadrilateral *ABCD* | The measure of the angle of square *KLMN*

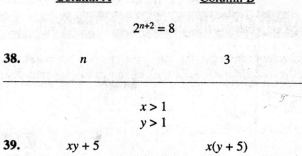

$$2^{n+2} = 8$$

38.   *n*   3

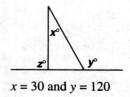

$x = 30$ and $y = 120$

35.   *z*   90

$x > 1$
$y > 1$

39. $xy + 5$ $x(y + 5)$

AC is the hypotenuse of $\triangle ABC$.

40. Measure of $\angle B$ | Sum of the measures of $\angle A$ and $\angle C$

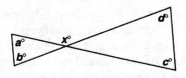

36. $a + b + c + d$ *x*

KL is a straight line.

37. $a + b$ 270

GO ON TO THE NEXT PAGE

PART II: STUDENT-PRODUCED RESPONSE QUESTIONS

Directions for Student-Produced Response Questions

Each of the remaining ten questions (41–50) requires you to solve the problem and enter your answer by marking the ovals in the special grid, as shown in the examples below.

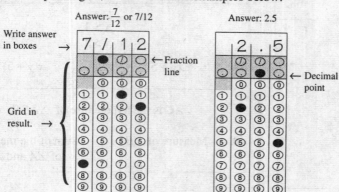

- Mark no more than one oval in any column.

- Because the answer sheet will be machine-scored, **you will receive credit only if the ovals are filled in correctly.**

- Although not required, it is suggested that you write your answer in the boxes at the top of the columns to help you fill in the ovals accurately.

- Some problems may have more than one correct answer. In such cases, grid only one answer.

- No question has a negative answer.

- **Mixed numbers** such as $2\frac{1}{2}$ much be gridded as 2.5 or 5/2. (If 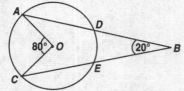 is gridded, it will be interpreted as $\frac{21}{2}$, not $\frac{21}{2}$.)

- <u>Decimal Accuracy</u>: If you obtain a decimal answer, enter the most accurate value that the grid will accommodate. For example, if you obtain an answer such as 0.6666..., you should record the result as .666 or .667. Less accurate values such as .66 or .67 are not acceptable.

Acceptable ways to grid $\frac{2}{3}$ = .6666. . .

---

41. A disease killed $\frac{2}{3}$ of the chickens on a farm. The owner then inoculated $\frac{1}{2}$ of the remaining chickens to prevent infection. If 100 were inoculated, how many chickens were lost before the treatment?

42. If 4% of motorists on the turnpike leave at a certain exit and 5% of these go to one particular motel for lodging, out of every 10,000 motorists how many motorists may be expected to go to this motel?

43. ADB and CEB are secants of circle O. If $\angle AOC \doteq 80$ and $\angle B \doteq 20$, how many degrees are in $\overset{\frown}{DE}$?

44. A rectangular field 50 meters in width and 120 meters in length is divided into two fields by a diagonal line. What is the length of fence (in meters) required to enclose one of these fields?

45. If there are 5 to 8 eggs in a pound, what is the maximum number of eggs in 40 pounds?

46. How many four-cent baseball cards can I purchase without receiving change for one dollar after buying 20 three-cent cards?

47. How many ounces are there in a cup of shredded coconut if 6 cups weigh one pound?

48. A man who owned $\frac{1}{4}$ share of a business sold $\frac{1}{3}$ of his control last year and sold $\frac{5}{12}$ of his remaining share this year. What part of the business does he now own?

49. If a score of 17 is added to a set of 10 data scores the mean (average) of the set becomes 14. What is the mean (average) of the original set of scores?

50. If $AB = 12$ and $BC = 6$, what is the length of a segment joining the midpoints of AB and BC? (Diagram is not to scale.)

IF YOU FINISH BEFORE 30 MINUTES, YOU MAY CHECK YOUR WORK ON THIS SECTION ONLY. DO NOT TURN TO ANY OTHER SECTION IN THE TEST.   **S T O P**

ANSWER KEY

Verbal Reasoning Section 1

1. A	6. B	11. B	16. C	21. A	26. E
2. B	7. A	12. C	17. D	22. C	27. A
3. A	8. C	13. D	18. D	23. E	28. D
4. C	9. D	14. B	19. A	24. A	29. B
5. D	10. E	15. B	20. E	25. E	30. C

Mathematical Reasoning Section 2

Note: Each correct answer to the mathematics questions is keyed by number to the corresponding topic in Chapters 8 and 9. These numerals refer to the topics listed below, with specific page references in parentheses.

1. Basic Fundamental Operations (179–182)
2. Algebraic Operations (182–183)
3. Using Algebra (182–184, 187)
4. Exponents, Roots, and Radicals (184–185)
5. Inequalities (188–189)
6. Fractions (182, 198)
7. Decimals (200)
8. Percent (200)
9. Averages (201)
10. Motion (203)
11. Ratio and Proportion (204–205)
12. Mixtures and Solution (178)
13. Work (206–207)
14. Coordinate Geometry (194)
15. Geometry (189–193, 195)
16. Quantitative Comparisons (211–212)
17. Data Interpretation (208)

1. E (1)	6. D (4)	11. B (2)	16. B (11)	21. B (15)
2. A (1)	7. D (14)	12. C (1)	17. B (1,17)	22. D (15)
3. C (3)	8. B (2)	13. B (6)	18. C (8)	23. E (1)
4. A (15)	9. B (1)	14. C (8)	19. A (8)	24. C (3)
5. B (1)	10. E (15)	15. D (8)	20. D (11)	25. C (8)

Writing Skills Section 3

1. D	8. B	15. D	22. D	29. B	36. A
2. D	9. E	16. A	23. D	30. D	37. C
3. C	10. B	17. E	24. B	31. A	38. D
4. A	11. C	18. D	25. E	32. C	39. C
5. E	12. C	19. B	26. D	33. A	
6. D	13. B	20. A	27. D	34. A	
7. E	14. B	21. E	28. E	35. E	

Verbal Reasoning Section 4

31. C	36. D	41. B	46. C	51. E	56. D
32. B	37. E	42. D	47. A	52. D	57. D
33. E	38. E	43. D	48. C	53. E	58. B
34. B	39. B	44. C	49. D	54. C	59. E
35. C	40. B	45. E	50. C	55. D	60. B

Mathematical Reasoning Section 5

26. C (6, 16)	29. D (2, 16)	32. A (8, 16)	35. C (15, 16)	38. B (4, 16)
27. A (4)	30. B (6, 16)	33. D (2, 16)	36. A (15, 16)	39. B (2, 16)
28. C (4)	31. C (2, 16)	34. C (15, 16)	37. C (15, 16)	40. C (15, 16)

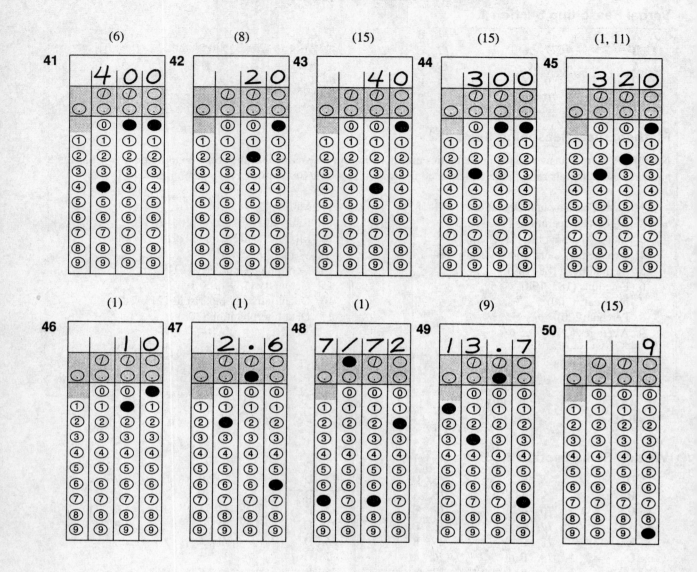

SCORING CHART — TYPICAL TEST B

Verbal Sections

Section 1   Questions 1–30
Number correct   _____ (A)
Number omitted   _____ (B)
Number incorrect   _____ (C)
$\frac{1}{4}$ (C) =   _____ (D)
Raw Score:
  (A) – (D) =   _____

Section 3   Questions 31–60
Number correct   _____ (A)
Number omitted   _____ (B)
Number incorrect   _____ (C)
$\frac{1}{4}$ (C) =   _____ (D)
Raw Score:
  (A) – (D) =   _____

Total Verbal Raw Score:
  (Section 1 +
  Section 3) =   _____

Mathematical Sections

Section 2   Questions 1–25
Number correct   _____ (A)
Number incorrect   _____ (B)
(A) – $\frac{1}{4}$ (B) =   _____ Raw Score I

Section 4   Questions 26–40
Number correct   _____ (C)
Number incorrect   _____ (D)
(C) – $\frac{1}{3}$ (D) =   _____ Raw Score II

Section 4   Questions 41–50
Number correct   _____ Raw Score III

Total Mathematical Raw Score:
  (Raw Scores I + II
  + III) =   _____

Writing Section

Section 3   Questions 1–39
Number correct   _____ (A)
Number incorrect   _____ (B)
$\frac{1}{4}$ (B) =   _____ (C)
(no penalty for omitted questions)
Writing Raw Score:
  (A) – (C) =   _____

EVALUATION CHART

Study your score. Your raw score on the Verbal and Mathematical Reasoning Sections is an indication of your probable achievement on the PSAT/NMSQT. As a guide to the amount of work you need or want to do with this book, study the following.

Raw Score			Self-rating
Verbal	*Mathematical*	*Writing*	
55–60	41–50	37–39	Superior
44–54	25–40	31–36	Very good
39–43	20–24	25–30	Satisfactory
35–38	16–19	19–24	Average
29–34	10–15	13–18	Needs further study
20–28	7–9	6–12	Needs intensive study
0–19	0–6	0–5	Probably inadequate

ANSWER EXPLANATIONS

Verbal Reasoning Section 1

1. **A** "Because" signals cause and effect. Because lightning victims are so battered and confused, they seem like assault victims. Remember to make your own guess before looking at the answer choices. *Mistaken for* fits best, when you know you're looking for a phrase that describes the resemblance between the two types of victim.

2. **B** The lack of drugs that are effective against viruses ("antiviral drugs") leaves virologists *helpless* to ease the suffering that viruses *cause*.

3. **A** Common sense suggests that an injury to their starting quarterback would stifle or suppress the team's joy, leaving it *muted*.

4. **C** We look for a negative word such as *over-priced* to describe the wines, because Ms. Sutcliffe gives "warnings" about them. At the same time, we need a positive word such as *trusty* to describe her book, since it contains helpful advice. Note that "trusty guide" is a cliché, a common expression.

5. **D** Though several answer choices express motion, only one choice conveys a *river's* motion as it winds along, wandering aimlessly: Choice D, *meandered*.

6. **B** The key word "developing" anticipates the description of the way a highway system changes and grows. The road network is described as similar to the brain, which also *evolves with* use, developing and changing.

7. **A** The book is organized by topic or theme: it is *thematically* organized.

8. **C** If episodes in the novel *resemble* or are like episodes Singer recounts in his autobiography (life story), then it appears they are based on *actual*, real occurrences in his life.

9. **D** Since the island generally receives no orders from its mother country, it is *autonomous* or self-governing.

10. **E** Fiction that involves "dream" and "mad invention" is *fantastic*: it presents fantasy.

11. **B** Compared to modern technological marvels like fax machines, the mimeograph machine seems to belong to a long ago period of history. It is an *anachronism,* so outmoded that it seems misplaced in time.

12. **C** A contrast is implied by the clause "that would have undone a lesser woman." Since Roosevelt was not a lesser woman, she was not undone; she *persevered* or continued striving. Just as she maintained her composure, she also maintained her dignity *unruffled* or undisturbed.

13. **D** A medicine that is said to "cure a wide variety of ailments" is by definition a *panacea.*

14. **B** The speech contained pompous language; therefore, it was *bombastic.* The sophisticated people were not impressed by this pretentious wordiness, so they *ridiculed* or mocked it.

15. **B** Note the key word "unfortunate." Miss Post liked the old-fashioned formality of addressing people by their last names: Miss Manners, Ms. Angelou, Mr. Nguyen. She *deprecated* or disapproved of the casual use of first names.

16. **C** *Rococo* style, by definition, is characterized by "scroll work and excessive decoration."

17. **D** A man too wedded to "orthodox theories" or doctrines can best be described as *doctrinaire* or dogmatic.

18. **D** The author is developing the military analogy in order to explain the immune system, the body's system of defense. Choice A is incorrect. The author is not critical of the analogy; he draws on it in order to explain a complex system. Choice B is incorrect. The passage is expository, not persuasive: it explains; it doesn't argue. Choice C is incorrect. The author compares the mass of the immune system to that of the brain. However, that is only a passing reference. Choice E is incorrect. In developing the military analogy, the author is clarifying our picture of the immune system; he is not correcting a view that is out of date.

19. **A** If you put together all the cells making up the immune system, you would have something about as big as the liver or brain. In other words, you'd have something that you could compare in mass or *bulk* to familiar body organs.

20. **E** Lines 3–4 state that the lymphocytes are "born in the bone marrow." This answers the question about where the body's lymphocytes *originate.*

21. **A** Cyclosporin is a drug that suppresses the body's immune system. The immune system protects the body from foreign invaders, such as viruses. Suppression or inhibition of the immune system might well make the body more susceptible to disease. It would not, however, make the body more likely to reject a transplanted organ, nor would it be likely to increase the effectiveness of antigens. Indeed, treatment by cyclosporin makes the body less likely to reject a transplanted organ. Presumably it also makes the immune system less responsive to the presence of antigens.

22. C Though the author mentions the Australian immunologist Sir Frank Macfarlane Burnet, he never directly quotes Burnet's words or those of any other medical authority. Choice A is incorrect. The author identifies lymphocytes as white blood cells. He states that antigens are protein molecules on a substance's surface that trigger the immune response. Choice B is incorrect. The passage is based on the comparison made between the immune system and an army. Choice D is incorrect. The author estimate the number of white blood cells available for mustering at approximately 200,000,000. Choice E is incorrect. By the use of military terminology ("troops," "billeted," "muster," "uniform") the author develops the central metaphor comparing the immune system to an army.

23. E Substitute the answer choices in the original sentence. The sergeant is a person who might have been a deputy sheriff before he joined the army—that is, in his civil or *nonmilitary* life.

24. A Farquhar agrees readily with the saying that all is fair in love and war. This implies he is willing to use underhanded or unfair methods to support the Southern cause.

25. E Farquhar has no objection to performing humble errands or undertaking dangerous tasks as long as these tasks are appropriate to someone who sees himself as a sort of "undercover soldier," a secret agent of the Confederacy. Anything he does must be consistent or *compatible* with his image of himself in this role.

26. E Earlier in the passage, Farquhar is described as frustrated by "the inglorious restraint" preventing his serving the Southern cause. He sees the life of the soldier as larger than that of the civilian, a life filled with opportunities for distinction, for renown. Thus, when he speaks about someone managing to sneak past the guards and accomplishing something for the cause, he is *envisioning himself in a heroic role.*

27. A Mrs. Farquhar's readiness to fetch water for the gray-clad Confederate soldier suggests some degree of sympathy on her part for the Confederate cause. Choices B and D are incorrect. There is nothing in the passage to suggest either of them. Choices C and E are incorrect. Mrs. Farquhar's action, in hospitably fetching water "with her own white hands," contradicts them.

28. D The phrase "burn like tow" and the reference to dry driftwood suggest that tow will catch fire readily. When asked to give the meaning of an unfamiliar word, look for nearby context clues.

29. B Farquhar wishes to prevent the Yankee advance. To do so, he must somehow damage the railroad, its bridges, its tunnels, or its trains. The soldier tells him that some highly flammable driftwood is piled up at the base of the wooden railroad bridge. Clearly, it would make sense for Farquhar to try to set fire to the driftwood in order to destroy the bridge.

30. C The scout is a Yankee soldier disguised as the enemy. By coming to the Farquhars' plantation in Confederate disguise, he is able to learn they are sympathetic to the enemy. By telling Farquhar of the work on the bridge, stressing both the lack of guards and the abundance of fuel, he is tempting Farquhar into an attack on the bridge (and into an ambush). The scout's job is to locate potential enemies and draw them out from cover.

Mathematical Reasoning Section 2

1. E Factor: $146(117 + 173 + 210)$
$146(500) = 73,000$

2. A Minimum weight of 1 dozen eggs = 24 ounces
Minimum weight of 1 egg = 2 ounces
Minimum weight of 69 eggs = 138 ounces

3. C Let x = number of nickels.
$12 - x$ = number of dimes.
$5x$ = value (in cents) of nickels
$10(12 - x)$ or $120 - 10x$ = value (in cents) of dimes
$5x + 120 - 10x = 85$
$-5x = -35$
$x = 7$

4. A (see diagram)

5. B Because $a - 1$ is even, a must be an odd integer. I is not correct: $a - 3$ is even and $3(a - 3)$ results in an even integer. II is correct: $2a$ is even and $2a + 1$ results in an odd integer. III is not correct: $(a - 1)$ is even and $a(a - 1)$ results in an even integer.

6. D The numerator, -1^n, has the value -1 for any positive integral value of n. The denominator, $(-1)^n$, equals 1 for any positive integral value of n that is even, but it equals -1 for any positive integral value of n that is odd. Thus, $-1 \div 1 = -1$, but $-1 \div (-1) = 1$.

7. D Since PO is a radius and $PO = 5$, OD is also a radius and therefore $OD = 5$. Since D is on the x-axis, OD is (5,0).

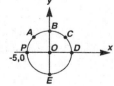

8. **B**   For $\frac{n}{d}$ to be greater than 1, we must have $n > d$. This is true only in choice **B**.

9. **B**   Cost – tax = $1.97 – .70 = $1.27
Cost of first 15 words = 85¢
Cost of additional words = 42¢
At $3\frac{1}{2}$ ¢ per word, 12 additional words were sent.
Total number of words = $15 + 12 = 27$

10. **E**   Since the lines are parallel, $c = f$ (alternate interior angles) (B); $e = a$ (corresponding angles) (C); and for the same reason $f = b$ (D). For (A), $d = a$ because they are vertical angles. In (E) the angles are supplementary.

11. **B** $\frac{2m}{3} = \frac{b}{a}$
$\frac{2m}{b} = \frac{3}{a}$ (exchange terms of the means)
Note that in either case product of means = product of extremes.

12. **C**   Because the diameter of the inscribed circle equals the length of the side of the square, radius of the circle is $\frac{1}{2}(8) = 4$.

P (lands inside circle) =

$$= \frac{\text{Area of Circle}}{\text{Area of Square}}$$
$$= \frac{\pi(4)^2}{8^2}$$
$$= \frac{16\pi}{64}$$
$$\frac{\pi}{4}$$

13. **B**   Substitute:
$$\frac{3(3)^2 - (-2)^2}{\frac{1}{2}(-1)^3}$$
$$\frac{3(9) - (4)}{(\frac{1}{2})(-1)} = \frac{27-4}{-\frac{1}{2}} = \frac{23}{-\frac{1}{2}} = 23 \div -\frac{1}{2}$$
$$= (23)(-2) = -46$$

14. **C** $260 = 130\%$ of the cost = 1.3 of the cost
Let x = cost.
$1.3x = \$260$
$13x = \$2600$
$x = \$200$ (cost)
40% of 200 = $80
New selling price = $200 + 80 = $280

15. **D** $\frac{1 \text{ yard}}{1 \text{ foot}} \times 100 = \%$
$\frac{3 \text{ feet}}{1 \text{ foot}} \times 10 = 300\%$

16. **B**   Let x = size of shadow of 35-foot tree.
$$\frac{\text{size of tree}}{\text{size of shadow}} = \frac{98'}{42'} = \frac{35'}{x}$$
$98x = (42)(35)$
$98x = 1470$
$x = 15$ ft.

17. **B**   Hint: Draw lines on the graph for 2 the departments involved. Meat = $25 million, Dairy = $15 million. The difference is $10 million.

18. **C**   Price during sale is 75% of normal price.
Change to original is 25%
$\frac{25\%}{75\%} = \frac{1}{3} = 33\frac{1}{3}\%$

19. **A**   Hint: Do the calculations and match the choices.
mestizos: $(22)(0.6) = 13.2$
Andian Indian $(22)(0.3) = 6.6$
whites: $(22)(0.1) = 2.2$
Choose **A**.

20. **D**   Old price for 2 pints was $2.40.
Present price for 2 pints is $3.00.
Ratio = $\frac{\$2.40}{\$3.00} = \frac{240}{300} = \frac{24}{30} = \frac{4}{5} = 4{:}5$

21. **B**   Let x = leg AB or leg BC.
Area $= \frac{1}{2}(x)(x)$
Area $= \frac{x^2}{2}$
Area $= \frac{x^2}{2} = 12.5$ [given]
$x^2 = 25$
$x = 5$ (each leg)
From the 45°-45°-90° triangle, $a = 5$, so
$a\sqrt{2} = 5\sqrt{2}$.

22. **D**   Since the diameter is 14, a radius OP is 7.
Since radius $OP \perp$ to tangent PX, OPX is a right $\triangle$.
$\therefore (PX)^2 + 7^2 = 25^2$
$(PX)^2 = 576$
$PX = 24$ feet

23. **E**   First test: $\frac{24}{25} = 96\%$
Second test: 48% and 48 correct
Let x = number of problems in the second test
$\frac{48}{x} = 48\%$
$\frac{48}{x} = \frac{48}{100}$
$x = 100$

24. **B**   It will take 5 times as much time.
5×25 minutes = 125 minutes
                        = 2 hours 5 minutes

25. **C**   The dealer remitted 95% of selling price.
Let x = the selling price
95% (or .95) of $x = \$4750$
$.95x = 4750$
$95x = 475000$
$x = \$5000$

Writing Skills Section 3

1. **D** Violation of parallel structure. Change *to attend* to *attending*.

2. **D** Faulty comparison. When comparing two persons or things, use the comparative form (*better*) instead of the superlative (*best*).

3. **C** Faulty diction. Use *behind* instead of *in back of*.

4. **A** Error in agreement. A system *has been incorporated* is correct.

5. **E** Sentence is correct.

6. **D** Error in agreement. The antecedent of *who* is *one*. Change *plan* to *plans*.

7. **E** Sentence is correct.

8. **B** Faulty diction. Change *amount of* to *number of*.

9. **E** Sentence is correct.

10. **B** Wrong tense. Change *is* to *has been*.

11. **C** Faulty diction. Delete *of*.

12. **C** Error in tense. Change *will go* to *would go*.

13. **B** Faulty comparison. Do not compare a person with a thing. Correct form: *Your argument is no different from that of the last speaker. . . .*

14. **B** Lack of agreement. Woman (singular) requires a singular pronoun. Change *their* to *her*.

15. **D** Faulty diction. The conjunction *than* helps to make a comparison, not *then*.

16. **A** Error in diction. Do not use *due to* when you mean *because of*.

17. **E** Sentence is correct.

18. **D** Faulty verbal. Change *in taking* to the infinitive *to take*.

19. **B** Wrong word. Use *lying* instead of *laying*.

20. **A** The sentence's use of parallel structure is effective and correct.

21. **E** This choice corrects the sentence fragment.

22. **D** *Do not use* calculate *when you mean* think.

23. **D** The additon of *when* makes the sentence more effective by tightening up the relationship between the clauses.

24. **B** Choice B expresses the author's meaning directly and concisely. All other choices are either indirect or ungrammatical.

25. **E** This choice corrects the sentence fragment.

26. **D** Changing *absenteeism is reduced* to *reduces absenteeism* maintains parallel structure.

27. **D** This choice eliminates the error in parallel structure.

28. **E** Omission of important word and error in verb tense are corrected in choice E.

29. **B** Choices A, D, and E are run-on sentences. Choice C is verbose.

30. **D** Choice A contains a sentence fragment. Choices B, C, and E are verbose.

31. **A** Sentence is correct.

32. **C** This sentence does not violate parallel structure.

33. **A** Sentence is correct.

34. **A** Only Choice A is concisely expressed in standard English. All the other choices are awkward or nonstandard.

35. **E** Choice A has a sentence fragment after the semicolon.
Choice B divides the main clause awkwardly.
Choice C is wordy and repetitious. It unnecessarily repeats *the English Channel*, the subject of sentence 7.
Choice D is an unclear, awkwardly constructed sentence.
Choice E is an accurate and logical revision. It is the best answer.

36. **A** Choice A succinctly and effectively combines the three sentences. It is the best answer.
Choice B contains a faulty comparison. The Nile cannot be longer than itself.
Choice C is similar to B.
Choice D is accurate but wordy and repetitious.
Choice E is awkwardly expressed.

37. **C** Although it is related to the topic of the paragraph, sentence 17 steers the discussion away from the paragraph's main topic, Egypt's dependence on the Nile. Therefore, C is the best answer.

38. **D** Sentence 11 states a complex idea that needs further explanation. The other sentences are facts that stand on their own. Therefore D is the best answer.

39. **C** Choice C does not describe the function of the last paragraph. The essay's main idea is validated by the contents of the essay's three main paragraphs, not by the final paragraph.

Verbal Reasoning Section 4

31. **C** A *thermometer* measures temperature. A *Geiger counter* measures *radiation*. (Function)

32. **B** *Fans* or spectators are seated in the bleachers. An *audience* is seated in the *seats*.
(Defining Characteristic)

33. **E** An *archipelago* is a group or chain of *islands*. A *constellation* is a group of *stars*. Beware of eyecatchers. Though you may associate islands and sand, a *dune* is not a group or chain of *sand*; it is a hill or ridge of sand.
(Part to Whole)

34. **B** A *glossary* or word list is composed of *words*. An *atlas* is composed of *maps*.
(Defining Characteristic)

35. **C** Something that is *buoyant* and tends to float is unlikely to *sink*. Something that is *adhesive* or sticky is unlikely to *loosen*. (Antonym Variant)

36. **D** Someone who is *vindictive* or vengeful is lacking in *mercy*. Someone who is *skeptical* or suspicious is lacking in *trustfulness*.
(Antonym Variant)

37. **E** Behind a *comet* stretches its glowing *tail*. Behind a *vessel* (ship) stretches its *wake,* a trail in the water. (Defining Characteristic)

38. **E** To *dampen enthusiasm* is to diminish it. To *mute* (muffle) *sound* is to diminish it. Note that Choice **C** is incorrect: to *distract attention* is not to diminish it but to divert it in a new direction. (Defining Characteristic)

39. **B** The *bouquet* of *wine* is its distinctive fragrance. It is analogous to the *aroma* of *coffee*. (Defining Characteristic)

40. **B** An *offhand* remark is made without forethought or *premeditation*. An *aboveboard* (open) deed is done without trickery or *guile*. (Antonym Variant)

41. **B** A *shard* is a broken fragment of *pottery*. A *splinter* may be a broken fragment of *bone*. (Part to Whole)

42. **D** Someone who is *refractory* (stubborn, unmanageable) is, by definition, hard to *manage*. Likewise, someone who is *lethargic* (sluggish, drowsy) is hard to *stimulate*. (Definition)

43. **D** A *snail* is not noted for *celerity* or speed. A *peacock* is not noted for *humility* or modesty. (Antonym Variant)

44. **C** The concluding sentence of the passage supports this point. For the slow spread of plant and animal life to have taken place as described, such a large land mass would have had to connect the continents.

45. **E** Throughout paragraph 1 the author contradicts the idea that human beings have existed in the Americas for as long as they have existed in the Old World; the life story of the human race begins long before the first human beings came to the New World.

46. **C** The sites of aboriginal habitation that have been uncovered have been *unearthed* or dug up. Remember, the passage comes from an anthropology text: anthropologists unearth or dig up relics of the past.

47. **A** In embracing an idea, the anthropologists *readily adopt it* as their own.

48. **C** Famine is not mentioned. The other four choices are mentioned in paragraph 3.

49. **D** Since the passage ends with the idea that plants and animals would have needed a road as wide as a continent in order to spread into North America, we may assume that the author would continue to explore this notion.

50. **C** The opening sentence states that Chaucer was considered a "rude versifier" until scholars learned to understand his technique. This suggests that people's failure to understand just what Chaucer was doing caused them to undervalue his poetic skill.

51. **E** A "rude versifier" is someone who composes rude (crude and *unpolished*) verse.

52. **D** By making a point of contrasting Chaucer the bookworm with Chaucer the unhackneyed observer of nature, the author clearly assumes that *it is unusual for someone so immersed in books to make original observations about nature as well.*

53. **E** The passage indicates Chaucer wrote on religion, ethics, rhetoric, and science. It does not indicate he wrote on *music*.

54. **C** The final paragraph presents a list or *catalog of examples* of the different verse types in which Chaucer wrote.

55. **D** Following the pattern for terza rima given in lines 28–30, you can see that if the rhyme pattern of the third stanza is cdc, then the rhyme pattern of the fourth stanza should be ded, and the rhyme pattern of the fifth stanza should be *efe*.

56. **D** The passage as a whole develops the idea of Chaucer's *far-ranging genius* as a poet of "wide learning" and equally wide "range of interest." Choice A is incorrect. The passage mentions Chaucer's skills as a satirist but does not dwell on them. Choice B is incorrect. Though great, Chaucer is not considered Shakespeare's superior: he is "surpassed by Shakespeare." Choice C is incorrect. The passage stresses Chaucer's technical expertise, not the supposed "crudities" of his verse. Choice E is incorrect. It is too narrow in scope to be a good title for the passage as a whole.

57. **D** The parents referred to are "otherwise obscure" because their only claim to fame is that they have famous children. Except as parents of famous children, they are *unrenowned* or obscure.

58. **B** President Clinton's mother has as her claim to fame the fame of her son. Had he not been elected president, she would not have been asked to appear on TV. Hers is clearly a derivative celebrity (fame).

59. **E** The author of Passage 2 says that the lines of Middle English verse "are an embodiment of what they state." What do they state? They state that language changes over time, that words that seemed appropriate a thousand years ago look odd and archaic today. As we look at the Middle English quotation, full of odd spellings (*nyce, straunge*) and archaic terms (*spedde* or sped, meaning managed or prospered), we see that the author has used the quote to *illustrate the degree of linguistic change that has occurred.*

60. **B** The author of Passage 2 begins his discussion by saying that it was unfortunate for Chaucer to have been christened the father of English poetry. He then goes on to explain why he dislikes the term. He dislikes it because of its implication of vicarious or derivative glory. In other words, he dislikes it because the term *implies Chaucer is important not as a great poet in his own right but as the somewhat outdated forerunner of the great poets of today.*

Mathematical Reasoning Section 5

26. **C** Note that multiplying both numerator and denominator of fraction B by 2 results in fraction A, and thus does not change the fraction's value.

27. **A** Because $0.000001 = 10^{-6}$, $\sqrt{x}, = \sqrt{10^{-6}} = 10^{-3} = 0.001$. Also, $100x = 100\,(0.000001) = 0.0001$. Because $0.001 > 0.0001$, $\sqrt{x}$ is greater than $100x$.

28. **C** Because $\sqrt[3]{(\sqrt{64})} = \sqrt[3]{8} = 2$ and $\sqrt{(^3\sqrt{64})} = \sqrt{4} = 2$, the two radical expressions are equal.

29. **D** $x^2 = 25$
    $x = +5$ and -5

30. **B** The denominator in $\frac{1}{q}$ is larger than the denominator in $\frac{1}{p}$.

31. **C** $4a + 2b - 3c^3 = (4)(2) + (2)(1) - 3(0) = 8 + 2 = 10$

32. **A** 105% of 500 = 525
    50% of 1000 = 500

33. **D** Two different equations are required to find two unknowns.

34. **C** The sum of the angles of any quadrilateral is 360°.
    $360° \div 4 = 90°$
    A square is a quadrilateral with sides equal and each angle $\overset{\triangle}{=} 90°$.

35. **C** Since $y = 120$, $a = 60$.
    Since the exterior angle of a triangle equals the sum of both remote interior angles, $z = x + a$.
    Since $x = 30$ [given], $z = 30 + 60$ or 90.

36. **A** $x = a + b$ (see answer 35)
    $x < a + b + c + d$ or, $a + b + c + d > x$

37. **C** $a + x = 180$
    $b + y = 180$
    $a + x + b + y = 360$
    Since $x + y = 90$, $a + b = 270$.

38. **B** Since $2^3 = 8$ and $2^{n+2} = 8$
    then $n + 2 = 3$
    $n = 1$

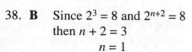

39. **B** $x(y + 5) = xy + 5x$
    Column A $= xy + 5$
    Column B $= xy + 5x$
    $5x > 5$ since $x > 1$

40. **C** (In a right triangle the right angle is opposite the hypotenuse)
    $\angle B \overset{\triangle}{=} 90$
    $\angle A + \angle C \overset{\triangle}{=} 90$

41. **400** 100 chickens $= \frac{1}{2}$ of $\frac{1}{3}$
    100 chickens $= \frac{1}{6}$
    $600 = \frac{6}{6}$
    600 = number before disease struck
    $\frac{2}{3}$ of $600 = 400$ (number of chickens lost before treatment)

42. **20** 5% of 4% $= (.05)(.04) = .0020 = .2\%$ or $\frac{.2}{100}$
    $\frac{.2}{100} = \frac{20}{10,000}$

43. **40** $\widehat{AC} = 80°$ since central $\angle \overset{\triangle}{=} 80$.
    Let x = number of degrees in $\widehat{DE}$.
    $\angle B \overset{\triangle}{=} \frac{1}{2}\,(\widehat{AC} - \widehat{DE})$
    $20° = \frac{1}{2}\,(80° - x)$
    $40° = 80° - x$
    $-40° = -x$
    $x = 40°$

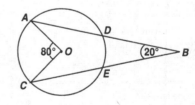

44. **300** Draw AC.
    Observe right $\triangle ABC$.
    Observe ratio of 5:12.
    $\triangle ABD$ is a 5:12:13 $\triangle$ with each dimension multiplied by 10.
    $AC = 130$ meters
    Perimeter $= 50 + 120 + 130 = 300$ meters

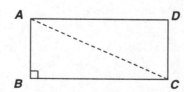

45. **320** Maximum number of eggs in one pound = 8
Maximum number of eggs in 40 pounds = 320

46. **10** Cost of twenty three-cent cards = 60¢
For 40¢, one can buy 10 four-cent cards.

47. **1.6** Let x = number of ounces in one cup.
$$\frac{6 \text{ cups}}{16 \text{ ounces}} = \frac{1 \text{ cup}}{x \text{ ounces}}$$
$6x = 16$
$x = 2.6+$
Therefore the best answer is 2.6.

48. $\frac{7}{72}$ Since he sold $\frac{1}{3}$ of $\frac{1}{4}$, he still held $\frac{2}{3}$ of $\frac{1}{4}$ or $\frac{1}{6}$. This year he sold $\frac{5}{12}$ of his remaining share, so he held $\frac{7}{12}$ of $\frac{1}{6}$ or he still holds $\frac{7}{72}$ of the business.

49. **13.7** Let S = sum of original set of scores.
x = mean of original set of scores.
$$\frac{S + 17}{11} = 14 \text{ or } S + 17 = 154 \text{ so } S = 137.$$

Therefore, mean of original set of 10 scores = $\frac{137}{10} = 13.7$

50. **9** Let X be the midpont of AB and Y be the midpoint of BC. $XB = 6$ and $BY = 3$. $XY = 9$.

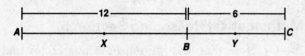

Answer Sheet

TYPICAL TEST C

Each mark should completely fill the appropriate space, and should be as dark as all other marks. Make all erasures complete. Traces of an erasure may be read as an answer. See pages vii and 27 for explanations of timing and number of questions.

Section 1 — Verbal
30 minutes

1 Ⓐ Ⓑ Ⓒ Ⓓ Ⓔ
2 Ⓐ Ⓑ Ⓒ Ⓓ Ⓔ
3 Ⓐ Ⓑ Ⓒ Ⓓ Ⓔ
4 Ⓐ Ⓑ Ⓒ Ⓓ Ⓔ
5 Ⓐ Ⓑ Ⓒ Ⓓ Ⓔ
6 Ⓐ Ⓑ Ⓒ Ⓓ Ⓔ
7 Ⓐ Ⓑ Ⓒ Ⓓ Ⓔ
8 Ⓐ Ⓑ Ⓒ Ⓓ Ⓔ
9 Ⓐ Ⓑ Ⓒ Ⓓ Ⓔ
10 Ⓐ Ⓑ Ⓒ Ⓓ Ⓔ
11 Ⓐ Ⓑ Ⓒ Ⓓ Ⓔ
12 Ⓐ Ⓑ Ⓒ Ⓓ Ⓔ
13 Ⓐ Ⓑ Ⓒ Ⓓ Ⓔ
14 Ⓐ Ⓑ Ⓒ Ⓓ Ⓔ
15 Ⓐ Ⓑ Ⓒ Ⓓ Ⓔ
16 Ⓐ Ⓑ Ⓒ Ⓓ Ⓔ
17 Ⓐ Ⓑ Ⓒ Ⓓ Ⓔ
18 Ⓐ Ⓑ Ⓒ Ⓓ Ⓔ
19 Ⓐ Ⓑ Ⓒ Ⓓ Ⓔ
20 Ⓐ Ⓑ Ⓒ Ⓓ Ⓔ
21 Ⓐ Ⓑ Ⓒ Ⓓ Ⓔ
22 Ⓐ Ⓑ Ⓒ Ⓓ Ⓔ
23 Ⓐ Ⓑ Ⓒ Ⓓ Ⓔ
24 Ⓐ Ⓑ Ⓒ Ⓓ Ⓔ
25 Ⓐ Ⓑ Ⓒ Ⓓ Ⓔ
26 Ⓐ Ⓑ Ⓒ Ⓓ Ⓔ
27 Ⓐ Ⓑ Ⓒ Ⓓ Ⓔ
28 Ⓐ Ⓑ Ⓒ Ⓓ Ⓔ
29 Ⓐ Ⓑ Ⓒ Ⓓ Ⓔ
30 Ⓐ Ⓑ Ⓒ Ⓓ Ⓔ

Section 2 — Math
30 minutes

1 Ⓐ Ⓑ Ⓒ Ⓓ Ⓔ
2 Ⓐ Ⓑ Ⓒ Ⓓ Ⓔ
3 Ⓐ Ⓑ Ⓒ Ⓓ Ⓔ
4 Ⓐ Ⓑ Ⓒ Ⓓ Ⓔ
5 Ⓐ Ⓑ Ⓒ Ⓓ Ⓔ
6 Ⓐ Ⓑ Ⓒ Ⓓ Ⓔ
7 Ⓐ Ⓑ Ⓒ Ⓓ Ⓔ
8 Ⓐ Ⓑ Ⓒ Ⓓ Ⓔ
9 Ⓐ Ⓑ Ⓒ Ⓓ Ⓔ
10 Ⓐ Ⓑ Ⓒ Ⓓ Ⓔ
11 Ⓐ Ⓑ Ⓒ Ⓓ Ⓔ
12 Ⓐ Ⓑ Ⓒ Ⓓ Ⓔ
13 Ⓐ Ⓑ Ⓒ Ⓓ Ⓔ
14 Ⓐ Ⓑ Ⓒ Ⓓ Ⓔ
15 Ⓐ Ⓑ Ⓒ Ⓓ Ⓔ
16 Ⓐ Ⓑ Ⓒ Ⓓ Ⓔ
17 Ⓐ Ⓑ Ⓒ Ⓓ Ⓔ
18 Ⓐ Ⓑ Ⓒ Ⓓ Ⓔ
19 Ⓐ Ⓑ Ⓒ Ⓓ Ⓔ
20 Ⓐ Ⓑ Ⓒ Ⓓ Ⓔ
21 Ⓐ Ⓑ Ⓒ Ⓓ Ⓔ
22 Ⓐ Ⓑ Ⓒ Ⓓ Ⓔ
23 Ⓐ Ⓑ Ⓒ Ⓓ Ⓔ
24 Ⓐ Ⓑ Ⓒ Ⓓ Ⓔ
25 Ⓐ Ⓑ Ⓒ Ⓓ Ⓔ

Section 3 — Writing
30 minutes

1 Ⓐ Ⓑ Ⓒ Ⓓ Ⓔ
2 Ⓐ Ⓑ Ⓒ Ⓓ Ⓔ
3 Ⓐ Ⓑ Ⓒ Ⓓ Ⓔ
4 Ⓐ Ⓑ Ⓒ Ⓓ Ⓔ
5 Ⓐ Ⓑ Ⓒ Ⓓ Ⓔ
6 Ⓐ Ⓑ Ⓒ Ⓓ Ⓔ
7 Ⓐ Ⓑ Ⓒ Ⓓ Ⓔ
8 Ⓐ Ⓑ Ⓒ Ⓓ Ⓔ
9 Ⓐ Ⓑ Ⓒ Ⓓ Ⓔ
10 Ⓐ Ⓑ Ⓒ Ⓓ Ⓔ
11 Ⓐ Ⓑ Ⓒ Ⓓ Ⓔ
12 Ⓐ Ⓑ Ⓒ Ⓓ Ⓔ
13 Ⓐ Ⓑ Ⓒ Ⓓ Ⓔ
14 Ⓐ Ⓑ Ⓒ Ⓓ Ⓔ
15 Ⓐ Ⓑ Ⓒ Ⓓ Ⓔ
16 Ⓐ Ⓑ Ⓒ Ⓓ Ⓔ
17 Ⓐ Ⓑ Ⓒ Ⓓ Ⓔ
18 Ⓐ Ⓑ Ⓒ Ⓓ Ⓔ
19 Ⓐ Ⓑ Ⓒ Ⓓ Ⓔ
20 Ⓐ Ⓑ Ⓒ Ⓓ Ⓔ
21 Ⓐ Ⓑ Ⓒ Ⓓ Ⓔ
22 Ⓐ Ⓑ Ⓒ Ⓓ Ⓔ
23 Ⓐ Ⓑ Ⓒ Ⓓ Ⓔ
24 Ⓐ Ⓑ Ⓒ Ⓓ Ⓔ
25 Ⓐ Ⓑ Ⓒ Ⓓ Ⓔ
26 Ⓐ Ⓑ Ⓒ Ⓓ Ⓔ
27 Ⓐ Ⓑ Ⓒ Ⓓ Ⓔ
28 Ⓐ Ⓑ Ⓒ Ⓓ Ⓔ
29 Ⓐ Ⓑ Ⓒ Ⓓ Ⓔ
30 Ⓐ Ⓑ Ⓒ Ⓓ Ⓔ
31 Ⓐ Ⓑ Ⓒ Ⓓ Ⓔ
32 Ⓐ Ⓑ Ⓒ Ⓓ Ⓔ
33 Ⓐ Ⓑ Ⓒ Ⓓ Ⓔ
34 Ⓐ Ⓑ Ⓒ Ⓓ Ⓔ
35 Ⓐ Ⓑ Ⓒ Ⓓ Ⓔ
36 Ⓐ Ⓑ Ⓒ Ⓓ Ⓔ
37 Ⓐ Ⓑ Ⓒ Ⓓ Ⓔ
38 Ⓐ Ⓑ Ⓒ Ⓓ Ⓔ
39 Ⓐ Ⓑ Ⓒ Ⓓ Ⓔ

Section 4 — Verbal
30 minutes

31 Ⓐ Ⓑ Ⓒ Ⓓ Ⓔ
32 Ⓐ Ⓑ Ⓒ Ⓓ Ⓔ
33 Ⓐ Ⓑ Ⓒ Ⓓ Ⓔ
34 Ⓐ Ⓑ Ⓒ Ⓓ Ⓔ
35 Ⓐ Ⓑ Ⓒ Ⓓ Ⓔ
36 Ⓐ Ⓑ Ⓒ Ⓓ Ⓔ
37 Ⓐ Ⓑ Ⓒ Ⓓ Ⓔ
38 Ⓐ Ⓑ Ⓒ Ⓓ Ⓔ
39 Ⓐ Ⓑ Ⓒ Ⓓ Ⓔ
40 Ⓐ Ⓑ Ⓒ Ⓓ Ⓔ
41 Ⓐ Ⓑ Ⓒ Ⓓ Ⓔ
42 Ⓐ Ⓑ Ⓒ Ⓓ Ⓔ
43 Ⓐ Ⓑ Ⓒ Ⓓ Ⓔ
44 Ⓐ Ⓑ Ⓒ Ⓓ Ⓔ
45 Ⓐ Ⓑ Ⓒ Ⓓ Ⓔ
46 Ⓐ Ⓑ Ⓒ Ⓓ Ⓔ
47 Ⓐ Ⓑ Ⓒ Ⓓ Ⓔ
48 Ⓐ Ⓑ Ⓒ Ⓓ Ⓔ
49 Ⓐ Ⓑ Ⓒ Ⓓ Ⓔ
50 Ⓐ Ⓑ Ⓒ Ⓓ Ⓔ
51 Ⓐ Ⓑ Ⓒ Ⓓ Ⓔ
52 Ⓐ Ⓑ Ⓒ Ⓓ Ⓔ
53 Ⓐ Ⓑ Ⓒ Ⓓ Ⓔ
54 Ⓐ Ⓑ Ⓒ Ⓓ Ⓔ
55 Ⓐ Ⓑ Ⓒ Ⓓ Ⓔ
56 Ⓐ Ⓑ Ⓒ Ⓓ Ⓔ
57 Ⓐ Ⓑ Ⓒ Ⓓ Ⓔ
58 Ⓐ Ⓑ Ⓒ Ⓓ Ⓔ
59 Ⓐ Ⓑ Ⓒ Ⓓ Ⓔ
60 Ⓐ Ⓑ Ⓒ Ⓓ Ⓔ

Section 5 — Math
30 minutes

26 Ⓐ Ⓑ Ⓒ Ⓓ Ⓔ
27 Ⓐ Ⓑ Ⓒ Ⓓ Ⓔ
28 Ⓐ Ⓑ Ⓒ Ⓓ Ⓔ
29 Ⓐ Ⓑ Ⓒ Ⓓ Ⓔ
30 Ⓐ Ⓑ Ⓒ Ⓓ Ⓔ
31 Ⓐ Ⓑ Ⓒ Ⓓ Ⓔ
32 Ⓐ Ⓑ Ⓒ Ⓓ Ⓔ
33 Ⓐ Ⓑ Ⓒ Ⓓ Ⓔ
34 Ⓐ Ⓑ Ⓒ Ⓓ Ⓔ
35 Ⓐ Ⓑ Ⓒ Ⓓ Ⓔ
36 Ⓐ Ⓑ Ⓒ Ⓓ Ⓔ
37 Ⓐ Ⓑ Ⓒ Ⓓ Ⓔ
39 Ⓐ Ⓑ Ⓒ Ⓓ Ⓔ
39 Ⓐ Ⓑ Ⓒ Ⓓ Ⓔ
40 Ⓐ Ⓑ Ⓒ Ⓓ Ⓔ

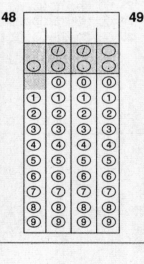

41 42 43 44 45 46 47 48 49 50

SECTION 1
Verbal Reasoning

Time—30 minutes
30 Questions

For each question in this section, select the best answer from among the choices given and fill in the corresponding oval on the answer sheet.

Directions

Each sentence below has one or two blanks, each blank indicating that something has been omitted. Beneath the sentence are five words or sets of words labeled A through E. Choose the word or set of words that, when inserted in the sentence, best fits the meaning of the sentence as a whole.

Example:

Medieval kingdoms did not become constitutional republics overnight; on the contrary, the change was ____ .

(A) unpopular
(B) unexpected
(C) advantageous
(D) sufficient
(E) gradual

Ⓐ Ⓑ Ⓒ Ⓓ ●

1. Criticism that tears down without suggesting areas of improvement is not ____ and should be avoided if possible.

   (A) representative   (B) constructive
   (C) mandatory   (D) pertinent   (E) sagacious

2. The wicked queen was filled with ____ delight when she gazed on the poisoned apple with which she planned to kill Snow White.

   (A) malicious   (B) innocent   (C) muted
   (D) ravenous   (E) heartwarming

3. Although weeks remain for concessions to be made and for new approaches to be attempted, negotiations have reached such a state that management and union leaders are ____ that their differences can no longer be reconciled.

   (A) encouraged   (B) bewildered
   (C) apprehensive   (D) relieved   (E) skeptical

4. Though editors often recommend major alterations in first novels, Hemingway's editors suggested he make only ____ changes in his manuscript.

   (A) naturalistic   (B) minute   (C) ambiguous
   (D) ineffective   (E) unexpected

5. Many educators believe that, far from being a temporary stopgap, useful only as a transitional measure, bilingual education has proved to have definite ____ education in any one tongue.

   (A) correlations with   (B) advantages over
   (C) connotations for   (D) limitations on
   (E) influence on

6. Although her early poetry was clearly ____ in nature, the critics thought she had promise and eventually would find her own voice.

   (A) conservative   (B) narrative
   (C) melodious   (D) derivative   (E) individual

7. If one task of biography is to cast as bright a light as possible over the ____ area of human behavior, then psychobiography doubles the effort, using the insights gleaned through psychological theory to ____ the full range of human experience.

   (A) murky..permeate   (B) shadowed..illumine
   (C) circumscribed..establish
   (D) broad..limit   (E) entire..hypothesize

8. In a time of general architectural simplicity and minimalism, the ornate new civic center was ____ for its flamboyance.

   (A) representative   (B) contemptible
   (C) conspicuous   (D) definitive
   (E) conventional

9. The columnist was very gentle when she mentioned her friends, but she was bitter and even ____ when she discussed people who ____ her.

   (A) laconic..infuriated   (B) acerbic..irritated
   (C) remorseful..encouraged
   (D) militant..distressed   (E) stoical..alienated

10. Like the theory of evolution, the Big Bang model of the universe's formation has undergone modification and ____, but it has ____ all serious challenges.

    (A) alteration..confirmed
    (B) refinement..resisted
    (C) transformation..ignored
    (D) evaluation..acknowledged
    (E) refutation..misdirected

11. There is an essential ____ in human gestures, and when someone raises the palms of his hands together, we do not know whether it is to bury himself in prayer or to throw himself into the sea.

    (A) economy   (B) dignity   (C) insincerity
    (D) reverence   (E) ambiguity

GO ON TO THE NEXT PAGE ⇒

12. Unable to ____ her wholehearted distaste for media events and unnecessary publicity, Dean Brower continued to make ____ comments throughout the entire ceremony.

    (A) control..garbled   (B) maintain..copious
    (C) conceal..effusive   (D) disguise..caustic
    (E) express..vitriolic

13. A ____ cannot recognize any faults in his country, no matter how flagrant they may be.

    (A) zealot   (B) patriarch   (C) chauvinist
    (D) renegade   (E) vigilante

14. Highly controversial at the time, Tynan's reviews were noted for their caustic attacks and general tone of ____ .

    (A) whimsy   (B) trepidation   (C) objectivity
    (D) truculence   (E) resignation

15. The term "rare earths" is in fact a ____, for, paradoxically, the rare-earth elements are in actuality ____, being present in low concentration in virtually all minerals.

    (A) truism..essential   (B) misnomer..ubiquitous
    (C) disclaimer..ephemeral (D) metaphor..figurative
    (E) mnemonic..unmemorable

16. The perpetual spinning of particles is much like that of a top, with one significant difference: unlike the top, the particles have no need to be wound up, for ____ is one of their ____ properties.

    (A) revolution..radical   (B) motion..intangible
    (C) rotation..intrinsic   (D) acceleration..lesser
    (E) collision..hypothetical

17. Slander is like counterfeit money: many people who would not coin it ____ it without qualms.

    (A) waste   (B) denounce   (C) circulate
    (D) withdraw   (E) invest

Directions

Each passage below is followed by questions based on its content. Answer the questions following each passage on the basis of what is <u>stated</u> or <u>implied</u> in that passage and in any introductory material that may be provided.

Questions 18–22 are based on the following passage.

The following passage is excerpted from a review of a book of literary criticism published in 1988.

"The emancipation of women," James Joyce told one of his friends, "has caused the greatest revolution in our time in the most important rela-
Line tionship there is—that between men and
5 women." Other modernists agreed: Virginia Woolf, claiming that in about 1910 "human character changed," and, illustrating the new balance between the sexes, urged, "Read the 'Agamemnon,' and see whether . . . your sympa-
10 thies are not almost entirely with Clytemnestra." D. H. Lawrence wrote, "Perhaps the deepest fight for 2000 years and more, has been the fight for women's independence."

But if modernist writers considered women's
15 revolt against men's domination one of their "greatest" and "deepest" themes, only recently— in perhaps the past 15 years—has literary criticism begun to catch up with it. Not that the images of sexual antagonism that abound in mod-
20 ern literature have gone unremarked; far from it. But what we are able to see in literary works depends on the perspectives we bring to them, and now that women—enough to make a difference— are reforming canons and interpreting literature,
25 the landscapes of literary history and the features of individual books have begun to change.

The War of the Words [by Sandra M. Gilbert and Susan Gubar] argues that modernism emerged from a battle of the sexes that began with
30 the demise of the Victorian feminine ideal and the rise of feminism in the late nineteenth century. Within this large-scale war, the authors chronicle periodic clashes between antagonists who seem to remain the same the more they change:
35 Victorian husbands and maddened wives, turn-of-the-century misogynists and militant suffragists, mid-century he-men and ambitious, independent women, contemporary masculinists and second-wave feminists.
40 Beyond narratives of physical and social violence between the sexes, Ms. Gilbert and Ms. Gubar document a war on women's words, waged by male writers who felt their tradition invaded by alien female talents. T. S. Eliot considered that
45 every masterpiece disturbs the order of those that precede it, but twentieth century women's writing seem to have thrown the tradition, and the traditionalists, into unusual disarray. Ms. Gilbert and Ms. Gubar attribute the revival of literary sex
50 wars in the twentieth century to the fact that never before had aspiring male writers had so many formidable literary foremothers to contend with—or, for that matter, so many female rivals for the power of the word who refused to wither under
55 their scorn. Men's defenses against women's words included ignoring women writers' achievements or patronizing them as "feminine," imposing derisive stereotypes on them, slandering them, "prescribing alternative ambitions for them,"
60 craftily appropriating their language, and identifying good writing with masculinity—as, for example, Williams's notion that "good poetry," like little boys, is made of "rats and snails and puppy dog tails."

GO ON TO THE NEXT PAGE

18. According to the passage, women are changing the nature of literary criticism by

(A) noting instances of hostility between men and women
(B) seeing literature from fresh points of view
(C) emphasizing the works of early twentieth-century writers
(D) limiting their criticism to books written by feminists
(E) resisting masculine authority and control

19. The reviewer quotes James Joyce, Virginia Woolf, and D. H. Lawrence primarily in order to show that

(A) they were too few for their views to make a difference
(B) although well-meaning, they were ineffectual
(C) before the twentieth century, there was little interest in women's literature
(D) modern literature is dependent on the women's movement
(E) the interest of writers in feminist issues is long standing

20. The reviewer's attitude toward women's emancipation can best be described as one of

(A) marked ambivalence   (B) qualified approval
(C) scientific detachment   (D) open endorsement
(E) warranted skepticism

21. The passage indicates that the response of many contemporary women writers to the scorn of their male peers has been one of

(A) dejection   (B) approbation   (C) defiance
(D) condescension   (E) tolerance

22. Williams makes his point about the masculine nature of good poetry (lines 55–64) through

(A) case histories   (B) textual analysis
(C) citations of authorities   (D) personal anecdote
(E) analogy

Questions 23–30 are based on the following passage.

The following excerpt is from Eyes on the Prize, *the companion guide to the public television series on America's civil rights struggle.*

During the 1930s National Association for the Advancement of Colored People (NAACP) attorneys Charles H. Houston, William Hastie, James
Line M. Nabrit, Leon Ransom, and Thurgood Marshall
5 charted a legal strategy designed to end segregation in education. They developed a series of legal cases challenging segregation in graduate and professional schools. Houston believed that the battle against segregation had to begin at the high-
10 est academic level in order to mitigate fear of race

mixing that could create even greater hostility and reluctance on the part of white judges. After establishing a series of favorable legal precedents in higher education, NAACP attorneys planned to
15 launch an all-out attack on the separate-but-equal doctrine in primary and secondary schools. The strategy proved successful. In four major United States Supreme Court decisions precedents were established that would enable the NAACP to con-
20 struct a solid legal foundation upon which the Brown case could rest: *Missouri ex rel. Gaines* v. *Canada,* Registrar of the University of Missouri (1938); *Sipuel* v. *Board of Regents of the University of Oklahoma* (1948); *McLaurin* v.
25 *Oklahoma State Regents for Higher Education* (1950); and *Sweatt* v. *Painter* (1950).

In the Oklahoma case, the Supreme Court held that the plaintiff was entitled to enroll in the university. The Oklahoma Regents responded by sep-
30 arating black and white students in cafeterias and classrooms. The 1950 *McLaurin* decision ruled that such internal separation was unconstitutional. In the *Sweatt* ruling, delivered on the same day, the Supreme Court held that the maintenance of
35 separate law schools for whites and blacks was unconstitutional. A year after Herman Sweatt entered the University of Texas law school, desegregation cases were filed in the states of Kansas, South Carolina, Virginia, and Delaware,
40 and in the District of Columbia asking the courts to apply the qualitative test of the Sweatt case to the elementary and secondary schools and to declare the separate-but-equal doctrine invalid in the area of public education.

45 The 1954 *Brown* v. *Board of Education* decision declared that a classification based solely on race violated the 14th Amendment to the United States Constitution. The decision reversed the 1896 *Plessy* v. *Ferguson* ruling that had estab-
50 lished the separate-but-equal doctrine. The *Brown* decision more than any other case launched the "equalitarian revolution" in American jurisprudence and signalled the emerging primacy of equality as a guide to constitutional decisions;
55 nevertheless, the decision did not end state-sanctioned segregation. Indeed, the second *Brown* decision, known as *Brown II* and delivered a year later, played a decisive role in limiting the effectiveness and impact of the 1954 case by providing
60 southern states with the opportunity to delay the implementation of desegregation.

The intervention of the federal government and the deployment of the National Guard in the 1954 Little Rock crisis, and again in 1963 when the
65 enrollment of James Meredith desegregated the University of Mississippi, highlights the role of federal power in promoting social change during this era. While black local and national leaders organized and orchestrated the legal struggles,
70 and students joined in freedom rides and staged

GO ON TO THE NEXT PAGE

sit-ins, another equally important dimension of the rights quest took shape: the battle between federal and state authority and the evolution of the doctrine of federalism. The fact remains that the United States Supreme Court lacked the power to enforce its decisions. President Dwight D. Eisenhower's use of federal troops in Little Rock was a major departure from the reluctance of past presidents to display federal power in the South, especially to protect the lives and rights of black citizens.

Black Americans had joyfully applauded the *Brown* decision, equating it with the Emancipation Proclamation. White southerners, on the other hand, almost universally denounced the ruling and even questioned the right of the Supreme Court to deliver such a blow to their way of life. It is possible to decipher two interlocking, mutually reinforcing strands in the southern reaction to *Brown*: massive resistance and interposition.

Massive resistance assumed many forms. In hundreds of communities local businessmen and social and political leaders organized White Citizens' Councils to undermine black pressure for desegregation of schools and civil rights. Council leaders employed economic sanctions, held rallies, and used intimidating rhetoric to instill fear in local blacks. Prominent southern politicians also demonstrated their displeasure.

An array of southern governors acquired national notoriety in their public displays of defiance to court-ordered desegregation of secondary schools and state universities. It was their obstinate adherence to the doctrine of interposition that provoked the confrontation between state and federal authority. This doctrine holds that a state may reject a federal mandate it considers to be an encroachment upon a state's rights. But this is only half of the explanation of how the confrontations originated, especially in the Meredith episode. The other half involves the protracted delays, futile negotiations, and considerable vacillation of the Kennedy administration before it finally began to act decisively to protect Meredith's life and right to attend "Ole Miss."

23. According to the passage, Houston aimed his legislative challenge at the graduate and professional school level on the basis of the assumption that

(A) the greatest inequities existed at the highest academic and professional levels
(B) the separate-but-equal doctrine applied solely to the highest academic levels
(C) there were clear precedents for reform in existence at the graduate school level
(D) the judiciary would feel less apprehensive about desegregation on the graduate level
(E) the consequences of desegregation would become immediately apparent at the graduate school level

24. The word "decision" in line 31 means
(A) firmness   (B) settlement   (C) ruling
(D) perseverance   (E) litigation

25. The passage suggests that the reaction of the Oklahoma Regents to the 1948 *Sipuel* decision was one of
(A) resigned tolerance   (B) avowed uncertainty
(C) moderate amusement   (D) distinct displeasure
(E) unquestioning approbation

26. The word "maintenance" in line 34 means
(A) repair   (B) livelihood   (C) firm assertion
(D) ongoing support   (E) continuity

27. Which of the following best describes the relationship between the *McLaurin* decision and the 1954 *Brown* v. *Board of Education* decision?
(A) The *McLaurin* decision superseded the *Brown* decision.
(B) The *Brown* decision provided a precedent for the *McLaurin* decision.
(C) The *Brown* decision reversed the *McLaurin* decision.
(D) The *McLaurin* decision limited the application of the *Brown* decision.
(E) The *McLaurin* decision provided legal authority for the *Brown* decision.

28. Which of the following titles best describes the content of the passage?
(A) Executive Intervention in the Fight Against Segregated Education
(B) The *Brown* Decision and the Equalitarian Revolution
(C) A Long War: The Struggle to Desegregate American Education
(D) The Emergence of Federalism and the Civil Rights Movement
(E) Education Reform and the Role of the NAACP

29. The aspect of Houston's work most clearly brought out in the passage is its
(A) psychological canniness
(B) judicial complexity
(C) fundamental efficiency
(D) radical intellectualism
(E) exaggerated idealism

30. The passage's attitude toward the Kennedy administration's handling of the Meredith case is one of
(A) grudging respect
(B) unmitigated disdain
(C) qualified forbearance
(D) marked ambivalence
(E) futile regret

IF YOU FINISH BEFORE 30 MINUTES, YOU MAY CHECK YOUR WORK ON THIS SECTION ONLY. DO NOT TURN TO ANY OTHER SECTION IN THE TEST.   **S T O P**

SECTION 2
Mathematical Reasoning

**Time—30 minutes
25 Questions**

Directions and Reference Information

In this section solve each problem, using any available space for scratchwork. Then decide which is the best of the choices given and fill in the corresponding oval on the answer sheet.

Notes:

(1) The use of a calculator is permitted. All numbers used are real numbers.

(2) Figures that accompany problems in this test are intended to provide information useful in solving the problems. They are drawn as accurately as possible EXCEPT when it is stated in a specific problem that the figure is not drawn to scale. All figures lie in a plane unless otherwise indicated.

Reference Information

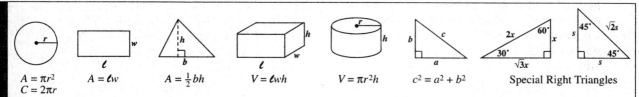

$A = \pi r^2$
$C = 2\pi r$

$A = \ell w$

$A = \frac{1}{2}bh$

$V = \ell w h$

$V = \pi r^2 h$

$c^2 = a^2 + b^2$

Special Right Triangles

The number of degrees of an arc in a circle is 360.
The measure in degrees of a straight angle is 180.
The sum of the measures in degrees of the angles of a triangle is 180.

---

1. How much is $\frac{1}{2}$ of $\frac{x}{2}$?

(A) x (B) $\frac{1}{x}$ (C) $\frac{1}{4}$ (D) $\frac{x}{4}$ (E) $4x$

2. If $\left(\frac{a}{2}\right)\left(\frac{b}{4}\right) = 8$, what is the value of $0.125\, ab$?

(A) 1   (B) 2   (C) 4   (D) 8   (E) 64

3. What percent of 7.5 is 0.075?

(A) 0.001%   (B) 0.01%   (C) 0.1%
(D) 1%   (E) 10%

4. In a graduating class having the same number of boys and girls, the guidance counselor finds that $\frac{1}{2}$ the boys and $\frac{1}{3}$ of the girls are going to college. What percent of the class is going to college?

(A) 33.3%   (B) 41.7%   (C) 58.3%
(D) 66%   (E) 83.3%

5. All of the following are equal EXCEPT

(A) $1 + \frac{x}{y}$ (B) $\frac{xy + x^2}{x^2}$ (C) $\frac{y^2 + xy}{xy}$

(D) $\frac{y}{x} + 1$ (E) $\frac{x + y}{x}$

6. $2x + t = 2$
$t =$

(A) x (B) $x - 1$ (C) $2x - 2$
(D) $2 - 2x$ (E) $1 - x$

7. The accompanying figure shows two vertices of square $ABCD$. Which of the following could be the coordinates of vertex C?

I. $(2, -2)$
II. $(4, -4)$
III. $(-2, 2)$

(A) I only
(B) II only
(C) I and II only
(D) I and III only
(E) II and III only

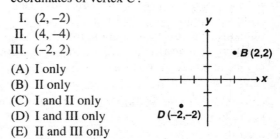

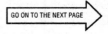GO ON TO THE NEXT PAGE

8. By allowing a discount of 30% on an article formerly selling for $150 a dealer finds he is making a profit of 5% of his cost. His cost was

(A) $52.50   (B) $98.50   (C) $100.00
(D) $105.00   (E) $142.50

9. A grocer paid $2600 for a secondhand delivery truck. At the end of $4\frac{1}{2}$ years he was allowed $440 for it toward the purchase of a new truck. What was the average yearly amount of depreciation?

(A) $220   (B) $450   (C) $480
(D) $550   (E) $2200

10. A diamond ring valued at $7000 was insured at 80% of its value. What was the premium, if the rate was $6 per $1000?

(A) $3.36   (B) $4.20   (C) $33.60
(D) $42.00   (E) $336.00

11. A can of food feeds 3 kittens or 2 dogs. If I have 8 cans of food and I feed 12 kittens, how many dogs can I feed?

(A) 2   (B) 4   (C) 8   (D) 12   (E) 18

12. How much more is $x - 2$ than 2?

(A) $-x$ (B) $x - 4$ (C) x (D) $2 - x$ (E) 0

13. A broad jumper makes an average standing jump of 8 feet. In how many jumps will he cover y yards?

(A) $\frac{3y}{8}$ (B) $\frac{8}{3y}$ (C) $24y$ (D) $\frac{1}{24y}$ (E) $\frac{24}{y}$

14. James is 30 years old and John is 3 years old. James will be five times as old as John in

(A) $3\frac{3}{4}$ years   (B) $6\frac{1}{2}$ years
(C) $11\frac{1}{4}$ years   (D) 37 years   (E) 38 years

15. Mrs. Lehman finds that her tax bill increased form $2500 to $3000. The percent increase is

(A) 5%   (B) 10%   (C) $16\frac{2}{3}$%
(D) 20%   (E) 25%

16. Mr. Liebow received 10 crates of fruit for which he paid $90. He finds that one crate is not suitable for sale because of spoilage. At what price should he sell each of the other crates in order to realize a 20% profit on the total cost?

(A) $1.80   (B) $3.00   (C) $10.80
(D) $12.00   (E) $18.00

17. At 10 A.M. water begins to pour into a cylindrical can 14 inches high and 4 inches in diameter at the rate of 8 cubic inches every 10 minutes. At what time will it being to overflow? $\left(\text{Use } \pi = \frac{22}{7}.\right)$

(A) 10:10 A.M.   (B) 11:40 A.M.   (C) 12:40 A.M.
(D) 1:40 P.M.   (E) 2:40 A.M.

18. The width of the ring (shaded portion of the figure) is exactly equal to the radius of the inner circle. What percent of the entire area is the area of the shaded portion?

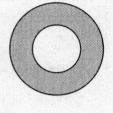

(A) 25%   (B) $33\frac{1}{3}$%
(C) 50%   (D) $66\frac{2}{3}$%   (E) 75%

19. Mr. Adams has a circular flower bed whose diameter is 4 feet. He wishes to increase the size of his bed so that it will have four times as much planting area. What must be the diameter of the new bed?

(A) 6 ft.   (B) 8 ft.   (C) 10 ft.
(D) 12 ft.   (E) 16 ft.

20. In circle O, $OA = 4$, and $\overset{\frown}{AB} =$ 112°. What is the measure of $\angle ABO$?

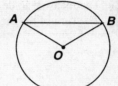

(A) 22°   (B) 34°   (C) 44°
(D) 45°   (E) 68°

21. An altitude h of a triangle is twice the base to which it is drawn. If the area of the triangle is 225 square inches, then altitude h is

(A) 15 in.   (B) 20 in.   (C) 25 in.
(D) 30 in.   (E) 35 in.

22. If the perimeter of a square is increased by 80%, by what percent is the area increased?

(A) 4%   (B) 20%   (C) 64%
(D) 80%   (E) 224%

23. In distributing milk at a summer camp it is found that a quart of milk will fill either 3 large glass tumblers or 5 small glass tumblers. How many small glass tumblers can be filled with one large glass tumbler?

(A) $\frac{3}{5}$ (B) $1\frac{2}{3}$ (C) $1\frac{2}{5}$ (D) 2   (E) $2\frac{1}{3}$

GO ON TO THE NEXT PAGE

24. Between what years did the sharpest drop in profits occur?

    (A) 1990–1991   (B) 1992–1993
    (C) 1993–1994   (D) 1995–1996
    (E) 1996–1997

25. How many persons in this city were engaged in transportation?

    (A) 7200   (B) 18,000   (C) 20,000
    (D) 36,000   (E) 72,000

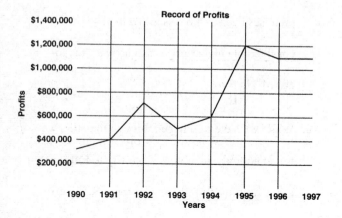

This graph shows the record of profits of the Beacon Co. for a period of 8 years.

This circle graph shows how 370,000 wage earners in a certain city earned their living during a given period.

IF YOU FINISH BEFORE 30 MINUTES, YOU MAY CHECK YOUR WORK ON THIS SECTION ONLY. DO NOT TURN TO ANY OTHER SECTION IN THE TEST.

S T O P

SECTION 3
Writing Skills

Time—30 minutes
39 Questions

Directions

The following sentences contain problems in grammar, usage, diction (choice of words), and idiom.

Some sentences are correct.
No sentence contains more than one error.

You will find that the error, if there is one, is underlined and lettered. Assume that elements of the sentence that are not underlined are correct and cannot be changed. In choosing answers, follow the requirements of standard written English.

If there is an error, select the <u>one underlined part</u> that must be changed to make the sentence correct and blacken the corresponding space on your answer sheet.

If there is no error, blacken answer space ⓔ .

Example:

The region has a climate <u>so severe that</u> plants
                          A

<u>growing there</u> rarely <u>had been</u> more than twelve
     B   C

inches <u>high</u>. <u>No error</u>
       D   E

Ⓐ Ⓑ ● Ⓓ Ⓔ

1. <u>After</u> his heart attack, he <u>was ordered</u> <u>to lay</u> in bed
   A   B   C

   and <u>rest for</u> two weeks. <u>No error</u>
        D   E

2. While <u>my</u> aunt and I <u>were traveling</u> <u>through</u> our
        A   B   C

   National Parks, my aunt was <u>frightened</u> by a bear.
                                 D

   <u>No error</u>
     E

3. <u>Only</u> recently, the <u>newly</u> organized football association
   A   B

   <u>added</u> two new teams to <u>their</u> league. <u>No error</u>
     C   D   E

4. <u>In view of</u> the controversy with the school board,
   A

   neither the teachers <u>nor</u> the principal <u>are being</u>
                         B   C

   considered for promotion <u>at this time</u>. <u>No error</u>
                             D   E

5. The <u>prospective purchaser</u> of the house left the
      A

   premises because he <u>was asked</u> to pay a
                        B

   <u>considerable higher</u> price <u>than</u> he was able to
      C   D

   afford. <u>No error</u>
            E

6. While we <u>have rummaged</u> <u>through</u> the attic, we
            A   B

   found <u>not only</u> an album of our trip to Europe, but
         C

   also a <u>multitude</u> of old news clippings. <u>No error</u>
          D   E

7. Of <u>all</u> the <u>members of</u> the United States team,
      A   B

   Greg Lemond <u>became</u> the first <u>to win</u> the
                C   D

   prestigious Tour de France bike race. <u>No error</u>
                                           E

8. <u>Neither</u> Carlos nor Mark <u>handed in</u> <u>their</u>
   A   B   C

   assignments <u>on time</u>. <u>No error</u>
                D   E

9. Before we <u>adopt</u> this legislation, we <u>ought to</u>
             A   B

   consider the <u>affect</u> the new law will have on <u>our</u>
                 C   D

   retired and disabled citizens. <u>No error</u>
                                    E

10. The legendary Henry Aaron <u>has established</u> an
                               A

    enviable <u>record, and it</u> probably will not
             B   C

    <u>be broken</u> during the next fifty years. <u>No error</u>
     D   E

11. Mathematics is not his <u>favorite subject</u>; he finds
                            A   B

    <u>them</u> <u>too</u> confusing. <u>No error</u>
     C   D   E

12. Toni Cade Bambara, <u>who</u> is a black American
                        A

    writer, <u>has been active</u> in civil rights and women's
             B

    issues, <u>nor is she</u> <u>attuned to</u> Afro-American
             C   D

    relationships. <u>No error</u>
                    E

GO ON TO THE NEXT PAGE

13. The boom of video cassette records <u>can be</u>
                                          A

<u>attributed to</u> <u>numerous</u> things, <u>including being</u> price
   B   C   D

reduction, time shift approval, and the growth of

rental stores. <u>No error</u>
                    E

14. With the <u>passage of</u> the Tax Reform Act of 1986,
                  A

the <u>most</u> comprehensive changes in the federal tax
      B

system <u>since</u> World War II <u>is</u> taking place. <u>No error</u>
        C   D   E

15. <u>After</u> a six-month study semester abroad, she <u>was</u>
        A   B

<u>happy</u> to get home to <u>comfortable familiar</u>
   C   D

surroundings and appetizing food. <u>No error</u>
                                      E

16. <u>Much more</u> experimental data <u>are</u> required <u>before</u>
        A   B   C

we can accept <u>this theory</u>. <u>No error</u>
               D   E

17. Because he <u>has been warned</u> <u>only</u> about the danger
                   A   B

of <u>walking</u> on the railroad trestle, he dared
   C

<u>several of</u> his friends to walk on the tracks. <u>No error</u>
   D   E

18. Where is it possible to find <u>if</u> <u>it</u> <u>was</u> Lowell <u>or</u>
                                   A   B   C

Longfellow <u>who</u> wrote "Hiawatha"? <u>No error</u>
            D   E

19. <u>Choosing</u> between you and <u>she</u> <u>is</u> very difficult;
        A   B   C

both of you are <u>fully qualified</u>. <u>No error</u>
                 D   E

20. Fifty-three thousand shouting <u>enthusiasts filled the stadium, they had come</u> to watch the first game of the season and to cheer the home team.

(A) enthusiasts filled the stadium, they had come
(B) enthusiasts filled the stadium to come
(C) enthusiasts, filling the stadium, had come
(D) enthusiasts filled the stadium; and had come
(E) enthusiasts filling the stadium, who had come

21. During the judging of the animals at the show, the judges could not decide <u>whether Brown's collie or Jones's terrier was the best</u> dog.

(A) whether Brown's collie or Jones's terrier was the best
(B) if Brown's collie or Jones's terrier was the better
(C) whether Brown's collie or Jones's terrier was the better
(D) if Brown's collie or Jones's terrier was the best
(E) whether Brown's collie or Jones's terrier had been the best

GO ON TO THE NEXT PAGE

22. Finally reviewing the extensive evidence against the defendant, he was found guilty.

    (A) Finally reviewing the extensive evidence against the defendant,
    (B) Reviewing the extensive evidence against the defendant,
    (C) The jury finally reviewed the extensive evidence against the defendant,
    (D) When the jury finally reviewed the extensive evidence against the defendant,
    (E) The jury finally reviewed the evidence against the defendant,

23. Paul Gauguin was married and had family responsibilities and he ran away to the South Seas to paint.

    (A) Paul Gauguin was married and had family responsibilities and he
    (B) Although being married and having family responsibilities, Paul Gauguin
    (C) Although Paul Gauguin was married and had family responsibilities, he
    (D) Being married, and therefore having family responsibilities, Paul Gauguin
    (E) Despite the fact that Paul Gauguin was married and had family responsibilities, he

24. A key difference between mice and moles is tail length, a mouse's tail is twice as long as the tail of a mole.

    (A) length, a mouse's tail is
    (B) length; a mouse's tail is
    (C) length, the tail of a mouse is
    (D) length; a mouse's tail, it is
    (E) length, mice's tails are

25. As a retired executive, he is now busier than ever; he makes his living by speaking before business and philanthropic groups, writing books and articles, and he is a director of three major corporations.

    (A) by speaking before business and philanthropic groups, writing books and articles, and he is a director of
    (B) by speaking before business and philanthropic groups, and he writes books and articles as well as being a director of
    (C) by speaking before business and philanthropic groups, and he writes books and articles, and directs
    (D) by speaking before business and philanthropic groups, writing books and articles, and directing
    (E) by speaking before business and philanthropic groups, in addition to writing books and articles, and he is a director of

26. The President has established a special commission for the space program; the purpose being to investigate the causes of the Challenger disaster.

    (A) program; the purpose being to
    (B) program; whose purpose being to
    (C) program, the purpose is to
    (D) program to
    (E) program; in order to

27. When Harriet Tubman decided to help runaway slaves escape to the North, she knew that her mission would bring her into danger in both South and North.

    (A) When Harriet Tubman decided to help runaway slaves escape
    (B) When Harriet Tubman decides to help runaway slaves escape
    (C) When Harriet Tubman decided about helping runaway slaves escape
    (D) After the decision by Harriet Tubman to help runaway slaves escape
    (E) After Harriet Tubman's making of the decision to help runaway slaves escape

28. The growing impoverishment of women and children in American society distresses Senator Moynihan, and he is also infuriated.

    (A) distresses Senator Moynihan, and he is also infuriated
    (B) distresses Senator Moynihan, infuriating him
    (C) distresses and infuriates Senator Moynihan
    (D) is distressing Senator Moynihan, making him infuriated
    (E) is a cause of distress to Senator Moynihan, and of a fury

29. Being a successful reporter demands powers of observation, fluency, and persistence.

    (A) Being a successful reporter demands
    (B) Being a successful reporter who demands
    (C) To be a successful reporter who demands
    (D) Being a successful reporter demanding
    (E) To be a successful reporter demanding

30. I don't object to John's bill payment if he doesn't expect any favors from me in return.

    (A) John's bill payment if he doesn't
    (B) whether John pays the bill but he mustn't not
    (C) having John pay the bill whether he doesn't
    (D) John's payment of the bill but he shouldn't
    (E) John's paying the bill as long as he doesn't

GO ON TO THE NEXT PAGE

31. <u>Had I been at the scene of the accident</u>, I could have administered first aid to the victims.

(A) Had I been at the scene of the accident
(B) If I were at the scene of the accident
(C) If I was at the scene of the accident
(D) I should have been at the scene of the accident
(E) I should have been at the scene of the accident, and

32. The Northern Lights, or Aurora Borealis, is so named <u>because it is a light display that takes place</u> in the northern skies.

(A) because it is a light display that takes place
(B) as a light display taking place
(C) because of taking place
(D) due to the fact that it is a light display
(E) contrary to the fact of taking place

33. It is not for you to assume responsibility; it is rather, <u>me who is</u> the guilty person in this matter.

(A) me who is
(B) me who am
(C) I who is
(D) I who are
(E) I who am

Directions

The passage below is the unedited draft of a student's essay. Some of the essay needs to be rewritten to make the meaning clearer and more precise. Read the essay carefully.

The essay is followed by six questions about changes that might improve all or part of its organization, development, sentence structure, use of language, appropriateness to the audience, or its use of standard written English. Choose the answer that most clearly and effectively expresses the student's intended meaning. Indicate your choice by filling in the corresponding space on the answer sheet.

ESSAY

[1] Although some people believe that certain celebrations have no point, celebrations are one of the few things that all people have in common. [2] They take place everywhere. [3] Listing all of them would be an impossible task. [4] People of all kinds look forward to celebrations for keeping traditions alive for generation after generation. [5] Those who criticize celebrations do not understand the human need to preserve tradition and culture.

[6] In the Muslim religion, the Ead is a celebration. [7] It begins as soon as Ramadan (the fasting month) is over. [8] During the Ead, families gather together. [9] New clothes are bought for children, and they receive money from both family and friends. [10] Also, each family, if they can afford it, slaughters a sheep or a cow. [11] They keep a small fraction of the meat, and the rest must give to the poor. [12] They also donate money to a mosque.

[14] Many celebrations involve eating meals. [15] In the United States, people gather together on Thanksgiving to say thank you for their blessings by having a huge feast with turkey, sweet potatoes, and cranberry sauce. [16] Christmas and Easter holiday dinners are a custom in the Christian religion. [17] They have a roast at Christmas. [18] At Easter they serve ham. [19] The Jewish people celebrate Passover with a big meal called a seder. [20] They say prayers, drink wine, and sing songs to remember how Jews suffered centuries ago when they escaped from slavery in Egypt.

[21] A celebration is held each year to honor great people like Dr. Martin Luther King. [22] His birthday is celebrated because of this man's noble belief in equality of all races. [23] People wish to remember not only his famous speeches, including "I Have A Dream," but also about him being assassinated in Memphis in 1968. [23] He died while fighting for the equality of minorities. [25] Unlike religious celebrations, celebrations for great heroes like Martin Luther King are for all people everywhere in the world. [26] He is a world-class hero and he deserved the Nobel Prize for Peace that he won.

34. To improve the unity of the first paragraph, which of the following is the best sentence to delete?

(A) Sentence 1
(B) Sentence 2
(C) Sentence 3
(D) Sentence 4
(E) Sentence 5

35. Which is the best revision of sentence 9 below?

New clothes are bought for children, and they receive money from both family and friends.

(A) New clothes are bought for children, and they receive money from both family and friends.
(B) The children, receive new clothes and gifts of money from family and friends.
(C) Receiving new clothes, money is also given by family and friends
(D) Gifts are given to the children of new clothes and money by family and friends.
(E) Parents buy new clothes for their children, and family and friends also give money to them.

GO ON TO THE NEXT PAGE

36. In the context of the third paragraph, which is the best way to combine sentences 16, 17, and 18?

    (A) A roast at Christmas, ham at Easter—that's what Christians eat.
    (B) Christians customarily serve a roast for Christmas dinner, at Easter ham is eaten.
    (C) At customary holiday dinners, Christians eat a roast at Christmas and ham is for Easter dinner.
    (D) Christians often celebrate the Christmas holiday with a roast for dinner and Easter with a traditional ham.
    (E) Christmas and Easter dinners are the custom in the Christian religion, where they have a roast at Christmas and ham at Easter.

37. In an effort to provide a more effective transition between paragraphs 3 and 4, which of the following would be the best revision of sentence 21 below?

    A celebration is held each year to honor great people like Dr. Martin Luther King.

    (A) There are also some celebrations to honor great people like Dr. Martin Luther King.
    (B) Martin Luther King is also celebrated in the United States.
    (C) In the United States, celebrating to honor great people like Dr. Martin Luther King has become a tradition.
    (D) In addition to observing religious holidays, people hold celebrations to honor great leaders like Dr. Martin Luther King
    (E) Besides holding religion-type celebrations, celebrations to honor great people like Dr. Martin Luther King are also held.

38. Which is the best revision of the underlined segment of sentence 23 below?

    People wish to remember not only his famous speeches, including "I Have A Dream," but also about his being assassinated in Memphis in 1968.

    (A) that his assassination occurred
    (B) about his being assassination
    (C) the fact that he was assassinated
    (D) about the assassination, too,
    (E) his assassination

39. Considering the essay as a whole, which one of the following best explains the main function of the last paragraph?

    (A) To summarize the main idea of the essay
    (B) To refute a previous argument stated in the essay
    (C) To give an example
    (D) To provide a solution to a problem.
    (E) To evaluate the validity of the essay's main idea

IF YOU FINISH BEFORE 30 MINUTES, YOU MAY CHECK YOUR WORK ON THIS SECTION ONLY. DO NOT TURN TO ANY OTHER SECTION IN THE TEST.   **S T O P**

SECTION **4**
Verbal Reasoning

Time—30 minutes
30 Questions

For each question in this section, select the best answer from among the choices given and fill in the corresponding oval on the answer sheet.

Directions

Each sentence below consists of a related pair of words or phrases, followed by five pairs of words or phrases labeled A through E. Select the pair that best expresses a relationship similar to that expressed in the original pair.

Example:

CRUMB:BREAD::
(A) ounce:unit
(B) splinter:wood
(C) water:bucket
(D) twine:rope
(E) cream:butter

31. FURNACE:HEAT::

    (A) sponge:moisture
    (B) thermometer:temperature
    (C) camera:exposure   (D) lamp:light
    (E) fan:warmth

32. PALOMINO:HORSE::

    (A) pecan:nut   (B) mongrel:collie
    (C) gander:goose   (D) gills:fish
    (E) saddle:stirrup

33. DROPCLOTH:FURNITURE::

    (A) banner:flagpole   (B) towel:rack
    (C) pillow:bedding   (D) curtain:theater
    (E) apron:clothing

34. YOLK:EGG::

    (A) rind:melon   (B) nucleus:cell
    (C) stalk:corn   (D) duck:fowl
    (E) web:spider

35. CONFINE:PRISONER::

    (A) impeach:governor   (B) trace:fugitive
    (C) detain:suspect   (D) testify:witness
    (E) ambush:sentry

36. SWATCH:FABRIC::

    (A) chip:paint   (B) slag:metal
    (C) mortar:brick   (D) essence:perfume
    (E) loaf:bread

37. TEPID:BOILING::

    (A) frugal:parsimonious
    (B) indifferent:apathetic
    (C) contemptuous:disdainful
    (D) cold:scorching   (E) pleasant:useful

38. CROW:BOASTFUL::

    (A) smirk:witty   (B) conceal:sly
    (C) pout:sulky   (D) blush:coarse
    (E) bluster:unhappy

39. LIBRETTO:POET::

    (A) aria:singer   (B) blueprint:draftsman
    (C) handwriting:author   (D) scalpel:surgeon
    (E) somersault:gymnast

40. SKIRMISH:BATTLE::

    (A) quiz:examination   (B) injury:scar
    (C) detour:road   (D) ambush:retreat
    (E) recital:concert

41. MEANDER:JOURNEY::

    (A) rehearse:performance
    (B) soar:flight   (C) observe:phenomenon
    (D) ramble:speech   (E) clarify:point

42. INDEPENDENT:AUTONOMY::

    (A) courageous:cowardice   (B) coy:silence
    (C) inventive:resourcefulness
    (D) nervous:equanimity   (E) prodigal:economy

43. PENITENT:CONTRITION::

    (A) pragmatist:resignation
    (B) hedonist:self-indulgence
    (C) skeptic:gullibility   (D) stoic:arrogance
    (E) zealot:trepidation

GO ON TO THE NEXT PAGE

The passage below is followed by questions based on its content. Answer the questions following the passage on the basis of what is <u>stated</u> or <u>implied</u> in that passage and in any introductory material that may be provided.

Questions 44–49 are based on the following passage.

In this excerpt from a recent autobiography, a black American writer is traveling to Africa to encounter his ancestral homeland.

An Arab sits beside me on the flight to Tunis. I take the aisle seat; he sits by the window. He wears black jeans and a black leather jacket and
Line he sweats a lot. He is more nervous even than I
5 am, more nervous than anyone ought to be. On his lap he clutches very tightly a brown leather satchel. It could easily fit under the seat in front of him, but he won't let go of it. He looks out the window for what must be the fiftieth time before
10 we take off. When he isn't looking out the window, he is looking around the plane, but not just glancing around; this man is nervous and looking for something, maybe the emergency exits. He is definitely in a hurry to take off. Is he a smuggler
15 and hiding from the police and the bag stuffed with jewels and money? He certainly doesn't seem like a Tunisian businessman merely returning home from a holiday in Italy.
  Then I realize. Arabs, Palestinians, they're all
20 the same.
  His hair is jet black and curly tight, tapering toward the back of his head. He wears a thick mustache and razor stubble covers his chin. He looks as if he hasn't slept any more than I have,
25 and he could use a cigarette.
  Of all the places to sit, why did I have to sit next to an Arab terrorist? And why did he, with all the empty seats on this flight, choose to sit next to me? To be over the wing, of course,
30 where an exploding bomb would do the most damage. In the satchel he must be carrying a bomb.
  I close my eyes and imagine the plane engulfed in a fireball after the explosion and streaking
35 through the sky and down into the sea. I will not hear the boom and I will feel nothing. I look over and silently thank this Arab terrorist for sitting so close to me. There will be no time for pain, no time to scream or panic or even to know what's
40 happening.
  We are already taxiing. I will go to my death calmly. I will see how brave I can be with death sitting right beside me, not just death but a violent explosion, being ripped out through a gaping hole
45 along with dozens of others, seats, baggage, shards of shattered and twisted metal, and plunging through the sky like a fallen angel.

  We are in the air and already out over the Mediterranean. The plane takes a violent dip. The
50 seat belt sign comes on. We are buffeted severely, knocked around in the sky. I grit my teeth, praying for a pilot who has trained with the U.S. Navy, wondering why I didn't fly to Tunisia on a real airline, like Pan Am.
55 I'm losing it, going crazy. I look over at my terrorist and he is going crazy too.
  The stewardess comes down the aisle. She is handing out landing cards for passengers to fill out and give to immigration officials once we
60 land. The Arab leans over to me.
  "Can you help me, please?" he asks.
  The look on my face. I wonder what it says to him.
  "Do you speak French?" he asks.
65 I shake off my stupor and answer him. He asks me to help him fill out his landing card. He cannot read or write. He hands me his passport—written in Arabic—and what he says in French I write for him.
70 He had been living and working in Naples, and now he was going home to be with his family in Tunis. He hated airplanes. Flying made him nervous.
  I nodded in agreement. "Me too," I said.
75 Tunis sprawled out below the plane and reached from the edge of the sea toward the desert, a huge city spreading endlessly, sand colored and white, reflecting sun and heat. The man beside me smiled the smile of a homecoming. To
80 him Tunis was beauty, tradition, home. To me it was just the beginning.
  I had eased into Africa all right, eased in with a jolt. The whole of Africa lay before me. And I was as racist as anyone else.

44. In lines 2–25, as the author observes his neighbor, his thoughts become increasingly

(A) figurative   (B) sardonic
(C) melodramatic   (D) abstract
(E) obscure

45. The author responds to the plane's dipping (line 49) by

(A) expressing gratitude for the pilot's skill
(B) feeling apprehension that the bomb will explode
(C) wishing he were back in American hands
(D) trying to prove his grit by keeping a calm appearance
(E) forgetting his worries about the terrorist

GO ON TO THE NEXT PAGE →

46. The author's immediate reaction to the Arab's question is one of

(A) indignation   (B) bafflement   (C) hostility
(D) impatience   (E) amusement

47. The author realizes that by assuming his neighbor was a terrorist he has been guilty of

(A) ethnicity   (B) discourtesy   (C) stereotyping
(D) rashness   (E) snobbery

48. In stating that he had "eased in with a jolt" (line 83), the author refers to the fact that

(A) the violent dipping of the plane had terrified him
(B) he had been unaware of terrorists before leaving America
(C) the existence of the bomb had shaken his confidence
(D) he had been shocked to find racist tendencies in himself
(E) traveling abroad is an inherently disconcerting experience

---

The passages below are followed by questions based on their content; questions following a pair of related passages may also be based on the relationship between the paired passages. Answer the questions on the basis of what is <u>stated</u> or <u>implied</u> in the passages and in any introductory material that may be provided.

Questions 50–60 are based on the following passages.

The following passages are exerpted from popular studies of dolphins.

PASSAGE 1

Most of the intelligent land animals have prehensile, grasping organs for exploring their environment—hands in human beings and their anthropoid relatives, the sensitive inquiring trunk in the elephant. One of the surprising things about the dolphin is that his superior brain is unaccompanied by any type of manipulative organ. He has, however, a remarkable range-finding ability involving some sort of echo-sounding. Perhaps this acute sense—far more accurate than any that human ingenuity has been able to devise artificially—brings him greater knowledge of his watery surroundings than might at first seem possible. Human beings think of intelligence as geared to things. The hand and the tool are to us the unconscious symbols of our intellectual attainment. It is difficult for us to visualize another kind of lonely, almost disembodied intelligence floating in the wavering green fairyland of the sea—an intelligence possibly near or comparable to our own but without hands to build, to transmit knowledge by writing, or to alter by one hairsbreadth the planet's surface. Yet at the same time there are indications that this is a warm, friendly, and eager intelligence quite capable of coming to the assistance of injured companions and striving to rescue them from drowning. Dolphins left the land when mammalian brains were still small and primitive. Without the stimulus provided by agile exploring fingers, these great sea mammals have yet taken a divergent road toward intelligence of a high order. Hidden in their sleek bodies is an impressively elaborated instrument, the reason for whose appearance is a complete enigma. It is as though both the human being and the dolphin were each part of some great eye that yearned to look both outward on eternity and inward to the sea's heart—that fertile entity like the mind in its swarming and grotesque life.

PASSAGE 2

Nothing about dolphins has been more widely or passionately discussed over the centuries than their supposed intelligence and communicative abilities. In fact, a persistent dogma holds that dolphins are among the most intelligent of animals and that they communicate with one another in complex ways. Implicit in this argument is the belief that dolphin cultures are at least as ancient and rich as our own.

To support the claim of high intelligence amongst dolphins, proponents note that they have large brains, live in societies marked as much by cooperative as by competitive interactions, and rapidly learn the artificial tasks given to them in captivity. Indeed, dolphins are clearly capable of learning through observation and have good memories. People who spend time with captive dolphins are invariably impressed by their sense of humor, playfulness, quick comprehension of body language, command of situations, mental agility, and emotional resilience. Individual dolphins have distinctive personalities and trainers often speak of being trained by their subjects, rather than the other way round.

The extremely varied repertoires of sounds made by dolphins are often invoked as *prima facie* evidence of advanced communication abilities. In addition, some "scientific" experiments done by John Lilly and his associates during the 1950s and 1960s were claimed to show that dolphins communicate not only with one another but also with humans, mimicking human speech and reaching out across the boundaries that divide us.

GO ON TO THE NEXT PAGE

These conclusions about dolphin intelligence and communication have not withstood critical
75 scrutiny. While they have fueled romantic speculation, their net impact has been to mislead. Rather than allowing dolphins to be discovered and appreciated for what they are, Lilly's vision has forced us to measure these animals' value
80 according to how close they come to equalling or exceeding our own intelligence, virtue, and spiritual development.

The issues of dolphin intelligence and communication have been inseparable in most people's
85 minds, and the presumed existence of one has been taken as proof of the other, a classic case of begging the question. Not surprisingly then, most experiments to evaluate dolphin intelligence have measured the animals' capacity for cognitive pro-
90 cessing as exhibited in their understanding of the rudiments of language.

From the early work of researchers like Dwight Batteau and Jarvis Bastian through the more recent work of Louis Herman and associ-
95 ates, dolphins have been asked to accept simple information, in the form of acoustic or visual symbols representing verbs and nouns, and then to act on the information following a set of commands from the experimenter.
100 The widely publicized results have been somewhat disappointing. Although they have demonstrated that dolphins do have the primary skills necessary to support understanding and use of a language, they have not distinguished the dol-
105 phins from other animals in this respect. For example, some seals, animals we do not normally cite as members of the intellectual or communicative elite, have been found to have the same basic capabilities.
110 What, then, do the results of experiments to date mean? Either we have not devised adequate tests to permit us to detect, measure, and rank intelligence as a measure of a given species' ability to communicate, or we must acknowledge that
115 the characteristics that we regard as rudimentary evidence of intelligence are held more commonly by many "lower" animals than we previously thought.

49. According to Passage 1, which of the following statements about dolphins is true?

   (A) They have always been water-dwelling creatures.
   (B) They at one time possessed prehensile organs.
   (C) They lived on land in prehistoric times.
   (D) Their brains are no longer mammalian in nature.
   (E) They developed brains to compensate for the lack of a prehensile organ.

50. The author of Passage 1 suggests that human failure to understand the intelligence of the dolphin is due to

   (A) the inadequacy of human range-finding equipment
   (B) a lack of knowledge about the sea
   (C) the want of a common language
   (D) the primitive origins of the human brain
   (E) our inclination to judge other life on the basis of our own experiences

51. In Passage 1, the author's primary purpose is apparently to

   (A) examine the dolphin's potential for surpassing humankind
   (B) question the need for prehensile organs in human development
   (C) refute the theory that dolphins are unable to alter their physical environment
   (D) reassess the nature and extent of dolphin intelligence
   (E) indicate the superiority of human intelligence over that of the dolphin

52. The word "acute" in line 10 means

   (A) excruciating   (B) severe   (C) keen
   (D) sudden and intense   (E) brief in duration

53. The "impressively elaborated instrument" referred to in line 33 is best interpreted to mean which of the following?

   (A) A concealed manipulative organ
   (B) An artificial range-finding device
   (C) A complex, intelligent brain
   (D) The dolphin's hidden eye
   (E) An apparatus for producing musical sounds

54. According to the author's simile in lines 34–39, the human mind and the heart of the sea are alike in that both

   (A) teem with exotic forms of life
   (B) argue in support of intelligence
   (C) are necessary to the evolution of dolphins
   (D) are directed outward
   (E) share a penchant for the grotesque

55. Which of the following best characterizes the tone of Passage 1?

   (A) Restrained skepticism
   (B) Pedantic assertion
   (C) Wondering admiration
   (D) Amused condescension
   (E) Ironic speculation

GO ON TO THE NEXT PAGE

56. The author of Passage 2 puts quotation marks around the word *scientific* in line 67 to indicate he

    (A) is faithfully reproducing Lilly's own words
    (B) intends to define the word later in the passage
    (C) believes the reader is unfamiliar with the word as used by Lilly
    (D) advocates adhering to the scientific method in all experiments
    (E) has some doubts as to how scientific those experiments were

57. The author of Passage 2 maintains that the writings of Lilly and his associates have

    (A) overstated the extent of dolphin intelligence
    (B) been inadequately scrutinized by critics
    (C) measured the worth of the dolphin family
    (D) underrated dolphins as intelligent beings
    (E) established criteria for evaluating dolphin intelligence

58. By calling the argument summarized in lines 73–82 a classic case of begging the question, the author of Passage 2 indicates he views it with

    (A) trepidation   (B) optimism   (C) detachment
    (D) skepticism   (E) credulity

59. Which of the following would most undercut the studies on which the author bases his conclusion in lines 110–118?

    (A) Evidence proving dolphin linguistic abilities to be far superior to those of other mammals
    (B) An article recording attempts by seals and walruses to communicate with human beings
    (C) The reorganization of current intelligence tests by species and level of difficulty
    (D) A reassessment of the definition of the term "lower animals"
    (E) The establishment of a project to develop new tests to detect intelligence in animals

60. The author of Passage 2 would find Passage 1

    (A) typical of the attitudes of Lilly and his associates
    (B) remarkable for the perspective it offers
    (C) indicative of the richness of dolphin culture
    (D) supportive of his fundamental point of view
    (E) intriguing for its far-reaching conclusions

IF YOU FINISH BEFORE 30 MINUTES, YOU MAY CHECK YOUR WORK ON THIS SECTION ONLY. DO NOT TURN TO ANY OTHER SECTION IN THE TEST.   **S T O P**

SECTION **5**
Mathematical Reasoning

Directions and Sample Questions

Notes:

(1) The use of a calculator is permitted. All numbers used are real numbers.

(2) Figures that accompany problems in this test are intended to provide information useful in solving the problems. They are drawn as accurately as possible EXCEPT when it is stated in a specific problem that the figure is not drawn to scale. All figures lie in a plane unless otherwise indicated.

Questions 1–15 each consist of two quantities in boxes, one in Column A and one in Column B. You are to compare the two quantities and on the answer sheet fill in oval

A if the quantity in Column A is greater;
B if the quantity in Column B is greater;
C if the two quantities are equal;
D if the relationship cannot be determined from the information given.

Notes:

1. In some questions, information is given about one or both of the quantities to be compared. In such cases, the given information is centered above the two columns and is not boxed.
2. In a given question, a symbol that appears in both columns represents the same thing in Column A as it does in Column B.
3. Letters such as x, n, and k stand for real numbers.

EXAMPLES		
Column A	Column B	Answers
E1 5^2	20	● Ⓑ Ⓒ Ⓓ

$150°\quad x°$

| E2 x | 30 | Ⓐ Ⓑ ● Ⓓ |

r and s are integers.

| E3 $r+1$ | $s-1$ | Ⓐ Ⓑ Ⓒ ● |

PART I: QUANTITATIVE COMPARISON QUESTIONS

SUMMARY DIRECTIONS FOR QUANTITATIVE COMPARISON QUESTIONS

Answer: A if the quantity in Column A is greater.
B if the quantity in Column B is greater.

C if the two quantities are equal.
D if the relationship cannot be determined from the information given.

Column A   Column B

In the state lottery 10% of the 2000 tickets sold won prizes ranging from $1.00 to $1000. Florence bought 20 tickets.

26. Number of winning tickets held by Florence   One winning ticket

$A > B$
$B > C$

27. $B + C$ $2A$

Column A   Column B

$a = 3$ and $b = 2$

28. $\dfrac{\dfrac{1}{ab}}{\dfrac{1}{a}+\dfrac{1}{b}}$ $\dfrac{1}{a+b}$

Ten cards numbered 2 through 11, one number on a card, are placed in a hat. A card is selected at random.

29. Probability of selecting a card having an even number on it.   Probability of selecting a card having a prime number on it.

GO ON TO THE NEXT PAGE →

Column A	Column B

30. $\dfrac{9x - 13}{8y - 7}$ $\dfrac{13 - 9x}{7 - 8y}$

$$0 < a < b < c$$

31. $\dfrac{c}{a}$ $\dfrac{c}{b}$

---

32. The percent increase from 50¢ to 70¢   The percent increase from 70¢ to 90¢

Mark, Philip, and Michael have a total of \$35. Mark and Philip have the same amount of money.

33. The amount of money Michael has.   The amount of money Philip has.

The diameter of the bicycle wheel is $\dfrac{7}{\pi}$ feet.

34. The number of revolutions made when going 70 feet.   10 revolutions

---

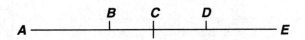

C is the midpoint of AE.
$AB = 90$ and $DE = 85$

35. BC CD

Column A	Column B

A cube with an edge length of s inches whose volume is numerically equal to its surface area.

36. s 8

In $\triangle ABC$, the measure of $\angle A$ is 86° and the measure of $\angle C$ is 66°.

37. Length of side AC Length of side AB

$$x > 0$$

38. $\dfrac{x + 6}{8}$ $\dfrac{x + 3}{4}$

In $\triangle ABC$
$AB = 4$ and $BC = 9$

39. Area of ABC 18

In $\triangle ABC$
$\angle A° = 48°$
$\angle B° = 72°$

40. Length of side AB Length of side AC

GO ON TO THE NEXT PAGE

PART II: STUDENT-PRODUCED RESPONSE QUESTIONS

Directions for Student-Produced Response Questions

Each of the remaining ten questions (41–50) requires you to solve the problem and enter your answer by marking the ovals in the special grid, as shown in the examples below.

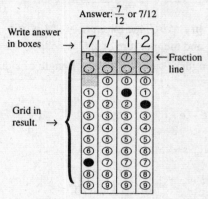

Answer: $\frac{7}{12}$ or 7/12

Write answer in boxes →

← Fraction line

Grid in result. →

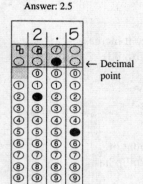

Answer: 2.5

← Decimal point

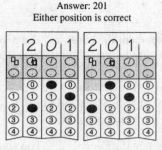

Answer: 201
Either position is correct

Note: You may start your answers in any column, space permitting. Columns not needed should be left blank.

- Mark no more than one oval in any column.
- Because the answer sheet will be machine-scored, **you will receive credit only if the ovals are filled in correctly.**
- Although not required, it is suggested that you write your answer in the boxes at the top of the columns to help you fill in the ovals accurately.
- Some problems may have more than one correct answer. In such cases, grid only one answer.
- No question has a negative answer.
- **Mixed numbers** such as $2\frac{1}{2}$ much be gridded as 2.5 or 5/2. (If [2 1 / 2] is gridded, it will be interpreted as $\frac{21}{2}$, not $\frac{21}{2}$.)

- Decimal Accuracy: If you obtain a decimal answer, enter the most accurate value that the grid will accommodate. For example, if you obtain an answer such as 0.6666..., you should record the result as .666 or .667. Less accurate values such as .66 or .67 are not acceptable.

Acceptable ways to grid $\frac{2}{3}$ = .6666. . .

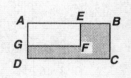

41. What does $3 + \frac{3}{0.3}$ equal?

42. How many 5-gallon cans of milk will be needed to fill 120 pint containers?

43. The first of four afternoon classes begins at 1 P.M. The last class ends at 3:52 P.M. Allowing 4 minutes between classes, how many minutes are there in each class period?

44. A group of soldiers forms a solid square with s soldiers on a side. If 56 soldiers are released, the remaining soldiers form a square with $(s - 2)$ soldiers on a side. What is the value of s?

45. The base of a rectangle is 20, which is twice its height. What part of the perimeter is the height?

46. At 3:55 P.M. a student begins to do her homework, which would take three hours to complete. At 4:15 P.M. she is interrupted by a telephone call and

does not resume work. What part of her homework is left uncompleted?

47. How many one-inch cubes can be put in a box 5 inches wide, 5 inches long, and 5 inches deep?

48. A solid block 1' × 2' × 3' weighs 4 pounds. What is the weight (in pounds) of a solid block of the same material 5' × 6' × 7'?

49. The length and width of a rectangle are each $\frac{2}{3}$ of the corresponding parts of $ABCD$. $AEB = 12$, $AGD = 6$. What is the area of the shaded part?

50. John's home is 6.3 miles due north of the community center. Dick's home is 5.5 miles due east of it. Find, to the nearest tenth of a mile, the shortest distance between their homes.

IF YOU FINISH BEFORE 30 MINUTES, YOU MAY CHECK YOUR WORK ON THIS SECTION ONLY. DO NOT TURN TO ANY OTHER SECTION IN THE TEST.

S T O P

ANSWER KEY

Verbal Reasoning Section 1

1. B	*6.* D	*11.* E	*16.* C	*21.* C	*26.* D
2. A	*7.* B	*12.* D	*17.* C	*22.* E	*27.* E
3. C	*8.* C	*13.* C	*18.* B	*23.* D	*28.* C
4. B	*9.* B	*14.* D	*19.* E	*24.* C	*29.* A
5. B	*10.* B	*15.* B	*20.* D	*25.* D	*30.* B

Mathematical Reasoning Section 2

Note: Each correct answer to the mathematics questions is keyed by number to the corresponding topic in Chapters 8 and 9. These numerals refer to the topics listed below, with specific page references in parentheses.

1. Basic Fundamental Operations (179–182)
2. Algebraic Operations (182–183)
3. Using Algebra (182–184, 187)
4. Exponents, Roots, and Radicals (184–185)
5. Inequalities (188–189)
6. Fractions (182, 198)
7. Decimals (200)
8. Percent (200)
9. Averages (201)
10. Motion (203)
11. Ratio and Proportion (204–205)
12. Mixtures and Solutions (178)
13. Work (206–207)
14. Coordinate Geometry (194)
15. Geometry (189–193, 195)
16. Quantitative Comparisons (211–212)
17. Data Interpretation (208)

1. D (1, 6)	*6.* D (2)	*11.* C (15)	*16.* D (15)	*21.* D (15)
2. D (3.6)	*7.* D (14)	*12.* B (3, 15)	*17.* D (15)	*22.* E (15)
3. D (8)	*8.* C (3, 8)	*13.* A (11)	*18.* E (15)	*23.* B (1)
4. B (6, 8)	*9.* C (1)	*14.* A (3)	*19.* B (3, 15)	*24.* B (17)
5. A (2)	*10.* C (8)	*15.* D (15)	*20.* B (15)	*25.* C (15, 17)

Writing Skills Section 3

1. C	*8.* C	*15.* D	*22.* D	*29.* A	*36.* D
2. E	*9.* C	*16.* E	*23.* C	*30.* E	*37.* D
3. D	*10.* C	*17.* A	*24.* B	*31.* A	*38.* E
4. C	*11.* C	*18.* A	*25.* D	*32.* A	*39.* C
5. C	*12.* C	*19.* B	*26.* D	*33.* E	
6. A	*13.* D	*20.* C	*27.* A	*34.* C	
7. E	*14.* D	*21.* C	*28.* C	*35.* B	

Verbal Reasoning Section 4

31. D	*36.* A	*41.* D	*46.* B	*51.* D	*56.* E
32. A	*37.* A	*42.* C	*47.* C	*52.* C	*57.* A
33. E	*38.* C	*43.* B	*48.* D	*53.* C	*58.* D
34. B	*39.* B	*44.* C	*49.* C	*54.* A	*59.* A
35. C	*40.* A	*45.* C	*50.* E	*55.* C	*60.* A

Mathematical Reasoning Section 5

26. D (8, 16)	*29.* C (1)	*32.* A (8, 16)	*35.* B (15. 16)	*38.* B (2, 16)
27. B (2, 16)	*30.* C (2, 16)	*33.* D (3, 16)	*36.* B (15)	*39.* D (15. 16)
28. C (2, 16)	*31.* A (6, 16)	*34.* C (15, 16)	*37.* B (15, 16)	*40.* B (15, 16)

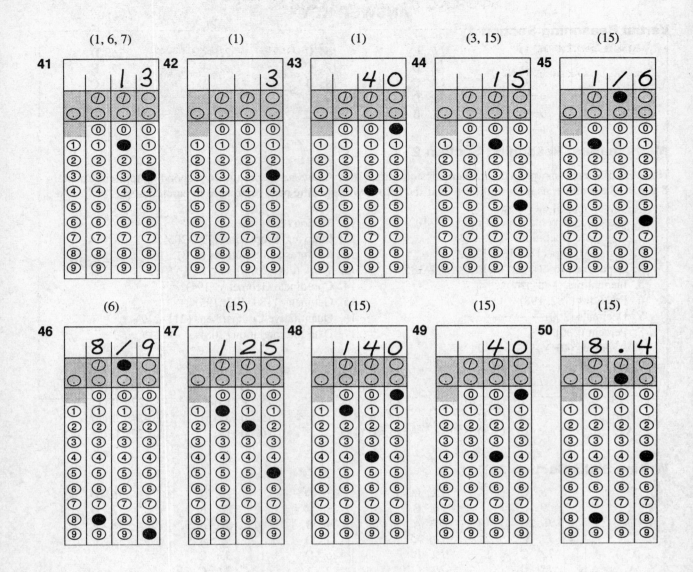

SCORING CHART — TYPICAL TEST C

Verbal Sections

Section 1   Questions 1–30
Number correct   _____ (A)
Number omitted   _____ (B)
Number incorrect   _____ (C)
$1/4$ (C) =   _____ (D)
Raw Score:
  (A) – (D) =   _____

Section 3   Questions 31–60
Number correct   _____ (A)
Number omitted   _____ (B)
Number incorrect   _____ (C)
$1/4$ (C) =   _____ (D)
Raw Score:
  (A) – (D) =   _____

Total Verbal Raw Score:
  (Section 1 +
  Section 3) =   _____

Mathematical Sections

Section 2   Questions 1–25
Number correct   _____ (A)
Number incorrect   _____ (B)
(A) – $1/4$ (B) =   _____ Raw Score I

Section 4   Questions 26–40
Number correct   _____ (C)
Number incorrect   _____ (D)
(C) – $1/3$ (D) =   _____ Raw Score II

Section 4   Questions 41–50
Number correct   _____ Raw Score III

Total Mathematical Raw Score:
  (Raw Scores I + II
  + III) =   _____

Writing Section

Section 3   Questions 1–39
Number correct   _____ (A)
Number incorrect   _____ (B)
$1/4$ (B) =   _____ (C)
(no penalty for omitted questions)
Writing Raw Score:
  (A) – (C) =   _____

EVALUATION CHART

Study your score. Your raw score on the Verbal and Mathematical Reasoning Sections is an indication of your probable achievement on the PSAT/NMSQT. As a guide to the amount of work you need or want to do with this book, study the following.

Raw Score			Self-rating
Verbal	*Mathematical*	*Writing*	
55–60	41–50	37–39	Superior
44–54	25–40	31–36	Very good
39–43	20–24	25–30	Satisfactory
35–38	16–19	19–24	Average
29–34	10–15	13–18	Needs further study
20–28	7–9	6–12	Needs intensive study
0–19	0–6	0–5	Probably inadequate

ANSWER EXPLANATIONS

Verbal Reasoning Section 1

1. **B** Criticism that suggests areas of improvement is said to be *constructive*. Before you look at the answer choices, read the sentence and try to think of a word that makes sense.

2. **A** The delight a wicked queen feels about poisoning someone is clearly *malicious* (spiteful, delighting in others' ills).

3. **C** The leaders would be *apprehensive* (worried) in such circumstances that they could not achieve their goal of reconciliation. Note that the phrase "negotiations have reached such a state" generally implies that they have reached a sorry state.

4. **B** "Though" signals a contrast, in this case a contrast between the huge changes most editors suggest and the *minute* (tiny) changes Hemingway's editors wanted.

5. **B** If bilingual education is more than a mere stop-gap (a somewhat negative description), it must possess certain positive qualities. Thus it has *advantages over* education in a single tongue. Note the use of *far from* to signal the contrast between the negative and positive views on bilingual education.

6. **D** "Although" signals a contrast. The critics believe the poet will find her own voice in time; in other words, she will sound like herself, not like other poets whose works she may have read. Now, however, she sounds like other poets; her work is *derivative*, lacking originality.

7. **B** The central metaphor of this sentence is the bright light. What does a bright light do? It lights up the darkness. The first missing word should be a synonym for *dark*. Choice A, *murky,* and Choice B, *shadowed,* both seem possible. The second missing word, however, also should reinforce the metaphor of light. Only Choice B does so: psychological insights *illumine* or make clear the range of human experience.

8. **C** *Ornate* means highly decorated. An ornate building would stand out from simple, unadorned neighbors: it would be *conspicuous* for its flamboyance.

9. **B** The columnist was *acerbic* (bitingly sarcastic) in writing of those who provoked or *irritated* her. Note the use of *but* to establish the contrast between the two clauses, and the use of *even* to indicate that the missing word is stronger than *bitter*.

10. **B** The writer concedes that the Big Bang theory has been changed somewhat: it has undergone *refinement* or polishing. However, he denies that its validity has been threatened seriously by any rival theories: it has *resisted* or defied all challenges. The use of the support signal *and* indicates that the first missing word is similar to "modification." The use of the contrast signal *but* indicates that the second missing word is contrary in meaning to "undergone modification."

11. **E** The statement that "we do not know" whether a gesture indicates devotion or despair suggests that gestures, by their nature, have *ambiguity* or lack of clarity.

12. **D** Because the dean was not able to *disguise* her distaste for the media barrage, she failed to stifle her *caustic* or sarcastically biting remarks about the event. Note the implicit cause and effect relationship between the opening phrase and the central clause of the sentence.

13. **C** According to the dictionary, if you're a *chauvinist,* you love your country to excess. Such excessive patriotism would prevent you from seeing your country's flaws.

14. **D** If Tynan's reviews were filled with sharp attacks, then they were clearly characterized by *truculence* (belligerence, harshness).

15. **B** If the rare earths are actually present to some degree in essentially all minerals, then they are not rare after all. Thus the term "rare earths" is a *misnomer* (incorrect designation), for the rare earths are actually *ubiquitous* (omnipresent; found everywhere). Watch out for words that signal the unexpected. Note the use of "paradoxically" here.

16. **C** Particles have no need to be wound up because the property of spinning (*rotation*) is built into their makeup; it is *intrinsic*.

17. **C** Whatever word you choose here must apply equally well both to slander and to counterfeit money. People who would not make up a slanderous statement *circulate* slander by passing it on. Similarly, people who would not coin or make counterfeit money *circulate* counterfeit money by passing it on. Note how the extended metaphor here influences the writer's choice of words.

18. **B** The correct answer, Choice B, is a simpler way of expressing the final sentence of the second paragraph. Note the parallel between "points of view" in the answer and "perspectives" in the passage. Choice A is incorrect. In lines 19–20, the author states that "images of sexual antagonism" have not been ignored in literary criticism. Choices C, D, and E are incorrect. They are not supported by the passage.

19. **E** Since these three authors were writing over half a century ago, they are mentioned to show that feminist issues are a concern of long standing to writers. Choices A and B are incorrect. They are contrary to the very positive tone of the passage. Choice C is incorrect. While it is noted that there was little interest in feminism before this century, the writer of the passage quotes modern authors to show the importance of the issue, not its previous lack of attention. Choice D is incorrect. It is not supported by the passage.

20. **D** The entire passage is an *endorsement* of or statement of support for women's emancipation. Note the first sentence of paragraph 2, in which it is described as one of the "greatest" and "deepest" themes of modern writers.

21. **C** In refusing "to wither under" the scorn of their male peers (line 54), the women writers are responding to their male contemporaries with *defiance.*

22. **E** Williams draws an *analogy* between little boys and good poetry, saying they are like one another in being made of earthy, allegedly "masculine" elements.

23. **D** Houston believed that the battle had to begin at the graduate level "to mitigate fear" (relieve *apprehension*) of race-mixing or miscegenation. Otherwise, the judges might have ruled against the NAACP-sponsored complaints.

24. **C** Note the immediate context of the quoted word. "The 1950 *McLaurin* decision ruled that . . ." In this legal context, *decision* and *ruling* are synonymous.

25. **D** The Regents responded to their defeat in *Sipuel* v. *Board of Regents of the University of Oklahoma* by separating black and white students in cafeterias and classrooms (thus undermining the effect of the decision). Hence it seems likely that their reaction to the decision was one of *distinct displeasure.*

26. **D** Maintenance for a law school involves providing ongoing *support* to ensure the school's continued existence.

27. **E** The 1950 *McLaurin* decision was one of the decisions which provided legal precedents for the 1954 *Brown* decision. Choice A is incorrect. *McLaurin* preceded *Brown* (1954). Therefore, it could not have superseded a decision that had yet to be made. Choice B is incorrect. *Brown I* followed *McLaurin.* Therefore, it could not have set a precedent for *McLaurin.* Choice C is incorrect. *Brown I* reversed *Plessy* v. *Ferguson.* It built on *McLaurin.* Choice D is incorrect. *McLaurin* preceded *Brown I.* Therefore, it could not have limited the application of a decision that had yet to be made.

28. **C** Taken as a whole, the passage deals with the entire struggle to desegregate U.S. education,

from the NAACP's legal maneuvers of the thirties to the executive actions of the fifties and sixties. Only this title is broad enough to cover the passage as a whole. Choice A is incorrect. The passage deals with the long legal maneuvers far more than it deals with executive intervention. Choice B is incorrect. The passage deals with much more than *Brown* v. *Board of Education.* Choices D and E are incorrect. They ignore the central subject of desegregation.

29. **A** In assessing the judges' possible reaction to race-mixing in the lower grades, Houston displayed *psychological canniness.* He was shrewd in seeing potential dangers and in figuring out strategies to avoid these dangers.

30. **B** In the final paragraph, the author assigns a share of the blame for the confrontation between state and federal authorities to the actions of the Kennedy administration, who engaged in "protracted delays, futile negotiations, and considerable vacillation" before acting to protect Meredith. Clearly, his attitude is one of *unmitigated disdain* (unrelieved scorn).

Mathematical Reasoning Section 2

1. **D** $\dfrac{1}{2} \cdot \dfrac{x}{2} = \dfrac{x}{4}$

2. **D** Because $\left(\dfrac{a}{2}\right)\left(\dfrac{b}{4}\right) = 8$

$$\dfrac{ab}{8} = 8$$
$$\text{and } ab = 64$$
$$\text{Because } 0.125 = \dfrac{1}{8}$$
$$\dfrac{1}{8}(64) = 8$$

3. **D** $\dfrac{0.075}{7.5} = \dfrac{75}{7500} = \dfrac{1}{100} = 1\%$

4. **B** $\dfrac{1}{2}$ of class are boys

$\dfrac{1}{2}$ of $\dfrac{1}{2}$ or $\dfrac{1}{4}$ of class are boys going to college.

$\dfrac{1}{2}$ of class are girls.

$\dfrac{1}{3}$ of $\dfrac{1}{2}$ or $\dfrac{1}{6}$ of class are girls going to college.

$\dfrac{1}{4} + \dfrac{1}{6} = \dfrac{5}{12} = 41.7\%$

5. **A** **(A)** $1 + \dfrac{x}{y} = \dfrac{y+x}{y}$

(B) $\dfrac{xy + x^2}{x^2} = \dfrac{x(y+x)}{x^2} = \dfrac{y+x}{x}$

(C) $\dfrac{y^2 + xy}{xy} = \dfrac{y(y+x)}{xy} = \dfrac{y+x}{x}$

(D) $\dfrac{y}{x} = 1 = \dfrac{y}{x} + \dfrac{x}{x} = \dfrac{y+x}{x}$

(E) $\dfrac{x+y}{x}$

6. **D** $2x + t = 2$
$t = 2 - 2x$

7. **D** See diagram; the square can have vertices lettered either clockwise or counterclockwise.

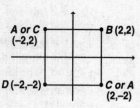

8. **C** A discount of 30% means he is getting 70% of former price.
70% or .7 of $150 = $105
Let x = cost.
$1.05x = \$105$
$105x = \$10500$
$x = \$100$

9. **C** $2600 - \$440 = \$2160$ (total depreciation)
$\$2160 \div 4\frac{1}{2}$ = average yearly depreciation
$\$2160 \div \frac{9}{2}$
$(\$2160)\left(\frac{2}{9}\right) = \$480$

10. **C** (80%) $7000
(.8) $7000 = $5600 (amount of insurance)
$6 per $1000 = $\frac{6}{1000} = \frac{.6}{100} = .006$

11. **C** 12 kittens consume 4 cans.
4 cans are left for the dogs.
4 cans will feed 8 dogs.

12. **B** $(x - 2) - 2 = x - 4$

13. **A** y yards = $3y$ feet
$\dfrac{\text{total distance}}{\text{distance of average jump}}$ = number of jumps
$\dfrac{3y}{8}$ [substitution]

14. **A** Let x = number of years when James will be five times as old as John will be.
James' age is now 30 years.
James' age at specified time = $30 + x$.
John's age is now 3 years.
John's age at specified time = $3 + x$.
$(30 + x) = 5(3 + x)$
$30 + x = 15 + 5x$
$15 = 4x$
$3\frac{3}{4} = x$

15. **D** Increase = $3000 - \$2500 = \$500$
$\dfrac{\text{increase}}{\text{original}} = \dfrac{\$500}{\$2500} = \dfrac{1}{5} = 20\%$

16. **D** He must realize a profit of 20% or $\frac{1}{5}$ of $90 or $18. He must sell the 9 crates for $108 or for $12 each.

17. **D** Volume $= \pi \cdot r^2 \cdot h$
If diameter = 4 inches, radius = 2 inches.
$\left(\frac{22}{7}\right)(2)(2)(14) = 176$ cubic inches
$\frac{176}{8} = 22$ ten-minute periods or 220 minutes
220 minutes = 3 hours 40 minutes
3 hours 40 minutes after 10 A.M. is 1:40 P.M.

18. **E** Let r = radius of inner circle.
r = width of shaded portion [given]
$2r$ = radius of large circle
Area of large circle – area of inner circle = area of shaded portion.
Area of circle $= \pi r^2$
Area of large circle $= \pi(2r)^2$ or $4\pi r^2$
Area of inner circle $= \pi(r)^2$ or πr^2
Area of shaded portion $= 3\pi r^2$
$\dfrac{3\pi r^2}{4\pi r^2} = \dfrac{3}{4} = 75\%$

19. **B** Diameter = 4 feet, radius = 2 feet.
Area of circle $= \pi r^2$ or 4π
Mr. Adams desires area of $4(4\pi)$ or 16π.
Let x = radius.
$\pi x^2 = 16\pi$
$x^2 = 16$
$x = 4$
diameter = 8 ft.

20. **B** $OA = OB$ [radii of same circle]
$\angle ABO = \angle ABO$
Since $\overarc{AB} = 112°$, central $\angle AOB \cong 112$.
$\angle ABO + \angle BAO + \angle AOB \cong 180$
$\angle ABO + \angle BAO = 68$
$\angle ABO \cong 34$

21. **D** It is easier to call base x and altitude $2x$.
Area of $\triangle = \frac{1}{2}(h)(b)$
Area of $\triangle = \left(\frac{1}{2}\right)(2x)(x)$
Area of $\triangle = x^2$
$x^2 = 225$ square inches [given]
$x = 15$ inches
$2x = 30$ inches [altitude]

22. **E** Let s = side of original.
$\therefore$ perimeter $= 4s$
$\therefore$ area $= s^2$
Increase in perimeter of new square = 80% (or 0.8) of $4s = 3.2s$
Perimeter of new square $= 3.2s + 4s = 7.2s$
Side of new square $= 7.2s \div 4 = 1.8s$
Area of new square $= (1.8s)^2 = 3.24s^2$
Difference in areas $= 3.24s^2 - s^2 = 2.24s^2$
$\dfrac{\text{difference}}{\text{original}} = \dfrac{2.24s^2}{1s^2} = 2.24 = 224\%$

23. **B** $\dfrac{\text{contents of large tumbler}}{\text{contents of small tumbler}} = \dfrac{3}{5}$

Let x = number of small glass tumblers that can be filled with one large glass tumbler.

$$\frac{3}{5} = \frac{x}{1}$$

$$5x = 3$$

$$x = 1\frac{2}{3}$$

24. **B** Choices **A** and **C** show rise. In Choice **E** there is no change. Choice **D** shows a slight drop. Choice **B** shows sharp drop.

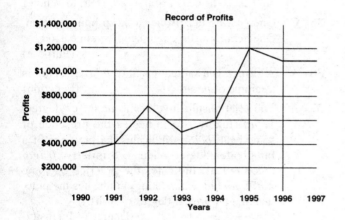

This graph shows the record of profits of the Beacon Co. for a period of 8 years.

25. **C** The sum of the measures of the angles around the center of the circle = 360°.

$$\frac{20°}{360°} = \frac{1}{18}$$

$$\left(\frac{1}{18}\right)(370,000) = 20,000$$

This circle graph shows how 370,000 wage earners in a certain city earned their living during a given period.

Writing Skills Section 3

1. **C** Wrong word. Use *lie* instead of *lay*.

2. **E** Sentence is correct.

3. **D** Error in agreement between pronoun and antecedent. Since antecedent is *association*, change *their* to *its*.

4. **C** Error in agreement. In a neither-nor construction the verb agrees with the noun or pronoun which comes immediately before the verb. *Principal is being considered* is correct.

5. **C** Misuse of adjective for adverb. Change *considerable* to *considerably*.

6. **A** Error in tense. Change *have rummaged* to *were rummaging*.

7. **E** Sentence is correct.

8. **C** Error in agreement. Change *their* to *his*.

9. **C** Error in diction. Use *effect* instead of *affect*.

10. **C** Error in subordination. Delete the comma and substitute *that* for *and it*. The second clause describes Aaron's record.

11. **C** Error in agreement. Change *them* to *it*.

12. **C** Incorrect coordinate conjunction. Change conjunction and word for *nor is she* to *and she is* to clarify the relationship between the clauses.

13. **D** Error in diction. The word *being* is unnecessary. Change *including being* to *including*.

14. **D** Error in agreement. *Changes* requires a plural verb. Change *is* to *are*.

15. **D** Misuse of adjective for adverb. Change *comfortable* to *comfortably*.

16. **E** Sentence is correct.

17. **A** Error in tense. Change *has been warned* to *had been warned*.

18. **A** Faulty diction. Use *if* to indicate a condition. Substitute *whether*.

19. **B** Error in case. Change *she* to *her*.

20. **C** Choices A, D, and E are run-on sentences. Choice B is constructed awkwardly.

21. **E** This choice corrects the sentence fragment.

22. **C** When comparing two things, you should use the comparative degree (*better*) rather than the superlative degree (*best*).

23. **C** The subordinating conjunction *Although* best connects the sentence's two clauses.

24. **B** Choices A, C, and E are run-on sentences; Choice D is unidiomatic.

25. **D** Parallel structure is maintained in Choice D. The parallelism is violated in the other choices.

26. **D** Choices A, B, and E contain sentence fragments; Choice C creates a comma splice.

27. **A** The past tense and the subordinating conjunction *When* are correctly used in Choice A.

28. **C** Choice C expresses the author's meaning directly and concisely. All other choices are either indirect or ungrammatical.

29. **A** Choices B, C, D, and E are sentence fragments.

30. **E** Choice E expresses the author's meaning directly and concisely. All other choices are either indirect or ungrammatical.

31. **A** The sentence uses the subjunctive mood correctly.

32. **A** Sentence is correct.

33. **E** The errors in case and agreement are corrected in Choice E. *I* should be used instead of *me* because it is the predicate nominative of the verb *is*. *Who*, having as its antecedent the pronoun *I*, is a first person singular pronoun. The first person singular verb *am* should be used.

34. **C** All sentences except sentence 3 contribute to the paragraph's main point, that celebrations help to unite people and keep traditions alive. Therefore, C is the best answer.

35. **B** Choice A is grammatically correct but is awkwardly expressed in the passive voice.
Choice B is clearly written and to the point. It is the best answer.
Choice C contains a dangling participle. The phrase *Receiving new clothes* should modify *children*, not *money*.
Choice D is awkwardly expressed.
Choice E is wordy and awkward.

36. **A** Choice A is fresh, but its tone is not consistent with the rest of the essay.
Choice B contains a comma splice between *dinner* and *at*.
Choice C emphasizes the idea properly, but contains an error in parallel construction.
Choice D places the emphasis where it belongs and expresses the idea effectively. It is the best answer.
Choice E is repetitious, and it contains an error in pronoun reference. The pronoun *they* has no specific referent.

37. **C** Choice A does not provide a significantly better transition.
Choice B does nothing to improve the relationship between paragraphs 3 and 4.
Choice C is awkwardly worded and does not include transitional material.
Choice D provides an effective transition between paragraphs. It is the best answer.
Choice E tries to provide a transition, but it is wordy and it contains a dangling participle.

38. **E** Choice A places emphasis on the location of the assassination instead of on the event itself, an emphasis that the writer did not intend.
Choice B contains a nonstandard usage. The phrase *to remember about* is not standard.
Choice C is grammatically correct but wordy.
Choice D is the same as B.
Choice E is a succinct and proper revision. It is the best answer.

39. **C** The main purpose of the last paragraph is to provide an example of a celebration that unites people and preserves tradition. Therefore, C is the best answer.

Verbal Reasoning Section 4

31. **D** A *furnace* provides *heat* and a *lamp* provides *light*.   (Function)

32. **A** A *palomino* is a type of *horse* and a *pecan* is a type of *nut*.   (Group and Member)

33. **E** A *dropcloth* protectively covers *furniture*. An *apron* protectively covers *clothing*. (Function)

34. **B** Just as the *yolk* is the center of the *egg*, the *nucleus* is the center of the *cell*. (Part to Whole)

35. **C** One *confines* a *prisoner* to keep him in prison. One *detains* a *suspect* to keep him in custody.   (Purpose)

36. **A** A *swatch* is a sample patch of *fabric*. A *chip* is a sample of *paint*.   (Function)

37. **A** The relationship involves a matter of degree. *Tepid* (lukewarm) indicates the presence of some heat; *boiling* indicates the presence of a far greater degree of heat. Similarly, *frugal* (economical) indicates the practice of some thrift; *parsimonious* (stingy) indicates the practice of a far greater degree of thrift.   (Degree of Intensity)

38. **C** To *crow* is to express oneself in a *boastful* fashion. To *pout* is to express oneself in a *sulky* fashion.   (Defining Characteristic)

39. **B** A *poet* creates a *libretto*. A *draftsman* creates a *blueprint*.   (Worker and Work Created)

40. **A** A *skirmish* (minor military engagement) is less important than a *battle*. A *quiz* is less important than an *examination*. (Degree of Intensity)

41. **D** To *meander* is to wander aimlessly during a *journey*. To *ramble* is to wander aimlessly during a *speech*.   (Manner)

42. **C** Someone who is *independent* has *autonomy* or freedom. Someone who is *inventive*, or creative, has *resourcefulness* (cleverness at solving problems).   (Synonym Variant)

43. **B** A *penitent* (person who repents) exhibits *contrition* (remorse). A *hedonist* (person devoted to the pursuit of pleasure as a way of life) exhibits *self-indulgence* (gratification of one's desires).   (Defining Characteristic)

44. **C** The author at first assumes his neighbor is simply a nervous flyer, though one even more nervous than he is himself. Next he speculates that his neighbor may be a smuggler. Finally he concludes that his seatmate must be an Arab terrorist. Clearly, as he observes his neighbor, his thoughts become increasingly *melodramatic* (theatrical; sensational).

45. **C** By praying for a pilot who had "trained with the U.S. Navy" and wishing he had traveled "on a real airline, like Pan Am" (then an active American firm), the author shows that in a crisis he mistrusts the expertise of foreigners and wishes *he were back in American hands.*

46. **B** The author is sitting there expecting to be blown up any minute by his terrorist seatmate. The last thing he expects is to have his neighbor politely ask him for help. Clearly, his immediate reaction is one of *bafflement* (total perplexity).

47. **C** In assuming his neighbor was a terrorist, in lumping together Arabs and Palestinians as if they were not individuals but "all the same," the author has been guilty of *stereotyping* his neighbor, seeing him not as an individual but as a type. In doing so, he has been "as racist as anyone else."

48. **D** The jolt the author talk about is the mental jolt he gets when he realizes that he has been making racist assumptions about his harmless neighbor. He has *been shocked to find racist tendencies in himself.*

49. **C** Passage 1 states: "Dolphins left the land when mammalian brains were still small and primitive." This indicates that dolphins were once land animals, mammals like ourselves, whose evolutionary development took them back into the sea.

50. **E** The passage indicates that human beings think of intelligence in terms of our own ability to manipulate our environment—our ability to build and do all sorts of things with our hands. Because dolphins have no hands, we have trouble appreciating their high level of intelligence.

51. **D** Passage 1 attempts to *reassess the nature and extent of dolphin intelligence,* first giving reasons why human beings may have trouble appreciating how intelligent dolphins really are and then, in the concluding sentence, reflecting how dolphin intelligence (that looks "inward to the sea's heart") may complement human intelligence (that looks "outward on eternity").

52. **C** The dolphin's acute echo-sounding sense is a sharp, *keen* sense that enables the dolphin to sound or measure the ocean depths by using echoes.

53. **C** The entire passage has concentrated on the dolphin's brain, so it is safe to assume that this is what is meant by the "impressively elaborated instrument." The items listed in the other answer choices have not been mentioned at all. Note that Choice B, an artificial range-finding device, is incorrect because the dolphin's range-finding ability is entirely natural, not artificial.

54. **A** The sea's heart is like the human mind in that it swarms or *teems* (abounds) with grotesque or exotic *forms of life.*

55. **C** The author's tone is distinctly admiring. The passage speaks of the dolphins' "remarkable range-finding ability," mentions their care for each other, and repeatedly praises dolphin intelligence.

56. **E** The quotation marks here indicate that the word in quotes is being used in a special sense (often an ironic one). In this case, as the next paragraph makes abundantly clear, the author is critical of both the results and the influence of Lilly's experiments. He *has some doubts as to how scientific those experiments were.*

57. **A** In claiming that "dolphins communicate not only with one another but also with humans, mimicking human speech and reaching out across the boundaries that divide us," Lilly and his associates have *overstated* their case, misrepresenting *the extent of dolphin intelligence.* Choice B is incorrect. In stating that Lilly's conclusions have not withstood (stood up against) critical scrutiny, the author indicates that they *have* been critically scrutinized to an appropriate degree.

58. **D** "Begging the question" refers to assuming the truth of the very point whose truth or falsehood you're trying to establish. The author of Passage 2 considers the reasoning in this argument flawed; he views it with doubt or *skepticism.*

59. **A** If dolphins were proven far superior in linguistic capability to seals and other lower animals, that clearly would contradict the results of the studies the author cites and would thus *undercut* or weaken their impact.

60. **A** In its glorification of dolphin intelligence as something that equals or possibly exceeds human intelligence, Passage 1 seems *typical of the attitudes of Lilly and his associates.*

Mathematical Reasoning Section 5

26. **D** The 10% winning tickets constitute a statistic true for all 2000 tickets and may not apply to the 20 particular tickets held by Florence.

27. **B** $A > B$
$A > C$
$2A > B + C$

28. **C** $\dfrac{1}{ab} = \dfrac{1}{6}$

$\dfrac{1}{a} + \dfrac{1}{b} = \dfrac{1}{3} + \dfrac{1}{2} = \dfrac{5}{6}$

[From Column A] $\dfrac{\frac{1}{6}}{\frac{5}{6}} = \dfrac{1}{6} \cdot \dfrac{6}{5} = \dfrac{1}{5}$

[From Column B] $\dfrac{1}{a + b} = \dfrac{1}{5}$

29. **C** There are 5 cards with even numbers (2, 4, 6, 8, and 10) and 5 cards with prime numbers (2, 3, 5, 7, and 11). Hence, the probabilities are equal.

30. **C** In Column B multiply by

$$\frac{-1}{-1} \cdot \frac{-13 + 9x}{-7 + 8y}$$

or $\frac{9x - 13}{8y - 7}$

31. **A** The numerators of both fractions are equal.

The denominator of $\frac{c}{a}$ is smaller than the denominator of $\frac{c}{b}$ since $a > b$.

Therefore the value of $\frac{c}{a} > \frac{c}{b}$.

32. **A** Percent increase is calculated by the difference as compared with the original.

In Column A: $\frac{20}{50}$ In Column B: $\frac{20}{70}$

The fraction with the smaller denominator is larger.

33. **D** If x = amount of money Michael has, and
    y = amount of money Mark has, then
    y = amount Philip has, and
$x + 2y = \$35$.
It is not possible to solve this equation with two unknowns.

34. **C** The circumference of the wheel = (π)(diameter)

or $(\pi)\left(\frac{7}{\pi}\right)$ or 7 feet

The number of revolutions = $\dfrac{\text{distance}}{\text{circumference}}$ = $\dfrac{70 \text{ feet}}{7 \text{ feet}}$ = 10 revolutions

35. **B** $AC = CE$; $90 + BC = CD + 85$; $CD > BC$

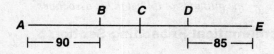

36. **B** Volume of cube = s^3 and surface area = $6s^2$. Hence, $s^3 = 6s^2$ or $s(s^2) = 6(s^2)$ so $s = 6$. Hence, $8 > s$.

37. **B** The measure of $\angle B$ = $180° - (86 + 66)$ or $28°$. $AB > AC$ since AB lies opposite the angle with a measure of 66°, and AC lies opposite the angle with a measure of 28°.

38. **B** $\dfrac{x + 6}{8} = \dfrac{x}{8} + \dfrac{3}{4}$

$\dfrac{x + 3}{4} = \dfrac{x}{4} + \dfrac{3}{4}$

$\dfrac{x}{4} > \dfrac{x}{8}$

39. **D** We may not assume that ABC is a right triangle. If it were a right triangle and AB and BC were legs, the area of ABC would be 4×9 divided by 2 or 18.

40. **B** $\angle C \stackrel{\circ}{=} 180 - (48 + 72)$
$\angle C \stackrel{\circ}{=} 180 - 120$ or 60
Therefore
Side AC (opposite $\angle B$) is larger than side AB (opposite $\angle C$).

41. **13** $\dfrac{3}{0.3} = \dfrac{30}{3} = 10$

$3 + 10 = 13$

42. **3** 4 quarts = 1 gallon
2 pints = 1 quart
8 pints = 1 gallon
40 pints = 5 gallons
120 pints = (3)5 gallons

43. **40** Time from 1 P.M. to 3:52 P.M. = 172 minutes. Time allowed between first and second class, second and third class, and third and last class = 12 minutes. Time for instruction in all four classes = $172 - 12 = 160$ minutes. Time for each class period = $160 \div 4 = 40$ minutes.

44. **15** $s^2 - 56 = (s - 2)^2$
$s^2 - 56 = s^2 - 4s + 4$
$4s = 60$
$s = 60$

45. $\frac{1}{6}$ Base = 20
Height = 10
Perimeter = 60
$\dfrac{10}{60} = \dfrac{1}{6}$

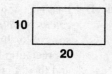

46. $\frac{8}{9}$ Twenty minutes (or $\frac{1}{3}$ hour) have elapsed before interruption.
$2\frac{2}{3}$ hours of work was not completed.

$2\frac{2}{3} = \dfrac{\frac{8}{3}}{3} = \dfrac{8}{3} \div 3 = \dfrac{8}{3} \cdot \dfrac{1}{3} = \dfrac{8}{9}$

47. **125** Volume = $5'' \times 5'' \times 5''$ = 125 cubic inches
$125 \div 1 = 125$ cubes

48. **140** $(1')(2')(3') = 6$ cubic feet = 4 pounds
$(5')(6')(7') = 210$ cubic feet = 140 pounds

49. **40** Area of shaded part = area of *ABCD* – area *AGFE*

Area of $ABCD = (12)(6) = 72$

$AE = \left(\frac{2}{3}\right)(12)$ or 8

$AG = \left(\frac{2}{3}\right)(6)$ or 4

Area $AGFE = (8)(4) = 32$

Area of shaded part = $72 - 32 = 40$

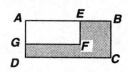

50. **8.4** A right triangle is formed, where the required distance is the hypotenuse. Apply the Pythagorean Theorem. Let x = shortest distance between their homes.

$x^2 = (6.3)^2 + (5.5)^2$
$x^2 = 39.69 + 30.25$ or 69.94
$x = \sqrt{69.94}$
$x = 8.36+ = 8.4$

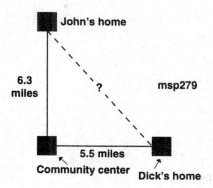

Answer Sheet

TYPICAL TEST D

Each mark should completely fill the appropriate space, and should be as dark as all other marks. Make all erasures complete. Traces of an erasure may be read as an answer. See pages vii and 27 for explanations of timing and number of questions.

Section 1 — Verbal
30 minutes

1 (A) (B) (C) (D) (E)
2 (A) (B) (C) (D) (E)
3 (A) (B) (C) (D) (E)
4 (A) (B) (C) (D) (E)
5 (A) (B) (C) (D) (E)
6 (A) (B) (C) (D) (E)
7 (A) (B) (C) (D) (E)
8 (A) (B) (C) (D) (E)
9 (A) (B) (C) (D) (E)
10 (A) (B) (C) (D) (E)
11 (A) (B) (C) (D) (E)
12 (A) (B) (C) (D) (E)
13 (A) (B) (C) (D) (E)
14 (A) (B) (C) (D) (E)
15 (A) (B) (C) (D) (E)
16 (A) (B) (C) (D) (E)
17 (A) (B) (C) (D) (E)
18 (A) (B) (C) (D) (E)
19 (A) (B) (C) (D) (E)
20 (A) (B) (C) (D) (E)
21 (A) (B) (C) (D) (E)
22 (A) (B) (C) (D) (E)
23 (A) (B) (C) (D) (E)
24 (A) (B) (C) (D) (E)
25 (A) (B) (C) (D) (E)
26 (A) (B) (C) (D) (E)
27 (A) (B) (C) (D) (E)
28 (A) (B) (C) (D) (E)
29 (A) (B) (C) (D) (E)
30 (A) (B) (C) (D) (E)

Section 2 — Math
30 minutes

1 (A) (B) (C) (D) (E)
2 (A) (B) (C) (D) (E)
3 (A) (B) (C) (D) (E)
4 (A) (B) (C) (D) (E)
5 (A) (B) (C) (D) (E)
6 (A) (B) (C) (D) (E)
7 (A) (B) (C) (D) (E)
8 (A) (B) (C) (D) (E)
9 (A) (B) (C) (D) (E)
10 (A) (B) (C) (D) (E)
11 (A) (B) (C) (D) (E)
12 (A) (B) (C) (D) (E)
13 (A) (B) (C) (D) (E)
14 (A) (B) (C) (D) (E)
15 (A) (B) (C) (D) (E)
16 (A) (B) (C) (D) (E)
17 (A) (B) (C) (D) (E)
18 (A) (B) (C) (D) (E)
19 (A) (B) (C) (D) (E)
20 (A) (B) (C) (D) (E)
21 (A) (B) (C) (D) (E)
22 (A) (B) (C) (D) (E)
23 (A) (B) (C) (D) (E)
24 (A) (B) (C) (D) (E)
25 (A) (B) (C) (D) (E)

Section 3 — Writing
30 minutes

1 (A) (B) (C) (D) (E)
2 (A) (B) (C) (D) (E)
3 (A) (B) (C) (D) (E)
4 (A) (B) (C) (D) (E)
5 (A) (B) (C) (D) (E)
6 (A) (B) (C) (D) (E)
7 (A) (B) (C) (D) (E)
8 (A) (B) (C) (D) (E)
9 (A) (B) (C) (D) (E)
10 (A) (B) (C) (D) (E)
11 (A) (B) (C) (D) (E)
12 (A) (B) (C) (D) (E)
13 (A) (B) (C) (D) (E)
14 (A) (B) (C) (D) (E)
15 (A) (B) (C) (D) (E)
16 (A) (B) (C) (D) (E)
17 (A) (B) (C) (D) (E)
18 (A) (B) (C) (D) (E)
19 (A) (B) (C) (D) (E)
20 (A) (B) (C) (D) (E)
21 (A) (B) (C) (D) (E)
22 (A) (B) (C) (D) (E)
23 (A) (B) (C) (D) (E)
24 (A) (B) (C) (D) (E)
25 (A) (B) (C) (D) (E)
26 (A) (B) (C) (D) (E)
27 (A) (B) (C) (D) (E)
28 (A) (B) (C) (D) (E)
29 (A) (B) (C) (D) (E)
30 (A) (B) (C) (D) (E)
31 (A) (B) (C) (D) (E)
32 (A) (B) (C) (D) (E)
33 (A) (B) (C) (D) (E)
34 (A) (B) (C) (D) (E)
35 (A) (B) (C) (D) (E)
36 (A) (B) (C) (D) (E)
37 (A) (B) (C) (D) (E)
38 (A) (B) (C) (D) (E)
39 (A) (B) (C) (D) (E)

Section 4 — Verbal
30 minutes

31 Ⓐ Ⓑ Ⓒ Ⓓ Ⓔ
32 Ⓐ Ⓑ Ⓒ Ⓓ Ⓔ
33 Ⓐ Ⓑ Ⓒ Ⓓ Ⓔ
34 Ⓐ Ⓑ Ⓒ Ⓓ Ⓔ
35 Ⓐ Ⓑ Ⓒ Ⓓ Ⓔ
36 Ⓐ Ⓑ Ⓒ Ⓓ Ⓔ
37 Ⓐ Ⓑ Ⓒ Ⓓ Ⓔ
38 Ⓐ Ⓑ Ⓒ Ⓓ Ⓔ
39 Ⓐ Ⓑ Ⓒ Ⓓ Ⓔ
40 Ⓐ Ⓑ Ⓒ Ⓓ Ⓔ
41 Ⓐ Ⓑ Ⓒ Ⓓ Ⓔ
42 Ⓐ Ⓑ Ⓒ Ⓓ Ⓔ
43 Ⓐ Ⓑ Ⓒ Ⓓ Ⓔ
44 Ⓐ Ⓑ Ⓒ Ⓓ Ⓔ
45 Ⓐ Ⓑ Ⓒ Ⓓ Ⓔ
46 Ⓐ Ⓑ Ⓒ Ⓓ Ⓔ
47 Ⓐ Ⓑ Ⓒ Ⓓ Ⓔ
48 Ⓐ Ⓑ Ⓒ Ⓓ Ⓔ
49 Ⓐ Ⓑ Ⓒ Ⓓ Ⓔ
50 Ⓐ Ⓑ Ⓒ Ⓓ Ⓔ
51 Ⓐ Ⓑ Ⓒ Ⓓ Ⓔ
52 Ⓐ Ⓑ Ⓒ Ⓓ Ⓔ
53 Ⓐ Ⓑ Ⓒ Ⓓ Ⓔ
54 Ⓐ Ⓑ Ⓒ Ⓓ Ⓔ
55 Ⓐ Ⓑ Ⓒ Ⓓ Ⓔ
56 Ⓐ Ⓑ Ⓒ Ⓓ Ⓔ
57 Ⓐ Ⓑ Ⓒ Ⓓ Ⓔ
58 Ⓐ Ⓑ Ⓒ Ⓓ Ⓔ
59 Ⓐ Ⓑ Ⓒ Ⓓ Ⓔ
60 Ⓐ Ⓑ Ⓒ Ⓓ Ⓔ

Section 5 — Math
30 minutes

26 Ⓐ Ⓑ Ⓒ Ⓓ Ⓔ
27 Ⓐ Ⓑ Ⓒ Ⓓ Ⓔ
28 Ⓐ Ⓑ Ⓒ Ⓓ Ⓔ
29 Ⓐ Ⓑ Ⓒ Ⓓ Ⓔ
30 Ⓐ Ⓑ Ⓒ Ⓓ Ⓔ
31 Ⓐ Ⓑ Ⓒ Ⓓ Ⓔ
32 Ⓐ Ⓑ Ⓒ Ⓓ Ⓔ
33 Ⓐ Ⓑ Ⓒ Ⓓ Ⓔ
34 Ⓐ Ⓑ Ⓒ Ⓓ Ⓔ
35 Ⓐ Ⓑ Ⓒ Ⓓ Ⓔ
36 Ⓐ Ⓑ Ⓒ Ⓓ Ⓔ
37 Ⓐ Ⓑ Ⓒ Ⓓ Ⓔ
39 Ⓐ Ⓑ Ⓒ Ⓓ Ⓔ
39 Ⓐ Ⓑ Ⓒ Ⓓ Ⓔ
40 Ⓐ Ⓑ Ⓒ Ⓓ Ⓔ

41, 42, 43, 44, 45, 46, 47, 48, 49, 50 — grid-in answer grids with digits 0–9.

SECTION 1
Verbal Reasoning

Time—30 minutes
30 Questions

For each question in this section, select the best answer from among the choices given and fill in the corresponding oval on the answer sheet.

Directions

Each sentence below has one or two blanks, each blank indicating that something has been omitted. Beneath the sentence are five words or sets of words labeled A through E. Choose the word or set of words that, when inserted in the sentence, best fits the meaning of the sentence as a whole.

Example:

Medieval kingdoms did not become constitutional republics overnight; on the contrary, the change was ____ .

(A) unpopular
(B) unexpected
(C) advantageous
(D) sufficient
(E) gradual   Ⓐ Ⓑ Ⓒ Ⓓ ●

1. Grown weary of constant crowds of reporters pursuing her, the candidate sought ____ at a family hideaway in Vermont.

   (A) company   (B) publicity   (C) seclusion
   (D) fulfillment   (E) diversion

2. Because his helping of food had been far too ____ , Oliver Twist beseeched the cook to give him more.

   (A) abundant   (B) savory   (C) generous
   (D) balanced   (E) meager

3. Although the coach was a tyrant who ____ his athletes regularly, the players were ____ as long as they won their games.

   (A) pampered..outspoken   (B) bullied..dissatisfied
   (C) browbeat..untroubled (D) oppressed..rebellious
   (E) neglected..intimidated

4. Sometimes making things clear for computers indirectly makes them more ____ to people, as when prices are not marked on electronically scanned merchandise.

   (A) appealing   (B) controversial   (C) manifest
   (D) obscure   (E) startling

5. Allowing women a voice in tribal government did not ____ Cherokee custom, for traditional Cherokee society was matrilineal, granting women the right to own property and to divorce their husbands.

   (A) violate   (B) emulate   (C) retrace
   (D) preclude   (E) fulfill

6. Though the assault victim had regained consciousness, he was not yet completely ____ , and so the police delayed questioning him until he seemed better able to tell a coherent tale.

   (A) listless   (B) impaired   (C) lucid
   (D) verbose   (E) inarticulate

7. In Renault's portrayal, the philosopher Aristotle, lacking breadth of vision and the ____ to inspire, proves an ____ tutor for the young Alexander of Macedon, whose spirit cried out for a counselor able to speak to his soul.

   (A) ability..illuminating   (B) power..inadequate
   (C) will..illustrious   (D) technique..acceptable
   (E) capacity..arbitrary

8. According to wildlife specialists, the few remaining pandas are so romantically ____ that their very survival as a species is threatened.

   (A) regarded   (B) disinclined   (C) camouflaged
   (D) displayed   (E) protected

9. In the course of learning to deal with the world of ideas, the adolescent gradually becomes able to express him- or herself in ____ such as courage and philosophy.

   (A) abstractions   (B) hypotheses   (C) proverbs
   (D) epigrams   (E) alliterations

10. In planting the kitchen garden, our goal was to become totally ____ so that we no longer needed to depend upon the ____ quality and inconsistencies of the commercial food wholesalers.

    (A) autonomous..undisputed
    (B) agrarian..admirable
    (C) cultivated..impeccable
    (D) self-sufficient..unreliable
    (E) egalitarian..unfailing

11. Gertrude Stein, the novelist and biographer, was the archetypal ____ American: dissatisfied with life in Oakland, she fled abroad, living in France till her death at the age of 72.

    (A) parochial   (B) conventional   (C) expatriate
    (D) territorial   (E) domestic

12. Since the propensity to migrate has persisted in every epoch, its explanation requires a theory ____ any particular period of time.

    (A) tailored to   (B) unconscious of
    (C) inapplicable to   (D) independent of
    (E) anomalous in

GO ON TO THE NEXT PAGE

13. Idealistic by nature, James disapproved of the ____ materialism of his classmates who boorishly considered only money and possessions worthy of respect.

    (A) crass   (B) altruistic   (C) ethical
    (D) cumbersome   (E) credulous

14. Relatively few politicians willingly forsake center stage, although a touch of ____ on their parts now and again might well increase their popularity with the voting public.

    (A) garrulity   (B) misanthropy
    (C) self-effacement   (D) self-dramatization
    (E) self-righteousness

15. In observing the ceremonies and rituals of worship, we must not make a show of our faith: the challenge of religion is to be ____ without becoming ____ .

    (A) reverent..relevant   (B) irreverent..blasphemous
    (C) heretical..caught   (D) pious..sanctimonious
    (E) indulgent..obvious

16. Although Mrs. Proudie ____ an interest in the spiritual well-being of the parishioners, in actuality her concern for their welfare was so ____ as to be practically nonexistent.

    (A) confessed..circumstantial
    (B) manifested..exemplary
    (C) simulated..profound
    (D) feigned..negligible
    (E) expressed..moribund

17. The term *baroque,* originally applied to the lavishly ornamented style of architecture that succeeded the Renaissance, is used generally in literary criticism to describe excessive or grandiloquent works that lack ____ of style.

    (A) diversity   (B) economy   (C) prolixity
    (D) adornment   (E) comprehension

Directions

Each passage below is followed by questions based on its content. Answer the questions following each passage on the basis of what is <u>stated</u> or <u>implied</u> in that passage and in any introductory material that may be provided.

Questions 18–22 are based on the following passage.

The following passage is taken from a book of popular history written in 1991.

The advantage of associating the birth of democracy with the Mayflower Compact is that it is easy to do so. The public loves a simple expla-
Line   nation, and none is simpler than the belief that on
5   November 11, 1620—the day the compact was approved—a cornerstone of American democracy was laid. Certainly it makes it easier on schoolchildren. Marking the start of democracy in 1620 relieves students of the responsibility of knowing
10   what happened in the hundred some years before, from the arrival of the *Santa Maria* to the landing of the *Mayflower.*

The compact, to be sure, demonstrated the Englishman's striking capacity for self-govern-
15   ment. And in affirming the principle of majority rule, the Pilgrims showed how far they had come from the days when the king's whim was law and nobody dared say otherwise.

But the emphasis on the compact is misplaced.
20   Scholarly research in the last half century indicates that the compact had nothing to do with the development of self-government in America. In truth, the Mayflower Compact was no more a cornerstone of American democracy than the Pilgrim
25   hut was the foundation of American architecture. As Samuel Eliot Morison so emphatically put it, American democracy "was not born in the cabin of the *Mayflower*."

The Pilgrims indeed are miscast as the heroes of
30   American democracy. They spurned democracy and would have been shocked to see themselves held up as its defenders. George Willison, regarded as one of the most careful students of the Pilgrims, states that "the merest glance at the history of
35   Plymouth" shows that they were not democrats.

The mythmakers would have us believe that even if the Pilgrims themselves weren't democratic, the Mayflower Compact itself was. But in fact the compact was expressly designed to curb free-
40   dom, not promote it. The Pilgrim governor and historian, William Bradford, from whom we have gotten nearly all of the information there is about the Pilgrims, frankly conceded as much. Bradford wrote that the purpose of the compact was to con-
45   trol renegades aboard the *Mayflower* who were threatening to go their own way when the ship reached land. Because the Pilgrims had decided to settle in an area outside the jurisdiction of their royal patent, some aboard the *Mayflower* had hint-
50   ed that upon landing they would "use their owne libertie, for none had power to command them." Under the terms of the compact, they couldn't; the compact required all who lived in the colony to "promise all due submission and obedience" to it.
55   Furthermore, despite the compact's mention of majority rule, the Pilgrim fathers had no intention of turning over the colony's government to the people. Plymouth was to be ruled by the elite. And the elite wasn't bashful in the least about
60   advancing its claims to superiority. When the Mayflower Compact was signed, the elite signed first. The second rank consisted of the "goodmen." At the bottom of the list came four servants' names. No women or children signed.

GO ON TO THE NEXT PAGE

65 Whether the compact was or was not actually hostile to the democratic spirit, it was deemed sufficiently hostile that during the Revolution the Tories put it to use as "propaganda for the crown." The monarchists made much of the fact
70 that the Pilgrims had chosen to establish an English-style government that placed power in the hands of a governor, not a cleric, and a governor who owed his allegiance not to the people or to a church but to "our dread Sovereign Lord King
75 James." No one thought it significant that the Tories had adopted the principle of majority rule. Tory historian George Chalmers, in a work published in 1780, claimed the central meaning of the compact was the Pilgrims' recognition of the
80 necessity of royal authority. This may have been not only a convenient argument but a true one. It is at least as plausible as the belief that the compact stood for democracy.

18. The author's attitude toward the general public (lines 3–7) can best be described as

(A) egalitarian (B) grateful (C) sympathetic
(D) envious (E) superior

19. The phrase "held up" in line 32 means

(A) delayed (B) cited (C) accommodated
(D) carried (E) waylaid

20. According to the passage (lines 44–56), the compact's primary purpose was to

(A) establish legal authority within the colony
(B) outlaw non-Pilgrims among the settlers
(C) preach against heretical thinking
(D) protect each individual's civil rights
(E) countermand the original royal patent

21. The author of the passage can best be described as

(A) an iconoclast (B) an atheist
(C) a mythmaker (D) an elitist
(E) an authoritarian

22. In lines 60–64, the details about the signers of the Mayflower Compact are used to emphasize

(A) the Pilgrims' respect for the social hierarchy
(B) the inclusion of servants among those signing
(C) their importance to American history
(D) the variety of social classes aboard
(E) the lack of any provision for minority rule

Questions 23–30 are based on the following passage.

In this excerpt from her autobiography, One Writer's Beginnings, *the short-story writer Eudora Welty introduces her parents.*

My father loved all instruments that would instruct and fascinate. His place to keep things was the drawer in the "library table" where, lying
Line on top of his folded maps, was a telescope with
5 brass extensions, to find the moon and the Big Dipper after supper in our front yard, and to keep appointments with eclipses. In the back of the drawer you could find a magnifying glass, a kaleidoscope, and a gyroscope kept in a black buckram
10 box, which he would set dancing for us on a string pulled tight. He had also supplied himself with an assortment of puzzles composed of metal rings and intersecting links and keys chained together, impossible for the rest of us, however patiently
15 shown, to take apart; he had an almost childlike love of the ingenious.

In time, a barometer was added to our dining room wall, but we didn't really need it. My father had the country boy's accurate knowledge of the
20 weather and its skies. He went out and stood on our front steps first thing in the morning and took a good look at it and a sniff. He was a pretty good weather prophet.

"Well, I'm *not*," my mother would say, with
25 enormous self-satisfaction.

He told us children what to do if we were lost in a strange country. "Look for where the sky is brightest along the horizon," he said. "That reflects the nearest river. Strike out for a river and you will
30 find habitation." Eventualities were much on his mind. In his care for us children he cautioned us to take measures against such things as being struck by lightning. He drew us all away from the windows during the severe electrical storms that are
35 common where we live. My mother stood apart, scoffing at caution as a character failing. "Why, I always loved a storm! High winds never bothered me in West Virginia! Just listen at that! I wasn't a bit afraid of a little lightning and thunder! I'd go
40 out on the mountain and spread my arms wide and *run* in a good big storm!"

So I developed a strong meteorological sensibility. In years ahead when I wrote stories, atmosphere took its influential role from the start.
45 Commotion in the weather and the inner feelings aroused by such a hovering disturbance emerged connected in dramatic form. (I tried a tornado first, in a story called "The Winds.")

From our earliest Christmas times, Santa Claus
50 brought us toys that instruct boys and girls (separately) how to build things—stone blocks cut to the castle-building style, Tinker Toys, and Erector

GO ON TO THE NEXT PAGE →

sets. Daddy made for us himself elaborate kites
that needed to be taken miles out of town to a pas-
55 ture long enough (and my father was not afraid of
horses and cows watching) for him to run with
and get up on a long cord to which my mother
held the spindle, and then we children were given
it to hold, tugging like something alive at our
60 hands. They were beautiful, sound, shapely box
kites, smelling delicately of office glue for their
entire short lives. And of course, as soon as the
boys attained anywhere near the right age, there
was an electric train, the engine with its pea-sized
65 working headlight, its line of cars, tracks
equipped with switches, semaphores, its station,
its bridges, and its tunnel, which blocked off all
other traffic in the upstairs hall. Even from down-
stairs, and through the cries of excited children,
70 the elegant rush and click of the train could be
heard through the ceiling, running around and
around its figure eight.

All of this, but especially the train, represents my
father's fondest beliefs—in progress, in the future.
75 With these gifts, he was preparing his children.

And so was my mother with her different gifts.

I learned from the age of two or three that any
room in our house, at any time of day, was there to
read in, or be read to. My mother read to me.
80 She'd read to me in the big bedroom in the morn-
ings, when we were in her rocker together, which
ticked in rhythm as we rocked, as though we had a
cricket accompanying the story. She'd read to me
in the dining room on winter afternoons in front of
85 the coal fire, with our cuckoo clock ending the
story with "Cuckoo," and at night when I'd got in
my own bed. I must have given her no peace.
Sometimes she read to me in the kitchen while she
sat churning, and the churning sobbed along with
90 *any* story. It was my ambition to have her read to
me while *I* churned; once she granted my wish, but
she read off my story before I brought her butter.
She was an expressive reader. When she was reading *Puss in Boots*, for instance, it was impossible
95 not to know that she distrusted *all* cats.

23. In saying that her father used the telescope to "keep
appointments with eclipses" (lines 6–7), Welty
means that

(A) the regularity of eclipses helped him avoid
missing engagements
(B) his attempts at astronomical observation met
with failure
(C) he made a point of observing major astronomical phenomena
(D) he tried to instruct his children in the importance of keeping appointments
(E) he invented ingenious new ways to use the telescope

24. We can infer from lines 18–23 that Welty's father
stood on the front steps and sniffed first thing in the
morning

(A) because he disapproved of the day's weather
(B) because he suffered from nasal congestion
(C) to enjoy the fragrance of the flowers
(D) to detect signs of changes in the weather
(E) in an instinctive response to fresh air

25. The word "measures" in line 32 means

(A) legislative actions   (B) preventative steps
(C) yardsticks   (D) food rations   (E) warnings

26. When Welty's mother exclaims "Just listen at that!"
(line 39), she wants everyone to pay attention to

(A) her husband's advice
(B) her memories of West Virginia
(C) the sounds of the storm
(D) her reasons for being unafraid
(E) the noise the children are making

27. Compared to Welty's father, her mother can best be
described as

(A) more literate and more progressive
(B) proud of her knowledge of the weather, but
imprudent about storms
(C) unafraid of ordinary storms, but deeply disturbed by tornados
(D) more protective of her children, but less patient
with them
(E) less apt to foresee problems, but more apt to
enjoy the moment

28. The word "fondest" in line 74 means

(A) most affectionate   (B) most foolish
(C) most radical   (D) most cherished
(E) most credulous

29. By the phrase "brought her butter" (line 93), Welty
means that she

(A) manufactured butter   (B) fetched butter
(C) spread butter   (D) purchased butter
(E) melted butter

30. Why does Welty recount these anecdotes about her
parents?

(A) She wishes to prove that theirs was an unhappy
marriage of opposites
(B) The anecdotes are vivid illustrations of truths
that she holds dear
(C) She seeks to provide advice for travelers lost in
the wilderness
(D) She envisions her parents chiefly as humorous
subjects for ironic characterization
(E) She wishes to provide background on early
influences on her as a writer

IF YOU FINISH BEFORE 30 MINUTES, YOU MAY CHECK YOUR WORK ON THIS
SECTION ONLY. DO NOT TURN TO ANY OTHER SECTION IN THE TEST.

S T O P

SECTION **2**
Mathematical Reasoning

**Time—30 minutes
25 Questions**

Directions and Reference Information

In this section solve each problem, using any available space for scratchwork. Then decide which is the best of the choices given and fill in the corresponding oval on the answer sheet.

Notes:

(1) The use of a calculator is permitted. All numbers used are real numbers.

(2) Figures that accompany problems in this test are intended to provide information useful in solving the problems. They are drawn as accurately as possible EXCEPT when it is stated in a specific problem that the figure is not drawn to scale. All figures lie in a plane unless otherwise indicated.

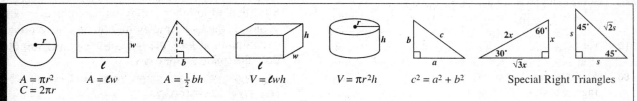

$A = \pi r^2$ $A = \ell w$ $A = \frac{1}{2} bh$ $V = \ell w h$ $V = \pi r^2 h$ $c^2 = a^2 + b^2$ Special Right Triangles
$C = 2\pi r$

The number of degrees of an arc in a circle is 360.
The measure in degrees of a straight angle is 180.
The sum of the measures in degrees of the angles of a triangle is 180.

1. If the mean (average) of a set of four scores is 18 and the mean (average) of a set of five scores is 27, what is the mean of the combined set of nine scores?

   (A) 19 (B) 21 (C) 22 (D) 23 (E) 24

2. Which of the following could represent the number of units in the lengths of the three sides of a right triangle?

   I. 9, 12, and 15
   II. 10, 26, and 24
   III. $1\frac{1}{2}$, 2, and $2\frac{1}{2}$
   (A) I only (B) II only (C) III only
   (D) I and II only (E) I, II and III

3. Mr. Benedict left half of his estate to his wife, one-fourth to his son, one-fifth to his daughter and the remainder, $5000, to his college. What is the total amount left by Mr. Benedict?

   (A) $9250 (B) $10,000 (C) $16,000
   (D) $50,000 (E) $100,000

4. A sweater marked $60 has a tag stating TAKE 10% OFF PRICE ON TAG. What must I pay for this sweater, taking advantage of this special price and paying the town 10% sales tax?

   (A) $48.60 (B) $54. (C) $57.60
   (D) $59.40 (E) $60.

5. One season a baseball team played g games and lost a total of l games. What part of their games did they win?

   (A) $\dfrac{l}{g}$ (B) $\dfrac{g}{l}$ (C) $\dfrac{g-l}{l}$
   (D) $\dfrac{l-g}{g}$ (E) $\dfrac{g-l}{g}$

6. What is the ratio of a 10-inch strip to a strip 2 yards long?

   (A) 5:1 (B) 1:5 (C) 20:1
   (D) 1:7.2 (E) 1:7.5

GO ON TO THE NEXT PAGE

7. The following is a report of defective parts reported by inspectors in 3 electronic factories:

   Brookline   3 per 10,000
   Brookville   5 per 100,000
   Brooklyn   13 per 1,000,000

   Which of the following best expresses the portion of defective parts in the three factories combined?

   (A) 5 per 10,000   (B) 66 per 10,000
   (C) 66 per 100,000   (D) 93 per 1,000,000
   (E) 363 per 1,000,000

8. Ten years ago Lori was y years old. How old will she be in x years from now?

   (A) $y - x + 10$ (B) $y + x - 10$ (C) $10 + y$
   (D) $x + y$ (E) $x + y + 10$

9. An efficiency expert has calculated that about 9.5% of the articles produced in a manufacturing plant are defective. This is equivalent to expressing the defective articles as

   (A) 9 out of 15   (B) 9 out of 50
   (C) 10 out of 95   (D) 19 out of 100
   (E) 19 out of 200

10. $x - 7 = 0$
    $y^2 = 25$
    $xy =$

    (A) $+35$ (B) ± 35 (C) -35 (D) 5   (E) 0

11. If k is the average of 10 and -14, then the average of k and -8 is

    (A) -24 (B) -12 (C) -11
    (D) -5 (E) $+5$

12. A father can do a job as fast as two sons working together. If one son does the job alone in three hours and the other does it alone in six hours, how many hours does it take the father to do the job alone?

    (A) 1   (B) 2   (C) 3   (D) 4   (E) $4\frac{1}{2}$

13. $9x - 12y = -21$
    $6x + 4y = 34$
    $3x - 4y$

    (A) -54 (B) -13 (C) -7
    (D) 7   (E) 13

14. A woman went shopping for sugar for canning. In one store sugar was 71¢ per pound and she found that she lacked 60¢ of having enough money to buy the number of pounds she needed. She bought the required amount of sugar at another store at 70¢ per pound and had 90¢ left. How much money did she have before making the purchase?

    (A) $105.00   (B) $105.90   (C) $106.00
    (D) $106.10   (E) more than $108.00

15. Which of the following is (are) true of the value of $(152)^3(783)(281) - (29)^5(0)(374)(2)^8$?

    I. The last digit in the answer is 4.
    II. The answer is an odd number.
    III. The answer is a negative number.
    (A) I only   (B) II only   (C) III only
    (D) I and II only   (E) I, II and III

16. How long would it take a car traveling at 30 miles per hour to cover a distance of 44 feet? (1 mi. = 5280 ft.)

    (A) 1 sec.   (B) 2.64 sec.   (C) 5.2 sec.
    (D) 1 min.   (E) 7.7 min.

17. $\angle a = \angle b$
    $\angle c \stackrel{\circ}{=} 60$
    $\angle d \stackrel{\circ}{=}$

    (A) 30   (B) 60
    (C) 120   (D) 180
    (E) none of these

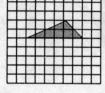

18. A pulley whose diameter is 9 inches in connected by a belt to another pulley whose diameter is 6 inches. If the larger pulley runs at 1200 revolutions per minute, at how many revolutions per minute does the smaller pulley run?

    (A) 800   (B) 1080   (C) 1600
    (D) 1800   (E) 2000

19. How many square units are there in the shaded triangle?

    (A) 3   (B) 4
    (C) 5   (D) 6
    (E) 9

20. In $\triangle ABC$, if $\angle A > \angle B$ and $\angle B > \angle C$, then each of the following can be true EXCEPT

    (A) $C < 40°$ (B) $A < 170°$ (C) $B > 60°$
    (D) $A > 90°$ (E) $C > 60°$

21. A rectangular piece of cardboard 9" × 12" is made into an open box by cutting a $2^{1}/_{2}$" square from each corner and bending up the sides. What is the volume of the box if no allowance is made for overlapping of the edges?

    (A) 70 cu. in.   (B) $154\frac{3}{8}$ cu. in.   (C) 195 cu. in.
    (D) 270 cu. in.   (E) 700 cu. in.

22. If the length and width of a rectangle are doubled, by what percent is the area increased?

    (A) 30%   (B) 75%   (C) 100%
    (D) 300%   (E) 400%

23. In pentagon $ABCDE$, $AB \perp BC$
    $\angle C + \angle D + \angle E + \angle A =$

    (A) 450°   (B) 540°
    (C) 630°   (D) 720°
    (E) 810°

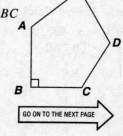

GO ON TO THE NEXT PAGE

24. This graph shows expenditures and profit for a firm with total sales of $240 million. How much (in millions of dollars) was spent for labor?

(A) 48   (B) 96   (C) 480
(D) 960   (E) 9600

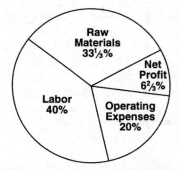

25. What percent of the wage earners are in trade and finance?

(A) 10   (B) 15   (C) 25
(D) 45   (E) 90

What Wage Earners Did

Personal Service 45°

Manufacturing 120°

All Others 60°

Trans 20°

Professions 25°

Trade and Finance 90°

IF YOU FINISH BEFORE 30 MINUTES, YOU MAY CHECK YOUR WORK ON THIS SECTION ONLY. DO NOT TURN TO ANY OTHER SECTION IN THE TEST.

S T O P

<table>
<tr><td>

SECTION 3
Writing Skills

</td><td>

Time—30 minutes
39 Questions

</td></tr>
</table>

Directions

The following sentences contain problems in grammar, usage, diction (choice of words), and idiom.

   Some sentences are correct.
   No sentence contains more than one error.

You will find that the error, if there is one, is underlined and lettered. Assume that elements of the sentence that are not underlined are correct and cannot be changed. In choosing answers, follow the requirements of standard written English.

If there is an error, select the one underlined part that must be changed to make the sentence correct and blacken the corresponding space on your answer sheet.

If there is no error, blacken answer space Ⓔ.

Example:

   The region has a climate <u>so severe that</u> plants
                            A

   <u>growing there</u> rarely <u>had been</u> more than twelve
       B   C

   inches <u>high</u>. <u>No error</u>
          D   E

Ⓐ Ⓑ ● Ⓓ Ⓔ

1. I <u>only</u> <u>bought</u> <u>what</u> was necessary; I was not
       A   B   C
    extravagant. <u>No error</u>
       D   E

2. <u>Bailing</u> <u>vigorously</u>, we managed <u>to remain</u> afloat
       A   B   C
    until we <u>were rescued</u> by the Coast Guard. <u>No error</u>
                D   E

3. We <u>had ought</u> to finish our trip before dark <u>because</u>
          A   B
    it gets very cold after the sun <u>goes down</u>. <u>No error</u>
    C   D   E

4. It is not you <u>who are</u> at fault; <u>rather</u>, it is <u>I</u> who <u>is</u>
                     A   B   C   D
    to blame. <u>No error</u>
                 E

5. <u>Because of</u> its efficacy in treating many ailments
       A
    and because <u>it has brought about</u> miraculous cures,
                     B
    penicillin <u>has become</u> an important <u>addition to</u> the
                  C   D
    druggist's stock. <u>No error</u>
                          E

6. After the rain <u>had fallen</u> <u>steadily</u> for five days,
                      A   B
    then the football field was a <u>massive sea</u> of mud.
    C   D
    <u>No error</u>
    E

7. I cannot force <u>myself</u> to like <u>that</u> <u>kind of a person</u>
                      A   B   C
    because his smugness <u>repels</u> me. <u>No error</u>
                            D   E

8. I believe <u>that</u> story about the fight <u>because</u> he
                 A   B
    <u>himself</u> had told us the story <u>was true</u>. <u>No error</u>
       C   D   E

9. The ship had <u>almost completely</u> <u>sank</u> <u>by the time</u>
                    A   B   C
    the rescuers <u>arrived</u> on the scene. <u>No error</u>
                    D   E

10. <u>Since</u> you do not participate in <u>any of</u> the class
       A   B
    activities, I <u>must conclude</u> that you are
                     C
    <u>disinterested</u>. <u>No error</u>
       D   E

11. Marc Chagall, <u>who</u> <u>recently</u> died, painted many
                     A   B
    <u>beautiful executed</u> fantasies <u>both</u> in the United
    C   D
    States and France. <u>No error</u>
                           E

12. <u>Although</u> many people complain about his attitude,
       A
    <u>it</u> <u>seems</u> perfectly all right to <u>myself</u>. <u>No error</u>
    B   C   D   E

13. The America's Cup, <u>which</u> was first won by the
                          A
    United States yacht *America,* <u>grew out of</u> the London
                                      B
    Exposition of 1951 and <u>now becoming</u> a world
                              C
    <u>yachting</u> championship. <u>No error</u>
       D   E

14. <u>On the contrary</u>, you <u>will find</u> that Ms. Keene is
       A   B
    <u>better</u> qualified than <u>him</u> for the executive position.
    C   D
    <u>No error</u>
    E

GO ON TO THE NEXT PAGE ⟶

15. Sometimes speed reading aids <u>in comprehension,</u>
                                         A
but remember that <u>turning</u> the pages <u>rapidly</u> does
  B   C   D
not guarantee rapid comprehension. <u>No error</u>
                                        E

16. The Salem witchcraft trials in 1692 inspired Arthur

Miller <u>to write</u> *The Crucible,* <u>to serve for</u> a parable
         A   B
for America <u>during</u> the <u>era of</u> McCarthyism.
               C   D

<u>No error</u>
    E

17. The <u>fishing fleet</u> <u>left</u> the harbor <u>when</u> the fishermen
            A   B   C
heard that a school of bluefish <u>were near</u> the wreck.
                                     D

<u>No error</u>
    E

18. After five years <u>of</u> booming markets and unparalleled
                         A
expansion, Wall Street's major securities firms

<u>planning</u> to slow <u>their</u> growth that has transformed
   B   C
them into <u>sprawling</u> global behemoths. <u>No error</u>
              D   E

19. <u>Neither</u> the reporters nor the editor <u>were</u> <u>satisfied with</u>
           A   B   C
the salary offer made <u>by</u> the publisher. <u>No error</u>
                         D   E

Directions

In each of the following sentences, some part or all of the sentence is underlined. Below each sentence you will find five ways of phrasing the underlined part. Select the answer that produces the most effective sentence, one that is clear and exact, without awkwardness or ambiguity, and fill in the corresponding oval on your answer sheet. In choosing answers, follow the requirements of standard written English. Choose the answer that best expresses the meaning of the original sentence.

Answer (A) is always the same as the underlined part. Choose Answer (A) if you think the original sentence needs no revision.

EXAMPLE:

Laura Ingalls Wilder published her first book <u>and she was sixty-five years old then</u>.

(A) and she was sixty-five years old then
(B) when she was sixty-five
(C) at age sixty-five years old
(D) upon reaching of sixty-five years
(E) at the time when she was sixty-five

SAMPLE ANSWER

Ⓐ ● Ⓒ Ⓓ Ⓔ

20. With the exception of <u>Frank and I, everyone in the class finished</u> the assignment before the bell rang.

(A) Frank and I, everyone in the class finished
(B) Frank and me, everyone in the class finished
(C) Frank and me, everyone in the class had finished
(D) Frank and I, everyone in the class had finished
(E) Frank and me everyone in the class finished

21. Many middle class individuals find that they cannot obtain good medical attention, <u>despite they need it badly</u>.

(A) despite they need it badly
(B) despite their bad need of it
(C) in spite of they need it badly
(D) however much their need of it were
(E) therefore, they need it badly

22. The form of terrorism that makes diplomats its target reached Sweden in <u>1975, the West German embassy in Stockholm was seized</u> by Germans linked to the Baader-Meinhof gang.

(A) 1975, the West German embassy in Stockholm was seized
(B) 1975, and the West German embassy in Stockholm was seized
(C) 1975, despite the West German embassy in Stockholm was seized
(D) 1975, when the West German embassy in Stockholm was seized
(E) 1975, the West German embassy in Stockholm's being seized

GO ON TO THE NEXT PAGE

23. Arlington National Cemetery, <u>the site of the Tomb of the Unknown Soldier, is located on</u> the former Custis estate in Virginia.

    (A) the site of the Tomb of the Unknown Soldier, is located on

    (B) being the cite of the Tomb of the Unknown Soldier, has been located at

    (C) where is located the Tomb of the Unknown Soldier, is at

    (D) being the site of the Tomb of the Unknown Soldier, is at

    (E) which includes the site of the Tomb of the Unknown Soldier, is located by

24. In the normal course of events, <u>Juan will graduate high school, he will enter</u> college in two years.

    (A) Juan will graduate high school, he will enter

    (B) Juan will graduate high school and enter

    (C) Juan will be graduated from high school and enter

    (D) Juan will have graduated from high school and enter

    (E) Juan will graduate high school; he will enter

25. It would have been <u>wrong, even had it been possible,</u> to force a parliamentary democracy down the throats of the Iranians.

    (A) wrong, even had it been possible,

    (B) wrong; even had it been possible,

    (C) wrong, it had been even possible,

    (D) wrong, even if possible it had been,

    (E) wrong: even had it been possible,

26. The number of California condors, decimated by increasing human intrusions into traditional condor breeding grounds, <u>are currently given as fewer than thirty.</u>

    (A) are currently given as fewer than thirty

    (B) currently are given as fewer than thirty

    (C) is currently given as fewer than thirty

    (D) were given currently as fewer than thirty

    (E) are currently going to be given as fewer than thirty

27. Many economists maintain that the current low interest rates not only promote investment in the stock market <u>but also made it more profitable.</u>

    (A) but also made it more profitable

    (B) but also makes it more profitable

    (C) but also made it more able to profit

    (D) but made it also more profitable

    (E) but also make it more profitable

28. Ever since the bombing of Cambodia, there has been much opposition <u>from they who maintain that it was an unauthorized war.</u>

    (A) from they who maintain that it was an unauthorized war

    (B) from they who maintain that it had been an unauthorized war

    (C) from those who maintain that it was an unauthorized war

    (D) from they maintaining that it was an unauthorized

    (E) from they maintaining that it had been an unauthorized war

29. During the winter of 1973, Americans <u>discovered the need to conserve energy and attempts were made to meet the crisis.</u>

    (A) discovered the need to conserve energy and attempts were made to meet the crisis

    (B) discovered the need to conserve energy and that the crisis had to be met

    (C) discovered the need to conserve energy and made attempts to meet the crisis

    (D) needed to conserve energy and to meet the crisis

    (E) needed to conserve energy and attempts were made to meet the crisis

30. <u>When one eats in this restaurant, you often find</u> that the prices are high and that the food is poorly prepared.

    (A) When one eats in this restaurant, you often find

    (B) When you eat in this restaurant, one often find

    (C) When you eat in this restaurant, you often find

    (D) If you eat in this restaurant, you often find

    (E) When one ate in this restaurant, he often found

31. The giving of foreign aid is a tool of national <u>policy, the hoped-for return is often indirect and long term.</u>

    (A) policy, the hoped-for return is often indirect and long term

    (B) policy, however the hoped-for return is often indirect and long term

    (C) policy, though the hoped-for return is often indirect and long term

    (D) policy, albeit the hoped-for return is often indirect and long term

    (E) policy, despite the hoped-for return is often indirect and long term

GO ON TO THE NEXT PAGE

32. Strict economic sanctions that have been imposed against the Union of South Africa <u>ban investments in that country and numerous metals may not be imported</u>.

    (A) ban investments in that country and numerous metals may not be imported

    (B) ban investments there and the importation of numerous metals

    (C) ban investing there and numerous metals may not be imported

    (D) ban investments in that country, also, numerous metals may not be imported

    (E) ban investing there and numerous metals have not imported

33. Feeling natural wildlife during fall migration <u>not advocated being that it entices them to stay and possibly starve</u> during the winter.

    (A) not advocated being that it entices them to stay and possibly starve

    (B) is not advocated since it entices them to stay and possibly starve

    (C) is not advocated being that it entices them to stay, perhaps starving

    (D) has not been advisable because of eating patterns

    (E) is not advocated; they can starve

Directions

The passage below is the unedited draft of a student's essay. Some of the essay needs to be rewritten to make the meaning clearer and more precise. Read the essay carefully.

The essay is followed by six questions about changes that might improve all or part of its organization, development, sentence structure, use of language, appropriateness to the audience, or its use of standard written English. Choose the answer that most clearly and effectively expresses the student's intended meaning. Indicate your choice by filling in the corresponding space on the answer sheet.

Essay

[1] At the beginning of the twentieth century, no one knew the technological developments that would be made by the 1990s. [2] The area of communication media is one of the significant developments in the twentieth century. [3] Also nuclear energy and great advancements in medicine and the treatment of disease.

[4] One important development was the invention of communication satellites which allow images and messages to be sent wirelessly around the world. [5] One advantage is that current events can be sent worldwide in seconds. [6] News used to travel by boat and take weeks or months to get overseas. [7] When a disaster struck the World Trade Center, the world saw it immediately and condemned the terrorists' actions. [8] One weak aspect of communication satellites is that they are launched from a space shuttle, and that is an extremely costly operation. [9] They also they cost millions of dollars to build and operate. [10] Therefore, many poor countries are left out of the so-called "Global Village."

[11] The invention and use of nuclear energy is another important technological development. [12] One positive feature of nuclear energy is that energy is cheaper, and can be made easy. [13] This is important in countries like France where almost all of the electricity is nuclear. [14] A negative consequence of nuclear energy is the probability of major nuclear accidents. [15] Watch out for human error and careless workmanship. [16] They were the cause of the meltdown in Chernobyl, which killed hundreds or maybe even thousands, and radiated half the Earth.

[17] There have been many significant technological advances in medicine in the twentieth century. [18] One development was the invention of the CAT scan. [19] The CAT scan allows doctors to make a picture of your brain to see if there is a growth on it. [20] One positive effect of the CAT scan is that doctors can diagnose brain tumors and brain cancer at an early stage. [21] One negative effect is that CAT scans are costly , so they are not used in third world countries.

34. Considering the main idea of the whole essay, which of the following is the best revision of sentence 1?

    (A) In 1900 no one could anticipate the technological developments in the 1990s.

    (B) Recent technological achievements would blow the minds of people at the beginning of the twentieth century.

    (C) The twentieth century has seen remarkable technological achievements, but there has also been a price to pay for progress.

    (D) No one knows if the twenty-first century will produce as much technological progress as the twentieth century did.

    (E) Technological progress in communications, nuclear energy, and medicine is wonderful, but in the process we are destroying ourselves and our environment.

35. Which is the best revision of the underlined segment of sentence 12 below?

One positive feature of nuclear <u>energy is that energy is cheaper, and can be made easy</u>.

    (A) energy is cheaper and can be made easily

    (B) energy is made cheaper and more easily made

    (C) it is cheap and easy to make

    (D) it is both cheap as well as made easily

    (E) it's more cheaper and easier to make

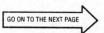

36. To improve the coherence of paragraph 2, which of the following is the best sentence to delete from the essay?

(A) Sentence 5
(B) Sentence 6
(C) Sentence 7
(D) Sentence 8
(E) Sentence 9

37. In the context of the sentences that precede and follow sentence 15, which is the best revision of sentence 15?

(A) Human error and careless workmanship are almost unavoidable.
(B) Especially human error and careless workmanship.
(C) There's hardly no foolproof way to prevent human error and careless workmanship.
(D) You must never put down your guard against human error and careless workmanship.
(E) Accidents can happen accidentally by human error and careless workmanship.

38. With regard to the entire essay, which of the following best explains the writer's intention in paragraphs 2, 3, and 4?

(A) To compare and contrast three technological achievements
(B) To provide examples of the pros and cons of technological progress
(C) To analyze the steps needed for achievement in three areas
(D) To convince the reader to be open to technological change
(E) To advocate more funds for technological research and development

39. Assume that sentences 17 and 18 were combined as follows: *A significant advance in medicine has been the invention of the CAT scan.* Which of the following is the best way to continue the paragraph?

(A) The CAT scan allows your doctors to make pictures of a brain to see if it has a growth on it, a cancer is growing, or tumors at an early stage.
(B) The CAT scan permits your doctors to make a picture and see if your brain has a growth on it, or whether or not you have brain tumors or brain cancer at an early stage.
(C) Taking pictures with a CAT scan, your brain is studied by doctors for growths, brain tumors, and cancer at an early stage.
(D) Doctors may make pictures of your brain to see if there is a growth, a tumor, or cancer at an early stage on it.
(E) With this device a doctor may look into a patient's brain to check for growths and to detect cancerous tumors at an early stage.

IF YOU FINISH BEFORE 30 MINUTES, YOU MAY CHECK YOUR WORK ON THIS SECTION ONLY. DO NOT TURN TO ANY OTHER SECTION IN THE TEST.   **S T O P**

SECTION 4
Verbal Reasoning

Time—30 minutes
30 Questions

For each question in this section, select the best answer from among the choices given and fill in the corresponding oval on the answer sheet.

Directions

Each sentence below consists of a related pair of words or phrases, followed by five pairs of words or phrases labeled A through E. Select the pair that best expresses a relationship similar to that expressed in the original pair.

Example:

CRUMB:BREAD::
(A) ounce:unit
(B) splinter:wood
(C) water:bucket
(D) twine:rope
(E) cream:butter

31. BOOK:CHAPTER::

    (A) painting:frame   (B) sentence:verb
    (C) building:story   (D) tree:root
    (E) movie:scenario

32. CLASP:BRACELET::

    (A) snap:hook   (B) buckle:belt
    (C) diamond:ring   (D) wrist:watch
    (E) cuff:trousers

33. FLEET:SHIPS::

    (A) team:coaches   (B) planet:satellites
    (C) shelf:books   (D) committee:meetings
    (E) pack:wolves

34. BANK:MONEY::

    (A) cask:wine   (B) ring:diamond
    (C) chain:link   (D) body:germ
    (E) transfusion:blood

35. FLIMSY:STRENGTH::

    (A) fancy:beauty   (B) hazardous:danger
    (C) wary:caution   (D) slippery:smoothness
    (E) clumsy:grace

36. OBSTINATE:MULISH::

    (A) gruff:doglike   (B) clever:dull
    (C) inanimate:beastly   (D) coy:kittenish
    (E) domestic:fawning

37. REFUGEE:ASYLUM::

    (A) patient:illness   (B) hermit:solitude
    (C) tutor:education   (D) convict:prison
    (E) judge:courtroom

38. INANE:MEANING::

    (A) vacant:space   (B) random:plan
    (C) affluent:wealth   (D) certain:direction
    (E) aesthetic:beauty

39. SAP:VITALITY::

    (A) sweeten:temperament   (B) divert:traffic
    (C) invest:income   (D) drain:wound
    (E) deplete:resources

40. COUNTESS:NOBILITY::

    (A) judge:jury   (B) celebrity:fans
    (C) professor:faculty   (D) miser:parsimony
    (E) nurse:surgery

41. CHAFF:WHEAT::

    (A) mote:dust   (B) gold:lead
    (C) dregs:wine   (D) roll:bread
    (E) vine:tomato

42. EPHEMERAL:PERMANENCE::

    (A) erratic:predictability
    (B) immaculate:cleanliness
    (C) commendable:reputation
    (D) spurious:emulation
    (E) mandatory:obedience

43. OGLE:OBSERVE::

    (A) haggle:outbid   (B) clamor:dispute
    (C) discern:perceive   (D) flaunt:display
    (E) glare:glower

The passage below is followed by questions based on its content. Answer the questions following the passage on the basis of what is <u>stated</u> or <u>implied</u> in that passage and in any introductory material that may be provided.

Questions 44–49 are based on the following passage.

The following passage, written in the twentieth century, is taken from a discussion of John Webster's seventeenth-century drama The Duchess of Malfi.

The curtain rises; the Cardinal and Daniel de Bosola enter from the right. In appearance, the Cardinal is something between an El Greco cardinal and a Van Dyke noble lord. He has the tall,
Line spare form—the elongated hands and features—
5 of the former; the trim pointed beard, the imperial repose, the commanding authority of the latter. But the El Greco features are not really those of asceticism or inner mystic spirituality. They are
10 the index to a cold, refined but ruthless cruelty in

GO ON TO THE NEXT PAGE →

a highly civilized controlled form. Neither is the imperial repose an aloof mood of proud detachment. It is a refined expression of satanic pride of place and talent.

15   To a degree, the Cardinal's coldness is artificially cultivated. He has defined himself against his younger brother Duke Ferdinand and is the opposite to the overwrought emotionality of the latter. But the Cardinal's aloof mood is not one of
20   bland detachment. It is the deliberate detachment of a methodical man who collects his thoughts and emotions into the most compact and formidable shape—that when he strikes, he may strike with the more efficient and devastating force. His
25   easy movements are those of the slowly circling eagle just before the swift descent with the exposed talons. Above all else, he is a man who never for a moment doubts his destined authority as a governor. He derisively and sharply rebukes
30   his brother the Duke as easily and readily as he mocks his mistress Julia. If he has betrayed his hireling Bosola, he uses his brother as the tool to win back his "familiar." His court dress is a long brilliant scarlet cardinal's gown with white cuffs
35   and a white collar turned back over the red, both collar and cuffs being elaborately scalloped and embroidered. He wears a small cape, reaching only to the elbows. His cassock is buttoned to the ground, giving a heightened effect to his already
40   tall presence. Richelieu would have adored his neatly trimmed beard. A richly jeweled and ornamented cross lies on his breast, suspended from his neck by a gold chain.

       Bosola, for his part, is the Renaissance "famil-
45   iar" dressed conventionally in somber black with a white collar. He wears a chain about his neck, a suspended ornament, and a sword. Although a "bravo," he must not be thought of as a leather-jacketed, heavy-booted tough, squat and swarthy.
50   Still less is he a sneering, leering, melodramatic villain of the Victorian gaslight tradition. Like his black-and-white clothes, he is a colorful contradiction, a scholar-assassin, a humanist-hangman; introverted and introspective, yet ruthless in
55   action; moody and reluctant, yet violent. He is a man of scholarly taste and subtle intellectual discrimination doing the work of a hired ruffian. In general effect, his impersonator must achieve suppleness and subtlety of nature, a highly complex,
60   compressed, yet well restrained intensity of temperament. Like Duke Ferdinand, he is inwardly

tormented, but not by undiluted passion. His dominant emotion is an intellectualized one: that of disgust at a world filled with knavery and folly,
65   but in which he must play a part and that a lowly, despicable one. He is the kind of rarity that Browning loved to depict in his Renaissance monologues.

44. The primary purpose of the passage appears to be to

(A) provide historical background on the Renaissance church
(B) describe ecclesiastical costuming and pageantry
(C) analyze the appearances and moral natures of two dramatic figures
(D) explain why modern audiences enjoy *The Duchess of Malfi*
(E) compare two interpretations of a challenging role

45. The word "spare" in line 5 means

(A) excessive   (B) superfluous
(C) pardonable   (D) lean   (E) inadequate

46. In lines 24–27, the author most likely compares the movements of the Cardinal to those of a circling eagle in order to emphasize his

(A) flightiness   (B) love of freedom
(C) eminence   (D) spirituality
(E) mercilessness

47. As used in the third paragraph, the word "bravo" most nearly means

(A) a courageous man   (B) a national hero
(C) a clergyman   (D) a humanist
(E) a mercenary killer

48. The word "discrimination" in lines 56–57 means

(A) prejudice   (B) villainy   (C) discretion
(D) favoritism   (E) discernment

49. The author of the passage assumes that the reader is

(A) familiar with the paintings of El Greco and Van Dyke
(B) disgusted with a world filled with cruelty and folly
(C) ignorant of the history of the Roman Catholic Church
(D) uninterested in psychological distinctions
(E) unacquainted with the writing of Browning

GO ON TO THE NEXT PAGE

The passages below are followed by questions based on their content; questions following a pair of related passages may also be based on the relationship between the paired passages. Answer the questions on the basis of what is <u>stated</u> or <u>implied</u> in the passages and in any introductory material that may be provided.

Questions 50–60 are based on the following passages.

The following passages deal with the exotic world of subatomic physics. Passage 1, written by a popularizer of contemporary physics, was published in 1985. Passage 2 appeared in a general magazine in 1993.

PASSAGE 1

The classical idea of matter was something with solidity and mass, like wet stone dust pressed in a fist. If matter was composed of atoms, then
Line the atoms too must have solidity and mass. At the
5 beginning of the twentieth century the atom was imagined as a tiny billiard ball or a granite pebble writ small. Then, in the physics of Niels Bohr, the miniature billiard ball became something akin to a musical instrument, a finely tuned Stradivarius 10
10 billion times smaller than the real thing. With the advent of quantum mechanics, the musical instrument gave way to pure music. On the atomic scale, the solidity and mass of matter dissolved into something light and airy. Suddenly physicists
15 were describing atoms in the vocabulary of the composer—"resonance," "frequency," "harmony," "scale." Atomic electrons sang in choirs like seraphim, cherubim, thrones, and dominions. Classical distinctions between matter and light
20 became muddled. In the new physics, light bounced about like particles, and matter undulated in waves like light.

In recent decades, physicists have uncovered elegant subatomic structures in the music of mat-
25 ter. They use a strange new language to describe the subatomic world: *quark, squark, gluon, gauge, technicolor, flavor, strangeness, charm.* There are *up* quarks and *down* quarks, *top* quarks and *bottom* quarks. There are particles with *truth*
30 and *antitruth,* and there are particles with *naked beauty.* The simplest of the constituents of ordinary matter—the proton, for instance—has taken on the character of a Bach fugue, a four-part counterpoint of matter, energy, space, and time.
35 At matter's heart there are arpeggios, chromatics, syncopation. On the lowest rung of the chain of being, Creation dances.

Already, the astronomers and the particle physicists are engaged in a vigorous dialogue.
40 The astronomers are prepared to recognize that the large-scale structure of the universe may have been determined by subtle interactions of particles in the first moments of the Big Bang. And the particle physicists are hoping to find confirmation of
45 their theories of subatomic structure in the astronomers' observations of deep space and time. The snake has bitten its tail and won't let go.

PASSAGE 2

Imagine an infinitesimal particle that is as heavy as a large atom and less tangible than a
50 shadow. For 15 years, hundreds of physicists have been chasing such an improbable phantom. Their quarry is the top quark, the sole missing member of a family of subatomic particles that form the basic building blocks of matter. Of six types of
55 quarks that are believed to exist, five have already been discovered. "The top," says Harvard University theorist Sheldon Glashow, "is not just another quark. It's the last blessed one, and the sooner we find it, the better everyone will feel."
60 Physicists will celebrate because the top is the absent jewel in the crown of the so-called Standard Model, a powerful theoretical synthesis that has reduced a once-bewildering zoo of particles to just a few fundamental constituents,
65 including three whimsically named couplets of quarks. Up and down quarks combine to create everyday protons and neutrons, while charm and strange quarks make up more esoteric particles, the kind produced by accelerators and high-ener-
70 gy cosmic rays. In 1977 physicists discovered a fifth quark they dubbed bottom, and they have been looking for its partner, top, ever since. Not finding it would amaze and befuddle particle physicists. Without the top, a large chunk of the
75 theoretical edifice, like an arch without a keystone, would come crashing down.

Theorists have already deduced that the top quark is heavier than any known particle. "A single top quark," exclaims Fermilab physicist Alvin
80 Tollestrup, "probably weighs at least as much as a whole silver atom does." (With an atomic weight of 108, a silver atom is made up of hundreds of up and down quarks.) Exactly how much top quarks weigh is a question scientists are anxious to
85 answer, but first they must find some to measure— a task considerably complicated by the fact that in nature these massive but ethereal entities made only a cameo appearance, just after the Big Bang.

Top quarks emerged from the primordial radia-
90 tion "around a thousandth of a billionth of a second after the Big Bang," estimates University of Michigan theorist Gordon Kane. But as the early universe expanded and cooled, they vanished. Their fleeting existence left behind a fundamental

GO ON TO THE NEXT PAGE

95 puzzle that physicists are struggling to solve:
What makes some particles so massive while others—photons, for example—have no mass at all?
Because of its boggling heft, the top quark should
help illuminate what mysterious mechanisms—
100 including perhaps other, still weightier particles—
are responsible for imparting mass, and hence
solidity, to the physical world.

50. Which of the following would be the most appropriate title for the Passage 1?

(A) Linguistic Implications of Particle Physics
(B) The Influence of Music on Particle Interactions
(C) Matter's Transformation: The Music of
     Subatomic Physics
(D) Trends in Physics Research: Eliminating the
     Quark
(E) The Impossible Dream: Obstacles to Proving
     the Existence of Matter

51. The author of Passage 1 refers to quarks, squarks,
and charms (paragraph 2) primarily in order to

(A) demonstrate the similarity between these parti-
     cles and earlier images of the atom
(B) make a distinction between appropriate and
     inappropriate terms
(C) object to suggestions of similar frivolous
     names
(D) provide examples of idiosyncratic nomencla-
     ture in contemporary physics
(E) cite preliminary experimental evidence sup-
     porting the existence of subatomic matter

52. The author's tone in the second paragraph of
Passage 1 can best be described as one of

(A) scientific detachment
(B) moderate indignation
(C) marked derision
(D) admiring wonder
(E) qualified skepticism

53. "Matter's heart" mentioned in line 35 is

(A) outer space
(B) the subatomic world
(C) the language of particle physics
(D) harmonic theory
(E) flesh and blood

54. In line 47, the image of the snake biting its tail is
used to emphasize

(A) the dangers of circular reasoning
(B) the vigor inherent in modern scientific dialogue
(C) the eventual triumph of the classical idea of
     matter
(D) the unity underlying the astronomers' and par-
     ticle physicists' theories
(E) the ability of contemporary scientific doctrine
     to swallow earlier theories

55. The author of Passage 2 describes the top quark as
"an improbable phantom" because it is

(A) nonexistent
(B) discoverable
(C) lively
(D) visionary
(E) elusive

56. Glashow's comment in lines 56–59 reflects his

(A) apprehension
(B) impatience
(C) imagination
(D) jubilation
(E) spirituality

57. From the term's use, we can infer that a "cameo
appearance" (line 88) is most likely

(A) noisy
(B) colorful
(C) explosive
(D) brief
(E) massive

58. The author of Passage 2 does all of the following
EXCEPT

(A) cite an authority
(B) use a simile
(C) define a term
(D) pose a question
(E) deny a possibility

59. The author of Passage 2 mentions the silver atom
(line 81) primarily to

(A) clarify the monetary value of the top quark
(B) explain what is meant by atomic weight
(C) illustrate how hefty a top quark is compared to
     other particles
(D) suggest the sorts of elements studied under
     cosmic ray bombardment
(E) demonstrate the malleability of silver as an
     element

60. As Passage 2 suggests, since the time Passage 1
was written, the Standard Model has

(A) determined even more whimsical names for the
     subatomic particles under discussion
(B) taken into account the confusion of the particle
     physicists
(C) ruled out some of the particles whose existence
     had been previously hypothesized
(D) refuted significant aspects of the Big Bang
     theory of the formation of the universe
(E) collapsed for lack of proof of the existence of
     top quarks

IF YOU FINISH BEFORE 30 MINUTES, YOU MAY CHECK YOUR WORK ON THIS
SECTION ONLY. DO NOT TURN TO ANY OTHER SECTION IN THE TEST.   **S T O P**

SECTION **5**
Mathematical Reasoning

Time—30 minutes
25 Questions

Directions and Sample Questions

Notes:

(1) The use of a calculator is permitted. All numbers used are real numbers.

(2) Figures that accompany problems in this test are intended to provide information useful in solving the problems. They are drawn as accurately as possible EXCEPT when it is stated in a specific problem that the figure is not drawn to scale. All figures lie in a plane unless otherwise indicated.

Questions 1–15 each consist of two quantities in boxes, one in Column A and one in Column B. You are to compare the two quantities and on the answer sheet fill in oval A if the quantity in Column A is greater; B if the quantity in Column B is greater; C if the two quantities are equal; D if the relationship cannot be determined from the information given. Notes: 1. In some questions, information is given about one or both of the quantities to be compared. In such cases, the given information is centered above the two columns and is not boxed. 2. In a given question, a symbol that appears in both columns represents the same thing in Column A as it does in Column B. 3. Letters such as x, n, and k stand for real numbers.	**EXAMPLES** Column A Column B Answers **E1** 5^2 20 ●Ⓑ©Ⓓ $150° \diagup x°$ **E2** x 30 Ⓐ Ⓑ ● Ⓓ *r* and *s* are integers. **E3** $r+1$ $s-1$ Ⓐ Ⓑ © ●

PART I: QUANTITATIVE COMPARISON QUESTIONS

SUMMARY DIRECTIONS FOR QUANTITATIVE COMPARISON QUESTIONS

Answer: A if the quantity in Column A is greater.   C if the two quantities are equal.
            B if the quantity in Column B is greater.   D if the relationship cannot be determined from the information given.

Column A	Column B		Column A	Column B
26. $\sqrt{\frac{1}{9}}$	$\left(\frac{1}{3}\right)^2$		$1 + x < 0$	
		28. x	0	
27. The number of integers from -5 to 5 inclusive	The number of integers from 5 to 15 inclusive		$-10 < a < -1$	
		29. $\dfrac{1}{a^4}$	$\dfrac{1}{a^5}$	

GO ON TO THE NEXT PAGE

Column A	Column B
30. $\quad 1 - x$	$1 + x$

$$\frac{1}{x} < 0$$

Column A	Column B
31. $\quad x$	0

$$2x = 24$$
$$2z = x$$

Column A	Column B
32. $\quad z$	12

$$1 \text{ kilometer} = \frac{5}{8} \text{ mile}$$

Column A	Column B
33. $\quad$ 5 miles	8 kilometers

$$\text{Area of circle} = \frac{\pi}{4}$$

Column A	Column B
34. $\quad$ Radius of circle	0.5

Perimeter of square
$ABCD = 4b + 4$

Column A	Column B
35. $\quad$ The length of $AB + BC$	$2b$

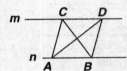

m is parallel to *n*.

Column A	Column B
36. $\quad$ Area of ABC	Area of ABD

In $\triangle ABC$, $BC = 12$,
$\angle A \cong \angle C$, and the
measure of $\angle A = 45$.

Column A	Column B
37. $\quad$ Area of ABC	72
38. $\quad \dfrac{t + n}{n}$	$\dfrac{t}{n} + 1$

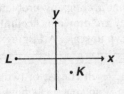

Column A	Column B
39. The x-coordinate of point K	The x-coordinate of point L

For any positive integer p, let $\boxed{P}$ represent the greatest perfect square that is less than or equal to p.

$$\boxed{p + 1} = 16$$

Column A	Column B
40. $\quad p$	24

PART II: STUDENT-PRODUCED RESPONSE QUESTIONS

Directions for Student-Produced Response Questions

Each of the remaining ten questions (41–50) requires you to solve the problem and enter your answer by marking the ovals in the special grid, as shown in the examples below.

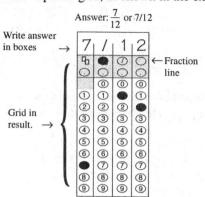

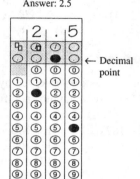

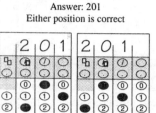

Note: You may start your answers in any column, space permitting. Columns not needed should be left blank.

- Mark no more than one oval in any column.
- Because the answer sheet will be machine-scored, **you will receive credit only if the ovals are filled in correctly.**
- Although not required, it is suggested that you write your answer in the boxes at the top of the columns to help you fill in the ovals accurately.
- Some problems may have more than one correct answer. In such cases, grid only one answer.
- No question has a negative answer.
- **Mixed numbers** such as $2\frac{1}{2}$ much be gridded as 2.5 or 5/2. (If $\boxed{2\ 1\ /\ 2}$ is gridded, it will be interpreted as $\frac{21}{2}$, not $2\frac{1}{2}$.)

- Decimal Accuracy: If you obtain a decimal answer, enter the most accurate value that the grid will accommodate. For example, if you obtain an answer such as 0.6666..., you should record the result as .666 or .667. Less accurate values such as .66 or .67 are not acceptable.

Acceptable ways to grid $\frac{2}{3} = .6666...$

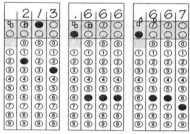

41. In the equation $\frac{3}{x} = \frac{x}{27}$, $x > 0$, what is the value of x?

42. If $\frac{1}{2} + \frac{2}{3} + \frac{3}{y} = \frac{23}{12}$, what does y equal?

43. An elevator has a capacity of 20 adults or 24 children. How many children can ride with 15 adults?

44. Joan does $\frac{2}{5}$ of her homework in an hour. How many additional hours will she have to work to complete her homework?

45. Lines ABC and EDC meet at an angle of 40° m $\angle CBD = 80°$, m $\angle AED = 60°$, $CD = 2$, $DE = 4$, $BD = 1$, What is the length of AE?

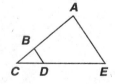

46. What is the maximum number of half-pint containers of cream that can be filled with a 4-gallon can of cream? (2 pts. = 1 qt. and 4 qts. = 1 gal.)

47. How many students are there in a class if two students remain after four rows of seats are filled, and nine students remain after three rows of seats are filled?

48. How many 2" squares can be cut from a rectangular sheet of paper that is $11" \times 5"$?

49. If $AB = BC$, $\overset{\frown}{AB} = 100°$, how many degrees does $\angle ABC$ equal?

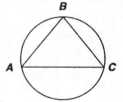

50. According to a recent survey, the average person in the United States consumes 0.03 gallons of olive oil per year, while in Italy the average person consumes 3.0 gallons of olive oil per year. How many times more olive oil is consumed by the average person in Italy than in the United States?

IF YOU FINISH BEFORE 30 MINUTES, YOU MAY CHECK YOUR WORK ON THIS SECTION ONLY. DO NOT TURN TO ANY OTHER SECTION IN THE TEST. **S T O P**

ANSWER KEY

Verbal Reasoning Section 1

1. C	6. C	11. C	16. D	21. A	26. C
2. E	7. B	12. D	17. B	22. A	27. E
3. C	8. B	13. A	18. E	23. C	28. D
4. D	9. A	14. C	19. B	24. D	29. A
5. A	10. D	15. D	20. A	25. B	30. E

Mathematical Reasoning Section 2

Note: Each correct answer to the mathematics questions is keyed by number to the corresponding topic in Chapters 8 and 9 These numerals refer to the topics listed below, with specific page references in parentheses.

1. Basic Fundamental Operations (179–182)
2. Algebraic Operations (182–183)
3. Using Algebra (182–184, 187)
4. Exponents, Roots, and Radicals (184–185)
5. Inequalities (188–189)
6. Fractions (182, 198)
7. Decimals (200)
8. Percent (200)
9. Averages (201)
10. Motion (203)
11. Ratio and Proportion (204–205)
12. Mixtures and Solutions (178)
13. Work (206–207)
14. Coordinate Geometry (194)
15. Geometry (189–193, 195)
16. Quantitative Comparisons (211–212)
17. Data Interpretation (208)

1. D (9)	6. D (11)	11. D (9)	16. A (10)	21. A (15)
2. E (15)	7. E (11)	12. B (13)	17. B (15)	22. D (15)
3. E (3, 6)	8. E (2)	13. C (2)	18. D (15)	23. A (15)
4. D (8)	9. E (8, 11)	14. B (1)	19. D (15)	24. B (8)
5. E (6)	10. B (2)	15. A (1, 2)	20. E (15)	25. C (8, 15)

Writing Skills Section 3

1. A	8. E	15. E	22. D	29. C	36. B
2. E	9. B	16. B	23. A	30. C	37. A
3. A	10. D	17. D	24. C	31. C	38. B
4. D	11. C	18. B	25. A	32. B	39. E
5. B	12. D	19. B	26. C	33. B	
6. C	13. C	20. C	27. E	34. C	
7. C	14. D	21. B	28. C	35. C	

Verbal Reasoning Section 4

31. C	36. D	41. C	46. E	51. D	56. B
32. B	37. B	42. A	47. E	52. D	57. D
33. E	38. B	43. D	48. E	53. B	58. E
34. A	39. E	44. C	49. A	54. D	59. C
35. E	40. C	45. D	50. C	55. E	60. C

Mathematical Reasoning Section 5

26. A (4, 6, 16)	29. A (6, 16)	32. B (2, 16)	35. A (15, 16)	38. C (2, 6, 16)
27. C (1, 16)	30. D (2, 16)	33. C (11, 16)	36. C (15, 16)	39. A (14, 16)
28. B (2, 16)	31. B (6, 16)	34. C (15, 16)	37. C (15, 16)	40. B (1, 3)

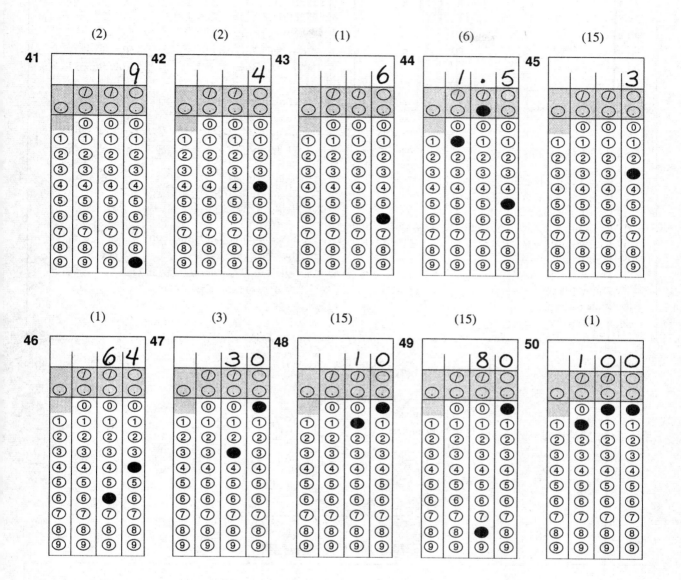

SCORING CHART — TYPICAL TEST D

Verbal Sections

Section 1   Questions 1–30
Number correct   _____ (A)
Number omitted   _____ (B)
Number incorrect   _____ (C)
$^1/_4$ (C) =   _____ (D)
Raw Score:
  (A) – (D) =   _____

Section 3   Questions 31–60
Number correct   _____ (A)
Number omitted   _____ (B)
Number incorrect   _____ (C)
$^1/_4$ (C) =   _____ (D)
Raw Score:
  (A) – (D) =   _____

Total Verbal Raw Score:
  (Section 1 +
  Section 3) =   _____

Mathematical Sections

Section 2   Questions 1–25
Number correct   _____ (A)
Number incorrect   _____ (B)
(A) – $^1/_4$ (B) =   _____ Raw Score I

Section 4   Questions 26–40
Number correct   _____ (C)
Number incorrect   _____ (D)
(C) – $^1/_3$ (D) =   _____ Raw Score II

Section 4   Questions 41–50
Number correct   _____ Raw Score III

Total Mathematical Raw Score:
  (Raw Scores I + II
  + III) =   _____

Writing Section

Section 3   Questions 1–39
Number correct   _____ (A)
Number incorrect   _____ (B)
$^1/_4$ (B) =   _____ (C)
(no penalty for omitted questions)
Writing Raw Score:
  (A) – (C) =   _____

EVALUATION CHART

Study your score. Your raw score on the Verbal and Mathematical Reasoning Sections is an indication of your probable achievement on the PSAT/NMSQT. As a guide to the amount of work you need or want to do with this book, study the following.

Raw Score			Self-rating
Verbal	*Mathematical*	*Writing*	
55–60	41–50	37–39	Superior
44–54	25–40	31–36	Very good
39–43	20–24	25–30	Satisfactory
35–38	16–19	19–24	Average
29–34	10–15	13–18	Needs further study
20–28	7–9	6–12	Needs intensive study
0–19	0–6	0–5	Probably inadequate

ANSWER EXPLANATIONS

Verbal Reasoning Section 1

1. **C**   Someone tired of being chased by reporters would logically seek to escape to *seclusion* (an isolated place of withdrawal).

2. **E**   Oliver asks for more because his first helping has been too *meager* (skimpy).

3. **C**   A tyrant or harsh ruler would *browbeat* or bully his subjects, yet if such methods helped players win games, they might be unworried or *untroubled* by them. Note the conjunction *although,* which signals a contrast.

4. **D**   The second clause gives an example of how making things clear for computers can make them more *obscure* or unclear to people. When stores use electronic bar codes to record the prices of items on sale, they often stop bothering to put price stickers on the items as well. However, when prices are not marked on electronically scanned merchandise, customers have no way of knowing how much items cost until they get to the checkout stand. In such cases, setting things up so that computers can read prices electronically has had the indirect effect of making it harder for people to comparison-shop.

5. **A**   Since Cherokee society already granted certain rights to women, it did not break with or *violate* Cherokee custom to allow women their rights.

6.. **C**   The police want the assault victim to give them a clear, understandable story; therefore, they're willing to wait until he's completely *lucid* (clearheaded; intelligible).

7. **B**   Because Aristotle lacked the *power* to inspire, he proved an *inadequate* or unsatisfactory tutor for Alexander, whose spirit longed for an inspiring teacher.

8. **B**   Animals that were "romantically *disinclined*" might therefore not be inclined to reproduce.

9. **A**   Words like "courage" and "philosophy" are *abstractions* (words representing ideas rather than concrete objects).

10. **D**   Because the commercial food wholesalers were inconsistent and provided *unreliable,* undependable products, the shoppers decided to depend on themselves, becoming *self-sufficient.*

11. **C**   By definition, an *expatriate* is one who lives in a foreign country in preference to living in his or her native land. Stein is a classic example of the expatriate American.

12. **D**   Because the tendency to migrate exists in all time periods, you cannot fully explain it on the basis of any single time period. Your explanation, like the phenomenon itself, must be *independent* of any particular period of time. The conjunction *since* is used here as a synonym for *because*; it indicates a cause and effect relationship.

13. **A**   People who consider only material goods worth their respect are guilty of *crass* (unrefined, grossly stupid) materialism. Note that the phrase "crass materialism" is a cliché, a commonplace expression.

14. **C**   The politicians do not forsake center stage. However, if they did forgo being the center of attention once in a while, the public might like them better for their *self-effacement* (withdrawal from attention).

15. **D**   Someone *sanctimonious* makes a show of religious faith; someone truly *pious* or devout does not.

16. **D**   Here the contrast is between reality and pretense. Mrs. Proudie *feigned* or pretended a great interest in the parishioners' welfare. However, her interest was *not* great but actually *negligible* or insignificant, so insignificant as to be almost nonexistent. Note that the conjunction *although* signals the contrast here. Note also that the phrase "so negligible as to be practically nonexistent" is a cliché, a literary commonplace.

17. **B**   By definition, an excessive or grandiloquent literary work lacks *economy* or conciseness in verbal expression. Note that you are dealing with a secondary meaning of *economy* here.

18. **E**   By stating that the public loves a simple explanation and by commenting on how much easier it is for schoolchildren to ignore what happened on the American continent from 1492 to 1620, the historian-author reveals a *superior* attitude toward the public at large, who are content with easy answers.

19. **B**   The democracy-rejecting Pilgrims would have been amazed to find themselves held up or *cited* as defenders of democracy.

20. **A**   The Pilgrims had been given a royal patent legally empowering them to settle in a certain area. Because they had decided to colonize a different area, some of the group felt that once they were ashore no laws would bind them. The compact bound the signers to obey the laws of the colony. It thus served to *establish legal authority within the colony.*

21. **A**   In debunking the image of the Mayflower Compact as the cornerstone of American democracy, the author reveals himself to be an *iconoclast,* an attacker of established beliefs.

22. **A**   According to the passage, the Pilgrims signed the Mayflower Compact in order of rank: first, the gentlemen; next, the "goodmen" or yeoman-farmers; finally, the servants. In doing so they showed their *respect for the social hierarchy.*

23. **C**   Welty's father used his telescope to observe the moon and the Big Dipper. An eager amateur astronomer, he clearly *made a point of observing* eclipses and other major astronomical phenomena.

24. **D**   Welty calls her father a "pretty good weather prophet," saying he had "the country boy's accurate knowledge of the weather and its skies." In support of this, she describes his going out on the porch first thing in the morning for a look at the weather and a sniff. This suggests he sniffed the air *to detect signs of changes in the weather*.

25. **B**   Caring for his children, the father warned them to take *preventative steps* (such as moving away from the windows during electrical storms) to avoid being hit by lightning.

26. **C**   Exhilarated by the thunderstorm (she "always loved a storm!"), the mother stands apart from the rest of the family, urging them to share her excitement over *the sounds of the storm*.

27. **E**   Running through thunderstorms unworried by lightning bolts, Welty's mother was clearly *less apt to foresee problems* than Welty's father was; she also was *more apt to enjoy the moment*.

28. **D**   Welty's father held dear his beliefs in progress and in the future; these were his fondest, *most cherished* beliefs.

29. **A**   Welty's ambition was to beat the milk in the churn and make butter while her mother read to her; her mother finished reading the story before Welty finished *manufacturing butter* for her.

30. **E**   Welty calls her autobiography *One Writer's Beginnings*. In this passage she shows how her father and mother, with their different gifts, were preparing her for life, especially for the life of a writer. Her father gave her his love of ingenious devices, his countryboy's knowledge of terrain. Her mother gave her books, a love of reading, a sense of the sound of words. Both parents helped form her "strong meteorological sensibility" that affected her later tales.

Mathematical Reasoning Section 2

1. **D**   Weighted average $= \dfrac{4(18) + 5(27)}{9} = \dfrac{207}{9} = 23$.

2. **E**   9, 12, and 15 represent the lengths of the sides of a 3-4-5 right triangle since $9 = 3(3)$, $12 = 3(4)$, and $15 = 3(5)$. Likewise, $1\frac{1}{2}$, 2, and $2\frac{1}{2}$ represent a 3-4-5 triangle since $1\frac{1}{2} = \frac{1}{2}(3)$, $2 = \frac{1}{2}(4)$, and $2\frac{1}{2} = \frac{1}{2}(5)$. 10, 26, and 24 represent the lengths of the sides of a 5-12-13 right triangle since $10 = 2(5)$, $24 = 2(12)$, and $26 = 2(13)$.

3. **E** $\frac{1}{2} + \frac{1}{4} + \frac{1}{5} = \frac{19}{20}$

   $\frac{1}{20}$ is left for his college

   Let x = amount left by Mr. Benedict.

   $\frac{1}{20} x = \$5000$

   $x = \$100{,}000$

4. **D**   Note that the sales tax is calculated on the actual selling price, which is $60 – $6. or $54. Since 10% of $54 = 5.40, the actual cost of the sweater is $54. + $5.40 or $59.40.

5. **E** $\dfrac{\text{games won}}{\text{games played}} = \dfrac{g - l}{g}$

6. **D** $\dfrac{10 \text{ inches}}{72 \text{ inches}} = \dfrac{1}{7.2}$ or 1:7.2

7. **E**   Brookline 3 per 10,000 or 300 per 1,000,000
   Brookville 5 per 100,000 or 50 per 1,000,000
   Brooklyn 13 per 1,000,000
   Total = 363 per 1,000,000

8. **E**   Today Lori is $10 + y$ years old. In x years she will be $10 + y + x$ years old.

9. **E** $9.5\% = \frac{9.5}{100} = \frac{19}{200}$ or 19 out of 200

10. **B** $x - 7 = 0$
    $x = 7$
    $y^2 = 25$
    $y = \pm 5$
    $xy = \pm 35$

11. **D**   The average of 10 and -14 is $-4 \div 2$ or $-2(k)$.
    $\dfrac{k + (-8)}{2} = \dfrac{-2 + (-8)}{2} = -5$

12. **B**   Determine how long it will take the two sons to do it together. That will be time required by father. Let x = time required if both boys work together.
    $\dfrac{x}{3} + \dfrac{x}{6} = 1$
    $2x + x = 6$
    $3x = 6$
    $x = 2$

13. **C**   Note that the required $3x - 4y$ is $\frac{1}{3}$ of first equation. This is easier than solving for x and y and substituting.
    $3x = \frac{1}{3}$ of $9x$
    $-4y = \frac{1}{3}$ of $-12y$
    $\therefore \ ? = \frac{1}{3}$ of -21 or -7

14. **B**   By making the purchase in the second store she saved 60¢ plus 90¢. She saved 1¢ per pound bought. Or she saved $1.50 on 150 pounds. She bought 150 pounds at 70¢ and had 90¢ left. Before the purchase she had 150 (.70) + .90 *or* $105.90.

15. **A** The second term contains a factor of 0 and hence that term equals 0; this rules out III as a possibility. Consider only the last digit in each factor in the first term. $2^3 = 8$; when 8 is multiplied by 3 and then by 1, the product is 24 (I). The value is even, thus ruling out II.

16. **A** $\dfrac{\text{distance (miles)}}{\text{rate (miles per hour)}} = \text{time (hours)}$

44 feet $= \frac{1}{120}$ of a mile

$\dfrac{\frac{1}{120}\ \text{mile}}{30\ \text{miles per hour}} = \dfrac{1}{120} \div 30 = \dfrac{1}{120} \cdot \dfrac{1}{30}$

$\qquad\qquad = \dfrac{1}{3600}$ hour $= 1$ second

17. **B** $\angle c = \angle x$ [vertical angles]
$\angle c = \angle x \overset{\circ}{=} 60$
$\angle a + \angle x + \angle b \overset{\circ}{=} 180$
$\angle a + \angle b \overset{\circ}{=} 120$
$\angle a = \angle b$ [given]
$\angle b \overset{\circ}{=} 60$
$\angle b = \angle d$ [vertical angles]
$\angle d \overset{\circ}{=} 60$

18. **D** Smaller pulleys make more revolutions per minute than larger pulleys. Therefore the number of revolutions per minute is inversely proportional to the circumference of the circle.
Circumference $= (\pi)(\text{diameter})$
Circumference of large pulley $= 9\pi$
Circumference of small pulley $= 6\pi$
Let x = number of revolutions per minute made by the smaller pulley.
$\dfrac{6\pi}{9\pi} = \dfrac{1200}{x}$
$\dfrac{6}{9} = \dfrac{1200}{x}$
$6x = 10800$
$x = 1800$ revolutions per minute

19. **D** Base of shaded $\triangle$ = 6 units
Altitude of shaded $\triangle$ = 2 units
Area = $\frac{1}{2}$(base)(altitude)
Area = $\frac{1}{2}$(6)(2) = 6

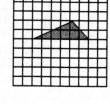

20. **E** Try values satisfying the relationship $A > B > C$ and $A + B + C = 180$.
(A) could be true if $C = 40$, $B = 50$, and $A = 90$.
(B) could be true if $A = 160$, $B = 11$ and $C = 90$.
(C) could be true if $A = 80$, $B = 70$ and $C = 30$.
(D) could be true with the same vlaues as in (B) above.
(E) If $C > 60$, there is less than 120 for A and B together. But each must be > 60 since each is > C.

21. **A** See diagram.

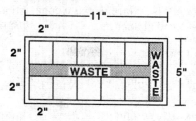

22. **D** Area of original rectangle $= lw$
Area of enlarged rectangle $= 4lw$
Increase $= 3lw$
$\dfrac{\text{increase}}{\text{original}} = \dfrac{3lw}{lw} = 3 = 300\%$

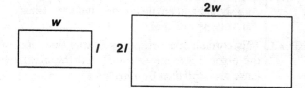

23. **A** $\angle A + \angle B + \angle C + \angle D + \angle E = 3(180°) = 540°$
Since $\angle B \overset{\circ}{=} 90$
$\angle C + \angle D + \angle E + \angle A \overset{\circ}{=} 450$

24. **B** 40% or 0.4(240) = 96

25. **C** $\dfrac{90}{360} = \dfrac{1}{4}$ or 25%

Writing Skills Section 3

1. **A** Misplaced modifier. *I bought only* is preferable.

2. **E** Sentence is correct.

3. **A** Error in diction. Change *had ought* to *ought*.

4. **D** Lack of agreement. The antecedent of *who* is *I. Who*, therefore, should be followed by *am*.

5. **B** Lack of parallel structure. Change clause to a phrase in order to parallel the preceding phrase. Change *it has brought about* to *of its*.

6. **C** Error in sentence connector. Both *after* and *then* are sentence connectors, but only one should be used to avoid redundancy. Delete *then*.

7. **C** Error in diction. Delete the article *a*.

8. **E** Sentence is correct.

9. **B** Error in tense. The past perfect tense of *sink* is *had sunk*.

10. **D** Error in diction. Use *uninterested* instead of *disinterested*.

11. **C** Misuse of adjective instead of adverb. Change *beautiful* to *beautifully*.

12. **D** Misuse of pronoun. *Myself* (reflexive pronoun) must be preceded in the same sentence by either the pronoun *I* or *me*. It should not be used in place of *me* (personal pronoun).

13. **C**   Error in tense. Change *now becoming* to *became.*

14. **D**   Error in case. Since *than* is a conjunction, a verb is understood after its use. Change *him* (*is*) to *he* (*is*).

15. **E**   Sentence is correct.

16. **B**   Error in diction. Change *to serve for* to *to serve as.*

17. **D**   Lack of agreement. *School* is singular and should be followed by *was* (singular).

18. **B**   Incomplete sentence. By changing *planning* to *plan,* we correct the error.

19. **B**   Lack of agreement. In a neither-nor construction the verb agrees with the noun or pronoun which comes immediately before the verb. The verb should agree with *editor* (singular). Change *were* to *was.*

20. **C**   This corrects the two errors in this sentence—the error in case (*me* for *I*) and the error in tense (*had finished* for *finished*).

21. **B**   *Despite* should be used as a preposition.

22. **D**   The addition of the conjunction *when* corrects the run-on sentence and shows the relationship between the two clauses.

23. **A**   Sentence is correct.

24. **C**   This corrects the two errors in the sentence—the idiom error *graduate high school* and the run-on sentence.

25. **A**   The inverted word order used with the subjunctive (*had it been*) is correct.

26. **C**   As the subject of a sentence *The number* generally is considered a singular noun and therefore requires a singular verb (*is given*).

27. **E**   Changing *made* to *make* corrects the sequence of tenses.

28. **C**   *From* is a preposition and requires a pronoun in the objective case—*from those* (*people*).

29. **C**   This corrects the lack of parallel structure.

30. **C**   Unnecessary shift of pronoun. Do not shift from *you* to *one.*

31. **C**   The addition of the conjunction *though* corrects the run-on sentence.

32. **B**   This corrects the lack of parallel structure.

33. **B**   Choice B expresses the author's meaning directly and concisely. All other choices are either indirect or ungrammatical.

34. **C**   Choice A implies that the essay's purpose is to admire the technological achievements of the twentieth century. The essay, however, has another purpose. Choice B is similar to A and also contains an inappropriate colloquialism. Choice C accurately captures the essay's theme—that technological progress is neither all good nor all bad. It is the best answer. Choice D suggests that the essay will discuss the prospects for continued technological progress, but the essay has a different purpose. Choice E names the three areas discussed in the essay but, contrary to the point of the essay, suggests that we would be better off without technological progress.

35. **C**   Choice A unnecessarily repeats *energy* and contains an incomplete comparison. Energy is cheaper than what? Choice B contains an incomplete comparison. Energy is cheaper than what? It also contains an error in parallel construction. Choice C is succinct and accurately expressed. It is the best answer. Choice D contains an error in parallel construction. Choice E also contains a faulty comparison. Cheaper and easier than what?

36. **B**   Although related to communications, the information contained in sentence 6 is not germane to the discussion of communication satellites. Therefore, B is the best answer.

37. **A**   Choice A is consistent in style and tone to the sentences preceding and following sentence 15. It is the best answer. Choice B is a sentence fragment. Choice C contains the nonstandard usage, *hardly no,* which is a double negative. Choice D contains a sudden shift to second person, which does not fit the tone and style of the preceding and following sentences. Choice E is needlessly repetitious.

38. **B**   Choice A does not accurately describe either the paragraph structure or the point of the essay. Choice B precisely describes the structure of each paragraph. It is the best answer. Choices C and D describe neither the paragraph structure nor the point of the essay. Choice E is an inference that might be drawn from the essay, but the writer never says so.

39. **E**   Choice A unnecessarily repeats *CAT scan* and contains faulty parallelism. Choice B unnecessarily repeats *CAT scan* and is needlessly wordy. Choice C contains a dangling participle. The phrase that begins *Taking pictures* should modify *doctors,* not *brain.* Choice D has no discernible connection with the previous sentence. Choice E is a succinct and error-free follow-up to the previous sentence. It is the best answer.

Verbal Reasoning Section 4

31. **C**   A *book* consists of several *chapters.* A *building* consists of several *stories.*   (Part to Whole)

32. **B**   A *clasp* is the fastening on a *bracelet.* A *buckle* is the fastening on a *belt.*   (Function)

33. **E**   A *fleet* is a group of *ships.* A *pack* is a group of *wolves.*   (Group and Member)

34. **A**   One stores *money* in a *bank.* One stores *wine* in a *cask.*   (Function)

35. **E**   *Flimsy* means weak and lacking in *strength.* *Clumsy* means awkward and lacking in *grace.*   (Antonym Variant)

36. **D**   A person who is *obstinate* or stubborn may be called *mulish* (like a mule). A person who is *coy* or pretends shyness may be called *kittenish* (like a kitten). (Definition)

37. **B**   A *refugee* seeks *asylum* or shelter. A *hermit* seeks *solitude* or isolation.
(Defining Characteristic)

38. **B**   Something that is *inane* or senseless lacks *meaning,* by definition. Something that is *random* or haphazard by definition lacks a *plan.*
(Antonym Variant)

39. **E**   To *sap vitality* is to weaken or exhaust liveliness. To *deplete resources* is to reduce supplies. (Defining Characteristic)

40. **C**   A *countess* is a member of the *nobility,* the aristocrats. A *professor* is a member of the *faculty,* the teaching staff. (Group and Member)

41. **C**   Just as the *wheat* is separated from the worthless straw or *chaff,* the *wine* is separated from the worthless sediment or *dregs.*
(Part to Whole)

42. **A**   Something that is *ephemeral* (fleeting, transient) lacks *permanence.* Something that is *erratic* (unpredictable) lacks *predictability.*
(Antonym Variant)

43. **D**   To *ogle* is to *observe* or look at someone provocatively (in an attention-getting manner). To *flaunt* is to *display* or show off something provocatively (in an attention-getting manner).
(Manner)

44. **C**   The author provides the reader both with physical details of dress and bearing and with comments about the motives and emotions of the Cardinal and Bosola. Choice A is incorrect. The passage scarcely mentions the church. Choice B is incorrect. The description of ecclesiastical costumes is only one item in the description of the Cardinal. Choice D is incorrect. While audiences today might well enjoy seeing the characters acted as described here, the author does not cite specific reasons why the play might appeal to modern audiences. Choice E is incorrect. The author's purpose is to describe two separate roles, not to compare two interpretations of a single role.

45. **D**   "Spare" is being used to describe the Cardinal's physical appearance. He is tall and lean.

46. **E**   The eagle is poised to strike "with exposed talons." It, like the Cardinal, gathers itself together to strike with greater force. The imagery suggests the Cardinal's *mercilessness.* Choice A is incorrect. The Cardinal is not *flighty* (light-headed and irresponsible); he is cold and calculating. Choice B is incorrect. He loves power, not freedom. Choice C is incorrect. An eagle poised to strike with bare claws suggests violence, not *eminence* (fame and high position). Choice D is incorrect. Nothing in the passage suggests he is spiritual. Beware of eye-catchers. "Eminence" is a title of honor applied to cardinals in the Roman Catholic church. Choice C may attract you for this reason.

47. **E**   Although Bosola is not a "leather-jacketed" hoodlum, he is a hired "assassin," a "hangman" (despite his scholarly taste and humanist disposition).

48. **E**   The author is contrasting the two sides of Bosola, the scholar and the assassin. As a scholar, he is a man of perceptive intellect, noted for discrimination or *discernment.*

49. **A**   The casual references to the elongated hands and features of El Greco's work and to the trim beards and commanding stances in the work of Van Dyke imply that the author assumes the reader has seen examples of both painters' art.

50. **C**   The opening paragraph discusses changes in the idea of matter, emphasizing the use of musical terminology to describe the concepts of physics. The second paragraph then goes on to develop the theme of the music of matter. Choice B is incorrect. Music does not directly influence the interactions of particles; physicists merely use musical terms to describe these interactions.

51. **D**   The author mentions these terms as examples of what he means by the strange new language or *idiosyncratic nomenclature* of modern particle physics.

52. **D**   In his references to the elegance of the newly discovered subatomic structures and to the dance of Creation, the author conveys his *admiration* and *wonder.*

53. **B**   "Matter's heart," where the physicist can observe the dance of Creation, is *the subatomic world,* the world of quarks and charms.

54. **D**   The image of the snake swallowing its tail suggests that the astronomers' and physicists' theories are, at bottom, one and the same. In other words, there is an *underlying unity* connecting them.

55. **E**   Like a ghost, the top quark evades its pursuers. It is *elusive.*

56. **B**   Glashow is eager for the end of the hunt. His words ("last blessed one," "the sooner . . . the better") reflect his *impatience.*

57. **D**   The fact that top quarks appeared just after the Big Bang and shortly thereafter vanished suggests that a cameo appearance must be *brief.*

58. **E**   The author of Passage 2 cites authorities (Glashow, Tollestrup, Kane) and use similes ("like an arch without a keystone"). She defines the top quark as the theoretical sixth member of the group of subatomic particles that make up the basic building blocks of matter. She poses a question about what makes certain particles more massive than others. However, she never *denies a possibility.*

59. **C** Physicists are familiar with the weight of a silver atom. In citing Tollestrup's statement that the top quark probably weighs as much as a silver atom, the author is illustrating just *how hefty* or massive a top quark is.

60. **C** Passage 2 states that the new theoretical model of the subatomic world "has reduced a once-bewildering zoo of particles to just a few fundamental constituents." Passage 1, for its part, lists all sorts of colorful terms—squark, gauge, technicolor, flavor—whose names fail to appear in Passage 2. This suggests that some of these specific particles whose existence had been previously hypothesized have been *ruled out* by the new theoretical synthesis.

Mathematical Reasoning Section 5

26. **A**
$$\sqrt{\frac{1}{9}} = \frac{1}{3}$$
$$\left(\frac{1}{3}\right)^2 = \frac{1}{9}$$
$$\frac{1}{3} > \frac{1}{9}$$

27. **C** From −5 to zero inclusive there are 6 integers, and from 1 to 5 there are 5 more integers, for a total of 11 integers. From 5 to 15 inclusive there are also 11 integers.

28. **B**
$$x + 1 < 0$$
$$\therefore x < -1$$

29. **A** Since a is negative, the denominator of $\frac{1}{a^4}$ will be positive for all its values, and the denominator of $\frac{1}{a^5}$ will be negative for all its values.

30. **D** The value of x may be zero, positive, or negative.

31. **B** The value of x must be negative for the value of the fraction $\frac{1}{x}$ to be less than zero (negative).

32. **B**
$$2x = 24$$
$$x = 12$$
$$2z = 12$$
$$z = 6$$

33. **C** This is a direct proportion. Let x = the number of miles in 8 kilometers
$$\frac{1 \text{ kilometer}}{\frac{5}{8}\text{ mile}} = \frac{8 \text{ kilometers}}{x \text{ miles}}$$
$$x = 5$$

34. **C** Area $= \pi r^2 = \frac{\pi}{4}$
$$r^2 = \frac{1}{4}$$
$$r = \frac{1}{2} \text{ or } 0.5$$

35. **A** Since the perimeter of square $= 4b + 4$, each side $= \frac{1}{4}(4b + 4)$ or $b + 1$, and the length of two sides $= 2b + 2$.
$$2b + 2 > 2b.$$

36. **C** Area of a $\triangle = \frac{1}{2}$ (base)(altitude). Both triangles share the same base (AB). Since distances between parallel lines are the same, the two triangles have equal altitudes.

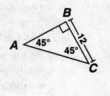

37. **C** Since $\angle A \overset{\circ}{=} \angle C$, $BC = AB$, $AB = 12$. Since the measure of $\angle B \overset{\circ}{=} 90$, ABC is a right $\triangle$ and the area equals $\frac{1}{2}$ (leg) (leg) or $(\frac{1}{2})(12)(12)$ or 72.

38. **C** $\frac{t + n}{n} = \frac{t}{n} + \frac{n}{n} = \frac{t}{n} + 1$

39. **A** The x-coordinate of K is a positive quantity. The x-coordinate of L is a negative quantity.

40. **B** Because $\boxed{24} = 16$ and $\boxed{25} = 25$, the greatest value of $p + 1$ is 24. Hence, p must be less than 24.

41. **9**
$$\frac{3}{x} = \frac{x}{27}$$
$$x^2 = 81$$
$$x = 9$$

42. **4**
$$\frac{1}{2} + \frac{2}{3} + \frac{3}{y} = \frac{23}{12}$$
$$\frac{6}{12} + \frac{8}{12} + \frac{3}{y} = \frac{23}{12}$$
$$\frac{14}{12} + \frac{3}{y} = \frac{23}{12}$$
$$\frac{3}{y} = \frac{9}{12}$$
$$\frac{3}{y} = \frac{3}{4}$$
$$y = 4$$

43. **6** The elevator carries 5 adults less than capacity when it carries 15 adults. Let x = number of children that can be carried with 15 adults.
$$\frac{20 \text{ adults}}{24 \text{ children}} = \frac{5 \text{ adults}}{x \text{ children}}$$
$$20x = 120$$
$$x = 6$$

44. **1.5** This is a direct proportion. The more Joan works, the more of her homework she accomplishes. Let x = time required to finish.

$$\frac{\text{part of work done}}{\text{time (in hours)}} = \frac{\frac{2}{5}}{1} = \frac{1}{x}$$

$$\frac{2}{5}x = 1$$

$$x = \frac{5}{2} = 2\frac{1}{2}$$

However, since Joan already worked 1 hour, she must work for $1\frac{1}{2}$ more hours, or 1.5 hours.

45. **3** Since $\angle C \triangleq 40$ and $\angle CBD \triangleq 80$,

$\angle BDC$ must $\triangleq 60$.

$\therefore BD \parallel AE$

$\therefore \triangle BCD \sim \triangle ACE$

$\frac{2}{6} = \frac{1}{?}$ [sides are proportional]

$? = 3$

46. **64** 4 gallons = 16 quarts = 32 pints = 64 half-pints

47. **30** Let x = number of pupils in each row.

$4x + 2 = 3x + 9$

$x = 7$ (in one row)

$4x + 2 = 28 + 2 = 30$

or, $3x + 9 = 21 + 9 = 30$

48. **10** See diagram.

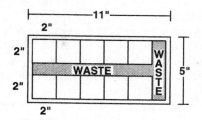

49. **80** $AB = BC$ [given]

$\therefore \overarc{AB} = \overarc{BC} = 100°$

$\therefore \overarc{AC} = 160°$

$\angle ABC \triangleq 80$

[inscribed angle]

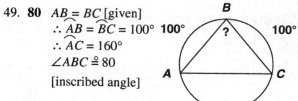

50. **100** $\frac{3.0}{0.03} = \frac{30}{0.3} = \frac{300}{3} = 100$

Answer Sheet

TYPICAL TEST E

Each mark should completely fill the appropriate space, and should be as dark as all other marks. Make all erasures complete. Traces of an erasure may be read as an answer. See pages vii and 27 for explanations of timing and number of questions.

Section 1 — Verbal
30 minutes

1 (A) (B) (C) (D) (E)
2 (A) (B) (C) (D) (E)
3 (A) (B) (C) (D) (E)
4 (A) (B) (C) (D) (E)
5 (A) (B) (C) (D) (E)
6 (A) (B) (C) (D) (E)
7 (A) (B) (C) (D) (E)
8 (A) (B) (C) (D) (E)
9 (A) (B) (C) (D) (E)
10 (A) (B) (C) (D) (E)
11 (A) (B) (C) (D) (E)
12 (A) (B) (C) (D) (E)
13 (A) (B) (C) (D) (E)
14 (A) (B) (C) (D) (E)
15 (A) (B) (C) (D) (E)
16 (A) (B) (C) (D) (E)
17 (A) (B) (C) (D) (E)
18 (A) (B) (C) (D) (E)
19 (A) (B) (C) (D) (E)
20 (A) (B) (C) (D) (E)
21 (A) (B) (C) (D) (E)
22 (A) (B) (C) (D) (E)
23 (A) (B) (C) (D) (E)
24 (A) (B) (C) (D) (E)
25 (A) (B) (C) (D) (E)
26 (A) (B) (C) (D) (E)
27 (A) (B) (C) (D) (E)
28 (A) (B) (C) (D) (E)
29 (A) (B) (C) (D) (E)
30 (A) (B) (C) (D) (E)

Section 2 — Math
30 minutes

1 (A) (B) (C) (D) (E)
2 (A) (B) (C) (D) (E)
3 (A) (B) (C) (D) (E)
4 (A) (B) (C) (D) (E)
5 (A) (B) (C) (D) (E)
6 (A) (B) (C) (D) (E)
7 (A) (B) (C) (D) (E)
8 (A) (B) (C) (D) (E)
9 (A) (B) (C) (D) (E)
10 (A) (B) (C) (D) (E)
11 (A) (B) (C) (D) (E)
12 (A) (B) (C) (D) (E)
13 (A) (B) (C) (D) (E)
14 (A) (B) (C) (D) (E)
15 (A) (B) (C) (D) (E)
16 (A) (B) (C) (D) (E)
17 (A) (B) (C) (D) (E)
18 (A) (B) (C) (D) (E)
19 (A) (B) (C) (D) (E)
20 (A) (B) (C) (D) (E)
21 (A) (B) (C) (D) (E)
22 (A) (B) (C) (D) (E)
23 (A) (B) (C) (D) (E)
24 (A) (B) (C) (D) (E)
25 (A) (B) (C) (D) (E)

Section 3 — Writing
30 minutes

1 (A) (B) (C) (D) (E)
2 (A) (B) (C) (D) (E)
3 (A) (B) (C) (D) (E)
4 (A) (B) (C) (D) (E)
5 (A) (B) (C) (D) (E)
6 (A) (B) (C) (D) (E)
7 (A) (B) (C) (D) (E)
8 (A) (B) (C) (D) (E)
9 (A) (B) (C) (D) (E)
10 (A) (B) (C) (D) (E)
11 (A) (B) (C) (D) (E)
12 (A) (B) (C) (D) (E)
13 (A) (B) (C) (D) (E)
14 (A) (B) (C) (D) (E)
15 (A) (B) (C) (D) (E)
16 (A) (B) (C) (D) (E)
17 (A) (B) (C) (D) (E)
18 (A) (B) (C) (D) (E)
19 (A) (B) (C) (D) (E)
20 (A) (B) (C) (D) (E)
21 (A) (B) (C) (D) (E)
22 (A) (B) (C) (D) (E)
23 (A) (B) (C) (D) (E)
24 (A) (B) (C) (D) (E)
25 (A) (B) (C) (D) (E)
26 (A) (B) (C) (D) (E)
27 (A) (B) (C) (D) (E)
28 (A) (B) (C) (D) (E)
29 (A) (B) (C) (D) (E)
30 (A) (B) (C) (D) (E)
31 (A) (B) (C) (D) (E)
32 (A) (B) (C) (D) (E)
33 (A) (B) (C) (D) (E)
34 (A) (B) (C) (D) (E)
35 (A) (B) (C) (D) (E)
36 (A) (B) (C) (D) (E)
37 (A) (B) (C) (D) (E)
38 (A) (B) (C) (D) (E)
39 (A) (B) (C) (D) (E)

Section 4 — Verbal
30 minutes

31 Ⓐ Ⓑ Ⓒ Ⓓ Ⓔ
32 Ⓐ Ⓑ Ⓒ Ⓓ Ⓔ
33 Ⓐ Ⓑ Ⓒ Ⓓ Ⓔ
34 Ⓐ Ⓑ Ⓒ Ⓓ Ⓔ
35 Ⓐ Ⓑ Ⓒ Ⓓ Ⓔ
36 Ⓐ Ⓑ Ⓒ Ⓓ Ⓔ
37 Ⓐ Ⓑ Ⓒ Ⓓ Ⓔ
38 Ⓐ Ⓑ Ⓒ Ⓓ Ⓔ
39 Ⓐ Ⓑ Ⓒ Ⓓ Ⓔ
40 Ⓐ Ⓑ Ⓒ Ⓓ Ⓔ
41 Ⓐ Ⓑ Ⓒ Ⓓ Ⓔ
42 Ⓐ Ⓑ Ⓒ Ⓓ Ⓔ
43 Ⓐ Ⓑ Ⓒ Ⓓ Ⓔ
44 Ⓐ Ⓑ Ⓒ Ⓓ Ⓔ
45 Ⓐ Ⓑ Ⓒ Ⓓ Ⓔ
46 Ⓐ Ⓑ Ⓒ Ⓓ Ⓔ
47 Ⓐ Ⓑ Ⓒ Ⓓ Ⓔ
48 Ⓐ Ⓑ Ⓒ Ⓓ Ⓔ
49 Ⓐ Ⓑ Ⓒ Ⓓ Ⓔ
50 Ⓐ Ⓑ Ⓒ Ⓓ Ⓔ
51 Ⓐ Ⓑ Ⓒ Ⓓ Ⓔ
52 Ⓐ Ⓑ Ⓒ Ⓓ Ⓔ
53 Ⓐ Ⓑ Ⓒ Ⓓ Ⓔ
54 Ⓐ Ⓑ Ⓒ Ⓓ Ⓔ
55 Ⓐ Ⓑ Ⓒ Ⓓ Ⓔ
56 Ⓐ Ⓑ Ⓒ Ⓓ Ⓔ
57 Ⓐ Ⓑ Ⓒ Ⓓ Ⓔ
58 Ⓐ Ⓑ Ⓒ Ⓓ Ⓔ
59 Ⓐ Ⓑ Ⓒ Ⓓ Ⓔ
60 Ⓐ Ⓑ Ⓒ Ⓓ Ⓔ

Section 5 — Math
30 minutes

26 Ⓐ Ⓑ Ⓒ Ⓓ Ⓔ
27 Ⓐ Ⓑ Ⓒ Ⓓ Ⓔ
28 Ⓐ Ⓑ Ⓒ Ⓓ Ⓔ
29 Ⓐ Ⓑ Ⓒ Ⓓ Ⓔ
30 Ⓐ Ⓑ Ⓒ Ⓓ Ⓔ
31 Ⓐ Ⓑ Ⓒ Ⓓ Ⓔ
32 Ⓐ Ⓑ Ⓒ Ⓓ Ⓔ
33 Ⓐ Ⓑ Ⓒ Ⓓ Ⓔ
34 Ⓐ Ⓑ Ⓒ Ⓓ Ⓔ
35 Ⓐ Ⓑ Ⓒ Ⓓ Ⓔ
36 Ⓐ Ⓑ Ⓒ Ⓓ Ⓔ
37 Ⓐ Ⓑ Ⓒ Ⓓ Ⓔ
39 Ⓐ Ⓑ Ⓒ Ⓓ Ⓔ
39 Ⓐ Ⓑ Ⓒ Ⓓ Ⓔ
40 Ⓐ Ⓑ Ⓒ Ⓓ Ⓔ

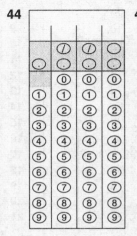

41

	/	/	
.	.	.	.
	0	0	0
1	1	1	1
2	2	2	2
3	3	3	3
4	4	4	4
5	5	5	5
6	6	6	6
7	7	7	7
8	8	8	8
9	9	9	9

42

	/	/	
.	.	.	.
	0	0	0
1	1	1	1
2	2	2	2
3	3	3	3
4	4	4	4
5	5	5	5
6	6	6	6
7	7	7	7
8	8	8	8
9	9	9	9

43

	/	/	
.	.	.	.
	0	0	0
1	1	1	1
2	2	2	2
3	3	3	3
4	4	4	4
5	5	5	5
6	6	6	6
7	7	7	7
8	8	8	8
9	9	9	9

44

	/	/	
.	.	.	.
	0	0	0
1	1	1	1
2	2	2	2
3	3	3	3
4	4	4	4
5	5	5	5
6	6	6	6
7	7	7	7
8	8	8	8
9	9	9	9

45

	/	/	
.	.	.	.
	0	0	0
1	1	1	1
2	2	2	2
3	3	3	3
4	4	4	4
5	5	5	5
6	6	6	6
7	7	7	7
8	8	8	8
9	9	9	9

46

	/	/	
.	.	.	.
	0	0	0
1	1	1	1
2	2	2	2
3	3	3	3
4	4	4	4
5	5	5	5
6	6	6	6
7	7	7	7
8	8	8	8
9	9	9	9

47

	/	/	
.	.	.	.
	0	0	0
1	1	1	1
2	2	2	2
3	3	3	3
4	4	4	4
5	5	5	5
6	6	6	6
7	7	7	7
8	8	8	8
9	9	9	9

48

	/	/	
.	.	.	.
	0	0	0
1	1	1	1
2	2	2	2
3	3	3	3
4	4	4	4
5	5	5	5
6	6	6	6
7	7	7	7
8	8	8	8
9	9	9	9

49

	/	/	
.	.	.	.
	0	0	0
1	1	1	1
2	2	2	2
3	3	3	3
4	4	4	4
5	5	5	5
6	6	6	6
7	7	7	7
8	8	8	8
9	9	9	9

50

	/	/	
.	.	.	.
	0	0	0
1	1	1	1
2	2	2	2
3	3	3	3
4	4	4	4
5	5	5	5
6	6	6	6
7	7	7	7
8	8	8	8
9	9	9	9

SECTION 1
Verbal Reasoning

Time—30 minutes
30 Questions

For each question in this section, select the best answer from among the choices given and fill in the corresponding oval on the answer sheet.

Directions

Each sentence below has one or two blanks, each blank indicating that something has been omitted. Beneath the sentence are five words or sets of words labeled A through E. Choose the word or set of words that, when inserted in the sentence, best fits the meaning of the sentence as a whole.

Example:

Medieval kingdoms did not become constitutional republics overnight; on the contrary, the change was ____ .

(A) unpopular
(B) unexpected
(C) advantageous
(D) sufficient
(E) gradual

Ⓐ Ⓑ Ⓒ Ⓓ ●

1. Impressed by the extraordinary potential of the new superconductor, scientists predict that its use will ___ the computer industry, creating new products overnight.

   (A) justify   (B) alienate   (C) nullify
   (D) revolutionize   (E) overestimate

2. In order that they may be able to discriminate wisely among the many conflicting arguments put before them, legislators must be trained to ____ the truth.

   (A) confuse   (B) condemn   (C) ignore
   (D) condone   (E) discern

3. By means of deft ____ , the mime can make the ____ air seem filled with objects.

   (A) trickery..musty   (B) gestures..empty
   (C) movements..innocuous
   (D) dexterity..refreshing   (E) staging..turbulent

4. People who find themselves unusually ____ and ready to drowse off at unexpected moments may be suffering from a hormonal imbalance.

   (A) lethargic   (B) distracted   (C) obdurate
   (D) benign   (E) perfunctory

5. In their new collections of lighthearted, provocative dresses, French fashion designers are gambling that even ____ professional women are ready for a bit of ____ in style.

   (A) strict..reticence   (B) serious..frivolity
   (C) elegant..tradition   (D) modern..harmony
   (E) unsentimental..propriety

6. Irony can, after a fashion, become a mode of escape: to laugh at the terrors of life is in some sense to ___ them.

   (A) exaggerate   (B) revitalize   (C) corroborate
   (D) evade   (E) justify

7. No matter how ____ the revelations of the coming year may be, they will be hard put to match those of the past decade, which have ____ transformed our view of the emergence of Mayan civilization.

   (A) minor..dramatically   (B) profound..negligibly
   (C) striking..radically   (D) bizarre..nominally
   (E) questionable..possibly

8. Few other plants can grow beneath the canopy of the sycamore tree, whose leaves and pods produce a natural herbicide that leaches into the soil, ____ other plants that might compete for water and nutrients.

   (A) inhibiting   (B) distinguishing   (C) nourishing
   (D) encouraging   (E) refreshing

9. Even when a judge does not say anything ____ , his or her tone of voice can signal a point of view to jurors and thus ____ the jury in a criminal trial.

   (A) coherent..circumvent   (B) questionable..perjure
   (C) prejudicial..influence   (D) material..convene
   (E) constructive..corrupt

10. Black women authors such as Zora Neale Hurston, originally ____ by both white and black literary establishments to obscurity as minor novelists, are being rediscovered by black feminist critics today.

    (A) inclined   (B) relegated   (C) subjected
    (D) diminished   (E) characterized

11. Unspoiled by more ____ entertainments, Margie was still ____ enough to view her first county fair with awe.

    (A) worldly..engaging
    (B) sophisticated..ingenuous
    (C) popular..garrulous
    (D) provincial..extravagant
    (E) intellectual..cosmopolitan

GO ON TO THE NEXT PAGE

12. The expression "he passed away" is ____ for "he died."

    (A) a reminder   (B) a commiseration
    (C) a simile   (D) a euphemism
    (E) an exaggeration

13. Despite the enormous popularity and influence of his book, *Thunder Out of China*, White's career ____ .

    (A) soared   (B) endured   (C) accelerated
    (D) revived   (E) foundered

14. Written just after King's assassination, Lomax's book has all the virtues of historical ____ , but lacks the greater virtue of historical ____ , which comes from long and mature reflection upon events.

    (A) precision..accuracy   (B) criticism..distance
    (C) immediacy..perspective
    (D) outlook..realism   (E) currency..testimony

15. Relishing his triumph, Costner especially ____ the chagrin of the critics who had predicted his ____ .

    (A) regretted..success
    (B) acknowledged..comeback
    (C) understated..bankruptcy
    (D) distorted..mortification
    (E) savored..failure

16. So intense was her ambition to attain the pinnacle of worldly success that not even the opulence and lavishness of her material possessions seemed ____ the ____ of that ambition.

    (A) necessary for..fulfillment
    (B) adequate to..fervor
    (C) appropriate to..ebullience
    (D) relevant to..languor
    (E) consonant with..insignificance

17. Critics of the movie version of *The Color Purple* ____ its saccharine, overoptimistic mood as out of keeping with the novel's more ____ tone.

    (A) applauded..somber   (B) condemned..hopeful
    (C) acclaimed..positive   (D) denounced..sanguine
    (E) decried..acerbic

Directions

Each passage below is followed by questions based on its content. Answer the questions following each passage on the basis of what is <u>stated</u> or <u>implied</u> in that passage and in any introductory material that may be provided.

Questions 18–22 are based on the following passage.

In the following passage from Jane Austen's novel Pride and Prejudice, *the heroine Elizabeth Bennet faces an unexpected encounter with her father's cousin (and prospective heir), the clergyman Mr. Collins.*

It was absolutely necessary to interrupt him now.

"You are too hasty, Sir," she cried. "You forget that I have made no answer. Let me do it without
Line   further loss of time. Accept my thanks for the
5   compliment you are paying me. I am very sensible of the honour of your proposals, but it is impossible for me to do otherwise than decline them."

"I am not now to learn," replied Mr. Collins
10   with a formal wave of the hand, "that it is usual with young ladies to reject the addresses of the man whom they secretly mean to accept, when he first applies for their favour; and that sometimes the refusal is repeated a second or even a third
15   time. I am therefore by no means discouraged by what you have just said, and shall hope to lead you to the altar ere long."

"Upon my word, Sir," cried Elizabeth, "your hope is rather an extraordinary one after my dec-
20   laration. I do assure you that I am not one of those young ladies (if such young ladies there are) who are so daring as to risk their happiness on the chance of being asked a second time. I am perfectly serious in my refusal. You could not make
25   *me* happy, and I am convinced that I am the last woman in the world who would make *you* so. Nay, were your friend Lady Catherine to know me, I am persuaded she would find me in every respect ill qualified for the situation."

30   "Were it certain that Lady Catherine would think so," said Mr. Collins very gravely—"but I cannot imagine that her ladyship would at all disapprove of you. And you may be certain that when I have the honour of seeing her again I shall
35   speak in the highest terms of your modesty, economy, and other amiable qualifications."

"Indeed, Mr. Collins, all praise of me will be unnecessary. You must give me leave to judge for myself, and pay me the compliment of believ-
40   ing what I say. I wish you very happy and very rich, and by refusing your hand, do all in my power to prevent your being otherwise. In making me the offer, you must have satisfied the delicacy of your feelings with regard to my family,
45   and may take possession of Longbourn estate whenever it falls, without any self-reproach. This matter may be considered, therefore, as finally settled." And, rising as she thus spoke, she would have quitted the room, had not Mr. Collins
50   thus addressed her.

"When I do myself the honour of speaking to you next on this subject I shall hope to receive a more favourable answer than you have now given me; though I am far from accusing you of cruelty
55   at present, because I know it to be the established custom of your sex to reject a man on the first application, and perhaps you have even now said as much to encourage my suit as would be consistent with the true delicacy of the female
60   character."

GO ON TO THE NEXT PAGE

"Really, Mr. Collins," cried Elizabeth with
some warmth, "you puzzle me exceedingly. If
what I have hitherto said can appear to you in the
form of encouragement, I know not how to
65   express my refusal in such a way as may convince
you of its being one."

18. It can be inferred that in the paragraphs immediately preceding this passage

(A) Elizabeth and Mr. Collins quarreled
(B) Elizabeth met Mr. Collins for the first time
(C) Mr. Collins asked Elizabeth to marry him
(D) Mr. Collins gravely insulted Elizabeth
(E) Elizabeth discovered that Mr. Collins was a fraud

19. The word "sensible" in line 6 means

(A) logical   (B) perceptible
(C) sound in judgment   (D) keenly aware
(E) appreciable

20. It can be inferred from lines 30–33 that Mr. Collins

(A) will take Elizabeth's words seriously
(B) admires Elizabeth's independence
(C) is very disappointed by her decision
(D) would accept Lady Catherine's opinion
(E) means his remarks as a joke

21. The reason Elizabeth insists all praise of her "will
be unnecessary" (lines 37–38) is because she

(A) feels sure Lady Catherine will learn to admire
    her in time
(B) is too shy to accept compliments readily
(C) has no intention of marrying Mr. Collins
(D) believes a clergyman should be less effusive
(E) values her own worth excessively

22. On the basis of his behavior in this passage, Mr.
Collins may best be described as

(A) malicious in intent
(B) both obtuse and obstinate
(C) unsure of his acceptance
(D) kindly and understanding
(E) sensitive to Elizabeth's wishes

Questions 23–30 are based on the following passage.

*African elephants now are an endangered species. The
following passage, taken from a newspaper article written in 1989, discusses the potential ecological disaster
that might occur if the elephant were to become extinct.*

The African elephant—mythic symbol of a
continent, keystone of its ecology and the largest
land animal remaining on earth—has become the
Line   object of one of the biggest, broadest international
5   efforts yet mounted to turn a threatened species

off the road to extinction. But it is not only the
elephant's survival that is at stake, conservationists say. Unlike the endangered tiger, unlike even
the great whales, the African elephant is in great
10   measure the architect of its environment. As a
voracious eater of vegetation, it largely shapes the
forest-and-savanna surroundings in which it lives,
thereby setting the terms of existence for millions
of other storied animals—from zebras to gazelles
15   to giraffes and wildebeests—that share its habitat.
And as the elephant disappears, scientists and
conservationists say, many other species will also
disappear from vast stretches of forest and savanna, drastically altering and impoverishing whole
20   ecosystems.

Just as the American buffalo was hunted
almost to extinction a century ago, so the African
elephant is now the victim of an onslaught of
commercial killing, stimulated in this case by
25   soaring global demand for ivory. Most of the
killing is illegal, and conservationists say that
although the pressure of human population and
development contributes to the elephants' decline,
poaching is by far the greatest threat. The ele-
30   phant may or may not be on the way to becoming
a mere zoological curiosity like the buffalo, but
the trend is clear.

In an atmosphere of mounting alarm among
conservationists, a new international coordinating
35   group backed by 21 ivory-producing and ivory-
consuming countries has met and adopted an
ambitious plan of action. Against admittedly long
odds, the multinational rescue effort is aimed both
at stopping the slaughter of the elephants in the
40   short term and at nurturing them as a vital "keystone species" in the long run.

It is the elephant's metabolism and appetite
that make it a disturber of the environment and
therefore an important creator of habitat. In a con-
45   stant search for the 300 pounds of vegetation it
must have every day, it kills small trees and
underbrush and pulls branches off big trees as
high as its trunk will reach. This creates innumerable open spaces in both deep tropical forests and
50   in the woodlands that cover part of the African
savannas. The resulting patchwork, a mosaic of
vegetation in various stages of regeneration, in
turn creates a greater variety of forage that attracts
a greater variety of other vegetation-eaters than
55   would otherwise be the case.

In studies over the last 20 years in southern
Kenya near Mount Kilimanjaro, Dr. David
Western has found that when elephants are
allowed to roam the savannas naturally and nor-
60   mally, they spread out at "intermediate densities."
Their foraging creates a mixture of savanna
woodlands (what the Africans call bush) and
grassland. The result is a highly diverse array of
other plant-eating species: those like the zebra,
65   wildebeest, and gazelle, that graze; those like the

GO ON TO THE NEXT PAGE

giraffe, bushbuck, and lesser kudu, that browse on tender shoots, buds, twigs and leaves; and plant-eating primates like the baboon and vervet monkey. These herbivores attract carnivores like
70   the lion and cheetah.

When the elephant population thins out, Dr. Western said, the woodlands become denser and the grazers are squeezed out. When pressure from poachers forces elephants to crowd more densely
75   onto reservations, the woodlands there are knocked out and the browsers and primates disappear.

Something similar appears to happen in dense tropical rain forests. In their natural state, because
80   the overhead forest canopy shuts out sunlight and prevents growth on the forest floor, rain forests provide slim pickings for large, hoofed plant-eaters. By pulling down trees and eating new growth, elephants enlarge natural openings in the
85   canopy, allowing plants to regenerate on the forest floor and bringing down vegetation from the canopy so that smaller species can get at it.

In such situations, the rain forest becomes hospitable to large plant-eating mammals such as
90   bongos, bush pigs, duikers, forest hogs, swamp antelopes, forest buffaloes, okapis, sometimes gorillas, and always a host of smaller animals that thrive on secondary growth. When elephants disappear and the forest reverts, the larger animals
95   give way to smaller, nimbler animals like monkeys, squirrels, and rodents.

23. The passage is primarily concerned with

(A) explaining why elephants are facing the threat of extinction
(B) explaining difficulties in providing sufficient forage for plant-eaters
(C) explaining how the elephant's impact on its surroundings affects other species
(D) distinguishing between savannas and rain forests as habitats for elephants
(E) contrasting elephants with members of other endangered species

24. In the opening paragraph, the author mentions tigers and whales in order to emphasize which point about the elephant?

(A) Like them, it faces the threat of extinction.
(B) It is herbivorous rather than carnivorous.
(C) It moves more ponderously than either the tiger or the whale.
(D) Unlike them, it physically alters its environment.
(E) It is the largest extant land mammal.

25. The word "mounting" in line 33 means

(A) ascended   (B) increased   (C) launched
(D) attached   (E) exhibited

26. A necessary component of the elephant's ability to transform the landscape is its

(A) massive intelligence
(B) fear of predators
(C) ravenous hunger
(D) lack of grace
(E) ability to regenerate

27. It can be inferred from the passage that

(A) the lion and the cheetah commonly prey upon elephants
(B) the elephant is dependent upon the existence of smaller plant-eating mammals for its survival
(C) elephants have an indirect effect on the hunting patterns of certain carnivores
(D) the floor of the tropical rain forest is too overgrown to accommodate larger plant-eating species
(E) the natural tendency of elephants is to crowd together in packs

28. The passage contains information that would answer which of the following questions?

I.   How does the elephant's foraging affect its surroundings?
II. How do the feeding patterns of gazelles and giraffes differ?
III. What occurs in the rain forest when the elephant population dwindles?

(A) I only   (B) II only   (C) I and II only
(D) II and III only   (E) I, II, and III

29. The word "host" in line 92 means

(A) food source for parasites
(B) very large number
(C) provider of hospitality
(D) military force
(E) angelic company

30. Which of the following statements best expresses the author's attitude toward the damage to vegetation caused by foraging elephants?

(A) It is a regrettable by-product of the feeding process.
(B) It is a necessary but undesirable aspect of elephant population growth.
(C) It fortuitously results in creating environments suited to diverse species.
(D) It has the unexpected advantage that it allows scientists access to the rain forest.
(E) It reinforces the impression that elephants are a disruptive force.

IF YOU FINISH BEFORE 30 MINUTES, YOU MAY CHECK YOUR WORK ON THIS SECTION ONLY. DO NOT TURN TO ANY OTHER SECTION IN THE TEST.   **S T O P**

SECTION **2**
Mathematical Reasoning

Time—30 minutes
25 Questions

Directions and Reference Information

In this section solve each problem, using any available space for scratchwork. Then decide which is the best of the choices given and fill in the corresponding oval on the answer sheet.

Notes:

(1) The use of a calculator is permitted. All numbers used are real numbers.

(2) Figures that accompany problems in this test are intended to provide information useful in solving the problems. They are drawn as accurately as possible EXCEPT when it is stated in a specific problem that the figure is not drawn to scale. All figures lie in a plane unless otherwise indicated.

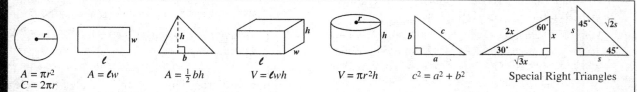

$A = \pi r^2$ $A = \ell w$ $A = \frac{1}{2}bh$ $V = \ell wh$ $V = \pi r^2 h$ $c^2 = a^2 + b^2$ Special Right Triangles
$C = 2\pi r$

The number of degrees of an arc in a circle is 360.
The measure in degrees of a straight angle is 180.
The sum of the measures in degrees of the angles of a triangle is 180.

1. $\left(\frac{4}{5} \div \frac{4}{5}\right) - \left(\frac{5}{6} \div \frac{5}{6}\right) =$
   (A) –2   (B) –1   (C) 0   (D) 1   (E) 2

2. For which of the following value(s) of x is it possible to obtain a value for $\frac{x}{3x + 5}$?

   I. $\frac{1}{2}$
   II. 0
   III. $-\frac{5}{3}$

   (A) I only   (B) II only   (C) III only
   (D) I and III only   (E) I, II and III

3. If $\widehat{x}$ is defined by the equation $\widehat{x} = \frac{\sqrt{x}}{2}$ then $\widehat{100}$ equals

   (A) 5   (B) 10   (C) 20   (D) 25   (E) 50

4. Which of the following has the largest numerical value?

   (A) $\frac{8}{0.8}$ (B) $\frac{0.8}{8}$ (C) $(0.8)^2$ (D) $\sqrt{0.8}$ (E) 0.8π

5. The number of washers $\frac{3}{32}$ inch thick that can be cut from a piece of stock $25\frac{1}{2}$ inches long, allowing $\frac{1}{16}$ inch for waste for each cut is

   (A) 160   (B) 163   (C) 260
   (D) 272   (E) 408

6. Mr. Grey left $\frac{1}{3}$ of his property to his wife and the remainder to be divided equally between his two children. If each child received $10,000, then the wife received

   (A) $3333.33   (B) $5000.00   (C) $6666.67
   (D) $10,000.00   (E) $20,000.00

7. Each of the following sets of three numbers could represent the lengths of the sides of a triangle EXCEPT

   (A) 9, 11, 14   (B) 5, 5, 8   (C) 8, 17, 8
   (D) 3, 4, 6   (E) 3, 2, 2

8. B equals 30% of
   (A) $30B$ (B) $\frac{B}{30}$ (C) $\frac{30}{B}$ (D) $\frac{3B}{10}$ (E) $\frac{10B}{3}$

GO ON TO THE NEXT PAGE

9. By how much is $\frac{3}{7}$ larger than 20% of 2?

(A) $\frac{1}{35}$ (B) $\frac{1}{7}$ (C) $\frac{4}{7}$ (D) $3\frac{3}{7}$ (E) $3\frac{4}{7}$

10. If 8 men can do a job in 12 days, what is the percentage increase in number of days required to do the job when 2 men are released?

(A) $16\frac{2}{3}$%   (B) 25%   (C) $33\frac{1}{3}$%
(D) 40%   (E) 48%

11. In a class of c pupils there are b boys. The ratio of girls to boys is:

(A) c:b (B) b:c (C) $\frac{c-b}{b}$
(D) $\frac{b-c}{b}$ (E) $\frac{b-c}{c}$

12. If in the number 4315 the digits representing tens and thousands were interchanged, the value of the new number formed in relation to the original number would be

(A) unchanged   (B) 280 more   (C) 280 less
(D) 2970 more   (E) 2970 less

13. $x + 2y = 1\frac{1}{3}$
$x - y = +\frac{1}{3}$
$3y =$

(A) 0   (B) $-\frac{1}{3}$ (C) $\frac{1}{3}$ (D) 1   (E) $1\frac{2}{3}$

14. The fraction $\frac{5Y3X}{2Y8}$, in which X and Y stand for two unknown digits, represents a division which results in a quotient that is a whole number. Which of the following is (are) true?

I. X may equal 2.
II. X may equal 6 or 0.
III. X may equal 4.
(A) I only   (B) II only   (C) III only
(D) I and III only   (E) I, II and III

15. $a - x = 1$
$b + 1 = x$
$ab =$

(A) $x^2 - 1$ (B) x^2 (C) $(x+1)^2$
(D) $(x-1)^2$ (E) $x^2 + 1$

16. When the radius of a circle is doubled, the area is multiplied by

(A) 2   (B) 2π (C) $2\pi r$ (D) 3.14   (E) 4

17. The area of a triangle whose legs are in the ratio of 2:3 is 48. The length of the hypotenuse is

(A) $\sqrt{13}$ (B) 8   (C) $4\sqrt{13}$ (D) 12   (E) 208

18. A picture frame is 1 foot long and 9 inches wide. How long will a larger picture frame of the same proportions be if it is 3 feet wide?

(A) 4 in.   (B) 4 ft.   (C) 12 ft.
(D) 36 in.   (E) 36 ft.

19. A cow is attached to a rope in a pasture bordered by two fences (each 60 feet long) which meet at an angle of 24°. If the rope attached to the cow is 15 feet long, over how many square feet can the cow graze?

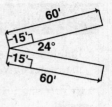

(A) 2π (B) 15π (C) 30π (D) 45π (E) 240π

20. The area of a circle is 154. What is the diameter of the circle? $\left(\text{Use } \pi = \frac{22}{7}.\right)$

(A) 3.14   (B) 7   (C) 14   (D) 21   (E) 49

21. In $\triangle ABC$, $AD = DB = 2$, $BE = EC = 3$, $DE = 4$, $AC =$

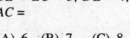

(A) 6   (B) 7   (C) 8
(D) 9   (E) 12

22. Find the vertex angle of an isosceles triangle if it exceeds each base angle by 30°.

(A) 50°   (B) 70°   (C) 75°   (D) 80°   (E) 105°

23. AB is parallel to CD. $EFGH$ is a straight line. If $\angle AFE$ is 4 times $\angle CGH$, what is the measure of $\angle HGD$?

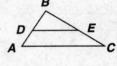

(A) 36   B) 120   (C) 135
(D) 144   (E) 160

24. Lines ABC and EDC meet at an angle of 30°. $BF = DF$, $AF = FE$. $\angle EDF = 80$. What is the measure of $\angle BFD$?

(A) 80°   (B) 100°   (C) 130°
(D) 150°   (E) 160°

25. To obtain a final average of 80% in a certain subject, what grade must a student earn in a test after having an average of 77.5% in four examinations?

(A) 85   (B) 87   (C) 89
(D) 90   (E) more than 90

IF YOU FINISH BEFORE 30 MINUTES, YOU MAY CHECK YOUR WORK ON THIS SECTION ONLY. DO NOT TURN TO ANY OTHER SECTION IN THE TEST.   **STOP**

SECTION 3
Writing Skills

Time—30 minutes
39 Questions

Directions

The following sentences contain problems in gram-mar, usage, diction (choice of words), and idiom.

  Some sentences are correct.
  No sentence contains more than one error.

You will find that the error, if there is one, is under-lined and lettered. Assume that elements of the sen-tence that are not underlined are correct and cannot be changed. In choosing answers, follow the requirements of standard written English.

If there is an error, select the one underlined part that must be changed to make the sentence correct and blacken the corresponding space on your answer sheet.

If there is no error, blacken answer space Ⓔ.

Example:

The region has a climate so severe that plants
                                 A
growing there rarely had been more than twelve
      B   C
inches high. No error
       D   E

Ⓐ Ⓑ ● Ⓓ Ⓔ

1. Notice the immediate affect this drug has on the
              A   B   C
behavior of the rats in the cage. No error
    D   E

2. I believe the commissioner and she to be honest:
                                 A
nevertheless, corruption by public officials and
   B
their staffs appears to be a continual political
            C   D
problem. No error
         E

3. In spite of official denials, news sources recently
   A
reported that the bombs that hit Tripoli in 1986
          B
were really intended to kill Muammar al-Qaddafi.
     C   D
No error
   E

4. Are you going to lie there all day and refuse to see
   A   B   C   D
your friends? No error
              E

5. Neither the teacher nor her pupils were enthused
    A   B   C
about going on the field trip. No error
    D   E

6. While Egyptian President Anwar El-Sadat was
   A
reviewing a military parade in 1981, a band of
                                    B
commandos had shot him and others in the vicinity.
          C   D
No error
   E

7. Please do not be aggravated by his bad manners
                   A   B
since he is merely trying to attract attention.
   C   D
No error
   E

8. Neither the opera singers or the general public
                          A
had seen as much glitter in years as they did
   B   C
during *Turandot,* the finale of the opera season.
                       D
No error
   E

9. His story about the strange beings in a space ship
                      A
was so incredulous that no one believed him.
   B   C   D
No error
   E

10. The hot air balloon had burst as they were preparing
                                      A
for launch, and the platform had broke as a result.
    B   C   D
No error
   E

11. I fail to understand why you are seeking my council
         A   B   C
after the way you ignored my advice last week.
                   D
No error
   E

12. Ann Landers, whose name is a household word
                  A
to millions of readers, are well-known for family
    B   C   D
advice. No error
        E

GO ON TO THE NEXT PAGE

13. Between you and I, the highway department must
               A
    review bridge construction across the country
                                    B
    in order to avoid major catastrophes resulting from
    C   D
    metal fatigue. No error
                   E

14. Child custody in surrogate mother cases is just

    one of the many controversial issues which are
    A   B   C
    currently being decided upon in the courts.
                    D

    No error
    E

15. John usually eats a quick lunch, ignoring the
                                      A
    question of whether what he eats is healthy or
               B   C   D
    not. No error
         E

16. If you continue to drive so recklessly, you are likely
    A   B   C
    to have a serious accident in the very near future.
                                     D

    No error
    E

17. The general along with the members of his
                 A
    general staff seem to favor immediate retaliation
    B   C   D
    at this time. No error
                  E

18. We resented him criticizing our efforts because
                 A   B
    he had ignored our requests for assistance
       C
    up to that time. No error
    D   E

19. Casey Jones, who was killed in the line of duty,
                 A   B
    became a hero to fellow railroad workers and
    C
    was to be immortalized by a ballad. No error
    D   E

Directions

In each of the following sentences, some part or all of the sentence is underlined. Below each sentence you will find five ways of phrasing the underlined part. Select the answer that produces the most effective sentence, one that is clear and exact, without awkwardness or ambiguity, and fill in the corresponding oval on your answer sheet. In choosing answers, follow the requirements of standard written English. Choose the answer that best expresses the meaning of the original sentence.

Answer (A) is always the same as the underlined part. Choose Answer (A) if you think the original sentence needs no revision.

EXAMPLE:

Laura Ingalls Wilder published her first book and she was sixty-five years old then.

(A) and she was sixty-five years old then
(B) when she was sixty-five
(C) at age sixty-five years old
(D) upon reaching of sixty-five years
(E) at the time when she was sixty-five

SAMPLE ANSWER

Ⓐ ● Ⓒ Ⓓ Ⓔ

20. The police officer refused to permit us to enter the apartment, saying that he had orders to stop him going into the building.

(A) stop him going
(B) prevent him going
(C) stop his going
(D) stop us going
(E) stop our going

21. After conducting the orchestra for six concerts, Beethoven's *Ninth Symphony* was scheduled.

(A) After conducting
(B) After he conducted
(C) Because he had conducted
(D) Although he conducted
(E) After he had conducted

22. Jackie Robinson became the first black player in major league baseball, he paved the way for black athletes to be accepted on the field.

(A) Jackie Robinson became the first black player in major league baseball, he
(B) Jackie Robinson, in becoming the first black player in major league baseball, he
(C) Jackie Robinson became the first black player in major league baseball; he
(D) Jackie Robinson, the first black player in major league baseball; he
(E) Jackie Robinson had become the first black player in major league baseball and he

GO ON TO THE NEXT PAGE →

23. Sitting in the Coliseum, the music couldn't hardly be heard because of the cheering and yelling of the spectators.

   (A) the music couldn't hardly be heard because of
   (B) the music couldn't hardly be heard due to
   (C) the music could hardly be heard due to
   (D) we could hardly be heard because of
   (E) the music could hardly hear the music because of

24. If I would have known about the traffic jam at the bridge, I would have taken an alternate route.

   (A) If I would have known about
   (B) If I could have known about
   (C) If I would of known about
   (D) If I was aware of
   (E) Had I known about

25. Across the nation, curricular changes sweeping the universities as schools reassess the knowledge that educated people should know

   (A) curricular changes sweeping the universities as schools
   (B) curricular changes are sweeping the universities as schools
   (C) changes are sweeping the curricular since schools
   (D) curricular changes sweeping the universities causing schools to
   (E) curricular changes sweep the universities, but schools

26. If you have enjoyed these kind of programs, write to your local public television station and ask for more.

   (A) these kind of programs
   (B) those kind of programs
   (C) these kinds of programs
   (D) these kind of a program
   (E) these kind of a program

27. In her critique of the newly opened restaurant, the reviewer discussed the elaborate menu, the impressive wine list, and how the waiters functioned.

   (A) list, and how the waiters functioned
   (B) list and how the waiters functioned
   (C) list, and the excellent service
   (D) list, and even the excellent service
   (E) list, and how the waiters usually function

28. Contemporary poets are not abandoning rhyme, but some avoiding it.

   (A) but some avoiding it
   (B) but it is avoided by some of them
   (C) but it is being avoided
   (D) but some are avoiding it
   (E) but it has been being avoided by some

29. Your complaint is no different from the last customer who expected a refund.

   (A) Your complaint is no different from the last customer
   (B) Your complaint is no different from that of the last customer
   (C) Your complaint is similar to the last customer
   (D) Your complaint is no different then that of the last customer
   (E) Your complaint is the same as the last customer

30. According to the review board, many laboratory tests were ordered by the staff of the hospital that had no medical justification.

   (A) many laboratory tests were ordered by the staff of the hospital that
   (B) many laboratory tests were ordered by the staff of the hospital who
   (C) the staff of the hospital ordered many laboratory tests that
   (D) the staff of the hospital, who ordered many laboratory tests that
   (E) the ordering of many laboratory tests by the staff of the hospital which

31. Confident about the outcome, President Clinton along with his staff are traveling to the conference.

   (A) Confident about the outcome, President Clinton along with his staff are traveling
   (B) Confident about the outcome, President Clinton's party are traveling
   (C) Confident about the outcome, President Clinton along with his staff is traveling
   (D) With confidence about the outcome, President Clinton along with his staff are traveling
   (E) President Clinton along with his staff is traveling confidently about the outcome,

32. Helen Keller was blind and deaf from infancy and she learned to communicate using both sign language and speech.

   (A) Helen Keller was blind and deaf from infancy and she
   (B) Although blind and deaf from infancy, Helen Keller
   (C) Although being blind and deaf from the time she was an infant, Helen Keller
   (D) Being blind and deaf from infancy, Helen Keller
   (E) Helen Keller, being blind and deaf from infancy, she

GO ON TO THE NEXT PAGE

33. Standing alone beside her husband's grave, <u>grief overwhelmed the widow and she wept inconsolably</u>.

    (A) grief overwhelmed the widow and she wept inconsolably

    (B) grief overwhelmed the widow, who wept inconsolably

    (C) grief overwhelmed the widow that wept inconsolably

    (D) the widow, overwhelmed by grief, wept inconsolably

    (E) the widow was overwhelmed by grief, she wept inconsolably

---

Directions

The passage below is the unedited draft of a student's essay. Some of the essay needs to be rewritten to make the meaning clearer and more precise. Read the essay carefully.

The essay is followed by six questions about changes that might improve all or part of its organization, development, sentence structure, use of language, appropriateness to the audience, or its use of standard written English. Choose the answer that most clearly and effectively expresses the student's intended meaning. Indicate your choice by filling in the corresponding space on the answer sheet.

Essay

[1] Members of our community have objected to the inclusion of various pieces of art in the local art exhibit. [2] They say that these pieces offend community values. [3] The exhibit in its entirety should be presented.

[4] The reason for this is that people have varied tastes, and those who like this form of art have a right to see the complete exhibit. [5] An exhibit like this one gives the community a rare chance to see the latest modern art nearby, and many people have looked forward to it with great anticipation. [6] It would be an unfortunate blow to those people for it not to be shown.

[7] The exhibit may contain pieces of art that tend to be slightly erotic, but what is being shown that most people haven't already seen? [8] So, give it an R or an X rating and don't let small children in. [9] But how many small children voluntarily go to see an art exhibit? [10] The exhibit includes examples of a new style of modern art. [11] The paintings show crowds of nude people. [12] The exhibit is at the library's new art gallery. [13] For centuries artists have been painting and sculpting people in the nude [14] Why are these works of art different? [15] Perhaps they are more graphic in some respects, but we live in a entirely different society than from the past. [16] It is strange indeed for people in this day and age to be offended by the sight of the human anatomy.

[17] If people don't agree with these pieces, they simply should just not go. [18] But they should not be allowed to prevent others from seeing it.

34. Taking into account the sentences which precede and follow sentence 3, which of the following is the best revision of sentence 3?

    (A) On the other hand, the whole exhibit should be presented.

    (B) The exhibit, however, should be presented in its entirety.

    (C) The exhibit should be entirely presented regardless of what the critics say.

    (D) But another point of view is that the exhibit should be presented in its entirety.

    (E) Still other members also say the whole exhibit should be presented in its entirety.

35. In the context of paragraph 3, which of the following is the best revision of sentence 8?

    (A) So, an R or X rating will warn people with small children to keep them out.

    (B) Therefore, giving it an R or an X rating and not letting small children in.

    (C) To satisfy everyone objecting to the exhibit, perhaps the exhibit could be given an R or an X rating to advise parents that some of the art on exhibit may not be suitable for young children.

    (D) Let an R or an X rating caution the public that some of the art may be offensive and be unsuitable for young children.

    (E) In conclusion, small children will be kept out by giving it an R or an X rating.

36. In the context of paragraph 3, which of the following is the best revision of sentences 10, 11, and 12?

    (A) Paintings on exhibit at the library showing crowds of nude people and done in a new style of modern art.

    (B) The exhibit, on display at the library, includes paintings of crowds of nude people done in a new style of modern art.

    (C) The exhibit includes paintings in a new style of modern art, which shows crowds of nude people at the library.

    (D) The library is the site of the exhibit which shows a new style of modern art, with paintings showing crowds of nude people

    (E) The new style of modern art includes examples of paintings showing crowds of nude people on exhibit in the library.

37. To improve the clarity and coherence of the whole essay, where is the best place to relocate the ideas contained in sentences 10, 11, and 12?

    (A) Before sentence 1
    (B) Between sentences 1 and 2
    (C) Between sentences 8 and 9
    (D) Between sentences 15 and 16
    (E) After sentence 18

38. Which of the following is the best revision the underlined segment of sentence 15 below?

    Perhaps they are more graphic in some respects, but we live in a entirely different society than from the past.

    (A) an entirely different society than of the past
    (B) a completely different society than the past
    (C) a society completely different than from past societies
    (D) a society which is entirely different from the way societies have been in the past
    (E) an entirely different society from that of the past

39. Which of the following revisions of sentence 17 provides the best transition between paragraphs 3 and 4?

    (A) If anyone doesn't approve of these pieces, they simply should not go to the exhibit.
    (B) Anyone disagreeing with the pieces in the exhibit shouldn't go to it.
    (C) Anyone who disapproves of nudity in art simply shouldn't go to the exhibit.
    (D) If anyone dislikes the sight of nudes in art, this show isn't for them.
    (E) Don't go if you disapprove of nudity in art.

IF YOU FINISH BEFORE 30 MINUTES, YOU MAY CHECK YOUR WORK ON THIS SECTION ONLY. DO NOT TURN TO ANY OTHER SECTION IN THE TEST.   **S T O P**

SECTION 4
Verbal Reasoning

**Time—30 minutes
30 Questions**

For each question in this section, select the best answer from among the choices given and fill in the corresponding oval on the answer sheet.

Directions

Each sentence below consists of a related pair of words or phrases, followed by five pairs of words or phrases labeled A through E. Select the pair that best expresses a relationship similar to that expressed in the original pair.

Example:

CRUMB:BREAD::
(A) ounce:unit
(B) splinter:wood
(C) water:bucket
(D) twine:rope
(E) cream:butter

 Ⓐ ● Ⓒ Ⓓ Ⓔ

31. PEBBLE:SLINGSHOT::

(A) arrow:quiver   (B) ball:cannon
(C) missile:target   (D) hilt:dagger
(E) barrel:rifle

32. DOOR:LATCH::

(A) window:pane   (B) necklace:clasp
(C) lock:key   (D) wall:plaster
(E) house:foundation

33. DRIZZLE:POUR::

(A) rumple:fold   (B) moisten:waterproof
(C) tingle:chill   (D) dam:flood
(E) smolder:blaze

34. CAPTION:PHOTOGRAPH::

(A) frame:painting   (B) subject:portrait
(C) signature:letter   (D) title:article
(E) stanza:poem

35. ERADICATE:ERROR::

(A) acknowledge:fault
(B) arbitrate:dispute
(C) penalize:foul
(D) uproot:weed
(E) erase:blackboard

36. TYRANNOSAUR:DINOSAUR::

(A) lizard:crocodile   (B) whale:fish
(C) condor:bird   (D) frog:tadpole
(E) tiger:leopard

37. GANDER:GOOSE::

(A) fawn:deer   (B) porpoise:whale
(C) mare:horse   (D) panda:bear
(E) ram:sheep

38. PROLIFIC:AUTHOR::

(A) melodious:singer   (B) veracious:witness
(C) dynamic:actor   (D) loquacious:speaker
(E) agile:acrobat

39. LOCOMOTION:FEET::

(A) perspiration:sweat   (B) amnesia:brain
(C) sensation:hands   (D) digestion:stomach
(E) sound:ears

40. MENTOR:PROTEGE::

(A) competitor:rival   (B) writer:plagiarist
(C) doctor:surgeon   (D) sponsor:candidate
(E) truant:dawdler

41. GARBLED:COMPREHEND::

(A) controversial:dispute
(B) negligible:disregard
(C) mangled:believe
(D) methodical:organize
(E) camouflaged:discern

42. TRAVELER:ITINERARY::

(A) lecturer:outline   (B) tourist:vacation
(C) pedestrian:routine   (D) explorer:safari
(E) soldier:furlough

43. PURIST:CORRECTNESS::

(A) miser:generosity   (B) saint:elevation
(C) nomad:refuge   (D) judge:accuracy
(E) martinet:discipline

The passage below is followed by questions based on its content. Answer the questions following the passage on the basis of what is <u>stated</u> or <u>implied</u> in that passage and in any introductory material that may be provided.

Questions 44–49 are based on the following passage.

The following passage is excerpted from a book on prominent black Americans during Franklin Delano Roosevelt's presidency.

Like her white friends Eleanor Roosevelt and Aubrey Williams, Mary Bethune believed in the fundamental commitment of the New Deal to
Line   assist the black American's struggle and in the

 GO ON TO THE NEXT PAGE ➡

5 need for blacks to assume responsibilities to help win that struggle. Unlike those of her white liberal associates, however, Bethune's ideas had evolved out of a long experience as a "race leader." Founder of a small black college in Florida, she
10 had become widely known by 1935 as an organizer of black women's groups and as a civil and political rights activist. Deeply religious, certain of her own capabilities, she held a relatively uncluttered view of what she felt were the New
15 Deal's and her own people's obligations to the cause of racial justice. Unafraid to speak her mind to powerful whites, including the president, or to differing black factions, she combined faith in the ultimate willingness of whites to discard their
20 prejudice and bigotry with a strong sense of racial pride and commitment to Negro self-help.

More than her liberal white friends, Bethune argued for a strong and direct black voice in initiating and shaping government policy. She pur-
25 sued this in her conversations with President Roosevelt, in numerous memoranda to Aubrey Williams, and in her administrative work as head of the National Youth Administration's Office of Negro Affairs. With the assistance of Williams,
30 she was successful in having blacks selected to NYA posts at the national, state, and local levels. But she also wanted a black presence throughout the federal government. At the beginning of the war she joined other black leaders in demanding
35 appointments to the Selective Service Board and to the Department of the Army; and she was instrumental in 1941 in securing Earl Dickerson's membership on the Fair Employment Practices Committee. By 1944, she was still making
40 appeals for black representation in "all public programs, federal, state, and local," and "in policy-making posts as well as rank and file jobs."

Though recognizing the weakness in the Roosevelt administration's response to Negro
45 needs, Mary Bethune remained in essence a black partisan champion of the New Deal during the 1930s and 1940s. Her strong advocacy of administration policies and programs was predicated on a number of factors: her assessment of the low
50 status of black Americans during the Depression; her faith in the willingness of some liberal whites to work for the inclusion of blacks in the government's reform and recovery measures; her conviction that only massive federal aid could elevate
55 the Negro economically; and her belief that the thirties and forties were producing a more self-aware and self-assured black population. Like a number of her white friends in government, Bethune assumed that the preservation of democ-
60 racy and black people's "full integration into the benefits and the responsibilities" of American life were inextricably tied together. She was convinced that, with the help of a friendly govern-

ment, a militant, aggressive "New Negro" would
65 emerge out of the devastation of depression and war, a "New Negro" who would "save America from itself," who would lead America toward the full realization of its democratic ideas.

44. The author's primary goal in the passage is to do which of the following?

(A) Criticize Mary Bethune for adhering too closely to New Deal policies

(B) Argue that Mary Bethune was too optimistic in her assessment of race relations

(C) Explore Mary Bethune's convictions and her influence on black progress in the Roosevelt years

(D) Point out the weaknesses of the white liberal approach to black needs during Roosevelt's presidency

(E) Summarize the attainments of blacks under the auspices of Roosevelt's New Deal

45. It can be inferred from the passage that Aubrey Williams was which of the following?

I. A man with influence in the National Youth Administration

II. A white liberal

III. A man of strong religious convictions

(A) I only   (B) II only   (C) III only
(D) I and II only   (E) I, II and III

46. The author mentions Earl Dickerson (line 37) primarily in order to

(A) cite an instance of Bethune's political impact

(B) contrast his career with that of Bethune

(C) introduce the subject of a subsequent paragraph

(D) provide an example of Bethune's "New Negro"

(E) show that Dickerson was a leader of his fellow blacks

47. The word "instrumental" in line 37 means

(A) subordinate   (B) triumphant   (C) musical
(D) gracious   (E) helpful

48. It can be inferred from the passage that Bethune believed the "New Negro" would "save America from itself" (lines 66–67) by

(A) joining the Army and helping America overthrow its Fascist enemies

(B) helping America accomplish its egalitarian ideals

(C) voting for administration anti-poverty programs

(D) electing other blacks to government office

(E) expressing a belief in racial pride

GO ON TO THE NEXT PAGE

The passages below are followed by questions based on their content; questions following a pair of related passages may also be based on the relationship between the paired passages. Answer the questions on the basis of what is <u>stated</u> or <u>implied</u> in the passages and in any introductory material that may be provided.

Questions 50–60 are based on the following passages.

The following passages are excerpted from two recent essays that relate writing to sports. The author of Passage 1 deals with having had a novel rejected by his publisher. The author of Passage 2 explores how his involvement in sports affected his writing career.

PASSAGE 1

In consigning this manuscript to a desk drawer, I am comforted by the behavior of baseball players. There are *no* pitchers who do not give up home
Line runs, there are *no* batters who do not strike out.
5 There are *no* major league pitchers or batters who have not somehow learned to survive giving up home runs and striking out. That much is obvious.

What seems to me less obvious is how these "failures" must be digested, or put to use, in the
10 overall experience of the player. A jogger once explained to me that the nerves of the ankle are so sensitive and complex that each time a runner sets his foot down, hundreds of messages are conveyed to the runner's brain about the nature of the
15 terrain and the requirements for weight distribution, balance, and muscle-strength. I'm certain that the ninth-inning home run that Dave Henderson hit off Donny Moore registered complexly and permanently in Moore's mind and
20 body and that the next time Moore faced Henderson, his pitching was informed by his awful experience of October 1986. Moore's continuing baseball career depended to some extent on his converting that encounter with Henderson
25 into something useful for his pitching. I can also imagine such an experience destroying an athlete, registering in his mind and body in such a negative way as to produce a debilitating fear.

Of the many ways in which athletes and artists
30 are similar, one is that, unlike accountants or plumbers or insurance salesmen, to succeed at all they must perform at an extraordinary level of excellence. Another is that they must be willing to extend themselves irrationally in order to achieve
35 that level of performance. A writer doesn't have to write all-out all the time, but he or she must be ready to write all-out any time the story requires it. Hold back and you produce what just about any literate citizen can produce, a "pretty good" piece
40 of work. Like the cautious pitcher, the timid writer can spend a lifetime in the minor leagues.

And what more than failure—the strike out, the crucial home run given up, the manuscript criticized and rejected—is more likely to produce cau-
45 tion or timidity? An instinctive response to painful experience is to avoid the behavior that produced the pain. To function at the level of

excellence required for survival, writers like athletes must go against instinct, must absorb their
50 failures and become stronger, must endlessly repeat the behavior that produced the pain.

PASSAGE 2

The athletic advantages of this concentration, particularly for an athlete who was making up for the absence of great natural skill, were consider-
55 able. Concentration gave you an edge over many of your opponents, even your betters, who could not isolate themselves to that degree. For example, in football if they were ahead (or behind) by several touchdowns, if the game itself seemed to have
60 been settled, they tended to slack off, to ease off a little, certainly to relax their own concentration. It was then that your own unwavering concentration and your own indifference to the larger point of view paid off. At the very least you could deal out
65 surprise and discomfort to your opponents.

But it was more than that. Do you see? The ritual of physical concentration, of acute engagement in a small space while disregarding all the clamor and demands of the larger world, was the
70 best possible lesson in precisely the kind of selfish intensity needed to create and to finish a poem, a story, or a novel. This alone mattered while all the world going on, with and without you, did not.

75 I was learning first in muscle, blood, and bone, not from literature and not from teachers of literature or the arts or the natural sciences, but from coaches, in particular this one coach who paid me enough attention to influence me to teach some
80 things to myself. I was learning about art and life through the abstraction of athletics in much the same way that a soldier is, to an extent, prepared for war by endless parade ground drill. His body must learn to be a soldier before heart, mind, and
85 spirit can.

Ironically, I tend to dismiss most comparisons of athletics to art and to "the creative process." But only because, I think, so much that is claimed for both is untrue. But I have come to believe—
90 indeed I have to believe it insofar as I believe in the validity and efficacy of art—that what comes to us first and foremost through the body, as a

GO ON TO THE NEXT PAGE

sensuous affective experience, is taken and transformed by mind and self into a thing of the spirit.
95   Which is only to say that what the body learns
and is taught is of enormous significance—at least
until the last light of the body fails.

49. Why does the author of Passage 1 consign his manuscript to a desk drawer?

(A) To protect it from the inquisitive eyes of his
family
(B) To prevent its getting lost or disordered
(C) Because his publisher wishes to take another
look at it
(D) Because he chooses to watch a televised base-
ball game
(E) To set it aside as unmarketable in its current state

50. Why is the author of Passage 1 "comforted by the
behavior of baseball players" (lines 2–3)?

(A) He treasures the timeless rituals of America's
national pastime.
(B) He sees he is not alone in having to confront
failure and move on.
(C) He enjoys watching the frustration of the batters who strike out.
(D) He looks at baseball from the viewpoint of a
behavioral psychologist.
(E) He welcomes any distraction from the task of
revising his novel.

51. What function in the passage is served by the discussion of the nerves in the ankle in lines 11–17?

(A) It provides a momentary digression from the
overall narrative flow.
(B) It emphasizes how strong a mental impact
Henderson's home run must have had on
Moore.
(C) It provides scientific confirmation of the neu-
romuscular abilities of athletes.
(D) It illustrates that the author's interest in sports
is not limited to baseball alone.
(E) It conveys a sense of how confusing it is for
the mind to deal with so many simultaneous
messages.

52. The word "registered" in line 19 means

(A) enrolled formally
(B) expressed without words
(C) corresponded exactly
(D) made an impression
(E) qualified officially

53. The attitude of the author of Passage 1 to accountants, plumbers, and insurance salesmen (lines
29–31) can best be described as

(A) respectful   (B) cautious   (C) superior
(D) cynical   (E) hypocritical

54. In the concluding paragraphs of Passage 1, the
author appears to

(A) romanticize the writer as someone heroic in his
or her accomplishments
(B) deprecate athletes for their inability to react to
experience instinctively
(C) minimize the travail that artists and athletes
endure to do their work
(D) advocate the importance of literacy to the common citizen
(E) suggest a cautious approach would reduce the
likelihood of future failure

55. The author of Passage 2 prizes

(A) his innate athletic talent
(B) the respect of his peers
(C) his ability to focus
(D) the gift of relaxation
(E) winning at any cost

56. The word "settled" in line 60 means

(A) judged
(B) decided
(C) reconciled
(D) pacified
(E) inhabited

57. What does the author mean by "indifference to the
larger point of view" (lines 63–64)?

(A) Inability to see the greater implications of the
activity in which you were involved
(B) Hostility to opponents coming from larger, better trained teams
(C) Reluctance to look beyond your own immediate concerns
(D) Refusing to care how greatly you might be hurt
by your opponents
(E) Being more concerned with the task at hand
than with whether you win or lose

58. What is the function of the phrase "to an extent" in
line 82?

(A) It denies a situation
(B) It conveys a paradox
(C) It qualifies a statement
(D) It represents a metaphor
(E) It minimizes a liability

GO ON TO THE NEXT PAGE

59. The author finds it ironic that he tends to "dismiss most comparisons of athletics to art" (lines 92–93) because

    (A) athletics is the basis for great art
    (B) he finds comparisons generally unhelpful
    (C) he is making such a comparison
    (D) he typically is less cynical
    (E) he rejects the so-called "creative process"

60. The authors of both passages would agree that

    (A) the lot of the professional writer is more trying than that of the professional athlete
    (B) athletics has little to do with the actual workings of the creative process
    (C) both artists and athletes learn hard lessons in the course of mastering their art
    (D) it is important to concentrate on the things that hurt us in life
    (E) participating in sports provides a distraction from the isolation of a writer's life

---

IF YOU FINISH BEFORE 30 MINUTES, YOU MAY CHECK YOUR WORK ON THIS SECTION ONLY. DO NOT TURN TO ANY OTHER SECTION IN THE TEST.   **S T O P**

SECTION 5
Mathematical Reasoning

Time—30 minutes
25 Questions

Directions and Sample Questions

Notes:

(1) The use of a calculator is permitted. All numbers used are real numbers.

(2) Figures that accompany problems in this test are intended to provide information useful in solving the problems. They are drawn as accurately as possible EXCEPT when it is stated in a specific problem that the figure is not drawn to scale. All figures lie in a plane unless otherwise indicated.

Questions 1–15 each consist of two quantities in boxes, one in Column A and one in Column B. You are to compare the two quantities and on the answer sheet fill in oval

A if the quantity in Column A is greater;
B if the quantity in Column B is greater;
C if the two quantities are equal;
D if the relationship cannot be determined from the information given.

Notes:

1. In some questions, information is given about one or both of the quantities to be compared. In such cases, the given information is centered above the two columns and is not boxed.
2. In a given question, a symbol that appears in both columns represents the same thing in Column A as it does in Column B.
3. Letters such as x, n, and k stand for real numbers.

	EXAMPLES		
	Column A	Column B	Answers
E1	5^2	20	● Ⓑ Ⓒ Ⓓ
E2	x	30	Ⓐ Ⓑ ● Ⓓ
E3	$r+1$	$s-1$	Ⓐ Ⓑ Ⓒ ●

E2: 150° / $x°$

E3: r and s are integers.

PART I: QUANTITATIVE COMPARISON QUESTIONS

SUMMARY DIRECTIONS FOR QUANTITATIVE COMPARISON QUESTIONS

Answer: A if the quantity in Column A is greater.
B if the quantity in Column B is greater.

C if the two quantities are equal.
D if the relationship cannot be determined from the information given.

	Column A	Column B			Column A	Column B
26.	$\dfrac{(624)(9)(8)}{(4)(3)(2)}$	$\dfrac{(4)(9)(642)}{(5)(4)(3)}$	**30.**	$2x+y=1$ y		$1-2x$
27.	$\dfrac{1}{\sqrt{81}}$	$\dfrac{1}{0.9}$	**31.**	$x \neq 0$ $\dfrac{\frac{x}{2}}{\frac{2}{x}}$		$\dfrac{x^2}{2}$
28.	$6R^6$	R^7	**32.**	$25 < \sqrt{x} < 36$ x		5
29.	$x^2+y^2=61$ x	y	**33.**	$(x+y)(x-y)$		x^2-y^2

GO ON TO THE NEXT PAGE

Column A	Column B

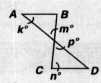

AB is parallel to CD and $p = 60$, $k = 40$

	Column A	Column B
34.	n	m

	Column A	Column B
35.	x^2	$z^2 - y^2$

perimeter of square $BCDE = 40$
$AB = BC$

	Column A	Column B
36.	Area of ABE	50

Column A	Column B

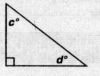

$a = 40$ and $c = 50$

	Column A	Column B
37.	b	d

$ab = 5$
$a^2 + b^2 = 7$

	Column A	Column B
38.	$(a + b)^2$	12

$z = 0$

	Column A	Column B
39.	$\dfrac{(2x)(xz)}{x + y}$	zero

$x^2 - 4x + 4 = 0$
$\dfrac{3}{4}y = \dfrac{4}{3}$

	Column A	Column B
40.	x	y

PART II: STUDENT-PRODUCED RESPONSE QUESTIONS

Directions for Student-Produced Response Questions

Each of the remaining ten questions (41–50) requires you to solve the problem and enter your answer by marking the ovals in the special grid, as shown in the examples below.

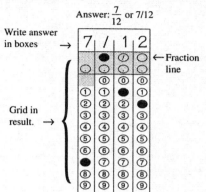

Answer: $\frac{7}{12}$ or 7/12

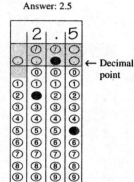

Answer: 2.5

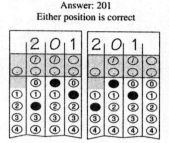

Answer: 201
Either position is correct

Note: You may start your answers in any column, space permitting. Columns not needed should be left blank.

- Mark no more than one oval in any column.
- Because the answer sheet will be machine-scored, **you will receive credit only if the ovals are filled in correctly.**
- Although not required, it is suggested that you write your answer in the boxes at the top of the columns to help you fill in the ovals accurately.
- Some problems may have more than one correct answer. In such cases, grid only one answer.
- No question has a negative answer.
- **Mixed numbers** such as $2\frac{1}{2}$ much be gridded as 2.5 or 5/2. (If [2 1 / 2] is gridded, it will be interpreted as $\frac{21}{2}$, not $\frac{21}{2}$.)

- Decimal Accuracy: If you obtain a decimal answer, enter the most accurate value that the grid will accommodate. For example, if you obtain an answer such as 0.6666..., you should record the result as .666 or .667. Less accurate values such as .66 or .67 are not acceptable.

Acceptable ways to grid $\frac{2}{3} = .6666...$

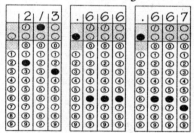

41. How many square units are there in the area of square *ABCD* with coordinates as follows: *A*(–4,4) *B*(4,4) *C*(4, –4) *D*(–4,–4)?

42. There are 216 couples competing in a dance contest. After each half hour one-third of the contestants are eliminated. How many couples will remain eligible for the prize after the first hour?

43. The drawing below represents 3 stacks of playing cards, each with 6 cards. What is the least number of cards that must be moved in order to have a ratio of 1:2:3 for the distribution of these cards in the stacks?

I   II   III

44. Lori, Meri, and Joan working at the same rate can complete a task in 5 days. What fraction of the task is performed by one of these people in one day?

45. A certain ore, when refined, yields an average of $1\frac{1}{4}$ pounds of metal to the ton. How many tons of ore will be needed to yield 200 pounds of metal?

46. What part of an hour do I work if I start at 2:50 and stop at 3:26 the same afternoon?

47. How many tiles (each one foot square) are necessary to form a one-foot border around the inside of a room that is 24 feet by 14 feet?

48. If the perimeter of a square is 16, what is its area?

GO ON TO THE NEXT PAGE

49. *AOC* is a diameter of circle *O*. Line *AB* = 12, *OA* = 10. Find the length of line *BC*.

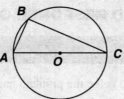

50. *AB* ‖ *CD*, *AB* = 32, *BC* = 10, *CD* = 20, *AD* = 10. What is the area of *ABCD*?

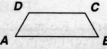

IF YOU FINISH BEFORE 30 MINUTES, YOU MAY CHECK YOUR WORK ON THIS SECTION ONLY. DO NOT TURN TO ANY OTHER SECTION IN THE TEST.   **S T O P**

ANSWER KEY

Verbal Reasoning Section 1

1. D	6. D	11. B	16. B	21. C	26. C
2. E	7. C	12. D	17. E	22. B	27. C
3. B	8. A	13. E	18. C	23. C	28. E
4. A	9. C	14. C	19. D	24. D	29. B
5. B	10. B	15. E	20. D	25. C	30. C

Mathematical Reasoning Section 2

Note: Each correct answer to the mathematics questions is keyed by number to the corresponding topic in Chapters 8 and 9. These numerals refer to the topics listed below, with specific page references in parentheses.

1. Basic Fundamental Operations (179–182)
2. Algebraic Operations (182–183)
3. Using Algebra (182–184, 187)
4. Exponents, Roots, and Radicals (184–185)
5. Inequalities (188–189)
6. Fractions (182–198)
7. Decimals (200)
8. Percent (200)
9. Averages (201)
10. Motion (203)
11. Ratio and Proportion (204–205)
12. Mixtures and Solutions (178)
13. Work (206–207)
14. Coordinate Geometry (194)
15. Geometry (189–193, 195)
16. Quantitative Comparisons (211–212)
17. Data Interpretation (208)

1. C (6)	6. D (6)	11. C (1)	16. E (15)	21. C (15)
2. D (2)	7. C (15)	12. E (1)	17. C (15)	22. D (15)
3. A (2, 4)	8. E (3, 8)	13. D (2)	18. B (15)	23. D (15)
4. A (4, 6, 7)	9. A (6, 8)	14. E (1)	19. B (15)	24. C (15)
5. B (1)	10. C (8, 11, 13)	15. A (2)	20. C (15)	25. D (8)

Writing Skills Section 3

1. B	8. A	15. E	22. C	29. B	36. B
2. A	9. C	16. E	23. E	30. C	37. A
3. E	10. C	17. C	24. E	31. C	38. E
4. E	11. C	18. A	25. B	32. B	39. C
5. C	12. C	19. D	26. C	33. D	
6. C	13. A	20. E	27. C	34. D	
7. A	14. D	21. E	28. D	35. D	

Verbal Reasoning Section 4

31. B	36. C	41. E	46. A	51. B	56. B
32. B	37. E	42. A	47. E	52. D	57. E
33. E	38. D	43. E	48. B	53. C	58. C
34. D	39. D	44. C	49. E	54. A	59. C
35. D	40. D	45. D	50. B	55. C	60. C

Mathematical Reasoning Section 5

26. A (1, 16)	29. D (2, 16)	32. A (4, 16)	35. C (15, 16)	38. A (2, 16)
27. B (4, 6, 7)	30. C (2, 16)	33. C (2, 16)	36. C (15, 16)	39. C (2, 16)
28. D (4, 16)	31. B (2, 6, 16)	34. A (15, 16)	37. A (15, 16)	40. A (3)

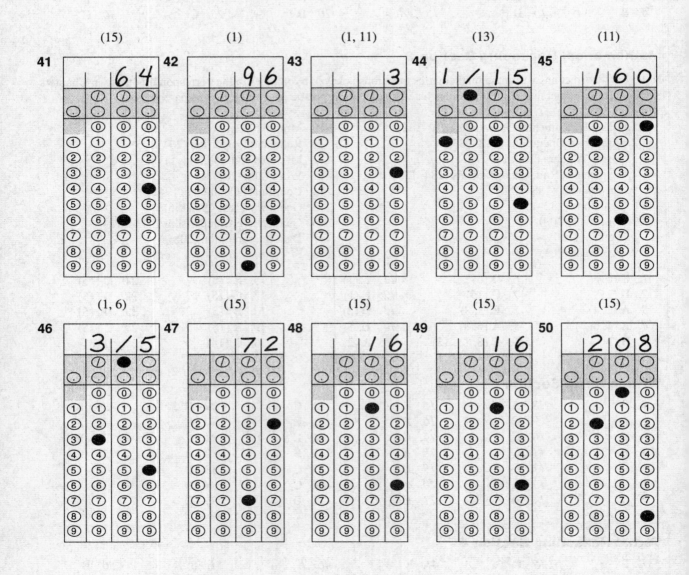

SCORING CHART — TYPICAL TEST E

Verbal Sections

Section 1   Questions 1–30
Number correct _____ (A)
Number omitted _____ (B)
Number incorrect _____ (C)
$1/4$ (C) = _____ (D)
Raw Score:
 (A) – (D) = _____

Section 3   Questions 31–60
Number correct _____ (A)
Number omitted _____ (B)
Number incorrect _____ (C)
$1/4$ (C) = _____ (D)
Raw Score:
 (A) – (D) = _____

Total Verbal Raw Score:
 (Section 1 +
 Section 3) = _____

Mathematical Sections

Section 2   Questions 1–25
Number correct _____ (A)
Number incorrect _____ (B)
(A) – $1/4$ (B) = _____ Raw Score I

Section 4   Questions 26–40
Number correct _____ (C)
Number incorrect _____ (D)
(C) – $1/3$ (D) = _____ Raw Score II

Section 4   Questions 41–50
Number correct _____ Raw Score III

Total Mathematical Raw Score:
 (Raw Scores I + II
 + III) = _____

Writing Section

Section 3   Questions 1–39
Number correct _____ (A)
Number incorrect _____ (B)
$1/4$ (B) = _____ (C)
(no penalty for omitted questions)
Writing Raw Score:
 (A) – (C) = _____

EVALUATION CHART

Study your score. Your raw score on the Verbal and Mathematical Reasoning Sections is an indication of your probable achievement on the PSAT/NMSQT. As a guide to the amount of work you need or want to do with this book, study the following.

Raw Score			Self-rating
Verbal	*Mathematical*	*Writing*	
55–60	41–50	37–39	Superior
44–54	25–40	31–36	Very good
39–43	20–24	25–30	Satisfactory
35–38	16–19	19–24	Average
29–34	10–15	13–18	Needs further study
20–28	7–9	6–12	Needs intensive study
0–19	0–6	0–5	Probably inadequate

ANSWER EXPLANATIONS

Verbal Reasoning Section 1

1. **D**   Such an extraordinarily useful material would *revolutionize* or make radical changes in an industry.

2. **E**   To make the correct decisions, the lawmakers must be able to *discern* or recognize the truth.

3. **B**   A mime (pantomime artist; performer who, without speaking, entertains through facial expressions and bodily movements) uses *gestures* (movements of the arms, head, hands, etc. that convey meaning) to fill the *empty* air.

4. **A**   If you started falling asleep at times you wouldn't normally wish to do so, you clearly would strike yourself as unusually *lethargic* (drowsily slow to respond; sluggish; listless).

5. **B**   There is a chance that *serious* women may not be attracted by an inappropriate *frivolity* or lightheartedness in style—hence the gamble.

6. **D**   If irony is a mode of escape, then the ironic person is *evading* or escaping life's terrors.

7. **C**   A contrast is set up here by the expression "no matter how." It tells us that, although future "revelations" (surprising news) may be *striking,* they will not equal past ones. These past revelations *radically* transformed or thoroughly changed our view.

8. **A**   Since "few other plants can grow beneath the canopy of the sycamore," it must be *inhibiting* or restraining the other plants.

9. **C**   Judges are not supposed to *influence* juries. The phrase "even when" signals a contrast: even when judges don't actually say injurious or *prejudicial* things, they may still affect the jury through their tone of voice.

10. **B**   Certain authors have been *relegated* or sent off to "obscurity," a state of being hidden or forgotten. There they must be "rediscovered."

11. **B**   Only someone *ingenuous* (naive; unsophisticated) whose taste had not been spoiled by worldly, *sophisticated* shows, would look at a local, relatively unpretentious county fair with wonder and awe.

12. **D**   A *euphemism* is by definition a mild expression used in place of a more unpleasant or distressing one. The blunt expression "he died" is unpleasantly direct for some people, who substitute the vague euphemism "he passed away."

13. **E**   *Despite* signals a contrast. If someone writes an enormously popular book, you would expect his career to prosper. Instead, White's career *foundered* or came to grief.

14. **C**   Because it was written immediately after the assassination, the book has *immediacy,* but it lacks *perspective;* the author had not had enough time to distance himself from his immediate reactions to the event and think about it.

15. **E**   The key word here is "chagrin." Because Costner has triumphed, the critics who predicted his *failure* feel chagrin (great annoyance mixed with disappointment or humiliation). Costner, for his part, greatly enjoys his success and especially enjoys or *savors* their embarrassment and vexation.

16. **B**   The phrase "not even" signals the contrast between the subject's "opulence" or wealth and her dissatisfaction with what she owned, her "material possessions." Not even all these possessions seemed *adequate* to the *fervor* (great intensity of feeling) of her ambition, her great desire to own even more.

17. **E**   Critics sometimes praise, but more often *decry* or condemn things. Here the critics see the "saccharine" (too sweet) mood of the movie as inconsistent with the *acerbic* (sour, bitter) tone of the book.

18. **C**   Among other clues, Mr. Collins states that he hopes to lead Elizabeth "to the altar ere long."

19. **D**   Elizabeth is "sensible of the honour" Mr. Collins is paying her by proposing. She is all too *keenly aware* of his intentions and wants nothing to do with them.

20. **D**   Mr. Collins breaks off in the middle of a sentence that begins: "Were it certain that Lady Catherine would think so — ." He then finishes it awkwardly by saying, "but I cannot imagine that her ladyship would at all disapprove of you." By implication, his unspoken thought was that, if Lady Catherine *didn't* approve of Elizabeth, then Mr. Collins wouldn't want to marry her after all.

21. **C**   Mr. Collins plans to praise Elizabeth to Lady Catherine in order to ensure Lady Catherine's approval of his bride. Elizabeth insists all such praise will be unnecessary because she *has no intention of marrying Mr. Collins* and thus has no need of Lady Catherine's approval.

22. **B**   *Obtuse* means thick-headed and *obstinate* means stubborn. Both apply to Mr. Collins, who can't seem to understand that Elizabeth is telling him "no."

23. **C**   The author's emphasis is on the elephant as an important "creator of habitat" for other creatures.

24. **D**   The elephant is the architect of its environment in that it *physically alters its environment*, transforming the landscape around it.

25. **C**   To mount an effort to rescue an endangered species is to *launch* or initiate a campaign.

26. **C** The author states that it is the elephant's metabolism and appetite—in other words, its voracity or *ravenous hunger*—that leads to its creating open spaces in the woodland and transforming the landscape.

27. **C** Since the foraging of elephants creates a varied landscape that attracts a diverse group of plant-eating animals and since the presence of these plant-eaters in turn attracts carnivores, it follows that elephants *have an indirect effect on the hunting patterns of carnivores.*

28. **E** You can arrive at the correct answer choice through the process of elimination.
Question I is answerable on the basis of the passage. The elephant's foraging opens up its surroundings by knocking down trees and stripping off branches. Therefore, you can eliminate Choices B and D.
Question II is answerable on the basis of the passage. Gazelles are grazers; giraffes are browsers. Therefore, you can eliminate Choice A.
Question III is answerable on the basis of the passage. The concluding sentence states that when elephants disappear the forest reverts. Therefore, you can eliminate Choice C.
Only Choice E is left. It is the correct answer.

29. **B** The author is listing the many species that depend on the elephant as a creator of habitat. Thus, the host of smaller animals is the *very large number* of these creatures that thrive in the elephant's wake.

30. **C** The author is in favor of the effect of elephants on the environment; he feels an accidental or *fortuitous result* of their foraging is that it allows a greater variety of creatures to exist in mixed-growth environments.

Mathematical Reasoning Section 2

1. **D** $\left(\frac{4}{5} \div \frac{4}{5}\right) = \left(\frac{4}{6} \div \frac{5}{4}\right) = 1$
$\frac{5}{6} \div \frac{5}{6} = 1$
$1 - 1 = 0$

2. **D** Since division by 0 is undefined no value can be obtained if the denominator of the fraction is 0. This occurs if $x = -\frac{5}{3}$. Therefore III cannot be used for x. I and II can; notice that when $x = 0$, the fraction has a value: 0.

3. **E** $\boxed{100} = \frac{\sqrt{100}}{2} = \frac{10}{2} = 5$

4. **A** $\frac{8}{0.8} = \frac{80}{8} = 10$
$\frac{0.8}{8} = \frac{8}{80} = \frac{1}{10}$
$(0.8)^2 = .64$
$\sqrt{0.8} = 0.89$
$0.8\pi = (0.8)(3.14) = 2.5+$

5. **B** Each washer consumes $\left(\frac{3}{32} + \frac{1}{16}\right)$ inch or $\frac{5}{32}$.
$25\frac{1}{2}$ inches $\div \frac{5}{32}$ = number of washers that can be cut
$\frac{51}{2} \div \frac{5}{32}$
$\frac{51}{2} \cdot \overset{16}{\cancel{32}} = \frac{816}{5} = 163\frac{1}{5} = 163$ washers

6. **D** Because $\frac{2}{3}$ was left for the two children and each received $\frac{1}{2}$ of $\frac{2}{3}$, each child received $\frac{1}{3}$. If $\frac{1}{3}$ = \$10,000, the wife also received \$10,000.

7. **C** The sum of two sides of a triangle must be greater than the third side. In (C), $8 + 8 < 17$.

8. **E** Let x equal the quantity desired.
$B = (30\%)(x)$
$B = \frac{30}{100} x$ or $\frac{3}{10} x$
$\left(\frac{10}{3}\right) B = \frac{3}{10} x \left(\frac{10}{3}\right)$
$\frac{10B}{3} = x$

9. **A** 20% or $\left(\frac{1}{5}\right)$ of 2 $= \frac{2}{5}$
$\frac{3}{7} - \frac{2}{5}$
$\frac{15}{35} - \frac{14}{35} = \frac{1}{35}$

10. **C** This is an inverse proportion. Let x = time required when 2 of 8 men are released.
$\frac{8 \text{ men}}{6 \text{ men}} = \frac{x}{12 \text{ days}}$
$6x = 96$
$x = 16$ days
Increase in time = 4 days
$\frac{\text{increase}}{\text{original}} = \frac{4}{12} = \frac{1}{3} = 33\frac{1}{3}\%$

11. **C** Number of girls = $c - b$.
Ratio of girls to boys = $\frac{c-b}{b}$

12. **B** The new number would be 1345.
$4315 - 1345 = 2970$

13. D $x + 2y = 1\frac{1}{3}$ (1)

$+x - y = +\frac{1}{3}$ (2)

$-x + y = -\frac{1}{3}$ [divide (2) by –1] (3)

$x + 2y = 1\frac{1}{3}$ (1)

$3y = 1$ [add (1) and (3)]

14. E   The last digit of the quotient must multiply by 8 to give a product whose last digit is X. $4 \times 8 = 32$ (I); $2 \times 8 = 16$ and $5 \times 8 = 40$ (II); $3 \times 8 = 24$ (III).

15. A $a - x = 1$
$a = x + 1$ (1)
$b + 1 = x$
$b = (x - 1)$ (2)
$ab = (x + 1)(x - 1)$ [multiply (1) and (2)]
$ab = x^2 - 1$

16. E   Let x = radius of original circle.
Then $2x$ = radius of enlarged circle
Area of original circle = πx^2
Area of enlarged circle = $\pi(2x)^2$ or $4\pi x^2$
Area of enlarged circle is four times that of the original circle.

17. C   Let legs = $2x$ and $3x$.

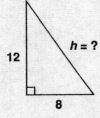

Area = $\dfrac{(2x)(3x)}{2} = 48$

$\dfrac{6x^2}{2} = 48$

$3x^2 = 48$

$x^2 = 16$

$x = 4$

Legs = 8 and 12
Apply the Pythagorean Theorem.
$h^2 = (8)^2 + (12)^2$
$h^2 = 64 + 144 = 208$
$h = \sqrt{208} = \sqrt{16}\sqrt{13} = 4\sqrt{13}$

18. B   The width of the larger frame is 3 feet (36 inches) wide, as compared with 9 inches of the smaller frame. The length must also be four times as much as the 1 foot of the smaller frame, or 4 feet.

19. B   The area of the sector over which the cow may graze is $\frac{24}{360}$ or $\frac{1}{15}$ of the area of the circle with the radius of 15. Since area of circle is $\pi(15)^2$ or 225π, the cow can graze over $\frac{1}{15}$ of 225π or 15π square feet.

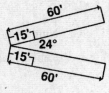

20. C   Area of circle = πr^2
$\pi r^2 = 154$
$\frac{22}{7} r^2 = 154$
$r^2 = (154)\left(\frac{7}{22}\right)$
$r^2 = 49$
$r = 7$
Diameter = 14

21. C   Recall: The line that joins the midpoints of two sides of a triangle is parallel to the third side and equal to one-half of it. Or observe $BDE \sim BAC$, since they have a common angle (B) and the two included sides are proportional.

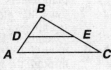

$\dfrac{DE}{AC} = \dfrac{1}{2}$

22. D   Let x = each base angle.
Then the vertex angle = $x + 30°$. Since the sum of the angles of a triangle equals a straight angle.

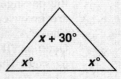

$x + x + x + 30° = 180°$
$3x + 30° = 180°$
$3x = 150°$
$x = 50°$
Vertex angle = $x + 30° = 80°$

23. D   Let $x \overset{\circ}{=} \angle CGH$. Then $4x \overset{\circ}{=} \angle AFE$.
$\angle AFE = \angle CGH$ [corresponding angles]
$\angle CFG = \angle HGD$ [vertical angles]
$\therefore \angle HGD = 4x$
$\angle HGD + \angle CGH \overset{\circ}{=} 180$ [supplementary angles]
or $4x + x \overset{\circ}{=} 180$
$5x \overset{\circ}{=} 180$
$x \overset{\circ}{=} 36$
Then $4x (\angle HGD) \overset{\circ}{=} 144$.

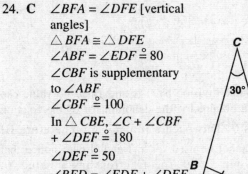

24. C $\angle BFA = \angle DFE$ [vertical angles]
$\triangle BFA \cong \triangle DFE$
$\angle ABF = \angle EDF \overset{\circ}{=} 80$
$\angle CBF$ is supplementary to $\angle ABF$
$\angle CBF \overset{\circ}{=} 100$
In $\triangle CBE$, $\angle C + \angle CBF + \angle DEF \overset{\circ}{=} 180$
$\angle DEF \overset{\circ}{=} 50$
$\angle BFD = \angle EDF + \angle DEF$ (exterior angle)
$\therefore \angle BFD = 50° + 80°$
$\angle BFD \overset{\circ}{=} 130$

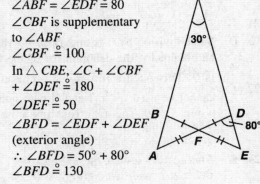

25. **D**   Sum of four examinations = (77.5)(4) = 310
Sum required for average of 80% after five examinations = (80)(5) = 400
Difference (or grade required on fifth test) = 90

Writing Skills Section 3

1. **A**   Error in diction. *Affect* is a verb and should not be used in place of *effect.*

2. **E**   Error in case. The subject of an infinitive (*to be*) should be in the objective case Therefore, change *commissioner and she* to *commissioner and her.*

3. **E**   Sentence is correct.

4. **E**   Sentence is correct.

5. **C**   Error in diction. There is no such verb as *enthuse.* Change *enthused* to *enthusiastic.*

6. **C**   Error in tense. Change *had not* to *shot.*

7. **A**   Error in diction. Use *irritated* instead of *aggravated.*

8. **A**   Incorrect correlative conjunction. Change *neither . . . or* to *neither . . . nor.*

9. **C**   Error in diction. Change *incredulous* to *incredible.*

10. **C**   Error in tense. Change *had broke* to *had broken.*

11. **C**   Error in diction. Change *council* to *counsel.*

12. **C**   Error in agreement. The subject, *Ann Landers,* is singular; the verb should be singular—*is.*

13. **A**   Error in case. The preposition *between* requires the objective case. Therefore, change *you and I* to *you and me.*

14. **D**   Error in diction. Issues are *decided* or settled. The actual choice made is what is *decided upon.* Delete *upon.*

15. **E**   Sentence is correct.

16. **E**   Sentence is correct.

17. **C**   Error in agreement. The subject, *general,* is singular; the verb should be singular—*seems.*

18. **A**   Error in case. The possessive pronoun precedes a gerund. Change *him* to *his.*

19. **D**   Error in tense. Change *was to be immortalized* to *was immortalized.*

20. **E**   The noun or pronoun preceding a gerund (*going*) should be in the possessive case.

21. **E**   The dangling modifier is best corrected in Choice E. Choices B and D introduce an error in tense. Choice C changes the meaning of the sentence.

22. **C**   Choices A and B are run-on sentences. Choices D and E are ungrammatical.

23. **E**   The dangling modifier and the double negative are corrected in Choice E.

24. **E**   The correct use of the subjunctive mood to indicate a condition contrary to fact is found in Choice E.

25. **B**   Choice B expresses the author's meaning directly and concisely. All other choices are indirect, ungrammatical, or fail to retain the meaning of the original statement.

26. **C**   *Kind* should be modified by *this* or *that; kinds,* by *these* or *those.*

27. **C**   Parallel structure is retained in Choice C.

28. **D**   This corrects the sentence fragment smoothly.

29. **B**   The faulty comparison is corrected in Choice B.

30. **C**   Choice C corrects the misplaced modifier and eliminates the unnecessary use of the passive voice.

31. **C**   The phrase *along with his staff* is not part of the subject of the sentence. The subject is *President Clinton* (singular); the verb should be *is traveling* (singular).

32. **B**   The use of the subordinating conjunction. *Although* and the deletion of unnecessary words strengthen this sentence.

33. **D**   Choices A, B, and C have dangling modifiers; Choice E creates a run-on sentence.

34. **D**   Choices A, B, and C abruptly state the contrasting point of view without regard to the context. Choice D takes the context into account and provides for a smooth progression of thought. It is the best answer.
Choice E is confusing. It is unclear until the end of the sentence whether the *other members* support or oppose the exhibit.

35. **D**   Choice A is not consistent in style and mood with the rest of the paragraph.
Choice B is a sentence fragment.
Choice C is excessively wordy.
Choice D fits the context of the paragraph and expresses the idea correctly. It is the best answer.
Choice E inappropriately uses *in conclusion* and contains the pronoun *it,* which lacks a specific referent.

36. **B**   Choice A lacks a main verb; therefore, it is a sentence fragment.
Choice B accurately combines the sentences. It is the best answer.
Choice C is expresses the idea in a way that the writer could not have intended.
Choice D subordinates important ideas and emphasizes a lesser one.
Choice E restates the idea in a manner that changes the writer's intended meaning.

37. **A**   Choice A is the best choice because the sentences contain basic information about the topic. Readers are left in the dark unless the information appears as early as possible in the essay.

38. **E**   Choice A contains faulty idiom; the phrase *than of the past* is nonstandard usage.
Choice B contains a faulty comparison; *society* and *the past* cannot be logically compared.

Choice C contains an error in idiom; the phrase *than from* is redundant.

Choice D is correct but excessively wordy.

Choice E is the best answer.

39. **C**   Choice A provides a reasonable transition, but it contains an error in pronoun-antecedent agreement. The pronoun *they* is plural; its antecedent *anyone* is singular.

Choice B contains an error in diction. One can *disapprove of* but not *disagree with* a piece of art.

Choice C alludes to the content of the previous paragraph and is clearly and succinctly expressed. It is the best answer.

Choice D contains an error in pronoun-antecedent agreement. The pronoun *them* is plural; the antecedent *anyone* is singular.

Choice E is inconsistent in tone and mood with the rest of the essay.

Verbal Reasoning Section 4

31. **B**   A *pebble* is shot from a *slingshot*; a *ball* is shot from a *cannon*.   (Function)

32. **B**   A *latch* is the part of the *door* that closes it; a *clasp* is the part of the *necklace* that closes it.   (Function)

33. **E**   To *drizzle* or rain lightly is less intense than to *pour*; to *smolder* or barely burn is less intense than to *blaze*.   (Degree of Intensity)

34. **D**   A *caption* is a title or explanatory heading for a *photograph*; a *title* is the equivalent for an *article*.   (Function)

35. **D**   To *eradicate* an *error* is to wipe it out or eliminate it; to *uproot* a *weed* is to pull it out or eliminate it.   (Purpose)

36. **C**   A *tyrannosaur* is a kind of *dinosaur*; a *condor* is a kind of *bird*.   (Class and Member)

37. **E**   A *gander* is a male *goose*; a *ram* is a male *sheep*.   (Sex)

38. **D**   An *author* who is *prolific* (highly productive) by definition writes a lot; a *speaker* who is *loquacious* (talkative) by definition talks a lot.   (Defining Characteristic)

39. **D**   *Locomotion* is a function of the *feet*; *digestion* is a function of the *stomach*.   (Function)

40. **D**   A *mentor*, by definition, aims to assist a *protégé*; a *sponsor*, by definition, aims to assist a *candidate*.   (Function)

41. **E**   Something *garbled* or confused is difficult to *comprehend*; something *camouflaged* or hidden is difficult to *discern* or perceive.   (Antonym Variant)

42. **A**   A *traveler* follows an *itinerary* or plan of his or her journey; a *lecturer* follows an *outline* or plan of his or her lecture.   (Worker and Tool)

43. **E**   A *purist* is concerned with strict *correctness*; a *martinet* is concerned with strict *discipline*.   (Defining Characteristic)

44. **C**   The entire passage examines Bethune's beliefs in the ultimate victory of racial justice and in the possibility of winning whites to her cause. In addition, it clearly shows Bethune, in her work to get her people represented in all public programs, having an impact on her people's progress.

45. **D**   You can arrive at the correct answer by the process of elimination. Williams assisted Bethune in influencing the advancement of blacks within the NYA. Therefore, you can eliminate Choices B and D. The opening sentence of the first paragraph indicates Williams was one of Bethune's white friends; references to him in the second paragraph suggest he was a liberal. Therefore, you can eliminate Choice A. Nothing in the passage suggests Williams was religious. Therefore, you can eliminate Choice E. Only Choice D is left. It is the correct answer.

46. **A**   Bethune's success in getting Dickerson's appointment is a clear example of her impact. Choice B is incorrect. The author is stressing how helpful Bethune was to Dickerson, not how different Bethune's career was from Dickerson's. Choice C is incorrect. Dickerson is not the subject of the paragraph that follows. Choice D is incorrect. The author brings up Bethune's belief in the "New Negro" well after he mentions her assistance to Dickerson. He draws no connection between Dickerson and the "New Negro." Choice E is incorrect. The author is making a point about Bethune, not about Dickerson.

47. **E**   Bethune was the intermediary who helped arrange for Dickerson's new position. She was instrumental or *helpful* in gaining this end.

48. **B**   By leading America to a "full realization of its democratic ideas," the New Negro would be *helping America accomplish its egalitarian goals*.

49. **E**   The italicized introduction states that the author has had his manuscript rejected by his publisher. He is consigning or committing it to a desk drawer *to set it aside as unmarketable*.

50. **B**   The rejected author identifies with these baseball players, who constantly must face "failure." *He sees he is not alone in having to confront failure and move on.*

51. **B**   The author uses the jogger's comment to make a point about the *mental impact Henderson's home run must have had on Moore*. He reasons that, if each step a runner takes sends so many complex messages to the brain, then Henderson's ninth-inning home run must have flooded Moore's brain with messages, impressing its image indelibly in Moore's mind.

52. **D**   The author is talking of the impact of Henderson's home run on Moore's mind. Registering in Moore's mind, the home run *made an impression* on him.

53. **C** The author looks on himself as someone who "to succeed at all . . . must perform at an extraordinary level of excellence." This level of excellence, he maintains, is not demanded of accountants, plumbers, and insurance salesmen, and he seems to pride himself on belonging to such a demanding profession. Thus, his attitude to members of less demanding professions can best be described as *superior*.

54. **A** The description of the writer defying his pain and extending himself irrationally to create a "masterpiece" despite the rejections of critics and publishers is a highly romantic one that elevates *the writer as someone heroic in his or her accomplishments*.

55. **C** The author of Passage 2 discusses the advantages of his ability to concentrate. Clearly, he prizes *his ability to focus* on the task at hand.

56. **B** When one football team is ahead of another by several touchdowns and there seems to be no way for the second team to catch up, the outcome of the game appears *decided* or settled.

57. **E** The "larger point of view" focuses on what to most people is the big question: the outcome of the game. The author is indifferent to this larger point of view. Concentrating on his own performance, he is *more concerned with the task at hand than with* winning or losing the game.

58. **C** Parade ground drill clearly does not entirely prepare a soldier for the reality of war. It does so only "to an extent." By using this phrase, the author is *qualifying his statement*, making it less absolute.

59. **C** One would expect someone who dismisses or rejects most comparisons of athletics to art to avoid making such comparisons. The author, however, *is making such a comparison*. This reversal of what would have been expected is an instance of irony.

60. **C** To learn to overcome failure, to learn to give one's all in performance, to learn to focus on the work of the moment, to learn "the selfish intensity needed to create and to finish a poem, a story, or a novel"—these are hard lessons that *both athletes and artists learn*.

Mathematical Reasoning Section 5

26. **A** $\dfrac{(624)(9)(8)}{(4)(3)(2)}$ $\dfrac{(4)(9)(642)}{(5)(4)(2)}$

$1 > \dfrac{1}{5}$

27. **B** $\dfrac{1}{\sqrt{81}} = \dfrac{1}{9}$

$\dfrac{1}{9} < \dfrac{1}{0.9}$ since the fraction with the greater denominator is smaller if the numerators are the same.

28. **D** If $R = 6$, $6R^6 = R^7$ but if R is negative, R^7 is negative and $6R^6$ is positive.

29. **D** $x^2 + y^2 = 61$
x and/or y may be negative, positive, or equal to zero.

30. **C** If $2x + y = 1$, then
$y = 1 - 2x$.

31. **B** $\dfrac{x}{2} \div \dfrac{2}{x}$ or $\dfrac{x}{2} \cdot \dfrac{x}{2} = \dfrac{x^2}{4}$

$\dfrac{x^2}{2} > \dfrac{x^2}{4}$ since x^2 must be positive.

32. **A** $\sqrt{x} > 25$; therefore $x > 5$.

33. **C** Factor $x^2 - y^2$: $(x + y)(x - y)$.

34. **A** Since AB is parallel to CD and $p = m$ [vertical angles] and $p = 60$, $m = 60$. Since $k = 40$, $x = 80$. Since $x = n$ [alternate interior angles of parallel lines], $n = 80$ and $n > m$.

35. **C** Applying the Pythagorean Theorem,
$x^2 + y^2 = z^2$
By subtraction,
$x^2 = z^2 - y^2$.

36. **C** Since the perimeter of the square = 40, each side = 10. ∴ $AB = BE = 10$
Area of $\triangle ABE = \frac{1}{2}(10)(10)$ or 50

37. **A** Since $a = 40$, $b = 50$. Since $c = 50$, $d = 40$. ∴ $b > d$

 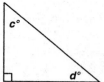

38. **A** $(a + b)^2 = a^2 + 2ab + b^2 = 17$

39. **C** Since $z = 0$, the numerator of the fraction in Column A = 0, and therefore the value of the fraction is zero.

40. **A** If $x^2 - 4x + 4 = 0$, then $(x - 2)^2 = 0$ and $x = 2$. If $\frac{3}{4} y = \frac{4}{3}$, then $y = \frac{16}{9}$. Because $2 > \frac{16}{9}$, $x > y$.

41. **64** Observe the diagram.
Each side equals 8 units.
The area equals 64 square units.

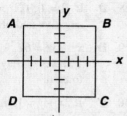

42. **96** At the end of the first half-hour, $\frac{1}{3}$ of 216 or 72 were eliminated, leaving 144 couples. During the second half-hour, $\frac{1}{3}$ of 144 or 48 were eliminated, leaving 96 couples.

43. **3** A distribution of 3 cards in I, 6 in II, and 9 in III will give a 1:2:3 ratio. Therefore, move 3 cards from stack I to stack III.

44. $\frac{1}{15}$ In one day the three of them do $\frac{1}{5}$ of the entire task. In that time each one does $\frac{1}{3}$ of $\frac{1}{5}$ or $\frac{1}{15}$ of the task.

45. **160** This is a direct proportion. Let x = number of tons of ore required to yield 200 pounds of metal.

$$\frac{\text{lbs. of metal}}{\text{tons of ore}} = \frac{1\frac{1}{4}}{1} = \frac{200}{x}$$

$$1\frac{1}{4}\, x = 200$$
$$\frac{5}{4}\, x = 200$$
$$x = 160$$

46. $\frac{3}{5}$ Time elapsed = 36 minutes
$\frac{36}{60} = \frac{3}{5}$ hour

47. **72** See diagram:

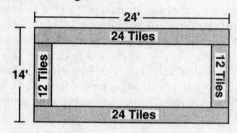

48. **16** Perimeter = 16
Each side = 4
Area = (side)^2 = 16

49. **16** $\angle B$ is inscribed in a semi-circle. Therefore $\angle B$ is a right $\angle$ and $\triangle ABC$ is a right $\triangle$.
Radius OA = 10; diameter (hypotenuse) = 20
Line AB = 12 [given]
$\triangle ABC$ is a 3-4-5 right $\triangle$ with AB = 4(3) and AC = 4(5).
$\therefore BC = 4(4) = 16$.

50. **208** Draw $DE \perp AB$.
Draw $CF \perp AB$.
DC = 20; AE = FB = 6
$\triangle AED$ is a 3-4-5 right triangle with AE = 2(3) and AD = 2(5).
$\therefore DE = 2(4) = 8$.
Area of trapezoid = $\frac{1}{2} h(DC + AB)$
Area of trapezoid = $\frac{1}{2}(8)(52)$
Area of trapezoid = 208

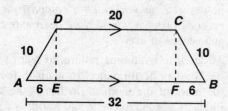

Answer Sheet

TYPICAL TEST F

Each mark should completely fill the appropriate space, and should be as dark as all other marks. Make all erasures complete. Traces of an erasure may be read as an answer. See pages vii and 27 for explanations of timing and number of questions.

Section 1 — Verbal
30 minutes

1 Ⓐ Ⓑ Ⓒ Ⓓ Ⓔ
2 Ⓐ Ⓑ Ⓒ Ⓓ Ⓔ
3 Ⓐ Ⓑ Ⓒ Ⓓ Ⓔ
4 Ⓐ Ⓑ Ⓒ Ⓓ Ⓔ
5 Ⓐ Ⓑ Ⓒ Ⓓ Ⓔ
6 Ⓐ Ⓑ Ⓒ Ⓓ Ⓔ
7 Ⓐ Ⓑ Ⓒ Ⓓ Ⓔ
8 Ⓐ Ⓑ Ⓒ Ⓓ Ⓔ
9 Ⓐ Ⓑ Ⓒ Ⓓ Ⓔ
10 Ⓐ Ⓑ Ⓒ Ⓓ Ⓔ
11 Ⓐ Ⓑ Ⓒ Ⓓ Ⓔ
12 Ⓐ Ⓑ Ⓒ Ⓓ Ⓔ
13 Ⓐ Ⓑ Ⓒ Ⓓ Ⓔ
14 Ⓐ Ⓑ Ⓒ Ⓓ Ⓔ
15 Ⓐ Ⓑ Ⓒ Ⓓ Ⓔ
16 Ⓐ Ⓑ Ⓒ Ⓓ Ⓔ
17 Ⓐ Ⓑ Ⓒ Ⓓ Ⓔ
18 Ⓐ Ⓑ Ⓒ Ⓓ Ⓔ
19 Ⓐ Ⓑ Ⓒ Ⓓ Ⓔ
20 Ⓐ Ⓑ Ⓒ Ⓓ Ⓔ
21 Ⓐ Ⓑ Ⓒ Ⓓ Ⓔ
22 Ⓐ Ⓑ Ⓒ Ⓓ Ⓔ
23 Ⓐ Ⓑ Ⓒ Ⓓ Ⓔ
24 Ⓐ Ⓑ Ⓒ Ⓓ Ⓔ
25 Ⓐ Ⓑ Ⓒ Ⓓ Ⓔ
26 Ⓐ Ⓑ Ⓒ Ⓓ Ⓔ
27 Ⓐ Ⓑ Ⓒ Ⓓ Ⓔ
28 Ⓐ Ⓑ Ⓒ Ⓓ Ⓔ
29 Ⓐ Ⓑ Ⓒ Ⓓ Ⓔ
30 Ⓐ Ⓑ Ⓒ Ⓓ Ⓔ

Section 2 — Math
30 minutes

1 Ⓐ Ⓑ Ⓒ Ⓓ Ⓔ
2 Ⓐ Ⓑ Ⓒ Ⓓ Ⓔ
3 Ⓐ Ⓑ Ⓒ Ⓓ Ⓔ
4 Ⓐ Ⓑ Ⓒ Ⓓ Ⓔ
5 Ⓐ Ⓑ Ⓒ Ⓓ Ⓔ
6 Ⓐ Ⓑ Ⓒ Ⓓ Ⓔ
7 Ⓐ Ⓑ Ⓒ Ⓓ Ⓔ
8 Ⓐ Ⓑ Ⓒ Ⓓ Ⓔ
9 Ⓐ Ⓑ Ⓒ Ⓓ Ⓔ
10 Ⓐ Ⓑ Ⓒ Ⓓ Ⓔ
11 Ⓐ Ⓑ Ⓒ Ⓓ Ⓔ
12 Ⓐ Ⓑ Ⓒ Ⓓ Ⓔ
13 Ⓐ Ⓑ Ⓒ Ⓓ Ⓔ
14 Ⓐ Ⓑ Ⓒ Ⓓ Ⓔ
15 Ⓐ Ⓑ Ⓒ Ⓓ Ⓔ
16 Ⓐ Ⓑ Ⓒ Ⓓ Ⓔ
17 Ⓐ Ⓑ Ⓒ Ⓓ Ⓔ
18 Ⓐ Ⓑ Ⓒ Ⓓ Ⓔ
19 Ⓐ Ⓑ Ⓒ Ⓓ Ⓔ
20 Ⓐ Ⓑ Ⓒ Ⓓ Ⓔ
21 Ⓐ Ⓑ Ⓒ Ⓓ Ⓔ
22 Ⓐ Ⓑ Ⓒ Ⓓ Ⓔ
23 Ⓐ Ⓑ Ⓒ Ⓓ Ⓔ
24 Ⓐ Ⓑ Ⓒ Ⓓ Ⓔ
25 Ⓐ Ⓑ Ⓒ Ⓓ Ⓔ

Section 3 — Writing
30 minutes

1 Ⓐ Ⓑ Ⓒ Ⓓ Ⓔ
2 Ⓐ Ⓑ Ⓒ Ⓓ Ⓔ
3 Ⓐ Ⓑ Ⓒ Ⓓ Ⓔ
4 Ⓐ Ⓑ Ⓒ Ⓓ Ⓔ
5 Ⓐ Ⓑ Ⓒ Ⓓ Ⓔ
6 Ⓐ Ⓑ Ⓒ Ⓓ Ⓔ
7 Ⓐ Ⓑ Ⓒ Ⓓ Ⓔ
8 Ⓐ Ⓑ Ⓒ Ⓓ Ⓔ
9 Ⓐ Ⓑ Ⓒ Ⓓ Ⓔ
10 Ⓐ Ⓑ Ⓒ Ⓓ Ⓔ
11 Ⓐ Ⓑ Ⓒ Ⓓ Ⓔ
12 Ⓐ Ⓑ Ⓒ Ⓓ Ⓔ
13 Ⓐ Ⓑ Ⓒ Ⓓ Ⓔ
14 Ⓐ Ⓑ Ⓒ Ⓓ Ⓔ
15 Ⓐ Ⓑ Ⓒ Ⓓ Ⓔ
16 Ⓐ Ⓑ Ⓒ Ⓓ Ⓔ
17 Ⓐ Ⓑ Ⓒ Ⓓ Ⓔ
18 Ⓐ Ⓑ Ⓒ Ⓓ Ⓔ
19 Ⓐ Ⓑ Ⓒ Ⓓ Ⓔ
20 Ⓐ Ⓑ Ⓒ Ⓓ Ⓔ
21 Ⓐ Ⓑ Ⓒ Ⓓ Ⓔ
22 Ⓐ Ⓑ Ⓒ Ⓓ Ⓔ
23 Ⓐ Ⓑ Ⓒ Ⓓ Ⓔ
24 Ⓐ Ⓑ Ⓒ Ⓓ Ⓔ
25 Ⓐ Ⓑ Ⓒ Ⓓ Ⓔ
26 Ⓐ Ⓑ Ⓒ Ⓓ Ⓔ
27 Ⓐ Ⓑ Ⓒ Ⓓ Ⓔ
28 Ⓐ Ⓑ Ⓒ Ⓓ Ⓔ
29 Ⓐ Ⓑ Ⓒ Ⓓ Ⓔ
30 Ⓐ Ⓑ Ⓒ Ⓓ Ⓔ
31 Ⓐ Ⓑ Ⓒ Ⓓ Ⓔ
32 Ⓐ Ⓑ Ⓒ Ⓓ Ⓔ
33 Ⓐ Ⓑ Ⓒ Ⓓ Ⓔ
34 Ⓐ Ⓑ Ⓒ Ⓓ Ⓔ
35 Ⓐ Ⓑ Ⓒ Ⓓ Ⓔ
36 Ⓐ Ⓑ Ⓒ Ⓓ Ⓔ
37 Ⓐ Ⓑ Ⓒ Ⓓ Ⓔ
38 Ⓐ Ⓑ Ⓒ Ⓓ Ⓔ
39 Ⓐ Ⓑ Ⓒ Ⓓ Ⓔ

Section 4 — Verbal
30 minutes

31 Ⓐ Ⓑ Ⓒ Ⓓ Ⓔ
32 Ⓐ Ⓑ Ⓒ Ⓓ Ⓔ
33 Ⓐ Ⓑ Ⓒ Ⓓ Ⓔ
34 Ⓐ Ⓑ Ⓒ Ⓓ Ⓔ
35 Ⓐ Ⓑ Ⓒ Ⓓ Ⓔ
36 Ⓐ Ⓑ Ⓒ Ⓓ Ⓔ
37 Ⓐ Ⓑ Ⓒ Ⓓ Ⓔ
38 Ⓐ Ⓑ Ⓒ Ⓓ Ⓔ
39 Ⓐ Ⓑ Ⓒ Ⓓ Ⓔ
40 Ⓐ Ⓑ Ⓒ Ⓓ Ⓔ
41 Ⓐ Ⓑ Ⓒ Ⓓ Ⓔ
42 Ⓐ Ⓑ Ⓒ Ⓓ Ⓔ
43 Ⓐ Ⓑ Ⓒ Ⓓ Ⓔ
44 Ⓐ Ⓑ Ⓒ Ⓓ Ⓔ
45 Ⓐ Ⓑ Ⓒ Ⓓ Ⓔ
46 Ⓐ Ⓑ Ⓒ Ⓓ Ⓔ
47 Ⓐ Ⓑ Ⓒ Ⓓ Ⓔ
48 Ⓐ Ⓑ Ⓒ Ⓓ Ⓔ
49 Ⓐ Ⓑ Ⓒ Ⓓ Ⓔ
50 Ⓐ Ⓑ Ⓒ Ⓓ Ⓔ
51 Ⓐ Ⓑ Ⓒ Ⓓ Ⓔ
52 Ⓐ Ⓑ Ⓒ Ⓓ Ⓔ
53 Ⓐ Ⓑ Ⓒ Ⓓ Ⓔ
54 Ⓐ Ⓑ Ⓒ Ⓓ Ⓔ
55 Ⓐ Ⓑ Ⓒ Ⓓ Ⓔ
56 Ⓐ Ⓑ Ⓒ Ⓓ Ⓔ
57 Ⓐ Ⓑ Ⓒ Ⓓ Ⓔ
58 Ⓐ Ⓑ Ⓒ Ⓓ Ⓔ
59 Ⓐ Ⓑ Ⓒ Ⓓ Ⓔ
60 Ⓐ Ⓑ Ⓒ Ⓓ Ⓔ

Section 5 — Math
30 minutes

26 Ⓐ Ⓑ Ⓒ Ⓓ Ⓔ
27 Ⓐ Ⓑ Ⓒ Ⓓ Ⓔ
28 Ⓐ Ⓑ Ⓒ Ⓓ Ⓔ
29 Ⓐ Ⓑ Ⓒ Ⓓ Ⓔ
30 Ⓐ Ⓑ Ⓒ Ⓓ Ⓔ
31 Ⓐ Ⓑ Ⓒ Ⓓ Ⓔ
32 Ⓐ Ⓑ Ⓒ Ⓓ Ⓔ
33 Ⓐ Ⓑ Ⓒ Ⓓ Ⓔ
34 Ⓐ Ⓑ Ⓒ Ⓓ Ⓔ
35 Ⓐ Ⓑ Ⓒ Ⓓ Ⓔ
36 Ⓐ Ⓑ Ⓒ Ⓓ Ⓔ
37 Ⓐ Ⓑ Ⓒ Ⓓ Ⓔ
39 Ⓐ Ⓑ Ⓒ Ⓓ Ⓔ
39 Ⓐ Ⓑ Ⓒ Ⓓ Ⓔ
40 Ⓐ Ⓑ Ⓒ Ⓓ Ⓔ

41
42

43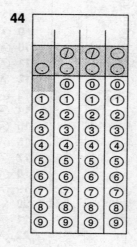
44
45

46
47
48
49
50

SECTION **1**
Verbal Reasoning

Time—30 minutes
30 Questions

For each question in this section, select the best answer from among the choices given and fill in the corresponding oval on the answer sheet.

Directions

Each sentence below has one or two blanks, each blank indicating that something has been omitted. Beneath the sentence are five words or sets of words labeled A through E. Choose the word or set of words that, when inserted in the sentence, <u>best</u> fits the meaning of the sentence as a whole.

Example:

Medieval kingdoms did not become constitutional republics overnight; on the contrary, the change was ____ .

(A) unpopular
(B) unexpected
(C) advantageous
(D) sufficient
(E) gradual
　　　　　　　Ⓐ Ⓑ Ⓒ Ⓓ ●

1. The distinctive qualities of African music were not appreciated or even ____ by Westerners until fairly recently.

(A) deplored   (B) revered   (C) ignored
(D) neglected   (E) perceived

2. Though typically interesting and original in both thought and expression, the author slips occasionally into unfortunate ____ that ____ her presentation.

(A) utterances..clarify   (B) platitudes..enhance
(C) banalities..revitalize   (D) clichés..mar
(E) moods..sustain

3. Even though previous reporters had lampooned the candidate throughout the campaign, he ____ further interviews.

(A) resisted   (B) halted   (C) sidestepped
(D) welcomed   (E) dreaded

4. Our parents expected us to treat our grandparents with proper ____ , paying attention to their wishes and showing respect for their years.

(A) sycophancy   (B) nostalgia   (C) effusiveness
(D) contempt   (E) deference

5. Geologists recognize that tiny ____ in the course of time become mighty chasms.

(A) grievances   (B) molecules   (C) fissures
(D) rivulets   (E) pebbles

6. To the cynic, there are no wholly altruistic, unselfish acts; every human deed is ____ an ulterior selfish motive.

(A) independent of   (B) emulated by
(C) disguised as   (D) founded upon   (E) similar to

7. Some tropical plants emit a ____ odor that has the distinct biological advantage of making them less attractive to potential ____ .

(A) savory..herbivores   (B) distasteful..biologists
(C) rank..predators   (D) fragrant..foragers
(E) fetid..vegetarians

8. Edison's remark that genius is "one percent inspiration and ninety-nine percent perspiration" implies the value of ____ .

(A) eagerness   (B) thoughtfulness
(C) eccentricity   (D) diligence   (E) intuition

9. Lacking a good understanding of what causes chronic pain or a good ____ to measure it, doctors, lawyers, and juries are forced to make largely ____ decisions about which patients will benefit from treatment and which claimants deserve compensation for their suffering.

(A) reason..judicious   (B) yardstick..arbitrary
(C) method..sound   (D) dimension..calculated
(E) authority..irrevocable

10. Whereas off-Broadway theater over the past several seasons has clearly ____ a talent for experimentation and improvisation, one deficiency in the commercial stage of late has been its marked incapacity for ____ .

(A) manifested..spontaneity
(B) accepted..theatricality
(C) cultivated..orthodoxy
(D) disavowed..histrionics
(E) betrayed..burlesque

11. As both a respected scholar in his own field and a leading theorist of evolution, columnist Gould packs a ____ few science writers can ____ .

(A) punch..acknowledge   (B) clout..match
(C) weapon..disarm   (D) prose..describe
(E) bag..carry

12. Unlike the gregarious Capote, who was never happier than when he was in the center of a crowd of celebrities, Faulkner in later years grew somewhat ____ and shunned company.

(A) congenial   (B) imperious   (C) dispassionate
(D) reclusive   (E) ambivalent

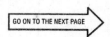

13. You may wonder how the expert on fossil remains is able to trace descent through teeth, which seem ____ pegs upon which to hang whole ancestries.

    (A) novel   (B) reliable   (C) specious
    (D) inadequate   (E) academic

14. She had taken the shocking news quietly, neither ____ fate nor ____ any word of bitterness.

    (A) conspiring with..heeding
    (B) submitting to..denying
    (C) railing against..uttering
    (D) dissenting from..retracting
    (E) mulling over..voicing

15. Having assumed that his wife's annoyance with young Pip would eventually ____ , Joe was startled when she delivered a lengthy ____ on the lad's manifold sins and wickedness.

    (A) escalate..harangue   (B) subside..tirade
    (C) abate..eulogy   (D) die down..refutation
    (E) erupt..discourse

16. Because the diffident young rookie felt out of place among the veteran players, he was ____ socializing with his teammates without an invitation.

    (A) fond of   (B) sanguine about   (C) chary of
    (D) obdurate about   (E) penalized for

17. In the tradition of scholarly ____ , the poet and scholar A.E. Housman once assailed a German rival for relying on manuscripts "as a drunkard relies on lampposts, for ____ rather than illumination."

    (A) animosity..current   (B) discourse..stability
    (C) erudition..shadow   (D) invective..support
    (E) competition..assistance

Directions

Each passage below is followed by questions based on its content. Answer the questions following each passage on the basis of what is <u>stated</u> or <u>implied</u> in that passage and in any introductory material that may be provided.

Questions 18–22 are based on the following passage.

There has been a great deal of scientific discussion about what happens when a star explodes. The following passage describes three types of stellar explosions.

The explosion of a star is an awesome event. The most violent of these cataclysms, which produce supernovae, probably destroys a star completely. Within our galaxy of roughly 100 billion
Line
5 stars the last supernova was observed in 1604. Much smaller explosions, however, occur quite frequently, giving rise to what astronomers call novae and dwarf novae. On the order of 25 novae occur in our galaxy every year, but only
10 two or three are near enough to be observed. About 100 dwarf novae are known altogether. If the exploding star is in a nearby part of the galaxy, it may create a "new star" that was not previously visible to the naked eye. The last new
15 star of this sort that could be observed clearly from the Northern Hemisphere appeared in 1946. In these smaller explosions the star loses only a minute fraction of its mass and survives to explode again.

20 Astrophysicists are fairly well satisfied that they can account for the explosions of supernovae. The novae and dwarf novae have presented more of a puzzle. From recent investigations that have provided important new information
25 about these two classes of exploding star, the picture that emerges is quite astonishing. It appears that every dwarf nova—and perhaps every nova—is a member of a pair of stars. The two stars are so close together that they revolve
30 around a point that lies barely outside the surface of the larger star. As a result the period of rotation is usually only a few hours, and their velocities range upward to within a two-hundredth of the speed of light.

35 Astronomers use the term "cataclysmic variable" to embrace the three general classes of exploding star: dwarf novae, novae, and supernovae. A cataclysmic variable is defined as a star that suddenly and unpredictably increases in
40 brightness by a factor of at least 10. Dwarf novae are stars that increase in brightness by a factor of 10 to 100 within a period of several hours and decline to their former brightness in two or three days. In this period they emit some 10.38 to 10.39
45 ergs of energy. At maximum brilliance a dwarf nova shines about as intensely as our sun; previously it had been only about a hundredth as bright. The number of outbursts ranges anywhere from three to 30 a year, but for any one star the
50 intervals have a fairly constant value. Moreover, the maximum brightness from outburst to outburst is the same within a factor of two for a given star. The dwarf novae are often referred to, after their prototypes, as U Geminorum or SS Cygni stars.
55 (The stars of each constellation are designated by letters or numbers.) A subgroup of dwarf novae, called Z Camelopardalis stars, do not always descend to minimum brightness between outbursts but may stay at some intermediate level for
60 several months.

GO ON TO THE NEXT PAGE →

18. The author's primary purpose in the passage is to

(A) compare the characteristics of novae with those of other stars

(B) explain why supernovae are so much less frequent than novae and dwarf novae

(C) account for the unpredictability of cataclysmic variables as a class

(D) describe the nature and range in scale of cataclysmic variables

(E) explain what happens during the stages of a star's destruction

19. According to the passage, our observations of novae are hampered by their

(A) extreme brightness   (B) loss of mass
(C) speed of rotation   (D) distance from earth
(E) tremendous violence

20. The word "embrace" in line 36 means

(A) clasp   (B) espouse   (C) corroborate
(D) differentiate   (E) include

21. The expression "cataclysmic variable" is an appropriate term for these stars because

(A) they are located at enormously varying distances from Earth

(B) they manifest themselves primarily in times of catastrophe

(C) their explosions differ in intensity and frequency

(D) astronomers can view them only under conditions of great difficulty

(E) they represent a particularly puzzling class of star

22. The passage provides information that would answer which of the following questions?

I. In what century were astronomers last able to observe the explosion of a supernova?

II. Why do the Z Camelopardalis stars remain at intermediate levels of brightness after some outbursts?

III. How rapidly after outburst do dwarf novae achieve their maximum level of brilliance?

(A) I only   (B) III only   (C) I and II only
(D) I and III only   (E) II and III only

Questions 23–30 are based on the following passage.

The following passage is from a book written by a New Mexico garlic farmer and novelist that was published in 1992.

The first summers at the Santa Fe and Los Alamos markets were trying. A customer who later became a friend described how I would sit or pace
Line   behind my little stand of onions and garlic, a tall
5   and forbidding presence, an angry or despairing
expression clouding my face. In fact, I was miserable. I was a solitary island of self-absorbed gloom surrounded by people buying and selling and having a good time at it. Eventually, after suf-
10   ficient pain, I learned to busy myself when things were slow by straightening the stand or the back of the truck and chatting with neighboring farmer-sellers. Eventually I learned not to put my ego out there on the stand with my produce, and to engage
15   with my customers as people, not as money dispensers, and to pay attention to what they were saying—or rather, how they were uttering the stock phrases and platitudes that accompany any exchange. It took me several seasons to see the
20   markets as places of sociability and conviviality, and thus as relief from the more regimented and solitary aspects of the farm. And as I relaxed, customers began to feel at ease and would stop to chat and browse through the produce. Whether
25   they bought or not became less important. What they were looking for or needed or liked or disliked became more interesting, and even whether they wanted to be pitched to or not, along with all those other signals they will emit, saying every-
30   thing from "I know exactly what I want" or "I just want to know how much I owe you" to "I need somebody to talk to."

At one of the markets not long ago I asked a twelve-year-old friend to mind the stand while his
35   father and I settled down on the tailgate to catch up with each other's news. There was a lull and I knew the boy was capable of dealing with the odd half-pound of garlic that might now and then be handed to him to weigh and price. But he object-
40   ed. In a slightly panicky voice, he said, "I've never sold anything before."

At his age, and even much later, it would have been my protest as well. In our society the young are trained early to buy. Selling comes later. We
45   also subscribe to the fiction that it's not something everybody has to do, preferring to think of ourselves as only buyers and consumers. Most people are perhaps unaware of the degree to which working at a job or a profession is selling
50   yourself by the hour, the week, the month, the year—no different in essence than selling yourself by the ounce, the pound, the ton, in tens of thousands of separate transactions individually conducted, face-to-face.

55   A taint of disrepute haunts all exchange, perhaps because most exchange is seen as inequitable or fraudulent or magical—or manipulated from afar by powerful interests and laden with hidden costs, overhead, kickbacks. The specialist at the
60   pinnacle of a professional career need never see the cash or checks that are banked in his name. It might be good social therapy if the analyst of the soul or the surgeon of the heart were obliged in

GO ON TO THE NEXT PAGE

65 person to receive fee and to write out receipt, so that it would remain clear throughout who was at whose service.

All this circles around the question of how to make a living—or more interestingly, an honest living, or a relatively honest living, in these times.

70 All human livings in industrial society are ultimately based on agricultural production and mineral extraction. One of the ways these processes are transferred upward and outward is through endless cycles of buying and selling. Which is to

75 say that one cannot live in this kind of world without being involved in these cycles, nearly or remotely. Something of this was in my mind when I decided to go back to peddling our produce off the back of the truck at the markets. I

80 wanted to be closer to an elemental process of human society, one which I had regarded with a degree of middle-class daintiness. Unconsciously, like many, I had aspired to the condition of always being a buyer, never a seller, always an

85 eater, never a washer of dishes, always a wearer of clothes, never a washer of laundry, which was why I found it so painful at first to be out there on the front line, on the other side of the business.

23. The author attributes his initial unhappiness at the market in large part to his

(A) self-preoccupation   (B) lack of training
(C) physical discomfort   (D) fear of competition
(E) need for money

24. By "sufficient pain" (lines 9–10) the author implies that

(A) the pain he had was more than enough to satisfy his masochistic tendencies
(B) it took him time and unhappiness before he could learn to change his ways
(C) he felt he did not deserve the unhappiness he had endured
(D) the other people at the market decided he had suffered enough
(E) any pain at all is far too much to bear

25. In lines 13–19, the author most likely describes the changes in his interactions with his customers in order to

(A) show how challenging the task of a salesperson can be
(B) reveal his motivation for becoming a garlic farmer
(C) indicate the adjustments the seller must make to meet the buyer's demands
(D) convey the importance of the social element in every transaction
(E) convince the reader of the improvement in his social skills

26. The phrase "pitched to" in line 28 means

(A) hurled at   (B) tilted toward
(C) played with   (D) fixed in place
(E) talked into buying

27. The word "odd" in line 37 means

(A) uneven   (B) occasional   (C) unpaired
(D) peculiar   (E) mysterious

28. The author's attitude toward the twelve-year-old's reaction to his request (lines 42–43) is one of

(A) righteous indignation
(B) grudging respect
(C) outright censure
(D) condescending amusement
(E) sympathetic comprehension

29. The reason the author thinks it would be good social therapy for surgeons and analysts to receive their fees in person (lines 61–66) is because many such professionals

(A) are fundamentally anti-social in nature
(B) act as if they're doing their patients a favor
(C) advocate a hands-on approach to therapy
(D) worry too little about collecting their fees
(E) lack skill in conducting financial transactions

30. In the final paragraph the author comes to realize that

(A) he too has been guilty of holding himself superior to those who take part in selling
(B) he no longer has the need to prove himself by peddling his produce in the marketplace
(C) not everyone is able to share his personal involvement in these elemental processes
(D) it is demeaning to engage in trade only if money is one's sole object
(E) he has the potential to develop his skills as a salesman without doing so at the expense of others

IF YOU FINISH BEFORE 30 MINUTES, YOU MAY CHECK YOUR WORK ON THIS SECTION ONLY. DO NOT TURN TO ANY OTHER SECTION IN THE TEST.   **S T O P**

<table>
<tr><td>

SECTION **2**
Mathematical Reasoning

</td><td>

Time—30 minutes
25 Questions

</td></tr>
</table>

Directions and Reference Information

In this section solve each problem, using any available space for scratchwork. Then decide which is the best of the choices given and fill in the corresponding oval on the answer sheet.

Notes:

(1) The use of a calculator is permitted. All numbers used are real numbers.

(2) Figures that accompany problems in this test are intended to provide information useful in solving the problems. They are drawn as accurately as possible EXCEPT when it is stated in a specific problem that the figure is not drawn to scale. All figures lie in a plane unless otherwise indicated.

Reference Information

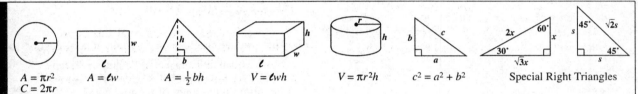

$A = \pi r^2$ $A = \ell w$ $A = \frac{1}{2}bh$ $V = \ell wh$ $V = \pi r^2 h$ $c^2 = a^2 + b^2$ Special Right Triangles
$C = 2\pi r$

The number of degrees of an arc in a circle is 360.
The measure in degrees of a straight angle is 180.
The sum of the measures in degrees of the angles of a triangle is 180.

---

1. How much more is $\frac{1}{3}$ of $\frac{1}{4}$ than $\frac{1}{4}$ of $\frac{1}{12}$?

   (A) $\frac{1}{4}$ (B) $\frac{1}{16}$ (C) $1\frac{2}{3}$ (D) 3   (E) 4

2. If $a^2 - b^2 = 36$ and $a - b = 4$, what is the value of $2a + 2b$?

   (A) 9   (B) 12   (C) 14   (D) 16   (E) 18

3. $\dfrac{5 + \frac{3}{4}}{1 - \frac{13}{36}}$ equals the square of what number?

   (A) $\sqrt{3}$ (B) $2\frac{1}{4}$ (C) 3   (D) 9   (E) 81

4. What is the largest integer that is a factor of all three of the following numbers: 2160, 1344, 1440?

   (A) 6   (B) 8   (C) 12   (D) 16   (E) 48

5. $n! = n(n-1)(n-2)(n-3) \ldots 1$

   In the product above n represent some positive integer and the three dots represent the missing factors in the product of all consecutive integers from n to 1, inclusive. Which of the following expressions is equivalent to $\dfrac{(n+1)!}{(n-1)!}$?

   (A) $n^2 + n$ (B) $n^2 - n$ (C) $n^2 - 1$

   (D) $n^2 + 1$ (E) $n^3 + n$

6. $2^x = \dfrac{\sqrt[4]{81}}{\sqrt{18}}$; $x =$

   (A) -1 (B) $-\frac{1}{2}$ (C) 0   (D) $\frac{1}{2}$ (E) 1

7. A man earns d dollars each week and spends s dollars a week. In how many weeks will he have Q dollars?

   (A) $\dfrac{ds}{Q}$ (B) $\dfrac{Q}{ds}$ (C) $\dfrac{Q}{s-d}$

   (D) $\dfrac{Q}{d-s}$ (E) $\dfrac{d-s}{Q}$

8. What percent of k is 10?

(A) $10k$ (B) $\dfrac{k}{10}$ (C) $\dfrac{10}{k}$

(D) $\dfrac{1000}{k}$ (E) $\dfrac{k}{1000}$

9. If 2 items are sold for 6¢, how many of these items can be bought for 36¢

(A) 6   (B) 12   (C) 18   (D) 36   (E) 72

10. During the drama society's performance in a school auditorium, with 750 seats in the orchestra and 400 seats in the balcony, $\dfrac{2}{3}$ of the seats in the orchestra and $\dfrac{3}{8}$ of the seats in the balcony are sold. What part of all the seats are left unsold?

(A) $\dfrac{10}{23}$ (B) $\dfrac{13}{23}$ (C) $\dfrac{23}{24}$ (D) $\dfrac{24}{25}$ (E) $\dfrac{13}{25}$

11. History of First-Class Letter Rates

1885–1917	2 cents	December 31, 1975	13 cents
1917–1919 (war years)	3 cents	May 29, 1978	15 cents
1919	2 cents	March 22, 1981	18 cents
July 6, 1932	3 cents	November 1, 1981	20 cents
August 1, 1958	4 cents	February 17, 1985	22 cents
January 7, 1963	5 cents	April 3, 1988	25 cents
January 7, 1968	6 cents	February 3, 1991	29 cents
May 16, 1971	8 cents	January 1, 1995	32 cents
March 2, 1974	10 cents		

The percentage increase of letter rates in 1978 as compared with the rate in 1932 was

(A) 8%   (B) 12%   (C) 40%
(D) 80%   (E) 400%

12. Flight #602 left Kennedy Airport at 1:00 P.M. and traveled south at an average rate of 200 miles per hour. Flight #302 left from the same point one-half hour later and traveled west at 320 miles per hour. How far apart are these planes at 4:00 P.M.?

(A) 1000 miles   (B) 1200 miles
(C) 1400 miles   (D) 1600 miles
(E) 2800 miles

13. Three men own a business establishment in the ratio of 19:5:3. What part of the total business does the man with the smallest interest control?

(A) 3%   (B) 9%   (C) 11.1%
(D) 16.6%   (E) 88.8%

14. If $x + y = 16$, what does $x - z$ equal?

(A) $z + 16$ (B) 8   (C) $16 - y$
(D) $z(16 - y)$ (E) $16 - y - z$

15. If a and b are positive integers and $\dfrac{a-b}{3.5} = \dfrac{4}{7}$, then which of the following is (are) correct?

I. $b < a$
II. $b \geq a$
III. $b \leq a$

(A) I only   (B) II only   (C) III only
(D) I and III only   (E) I, II and III

16. 10^x means that 10 is to be used as a factor x times, and 10^{-x} means $\dfrac{1}{10^x}$. Very large and very small numbers, therefore, are frequently written as decimals multipled by 10^x, where x is a positive or a negative integer. All of the following are correct EXCEPT

(A) $470,000 = 4.7 \times 10^5$
(B) 450 billion $= 4.5 \times 10^{11}$
(C) $0.00000000075 = 7.5 \times 10^{-10}$
(D) 86 hundred-thousandths $= 8.6 \times 10^{-2}$
(E) 26 million $= 2.6 \times 10^7$

17. The graduating class of a certain school desires to leave as a memorial two prizes of $50 each to be awarded annually for the two best essays. What is the minimum amount of money that must be invested in 10% bonds to ensure the necessary income?

(A) $1000   (B) $10,000   (C) $4000
(D) $5000   (E) more than $10,000

18. A farmer has enough feed to take care of 60 chickens for 8 days. How long will this feed last if he purchases 20 additional chickens?

(A) 2 days   (B) 5 days   (C) 6 days
(D) $10 \dfrac{2}{3}$ days   (E) 24 days

19. A rectangular fish tank 25" by 9" has water in it to a level of 2". This water is carefully poured into a cylindrical container with a diameter of 10". How high (in terms of π) will the water reach in the cylindrical container?

(A) 18π (B) $\dfrac{\pi}{18}$ (C) $\dfrac{18}{\pi}$ (D) $\dfrac{9}{2\pi}$ (E) $\dfrac{9\pi}{2}$

20. AB and CD are chords of a circle intersecting at E. If $\overset{\frown}{AD} = 60°$ and $\angle AED \triangleq 45$, what is the measure of $\angle EDB$?

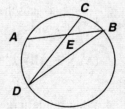

(A) 15°   (B) 20°   (C) 30°
(D) 45°   (E) 60°

GO ON TO THE NEXT PAGE

21. If $\boxed{\times}$ is defined by the equation $x\boxed{\times}y = x + xy + y$ for all numbers x and y, what is the value of a if $8\boxed{\times}a = 3$?

(A) –5   (B) $-\frac{5}{9}$ (C) $\frac{3}{8}$ (D) $\frac{5}{9}$ (E) 5

22. $\angle BAD = \angle CAD$, $BA = BC$, $DA = DC$, and $\angle B \triangleq 120$. $\angle ADC$ has a measure of

(A) 60°   (B) 120°
(C) 150°   (D) 160°
(E) 165°

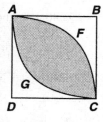

23. $ABCD$ is a square of side 10. AFC is an arc of a circle with the center at D. AGC is an arc of a circle with the center at B. Which of the following correctly express(es) the area of the shaded portion?

   I. $50\pi - 100$
  II. $100 - 50\pi$
 III. $100\pi - 100$

(A) I only   (B) II only   (C) III only
(D) I and III only   (E) I, II and III

24. This graph represents the assets of a savings bank. For which of these assets would the measure of the central angle be about 100 degrees?

(A) Mortgages   (B) Bonds
(C) Cash on Hand   (D) Stocks
(E) Other Assets

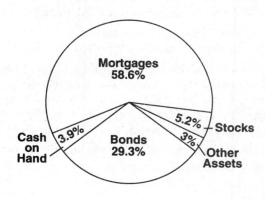

This graph represents data collected from six cities showing the average maximum and the average minimum temperatures for a 12-month period.

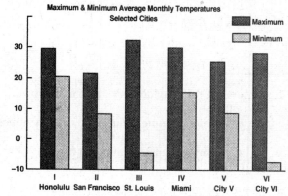

25. Of the following, which location has the highest average maximum monthly temperature?
(A) I   (B) II   (C) III   (D) IV   (E) V

IF YOU FINISH BEFORE 30 MINUTES, YOU MAY CHECK YOUR WORK ON THIS SECTION ONLY. DO NOT TURN TO ANY OTHER SECTION IN THE TEST.

S T O P

SECTION 3
Writing Skills

Time—30 minutes
39 Questions

Directions

The following sentences contain problems in grammar, usage, diction (choice of words), and idiom.

    Some sentences are correct.
    No sentence contains more than one error.

You will find that the error, if there is one, is underlined and lettered. Assume that elements of the sentence that are not underlined are correct and cannot be changed. In choosing answers, follow the requirements of standard written English.

If there is an error, select the <u>one underlined part</u> that must be changed to make the sentence correct and blacken the corresponding space on your answer sheet.

If there is no error, blacken answer space Ⓔ .

Example:
    The region has a climate <u>so severe that</u> plants
                      A

    <u>growing there</u> rarely <u>had been</u> more than twelve
        B   C

    inches <u>high</u>. <u>No error</u>
         D   E

Ⓐ Ⓑ ● Ⓓ Ⓔ

1. As <u>some of</u> the conglomerates gain more power,
   A   B
the legal codes <u>regarding</u> bankruptcy and monopoly
            C
<u>will need</u> further consideration. <u>No error</u>
   D   E

2. In 1777, the Second Continental Congress

<u>has adopted</u> a resolution <u>to designate</u> the design
    A   B
for the American flag, <u>but</u> no flags were issued
                C
<u>until</u> 1783. <u>No error</u>
   D   E

3. The Joneses moved to Arizona <u>because</u> <u>they</u>
                  A   B
thought the climate in that state <u>was</u> very <u>healthful</u>.
                  C   D

<u>No error</u>
 E

4. He <u>dashed into</u> the burning building, <u>irregardless</u> of
     A   B
the risk <u>involved</u>, to warn the <u>sleeping occupants</u>.
       C   D
<u>No error</u>
 E

5. <u>According to</u> Ms. Lynch's portfolio, <u>there</u> is little
   A   B
doubt that she and her staff <u>is</u> <u>eminently qualified</u>
                C   D
for the assignment. <u>No error</u>
            E

6. Neither the Republican members of the committee

<u>who</u> supported the proposed legislation <u>or</u> the
 A   B
Democratic members who opposed it controlled

a <u>clear majority</u>; the votes of the independents
    C
<u>were</u> crucial. <u>No error</u>
 D   E

7. <u>No one</u> can predict <u>what</u> the <u>affect</u> of the
   A   B   C
Iran-Contra disclosures <u>will be</u> on American
                 D
politics in the near future. <u>No error</u>
                 E

8. <u>In order to</u> give adequate attention to all students,
   A
many teachers <u>prefer</u> team teaching, <u>which</u> divides
        B   C
students according to <u>his and her</u> abilities. <u>No error</u>
           D   E

9. I was <u>irritated by you</u> coming into the room <u>as you</u>
      A   B   C
did—<u>shouting</u> and screaming. <u>No error</u>
     D   E

10. He <u>has lain</u> down his book and is sleeping; <u>reading</u>
     A   B
in a <u>dimly lit</u> room can be <u>very</u> tiring. <u>No error</u>
    C   D   E

11. He worked <u>very hard</u> in order to <u>provide</u> for <u>their</u>
        A   B   C
family's comfort <u>and</u> his children's educations.
           D
<u>No error</u>
 E

12. That <u>kind of a</u> compromise is repugnant to me
     A
<u>because</u> <u>it</u> violates the basic <u>principles</u> of our party.
   B   C   D
<u>No error</u>
 E

GO ON TO THE NEXT PAGE

13. Just <u>like</u> prehistoric man, some <u>groups of</u> south-
    　　　A　　　　　　　　　　　　　　B
    western Indians <u>have dwelled</u> in caves along
    　　　　　　　　　C
    <u>steep, rocky</u> ledges. <u>No error</u>
    　　　D　　　　　　　　E

14. I <u>find</u> that sculpture <u>more unusual</u> <u>than</u> any of the
    　　A　　　　　　　　B　　　　C
    other sculptures exhibited <u>during</u> this special exhibit.
    　　　　　　　　　　　　D

    <u>No error</u>
    　　E

15. <u>One</u> of the basic economic reactions is <u>that</u> as
    　A　　　　　　　　　　　　　　　　　B
    bond prices fall, stock prices <u>rise</u>, and
    　　　　　　　　　　　　　　C
    <u>an increase in interest rates.</u> <u>No error</u>
    　　　　　D　　　　　　　　　E

16. Some of the major networks <u>have created</u>
    　A　　　　　　　　　　　B
    <u>special prepared</u> news stories about life on city
    　　　C
    streets <u>to publicize</u> the plight of the homeless.
    　　　　　D

    <u>No error</u>
    　　E

17. <u>Some women</u> have made a <u>clear-cut choice</u>
    　　A　　　　　　　　　　B
    between a career and motherhood; others have

    <u>been creating</u> a <u>balance between</u> the two. <u>No error</u>
    　　C　　　　　　　D　　　　　　　　E

18. The renter of the car <u>initialed</u> the clause in the contract
    　　　　　　　　　　A
    <u>to show</u> that he was <u>aware</u> that he <u>was liable</u> for the
    　B　　　　　　　　C　　　　　　D
    first fifty dollars of any damages to the automobile.

    <u>No error</u>
    　　E

19. The population explosion, <u>rather</u> unexpected
    　　　　　　　　　　　　　A
    <u>according to</u> educators, <u>have caught</u> them at a
    　　B　　　　　　　　C
    disadvantage with <u>a dearth of</u> classrooms.
    　　　　　　　　　D

    <u>No error</u>
    　　E

20. <u>If I would have realized</u> the danger involved in this assignment, I would not have asked you to undertake it.

    (A) If I would have realized
    (B) If I should have realized
    (C) If I had realized
    (D) When I realized
    (E) Because I did not realize

21. The <u>imminent historian stood</u> in bed, recuperating from a viral infection, while his paper was being read at the convention.

    (A) imminent historian stood
    (B) imminent historian remained
    (C) eminent historian stayed
    (D) eminent historian stood
    (E) eminent historian had remained

22. At the zoo, the brightly-plumaged <u>birds that fluttered</u> overhead like tropical flowers in a breeze.

    (A) birds that fluttered
    (B) birds fluttering
    (C) birds which fluttered
    (D) birds fluttered
    (E) birds aflutter

GO ON TO THE NEXT PAGE ⇨

23. In India, Mahatma Gandhi was more than a political leader he was the enlightened one embodying the soul of the nation.

    (A) political leader he was
    (B) political leader; he was
    (C) political leader, he was
    (D) political leader which was
    (E) political leader, although he was

24. When the National Association for the Advancement of Colored People examined discrimination in the music business recently, its report concentrating on offstage employment opportunities.

    (A) its report concentrating on offstage employment opportunities
    (B) its report having concentrated on offstage employment opportunities
    (C) its report concentrated on offstage employment opportunities
    (D) its report concentrating in offstage employment opportunities
    (E) its report concentrated in offstage employment opportunities

25. Some doctors volunteer to serve the poor in addition to their regular practices, they find healing the poor provides different insights than healing the rich.

    (A) Some doctors volunteer to serve the poor in addition to their regular practices, they find
    (B) Besides their regular practices, some doctors serve the poor to find
    (C) In addition to running their regular practices, some doctors volunteer to serve the poor; they find that
    (D) Some doctors, in volunteering to serve the poor, find
    (E) Running their regular practices and serving the poor help some doctors realize that

26. Because of a teacher shortage in the math and science disciplines, educators are encouraging retired scientists and engineers to pursue a second career in teaching.

    (A) Because of a teacher shortage in the math and science disciplines, educators are encouraging
    (B) Educators, faced with a teacher shortage in technical disciplines have encouraged
    (C) In addition to a teacher shortage in the math and science areas, educators encourage
    (D) Teacher shortages in the math and science disciplines have forced educators to hire
    (E) Because there is a teacher shortage in the math and science disciplines, educators encourage

27. Neither the principal or the teachers had been satisfied with the addition of a crossing guard, and wanted a traffic light installed at the street crossing.

    (A) Neither the principal or the teachers had been satisfied with the addition of a crossing guard, and
    (B) Neither the principal nor the teachers were satisfied with the addition of a crossing guard; they
    (C) Because neither the principal or the teachers had been satisfied with the addition of a crossing guard, they
    (D) As a result of the addition of a crossing guard, the principal and the teachers
    (E) Neither the principal nor the teachers feels the crossing guard is sufficient; and they

28. Most of the students like to read these kind of detective stories for their supplementary reading.

    (A) these kind of detective stories
    (B) these kind of detective story
    (C) this kind of detective story
    (D) this kinds of detective story
    (E) those kind of detective story

29. Because of his throat ailment, the tenor has not and apparently never will sing again.

    (A) had not and apparently never will sing
    (B) has not sung and apparently never will sing
    (C) has not and apparently never would sing
    (D) has not sung and apparently never will sing
    (E) had not and apparently never will sing

30. Having the best record for attendance, the school awarded him a medal at graduation.

    (A) the school awarded him a medal
    (B) the school awarded a medal to him
    (C) he was awarded a medal by the school
    (D) a medal was awarded to him by the school
    (E) a school medal was awarded to him

31. Several regulations were proposed by the president of the university that had a sexist bias, according to women students.

    (A) Several regulations were proposed by the president of the university that
    (B) Several regulations were proposed by the president of the university who
    (C) The proposal of several regulations by the president of the university which
    (D) The president of the university, who proposed several regulations that
    (E) The president of the university, proposed several regulations that

GO ON TO THE NEXT PAGE

32. The difference between the candidates is that <u>one is radical; the other, conservative.</u>

    (A) one is radical; the other, conservative
    (B) one is radical; the other being conservative
    (C) while one is radical; the other, conservative
    (D) one is radical, the other, conservative
    (E) one is radical, although the other is more conservative

33. Police academies, <u>on seeing as how new recruits lack basic driving skills, are teaching</u> recruits the basics on test fields and neighborhood streets.

    (A) Police academies, on seeing as how new recruits lack basic driving skills, are teaching
    (B) Since new police recruits lack basic driving skills, police academies are teaching
    (C) Police academies, because new recruits are lacking basic driving skills, teach
    (D) As a result of new recruits lacking basic driving skills, police academies are teaching
    (E) Even though new recruits lack basic driving skills, police academies are teaching

---

Directions

The passage below is the unedited draft of a student's essay. Some of the essay needs to be rewritten to make the meaning clearer and more precise. Read the essay carefully.

The essay is followed by six questions about changes that might improve all or part of its organization, development, sentence structure, use of language, appropriateness to the audience, or its use of standard written English. Choose the answer that most clearly and effectively expresses the student's intended meaning. Indicate your choice by filling in the corresponding space on the answer sheet.

Essay

[1] For two hundred years United States citizens have taken for granted their right to life, liberty, and the pursuit of happiness. [2] From the experiences in the former Yugoslavia to the repressive regime in the People's Republic of China, Americans should know, however, that human rights are always in danger.

[3] During the period of the conquistadores and Spanish colonial rule of Latin America, for example. [4] Latin American natives were often violated and repressed by European settlers, an example of this is the fact that the land formerly owned by the native Latin Americans was taken away from them so the people lost the right to own land. [5] Secondly, the Latin American people were forced to work this land as slaves on their own land. [6] These human rights violations were overcome by the

independence movements led by such freedom fighters as Bolivar and San Martin in the late 1800s.

[7] In the Soviet Union, the extremely repressive Stalinist regime after WW II violated the rights of the Russian peasants, known as kulaks. [8] Collectivizing their farmlands by force, their rights were violated by Stalin. [9] Therefore, their private possessions were lost. [10] Another way by which they had their human rights violated was by forcing political opponents to remain silent, to work in labor camps, or to be killed. [11] After Stalin's death in 1953, one of his successors, Nikita Kruschev, attempted to denounce the Stalinist regime. [12] However, it took another thirty years and the collapse of the Soviet Union to bring about basic human rights in Russia.

[13] About the history of human rights violations, the Serbs in the former Yugoslavia and the leaders of Communist China should know that they can't go on forever. [14] Eventually, their power will be usurped, or the people will rise up to claim their God-given human rights.

34. Taking into account the sentences which precede and follow sentence 3, which of the following is the best revision of sentence 3?

    (A) As an example, the time that the Spanish were expanding their empire and searching for gold.
    (B) Take, for example, during the era of the conquistadores and Spanish colonial rule in Latin America.
    (C) Consider, for example, the period of the conquistadores and Spanish colonial rule in Latin America.
    (D) The Spanish expanded their empire into Latin America in the 16th century.
    (E) For instance, the period of Spanish colonialism in Latin America, for example.

35. Which of the following is the best revision of sentence 4?

    (A) The land of Latin American natives was confiscated by European settlers. In fact, the rights of the natives to own land was violated and repressed.
    (B) European settlers in Latin America have seized the land and the natives had repressed the right to own property.
    (C) The colonial rulers confiscated the natives' property and denied them the right to own land.
    (D) Having their rights violated, the natives of Latin America had their land taken away. Then the European settlers repress their right to own any land at all.
    (E) The rights of the Latin American natives were violated and repressed. For example, they took their land and they prohibited them from owning land.

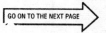

GO ON TO THE NEXT PAGE

36. In the context of paragraph 3, which is the best revision of sentences 8 and 9?

   (A) Forcing them to collectivize their farmlands, Stalin confiscated their private property.

   (B) One of the ways by which Stalin violated their rights was by forcing people to collectivize their farmlands, thus causing them to lose their right to hold private possessions.

   (C) One way in which the kulaks had their rights violated was Stalin forcing them to collectivize their farmlands and therefore, surrender private property.

   (D) Having lost the right to own private property, Stalin collectivized the kulaks' farmland.

   (E) The loss of private property and the collectivization of farmland was one way by which Stalin violated their rights.

37. Which of the following is the best revision the underlined segment of sentence 10 below?

Another way by which they had their human rights violated was by forcing political opponents to remain silent, to work in labor camps, or to be killed.

   (A) A second method by which political opponents had their human rights violated was

   (B) Stalin also violated the human rights of political opponents

   (C) Stalin also violated human rights

   (D) Stalin's violation of the human rights of political opponents was

   (E) Political opponents' human rights were also violated by Stalin

38. Considering the content of the entire essay, which revision of the underlined segment of sentence 13 below provides the best transition between paragraphs 3 and 4?

About the history of human rights violations, the Serbs in the former Yugoslavia and the leaders of Communist China should know that they can't go on forever.

   (A) In conclusion,

   (B) Finally,

   (C) Last but not least,

   (D) Based on the history of international agreements on human rights,

   (E) If the experience of Latin America and the Soviet Union means anything,

39. Based on the essay as a whole, which of the following describes the writer's intention in the last paragraph?

   (A) To draw a conclusion based on the evidence in the passage

   (B) To prepare readers for the future

   (C) To instruct readers about the past

   (D) To offer solutions to the problem posed by the essay

   (E) To give an example

IF YOU FINISH BEFORE 30 MINUTES, YOU MAY CHECK YOUR WORK ON THIS SECTION ONLY. DO NOT TURN TO ANY OTHER SECTION IN THE TEST. **S T O P**

SECTION **4**
Verbal Reasoning

**Time—30 minutes
30 Questions**

For each question in this section, select the best answer from among the choices given and fill in the corresponding oval on the answer sheet.

Directions

Each sentence below consists of a related pair of words or phrases, followed by five pairs of words or phrases labeled A through E. Select the pair that best expresses a relationship similar to that expressed in the original pair.

Example:

CRUMB:BREAD::
(A) ounce:unit
(B) splinter:wood
(C) water:bucket
(D) twine:rope
(E) cream:butter

31. LAWN:MOWER::

    (A) forest:timber   (B) flower:petal
    (C) garden:weed   (D) nail:clipper
    (E) corral:fence

32. AUDIT:BOOKS::

    (A) hear:records   (B) inspect:buildings
    (C) publish:texts   (D) perform:plays
    (E) distribute:films

33. BOBBIN:THREAD::

    (A) swatch:fabric   (B) sweater:yarn
    (C) shoe:lace   (D) bow:string
    (E) reel:tape

34. BUNGALOW:BUILDING::

    (A) cathedral:chapel   (B) engine:automobile
    (C) dinghy:boat   (D) index:book   (E) flap:tent

35. LAIR:BEAR::

    (A) fang:rattlesnake   (B) viper:reptile
    (C) vixen:fox   (D) pack:wolf
    (E) burrow:rabbit

36. HEFTY:WEIGHT::

    (A) lofty:height   (B) narrow:distance
    (C) thin:texture   (D) olfactory:smell
    (E) agile:bulk

37. DEPOSE:MONARCH::

    (A) propose:suitor   (B) dismiss:employee
    (C) defend:claim   (D) support:candidate
    (E) deride:heckler

38. ARSONIST:CONFLAGRATION::

    (A) kleptomaniac:arrest   (B) thug:assault
    (C) felon:collusion   (D) pyromaniac:burial
    (E) orator:mob

39. PENSIVE:REFLECT::

    (A) retiring:exhaust   (B) melancholy:gladden
    (C) unruly:disobey   (D) irate:pacify
    (E) tactful:offend

40. SPECTACLES:SEEING::

    (A) dictaphone:speaking   (B) paper:writing
    (C) hurdles:running   (D) flippers:swimming
    (E) manacles:freeing

41. ENIGMATIC:TEXT::

    (A) reckless:conduct   (B) wordy:prose
    (C) brusque:manner   (D) obscure:remark
    (E) cursory:investigation

42. APLOMB:NONCHALANT::

    (A) composure:indefatigable
    (B) wariness:petulant   (C) disdain:unworthy
    (D) affability:cordial   (E) ardor:indifferent

43. JUGGERNAUT:UNSTOPPABLE::

    (A) catastrophe:unnatural
    (B) turncoat:treacherous
    (C) charlatan:knowledgeable
    (D) killjoy:insufferable
    (E) astronaut:robust

The passage below is followed by questions based on its content. Answer the questions following the passage on the basis of what is <u>stated</u> or <u>implied</u> in that passage and in any introductory material that may be provided.

Questions 44–48 are based on the following passage.

The following passage on American popular songs is excerpted from a magazine article written in 1991 by the novelist E.L. Doctorow.

With Tin Pan Alley, songs became a widely distributed industrial spiritual product. The standards that emerged from this manufactory release us into a flow of imagery that whirls us through
Line our decades, our eras, our changing landscape.
5   For a long while industrialized America looks back longingly at its rural past: "When You Were Sweet Sixteen," it sighs, "In the Evening by the

GO ON TO THE NEXT PAGE ➔

Moonlight," "On the Banks of the Wabash," "In
the Good Old Summertime." Then the spirit
changes; defiance, rebelliousness is encoded in
the sophistications of the double entendre: "(You
Can Go as Far as You Like With Me) In My
Merry Oldsmobile," "There'll Be a Hot Time (In
the Old Town, Tonight)," "It Don't Mean a Thing
If It Ain't Got That Swing."

When a song is a standard it can reproduce
itself from one of its constituent parts. If you
merely recite the words you will hear the melody.
If you hum the melody the words will articulate
themselves in your mind. This is an indication of
an unusual self-referential power—the physical
equivalent would be regeneration of a severed
limb, or cloning an entire being from one cell.
Standards from every period of our lives remain
cross-indexed in our brains to be called up in
whole, or in part, or, in fact, to come to mind
unbidden. Nothing else can as suddenly and
poignantly evoke the look, the feel, the smell of
our times past. We use standards in the privacy of
our minds as signifiers of our actions and relationships. They can be a cheap means of therapeutic
self-discovery. If, for example, you are deeply in
love and thinking about her and looking forward
to seeing her, pay attention to the tune you're
humming. Is it "Just One of Those Things"? You
will soon end the affair.

Of Great Songs, the men who wrote them will
tell you their basic principle of composition. Keep
it simple. The simpler, the better. You want
untrained voices to handle it in the shower, in the
kitchen. Try to keep the tune in one octave. Stick
with the four basic chords and avoid tricky
rhythms. They may not know that this is the aesthetic of the church hymn. They may not know
that hymns were the first hits. But they know that
hymns and their realm of discourse ennoble or
idealize life, express its pieties, and are in themselves totally proper and appropriate for all ears.
And so most popular ballads are, in their characteristic romanticism, secularized hymns.

The principle of keeping it simple suggests
why many standards sound alike. One might even
say a song can't become a standard unless it is
reminiscent of existing standards. Maybe this is
why we feel a new good song has the characteristic of seeming, on first hearing, always to have
existed. In a sense it has. Just as we in our own
minds seem to have always existed, regardless of
the date of our birth. A standard suggests itself as
having been around all along, and waiting only
for the proper historical moment in which to
reveal itself.

When people say "our song," they mean they
and the song exist together as some sort of gener-
ational truth. They are met to make a common

destiny. The song names them, it rescues them
from the accident of a historical genetic existence.
They are located in cultural time. A crucial event,
a specific setting, a certain smile, a kind of lingo,
a degree of belief or skepticism, a particular
humor, or a dance step goes with the song. And
from these ephemera we make our place in civilization. For good or bad, we have our timely
place.

44. From the song titles in lines 7–16, we can see that
double entendres have two meanings, one of which
is often

(A) industrial   (B) historical   (C) sexual
(D) philosophic   (E) geographic

45. The word "standard" in line 17 refers to

(A) a distinctive banner
(B) a model for personal behavior
(C) an authoritative rule for composing songs
(D) a well-established musical piece
(E) carefully drawn manufacturing specifications

46. From lines 36–37, we can infer that the song "Just
One of Those Things" most likely describes

(A) a single encounter in a relationship
(B) an instance of self-discovery
(C) the termination of a love affair
(D) an unwelcome revelation
(E) an ongoing profound attachment

47. Would-be composers most probably are given the
advice to keep things simple (lines 39–40)

(A) because the author assumes complexity is
    beyond their current level of ability
(B) so that their tunes will appeal to the majority of
    the population
(C) to set them apart from most composers of con-
    temporary music
(D) as a challenge to their ability to adapt their
    musical styles to meet different needs
(E) because the author personally dislikes intricate
    pieces of music

48. According to lines 67–72, the songs we adopt

(A) are the product of purely commercial forces
(B) are fictional substitutes for the truth
(C) prepare us to meet accidents and sudden disasters
(D) help define us and evoke the attitudes of our age
(E) are hackneyed responses to rapidly-evolving
    situations

GO ON TO THE NEXT PAGE

The passages below are followed by questions based on their content; questions following a pair of related passages may also be based on the relationship between the paired passages. Answer the questions on the basis of what is stated or implied in the passages and in any introductory material that may be provided.

Questions 50–60 are based on the following passages.

The following passages are excerpted from recent works that discuss the survival of the city in our time. Passage 1 was written by a literary critic and philosopher; Passage 2, by an urban planner and sociologist.

PASSAGE 1

When musing on cities over time and in our time, from the first (whenever it was) to today, we must always remember that cities are artifacts.
Line Forests, jungles, deserts, plains, oceans—the
5 organic environment is born and dies and is reborn endlessly, beautifully, and completely without moral constraint or ethical control. But cities—despite the metaphors that we apply to them from biology or nature ("The city dies when
10 industry flees"; "The neighborhoods are the vital cells of the urban organism"), despite the sentimental or anthropomorphic devices we use to describe cities—are artificial. Nature has never made a city, and what Nature makes that may
15 seem like a city—an anthill, for instance—only *seems* like one. It is not a city.

Human beings made and make cities, and only human beings kill cities, or let them die. And human beings do both—make cities and unmake
20 them—by the same means: by acts of choice. We enjoy deluding ourselves in this as in other things. We enjoy believing that there are forces out there completely determining our fate, natural forces— or forces so strong and overwhelming as to be like
25 natural forces—that send cities through organic or biological phases of birth, growth, and decay. We avoid the knowledge that cities are at best works of art, and at worst ungainly artifacts—but never flowers or even weeds—and that we, not some
30 mysterious force or cosmic biological system, control the creation and life of a city.

We control the creation and life of a city by the choices and agreements we make—the basic choice being, for instance, not to live alone, the
35 basic agreement being to live together. When people choose to settle, like the stars, not wander like the moon, they create cities as sites and symbols of their choice to stop and their agreement not to separate. Now stasis and proximity, not move-
40 ment and distance, define human relationships. Mutual defense, control of a river or harbor, shelter from natural forces—all these and other reasons may lead people to aggregate, but once congregated, they then live differently and become
45 different.

A city is not an extended family. That is a tribe or clan. A city is a collection of disparate families who agree to a fiction: They agree to live *as if*
50 they were as close in blood or ties of kinship as in fact they are in physical proximity. Choosing life in an artifact, people agree to live in a state of similitude. A city is a place where ties of proximity, activity, and self-interest assume the role of
55 family ties. It is a considerable pact, a city. If a family is an expression of continuity through biology, a city is an expression of continuity through will and imagination—through mental choices making artifice, not through physical
60 reproduction.

PASSAGE 2

It is because of this centrality [of the city] that the financial markets have stayed put. It had been widely forecast that they would move out en masse, financial work being among the most
65 quantitative and computerized of functions. A lot of the back-office work has been relocated. The main business, however, is not record keeping and support services; it is people sizing up other people, and the center is the place for that.

70 The problems, of course, are immense. To be an optimist about the city, one must believe that it will lurch from crisis to crisis but somehow survive. Utopia is nowhere in sight and probably never will be. The city is too mixed up for that. Its
75 strengths and its ills are inextricably bound together. The same concentration that makes the center efficient is the cause of its crowding and the destruction of its sun and its light and its scale.
80 Many of the city's problems, furthermore, are external in origin—for example, the cruel demographics of peripheral growth, which are difficult enough to forecast, let alone do anything about.

What has been taking place is a brutal simplifi-
85 cation. The city has been losing those functions for which it is no longer competitive. Manufacturing has moved toward the periphery; the back offices are on the way. The computers are already there. But as the city has been losing
90 functions it has been reasserting its most ancient one: a place where people come together, face-to-face.

More than ever, the center is the place for news and gossip, for the creation of ideas, for market-
95 ing them and swiping them, for hatching deals, for starting parades. This is the stuff of the public life of the city—by no means wholly admirable, often abrasive, noisy, contentious, without apparent purpose.

GO ON TO THE NEXT PAGE →

100   But this human congress is the genius of the place, its reason for being, its great marginal edge. This is the engine, the city's true export. Whatever makes this congress easier, more spontaneous, more enjoyable is not at all a frill. It is
105   the heart of the center of the city.

49. The author's purpose in Passage 1 is primarily to

(A) identify the sources of popular discontent with cities
(B) define the city as growing out of a social contract
(C) illustrate the difference between cities and villages
(D) compare cities with blood families
(E) persuade the reader to change his behavior

50. The author cites the sentence "The neighborhoods are the vital cells of the urban organism" (lines 10–11) as

(A) an instance of prevarication
(B) a simple statement of scientific fact
(C) a momentary digression from his central thesis
(D) an example of one type of figurative language
(E) a paradox with ironic implications

51. The author's attitude toward the statements quoted in lines 7–13 is

(A) respectful   (B) ambivalent   (C) pragmatic
(D) skeptical   (E) approving

52. According to the author of Passage 1, why is an ant hill by definition unlike a city?

(A) It can be casually destroyed by human beings.
(B) Its inhabitants outnumber the inhabitants of even the largest city.
(C) It is the figurative equivalent of a municipality.
(D) It is a work of instinct rather than of imagination.
(E) It exists on a far smaller scale than any city does.

53. Mutual defense, control of waterways, and shelter from the forces of nature (lines 42–43) are presented primarily as examples of motives for people to

(A) move away from their enemies
(B) build up their supplies of armament
(C) gather together in settlements
(D) welcome help from their kinfolk
(E) redefine their family relationships

54. We can infer from lines 35–40 that roving tribes differ from city dwellers in that these nomads

(A) have not chosen to settle in one spot
(B) lack ties of activity and self-interest
(C) are willing to let the cities die
(D) have no need for mutual defense
(E) define their relationships by proximity

55. By saying a city "is a considerable pact" (line 55), the author primarily stresses

(A) its essential significance
(B) its speculative nature
(C) the inevitable agreement
(D) the moral constraints
(E) its surprising growth

56. To the author of Passage 1, to live in a city is

(A) an unexpected outcome
(B) an opportunity for profit
(C) an act of volition
(D) a pragmatic solution
(E) an inevitable fate

57. Underlying the forecast mentioned in lines 2–4 is the assumption that

(A) the financial markets are similar to the city in their need for quantitative data
(B) computerized tasks such as record keeping can easily be performed at remote sites
(C) computerized functions are not the main activity of these firms
(D) the urban environment is inappropriate for the proper performance of financial calculations
(E) either the markets would all move or none of them would relocate

58. The word "scale" in line 79 means

(A) series of musical tones
(B) measuring instrument
(C) relative dimensions
(D) thin outer layer
(E) means of ascent

59. The "congress" referred to in line 101 is

(A) a city council
(B) the supreme legislative body
(C) a meeting of minds
(D) an enjoyable luxury
(E) an intellectual giant

60. The author of Passage 2 differs from the author of Passage 1 in that he

(A) argues in favor of choosing to live alone
(B) disapproves of relocating support services to the outskirts of the city
(C) has no patience with the harshness inherent in public life
(D) believes that in the long run the city as we know it will not survive
(E) is more outspoken about the city's difficulties

IF YOU FINISH BEFORE 30 MINUTES, YOU MAY CHECK YOUR WORK ON THIS SECTION ONLY. DO NOT TURN TO ANY OTHER SECTION IN THE TEST.   **S T O P**

SECTION 5
Mathematical Reasoning

**Time—30 minutes
25 Questions**

Directions and Sample Questions

Notes:

(1) The use of a calculator is permitted. All numbers used are real numbers.

(2) Figures that accompany problems in this test are intended to provide information useful in solving the problems. They are drawn as accurately as possible EXCEPT when it is stated in a specific problem that the figure is not drawn to scale. All figures lie in a plane unless otherwise indicated.

Questions 1–15 each consist of two quantities in boxes, one in Column A and one in Column B. You are to compare the two quantities and on the answer sheet fill in oval

A if the quantity in Column A is greater;
B if the quantity in Column B is greater;
C if the two quantities are equal;
D if the relationship cannot be determined from the information given.

Notes:

1. In some questions, information is given about one or both of the quantities to be compared. In such cases, the given information is centered above the two columns and is not boxed.
2. In a given question, a symbol that appears in both columns represents the same thing in Column A as it does in Column B.
3. Letters such as x, n, and k stand for real numbers.

EXAMPLES		
Column A	Column B	Answers
E1 5^2	20	● Ⓑ Ⓒ Ⓓ
150° $x°$		
E2 x	30	Ⓐ Ⓑ ● Ⓓ
r and s are integers.		
E3 $r + 1$	$s - 1$	Ⓐ Ⓑ Ⓒ ●

PART I: QUANTITATIVE COMPARISON QUESTIONS

SUMMARY DIRECTIONS FOR QUANTITATIVE COMPARISON QUESTIONS

Answer: A if the quantity in Column A is greater.   C if the two quantities are equal.
         B if the quantity in Column B is greater.   D if the relationship cannot be determined from the information given.

	Column A	Column B
	$\dfrac{(7)(7)(21)}{x} = (7)(3)$	
26.	21	x
27.	$\sqrt{\dfrac{1}{4}}$	$(0.25)^2$
	$2^{n+1} = 32$	
28.	n	5

	Column A	Column B
	Length of a diameter of circle O equals the length of a diagonal of square $ABCD$.	
29.	Area of circle O	Area of square $ABCD$
	$x^2 - y^2 = 0$	
30.	$x + y$	0
31.	$\dfrac{a + b}{b}$	$\dfrac{a}{b} + 1$

GO ON TO THE NEXT PAGE

	Column A	Column B		Column A	Column B

$a + 3 = 5$
$b + 3 = 7$

32. $b - a$ a

City A is 10 miles from City B
and City C is 5 miles from City B.

33.   Distance from   15 miles
City A to City C

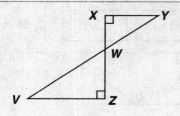

34.   The average of a, b, and c x

$XY = 8$, $WY = 10$, $VZ = 16$
$ZX \perp XY$ and $XZ \perp VZ$

35.   Length of XWZ $XY + WY$

$abc = 0$ and $a = 1$

36.   1 bc

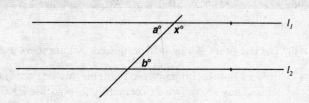

$a + b = 110°$

37. x 110

$4x > 3y$

38. x y

$a^4 = b^4$ $(a, b \neq 0)$

39. a^2b ab^2

x is an integer.

40.   The maximum value   11
of $10 - x^2$

GO ON TO THE NEXT PAGE

PART II: STUDENT-PRODUCED RESPONSE QUESTIONS

Directions for Student-Produced Response Questions

Each of the remaining ten questions (41–50) requires you to solve the problem and enter your answer by marking the ovals in the special grid, as shown in the examples below.

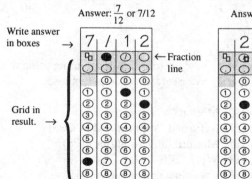

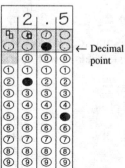

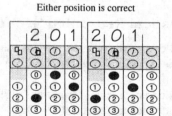

Note: You may start your answers in any column, space permitting. Columns not needed should be left blank.

- Mark no more than one oval in any column.

- Because the answer sheet will be machine-scored, **you will receive credit only if the ovals are filled in correctly.**

- Although not required, it is suggested that you write your answer in the boxes at the top of the columns to help you fill in the ovals accurately.

- Some problems may have more than one correct answer. In such cases, grid only one answer.

- No question has a negative answer.

- **Mixed numbers** such as $2\frac{1}{2}$ much be gridded as 2.5 or 5/2. (If $\boxed{2\,1/2}$ is gridded, it will be interpreted as $\frac{21}{2}$, not $\frac{21}{2}$.)

- Decimal Accuracy: If you obtain a decimal answer, enter the most accurate value that the grid will accommodate. For example, if you obtain an answer such as 0.6666..., you should record the result as .666 or .667. Less accurate values such as .66 or .67 are not acceptable.

Acceptable ways to grid $\frac{2}{3}$ = .6666. . .

41. What part of $3.00 is a dime?

42. A school now has a registration of $850, which represents a $6\frac{1}{4}$% increase over the previous year. What was the registration in the previous year?

43. Three boys have marbles in the ratio of 19:5:3. If the boy with the least number has 9 marbles, how many marbles does the boy with the greatest number have?

44. A bowler has an average of 150 points a game for 12 games. If he bowls 6 more games, how high an average must he make in these games to raise his average for the 18 games to 160?

45. On a certain map the scale is given as 1 inch = 1 mile. A boy copies the map, making each dimension three times as large as the given dimensions. On his map how many miles will 6 inches represent?

46. A store is selling two brands of hose. One brand is marked "$4 a pair." The other brand sells for $3 a pair. How many combinations of these two brands can be purchased for $25 without receiving change?

47. *AOC* is a diameter of circle *O*. $\angle BAC \stackrel{\circ}{=} 30$. $\overset{\frown}{BC} = \overset{\frown}{CD}$. How many degrees are there in the measure of $\overset{\frown}{AD}$?

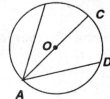

48. *AD* = 10, AE = 8, $\angle B = \angle C \stackrel{\circ}{=} 45$. What does *BC* equal?

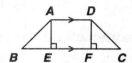

49. The base of a 39-foot ladder is placed 15 feet from a building which is 200 feet tall. How many feet up the building will the ladder extend?

50. A box was made in the form of a cube. If a second cubical box has inside dimensions three times those of the first box, how many times as much does it contain?

IF YOU FINISH BEFORE 30 MINUTES, YOU MAY CHECK YOUR WORK ON THIS SECTION ONLY. DO NOT TURN TO ANY OTHER SECTION IN THE TEST.

STOP

ANSWER KEY

Verbal Reasoning Section 1

1. E	6. D	*11.* B	16. C	21. C	26. E
2. D	7. C	*12.* D	17. D	22. D	27. B
3. D	8. D	*13.* D	18. D	23. A	28. E
4. E	9. B	*14.* C	19. D	24. B	29. B
5. C	*10.* A	*15.* B	20. E	25. D	30. A

Mathematical Reasoning Section 2

Note: Each correct answer to the mathematics questions is keyed by number to the corresponding topic in Chapters 8 and 9. These numerals refer to the topics listed below, with specific page references in parentheses.

1. Basic Fundamental Operations (179–182)
2. Algebraic Operations (182–183)
3. Using Algebra (182–184, 187)
4. Exponents, Roots, and Radicals (184–185)
5. Inequalities (188–189)
6. Fractions (182, 198)
7. Decimals (200)
8. Percent (200)
9. Averages (201)
10. Motion (203)
11. Ratio and Proportion (204–205)
12. Mixtures and Solutions (178)
13. Work (206–207)
14. Coordinate Geometry (194)
15. Geometry (189–193, 195)
16. Quantitative Comparisons (211–212)
17. Data Interpretation (208)

1. B (1, 6)	6. B (4)	*11.* E (8)	16. D (4, 7)	21. B (2)
2. E (3)	7. D (2)	*12.* A (10)	17. A (2)	22. C (15)
3. C (1, 6)	8. D (8)	*13.* C (11)	18. C (11)	23. A (2, 15)
4. E (1)	9. B (11)	*14.* E (2)	19. C (15)	24. B (8, 15)
5. A (3)	*10.* A (6)	*15.* A (5)	20. A (15)	25. C (17)

Writing Skills Section 3

1. E	8. D	*15.* D	22. D	29. D	36. A
2. A	9. B	16. C	23. B	30. C	37. C
3. E	*10.* A	17. C	24. C	*31.* E	38. E
4. B	*11.* C	18. E	25. C	32. A	39. A
5. C	*12.* A	19. C	26. A	33. B	
6. B	*13.* E	20. C	27. B	34. C	
7. C	*14.* E	21. C	28. C	35. C	

Verbal Reasoning Section 4

31. D	36. A	*41.* D	46. C	51. D	56. C
32. B	37. B	42. D	47. B	52. D	57. B
33. E	38. B	43. B	48. D	53. C	58. C
34. C	39. C	44. C	49. B	54. A	59. C
35. E	40. D	45. D	50. D	55. A	60. E

Mathematical Reasoning Section 5

26. B (6, 16)	29. A (15, 16)	32. C (2, 16)	35. C (15, 16)	38. D (5, 16)
27. A (4, 5, 7, 16)	30. D (2, 16)	33. D (15, 16)	36. A (2, 16)	39. D (3, 16)
28. B (4, 16)	*31.* C (2, 16)	34. C (15, 16)	37. A (15, 16)	40. B (4, 16)

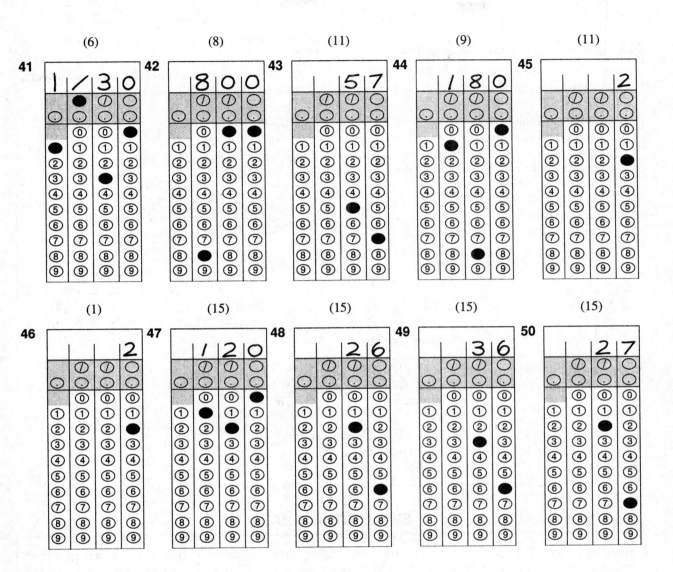

SCORING CHART — TYPICAL TEST F

Verbal Sections

Section 1   Questions 1–30
Number correct   _____ (A)
Number omitted   _____ (B)
Number incorrect   _____ (C)
$1/4$ (C) =   _____ (D)
Raw Score:
  (A) – (D) =   _____

Section 3   Questions 31–60
Number correct   _____ (A)
Number omitted   _____ (B)
Number incorrect   _____ (C)
$1/4$ (C) =   _____ (D)
Raw Score:
  (A) – (D) =   _____

Total Verbal Raw Score:
  (Section 1 +
  Section 3) =   _____

Mathematical Sections

Section 2   Questions 1–25
Number correct   _____ (A)
Number incorrect   _____ (B)
(A) – $1/4$ (B) =   _____ Raw Score I

Section 4   Questions 26–40
Number correct   _____ (C)
Number incorrect   _____ (D)
(C) – $1/3$ (D) =   _____ Raw Score II

Section 4   Questions 41–50
Number correct   _____ Raw Score III

Total Mathematical Raw Score:
  (Raw Scores I + II
  + III) =   _____

Writing Section

Section 3   Questions 1–39
Number correct   _____ (A)
Number incorrect   _____ (B)
$1/4$ (B) =   _____ (C)
(no penalty for omitted questions)
Writing Raw Score:
  (A) – (C) =   _____

EVALUATION CHART

Study your score. Your raw score on the Verbal and Mathematical Reasoning Sections is an indication of your probable achievement on the PSAT/NMSQT. As a guide to the amount of work you need or want to do with this book, study the following.

Raw Score			Self-rating
Verbal	*Mathematical*	*Writing*	
55–60	41–50	37–39	Superior
44–54	25–40	31–36	Very good
39–43	20–24	25–30	Satisfactory
35–38	16–19	19–24	Average
29–34	10–15	13–18	Needs further study
20–28	7–9	6–12	Needs intensive study
0–19	0–6	0–5	Probably inadequate

ANSWER EXPLANATIONS

Verbal Reasoning Section 1

1. **E** The phrase "or even" indicates that the missing word is less intense than "appreciated," yet not negative, because the speaker's attitude is favorable toward African music. *Perceived* fits the sentence, while Choice B, *revered*, would be too positive and the other choices too negative.

2. **D** *Though* signals a contrast. The author is usually an original writer. However, sometimes she falls into *clichés* (hackneyed, trite expressions) that damage or *mar* what she writes.

3. **D** In contrast to what might have been expected, the candidate *welcomed* further interviews. Note how the use of "even though" indicates a contrast between one idea and another, setting up a reversal of thought.

4. **E** To show respect for one's elders is to pay them proper *deference* (courteous regard).

5. **C** *Fissures* are small cracks. "Chasms," which some fissures turn into, are gorges or ravines.

6. **D** To the cynic (a person who expects nothing but the worst of human actions and motives), human actions are *founded* or based upon selfish motives.

7. **C** Biologically, it would be an advantage *not* to attract *predators* (animal that preys on or devours other creatures); a *rank* or offensive smell that drives off its predators would be advantageous to a plant.

8. **D** *Diligence* is steady effort or energy: when you work with diligence you tend to produce perspiration.

9. **B** People need some sort of *yardstick* (literally, a stick one yard long; figuratively, a standard for measurement) to measure pain. Without such a standard, they wind up making *arbitrary*, unsupported decisions about the treatment and compensation of individuals suffering from pain.

10. **A** The off-Broadway and Broadway theaters are contrasted here. The former has *manifested* or shown a talent for improvisation, extemporaneous or spontaneous performance. The latter has manifested no such talent for *spontaneity*. Note the use of "whereas" to establish the contrast.

11. **B** Because he is so highly respected, Gould packs a *clout* (wields an influence; has an impact) few other science writers can *match*.

12. **D** Capote was *gregarious* or social and companionable; since Faulkner is contrasted with him, Faulkner must have been *reclusive*, preferring to lead a solitary life.

13. **D** If "you may wonder" how the expert reaches his or her conclusions, it appears that it is questionable to rely on teeth for guidance in interpreting fossils. Choice D, *inadequate*, creates the element of doubt that the clause tries to develop. Choice C, *specious*, also creates an element of doubt; however, nothing in the context justifies the idea that the reasoning is specious or false. Note that here you are dealing with an extended metaphor. Picture yourself hanging a heavy winter coat on a slim wooden peg. Wouldn't you worry that the peg might prove inadequate or flimsy?

14. **C** To *rail against* fate would be to complain angrily about it or utter words of bitterness about it. Note how the use of parallel structure (*neither . . . nor*) indicates that the two principal phrases linked together are similar in meaning.

15. **B** The key word here is *startled.* Joe assumes that his wife's annoyance with Pip will lessen or *subside* in time. Surprisingly, it does not: she delivers a long *tirade* (harshly critical speech) on the boy's misdeeds.

16. **C** *Because* signals cause and effect. The new player feels as if he doesn't belong among the veterans. For this reason, he is *chary* or cautious about hanging around with them uninvited.

17. **D** The key word here is *assailed.* Housman is attacking his rival. Thus he is in the tradition of scholarly *invective* (vehement verbal attack). He criticizes his foe for turning to manuscripts merely for confirmation or *support* of old theories and not for enlightenment or illumination. Note the use of figurative language, in this case the simile of a drunkard leaning against a post.

18. **D** The author states what cataclysmic variables are and describes how the three general classes of exploding stars range in magnitude and other characteristics. Choice A is incorrect. The author gives far more emphasis to dwarf novae than to novae. Choice B is incorrect. The author offers no such explanation. Choice C is incorrect. He states their unpredictability; he does not explain or account for it. Choice E is incorrect. The author offers no such explanation.

19. **D** In the first paragraph, it says "25 novae occur in our galaxy every year, but only two or three are *near enough* to be observed." Thus, our observations of novae are hampered by their *distance.*

20. **E** In embracing three general classes of exploding star, the term *includes* them all.

21. **C** *Cataclysmic* means relating to violent explosions. *Variable* means changing. Cataclysmic variables were given their name because *their explosions differ in intensity and frequency.*

22. **D** You can arrive at the correct answer by the process of elimination. Question I is answerable on the basis of the passage. Line 5 states that the last supernova was observed in 1604. Therefore, you can eliminate Choices B and E. Question II is unanswerable on the basis of the passage. No reason for the phenomenon is given in the passage. Therefore, you can eliminate Choice C. Question III is answerable on the basis of the passage. Lines 40–42 state that dwarf novae increase in brightness "within a period of several hours" and then decline from this maximum level of brilliance over a period of two to three days. Therefore, you can eliminate Choice A. Only Choice D is left. It is the correct answer.

23. **A** Describing himself as "a solitary island of self-absorbed gloom," the author clearly attributes his initial unhappiness at the market in large part to his self-absorption or *self-preoccupation.*

24. **B** The author had to go through a certain amount of *time and unhappiness* before he was ready to get over his self-absorption and change his ways.

25. **D** In describing how he learned to deal with his customers as people, to chat with them and meet their human, social needs, the author *conveys the importance of the social element in every transaction.*

26. **E** If a customer is unwilling to be "pitched to," he is reluctant to have the salesperson deliver his sales pitch. In other words, the customer doesn't want to be *talked into buying* anything.

27. **B** Because of the pause or lull in shopping, the author doesn't expect the boy to have to sell very much. The lad would only have to weigh and price an *occasional* or odd half-pound of garlic.

28. **E** By saying that, as a teenager, he would have reacted in the same way his friend's son did ("'I've never sold anything before'. . . would have been my protest as well"), the author shows he is both sympathetic and understanding.

29. **B** By never having to see or touch the physical cash and checks with which their patients purchase their services, surgeons and analysts seem to hold themselves above their customers, acting *as if they're doing their patients a favor* by treating them, when, instead, the doctors should be at their patients' service.

30. **A** The author states that "unconsciously . . . (he) had aspired to the condition of always being a buyer, never a seller." In other words, he too had *been guilty of holding himself superior to those who take part in selling.*

Mathematical Reasoning Section 2

1. **B** $\frac{1}{3}$ of $\frac{1}{4}$ $= \frac{1}{12} = \frac{4}{48}$

   $\frac{1}{4}$ of $\frac{1}{12}$ $= \frac{1}{48}$

   $\frac{4}{48} - \frac{1}{48} = \frac{3}{48} = \frac{1}{16}$

2. **E** Because $(a - b)(a + b) = a^2 - b^2$,

   $a + b = \dfrac{a^2 - b^2}{a - b} = \dfrac{36}{4} = 9$

   Hence, $2a + 2b = 2(a + b) = 2(9) = 18.$

3. **C** $\dfrac{5\frac{3}{4}}{1 - \frac{13}{36}} = \dfrac{5\frac{3}{4}}{\frac{23}{36}} = \dfrac{\frac{23}{4}}{\frac{23}{36}} = \dfrac{23}{4} \div \dfrac{23}{36} = \dfrac{23}{\cancel{4}} \cdot \dfrac{\cancel{36}^{9}}{\cancel{23}} = 9$

   $(?)^2 = 9$

   $? = 3$

4. **E** Since 2160, 1344, and 1440 are divisible by the largest number (48), the correct answer is (**E**). It may be easier to discover that all are divisble by both 6 and 8, and hence by 48, without actually dividing by 48.

5. **A** $\dfrac{(n + 1)!}{(n - 1)!} = \dfrac{(n + 1)n \cancel{(n - 1)!}^{1}}{\cancel{(n - 1)!}}$

   $= (n + 1)n$

   $= n^2 + n$

6. **B** $\sqrt[4]{81} = 3$

   $\sqrt{18} = \sqrt{9}\sqrt{2} = 3\sqrt{2}$

   $2^x = \dfrac{3}{3\sqrt{2}} = \dfrac{1}{\sqrt{2}} = 2^{-\frac{1}{2}}$

   $2^x = 2^{-\frac{1}{2}}$

   $x = -\dfrac{1}{2}$

7. **D** He saves $d - s$ dollars per week.

   In $\dfrac{Q}{d - s}$ weeks he will have Q dollars.

8. **D** $\dfrac{?}{100} \cdot k = 10$

   $\dfrac{?}{100} = \dfrac{10}{k}$

   $? = \dfrac{1000}{k}$

9. **B** This is a direct proportion. Let $x =$ the number of items that can be bought for 36¢.

   $\dfrac{\text{number of items}}{\text{cost in ¢}} = \dfrac{2}{6} = \dfrac{x}{36}$

   $6x = 72$

   $x = 12$

10. **A** $\frac{1}{3}$ of $750 = 250$ unsold seats in orchestra

    $\frac{5}{8}$ of $400 = 250$ unsold seats in balcony

    $500 =$ total unsold seats

    $\dfrac{500}{1150} = \dfrac{10}{23}$

11. **E** The change is 15¢ – 3¢ or 12¢.
Change ÷ original × 100 = percentage change.
$\frac{12}{3} = 4 = 400\%$

12. **A** Time in flight for #602 = 3 hours. 200 × 3 = 600 miles covered by #602. Time in flight for #302 = $2\frac{1}{2}$ hours. 320 × $2\frac{1}{2}$ = 800 miles covered by #302. This forms a right triangle. Observe 3, 4, 5 ratio, with each dimension multiplied by 200.

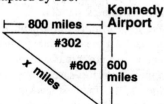

$x = 1000$. ∴ Distance = 1000 miles

13. **C** Total = 27
$\frac{3}{27} = \frac{1}{9} = 11.1\%$

14. **E** $x + y = 16$
$x = 16 - y$
$(16 - y) - z = 16 - y - z$

15. **A** $\frac{a-b}{3.5} = \frac{4}{7}$

Since $3.5 = \frac{1}{2}$ of 7, $a - b = \frac{1}{2}$ of $4 = 2$.
Since $a - b = 2$, $b < a$.

16. **D** $10^x = \underbrace{(10)(10)(10) \ldots \ldots \ldots (10)}_{x \text{ times}}$

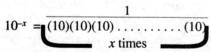

$10^{-x} = \dfrac{1}{\underbrace{(10)(10)(10) \ldots \ldots \ldots (10)}_{x \text{ times}}}$

(A) is true.
470,000 = (4.7)(10)(10)(10)(10) = 4.7×10^5
(B) is true. 450 billion = 4.5×10^{11}
(C) is true. 0.00000000075 = 7.5×10^{-10}
(D) is not true. $\frac{86}{100,000} = \frac{8.6}{10,000} = 8.6 \times 10^{-4}$
(E) is true. 26 million = 2.6×10^7

17. **A** Necessary money = 2 × $50 = $100.
Let x = amount of money to be invested to yield $100 per year.
10% or (.10) of x = 100
$.10x = 100$
$x = \$1000$

18. **C** This is an inverse proportion, since the more chickens you feed the less time it will last.
Let x = number of days food will last for 80 chickens.
$\dfrac{60 \text{ chickens}}{80 \text{ chickens}} = \dfrac{x}{8 \text{ days}}$
$80x = 480$
$x = 6 \text{ days}$

19. **C** Volume of water in rectangular tank = (25")(9")(2")
Let x = height of this volume of water in cylindrical container.
Volume in cylindrical container = $(\pi)(\text{radius})^2(\text{height})$ or $(\pi)(5)^2(x)$ or $(25)(x)(\pi)$
Since volumes are equal,
$(25")(9")(2") = (25)(x)(\pi)$
$18 = \pi x$
$\dfrac{18}{\pi} = x$

20. **A** $\angle EDB \triangleq \frac{1}{2}\widehat{CB}$
$\angle AED \triangleq$
$\frac{1}{2}(\widehat{AD} + \widehat{CB})$
Let $x \triangleq \widehat{CB}$.
$45° = \frac{1}{2}(60 + x)$
$90 = 60 + x$
$30° = x$
Since $\widehat{CB} = 30°$, then $\angle EDB = 15$.

21. **B** $8 + 8a + a = 3$
$9a = -5$
$a = -\frac{5}{9}$

22. **C** $\angle BAC + \angle BCA = 180° - 120° = 60°$
Since $BA = BC$,
$\angle BAC + \angle BCA \triangleq 30$
DA bisects $\angle BAC$ [given].
$\angle DAC \triangleq 15$
Since $DA = DC$, $\angle DCA \triangleq 15$.
$\angle ADC = 180° - (\angle DCA + \angle DAC)$
$\angle ADC \triangleq 180 - 30 = 150$

23. **A** Draw AC.
Area of $\triangle ADC$
$= \frac{10 \times 10}{2} = 50$
$AFCD = \frac{1}{4}$ of circle
Area of this $\frac{1}{4}$ of circle
$= \frac{\pi(10)^2}{4} = 25\pi$
Shaded half below $AC = 25\pi - \triangle ADC$ or $25\pi - 59$
Likewise shaded half above $AC = 25\pi - 50$
Entire shaded area = $50\pi - 100$

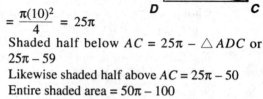

24. **B** Bonds are almost 30%. (30%)(360 degrees) or (.3)(360) = 180° degrees. Mortgages are almost double. The other assets are far less. You don't need the calculator for this problem. ESTIMATE!

25. **C** The solid bar for St. Louis is the tallest.

Writing Skills Section 3

1. **E** Sentence is correct.

2. **A** Error in tense. Change *has adopted* to *adopted*.

3. **E** Sentence is correct.

4. **B** Error in diction. Change *irregardless* to *regardless*.

5. **C** Error in agreement. The subject *she and her staff* is plural; the verb should be plural—*are*.

6. **B** Error in diction. Change *or* to *nor*.

7. **C** Error in diction. Change *affect* to *effect*.

8. **D** Error in agreement. Change *his and her* to *their*.

9. **B** Error in case. Change *you* to *your*.

10. **A** Error in tense. The verb *lie* (past participle is *lain*) means to recline; the verb *to lay* (past participle is *laid*) means to put or place. Therefore, change *has lain* to *has laid*.

11. **C** Error in agreement. Change *their* to *his*.

12. **A** Error in diction. Omit *a*.

13. **E** Sentence is correct.

14. **E** Sentence is correct.

15. **D** Lack of parallel structure. Change *an increase in interest rates* to *interest rates increase*.

16. **C** Misuse of adjective for adverb. Change *special prepared* to *specially prepared*.

17. **C** Error in tense. Change *been creating* to *created*.

18. **E** Sentence is correct.

19. **C** Error in agreement. The subject *explosion* is singular. Therefore, change *have caught* to *has caught*.

20. **C** The past perfect tense is required in an "if" clause.

21. **C** The two errors in diction (*imminent* for *eminent* and *stood* for *stayed*) are corrected in Choice C.

22. **D** This corrects the sentence fragment.

23. **B** Choice B corrects the run-on sentence.

24. **C** Choice C corrects the sentence fragment.

25. **C** Choice C corrects the run-on sentence and expresses the author's meaning directly and concisely. All other choices are indirect, ungrammatical, or do not retain the meaning of the original sentence.

26. **A** Sentence is correct as given.

27. **B** Choice B corrects the conjunction *neither . . . nor* (not *neither. . . or*) as well as the run-on sentence, and retains the meaning of the original sentence.

28. **C** Use *this kind of story* or *these kinds of stories.*

29. **D** The omission of the correct verb form is corrected in Choice D.

30. **C** The dangling participle construction is corrected in C.

31. **E** Choice E corrects the misplaced modifier and eliminates the unnecessary use of the passive voice.

32. **A** The use of the semicolon to separate the pair of clauses is correct.

33. **B** Choice B expresses the author's meaning directly and concisely. All other choices are indirect, ungrammatical, or do not retain the meaning of the original sentence.

34. **C** Choice A is a sentence fragment.
Choice B violates standard English idiom. The phrase *for example* should be followed by a noun, not by a prepositional phrase.
Choice C is a complete sentence and serves as an appropriate topic sentence for the second paragraph. It is the best answer.
Choice D serves neither as a good transition from the first to the second paragraph, nor as an effective topic sentence for the second paragraph.
Choice E is a sentence fragment; also the phrases *for instance* and *for example* are redundant.

35. **C** Choice A contains an error in subject-verb agreement. The plural subject *rights* should have a plural verb, *were*.
Choice B shifts verb tenses from present perfect (*have seized*) to past perfect (*had repressed*). Confusion ensues.
Choice C succinctly and accurately revises the original sentence. It is the best answer.
Choice D is a confusion of verb tenses, which renders the sentence almost incomprehensible.
Choice E has a severe pronoun reference problem. It is unclear to whom the pronouns *they, their,* and *them* refer.

36. **A** Choice A clearly and succinctly explains the fate of the kulaks. It is the best answer.
Choice B is wordy and awkwardly expressed.
Choice C is wordy and contains a usage error. Because *forcing* is a gerund, *Stalin* should be possessive (*Stalin's*).
Choice D contains a dangling participle. It says that Stalin lost this right to own private property, an idea contrary to what the writer intended.
Choice E is not accurately expressed and contains an error in subject-verb agreement. The compound subject *loss* and *collectivization* requires a plural verb.

37. **C** Choice A is wordy and repetitious. It also contains an error in idiom. The word *by* should be *in*.
Choice B unnecessarily repeats the phrase *political opponents.*
Choice C is succinctly and accurately expressed. It is the best answer.
Choice D is awkward and, like B, repetitious.
Choice E is in the passive voice and is awkwardly expressed.

38. **E**   Choices A, B, and C are trite and abrupt transitions. They should be avoided.

Choice D is not a good answer because the essay does not discuss international agreements on human rights.

Choice E accurately and smoothly provides a link between the content of the essay and the concluding paragraph. It is the best answer.

39. **A**   Only Choice A accurately describes the function of the last paragraph. The conclusion—that people will eventually claim their rights—grows out of the discussion in paragraphs 1, 2, and 3. Therefore, Choice A is the best answer.

Verbal Reasoning Section 4

31. **D**   A *mower* cuts *lawns*; a *clipper* cuts *nails*.
(Function)

32. **B**   One *audits* or examines *books* (financial records) to find errors; one *inspects buildings* to find flaws.   (Purpose)

33. **E**   A *bobbin* is a spool on which *thread* is wound; a *reel* is a spool on which *tape* is wound.
(Definition)

34. **C**   A *bungalow* is a small *building*; a *dinghy* is a small *boat*. Beware of eye-catchers. Though cathedrals and chapels are buildings, a cathedral is not a kind of chapel.   (Class and Member)

35. **E**   A *bear's* home is a *lair;* a *rabbit's* home is a *burrow*.   (Function)

36. **A**   A thing that is *hefty* has a lot of *weight*; a thing that is *lofty* has a lot of *height*.
(Synonym Variant)

37. **B**   To *depose* a *monarch* is to get rid of him; to *dismiss* an *employee* is to get rid of or fire him.
(Function)

38. **B**   An *arsonist* is a criminal who makes a fire or *conflagration*; a *thug* is a criminal who makes an *assault* or attack on someone.   (Definition)

39. **C**   Someone who is *pensive* or thoughtful will *reflect* on things or ponder them; someone who is *unruly* or undisciplined will *disobey* or refuse to follow orders.   (Synonym Variant)

40. **D**   People use *spectacles* for *seeing* better; people use *flippers* for *swimming* better. (Function)

41. **D**   An *enigmatic text* is a piece of writing that is mysterious and hard to understand; an *obscure remark* is an utterance that is vague and hard to understand.   (Manner)

42. **D**   Someone with *aplomb* (self-confidence, poise) is *nonchalant* (casual, without concern); someone with *affability* (friendliness) is *cordial* (friendly, warm).   (Synonym Variant)

43. **B**   A *juggernaut* is a dangerous force or object that is *unstoppable* and crushes everything in its path; a *turncoat* is a dangerous person who is *treacherous,* who turns against her friends.
(Definition)

44. **C**   "Going far" with someone clearly has *sexual* connotations. Such risque interpretations are characteristic of double entendres.

45. **D**   The dictionary defines a musical standard as a musical composition that has become part of the standard repertoire, in other words, *a well-established musical piece.*

46. **C**   If humming "Just One of Those Things" suggests you will soon end your current romance, this implies that the song recounts the end or *termination of a love affair.*

47. **B**   The simpler the tune, the wider its potential appeal. Established composers counsel beginners to keep things simple in order to maximize their potential audience (and potential song royalties).

48. **D**   By locating us in cultural time, the songs we adopt name us (*help define us*) and bring to mind the turns of phrase and particular outlook of our day (*evoke the attitudes of our age*).

49. **B**   Throughout Passage 1 the author reiterates that human beings make cities, that the creation of a city is an act of choice, that a city is the result of an agreement or pact. In all these ways, he *defines the city as growing out of a social contract* by which human beings choose to bind themselves.

50. **D**   The sentences quoted within the parenthesis are illustrations of the sort of metaphors we use in describing cities. Thus, they are examples *of one type of figurative language.*

51. **D**   Insisting that cities are not natural but artificial, the author rejects these metaphors as inaccurate. His attitude toward the statements he quotes is clearly *skeptical.*

52. **D**   An ant hill is the work of insects rather than of human beings. *It is a work of instinct rather than of imagination* and human intelligence; therefore, by his definition, it is not like a city.

53. **C**   The author cites these factors as "reasons (that) may lead people to aggregate" or *gather together in settlements.*

54. **A**   The nomads have chosen to wander like the moon. The logical corollary of that is that they *have not chosen to settle in one spot.*

55. **A**   The author clearly is impressed by the magnitude of the choice people make when they agree to live as if mere geographical links, "ties of proximity," can be as strong as blood relationships. In proclaiming a city "a considerable pact," he stresses the *essential significance* or weightiness of this agreement.

56. **C**   To the author, "a city is an expression of continuity through will and imagination." Thus, to live in a city is *an act of volition* (will).

57. **B**   One would predict such a mass exodus of financial firms only if one assumed that the firms could do their work just as well at distant

locations as they could in the city. Thus, the basic assumption underlying the forecast is that *computerized tasks such a record keeping* (the major task of most financial institutions) *can easily be performed at remote sites.*

58. **C**   The city's concentration of people necessitates the enormous size of its buildings. These outsized building destroy the scale or *relative dimensions* of the city as it was originally envisioned by its planners.

59. **C**   The human congress is described in the next-to-last paragraph. It is the *meeting of minds*, the vital exchange of ideas and opinions, that the city makes possible.

60. **E**   While the author of Passage 1 talks in terms of abstractions that keep people dwelling together in cities (the city as pact, the city as an expression of will and imagination), the author of Passage 2 openly mentions the concrete ills that threaten the city: overcrowding, overbuilding of outsize skyscrapers that block the sun, loss of businesses to the suburbs (with the attendant loss of tax revenues). Given his perspective as an urban planner and sociologist, he is inevitably moved to talk about the city's difficulties.

Mathematical Reasoning Section 5

26. **B** $\dfrac{(7)(7)(21)}{x} = (7)(3)$

$(7)(7)(21) = (7)(3)(x)$

$49 = x$

27. **A** $\sqrt{\dfrac{1}{4}} = \dfrac{1}{2}$

$(.25)^2 = \left(\dfrac{1}{4}\right)^2 = \dfrac{1}{16}$

$\dfrac{1}{2} > \dfrac{1}{16}$

28. **B** $2^{n+1} = 32$

$2^5 = 32$

$n + 1 = 5$

$n = 4$

29. **A**   Let d = diameter of circle O = length of a diagonal of square $ABCD$.

Area circle $O = \pi\left(\dfrac{d}{2}\right)^2 = \dfrac{\pi}{4}d^2$.

Because the area of a square is equal to one-half the product of the lengths of its diagonals, the area of square $ABCD = \dfrac{1}{2}d^2$. Because $\dfrac{\pi}{4} > \dfrac{1}{2}$, the area of the circle is greater than the area of the square.

30. **D** $x^2 - y^2 = 0$

$(x + y)(x - y) = 0$

$x + y = 0$ or $x - y = 0$

Therefore we cannot tell if Column A = Column B or is greater or less than it.

31. **C** $\dfrac{a + b}{b} = \dfrac{a}{b} + \dfrac{b}{b} = \dfrac{a}{b} + 1$

32. **C** $a + 3 = 5 \qquad b + 3 = 7$

$a = 2 \qquad\qquad b = 4$

$b - a = 4 - 2 = 2$

33. **D**   City C could be at any point on the circumference of the circle with radius 5 miles. City A could be at any point on the circumference of the circle with radius 10 miles.

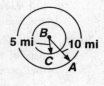

34. **C** $a + b + c = 180°$, with average of $60°$. Since triangle ABC is equilateral, $x = 60°$.

35. **C** $\triangle$s XWY and WVZ are right triangles, $a = b$ [vertical angles]. $\triangle XWY \sim WVZ$.

$\dfrac{XY}{VZ} = \dfrac{8}{16} = \dfrac{1}{2} = \dfrac{WY}{VW} = \dfrac{10}{20}$

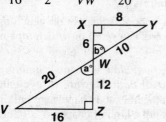

Right $\triangle WXY$ is a 3-4-5 triangle with all dimensions multiplied by 2, so $WX = 6$. Right $\triangle WVZ$ is a 3-4-5 triangle with all dimensions multiplied by 4, so $WZ = 12$.

$XWZ = 18$

$XY + WY = 8 + 10 = 18$

36. **A**   Either b or c must equal zero. Therefore $bc = 0$.

37. **A**   Alternate interior angles a and b are equal.

$a = b = \dfrac{1}{2}(110°) = 55°$

$x + 55° = 180°$

$x = 125$

38. **D**   Many different values may be substituted for x and for y in the inequality, producing different values and relationships. We know only that $x > \dfrac{3}{4}y$.

39. **D**   Since $a^4 = b^4$, $(a^2)^2 = (b^2)^2$ so $a^2 = b^2$. Therefore, the expressions a^2b and ab^2 will have the same value only if a and b are equal. However, a and b are not necessarily equal since a and b may have opposite signs.

40. **B**   Because x is squared, x^2 has a positive value. Ten minus any positive value is less than 11.

41. $\dfrac{1}{30}$ $\dfrac{1 \text{ dime}}{\$3.00} = \dfrac{10¢}{300¢} = \dfrac{10}{300} = \dfrac{1}{30}$

42. **800**   Let x = registration of previous year.

        of x = increase over previous year.

        of $x + x$ = present registration.

$$0.0625x + x = 850$$
$$10625x = 850$$
$$10625x = 8500000$$
$$x = 800$$

43. **57**   Basic ratio = $19x:5x:3x$
If $3x = 9$, then $19x = (19)(3) = 57$.

44. **180**   To have average of 160 for 18 games, sum = 2880.
He has average of 150 for 12 games, sum = 1800.
Required additional points = 1080
Average for 6 more games = $1080 \div 6 = 180$

45. **2**   6 inches on the boy's map = 2 inches on original map
2 inches = 2 miles on original scale

46. **2**   Possibilities are
three 3¢ + four 4¢ = 25
seven 3¢ + one 4¢ = 25

47. **120**   If $\angle BAC \stackrel{\circ}{=} 30$, then
$\widehat{BC} = 60°$
If $\widehat{BC} = \widehat{CD}$,
$\widehat{CD} = 60°$.
Since AOC is the diameter, $\widehat{ADC} = 180°$.
Since $\widehat{CD} = 60°$,
$\widehat{AD} = 120°$.

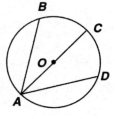

48. **26** $\angle BAE \stackrel{\circ}{=} 45$, since $\angle AEB$ is a right angle, and $\angle ABE \stackrel{\circ}{=} 45$.
∴ $AE = EB = 8$
Likewise $FC = 8$
$EF = AD = 10$
$BC = 8 + 10 + 8 = 26$

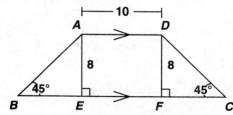

49. **36**   Let x = number of feet ladder will extend up the building. The right triangle formed is a 5-12-13 triangle with all dimensions multiplied by 3. $39 = 3(13)$, $15 = 3(5)$, so $x = 3(12) = 36$.

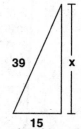

50. **27**   Assume x, x, x are, respectively, the sides of the original cube.
Then $3x$, $3x$, $3x$ will be the sides of the enlarged box.
Volume of original box = x^2
Volume of enlarged box = $(3x)(3x)(3x)$ or $27x^3$

Answer Sheet

TYPICAL TEST G

Each mark should completely fill the appropriate space, and should be as dark as all other marks. Make all erasures complete. Traces of an erasure may be read as an answer. See pages vii and 27 for explanations of timing and number of questions.

Section 1 — Verbal
30 minutes

1 Ⓐ Ⓑ Ⓒ Ⓓ Ⓔ
2 Ⓐ Ⓑ Ⓒ Ⓓ Ⓔ
3 Ⓐ Ⓑ Ⓒ Ⓓ Ⓔ
4 Ⓐ Ⓑ Ⓒ Ⓓ Ⓔ
5 Ⓐ Ⓑ Ⓒ Ⓓ Ⓔ
6 Ⓐ Ⓑ Ⓒ Ⓓ Ⓔ
7 Ⓐ Ⓑ Ⓒ Ⓓ Ⓔ
8 Ⓐ Ⓑ Ⓒ Ⓓ Ⓔ
9 Ⓐ Ⓑ Ⓒ Ⓓ Ⓔ
10 Ⓐ Ⓑ Ⓒ Ⓓ Ⓔ
11 Ⓐ Ⓑ Ⓒ Ⓓ Ⓔ
12 Ⓐ Ⓑ Ⓒ Ⓓ Ⓔ
13 Ⓐ Ⓑ Ⓒ Ⓓ Ⓔ
14 Ⓐ Ⓑ Ⓒ Ⓓ Ⓔ
15 Ⓐ Ⓑ Ⓒ Ⓓ Ⓔ
16 Ⓐ Ⓑ Ⓒ Ⓓ Ⓔ
17 Ⓐ Ⓑ Ⓒ Ⓓ Ⓔ
18 Ⓐ Ⓑ Ⓒ Ⓓ Ⓔ
19 Ⓐ Ⓑ Ⓒ Ⓓ Ⓔ
20 Ⓐ Ⓑ Ⓒ Ⓓ Ⓔ
21 Ⓐ Ⓑ Ⓒ Ⓓ Ⓔ
22 Ⓐ Ⓑ Ⓒ Ⓓ Ⓔ
23 Ⓐ Ⓑ Ⓒ Ⓓ Ⓔ
24 Ⓐ Ⓑ Ⓒ Ⓓ Ⓔ
25 Ⓐ Ⓑ Ⓒ Ⓓ Ⓔ
26 Ⓐ Ⓑ Ⓒ Ⓓ Ⓔ
27 Ⓐ Ⓑ Ⓒ Ⓓ Ⓔ
28 Ⓐ Ⓑ Ⓒ Ⓓ Ⓔ
29 Ⓐ Ⓑ Ⓒ Ⓓ Ⓔ
30 Ⓐ Ⓑ Ⓒ Ⓓ Ⓔ

Section 2 — Math
30 minutes

1 Ⓐ Ⓑ Ⓒ Ⓓ Ⓔ
2 Ⓐ Ⓑ Ⓒ Ⓓ Ⓔ
3 Ⓐ Ⓑ Ⓒ Ⓓ Ⓔ
4 Ⓐ Ⓑ Ⓒ Ⓓ Ⓔ
5 Ⓐ Ⓑ Ⓒ Ⓓ Ⓔ
6 Ⓐ Ⓑ Ⓒ Ⓓ Ⓔ
7 Ⓐ Ⓑ Ⓒ Ⓓ Ⓔ
8 Ⓐ Ⓑ Ⓒ Ⓓ Ⓔ
9 Ⓐ Ⓑ Ⓒ Ⓓ Ⓔ
10 Ⓐ Ⓑ Ⓒ Ⓓ Ⓔ
11 Ⓐ Ⓑ Ⓒ Ⓓ Ⓔ
12 Ⓐ Ⓑ Ⓒ Ⓓ Ⓔ
13 Ⓐ Ⓑ Ⓒ Ⓓ Ⓔ
14 Ⓐ Ⓑ Ⓒ Ⓓ Ⓔ
15 Ⓐ Ⓑ Ⓒ Ⓓ Ⓔ
16 Ⓐ Ⓑ Ⓒ Ⓓ Ⓔ
17 Ⓐ Ⓑ Ⓒ Ⓓ Ⓔ
18 Ⓐ Ⓑ Ⓒ Ⓓ Ⓔ
19 Ⓐ Ⓑ Ⓒ Ⓓ Ⓔ
20 Ⓐ Ⓑ Ⓒ Ⓓ Ⓔ
21 Ⓐ Ⓑ Ⓒ Ⓓ Ⓔ
22 Ⓐ Ⓑ Ⓒ Ⓓ Ⓔ
23 Ⓐ Ⓑ Ⓒ Ⓓ Ⓔ
24 Ⓐ Ⓑ Ⓒ Ⓓ Ⓔ
25 Ⓐ Ⓑ Ⓒ Ⓓ Ⓔ

Section 3 — Writing
30 minutes

1 Ⓐ Ⓑ Ⓒ Ⓓ Ⓔ
2 Ⓐ Ⓑ Ⓒ Ⓓ Ⓔ
3 Ⓐ Ⓑ Ⓒ Ⓓ Ⓔ
4 Ⓐ Ⓑ Ⓒ Ⓓ Ⓔ
5 Ⓐ Ⓑ Ⓒ Ⓓ Ⓔ
6 Ⓐ Ⓑ Ⓒ Ⓓ Ⓔ
7 Ⓐ Ⓑ Ⓒ Ⓓ Ⓔ
8 Ⓐ Ⓑ Ⓒ Ⓓ Ⓔ
9 Ⓐ Ⓑ Ⓒ Ⓓ Ⓔ
10 Ⓐ Ⓑ Ⓒ Ⓓ Ⓔ
11 Ⓐ Ⓑ Ⓒ Ⓓ Ⓔ
12 Ⓐ Ⓑ Ⓒ Ⓓ Ⓔ
13 Ⓐ Ⓑ Ⓒ Ⓓ Ⓔ
14 Ⓐ Ⓑ Ⓒ Ⓓ Ⓔ
15 Ⓐ Ⓑ Ⓒ Ⓓ Ⓔ
16 Ⓐ Ⓑ Ⓒ Ⓓ Ⓔ
17 Ⓐ Ⓑ Ⓒ Ⓓ Ⓔ
18 Ⓐ Ⓑ Ⓒ Ⓓ Ⓔ
19 Ⓐ Ⓑ Ⓒ Ⓓ Ⓔ
20 Ⓐ Ⓑ Ⓒ Ⓓ Ⓔ
21 Ⓐ Ⓑ Ⓒ Ⓓ Ⓔ
22 Ⓐ Ⓑ Ⓒ Ⓓ Ⓔ
23 Ⓐ Ⓑ Ⓒ Ⓓ Ⓔ
24 Ⓐ Ⓑ Ⓒ Ⓓ Ⓔ
25 Ⓐ Ⓑ Ⓒ Ⓓ Ⓔ
26 Ⓐ Ⓑ Ⓒ Ⓓ Ⓔ
27 Ⓐ Ⓑ Ⓒ Ⓓ Ⓔ
28 Ⓐ Ⓑ Ⓒ Ⓓ Ⓔ
29 Ⓐ Ⓑ Ⓒ Ⓓ Ⓔ
30 Ⓐ Ⓑ Ⓒ Ⓓ Ⓔ
31 Ⓐ Ⓑ Ⓒ Ⓓ Ⓔ
32 Ⓐ Ⓑ Ⓒ Ⓓ Ⓔ
33 Ⓐ Ⓑ Ⓒ Ⓓ Ⓔ
34 Ⓐ Ⓑ Ⓒ Ⓓ Ⓔ
35 Ⓐ Ⓑ Ⓒ Ⓓ Ⓔ
36 Ⓐ Ⓑ Ⓒ Ⓓ Ⓔ
37 Ⓐ Ⓑ Ⓒ Ⓓ Ⓔ
38 Ⓐ Ⓑ Ⓒ Ⓓ Ⓔ
39 Ⓐ Ⓑ Ⓒ Ⓓ Ⓔ

Section 4 — Verbal
30 minutes

31 Ⓐ Ⓑ Ⓒ Ⓓ Ⓔ
32 Ⓐ Ⓑ Ⓒ Ⓓ Ⓔ
33 Ⓐ Ⓑ Ⓒ Ⓓ Ⓔ
34 Ⓐ Ⓑ Ⓒ Ⓓ Ⓔ
35 Ⓐ Ⓑ Ⓒ Ⓓ Ⓔ
36 Ⓐ Ⓑ Ⓒ Ⓓ Ⓔ
37 Ⓐ Ⓑ Ⓒ Ⓓ Ⓔ
38 Ⓐ Ⓑ Ⓒ Ⓓ Ⓔ
39 Ⓐ Ⓑ Ⓒ Ⓓ Ⓔ
40 Ⓐ Ⓑ Ⓒ Ⓓ Ⓔ
41 Ⓐ Ⓑ Ⓒ Ⓓ Ⓔ
42 Ⓐ Ⓑ Ⓒ Ⓓ Ⓔ
43 Ⓐ Ⓑ Ⓒ Ⓓ Ⓔ
44 Ⓐ Ⓑ Ⓒ Ⓓ Ⓔ
45 Ⓐ Ⓑ Ⓒ Ⓓ Ⓔ
46 Ⓐ Ⓑ Ⓒ Ⓓ Ⓔ
47 Ⓐ Ⓑ Ⓒ Ⓓ Ⓔ
48 Ⓐ Ⓑ Ⓒ Ⓓ Ⓔ
49 Ⓐ Ⓑ Ⓒ Ⓓ Ⓔ
50 Ⓐ Ⓑ Ⓒ Ⓓ Ⓔ
51 Ⓐ Ⓑ Ⓒ Ⓓ Ⓔ
52 Ⓐ Ⓑ Ⓒ Ⓓ Ⓔ
53 Ⓐ Ⓑ Ⓒ Ⓓ Ⓔ
54 Ⓐ Ⓑ Ⓒ Ⓓ Ⓔ
55 Ⓐ Ⓑ Ⓒ Ⓓ Ⓔ
56 Ⓐ Ⓑ Ⓒ Ⓓ Ⓔ
57 Ⓐ Ⓑ Ⓒ Ⓓ Ⓔ
58 Ⓐ Ⓑ Ⓒ Ⓓ Ⓔ
59 Ⓐ Ⓑ Ⓒ Ⓓ Ⓔ
60 Ⓐ Ⓑ Ⓒ Ⓓ Ⓔ

Section 5 — Math
30 minutes

26 Ⓐ Ⓑ Ⓒ Ⓓ Ⓔ
27 Ⓐ Ⓑ Ⓒ Ⓓ Ⓔ
28 Ⓐ Ⓑ Ⓒ Ⓓ Ⓔ
29 Ⓐ Ⓑ Ⓒ Ⓓ Ⓔ
30 Ⓐ Ⓑ Ⓒ Ⓓ Ⓔ
31 Ⓐ Ⓑ Ⓒ Ⓓ Ⓔ
32 Ⓐ Ⓑ Ⓒ Ⓓ Ⓔ
33 Ⓐ Ⓑ Ⓒ Ⓓ Ⓔ
34 Ⓐ Ⓑ Ⓒ Ⓓ Ⓔ
35 Ⓐ Ⓑ Ⓒ Ⓓ Ⓔ
36 Ⓐ Ⓑ Ⓒ Ⓓ Ⓔ
37 Ⓐ Ⓑ Ⓒ Ⓓ Ⓔ
39 Ⓐ Ⓑ Ⓒ Ⓓ Ⓔ
39 Ⓐ Ⓑ Ⓒ Ⓓ Ⓔ
40 Ⓐ Ⓑ Ⓒ Ⓓ Ⓔ

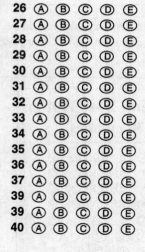

41 42 43 44 45 46 47 48 49 50

SECTION 1
Verbal Reasoning

For each question in this section, select the best answer from among the choices given and fill in the corresponding oval on the answer sheet.

Directions

Each sentence below has one or two blanks, each blank indicating that something has been omitted. Beneath the sentence are five words or sets of words labeled A through E. Choose the word or set of words that, when inserted in the sentence, best fits the meaning of the sentence as a whole.

Example:

Medieval kingdoms did not become constitutional republics overnight; on the contrary, the change was ____ .

(A) unpopular
(B) unexpected
(C) advantageous
(D) sufficient
(E) gradual   Ⓐ Ⓑ Ⓒ Ⓓ ●

1. Because of the recent flood of counterfeit twenty dollar bills, the teller carefully ____ each bill handed him by a customer.

   (A) rescinded   (B) squandered   (C) repudiated
   (D) returned   (E) scrutinized

2. Among naturalists, the statistics of elephant population decline have prompted a cry of ____ , with newspaper articles and even a television special ____ the species' slow extinction.

   (A) warning..celebrating
   (B) alarm..deploring
   (C) jubilation..hastening
   (D) desperation..boycotting
   (E) anxiety..refuting

3. Advances in health care have lengthened life spans, lowered infant mortality rates, and, thus, ____ the overpopulation problem.

   (A) eliminated   (B) aggravated   (C) minimized
   (D) distorted   (E) discouraged

4. They greeted his proposal with ____ and refused to give it serious study.

   (A) acclaim   (B) detachment   (C) fervor
   (D) derision   (E) approbation

5. While some scientists point to the vast uncertainties about global warming as reason to delay action in confronting the greenhouse effect, many experts argue that the possibility of ____ damage ____ strong measures now to reduce the human impact on global systems.

   (A) excessive..precludes
   (B) aggravated..sidetracks
   (C) accelerated..warrants
   (D) illusory..justifies
   (E) ambiguous..demands

6. Articulate, witty, intellectually vigorous, with rock-solid self-confidence and a clear sense of values, he has all the qualities one associates with corporate ____ .

   (A) bankruptcy   (B) conservatism   (C) stagnation
   (D) leadership   (E) loyalty

7. Even Republican members of the committee, who normally would have defended the administration's actions, found themselves forced to ____ the secret plans to raise money for the contras.

   (A) deprecate   (B) conceal   (C) explicate
   (D) implement   (E) validate

8. The epiphyte plants of the rain forest use trees for physical support but do not, like ____ , sap nutrients from their hosts.

   (A) fauna   (B) predators   (C) parasites
   (D) insectivores (E) stumps

9. Holroyd manages to make each successive phase of Shaw's life seem significant of itself, rather than simply as ____ of what was to come or as raw material for Shaw's plays.

   (A) an application   (B) a foretoken
   (C) a predilection   (D) a plagiarism
   (E) a recollection

10. The renovation of historic Union Station is salutary not just as an example of ____ restoration but also as a reminder that in this age of retrenchment and diminished dreams, ambitious federal public works programs can still ____ .

   (A) impeccable..succeed   (B) inadequate..inspire
   (C) flawless..terminate   (D) archaic..flourish
   (E) partial..impede

11. Unlike the archetypal reclusive scientist-scholar, lost in a fog of abstruse speculations, Feynman was _____ soul much given to convivial company.

   (A) a gregarious   (B) a recondite
   (C) a dispassionate   (D) a pragmatic
   (E) an introverted

12. Though Islam has factions hostile to science, it has _____ quite a few of its own research scientists.

   (A) maligned   (B) misinterpreted   (C) eliminated
   (D) spawned   (E) rebuked

13. For centuries, physicists have had good reason to believe in the principle of equivalence propounded by Galileo: it has _____ many rigorous tests that _____ its accuracy to extraordinary precision.

   (A) endured..compromised
   (B) passed..presupposed   (C) borne..postulated
   (D) survived..proved   (E) inspired..equated

14. To the embittered ex-philanthropist, all the former recipients of her charity were _____ , as stingy with their thanks as they were wasteful of her largesse.

   (A) louts   (B) misers   (C) ingrates
   (D) prigs   (E) renegades

15. Among contemporary writers of fiction, Mrs. Woolf is _____ figure, in some ways as radical as James Joyce, in others no more modern than Jane Austen.

   (A) a doctrinaire   (B) an introspective
   (C) a peripheral   (D) a disinterested
   (E) an anomalous

16. _____ stereotypes that depict Latinos as cut off from the American mainstream, the Latino National Political Survey found a high degree of _____ the mainstream among people of Hispanic descent.

   (A) Supporting..familiarity with
   (B) Debunking..assimilation into
   (C) Creating..commitment to
   (D) Dismantling..indifference to
   (E) Subverting..hostility toward

17. Physicists dream of a unified theory of matter that could replace the current _____ of mutually inconsistent theories that clutter the field.

   (A) bonanza   (B) concord   (C) dearth
   (D) integration   (E) welter

Directions

Each passage below is followed by questions based on its content. Answer the questions following each passage on the basis of what is <u>stated</u> or <u>implied</u> in that passage and in any introductory material that may be provided.

Questions 18–23 are based on the following passage.

In this autobiographical excerpt, the author, the daughter of migrant workers, describes a childhood incident whose significance she came to understand only with the passage of time.

When school was out, I hurried to find my sister and get out of the schoolyard before seeing anybody in my class. But Barbara and her friends had
Line beaten us to the playground entrance and they
5 seemed to be waiting for us. Barbara said, "So now you're in the A class." She sounded impressed.
   "What's the A class?" I asked.
   Everybody made superior yet faintly envious giggling sounds. "Well, why did you think the
10 teacher moved you to the front of the room, dopey? Didn't you know you were in the C class before, way in the back of the room?"
   Of course I hadn't known. The Wenatchee fifth grade was bigger than my whole school had been
15 in North Dakota, and the idea of subdivisions within a grade had never occurred to me. The subdividing for the first marking period had been done before I came to the school, and I had never, in the six weeks I'd been there, talked to anyone long
20 enough to find out about the A, B, and C classes.
   I still could not understand why that had made such a difference to Barbara and her friends. I didn't yet know that it was disgraceful and dirty to be a transient laborer and ridiculous to be from
25 North Dakota. I thought living in a tent was more fun than living in a house. I didn't know that we were gypsies, really (how that thought would have thrilled me then!), and that we were regarded with the suspicion felt by those who plant toward those who do not plant. It didn't occur to me that
30 those who do not plant. It didn't occur to me that we were all looked upon as one more of the untrustworthy natural phenomena, drifting here and there like mists or winds, that farmers of certain crops are resentfully forced to rely on. I
35 didn't know that I was the only child who had camped on the Baumanns' land ever to get out of the C class. I did not know that school administrators and civic leaders held conferences to talk about the problem of transient laborers.
40 I only knew that for two happy days I walked to school with Barbara and her friends, played hopscotch and jump rope with them at recess, and was even invited into the house for some ginger ale—an exotic drink I had never tasted before.

GO ON TO THE NEXT PAGE →

18. The tone of this passage as a whole is

(A) reflective   (B) joyful   (C) impersonal
(D) pessimistic   (E) suspicious

19. This passage is presented from the point of view of

(A) an understanding teacher   (B) a younger sister
(C) a mature adult   (D) a helpful parent
(E) an envious pupil

20. The narrator had most probably been placed in the C class because

(A) she was a poor reader
(B) she had come from a small school
(C) the marking system confused her
(D) all migrant children were placed in the C class
(E) all migrant children lived in tents

21. The author's tone in listing all the items she "didn't yet know" (lines 23–36) is

(A) embarrassed   (B) arrogant   (C) objective
(D) gloomy   (E) ironic

22. In lines 43–44, the author refers to her first taste of ginger ale to emphasize

(A) her eventual dependence on soft drinks
(B) the rarity of ginger ale in the town of Wenatchee
(C) how exceptionally refreshing a soft drink can be
(D) Barbara's generosity in giving the author a treat
(E) her lack of everyday experiences we take for granted

23. After the narrator was moved to the A class, what was the attitude of Barbara and Barbara's friends toward her?

(A) Dislike   (B) Acceptance   (C) Dismay
(D) Apology   (E) Jealousy

Questions 24–30 are based on the following passage.

Students of the modern civil rights movement regularly contrast the figures of Malcolm X and Martin Luther King. The black protest movement in America has always had strong, controversial leaders. Two of the strongest, Booker T. Washington and W.E.B. Du Bois, who shaped the course of the movement in the early part of the century, are discussed in this excerpt from a black studies text published in 1982.

During the nineteenth century and the early decades of the twentieth, when blacks were virtually powerless, propagandists like Frederick
Line Douglass, Booker T. Washington, and W.E.B. Du
5 Bois naturally loomed large in the pantheon of black leaders. The term propagandist—used here in its neutral meaning as denoting one who employs symbols to influence the feelings and behavior of an audience—is a particularly apt
10 description of the role played by Du Bois, the leading black intellectual and the most important black protest spokesman in the first half of the twentieth century. As platform lecturer and particularly as editor of several publications, Du Bois
15 was a caustic and prophetic voice, telling whites that racist social institutions oppressed blacks and telling blacks that change in their subordinate status was impossible unless they demanded it insis-
tently and continuously. Du Bois himself in his
20 noted autobiographical work, *Dusk of Dawn*, aptly evaluated his principal contribution when he wrote of "my role as a master of propaganda."

Central to Du Bois's role as a propagandist were the ideologies that he articulated. And Du
25 Bois's ideas reflected most of the diverse themes in black thinking about how to assault the bas-
tions of prejudice and discrimination. Most important, he articulated the blacks' desire for full participation in the larger American society and
30 demanded "the abolition of all caste distinctions based simply on race and color." On the other hand, he also exhibited a nationalist side—a strong sense of group pride, advocacy of racial unity, and a profound identification with blacks in
35 other parts of the world. As he said in one of his oft-quoted statements,

"One ever feels his twoness—an American, a Negro: two souls, two thoughts, two unreconciled strivings; two warring ideals
40 in one dark body, whose dogged strength alone keeps it from being torn asunder. The history of the American Negro is the history of this strife—this longing to attain self-
conscious manhood, to merge his double
45 self into a better and truer self. In this merg-
ing he wishes neither of the older selves to be lost. . . .He simply wishes to make it possible for a man to be both a Negro and an American without being cursed and spit
50 upon by his fellows, without having the doors of opportunity closed roughly in his face."

In addition, Du Bois was both a pioneering advocate of black capitalism, and later was one of the
55 country's most prominent black Marxists. Essentially a protest leader, he was also criticized at times for enunciating tactics of accommoda-
tion. An elitist who stressed the leadership role of a college-educated Talented Tenth, he articulated
60 a fervent commitment to the welfare of the black masses.

Given the persistent and intransigent nature of the American race system, which proved quite impervious to black attacks, Du Bois in his
65 speeches and writings moved from one proposed solution to another, and the salience of various

GO ON TO THE NEXT PAGE

parts of his philosophy changed as his perceptions of the needs and strategies of black America shift-
70   ed over time. Aloof and autonomous in his per-
sonality, Du Bois did not hesitate to depart markedly from whatever was the current main-stream of black thinking when he perceived that the conventional wisdom being enunciated by black spokesmen was proving inadequate to the
75   task of advancing the race. His willingness to seek different solutions often placed him well in advance of his contemporaries, and this, com-bined with a strong-willed, even arrogant person-ality, made his career as a black leader essentially
80   a series of stormy conflicts.

Thus Du Bois first achieved his role as a major black leader in the controversy that arose over the program of Booker T. Washington, the most prominent and influential black leader at the
85   opening of the twentieth century. Amidst the wave of lynchings, disfranchisement, and segregation laws, Washington, seeking the good will of pow-erful whites, taught blacks not to protest against discrimination, but to elevate themselves through
90   industrial education, hard work, and property accumulation; then, they would ultimately obtain recognition of their citizenship rights. At first Du Bois agreed with this gradualist strategy, but in 1903 with the publication of his most influential
95   book, *Souls of Black Folk*, he became the chief leader of the onslaught against Washington that polarized the black community into two wings— the "conservative" supporters of Washington and his "radical" critics.

24. Judging from lines 19–22, Du Bois regarded his work as a propagandist as

(A) a necessary evil
(B) a temporary distraction
(C) an academic failure
(D) a particular achievement
(E) an inappropriate occupation

25. In lines 37–52, Du Bois emphasizes the American Negro's

(A) origins   (B) duality   (C) opportunity
(D) manliness   (E) idealism

26. The word "dogged" in line 40 means

(A) brutal and ruthless
(B) tenacious and unyielding
(C) loyal and domesticated
(D) hunted down
(E) canine

27. The author's attitude towards Du Bois's departure from conventional black policies can best be described as

(A) skeptical   (B) derisive   (C) shocked
(D) approving   (E) resigned

28. The author's primary purpose in the closing para-graph is to

(A) explain how Du Bois was influenced by Washington
(B) compare the personalities of Du Bois and Washington
(C) explain why Du Bois gained power in the black community
(D) describe Du Bois's role in early twentieth cen-tury black leadership
(E) correct the misconception that Du Bois shunned polarization

29. Which of the following statements about Du Bois does the passage best support?

(A) He sacrificed the proven strategies of earlier black leaders to his craving for political novelty.
(B) Preferring conflict to harmony, he followed a disruptive course that alienated him from the bulk of his followers.
(C) He proved unable to change with the times in mounting fresh attacks against white racism.
(D) He relied on the fundamental benevolence of the white population for the eventual success of his movement.
(E) Once an adherent of Washington's policies, he ultimately lost patience with them for their ineffectiveness.

30. It can be inferred that Booker T. Washington in comparison with Du Bois could be described as all of the following EXCEPT

(A) submissive to the majority
(B) concerned with financial success
(C) versatile in adopting strategies
(D) traditional in preaching industry
(E) respectful of authority

IF YOU FINISH BEFORE 30 MINUTES, YOU MAY CHECK YOUR WORK ON THIS SECTION ONLY. DO NOT TURN TO ANY OTHER SECTION IN THE TEST.

S T O P

SECTION 2
Mathematical Reasoning

Time—30 minutes
25 Questions

Directions and Reference Information

In this section solve each problem, using any available space for scratchwork. Then decide which is the best of the choices given and fill in the corresponding oval on the answer sheet.

Notes:

(1) The use of a calculator is permitted. All numbers used are real numbers.

(2) Figures that accompany problems in this test are intended to provide information useful in solving the problems. They are drawn as accurately as possible EXCEPT when it is stated in a specific problem that the figure is not drawn to scale. All figures lie in a plane unless otherwise indicated.

Reference Information

$A = \pi r^2$ $A = \ell w$ $A = \frac{1}{2}bh$ $V = \ell wh$ $V = \pi r^2 h$ $c^2 = a^2 + b^2$ Special Right Triangles
$C = 2\pi r$

The number of degrees of an arc in a circle is 360.
The measure in degrees of a straight angle is 180.
The sum of the measures in degrees of the angles of a triangle is 180.

---

1. $z + \dfrac{1}{z} = 2;\ z =$

(A) $\sqrt{3}$ (B) $\frac{1}{2}$ (C) 1   (D) $1\frac{1}{2}$ (E) 2

2. If $2x = 3(a + b)$, then $\dfrac{3}{2x}$ equals

(A) $\dfrac{1}{a + b}$ (B) $a + b$ (C) $2(a + b)$

(D) $3(a + b)$ (E) $2x(a + b)$

3. A tailor cuts a 2-yard piece of ribbon into three equal parts. How can the length of each part be expressed?

  I. 24 inches

  II. $\frac{2}{3}$ yard

  III. 1.5 feet

(A) I only   (B) II only   (C) III only
(D) I and II only   (E) I, II and III

4. A part-time salesperson receives a salary of $50 for working 3 evenings and a commission of 4% on all sales. This salesperson earned $200 for working 3 evenings. What was the amount of sales?

(A) $375   (B) $600   (C) $650
(D) $850   (E) $3750

5. One-half of the students in a city school plan to enter liberal arts colleges and one-third of the students plan to go to junior college. The remaining 300 pupils expect to seek permanent employment after graduation. How many students are there in this school?

(A) 360   (B) 350   (C) 900
(D) 1350   (E) 1800

6. A typist has a task that is normally completed in three hours. What part of this task can be completed from 8:55 A.M. to 9:15 A.M.?

(A) $\frac{1}{6}$ (B) $\frac{1}{3}$ (C) $\frac{2}{3}$ (D) $\frac{1}{5}$ (E) $\frac{1}{9}$

GO ON TO THE NEXT PAGE

7. A motorist paid $9.24 for six gallons of gasoline. This included a tax of 4¢ per gallon. The basic price (per gallon) of the gasoline before inclusion of the tax is

   (A) $1.50   (B) $1.54   (C) $1.56

   (D) $1.60   (E) more than $1.60

8. If x is an odd integer, which of the following is (are) always true?

   I. $(x + 1)(x - 1)$ is even.
   II. $x + 483$ is even.
   III. $x^2 + 2$ is even.

   (A) I only   (B) II only   (C) III only
   (D) I and II only   (E) I, II and III

9. A salesperson operates a car that averaged 15 miles to a gallon of gasoline. By installing a new carburetor, mileage was impoved by $\frac{1}{5}$. How much will be saved on gasoline during a year in which 5400 miles were covered, if the average cost of gasoline is $1.35 per gallon?

   (A) $25.92   (B) $64.80   (C) $81.00
   (D) $108.00   (E) $810.00

10.

x	-7	-3	1	?
y	0	1	2	3

   The table shows values of x and y that satisfy a first-degree equation. What is the missing value of x?

   (A) -3 (B) -2 (C) 2 (D) 4 (E) 5

11. After a 40% reduction is allowed, a painting is sold for $48. The original marked price was

   (A) $67.50   (B) $80.00   (C) $120.00
   (D) $128.00   (E) $192.00

12. If 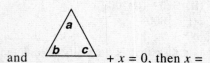 is defined to equal $ab - c$

   and 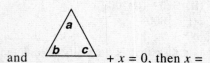 $+ x = 0$, then $x =$

   (A) $ac - b$ (B) $ac + b$ (C) $c - ab$
   (D) $ab - c$ (E) $ab + c$

13. How many degrees are there in an angle formed by the hands of a clock at 2:30?

   (A) 100°   (B) 105°   (C) 110°
   (D) 115°   (E) 120°

14. AB is parallel to DC, $\overset{\frown}{AD}$ equals 110° and $\overset{\frown}{AB}$ equals 30°. The measure of $\angle CED$ equals

   (A) 40°   (B) 70°
   (C) 80°   (D) 110°
   (E) 140°

   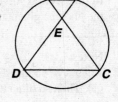

15. CB and AB are tangent to circle O. If $\angle COA \overset{\circ}{=} 140$, what is the measure of $\angle B$?

   (A) 30°   (B) 40°
   (C) 70°   (D) 110°
   (E) 140°

   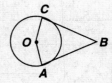

16. $\overset{\frown}{AB}$ of circle O contains 72° and is 6π long. Find the area of circle O.

   (A) 9   (B) 36   (30) 30π (D) 225π (E) 900

17. In $\triangle ABC$, $\angle B = 3\angle A$, and $\angle C = 8\angle A$. What is the measure of $\angle B$?

   (A) 15°   (B) 30°   (C) 45°   (D) 60°   (E) 120°

18. The graphs of $x + 3y = 4$ and $2x + 6y = 8$ are drawn on the same axes. Which of the following will be true?

   I.   If the coordinates of any point on the graph of the first equation are doubled, the result will be the coordinates of a point on the graph of the second equation.
   II. The two graphs will intersect in only one point.
   III. The two graphs have the same y-intercept.

   (A) I only   (B) II only   (C) III only
   (D) I and II only   (E) I, II and III

19. $ABCDEF$ is a regular hexagon. If the perimeter $= 12$, find the area of $ABCDEF$.

   (A) $6\sqrt{3}$ (B) $12\sqrt{3}$ (C) 12
   (D) 24   (E) 36

GO ON TO THE NEXT PAGE

20. A radian is an angle of such size that, when its vertex is placed at the center of any circle, its sides will cut off an arc equal in length to the radius of the circle. One radian is exactly equal to

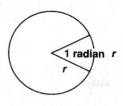

(A) 57° (B) 60° (C) 90°

(D) $\dfrac{180°}{\pi}$ (E) $\dfrac{360°}{\pi}$

21. If the hypotenuse of a right triangle is 10 and one leg is $5\sqrt{3}$, then the area of the triangle is

(A) 5 (B) $25\sqrt{3}$ (C) 25

(D) $50\sqrt{3}$ (E) $12.5\sqrt{3}$

22. Square *ABCD* is inscribed in circle *O*. If the side of the square is 2, find the area of circle *O*.

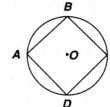

(A) π (B) 2π (C) 4π

(D) 8π (E) 16π

23. The length of a rectangle is represented by the numerical value of $5V^3$. If the rectangle is equal in area to a square with a side represented by $4V$, what is the width of the rectangle in terms of V?

(A) $\dfrac{1}{80V^5}$ (B) $\dfrac{4}{5V}$ (C) $\dfrac{16}{5V}$

(D) $\dfrac{16}{5V^2}$ (E) $\dfrac{5V}{16}$

24. Mr. Sutton, the driver of the oil delivery truck, finds that his customer's oil tank is $^3/_{10}$ full. He fills the oil tank with 420 gallons of oil. What is the capacity of this oil tank (in gallons)?

(A) 480 (B) 600 (C) 1000
(D) 1260 (E) 1800

VOLUMES OF SALES FOR A
10-MONTH PERIOD FOR
TWO SALES PEOPLE

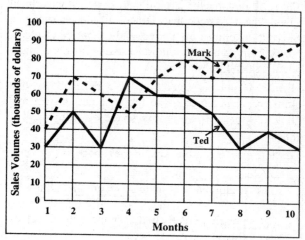

25. During what month did Mark's sales exceed Ted's sales by more than $40,000?

(A) 3 (B) 5 (C) 7 (D) 8 (E) 9

IF YOU FINISH BEFORE 30 MINUTES, YOU MAY CHECK YOUR WORK ON THIS SECTION ONLY. DO NOT TURN TO ANY OTHER SECTION IN THE TEST.   **S T O P**

SECTION 3
Writing Skills

Time—30 minutes
39 Questions

Directions

The following sentences contain problems in grammar, usage, diction (choice of words), and idiom.

> Some sentences are correct.
> No sentence contains more than one error.

You will find that the error, if there is one, is underlined and lettered. Assume that elements of the sentence that are not underlined are correct and cannot be changed. In choosing answers, follow the requirements of standard written English.

If there is an error, select the <u>one underlined part</u> that must be changed to make the sentence correct and blacken the corresponding space on your answer sheet.

If there is no error, blacken answer space Ⓔ.

Example:

The region has a climate <u>so severe that</u> plants
                              A
<u>growing there</u> rarely <u>had been</u> more than twelve
    B   C
inches <u>high</u>. <u>No error</u>
       D   E

1. It <u>was reported</u> that the identities <u>of them</u> to be
        A   B
called <u>as</u> witnesses would be released on Tuesday
       C
<u>by</u> the district attorney. <u>No error</u>
 D   E

2. The ad <u>stated</u> that a piano <u>was needed</u> for the
            A   B
<u>school play</u> <u>in good condition</u>. <u>No error</u>
    C   D   E

3. The fishing <u>fleet</u> <u>left</u> the harbor when the fishermen
               A   B
heard that a school of bluefish <u>were</u> <u>near</u> the wreck.
                                 C   D
<u>No error</u>
 E

4. In consideration <u>about</u> his long service to the
                      A
theater, the Tony Awards committee made a special

presentation <u>honoring</u> the producer George Abbott
              B
who had <u>recently celebrated</u> his <u>hundredth</u> birthday.
         C   D
<u>No error</u>
 E

5. A minority group <u>comprising</u> 30% of the community
                     A
and represented by <u>only</u> one member <u>out of 25</u> on
 B   C   D
the City Council. <u>No error</u>
                   E

6. In spite of a superficial simplicity, there <u>are</u> still
                                                A
many <u>aspects</u> of the prose style of Ernest
      B
Hemingway <u>that</u> would be profitable subjects
            C
for <u>further</u> study. <u>No error</u>
     D   E

7. <u>Among</u> George, Henry, <u>and I,</u> <u>there</u> can be <u>no</u>
    A   B   C   D
secrets. <u>No error</u>
          E

8. <u>Neither</u> the reporters <u>nor</u> the editor <u>were</u> satisfied
    A   B   C
with the salary offer made <u>by</u> the publisher.
                             D
<u>No error</u>
 E

9. The workers <u>who</u> I see in the subway <u>every</u>
                A   B
afternoon <u>seem tired</u> and <u>dejected</u>. <u>No error</u>
            C   D   E

10. The article <u>was rejected</u> because of its length,
                 A
verbosity, and <u>it presented</u> <u>only</u> one point of
                 B   C   D
view. <u>No error</u>
       E

11. Mr. Jones's <u>decision</u> to retire <u>came</u> <u>as a shock</u> to all
                 A   B   C
who respected his ability. <u>No error</u>
 D   E

12. When she spoke with the police, she reported her

loss; <u>she</u> stated that a <u>large quantity</u> of clothing and
       A   B
valuable books <u>were missing</u>. <u>No error</u>
                C   D   E

GO ON TO THE NEXT PAGE

13. Between the small shops and boutiques of
     A
Greenwich Village and the giant department stores
               B
of midtown Manhattan lie the ethnically-varied
             C
residential neighborhood of Chelsea. No error
             D   E

14. Bailing vigorously, we managed to remain afloat
   A   B   C   D
until we were rescued by the Coast Guard. No error
                             E

15. We had ought to finish our trip before dark because
     A   B
it gets very cold after the sun goes down. No error
C   D   E

16. Does that remark infer that you are displeased with
   A   B   C
the way I am managing the business? No error
      D   E

17. I am sure that he has been here and did what was
    A   B   C   D
expected of him. No error
            E

18. Because of its efficacy in treating many ailments
          A
and because it has brought about miraculous cures,
           B
penicillin has become an important addition to
          C   D
the druggist's stock. No error
              E

19. Despite the efforts of the International Red Cross,
          A
maltreatment takes place in refugee camps where
          B
they must wait for months in deplorable living
C   D
conditions. No error
     E

Directions

In each of the following sentences, some part or all of the sentence is underlined. Below each sentence you will find five ways of phrasing the underlined part. Select the answer that produces the most effective sentence, one that is clear and exact, without awkwardness or ambiguity, and fill in the corresponding oval on your answer sheet. In choosing answers, follow the requirements of standard written English. Choose the answer that best expresses the meaning of the original sentence.

Answer (A) is always the same as the underlined part. Choose Answer (A) if you think the original sentence needs no revision.

EXAMPLE:

Laura Ingalls Wilder published her first book and she was sixty-five years old then.

(A) and she was sixty-five years old then
(B) when she was sixty-five
(C) at age sixty-five years old
(D) upon reaching of sixty-five years
(E) at the time when she was sixty-five

SAMPLE ANSWER

Ⓐ ● Ⓒ Ⓓ Ⓔ

20. In the tennis match Don was paired with Bill; Ed with Al.

  (A) was paired with Bill; Ed with Al
  (B) was paired with Bill; but Ed was paired with Al
  (C) was paired with Bill, and it was Ed with Al
  (D) pairing with Bill; Ed being with Al
  (E) pairing with Bill; Ed was with Al

21. In the Middle Ages, a lord's intricate wall hangings were more than mere tapestries they were a measure of his consequence and wealth.

  (A) mere tapestries they were a measure
  (B) merely tapestries they were a measure
  (C) mere tapestries and were a measure
  (D) mere tapestries; they were a measure
  (E) mere tapestries, while they were a measure

22. With the exception of Frank and I, everyone in the class finished the assignment before the bell rang.

  (A) Frank and I, everyone in the class finished
  (B) Frank and me, everyone in the class finished
  (C) Frank and me, everyone in the class had finished
  (D) Frank and I, everyone in the class had finished
  (E) Frank and me everyone in the class finished

GO ON TO THE NEXT PAGE ▷

23. Many middle class individuals find that they cannot obtain good medical attention, <u>despite they need it badly</u>.

    (A) despite they need it badly
    (B) despite their bad need of it
    (C) in spite of they need it badly
    (D) however much they need it
    (E) therefore, they need it badly

24. It is possible for a student to do well in class all semester and <u>then you fail</u> because of a poor performance on the final examination.

    (A) then you fail
    (B) then one fails
    (C) then you get a failing grade
    (D) later he fails
    (E) then to fail

25. <u>When one eats in this restaurant, you often find</u> that the prices are high and that the food is poorly prepared.

    (A) When one eats in this restaurant, you often find
    (B) When you eat in this restaurant, one often finds
    (C) When one eats in this restaurant, one often finds
    (D) If you eat in this restaurant, you often find
    (E) When one ate in this restaurant, he often found

26. Ever since the bombing of Cambodia, there has been much opposition <u>from they who maintain that it was unauthorized</u>.

    (A) from they who maintain that it was unauthorized
    (B) from they who maintain that it had been unauthorized
    (C) from those who maintain that it was unauthorized
    (D) from they maintaining that it was unauthorized
    (E) from they maintaining that it had been unauthorized

27. As the protest mounted, small <u>skirmishes between students and police that broke</u> out everywhere, flaring up like sudden brush fires on all sides.

    (A) skirmishes between students and police that broke
    (B) skirmishes between students and police which broke
    (C) skirmishes between students and police broke
    (D) skirmishes between students and police which were breaking
    (E) skirmishes between students and police breaking

28. <u>Great plans for the future were made by Huck and Tom that</u> depended on their finding the gold hidden in the cave.

    (A) Great plans for the future were made by Huck and Tom that
    (B) Great plans for the future were made by Huck and Tom which
    (C) Huck and Tom, who made great plans for the future that
    (D) Huck and Tom made great plans for the future that
    (E) Great plans for the future were being made by Huck and Tom that

29. <u>Many classic recordings have been reissued</u> in compact disk format, some perennial favorites have not

    (A) Many classic recordings have been reissued
    (B) Many classic recordings have reissued
    (C) Many a classic recording have been reissued
    (D) Despite many classic recordings which have been reissued
    (E) Although many classic recordings have been reissued

30. The method <u>of how different viruses being transmitted</u> from one patient to another depends on the particular viruses involved

    (A) of how different viruses being transmitted
    (B) whereby the transmission of different viruses is
    (C) by which different viruses are transmitted
    (D) for different viruses that are being transmitted
    (E) when different viruses being transmitted

31. <u>Because he wished to help alleviate the famine that followed the Russian civil was why Armand Hammer, a young American millionaire, decided that he had to go to Moscow.</u>

    (A) Because he wished to help alleviate the famine that followed the Russian civil war was why Armand Hammer, a young American millionaire, decided that he had to go to Moscow.
    (B) Because he wished to help alleviate the famine that followed the Russian civil war, a young American millionaire named Armand Hammer, decided that this was why he had to go to Moscow.
    (C) Armand Hammer, a young American millionaire, decided that he had to go to Moscow to help alleviate the famine that followed the Russian civil war.
    (D) Armand Hammer, a young American millionaire, deciding that he had to go to Moscow because he wished to help alleviate the famine that followed the Russian civil war.
    (E) A young American millionaire named Armand Hammer decided that he had to go to Moscow and he wished to help alleviate the famine that followed the Russian civil war.

GO ON TO THE NEXT PAGE →

32. Wildly unscientific medical remedies, such as bleeding people with leeches, were practiced for <u>centuries, and they showed</u> no sign of doing the patients any good.

- (A) centuries, and they showed
- (B) centuries that showed
- (C) centuries, they showed
- (D) centuries, however, they showed
- (E) centuries though they showed

33. <u>The novelist Graham Greene is one of Britain's finest authors and the most important</u> collection of his manuscripts is located in Texas, not in England.

- (A) The novelist Graham Greene is one of Britain's finest authors and the most important
- (B) The novelist Graham Greene being one of Britain's finest authors and the most important
- (C) Although the novelist Graham Greene is one of Britain's finest authors, and the most important
- (D) Although the novelist Graham Greene is one of Britain's finest authors, the most important
- (E) The novelist Graham Greene is one of Britain's finest authors; furthermore, the most important

Directions

The passage below is the unedited draft of a student's essay. Some of the essay needs to be rewritten to make the meaning clearer and more precise. Read the essay carefully.

The essay is followed by six questions about changes that might improve all or part of its organization, development, sentence structure, use of language, appropriateness to the audience, or its use of standard written English. Choose the answer that most clearly and effectively expresses the student's intended meaning. Indicate your choice by filling in the corresponding space on the answer sheet.

Essay

[1] Teenagers under eighteen can now receive a major credit card as long as the credit card's use is supervised by a parent or guardian. [2] This is a good idea since it gives these teenagers the responsibility of managing their money. [3] Another is because teenagers can develop good habits of spending that will be useful later in life.

[4] A teenager can legally hold a job at age sixteen. [5] This means that many teenagers have a steady income, which they should be able to spend as they wish. [6] Being in control of their own finances not only teaches them the value of money but how to spend it wisely.

[7] An example of a teenager with a credit card is Bonita Robbins. [8] Bonita is junior in high school. [9] She is seventeen years old. [10] She works after school in a real estate office. [11] She earns about $100 a week. [12] After three months of work she applied for a credit card. [13] Her bank gave her one but said that there will be a "trial period" in which her parent will be responsible. [14] Most of the time Bonita paid her bills punctually and on time. [15] However, during one month Bonita charged more than she could pay, so her parents loaned her the money. [16] The next month Bonita saved her income and paid it back. [17] This was a good lesson for Bonita, because next time she'll probably be more careful about spending money.

[18] This plan also lets the parents and the teenagers plan how the credit card will be used. [19] Teenagers might use the card freely to buy things for less than $25. [20] For items costing more, talk to your parents before buying them. [21] Parents could help their teenager to plan a budget or set priorities for spending money. [22] Since parents are going to assume responsibility for the card's use or abuse, they will want to have some input on how it will be used.

34. Which is the best revision of the underlined segment of sentence 3 below?

Another <u>is because teenagers can develop</u> good habits of spending that will be useful later in life.

- (A) reason is because teenagers develop
- (B) reason is because teenagers may develop
- (C) idea is due to the fact that teenagers may develop
- (D) may come about due to teenagers' developing
- (E) idea may be because teenagers develop

35. Given the context of paragraph 3, which revision of sentences 8, 9, 10, and 11 is the most effective?

- (A) Bonita, a junior in high school, earning about $100 a week by working after school in a real estate office, is seventeen years old.
- (B) As a junior in high school and being seventeen, she works after school in a real estate office, earns about $100 a week.
- (C) A seventeen-year-old high school junior, she earns $100 a week at an after-school job in a real estate office.
- (D) Bonita Robbins earns about $100 a week, being employed after school in a real estate office; she is seventeen and is a high school junior.
- (E) Being a junior in high school, Bonita, seventeen years old, earning about $100 week in a real estate office at an after-school job.

GO ON TO THE NEXT PAGE

36. Which of the following is the best revision of sentence 14?

   (A) Bills were paid punctually.
   (B) Usually Bonita had paid her bills on time.
   (C) Most of the time the bills were paid by Bonita on time.
   (D) Usually Bonita paid her bills punctually and on time.
   (E) Usually Bonita paid her bills when they were due.

37. With regard to the whole essay, which of the following best describes the function of paragraph 3?

   (A) To summarize the discussion presented in earlier paragraphs
   (B) To persuade readers to change their point of view
   (C) To provide an example
   (D) To ridicule an idea presented earlier in the essay
   (E) To draw a conclusion

38. Which revision of the underlined segment of sentence 18 below provides the best transition between the third and fourth paragraphs?

This plan also lets the parents and the teenagers plan how the credit card will be used.

   (A) Another advantage of this plan is that it
   (B) Another advantage of a "trial" credit card program like Bonita's is that it
   (C) A different advantage to Bonita's experience
   (D) All of a sudden, it
   (E) Together, it

39. In the context of the fourth paragraph, which is the best revision of sentence 20?

   (A) Before buying items worth more, teenagers might consult a parent.
   (B) Teenagers should be talking to their parents before buying something that costs more than $25.
   (C) But first talking about things costing more than $25 between parents and teenagers.
   (D) First teenagers and parents must talk before buying something that costs more than $25.
   (E) Buying something that costs more than $25 to purchase must be talked over between parents and teenagers beforehand.

IF YOU FINISH BEFORE 30 MINUTES, YOU MAY CHECK YOUR WORK ON THIS SECTION ONLY. DO NOT TURN TO ANY OTHER SECTION IN THE TEST.   **STOP**

SECTION 4
Verbal Reasoning

Time—30 minutes
30 Questions

For each question in this section, select the best answer from among the choices given and fill in the corresponding oval on the answer sheet.

Directions

Each sentence below consists of a related pair of words or phrases, followed by five pairs of words or phrases labeled A through E. Select the pair that best expresses a relationship similar to that expressed in the original pair.

Example:

CRUMB:BREAD::
(A) ounce:unit
(B) splinter:wood
(C) water:bucket
(D) twine:rope
(E) cream:butter

31. SCHOOL:TRUANT::
(A) university:teacher   (B) hospital:patient
(C) courtroom:defendant   (D) jail:convict
(E) army:deserter

32. STROLLER:BABY::
(A) moving van:mover   (B) ambulance:driver
(C) bus:passenger   (D) shopping cart:cashier
(E) carriage:horse

33. FLURRY:BLIZZARD::
(A) mud:slide   (B) mist:snow
(C) geyser:steam   (D) breeze:gale
(E) avalanche:waterfall

34. CARPET:FLOOR::
(A) mosaic:tile   (B) tapestry:wall
(C) beam:ceiling   (D) rug:fringe
(E) knob:door

35. TREATY:NATIONS::
(A) map:mountains   (B) contract:individuals
(C) reconciliation:ideas   (D) agreement:terms
(E) boundary:states

36. KANGAROO:MARSUPIAL::
(A) rose:hybrid   (B) mushroom:fungus
(C) antelope:gazelle   (D) alligator:swamp
(E) dog:flea

37. SNICKER:DISRESPECT::
(A) chortle:grief   (B) coax:petulance
(C) swagger:movement   (D) moan:suffering
(E) bellow:disgust

38. CHOREOGRAPHER:DANCE::
(A) astrologer:stars   (B) calligrapher:pen
(C) director:film   (D) driver:automobile
(E) photographer:camera

39. TASTE:GUSTATORY::
(A) touch:furtive   (B) eyes:visionary
(C) hearing:impaired   (D) smell:olfactory
(E) remark:derogatory

40. POVERTY:PAUPER::
(A) hunger:gourmet   (B) modesty:braggart
(C) ignorance:tutor   (D) slowness:sluggard
(E) wealth:jeweler

41. SERMON:SPEECH::
(A) stanza:poetry   (B) minister:congregation
(C) pilgrimage:journey   (D) lectern:lecture
(E) repentance:prayer

42. MERCURIAL:MOOD::
(A) jovial:wrath   (B) hypocritical:conduct
(C) ominous:weather   (D) frugal:economy
(E) erratic:course

43. COMMUTE:SENTENCE::
(A) travel:journal   (B) reduce:fine
(C) convict:crime   (D) refurbish:house
(E) transcribe:copy

The passage below is followed by questions based on its content. Answer the questions following the passage on the basis of what is <u>stated</u> or <u>implied</u> in that passage and in any introductory material that may be provided.

Questions 44–48 are based on the following passage.

For the past thirty years, one of the most exciting areas of modern geology has been plate tectonics, the study of the movements of the plates that make up the earth's outer shell. The following passage, taken from an article published in 1975, discusses one way in which the lithosphere, or outer crust of the earth, is affected by plate tectonics.

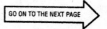 GO ON TO THE NEXT PAGE

The lithosphere, or outer shell, of the earth is made up of about a dozen rigid plates that move with respect to one another. New lithosphere is created at mid-ocean ridges by the upwelling and cooling of magma from the earth's interior. Since new lithosphere is continuously being created and the earth is not expanding to any appreciable extent, the question arises: What happens to the "old" lithosphere?

The answer came in the late 1960s as the last major link in the theory of sea-floor spreading and plate tectonics that has revolutionized our understanding of tectonic processes, or structural deformations, in the earth and has provided a unifying theme for many diverse observations of the earth sciences. The old lithosphere is subducted, or pushed down, into the earth's mantle (the thick shell of red-hot rock beneath the earth's thin, cooler crust and above its metallic, partly melted core). As the formerly rigid plate descends it slowly heats up, and over a period of millions of years it is absorbed into the general circulation of the earth's mantle.

The subduction of the lithosphere is perhaps the most significant phenomenon in global tectonics. Subduction not only explains what happens to old lithosphere but also accounts for many of the geologic processes that shape the earth's surface. Most of the world's volcanoes and earthquakes are associated with descending lithospheric plates. The prominent island arcs—chains of islands such as the Aleutians, the Kuriles, the Marianas, and the islands of Japan—are surface expressions of the subduction process. The deepest trenches of the world's oceans, including the Java and Tonga trenches and all others associated with island arcs, mark the seaward boundary of subduction zones. Major mountain belts, such as the Andes and the Himalayas, have resulted from the convergence and subduction of lithospheric plates.

To understand the subduction process it is necessary to look at the thermal regime of the earth. The temperatures within the earth at first increase rapidly with depth, reaching about 1,200 degrees Celsius at a depth of 100 kilometers. Then they increase more gradually, approaching 2,000 degrees C. at about 500 kilometers. The minerals in peridotite, the major constituent of the upper mantle, start to melt at about 1,200 C., or typically at a depth of 100 kilometers. Under the oceans the upper mantle is fairly soft and may contain some molten material at depths as shallow as 80 kilometers. The soft region of the mantle, over which the rigid lithospheric plate normally moves, is the asthenosphere. It appears that in certain areas convection currents in the asthenosphere may drive the plates, and that in other regions the plate motions may drive the convection currents.

44. Each of the following geological phenomena is mentioned in the passage as being relevant to the subduction of the lithosphere EXCEPT

(A) principal archipelagoes
(B) significant rifts in the sea bottom
(C) deserts in process of formation
(D) prominent mountain ranges
(E) volcanic eruptions

45. The style of the passage can best be described as

(A) oratorical   (B) argumentative   (C) expository
(D) meditative   (E) deprecatory

46. According to the passage, which of the following statements is (are) true of the earth's mantle?

I.   It is in a state of flux.
II. Its temperature is far greater than that of the lithosphere.
III. It eventually incorporates the subducted lithosphere.

(A) I only   (B) II only   (C) I and II only
(D) II and III only   (E) I, II, and III

47. The word "prominent" in line 31 means

(A) renowned   (B) flagrant   (C) diverse
(D) projecting   (E) immutable

48. Lines 55–58 suggest that the author regards current knowledge about the relationship between lithospheric plate motions and the convection currents in the asthenosphere as

(A) obsolete   (B) unfounded   (C) derivative
(D) definitive   (E) tentative

GO ON TO THE NEXT PAGE

The passages below are followed by questions based on their content; questions following a pair of related passages may also be based on the relationship between the paired passages. Answer the questions on the basis of what is <u>stated</u> or <u>implied</u> in the passages and in any introductory material that may be provided.

Questions 50–60 are based on the following passages.

The following passages, written in the mid-twentieth century, present two views of satire. Passage 1, written during World War II, sees satire as a powerful civilizing force. Passage 2, written a decade or so later, views it as an art now fallen into disuse.

PASSAGE 1

One thing is clear: the satiric note is a characteristic strain in the babel of the modern world. As the pace of our lives has accelerated, as science
Line has made the bare description of our universe
5 more complicated, and modern industry diversified the structure of society and sharpened the conflicts of its economic interests, there has taken place a no less desperate struggle of minds. It still continues and, since the pace of change is not in
10 any way slackening, seems destined to continue. Traditional ways of acting and believing lie around us in all degrees of repair, usefulness, and obstructiveness. New developments have shot up among them, some clearly conceived and good,
15 others incredibly makeshift or destructive. Satire calls attention to these confusions and sharpens the need for clarifying them.

It is no easy job to tidy up our intellectual and spiritual universe. But to live in chaos is to admit
20 defeat. We all want order in our lives and meaning in our world. Nature plays cruel and bitter jokes on us. We inflict stupid and bitter miseries on each other. We make wild blunders, but, as Thornton Wilder points out, we come through "by
25 the skin of our teeth." We clear away the wreckage of blitzed cities, we reclaim the dust bowl and control floods, we try to imagine and then create love and justice. To do so, we have to hew a path through the absurdities and empty-headed
30 mouthings of conventional formulas, through old and new fanaticisms, through muddle and deliberate misrepresentation, through needless cruelty and suffering.

Satire can help at these tasks because people
35 will let satire say things they will not permit the outright preacher or philosopher or social reformer to say. Not that they want to let the satirist say such things, or always know that they are letting him, but that in various ways he gets
40 around them. It is a sound instinct that has led modern artists and writers into the realm of satire. If the satirist himself has a critical eye, an undeluded mind, satire can enable him to persuade others to see with his eyes, to analyze with his mind.
45 With satire he can drown the nonsensical in ridicule and bathe our crimes in acid.

Satire is a powerful civilizing agent: if we ever become civilized it will probably be satire almost as much as poetry that will have accomplished it.
50 Because the great criteria of satire are always truth and sanity. Even the minor satire of deriding foibles, affectations, crazes, and fashions strikes its sparks from the flint of fact. But satire may deepen into being a criticism of humanity and of
55 life itself. When it does, it depends for its dignity upon the principles it invokes, and upon the depth, breadth, and sanity of the satirist's vision. Grace, wit, and virtuosity are all delightful adjuncts without which would-be satirists may
60 find themselves only would-be. Flippancy, shallowness, and insincerity, however, are fatal. The great satirists see straight, they see far, and they see deep. That is what makes them great.

It is also what makes satire valuable. Not that
65 we want satire all the time, or that everything is in need of being satirized. Men and women and God's world need to be praised and loved, too, and deserve to be. But sometimes they need to be knocked off their perch, and even, on occasion, to
70 have their blocks knocked off. They need to have their eyes opened to their own blindness and foolishness. And when they are mean, cruel, or revengeful, their failings need to be beaten to a pulp.

PASSAGE 2

75 We still have, in short, all the weapons in the arsenal of satire: the rapier of wit, the broadsword of invective, the stiletto of parody, the Damoclean swords of sarcasm and irony. Their cutting edges are bright and sharp; they glisten with barbs guar-
80 anteed to stick and stay stuck in the thickest hide, or stab the most inflated Polonius in the arras. Yet though they hang well-oiled and ready to our hands, we tend to use them separately and gingerly. We are afraid of hurting someone's feelings or
85 of being hurt in a return bout. We tremble at the prospect of treading on someone's moral corns. We are too full of the milquetoast of human kindness. We always see the Other Side of the Case, always remember that our Victim may have a
90 Mom who loves him, always fear that we may be setting him back a few hundred hours in his psychiatric adjustment. Oh, yes. We poke and pry a bit. We pin an errant butterfly to a board or two. But for real lessons in the ungentlest of the arts
95 we must turn back to the older masters.

GO ON TO THE NEXT PAGE →

49. According to lines 2–17, as the world becomes more complex and our intellectual universe more chaotic, satire becomes

(A) confusing because of its makeshift nature
(B) helpful in promoting clarity of thought
(C) useful in distracting us from our confusions
(D) diverting in its mockery of our follies
(E) destructive because it undermines our faith in the possibility of reform

50. To "reclaim the dust bowl" (line 26) is to

(A) declare kinship with the past
(B) recover useful material from scraps
(C) make barren land fit for use
(D) redeem a pledge to our ancestors
(E) assert ownership of vacant property

51. Passage 1's author looks on satire's ability to get around people (lines 37–41) with

(A) consternation   (B) indifference
(C) skepticism   (D) satisfaction   (E) awe

52. The author regards poetry (lines 47–49) as

(A) an inferior genre to satire
(B) a major civilizing influence
(C) diametrically opposed to satire
(D) great because of its vision of humanity
(E) the equal of satire

53. The phrase "strikes its sparks from the flint of fact" (line 53) is best taken to mean that even minor satire

(A) is easy to ignite
(B) has a striking appearance
(C) is as short-lived as a spark
(D) has a factual basis
(E) is hardhearted

54. In lines 68–70, the author is speaking

(A) vindictively   (B) hypothetically
(C) metaphorically   (D) directly   (E) formally

55. According to Passage 2, we avoid using satire because we

(A) are apprehensive of its sting
(B) do not comprehend its character
(C) feel inferior to the older masters
(D) are not inquisitive by nature
(E) are too uneducated in its use

56. As used in lines 83–84, the word "gingerly" most nearly means

(A) insincerely   (B) effectively   (C) clumsily
(D) carefully   (E) unhappily

57. Passage 2 suggests that people today ("we") chiefly aspire to

(A) a sense of emotional security
(B) a feeling of aggressiveness
(C) material wealth
(D) freedom from hunger
(E) protection from satire

58. By the metaphor "the broadsword of invective" the author most likely intends to imply that invective

(A) cuts less than other forms of satire
(B) is a relatively crude form of satire
(C) deserves greater respect than other forms of satire
(D) represents an older tradition of satire
(E) is an immensely popular form of satire

59. The tone of the latter part of Passage 2 is one of

(A) outraged dignity   (B) pronounced irony
(C) growing distrust   (D) calm resignation
(E) happy abandon

60. The author of Passage 1 would most likely react to the characterization of satire as pinning "an errant butterfly to a board or two" (line 93) by asserting that

(A) butterflies are graceful creatures deserving praise
(B) the beauty of satire is that it is pointless
(C) it is wrong to inflict needless pain on insects
(D) satirists must be wary of hurting people's feelings
(E) satire needs to take on more important targets

IF YOU FINISH BEFORE 30 MINUTES, YOU MAY CHECK YOUR WORK ON THIS
SECTION ONLY. DO NOT TURN TO ANY OTHER SECTION IN THE TEST.   **S T O P**

SECTION 5
Mathematical Reasoning

Directions and Sample Questions

Notes:

(1) The use of a calculator is permitted. All numbers used are real numbers.

(2) Figures that accompany problems in this test are intended to provide information useful in solving the problems. They are drawn as accurately as possible EXCEPT when it is stated in a specific problem that the figure is not drawn to scale. All figures lie in a plane unless otherwise indicated.

Questions 1–15 each consist of two quantities in boxes, one in Column A and one in Column B. You are to compare the two quantities and on the answer sheet fill in oval

A if the quantity in Column A is greater;
B if the quantity in Column B is greater;
C if the two quantities are equal;
D if the relationship cannot be determined from the information given.

Notes:

1. In some questions, information is given about one or both of the quantities to be compared. In such cases, the given information is centered above the two columns and is not boxed.
2. In a given question, a symbol that appears in both columns represents the same thing in Column A as it does in Column B.
3. Letters such as x, n, and k stand for real numbers.

EXAMPLES		
Column A	Column B	Answers
E1 $\quad 5^2$	20	● Ⓑ Ⓒ Ⓓ

$150° \quad x°$

E2 $\quad x$	30	Ⓐ Ⓑ ● Ⓓ

r and s are integers.

E3 $\quad r+1$	$s-1$	Ⓐ Ⓑ Ⓒ ●

PART I: QUANTITATIVE COMPARISON QUESTIONS

SUMMARY DIRECTIONS FOR QUANTITATIVE COMPARISON QUESTIONS

Answer: A if the quantity in Column A is greater.   C if the two quantities are equal.
B if the quantity in Column B is greater.   D if the relationship cannot be determined from the information given.

	Column A	Column B
26.	$\frac{1}{8}$	$\left(\frac{1}{0.08}\right)^2$
27.	$x+y$	$x-y$
28.	$x^2 = xy$	
	x	y

	Column A	Column B
	$\dfrac{1}{x} < 1$	
29.	x	0
	$xyz = 0$	
30.	x	y
	$p = 9 - x^2$ and $q = 9y^2$	
	x and y are positive integers.	
31.	The greatest possible value of p.	The smallest possible value of q.

GO ON TO THE NEXT PAGE

	Column A	Column B		Column A	Column B

32. $20\%x$ 10% of $\dfrac{x}{2}$

$$x = 2 \text{ and } y = 3$$

33. $x + y$ $\dfrac{\dfrac{1}{xy}}{\dfrac{1}{x}+\dfrac{1}{y}}$

34. The time required to travel a mile and a half at 20 miles per hour   The time required to travel $^3/_4$ mile at 10 miles per hour

---

The sum of the sides of a square $= s$.
The length of a rectangle is $\dfrac{s}{2}$, which is 4 times its width.

35. The area of the square   The area of the rectangle

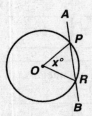

O is the center of the circle.
$$PR = OP$$

36. x $60°$

37. AB BC

$$x > 0$$

38. $24x\%$ $\dfrac{6x}{25}$

$$x > 0 > y$$

39. $x + y$ y

40. $\dfrac{6a-5}{2}$ $3a - 3$

PART II: STUDENT-PRODUCED RESPONSE QUESTIONS

Directions for Student-Produced Response Questions

Each of the remaining ten questions (41–50) requires you to solve the problem and enter your answer by marking the ovals in the special grid, as shown in the examples below.

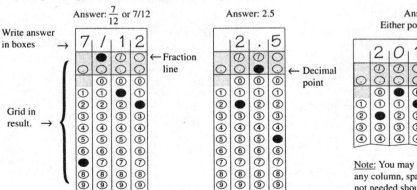

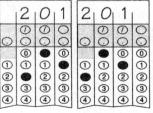

Note: You may start your answers in any column, space permitting. Columns not needed should be left blank.

- Mark no more than one oval in any column.
- Because the answer sheet will be machine-scored, **you will receive credit only if the ovals are filled in correctly.**
- Although not required, it is suggested that you write your answer in the boxes at the top of the columns to help you fill in the ovals accurately.
- Some problems may have more than one correct answer. In such cases, grid only one answer.
- No question has a negative answer.
- **Mixed numbers** such as $2\frac{1}{2}$ much be gridded as 2.5 or 5/2. (If is gridded, it will be interpreted as $\frac{21}{2}$, not $\frac{21}{2}$.)

- Decimal Accuracy: If you obtain a decimal answer, enter the most accurate value that the grid will accommodate. For example, if you obtain an answer such as 0.6666..., you should record the result as .666 or .667. Less accurate values such as .66 or .67 are not acceptable.

Acceptable ways to grid $\frac{2}{3}$ = .6666. . .

41. What whole number does $\dfrac{\frac{2}{3} + \frac{1}{4}}{\frac{1}{6} + \frac{2}{3} + \frac{1}{12}}$ equal?

42. If $13 = \dfrac{13w}{1-w}$, what whole number does $(2w)^2$ equal?

43. If $r = \sqrt{\dfrac{3V}{\pi h}}$, by what number must we multiply V in order to multiply r by 9?

44. How many posts are needed for a 50-foot fence if each post is 5 feet from the next post?

45. A fish tank $1' \times 1\frac{1}{2}' \times \frac{1}{2}'$ is carefully used to fill a large tank which has a capacity of 15 cubic feet. How many times will the contents of the smaller tank be required to be emptied into the larger tank to completely fill the tank?

46. $X = 66\frac{2}{3}\% \ Y$

$Y = 33\frac{1}{3}\% \ Z$
What percent of X is Z?

47. A man works 5 days a week and binds 35 sets of books each week. If there are 7 books in a set, what is the number of books he binds each day?

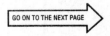

48. In the accompanying figure, the area of square *ABCD* is 36 and points *L* and *M* are the midpoints of sides *AB* and *AD*, respectively. What is the area of quadrilateral *BLMD*?

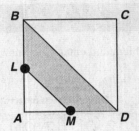

49. A map measuring 8" × 10" and drawn to the scale 1" = 50 miles is pasted on a sheet of paper of the same size. Find the least number of sheets of this paper that would have to be taped together to hold this same map if it were drawn to the scale 2" = 25 miles.

50. In △*ABC*, *AF* and *CE* meet in *D*. If *AE* = *EB*, *BF* = *FC*, then what does $\dfrac{AD \times CD}{FD \times ED}$ equal?

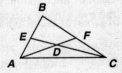

IF YOU FINISH BEFORE 30 MINUTES, YOU MAY CHECK YOUR WORK ON THIS SECTION ONLY. DO NOT TURN TO ANY OTHER SECTION IN THE TEST.

S T O P

ANSWER KEY

Verbal Reasoning Section 1

1. E	*6.* D	*11.* A	*16.* B	*21.* E	*26.* B
2. B	*7.* A	*12.* D	*17.* E	*22.* E	*27.* D
3. B	*8.* C	*13.* D	*18.* A	*23.* B	*28.* D
4. D	*9.* B	*14.* C	*19.* C	*24.* D	*29.* E
5. C	*10.* A	*15.* E	*20.* D	*25.* B	*30.* C

Mathematical Reasoning Section 2

Note: Each correct answer to the mathematics questions is keyed by number to the corresponding topic in Chapters 8 and 9. These numerals refer to the topics listed below, with specific page references in parentheses.

1. Basic Fundamental Operations (179–182)
2. Algebraic Operations (182–183)
3. Using Algebra (182–184, 187)
4. Exponents, Roots, and Radicals (184–185)
5. Inequalities (188–189)
6. Fractions (182, 198)
7. Decimals (200)
8. Percent (200)
9. Averages (201)
10. Motion (203)
11. Ratio and Proportion (204–205)
12. Mixtures and Solutions (178)
13. Work (206–207)
14. Coordinate Geometry (194)
15. Geometry (189–193, 195)
16. Quantitative Comparisons (211–212)
17. Data Interpretation (208)

1. C (2)	*6.* E (6)	*11.* B (8)	*16.* D (15)	*21.* E (4, 14)
2. A (2)	*7.* A (1)	*12.* C (2)	*17.* C (15)	*22.* B (15)
3. D (1)	*8.* D (1, 21)	*13.* B (15)	*18.* C (15)	*23.* C (15)
4. E (8)	*9.* C (6)	*14.* B (15)	*19.* A (15)	*24.* B (6)
5. E (3, 6)	*10.* E (3)	*15.* B (15)	*20.* D (15)	*25.* D (17)

Writing Skills Section 3

1. B	*8.* C	*15.* A	*22.* C	*29.* E	*36.* E
2. D	*9.* A	*16.* B	*23.* B	*30.* C	*37.* C
3. C	*10.* C	*17.* C	*24.* E	*31.* C	*38.* B
4. A	*11.* E	*18.* B	*25.* C	*32.* E	*39.* A
5. B	*12.* D	*19.* C	*26.* C	*33.* D	
6. E	*13.* C	*20.* A	*27.* C	*34.* B	
7. B	*14.* E	*21.* D	*28.* D	*35.* C	

Verbal Reasoning Section 4

31. E	*36.* B	*41.* C	*46.* E	*51.* D	*56.* D
32. C	*37.* D	*42.* E	*47.* D	*52.* B	*57.* A
33. D	*38.* C	*43.* B	*48.* E	*53.* D	*58.* B
34. B	*39.* D	*44.* C	*49.* B	*54.* C	*59.* B
35. B	*40.* D	*45.* C	*50.* C	*55.* A	*60.* E

Mathematical Reasoning Section 5

26. B (4, 6, 7, 16)	*29.* D (6, 16)	*32.* D (8, 16)	*35.* C (15, 16)	*38.* C (6, 8, 16)
27. D (2, 16)	*30.* D (1, 16)	*33.* A (2, 6, 16)	*36.* C (15, 16)	*39.* B (5, 16)
28. D (6, 16)	*31.* B (3)	*34.* C (10, 16)	*37.* C (15, 16)	*40.* A (2, 6, 16)

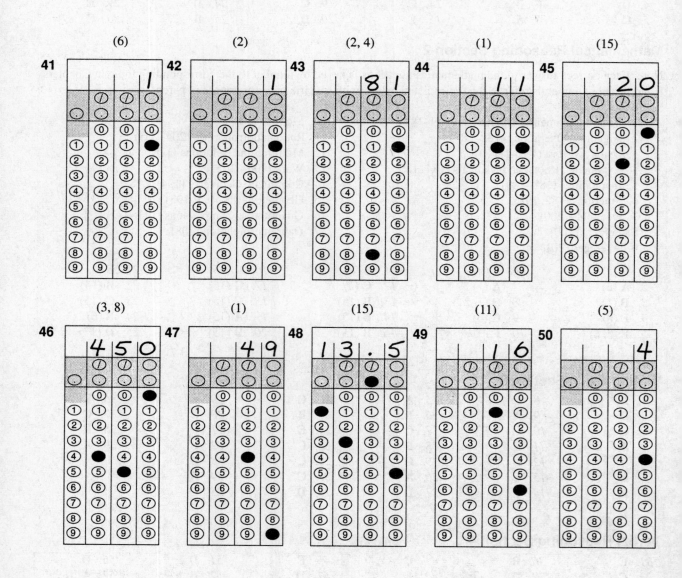

SCORING CHART — TYPICAL TEST G

Verbal Sections

Section 1   Questions 1–30
Number correct _____ (A)
Number omitted _____ (B)
Number incorrect _____ (C)
$\frac{1}{4}$ (C) = _____ (D)
Raw Score:
  (A) – (D) = _____

Section 3   Questions 31–60
Number correct _____ (A)
Number omitted _____ (B)
Number incorrect _____ (C)
$\frac{1}{4}$ (C) = _____ (D)
Raw Score:
  (A) – (D) = _____

Total Verbal Raw Score:
  (Section 1 +
  Section 3) = _____

Mathematical Sections

Section 2   Questions 1–25
Number correct _____ (A)
Number incorrect _____ (B)
(A) – $\frac{1}{4}$ (B) = _____ Raw Score I

Section 4   Questions 26–40
Number correct _____ (C)
Number incorrect _____ (D)
(C) – $\frac{1}{3}$ (D) = _____ Raw Score II

Section 4   Questions 41–50
Number correct _____ Raw Score III

Total Mathematical Raw Score:
  (Raw Scores I + II
  + III) = _____

Writing Section

Section 3   Questions 1–39
Number correct _____ (A)
Number incorrect _____ (B)
$\frac{1}{4}$ (B) = _____ (C)
(no penalty for omitted questions)
Writing Raw Score:
  (A) – (C) = _____

EVALUATION CHART

Study your score. Your raw score on the Verbal and Mathematical Reasoning Sections is an indication of your probable achievement on the PSAT/NMSQT. As a guide to the amount of work you need or want to do with this book, study the following.

| **Raw Score** | | | **Self-rating** |
Verbal	Mathematical	Writing	
55–60	41–50	37–39	Superior
44–54	25–40	31–36	Very good
39–43	20–24	25–30	Satisfactory
35–38	16–19	19–24	Average
29–34	10–15	13–18	Needs further study
20–28	7–9	6–12	Needs intensive study
0–19	0–6	0–5	Probably inadequate

ANSWER EXPLANATIONS

Verbal Reasoning Section 1

1. **E** A marked increase in counterfeiting would motivate banks to order their tellers to take a close look at or *scrutinize* any bills that might be fake.

2. **B** Naturalists would be *alarmed* by the idea that the elephant population might be decreasing. They would *deplore* (disapprove of, lament) the notion that the species was slowly dying out.

3. **B** To *aggravate* a problem is to make it worse. When people live longer and fewer babies die, overpopulation is made worse.

4. **D** *Derision* is making fun of something. Since they did not take his proposal seriously, they treated it with derision. Choice B is a less appropriate answer because *detachment* or indifference is not so nearly opposite to "serious study."

5. **C** This sentence contrasts the opinion of "some scientists" with that of "many experts." The first group thinks that action should be delayed. Therefore, the second group must want action soon: because damage is *accelerated*, it "*warrants* strong measures now." Choice D is incorrect because *illusory* means not real; if the damage were not real, then there would be no reason to take action.

6. **D** The qualities listed are highly positive ones. All would be helpful to someone in a position of *leadership*. Choice E is incorrect. Though *loyalty* has positive associations, it is not particularly related to articulateness (clarity in speech; fluency), wit, or intellectual vigor.

7. **A** The structure of the sentence ("Even...who normally would") signals a contrast. The Republican committee members did *not* defend the administration's actions. Instead, they *deprecated* (condemned; disapproved) them.

8. **C** By definition, *parasites* sap or drain nutrients from their hosts.

9. **B** A *foretoken* is an advance indication. Earlier phases of one's life may be foretokens of later stages.

10. **A** Both missing words must be positive. The speaker is praising the installation as *impeccable* (without fault) and saying that, despite recent drawbacks, such programs can still *succeed.*

11. **A** *Unlike* signals a contrast. Feynman was not reclusive or solitary. Instead, he was *gregarious* or sociable.

12. **D** *Though* signals a contrast. Parts of Islam hate science. However, despite this, Islam has produced or *spawned* scientists in its own ranks.

13. **D** The physicists have had good reason to believe in the principle because it has *survived* rigorous or strict tests. These tests have *proved* that the principle is accurate. Note how the second clause supports the first, explaining why the physicists have had reason to be confident in the principle.

14. **C** The embittered benefactor thinks of the former recipients as *ingrates* (ungrateful persons) because they did not thank her sufficiently for her generosity. She does not think of them as *misers* (hoarders of wealth): although they are stingy in expressing thanks, they are extravagant in spending money. She certainly does not think of them as *louts* (clumsy oafs), *prigs* (self-righteous fussbudgets), or *renegades* (traitors) : what she specifically resents in them is ingratitude, not cloddishness, self-satisfaction, or treachery.

15. **E** If Mrs. Woolf combines both modern radical and old-fashioned nonradical elements in her fictions, then she presents *an anomalous* or contradictory image.

16. **B** If Latinos have been *assimilated* or absorbed into the American mainstream, then that *debunks* (exposes as false; reveals the foolishness of) the idea that Latinos are cut off from the mainstream.

17. **E** The field is cluttered by a *welter* or chaotic jumble of contradictory theories. Choice A is incorrect. While *bonanza* means abundance, it is an abundance of good things, a desired abundance. Here the abundance of theories is undesired; it is a confusion, not a blessing.

18. **A** The author is *reflecting on* or considering her childhood. She is remembering and analyzing past events.

19. **C** The speaker is an *adult*, looking back in time. Her description implies that she did not understand the prejudice of the other children, because she was young and innocent. As an adult, she is clear about the attitude of the other pupils; as a child, it made no sense to her.

20. **D** Paragraph 5 states: "I was the only child who had camped on the Baumanns' land ever to get out of the C class." This suggests that the school administrators dealt with the "problem of transient laborers" by *placing all migrant children in the C class.*

21. **E** The author does not personally believe that being a migrant worker is disgraceful. That is what the townsfolk believed. She uses the townsfolk's own words ("disgraceful and dirty," "gypsies," "untrustworthy") to imply the exactly opposite beliefs. In doing so, her tone is clearly *ironic.*

22. **E** Most people would agree that ginger ale is a common beverage, not "an exotic drink." By referring to it as exotic, the author underscores how unfamiliar she was as the child of migrant workers with *everyday experiences we take for granted.*

23. **B** Barbara and her friends began to play with the narrator and invite her to one of their homes because of her transfer to the A class. This upward change in her academic status led to a similar change in her social status: the other children began to treat her with *acceptance.*

24. **D** Given that Du Bois chose to describe himself as "a master of propaganda," he most probably regarded his work as a propagandist as *a particular achievement* on his part.

25. **B** Du Bois describes at length the sense of "twoness" he feels as a black American. In other words, he emphasizes the American Negro's *duality.*

26. **B** The body's dogged strength enables it to resist being pulled apart. In stubbornly resisting the forces that threaten to tear him in two, the black American is *tenacious* (persistent) and *unyielding* (resolute).

27. **D** Although the author points out that Du Bois's methods led him into conflicts, he describes Du Bois as "often . . . well in advance of his contemporaries" and stresses that his motives for departing from the mainstream were admirable. Thus, his attitude can best be described as *approving.*

28. **D** The final two paragraphs discuss Du Bois in relationship to black leaders in general and then provide the specific example of his relationship to Booker T. Washington. Choice A is incorrect. The author mentions Du Bois's early support of Washington's gradualist approach in order to contrast it with his later departure from Washington's conservatism. Choice B is incorrect. The author discusses Du Bois's personality only in passing; he discusses Washington's personality not at all. Choice C is incorrect. The author's chief concern is to describe Du Bois's position, not analyze what lay behind his achieving this position. He spends more time showing why Du Bois angered his fellow blacks than he does showing why Du Bois attracted them. Choice E is incorrect. It is unsupported by the passage.

29. **E** The last sentence points out that Du Bois originally agreed with Washington's program. Choice A is incorrect. Nothing in the passage suggests that Du Bois sacrificed effective strategies out of a desire to try something new. Choice B is incorrect. Du Bois gained in influence, effectively winning away large numbers of blacks from Washington's policies. Choice

C is incorrect. Du Bois's quickness to depart from conventional black wisdom when it proved inadequate to the task of advancing the race shows him to be well able to change with the times. Choice D is incorrect. Washington, not Du Bois, is described as seeking the good will of powerful whites.

30. **C** The author does *not* portray Washington as versatile. Instead, he portrays Du Bois as versatile. Choice A is incorrect. The author portrays Washington as submissive to the majority; he shows him teaching blacks not to protest. Choice B is incorrect. The author portrays Washington as concerned with financial success; he shows him advocating property accumulation. Choice D is incorrect. The author portrays Washington as traditional in preaching industry; he shows him advocating hard work. Choice E is incorrect. The author portrays Washington as respectful of authority; he shows him deferring to powerful whites.

Mathematical Reasoning Section 2

1. **C** $z + \dfrac{1}{z} = 2$

$$\frac{z^2 + 1}{z} = 2$$

$$z^2 + 1 = 2z$$
$$z^2 - 2z + 1 = 0$$
$$(z - 1)(z - 1) = 0 \text{ [factoring]}$$
$$z = 1$$

2. **A** $2x = 3(a + b)$

$$\frac{2x}{(a + b)} = \frac{3(a + b)}{(a + b)} \text{ [divide by } (a + b)]$$

$$\frac{2x}{(a + b)} = 3$$

$$\frac{2x}{(a + b)(2x)} = \frac{3}{2x} \text{ [divide by } 2x]$$

$$\frac{1}{a + b} = \frac{3}{2x}$$

3. **D** 2 yards = 72 inches
$72 \div 3 = 24$ inches $= \dfrac{24}{36}$ or $\dfrac{2}{3}$ yard.

4. **E** Total salary = $200
Income from commission = $150
Let x = amount of sales.
4% or (.04) of x = $150
$$.04x = 150$$
$$4x = 15000$$
$$x = \$3750$$

5. **E** $\frac{1}{2} + \frac{1}{3} = \frac{5}{6}$ accounts for part of students going on for further education. Therefore $\frac{1}{6}$ expect to seek permanent employment.

Let x = number of students in this school.

$\frac{1}{6} x = 300$

$x = 1800.$

6. **E**   Time elapsed from 8:55 to 9:15 = 20 minutes $\left(\frac{1}{3} \text{ hour}\right)$

$\dfrac{\text{time actually put in on task}}{\text{time required to complete task}} = \dfrac{\text{part of task}}{\text{completed}}$

$\dfrac{\frac{1}{3} \text{ hour}}{3 \text{ hours}} = \frac{1}{3} \div 3 = \left(\frac{1}{3}\right)\left(\frac{1}{3}\right) = \frac{1}{9}$

7. **A**   Total cost = $9.24
Cost of tax = $.24
Basic price = $9.00
Basic price per gallon = $9.00 ÷ 6 gallons = 1.50 per gallon

8. **D**   If x is odd, $x + 1$ and $x - 1$ are both even; their product, $(x + 1)(x - 1)$, will also be even (I). $x + 483$ is the sum of two odd numbers, and is therefore even (II). If x is odd, x^2, the product of two odd numbers, is also odd; when 2 is added to it, the sum is odd (III).

9. **C**   Improvement = 3 miles to the gallon for a total of 18 miles per gallon
Consumption for 5400 miles with old carburetor = 360 gallons
Consumption for 5400 miles with new carburetor = 300 gallons
Saving = 60 gallons at $1.35 per gallon = $81.00

10. **E**   Observe the values of y: 0 + 1 = 1; 1 + 1 = 2. 2 + 1 = 3.
Observe the values of x: −7 + 4 = −3; −3 + 4 = 1. ∴ 1 + 4 = 5

11. **B**   The painting was sold for 60% of the original marked price.
Let x = original marked price.
60% of x or $.6x$ = $48.
$6x = 480$
$x = \$80$

12. **C** $ab - c + x = 0$
$x = c - ab$

13. **B**   The angle between two minute units on a clock $= \frac{360°}{60} = 6°.$
At half past 2 the hour hand is midway between 2 and 3.
The distance from this point to the 6 on the clock is 17.5 minutes $(17.5)(6°) = 105°.$

14. **B**   Recall: parallel chords intercept equal arcs.
$\widehat{AD} = \widehat{BC} = 110°$
$\widehat{CD} = 360° - (\widehat{AD} + \widehat{AB} + \widehat{BC})$
or $360° - (110° + 30° + 110°) = 110°$
$\angle CED \overset{\circ}{=} \frac{1}{2}(\widehat{CD} + \widehat{AB})$
or $\frac{1}{2}(30° + 110°) = 70°$

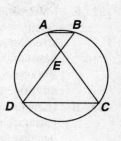

15. **B**   Draw OB. $\angle OCB$ is a right angle (radius drawn to tangent at point of contact of tangent). OB bisects angle COA. $\angle COB \overset{\circ}{=} 70$.
∴ $\angle CBO \overset{\circ}{=} 20$. Likewise, $\angle OBA \overset{\circ}{=} 20$.
$\angle B = 40$.

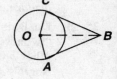

16. **D** $\widehat{AB} = 72° = \frac{1}{5}$ of 360° (circumference)
$5(6\pi) = 30\pi$ = circumference.
Let d = diameter and r = radius.
$\pi d = 30\pi$
$d = 30$
$r = 15$
Area = πr^2
Area = $\pi(15)^2 = 225\pi$

17. **C**   Let x = number of degrees in $\angle A$ (the smallest of the angles).
Then $3x$ = number of degrees in $\angle B$ (the desired quantity).
Then $8x$ = number of degrees in $\angle C$ (necessary to find the sum of the angles of the triangle).
Since the sum of the angles of a triangle equals a straight angle,
$x + 3x + 8x \overset{\circ}{=} 180.$
$12x \overset{\circ}{=} 180$
$x \overset{\circ}{=} 15$
$3x \overset{\circ}{=} 45 \ (\angle B)$

18. **C**   Multiplying each term of the first equation by 2 shows that it is equivalent to the second equation. The graphs of the two equations are identical, so only III is true.

19. **A** Draw OC, OD.

$\triangle OCD = \frac{1}{6}$ of $ABCDEF$

Since perimeter = 12,

$CD = 2$.

O is center of circum-
scribed circle.

$OC = OD$ (radii)

$\angle COD = \frac{1}{6}(360°) = 60°$

$\therefore \triangle OCD$ is equilateral.

Area of equilateral $\triangle = \frac{s^2}{4}\sqrt{3}$

Area $= \frac{2^2}{4}\sqrt{3} = \sqrt{3}$

Area of hexagon $= 6(\sqrt{3}) = 6\sqrt{3}$

20. **D** Let x = central angle of a radian

Length of arc of one radian $= r$

Radius $= r$

Circumference $= 2\pi r$

$\dfrac{\text{central angle}}{360°} = \dfrac{\text{length of arc}}{\text{circumference}}$

or $\dfrac{x}{360°} = \dfrac{r}{2\pi r}$

$2\pi x = 360°$

$x = \dfrac{360°}{2\pi}$

$x = \dfrac{180°}{\pi}$

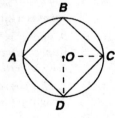
1 radian

21. **E** Let the hypotenuse be a; $a = 10$ and one leg,

$5\sqrt{3}$, is $\frac{a}{2}\sqrt{3}$. Thus, the triangle is a 30°-
60°-90° triangle. The other leg is the one oppo-
site 30°, or $\frac{a}{2}$.

$\frac{a}{2} = \frac{10}{2} = 5$

Area of $\triangle = \dfrac{(5\sqrt{3})(5)}{2} = 12.5\sqrt{3}$

22. **B** Draw OD and OC radii
of circle.

$\triangle DOC$ is a right isosceles triangle.

$DC = 2$ [given]

Let r = radii, OD, OC.

Using the Pythagorean
Theorem,

$r^2 + r^2 = 2r^2$

$2r^2 = 4$

$r^2 = 2$.

Area of circle $(\pi r^2) = 2\pi$

23. **C** Area of square $= (4V)^2 = 16V^2$

Length of rectangle $= 5V^3$ [given]

Let w = width of rectangle

Area of rectangle = (length)(width)

$16V^2 = 5V^3 w$

$\dfrac{16V^2}{5V^3} = w$ or $w = \dfrac{16}{5V}$

24. **B** Let x = the capacity of the oil tank

$\frac{7}{10}x = 420$

$x = (420)(\frac{10}{7}) =$

$x = (60)(10) = 600$

25. **D** The chart indicates the differences as follows:

#3: $30,000   #5: $10,000   #7: $20,000   #8:
$60,000   #9: $40,000

Writing Skills Section 3

1. **B** Error in case. Change *of them* to *of those* (people).

2. **D** Misplaced modifier. The phrase *in good condition* should come after the word *piano*.

3. **C** Lack of agreement. *School* is singular and
should be followed by *was* (singular).

4. **A** Error in diction. Use *In consideration of*
instead of *In consideration about*.

5. **B** Incomplete sentence. By changing *and* to *was*
or *is*, we correct the error.

6. **E** Sentence is correct.

7. **B** Error in case. Change *I* to *me* because the pronoun is the object of the preposition *among*.

8. **C** Lack of agreement. The verb should agree with
editor (singular). Change *were* to *was*.

9. **A** Error in case. The pronoun should be *whom*
because it is the object of the verb *see*.

10. **C** Lack of parallel structure. Change *it presented*
to *presentation of*.

11. **E** Sentence is correct.

12. **D** Lack of agreement. The subject is *quantity*
(singular) and requires a singular verb *was
missing*.

13. **C** Lack of agreement. The subject is *neighborhood*
(singular) and requires a singular verb *lies*.

14. **E** Sentence is correct.

15. **A** Error in diction. Change *had ought* to *ought*.

16. **B** Error in diction. Change *infer* to *imply*.

17. **C** Error in tense. Change *did* to *has done*.

18. **B** Lack of parallel structure. Change clause to a
phrase in order to parallel the preceding
phrase. Change *it has brought about* to *if it*.

19. **C** Reference error. The pronoun *they* must refer
to a particular plural noun in the sentence or be
unclear. Substitute *refugees* for *they*.

20. **A**   The original answer provides the most effective and concise sentence.

21. **D**   The use of the semi-colon both corrects the run-on sentence and effectively contrasts the two clauses.

22. **C**   This corrects the two errors in this sentence—the error in case (*me* for *I*) and the error in tense (*had finished* for *finished*).

23. **B**   *Despite* should be used as a preposition.

24. **E**   This corrects the lack of parallel structure.

25. **C**   Unnecessary shift of pronoun. Do not shift from *you* to *one*.

26. **C**   *From* is a preposition and requires a pronoun in the objective case—*from those* (*people*).

27. **C**   This corrects the sentence fragment.

28. **D**   The shift to active voice and placement of the dependent clause closer to the noun it modifies both strengthen the sentence.

29. **E**   The introduction of the conjunction *although* corrects the run-on sentence and provides a logical relationship between the clauses.

30. **C**   This corrects the error in verb form in the original sentence.

31. **C**   This rearrangement of the sentence both eliminate wordiness and presents the ideas in a clear, straightforward manner.

32. **E**   The introduction of the conjunction *though* clarifies the relationship between the clauses.

33. **D**   The relationship between the two clauses is one of contrast. It is made clear by the use of *although*.

34. **B**   Choice A contains the nonstandard usage *is because*.
Choice B is correctly worded and concise. It is the best answer.
Choices C, D, and E are wordy, awkward, or both.

35. **C**   Choice A subordinates the important information about Bonita (her job and earnings), and emphasizes the fact that Bonita is seventeen.
Choice B lacks parallelism and is awkwardly worded.
Choice C accurately and economically combines the sentences. It is the best answer.
Choice D fails to subordinate the less important information about Bonita. It also unnecessarily repeats Bonita's full name.
Choice E lacks a main verb; therefore, it is a sentence fragment.

36. **E**   Choice A contains too little information. Exactly who paid the bills remains unclear.
Choice B contains a verb in the past perfect tense, which is inconsistent with the rest of the essay.
Choice C is awkwardly written in passive voice.
Choice D contains a redundancy: *punctually* and *on time*.
Choice E is clear and accurate. It is the best answer.

37. **C**   Only Choice C is correct. The paragraph gives a specific example of a teenager with a credit card.

38. **B**   Choice A is a reasonable transition except that the phrase *this plan* does not have a specific referent.
Choice B effectively links the two paragraphs by alluding specifically to material in previous paragraphs. It is the best answer.
Choice C is almost incomprehensible.
Choice D is inappropriate in the context.
Choice E fails to include an appropriate transitional word or phrase.

39. **A**   Choice A is consistent in style, tone, and content with the previous sentence. It is the best answer.
Choice B is awkwardly expressed, and by using *should,* changes the passage from the indicative to the imperative mood.
Choice C is a sentence fragment.
Choice D is awkwardly worded. The imperative *must* is inconsistent with the rest of the paragraph.
Choice E is wordy and, like B and D, changes the mood of the passage from indicative to imperative.

Verbal Reasoning Section 4

31. **E**   A *truant* runs away from *school*; a *deserter* runs away from the *army*.   (Definition)

32. **C**   A *stroller* carries a *baby;* a *bus* carries a *passenger.*   (Function)

33. **D**   A *flurry* is a short, light snowfall, while a *blizzard* is a very heavy fall of snow; a *breeze* is a light gust of wind, while a *gale* is an extremely strong wind.   (Degree of Intensity)

34. **B**   A *carpet* is a textile fabric that lies on the *floor*; a *tapestry* is a textile fabric that hangs on the *wall.*   (Function)

35. **B**   A formal agreement between *nations* is a *treaty;* a formal agreement between *individuals* is a *contract.*   (Defining Characteristic)

36. **B**   A *kangaroo* is a kind of *marsupial*; a *mushroom* is a kind of *fungus.*   (Class and Member)

37. **D**   A *snicker* is a noise people make that shows *disrespect*; a *moan* is a noise people make that indicates *suffering.*   (Action and Its Significance)

38. **C**   A *choreographer* designs a *dance*; a *director* designs a *film.*   (Worker and Work Created)

39. **D**   *Gustatory* means of or relating to the sense of *taste*; *olfactory* means of or relating to the sense of *smell.* Choice B is incorrect. *Visionary* means seeing visions; it does not mean relating to the sense of sight.   (Defining Characteristic)

40. **D**   A *pauper* is a poor person, someone characterized by *poverty*; a *sluggard* is a sluggish person, someone characterized by *slowness.* Beware eye-catchers. Choice E is incorrect. Though a

jeweler deals in gems and other valuable items, a jeweler is not necessarily characterized by *wealth.*   (Defining Characteristic)

41. **C** A *sermon* is a religious *speech*; a *pilgrimage* is a religious *journey.*   (Class and Member)

42. **E** Frequently shifting emotions indicate a *mercurial mood*; frequently shifting directions indicate an *erratic course.*   (Manner)

43. **B** A judge may *commute* a prisoner's *sentence,* making it shorter; a judge may *reduce* a convicted person's *fine,* making it smaller.   (Function)

44. **C** Only deserts are not mentioned as related to the subduction of the lithosphere.

45. **C** The author is concerned with explaining what happens in a geological phenomenon. His style is, by definition, *expository.*

46. **E** All three statements are true. The general circulation or flow of the earth's mantle, mentioned in the second paragraph, is an indication that the mantle *is in a state of flux* or flow. The second paragraph also indicates that the lithosphere or crust is cooler than the mantle and that the subducted lithosphere is absorbed or incorporated by the mantle.

47. **D** The island arcs are prominent in *projecting* above the ocean's surface.

48. **E** In the last sentence of paragraph 4, the author states that *it appears* that the convection currents may in some regions drive the plates, and in other regions be driven by the plates. However, this is merely a hypothesis. Thus, current knowledge of the relationship between the plate motions and the currents is clearly *tentative* or hypothetical.

49. **B** By making people aware of contemporary ideological and ethical follies and confusions, satire helps clear up their intellectual and spiritual universe, *promoting clarity of thought.*

50. **C** Reclaiming the dust bowl is like clearing away the rubble of bombed cities or like controlling floods: it is a major physical effort to restore land that has been ravaged by nature or by man. Specifically, it is the attempt to *make the barren land* destroyed by drought and dust storms *fit for use.*

51. **D** To the author, satire's ability to get around people and tell them things they need to hear (even if they would prefer to hear nothing of the kind) is a very good thing. He looks on it with *satisfaction.*

52. **B** By stating that "if we ever become civilized it will probably be satire almost as much as poetry that will have accomplished it," the author indicates that poetry has an even stronger civilizing effect than satire itself does. Thus, he regards poetry as *a major civilizing influence.*

53. **D** You can write all you want, but your satire will stir no one unless it is based on something true. For satire to strike sparks, it must *have a factual basis.*

54. **C** In talking about people needing to be knocked off their perch, the author means that they should be jolted by the truth, not that they should be physically struck down. He is speaking figuratively or *metaphorically,* not literally.

55. **A** The fourth sentence indicates that we fail to speak or write satirically because we are afraid or *apprehensive.*

56. **D** The fear of hurting someone's feelings makes us act carefully or *gingerly.*

57. **A** According to the passage, we are afraid of delaying people in their progress toward a perfect psychological readjustment. This suggests that it is of great importance for people to gain such a *sense of emotional security.*

58. **B** A broadsword is a somewhat heavy sword with a broad blade, one used for cutting rather than for thrusting or pricking. It is a less "refined" weapon than the light, pointed rapier. Thus, it is an apt metaphor for invective (violent verbal abuse), *a relatively crude form of satire.*

59. **B** The author is clearly mocking the foibles and follies of modern man. His tone is one of *pronounced* (noticeable; definite) *irony.*

60. **E** The metaphor of pinning an errant butterfly to a board suggests that the target of such satire is a minor one indeed—a mere foible or affectation, not a major vice. While the author of Passage 1 appreciates minor satire, he also has a very strong sense of what makes great satire great and would be very likely to assert that *satire needs to take on more important targets* than wayward butterflies.

Mathematical Reasoning Section 5

26. **B** $\left(\frac{1}{0.08}\right)^2 = \frac{1}{0.0064}$

    If two fractions have the same numerator, the one with the smaller denominator is larger.

27. **D** x and/or y may be negative, or equal to zero

28. **D** $x^2 = xy$. Dividing by x give $x = y$, but this is possible only if x does not equal 0. If $x = 0$, y can have any value.

29. **D** Since $\frac{1}{x} < 1$, x can have any value greater than 1 or any negative value, but may not have a value between 0 and 1 inclusive.

30. **D** At least one of the factors (x, y, or z) must be equal to zero, regardless of the value of the other factor(s), which are then completely unrestricted.

31. **B** Because x and y are positive integers, the greatest possible value of p is obtained by letting x have its smallest value: $p = 9 - 1^2 = 8$. The smallest possible value of q is obtained by letting y have it smallest value: $q = 9y^2 = 9(1^2) = 9$. Hence, the smallest possible value of q is greater than the greatest possible value of p.

32. **D** 20% of $x = \left(\dfrac{1}{5}\right)(x) = \dfrac{x}{5}$

    10% of $\dfrac{x}{2} = \left(\dfrac{1}{10}\right)\left(\dfrac{x}{2}\right) = \dfrac{x}{20}$

    Since x can have any value, $\dfrac{x}{5} > \dfrac{x}{20}$ if x is positive, $\dfrac{x}{5} = \dfrac{x}{20}$ if $x = 0$ and $\dfrac{x}{5} < \dfrac{x}{20}$ if x is negative.

33. **A** $x + y = 5$ [Column A]

    $\dfrac{1}{xy} = \dfrac{1}{6}$ [Column B]

    $\dfrac{1}{x} + \dfrac{1}{y} = \dfrac{1}{2} + \dfrac{1}{3} = \dfrac{5}{6}$

    $\dfrac{\frac{1}{6}}{\frac{5}{6}} = \dfrac{1}{6} \cdot \dfrac{6}{5} = \dfrac{1}{5}$

    $5 > \dfrac{1}{5}$

34. **C** The time required for each would be the same since one is traveling twice as fast but is also covering twice as much distance.

35. **C** Since the perimeter of the square $= s$, each side equals $\dfrac{s}{4}$; the area $= \dfrac{s^2}{16}$. The length of the rectangle $= \dfrac{s}{2}$ and its width is $\dfrac{1}{4}$ of $\dfrac{s}{2}$ or $\dfrac{s}{8}$; its area $= \left(\dfrac{s}{2}\right)\left(\dfrac{s}{8}\right)$ or $\dfrac{s^2}{16}$.

36. **C** Since $OP = OR$, $PR = OP = OR$. $\therefore \triangle OPR$ is equilateral. $\therefore \angle C \overset{\circ}{=} 60$.

37. **C** If one acute angle of a right triangle has a measure of 45°, then the other acute angle has a measure of 45°. $\therefore ABC$ is an isosceles right $\triangle$.

38. **C** $24x\% = \dfrac{24x}{100} = \dfrac{6x}{25}$

39. **B** Subtract y from both columns
    $x > 0$

40. **A** $\dfrac{6a - 5}{2} = 3a - \dfrac{5}{2}$ or $3a - 2\dfrac{1}{2} > 3a - 3$

41. **1** $\dfrac{\frac{2}{3} + \frac{1}{4}}{\frac{1}{6} + \frac{2}{3} + \frac{1}{12}}$ Multiply all terms in numerator and denominator by 12 to clear fractions:

    $\dfrac{8 + 3}{2 + 8 + 1} = \dfrac{\cancel{11}}{\cancel{11}} = 1$

42. **1** $13 = \dfrac{13w}{1 - w}$

    $13(1 - w) = 13w$

    $13 - 13w = 13w$

    $13 = 26w$

    $\dfrac{1}{2} = w$

    $(2w)^2 = (2 \cdot \tfrac{1}{2})^2 = (1)^2 = 1$

43. **81** If r is multiplied by 9, V must be multiplied by 81, since $\sqrt{81} = 9$. Recall: If equals be multiplied by equals, the results are equal.

44. **11** $\dfrac{\text{50-foot fence}}{\text{5-foot spaces}} = 10$ spaces

    This will require 11 posts. Observe that there will be a post at the point where the fence begins.

45. **20** Volume of small fish tank $= (1')\left(1\tfrac{1}{2}'\right)\left(\tfrac{1}{2}'\right)$

    $= (1')\left(\dfrac{3}{2}'\right)\left(\dfrac{1}{2}'\right) = \dfrac{3}{4}$ cubic foot

    15 cubic feet $\div \dfrac{3}{4}$ cubic foot

    $15 \cdot \dfrac{4}{3}$

    $\overset{5}{\cancel{15}} \cdot \dfrac{4}{\cancel{3}} = 20$ times

46. **450** $X = 66\tfrac{2}{3}\% \, Y$ or $X = \dfrac{2}{3}Y$ (1)

    $Y = 33\tfrac{1}{3}\% \, Z$ or $Y = \dfrac{1}{3}Z$ (2)

    $\dfrac{3}{2}X = Y$ [multiply (1) by $\tfrac{3}{2}$]

    $\dfrac{1}{3}Z = Y$ (2)

    $\dfrac{1}{3}Z = \dfrac{3}{2}X$ [both are equal to Y]

    $Z = \dfrac{9}{2}X$ [multiply by 3]

    $Z = 4\tfrac{1}{2}X$ or $Z = 450\%X$

47. **49** 5 days = 35 sets
    1 day = 7 sets
    7 books = 1 set
    49 books = 7 sets

48. **13.5** Area square $ABCD$ = (side)^2 = 36, so side AB = AD = 6 and area right $\triangle BAD$ = $\frac{1}{2}$ (6)(6) = 18. Since AL = AM = 3, area right $\triangle LAM$ = $\frac{1}{2}$(3)(3) = 4.5.

Area quadrilateral $BLMD$ =

area $\triangle BAD$ – area $\triangle LAM$

= 18 – 4.5

= 13.5

49. **16** Original scale = 1" = 50 miles
Since new scale 2" = 25 miles
Then 4" = 50 miles
Since the new linear scale is four times the old, four times as much paper is needed in the width and four times as much in the length. Therefore 4 × 4 or 16 sheets would have to be taped together to hold the map.

50. **4** Draw EF.

$EF \parallel AC$, $EF = \frac{1}{2}AC$ [line joining the midpoints of 2 sides of a triangle is parallel to the third and equal to $\frac{1}{2}$ of it]

$< FED = < DCA$ [alternate interior angles of parallel lines]

Also, $\angle EFD = \angle DAC$

$\triangle EDF \sim \triangle ADC$

Since $EF = \frac{1}{2}AC$, $ED = \frac{1}{2}DC$ and $DF = \frac{1}{2}AD$ [corresponding sides of similar triangles]

Let $DE = a$.

Then $DC = 2a$.

Let $DF = b$.

Then $AD = 2b$.

Substitute: $\dfrac{(2b)(2a)}{(b)(a)} = \dfrac{4\,ab}{ab} = 4$

Answer Sheet

TYPICAL TEST H

Each mark should completely fill the appropriate space, and should be as dark as all other marks. Make all erasures complete. Traces of an erasure may be read as an answer. See pages vii and 27 for explanations of timing and number of questions.

Section 1 — Verbal
30 minutes

1 Ⓐ Ⓑ Ⓒ Ⓓ Ⓔ
2 Ⓐ Ⓑ Ⓒ Ⓓ Ⓔ
3 Ⓐ Ⓑ Ⓒ Ⓓ Ⓔ
4 Ⓐ Ⓑ Ⓒ Ⓓ Ⓔ
5 Ⓐ Ⓑ Ⓒ Ⓓ Ⓔ
6 Ⓐ Ⓑ Ⓒ Ⓓ Ⓔ
7 Ⓐ Ⓑ Ⓒ Ⓓ Ⓔ
8 Ⓐ Ⓑ Ⓒ Ⓓ Ⓔ
9 Ⓐ Ⓑ Ⓒ Ⓓ Ⓔ
10 Ⓐ Ⓑ Ⓒ Ⓓ Ⓔ
11 Ⓐ Ⓑ Ⓒ Ⓓ Ⓔ
12 Ⓐ Ⓑ Ⓒ Ⓓ Ⓔ
13 Ⓐ Ⓑ Ⓒ Ⓓ Ⓔ
14 Ⓐ Ⓑ Ⓒ Ⓓ Ⓔ
15 Ⓐ Ⓑ Ⓒ Ⓓ Ⓔ
16 Ⓐ Ⓑ Ⓒ Ⓓ Ⓔ
17 Ⓐ Ⓑ Ⓒ Ⓓ Ⓔ
18 Ⓐ Ⓑ Ⓒ Ⓓ Ⓔ
19 Ⓐ Ⓑ Ⓒ Ⓓ Ⓔ
20 Ⓐ Ⓑ Ⓒ Ⓓ Ⓔ
21 Ⓐ Ⓑ Ⓒ Ⓓ Ⓔ
22 Ⓐ Ⓑ Ⓒ Ⓓ Ⓔ
23 Ⓐ Ⓑ Ⓒ Ⓓ Ⓔ
24 Ⓐ Ⓑ Ⓒ Ⓓ Ⓔ
25 Ⓐ Ⓑ Ⓒ Ⓓ Ⓔ
26 Ⓐ Ⓑ Ⓒ Ⓓ Ⓔ
27 Ⓐ Ⓑ Ⓒ Ⓓ Ⓔ
28 Ⓐ Ⓑ Ⓒ Ⓓ Ⓔ
29 Ⓐ Ⓑ Ⓒ Ⓓ Ⓔ
30 Ⓐ Ⓑ Ⓒ Ⓓ Ⓔ

Section 2 — Math
30 minutes

1 Ⓐ Ⓑ Ⓒ Ⓓ Ⓔ
2 Ⓐ Ⓑ Ⓒ Ⓓ Ⓔ
3 Ⓐ Ⓑ Ⓒ Ⓓ Ⓔ
4 Ⓐ Ⓑ Ⓒ Ⓓ Ⓔ
5 Ⓐ Ⓑ Ⓒ Ⓓ Ⓔ
6 Ⓐ Ⓑ Ⓒ Ⓓ Ⓔ
7 Ⓐ Ⓑ Ⓒ Ⓓ Ⓔ
8 Ⓐ Ⓑ Ⓒ Ⓓ Ⓔ
9 Ⓐ Ⓑ Ⓒ Ⓓ Ⓔ
10 Ⓐ Ⓑ Ⓒ Ⓓ Ⓔ
11 Ⓐ Ⓑ Ⓒ Ⓓ Ⓔ
12 Ⓐ Ⓑ Ⓒ Ⓓ Ⓔ
13 Ⓐ Ⓑ Ⓒ Ⓓ Ⓔ
14 Ⓐ Ⓑ Ⓒ Ⓓ Ⓔ
15 Ⓐ Ⓑ Ⓒ Ⓓ Ⓔ
16 Ⓐ Ⓑ Ⓒ Ⓓ Ⓔ
17 Ⓐ Ⓑ Ⓒ Ⓓ Ⓔ
18 Ⓐ Ⓑ Ⓒ Ⓓ Ⓔ
19 Ⓐ Ⓑ Ⓒ Ⓓ Ⓔ
20 Ⓐ Ⓑ Ⓒ Ⓓ Ⓔ
21 Ⓐ Ⓑ Ⓒ Ⓓ Ⓔ
22 Ⓐ Ⓑ Ⓒ Ⓓ Ⓔ
23 Ⓐ Ⓑ Ⓒ Ⓓ Ⓔ
24 Ⓐ Ⓑ Ⓒ Ⓓ Ⓔ
25 Ⓐ Ⓑ Ⓒ Ⓓ Ⓔ

Section 3 — Writing
30 minutes

1 Ⓐ Ⓑ Ⓒ Ⓓ Ⓔ
2 Ⓐ Ⓑ Ⓒ Ⓓ Ⓔ
3 Ⓐ Ⓑ Ⓒ Ⓓ Ⓔ
4 Ⓐ Ⓑ Ⓒ Ⓓ Ⓔ
5 Ⓐ Ⓑ Ⓒ Ⓓ Ⓔ
6 Ⓐ Ⓑ Ⓒ Ⓓ Ⓔ
7 Ⓐ Ⓑ Ⓒ Ⓓ Ⓔ
8 Ⓐ Ⓑ Ⓒ Ⓓ Ⓔ
9 Ⓐ Ⓑ Ⓒ Ⓓ Ⓔ
10 Ⓐ Ⓑ Ⓒ Ⓓ Ⓔ
11 Ⓐ Ⓑ Ⓒ Ⓓ Ⓔ
12 Ⓐ Ⓑ Ⓒ Ⓓ Ⓔ
13 Ⓐ Ⓑ Ⓒ Ⓓ Ⓔ
14 Ⓐ Ⓑ Ⓒ Ⓓ Ⓔ
15 Ⓐ Ⓑ Ⓒ Ⓓ Ⓔ
16 Ⓐ Ⓑ Ⓒ Ⓓ Ⓔ
17 Ⓐ Ⓑ Ⓒ Ⓓ Ⓔ
18 Ⓐ Ⓑ Ⓒ Ⓓ Ⓔ
19 Ⓐ Ⓑ Ⓒ Ⓓ Ⓔ
20 Ⓐ Ⓑ Ⓒ Ⓓ Ⓔ
21 Ⓐ Ⓑ Ⓒ Ⓓ Ⓔ
22 Ⓐ Ⓑ Ⓒ Ⓓ Ⓔ
23 Ⓐ Ⓑ Ⓒ Ⓓ Ⓔ
24 Ⓐ Ⓑ Ⓒ Ⓓ Ⓔ
25 Ⓐ Ⓑ Ⓒ Ⓓ Ⓔ
26 Ⓐ Ⓑ Ⓒ Ⓓ Ⓔ
27 Ⓐ Ⓑ Ⓒ Ⓓ Ⓔ
28 Ⓐ Ⓑ Ⓒ Ⓓ Ⓔ
29 Ⓐ Ⓑ Ⓒ Ⓓ Ⓔ
30 Ⓐ Ⓑ Ⓒ Ⓓ Ⓔ
31 Ⓐ Ⓑ Ⓒ Ⓓ Ⓔ
32 Ⓐ Ⓑ Ⓒ Ⓓ Ⓔ
33 Ⓐ Ⓑ Ⓒ Ⓓ Ⓔ
34 Ⓐ Ⓑ Ⓒ Ⓓ Ⓔ
35 Ⓐ Ⓑ Ⓒ Ⓓ Ⓔ
36 Ⓐ Ⓑ Ⓒ Ⓓ Ⓔ
37 Ⓐ Ⓑ Ⓒ Ⓓ Ⓔ
38 Ⓐ Ⓑ Ⓒ Ⓓ Ⓔ
39 Ⓐ Ⓑ Ⓒ Ⓓ Ⓔ

Section 4 — Verbal
30 minutes

31 Ⓐ Ⓑ Ⓒ Ⓓ Ⓔ
32 Ⓐ Ⓑ Ⓒ Ⓓ Ⓔ
33 Ⓐ Ⓑ Ⓒ Ⓓ Ⓔ
34 Ⓐ Ⓑ Ⓒ Ⓓ Ⓔ
35 Ⓐ Ⓑ Ⓒ Ⓓ Ⓔ
36 Ⓐ Ⓑ Ⓒ Ⓓ Ⓔ
37 Ⓐ Ⓑ Ⓒ Ⓓ Ⓔ
38 Ⓐ Ⓑ Ⓒ Ⓓ Ⓔ
39 Ⓐ Ⓑ Ⓒ Ⓓ Ⓔ
40 Ⓐ Ⓑ Ⓒ Ⓓ Ⓔ
41 Ⓐ Ⓑ Ⓒ Ⓓ Ⓔ
42 Ⓐ Ⓑ Ⓒ Ⓓ Ⓔ
43 Ⓐ Ⓑ Ⓒ Ⓓ Ⓔ
44 Ⓐ Ⓑ Ⓒ Ⓓ Ⓔ
45 Ⓐ Ⓑ Ⓒ Ⓓ Ⓔ
46 Ⓐ Ⓑ Ⓒ Ⓓ Ⓔ
47 Ⓐ Ⓑ Ⓒ Ⓓ Ⓔ
48 Ⓐ Ⓑ Ⓒ Ⓓ Ⓔ
49 Ⓐ Ⓑ Ⓒ Ⓓ Ⓔ
50 Ⓐ Ⓑ Ⓒ Ⓓ Ⓔ
51 Ⓐ Ⓑ Ⓒ Ⓓ Ⓔ
52 Ⓐ Ⓑ Ⓒ Ⓓ Ⓔ
53 Ⓐ Ⓑ Ⓒ Ⓓ Ⓔ
54 Ⓐ Ⓑ Ⓒ Ⓓ Ⓔ
55 Ⓐ Ⓑ Ⓒ Ⓓ Ⓔ
56 Ⓐ Ⓑ Ⓒ Ⓓ Ⓔ
57 Ⓐ Ⓑ Ⓒ Ⓓ Ⓔ
58 Ⓐ Ⓑ Ⓒ Ⓓ Ⓔ
59 Ⓐ Ⓑ Ⓒ Ⓓ Ⓔ
60 Ⓐ Ⓑ Ⓒ Ⓓ Ⓔ

Section 5 — Math
30 minutes

26 Ⓐ Ⓑ Ⓒ Ⓓ Ⓔ
27 Ⓐ Ⓑ Ⓒ Ⓓ Ⓔ
28 Ⓐ Ⓑ Ⓒ Ⓓ Ⓔ
29 Ⓐ Ⓑ Ⓒ Ⓓ Ⓔ
30 Ⓐ Ⓑ Ⓒ Ⓓ Ⓔ
31 Ⓐ Ⓑ Ⓒ Ⓓ Ⓔ
32 Ⓐ Ⓑ Ⓒ Ⓓ Ⓔ
33 Ⓐ Ⓑ Ⓒ Ⓓ Ⓔ
34 Ⓐ Ⓑ Ⓒ Ⓓ Ⓔ
35 Ⓐ Ⓑ Ⓒ Ⓓ Ⓔ
36 Ⓐ Ⓑ Ⓒ Ⓓ Ⓔ
37 Ⓐ Ⓑ Ⓒ Ⓓ Ⓔ
39 Ⓐ Ⓑ Ⓒ Ⓓ Ⓔ
39 Ⓐ Ⓑ Ⓒ Ⓓ Ⓔ
40 Ⓐ Ⓑ Ⓒ Ⓓ Ⓔ

41

42

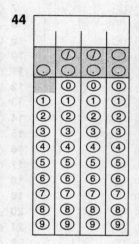

43

44

45

46 47 48 49 50

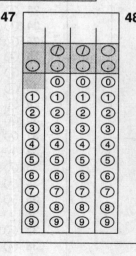

SECTION 1
Verbal Reasoning

Time—30 minutes
30 Questions

For each question in this section, select the best answer from among the choices given and fill in the corresponding oval on the answer sheet.

Directions

Each sentence below has one or two blanks, each blank indicating that something has been omitted. Beneath the sentence are five words or sets of words labeled A through E. Choose the word or set of words that, when inserted in the sentence, best fits the meaning of the sentence as a whole.

Example:

Medieval kingdoms did not become constitutional republics overnight; on the contrary, the change was ____ .

(A) unpopular
(B) unexpected
(C) advantageous
(D) sufficient
(E) gradual

Ⓐ Ⓑ Ⓒ Ⓓ ●

1. Though he was reputedly a skilled craftsman, the judging committee found his work ____ and lacking in polish.

   (A) crude
   (B) accomplished
   (C) distinguished
   (D) adequate
   (E) conceptual

2. The dean tried to retain control of the situation on campus, but her attempt was ____ by the board of trustees.

   (A) endorsed   (B) frustrated   (C) disclosed
   (D) witnessed   (E) justified

3. Taxonomy—the branch of biology that describes and classifies living creatures—has ____ for approximately 1.4 million creatures.

   (A) need   (B) names   (C) sanctions
   (D) relevance   (E) scope

4. The extended heat wave left many people ____ , lacking their usual energy and interest in life.

   (A) isolated   (B) fervid   (C) intemperate
   (D) listless   (E) nomadic

5. Though Mark had reservations about many of the fraternity's policies, he diplomatically kept them to himself and allowed his fellow members to interpret his ____ as a sign of ____ on his part.

   (A) complaints..reluctance
   (B) silence..acquiescence
   (C) arguments..pugnacity
   (D) comments..inarticulateness
   (E) selfishness..wisdom

6. During the height of the mating season, disputes often erupt in the small rookery where space is ____ and male egrets must ____ a patch on which to build their nests.

   (A) inadequate..mull over
   (B) circumscribed..rule out
   (C) unavailable..pick through
   (D) unconditional..seek out
   (E) limited..vie for

7. Although I am not an ardent admirer of the work of George Eliot, simple justice demands a prefatory ____ her many admirable qualities.

   (A) skepticism regarding
   (B) effusion over
   (C) denial of
   (D) tribute to
   (E) dismissal of

8. Just as avarice is the mark of the miser, indulgence is the mark of the ____ .

   (A) pauper   (B) philanthropist   (C) coward
   (D) martinet   (E) glutton

9. Bernard Shaw's goal as an anchorman is ____ ; when he covered the attempted assassination of President Reagan in 1981, his eyes were not enlarged and his voice was not high-pitched.

   (A) accuracy   (B) eloquence   (C) dispassion
   (D) credibility   (E) sensitivity

10. Upon realizing that their position was ____ , the general ____ the troops to retreat to a neighboring hill.

    (A) valuable..remonstrated
    (B) untenable..ordered
    (C) evident..urged
    (D) exposed..neglected
    (E) salubrious..commanded

GO ON TO THE NEXT PAGE

11. Given the many areas of conflict still awaiting
____, the outcome of the peace talks remains ____.

(A) justification..pragmatic
(B) settlement..permanent
(C) resolution..problematic
(D) compromise..plausible
(E) arbitration..pacific

12. Because he could not support the cures he obtained
with scientific data, he was accused by some skeptics of being ____ .

(A) a zealot   (B) an artist   (C) a mendicant
(D) a charlatan   (E) a dilettante

13. To progress from nature's despoiler to its ____ , we
must resist the temptation technology affords us to
mold a world responsive to our ____ alone.

(A) conservator..whims   (B) prey..desires
(C) creator..voices   (D) ravager..needs
(E) savior..threats

14. While some people take satisfaction from a religious or mystical explanation of human intelligence, for Bonner, the more ____ and ____ the
explanation, the better she likes it.

(A) rational..materialistic   (B) logical..spiritual
(C) pragmatic..dubious
(D) theoretical..rudimentary   (E) occult..viable

15. Mr. Southern is a historian who has entered so thoroughly into the spirit of the age that even its paradoxes leave him ____ .

(A) nonplussed   (B) indifferent   (C) undaunted
(D) ambivalent   (E) intransigent

16. Unfortunately, the book comes down so firmly on
the nature side of the nature-nurture debate that it
tends to ____ many of the subtleties of the argument, leaving the reader with a highly ____ view of
the issue.

(A) carry through..lucid   (B) skim over..simplistic
(C) go beyond..dogmatic   (D) sidestep..cerebral
(E) highlight..arbitrary

17. Critics have been misled by Williams's obvious
____ exaggerated theatrical gestures into ____ his
plays as mere melodramas, "full of sound and fury,
signifying nothing."

(A) disinclination for..disparaging
(B) repudiation of..misrepresenting
(C) indulgence in..acclaiming
(D) propensity for..denigrating
(E) indifference to..lauding

GO ON TO THE NEXT PAGE

Directions

Each passage below is followed by questions based on
its content. Answer the questions following each passage on the basis of what is <u>stated</u> or <u>implied</u> in that
passage and in any introductory material that may be
provided.

Questions 18–22 are based on the following passage.

*Noted for their destructiveness, tornadoes have long
fascinated both scientists and the public at large. The
following passage is from a magazine article on tornadoes written in 1984.*

A tornado is the product of a thunderstorm,
specifically of the interaction of a strong thunderstorm with winds in the troposphere (the active
layer of the atmosphere that extends nine to seventeen kilometers up from the ground). The
process by which a tornado is formed is one in
which a small fraction of the tremendous energy
of the thunderstorm, whose towering cumulonimbus cloud can be ten to twenty kilometers across
and more than seventeen kilometers high, is concentrated in an area no more than several hundred
meters in diameter. Before going into the process
in detail let me first describe the phenomenon
itself.

A tornado is a vortex; air rotates around the tornado's axis about as fast as it moves toward and
along the axis. Drawn by greatly reduced atmos-
pheric pressure in the central core, air streams into
the base of the vortex from all directions through a
shallow layer a few tens of meters deep near the
ground. In the base the air turns abruptly to spiral
upward around the core and finally merges, at the
hidden upper end of the tornado, with the airflow
in the parent cloud. The pressure within the core
may be as much as ten percent less than that of the
surrounding atmosphere; about the same difference as that between sea level and an altitude of
one kilometer. Winds in a tornado are almost
always cyclonic, which in the Northern Hemisphere
means counterclockwise.

The vortex frequently—not always—becomes
visible as a funnel cloud hanging part or all of the
way to the ground from the generating storm. A
funnel cloud forms only if the pressure drop in the
core exceeds a critical value that depends on the
temperature and the humidity of the inflowing air.
As air flows into the area of lower pressure, it
expands and cools; if it cools enough, the water
vapor in it condenses and forms droplets. The
warmer and drier the inflowing air is, the greater
the pressure drop must be for condensation to
occur and a cloud to form. Sometimes no condensation funnel forms, in which case the tornado
reveals itself only through the dust and debris it
carries aloft.

Line numbers: 5, 10, 15, 20, 25, 30, 35, 40, 45

A funnel can be anywhere from tens of meters to several kilometers long, and where it meets the parent cloud its diameter ranges from a few meters to hundreds of meters. Usually it is cone-shaped, but short, broad, cylindrical pillars are
50 formed by very strong tornadoes, and long, rope-like tubes that trail off horizontally are also common. Over a tornado's brief lifetime (never more than a few hours) the size and shape of the funnel
55 may change markedly, reflecting changes in the intensity of the winds or in the properties of the inflowing air. Its color varies from a dirty white to gray to dark blue gray when it consists mostly of water droplets, but if the core fills with dust, the
60 funnel may take on a more exotic hue, such as the red of west Oklahoma clay. Tornadoes can also be noisy, often roaring like a freight train or a jet engine. This may result from the interaction of the concentrated high winds with the ground.

18. Tornadoes are characterized by which of the following?

    I. Brevity of duration
    II. Intense concentration of energy
    III. Uniformity of shape

(A) I only   (B) II only   (C) I and II only
(D) II and III only   (E) I, II, and III

19. Which of the following titles best summarizes the content of this passage?

(A) The Composition and Nature of Tornadoes
(B) Predicting the Tornado's Path
(C) The Destructive Impact of Tornadoes
(D) Harnessing the Tornado's Energy
(E) Facts and Fictions About Tornadoes

20. Lines 39–42 suggest that which of the following is true of a tornado?

(A) Its winds are invariably counterclockwise.
(B) It can last for days at a time.
(C) Its funnel cloud will not form if the air is cool and dry.
(D) It exceeds its parent cloud in size.
(E) It responds to changes in temperature and humidity.

21. According to the author, a direct relation may exist between the color a tornado takes on and

(A) the composition of the terrain it passes over
(B) the intensity of the winds it concentrates
(C) the particular shape of funnel it forms
(D) the direction in which its winds rotate
(E) the degree of noise involved

22. In the final paragraph the author does all of the following EXCEPT

(A) suggest a hypothesis
(B) provide a concrete example
(C) indicate a time span
(D) argue a viewpoint
(E) use a simile

Questions 23–30 are based on the following passage.

The following passage is an excerpt from An American Childhood, *the autobiography of the writer Annie Dillard published in 1987.*

Outside in the neighborhoods, learning our way around the streets, we played among the enormous stone monuments of the millionaires—
Line both those tireless Pittsburgh founders of the
5 heavy industries from which the nation's wealth derived (they told us at school) and the industrialists' couldn't-lose bankers and backers, all of whom began as canny boys, the stories of whose rises to riches adults still considered inspirational
10 to children.
    We were unthinkingly familiar with the moguls' immense rough works as so much weird scenery on long drives. We saw the long, low-slung stripes of steel factories by the rivers; we saw pyramidal
15 heaps of yellow sand at glassworks by the shining railroad tracks; we saw rusty slag heaps on the outlying hilltops, and coal barges tied up at the docks. We recognized, on infrequent trips downtown, the industries' smooth corporate headquarters, each to
20 its own soaring building—Gulf Oil, Alcoa, U.S. Steel, Koppers Company, Pittsburgh Plate Glass, Mellon Bank. Our classmates' fathers worked in these buildings, or at nearby corporate headquarters for Westinghouse Electric, Jones & Laughlin Steel,
25 Allegheny Ludlum, Westinghouse Air Brake, and H. J. Heinz.
    The nineteenth-century industrialists' institutions—galleries, universities, hospitals, churches, Carnegie libraries, the Carnegie Museum, Frick
30 Park, Mellon Park—were, many of them, my stomping grounds. These absolute artifacts of philanthropy littered the neighborhoods with marble. Millionaires' encrusted mansions, now obsolete and turned into parks or art centers, weighed
35 on every block. They lent their expansive, hushed moods to the Point Breeze neighborhoods where we children lived and where those fabulous men had lived also, or rather had visited at night in order to sleep. Everywhere I looked, it was the
40 Valley of the Kings, their dynasty just ended, and their monuments intact but already out of fashion.
    All these immensities wholly dominated the life of the city. So did their several peculiar social legacies: their powerful Calvinist mix of piety and
45 acquisitiveness, which characterized the old and new Scotch-Irish families and the nation they helped found; the wall-up hush of what was, by my day, old money—amazing how fast it ages if you let it alone—and the clang and roar of
50 making that money; the owners' Presbyterian churches, their anti-Catholicism, anti-Semitism, Republicanism, and love of continuous work; their dogmatic practicality; their easy friendliness; their Pittsburgh-centered innocence, and, paradox-
55 ically, their egalitarianism.

GO ON TO THE NEXT PAGE

For all the insularity of the old guard, Pittsburgh was always an open and democratic town. "Best-natured people I ever went among," a Boston visitor noted two centuries earlier. In colo-
60 nial days, everybody went to balls, regardless of rank. No one had any truck with aristocratic pretensions—hadn't they hated the British lords in Ulster? People who cared to rave about their bloodlines, Mother told us, had stayed in Europe,
65 which deserved them. We were vaguely proud of living in a city so full of distinctive immigrant groups, among which we never thought to number ourselves. We had no occasion to visit the steep hillside neighborhoods—Polish, Hungarian,
70 Rumanian, Italian, Slav—of the turn-of-the-century immigrants who poured the steel and stirred the glass and shoveled the coal.

We children played around the moguls' enormous pale stone houses, restful as tombs, set back
75 just so on their shaded grounds. Henry Clay Frick's daughter, unthinkably old, lived alone in her proud, sinking mansion; she had lived alone all her life. No one saw her. Men mowed the wide lawns and seeded them, and pushed rollers over
80 them, over the new grass seed and musket balls and arrowheads, over the big trees' roots, bones, shale, coal.

We knew bits of this story, and we knew none of it. We knew that before big industry there had
85 been small industry here—H. J. Heinz setting up a roadside stand to sell horseradish roots from his garden. There were the makers of cannonballs for the Civil War. There were the braggart and rowdy flatboat men and keelboat men, and the honored
90 steamboat builders and pilots. There were local men getting rich in iron and glass manufacturing and trade downriver. There was a whole continentful of people passing through, native-born and immigrant men and women who funneled
95 down Pittsburgh, where two rivers converged to make a third river. It was the gateway to the West; they piled onto flatboats and launched out into the Ohio River singing, to head for new country. There had been a Revolutionary War, and before
100 that the French and Indian War. And before that, and first of all, had been those first settlers come walking bright-eyed in, into nowhere from out of nowhere, the people who, as they said, "broke wilderness," the pioneers. This was the history.

23. The opening paragraph suggests the author regards the inspirational tales of the lives of the industrialists with a sense of

(A) optimism   (B) reverence   (C) discomfort
(D) irony   (E) envy

24. The author and her fellow children regarded the enormous buildings as

(A) unnatural phenomena to observe
(B) a backdrop to their lives
(C) a challenge to the imagination
(D) signs of excessive consumption
(E) intimations of immortality

25. The author calls the moguls fabulous (line 37) because they were

(A) fictitious   (B) celebrated   (C) wonderful
(D) startling   (E) affluent

26. By "People who cared to rave about their bloodlines...had stayed in Europe, which deserved them," the author's mother means

(A) only Europe was worthy enough to have citizens descended from noble blood
(B) aristocrats tended to be disinclined to travel
(C) Americans were ashamed of their lack of noble birth, and therefore avoided Europe
(D) it served Europe right if all those snobs who boasted about their lineage stayed right there
(E) it was madness for an American to try to trace his bloodlines; only a European could succeed

27. The author uses the description of the Frick lawns in lines 78–82 chiefly to help

(A) indicate the opulence of the moguls' lifestyle
(B) counteract the isolation of Henry Clay Frick's daughter
(C) convey a sense of Pittsburgh's buried past
(D) highlight the distinction between the moguls and their employees
(E) argue in favor of preserving open spaces in cities

28. The opening sentence of the last paragraph (lines 83–84) presents the reader with

(A) a euphemism   (B) an epitaph   (C) a simile
(D) a paradox   (E) a reminiscence

29. In the phrase "broke wilderness" (lines 103–104), "broke" most likely means

(A) shattered   (B) bankrupted   (C) unraveled
(D) interrupted   (E) penetrated

30. The passage's closing paragraph is organized according to

(A) geographical principles
(B) reverse chronological order
(C) cause and effect
(D) personal recollections
(E) extensive quotations

IF YOU FINISH BEFORE 30 MINUTES, YOU MAY CHECK YOUR WORK ON THIS SECTION ONLY. DO NOT TURN TO ANY OTHER SECTION IN THE TEST.   **S T O P**

SECTION **2**
Mathematical Reasoning

Time—30 minutes
25 Questions

Directions and Reference Information

In this section solve each problem, using any available space for scratchwork. Then decide which is the best of the choices given and fill in the corresponding oval on the answer sheet.

Notes:

(1) The use of a calculator is permitted. All numbers used are real numbers.

(2) Figures that accompany problems in this test are intended to provide information useful in solving the problems. They are drawn as accurately as possible EXCEPT when it is stated in a specific problem that the figure is not drawn to scale. All figures lie in a plane unless otherwise indicated.

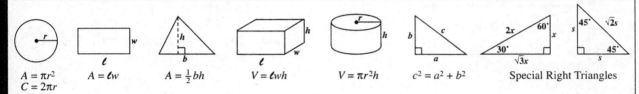

$A = \pi r^2$
$C = 2\pi r$

$A = \ell w$

$A = \frac{1}{2}bh$

$V = \ell wh$

$V = \pi r^2 h$

$c^2 = a^2 + b^2$

Special Right Triangles

The number of degrees of an arc in a circle is 360.
The measure in degrees of a straight angle is 180.
The sum of the measures in degrees of the angles of a triangle is 180.

---

1. $\frac{1}{2} + \frac{3}{4} \div \left(\frac{5}{6} \times \frac{7}{8}\right) - \frac{9}{10} =$

    (A) $\frac{18}{35}$ (B) $\frac{22}{35}$ (C) $\frac{57}{70}$ (D) $\frac{7}{12}$ (E) $1\frac{5}{7}$

2. A prime number is an integer greater than 1 that is evenly divisible only by itself and 1. Which of the following represents a prime number when $n = 5$?

    (A) $n^2 + n$ (B) $7n$ (C) $n^2 - 2$
    (D) $n^2 + 2$ (E) $3n + 1$

3. How many thirds are there in 75% of an apple pie?

    (A) $\frac{1}{4}$ (B) 1 (C) 2 (D) $2\frac{1}{4}$ (E) 3

4. If $i^2 = -1$, then i^{39} equals:

    (A) 1 (B) –1 (C) i (D) $-i$ (E) $3i$

5. Ed Walsh left his estate to his three children to be distributed in the ratio of 1:2:1. If the value of the estate was $40,000, how much did the child with the greatest share receive?

    (A) $2000   (B) $13,333.33   (C) $13,334
    (D) $20,000   (E) $30,000

6. A dealer bought a chair for $60. What price should be put on this chair in order to offer a 10% discount and still make a 20% profit for this dealer?

    (A) $72.00   (B) $78.00   (C) $79.20
    (D) $80.00   (E) $85.00

7. If, after successive discounts of 15% and 10% have been allowed on the marked price, the net price of a certain article is $306, the marked price is

    (A) $230.00   (B) $234.09   (C) $382.50
    (D) $400.00   (E) $408.00

GO ON TO THE NEXT PAGE

8. How much can be saved by purchasing a radio for cash at $72 instead of paying $15 down and five monthly payments of $13 each?

    (A) $7   (B) $8   (C) $9   (D) $10
    (E) none of these

9. Point M is the midpoint of line KL, and point C is the midpoint of line AB. If $KM > AC$, then which of the following is (are) true?

    I. $KL < AB$
    II. $KL > AB$
    III. $KM < AC$

    (A) I only   (B) II only   (C) III only
    (D) I and III only   (E) I, II, and III

10. Which of the following statements is (are) true of the length of segments on line l?

    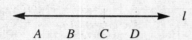

    I. $AB + BC = AD - CD$
    II. $AD - BC = AB + CD$
    III. $AB + CD = AD$

    (A) I only   (B) II only   (C) III only
    (D) I and II only   (E) I, II, and III

11. The length of a rectangle is 3 inches greater than its width and its area is 88 square inches. An equation that may be used to find the width w of the rectangle is

    (A) $3w^2 = 88$ (B) $\dfrac{w^2}{3} = 88$
    (C) $w^2 + 3w - 88 = 0$ (D) $w^2 - 3w = 88$
    (E) $w = 29.3$

12. On the average, 800 pounds of valuable oxides are obtained from every 2 tons of ore mined. What is the ratio of valuable oxides to other material in 100 tons of ore? (1 ton = 2000 pounds)

    (A) 1:400   (B) 1:5   (C) 1:4
    (D) 2:1   (E) 4:1

13. How many pints of flour should be used with 3 pints of milk in a recipe which calls for 2 parts of milk and 3 parts of flour?

    (A) 2   (B) 3   (C) $4\frac{1}{2}$ (D) 5   (E) 6

14. $\sqrt{\dfrac{2 + x^2}{2}} = 3$

    What is the value of x?

    (A) ±2 (B) ±3 (C) ±4 (D) ±5 (E) ±6

15. A motorist travels D miles in T hours and then travels d miles at t hours. His average rate for the entire trip is

    (A) $\dfrac{1}{2}\left(\dfrac{D}{T} + \dfrac{d}{t}\right)$ (B) $\dfrac{2Dd}{Tt}$ (C) $\dfrac{D + d}{T + t}$

    (D) $\dfrac{Dt + dT}{2Tt}$ (E) $\dfrac{d}{t} + \dfrac{D}{T}$

16. 1500 is greater than 1200 by

    (A) 2.5%   (B) 3%   (C) 11.9%
    (D) 20%   (E) 25%

17. Melinda has 10 problems to do before watching a television program scheduled for 9 P.M. She takes 10 minutes on the average to do a problem. What is the latest time she could begin to do her homework and have her work done by the time the television program begins?

    (A) 7:10 P.M.   (B) 7:20 P.M.   (C) 7:30 P.M.
    (D) 7:45 P.M.   (E) 8:00 P.M.

18. For $X \neq 0$, let X be defined by $\boxed{X} = X^2 + \dfrac{1}{X^2}$

    Then $\boxed{2} =$

    (A) 1   (B) 2   (C) 4   (D) $4\frac{1}{4}$ (E) $4\frac{1}{2}$

19. In a right triangle, sides x, y, z have values such that $x < y < z$. Which of the following expresses the value of z^2?

    (A) $x^2 + y^2$ (B) $x^2 - y^2$ (C) $x - y$
    (D) $x + y$ (E) $y^2 - x^2$

20. A pond 100 feet in diameter is surrounded by a circular grass walk which is 2 feet wide. The number of square feet of grass on the walk is

    (A) 4π (B) 20π (C) 196π
    (D) 204π (E) 270π

21. Which of the following is the equation of line RS in the figure?

    (A) $y = x$
    (B) $y = -x$
    (C) $y = 4 - x$
    (D) $y = x - 4$
    (E) $y = x \neq 4$

    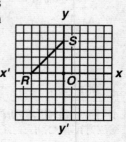

22. *RS* and *RT* are tangent to circle *O*. ∠*SRT* ≅ 30.
∠*SOT* ≅

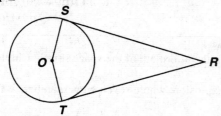

(A) 110   (B) 120   (C) 150
(D) 250   (E) 300

23. In △ *ABC*, *AP* is drawn so that ∠1 = ∠2. All of the
following are true EXCEPT

(A) *AB > AP*
(B) *AP < AB*
(C) *AP = AC*
(D) The measure of
∠2 is greater
than the measure
of ∠3.
(E) *AP > AB*

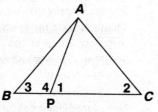

24. Out of every dollar, how much does the average
American spend for housing?

(A) 5¢   (B) 7$\frac{1}{2}$ ¢   (C) 10¢

(D) 12$\frac{1}{2}$ ¢ (E) 15¢

HOW THE AVERAGE AMERICAN SPENDS MONEY

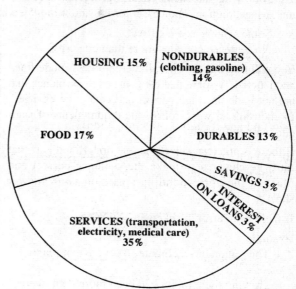

25. Of all the taxes collected, what percent comes
from income taxes (to the nearest percent)?

(A) 25%   (B) 33$\frac{1}{3}$ %   (C) 40%

(D) 50%   (E) 75%

WHERE THE TAX DOLLAR COMES FROM

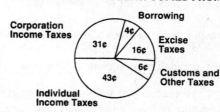

IF YOU FINISH BEFORE 30 MINUTES, YOU MAY CHECK YOUR WORK ON THIS
SECTION ONLY. DO NOT TURN TO ANY OTHER SECTION IN THE TEST.

S T O P

SECTION 3
Writing Skills

Time—30 minutes
39 Questions

Directions

The following sentences contain problems in grammar, usage, diction (choice of words), and idiom.

> Some sentences are correct.
> No sentence contains more than one error.

You will find that the error, if there is one, is underlined and lettered. Assume that elements of the sentence that are not underlined are correct and cannot be changed. In choosing answers, follow the requirements of standard written English.

If there is an error, select the one underlined part that must be changed to make the sentence correct and blacken the corresponding space on your answer sheet.

If there is no error, blacken answer space Ⓔ.

Example:

> The region has a climate so severe that plants
>   A
>
> growing there rarely had been more than twelve
>   B   C
>
> inches high. No error
>   D   E

Ⓐ Ⓑ ● Ⓓ Ⓔ

1. I can hardly believe your tale of military intrigue;
              A
the sophisticated secret weapons and the

increasing violent actions that were exhibited
        B   C
by just one man seem incredible. No error
              D   E

2. The animals who were chosen to represent the
            A   B
Democratic and Republican parties, the donkey and

the elephant, were created by the renowned cartoonist
            C   D
Thomas Nast. No error
        E

3. I should like you and he to supply the necessary data
   A   B   C
for the annual statement which must be prepared

in advance of the spring meeting. No error
    D   E

4. In the aftermath of the space shuttle Challenger
          A
explosion, where seven crew members were killed,
         B   C
the NASA program underwent a massive examination
                   D
of priorities. No error
       E

5. Twenty-five restless five-year-olds were throwing
          A   B
paper clips, were drawing on the blackboard, and

called to one another while their teacher went
  C   D
searching for milk and cookies. No error
              E

6. Recent medical breakthroughs, including the

discovery of a vaccine to slow the AIDS virus,
  A
have encouraged researchers; and a cure is still
     B   C
eluding them. No error
  D   E

7. Before the producer took the musical to Broadway,
  A
he tried to get the show with all their actors and
    B   C
actresses booked in summer stock theaters for

last-minute revisions. No error
    D   E

8. Neither the mid-life career change applicant nor the
                       A
young, inexperienced applicant are finding it easy
                 B
to begin a career in data processing because of a
  C   D
shortage of job openings. No error
           E

9. Even after you have endured a cold winter in sub-zero
    A
weather, one finds it possible to become acclimated
     B C   D
to tropical temperatures in the summer. No error
                   E

GO ON TO THE NEXT PAGE

10. When you buy a condominium, you will have
    A
    less work than owning a house entails, but you
    B
    have not had the intrinsic rewards. No error
    C   D   E

11. We have come to the conclusion that we can end
    A
    hostilities in that area of the world by providing
    B
    food to both sides, bringing the opposing forces to
    the negotiation table, and to guarantee financial aid
    C   D
    to both sides once peace is established. No error
    E

12. Numerous collections of short stories include works
    A
    by Isaac Bashevis Singer who, despite living in the
    B
    United States over fifty years, continues to write
    C   D
    primarily in Yiddish. No error
    E

13. Public television has succeeded admirably in raising
    A   B
    money for its future programs through marathon
    C
    fund-raising projects. No error
    D   E

14. By the time the bank guard closed the doors, a riot
    A
    had erupted due to the long lines and shortage of
    B   C   D
    tellers. No error
    E

15. The ancient concept which states that the sun
    A   B
    revolves around the earth is questioned by
    C   D
    Copernicus in the sixteenth century. No error
    E

16. If the bystander had not been familiar with first-
    A   B
    aid techniques, the young diver which had the bad
    C
    fall might have been paralyzed. No error
    D   E

17. The article was rejected because of its length,
    A   B
    verbosity, and because it presented only one point
    C   D
    of view. No error
    E

18. Because of the triage practice used in hospitals,
    A
    some of them waiting in the emergency room
    B
    had been there for more than an hour. No error
    C   D   E

19. Neither of the defendants were prepared for
    A
    several of the arguments brought into the open
    B   C
    and deftly handled by the prosecution. No error
    D   E

Directions

In each of the following sentences, some part or all of the sentence is underlined. Below each sentence you will find five ways of phrasing the underlined part. Select the answer that produces the most effective sentence, one that is clear and exact, without awkwardness or ambiguity, and fill in the corresponding oval on your answer sheet. In choosing answers, follow the requirements of standard written English. Choose the answer that best expresses the meaning of the original sentence.

Answer (A) is always the same as the underlined part. Choose Answer (A) if you think the original sentence needs no revision.

EXAMPLE:

Laura Ingalls Wilder published her first book and she was sixty-five years old then.

(A) and she was sixty-five years old then
(B) when she was sixty-five
(C) at age sixty-five years old
(D) upon reaching of sixty-five years
(E) at the time when she was sixty-five

SAMPLE ANSWER

Ⓐ ● Ⓒ Ⓓ Ⓔ

20. Complaining that he couldn't hear hardly anything, he asked Dr. Brown, the otologist, whether he should get a hearing aid.

    (A) Complaining that he couldn't hear hardly anything,
    (B) Complaining that he couldn't hardly hear anything,
    (C) He complained that he couldn't hear hardly anything,
    (D) Complaining that he could hear hardly anything,
    (E) Because he couldn't hear hardly anything,

21. Shakespeare wrote many plays, they are now being presented on public television.

(A) Shakespeare wrote many plays, they are now being presented on public television.
(B) Shakespeare wrote many plays, and they have been presented on public television.
(C) Shakespeare wrote many plays, which public television has now presented.
(D) The many plays of Shakespeare have now been presented on public television.
(E) Shakespeare wrote many plays; they are now being presented on public television.

22. Many alcoholics attempt to conceal their problem from their fellow workers, but invariably failing to keep their secret.

(A) but invariably failing to keep their secret
(B) but they invariably fail to keep their secret
(C) but fail, invariably, to keep their secret
(D) who invariably fail to keep their secret
(E) who they invariably fail to keep their secret from

23. Upon considering the facts of the case, the solution was obvious; consequently, Holmes sent for the police.

(A) Upon considering
(B) When considering
(C) Considering
(D) On consideration of
(E) When he considered

24. Familiar with the terrain from previous visits, the explorer's search for the abandoned mine site was a success.

(A) the explorer's search for the abandoned mine site was a success
(B) the success of the explorer's search for the abandoned mine site was assured
(C) the explorer succeeded in finding the abandoned mine site
(D) the search by the explorer for the abandoned mine site was successful
(E) the explorer in his search for the abandoned mine site was a success

25. Economic conditions demand not only cutting wages and prices but also to reduce inflation-raised tax rates.

(A) not only cutting wages and prices but also to reduce
(B) we not only cut wages and prices but also reduce
(C) to not only cut wages and prices but also to reduce
(D) not only to cut wages and prices but also to reduce
(E) not only a cut in wages and prices but also to reduce

26. He interviewed several candidates who he thought had the experience and qualifications he required.

(A) who he thought
(B) whom he thought
(C) of whom he thought
(D) he thought who
(E) which he thought

27. A person's true character, it seems, is revealed in a situation which is similar to this.

(A) in a situation which is similar to this
(B) in a situation like this is
(C) in a situation such as this
(D) in such a situation like this is
(E) from a situation such as this

28. It is typical of military service for a skilled technician to be inducted and then you spend your whole tour of duty peeling potatoes and cleaning latrines.

(A) then you spend your whole tour of duty
(B) to spend your whole tour of duty
(C) then they spend their whole tour of duty
(D) to spend their whole tour of duty
(E) then spend his whole tour of duty

29. Being that he is that kind of a boy, he should not be blamed for his mistakes.

(A) Being that he is that kind of a boy,
(B) Being that he is that kind of boy,
(C) Since he is that kind of boy,
(D) Since that he is that sort of a boy,
(E) Because he is that sort of a boy,

30. At an early stage in his travels, Henry James writing from abroad described the subtle differences distinguishing Americans from Europeans.

(A) At an early stage in his travels, Henry James writing
(B) At an early stage in his travels, Henry James wrote
(C) At an early stage in his travels, Henry James while writing
(D) At an early stage in his travels, Henry James was writing
(E) Henry James, whose writing at an early stage in his travels

31. Fame as well as fortune were his goals in life.

(A) Fame as well as fortune were his goals in life.
(B) Fame as well as fortune was his goals in life.
(C) Fame as well as fortune were his goal in life.
(D) Fame and fortune were his goals in life.
(E) Fame also fortune were his goals in life.

GO ON TO THE NEXT PAGE

32. For recreation I like to watch <u>these kind of</u> programs in the evening.

    (A) these kind of
    (B) these sort of
    (C) these kinds of
    (D) them kinds of
    (E) this kinds of

33. Whatever the surface indications of the moment may be, modern men are basically <u>less tolerant of despots then men of old.</u>

    (A) less tolerant of despots then men of old
    (B) less tolerant of despots than older men
    (C) less tolerant of despots than men of old
    (D) more intolerant of despots then in former years
    (E) less tolerant of despots than the men of old

Directions

The passage below is the unedited draft of a student's essay. Some of the essay needs to be rewritten to make the meaning clearer and more precise. Read the essay carefully.

The essay is followed by six questions about changes that might improve all or part of its organization, development, sentence structure, use of language, appropriateness to the audience, or its use of standard written English. Choose the answer that most clearly and effectively expresses the student's intended meaning. Indicate your choice by filling in the corresponding space on the answer sheet.

Essay

[1] It is difficult to deny that the world of music has changed greatly in the past thirty years. [2] The style, sound, technology, and lyrics of music have been altered greatly. [3] In the last three decades, several new categories of music have come into being.

[4] One reason why music has changed so greatly is that artists use music as a tool to publicize certain social messages. [5] Although many artists of the 1970s used this method as well, their issues were not as severe that banning their album was possible. [6] For example, one rap-singer, Ice-T, used his album to promote "cop-killing." [7] The idea was so offensive that many believed the album should be banned. [8] The controversy caused by Ice-T made the Arista record company refuse to continue production of the album.

[9] Another way in which music has changed is lyrics. [10] When you listen to certain heavy metal or rap groups, one may notice foul and obscene language used. [11] Some of the references to sex are shocking. [12] In past eras, such language in recorded music was unheard of.

[13] Technological changes in music have occurred. [14] With the advent of highly advanced musical devices and many digital effects, the sounds of music have been completely altered. [15] Rock and roll was invented in early 1950s. [16] When you listen to heavy metal, you hear more distorted guitar sounds than in music of the 60s and 70s. [17] In the era of electronic instruments, the variety of possible sounds is incredible. [18] Present day sounds could never have been achieved in previous years because the technology was not at hand. [19] New music utilizes electronically produced sounds never heard before. [20] Computers generate everything from the human voice under water to the sound of whales. [21] There are no limits to what the music of the future will sound like.

34. Which of the following is the best revision of the underlined segment of sentence 5 below?

Although many artists of the 1970s used this method as well, <u>their issues were not as severe that banning their album was possible.</u>

    (A) the issues were less severe than those which caused banning their album to be possible.
    (B) their issues were not as severe that their albums were in danger of being banned.
    (C) they never raised issues that could have caused their albums to be banned.
    (D) the issues they raised were not serious enough that banning their album was a possibility.
    (E) they raised less serious issues and banning their albums was not likely.

35. Taking into account the sentences which precede and follow sentence 10, which is the most effective revision of sentence 10?

    (A) Listening to certain heavy metal or rap groups, lyrics containing obscenities are often heard.
    (B) Obscene language is common in the songs of heavy metal and rap groups.
    (C) Certain heavy metal and rap groups use foul and obscene language.
    (D) Obscenities are often heard when one listens to the lyrics of certain heavy metal or rap groups.
    (E) Listening to obscene language and listening to the lyrics of certain heavy metal and rap groups.

36. In the context of the entire essay, which revision of sentence 13 provides the most effective transition between paragraphs 3 and 4?

    (A) Technological changes in music also have occurred.
    (B) Also, technology has changed musical sounds.
    (C) Noticeable changes in music's sounds have come about through technological changes.
    (D) Changes in musical technology has changed musical sound, too.
    (E) But the most noticeable change in music has been its sound.

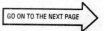
GO ON TO THE NEXT PAGE

37. In a revision of the entire essay, which of the following sentences most needs further development?

    (A) Sentence 3
    (B) Sentence 7
    (C) Sentence 8
    (D) Sentence 19
    (E) Sentence 20

38. Which of the following sentences should be deleted to improve the unit and coherence of paragraph 4?

    (A) Sentence 14
    (B) Sentence 15
    (C) Sentence 16
    (D) Sentence 17
    (E) Sentence 18

39. Taking into account the organization of the entire essay, which is the best revision of sentence 2 in the introductory paragraph?

    (A) In the past thirty years, not only the style, sound, and technology has changed, but the lyrics have, too.
    (B) Having undergone a change in the style, sound, technology, musical lyrics have altered also.
    (C) Changes in musical sound have occurred, while the technology and lyrics have tremendously altered the style of music.
    (D) Musicians have changed the purpose and the lyrics of music, and technology has changed its sound.
    (E) Along with changes in sound and technology, the lyrics of music have changed, too.

IF YOU FINISH BEFORE 30 MINUTES, YOU MAY CHECK YOUR WORK ON THIS SECTION ONLY. DO NOT TURN TO ANY OTHER SECTION IN THE TEST.   **S T O P**

SECTION 4
Verbal Reasoning

Time—30 minutes
30 Questions

For each question in this section, select the best answer from among the choices given and fill in the corresponding oval on the answer sheet.

Directions

Each sentence below consists of a related pair of words or phrases, followed by five pairs of words or phrases labeled A through E. Select the pair that best expresses a relationship similar to that expressed in the original pair.

Example:

CRUMB:BREAD::
(A) ounce:unit
(B) splinter:wood
(C) water:bucket
(D) twine:rope
(E) cream:butter

Ⓐ ● Ⓒ Ⓓ Ⓔ

31. MUFFLER:NECK::
   (A) lace:collar   (B) elbow:arm
   (C) sash:waist   (D) cuticle:finger
   (E) skirt:hem

32. BARGE:VESSEL::
   (A) cargo:hold   (B) brake:automobile
   (C) shovel:implement   (D) squadron:plane
   (E) link:chain

33. LAUREL WREATH:VICTORY::
   (A) rosebud:charity   (B) maple leaf:sweetness
   (C) blindfold:visibility   (D) palm tree:idleness
   (E) olive branch:peace

34. GRATING:EAR::
   (A) warm:touch   (B) smooth:skin
   (C) garish:eye   (D) beating:heart
   (E) peeling:nose

35. INVENTOR:PATENT::
   (A) architect:blueprint   (B) librarian:catalog
   (C) author:copyright   (D) editor:manuscript
   (E) engineer:bridge

36. LEOPARD:CARNIVOROUS::
   (A) tiger:striped   (B) quadruped:omnivorous
   (C) cow:herbivorous   (D) cat:feline
   (E) seal:trained

37. BREEZE:CYCLONE::
   (A) ripple:tidal wave   (B) gust:wind
   (C) dune:sandstorm   (D) warning:forecast
   (E) weather:phenomenon

38. RAMSHACKLE:SOUNDNESS::
   (A) garbled:clarity   (B) decrepit:demolition
   (C) humdrum:monotony
   (D) flimsy:transparency   (E) steadfast:speed

39. AGITATOR:FIREBRAND::
   (A) miser:spendthrift   (B) renegade:turncoat
   (C) anarchist:backslider
   (D) maverick:scapegoat   (E) reprobate:hothead

40. CALLOW:MATURITY::
   (A) incipient:fruition   (B) eager:anxiety
   (C) youthful:senility   (D) apathetic:disinterest
   (E) pallid:purity

41. TIRADE:ABUSIVE::
   (A) diatribe:political   (B) satire:pungent
   (C) panegyric:laudatory   (D) eulogy:lamentable
   (E) elegy:religious

42. SKULDUGGERY:SWINDLER::
   (A) surgery:quack   (B) quandary:craven
   (C) chicanery:trickster   (D) forgery:speculator
   (E) cutlery:butcher

43. SELF-RESPECTING:VAINGLORIOUS::
   (A) loyal:perfidious   (B) healthful:salubrious
   (C) querulous:cantankerous
   (D) modest:lascivious   (E) careful:punctilious

The passage below is followed by questions based on its content. Answer the questions following the passage on the basis of what is <u>stated</u> or <u>implied</u> in that passage and in any introductory material that may be provided.

Questions 44–48 are based on the following passage.

Are Americans today overworked? The following passage is excerpted from a book published in 1991 on the unexpected decline of leisure in American life.

Faith in progress is deep within our culture. We have been taught to believe that our lives are better than the lives of those who came before us. The ideology of modern economics suggests that material progress has yielded enhanced satisfaction and well-being. But much of our confidence about our own well being comes from the assumption that our lives are easier than those of earlier generations. I have already disputed the notion that we work less than medieval European

Line 5

10

GO ON TO THE NEXT PAGE ▶

peasants, however poor they may have been. The field research of anthropologists gives another view of the conventional wisdom.

15 The lives of so-called primitive peoples are commonly thought to be harsh—their existence dominated by the "incessant quest for food." In fact, primitives do little work. By contemporary standards, we'd have to judge them very lazy. If the Kapauku of Papua work one day, they do no
20 labor on the next. !Kung Bushmen put in only two and a half days per week and six hours per day. In the Sandwich Islands of Hawaii, men work only four hours per day. And Australian aborigines have similar schedules. The key to understanding why
25 these "stone age peoples" fail to act like us— increasing their work effort to get more things—is that they have limited desires. In the race between wanting and having, they have kept their wanting low—and, in this way, ensure their own kind of
30 satisfaction. They are materially poor by contemporary standards, but in at least one dimension— time—we have to count them richer.

I do not raise these issues to imply that we would be better off as Polynesian natives or
35 medieval peasants. Nor am I arguing that "progress" has made us worse off. I am, instead, making a much simpler point. We have paid a price for prosperity. Capitalism has brought a dramatically increased standard of living, but at the
40 cost of a much more demanding worklife. We are eating more, but we are burning up those calories at work. We have color televisions and compact disc players, but we need them to unwind after a stressful day at the office. We take vacations, but
45 we work so hard throughout the year that they become indispensable to our sanity. The conventional wisdom that economic progress has given us more things *as well as* more leisure is difficult to sustain.

44. According to the author, we base our belief that American people today are well off on the assumption that

(A) America has always been the land of opportunity
(B) Americans particularly deserve to be prosperous
(C) people elsewhere have an inferior standard of living
(D) people elsewhere envy the American way of life
(E) our faith in progress will protect us as a nation

45. The author regards "the conventional wisdom" (line 13) with

(A) resentment
(B) skepticism
(C) complacency
(D) apprehension
(E) bewilderment

46. In lines 18–27, the Kapauku tribesmen and the !Kung Bushmen are presented as examples of

(A) malingerers who turn down opportunities to work
(B) noble savages with little sense of time
(C) people who implicitly believe in progress
(D) people unmotivated by a desire for consumer goods
(E) people obsessed by their constant search for food

47. The primary purpose of the passage is to

(A) dispute an assumption
(B) highlight a problem
(C) ridicule a theory
(D) answer a criticism
(E) counter propaganda

48. The last four sentences of the passage (lines 40–49) provide

(A) a recapitulation of a previously made argument
(B) an example of the argument that has been proposed earlier
(C) a series of assertions and qualifications with a conclusion
(D) a reconciliation of two opposing viewpoints
(E) a reversal of the author's original position

GO ON TO THE NEXT PAGE

The passages below are followed by questions based on their content; questions following a pair of related passages may also be based on the relationship between the paired passages. Answer the questions on the basis of what is <u>stated</u> or <u>implied</u> in the passages and in any introductory material that may be provided.

Questions 49–60 are based on the following passages.

In the following passages, the novelist Virginia Woolf and a contemporary literary critic separately discuss the relationship between women and fiction.

PASSAGE 1

The most superficial inquiry into women's writing instantly raises a host of questions. Why, we ask at once, was there no continuous writing done
Line by women before the eighteenth century? Why did
5 they then write almost habitually as men, and in the course of that writing produce, one after another, some of the classics of English fiction? And why did their art then, and why to some extent does their art still, take the form of fiction?
10 A little thought will show us that we are asking questions to which we shall get, as answer, only further fiction. The answer lies at present locked in old diaries, stuffed away in old drawers, half obliterated in the memories of the aged. It is to be found in the
15 lives of the obscure—in those almost unlit corridors of history where the figures of generations of women are so dimly, so fitfully perceived. For very little is known about women. The history of England is the history of the male line, not of the
20 female. Of our fathers we know always some fact, some distinction. They were soldiers or they were sailors; they filled that office or they made that law. But of our mothers, our grandmothers, our great-grandmothers, what remains? Nothing but a tradi-
25 tion. One was beautiful; one was red-haired; one was kissed by a Queen. We know nothing of them except their names and the dates of their marriages and the number of children they bore.
Thus, if we wish to know why at any particular
30 time women did this or that, why they wrote nothing, why on the other hand they wrote masterpieces, it is extremely difficult to tell. Anyone who should seek among those old papers, who should turn history wrong side out and so construct a
35 faithful picture of the daily life of the ordinary woman in Shakespeare's time, in Milton's time, in Johnson's time, would not only write a book of astonishing interest, but would furnish the critic with a weapon that he now lacks. The extraordi-
40 nary woman depends on the ordinary woman. It is only when we know what were the conditions of the average woman's life—the number of her children, whether she had money of her own, if she had a room to herself, whether she had help in
45 bringing up her family, if she had servants, whether part of the housework was her task—it is only when we can measure the way of life and the experience of life made possible to the ordinary woman that we can account for the success or fail-
50 ure of the extraordinary woman as writer.

PASSAGE 2

As the works of dozens of women writers have been rescued from what E.P. Thompson calls "the enormous condescension of posterity," and considered in relation to each other, the lost continent of
55 the female tradition has risen like Atlantis from the sea of English literature. It is now becoming clear that, contrary to Mill's theory, women have had a literature of their own all along. The woman novelist, according to Vineta Colby, was "really nei-
60 ther single nor anomalous," but she was also more than a "register and spokesman for her age." She was part of a tradition that had its origins before her age, and has carried on through our own.
Many literary historians have begun to reinter-
65 pret and revise the study of women writers. Ellen Moers sees women's literature as an international movement, "apart from, but hardly subordinate to the mainstream: an undercurrent, rapid and powerful. This 'movement' began in the late eigh-
70 teenth century, was multinational, and produced some of the greatest literary works of two centuries, as well as most of the lucrative potboilers." Other critics are beginning to agree that when we look at women writers collectively we can see an
75 imaginative continuum, the recurrence of certain patterns, themes, problems, and images from generation to generation.
This book is an effort to describe the female literary tradition in the English novel from the
80 generation of the Brontes to the present day, and to show how the development of this tradition is similar to the development of any literary subculture. It is important to see the female literary tradition in these broad terms, in relation to the
85 wider evolution of women's self-awareness and to the ways any minority group finds its direction of self-expression relative to a dominant society, because we cannot show a pattern of deliberate progress and accumulation. It is true, as Ellen
90 Moers writes, that "women studied with a special closeness the works written by their own sex"; in terms of influences, borrowings, and affinities, the tradition is strongly marked. But it is also full of holes and hiatuses, because of what Germaine
95 Greer calls the "phenomenon of the transience of female literary fame"; "almost uninterruptedly since the Interregnum, a small group of women have enjoyed dazzling literary prestige during their own lifetimes, only to vanish without trace
100 from the records of posterity." Thus each genera-

GO ON TO THE NEXT PAGE

tion of women writers has found itself, in a sense, without a history, forced to rediscover the past anew, forging again and again the consciousness of their sex. Given this perpetual disruption, and
105 also the self-hatred that has alienated women writers from a sense of collective identity, it does not seem possible to speak of a movement.

49. The questions in lines 2–9 chiefly serve to

(A) suggest how the author defines women's writing
(B) outline the direction of the author's research
(C) underscore how little is known about the subject
(D) divert the reader's attention from the central issue
(E) express the author's reluctance to appear dogmatic

50. The word "filled" in line 22 means

(A) inflated   (B) blocked   (C) furnished
(D) held   (E) pervaded

51. Woolf's point in lines 17–28 about how little is known about women is made primarily through

(A) case histories   (B) examples
(C) statistics   (D) metaphors
(E) repeated quotations

52. The individual women mentioned in lines 25–26 are presented primarily as instances of people who

(A) encountered royalty
(B) gave birth to children
(C) observed family traditions
(D) sought to become writers
(E) lived largely unrecorded lives

53. Which of the following would be the most appropriate title for Passage 2?

(A) A Unique Phenomenon: Nineteenth- and Twentieth-Century Feminine Literary Movements
(B) A Literature of Their Own: The Female Literary Tradition
(C) The Role of The Ordinary Woman in Modern Literature
(D) The Emergence of the Contemporary Women's Novel
(E) Fame Versus Fortune: The Dilemma of the Woman Writer

54. In the first paragraph of Passage 2, the author makes use of all the following techniques EXCEPT

(A) extended metaphor
(B) enumeration and classification
(C) classical allusion   (D) direct quotation
(E) comparison and contrast

55. The metaphor of the newly-arisen "lost continent" (lines 54–56) is used primarily to convey

(A) the vast degree of effort involved in reinterpreting women's literature
(B) the number of works of literature that have been created by women
(C) the way forgotten literary works have resurfaced after many years
(D) the extent to which books written by women appeared unrelated
(E) the overwhelming size of the problem confronting the author

56. In the second paragraph of Passage 2, the author's attitude toward the literary critics cited can best be described as one of

(A) irony   (B) ambivalence   (C) disparagement
(D) receptiveness   (E) awe

57. The word "closeness" in line 91 means

(A) proximity in space
(B) narrow margin of victory
(C) disposition to secrecy
(D) cautiousness about expenditures
(E) minute attention to details

58. Which of the following words could best be substituted for "forging" (line 103) without substantially changing the author's meaning?

(A) Counterfeiting   (B) Creating   (C) Exploring
(D) Diverting   (E) Straining

59. It can be inferred from Passage 2 that the author considers Moers's work to be

(A) fallacious and misleading
(B) scholarly and definitive
(C) admirable, but inaccurate in certain of its conclusions
(D) popular, but irrelevant to mainstream female literary criticism
(E) idiosyncratic, but of importance historically

60. Compared to the author of Passage 2, the author of Passage 1 is

(A) more academic and less colloquial
(B) less effusive and more detached
(C) less didactic and more dogmatic
(D) less scholarly and more descriptive
(E) more radical and less entertaining

IF YOU FINISH BEFORE 30 MINUTES, YOU MAY CHECK YOUR WORK ON THIS SECTION ONLY. DO NOT TURN TO ANY OTHER SECTION IN THE TEST.   **STOP**

SECTION 5
Mathematical Reasoning

Directions and Sample Questions

Notes:

(1) The use of a calculator is permitted. All numbers used are real numbers.

(2) Figures that accompany problems in this test are intended to provide information useful in solving the problems. They are drawn as accurately as possible EXCEPT when it is stated in a specific problem that the figure is not drawn to scale. All figures lie in a plane unless otherwise indicated.

Questions 1–15 each consist of two quantities in boxes, one in Column A and one in Column B. You are to compare the two quantities and on the answer sheet fill in oval

A if the quantity in Column A is greater;
B if the quantity in Column B is greater;
C if the two quantities are equal;
D if the relationship cannot be determined from the information given.

Notes:

1. In some questions, information is given about one or both of the quantities to be compared. In such cases, the given information is centered above the two columns and is not boxed.

2. In a given question, a symbol that appears in both columns represents the same thing in Column A as it does in Column B.

3. Letters such as x, n, and k stand for real numbers.

	EXAMPLES		
	Column A	Column B	Answers
E1	5^2	20	● Ⓑ Ⓒ Ⓓ
E2	x	30	Ⓐ Ⓑ ● Ⓓ
E3	$r + 1$	$s - 1$	Ⓐ Ⓑ Ⓒ ●

For E2: $150°$ / $x°$

For E3: r and s are integers.

PART I: QUANTITATIVE COMPARISON QUESTIONS

SUMMARY DIRECTIONS FOR QUANTITATIVE COMPARISON QUESTIONS

Answer: A if the quantity in Column A is greater.
B if the quantity in Column B is greater.
C if the two quantities are equal.
D if the relationship cannot be determined from the information given.

	Column A	Column B
26.	$10 - \frac{10}{0.1}$	-9
27.	$\sqrt{4}$	$\frac{1}{0.5}$
28.	0.6%	$\frac{6}{1000}$
29.	$\frac{2548}{14}$ inches	5 yards 2 inches

	Column A	Column B
	$x = y = 5$	
30.	$\dfrac{1}{x} \div \dfrac{1}{\frac{1}{x}}$	$\dfrac{1}{y}$
31.	$(y + 160) - (120 - y)$	$(x + 10) - (x - 2y - 30)$
	$a = b^2 - 1$	
32.	a	b

GO ON TO THE NEXT PAGE →

Column A	Column B

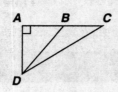

$AB = BC$
$AD \perp AC$

33.   Area of *ABD*   Area of *BCD*

34. $\dfrac{a+b}{2}$ $\dfrac{1}{2}(c+d)$

$x > 0$ and $y > 0$

$x = \dfrac{y}{2}$

35. $y + 2$ $2x + 2$

36. $\dfrac{1}{2}$ $\sqrt{\dfrac{1}{4}}$

Column A	Column B

$7x = 35 + 7y$

37. y $x - 7$

x is 25% of y and
y is 50% of z.

38.   Average of x, y, and z $4x$

39.   The original price of a TV set, including delivery charge.   The reduced price of the same set during a sale at a 10% reduction but a 10% delivery charge.

40.   Lori's rate driving to school was 30 miles per hour. Going home her average speed was 40 miles per hour.   Average rate of 35 miles per hour.

GO ON TO THE NEXT PAGE

PART II: STUDENT-PRODUCED RESPONSE QUESTIONS

Directions for Student-Produced Response Questions

Each of the remaining ten questions (41–50) requires you to solve the problem and enter your answer by marking the ovals in the special grid, as shown in the examples below.

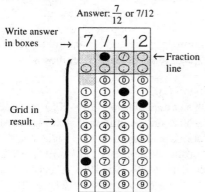

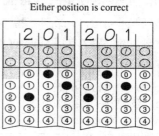

Answer: $\frac{7}{12}$ or 7/12

Answer: 2.5

Answer: 201
Either position is correct

Write answer in boxes →

← Fraction line

← Decimal point

Grid in result. →

<u>Note:</u> You may start your answers in any column, space permitting. Columns not needed should be left blank.

- Mark no more than one oval in any column.
- Because the answer sheet will be machine-scored, **you will receive credit only if the ovals are filled in correctly.**
- Although not required, it is suggested that you write your answer in the boxes at the top of the columns to help you fill in the ovals accurately.
- Some problems may have more than one correct answer. In such cases, grid only one answer.
- No question has a negative answer.
- **Mixed numbers** such as $2\frac{1}{2}$ much be gridded as 2.5 or 5/2. (If [2 1 / 2] is gridded, it will be interpreted as $\frac{21}{2}$, not $\frac{21}{2}$.)

- <u>Decimal Accuracy:</u> If you obtain a decimal answer, enter the most accurate value that the grid will accommodate. For example, if you obtain an answer such as 0.6666..., you should record the result as .666 or .667. Less accurate values such as .66 or .67 are not acceptable.

Acceptable ways to grid $\frac{2}{3}$ = .6666. . .

---

41. What number placed within the parentheses will make the following statement true?
$\frac{(\quad)}{5}$ cubic feet = $\frac{1}{3}$ cubic yard

42. A farmer sold $\frac{3}{8}$ of his strawberries for $60. At that rate what would he receive (in dollars) for the remainder of his crop?

43. If $5x - 3y = 3$ and $2x - 4y = -10$, what does $3x + y$ equal?

44. Five candidates run for office in a club that has a membership of 356. What is the least number of votes the successful candidate must receive to be victorious?

45. A bus has a capacity of 20 adults or 24 children. How many children can ride with 15 adults?

46. How many squares 2" × 2" can be cut from a piece of cardboard 8" × 4"?

47. If $3x - 6 = 1$, what is the value of $x - 2$?

48. AB is a diameter.
If $OC = BC$, then what does $\frac{x}{2}$ equal?

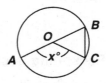

49. If a square with an area 144 is equal in perimeter to an equilateral triangle, what is a side of the triangle?

50. Quadrilateral $ABCD$ is inscribed in circle O.
$\angle DAB \stackrel{\circ}{=} 80$ and $\angle ABC \stackrel{\circ}{=} 120$. What is the measure of $\angle ADC$?

IF YOU FINISH BEFORE 30 MINUTES, YOU MAY CHECK YOUR WORK ON THIS SECTION ONLY. DO NOT TURN TO ANY OTHER SECTION IN THE TEST.

S T O P

ANSWER KEY

Verbal Reasoning Section 1

1. **A**	*6.* **E**	*11.* **C**	*16.* **B**	*21.* **A**	*26.* **D**
2. **B**	*7.* **D**	*12.* **D**	*17.* **D**	*22.* **D**	*27.* **C**
3. **B**	*8.* **E**	*13.* **A**	*18.* **C**	*23.* **D**	*28.* **D**
4. **D**	*9.* **C**	*14.* **A**	*19.* **A**	*24.* **B**	*29.* **E**
5. **B**	*10.* **B**	*15.* **C**	*20.* **E**	*25.* **B**	*30.* **B**

Mathematical Reasoning Section 2

Note: Each correct answer to the mathematics questions is keyed by number to the corresponding topic in Chapters 8 and 9. These numerals refer to the topics listed below, with specific page references in parentheses.

1. Basic Fundamental Operations (179–182)
2. Algebraic Operations (182–183)
3. Using Algebra (182–184, 187)
4. Exponents, Roots, and Radicals (184–185)
5. Inequalities (188–189)
6. Fractions (182, 198)
7. Decimals (200)
8. Percent (200)
9. Averages (201)
10. Motion (203)
11. Ratio and Proportion (204–205)
12. Mixtures and Solutions (178)
13. Work (206–207)
14. Coordinate Geometry (194)
15. Geometry (189–193, 195)
16. Quantitative Comparisons (211–212)
17. Data Interpretation (208)

1. **B** (1, 6)	*6.* **D** (3, 8)	*11.* **C** (3)	*16.* **E** (8)	*21.* **E** (14)
2. **C** (1, 3)	*7.* **D** (3, 8)	*12.* **C** (11)	*17.* **B** (1)	*22.* **C** (15)
3. **D** (8)	*8.* **B** (8)	*13.* **C** (11)	*18.* **D** (2)	*23.* **E** (5, 15)
4. **D** (4)	*9.* **B** (5, 15)	*14.* **C** (4)	*19.* **A** (15)	*24.* **E** (8, 17)
5. **D** (11)	*10.* **D** (15)	*15.* **C** (10)	*20.* **D** (15)	*25.* **E** (17)

Writing Skills Section 3

1. **B**	*8.* **B**	*15.* **D**	*22.* **B**	*29.* **C**	*36.* **E**
2. **A**	*9.* **B**	*16.* **C**	*23.* **E**	*30.* **A**	*37.* **A**
3. **B**	*10.* **C**	*17.* **C**	*24.* **C**	*31.* **D**	*38.* **B**
4. **B**	*11.* **D**	*18.* **B**	*25.* **B**	*32.* **C**	*39.* **D**
5. **C**	*12.* **E**	*19.* **A**	*26.* **A**	*33.* **E**	
6. **C**	*13.* **E**	*20.* **D**	*27.* **C**	*34.* **C**	
7. **C**	*14.* **C**	*21.* **E**	*28.* **E**	*35.* **B**	

Verbal Reasoning Section 4

31. **C**	*36.* **C**	*41.* **C**	*46.* **D**	*51.* **B**	*56.* **D**
32. **C**	*37.* **A**	*42.* **C**	*47.* **A**	*52.* **E**	*57.* **E**
33. **E**	*38.* **A**	*43.* **E**	*48.* **C**	*53.* **B**	*58.* **B**
34. **C**	*39.* **B**	*44.* **C**	*49.* **C**	*54.* **B**	*59.* **C**
35. **C**	*40.* **A**	*45.* **B**	*50.* **D**	*55.* **C**	*60.* **D**

Mathematical Reasoning Section 5

26. **B** (6, 7, 16)	*29.* **C** (11, 16)	*32.* **D** (2, 16)	*35.* **C** (2, 16)	*38.* **C** (3, 16)
27. **C** (4, 6, 7, 16)	*30.* **B** (2, 16)	*33.* **C** (15, 16)	*36.* **C** (4, 16)	*39.* **A** (8, 16)
28. **C** (6, 8, 16)	*31.* **C** (2, 16)	*34.* **C** (15, 16)	*37.* **A** (2, 16)	*40.* **D** (10, 16)

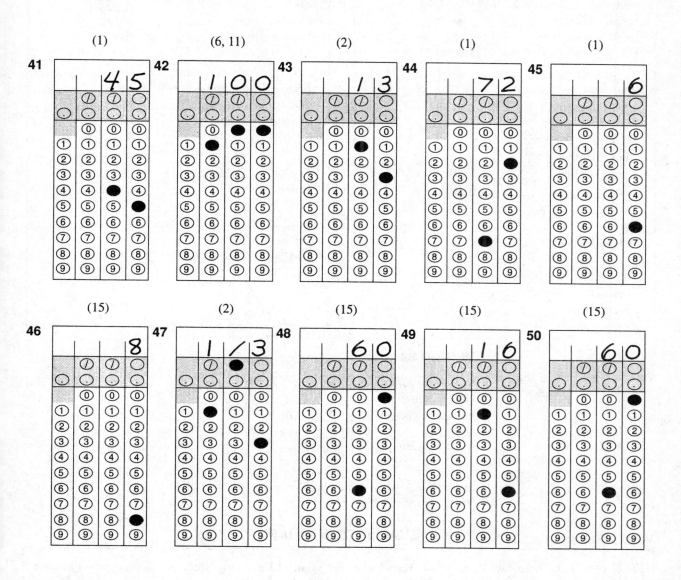

SCORING CHART — TYPICAL TEST H

Verbal Sections

Section 1   Questions 1–30
Number correct _____ (A)
Number omitted _____ (B)
Number incorrect _____ (C)
$\frac{1}{4}$ (C) =   _____ (D)
Raw Score:
   (A) – (D) =   _____

Section 3   Questions 31–60
Number correct _____ (A)
Number omitted _____ (B)
Number incorrect _____ (C)
$\frac{1}{4}$ (C) =   _____ (D)
Raw Score:
   (A) – (D) =   _____

Total Verbal Raw Score:
   (Section 1 +
   Section 3) =   _____

Mathematical Sections

Section 2   Questions 1–25
Number correct _____ (A)
Number incorrect _____ (B)
(A) – $\frac{1}{4}$ (B) =   _____ Raw Score I

Section 4   Questions 26–40
Number correct _____ (C)
Number incorrect _____ (D)
(C) – $\frac{1}{3}$ (D) =   _____ Raw Score II

Section 4   Questions 41–50
Number correct   _____ Raw Score III

Total Mathematical Raw Score:
   (Raw Scores I + II
   + III) =   _____

Writing Section

Section 3   Questions 1–39
Number correct _____ (A)
Number incorrect _____ (B)
$\frac{1}{4}$ (B) =   _____ (C)
(no penalty for omitted questions)
Writing Raw Score:
   (A) – (C) =   _____

EVALUATION CHART

Study your score. Your raw score on the Verbal and Mathematical Reasoning Sections is an indication of your probable achievement on the PSAT/NMSQT. As a guide to the amount of work you need or want to do with this book, study the following.

Raw Score			Self-rating
Verbal	Mathematical	Writing	
55–60	41–50	37–39	Superior
44–54	25–40	31–36	Very good
39–43	20–24	25–30	Satisfactory
35–38	16–19	19–24	Average
29–34	10–15	13–18	Needs further study
20–28	7–9	6–12	Needs intensive study
0–19	0–6	0–5	Probably inadequate

ANSWER EXPLANATIONS

Verbal Reasoning Section 1

1. **A** *Though* calls for a contrast. From someone with the reputation of a skilled craftsman we expect fine work; instead, the work here is not polished but *crude*.

2. **B** The use of *but* indicates that the dean's attempt to keep control failed. It did so because it was *frustrated* by the board of trustees. None of the other possible actions of the board of trustees would necessarily have caused the dean's attempt to fail.

3. **B** According to the definition set off by the hyphens, the science of taxonomy is to classify or categorize living creatures, sorting them into groups with individual *names*.

4. **D** To lack one's usual energy and interest in life is by definition to be *listless* (languid, spiritless). Note how the phrase following the comma serves to define the missing word.

5. **B** Mark keeps his reservations or reluctance to go along with his fraternity's policies to himself: he says nothing. By saying nothing, he lets his fraternity brothers assume his *silence* is a sign of *acquiescence* or agreement.

6. **E** Why would fights break out in a small rookery? They would do so because there is not enough room to accommodate all the birds that need to build a nest. Because space is *limited*, each bird therefore must *vie for* (struggle or fight for) its own patch of land.

7. **D** *Although* the writer does not personally enjoy Eliot's novels, before he criticizes her he feels he should, to be fair, pay *tribute* or give due recognition to her literary virtues.

8. **E** A *glutton* is by definition a person who eats or drinks excessively, someone who indulges his or her appetites without restraint.

9. **C** While all the answer choices are plausible goals for an anchorman, only one is acceptable in light of the second clause: *dispassion* or calm. Shaw's maintenance of his composure is illustrated by his ability to maintain the normal pitch of his voice.

10. **B** If the general realized that he could not maintain his position because it was *untenable* (indefensible), he would *order* his troops to retreat.

11. **C** The phrase "given the . . ." signals cause and effect. Because many areas of conflict are still in need of *resolution* or settlement, we do not know what the outcome of the peace talks will be. In other words, the end result of the talks remains *problematic* (unclear and unsettled; perplexing).

12. **D** A person who could not support his claims for alleged cures with hard scientific data might as a consequence be called a *charlatan* (a faker or quack) by skeptics or disbelievers in his powers.

13. **A** To progress from nature's despoiler (looter; plunderer) is to move in a positive direction, to go from harming nature to helping it. Examine the first word of each answer choice. Only Choice A, *conservator* (protector; preserver), and Choice E, *savior*, have this positive sense. The correct answer is Choice A. If we want to be nature's *conservator*, then we must fight the temptation to use our technology to shape the world to make it respond to our *whims* or sudden fancies.

14. **A** *While* signals a contrast. Bonner does not like religious or mystical (spiritual; not apparent to the senses) explanations of intelligence. Instead she likes *rational* (logical) and *materialistic* ones that define reality as explainable only in terms of physical matter.

15. **C** Because Mr. Southern so understands the spirit of the age, he is unafraid of or *undaunted by* its paradoxes. To say that a historian has entered thoroughly into the spirit of an age is a compliment. Thus, the missing word must be complimentary in meaning.

16. **B** It would be unfortunate for a book to come down very firmly on one side of a debate if, in the process, it *skimmed over* (examined superficially or missed entirely) tricky spots in the argument and gave the reader a *simplistic*, oversimplified picture of the subject.

17. **D** It is Williams's *propensity* or liking for theatricality that causes critics to *denigrate* or belittle his plays as mere melodrama. Note how the use of *mere* and the sense of the Shakespearean quotation convey the idea that Williams's plays have been sullied or belittled.

18. **C** You can arrive at the correct answer by the process of elimination. Statement I is true. The passage states that the tornado's lifetime is never more than a few hours. Therefore, you can eliminate Choices B and D. Statement II is true. The first paragraph indicates that a fraction of the thunderstorm's tremendous energy "is concentrated into an area no more than several hundred meters in diameter." A later portion of the passage refers to the tornado's "concentrated high winds." Therefore, you can eliminate Choice A. Statement III is untrue. The passage indicates that tornadoes may vary markedly in size and shape. Therefore, you can eliminate Choice E. Only Choice C is left. It is the correct answer.

19. **A** The passage describes tornadoes as the product of thunderstorms and goes on to discuss various aspects of their nature (energy concentration, pressure drops, intense winds, funnel clouds, etc.)

20. **E** Paragraph 3 states that the "warmer and drier the inflowing air is, the greater the pressure drop must be for condensation to occur and a cloud to form." This suggests that temperature and humidity affect the tornado, and that *it responds to changes in temperature and humidity.* Choice A is incorrect. The passage indicates that in the Northern Hemisphere a tornado's winds may be counterclockwise; it never suggests that a tornado's winds are *invariably* counterclockwise. Choice B is incorrect. Paragraph 4 states that a tornado's lifetime is never more than a few hours. Choice C is incorrect. The *warmer* and *drier* the air is, the greater the pressure drop has to be for the funnel cloud to form. This does not suggest that the cloud will not form if the air is cool and dry. Choice D is incorrect. A thunderstorm's cumulonimbus cloud can be more than seventeen kilometers high. A tornado's funnel cloud is described as smaller than this.

21. **A** The author states that "if the core fills with dust, the funnel may take on a more exotic hue, such as the red of west Oklahoma clay." The hue or color of the funnel thus depends on what the soil in that region is made of.

22. **D** The author suggests a hypothesis (tornado noise "may result from the interaction of the concentrated high winds with the ground"). He provides a concrete example ("the red of west Oklahoma clay"). He indicates a time span ("never more than a few hours"). He uses similes ("roaring like a freight train"). He does not, however, argue a particular point of view.

23. **D** The author calls the industrialists and their "couldn't-lose" bankers and backers "canny boys" (shrewd fellows) and says the adults considered stories about these wheelers and dealers "inspirational to children." Clearly, she finds neither the stories nor the men inspirational: she looks on both with irony.

24. **B** In stating that she and the other children were "unthinkingly familiar" with the moguls' enormous buildings "as so much weird scenery on long drives," the author reveals that the children viewed these buildings as an accepted *backdrop to their lives,* something they saw in passing without giving it much thought.

25. **B** The moguls were fabulous men in being *celebrated* or famed for their wealth and philanthropy.

26. **D** The mother's tone in this comment is highly sardonic. Clearly, she is not someone who cares to rave or talk boastfully about her good birth and noble connections. Instead, she dismisses such people as snobs and dismisses Europe as a fit home for snobs.

27. **C** Beneath the lawns lie musket balls and arrowheads and bones, all relics of *Pittsburgh's buried past.* Note that in the paragraph that immediately follows this description the author cites details from Pittsburgh's history.

28. **D** To say that one knows something and does not know it is to state a *paradox,* an apparently self-contradictory declaration.

29. **E** In breaking the wilderness, the first white settlers *penetrated* the forest, bursting through the undergrowth into territory known only to the native Americans.

30. **B** Summing up Pittsburgh's history, the author starts with modern big industry and works her way back in time till she concludes citing the pioneers who were the first white settlers in the region. Thus, she organizes the paragraph in *reverse chronological order.*

Mathematical Reasoning Section 2

1. **B** $\frac{1}{2} + \frac{3}{4} \div \left(\frac{5}{6} \times \frac{7}{8}\right) - \frac{9}{10}$

    $\frac{1}{2} + \frac{3}{4} \div \left(\frac{35}{48}\right) - \frac{9}{10}$

    $\frac{1}{2} + \frac{3}{4} \cdot \frac{\overset{12}{48}}{35} - \frac{9}{10}$

    $\frac{1}{2} + \frac{36}{35} - \frac{9}{10}$

    $\frac{35}{70} + \frac{72}{70} - \frac{63}{70} = \frac{44}{70} = \frac{22}{35}$

2. **C** For $n = 5$, $n^2 - 2 = 25 - 2 = 23$ and 23 is evenly divisible only by itself and 1.

3. **D** Let x = number of thirds in 75%.

    $\frac{x}{3} = 75\%$

    $\frac{x}{3} = \frac{3}{4}$

    $4x = 9$

    $x = \frac{9}{4} = 2\frac{1}{4}$

4. **D** $i^{39} = (i^2)^{19} \; i = (-1)^{19} \; i$. Since -1 raised to an odd integer power is always equal to -1, $i^{39} = -i$.

5. **D** The child with the greatest share would receive $\frac{2}{4}$ or $\frac{1}{2}$ of $40,000 = $20,000.

6. **D** Cost = $60   Profit = $12
    Actual selling price = $72
    Actual selling price ($72) = 90% of marked price
    Let x = marked price.
    90% of x or $.9x = 72
    $9x = 720
    $x = 80$

7. **D**   Let x = marked price.
$0.85x$ = price after first discount of 15%
$0.9(0.85x)$ = price after second discount of 10%
$0.765x = \$306$
$765x = 306000$
$x = \$400$

8. **B**   5 payments of $13 each = $65 + $15 (down payment) = $80
$80 – $72 = $8 saving

9. **B** $KM = \frac{1}{2} KL$ and $AC = \frac{1}{2} AB$. Since $KM > AC$, $KL > AB$ since doubles, triples, etc. of unequal quantities are unequal in the same order.

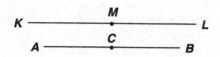

10. **D**   I. $AD – CD = AC$, and $AB + BC = AC$
II. $AD – BC = AB + CD$
III. This is not true because $AB + CD = AD – BC$.

11. **C**   Let w = width.
Then $w + 3$ = length [given].
$(w)(w +3)$ = area
$w^2 + 3w = 88$ [given]
$w^2 + 3w – 88 = 0$ [subtraction]

12. **C**   800 pounds of valuable oxide + 3200 pounds of other material = 4000 pounds of ore.
Ratio $= \frac{800}{3200} = \frac{8}{32} = \frac{1}{4}$ or 1:4. The ratio is the same for any number of tons.

13. **C**   Let x = number of pints of flour to be used with 3 pints of milk.
$\frac{\text{milk}}{\text{flour}} = \frac{2 \text{ parts}}{3 \text{ parts}} = \frac{3 \text{ pints}}{x}$
$2x = 9$; $x = 4\frac{1}{2}$ pints of flour

14. **C** $\left(\sqrt{\frac{2 + x^2}{2}}\right)^2 = (3)^2$

$\frac{2 + x^2}{2} = (3)^2$
$2 + x^2 = 18$
$x^2 = 16$
$x = \pm4$

15. **C**   Total Distance $= (D + d)$ miles
Total time $= (T + t)$ hours

Average rate for entire trip $= \dfrac{D + d}{T + t}$

16. **E**   Difference = 300
$\dfrac{\text{difference}}{\text{original}} = \dfrac{300}{1200} = \dfrac{1}{4} = 25\%$

17. **B**   Time required for homework = (10)(10 minutes) = 100 minutes = 1 hour and 40 minutes. She must begin to work 1 hour and 40 minutes before 9 P.M. or at 7:20 P.M.

18. **D**   Substitute: $②= 2^2 + \frac{1}{2^2} = 4 + \frac{1}{4}$ or $4\frac{1}{4}$

19. **A**   Size z is the longest side and must be the hypotenuse—the Pythagorean Theorem.

20. **D**   Diameter of outer circle = 104 feet
Radius of outer circle = 52 feet
Area of outer circle = $\pi r^2 = (52)^2\pi = 2704\pi$
Radius of inner circle = 50 feet
Area of inner circle = $\pi r^2 = (52)^2\pi = 2500\pi$
Difference = area of circular grass walk = $2704\pi – 2500\pi = 204\pi$

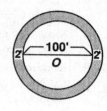

21. **E**   From the graph we observe:
At, S, $x = 0$, $y = +4$.
At R, $x = –4$, $y = 0$.
$\therefore y = x + 4$
Or apply formula
$y = mx + b$.
Since $x = 0$ when $y = 4$ (at 0.4)
$4 = m(0) + b$
$b = 4$, and since $x = –4$ when $y = 0$
(at –4,0) $0 = m(–4) + 4$
$m = 1$.
Substituting values of m and b: $y = x + 4$.

22. **C**   Let minor $\overarc{ST} = x$.
Let major $\overarc{SR} = y$.
$x + y = 360°$
$\angle SRT = \frac{1}{2}(y – x)$
$30° = \frac{1}{2}(y – x)$
or $60° = y – x$
or $x – y = –60°$
Since $x + y = 360°$,
$2x = 300°$ [addition]
$x = 150°$

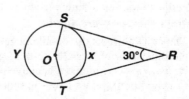

23. **E** $AP = AC$ since $\angle 1 = \angle 2$ (C), $\angle 1 > \angle 3$ (exterior $\angle$). Therefore, $\angle 2 > \angle 3$ (D), and in $\triangle BAC$, $AB > AC$. If $AB > AC$, then also $AB > AP$ (or $AP < AB$) (B) and (A), (E) contradicts (A) and (B) and is therefore incorrect.

24. **E** $15\% = \frac{15}{100}$ or $15¢$

25. **E** $31¢ + 43¢ = 74¢$
$\frac{74}{100} = 74\%$, which is the closest to 75%

Writing Skills Section 3

1. **B**   Error in using an adjective in place of an adverb. Change *increasing* to *increasingly*.

2. **A**   Misuse of relative pronoun. Change *who* (that refers to people) to *which* (that refers to things).

3. **B**   Error in case. Change *he* to *him*.

4. **B**   Incorrect introduction to noun clause. Change *where* to *in which* to modify *explosion*.

5. **C**   Lack of parallel structure. Change *called* to *were calling*.

6. **C**   Incorrect coordinating conjunction. Change *and* to *but*.

7. **C**   Error in agreement. Change *their* to *its*.

8. **B**   Error in agreement. Change *are finding* to *is finding*.

9. **B**   Error in case. The pronoun should be *whom* because it is the object of the verb *see*.

10. **C**   Error in tense. Change *have not had* to *will not have*.

11. **D**   Lack of parallel structure. Change *to guarantee* to *guaranteeing*.

12. **E**   Sentence is correct.

13. **E**   Sentence is correct.

14. **C**   Error in diction. Change *due to* to *as a result*.

15. **D**   Error in tense. Change *is questioned by* to *was questioned by*.

16. **C**   Misuse of relative pronoun. Change *which* (that refers to things) to *who* (that refers to people).

17. **C**   Lack of parallel structure. Change *because it presented* to *presentation of*.

18. **B**   Misuse of pronoun. Change *them* (personal pronoun) to *those* (indefinite demonstrative pronoun).

19. **A**   Error in agreement. The indefinite pronoun *neither* requires a singular verb. Change *were prepared* to *was prepared*.

20. **D**   Choice D corrects the double negative found in the other four choices. Note that, grammatically, *hardly* is considered a negative word. Choice C, in addition, creates a run-on sentence.

21. **E**   Choice A is a run-on sentence. Choices B, C, and D change the meaning of the original sentence. They indicate that the plays have already been esented; the original sentence

states that these plays are being presented at the present time. Choice E corrects the run-on without altering the meaning of the sentence.

22. **B**   In choice A, the conjunction *but* should be followed by a clause to parallel the clause in the first half of the sentence. Choice B provides such a clause. The awkward placement of the word *invariably* in Choice C makes the sentence very unclear. The use of *who* in Choices D and E leads to ambiguity because it may be taken to refer to *workers*.

23. **E**   Choices A, B, and C are incorrect because of the dangling participle *considering*. Choice D changes the meaning of the sentence.

24. **C**   In Choices A, B, and D, the modifier *familiar* is dangling. The wording in Choice E suggests that the explorer was a success, whereas the original sentence states that the search was a success—a somewhat different meaning. Choice C corrects the error and retains the original meaning of the sentence.

25. **B**   Choices A, C, and E do not maintain parallel structure. Choice B corrects this weakness. The infinitive *to cut* cannot be an object of *demand*, as in Choice D; a noun clause like the one in Choice B corrects this error.

26. **A**   Choice A is correct because the subject of the verb *had* must be *who* and not *whom*. *Which* in Choice E should not be used to refer to a person.

27. **C**   In Choices B and D, the preposition *like* is used incorrectly as a conjunction. The use of *from* in Choice E is idiomatically incorrect. Choice A creates an awkward and needlessly wordy sentence.

28. **E**   The pronouns *you* and *your* in the second clause of the sentence refer to *technician*, which is a third person singular noun. The pronoun, therefore, should be the third person singular *his*.

29. **C**   There are two errors in the underlined portion of this sentence: the expression *being that* is nonstandard, and the phrase *kind of* or *sort of* should not be followed by *a* or *an*.

30. **A**   As used in Choice A, *writing* is a participle modifying *James*. In Choices B, C, and D, the use of a verb (*wrote, was written,* or *was writing*) without the use of a conjunction to connect with *described* creates a grammatically incorrect sentence. The change in Choice E results in a sentence fragment.

31. **D**   In the original sentence, the subject is *fame*, a singular noun. Therefore, the verb should also be singular. This eliminates Choices A and C. In Choice B, *goals* should be *goal*. The word *also* in Choice E should not be used as a conjunction.

32. **C**   The plural expressions *kinds of* and *sorts of* should be modified by *these* and *those*.

33. **E** *Then* is incorrectly used in this sentence. The correct word is *than.* Choices B and C change the meaning of the sentence.

34. **C** Choice A contains an awkwardly expressed clause that begins *which caused.* Choice B contains a faulty comparison: *not as severe that.* Choice C accurately revises the sentence. It is the best answer. Choice D contains an awkwardly expressed clause that begins *that banning.* Choice E contains faulty diction. The conjunction *and* is not an effective connecting word in the context.

35. **B** Choice A contains a dangling participle and a weak passive construction. Choice B accurately continues the thought begun in sentence 9. It is the best answer. Choice C contains redundant language; *foul* and *obscene* are redundant. Choice D contains a weak passive construction (*Obscenities are heard*) and is wordy. Choice E lacks a main verb; therefore, it is a sentence fragment.

36. **E** Choices A and B are adequate, but dull, transitional statements. Choice C is a wordier version of A and B. Choice D contains an error in subject-verb agreement; the subject *changes* is plural, but the verb *has* is singular. Choice E serves as a good transitional statement that highlights the most important change in music discussed in the essay. It is the best answer.

37. **A** Only Choice A requires development, since no mention is made in the essay of "new categories" of music. All the others choices are factual statements that require no further elaboration.

38. **B** All choices except B contribute to the discussion of changes in musical sounds brought about by technology. Choice B, however, wanders from the topic.

39. **D** Choice A unnecessarily repeats the phrase *in the past thirty years* and fails to list the changes in music in the order they are discussed in the essay. Choice B is awkwardly expressed and confusing. Choice C fails to list the changes in music in the proper order. Also, *technology and lyrics* appear to be a single item. Choice D succinctly and accurately states the main idea of the essay. It is the best answer. Choice E, by subordinating the initial clause, gives lyrics in music undeserved importance.

Verbal Reasoning Section 4

31. **C** One wears a *muffler* around one's *neck*; one wears a *sash* around one's *waist.*
(Defining Characteristic)

32. **C** A *barge* is a kind of *vessel* or ship; a *shovel* is a kind of *implement* or tool.
(Class and Member)

33. **E** A *laurel wreath* is the symbol of *victory.* An *olive branch* is the symbol of *peace.* Beware of

eye-catchers. We may associate *idleness* with the notion of lying under a *palm tree;* however, this is not an essential or necessary relationship. (Symbol and Abstraction It Represents)

34. **C** A *grating* sound by definition offends the *ear;* a *garish* appearance offends the *eye.*
(Defining Characteristic)

35. **C** An *inventor* protects his or her invention by obtaining a *patent;* an *author* protects his or her literary work by obtaining a *copyright.*
(Function)

36. **C** A *leopard* is by definition a *carnivorous* (meat-eating) animal; a *cow* is by definition a *herbivorous* (grass-eating) animal.
(Defining Characteristic)

37. **A** A *breeze* is less forceful than a *cyclone;* a *ripple* is less forceful than a *tidal wave.*
(Degree of Intensity)

38. **A** Something *ramshackle* or rickety lacks *soundness* or solidity. Something *garbled* or jumbled lacks *clarity.* (Antonym Variant)

39. **B** *Agitator* (trouble-maker) is a synonym for *firebrand. Renegade* (traitor) is a synonym for *turncoat.* (Synonym)

40. **A** Someone *callow* is immature and will not reach full development until *maturity.* Something *incipient* is beginning to become apparent and will not reach full development until *fruition.* (Antonym Variant)

41. **C** A *tirade* (scolding, denunciatory speech) is by definition *abusive;* a *panegyric* (eulogy) is by definition *laudatory* (full of praise).
(Defining Characteristic)

42. **C** *Skulduggery* or dishonest, unscrupulous behavior is the mark of the *swindler. Chicanery* or trickery is the mark of the *trickster.*
(Defining Characteristic)

43. **E** *Self-respecting* is less extreme than *vainglorious* or excessively proud. *Careful* is less extreme than *punctilious* or excessively attentive to fine points. (Degree of Intensity)

44. **C** According to the author, "We have been taught to believe that our lives are better than the lives of those who came before us" and the lives of those today who live in similarly "primitive" circumstances. We base our belief that we Americans are well off today on the assumption that people in earlier generations and people living in "primitive" circumstances *have an inferior standard of living.*

45. **B** The conventional wisdom is that the lives of primitive peoples are filled with toil. The author, however, states that primitives do little work. Thus, she regards the conventional wisdom with *skepticism* or doubt.

46. **D** According to the author, these "stone age peoples" have limited desires. They are not motivated

by any particular *desire for consumer goods* or other material comforts.

47. **A** Throughout the passage the author *disputes the assumption* made by the conventional wisdom that our economic progress has been an unmitigated blessing. She argues instead that we "have paid a price of prosperity."

48. **C** The author makes an assertion: "We are eating more." She then qualifies or limits her assertion: "but we are burning up those calories at work." She repeats this pattern of assertion followed by qualification. She then draws her conclusion: it is hard to support the conventional wisdom that economic progress has been an unmixed blessing for us.

49. **C** Repetition often is used rhetorically for emphasis. By asking question after question about why women's writing has taken the shape it has, the author *underscores* or emphasizes *how little is known about* a significant subject.

50. **D** To fill an office is to work in or *hold* that job.

51. **B** To make her point, Woolf gives *examples* of three women about whom little is known.

52. **E** "One was beautiful; one was red-haired; one was kissed by a queen." What did these women have in common? They all led *largely unrecorded lives:* their grandchildren know only stray fragments about the history of these women's lives.

53. **B** Both the author's use of the phrase "a literature of their own" in the opening paragraph and her ongoing exploration of what she means by the female literary tradition in the English novel support this choice. Choice A is incorrect. It is not the uniqueness of the phenomenon but the traditional nature of the phenomenon that interests the author. Choice C is incorrect. The passage deals specifically with women's *literary* tradition. Choice D is incorrect. The passage is concerned with the roots of female writing, not with its present-day manifestation. Choice E is incorrect. The author presents no such choice.

54. **B** The writer neither lists (*enumerates*) nor sorts (*classifies*) anything in the opening paragraph. Choice A is incorrect. The writer likens the female tradition to a lost continent and develops the metaphor by describing the continent "rising . . . from the sea of English literature." Choice C is incorrect. The author refers or *alludes* to the classical legend of Atlantis. Choice D is incorrect. The author quotes Colby and Thompson. Choice E is incorrect. The author contrasts the revised view of women's literature with Mill's view.

55. **C** The legend of Atlantis tells of a continent that sank beneath the sea, only to rise again. The author uses the metaphor of the newly arisen lost continent to give the reader a sense of how

an enormous body of *literary works written by women* has once more come to public attention, *resurfacing after many years.*

56. **D** The author opens the paragraph by stating that many literary critics have begun reinterpreting the study of women's literature. She then goes on to cite individual comments that support her assertion. Clearly, she is *receptive* or open to the ideas of these writers, for they and she share a common sense of the need to reinterpret their common field. Choices A and B are incorrect. The author cites the literary critics straightforwardly, presenting their statements as evidence supporting her thesis. Choice C is incorrect. The author does not *disparage* or belittle these critics. By quoting them respectfully she implicitly acknowledges their competence. Choice E is incorrect. The author quotes the critics as acknowledged experts in the field. However, she is quite ready to disagree with their conclusions (as she disagrees with Moers's view of women's literature as an international movement). Clearly, she does not look on these critics with *awe.*

57. **E** To study something with a special closeness is to pay *minute attention to details.*

58. **B** If women writers have no history, they have to rediscover the past. In the process, they *create* or forge their consciousness of what their sex has achieved. Here *forge* is used with its meaning of *fashion* or *make*, as blacksmiths forge metal by hammering it into shape. It is in this sense that James Joyce used *forge* in *A Portrait of the Artist as a Young Man,* whose hero goes forth to "forge in the smithy of (his) soul the uncreated conscience of (his) race."

59. **C** The author both cites Moers's work in support of her own assertions and argues against the validity of Moers's conclusion that women's literature is an international movement. Thus, while she finds Moers's work basically *admirable* and worthy of respect, she considers it *inaccurate* in some of the conclusions it draws. Choice A is incorrect. The author would not cite Moers as she does in the second paragraph if she believed Moers to be wholly *misleading.* Choice B is incorrect. Since the author disagrees with at least one of Moers's conclusions, she obviously does not find Moers's work the *definitive* or final word. Choices D and E are incorrect. Neither is supported by the author's mentions of Moers.

60. **D** Woolf does not document her argument with extensive quotations from literary critics. Instead, she uses telling examples ("One was beautiful; one was red-haired; one was kissed by a queen") to show how little we know about our grandmothers' actual lives. She is *less scholarly and more descriptive* in her approach to the subject.

Mathematical Reasoning Section 5

26. **B** $\frac{10}{0.1} = \frac{100}{1} = 100$

    $10 - 100 = -90$
    $-9 > -90$

27. **C** $\sqrt{4} = 2$
    $\frac{1}{0.5} = \frac{10}{5} = 2$

28. **C** $0.6\% = \frac{0.6}{100} = \frac{6}{1000}$

29. **C** $\frac{2548}{14}$ inches = 182 inches

    5 yards 2 inches = 182 inches

30. **B** $\frac{1}{5} \div \frac{5}{1}$ [Column A] $\frac{1}{y} = \frac{1}{5}$ [Column B]

    $\frac{1}{5} \div \frac{1}{1}$

    $\frac{1}{5} \cdot \frac{1}{5} = \frac{1}{25}$

31. **C** $(y + 160) - (120 - y) =$
    $y + 160 - 120 + y = 2y + 40$
    $(x + 10) - (x - 2y - 30) =$
    $x + 10 - x + 2y + 30 = 2y + 40$

32. **D** To solve for a and b we need 2 equations involving a and b.

33. **C** The two triangles have the same altitude (AD) and have equal bases ($AB = BC$).

    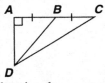

34. **C** The acute angles of a right triangle are complementary.

35. **C** $x = \frac{y}{2}$
    $y = 2x$ (cross multiplication)
    $y + 2 = 2x + 2$ (addition of 2)

36. **C** $\sqrt{\frac{1}{4}} = \frac{1}{2}$

37. **A** $7x = 35 + 7y$
    $7x - 35 = 7y$
    $x - 5 = y$ (division by 7)
    Since $x - 5 > x - 7$, then $y > x - 7$.

38. **A** Because x is 25% of y, $x = 0.25y$ or, equivalently, $y = 4x$. Since y is 50% of z, $y = 0.50z$ or, equivalently, $z = 2y = 2(4x) = 8x$. Average of x, y, and $z = \frac{x + y + z}{3} = \frac{x + 4x + 8x}{3} = \frac{13x}{3}$, which is greater than $4x$.

39. **A** Experiment with convenient values. If the original price was $100, then the reduced price is $100 – $10 or $90 plus 10% of $90 or $9, for a total of $99.

40. **D** We may not assume that Lori used the same route (with the exact same distance) on both trips.

41. **45** 27 cubic feet = 1 cubic yard
    9 cubic feet = $\frac{1}{3}$ cubic yard
    or $\frac{45}{5}$ cubic feet = $\frac{1}{3}$ cubic yard

42. **100** $\frac{3}{8}$ = $60
    $\frac{1}{8}$ = $20
    Remainder of crop $\left(\frac{5}{8}\right)$ = $100

43. **13** $5x - 3y = 3$ (1)
    $2x - 4y = -10$ (2)
    Subtract equation (2) from equation (1):
    $3x + y = 13$

44. **72** $\frac{356}{5} = 71 +$.

    If one candidate gets 72 votes he can be a winner, because we have 356 – 72 = 284 votes to be divided among four other candidates and it is possible for each of these four to receive 71 votes. If a candidate gets 71 votes, it is not possible to be the winner, since 356 – 71 = 285 votes remaining to be divided among the other four candidates. One of these four must receive more than 71 and would thus be the winner.

45. **6** When 15 adults ride the bus, they are using $\frac{15}{20}$ or $\frac{3}{4}$ of capacity, leaving $\frac{1}{4}$ of capacity unused. We therefore can add $\frac{1}{4}$ capacity of bus when children ride, or $\frac{1}{4}$ of 24 = 6.

46. **8** Four of the 2" squares can fit along the 8" side, and two along the 4" side.
    $4 \times 2 = 8$ squares.

47. **$\frac{1}{3}$** $3x - 6 = 1$
    $x - 2 = \frac{1}{3}$ [divide by 3]

48. **60** Radii OC and OB are equal. Since $OC = BC$, OBC is an equilateral triangle; $\angle BOC$ has a measure of 60° and x, its supplement, has a measure of 120°.
    $\frac{x}{2} = 60$

49. **16** Area of square = $s^2 = 144$
    Side = 12 and perimeter of square = 48
    Perimeter of equilateral triangle = 48 [given]
    Side of triangle = 48 ÷ 3 = 16

50. **60** If $\angle ABC \stackrel{\circ}{=} 120$, then $\overparen{ADC} = 240°$.
    $\angle ADC \stackrel{\circ}{=} \frac{1}{2} \overparen{ABC} = 360° - \overparen{ADC}(240°) = 120°$
    $\angle ADC \stackrel{\circ}{=} \frac{1}{2} \overparen{ABC}$
    $\angle ADC \stackrel{\circ}{=} 60$

    Recall: An inscribed angle is measured by one-half of its intercepted arc.

    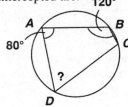

Answer Sheet
TYPICAL TEST I

Each mark should completely fill the appropriate space, and should be as dark as all other marks. Make all erasures complete. Traces of an erasure may be read as an answer. See pages vii and 27 for explanations of timing and number of questions.

Section 1 — Verbal
30 minutes

1 Ⓐ Ⓑ Ⓒ Ⓓ Ⓔ
2 Ⓐ Ⓑ Ⓒ Ⓓ Ⓔ
3 Ⓐ Ⓑ Ⓒ Ⓓ Ⓔ
4 Ⓐ Ⓑ Ⓒ Ⓓ Ⓔ
5 Ⓐ Ⓑ Ⓒ Ⓓ Ⓔ
6 Ⓐ Ⓑ Ⓒ Ⓓ Ⓔ
7 Ⓐ Ⓑ Ⓒ Ⓓ Ⓔ
8 Ⓐ Ⓑ Ⓒ Ⓓ Ⓔ
9 Ⓐ Ⓑ Ⓒ Ⓓ Ⓔ
10 Ⓐ Ⓑ Ⓒ Ⓓ Ⓔ
11 Ⓐ Ⓑ Ⓒ Ⓓ Ⓔ
12 Ⓐ Ⓑ Ⓒ Ⓓ Ⓔ
13 Ⓐ Ⓑ Ⓒ Ⓓ Ⓔ
14 Ⓐ Ⓑ Ⓒ Ⓓ Ⓔ
15 Ⓐ Ⓑ Ⓒ Ⓓ Ⓔ
16 Ⓐ Ⓑ Ⓒ Ⓓ Ⓔ
17 Ⓐ Ⓑ Ⓒ Ⓓ Ⓔ
18 Ⓐ Ⓑ Ⓒ Ⓓ Ⓔ
19 Ⓐ Ⓑ Ⓒ Ⓓ Ⓔ
20 Ⓐ Ⓑ Ⓒ Ⓓ Ⓔ
21 Ⓐ Ⓑ Ⓒ Ⓓ Ⓔ
22 Ⓐ Ⓑ Ⓒ Ⓓ Ⓔ
23 Ⓐ Ⓑ Ⓒ Ⓓ Ⓔ
24 Ⓐ Ⓑ Ⓒ Ⓓ Ⓔ
25 Ⓐ Ⓑ Ⓒ Ⓓ Ⓔ
26 Ⓐ Ⓑ Ⓒ Ⓓ Ⓔ
27 Ⓐ Ⓑ Ⓒ Ⓓ Ⓔ
28 Ⓐ Ⓑ Ⓒ Ⓓ Ⓔ
29 Ⓐ Ⓑ Ⓒ Ⓓ Ⓔ
30 Ⓐ Ⓑ Ⓒ Ⓓ Ⓔ

Section 2 — Math
30 minutes

1 Ⓐ Ⓑ Ⓒ Ⓓ Ⓔ
2 Ⓐ Ⓑ Ⓒ Ⓓ Ⓔ
3 Ⓐ Ⓑ Ⓒ Ⓓ Ⓔ
4 Ⓐ Ⓑ Ⓒ Ⓓ Ⓔ
5 Ⓐ Ⓑ Ⓒ Ⓓ Ⓔ
6 Ⓐ Ⓑ Ⓒ Ⓓ Ⓔ
7 Ⓐ Ⓑ Ⓒ Ⓓ Ⓔ
8 Ⓐ Ⓑ Ⓒ Ⓓ Ⓔ
9 Ⓐ Ⓑ Ⓒ Ⓓ Ⓔ
10 Ⓐ Ⓑ Ⓒ Ⓓ Ⓔ
11 Ⓐ Ⓑ Ⓒ Ⓓ Ⓔ
12 Ⓐ Ⓑ Ⓒ Ⓓ Ⓔ
13 Ⓐ Ⓑ Ⓒ Ⓓ Ⓔ
14 Ⓐ Ⓑ Ⓒ Ⓓ Ⓔ
15 Ⓐ Ⓑ Ⓒ Ⓓ Ⓔ
16 Ⓐ Ⓑ Ⓒ Ⓓ Ⓔ
17 Ⓐ Ⓑ Ⓒ Ⓓ Ⓔ
18 Ⓐ Ⓑ Ⓒ Ⓓ Ⓔ
19 Ⓐ Ⓑ Ⓒ Ⓓ Ⓔ
20 Ⓐ Ⓑ Ⓒ Ⓓ Ⓔ
21 Ⓐ Ⓑ Ⓒ Ⓓ Ⓔ
22 Ⓐ Ⓑ Ⓒ Ⓓ Ⓔ
23 Ⓐ Ⓑ Ⓒ Ⓓ Ⓔ
24 Ⓐ Ⓑ Ⓒ Ⓓ Ⓔ
25 Ⓐ Ⓑ Ⓒ Ⓓ Ⓔ

Section 3 — Writing
30 minutes

1 Ⓐ Ⓑ Ⓒ Ⓓ Ⓔ
2 Ⓐ Ⓑ Ⓒ Ⓓ Ⓔ
3 Ⓐ Ⓑ Ⓒ Ⓓ Ⓔ
4 Ⓐ Ⓑ Ⓒ Ⓓ Ⓔ
5 Ⓐ Ⓑ Ⓒ Ⓓ Ⓔ
6 Ⓐ Ⓑ Ⓒ Ⓓ Ⓔ
7 Ⓐ Ⓑ Ⓒ Ⓓ Ⓔ
8 Ⓐ Ⓑ Ⓒ Ⓓ Ⓔ
9 Ⓐ Ⓑ Ⓒ Ⓓ Ⓔ
10 Ⓐ Ⓑ Ⓒ Ⓓ Ⓔ
11 Ⓐ Ⓑ Ⓒ Ⓓ Ⓔ
12 Ⓐ Ⓑ Ⓒ Ⓓ Ⓔ
13 Ⓐ Ⓑ Ⓒ Ⓓ Ⓔ
14 Ⓐ Ⓑ Ⓒ Ⓓ Ⓔ
15 Ⓐ Ⓑ Ⓒ Ⓓ Ⓔ
16 Ⓐ Ⓑ Ⓒ Ⓓ Ⓔ
17 Ⓐ Ⓑ Ⓒ Ⓓ Ⓔ
18 Ⓐ Ⓑ Ⓒ Ⓓ Ⓔ
19 Ⓐ Ⓑ Ⓒ Ⓓ Ⓔ
20 Ⓐ Ⓑ Ⓒ Ⓓ Ⓔ
21 Ⓐ Ⓑ Ⓒ Ⓓ Ⓔ
22 Ⓐ Ⓑ Ⓒ Ⓓ Ⓔ
23 Ⓐ Ⓑ Ⓒ Ⓓ Ⓔ
24 Ⓐ Ⓑ Ⓒ Ⓓ Ⓔ
25 Ⓐ Ⓑ Ⓒ Ⓓ Ⓔ
26 Ⓐ Ⓑ Ⓒ Ⓓ Ⓔ
27 Ⓐ Ⓑ Ⓒ Ⓓ Ⓔ
28 Ⓐ Ⓑ Ⓒ Ⓓ Ⓔ
29 Ⓐ Ⓑ Ⓒ Ⓓ Ⓔ
30 Ⓐ Ⓑ Ⓒ Ⓓ Ⓔ
31 Ⓐ Ⓑ Ⓒ Ⓓ Ⓔ
32 Ⓐ Ⓑ Ⓒ Ⓓ Ⓔ
33 Ⓐ Ⓑ Ⓒ Ⓓ Ⓔ
34 Ⓐ Ⓑ Ⓒ Ⓓ Ⓔ
35 Ⓐ Ⓑ Ⓒ Ⓓ Ⓔ
36 Ⓐ Ⓑ Ⓒ Ⓓ Ⓔ
37 Ⓐ Ⓑ Ⓒ Ⓓ Ⓔ
38 Ⓐ Ⓑ Ⓒ Ⓓ Ⓔ
39 Ⓐ Ⓑ Ⓒ Ⓓ Ⓔ

Section 4 — Verbal
30 minutes

31 Ⓐ Ⓑ Ⓒ Ⓓ Ⓔ
32 Ⓐ Ⓑ Ⓒ Ⓓ Ⓔ
33 Ⓐ Ⓑ Ⓒ Ⓓ Ⓔ
34 Ⓐ Ⓑ Ⓒ Ⓓ Ⓔ
35 Ⓐ Ⓑ Ⓒ Ⓓ Ⓔ
36 Ⓐ Ⓑ Ⓒ Ⓓ Ⓔ
37 Ⓐ Ⓑ Ⓒ Ⓓ Ⓔ
38 Ⓐ Ⓑ Ⓒ Ⓓ Ⓔ
39 Ⓐ Ⓑ Ⓒ Ⓓ Ⓔ
40 Ⓐ Ⓑ Ⓒ Ⓓ Ⓔ
41 Ⓐ Ⓑ Ⓒ Ⓓ Ⓔ
42 Ⓐ Ⓑ Ⓒ Ⓓ Ⓔ
43 Ⓐ Ⓑ Ⓒ Ⓓ Ⓔ
44 Ⓐ Ⓑ Ⓒ Ⓓ Ⓔ
45 Ⓐ Ⓑ Ⓒ Ⓓ Ⓔ
46 Ⓐ Ⓑ Ⓒ Ⓓ Ⓔ
47 Ⓐ Ⓑ Ⓒ Ⓓ Ⓔ
48 Ⓐ Ⓑ Ⓒ Ⓓ Ⓔ
49 Ⓐ Ⓑ Ⓒ Ⓓ Ⓔ
50 Ⓐ Ⓑ Ⓒ Ⓓ Ⓔ
51 Ⓐ Ⓑ Ⓒ Ⓓ Ⓔ
52 Ⓐ Ⓑ Ⓒ Ⓓ Ⓔ
53 Ⓐ Ⓑ Ⓒ Ⓓ Ⓔ
54 Ⓐ Ⓑ Ⓒ Ⓓ Ⓔ
55 Ⓐ Ⓑ Ⓒ Ⓓ Ⓔ
56 Ⓐ Ⓑ Ⓒ Ⓓ Ⓔ
57 Ⓐ Ⓑ Ⓒ Ⓓ Ⓔ
58 Ⓐ Ⓑ Ⓒ Ⓓ Ⓔ
59 Ⓐ Ⓑ Ⓒ Ⓓ Ⓔ
60 Ⓐ Ⓑ Ⓒ Ⓓ Ⓔ

Section 5 — Math
30 minutes

26 Ⓐ Ⓑ Ⓒ Ⓓ Ⓔ
27 Ⓐ Ⓑ Ⓒ Ⓓ Ⓔ
28 Ⓐ Ⓑ Ⓒ Ⓓ Ⓔ
29 Ⓐ Ⓑ Ⓒ Ⓓ Ⓔ
30 Ⓐ Ⓑ Ⓒ Ⓓ Ⓔ
31 Ⓐ Ⓑ Ⓒ Ⓓ Ⓔ
32 Ⓐ Ⓑ Ⓒ Ⓓ Ⓔ
33 Ⓐ Ⓑ Ⓒ Ⓓ Ⓔ
34 Ⓐ Ⓑ Ⓒ Ⓓ Ⓔ
35 Ⓐ Ⓑ Ⓒ Ⓓ Ⓔ
36 Ⓐ Ⓑ Ⓒ Ⓓ Ⓔ
37 Ⓐ Ⓑ Ⓒ Ⓓ Ⓔ
39 Ⓐ Ⓑ Ⓒ Ⓓ Ⓔ
39 Ⓐ Ⓑ Ⓒ Ⓓ Ⓔ
40 Ⓐ Ⓑ Ⓒ Ⓓ Ⓔ

Grid-in answer boxes numbered 41, 42, 43, 44, 45, 46, 47, 48, 49, 50, each with four columns of bubbles (fraction bar ⁄, decimal point ·, and digits 0–9).

SECTION 1
Verbal Reasoning

Time—30 minutes
30 Questions

For each question in this section, select the best answer from among the choices given and fill in the corresponding oval on the answer sheet.

Directions

Each sentence below has one or two blanks, each blank indicating that something has been omitted. Beneath the sentence are five words or sets of words labeled A through E. Choose the word or set of words that, when inserted in the sentence, best fits the meaning of the sentence as a whole.

Example:

Medieval kingdoms did not become constitutional republics overnight; on the contrary, the change was ____ .

(A) unpopular
(B) unexpected
(C) advantageous
(D) sufficient
(E) gradual   Ⓐ Ⓑ Ⓒ Ⓓ ●

1. Her audacious approach won her an interview when a less ____ method would have been sure to fail.

   (A) daring   (B) ingratiating   (C) conventional
   (D) intelligent   (E) arrogant

2. The plot of the motion picture *Hoosiers* is ____ ; we have all seen this story, the tale of an underdog team going on to win a championship, in one form or another countless times.

   (A) inept   (B) absorbing   (C) intricate
   (D) controversial   (E) trite

3. Whenever Ginger's brother played a trick on her, she would spend hours thinking up diabolical ways in which to ____ .

   (A) retaliate   (B) retrench   (C) prevaricate
   (D) sublimate   (E) reconcile

4. The term *metaphysics* has long had a bad name in scientific circles, and the ____ hasn't quite faded.

   (A) bloom   (B) glory   (C) taint
   (D) idiom   (E) appeal

5. Because both male and female egrets display the same plumage during breeding season, ____ the two sexes is extremely difficult.

   (A) evolving from   (B) distinguishing between
   (C) generalizing about   (D) maneuvering around
   (E) accommodating to

6. Although there are still ____ outbreaks of typhoid fever from time to time, no persistent, extended typhoid epidemic has occurred in the past forty years.

   (A) therapeutic   (B) synchronized
   (C) devastating   (D) sedentary   (E) sporadic

7. Knowing that the results of future experiments might well cause her to ____ her hypothesis, she voiced ____ opinion which she insisted was subject to change.

   (A) modify..an unqualified   (B) qualify..a definitive
   (C) abandon..a dogmatic   (D) alter..a blunt
   (E) rethink..a tentative

8. Although he was ____ by nature, he ____ contact with others during the period of his trial.

   (A) gracious..sought   (B) magnanimous..attempted
   (C) altruistic..evaded   (D) gregarious..shunned
   (E) prodigal..avoided

9. Picasso was never early and never late; it was his pride that ____ was the politeness of kings.

   (A) condescension   (B) deference
   (C) minuteness   (D) punctuality   (E) temperance

10. Although Maria Montessori gained fame for her innovations in ____ , it took years before her teaching techniques were common practice in American schools.

    (A) democracy   (B) sophistry   (C) philanthropy
    (D) technology   (E) pedagogy

11. Language, culture, and personality may be considered independently of each other in thought, but they are ____ in fact.

    (A) autonomous   (B) pervasive   (C) equivocal
    (D) inseparable   (E) immutable

12. Since depression seems to result when certain cells in the brain receive too little of two key chemicals, the neurotransmitters norepinephrine and serotonin, one goal of treatment is to make more of the chemicals ____ the nerve cells that need them.

    (A) analogous to   (B) dependent on
    (C) available to   (D) regardless of
    (E) interchangeable with

13. The sudden shift from ____ to ____ in Hugo's novels can startle readers, especially when he abruptly juxtaposes a scene of chaste and holy love with one of coarse and profane licentiousness.

    (A) devotion..frivolity   (B) piety..ribaldry
    (C) vulgarity..adultery   (D) decorum..salubrity
    (E) purity..maturity

GO ON TO THE NEXT PAGE

14. In the end, the *Normandie* lacked even the dignity of being sunk by the enemy at sea; she burned and went down ____ at her Manhattan pier in 1942, while incompetents were transforming her into a troop ship.

(A) majestically   (B) ignominiously
(C) militantly   (D) negligently   (E) auspiciously

15. Hoving ____ refers to the smuggled Greek urn as the "hot pot," not because there were doubts about its authenticity or even great reservations as to its price, but because its ____ was open to question.

(A) mendaciously..exorbitance
(B) characteristically..genuineness
(C) colloquially..origin
(D) repeatedly..fraudulence
(E) cheerfully..function

16. This psychological biography presents a picture of a deeply ____ individual, unable to ____ anyone else's success, whose ruthless pursuit of recognition and fame has been marked by hypocritical gestures of openness and affection.

(A) altruistic..comprehend   (B) egotistical..tolerate
(C) modest..admit   (D) apathetic..match
(E) indolent..vilify

17. She conducted the interrogation not only with dispatch but with ____ , being a person who is ____ in manner yet subtle in discrimination.

(A) elan..enthusiastic   (B) equanimity..abrupt
(C) finesse..expeditious   (D) zeal..doctrinaire
(E) trepidation..cursory

Directions

Each passage below is followed by questions based on its content. Answer the questions following each passage on the basis of what is stated or implied in that passage and in any introductory material that may be provided.

Questions 18–22 are based on the following passage.

In the following passage, the celebrated author and chef M.F.K. Fisher considers the greater implications of a small shipboard incident.

The Captain's Dinner was strange. We were off the coast of Lower California. The water was so calm that we could hear flying fish slap against it.
Line We ate at a long table out on deck, under an
5 awning between us and the enormous stars.
The Captain looked well in his white uniform, and smiled almost warmly at us all, probably thanking God that most of us would leave him in a few days. The waiters were excited, the way the
10 Filipino boys used to be at boarding school when there was a Christmas party, and the table looked like something from a Renaissance painting.

There were galantines and aspics down the center, with ripe grapes brought from Italy and
15 stranger fruits from all the ports we'd touched, and crowning everything, two stuffed pheasants in their dulled but still dashing feathers. There were wineglasses on stems, and little printed menus, proof that this masterpiece of a meal was known
20 about in Rome, long since.

We ate and drank and heard our own suddenly friendly voices over the dark waters. The waiters glided deftly, perhaps dreaming that they served at Maxim's instead of on this fifth-rate freighter, and
25 we drank Asti Spumanti, undated but delightful.

And finally, while we clapped, the chef stood before us, bowing in the light from the narrow stairs. He wore his high bonnet and whites, and a long-tailed morning coat, and looked like a draw-
30 ing by Ludwig Bemelmans, with oblique sadness in his pasty outlines.

There was a silence after our applause. He turned nervously toward the light, and breathed not at all. We heard shufflings and bumps. Then,
35 up through the twisting white closeness of the stairway, borne on the backs and arms of three awestruck kitchen boys, rose something almost too strange to talk about.

The chef stood back, bowing, discreetly wiping
40 the sweat from his white face. The Captain applauded. We all clapped, and even cheered. The three boys set the thing on a special table.

It was a replica, about as long as a man's cof-fin, of the cathedral at Milano. It was made in
45 white and pink sugar. There was a light inside, of course, and it glowed there on the deck of the lit-tle ship, trembling in every flying buttress with the Mexican ground swell, pure and ridiculous; and something about it shamed me.

50 It was a little dusty. It had undoubtedly been mended, after mighty storms, in the dim galleys of a hundred ships, better but never worse than this. It was like a flag flying for the chef, a bul-wark all in spun sugar against the breath of cor-
55 ruption. It was his masterpiece, made years ago in some famous kitchen, and he showed it to us now with dignity.

18. It can be inferred from the passage that the author is most likely

(A) a student at a boarding school
(B) an officer of a vessel at anchor
(C) an enemy of the ship's captain
(D) a passenger near the end of a voyage
(E) a newcomer on board the vessel

GO ON TO THE NEXT PAGE

19. The author's general attitude toward the freighter in the third and fourth paragraphs is best described as

(A) condescending   (B) suspicious   (C) bitter
(D) apathetic   (E) admiring

20. It can be inferred from the passage that Maxim's (paragraph 4) was most likely which of the following?

 I. A renowned restaurant
 II. An eminent cargo vessel
 III. A desirable place to work

(A) I only   (B) II only   (C) I and III only
(D) II and III only   (E) I, II, and III

21. The evidence in the passage suggests that the chef most likely sweats

(A) from his labors in transporting the replica
(B) from the heat of the kitchen
(C) because he is afflicted with shortness of breath
(D) out of fear for his irreplaceable creation
(E) from his exertions in constructing the cathedral

22. Which of the following statements best expresses the author's impression of the chef?

(A) Reduced to working on cargo vessels, he is ashamed of his loss of professional prestige.
(B) Although he has come down in the world, he retains the memory of his youthful achievements.
(C) He applies himself with diligence to new creations, hoping to gain renown.
(D) He prefers heading his own kitchen to working as an underling in a more famous establishment.
(E) Despite his early promise, he is unable to create an original work of art.

Questions 23–30 are based on the following passage.

The following passage is taken from a book documenting the women's rights movement in the United States.

During the decade of 1880–1890 it was becoming increasingly evident that the factors that had brought about the existence of two sepa-
Line rate suffrage institutions were steadily diminish-
5 ing in importance.

The National Woman Suffrage Association had been launched by the intellectually irrepressible Elizabeth Cady Stanton and the ever catholic Susan B. Anthony. Both were ready to work with
10 anyone, whatever their views on other matters, as long as they wholeheartedly espoused woman suffrage. Consequently, in its earlier years the National was both aggressive and unorthodox. It damned both Republicans and Democrats who
15 brushed the suffrage question aside. It was willing to take up the cudgels for distressed women whatever their circumstances, be they "fallen women," divorce cases, or underpaid seamstresses.

The American Woman Suffrage Association,
20 by contrast, took its tone and outlook from a New England that had turned its back on those fiery days when abolitionists, men and women alike, had stood up to angry mobs. Its advocacy of worthy causes was highly selective. Lucy Stone
25 was not interested in trade unionism and wished to keep the suffrage cause untarnished by concern with divorce or "the social evil." The very epitome of the American's attitude was its most distinguished convert and leader, Julia Ward Howe—
30 erudite, honored lay preacher, the revered author of "The Battle Hymn of the Republic," who cast a highly desirable aura of prestige and propriety over the women's cause.

It was not that Mrs. Howe in herself made suf-
35 frage respectable; she was a symbol of the forces that were drawing the suffrage movement into the camp of decorum. American society was becoming rapidly polarized. The middle class was learning to identify organized labor with social turmoil.
40 A succession of strikes during the depression of 1873–1878, in textiles, mining, and railroads, culminated in the Great Railroad Strike of 1877 involving nearly 100,000 workers from the Atlantic coast to the Mississippi valley; they did
45 not help to reassure women taught by press and pulpit to identify any type of militancy with radicalism. Nor was this trend allayed by the hysteria whipped up over the Molly Maguire trials for secret conspiracy among Pennsylvania coal min-
50 ers, or the alleged communistic influences at work in such growing organizations as the Knights of Labor and the A. F. of L. The existence of a small number of socialists was used to smear all organized labor with the taint of "anarchism." The
55 crowning touch took place during the widespread agitation for an eight-hour day in 1886 when a bomb, thrown by a hand unknown to this day into a radical meeting in Chicago's Haymarket Square, touched off a nation-wide wave of panic.

60 The steady trend of the suffrage movement toward the conservative and the conventional during the last twenty years of the nineteenth century must be viewed in this setting, in order to avoid the misconception that a few conservative women
65 took it over, through their own superior ability and the passivity of the former militants. Even the latter were changing their views, judging by their actions. It was one thing to challenge the proprieties at the Centennial of 1876; ten years later it
70 would have been inconceivable even to the women who took part in the demonstration. Susan Anthony herself would have thought twice about flouting federal election laws and going to jail in an era that witnessed the Haymarket hysteria.

75 Moreover the social makeup of the suffrage leadership was changing perceptibly. There were fewer housewives or women who did the greater part of their own work, and more professionals, writers, and women of substantial means. Those
80 who had begun the struggle in want and penury—

GO ON TO THE NEXT PAGE →

living, like Lucy Stone and Abby Kelley, on whatever pittance they could wring out of their lecturing—had by now achieved some measure of comfort and ease. Even the spartan Susan Anthony,
who dipped continually into her meager finances
for the sake of the cause, had comfortably situated
friends in most cities, who cared for her on her
endless lecture and campaign trips; whenever she
was in Washington she stayed at the Riggs Hotel,
whose owners put a suite at her disposal, sometimes for months at a time.

Along with increased means (always more evident in the lives of the individual women than in
the suffrage organizations' finances, which continued on a deplorable hand-to-mouth basis) came
greater influence and prestige. Twenty years had
seen a profound change of public attitude. Woman
suffrage was not yet generally accepted, but it was
no longer considered the province of eccentrics
and crackpots. It boasted influential friends in
Congress, and the annual conventions of the
National Association in Washington were the
occasion, not only of hearings before Congres-
sional committees and lobbying "on the hill," but
of White House teas and receptions.

23. The author's primary purpose in the passage is to

(A) contrast Susan B. Anthony with Julia Ward Howe
(B) recount the advances in the suffrage movement from 1880 to 1890
(C) account for the changes occurring in the suffrage movement from 1880 to 1890
(D) explain the growing divisions within the women's movement
(E) point out aspects of the suffrage movement which exist in contemporary feminism

24. The word "espoused" in line 11 means

(A) married   (B) championed   (C) reconciled
(D) despised   (E) endowed

25. Which of the following statements is most compatible with the early principles of the National as described in the passage?

(A) Advocates of suffrage should maintain their distance from socially embarrassing "allies."
(B) Marital and economic issues are inappropriate concerns for the suffrage movement.
(C) Propriety of behavior should characterize representatives of the women's cause.
(D) A nominal espousal of woman suffrage is worthy of suffragist support.
(E) The concerns of all afflicted women are the concerns of the suffrage movement.

26. The passage singles out Julia Ward Howe as an example of

(A) a venerated figurehead
(B) an overzealous advocate
(C) a heterodox thinker
(D) an ordained cleric
(E) a militant activist

27. The word "touch" in line 55 means

(A) physical contact
(B) slight amount
(C) close personal communication
(D) request for additional funds
(E) detail completing an effect

28. The author's attitude toward the public reaction to the Molly Maguire trials is that the reaction was

(A) appropriate   (B) disorganized
(C) overwrought   (D) necessary
(E) understated

29. The author stresses the growing antiradical bias of the American middle class during the decade 1880–1890 in order to

(A) question a trend that proved destructive to the suffrage movement
(B) explain the unexpected emergence of an able body of radical leaders
(C) refute the contention that Anthony was unchanged by her experiences
(D) correct a misapprehension about changes in the suffrage movement
(E) excuse the growing lack of militancy on the part of the National

30. The passage suggests that, by 1890, attempts to effect woman suffrage by violating the proprieties and defying Federal laws would probably have been viewed even by movement members with

(A) indifference
(B) defiance
(C) disapprobation
(D) respect
(E) optimism

IF YOU FINISH BEFORE 30 MINUTES, YOU MAY CHECK YOUR WORK ON THIS SECTION ONLY. DO NOT TURN TO ANY OTHER SECTION IN THE TEST.   **STOP**

SECTION **2**
Mathematical Reasoning

Time—30 minutes
25 Questions

Directions and Reference Information

In this section solve each problem, using any available space for scratchwork. Then decide which is the best of the choices given and fill in the corresponding oval on the answer sheet.

Notes:

(1) The use of a calculator is permitted. All numbers used are real numbers.

(2) Figures that accompany problems in this test are intended to provide information useful in solving the problems. They are drawn as accurately as possible EXCEPT when it is stated in a specific problem that the figure is not drawn to scale. All figures lie in a plane unless otherwise indicated.

$A = \pi r^2$ $A = \ell w$ $A = \frac{1}{2}bh$ $V = \ell wh$ $V = \pi r^2 h$ $c^2 = a^2 + b^2$ Special Right Triangles
$C = 2\pi r$

The number of degrees of an arc in a circle is 360.
The measure in degrees of a straight angle is 180.
The sum of the measures in degrees of the angles of a triangle is 180.

1. How much less is $\frac{1}{2}$ of $\frac{4}{7}$ than $\frac{5}{7}$ of $\frac{1}{2}$?

   (A) $\frac{1}{7}$ (B) $\frac{2}{7}$ (C) $\frac{3}{7}$ (D) $\frac{1}{14}$ (E) $\frac{3}{14}$

2. $\sqrt{\frac{16}{35} + \frac{1}{4}} =$

   (A) $\frac{3}{5}$ (B) $\frac{6}{7}$ (C) $\frac{25}{36}$ (D) $\frac{5}{6}$ (E) $\frac{7}{6}$

3. The lengths of each of the sides of $\triangle ABC$ are whole numbers. If $AB = BC$ and $AC = 9$, what is the shortest possible length of side $\overline{AB}$?

   (A) 4   (B) 5   (C) 6   (D) 7   (E) 8

4. If $\boxed{K}$ is defined by the equation

   $\boxed{K} = \dfrac{\sqrt{K}}{2}$ for all numbers K, which of the following equals 5?

   (A) $\boxed{10}$ (B) $\boxed{20}$ (C) $\boxed{25}$ (D) $\boxed{50}$ (E) $\boxed{100}$

5. The number of pupils in a school increased from 2500 to 3000. The percent of increase is

   (A) 0.05%   (B) 0.5%   (C) 5%
   (D) 20%   (E) 25%

6. A round-trip ticket cost \$54.50 while a one-way ticket cost \$29.00. How much will be saved by buying 3 round-trip tickets instead of buying one-way tickets?

   (A) \$10.50   (B) \$10.65   (C) \$11.50
   (D) \$31.00   (E) \$35.50

7. There are 10 automobiles waiting to enter a toll-gate. If the average length of each car is 16 feet and the average space between each car is 6 inches, what is the length (in feet) of the distance between the front of the first car and the rear of the last vehicle?

   (A) 164   (B) $164\frac{1}{2}$ (C) 165   (D) 166   (E) 220

GO ON TO THE NEXT PAGE

8. If y represents the tens digit and x the units digit of a two-digit number, then the number is represented by

(A) $y + x$ (B) yx (C) $10x + y$
(D) $10y + x$ (E) $10yx$

9. The expression $\sqrt{4 - 3x}$ has a real value for each of the following values of x EXCEPT

(A) -4 (B) 0 (C) $\frac{2}{3}$ (D) 1 (E) 2

10. If $\dfrac{1}{x} = \dfrac{a}{b}$ then x equals the

(A) sum of a and b (B) product of a and b
(C) difference of a and b (D) quotient of b and a
(E) quotient of a and b

11. A circular pond 40 feet in diameter is surrounded by a patch of grass 2 feet wide. What is the area of the grass?

(A) 4π sq. ft.   (B) 84π sq. ft.
(C) 164π sq. ft.   (D) 336π sq. ft.
(E) 400π sq. ft.

12. $\dfrac{9K^3 - 9m^2K}{3K^2 - 3mK}$ is equivalent to $3K +$

(A) m (B) $3m$ (C) 1 (D) 2 (E) 3

13. In $\triangle CDE$, $CE > CD$. Point A bisects side CD, and point B bisects side CE. Which of the following is (are) true?

   I. $CB = AD$
  II. $AC = BC$
 III. $CB > CA$

(A) I only   (B) II only   (C) III only
(D) I and II only   (E) I, II, and III

14. A certain radio costs a merchant $72, which includes overhead and selling expenses. At what price must he sell it if he is to make a profit of 20% on the selling price?

(A) $86.40   (B) $90.00   (C) $92.00
(D) $100.00   (E) $144.00

15. A merchant bought cloth at $1.60 a yard. The merchant would like to make a profit of 20%. What price should he mark the sales tag, which in addition to the price includes the statement: *TAKE 20% OFF THIS PRICE*?

(A) $2.00   (B) $2.24   (C) $2.40
(D) $2.50   (E) $2.60

16. A metal cube with an edge of one foot is melted into a rectangular solid one-eighth of a foot in height. What is the area of the top of the new solid?

(A) $\frac{1}{64}$ sq. ft.   (B) $\frac{1}{8}$ sq. ft.   (30)$\frac{1}{4}$ sq. ft.
(D) 4 sq. ft.   (E) 8 sq. ft.

17. In the accompanying diagram (not drawn to scale), which of the following is (are) always true?

   I. $d > b$
  II. $a > d$
 III. $d > c$

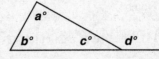

(A) I only   (B) II only   (C) III only
(D) I and II only   (E) I, II, and III

18. The ratio of boys to girls in a senior class is 5:3. If $\frac{9}{10}$ of the boys may graduate and all the girls may or may not graduate, what is the minimum part of the senior class that may graduate?

(A) $\frac{3}{5}$ (B) $\frac{7}{8}$ (C) $\frac{15}{16}$ (D) $\frac{2}{3}$ (E) $\frac{27}{50}$

19. Given a circle A whose diameter is 2 feet and a rectangular piece of tin B, 10 feet by 4 feet, find, correct to the nearest square foot, the tin that will be left after the greatest possible number of circles of the size of A have been cut from B.

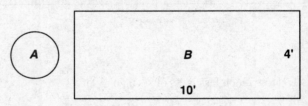

(A) zero   (B) 1 sq. ft.   (C) 2 sq. ft.
(D) 9 sq. ft.   (E) 20 sq. ft.

20. The sum of three sides of a square equals x. The area of this square, in terms of x, equals

(A) $3x$ (B) $\dfrac{x}{3}$ (C) $\dfrac{3}{x}$ (D) $\dfrac{x^2}{3}$ (E) $\dfrac{x^2}{9}$

21. The distance between point P (3,0) and point Q is 5. The coordinates of point Q could be any of the following EXCEPT

(A) $(-8,0)$ (B) $(3, -5)$ (C) $(3,5)$
(D) $(8,0)$ (E) $(-2,0)$

22. What part of the large circle is shaded?

(A) $\frac{1}{5}$ (B) $\frac{1}{4}$ (C) $\frac{1}{3}$
(D) $\frac{1}{2}$ (E) none of these

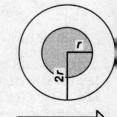

GO ON TO THE NEXT PAGE

23. A rectangle is revolved through 360° about its longer side as an axis. If the longer side is a units and the shorter side is b units, the volume of the resulting solid in cubic units is

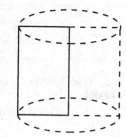

(A) πab^2 (B) $\pi a^2 b$
(C) $2\pi ab$ (D) $2\pi ab^2$
(E) πab

24. On this graph, what is the measure of the central angle of the sector for women in the navy?

(A) 32°   (B) 73°   (C) 90°
(D) 115°   (E) 133°

AREAS OF SERVICE OF THE
APPROXIMATELY 223,297 WOMEN IN THE
U.S. ARMED FORCES

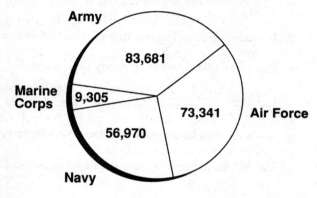

25. According to this graph, which of the following age group has the best driving record?

(A) 25–29   (B) 30–34   (C) 34–39
(D) 45–49   (E) 65–69

Danger on the Road
Fatalities per one million licensed drivers
in each age group in 1990.

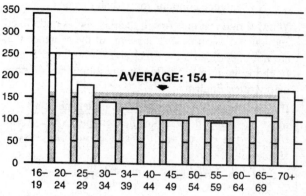

Source: National Highway Traffic Safety Administration

IF YOU FINISH BEFORE 30 MINUTES, YOU MAY CHECK YOUR WORK ON THIS
SECTION ONLY. DO NOT TURN TO ANY OTHER SECTION IN THE TEST.   **S T O P**

SECTION 3
Writing Skills

Time—30 minutes
39 Questions

Directions

The following sentences contain problems in grammar, usage, diction (choice of words), and idiom.

　　Some sentences are correct.
　　No sentence contains more than one error.

You will find that the error, if there is one, is underlined and lettered. Assume that elements of the sentence that are not underlined are correct and cannot be changed. In choosing answers, follow the requirements of standard written English.

If there is an error, select the <u>one underlined part</u> that must be changed to make the sentence correct and blacken the corresponding space on your answer sheet.

If there is no error, blacken answer space Ⓔ .

Example:

　　The region has a climate <u>so severe that</u> plants
　　　　　　　　　　　　　　　　　A

　　<u>growing there</u> rarely <u>had been</u> more than twelve
　　　　B　　　　　　　　　　C

　　inches <u>high</u>. <u>No error</u>
　　　　　D　　　　E

1. The lieutenant <u>reminded</u> his men that the
　　　　　　　　　　A

　　only information <u>to be given</u> to the captors
　　　　　　　　　　B

　　was <u>each</u> individual's name, rank, and
　　　　　C

　　<u>what his serial number was</u>. <u>No error</u>
　　　　　　　D　　　　　　　　　E

2. When the teacher ordered the student <u>to go to</u> the
　　　A　　　　　　　　　　　　　　　　　　　　B

　　dean's office <u>as a result of</u> the class disruption, she
　　　　　　　　　　C

　　surprised us because she usually <u>will handle</u> her
　　　　　　　　　　　　　　　　　　　　D

　　own discipline problems. <u>No error</u>
　　　　　　　　　　　　　E

3. He was the author <u>whom</u> I <u>believed</u> was <u>most likely</u>
　　　　　　　　　　A　　　B　　　　C

　　to receive the <u>coveted</u> award. <u>No error</u>
　　　　　　　D　　　　　　　E

4. Please give this scholarship <u>to whoever</u> in the
　　　　　　　　　　　　　　　　A

　　graduating class <u>has done</u> the most to <u>promote</u>
　　　　　　　　　B　　　　　　　　　　C

　　<u>goodwill</u> in the community. <u>No error</u>
　　　D　　　　　　　　　　　E

5. Both lawyers <u>interpreted</u> the statute <u>differently</u>, <u>and</u>
　　　　　　　　A　　　　　　　　　B　　　　C

　　they needed a judge to settle <u>its</u> dispute. <u>No error</u>
　　　　　　　　　　　　　　D　　　　　　E

6. All of the team members, except <u>him</u>, <u>has</u> anticipated
　　　　　　　　　　　　　　　　A　　B

　　interest from the national leagues, and now practice
　　　　C

　　twice <u>as long</u>. <u>No error</u>
　　　　　D　　　E

7. Everybody <u>but</u> him has paid <u>their</u> dues; we
　　　　　　A　　　　　　　　B

　　<u>must seek</u> ways to make him understand the
　　　C

　　<u>need for</u> prompt payment. <u>No error</u>
　　　D　　　　　　　　　E

8. <u>In order to be sure</u> <u>that</u> the mattress was firm before
　　　A　　　　　　　　B

　　placing an order, the man gingerly <u>sat down</u> and
　　　　　　　　　　　　　　　　　　C

　　<u>laid back</u>. <u>No error</u>
　　　D　　　　E

9. <u>Since</u> she found the climate of Arizona <u>very healthy</u>,
　　A　　　　　　　　　　　　　　　　　　B

　　she decided <u>to move</u> to Phoenix <u>as soon as</u> possible.
　　　　　　　C　　　　　　　　　D

　　<u>No error</u>
　　　E

10. The data <u>which</u> he presented <u>was</u> not <u>pertinent</u> to
　　　　　　A　　　　　　　B　　　C

　　the matter <u>under discussion</u>. <u>No error</u>
　　　　　　　D　　　　　　E

11. In order for <u>he and I</u> to be able <u>to attend</u>, we
　　　　　　A　　B　　　　　　　C

　　<u>will need</u> to receive tickets within the week.
　　　D

　　<u>No error</u>
　　　E

12. I <u>feel badly</u> about the present conflict <u>because</u> I do
　　　A　　　　　　　　　　　　　　　B

　　not know how to resolve it without <u>hurting</u> either
　　　　　　　　　　　　　　　　　　C

　　you or <u>him</u>. <u>No error</u>
　　　　　D　　　E

13. A new production of the opera *Aida* has <u>just</u> been
　　　　　　　　　　　　　　　　　　　　A

　　announced; <u>it</u> will be <u>sang</u> on an outdoor stage
　　　　　　　B　　　　　C

　　with live animals. <u>No error</u>
　　　D　　　　　　E

GO ON TO THE NEXT PAGE →

14. Unless two or more members object to <u>him joining</u>
      A   B

the club, we shall have <u>to accept</u> his application <u>for</u>
                        C   D

membership. <u>No error</u>
              E

15. Thurgood Marshall <u>made history by</u> <u>becoming</u> the
                      A   B

first black Supreme Court Justice <u>when</u> he was
                                   C

<u>appointed of</u> this position by President Lyndon
  D

Johnson. <u>No error</u>
          E

16. <u>When</u> she spoke with the police, she reported her
   A

loss, stating that a <u>large quantity of</u> clothing and
                  B

<u>of valuable books</u> <u>were</u> missing. <u>No error</u>
     C   D   E

17. "Babbittry," a term used to <u>describe</u> a <u>typically</u>
                     A   B

conservative businessman, <u>was</u> <u>derived from</u>
                    C   D

Sinclair Lewis' novel *Babbitt.* <u>No error</u>
                    E

18. For such a long trip, someone should <u>have chosen</u> a
                                 A

different bus line, <u>for</u> this bus has <u>fewer comforts</u>
             B   C

<u>then</u> any of the others. <u>No error</u>
  D   E

19. <u>After</u> the incident was over, <u>neither</u> the passengers
   A   B

nor the bus driver <u>were</u> able to identify the youngster
               C

who <u>had created</u> the disturbance. <u>No error</u>
      D   E

Directions

In each of the following sentences, some part or all of the sentence is underlined. Below each sentence you will find five ways of phrasing the underlined part. Select the answer that produces the most effective sentence, one that is clear and exact, without awkwardness or ambiguity, and fill in the corresponding oval on your answer sheet. In choosing answers, follow the requirements of standard written English. Choose the answer that best expresses the meaning of the original sentence.

Answer (A) is always the same as the underlined part. Choose Answer (A) if you think the original sentence needs no revision.

EXAMPLE:

Laura Ingalls Wilder published her first book <u>and she was sixty-five years old then.</u>

(A) and she was sixty-five years old then
(B) when she was sixty-five
(C) at age sixty-five years old
(D) upon reaching of sixty-five years
(E) at the time when she was sixty-five

SAMPLE ANSWER
Ⓐ ● Ⓒ Ⓓ Ⓔ

20. By the time we arrive in Italy, <u>we have traveled through four countries.</u>

(A) we have traveled through four countries
(B) we had traveled through four countries
(C) we will have traveled through four countries
(D) four countries will have been traveled through
(E) we through four countries shall have traveled

21. To say "My lunch was satisfactory" <u>is complimentary, to say</u> "My lunch is adequate" is not.

(A) complimentary, to say
(B) complementary, to say
(C) complementary, however, to say
(D) complimentary, but to say
(E) complementary to saying

22. When one debates the merits of the proposed reduction in our tax base, <u>you should take into consideration the effect</u> it will have on the schools and the other public services.

(A) you should take into consideration the effect
(B) you should consider the effect
(C) he should take the affect
(D) he takes into consideration the affect
(E) he should take into consideration the effect

23. We were afraid of the teacher's <u>wrath, due to this</u> <u>statement that</u> he would penalize <u>anyone who failed</u> to hand in his term paper on time.

    (A) wrath, due to this statement that,
    (B) wrath due to this statement that,
    (C) wrath, inasmuch as his statement that,
    (D) wrath because of his statement that,
    (E) wrath and his statement that,

24. Although the doctors had put the patient through a series of tests, including X-rays and cytoscopy, <u>they have found no explanation of her mysterious</u> <u>ailment</u>.

    (A) they have found no explanation of her mysterious ailment
    (B) no explanation of her mysterious ailment has been found
    (C) no explanation was found of her mysterious ailment
    (D) they did not explain her mysterious ailment
    (E) they found no explanation of her mysterious ailment

25. <u>Originally referring to an excess of patriotic fervor,</u> the term "chauvinism" has come to signify devotion to the theory of masculine superiority.

    (A) Originally referring to an excess of patriotic fervor,
    (B) In its original reference to an excess of patriotic fervor,
    (C) Originally it referred to an excess of patriotic fervor,
    (D) Originally it was referring to excessive patriotic fervor,
    (E) An excess of patriotic fervor being originally referred to,

26. Exercise offers both physical and emotional benefits: a sense of control over one's body, a feeling of accomplishment <u>and it is a release of pent-up frus-</u> <u>trations</u>.

    (A) and it is a release of pent-up frustrations
    (B) and it releases pent-up frustrations
    (C) by releasing pent-up frustrations
    (D) and a release of pent-up frustrations
    (E) and a release from pent-up frustrations

27. <u>If the Confederate Army would have carried the day</u> <u>at Gettysburg</u>, the history of America during the past century would have been profoundly altered.

    (A) If the Confederate Army would have carried the day at Gettysburg,
    (B) Had the Confederate Army carried the day at Gettysburg,
    (C) The Confederate Army having carried the day at Gettysburg,
    (D) If the Confederate Army would have won at Gettysburg,
    (E) If the Battle of Gettysburg would have been won by the Confederate Army,

28. I have discovered that the subways in New York are <u>as clean as any other city I have visited</u>.

    (A) as clean as any other city I have visited
    (B) as clean as those in any other city I have visited
    (C) as clean as those in any city I visited
    (D) cleaner than any city I visited
    (E) cleaner than any other city I have visited

29. Inflation in the United States <u>has not and, we hope,</u> <u>never will reach</u> a rate of 20 percent a year.

    (A) has not and, we hope, never will reach
    (B) has not reached and, we hope, never will
    (C) has not and hopefully never will reach
    (D) has not reached and, we hope, never will reach
    (E) has not reached and hopefully never will

30. <u>Arriving at the scene of the accident, the victims of</u> <u>the crash were treated by the paramedics.</u>

    (A) Arriving at the scene of the accident, the victims of the crash were treated by the paramedics
    (B) At the scene of the accident, the paramedics treated the victims of the crash
    (C) As soon as they had arrived at the scene of the accident, the paramedics treated the crash victims
    (D) Arriving at the scene of the accident, the paramedics will treat the victims of the crash
    (E) Arriving at the scene of the accident, the paramedics treated the victims of the crash

31. <u>Since all the tickets to the show had been sold</u>, we went to a concert at Carnegie Hall.

    (A) Since all the tickets to the show had been sold
    (B) Being that all the tickets to the show had been sold
    (C) All the tickets to the show having been sold
    (D) Because they sold all the tickets to the show
    (E) Being that all the tickets to the show were sold

32. Although I understand why airlines have to serve frozen foods to their passengers, I do not understand why I was served <u>a meal by a flight attendant</u> <u>that had been only partially defrosted</u>.

    (A) a meal by a flight attendant that had been only partially defrosted
    (B) an only partially defrosted meal by a flight attendant
    (C) a meal that had been only partially defrosted by a flight attendant
    (D) by a flight attendant a meal that had been only partially defrosted
    (E) by a flight attendant of a partially defrosted meal

GO ON TO THE NEXT PAGE

33. If anyone asks for an application, send them to room 1134 to see the personnel director.

(A) If anyone asks for an application, send them
(B) Send anyone who asks for an application
(C) When anyone asks for an application, send them
(D) If anyone asks for an application, they should be sent
(E) As soon as anyone asks for an application, send them

Directions

The passage below is the unedited draft of a student's essay. Some of the essay needs to be rewritten to make the meaning clearer and more precise. Read the essay carefully.

The essay is followed by six questions about changes that might improve all or part of its organization, development, sentence structure, use of language, appropriateness to the audience, or its use of standard written English. Choose the answer that most clearly and effectively expresses the student's intended meaning. Indicate your choice by filling in the corresponding space on the answer sheet.

Essay

[1] From the colonial times until today, the appeal of the underdog has retained a hold on Americans. [2] It is a familiar sight today to see someone rooting for the underdog while watching a sports event on television. [3] Though that only happens if they don't already have a favorite team. [4] Variations of the David and Goliath story are popular in both fact and fiction. [5] Horatio Alger stories, wondrous tales of conquering the West, and the way that people have turned rags-to-riches stories such as Vanderbilt into national myths are three examples of America's fascination with the underdog.

[6] This appeal has been spurred by American tradition as well as an understandably selfish desire to feel good about oneself and life. [7] Part of the aura America has held since its creation is that the humblest and poorest person can make it here in America. [8] That dream is ingrained in the history of America. [9] America is made up of immigrants. [10] Most were poor when they came here. [11] They thought of America as the land of opportunity, where any little guy could succeed. [12] All it took was the desire to lift oneself up and some good honest work. [13] Millions succeeded on account of the American belief to honor and support the underdog in all its efforts.

[14] The underdog goes against all odds and defeats the stronger opponent with hope. [15] It makes people feel that maybe one day they too will triumph against the odds. [16] It changes their view of life's struggles because they trust that in the end all their hardships will amount to something. [17] Despair has no place in a society where everyone knows that they can succeed. [18] It's no wonder that the underdog has always had a tight hold upon American hopes and minds.

34. Which of the following is the best revision of the underlined sections of sentences 1 and 2 (below), so that the two sentences are combined into one?

From the colonial times until today, the appeal of the underdog has retained a hold on Americans. It is a familiar sight today to see someone rooting for the underdog while watching a sports event on television.

(A) the appeal of the underdog has retained a hold on Americans, and it is a familiar sight today to see underdogs being the one rooted for
(B) the appeal of the underdog has retained a hold on Americans, but it is a familiar sight today to see someone rooting for the underdog
(C) the underdog has retained a hold on Americans, who commonly root for the underdog, for example,
(D) the underdog has retained a hold on Americans, commonly rooting for the underdog
(E) the underdog's appeal has retained a hold on Americans, for example, they commonly root for the underdog

35. To improve the coherence of paragraph 1, which of the following sentences should be deleted?

(A) Sentence 1
(B) Sentence 2
(C) Sentence 3
(D) Sentence 4
(E) Sentence 5

36. Considering the content of paragraph 2, which of the following is the best revision of the paragraph's topic sentence, sentence 6?

(A) This appeal got spurred by American tradition as well as by an understandably selfish desire to feel good about oneself and one's life.
(B) The appeal of the underdog has been spurred by American tradition.
(C) The appeal has been spurred by Americans' traditional and selfish desire to feel good about themselves and life.
(D) American tradition as well as Americans' desire to feel good about oneself and their life has spurred the appeal of underdogs.
(E) American traditions include an understandably selfish desire to feel good about themselves and the appeal of the underdog.

GO ON TO THE NEXT PAGE

37. In the context of paragraph 2, which of the following is the best way to combine sentences 8, 9, 10, and 11?

(A) That dream is ingrained in the experience of America, a country made up of poor immigrants who believed that in this land of opportunity any little guy had a chance to succeed.

(B) That dream was ingrained in our history, a country made up of immigrants, poor and hopeful that any little guy is able to succeed in America, the land of opportunity.

(C) That dream has been ingrained America's history that poor immigrants look on America as a land of opportunity, which any little guy had been able to succeed in.

(D) The American experience has ingrained in it the dream that by immigrants coming to this country poorly could succeed because America is the land of opportunity.

(E) Ingrained in the American experience is the dream of poor immigrants that they could succeed here, after all, this is the land of opportunity.

38. Taking into account the sentences that precede and follow sentence 13, which of the following is the most effective revision of sentence 13?

(A) Americans believe that the underdog should be honored and supported, which led to their success.

(B) Because America believed in honoring and supporting the underdog, they succeed.

(C) And succeed they did because of America's commitment to honor and support the underdog.

(D) Honoring and supporting underdogs is a firmly held value in America, and it led to the success of underdogs.

(E) They succeeded with their efforts to be supported and honored by America.

39. Which of the following revisions of sentence 14 is the best transition between paragraphs 3 and 4?

(A) Underdogs, in addition, went against all odds and with hope defeat stronger opponents.

(B) The underdog, feeling hopeful, going against all odds, and defeating stronger opponents.

(C) It is the hope of the underdog who goes against the odds and defeats the stronger opponent.

(D) The triumph of the underdog over a strong opponent inspires hope.

(E) The underdog triumphs against all odds and defeats the stronger opponents.

IF YOU FINISH BEFORE 30 MINUTES, YOU MAY CHECK YOUR WORK ON THIS
SECTION ONLY. DO NOT TURN TO ANY OTHER SECTION IN THE TEST.

S T O P

SECTION **4**
Verbal Reasoning

Time—30 minutes
30 Questions

For each question in this section, select the best answer from among the choices given and fill in the corresponding oval on the answer sheet.

Directions

Each sentence below consists of a related pair of words or phrases, followed by five pairs of words or phrases labeled A through E. Select the pair that best expresses a relationship similar to that expressed in the original pair.

Example:

CRUMB:BREAD::
(A) ounce:unit
(B) splinter:wood
(C) water:bucket
(D) twine:rope
(E) cream:butter

31. PRY:CROWBAR::

(A) peek:curtain   (B) skate:rink
(C) leap:frog   (D) perch:rooster
(E) dig:shovel

32. TROUGH:PIGS::

(A) carton:eggs   (B) den:bears
(C) manger:cattle   (D) flock:sheep
(E) corral:horses

33. SIDEWALK:PEDESTRIAN::

(A) hangar:plane   (B) sidecar:motorcycle
(C) highway:robber   (D) boardwalk:shore
(E) waterway:boat

34. STUDIO:SCULPTOR::

(A) gallery:painting   (B) smithy:blacksmith
(C) gymnasium:spectator   (D) park:monument
(E) apartment:renter

35. INTIMIDATE:FEAR::

(A) mitigate:pain   (B) commiserate:sorrow
(C) exasperate:irritation   (D) exonerate:guilt
(E) remunerate:poverty

36. INSIPID:FOOD::

(A) savory:potions   (B) musky:aroma
(C) vapid:remarks   (D) horrendous:noise
(E) spectacular:views

37. HAWK:TALONS::

(A) monkey:tail   (B) eagle:wings
(C) lion:claws   (D) tiger:stripes
(E) rhinoceros:horn

38. ARIA:DIVA::

(A) opera:librettist   (B) soliloquy:actor
(C) compound:chemist   (D) air:melody
(E) duet:conductor

39. OPHTHALMOLOGIST:EYES::

(A) entomologist:ears   (B) apologist:tongue
(C) dermatologist:skin   (D) philatelist:coins
(E) geologist:genes

40. IRKSOME:CHAFE::

(A) awesome:distress   (B) tiresome:endure
(C) fulsome:praise   (D) lurid:shock
(E) pallid:allure

41. SLAG:METAL::

(A) veneer:wood   (B) dregs:wine
(C) lawn:grass   (D) chapter:book
(E) pedestal:statue

42. MALINGERER:WORK::

(A) recluse:company   (B) thief:plunder
(C) arbitrator:negotiation
(D) benefactor:philanthropy
(E) counselor:client

43. OGLE:FLIRTATIOUSNESS::

(A) observe:nonchalance   (B) mute:intensity
(C) gape:astonishment   (D) squint:diffidence
(E) peer:effrontery

The passage below is followed by questions based on its content. Answer the questions following the passage on the basis of what is <u>stated</u> or <u>implied</u> in that passage and in any introductory material that may be provided.

Questions 44–49 are based on the following passage.

The following passage on the formation of oil is excerpted from a novel about oil exploration written by Alistair MacLean.

　　Five main weather elements act upon rock. Frost and ice fracture rock. It can be gradually eroded by airborne dust. The action of the seas, whether through the constant movement of tides or Line the pounding of heavy storm waves, remorselessly

5

wears away the coastlines. Rivers are immensely powerful destructive agencies—one has but to look at the Grand Canyon to appreciate their enor-
10 mous power. And such rocks as escape all these influences are worn away over the eons by the effect of rain.

Whatever the cause of erosion, the net result is the same. The rock is reduced to its tiniest possi-
15 ble constituents—rock particles or, simply, dust. Rain and melting snow carry this dust down to the tiniest rivulets and the mightiest rivers, which, in turn, transport it to lakes, inland seas, and the coastal regions of the oceans. Dust, however fine and powdery, is still heavier than water, and
20 whenever the water becomes sufficiently still, it will gradually sink to the bottom, not only in lakes and seas but also in the sluggish lower reaches of rivers and where flood conditions exist, in the form of silt.

25 And so, over unimaginably long reaches of time, whole mountain ranges are carried down to the seas, and in the process, through the effects of gravity, new rock is born as layer after layer of dust accumulates on the bottom, building up to a
30 depth of ten, a hundred, perhaps even a thousand feet, the lowermost layers being gradually com-pacted by the immense and steadily increasing pressures from above, until the particles fuse together and reform as new rock.

35 It is in the intermediate and final processes of the new rock formation that oil comes into being. Those lakes and seas of hundreds of millions of years ago were almost choked by water plants and the most primitive forms of aquatic life. On
40 dying, they sank to the bottom of the lakes and seas along with the settling dust particles and were gradually buried deep under the endless lay-ers of more dust and more aquatic and plant life that slowly accumulated above them. The passing
45 of millions of years and the steadily increasing pressures from above gradually changed the decayed vegetation and dead aquatic life into oil.

Described this simply and quickly, the process sounds reasonable enough. But this is where the
50 gray and disputatious area arises. The conditions necessary for the formation of oil are known; the cause of the metamorphosis is not. It seems prob-able that some form of chemical catalyst is involved, but this catalyst has not been isolated.
55 The first purely synthetic oil, as distinct from sec-ondary synthetic oils such as those derived from

coal, has yet to be produced. We just have to accept that oil is oil, that it is there, bound up in rock strata in fairly well-defined areas throughout
60 the world but always on the sites of ancient seas and lakes, some of which are now continental land, some buried deep under the encroachment of new oceans.

44. According to the author, which of the following statements is (are) true?

   I. The action of the seas is the most important factor in erosion of the earth's surface.
   II. Scientists have not been able to produce a purely synthetic oil in the laboratory.
   III. Gravity plays an important role in the forma-tion of new rock.

(A) I only   (B) II only   (C) III only
(D) II and III only   (E) I, II, and III

45. The Grand Canyon is mentioned in the first para-graph to illustrate

(A) the urgent need for dams
(B) the devastating impact of rivers
(C) the effect of rain
(D) a site where oil may be found
(E) the magnificence of nature

46. According to the author, our understanding of the process by which oil is created is

(A) biased   (B) systematic   (C) erroneous
(D) deficient   (E) adequate

47. We can infer that prospectors should search for oil deposits

(A) wherever former seas existed
(B) in mountain streambeds
(C) where coal deposits are found
(D) in the Grand Canyon
(E) in new rock formations

48. The author does all of the following EXCEPT

(A) describe a process   (B) state a possibility
(C) cite an example   (D) propose a solution
(E) mention a limitation

49. The word "reaches" in line 25 means

(A) grasps   (B) unbroken stretches
(C) range of knowledge   (D) promontories
(E) juxtapositions

GO ON TO THE NEXT PAGE

The passages below are followed by questions based on their content; questions following a pair of related passages may also be based on the relationship between the paired passages. Answer the questions on the basis of what is <u>stated</u> or <u>implied</u> in the passages and in any introductory material that may be provided.

Questions 50–60 are based on the following passages.

In Passage 1, the author discusses British attitudes toward Americanisms. In Passage 2, the author deals with the same topic, but in a somewhat different manner. The authors of both passages are American.

PASSAGE 1

Twenty years before the Revolution, Samuel Johnson was already denouncing a book by an American as "a tract of corruption, to which every
Line language widely diffused must always be
5 exposed." Johnson's own experience and common sense certainly told him that linguistic change was inevitable, but his intense conservatism also told him that any change was likely to be for the worse—especially if it was the work of ignorant
10 provincials, remote from the civilizing influence of London. Johnson considered even the Scots semibarbarous; it would have been surprising had he viewed the Americans any less sourly.

Johnson's view of American English remained
15 typical of English literary opinion for well over a century. Thus in 1808, an English magazine denounced the "torrent of barbarous phraseology" that threatened to "destroy the purity of the English language." Another critic found American
20 writing loaded with "a great multitude of words that are. . .as utterly foreign as if they had been adopted from Chinese or Hebrew." The first criticism was obviously fatuous: how can one talk of the "purity" of a language that had been borrow-
25 ing from foreign tongues, with both hands, for centuries? The second was simply ignorant: the much-deplored "Americanisms" of the early nineteenth century were, in their great majority, English, not borrowed. Some were English words
30 that had fallen out of cultivated use in the old country; thus Americans said "fall" where educated Englishmen said "autumn." Indeed, of the two, "fall" was the more authentically "English"—if the term means anything—being directly derived
35 from Old English, while "autumn" was a French import. Likewise, the phrase "I guess" meaning "I suppose," used by English writers until well into this century as a virtual trademark of eccentric American speech, goes back to Chaucer (*Of twen-*
40 *ty yeer of age he was, I gesse.*) Others, as we've seen, were old English words with new meanings, while still others were new compounds—but compounded out of English elements, according to the rules of English syntax. "Belittle," target of
45 several critics, was modeled on such respectable English verbs as "befoul," used since the fourteenth century, while "lengthy," another supposed barbarism, was equally analogous to "weighty," used since around 1500.

50 American commentators, then and later, repeatedly made these points—with an occasional assist from colleagues across the Atlantic—but it made no difference to most English travelers and critics, who continued to berate American
55 English, along with American manners and morals, in terms that were at best unreasonable and at worst viciously dishonest. Frances Trollope, mother of the novelist, reported in 1832 that during her entire stay in America she had
60 seldom "heard a sentence elegantly turned and correctly pronounced." A few years later, Dickens, after his fabulously successful American tour, wrote that outside New York and Boston, grammar was "more than doubtful" and that "the oddest vul-
65 garisms" were acceptable. Perhaps the lowest blow came in 1863, from Henry Alford, Dean of Canterbury. Though he had never visited America, he bewailed "the process of deterioration which our Queen's English has undergone at the hands
70 of the Americans," and finished by denouncing them for conducting "the most cruel and unprincipled war in the history of the world." Since earlier writers had denounced America for tolerating the slavery that the unprincipled war would abolish, it
75 was clear that for a certain type of Englishman, *anything* America did, in language or politics, was wrong.

Though nobody has conducted a poll on the subject, my own feeling is that most British writers
80 today take a less jaundiced view of American English. They may or may not use Americanisms themselves, but see no reason why Americans should not use them. Many, perhaps the majority, would agree with the view put forward by the
85 American critic Brander Matthews nearly a century ago: "A Briticism is none the worse because it is known only to the inhabitants of the British Isles, and an Americanism is not to be despised because it is current only in America. The question is not
90 where it was born, but whether it is worthy to live."

PASSAGE 2

In the field of language an Americanism is generally regarded by the English as ipso facto obnoxious, and when a new one of any pungency begins to force its way into British usage the guardians of
95 the national linguistic chastity belabor it with great vehemence and predict calamitous consequences if it is not put down. If it makes progress despite

GO ON TO THE NEXT PAGE

these alarms, they often switch to the doctrine that
it is really old English and search the Oxford
100 Dictionary for examples of its use in Chaucer's
time; but while it is coming in they give it no quarter. Here the unparalleled English talent for discovering moral obliquity comes into play, and
what begins as an uproar over a word sometimes
105 ends as a holy war to keep the knavish Yankee
from undermining and ruining the English Kultur
and overthrowing the British Empire.

50. The corruption to which Johnson refers (line 3) is

(A) philosophical   (B) moral   (C) physical
(D) linguistic   (E) financial

51. The author of Passage 1 is unsurprised by Johnson's
sour view of Americans because

(A) Americans are descended from the Scots,
whom Johnson also despised
(B) given America's even greater distance from
London than Scotland's, Johnson was sure to
find anything American barbarous
(C) as a British writer, Johnson despised Americans
for stealing many of their common phrases
from his fellow authors
(D) Johnson was still smarting from the American
colonies' rebellion against the British crown
(E) in sharp contrast to Johnson, Americans are
determined proponents of change

52. By the phrase "with both hands" (line 25), the author
most likely intends to suggest that the borrowing has
been

(A) evenhanded   (B) immoderate   (C) foolish
(D) enervating   (E) ambidextrous

53. Passage 1's author states in defense of Americanisms that many of the new compound words
coined by Americans

(A) are patterned on traditional English usage
(B) possess a liveliness unmatched by comparable
English words
(C) have fallen out of cultivated use in America
(D) are actually Latinate in derivation
(E) are less barbarous than Chaucerian spelling

54. The word "turned" in line 60 means

(A) revolved   (B) transformed   (C) shifted
(D) phrased   (E) diagrammed

55. The author of Passage 1 quotes Brander Matthews
(lines 86–90) in order to

(A) cite a contemporary viewpoint
(B) present a measured judgment
(C) provide a happy ending
(D) propose a hypothesis
(E) expose a logical fallacy

56. According to Passage 2, if an Americanism finds
acceptance in British usage, the English

(A) refuse to allow the word to be included in the
dictionaries
(B) deny that it really is an Americanism
(C) feel that their cultural level is lowered
(D) will not admit that it is accepted
(E) claim that it is not American slang but good
American usage

57. With which one of the following statements about
British English would the author of Passage 2 be
most likely to agree?

(A) British English contains less slang than
American English.
(B) British English is lacking in humor.
(C) British English is no longer a growing language.
(D) The alertness of literary critics has preserved
the purity of British English.
(E) The absorption of Americanisms into British
English is inevitable.

58. The author of Passage 2 regards the British
assumption of American linguistic inferiority with

(A) wholehearted approval
(B) grudging acceptance   (C) bitter resentment
(D) sardonic humor   (E) watchful concern

59. The phrase "put down" in line 97 is best taken to
mean that Americanisms should be

(A) written down   (B) set in an appropriate context
(C) ranked below foreign phrases
(D) thoroughly suppressed   (E) badly expressed

60. The author of Passage 2 would most likely react to
the opinion voiced in lines 79–81 that most British
writers today take a less jaundiced view of American
English with

(A) marked relief   (B) grudging approval
(C) deceptive caution   (D) wholehearted regret
(E) outright incredulity

IF YOU FINISH BEFORE 30 MINUTES, YOU MAY CHECK YOUR WORK ON THIS
SECTION ONLY. DO NOT TURN TO ANY OTHER SECTION IN THE TEST.   **S T O P**

SECTION 5
Mathematical Reasoning

Directions and Sample Questions

Notes:

(1) The use of a calculator is permitted. All numbers used are real numbers.

(2) Figures that accompany problems in this test are intended to provide information useful in solving the problems. They are drawn as accurately as possible EXCEPT when it is stated in a specific problem that the figure is not drawn to scale. All figures lie in a plane unless otherwise indicated.

Questions 1–15 each consist of two quantities in boxes, one in Column A and one in Column B. You are to compare the two quantities and on the answer sheet fill in oval

A if the quantity in Column A is greater;
B if the quantity in Column B is greater;
C if the two quantities are equal;
D if the relationship cannot be determined from the information given.

Notes:

1. In some questions, information is given about one or both of the quantities to be compared. In such cases, the given information is centered above the two columns and is not boxed.
2. In a given question, a symbol that appears in both columns represents the same thing in Column A as it does in Column B.
3. Letters such as x, n, and k stand for real numbers.

	EXAMPLES		
	Column A	Column B	Answers
E1	5^2	20	● Ⓑ Ⓒ Ⓓ
E2	x	30	Ⓐ Ⓑ ● Ⓓ
E3	$r + 1$	$s - 1$	Ⓐ Ⓑ Ⓒ ●

For E2: $150°$ $x°$

For E3: r and s are integers.

PART I: QUANTITATIVE COMPARISON QUESTIONS

SUMMARY DIRECTIONS FOR QUANTITATIVE COMPARISON QUESTIONS

Answer: A if the quantity in Column A is greater.
          B if the quantity in Column B is greater.

C if the two quantities are equal.
D if the relationship cannot be determined from the information given.

	Column A	Column B
26.	$(2)(4)(6)(8)(10)(12)$	$(24)(40)(8)(6)$

$$x^2 - 25 = 0$$

	Column A	Column B
27.	x	5

$$5y + 15 = 3x + 5y$$

	Column A	Column B
28.	y	0
29.	$\sqrt{\frac{1}{9}} + \sqrt{\frac{1}{16}}$	$\sqrt{\frac{1}{16} + \frac{1}{9}}$

$x = 0$, $y > 1$, and $z > 1$

	Column A	Column B
30.	$2x(y + z)$	$y(x + z)$
31.	The largest integer less than $\frac{15}{7}$	The largest integer less than $\frac{41}{14}$

$a = 5, 10$
$b = 2, 3$

	Column A	Column B
32.	a^2	b^3

GO ON TO THE NEXT PAGE →

Column A	Column B

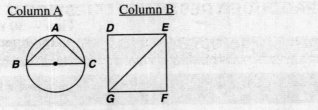

Diameter $BC = 10$
$AB = AC$
Perimeter of square $DEFG = 20$

33.   Area of ABC Area of $DEFG$

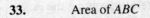

In $\triangle KML$, the measure of $\angle L$
equals the measure of $\angle M$.

34.   Measure of $\angle K$ $60°$

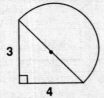

35.   The perimeter of this $5 + 2.5\pi$
semicircle

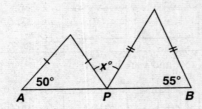

P is a point on line segment AB.

36.   Value of x $75°$

Column A	Column B

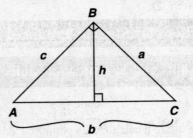

37. $\dfrac{bh}{2}$ $\dfrac{ac}{2}$

Let $[x]$ represent the greatest integer
that is less than or equal to x.

38. $[-2,1]$ $[-3]$

$$x^2 + y^2 = 100$$

39. x y

$1 \text{ kilometer} = \dfrac{5}{8} \text{ mile}$

40. 1 mile $\dfrac{5}{8}$ kilometer

GO ON TO THE NEXT PAGE

PART II: STUDENT-PRODUCED RESPONSE QUESTIONS

Directions for Student-Produced Response Questions

Each of the remaining ten questions (41–50) requires you to solve the problem and enter your answer by marking the ovals in the special grid, as shown in the examples below.

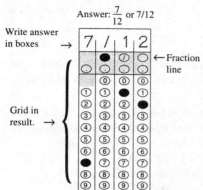

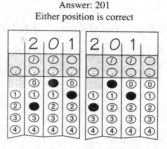

Note: You may start your answers in any column, space permitting. Columns not needed should be left blank.

- Mark no more than one oval in any column.
- Because the answer sheet will be machine-scored, **you will receive credit only if the ovals are filled in correctly.**
- Although not required, it is suggested that you write your answer in the boxes at the top of the columns to help you fill in the ovals accurately.
- Some problems may have more than one correct answer. In such cases, grid only one answer.
- No question has a negative answer.
- **Mixed numbers** such as $2\frac{1}{2}$ much be gridded as 2.5 or 5/2. (If ⬜ is gridded, it will be interpreted as $\frac{21}{2}$, not $\frac{21}{2}$.)

- Decimal Accuracy: If you obtain a decimal answer, enter the most accurate value that the grid will accommodate. For example, if you obtain an answer such as 0.6666..., you should record the result as .666 or .667. Less accurate values such as .66 or .67 are not acceptable.

Acceptable ways to grid $\frac{2}{3}$ = .6666...

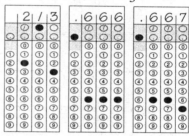

41. 32 is $\frac{2}{7}$ of what number?

42. Half of the members of a graduating class are going to college. One-fourth of these are going to the local municipal college. What part of the graduating class is going to the municipal college?

43. If books bought at prices ranging from $2.00 to $3.50 are sold at prices ranging from $3.00 to $4.25, what is the greatest possible profit that might be made by selling 8 books? (Omit the $ sign in your answer.)

44. Find the area of *ABCD*.

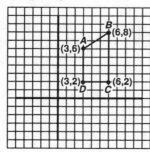

45. The distance *s* in feet that a body falls in *t* seconds is given by the formula $s = 16t^2$. If a body has been falling for 5 seconds, how far (in feet) will it fall during the 6th second?

46. How long is the shadow of a 30-foot tree when a 20-foot pole casts a 14-foot shadow?

47. A cup of oatmeal weighs 3 ounces. A cup of pancake mix weighs 5 ounces. How many cups of oatmeal will have the same weight as 3 cups of pancake mix?

48. Abe can mow the lawn in 15 minutes. Ben can mow the lawn in 20 minutes. Carl can mow the lawn in 30 minutes. They work together for 5 minutes. What part of the lawn was mowed?

49. The sum of the base angles of an isosceles triangle is one-half the vertex angle. How many degrees are there in the vertex angle?

50. In $\triangle ABC$, $AB = 2\sqrt{2}$, $BC = 8$, $\angle ABC \stackrel{\circ}{=} 45$. Find area *ABC*.

IF YOU FINISH BEFORE 30 MINUTES, YOU MAY CHECK YOUR WORK ON THIS SECTION ONLY. DO NOT TURN TO ANY OTHER SECTION IN THE TEST.

STOP

ANSWER KEY

Verbal Reasoning Section 1

1. A	*6.* E	*11.* D	*16.* B	*21.* D	*26.* A
2. E	*7.* E	*12.* C	*17.* C	*22.* B	*27.* E
3. A	*8.* D	*13.* B	*18.* D	*23.* C	*28.* C
4. C	*9.* D	*14.* B	*19.* A	*24.* B	*29.* D
5. B	*10.* E	*15.* C	*20.* C	*25.* E	*30.* C

Mathematical Reasoning Section 2

Note: Each correct answer to the mathematics questions is keyed by number to the corresponding topic in Chapters 8 and 9. These numerals refer to the topics listed below, with specific page references in parentheses.

1. Basic Fundamental Operations (179–182)
2. Algebraic Operations (182–183)
3. Using Algebra (182–184, 187)
4. Exponents, Roots, and Radicals (184–185)
5. Inequalities (188–189)
6. Fractions (182, 198)
7. Decimals (200)
8. Percent (200)
9. Averages (201)
10. Motion (203)
11. Ratio and Proportion (204–205)
12. Mixtures and Solutions (178)
13. Work (206–207)
14. Coordinate Geometry (194)
15. Geometry (189–193, 195)
16. Quantitative Comparisons (211–212)
17. Data Interpretation (208)

1. **D** (1, 6)	*6.* **A** (1)	*11.* **B** (15)	*16.* **E** (15)	*21.* **A** (14)
2. **D** (4, 6)	*7.* **B** (1)	*12.* **B** (2)	*17.* **A** (5, 15)	*22.* **B** (15)
3. **B** (15)	*8.* **D** (3)	*13.* **C** (5, 15)	*18.* **C** (11)	*23.* **A** (15)
4. **E** (2)	*9.* **E** (4)	*14.* **B** (3, 8)	*19.* **D** (15)	*24.* **C** (1, 15)
5. **D** (8)	*10.* **D** (2)	*15.* **D** (3, 8)	*20.* **E** (15)	*25.* **D** (17)

Writing Skills Section 3

1. D	*8.* D	*15.* D	*22.* E	*29.* D	*36.* B
2. D	*9.* E	*16.* D	*23.* D	*30.* E	*37.* A
3. A	*10.* B	*17.* E	*24.* E	*31.* A	*38.* C
4. E	*11.* B	*18.* D	*25.* A	*32.* B	*39.* D
5. D	*12.* A	*19.* C	*26.* D	*33.* B	
6. B	*13.* C	*20.* C	*27.* B	*34.* C	
7. B	*14.* B	*21.* D	*28.* B	*35.* C	

Verbal Reasoning Section 4

31. E	*36.* C	*41.* B	*46.* D	*51.* B	*56.* B
32. C	*37.* C	*42.* A	*47.* A	*52.* B	*57.* E
33. E	*38.* B	*43.* C	*48.* D	*53.* A	*58.* D
34. B	*39.* C	*44.* D	*49.* B	*54.* D	*59.* D
35. C	*40.* D	*45.* B	*50.* D	*55.* B	*60.* E

Mathematical Reasoning Section 5

26. **C** (1, 16)	*29.* **A** (4, 6, 16)	*32.* **D** (2, 16)	*35.* **C** (15, 16)	*38.* **C** (3, 16)
27. **D** (2, 16)	*30.* **B** (2, 16)	*33.* **C** (15, 16)	*36.* **C** (15, 16)	*39.* **D** (2, 16)
28. **D** (2, 16)	*31.* **C** (1, 16)	*34.* **D** (15, 16)	*37.* **C** (15, 16)	*40.* **A** (11, 16)

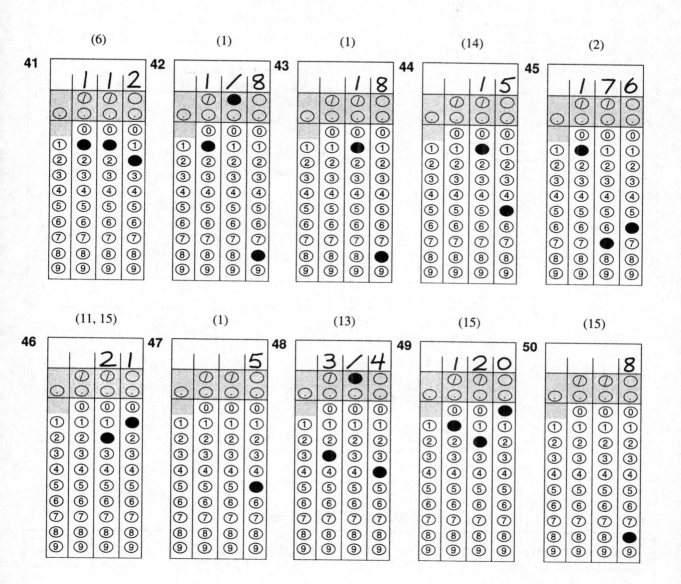

SCORING CHART — TYPICAL TEST I

Verbal Sections

Section 1   Questions 1–30
Number correct   _____ (A)
Number omitted   _____ (B)
Number incorrect   _____ (C)
$1/4$ (C) =   _____ (D)
Raw Score:
  (A) – (D) =   _____

Section 3   Questions 31–60
Number correct   _____ (A)
Number omitted   _____ (B)
Number incorrect   _____ (C)
$1/4$ (C) =   _____ (D)
Raw Score:
  (A) – (D) =   _____

Total Verbal Raw Score:
  (Section 1 +
  Section 3) =   _____

Mathematical Sections

Section 2   Questions 1–25
Number correct   _____ (A)
Number incorrect   _____ (B)
(A) – $1/4$ (B) =   _____ Raw Score I

Section 4   Questions 26–40
Number correct   _____ (C)
Number incorrect   _____ (D)
(C) – $1/3$ (D) =   _____ Raw Score II

Section 4   Questions 41–50
Number correct   _____ Raw Score III

Total Mathematical Raw Score:
  (Raw Scores I + II
  + III) =   _____

Writing Section

Section 3   Questions 1–39
Number correct   _____ (A)
Number incorrect   _____ (B)
$1/4$ (B) =   _____ (C)
(no penalty for omitted questions)
Writing Raw Score:
  (A) – (C) =   _____

EVALUATION CHART

Study your score. Your raw score on the Verbal and Mathematical Reasoning Sections is an indication of your probable achievement on the PSAT/NMSQT. As a guide to the amount of work you need or want to do with this book, study the following.

Raw Score			Self-rating
Verbal	Mathematical	Writing	
55–60	41–50	37–39	Superior
44–54	25–40	31–36	Very good
39–43	20–24	25–30	Satisfactory
35–38	16–19	19–24	Average
29–34	10–15	13–18	Needs further study
20–28	7–9	6–12	Needs intensive study
0–19	0–6	0–5	Probably inadequate

ANSWER EXPLANATIONS

Verbal Reasoning Section 1

1. **A**   An audacious or *daring* approach succeeded; a less daring approach would have failed.

2. **E**   A plot that people have seen over and over again is by definition *trite* (stale; overdone). Note that the second clause gives you the information you need to fill in the word missing in the first clause.

3. **A**   Ginger spent hours thinking up wicked ways to pay her brother back for his trick. In other words, she tried to *retaliate*.

4. **C**   A bad name stains or *taints* one's reputation.

5. **B**   Plumes are feathers. If the male and female birds have the same plumage, they must look alike. Therefore, *distinguishing between* the males and females, telling them apart, must be difficult.

6. **E**   *Although* signals a contrast. You are looking for a word that is an antonym or near-antonym for *persistent* and *extended*. That word is *sporadic* (occasional; intermittent).

7. **E**   The scientist is aware that future data may cause her to change her opinion. Therefore, she is willing to express only a *tentative* (temporary; provisional) opinion.

8. **D**   A *gregarious* or sociable person normally seeks the company of others. However, because of his legal problems, this usually sociable individual is *shunning* or avoiding others. Note how the signal word *although* sets up a contrast.

9. **D**   Picasso always was exactly on time. He prided himself on his *punctuality* (promptness).

10. **E**   The innovations for which Maria Montessori became famous were creative teaching techniques; they transformed the field of *pedagogy* (teaching; art of education).

11. **D**   The statement asserts that the three are not in fact independent or separate but are instead *inseparable*. Again, the signal word (in this case, *but*) sets up a contrast that lets you know you are looking for an antonym or near-antonym of *independent*.

12. **C**   If depression occurs when nerve cells get too little of certain chemicals, it makes sense to have these cells get more of the chemicals. This can be done by making more of the chemicals *available to* the cells.

13. **B**   The contrast in Hugo is between *piety* or devotion ("a scene of chaste and holy love") and *ribaldry* or indecency (a scene of "coarse and profane licentiousness"). Note that the sentence's parallelism demands that the two missing words be antonyms or near-antonyms.

14. **B**   To sink *ignominiously* is to do so shamefully or disgracefully. Such an end lacks dignity or honor. Note again how the clue to the missing word in one clause can be found in the clause without the blank. In this case, the key phrase is "lacked. . .the dignity of being sunk."

15. **C**   In calling the smuggled urn a "hot pot," Hoving is speaking informally or *colloquially*. (*Hot* here is a slang term meaning stolen or illegally obtained.) Because the urn had been smuggled into the country, there clearly were unresolved questions about its *origin*.

16. **B**   An *egotistical* or self-centered and conceited person would find it difficult to *tolerate* or bear someone else's success.

17. **C**   That the interrogator is subtle in discrimination or judgment shows she can conduct matters with *finesse* (tact; delicacy); that she is *expeditious* (efficient and prompt) in manner shows she can conduct matters with *dispatch* (speed). Note the use of parallel structure in this sentence.

18. **D**   The author is a passenger who has been aboard while the boat has touched at several ports (line 15).

19. **A**   The author is condescending in commenting on dulled feathers and fifth-rate freighters.

20. **C**   Since the waiters are said to be dreaming they served at Maxim's, it is most likely that Maxim's is both a famous restaurant and a desirable place to work.

21. **D**   The chef sweats because he is nervous while his delicate sugar cathedral is being carried up the stairs.

22. **B**   The chef originally made the sugar cathedral in a famous kitchen. He has come down in the world, but retains his self-esteem.

23. **C**   The passage points out that in this period the differences between the two branches of the suffrage movement were diminishing in importance. Thus, it is *accounting for changes* occurring in the movement. Choice A is incorrect. Both are mentioned (along with other suffragist leaders) in the context of the movements they led, but, while the movements are directly contrasted, Anthony and Howe are not directly contrasted. Choice B is incorrect. The movement did not advance in this period. Choice D is incorrect. The divisions were becoming less important, not more so, as the two branches became increasingly alike in nature. Choice E is incorrect. It is unsupported by the passage.

24. **B**   Fighting to win women the right to vote, Stanton and Anthony were willing to work with anyone who espoused or *championed* their cause.

25. **E** The National took up the cudgels and fought for *all* women in distress, whatever their social or economic standing.

26. **A** The revered Mrs. Howe stood for the forces of propriety that were engulfing the suffragist movement. The embodiment of decorum, she was a *venerated figurehead* to be admired and respected, not a revolutionary firebrand to be followed into the battle. Choice B is incorrect. Nothing in the passage suggests Mrs. Howe was overzealous. Choice C is incorrect. Mrs. Howe was orthodox in her thinking, not heterodox. Choice D is incorrect. A lay preacher is by definition not a member of the clergy. Therefore, Mrs. Howe was not an ordained cleric. Choice E is incorrect. Mrs. Howe was characterized by a lack of militancy.

27. **E** The author describes the Haymarket incident as the crowning touch in the antilabor smear campaign because the bombing was the final *detail completing* the image of organized labor as a hotbed of terrorists and radicals.

28. **C** The author refers to the public's reaction to the Molly Maguire trials as "hysteria" that was "whipped up" or deliberately incited. Clearly, her attitude towards it is that it was *overwrought* or overexcited. Note how the use of words that convey emotion ("hysteria") help you to determine the author's attitude to the subject.

29. **D** The first sentence of the fourth paragraph indicates that the author's concern is to avoid a misconception or *correct a misapprehension* about what caused the trend toward conservatism in the suffrage movement.

30. **C** If even the radical Susan B. Anthony would have had second thoughts about flouting or disregarding federal election laws, we may logically infer that the ordinary, not quite so militant movement member would have viewed such actions with disapproval or *disapprobation*.

Mathematical Reasoning Section 2

1. **D** $\frac{1}{2} \cdot \frac{4}{7} = \frac{2}{7}$ or $\frac{4}{14}$

   $\frac{5}{7} \cdot \frac{1}{2} = \frac{5}{14}$

   Difference = $\frac{1}{14}$

2. **D** $\sqrt{\frac{16}{36} + \frac{1}{4}}$

   $\sqrt{\frac{16}{36} + \frac{9}{36}}$

   $\sqrt{\frac{25}{36}} = \frac{5}{6}$

3. **B**

   $x + x > 9$
   $2x > 9$
   $x > \frac{9}{2}$
   $x > 4.5$

   Because x is a whole number, the shortest possible length of side $\overline{AB}$ is 5.

4. **E** $100 = \frac{\sqrt{100}}{2} = \frac{10}{2} = 5$

5. **D** Increase = 500

   $\frac{\text{increase}}{\text{original}} = \frac{500}{2500} = \frac{1}{5} = 20\%$

6. **A** Saving on one round-trip = $58.00 - $54.50 = $3.50

   Savings on 3 round-trips = $10.50

7. **B** Length of all cars = 10×16 feet = 160 feet. Observe that there are nine spaces between 10 automobiles. Distance of these nine spaces = 6 inches $\times 9$ = 54 inches or $4\frac{1}{2}$ feet. Distance from front of first car to rear of last vehicle = $160 + 4\frac{1}{2} = 164\frac{1}{2}$ feet.

8. **D** Any two-digit number = ten times the tens digit plus the units digit.
   y = tens digit [given]
   x = units digit [given]
   $10y + x$ = the number

9. **E** $\sqrt{4} - 3x$ will have a real value unless $4 - 3x$ is negative. This will occur if $3x > 4$. Of the choices given, only $x = 2$ makes $3x > 4$.

10. **D** $\frac{1}{x} = \frac{a}{b}$

    $ax = b$ [product of means = product of extremes]

    $x = \frac{b}{a}$

11. **B** Diameter of outer circle = 44 feet
    Radius = 22 feet
    Area of outer circle = $\pi r^2 = \pi(22)^2 = 484\pi$ square feet
    Diameter of inner circle = 40 feet
    Radius = 20 feet
    Area of inner circle = $\pi r^2 = \pi(20)^2 = 400\pi$ square feet
    Area of patch (difference of two circles) = $484\pi - 400\pi = 84\pi$ square feet

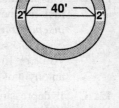

12. **B** Factor and cancel:

$$\frac{9K^3 - 9m^2K}{3K^2 - 3mK}$$

$$\frac{9K(K^2 - m^2)}{3K(K - m)}$$

$$\frac{3K(K + m)(K-m)}{3K(K-m)} = 3K + 3m$$

13. **C** $CB = \frac{1}{2} CE$ and $AD = \frac{1}{2} CD$, but since $CE > CD$, CB cannot equal AD. For the same reason II is not correct. However, consider the following: CB is one half of CE, and CA is one half of CD. Since $CE > CD$, one half of CE (or CB) > one half of CD (or CA). Doubles, triples, halves, thirds, etc., of unequal quantities are unequal in the same order.

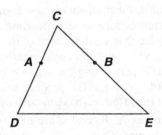

14. **B** Let x = selling price.
$0.20x$ = profit [given]
Cost + profit = selling price
$\$72 + 0.20x = x$
$72 = x - 0.20x$
$7200 = 100x - 20x$ [multiply by 100]
$7200 = 80x$
$\$90 = x$

15. **D** Marked price less 20% = selling price   (1)
20% of selling price = profit   (2)
Cost = $1.60   (3)
Cost + profit = selling price   (4)
Let x = marked price.
$x - 0.20x$ = selling price   (1)
$0.20 (x - 0.20x)$ or $(0.20x - 0.04x)$ = profit   (2)
$1.60 + 0.20x - 0.04x = x - 0.20x$ (4)
$0.20x - 0.04x - x + 0.20x = -1.60$
[multiply by 100]
$20x - 4x - 100x + 20x = -160$
$-64x = -160$
$64x = 160$
$x = \$2.50$

16. **E** Let x = area of top of melted cube in the rectangular solid (in square feet).
Volume in rectangular solid = area of top of melted surface x height $= (x)\left(\frac{1}{8} \text{ foot}\right) = \frac{x}{8}$ cubic feet
Volume of original cube = 1' × 1" × 1' = 1 cubic foot
Since the amount (volume) of metal cube is equal to melted material,
$\frac{x}{8} = 1$ and
$x = 8$ square feet.

17. **A** The exterior angle of a triangle is equal to the sum of both remote interior angles, or $d = a + b$. Therefore I is correct and II is incorrect. III is incorrect becuase $d + c = 180$ in various combinations.

18. **C** $\frac{5}{8}$ of the class consists of boys.
$\frac{3}{8}$ of the class consists of girls.
According to the data, the only ones that may not graduate are the $\frac{1}{10}$ of the boys. They make up $\frac{1}{10}$ of $\frac{5}{8}$ of the class or $\frac{1}{16}$ of the class. Therefore the remaining $\frac{15}{16}$ may graduate.

19. **D** Because the diameter of each circle equals 2 feet, the maximum number of circles along the width is 2. Total number of circles equals 10.
Area of circle = πr^2 or area of each circle = $\pi(1)^2 = 3.14$ square feet
Area of all 10 circles = 31.4 square feet
Area of rectangle = bh or 10 × 4 = 40 square feet
Area of tin left over = 40 − 31.4 = 8.6 square feet
The answer to the nearest square foot is 9.

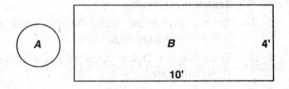

20. **E** Each side $= \frac{x}{3}$
Area = (side)^2 or $\frac{x^2}{9}$

21. **A** If two points have one coordinate the same, the distance between them is the difference between the two other coordinates
(A) $3 - (-8) \neq 5$;   (B) $0 - (-5) = 5$;
(C) $5 - 0 = 5$;   (D) $8 - 3 = 5$;
(E) $3 - (-2) = 5$

22. **B**   Area of large circle
= π(radius)^2
$\pi(2r)^2 = 4\pi r^2$
Area of shaded circle
= πr^2
$\dfrac{\text{shaded circle}}{\text{large circle}} = \dfrac{\pi r^2}{4\pi r^2}$

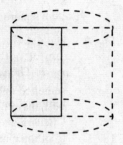

$= \dfrac{\pi r^2}{4\pi r^2} = \dfrac{1}{4}$

23. **A**   The resulting solid is a circular cylinder of height *a* and radius of circular base equal to *b*. The volume of the cylinder is equal to the area of the circular base multiplied by the altitude.
$V = \pi r^2 h$
When $r = b$ and $h = a$,
$V = (\pi)(b^2)(a)$
$V = \pi ab^2$.

24. **C**   Estimate or use a calculator. Approximately 57,000 of a total of about 224,000 are in the navy. $\frac{57}{224} = 0.25 +$ or $\frac{1}{4}$. $\left(\frac{1}{4}\right)$ (360 degrees) = 90 degrees.

25. **D**   Fatalities by group: (per 1 million)
(A) 175 (B) 148 (C) 125 (D) 100 (E) 102

Writing Skills Section 3

1. **D**   Lack of parallel structure. Change the clause *what his serial number was* to a noun (*serial number*) to match the other items in the list.

2. **D**   Error in tense. Change *will handle* to *handled*.

3. **A**   Error in case. Change *whom* to *who*.

4. **E**   Sentence is correct.

5. **D**   Error in agreement. Since the antecedent of *its* is *lawyers* change *its* to *their*.

6. **B**   Error in tense. Delete the word *has* to make the verb *anticipated*.

7. **B**   Error in agreement. *Everybody* is a singular pronoun. Change *their* to *his* or *her*.

8. **D**   Error in diction. The verb *to lay* (past tense is *laid*) means to put or to place; the verb *to lie* (past tense is *lay*) means to recline. Therefore, change *laid back* to *lay back*.

9. **E**   Sentence is correct.

10. **B**   Error in agreement. *Data* is a plural noun. Change *was* to *were*.

11. **B**   Error in case. Change *he and I* to *him and me*.

12. **A**   The verb *feels* should be followed by an adjective (*bad*).

13. **C**   Error in tense. Change *will be sang* to *will be sung*.

14. **B**   Error in case. Change *him* to *his*.

15. **D**   Error in diction. Change *appointed of* to *appointed to*.

16. **D**   Lack of agreement. The subject is *quantity* (singular) and requires a singular verb *was missing*.

17. **E**   Sentence is correct.

18. **D**   Faulty diction. The conjunction *than* helps to make a comparison, not *then*.

19. **C**   Error in agreement. In a neither-nor construction the verb agrees with the noun or pronoun which comes immediately before the verb. *Driver was able to identify* is correct.

20. **C**   This sentence illustrates the use of the future perfect tense. The present perfect tense, as used in Choice A, and the past perfect tense, as used in Choice B, are incorrect. Choice C correctly indicates that an anticipated event will be completed before a definite time in the future. Choice D is weak because of the use of the passive voice and the consequent vagueness as to who is performing the action. Choice E is awkward because of the needless separation of subject (*we*) from verb (*shall have traveled*).

21. **D**   Choices A, B, and C are examples of run-on sentences. Choices B, C, and E also confuse the meanings of *complementary* and *complimentary*. Choice E leaves the verb *is not* without a subject. Choice D corrects the run-on sentence and adds no other errors.

22. **E**   In Choices A and B we find an unwarranted shift from the third person pronoun *one* to the second person pronoun *you*. Choices C and D improperly use *affect* instead of *effect*.

23. **D**   Choices A and B illustrate the incorrect use of *due to*. The change to *inasmuch* as in Choice C creates a sentence fragment. Choice E is poor because it omits the causal relationship implied by the original sentence.

24. **E**   Choices A and B improperly use the present perfect tense. In Choice C we find an unnecessary separation of the noun (*explanation*) and its modifier (*of her mysterious ailment*). Choice D changes the original meaning of the sentence.

25. **A**   Choices C and D create run-on sentences. Choice B changes the meaning of the sentence. Choice E makes an unwarranted shift to the passive voice, resulting in a vague and awkward sentence.

26. **D**   Choices A and B violate parallel structure. Choices C and E change the meaning of the original sentence.

27. **B** The *if* clause with which the sentence begins expresses a condition contrary to fact and therefore requires the subjunctive mood. Choice B provides the necessary subjunctive. Choice C changes the meaning of the sentence.

28. **B** Choices A, D, and E compare two things which cannot be directly compared—subways and cities. In Choice C, the omission of *other* changes the meaning of the sentence.

29. **D** Choices A, B, and E omit important parts of the verb. *Hopefully* in Choices C and E is wrong; although many people use it this way, most grammarians do not accept it as a substitute for *we hope*. (Strictly speaking, *hopefully* should only be used to mean *in a hopeful way*, as in *The farmer searched the skies hopefully looking for signs of rain*.)

30. **E** Choice A, has a dangling participle. Choices B, C, and D change the meaning of the sentence.

31. **A** *Being that* in Choices B and E is nonstandard and therefore incorrect. Choices C and D make slight changes in the meaning of the sentence.

32. **B** Choice A contains a misplaced modifier. Was the flight attendant partially defrosted? So Choice A would imply. In Choices C and D, the word *only* should come immediately before *partially*. In Choice E, the transitive verb *served* does not have an object.

33. **B** Choices A, C, D, and E suffer from the lack of agreement between the pronouns *they* and *them* (plural) and their antecedent *anyone* (singular).

34. **C** Choice A contains the extremely awkward phrase *to see underdogs being the one rooted for*. Choice B uses the coordinating conjunction *but*, which makes no sense in the context. Choice C clearly and concisely combines the thoughts contained in the two sentences. It is the best answer. Choice D contains a clause and a phrase that have no grammatical relationship. Choice E contains a comma splice between *Americans* and *for example*.

35. **C** All sentences except 3 contribute to the discussion of the underdog. Sentence 3 is an unnecessary digression. Therefore, it is the best answer.

36. **B** Choice A is grammatically correct, but it refers to Americans' desire to feel good, a topic not discussed in paragraph 2. Choice B accurately introduces the topic of the paragraph. It is the best answer. Choices C and D are similar to A. Choice E is awkwardly expressed and contains the pronoun *themselves*, which refers grammatically to *traditions* instead of to *Americans*.

37. **A** Choice A clearly and accurately combines the sentences. It is the best answer. Choice B is awkward and cumbersome. Choice C contains an awkward shift in verb tense from present (*look*) to past perfect (*had been*). Choice D contains the adverb *poorly*, which should be an adjective and should modify *immigrants* instead of *coming*.

38. **C** Choice A is not an effective revision. It changes the focus of the discussion and contains a pronoun *their*, which refers grammatically to *Americans* instead of to *underdog*. Choice B contains an awkward shift in verb tense from past (*believed*) to present (*succeed*). Choice C follows naturally from the preceding sentence and is accurately expressed. It is the best answer. Choice D is grammatical, but it shifts the focus of the discussion. Choice E is confusing and contains the pronouns *they* and *their*, which lack a specific referent.

39. **D** Choice A contains some transitional material but shifts verb tenses from past (*went*) to present (*defeat*). Choice B, which lacks a main verb, is a sentence fragment. Choice C, although grammatically correct, seems incomplete because the pronoun *it* lacks a specific referent. Choice D provides a smooth transition between paragraphs and introduces the topic of paragraph 3. It is the best answer. Choice E lacks any meaningful transitional material.

Verbal Reasoning Section 4

31. **E** A *crowbar* is a tool used for *prying*; a *shovel* is a tool used for *digging*. (Definition)

32. **C** A *trough* is a feeding bin for *pigs*; a *manger* is a feeding bin for *cattle*. (Function)

33. **E** A *pedestrian* travels along a *sidewalk*; a *boat* travels along a *waterway*. (Function)

34. **B** A *sculptor* works in a *studio*; a *blacksmith* works in a *smithy*. (Worker and Workplace)

35. **C** To *intimidate* someone is to cause that person *fear*; to *exasperate* someone is to cause that person *irritation*. (Cause and Effect)

36. **C** By definition, *food* that is *insipid* (dull; tasteless) lacks flavor; *remarks* that are *vapid* (inane; empty) lack sense. (Defining Characteristic)

37. **C** A *hawk* seizes its prey with its *talons*; a *lion*, with its *claws*. (Part to Whole)

38. **B** A *diva* (singer) performs an *aria*; an *actor* performs a *soliloquy*. (Defining Characteristic)

39. **C** An *ophthalmologist* is a physician who specializes in the treatment of disorders of the *eyes*; a *dermatologist* is a physician who specializes in the treatment of disorders of the *skin*.
(Defining Characteristic)

40. **D** Something *irksome* (annoying; vexing) by definition *chafes*; something *lurid* (revolting; horrifying) by definition *shocks*.   (Definition)

41. **B** *Slag* is the waste matter or residue left over when *metal* is made; the *dregs* are the waste matter or residue left over when *wine* is made.
(Part to Whole)

42. **A** A *malingerer* (someone who goofs off) shuns *work*; a *recluse* (hermit) shuns *company*.
(Defining Characteristic)

43. **C** To *ogle* (look at someone coquettishly) indicates *flirtatiousness*; to *gape* (stare at in wonder) indicates *astonishment*.
(Action and Its Significance)

44. **D** You can arrive at the correct answer by the process of elimination. Statement I is false. While sea action plays a part in erosion, the author does not say it is the most important factor in erosion. Therefore, you can eliminate Choices A and E. Statement II is true. The first purely synthetic oil "has yet to be produced." Therefore, you can eliminate Choice C. Statement III is true. New rock is born or created "through the effects of gravity." Therefore, you can eliminate Choice B. Only Choice D is left. It is the correct answer.

45. **B** The author mentions the Grand Canyon in the context of speaking of rivers as "immensely powerful destructive agencies." The dramatic canyon illustrates the *devastating impact* a river can have.

46. **D** In the last paragraph the author states that "the cause of the metamorphosis" of decayed vegetation and dead aquatic life into oil is not known. We lack full understanding of the process by which oil is created; therefore, our understanding is *deficient*. Choice C is incorrect. Our knowledge is not *erroneous* or false; it is simply incomplete.

47. **A** The last sentence states that oil is always found "on the sites of ancient seas and lakes."

48. **D** The author describes several processes (erosion, rock formation, oil formation). He states the possibility that a chemical catalyst is involved in oil formation. He cites the Grand Canyon as an example of what a river can do to the land. He mentions the limitation of our ability to produce oil synthetically. However, he never proposes a solution to any problem.

49. **B** The term *reaches* here refers to the vast, *unbroken stretches* of time it takes for the mountains to erode and, out of their dust, for new rock to be formed at the bottom of the sea.

50. **D** Johnson is writing of exposing languages to corruption. The corruption to which he refers is therefore *linguistic*.

51. **B** The author judges Johnson's view of Americans on the basis of Johnson's well-known views of the Scots. Because the Scots lived relatively far from London ("civilization" to Johnson), he considered them less than civilized. *Given America's even greater distance from London,* to Johnson anything American would inevitably have seemed wholly barbarous.

52. **B** Think of a child using both hands to grab as many toys as he possibly can hold. The author is suggesting that the English language has borrowed many, many words from foreign languages. In other words, the borrowing has been unrestrained or *immoderate*.

53. **A** Even the new terms, says the author, are "compounded out of English elements, according to the rules of English syntax." In other words, they are *patterned on traditional English usage*.

54. **D** To turn a sentence is to fashion or *phrase* it, giving it shape.

55. **B** The author takes Matthews' view to represent the majority viewpoint held by responsible, "less jaundiced" authorities today. Thus he quotes Matthews in order to *present a measured judgment*.

56. **B** Sentence 2 indicates that those Americanisms that make progress with the British public (that is, find acceptance and are popularly used) are co-opted by the British, who say such terms are really old English and therefore not really Americanisms at all.

57. **E** Since the British, according to this passage, justify their adoption of Americanisms by maintaining they are actually British terms whose use dates back to ancient days ("Chaucer's time"), it is clear that these terms are being incorporated into British English and that this absorption of Americanisms is inevitable.

58. **D** Obviously, the author does not take the British attitude of superiority seriously. He exaggerates their position, talking about holy wars, and poking fun at them with such terms as "guardians of the national linguistic chastity." He looks on their assumption of American linguistic inferiority with *humor*, but there is an edge to his amusement: he is *sardonic* (mocking) in ridiculing them.

59. **D** The author uses "put down" here in much the same way one would use it in the phrase "putting down a riot." He believes the British authorities want all Americanisms *thoroughly suppressed*.

60. **E** Given the extreme stand he takes about the British "guardians of the national linguistic chastity" engaging in a holy war against those

who violate the noble English language, the author of Passage 2 seems very unlikely to believe that any such moderate view of American English could prevail. His most likely reaction, therefore, would be one of *outright incredulity* or disbelief.

Mathematical Reasoning Section 5

26. C Note both columns have the factors (8) and (6). Consider the other factors. (4)(10) in Column A cancel (40) in Column B. Also the factors (2)(12) in Column A cancel (24) in Column B.

27. D $x^2 - 25 = 0$
$$x^2 = 25$$
$$x = +5 \text{ and } -5$$

28. D In this equation $x = 5$. Any value of y will satisfy this equation.

29. A $\sqrt{\frac{1}{9}} + \sqrt{\frac{1}{16}} = \frac{1}{3} + \frac{1}{4} = \frac{7}{12}$

$$\sqrt{\frac{1}{16} + \frac{1}{9}} = \sqrt{\frac{25}{144}} = \frac{5}{12}$$
$$\frac{7}{12} > \frac{5}{12}$$

30. B If $x = 0$, $2x(y + z) = 0$.
For Column B, $y(x + z) = y(0 + z)$.
Since y and z are positive, the value of $y(x + z)$ is positive.

31. C Since $\frac{15}{7} = 2\frac{1}{7}$ and $\frac{41}{14} = 2\frac{13}{14}$, the largest integer less than $\frac{15}{7}$ is 2 and the largest integer less than $\frac{41}{14}$ is also 2.

32. D If $a = 5$, $a^2 = 25$.
If $a = 10$, $a^2 = 100$.
If $b = 2$, $b^3 = 8$.
If $b = 3$, $b^3 = 27$.

33. C $\triangle ABC$ is inscribed in a semicircle. $\therefore ABC$ is a right triangle. Since $AB = AC$, ABC is an isosceles right triangle. Since $BC = 10$, $AC = AB = 5\sqrt{2}$. The area of $ABC = \frac{1}{2}(AC)(AB)$ or $\frac{1}{2}(5\sqrt{2})(5\sqrt{2})$ or 25. The perimeter of the square equals 20. Therefore each side equals 5 and the area of the square is 5^2 or 25.

34. D Only if $\triangle KML$ is equilateral would the vertex angle K be equal to the measures of angles L and M. If $\triangle KML$ is isosceles, then K could be more than or less than 60°.

35. C The perimeter of the semicircle equals the diameter plus half the circumference of the circle. The diameter, the hypotenuse of a 3:4:5 triangle, equals 5. The circumference equals 5π. One-half the circumference (2.5π) plus 5 equals the perimeter of the semicircle.

36. C The value of
$$x = 180 - (55 + 50)$$
$$= 180 - 105$$
$$= 75°$$

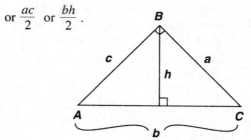

37. C Since $AB \perp BC$, the area of
$ABC = \frac{1}{2}(AB)(BC)$ or $\frac{1}{2}ac$
or $\frac{ac}{2}$ or $\frac{bh}{2}$.

38. A Because x is 25% of y, $x = 0.25y$ or, equivalently, $y = 4x$. Since y is 50% of z, $y = 0.50z$ or, equivalently, $z = 2y = 2(4x) = 8x$. Average of x, y, and $z = \frac{x + y + z}{3} = \frac{x + 4x + 8x}{3} = \frac{13x}{3}$, which is greater than $4x$.

39. D With negative values as well as positive values for x and for y the sum of their squares would equal 10.

40. A If 1 kilometer $= \frac{5}{8}$ mile, then
$\frac{5}{8}$ of a kilometer $= \left(\frac{5}{8}\right)\left(\frac{5}{8}\right)$ mile or $\frac{25}{64}$ mile, which is less than 1 mile.

41. 112 Let $x =$ the number.
$$\frac{2}{7}x = 32$$
$$x = 112$$

42. $\frac{1}{8}$ $\frac{1}{4}$ of $\frac{1}{2} = \frac{1}{8}$

43. 18 Greatest profit will be made when they are purchased at lowest price ($2.00) and sold for the maximum price ($4.25). Maximum profit for each book is $2.25. Therefore for 8 books, maximum profit = $18.00

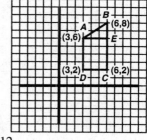

44. 15 Draw $AE \perp BC$.
Area of rectangle formed equals base (3) × altitude (4) = 12.
Area of triangle AEB equals $\frac{1}{2}$ (base 2 × altitude 3) = 3.
Area of $ABCD = 12 + 3 = 15$.

45. 176 $s = 16t^2$ [given]

$s = 16(5)^2$ [substitution]

$s = 16(25) = 400$ feet covered in 5 seconds

For 6 seconds, $t = 6$

$s = 16t^2$

$s = 16(6)^2$

$s = 16(36) = 576$ feet

$576 - 400 = 176$ feet

46. 21   Let x = size of shadow of the tree.

$$\frac{\text{size of object}}{\text{size of shadow}} = \frac{20\text{-foot pole}}{14\text{-foot shadow}} = \frac{30\text{-foot tree}}{x}$$

$20x = (30)(14)$

$20x = 420$

$x = 21$ feet

47. 5   1 cup pancake mix = 5 ounces

3 cups pancake mix = 15 ounces

3 ounces oatmeal = 1 cup

$\therefore$ 15 ounces oatmeal = 5 cups

48. $\frac{3}{4}$ In 5 minutes Abe does $\frac{5}{15}$ or $\frac{1}{3}$ of the lawn.

In 5 minutes Ben does $\frac{5}{20}$ or $\frac{1}{4}$ of the lawn.

In 5 minutes Carl does $\frac{5}{30}$ or $\frac{1}{6}$ of the lawn.

Total done = $\frac{1}{3} + \frac{1}{4} + \frac{1}{6} = \frac{3}{4}$

49. 120   Let x = vertex angle.

Let y = each base angle of the isosceles triangle.

$x + y + y = 180°$. [The sum of the angles of a triangle equals a straight angle.]

$(y + y) = \frac{1}{2} x$ [given]

$2y = \frac{x}{2}$

$4y = x$

$4y + y + y = 180°$ [substitution]

$6y = 180°$

$y = 30°$

$x = 4y = 120°$

50. 8   Draw $AD \perp BC$.

In $\triangle ABC$, $\angle BAD \stackrel{\circ}{=} 45$

$\therefore BD = AD$;

$AB = 2\sqrt{2}$ [given]

$\triangle ABD$ is a 45°-45°-90° triangle. The hypotenuse,

$a\sqrt{2}$, equals $2\sqrt{2}$, so

$a = 2$. Thus, $AD = 2$.

Area of $\triangle ABC = \frac{bh}{2} = \frac{(8)(2)}{(2)} = 8$

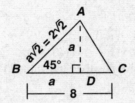

Answer Sheet
TYPICAL TEST J

Each mark should completely fill the appropriate space, and should be as dark as all other marks. Make all erasures complete. Traces of an erasure may be read as an answer. See pages vii and 27 for explanations of timing and number of questions.

Section 1 — Verbal
30 minutes

1 Ⓐ Ⓑ Ⓒ Ⓓ Ⓔ
2 Ⓐ Ⓑ Ⓒ Ⓓ Ⓔ
3 Ⓐ Ⓑ Ⓒ Ⓓ Ⓔ
4 Ⓐ Ⓑ Ⓒ Ⓓ Ⓔ
5 Ⓐ Ⓑ Ⓒ Ⓓ Ⓔ
6 Ⓐ Ⓑ Ⓒ Ⓓ Ⓔ
7 Ⓐ Ⓑ Ⓒ Ⓓ Ⓔ
8 Ⓐ Ⓑ Ⓒ Ⓓ Ⓔ
9 Ⓐ Ⓑ Ⓒ Ⓓ Ⓔ
10 Ⓐ Ⓑ Ⓒ Ⓓ Ⓔ
11 Ⓐ Ⓑ Ⓒ Ⓓ Ⓔ
12 Ⓐ Ⓑ Ⓒ Ⓓ Ⓔ
13 Ⓐ Ⓑ Ⓒ Ⓓ Ⓔ
14 Ⓐ Ⓑ Ⓒ Ⓓ Ⓔ
15 Ⓐ Ⓑ Ⓒ Ⓓ Ⓔ
16 Ⓐ Ⓑ Ⓒ Ⓓ Ⓔ
17 Ⓐ Ⓑ Ⓒ Ⓓ Ⓔ
18 Ⓐ Ⓑ Ⓒ Ⓓ Ⓔ
19 Ⓐ Ⓑ Ⓒ Ⓓ Ⓔ
20 Ⓐ Ⓑ Ⓒ Ⓓ Ⓔ
21 Ⓐ Ⓑ Ⓒ Ⓓ Ⓔ
22 Ⓐ Ⓑ Ⓒ Ⓓ Ⓔ
23 Ⓐ Ⓑ Ⓒ Ⓓ Ⓔ
24 Ⓐ Ⓑ Ⓒ Ⓓ Ⓔ
25 Ⓐ Ⓑ Ⓒ Ⓓ Ⓔ
26 Ⓐ Ⓑ Ⓒ Ⓓ Ⓔ
27 Ⓐ Ⓑ Ⓒ Ⓓ Ⓔ
28 Ⓐ Ⓑ Ⓒ Ⓓ Ⓔ
29 Ⓐ Ⓑ Ⓒ Ⓓ Ⓔ
30 Ⓐ Ⓑ Ⓒ Ⓓ Ⓔ

Section 2 — Math
30 minutes

1 Ⓐ Ⓑ Ⓒ Ⓓ Ⓔ
2 Ⓐ Ⓑ Ⓒ Ⓓ Ⓔ
3 Ⓐ Ⓑ Ⓒ Ⓓ Ⓔ
4 Ⓐ Ⓑ Ⓒ Ⓓ Ⓔ
5 Ⓐ Ⓑ Ⓒ Ⓓ Ⓔ
6 Ⓐ Ⓑ Ⓒ Ⓓ Ⓔ
7 Ⓐ Ⓑ Ⓒ Ⓓ Ⓔ
8 Ⓐ Ⓑ Ⓒ Ⓓ Ⓔ
9 Ⓐ Ⓑ Ⓒ Ⓓ Ⓔ
10 Ⓐ Ⓑ Ⓒ Ⓓ Ⓔ
11 Ⓐ Ⓑ Ⓒ Ⓓ Ⓔ
12 Ⓐ Ⓑ Ⓒ Ⓓ Ⓔ
13 Ⓐ Ⓑ Ⓒ Ⓓ Ⓔ
14 Ⓐ Ⓑ Ⓒ Ⓓ Ⓔ
15 Ⓐ Ⓑ Ⓒ Ⓓ Ⓔ
16 Ⓐ Ⓑ Ⓒ Ⓓ Ⓔ
17 Ⓐ Ⓑ Ⓒ Ⓓ Ⓔ
18 Ⓐ Ⓑ Ⓒ Ⓓ Ⓔ
19 Ⓐ Ⓑ Ⓒ Ⓓ Ⓔ
20 Ⓐ Ⓑ Ⓒ Ⓓ Ⓔ
21 Ⓐ Ⓑ Ⓒ Ⓓ Ⓔ
22 Ⓐ Ⓑ Ⓒ Ⓓ Ⓔ
23 Ⓐ Ⓑ Ⓒ Ⓓ Ⓔ
24 Ⓐ Ⓑ Ⓒ Ⓓ Ⓔ
25 Ⓐ Ⓑ Ⓒ Ⓓ Ⓔ

Section 3 — Writing
30 minutes

1 Ⓐ Ⓑ Ⓒ Ⓓ Ⓔ
2 Ⓐ Ⓑ Ⓒ Ⓓ Ⓔ
3 Ⓐ Ⓑ Ⓒ Ⓓ Ⓔ
4 Ⓐ Ⓑ Ⓒ Ⓓ Ⓔ
5 Ⓐ Ⓑ Ⓒ Ⓓ Ⓔ
6 Ⓐ Ⓑ Ⓒ Ⓓ Ⓔ
7 Ⓐ Ⓑ Ⓒ Ⓓ Ⓔ
8 Ⓐ Ⓑ Ⓒ Ⓓ Ⓔ
9 Ⓐ Ⓑ Ⓒ Ⓓ Ⓔ
10 Ⓐ Ⓑ Ⓒ Ⓓ Ⓔ
11 Ⓐ Ⓑ Ⓒ Ⓓ Ⓔ
12 Ⓐ Ⓑ Ⓒ Ⓓ Ⓔ
13 Ⓐ Ⓑ Ⓒ Ⓓ Ⓔ
14 Ⓐ Ⓑ Ⓒ Ⓓ Ⓔ
15 Ⓐ Ⓑ Ⓒ Ⓓ Ⓔ
16 Ⓐ Ⓑ Ⓒ Ⓓ Ⓔ
17 Ⓐ Ⓑ Ⓒ Ⓓ Ⓔ
18 Ⓐ Ⓑ Ⓒ Ⓓ Ⓔ
19 Ⓐ Ⓑ Ⓒ Ⓓ Ⓔ
20 Ⓐ Ⓑ Ⓒ Ⓓ Ⓔ
21 Ⓐ Ⓑ Ⓒ Ⓓ Ⓔ
22 Ⓐ Ⓑ Ⓒ Ⓓ Ⓔ
23 Ⓐ Ⓑ Ⓒ Ⓓ Ⓔ
24 Ⓐ Ⓑ Ⓒ Ⓓ Ⓔ
25 Ⓐ Ⓑ Ⓒ Ⓓ Ⓔ
26 Ⓐ Ⓑ Ⓒ Ⓓ Ⓔ
27 Ⓐ Ⓑ Ⓒ Ⓓ Ⓔ
28 Ⓐ Ⓑ Ⓒ Ⓓ Ⓔ
29 Ⓐ Ⓑ Ⓒ Ⓓ Ⓔ
30 Ⓐ Ⓑ Ⓒ Ⓓ Ⓔ
31 Ⓐ Ⓑ Ⓒ Ⓓ Ⓔ
32 Ⓐ Ⓑ Ⓒ Ⓓ Ⓔ
33 Ⓐ Ⓑ Ⓒ Ⓓ Ⓔ
34 Ⓐ Ⓑ Ⓒ Ⓓ Ⓔ
35 Ⓐ Ⓑ Ⓒ Ⓓ Ⓔ
36 Ⓐ Ⓑ Ⓒ Ⓓ Ⓔ
37 Ⓐ Ⓑ Ⓒ Ⓓ Ⓔ
38 Ⓐ Ⓑ Ⓒ Ⓓ Ⓔ
39 Ⓐ Ⓑ Ⓒ Ⓓ Ⓔ

Section 4 — Verbal
30 minutes

31 Ⓐ Ⓑ Ⓒ Ⓓ Ⓔ
32 Ⓐ Ⓑ Ⓒ Ⓓ Ⓔ
33 Ⓐ Ⓑ Ⓒ Ⓓ Ⓔ
34 Ⓐ Ⓑ Ⓒ Ⓓ Ⓔ
35 Ⓐ Ⓑ Ⓒ Ⓓ Ⓔ
36 Ⓐ Ⓑ Ⓒ Ⓓ Ⓔ
37 Ⓐ Ⓑ Ⓒ Ⓓ Ⓔ
38 Ⓐ Ⓑ Ⓒ Ⓓ Ⓔ
39 Ⓐ Ⓑ Ⓒ Ⓓ Ⓔ
40 Ⓐ Ⓑ Ⓒ Ⓓ Ⓔ
41 Ⓐ Ⓑ Ⓒ Ⓓ Ⓔ
42 Ⓐ Ⓑ Ⓒ Ⓓ Ⓔ
43 Ⓐ Ⓑ Ⓒ Ⓓ Ⓔ
44 Ⓐ Ⓑ Ⓒ Ⓓ Ⓔ
45 Ⓐ Ⓑ Ⓒ Ⓓ Ⓔ
46 Ⓐ Ⓑ Ⓒ Ⓓ Ⓔ
47 Ⓐ Ⓑ Ⓒ Ⓓ Ⓔ
48 Ⓐ Ⓑ Ⓒ Ⓓ Ⓔ
49 Ⓐ Ⓑ Ⓒ Ⓓ Ⓔ
50 Ⓐ Ⓑ Ⓒ Ⓓ Ⓔ
51 Ⓐ Ⓑ Ⓒ Ⓓ Ⓔ
52 Ⓐ Ⓑ Ⓒ Ⓓ Ⓔ
53 Ⓐ Ⓑ Ⓒ Ⓓ Ⓔ
54 Ⓐ Ⓑ Ⓒ Ⓓ Ⓔ
55 Ⓐ Ⓑ Ⓒ Ⓓ Ⓔ
56 Ⓐ Ⓑ Ⓒ Ⓓ Ⓔ
57 Ⓐ Ⓑ Ⓒ Ⓓ Ⓔ
58 Ⓐ Ⓑ Ⓒ Ⓓ Ⓔ
59 Ⓐ Ⓑ Ⓒ Ⓓ Ⓔ
60 Ⓐ Ⓑ Ⓒ Ⓓ Ⓔ

Section 5 — Math
30 minutes

26 Ⓐ Ⓑ Ⓒ Ⓓ Ⓔ
27 Ⓐ Ⓑ Ⓒ Ⓓ Ⓔ
28 Ⓐ Ⓑ Ⓒ Ⓓ Ⓔ
29 Ⓐ Ⓑ Ⓒ Ⓓ Ⓔ
30 Ⓐ Ⓑ Ⓒ Ⓓ Ⓔ
31 Ⓐ Ⓑ Ⓒ Ⓓ Ⓔ
32 Ⓐ Ⓑ Ⓒ Ⓓ Ⓔ
33 Ⓐ Ⓑ Ⓒ Ⓓ Ⓔ
34 Ⓐ Ⓑ Ⓒ Ⓓ Ⓔ
35 Ⓐ Ⓑ Ⓒ Ⓓ Ⓔ
36 Ⓐ Ⓑ Ⓒ Ⓓ Ⓔ
37 Ⓐ Ⓑ Ⓒ Ⓓ Ⓔ
39 Ⓐ Ⓑ Ⓒ Ⓓ Ⓔ
39 Ⓐ Ⓑ Ⓒ Ⓓ Ⓔ
40 Ⓐ Ⓑ Ⓒ Ⓓ Ⓔ

Grid-in answer boxes 41, 42, 43, 44, 45, 46, 47, 48, 49, 50 (each with the same grid):

	/	/	
.	.	.	.
	0	0	0
1	1	1	1
2	2	2	2
3	3	3	3
4	4	4	4
5	5	5	5
6	6	6	6
7	7	7	7
8	8	8	8
9	9	9	9

For each question in this section, select the best answer from among the choices given and fill in the corresponding oval on the answer sheet.

Directions

Each sentence below has one or two blanks, each blank indicating that something has been omitted. Beneath the sentence are five words or sets of words labeled A through E. Choose the word or set of words that, when inserted in the sentence, best fits the meaning of the sentence as a whole.

Example:

Medieval kingdoms did not become constitutional republics overnight; on the contrary, the change was ____ .

(A) unpopular
(B) unexpected
(C) advantageous
(D) sufficient
(E) gradual   Ⓐ Ⓑ Ⓒ Ⓓ ●

1. Concern over the effects of estrogen has ____ in recent weeks as three new studies suggest that birth control pills, which contain estrogen, may increase women's risk of developing breast cancer.

    (A) heightened   (B) dissipated   (C) lapsed
    (D) suffered   (E) alternated

2. The traditional French cafe is slowly becoming ____ , a victim to the growing popularity of *le fast food*.

    (A) celebrated   (B) indispensable   (C) prevalent
    (D) extinct   (E) fashionable

3. Once known only to importers of exotic foreign delicacies, the kiwi fruit has been transplanted successfully to America and is now ____ a much wider market.

    (A) accessible to   (B) unknown to
    (C) perplexing to   (D) comparable to
    (E) uncultivated by

4. Although we expected the women's basketball coach to be ____ over the recent victory of the team, we found her surprisingly ____ .

    (A) ecstatic..gleeful   (B) ambivalent..devious
    (C) triumphant..responsive   (D) elated..naive
    (E) jubilant..disheartened

5. Continuously looking for new ways of presenting his material, for fresh methods of capturing his students' attention, he has been ____ in the classroom.

    (A) a pedant   (B) a misfit   (C) an innovator
    (D) a stoic   (E) a martinet

6. Surveying the historic monuments that lined the Mall, she was overcome with a sense of how ____ history and tradition this city of Washington was.

    (A) superseded by   (B) saturated with
    (C) irrelevant to   (D) devoid of
    (E) unadorned by

7. The debate coach suggested that he eliminate his ____ remarks in his otherwise serious speech because they were ____ .

    (A) bantering..inappropriate   (B) jesting..accurate
    (C) solemn..irrelevant   (D) tacit..digressive
    (E) perfunctory..inconsiderate

8. Measurement is, like any other human endeavor, a complex activity, subject to error, not always used ____ , and frequently misinterpreted and ____.

    (A) mistakenly..derided   (B) erratically..analyzed
    (C) systematically..organized
    (D) innovatively..refined
    (E) properly..misunderstood

9. This coming trip to France should provide me with ____ test of the value of my conversational French class.

    (A) an intimate   (B) an uncertain
    (C) a pragmatic   (D) a pretentious
    (E) an arbitrary

10. Many young people and adults, uncomfortable with math, feel it is a subject best ____ engineers, scientists, and that small, elite group endowed at birth with a talent for the ____ world of numbers.

    (A) ignored by..abstract   (B) suited to..accessible
    (C) studied by..interminable   (D) left to..esoteric
    (E) avoided by..abstruse

11. In a shocking instance of ____ research, one of the most influential researchers in the field of genetics reported on experiments that were never carried out and published deliberately ____ scientific papers on his nonexistent work.

    (A) comprehensive..abstract
    (B) theoretical..challenging
    (C) erroneous..impartial
    (D) derivative..authoritative
    (E) fraudulent..deceptive

GO ON TO THE NEXT PAGE

12. Many of the characters portrayed by Clint Eastwood are strong but ____ types, rugged men of few words.

    (A) ruthless   (B) equivocal   (C) laconic
    (D) stingy   (E) vociferous

13. Like sauces, without a certain amount of spice, conversations grow ____ .

    (A) eloquent   (B) heated   (C) elaborate
    (D) straightforward   (E) insipid

14. James Bryce and Harold Laski, household names to intellectuals in another era, appear to have ____ that decent ____ reserved for those whose major works, still in print, are rarely read.

    (A) aspired to..popularity
    (B) escaped from..notoriety
    (C) receded into..obscurity
    (D) responded to..privacy
    (E) stumbled upon..nirvana

15. Her novel published to universal acclaim, her literary gifts acknowledged by the chief figures of the Harlem Renaissance, her reputation as yet ____ by envious slights, Hurston clearly was at the ____ of her career.

    (A) undamaged..ebb   (B) untarnished..zenith
    (C) untainted..end   (D) blackened..mercy
    (E) unmarred..whim

16. Because he had assumed that the child's first, fierce rush of grief would quickly ____ , Murdstone was astonished to find him still ____ .

    (A) subside..disconsolate   (B) fade..irresolute
    (C) elapse..disingenuous   (D) escalate..forlorn
    (E) dwindle..dormant

17. Both ____ and ____ , Scrooge seldom smiled and never gave away a halfpenny.

    (A) sanguine..miserly   (B) acerbic..magnanimous
    (C) morose..munificent   (D) crabbed..parsimonious
    (E) sullen..philanthropic

Directions

Each passage below is followed by questions based on its content. Answer the questions following each passage on the basis of what is stated or implied in that passage and in any introductory material that may be provided.

Questions 18–22 are based on the following passage.

One major legacy of the civil rights movement was the establishment of black studies programs in schools throughout the nation. The following excerpt, taken from a text published in 1986, discusses that development.

Paralleling the growth of interest among professional historians during the early 1960s was a simultaneous groundswell of popular interest in the Afro-American past that was directly stimulated by the drama of the protest movement. Sensing the "Negro Mood," the journalist Lerone Bennett wrote a series of articles on Afro-American history for *Ebony* and soon after brought them together in his popular volume, *Before the Mayflower* (1962). As the nonviolent direct action movement attained its crest in 1963–64, movement activists introduced black history units into the curricula of the "freedom schools" that accompanied the school integration boycotts. Meanwhile, boards of education began to address themselves to "the racial imbalance and neutralism of pusillanimous textbooks designed to appeal to Southern as well as Northern school adoption committees." In 1964 New York City's school board published *The Negro in American History;* Detroit's social studies teachers produced *The Struggle for Freedom and Rights: Basic Facts about the Negro in American History.* Franklin, surveying the activities among publishers, teachers, and school boards, called these beginnings of curriculum revision "one of the most significant by-products of the current Civil Rights Revolution."

The relationship between these developments at the grass roots level and what was occurring in the scholarly world is of course indirect. Yet, given the context of social change in the early 1960s, Negro history was now the object of unprecedented attention among wide segments of the American population, black and white. In academe nothing demonstrated this growing legitimacy of black history better than the way in which certain scholars of both races, who had previously been ambivalent about being identified as specialists in the field, now reversed themselves.

Thus Frenise Logan, returning to an academic career, decided to attempt to publish his doctoral dissertation on blacks in late nineteenth-century North Carolina. A 1960 award encouraged him to do further research, and his expanded *The Negro in North Carolina, 1876–1894* appeared in 1964. It is true that as late as 1963 a white professor advised John W. Blassingame to avoid black history if he wanted to have "a future in the historical profession." Yet more indicative of how things were going was that 1964–65 marked a turning point for two of Kenneth Stampp's former students—Nathan Huggins and Leon Litwack. The changing intellectual milieu seems to have permitted Huggins, whose original intention of specializing in African and Afro-American history had been overruled by practical concerns, to move into what became his long-range commitment to the field. By 1965 when his interest in intellectual

GO ON TO THE NEXT PAGE

60 history found expression in the idea of doing a book on the Harlem Renaissance, the factors that earlier would have discouraged him from such a study had dissipated. For Litwack the return to Negro history was an especially vivid experience,
65 and he recalls the day he spoke at the University of Rochester, lecturing on Jacksonian democracy. Some students in the audience, sensing that his heart was just not in that topic, urged him to undertake research once again in the field to
70 which he had already contributed so significantly. He settled on the study that became *Been in the Storm So Long* (1979). In short, both Huggins and Litwack now felt able to dismiss the professional considerations that had loomed so large in their
75 earlier decision to work in other specialties and to identify themselves with what had hitherto been a marginal field of inquiry.

18. The author indicates that the growth of scholarly involvement in the study of black history was
(A) unappreciated in academic circles
(B) encouraged by the civil rights movement
(C) systematically organized
(D) unaffected by current events
(E) motivated by purely financial concerns

19. The author cites Logan, Huggins, and Litwack for their
(A) work on curriculum reform in the public schools
(B) participation in the Freedom Summer in Mississippi
(C) return to the field of Afro-American history
(D) research on blacks in nineteenth century North Carolina
(E) identification with nonviolent direct action

20. It can be inferred that prior to 1950 for a historian to choose to specialize in black history
(A) was encouraged by the academic establishment
(B) established his academic conventionality
(C) afforded him special opportunities for publication
(D) was detrimental to his professional career
(E) enhanced his contact with his colleagues

21. Which of the following best describes the purpose of the passage?
(A) To document the sacrifices made by black and white scholars in the field
(B) To defend the validity of black history as a legitimate scholarly pursuit
(C) To investigate the origins of Afro-American studies in American universities
(D) To encourage the return to the study of black history at the grass roots level
(E) To describe black history's coming of age as an academically respectable field

22. The passage suggests that Bennett's work was similar to Logan's work in which of the following ways?

I. Both Bennett's and Logan's books recorded a then relatively unfamiliar aspect of Afro-American history.
II. Both Bennett's and Logan's works were designed to appeal to a primarily academic audience.
III. Both Bennett's and Logan's works were published in a variety of formats.

(A) I only   (B) III only   (C) I and II only
(D) I and III only   (E) II and III only

Questions 23–30 are based on the following passage.

The following passage is taken from a book written in 1988 by the molecular biologist Francis Crick, best known as the discoverer of DNA.

Even a cursory look at the world of living things shows its immense variety. Though we find many different animals in zoos, they are only a
Line tiny fraction of the animals of similar size and
5 type. J. B. S. Haldane was once asked what the study of biology could tell one about the Almighty. "I'm really not sure," said Haldane, "except that he must be inordinately fond of beetles." There are thought to be at least 300,000
10 species of beetles. By contrast, there are only about 10,000 species of birds. We must also take into account all the different types of plants, to say nothing of microorganisms such as yeasts and bacteria. In addition, there are all the extinct
15 species, of which the dinosaurs are the most dramatic example, numbering in all perhaps as many as a thousand times all those alive today.
    The second property of almost all living things is their complexity and, in particular, their highly
20 organized complexity. This so impressed our forebears that they considered it inconceivable that such intricate and well-organized mechanisms would have arisen without a designer. Had I been living 150 years ago I feel sure I would have been
25 compelled to agree with this Argument from Design. Its most thorough and eloquent protagonist was the Reverend William Paley whose book, *Natural Theology—or Evidence of the Existences and Attributes of the Deity Collected from the*
30 *Appearances of Nature*, was published in 1802. Imagine, he said, that crossing a heath one found on the ground a watch in good working condition. Its design and its behavior could only be explained by invoking a maker. In the same way,
35 he argued, the intricate design of living organisms forces us to recognize that they too must have had a Designer.
    This compelling argument was shattered by Charles Darwin, who believed that the *appear-*
40 *ance* of design is due to the process of natural

GO ON TO THE NEXT PAGE

selection. This idea was put forward both by
Darwin and by Alfred Wallace, essentially independently. Their two papers were read before the
Linnean Society of July 1, 1858, but did not
45 immediately produce much reaction. In fact, the
president of the society, in his annual review,
remarked that the year that had passed had not
been marked by any striking discoveries. Darwin
wrote up a "short" version of his ideas (he had
50 planned a much longer work) as *The Origin of
Species*. When this was published in 1859, it
immediately ran through several reprintings and
did indeed produce a sensation. As well it might,
because it is plain today that it outlined the essen-
55 tial feature of the "Secret of Life." It needed only
the discovery of genetics, originally made by
Gregor Mendel in the 1860s, and, in this century,
of the molecular basis of genetics, for the secret to
stand before us in all its naked glory. It is all the
60 more astonishing that today the majority of
human beings are not aware of all this. Of those
who are aware of it, many feel (with Ronald
Reagan) that there must be a catch in it somewhere. A surprising number of highly educated
65 people are indifferent to these discoveries, and in
western society a rather vocal minority are active-
ly hostile to evolutionary ideas.

To return to natural selection. Perhaps the first
point to grasp is that a complex creature, or even a
70 complex part of a creature, such as the eye, did
not arise in one evolutionary step. Rather it
evolved through a series of small steps. Exactly
what is meant by small is not necessarily obvious
since the growth of an organism is controlled by
75 an elaborate program written in its genes. A small
change in a key part of the program can make a
large difference. For example, an alteration in one
gene in *Drosophila* can produce a fruit fly with
legs in place of its antennae.

80 Each small step is caused by a random alteration in the genetic instructions. Many of these
random alterations may do the organism no good
(some may even kill it before it is born), but occasionally a particular chance alteration may give
85 that particular organism a selective advantage.
This means that in the last analysis the organism
will, on average, leave more offspring than it
would otherwise. If this advantage persists in its
descendants then this beneficial mutant will grad-
90 ually, over many generations, spread through the
population. In favorable cases, every individual
will come to possess the improved version of the
gene. The older version will have been eliminated. Natural selection is thus a beautiful mecha-
95 nism for turning rare events (strictly, favorable
rare events) into common ones.

23. Haldane's remark about beetles (lines 7–9) emphasizes their

(A) tininess and fragility
(B) underlying holiness
(C) capacity for affection
(D) diversity and abundance
(E) physical similarity

24. The word "property" in line 18 means

(A) riches   (B) grounds   (C) trait
(D) belongings   (E) effect

25. The Argument from Design (lines 18–26) argues in
favor of the existence of

(A) nature   (B) complexity   (C) natural selection
(D) a protagonist   (E) a creator

26. Crick's comments about Ronald Reagan and others
aware of evolutionary ideas (lines 59–67) can best
be described as a

(A) touching commendation
(B) pointed digression
(C) blunt acknowledgment
(D) provocative hypothesis
(E) clever euphemism

27. Crick's attitude towards the process of natural
selection can best be described as one of

(A) mild skepticism
(B) puzzled fascination
(C) controlled apprehension
(D) appreciative admiration
(E) lofty detachment

28. Crick's primary purpose in introducing the reference to *Drosophila* (lines 77–79) is to

(A) indicate his familiarity with laboratory experiments on fruit flies
(B) describe the process by which a genetic alteration changes the body
(C) provide a vivid illustration of extreme effects of
a slight genetic change
(D) give an example of a favorable genetic mutation
(E) demonstrate that it took several evolutionary
steps for the fruit fly to reach its present form

29. The word "chance" in line 84 means

(A) fortunate   (B) probable   (C) accidental
(D) speculative   (E) risky

30. The passage indicates that the advantage referred to
in the term "selective advantage" (line 85) is

(A) immutable   (B) reproductive   (C) limited
(D) mental   (E) inequitable

IF YOU FINISH BEFORE 30 MINUTES, YOU MAY CHECK YOUR WORK ON THIS
SECTION ONLY. DO NOT TURN TO ANY OTHER SECTION IN THE TEST.   **S T O P**

SECTION **2**
Mathematical Reasoning

Time—30 minutes
25 Questions

Directions and Reference Information

In this section solve each problem, using any available space for scratchwork. Then decide which is the best of the choices given and fill in the corresponding oval on the answer sheet.

Notes:

(1) The use of a calculator is permitted. All numbers used are real numbers.

(2) Figures that accompany problems in this test are intended to provide information useful in solving the problems. They are drawn as accurately as possible EXCEPT when it is stated in a specific problem that the figure is not drawn to scale. All figures lie in a plane unless otherwise indicated.

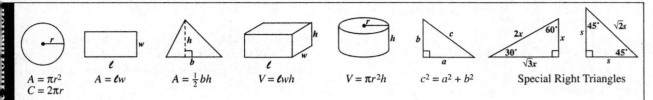

$A = \pi r^2$ $A = \ell w$ $A = \frac{1}{2}bh$ $V = \ell wh$ $V = \pi r^2 h$ $c^2 = a^2 + b^2$ Special Right Triangles
$C = 2\pi r$

The number of degrees of an arc in a circle is 360.
The measure in degrees of a straight angle is 180.
The sum of the measures in degrees of the angles of a triangle is 180.

---

1. $\dfrac{\frac{1}{2} + \frac{1}{3}}{1.2} =$

(A) $\frac{1}{30}$ (B) $\frac{5}{6}$ (C) $\frac{25}{36}$ (D) 1   (E) $4\frac{4}{5}$

2. Which of the following is largest?

(A) $\left(\frac{1}{5}\right)^2$ (B) $\frac{5}{0.5}$ (C) 5.5   (D) $\frac{0.5}{5}$ (E) $\sqrt{5}$

3. Which of the following is equal to $\dfrac{(9^{-2}) + (9^{-1})}{(81^\circ)(9^{-2})}$?

(A) 0   (B) $\frac{1}{10}$ (C) $\frac{1}{9}$ (D) $\frac{3}{2}$ (E) 10

4. $0.005 =$

(A) 0.05% (B) $\frac{1}{10}\%$ (C) $\frac{1}{2}\%$
(D) 5% (E) 50%

5. $\dfrac{x + n}{n}$ equals

(A) x (B) nx (C) $x + 1$

(D) $\frac{x}{n} + 1$ (E) $nx + 1$

6. For which of the following values of x and y is $\dfrac{x}{y} > 1$?

(A) $x = 0, y = 1$ (B) $x = 1, y = 1$
(C) $x = 1, y = 2$ (D) $x = 3, y = 2$
(E) $x = 3, y = 4$

7. Ten years ago I was x years old. How old will I be ten years from now?

(A) $10x$ (B) $20x$ (C) $x + 10$
(D) $x + 20$ (E) $2x - 20$

8. How many 4-cent baseball cards can be purchased for $4D$ dollars?

(A) D (B) $16D$ (C) $400D$

(D) $100D$ (E) $\dfrac{16D}{100}$

9. If $n\left[\begin{smallmatrix}-3\\+5\end{smallmatrix}\right.$ means that both $n - 3$ and $n + 5$ are divisible by 8, n could have any one of the following values EXCEPT

(A) 51   (B) 59   (C) 64   (D) 67   (E) 75

GO ON TO THE NEXT PAGE

10. Martin rides to Cambridge, 30 miles away from home, at the average rate of 10 miles per hour. He returns on a better road that is 50% longer where he can increase his rate by 100%. How much time does he save by taking the better road on his return trip?

(A) $2\frac{1}{4}$ minutes   (B) 15 minutes
(C) 45 minutes   (D) 2 hours 15 minutes
(E) 2 hours 45 minutes

11. A man buys a boat for $16,000. He wishes to sell it at a profit of $1000 after paying the legal fees of $100 and a commission of 5% of the selling price. He must sell the boat for

(A) $17,100   (B) $17,800   (C) $17,900
(D) $18,000   (E) $18,850

12. Formerly, $\frac{1}{6}$ of a pie cost 20¢. Now the price of $\frac{1}{8}$ of a pie is 30¢. The percent increase is

(A) 10%   (B) 20%   (C) $33\frac{1}{3}$%
(D) 50%   (E) 100%

13. Which of the following is (are) always true for $\triangle ABC$?

I. $AB + BC = AC$
II. $BC + AC > AB$
III. $AB + BC > AC + BC$

(A) I only   (B) II only   (C) III only
(D) I and II only   (E) I, II, and III

14. The oil burner in a certain house is used to heat the house and to heat the hot water. During the seven cold months when the house is heated, an average of 200 gallons of oil a month is used. In the remaining five months, when the house is not heated, a total of 200 gallons of oil is used. What percentage of the year's oil supply is required to heat water during these five months?

(A) $\frac{1}{8}$%   (B) 7%   (C) 8%

(D) $12\frac{1}{2}$%   (E) 14%

15. A man pays $8.00 at the box office for 3 adult admission tickets and 4 children admission tickets. If children pay half the admission fee charged for adults, the fee for adults must be

(A) 80¢   (B) $1.00   (C) $1.60
(D) $1.80   (E) $3.20

16. On a rectangular graph, which of the following points will be the same distance from the origin at (3,0)?

I. (0,3)
II. (−3,0)
III. (3,3)

(A) I only   (B) II only   (C) III only
(D) I and II only   (E) I, II, and III

17. If $A = \frac{2}{3}B$, $B = \frac{2}{3}C$, and $C = \frac{2}{3}D$, what part of D is B?

(A) $\frac{8}{27}$ (B) $\frac{4}{9}$ (C) $\frac{2}{3}$ (D) 75   (E) $\frac{4}{3}$

18. Candy formerly sold at $1.76 for a one-pound box is now sold in eight-ounce packages for 96¢. The ratio of the old price to the new price is

(A) 11:6   (B) 6:11   (C) 1.7:1
(D) 11:12   (E) 12:11

19. The number of telephones in a certain town is 48,000. If this represents 12.8 telephones per 100 of population, the population of this town to the nearest thousand is

(A) 128,000   (B) 375,000   (C) 378,000
(D) 566,000   (E) 560,000

20. AOD is a diameter of circle O. The coordinates of points A and D are (−11, −5) and (−3, −5). Find the area of circle O.

(A) 9π (B) 16π (C) 25π
(D) 64π (E) 116π

21. In $\triangle ABC$ $AB = 1.37$, $BC = 5.19$; AC may equal

(A) 6.55   (B) 6.57   (C) 6.59
(D) 6.61   (E) 6.63

22. $AB \perp BC$, $BD \perp ADC$. $AD = 9$, $DC = 16$. Find AB.

(A) 7   (B) 12   (C) 15
(D) $\sqrt{237}$

(E)   cannot be determined
from given information

23. Which two of the following are equal?

I. $1 + \dfrac{x}{y}$

II. y

III. $\dfrac{y^2 + 2xy}{xy}$

IV. $\dfrac{y}{x}$

V. $\dfrac{2x + y}{x}$

(A) I and III   (B) I and IV   (C) I and V
(D) III and V   (E) II and V

24. Of the following periods, which shows the greatest decrease in the volume of Bulk-Rate mail?

(A) 1982–1984   (B) 1986–1987
(C) 1987–1989   (D) 1989–1990
(E) 1991–5/29/92

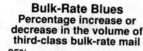
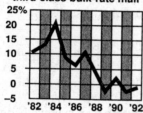

Bulk-Rate Blues
Percentage increase or decrease in the volume of third-class bulk-rate mail

Through May 29
Source: U.S. Postal Service

25. What part of the expenditures went for medical insurance by the Browns?

(A) $\dfrac{3}{70}$ (B) $\dfrac{3}{7}$ (C) $\dfrac{13}{35}$ (D) $\dfrac{3}{35}$ (E) $\dfrac{67}{70}$

HOW THE BROWNS SPENT THEIR MONEY LAST YEAR

Expenditures	
Housing (mortgage, taxes, insurance, utilities)	$13,750
Clothing	1,300
Medical insurance	1,500
Medical costs	2,600
Student loan repayments	4,200
Household furniture and appliances	1,700
Contributions (charitable, political)	750
Entertainment	2,200
Food	4,000
Transportation	3,300
Total expenditures	**$35,000**

IF YOU FINISH BEFORE 30 MINUTES, YOU MAY CHECK YOUR WORK ON THIS SECTION ONLY. DO NOT TURN TO ANY OTHER SECTION IN THE TEST.

S T O P

SECTION 3
Writing Skills

Time—30 minutes
39 Questions

Directions

The following sentences contain problems in grammar, usage, diction (choice of words), and idiom.

Some sentences are correct.

No sentence contains more than one error.

You will find that the error, if there is one, is underlined and lettered. Assume that elements of the sentence that are not underlined are correct and cannot be changed. In choosing answers, follow the requirements of standard written English.

If there is an error, select the one underlined part that must be changed to make the sentence correct and blacken the corresponding space on your answer sheet.

If there is no error, blacken answer space Ⓔ .

Example:

The region has a climate <u>so severe that</u> plants
                          A
<u>growing there</u> rarely <u>had been</u> more than twelve
     B   C
inches <u>high</u>. <u>No error</u>
       D   E

Ⓐ Ⓑ ● Ⓓ Ⓔ

1. I <u>have been thinking</u> lately about the monsters—or
            A
fantasies <u>or</u> whatever—<u>that</u> frightened <u>myself</u> as a
          B   C   D
child. <u>No error</u>
            E

2. We <u>admired</u> his <u>many</u> attempts <u>bravely</u> <u>to enter</u> the
          A   B   C   D
burning building. <u>No error</u>
                       E

3. He worked in the lumber camps <u>during</u> the summer
                                  A
not <u>because of</u> the money <u>but</u> because he wanted to
       B   C
strengthen his muscles by doing <u>hard</u> physical
                                  D
labor. <u>No error</u>
            E

4. That book is <u>liable</u> to become a best seller because
       A   B
it is well-written, <u>full of suspense</u>, and <u>very</u> enter-
                         C   D
taining. <u>No error</u>
              E

5. <u>According to</u> a random poll <u>taken by</u> *National*
        A   B
Wildlife, the top three threats to the environment <u>is</u>
                                                      C
water pollution, air pollution, and <u>hazardous</u> wastes.
                                        D
<u>No error</u>
   E

6. His three children, Ruth, Frank, and Ellis, are very
talented youngsters, <u>but</u> the <u>latter</u> <u>shows</u> the <u>most</u>
                      A   B   C   D
promise. <u>No error</u>
              E

7. <u>Passing</u> antidrug legislation, calling for more
    A
education, and <u>to aid</u> Bolivia in raids on cocaine
                   B
dealers are <u>all ways</u> that the United States is fighting
                C
back <u>against</u> "crack" use. <u>No error</u>
         D   E

8. Cajun cooking, which uses <u>special prepared</u> spices,
                                  A
has always been well-known in Louisiana, <u>but it is</u>
                                               B
<u>only</u> now becoming known in other <u>parts of</u> the
   C   D
country. <u>No error</u>
              E

9. It seems strange <u>to realize that</u> when Harvey
                         A
Firestone <u>organized</u> the Firestone Tire and Rubber
                B
Company in <u>1900,</u> rubber tires <u>had been</u> a novelty.
               C   D
<u>No error</u>
   E

10. The same laser technology that is <u>being used</u> on
                                          A
compact disks <u>is</u> also <u>under application</u> to computers
                  B   C
<u>to achieve</u> additional memory. <u>No error</u>
    D   E

11. The <u>suspenseful</u> play "The Mystery of Edwin Drood"
         A
permits <u>its</u> audience to determine the ending;
            B
<u>unfortunately,</u> the play has a <u>new unique</u> ending for
    C   D
each performance. <u>No error</u>
                       E

GO ON TO THE NEXT PAGE →

12. The Philippine government <u>changed hands</u> <u>when</u>
<u>A</u>　　　<u>B</u>

Marcos failed <u>satisfying</u> his countrymen that he had
C

won the presidential election, and Corazon Aquino

<u>took over.</u>   <u>No error</u>
D　　　　　E

13. <u>Was</u> <u>it</u> <u>they</u> who were involved in the recent <u>unruly</u>
A　B　C　　　　　　　　　　　　D
<u>demonstration?</u>   <u>No error</u>
E

14. We <u>must regard</u> any statement about this controversy,
　　A

<u>whatever</u> the source, <u>as</u> gossip until <u>they are</u>
B　　　　　　　C　　　　　　D

confirmed.   <u>No error</u>
E

15. She is the <u>only</u> one of the applicants <u>who</u> <u>are</u>
　　　　　A　　　　　　　　　　B　C

<u>fully qualified</u> for the position.   <u>No error</u>
D　　　　　　　　　　　　E

16. <u>In order to</u> meet publication schedules, publishers
　A

often <u>find</u> <u>it necessary</u> to trim everyone's schedule
B　　C

and <u>leaving room</u> for unexpected problems.
　　　D

<u>No error</u>
E

17. <u>If</u> the flag <u>is given</u> to him, Juan and <u>him</u> should be
A　　　　B　　　　　　　　　　C

at the <u>beginning</u> of the processional.   <u>No error</u>
　　　D　　　　　　　　　　　　E

18. People often forget <u>during</u> the winter that lawn
A

maintenance <u>must be started</u> <u>at the onset</u> of spring,
　　　　B　　　　　C

<u>in fact</u> they soon remember.   <u>No error</u>
D　　　　　　　　　　E

19. We <u>must come</u> to the realization <u>that</u> it is our
　　A　　　　　　　　　　　B

obligation <u>to look after</u> the poorer nations by
　　　　C

providing medical care, establishing hospitals

and schools, and <u>to insure</u> adequate food supplies.
D

<u>No error</u>
E

Directions

In each of the following sentences, some part or all of the sentence is underlined. Below each sentence you will find five ways of phrasing the underlined part. Select the answer that produces the most effective sentence, one that is clear and exact, without awkwardness or ambiguity, and fill in the corresponding oval on your answer sheet. In choosing answers, follow the requirements of standard written English. Choose the answer that best expresses the meaning of the original sentence.

Answer (A) is always the same as the underlined part. Choose Answer (A) if you think the original sentence needs no revision.

EXAMPLE:

Laura Ingalls Wilder published her first book <u>and she was sixty-five years old then.</u>

(A) and she was sixty-five years old then
(B) when she was sixty-five
(C) at age sixty-five years old
(D) upon reaching of sixty-five years
(E) at the time when she was sixty-five

SAMPLE ANSWER

Ⓐ ● Ⓒ Ⓓ Ⓔ

20. <u>Because he spoke out against Hitler's policies was why Dietrich Bonhoeffer, a Lutheran pastor in Nazi Germany, was arrested and eventually hanged by the Gestapo.</u>

(A) Because he spoke out against Hitler's policies was why Dietrich Bonhoeffer, a Lutheran pastor in Nazi Germany, was arrested and eventually hanged by the Gestapo.
(B) Dietrich Bonhoeffer, a Lutheran pastor in Nazi Germany, was arrested and eventually hanged by the Gestapo because he spoke out against Hitler's policies.
(C) Because he spoke out against Hitler's policies, Dietrich Bonhoeffer, a Lutheran pastor in Nazi Germany, was arrested and eventually hanged by the Gestapo.
(D) Dietrich Bonhoeffer, a Lutheran pastor in Nazi Germany, being arrested and eventually hung because he spoke out against Hitler's policies.
(E) A Lutheran pastor in Nazi Germany, Dietrich Bonhoeffer, spoke out against Hitler's policies so that he arrested and eventually hung.

GO ON TO THE NEXT PAGE →

21. The difference between Liebniz and Schopenhauer is that the former is optimistic; the latter, pessimistic.

    (A) the former is optimistic; the latter, pessimistic
    (B) the former is optimistic, the latter, pessimistic
    (C) while the former is optimistic; the latter, pessimistic
    (D) the former one is optimistic; the latter one is a pessimistic
    (E) the former is optimistic; the latter being pessimistic

22. Most students like to read these kind of books during their spare time.

    (A) these kind of books
    (B) these kind of book
    (C) this kind of books
    (D) this kinds of books
    (E) those kind of books

23. John was imminently qualified for the position because he had studied computer programming and how to operate an IBM machine.

    (A) imminently qualified for the position because he had studied computer programming and how to operate an IBM machine.
    (B) imminently qualified for the position since studying computer programming and the operation of an IBM machine.
    (C) eminently qualified for the position because he had studied computer programming and how to operate an IBM machine.
    (D) eminently qualified for the position because he had studied computer programming and the operation of an IBM machine.
    (E) eminently qualified for the position because he has studied computer programming and how to operate an IBM machine.

24. The idea of inoculating people with smallpox to protect them from later attacks was introduced into Europe by Mary Wortley Montagu, who learned of it in Asia.

    (A) Mary Wortley Montagu, who learned of it in Asia
    (B) Mary Wortley Montagu, who learned of them in Asia
    (C) Mary Wortley Montagu, who learned it of those in Asia
    (D) Mary Wortley Montagu, learning of it in Asia
    (E) Mary Wortley Montagu, because she learned of it in Asia

25. In general, the fate of Latin American or East Asian countries will affect America more than it does Britain or France.

    (A) will affect America more than it does
    (B) will effect America more than it does
    (C) will affect America more than they do
    (D) will effect America more than they do
    (E) will affect America more than they would

26. While campaigning for President, Dole nearly exhausted his funds and must raise money so that he could pay for last-minute television commercials.

    (A) exhausted his funds and must raise money so that he could pay
    (B) would exhaust his funds to raise money so that he could pay
    (C) exhausted his funds and had to raise money so that he can pay
    (D) exhausted his funds and had to raise money so that he could pay
    (E) exhausted his funds and must raise money so that he can pay

27. Athletic coaches stress not only eating nutritious meals but also to get adequate sleep.

    (A) not only eating nutritious meals but also to get
    (B) to not only eat nutritious meals but also getting,
    (C) not only to eat nutritious meals but also getting,
    (D) not only the eating of nutritious meals but also getting
    (E) not only eating nutritious meals but also getting

28. Oakland, California is where the American novelist Jack London spent his early manhood; it was a busy waterfront town.

    (A) is where the American novelist Jack London spent his early manhood; it was a busy waterfront town
    (B) was the busy waterfront town where the American novelist Jack London spent his early manhood
    (C) is the place where the American novelist Jack London spent his early manhood in a busy waterfront town
    (D) is the site of the busy waterfront which was where the American novelist Jack London was situated in early manhood
    (E) is where the American novelist Jack London spent his early manhood in a busy waterfront town

29. The goal of the remedial program was that it enables the students to master the basic skills they need to succeed in regular coursework.

    (A) that it enables
    (B) by enabling
    (C) to enable
    (D) where students are enabled
    (E) where it enables

GO ON TO THE NEXT PAGE

30. Her coach along with her parents and friends are confident she will win the tournament.

(A) along with her parents and friends are confident she

(B) along with her parents and friends are confident that she

(C) along with her parents and friends have been confident she

(D) together with her parents and friends are confident she

(E) along with her parents and friends is confident she

31. The referee would of stopped the fight if the battered boxer would of risen to his feet.

(A) would of stopped the fight if the battered boxer would of risen

(B) would have stopped the fight if the battered boxer would of risen

(C) would have stopped the fight if the battered boxer had risen

(D) would of stopped the fight if the battered boxer would of rose

(E) would have stopped the fight if the battered boxer had rose

32. When the waitress told me that I could have my choice of vanilla, chocolate, or pistachio ice cream, I selected the former even though I prefer the latter.

(A) the former even though I prefer the latter

(B) the first even though I prefer the latter

(C) the former even though I prefer the last

(D) the former even though it is the latter that I prefer

(E) the first even though I prefer the last

33. In visiting the Tower of London, Mrs. Pomeroy's hat was blown off her head into the river.

(A) In visiting the Tower of London, Mrs. Pomeroy's hat was blown off her head into the river.

(B) Mrs. Pomeroy visited the Tower of London, her hat blew off her head into the river.

(C) Mrs. Pomeroy, who was visiting the Tower of London when her hat blew off her head, saw it fall into the river.

(D) When Mrs. Pomeroy visited the Tower of London, her hat was blown off her head and fell into the river.

(E) Mrs. Pomeroy visited the Tower of London; suddenly her hat was blown off her head which fell into the river.

GO ON TO THE NEXT PAGE

Directions

The passage below is the unedited draft of a student's essay. Some of the essay needs to be rewritten to make the meaning clearer and more precise. Read the essay carefully.

The essay is followed by six questions about changes that might improve all or part of its organization, development, sentence structure, use of language, appropriateness to the audience, or its use of standard written English. Choose the answer that most clearly and effectively expresses the student's intended meaning. Indicate your choice by filling in the corresponding space on the answer sheet.

Essay

[1] When you turn on the radio or pop in a tape while the house is quiet or going to work or school in your car, you have several choices of music to listen to. [2] Although, in recent years, CDs have become the medium of choice over records and even tapes. [3] On the radio you have your rap on one station, your classical on another, your New Wave music on another, and then you have your Country. [4] Some young people feel that country is for fat old people, but it isn't. [5] It is music for all ages, fat or thin.

[6] Country music is "fun" music. [7] It has an unmistakable beat and sound that gets you up and ready to move. [8] You can really get into country, even if it is just the clapping of the hands or the stamping of the feet. [9] You can't help feeling cheerful watching the country performers, who all seem so happy to be entertaining their close "friends," although there may be 10,000 of them in the stadium or concert hall. [10] The musicians love it, and audience flips out with delight. [11] The interpersonal factors in evidence cause a sudden psychological bond to develop into a temporary, but nevertheless tightly knit, family unit. [12] For example, you can imagine June Carter Cash as your favorite aunt and Randy Travis as your long lost cousin.

[13] Some people spurn country music. [14] Why, they ask, would anyone want to listen to singers whine about their broken marriages or their favorite pet that was run over by an 18-wheeler? [15] They claim that Willie Nelson, one of today's country legends, can't even keep his income taxes straight. [16] Another "dynamic" performer is Dolly Parton, whose most famous feature is definitely not her voice. [17] How talented could she be if her body is more famous than her singing?

[18] Loretta Lynn is the greatest. [19] Anyone's negative feelings towards country music would change after hearing Loretta's strong, emotional, and haunting voice. [20] Look, it can't hurt to give a listen. [21] You never know, you might even like it so much that you will go out, pick up a secondhand guitar and learn to strum a few chords.

34. Which is the best revision of the underlined segment of sentence 1 below?

When you turn on the radio or pop in a tape while the house is quiet or going to work or school in your car, you have several choices of music to listen to.

(A) while the house is quiet or in your car going to work or school

(B) driving to work or school while the house is quiet

(C) while the house is quiet or you are driving to work or school

(D) while driving to work or school in your car, and the house is quiet

(E) while there's quiet in the house or you go to work or school in your car

35. To improve the coherence of paragraph 1, which of the following sentences should be deleted?

(A) Sentence 1

(B) Sentence 2

(C) Sentence 3

(D) Sentence 4

(E) Sentence 5

36. Taking into account the sentences that precede and follow sentence 8, which of the following is the best revision of sentence 8?

(A) Clap your hands and stamp your feet is what to do to easily get into country.

(B) You're really into country, even if it is just clapping of the hands or stamping of the feet.

(C) You can easily get into country just by clapping your hands or stamping your feet.

(D) One can get into country music rather easily; one must merely clap one's hands or stamp one's feet.

(E) Getting into country is easy, just clap your hands and stamp your feet.

37. With regard to the writing style and tone of the essay, which is the best revision of sentence 11?

(A) The interpersonal relationship that develops suddenly creates a temporary, but nevertheless a closely knit, family unit.

(B) A family-like relationship develops quickly and rapidly.

(C) A close family-type relation is suddenly very much in evidence between the performer and his or her audience.

(D) All of a sudden you feel like a member of a huge, but tight, family.

(E) A sudden bond develops between the entertainer and the audience that might most suitably be described as a "family," in the best sense of the term.

38. Considering the essay as a whole, which of the following best describes the function of paragraph 3?

(A) To present some objective data in support of another viewpoint

(B) To offer a more balanced view of the essay's subject matter

(C) To ridicule those readers who don't agree with the writer

(D) To lend further support to the essay's main idea

(E) To divert the reader's attention from the main idea of the essay

39. Which of the following revisions of sentence 18 provides the smoothest transition between paragraphs 3 and 4?

(A) Loretta Lynn is one of the great singers of country music.

(B) Loretta Lynn, however, is the greatest country singer yet.

(C) But you can bet they've never heard Loretta Lynn.

(D) The sounds of Loretta Lynn tells a different story, however.

(E) Loretta Lynn, on the other hand, is superb.

IF YOU FINISH BEFORE 30 MINUTES, YOU MAY CHECK YOUR WORK ON THIS SECTION ONLY. DO NOT TURN TO ANY OTHER SECTION IN THE TEST.

S T O P

SECTION 4
Verbal Reasoning

**Time—30 minutes
30 Questions**

For each question in this section, select the best answer from among the choices given and fill in the corresponding oval on the answer sheet.

Directions

Each sentence below consists of a related pair of words or phrases, followed by five pairs of words or phrases labeled A through E. Select the pair that best expresses a relationship similar to that expressed in the original pair.

Example:

CRUMB:BREAD::
(A) ounce:unit
(B) splinter:wood
(C) water:bucket
(D) twine:rope
(E) cream:butter

31. CONDUCTOR:ORCHESTRA::

    (A) ballerina:ballet   (B) surgeon:hospital
    (C) director:cast   (D) lawyer:courtroom
    (E) tenor:chorus

32. ALPHABET:LETTER::

    (A) preface:book   (B) piano:music
    (C) ruler:distance   (D) deck:card
    (E) latch:door

33. ESSAYIST:WORDS::

    (A) sculptor:chisel   (B) painter:easel
    (C) baker:batter   (D) soldier:uniform
    (E) butcher:meat

34. SANCTUARY:REFUGE::

    (A) oasis:desert   (B) church:pew
    (C) departure:flight   (D) tree:shade
    (E) holiday:resort

35. INAUGURATE:PRESIDENT::

    (A) abdicate:king   (B) promote:student
    (C) campaign:candidate   (D) install:officer
    (E) succeed:governor

36. RUSTLE:CATTLE::

    (A) bleat:sheep   (B) swim:fish
    (C) pan:gold   (D) speculate:stock
    (E) hijack:cargo

37. AVARICE:VICE::

    (A) charity:virtue   (B) greed:devil
    (C) motive:suspicion   (D) penury:crime
    (E) frugality:economy

38. OUTFOX:CUNNING::

    (A) outline:thought   (B) outstrip:speed
    (C) outreach:charity   (D) outrank:bravery
    (E) outrage:wrath

39. GLINT:LIGHT::

    (A) blare:sound   (B) whiff:scent
    (C) shade:color   (D) glut:food
    (E) wave:tide

40. MERCURIAL:CONSTANCY

    (A) sturdy:durability   (B) genial:loyalty
    (C) ephemeral:permanence
    (D) quixotic:idealism   (E) diffident:fidelity

41. CACOPHONOUS:HEAR::

    (A) intangible:touch   (B) unsavory:taste
    (C) olfactory:smell   (D) palpable:feel
    (E) credulous:believe

42. IMPERTURBABLE:DISCOMPOSE::

    (A) amenable:sway   (B) laconic:interpret
    (C) boorish:provoke   (D) incredulous:convince
    (E) egregious:intrude

43. SCOTCH:RUMOR::

    (A) divert:traffic   (B) broach:topic
    (C) suppress:riot   (D) singe:fire
    (E) spread:gossip

The passage below is followed by questions based on its content. Answer the questions following the passage on the basis of what is <u>stated</u> or <u>implied</u> in that passage and in any introductory material that may be provided.

Questions 44–49 are based on the following passage.

In this excerpt from the novel "Hard Times" by Charles Dickens, the reader is introduced to Thomas Gradgrind, headmaster of a so-called model school.

Thomas Gradgrind, sir. A man of realities. A man of facts and calculations. A man who proceeds upon the principle that two and two are four, and nothing over, and who is not to be talked into allowing for anything over. Thomas Gradgrind,

Line
5

GO ON TO THE NEXT PAGE

sir—peremptorily Thomas—Thomas Gradgrind.
With a rule and a pair of scales, and the multiplication table always in his pocket, sir, ready to
weigh and measure any parcel of human nature,
10 and tell you exactly what it comes to. It is a mere
question of figures, a case of simple arithmetic.
You might hope to get some other nonsensical
belief into the head of George Gradgrind, or
Augustus Gradgrind, or John Gradgrind, or
15 Joseph Gradgrind (all suppositions, nonexistent
persons), but into the head of Thomas
Gradgrind—no, sir!

Mr. Gradgrind walked homeward from the
school in a state of considerable satisfaction. It
20 was his school, and he intended it to be a model.
He intended every child in it to be a model—just
as the young Gradgrinds were all models.

There were five young Gradgrinds, and they
were models every one. They had been lectured at
25 from their tenderest years; coursed, like little
hares. Almost as soon as they could run alone,
they had been made to run to the lecture-room.
The first object with which they had an association, or of which they had a remembrance, was a
30 large blackboard with a dry Ogre chalking ghastly
white figures on it.

Not that they knew, by name or nature, anything about an Ogre. Fact forbid! I only use the
word to express a monster in a lecturing castle,
35 with Heaven knows how many heads manipulated
into one, taking childhood captive, and dragging it
into gloomy statistical dens by the hair.

No little Gradgrind had ever seen a face in the
moon; it was up in the moon before it could speak
40 distinctly. No little Gradgrind had ever learnt the
silly jingle, Twinkle, twinkle, little star; how I
wonder what you are! No little Gradgrind had
ever known wonder on the subject of the stars,
each little Gradgrind having at five years old dis-
45 sected the Great Bear like a Professor Owen, and
driven Charles's Wain like a locomotive engine-
driver. No little Gradgrind had ever associated a
cow in a field with that famous cow with the
crumpled horn who tossed the dog who worried
50 the cat who killed the rat who ate the malt, or with
that yet more famous cow who swallowed Tom
Thumb: it had never heard of those celebrities,
and had only been introduced to a cow as a
graminivorous ruminating quadruped with several
55 stomachs.

44. The phrase "peremptorily Thomas" in line 6
emphasizes Gradgrind's

(A) absolute insistence upon facts
(B) dislike of the name Augustus
(C) need to remind himself of the simplest details
(D) desire to be on a first name basis with others
(E) inability to introduce himself properly

45. The word "rule" in line 7 means

(A) legal regulation   (B) academic custom
(C) scientific principle
(D) dominion over schoolchildren
(E) straightedge used in measuring

46. The author's tone in describing Thomas Gradgrind's
educational methodology is

(A) openly admiring   (B) acutely concerned
(C) bitterly scornful   (D) broadly satirical
(E) warmly nostalgic

47. The passage suggests that Gradgrind rejects from
his curriculum anything that is in the least

(A) analytical   (B) mechanical   (C) fanciful
(D) dogmatic   (E) pragmatic

48. It can be inferred from the passage that the Great
Bear and Charles's Wain most likely are

(A) subjects of nursery rhymes
(B) groupings of stars
(C) zoological phenomena
(D) themes of popular songs
(E) popular toys for children

49. Which of the following axioms is closest to
Gradgrind's view of education as presented in the
passage?

(A) Experience keeps a dear school, but fools will
learn in no other.
(B) Let early education be a sort of amusement,
that you may be better able to find out the natural bent.
(C) Education is what you have left over after you
have forgotten everything you have learned.
(D) A teacher who can arouse a feeling for one single good action accomplishes more than one
who fills our memory with rows on rows of
natural objects, classified with name and form.
(E) Modern science, as training the mind to an
exact and impartial analysis of fact, is an
education specially fitted to promote sound
citizenship.

GO ON TO THE NEXT PAGE

The passages below are followed by questions based on their content; questions following a pair of related passages may also be based on the relationship between the paired passages. Answer the questions on the basis of what is <u>stated</u> or <u>implied</u> in the passages and in any introductory material that may be provided.

Questions 50–60 are based on the following passages.

The following passages are excerpted from recent essays about flying.

PASSAGE 1

Flying alone in an open plane is the purest experience of flight possible. That pure experience is felt at its most intense in acrobatic flying,
Line when you are upside down, or pointed at the sky
5 or at the earth, and moving in ways that you can only in the unsubstantial medium of the air. Acrobatic flying is a useless skill in its particulars—nobody *needs* to do a loop or a roll, not even a fighter pilot—but this skill extends your
10 control of the plane and yourself and makes extreme actions in the sky comfortable. When you reach the top of a loop, upside down and engine at full throttle, and tilt your head back to pick up the horizon line behind you, you are as
15 far outside instinctive human behavior as you can go—hanging in space, the sky below you and the earth above, inscribing a circle on emptiness. And then the nose drops across the horizon; your speed increases and the plane scoops through into
20 normal flight, and you are back in the normal world, with the earth put back in its place. The going out and coming back are what makes a loop so satisfying.

After a while, that is. At first it was terrifying,
25 like being invited to a suicide that you didn't want to commit. "This is a loop," my instructor said casually. He lowered the plane's nose to gain airspeed, and then pulled sharply up. The earth, and my stomach, fell away from me; and we were
30 upside down, and I could feel gravity clawing at me, pulling me out into the mile of empty space between me and the ground. I grabbed at the sides of the cockpit and hung on until gravity was on my side again.
35 "You seemed a little nervous that time," the instructor said when the plane was right side up again. "You've got to have confidence in that seat belt, or you'll never do a decent loop. So this time, when we get on top, I want you to put both
40 arms out of the cockpit." And I did it. It was like stepping off a bridge, but I did it, and the belt held, and the plane came round. And after that I could fly a loop. It was, as I said, satisfying.

PASSAGE 2

The black plane dropped spinning, and flat-
45 tened out spinning the other way; it began to carve the air into forms that built wildly and musically on each other and never ended. Reluctantly, I started paying attention. Rahm drew high above the world an inexhaustibly glo-
50 rious line; it piled over our heads in loops and arabesques. The plane moved every way a line can move, and it controlled three dimensions, so the line carved massive and subtle slits in the air like sculptures. The plane looped the loop, seem-
55 ing to arch its back like a gymnast; it stalled, dropped, and spun out of it climbing; it spiraled and knifed west on one side's wings and back east on another; it turned cartwheels, which must be physically impossible; it played with its own
60 line like a cat with yarn. How did the pilot know where in the air he was? If he got lost, the ground would swat him.

His was pure energy and naked spirit. I have thought about it for years. Rahm's line unrolled in
65 time. Like music, it split the bulging rim of the future along its seam. It pried out the present. We watchers waited for the split-second curve of beauty in the present to reveal itself. The human pilot, Dave Rahm, worked in the cockpit right at
70 the plane's nose; his very body tore into the future for us and reeled it down upon us like a curling peel.

Like any fine artist, he controlled the tension of the audience's longing. You desired, unwitting-
75 ly, a certain kind of roll or climb, or a return to a certain portion of the air, and he fulfilled your hope slantingly, like a poet, or evaded it until you thought you would burst, and then fulfilled it surprisingly, so you gasped and cried out.
80 The oddest, most exhilarating and exhausting thing was this: he never quit. The music had no periods, no rests or endings; the poetry's beautiful sentence never ended; the line had no finish; the sculptured forms piled overhead, one into another
85 without surcease. Who could breathe, in a world where rhythm itself had no periods?

I went home and thought about Rahm's performance that night, and the next day, and the next.

GO ON TO THE NEXT PAGE ⟩

I had thought I knew my way around beauty a
90 little bit. I knew I had devoted a good part of my
life to it, memorizing poetry and focusing my
attention on complexity of rhythm in particular,
on force, movement, repetition, and surprise, in
both poetry and prose. Now I had stood among
95 dandelions between two asphalt runways in
Bellingham, Washington, and begun learning
about beauty. Even the Boston Museum of Fine
Arts was never more inspiring than this small
northwestern airport on this time-killing Sunday
100 afternoon in June. Nothing on earth is more glad-
dening than knowing we must roll up our sleeves
and move back the boundaries of the humanly
possible once more.

50. According to the author of Passage 1, training in
acrobatic flying

(A) has only theoretical value
(B) expands a pilot's range of capabilities
(C) is an essential part of general pilot training
(D) comes naturally to most pilots
(E) should only be required of fighter pilots

51. The word "medium" in line 6 means

(A) midpoint   (B) appropriate occupation
(C) method of communication
(D) environment   (E) compromise

52. To "pick up the horizon line" (line 14) is to

(A) lift it higher   (B) spot it visually
(C) measure its distance   (D) choose it eagerly
(E) increase its visibility

53. Passage 1 suggests that the author's grabbing at the
sides of the cockpit (lines 32–33) was

(A) instinctive   (B) terrifying   (C) essential
(D) habit-forming   (E) life-threatening

54. By putting both arms out of the cockpit (lines
39–40), the author

(A) chooses the path of least resistance
(B) enables himself to steer the plane more freely
(C) relies totally on his seat belt to keep him safe
(D) allows himself to give full expression to his
nervousness
(E) is better able to breathe deeply and relax

55. The author's use of the word "satisfying" (line 43)
represents

(A) a simile   (B) an understatement
(C) a fallacy   (D) a euphemism   (E) a hypothesis

56. The author of Passage 2 mentions her initial reluctance to watch the stunt flying (line 48) in order to

(A) demonstrate her hostility to commercial enter-
tainment
(B) reveal her fear of such dangerous enterprises
(C) minimize her participation in aerial acrobatics
(D) indicate how captivating the demonstration was
(E) emphasize the acuteness of her perceptions

57. By fulfilling "your hope slantingly, like a poet"
(lines 76–77), the author means that

(A) the pilot flew the plane on a diagonal
(B) Rahm was a writer of popular verse
(C) the pilot had a bias against executing certain
kinds of rolls
(D) Rahm refused to satisfy your expectations
directly
(E) the pilot's sense of aesthetic judgment was
askew

58. At the end of Passage 2, the author is left feeling

(A) empty in the aftermath of the stunning performance she has seen
(B) jubilant at the prospect of moving from Boston
to Washington
(C) exhilarated by her awareness of new potentials
for humanity
(D) glad that she has not wasted any more time
memorizing poetry
(E) surprised by her response to an art form she
had not previously believed possible

59. Compared to Passage 2, Passage 1 is

(A) less informative   (B) more tentative
(C) more argumentative   (D) more speculative
(E) less lyrical

60. How would the author of Passage 2 most likely react
to the assessment of acrobatic flying in lines 7–11?

(A) She would consider it too utilitarian an assessment of an aesthetic experience.
(B) She would reject it as an inaccurate description
of the pilot's technique.
(C) She would admire it as a poetic evocation of
the pilot's art.
(D) She would criticize it as a digression from the
author's main point.
(E) She would regard it as too effusive to be appropriate to its subject.

IF YOU FINISH BEFORE 30 MINUTES, YOU MAY CHECK YOUR WORK ON THIS
SECTION ONLY. DO NOT TURN TO ANY OTHER SECTION IN THE TEST.

S T O P

SECTION 5
Mathematical Reasoning

Time—30 minutes
25 Questions

Directions and Sample Questions

Notes:

(1) The use of a calculator is permitted. All numbers used are real numbers.

(2) Figures that accompany problems in this test are intended to provide information useful in solving the problems. They are drawn as accurately as possible EXCEPT when it is stated in a specific problem that the figure is not drawn to scale. All figures lie in a plane unless otherwise indicated.

Questions 1–15 each consist of two quantities in boxes, one in Column A and one in Column B. You are to compare the two quantities and on the answer sheet fill in oval

A if the quantity in Column A is greater;
B if the quantity in Column B is greater;
C if the two quantities are equal;
D if the relationship cannot be determined from the information given.

Notes:

1. In some questions, information is given about one or both of the quantities to be compared. In such cases, the given information is centered above the two columns and is not boxed.
2. In a given question, a symbol that appears in both columns represents the same thing in Column A as it does in Column B.
3. Letters such as x, n, and k stand for real numbers.

	EXAMPLES		
	Column A	Column B	Answers
E1	5^2	20	● Ⓑ Ⓒ Ⓓ
E2	x	30	Ⓐ Ⓑ ● Ⓓ
E3	$r+1$	$s-1$	Ⓐ Ⓑ Ⓒ ●

E2: $150°$ $x°$

E3: r and s are integers.

PART I: QUANTITATIVE COMPARISON QUESTIONS

SUMMARY DIRECTIONS FOR QUANTITATIVE COMPARISON QUESTIONS

Answer: A if the quantity in Column A is greater.
B if the quantity in Column B is greater.
C if the two quantities are equal.
D if the relationship cannot be determined from the information given.

	Column A	Column B
26.	2^3	3^2
27.	$a+b=-7$ $b-a=3$	
	$a+b$	$a-b$
28.	$\frac{1}{x}>1$	
	x	1
29.	$81<x<100$	
	$\sqrt{x}$	9

	Column A	Column B
	The average of 5 and a is 5	
30.	a	5
31.	The square of 0.5	The reciprocal of 4
32.	$3x-6=1$	
	$x-2$	$\frac{1}{3}$
33.	$\frac{1}{\sqrt{25}}$	20%

GO ON TO THE NEXT PAGE →

| Column A | Column B | | Column A | Column B |

$$\frac{a}{3} = b$$

34. $3a$ $9b$

$x < 5$

35. $(x + 5)(x - 5)$ $x^2 - 25$

$abc = 0$ and $a = 1$

36. bc 1

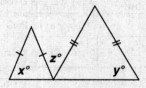

$x = 70$ and $y = 40$

37. x z

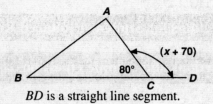

BD is a straight line segment.

38. x 30

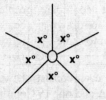

Five line segments meet at point *O*.

39. $2x$ 72

The operation $\triangle$ is defined by the equation
$$a \triangle b = a^2 + b^2$$

$xy \neq 0$

40. $(x \triangle y)^2$ $x^2 \triangle y^2$

GO ON TO THE NEXT PAGE

PART II: STUDENT-PRODUCED RESPONSE QUESTIONS

Directions for Student-Produced Response Questions

Each of the remaining ten questions (41–50) requires you to solve the problem and enter your answer by marking the ovals in the special grid, as shown in the examples below.

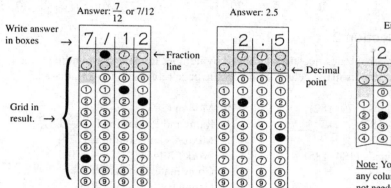

- Mark no more than one oval in any column.
- Because the answer sheet will be machine-scored, **you will receive credit only if the ovals are filled in correctly.**
- Although not required, it is suggested that you write your answer in the boxes at the top of the columns to help you fill in the ovals accurately.
- Some problems may have more than one correct answer. In such cases, grid only one answer.
- No question has a negative answer.
- **Mixed numbers** such as $2\frac{1}{2}$ much be gridded as 2.5 or 5/2. (If [2 1 / 2] is gridded, it will be interpreted as $\frac{21}{2}$, not $2\frac{1}{2}$.)

- Decimal Accuracy: If you obtain a decimal answer, enter the most accurate value that the grid will accommodate. For example, if you obtain an answer such as 0.6666..., you should record the result as .666 or .667. Less accurate values such as .66 or .67 are not acceptable.

Acceptable ways to grid $\frac{2}{3}$ = .6666...

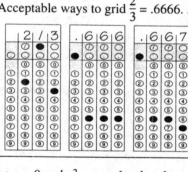

41. What is the minimum weight in ounces of 69 eggs taken from a crate containing a grade of eggs weighing 24 to 26 ounces per dozen?

42. At the end of spring training a football coach discharged $\frac{1}{5}$ of his squad and asked the remaining 32 boys to report on Labor Day. How many boys were on the squad during spring training?

43. A stick 35 inches long is to be cut so that one piece is $\frac{1}{4}$ as long as the other. How many inches long must the shorter piece be?

44. A baseball team has won 15 games and lost 9. If these games represent $16\frac{2}{3}\%$ of the games to be played, how many more games must the team win to average .750 for the season?

45. If $x^2 + y = 9$ and $x^2 - y = -1$, what does y equal?

46. If $17xy = 22xy - 5$, what does x^2y^2 equal?

47. What is the area of a triangle whose sides are 5, 8, and 5?

48. If O is the center of a circle, $AO = 3x + 2$ and $OB = 5x - 4$, find the diameter AOB of the circle.

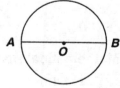

49. If the area of a circle is twice the area of a triangle whose base is 4π and whose altitude is 4, what does the radius of the circle equal?

50. In parallelogram $ABCD$ $\angle B \cong \angle A + \angle C$. What is the measure, in degrees, of $\angle D$?

IF YOU FINISH BEFORE 30 MINUTES, YOU MAY CHECK YOUR WORK ON THIS SECTION ONLY. DO NOT TURN TO ANY OTHER SECTION IN THE TEST.   **STOP**

ANSWER KEY

Verbal Reasoning Section 1

1. A	*6.* B	*11.* E	*16.* A	*21.* E	*26.* B
2. D	*7.* A	*12.* C	*17.* D	*22.* D	*27.* D
3. A	*8.* E	*13.* E	*18.* B	*23.* D	*28.* C
4. E	*9.* C	*14.* C	*19.* C	*24.* C	*29.* C
5. C	*10.* D	*15.* B	*20.* D	*25.* E	*30.* B

Mathematical Reasoning Section 2

Note: Each correct answer to the mathematics questions is keyed by number to the corresponding topic in Chapters 8 and 9. These numerals refer to the topics listed below, with specific page references in parentheses.

1. Basic Fundamental Operations (179–182)
2. Algebraic Operations (182–183)
3. Using Algebra (182–184, 187)
4. Exponents, Roots, and Radicals (184–185)
5. Inequalities (188–189)
6. Fractions (182, 198)
7. Decimals (200)
8. Percent (200)
9. Averages (201)

10. Motion (203)
11. Ratio and Proportion (204–205)
12. Mixtures and Solutions (178)
13. Work (206–207)
14. Coordinate Geometry (194)
15. Geometry (189–193, 195)
16. Quantitative Comparisons (211–212)
17. Data Interpretation (208)

1. C (6, 7)	*6.* D (6)	*11.* D (3, 8)	*16.* D (14)	*21.* A (15)
2. B (4, 6, 7)	*7.* D (2)	*12.* E (8)	*17.* B (1, 6)	*22.* C (15)
3. E (4, 6)	*8.* D (3)	*13.* B (15)	*18.* D (11)	*23.* D (2, 6)
4. C (7, 8)	*9.* C (1)	*14.* D (8)	*19.* B (11)	*24.* C (17)
5. D (2, 6)	*10.* C (8, 10)	*15.* C (3)	*20.* B (15)	*25.* A (6, 17)

Writing Skills Section 3

1. D	*8.* A	*15.* C	*22.* C	*29.* C	*36.* C
2. C	*9.* D	*16.* D	*23.* D	*30.* E	*37.* D
3. B	*10.* C	*17.* C	*24.* A	*31.* C	*38.* B
4. B	*11.* C	*18.* D	*25.* A	*32.* E	*39.* C
5. C	*12.* C	*19.* D	*26.* D	*33.* D	
6. B	*13.* E	*20.* B	*27.* E	*34.* C	
7. B	*14.* D	*21.* A	*28.* B	*35.* B	

Verbal Reasoning Section 4

31. C	*36.* E	*41.* B	*46.* D	*51.* D	*56.* D
32. D	*37.* A	*42.* D	*47.* C	*52.* B	*57.* D
33. C	*38.* B	*43.* C	*48.* B	*53.* A	*58.* C
34. D	*39.* B	*44.* A	*49.* E	*54.* C	*59.* E
35. D	*40.* C	*45.* E	*50.* B	*55.* B	*60.* A

Mathematical Reasoning Section 5

26. B (4, 16)	*29.* A (4, 16)	*32.* C (2, 16)	*35.* C (2, 16)	*38.* C (15, 16)
27. B (2, 16)	*30.* B (9, 16)	*33.* C (2, 4, 8, 16)	*36.* B (2, 16)	*39.* A (15, 16)
28. D (6, 16)	*31.* C (4, 6, 16)	*34.* C (2, 16)	*37.* C (15, 16)	*40.* A (2, 16)

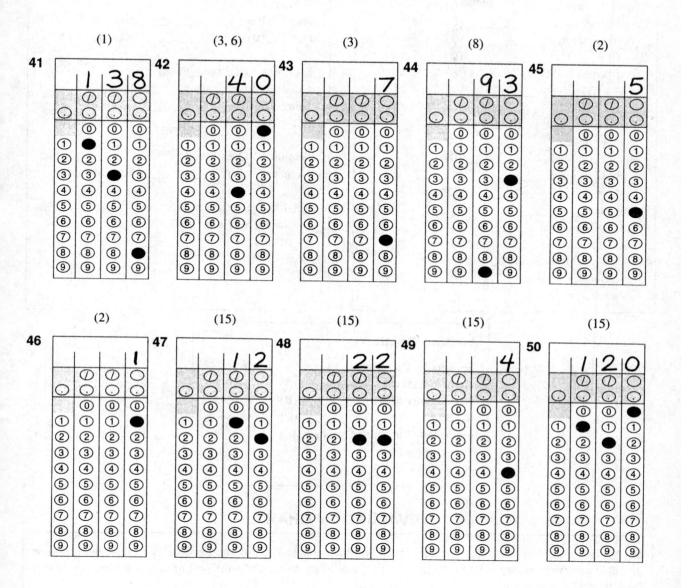

SCORING CHART — TYPICAL TEST J

Verbal Sections

Section 1   Questions 1–30
Number correct _____ (A)
Number omitted _____ (B)
Number incorrect _____ (C)
$1/4$ (C) = _____ (D)
Raw Score:
  (A) – (D) = _____

Section 3   Questions 31–60
Number correct _____ (A)
Number omitted _____ (B)
Number incorrect _____ (C)
$1/4$ (C) = _____ (D)
Raw Score:
  (A) – (D) = _____

Total Verbal Raw Score:
  (Section 1 +
  Section 3) = _____

Mathematical Sections

Section 2   Questions 1–25
Number correct _____ (A)
Number incorrect _____ (B)
(A) – $1/4$ (B) = _____ Raw Score I

Section 4   Questions 26–40
Number correct _____ (C)
Number incorrect _____ (D)
(C) – $1/3$ (D) = _____ Raw Score II

Section 4   Questions 41–50
Number correct _____ Raw Score III

Total Mathematical Raw Score:
  (Raw Scores I + II
  + III) = _____

Writing Section

Section 3   Questions 1–39
Number correct _____ (A)
Number incorrect _____ (B)
$1/4$ (B) = _____ (C)
(no penalty for omitted questions)
Writing Raw Score:
  (A) – (C) = _____

EVALUATION CHART

Study your score. Your raw score on the Verbal and Mathematical Reasoning Sections is an indication of your probable achievement on the PSAT/NMSQT. As a guide to the amount of work you need or want to do with this book, study the following.

| Raw Score | | | Self-rating |
Verbal	Mathematical	Writing	
55–60	41–50	37–39	Superior
44–54	25–40	31–36	Very good
39–43	20–24	25–30	Satisfactory
35–38	16–19	19–24	Average
29–34	10–15	13–18	Needs further study
20–28	7–9	6–12	Needs intensive study
0–19	0–6	0–5	Probably inadequate

ANSWER EXPLANATIONS

Verbal Reasoning Section 1

1. **A** Logically, such bleak information would make people more worried about using pills containing estrogen. Thus, concern over the effects of estrogen would *heighten.*

2. **D** Fast food restaurants are growing more popular in France. The traditional cafe is therefore growing less popular (falling "victim to the growing popularity" of McBurgers) and is slowly *becoming extinct* (vanishing, disappearing; dying out).

3. **A** Because it can now be grown successfully in America, the once-rare fruit is now *accessible* or readily available to American consumers.

4. **E** *Although* signals a contrast. You would expect the coach to be *jubilant* (extremely joyful) about her team's victory. Instead, she was *disheartened* (discouraged).

5. **C** Someone always searching for new ways to do things is by definition *an innovator* (someone who introduces changes into the existing ways of doing things).

6. **B** With its abundance of historic buildings, Washington seems *saturated* (soaked through and through; thoroughly permeated) with the spirit of American history. Note how *saturated* is used here in a figurative sense; the city isn't *literally* soaked with anything (except for an occasional rainstorm).

7. **A** *Bantering* or joking remarks are clearly *inappropriate* in a serious speech.

8. **E** The sentence lists negative aspects of measurement. One is that it is *not* always used *properly* or correctly. Another is that it is often *misunderstood.* Note that, while the first missing word must be positive, the second must be negative.

9. **C** A trip to France, with all the chances for talking in French it would provide, would be a practical or *pragmatic* test of how much you had learned of conversational French.

10. **D** People uncomfortable with math would be likely to think the field should be *left to* those gifted in such an *esoteric* (hard to understand; known only to a chosen few) subject.

11. **E** Though scientists might be upset by *erroneous* (faulty) or *derivative* (unoriginal) work, the scientific community would be most shocked by *fraudulent* or faked research that was intentionally *deceptive* or deceitful.

12. **C** The key phrase "of few words" indicates that Eastwood's characters are *laconic,* untalkative types.

13. **E** *Insipid* (flavorless; dull and uninteresting) is a term that applies equally well to food and to conversations.

14. **C** If Bryce's and Laski's works are now rarely read, these once-prominent figures have *receded into obscurity.* Here *obscurity* is the opposite of *fame.*

15. **B** A writer whose work was universally acclaimed or applauded and whose reputation was not yet *tarnished* or stained would be at the *zenith* or high point of her career.

16. **A** If you expected someone's grief to die down or *subside* quickly, you would be surprised to find that he continued to grieve and was hopelessly unhappy (*disconsolate*).

17. **D** Someone *crabbed* (bad-humored; harsh; morose) seldom smiles; someone *parsimonious* (stingy; miserly) never gives away money. Note how parallel structure determines word order: the first missing adjective relates to the first verb ("seldom smiled"); the second missing adjective relates to the second verb ("never gave away").

18. **B** The opening sentence maintains the growth of scholarly activity was stimulated by the protest movement. The protest movement caused an upsurge of popular interest in the African American past. It also created a climate in which professional studies of black history were legitimized.

19. **C** The three men are cited as examples of scholars who were encouraged to resume their earlier researches in black history. Choices A, B and E are incorrect. None of the three men were identified in the passage with these concerns. Choice D is incorrect. Only Logan is identified with research on blacks in nineteenth-century North Carolina.

20. **D** According to the passage, prior to the early 1960s Negro history was not an object of particularly great renown in academe. In the 1950s, the advice given to Blassingame to avoid black history if he desired "a future in the historical profession" seemed wise—graduate students of the caliber of Huggins and Litwack felt an ambivalence about entering the field because of "practical concerns." What these concerns boiled down to was the sense that to choose black history as one's specialization would be *detrimental* or harmful to one's career.

21. **E** The author is describing what occurred during the period to change black history from a marginal field to a vital field of specialization.

22. **D** You can arrive at the correct answer by the process of elimination. Statement I is supported by the passage. At the time Bennett and Logan wrote, both the pre-Mayflower period of black history and the nineteenth-century life of blacks in North Carolina were relatively

unexplored. Therefore, you can eliminate Choices B and E. Statement II is unsupported by the passage. Bennett's work was a popularization intended for a wide general audience. It was not aimed at academics. Therefore, you can eliminate Choice C. Statement III is supported by the passage. Bennett's work appeared first as a series of magazine articles, then as a book. Logan's work first appeared as a doctoral thesis, then (with revisions) as a book. Therefore, you can eliminate Choice A. Only Choice D is left. It is the correct answer.

23. **D** Following the logic of Haldane's remark, God must be inordinately (excessively) fond of beetles because he made so many of them. Thus, Haldane's remark underscores the *diversity and abundance* of beetles.

24. **C** In discussing properties of living things, Crick is describing their *traits* or characteristics.

25. **E** The Argument from Design maintains that, if you find a complex working object like a watch, the only way you can explain its existence is to assume that it was made by a watchmaker. In the same way, it argues that when you look at the complex living organisms around you, the only way you can explain their existence is to assume that they were made by a designer or *creator.*

26. **B** Crick's comments about Ronald Reagan and other doubters of evolutionary ideas are quite *pointed* (sharp): he is nonplussed that more than a century after Darwin and Mendel people of Reagan's education and stature still doubt these ideas or reject them outright. However, they are clearly a *digression* (wandering away) from the subject at hand. He openly acknowledges as much when he begins the following paragraph with "To return to natural selection."

27. **D** The author's attitude is most evident in the concluding sentence, in which natural selection is described as "a beautiful mechanism" that increases favorable events. He clearly regards the process with *appreciative admiration.*

28. **C** Scanning the passage, you easily find the one sentence that mentions *Drosophila.* The sentence immediately before it tells us the point the author is trying to make with this example: "A small change in a key part of the program can make a large difference."

29. **C** A chance alteration is a random, *accidental* one: it comes about through chance, not through planning.

30. **B** In the final paragraph, we find that an organism with a "selective advantage" will reproduce more, that is, "on the average, leave more offspring." Thus, its advantage is a *reproductive* one.

Mathematical Reasoning Section 2

1. **C** $\frac{1}{2} + \frac{1}{3} = \frac{5}{6}$

   $\frac{5}{6} \div 1.2 = \frac{5}{6} \div 1\frac{1}{5} = \frac{5}{6} \div \frac{6}{5} = \frac{5}{6} \cdot \frac{5}{6} = \frac{25}{36}$

2. **B** (A) $\left(\frac{1}{5}\right)^2 = \frac{1}{25}$

   (B) $\frac{5}{0.5} = \frac{50}{5} = 10$

   (C) 5.5

   (D) $\frac{0.5}{.5} = \frac{5}{50} = \frac{1}{10}$

   (E) $\sqrt{5} = 2+$

3. **E** $\frac{(9^{-2}) + (9^{-1})}{(81^0)(9^{-2})} = \frac{\frac{1}{9^2} + \frac{1}{9}}{(1)\left(\frac{1}{9^2}\right)} = \frac{\frac{1}{81} + \frac{1}{9}}{\frac{1}{81}} = \frac{\frac{10}{81}}{\frac{1}{81}} = 10$

4. **C** $5\% = \frac{5}{100}$

   $0.005 = \frac{5}{1000}$

   $0.005 = \frac{0.5}{100} = 0.5\% = \frac{1}{2}\%$

5. **D** $\frac{x + n}{n} = \frac{x}{n} + \frac{n}{n} = \frac{x}{n} + 1$

6. **D** In order for $\frac{x}{y}$ to be greater than 1, x must be greater than y. This is true only in (D).

7. **D** If my age was x years ten years ago, then I am now $x + 10$ years old. In ten years I will be $x + 10 + 10$ or $x + 20$ years old.

8. **D** This is a direct proportion. Let x = number of cards that can be purchased for $4D$ dollars.

   $\frac{\text{number of stamps}}{\text{dollars}} \quad \frac{25}{1} = \frac{x}{4D}$

   $x = 100D$

9. **C** Notice that 64 is divisible by 8; therefore a number 3 less than 64 or 5 greater than 64 cannot be divisible by 8. You can also test each choice; if you use this strategy, notice that it is necessary to test only one of the requirements, for if $n - 3$ is divisible by 8, then $n + 5$ must also be since it exceeds $n - 3$ by 8.

10. **C** Distance ÷ rate = time
    Trip to Cambridge: 30 miles ÷ 10 miles per hour = 3 hours
    Trip from Cambridge: 45 miles ÷ 20 miles per hour = $2\frac{1}{4}$ hours
    Saving = $\frac{3}{4}$ hour = 45 minutes

11. D Selling price = cost + \$1000 + \$100 + 5% of selling price

Let x = selling price

$$x = \$16{,}000 + 1000 + 100 + 0.05x$$
$$x - 0.05x = 17100$$
$$0.95x = 17100$$
$$95x = 1710000$$
$$x = \$18{,}000$$

12. E Formerly, $\frac{1}{6}$ pie cost 20¢. A pie cost \$1.20

Now $\frac{1}{8}$ pie costs 30¢. A pie costs \$2.40

$$\frac{\text{change}}{\text{original}} = \frac{\$1.20}{\$1.20} = 1 = 100\%$$

13. B I is not correct. The sum of two sides of a triangle is greater than the third. Also, recall that a straight line is the shortest distance between two points. Therefore II is correct. III can be reduced to the statement $AB > AC$. This may not be assumed from the information given.

14. D During heating season (200 gallons)(7 months) = 1400 gallons used

During remaining season amount used = 200 gallons

Total for year = 1600 gallons

$$\frac{200}{1600} = \frac{1}{8} = 12\frac{1}{2}\%$$

15. C Let x = price for children's admission ticket.

Then $2x$ = price for adults' admission ticket.

$3(2x)$ = cost of 3 adults' tickets

$4(x)$ = cost of 4 children's tickets

$$6x + 4x = \$8.00$$
$$10x = \$8.00$$
$$x = .80$$
$$2x = \$1.60$$

16. D The distance of (3,0) from the origin is 3 units. This is also true for the coordinates described in I and II. To calculate the distance for the coordinates of III, consider as the distance the hypotenuse of a triangle with legs 3 and 3. It is a 45°-45°-90° triangle, so the hypotenuse = $3\sqrt{2}$.

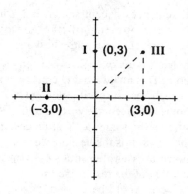

17. B "What part of D is B" means $\frac{B}{D} = ?$

$$B = \tfrac{2}{3}C$$
$$C = \tfrac{2}{3}D$$
$$\tfrac{3}{2}C = D$$

Substitute:

$$\frac{B}{D} = \frac{\tfrac{2}{3}C}{\tfrac{3}{2}C} = \tfrac{2}{3}C \div \tfrac{3}{2}C = \tfrac{2}{3} \div \tfrac{3}{2} = \tfrac{2}{3} \cdot \tfrac{2}{3} = \tfrac{4}{9}$$

18. D Former price was \$1.76 for 16 ounces.
New price is \$1.92 for 16 ounces.

Ratio is $\frac{1.76}{1.92} = \frac{176}{192} = \frac{11}{12} = 11{:}12$

19. B Let x = population of town.

$$\frac{12.8}{100} = \frac{48000}{x}$$
$$12.8x = 4800000$$
$$128x = 48000000$$
$$x = 375{,}000$$

20. B Length of $AOD = 8[11 - 3]$

$\therefore$ radius = 4

Area = $\pi(4)^2$

Area = 16π

21. A Because a straight line is the shortest distance between points, the third side must be less than $1.37 + 5.19$ or 6.56. Only choice A is less than 6.56.

22. C Let $x = AB$.

$$\frac{25}{x} = \frac{x}{9}$$

[When an altitude is drawn on the hypotenuse, a leg is the mean proportional between the whole hypotenuse and the segment adjacent to it.]

$$x^2 = 225$$
$$x = 15$$

23. D I. $1 + \dfrac{x}{y} = \dfrac{y + x}{y}$

II. y

III. $\dfrac{y^2 + 2xy}{xy} = \dfrac{y(y + 2x)}{xy} = \dfrac{y + 2x}{y}$

IV. $\dfrac{y}{x}$

V. $\dfrac{2x + y}{x}$ or $\dfrac{y + 2x}{x}$

III and V are equal.

24. C All except the 1987–1989 period showed a rise in the solid line.

25. A $\dfrac{1500}{35000} = \dfrac{15}{350} = \dfrac{3}{70}$

Writing Skills Section 3

1. **D** The reflexive pronoun *myself* cannot be used as the object of the verb *frightened.* Change *myself* to *me.*

2. **C** Misuse of adverb for adjective. Change *his many attempts bravely to enter* to *his many brave attempts to enter.*

3. **B** Lack of parallel structure. Change *not because of the money* to *not because he needed the money* (a clause) to parallel the clause that follows *but.*

4. **B** Error in diction. Change *liable* to *likely.*

5. **C** Error in agreement. Change *is* to *are.*

6. **B** Error in diction. *Latter* should not be used to refer to more than two items. Change *latter* to *last.*

7. **B** Lack of parallel structure. Change *to aid* to *aiding.*

8. **A** Misuse of adverb for adjective. Change *special prepared* to *specially prepared.*

9. **D** Error in tense. Change *had been* to *were.*

10. **C** Lack of parallel structure. Change *under application* to *being applied.*

11. **C** Incorrect sentence connector. Change the conjunctive adverb *unfortunately* to *therefore* to clarify the relationship between the clauses.

12. **C** Faulty verbal. Change *satisfying* to the infinitive *to satisfy.*

13. **E** Sentence is correct.

14. **D** Error in agreement. Change *they are* to *it is.*

15. **C** Error in agreement. The antecedent of *who* is *one.* Therefore, *who is* is correct.

16. **D** Lack of parallel structure. Change *leaving room for* to *to leave room for.*

17. **C** Error in case. Change *him* to *he.*

18. **D** Error in sentence connector. Change *in fact* to *but* in order to clarify the relationship between the clauses.

19. **D** Error in parallel structure. Change *to insure* to *insuring.*

20 **B** Choice B eliminates the excessive wordiness of the original sentence without introducing any errors in diction.

21. **A** The use of the semicolon to separate the pair of clauses is correct.

22. **C** Error in agreement. *Kind* is singular and requires a singular modifier (*this*).

23. **D** Choice D corrects the error in diction and the error in parallel structure.

24. **A** The original answer provides the most effective and concise sentence.

25. **A** The original sentence is correct. The singular pronoun *it* refers to the subject of the main clause, *fate* (singular).

26. **D** Choices A, B, C, and E suffer from errors in the sequence of tenses.

27. **E** A lack of parallel structure is found in the other four choices.

28. **B** Choice B is the clearest, most graceful, and most concise way of expressing the ideas being described.

29. **C** Choice A provides us with the result of the program rather than the goal. Choice B results in a sentence fragment. Choices D and E use the *was where* construction, which is unclear and should be avoided.

30. **E** Choices A, B, C, and D suffer from an error in agreement between the subject and the verb. Remember that the prepositional phrase *along with her parents and friends* is not part of the subject. The subjects is the singular word *coach;* it should be followed by the singular verb *is.*

31. **C** The use of *of* instead of *have* in Choices A and D is incorrect. The *if* clause requires the subjective mood *had risen* instead of *would have risen* in Choice B. Choices D and E are incorrect, because the past participle of *rise* is *risen.*

32. **E** *Former* and *latter* should be used only when two items are under consideration. When three or more items are discussed, as in this sentence, use *first* and *last.*

33. **D** Choice A is unacceptable because of the dangling modifier. Choice B is a run-on sentence. Choice C changes the meaning of the sentence. Choice E suffers from a misplaced modifier. Did her head fall into the river? So Choice E would imply.

34. **C** Choice A says that the house is *in your car,* an unlikely place for it to be.
Choice B contains an idea that the writer could not have intended.
Choice C accurately states the intended idea. It is the best answer.
Choice D, like B, contains an idea that is quite absurd.
Choice E is wordy and awkwardly expressed.

35. **B** All sentences except sentence 2 contribute to the development of the essay's topic. Therefore, choice B is the best answer.

36. **C** Choice A is awkwardly expressed.
Choice B is awkward and contains the pronoun *it,* which has no specific referent.
Choice C is accurately expressed and is consistent with the sentences that precede and follow sentence 8. It is the best answer.
Choice D is written in a style that is different from that of the rest of the essay.
Choice E would be a good choice, but it contains a comma splice. A comma may not be used to join two independent clauses.

37. **D** Choice A is quite formal and is not in keeping with the style and tone of the essay.

Choice B is close to the style and tone of the essay, but it contains the redundance, *quickly and rapidly.*

Choice C has a formal tone inconsistent with the rest of the essay.

Choice D uses the second person pronoun and is consistent with the folksy, conversational style of the essay. It is the best answer.

Choice E uses an objective tone far different from the writing in the rest of the essay.

38. **B** Choice A is only partly true. While the paragraph gives another viewpoint, the data it contains are hardly objective.

Choice B accurately states the writer's intention. It is the best answer.

Choices C, D, and E in no way describe the function of paragraph 3.

39. **C** Choice A provides no particular link to the previous paragraph.

Choice B provides a rather weak transition between paragraphs.

Choice C creates a strong bond between paragraphs by alluding to material in paragraph 3 and introducing the topic of paragraph 4. It is the best answer.

Choice D could be a good transition were it not for the error in subject-verb agreement. The subject *sounds* is plural; the verb *tells* is singular.

Choice E provides a weak transition and its writing style is not consistent with the rest of the essay.

Verbal Reasoning Section 4

31. **C** A *conductor* leads or directs an *orchestra*; a *director* guides or directs a *cast.* (Function)

32. **D** An *alphabet* is made up of individual *letters*; a *deck* is made up of individual *cards.*
(Part to Whole)

33. **C** *Words* are the medium an *essayist* employs when creating an essay; *batter* is the material a *baker* uses when preparing a cake.
(Worker and Material)

34. **D** A *sanctuary* (place of safety) provides one with shelter or *refuge*; a *tree* provides one with shelter or *shade.* (Function)

35. **D** To *inaugurate* a *president* is to introduce him or her into office. To *install* an *officer* is to do the same. (Function)

36. **E** To *rustle cattle* is to steal them. To *hijack cargo* is to steal it. Note that you are dealing with a secondary meaning of the verb *rustle* here.
(Defining Characteristic)

37. **A** *Avarice* or greed is the name of a particular *vice* (evil quality); *charity* or love is the name of a particular *virtue* (good quality).
(Class and Member)

38. **B** To *outfox* someone is to surpass that person in *cunning*; to *outstrip* someone is to surpass that person in *speed.* (Defining Characteristic)

39. **B** A *glint* is a small gleam of *light.* A *whiff* is a slight puff of *scent.*
(Degree of Intensity)

40. **C** *Mercurial* (flighty; changeable) by definition means lacking *constancy*; *ephemeral* (temporary; fleeting) by definition means lacking *permanence.* Beware of eye-catchers. Choice **E** is incorrect. *Diffident* by definition means lacking faith in oneself, not lacking *fidelity* or loyalty to others. (Antonym Variant)

41. **B** Something *cacophonous* (discordant; harsh-sounding) is unpleasant to *hear*; something *unsavory* (unpalatable; disagreeable in taste) is unpleasant to *taste.* (Defining Characteristic)

42. **D** Someone *imperturbable* (unexcitable; calm) is difficult to *discompose* or agitate; someone *incredulous* (disbelieving) is difficult to convince. (Antonym Variant)

43. **C** To *scotch* or block a *rumor* is to crush it. To *suppress* or quell a *riot* is to crush it.
(Defining Characteristic)

44. **A** Dickens implies that Gradgrind is so peremptory (absolute; dogmatic) about facts that he would insist upon the fact that his given name was, in fact, Thomas.

45. **E** Gradgrind carries scales and a rule in his pocket to "weigh and measure any parcel of human nature." Though Dickens plays upon several meanings of *rule* here, the word basically refers to a ruler or measuring stick.

46. **D** Dickens is poking fun at Gradgrind's teaching methods and is thus *broadly satirical* (full of ridicule).

47. **C** Gradgrind never introduces his pupils to nursery rhymes or to fantasy creatures such as ogres. This suggests that he rejects from his curriculum anything that is in the least *fanciful* or imaginative.

48. **B** The little Gradgrinds, having studied the Great Bear and Charles's Wain, had never "known wonder on the subject of stars." This suggests that the Great Bear and the Wain are constellations, or *groupings of stars.*

49. **E** Gradgrind's main idea is to fill his pupils full of *facts,* particularly facts about *science* (statistics, constellations, graminivorous quadrupeds, etc.).

50. **B** In extending the pilot's control of the plane and making extreme actions (loops, sudden swerves, dives, etc.) comfortable, acrobatic flying *extends a pilot's range of capabilities.*

51. **D** The medium of the air is the *environment* in which flying creatures function.

52. **B** In the course of doing a loop, you lose sight of the horizon and must tilt your head backward

to catch sight of the horizon line again. Thus, to pick up the horizon line is to *spot it visually.*

53. **A**   Earlier in the passage, the author describes the experience of doing a loop as being "as far outside instinctive human behavior as you can go." In grabbing at the sides of the cockpit during the loop, the author is reverting to *instinctive,* involuntary behavior. Choice B is incorrect. The experience of doing a loop was terrifying; grabbing the sides of the cockpit was not. Choice C is incorrect. It was not essential for the author to grab the sides of the cockpit; his seat belt was strong enough to keep him from falling out of the plane. Choice D is incorrect. The author did not wind up making a habit of grabbing the sides of the cockpit; he did it only that once. Choice E is incorrect. The experience of doing a loop may have seemed life-threatening; grabbing the sides of the cockpit was not.

54. **C**   The instructor tells the author to put his arms out of the cockpit so that he can learn to have confidence in his seat belt's ability to hold him in the plane. He does so, *relying totally on his seat belt to keep him safe.*

55. **B**   By stressing the terror that went into learning how to fly a loop, the author makes you feel that *satisfying* is an extremely mild word to describe the exhilaration of overcoming such an extreme fear and mastering such an unnatural skill. It is clearly an *understatement.*

56. **D**   The author was not a fan of stunt-flying; she was reluctant to pay attention to the aerial display. Therefore, this particular aerial display must have been unusually *captivating* to capture her attention.

57. **D**   The author describes the audience's longing for a particular effect in the stunt-flying demonstration ("a certain kind of roll or climb, or a return to a certain portion of the air"). This is akin to a reader's longing for a particular effect in a poem—for example, a certain kind of image or rhyme, or the return of an earlier refrain. Poets, however, play with their readers' expectations, sometimes varying exact end-rhymes with an occasional assonance or consonance (*slant* rhymes), as when Emily Dickinson unexpectedly rhymes *came* with *home.* Thus, in saying that Rahm "fulfilled your hope slantingly, like a poet," the author means that he *refused to satisfy your expectations directly* but gave you something unexpected instead.

58. **C**   By "moving back the boundaries of the humanly possible" the author is talking about becoming aware *of new potentials for humanity.* This new knowledge leaves her gladdened and *exhilarated.*

59. **E**   Passage 1 is both descriptive and informative. In recounting the story of the flying lesson, it is anecdotal. However, in comparison with Passage 2, it is not particularly poetic or *lyrical.*

60. **A**   The author of Passage 1 talks about how useful acrobatic flying is in improving the skills of pilots. The author of Passage 2, however, looks on acrobatic flying as *an aesthetic experience*: she responds to Rahm's aerial demonstration as a new form of beauty, a performance that engages her aesthetically. Therefore, she would most likely consider the assessment of aerial flying in Passage 1 *too utilitarian* (concerned with practical usefulness) to be appropriate for an aesthetic experience.

Mathematical Reasoning Section 5

26. **B** $2^3 = (2)(2)(2) = 8$
$3^2 = (3)(3) = 9$

27. **B**   Because $b - a = 3$, $-(b - a) = -3$, or $a - b = 3$. Because $-3 > -7$, $a - b > a + b$.

28. **D**   If x has a negative value, the correct answer would be **B**. If x is positive, the correct answer would be **A**. Therefore the correct answer is **D**.

29. **A** $\sqrt{81} = 9$
$\sqrt{100} = 9$
The square root of x is more than 9 but less than 10. $9+ > 9$

30. **C**   Because the average of these two quantities is 5, the sum of these quantities must be 10. Therefore, $5 + a = 10$ and $a = 5$.

31. **C** $(0.5)^2 = 0.25$
The reciprocal of 4 is $\frac{1}{4}$ or 0.25.

32. **C** $3x - 6 = 1$
Divide each term of the equation by 3:
$x - 2 = \frac{1}{3}$.

33. **C** $\frac{1}{\sqrt{25}} = \frac{1}{5} = 20\%$

34. **C** $\frac{a}{3} = b$
$a = 3b$
$3a = 9b$

35. **C**   Factor: $x^2 - 25 = (x + 5)(x - 5)$. Even though $x < 5$ makes $x^2 - 25$ negative, the above equation is true.

36. **B**   If $a = 1$, b and/or $c = 0$.

37. **C** $x + y + z = 180$
$70 + 40 + z = 180$
$z = 70$

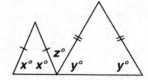

38. **C** $\angle BCA + \angle ACD \overset{\circ}{=} 180$
$(x + 70)° = 100°$
$x = 30°$

39. **A** $x = \frac{1}{5}$ of $360° = 72$

$2x = 144$

40. **A**   In Column B, $x^2 \triangle y^2 = x^4 + y^4$
In Column A, $(x \triangle y)^2 = (x^2 + y^2)^2$ or
$(x^2 + y^2)(x^2 + y^2)$ or $x^4 + 2x^2y^2 + y^4$
Since x^2 and y^2 are NOT negative, the value in
Column A is greater by $2x^2y^2$; also $2x^2y^2 \neq 0$
since $xy \neq 0$.

41. **138** Minimum weight of 1 dozen eggs = 24 ounces
Minimum weight of 1 egg = 2 ounces
Minimum weight of 69 eggs = 138 ounces

42. **40**   Let x = number of boys on the squad at the end
of spring training.
$\frac{4}{5}x = 32$
$x = 40$

43. **7**   Let x = length (inches) of shorter piece
Then $4x$ = length (inches) of longer piece.
$4x + x = 35$
$5x = 35$
$x = 7$

44. **93**   If $16\frac{2}{3}$% or $\frac{1}{6}$ of the total = 24 games, 100% =
144 games = total games for season.
.750 average = $\frac{3}{4}$ (144) = 108 games to win
Number of games already won = 15
Games still to win = $108 - 15 = 93$

45. **5** $x^2 + y = 9$ (1)
$x^2 - y = -1$ (2)
$-x^2 + y = 1$ [divide (2) by -1]
$x^2 + y = 9$ (1)
$2y = 10$ [addition]
$y = 5$

46. **1** $17xy = 22xy - 5$
$-5xy = -5$
$xy = 1$ [divide by -5]
$x^2y^2 = 1$ [square both sides of equation]

47. **12** $\triangle ABC$ is isosceles.
Draw altitude AD.
$BD = DC$
$\triangle ABD$ is a 3:4:5
triangle; $AD = 3$.
Area = $(h)(b)$
Area = $(3)(8) = 12$

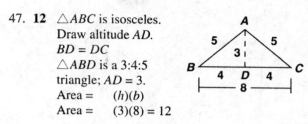

48. **22** $AO = OB$
$3x + 2 = 5x - 4$
$6 = 2x$
$3 = x$
$AO = 11$ [radius]
Diameter = 22

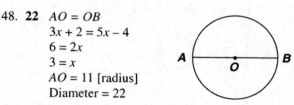

49. **4**   Length of $AOD = 8[11 - 3]$
$\therefore$ radius = 4
Area = $\pi(4)^2$
Area = 16π
Area of triangle = $\frac{1}{2}$ (altitude)(base) or
$\frac{1}{2}$ (4)(4π) or 8π
Area of circle = $2(8\pi)$ [given]
Area of circle = 16π or πr^2
$\pi r^2 = 16\pi$
$r^2 = 16$
$r = 4$

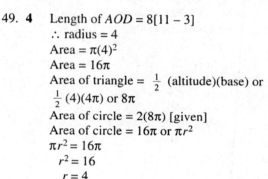

50. **120** Because opposite angles of a
parallelogram are equal,
$\angle B = \angle D$.
$\therefore \angle D = \angle A + \angle C$.
Let $x \overset{\circ}{=} \angle A$.
Then $x \overset{\circ}{=} \angle C$.
Then $2x \overset{\circ}{=} \angle D$ and
$2x \overset{\circ}{=} \angle B$; $6x \overset{\circ}{=} 360$
[sum of the angles of a quadrilateral = 360°].
$x \overset{\circ}{=} 60$, $\angle D$ or $2x \overset{\circ}{=} 120$

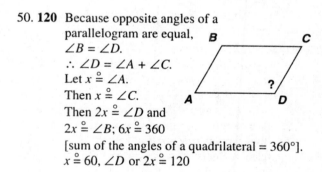

Answer Sheet
Use these Answer Sheets for additional practice.

Each mark should completely fill the appropriate space, and should be as dark as all other marks. Make all erasures complete. Traces of an erasure may be read as an answer. See pages vii and 27 for explanations of timing and number of questions.

Section 1 — Verbal
30 minutes

1. Ⓐ Ⓑ Ⓒ Ⓓ Ⓔ
2. Ⓐ Ⓑ Ⓒ Ⓓ Ⓔ
3. Ⓐ Ⓑ Ⓒ Ⓓ Ⓔ
4. Ⓐ Ⓑ Ⓒ Ⓓ Ⓔ
5. Ⓐ Ⓑ Ⓒ Ⓓ Ⓔ
6. Ⓐ Ⓑ Ⓒ Ⓓ Ⓔ
7. Ⓐ Ⓑ Ⓒ Ⓓ Ⓔ
8. Ⓐ Ⓑ Ⓒ Ⓓ Ⓔ
9. Ⓐ Ⓑ Ⓒ Ⓓ Ⓔ
10. Ⓐ Ⓑ Ⓒ Ⓓ Ⓔ
11. Ⓐ Ⓑ Ⓒ Ⓓ Ⓔ
12. Ⓐ Ⓑ Ⓒ Ⓓ Ⓔ
13. Ⓐ Ⓑ Ⓒ Ⓓ Ⓔ
14. Ⓐ Ⓑ Ⓒ Ⓓ Ⓔ
15. Ⓐ Ⓑ Ⓒ Ⓓ Ⓔ
16. Ⓐ Ⓑ Ⓒ Ⓓ Ⓔ
17. Ⓐ Ⓑ Ⓒ Ⓓ Ⓔ
18. Ⓐ Ⓑ Ⓒ Ⓓ Ⓔ
19. Ⓐ Ⓑ Ⓒ Ⓓ Ⓔ
20. Ⓐ Ⓑ Ⓒ Ⓓ Ⓔ
21. Ⓐ Ⓑ Ⓒ Ⓓ Ⓔ
22. Ⓐ Ⓑ Ⓒ Ⓓ Ⓔ
23. Ⓐ Ⓑ Ⓒ Ⓓ Ⓔ
24. Ⓐ Ⓑ Ⓒ Ⓓ Ⓔ
25. Ⓐ Ⓑ Ⓒ Ⓓ Ⓔ
26. Ⓐ Ⓑ Ⓒ Ⓓ Ⓔ
27. Ⓐ Ⓑ Ⓒ Ⓓ Ⓔ
28. Ⓐ Ⓑ Ⓒ Ⓓ Ⓔ
29. Ⓐ Ⓑ Ⓒ Ⓓ Ⓔ
30. Ⓐ Ⓑ Ⓒ Ⓓ Ⓔ

Section 2 — Math
30 minutes

1. Ⓐ Ⓑ Ⓒ Ⓓ Ⓔ
2. Ⓐ Ⓑ Ⓒ Ⓓ Ⓔ
3. Ⓐ Ⓑ Ⓒ Ⓓ Ⓔ
4. Ⓐ Ⓑ Ⓒ Ⓓ Ⓔ
5. Ⓐ Ⓑ Ⓒ Ⓓ Ⓔ
6. Ⓐ Ⓑ Ⓒ Ⓓ Ⓔ
7. Ⓐ Ⓑ Ⓒ Ⓓ Ⓔ
8. Ⓐ Ⓑ Ⓒ Ⓓ Ⓔ
9. Ⓐ Ⓑ Ⓒ Ⓓ Ⓔ
10. Ⓐ Ⓑ Ⓒ Ⓓ Ⓔ
11. Ⓐ Ⓑ Ⓒ Ⓓ Ⓔ
12. Ⓐ Ⓑ Ⓒ Ⓓ Ⓔ
13. Ⓐ Ⓑ Ⓒ Ⓓ Ⓔ
14. Ⓐ Ⓑ Ⓒ Ⓓ Ⓔ
15. Ⓐ Ⓑ Ⓒ Ⓓ Ⓔ
16. Ⓐ Ⓑ Ⓒ Ⓓ Ⓔ
17. Ⓐ Ⓑ Ⓒ Ⓓ Ⓔ
18. Ⓐ Ⓑ Ⓒ Ⓓ Ⓔ
19. Ⓐ Ⓑ Ⓒ Ⓓ Ⓔ
20. Ⓐ Ⓑ Ⓒ Ⓓ Ⓔ
21. Ⓐ Ⓑ Ⓒ Ⓓ Ⓔ
22. Ⓐ Ⓑ Ⓒ Ⓓ Ⓔ
23. Ⓐ Ⓑ Ⓒ Ⓓ Ⓔ
24. Ⓐ Ⓑ Ⓒ Ⓓ Ⓔ
25. Ⓐ Ⓑ Ⓒ Ⓓ Ⓔ

Section 3 — Writing
30 minutes

1. Ⓐ Ⓑ Ⓒ Ⓓ Ⓔ
2. Ⓐ Ⓑ Ⓒ Ⓓ Ⓔ
3. Ⓐ Ⓑ Ⓒ Ⓓ Ⓔ
4. Ⓐ Ⓑ Ⓒ Ⓓ Ⓔ
5. Ⓐ Ⓑ Ⓒ Ⓓ Ⓔ
6. Ⓐ Ⓑ Ⓒ Ⓓ Ⓔ
7. Ⓐ Ⓑ Ⓒ Ⓓ Ⓔ
8. Ⓐ Ⓑ Ⓒ Ⓓ Ⓔ
9. Ⓐ Ⓑ Ⓒ Ⓓ Ⓔ
10. Ⓐ Ⓑ Ⓒ Ⓓ Ⓔ
11. Ⓐ Ⓑ Ⓒ Ⓓ Ⓔ
12. Ⓐ Ⓑ Ⓒ Ⓓ Ⓔ
13. Ⓐ Ⓑ Ⓒ Ⓓ Ⓔ
14. Ⓐ Ⓑ Ⓒ Ⓓ Ⓔ
15. Ⓐ Ⓑ Ⓒ Ⓓ Ⓔ
16. Ⓐ Ⓑ Ⓒ Ⓓ Ⓔ
17. Ⓐ Ⓑ Ⓒ Ⓓ Ⓔ
18. Ⓐ Ⓑ Ⓒ Ⓓ Ⓔ
19. Ⓐ Ⓑ Ⓒ Ⓓ Ⓔ
20. Ⓐ Ⓑ Ⓒ Ⓓ Ⓔ
21. Ⓐ Ⓑ Ⓒ Ⓓ Ⓔ
22. Ⓐ Ⓑ Ⓒ Ⓓ Ⓔ
23. Ⓐ Ⓑ Ⓒ Ⓓ Ⓔ
24. Ⓐ Ⓑ Ⓒ Ⓓ Ⓔ
25. Ⓐ Ⓑ Ⓒ Ⓓ Ⓔ
26. Ⓐ Ⓑ Ⓒ Ⓓ Ⓔ
27. Ⓐ Ⓑ Ⓒ Ⓓ Ⓔ
28. Ⓐ Ⓑ Ⓒ Ⓓ Ⓔ
29. Ⓐ Ⓑ Ⓒ Ⓓ Ⓔ
30. Ⓐ Ⓑ Ⓒ Ⓓ Ⓔ
31. Ⓐ Ⓑ Ⓒ Ⓓ Ⓔ
32. Ⓐ Ⓑ Ⓒ Ⓓ Ⓔ
33. Ⓐ Ⓑ Ⓒ Ⓓ Ⓔ
34. Ⓐ Ⓑ Ⓒ Ⓓ Ⓔ
35. Ⓐ Ⓑ Ⓒ Ⓓ Ⓔ
36. Ⓐ Ⓑ Ⓒ Ⓓ Ⓔ
37. Ⓐ Ⓑ Ⓒ Ⓓ Ⓔ
38. Ⓐ Ⓑ Ⓒ Ⓓ Ⓔ
39. Ⓐ Ⓑ Ⓒ Ⓓ Ⓔ

Section 4 — Verbal
30 minutes

31 Ⓐ Ⓑ Ⓒ Ⓓ Ⓔ
32 Ⓐ Ⓑ Ⓒ Ⓓ Ⓔ
33 Ⓐ Ⓑ Ⓒ Ⓓ Ⓔ
34 Ⓐ Ⓑ Ⓒ Ⓓ Ⓔ
35 Ⓐ Ⓑ Ⓒ Ⓓ Ⓔ
36 Ⓐ Ⓑ Ⓒ Ⓓ Ⓔ
37 Ⓐ Ⓑ Ⓒ Ⓓ Ⓔ
38 Ⓐ Ⓑ Ⓒ Ⓓ Ⓔ
39 Ⓐ Ⓑ Ⓒ Ⓓ Ⓔ
40 Ⓐ Ⓑ Ⓒ Ⓓ Ⓔ
41 Ⓐ Ⓑ Ⓒ Ⓓ Ⓔ
42 Ⓐ Ⓑ Ⓒ Ⓓ Ⓔ
43 Ⓐ Ⓑ Ⓒ Ⓓ Ⓔ
44 Ⓐ Ⓑ Ⓒ Ⓓ Ⓔ
45 Ⓐ Ⓑ Ⓒ Ⓓ Ⓔ
46 Ⓐ Ⓑ Ⓒ Ⓓ Ⓔ
47 Ⓐ Ⓑ Ⓒ Ⓓ Ⓔ
48 Ⓐ Ⓑ Ⓒ Ⓓ Ⓔ
49 Ⓐ Ⓑ Ⓒ Ⓓ Ⓔ
50 Ⓐ Ⓑ Ⓒ Ⓓ Ⓔ
51 Ⓐ Ⓑ Ⓒ Ⓓ Ⓔ
52 Ⓐ Ⓑ Ⓒ Ⓓ Ⓔ
53 Ⓐ Ⓑ Ⓒ Ⓓ Ⓔ
54 Ⓐ Ⓑ Ⓒ Ⓓ Ⓔ
55 Ⓐ Ⓑ Ⓒ Ⓓ Ⓔ
56 Ⓐ Ⓑ Ⓒ Ⓓ Ⓔ
57 Ⓐ Ⓑ Ⓒ Ⓓ Ⓔ
58 Ⓐ Ⓑ Ⓒ Ⓓ Ⓔ
59 Ⓐ Ⓑ Ⓒ Ⓓ Ⓔ
60 Ⓐ Ⓑ Ⓒ Ⓓ Ⓔ

Section 5 — Math
30 minutes

26 Ⓐ Ⓑ Ⓒ Ⓓ Ⓔ
27 Ⓐ Ⓑ Ⓒ Ⓓ Ⓔ
28 Ⓐ Ⓑ Ⓒ Ⓓ Ⓔ
29 Ⓐ Ⓑ Ⓒ Ⓓ Ⓔ
30 Ⓐ Ⓑ Ⓒ Ⓓ Ⓔ
31 Ⓐ Ⓑ Ⓒ Ⓓ Ⓔ
32 Ⓐ Ⓑ Ⓒ Ⓓ Ⓔ
33 Ⓐ Ⓑ Ⓒ Ⓓ Ⓔ
34 Ⓐ Ⓑ Ⓒ Ⓓ Ⓔ
35 Ⓐ Ⓑ Ⓒ Ⓓ Ⓔ
36 Ⓐ Ⓑ Ⓒ Ⓓ Ⓔ
37 Ⓐ Ⓑ Ⓒ Ⓓ Ⓔ
39 Ⓐ Ⓑ Ⓒ Ⓓ Ⓔ
39 Ⓐ Ⓑ Ⓒ Ⓓ Ⓔ
40 Ⓐ Ⓑ Ⓒ Ⓓ Ⓔ

41   42   43   44   45   46   47   48   49   50

(grid-in answer bubbles, digits 0–9)

Answer Sheet
Use these Answer Sheets for additional practice.

Each mark should completely fill the appropriate space, and should be as dark as all other marks. Make all erasures complete. Traces of an erasure may be read as an answer. See pages vii and 27 for explanations of timing and number of questions.

Section 1 — Verbal
30 minutes

1 Ⓐ Ⓑ Ⓒ Ⓓ Ⓔ
2 Ⓐ Ⓑ Ⓒ Ⓓ Ⓔ
3 Ⓐ Ⓑ Ⓒ Ⓓ Ⓔ
4 Ⓐ Ⓑ Ⓒ Ⓓ Ⓔ
5 Ⓐ Ⓑ Ⓒ Ⓓ Ⓔ
6 Ⓐ Ⓑ Ⓒ Ⓓ Ⓔ
7 Ⓐ Ⓑ Ⓒ Ⓓ Ⓔ
8 Ⓐ Ⓑ Ⓒ Ⓓ Ⓔ
9 Ⓐ Ⓑ Ⓒ Ⓓ Ⓔ
10 Ⓐ Ⓑ Ⓒ Ⓓ Ⓔ
11 Ⓐ Ⓑ Ⓒ Ⓓ Ⓔ
12 Ⓐ Ⓑ Ⓒ Ⓓ Ⓔ
13 Ⓐ Ⓑ Ⓒ Ⓓ Ⓔ
14 Ⓐ Ⓑ Ⓒ Ⓓ Ⓔ
15 Ⓐ Ⓑ Ⓒ Ⓓ Ⓔ
16 Ⓐ Ⓑ Ⓒ Ⓓ Ⓔ
17 Ⓐ Ⓑ Ⓒ Ⓓ Ⓔ
18 Ⓐ Ⓑ Ⓒ Ⓓ Ⓔ
19 Ⓐ Ⓑ Ⓒ Ⓓ Ⓔ
20 Ⓐ Ⓑ Ⓒ Ⓓ Ⓔ
21 Ⓐ Ⓑ Ⓒ Ⓓ Ⓔ
22 Ⓐ Ⓑ Ⓒ Ⓓ Ⓔ
23 Ⓐ Ⓑ Ⓒ Ⓓ Ⓔ
24 Ⓐ Ⓑ Ⓒ Ⓓ Ⓔ
25 Ⓐ Ⓑ Ⓒ Ⓓ Ⓔ
26 Ⓐ Ⓑ Ⓒ Ⓓ Ⓔ
27 Ⓐ Ⓑ Ⓒ Ⓓ Ⓔ
28 Ⓐ Ⓑ Ⓒ Ⓓ Ⓔ
29 Ⓐ Ⓑ Ⓒ Ⓓ Ⓔ
30 Ⓐ Ⓑ Ⓒ Ⓓ Ⓔ

Section 2 — Math
30 minutes

1 Ⓐ Ⓑ Ⓒ Ⓓ Ⓔ
2 Ⓐ Ⓑ Ⓒ Ⓓ Ⓔ
3 Ⓐ Ⓑ Ⓒ Ⓓ Ⓔ
4 Ⓐ Ⓑ Ⓒ Ⓓ Ⓔ
5 Ⓐ Ⓑ Ⓒ Ⓓ Ⓔ
6 Ⓐ Ⓑ Ⓒ Ⓓ Ⓔ
7 Ⓐ Ⓑ Ⓒ Ⓓ Ⓔ
8 Ⓐ Ⓑ Ⓒ Ⓓ Ⓔ
9 Ⓐ Ⓑ Ⓒ Ⓓ Ⓔ
10 Ⓐ Ⓑ Ⓒ Ⓓ Ⓔ
11 Ⓐ Ⓑ Ⓒ Ⓓ Ⓔ
12 Ⓐ Ⓑ Ⓒ Ⓓ Ⓔ
13 Ⓐ Ⓑ Ⓒ Ⓓ Ⓔ
14 Ⓐ Ⓑ Ⓒ Ⓓ Ⓔ
15 Ⓐ Ⓑ Ⓒ Ⓓ Ⓔ
16 Ⓐ Ⓑ Ⓒ Ⓓ Ⓔ
17 Ⓐ Ⓑ Ⓒ Ⓓ Ⓔ
18 Ⓐ Ⓑ Ⓒ Ⓓ Ⓔ
19 Ⓐ Ⓑ Ⓒ Ⓓ Ⓔ
20 Ⓐ Ⓑ Ⓒ Ⓓ Ⓔ
21 Ⓐ Ⓑ Ⓒ Ⓓ Ⓔ
22 Ⓐ Ⓑ Ⓒ Ⓓ Ⓔ
23 Ⓐ Ⓑ Ⓒ Ⓓ Ⓔ
24 Ⓐ Ⓑ Ⓒ Ⓓ Ⓔ
25 Ⓐ Ⓑ Ⓒ Ⓓ Ⓔ

Section 3 — Writing
30 minutes

1 Ⓐ Ⓑ Ⓒ Ⓓ Ⓔ
2 Ⓐ Ⓑ Ⓒ Ⓓ Ⓔ
3 Ⓐ Ⓑ Ⓒ Ⓓ Ⓔ
4 Ⓐ Ⓑ Ⓒ Ⓓ Ⓔ
5 Ⓐ Ⓑ Ⓒ Ⓓ Ⓔ
6 Ⓐ Ⓑ Ⓒ Ⓓ Ⓔ
7 Ⓐ Ⓑ Ⓒ Ⓓ Ⓔ
8 Ⓐ Ⓑ Ⓒ Ⓓ Ⓔ
9 Ⓐ Ⓑ Ⓒ Ⓓ Ⓔ
10 Ⓐ Ⓑ Ⓒ Ⓓ Ⓔ
11 Ⓐ Ⓑ Ⓒ Ⓓ Ⓔ
12 Ⓐ Ⓑ Ⓒ Ⓓ Ⓔ
13 Ⓐ Ⓑ Ⓒ Ⓓ Ⓔ
14 Ⓐ Ⓑ Ⓒ Ⓓ Ⓔ
15 Ⓐ Ⓑ Ⓒ Ⓓ Ⓔ
16 Ⓐ Ⓑ Ⓒ Ⓓ Ⓔ
17 Ⓐ Ⓑ Ⓒ Ⓓ Ⓔ
18 Ⓐ Ⓑ Ⓒ Ⓓ Ⓔ
19 Ⓐ Ⓑ Ⓒ Ⓓ Ⓔ
20 Ⓐ Ⓑ Ⓒ Ⓓ Ⓔ
21 Ⓐ Ⓑ Ⓒ Ⓓ Ⓔ
22 Ⓐ Ⓑ Ⓒ Ⓓ Ⓔ
23 Ⓐ Ⓑ Ⓒ Ⓓ Ⓔ
24 Ⓐ Ⓑ Ⓒ Ⓓ Ⓔ
25 Ⓐ Ⓑ Ⓒ Ⓓ Ⓔ
26 Ⓐ Ⓑ Ⓒ Ⓓ Ⓔ
27 Ⓐ Ⓑ Ⓒ Ⓓ Ⓔ
28 Ⓐ Ⓑ Ⓒ Ⓓ Ⓔ
29 Ⓐ Ⓑ Ⓒ Ⓓ Ⓔ
30 Ⓐ Ⓑ Ⓒ Ⓓ Ⓔ
31 Ⓐ Ⓑ Ⓒ Ⓓ Ⓔ
32 Ⓐ Ⓑ Ⓒ Ⓓ Ⓔ
33 Ⓐ Ⓑ Ⓒ Ⓓ Ⓔ
34 Ⓐ Ⓑ Ⓒ Ⓓ Ⓔ
35 Ⓐ Ⓑ Ⓒ Ⓓ Ⓔ
36 Ⓐ Ⓑ Ⓒ Ⓓ Ⓔ
37 Ⓐ Ⓑ Ⓒ Ⓓ Ⓔ
38 Ⓐ Ⓑ Ⓒ Ⓓ Ⓔ
39 Ⓐ Ⓑ Ⓒ Ⓓ Ⓔ

Section 4 — Verbal
30 minutes

31 Ⓐ Ⓑ Ⓒ Ⓓ Ⓔ
32 Ⓐ Ⓑ Ⓒ Ⓓ Ⓔ
33 Ⓐ Ⓑ Ⓒ Ⓓ Ⓔ
34 Ⓐ Ⓑ Ⓒ Ⓓ Ⓔ
35 Ⓐ Ⓑ Ⓒ Ⓓ Ⓔ
36 Ⓐ Ⓑ Ⓒ Ⓓ Ⓔ
37 Ⓐ Ⓑ Ⓒ Ⓓ Ⓔ
38 Ⓐ Ⓑ Ⓒ Ⓓ Ⓔ
39 Ⓐ Ⓑ Ⓒ Ⓓ Ⓔ
40 Ⓐ Ⓑ Ⓒ Ⓓ Ⓔ
41 Ⓐ Ⓑ Ⓒ Ⓓ Ⓔ
42 Ⓐ Ⓑ Ⓒ Ⓓ Ⓔ
43 Ⓐ Ⓑ Ⓒ Ⓓ Ⓔ
44 Ⓐ Ⓑ Ⓒ Ⓓ Ⓔ
45 Ⓐ Ⓑ Ⓒ Ⓓ Ⓔ
46 Ⓐ Ⓑ Ⓒ Ⓓ Ⓔ
47 Ⓐ Ⓑ Ⓒ Ⓓ Ⓔ
48 Ⓐ Ⓑ Ⓒ Ⓓ Ⓔ
49 Ⓐ Ⓑ Ⓒ Ⓓ Ⓔ
50 Ⓐ Ⓑ Ⓒ Ⓓ Ⓔ
51 Ⓐ Ⓑ Ⓒ Ⓓ Ⓔ
52 Ⓐ Ⓑ Ⓒ Ⓓ Ⓔ
53 Ⓐ Ⓑ Ⓒ Ⓓ Ⓔ
54 Ⓐ Ⓑ Ⓒ Ⓓ Ⓔ
55 Ⓐ Ⓑ Ⓒ Ⓓ Ⓔ
56 Ⓐ Ⓑ Ⓒ Ⓓ Ⓔ
57 Ⓐ Ⓑ Ⓒ Ⓓ Ⓔ
58 Ⓐ Ⓑ Ⓒ Ⓓ Ⓔ
59 Ⓐ Ⓑ Ⓒ Ⓓ Ⓔ
60 Ⓐ Ⓑ Ⓒ Ⓓ Ⓔ

Section 5 — Math
30 minutes

26 Ⓐ Ⓑ Ⓒ Ⓓ Ⓔ
27 Ⓐ Ⓑ Ⓒ Ⓓ Ⓔ
28 Ⓐ Ⓑ Ⓒ Ⓓ Ⓔ
29 Ⓐ Ⓑ Ⓒ Ⓓ Ⓔ
30 Ⓐ Ⓑ Ⓒ Ⓓ Ⓔ
31 Ⓐ Ⓑ Ⓒ Ⓓ Ⓔ
32 Ⓐ Ⓑ Ⓒ Ⓓ Ⓔ
33 Ⓐ Ⓑ Ⓒ Ⓓ Ⓔ
34 Ⓐ Ⓑ Ⓒ Ⓓ Ⓔ
35 Ⓐ Ⓑ Ⓒ Ⓓ Ⓔ
36 Ⓐ Ⓑ Ⓒ Ⓓ Ⓔ
37 Ⓐ Ⓑ Ⓒ Ⓓ Ⓔ
39 Ⓐ Ⓑ Ⓒ Ⓓ Ⓔ
39 Ⓐ Ⓑ Ⓒ Ⓓ Ⓔ
40 Ⓐ Ⓑ Ⓒ Ⓓ Ⓔ

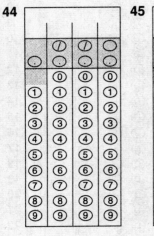

Grid-in questions 41, 42, 43, 44, 45, 46, 47, 48, 49, 50 — each with the following grid:

	/	/	
.	.	.	.
	0	0	0
1	1	1	1
2	2	2	2
3	3	3	3
4	4	4	4
5	5	5	5
6	6	6	6
7	7	7	7
8	8	8	8
9	9	9	9

Answer Sheet
Use these Answer Sheets for additional practice.

Each mark should completely fill the appropriate space, and should be as dark as all other marks. Make all erasures complete. Traces of an erasure may be read as an answer. See pages vii and 27 for explanations of timing and number of questions.

Section 1 — Verbal
30 minutes

1 Ⓐ Ⓑ Ⓒ Ⓓ Ⓔ
2 Ⓐ Ⓑ Ⓒ Ⓓ Ⓔ
3 Ⓐ Ⓑ Ⓒ Ⓓ Ⓔ
4 Ⓐ Ⓑ Ⓒ Ⓓ Ⓔ
5 Ⓐ Ⓑ Ⓒ Ⓓ Ⓔ
6 Ⓐ Ⓑ Ⓒ Ⓓ Ⓔ
7 Ⓐ Ⓑ Ⓒ Ⓓ Ⓔ
8 Ⓐ Ⓑ Ⓒ Ⓓ Ⓔ
9 Ⓐ Ⓑ Ⓒ Ⓓ Ⓔ
10 Ⓐ Ⓑ Ⓒ Ⓓ Ⓔ
11 Ⓐ Ⓑ Ⓒ Ⓓ Ⓔ
12 Ⓐ Ⓑ Ⓒ Ⓓ Ⓔ
13 Ⓐ Ⓑ Ⓒ Ⓓ Ⓔ
14 Ⓐ Ⓑ Ⓒ Ⓓ Ⓔ
15 Ⓐ Ⓑ Ⓒ Ⓓ Ⓔ
16 Ⓐ Ⓑ Ⓒ Ⓓ Ⓔ
17 Ⓐ Ⓑ Ⓒ Ⓓ Ⓔ
18 Ⓐ Ⓑ Ⓒ Ⓓ Ⓔ
19 Ⓐ Ⓑ Ⓒ Ⓓ Ⓔ
20 Ⓐ Ⓑ Ⓒ Ⓓ Ⓔ
21 Ⓐ Ⓑ Ⓒ Ⓓ Ⓔ
22 Ⓐ Ⓑ Ⓒ Ⓓ Ⓔ
23 Ⓐ Ⓑ Ⓒ Ⓓ Ⓔ
24 Ⓐ Ⓑ Ⓒ Ⓓ Ⓔ
25 Ⓐ Ⓑ Ⓒ Ⓓ Ⓔ
26 Ⓐ Ⓑ Ⓒ Ⓓ Ⓔ
27 Ⓐ Ⓑ Ⓒ Ⓓ Ⓔ
28 Ⓐ Ⓑ Ⓒ Ⓓ Ⓔ
29 Ⓐ Ⓑ Ⓒ Ⓓ Ⓔ
30 Ⓐ Ⓑ Ⓒ Ⓓ Ⓔ

Section 2 — Math
30 minutes

1 Ⓐ Ⓑ Ⓒ Ⓓ Ⓔ
2 Ⓐ Ⓑ Ⓒ Ⓓ Ⓔ
3 Ⓐ Ⓑ Ⓒ Ⓓ Ⓔ
4 Ⓐ Ⓑ Ⓒ Ⓓ Ⓔ
5 Ⓐ Ⓑ Ⓒ Ⓓ Ⓔ
6 Ⓐ Ⓑ Ⓒ Ⓓ Ⓔ
7 Ⓐ Ⓑ Ⓒ Ⓓ Ⓔ
8 Ⓐ Ⓑ Ⓒ Ⓓ Ⓔ
9 Ⓐ Ⓑ Ⓒ Ⓓ Ⓔ
10 Ⓐ Ⓑ Ⓒ Ⓓ Ⓔ
11 Ⓐ Ⓑ Ⓒ Ⓓ Ⓔ
12 Ⓐ Ⓑ Ⓒ Ⓓ Ⓔ
13 Ⓐ Ⓑ Ⓒ Ⓓ Ⓔ
14 Ⓐ Ⓑ Ⓒ Ⓓ Ⓔ
15 Ⓐ Ⓑ Ⓒ Ⓓ Ⓔ
16 Ⓐ Ⓑ Ⓒ Ⓓ Ⓔ
17 Ⓐ Ⓑ Ⓒ Ⓓ Ⓔ
18 Ⓐ Ⓑ Ⓒ Ⓓ Ⓔ
19 Ⓐ Ⓑ Ⓒ Ⓓ Ⓔ
20 Ⓐ Ⓑ Ⓒ Ⓓ Ⓔ
21 Ⓐ Ⓑ Ⓒ Ⓓ Ⓔ
22 Ⓐ Ⓑ Ⓒ Ⓓ Ⓔ
23 Ⓐ Ⓑ Ⓒ Ⓓ Ⓔ
24 Ⓐ Ⓑ Ⓒ Ⓓ Ⓔ
25 Ⓐ Ⓑ Ⓒ Ⓓ Ⓔ

Section 3 — Writing
30 minutes

1 Ⓐ Ⓑ Ⓒ Ⓓ Ⓔ
2 Ⓐ Ⓑ Ⓒ Ⓓ Ⓔ
3 Ⓐ Ⓑ Ⓒ Ⓓ Ⓔ
4 Ⓐ Ⓑ Ⓒ Ⓓ Ⓔ
5 Ⓐ Ⓑ Ⓒ Ⓓ Ⓔ
6 Ⓐ Ⓑ Ⓒ Ⓓ Ⓔ
7 Ⓐ Ⓑ Ⓒ Ⓓ Ⓔ
8 Ⓐ Ⓑ Ⓒ Ⓓ Ⓔ
9 Ⓐ Ⓑ Ⓒ Ⓓ Ⓔ
10 Ⓐ Ⓑ Ⓒ Ⓓ Ⓔ
11 Ⓐ Ⓑ Ⓒ Ⓓ Ⓔ
12 Ⓐ Ⓑ Ⓒ Ⓓ Ⓔ
13 Ⓐ Ⓑ Ⓒ Ⓓ Ⓔ
14 Ⓐ Ⓑ Ⓒ Ⓓ Ⓔ
15 Ⓐ Ⓑ Ⓒ Ⓓ Ⓔ
16 Ⓐ Ⓑ Ⓒ Ⓓ Ⓔ
17 Ⓐ Ⓑ Ⓒ Ⓓ Ⓔ
18 Ⓐ Ⓑ Ⓒ Ⓓ Ⓔ
19 Ⓐ Ⓑ Ⓒ Ⓓ Ⓔ
20 Ⓐ Ⓑ Ⓒ Ⓓ Ⓔ
21 Ⓐ Ⓑ Ⓒ Ⓓ Ⓔ
22 Ⓐ Ⓑ Ⓒ Ⓓ Ⓔ
23 Ⓐ Ⓑ Ⓒ Ⓓ Ⓔ
24 Ⓐ Ⓑ Ⓒ Ⓓ Ⓔ
25 Ⓐ Ⓑ Ⓒ Ⓓ Ⓔ
26 Ⓐ Ⓑ Ⓒ Ⓓ Ⓔ
27 Ⓐ Ⓑ Ⓒ Ⓓ Ⓔ
28 Ⓐ Ⓑ Ⓒ Ⓓ Ⓔ
29 Ⓐ Ⓑ Ⓒ Ⓓ Ⓔ
30 Ⓐ Ⓑ Ⓒ Ⓓ Ⓔ
31 Ⓐ Ⓑ Ⓒ Ⓓ Ⓔ
32 Ⓐ Ⓑ Ⓒ Ⓓ Ⓔ
33 Ⓐ Ⓑ Ⓒ Ⓓ Ⓔ
34 Ⓐ Ⓑ Ⓒ Ⓓ Ⓔ
35 Ⓐ Ⓑ Ⓒ Ⓓ Ⓔ
36 Ⓐ Ⓑ Ⓒ Ⓓ Ⓔ
37 Ⓐ Ⓑ Ⓒ Ⓓ Ⓔ
38 Ⓐ Ⓑ Ⓒ Ⓓ Ⓔ
39 Ⓐ Ⓑ Ⓒ Ⓓ Ⓔ

Section 4 — Verbal
30 minutes

31 Ⓐ Ⓑ Ⓒ Ⓓ Ⓔ
32 Ⓐ Ⓑ Ⓒ Ⓓ Ⓔ
33 Ⓐ Ⓑ Ⓒ Ⓓ Ⓔ
34 Ⓐ Ⓑ Ⓒ Ⓓ Ⓔ
35 Ⓐ Ⓑ Ⓒ Ⓓ Ⓔ
36 Ⓐ Ⓑ Ⓒ Ⓓ Ⓔ
37 Ⓐ Ⓑ Ⓒ Ⓓ Ⓔ
38 Ⓐ Ⓑ Ⓒ Ⓓ Ⓔ
39 Ⓐ Ⓑ Ⓒ Ⓓ Ⓔ
40 Ⓐ Ⓑ Ⓒ Ⓓ Ⓔ
41 Ⓐ Ⓑ Ⓒ Ⓓ Ⓔ
42 Ⓐ Ⓑ Ⓒ Ⓓ Ⓔ
43 Ⓐ Ⓑ Ⓒ Ⓓ Ⓔ
44 Ⓐ Ⓑ Ⓒ Ⓓ Ⓔ
45 Ⓐ Ⓑ Ⓒ Ⓓ Ⓔ
46 Ⓐ Ⓑ Ⓒ Ⓓ Ⓔ
47 Ⓐ Ⓑ Ⓒ Ⓓ Ⓔ
48 Ⓐ Ⓑ Ⓒ Ⓓ Ⓔ
49 Ⓐ Ⓑ Ⓒ Ⓓ Ⓔ
50 Ⓐ Ⓑ Ⓒ Ⓓ Ⓔ
51 Ⓐ Ⓑ Ⓒ Ⓓ Ⓔ
52 Ⓐ Ⓑ Ⓒ Ⓓ Ⓔ
53 Ⓐ Ⓑ Ⓒ Ⓓ Ⓔ
54 Ⓐ Ⓑ Ⓒ Ⓓ Ⓔ
55 Ⓐ Ⓑ Ⓒ Ⓓ Ⓔ
56 Ⓐ Ⓑ Ⓒ Ⓓ Ⓔ
57 Ⓐ Ⓑ Ⓒ Ⓓ Ⓔ
58 Ⓐ Ⓑ Ⓒ Ⓓ Ⓔ
59 Ⓐ Ⓑ Ⓒ Ⓓ Ⓔ
60 Ⓐ Ⓑ Ⓒ Ⓓ Ⓔ

Section 5 — Math
30 minutes

26 Ⓐ Ⓑ Ⓒ Ⓓ Ⓔ
27 Ⓐ Ⓑ Ⓒ Ⓓ Ⓔ
28 Ⓐ Ⓑ Ⓒ Ⓓ Ⓔ
29 Ⓐ Ⓑ Ⓒ Ⓓ Ⓔ
30 Ⓐ Ⓑ Ⓒ Ⓓ Ⓔ
31 Ⓐ Ⓑ Ⓒ Ⓓ Ⓔ
32 Ⓐ Ⓑ Ⓒ Ⓓ Ⓔ
33 Ⓐ Ⓑ Ⓒ Ⓓ Ⓔ
34 Ⓐ Ⓑ Ⓒ Ⓓ Ⓔ
35 Ⓐ Ⓑ Ⓒ Ⓓ Ⓔ
36 Ⓐ Ⓑ Ⓒ Ⓓ Ⓔ
37 Ⓐ Ⓑ Ⓒ Ⓓ Ⓔ
39 Ⓐ Ⓑ Ⓒ Ⓓ Ⓔ
39 Ⓐ Ⓑ Ⓒ Ⓓ Ⓔ
40 Ⓐ Ⓑ Ⓒ Ⓓ Ⓔ

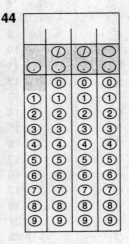

41 42
43 44 45
46 47 48 49 50

Answer Sheet
Use these Answer Sheets for additional practice.

Each mark should completely fill the appropriate space, and should be as dark as all other marks. Make all erasures complete. Traces of an erasure may be read as an answer. See pages vii and 27 for explanations of timing and number of questions.

Section 1 — Verbal
30 minutes

1 (A) (B) (C) (D) (E)
2 (A) (B) (C) (D) (E)
3 (A) (B) (C) (D) (E)
4 (A) (B) (C) (D) (E)
5 (A) (B) (C) (D) (E)
6 (A) (B) (C) (D) (E)
7 (A) (B) (C) (D) (E)
8 (A) (B) (C) (D) (E)
9 (A) (B) (C) (D) (E)
10 (A) (B) (C) (D) (E)
11 (A) (B) (C) (D) (E)
12 (A) (B) (C) (D) (E)
13 (A) (B) (C) (D) (E)
14 (A) (B) (C) (D) (E)
15 (A) (B) (C) (D) (E)
16 (A) (B) (C) (D) (E)
17 (A) (B) (C) (D) (E)
18 (A) (B) (C) (D) (E)
19 (A) (B) (C) (D) (E)
20 (A) (B) (C) (D) (E)
21 (A) (B) (C) (D) (E)
22 (A) (B) (C) (D) (E)
23 (A) (B) (C) (D) (E)
24 (A) (B) (C) (D) (E)
25 (A) (B) (C) (D) (E)
26 (A) (B) (C) (D) (E)
27 (A) (B) (C) (D) (E)
28 (A) (B) (C) (D) (E)
29 (A) (B) (C) (D) (E)
30 (A) (B) (C) (D) (E)

Section 2 — Math
30 minutes

1 (A) (B) (C) (D) (E)
2 (A) (B) (C) (D) (E)
3 (A) (B) (C) (D) (E)
4 (A) (B) (C) (D) (E)
5 (A) (B) (C) (D) (E)
6 (A) (B) (C) (D) (E)
7 (A) (B) (C) (D) (E)
8 (A) (B) (C) (D) (E)
9 (A) (B) (C) (D) (E)
10 (A) (B) (C) (D) (E)
11 (A) (B) (C) (D) (E)
12 (A) (B) (C) (D) (E)
13 (A) (B) (C) (D) (E)
14 (A) (B) (C) (D) (E)
15 (A) (B) (C) (D) (E)
16 (A) (B) (C) (D) (E)
17 (A) (B) (C) (D) (E)
18 (A) (B) (C) (D) (E)
19 (A) (B) (C) (D) (E)
20 (A) (B) (C) (D) (E)
21 (A) (B) (C) (D) (E)
22 (A) (B) (C) (D) (E)
23 (A) (B) (C) (D) (E)
24 (A) (B) (C) (D) (E)
25 (A) (B) (C) (D) (E)

Section 3 — Writing
30 minutes

1 (A) (B) (C) (D) (E)
2 (A) (B) (C) (D) (E)
3 (A) (B) (C) (D) (E)
4 (A) (B) (C) (D) (E)
5 (A) (B) (C) (D) (E)
6 (A) (B) (C) (D) (E)
7 (A) (B) (C) (D) (E)
8 (A) (B) (C) (D) (E)
9 (A) (B) (C) (D) (E)
10 (A) (B) (C) (D) (E)
11 (A) (B) (C) (D) (E)
12 (A) (B) (C) (D) (E)
13 (A) (B) (C) (D) (E)
14 (A) (B) (C) (D) (E)
15 (A) (B) (C) (D) (E)
16 (A) (B) (C) (D) (E)
17 (A) (B) (C) (D) (E)
18 (A) (B) (C) (D) (E)
19 (A) (B) (C) (D) (E)
20 (A) (B) (C) (D) (E)
21 (A) (B) (C) (D) (E)
22 (A) (B) (C) (D) (E)
23 (A) (B) (C) (D) (E)
24 (A) (B) (C) (D) (E)
25 (A) (B) (C) (D) (E)
26 (A) (B) (C) (D) (E)
27 (A) (B) (C) (D) (E)
28 (A) (B) (C) (D) (E)
29 (A) (B) (C) (D) (E)
30 (A) (B) (C) (D) (E)
31 (A) (B) (C) (D) (E)
32 (A) (B) (C) (D) (E)
33 (A) (B) (C) (D) (E)
34 (A) (B) (C) (D) (E)
35 (A) (B) (C) (D) (E)
36 (A) (B) (C) (D) (E)
37 (A) (B) (C) (D) (E)
38 (A) (B) (C) (D) (E)
39 (A) (B) (C) (D) (E)

Section 4 — Verbal
30 minutes

31 Ⓐ Ⓑ Ⓒ Ⓓ Ⓔ
32 Ⓐ Ⓑ Ⓒ Ⓓ Ⓔ
33 Ⓐ Ⓑ Ⓒ Ⓓ Ⓔ
34 Ⓐ Ⓑ Ⓒ Ⓓ Ⓔ
35 Ⓐ Ⓑ Ⓒ Ⓓ Ⓔ
36 Ⓐ Ⓑ Ⓒ Ⓓ Ⓔ
37 Ⓐ Ⓑ Ⓒ Ⓓ Ⓔ
38 Ⓐ Ⓑ Ⓒ Ⓓ Ⓔ
39 Ⓐ Ⓑ Ⓒ Ⓓ Ⓔ
40 Ⓐ Ⓑ Ⓒ Ⓓ Ⓔ
41 Ⓐ Ⓑ Ⓒ Ⓓ Ⓔ
42 Ⓐ Ⓑ Ⓒ Ⓓ Ⓔ
43 Ⓐ Ⓑ Ⓒ Ⓓ Ⓔ
44 Ⓐ Ⓑ Ⓒ Ⓓ Ⓔ
45 Ⓐ Ⓑ Ⓒ Ⓓ Ⓔ
46 Ⓐ Ⓑ Ⓒ Ⓓ Ⓔ
47 Ⓐ Ⓑ Ⓒ Ⓓ Ⓔ
48 Ⓐ Ⓑ Ⓒ Ⓓ Ⓔ
49 Ⓐ Ⓑ Ⓒ Ⓓ Ⓔ
50 Ⓐ Ⓑ Ⓒ Ⓓ Ⓔ
51 Ⓐ Ⓑ Ⓒ Ⓓ Ⓔ
52 Ⓐ Ⓑ Ⓒ Ⓓ Ⓔ
53 Ⓐ Ⓑ Ⓒ Ⓓ Ⓔ
54 Ⓐ Ⓑ Ⓒ Ⓓ Ⓔ
55 Ⓐ Ⓑ Ⓒ Ⓓ Ⓔ
56 Ⓐ Ⓑ Ⓒ Ⓓ Ⓔ
57 Ⓐ Ⓑ Ⓒ Ⓓ Ⓔ
58 Ⓐ Ⓑ Ⓒ Ⓓ Ⓔ
59 Ⓐ Ⓑ Ⓒ Ⓓ Ⓔ
60 Ⓐ Ⓑ Ⓒ Ⓓ Ⓔ

Section 5 — Math
30 minutes

26 Ⓐ Ⓑ Ⓒ Ⓓ Ⓔ
27 Ⓐ Ⓑ Ⓒ Ⓓ Ⓔ
28 Ⓐ Ⓑ Ⓒ Ⓓ Ⓔ
29 Ⓐ Ⓑ Ⓒ Ⓓ Ⓔ
30 Ⓐ Ⓑ Ⓒ Ⓓ Ⓔ
31 Ⓐ Ⓑ Ⓒ Ⓓ Ⓔ
32 Ⓐ Ⓑ Ⓒ Ⓓ Ⓔ
33 Ⓐ Ⓑ Ⓒ Ⓓ Ⓔ
34 Ⓐ Ⓑ Ⓒ Ⓓ Ⓔ
35 Ⓐ Ⓑ Ⓒ Ⓓ Ⓔ
36 Ⓐ Ⓑ Ⓒ Ⓓ Ⓔ
37 Ⓐ Ⓑ Ⓒ Ⓓ Ⓔ
39 Ⓐ Ⓑ Ⓒ Ⓓ Ⓔ
39 Ⓐ Ⓑ Ⓒ Ⓓ Ⓔ
40 Ⓐ Ⓑ Ⓒ Ⓓ Ⓔ

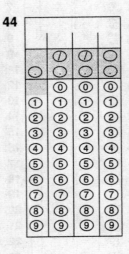

Grid-in answer boxes (each: four columns with / and . rows, and bubbles 0–9):

	Col 1	Col 2	Col 3	Col 4
/		/	/	
.	.	.	.	.
0		0	0	0
1	1	1	1	1
2	2	2	2	2
3	3	3	3	3
4	4	4	4	4
5	5	5	5	5
6	6	6	6	6
7	7	7	7	7
8	8	8	8	8
9	9	9	9	9

41

42

43

44

45

46

47

48

49

50

Answer Sheet

Use these Answer Sheets for additional practice.

Each mark should completely fill the appropriate space, and should be as dark as all other marks. Make all erasures complete. Traces of an erasure may be read as an answer. See pages vii and 27 for explanations of timing and number of questions.

Section 1 — Verbal
30 minutes

1 (A) (B) (C) (D) (E)
2 (A) (B) (C) (D) (E)
3 (A) (B) (C) (D) (E)
4 (A) (B) (C) (D) (E)
5 (A) (B) (C) (D) (E)
6 (A) (B) (C) (D) (E)
7 (A) (B) (C) (D) (E)
8 (A) (B) (C) (D) (E)
9 (A) (B) (C) (D) (E)
10 (A) (B) (C) (D) (E)
11 (A) (B) (C) (D) (E)
12 (A) (B) (C) (D) (E)
13 (A) (B) (C) (D) (E)
14 (A) (B) (C) (D) (E)
15 (A) (B) (C) (D) (E)
16 (A) (B) (C) (D) (E)
17 (A) (B) (C) (D) (E)
18 (A) (B) (C) (D) (E)
19 (A) (B) (C) (D) (E)
20 (A) (B) (C) (D) (E)
21 (A) (B) (C) (D) (E)
22 (A) (B) (C) (D) (E)
23 (A) (B) (C) (D) (E)
24 (A) (B) (C) (D) (E)
25 (A) (B) (C) (D) (E)
26 (A) (B) (C) (D) (E)
27 (A) (B) (C) (D) (E)
28 (A) (B) (C) (D) (E)
29 (A) (B) (C) (D) (E)
30 (A) (B) (C) (D) (E)

Section 2 — Math
30 minutes

1 (A) (B) (C) (D) (E)
2 (A) (B) (C) (D) (E)
3 (A) (B) (C) (D) (E)
4 (A) (B) (C) (D) (E)
5 (A) (B) (C) (D) (E)
6 (A) (B) (C) (D) (E)
7 (A) (B) (C) (D) (E)
8 (A) (B) (C) (D) (E)
9 (A) (B) (C) (D) (E)
10 (A) (B) (C) (D) (E)
11 (A) (B) (C) (D) (E)
12 (A) (B) (C) (D) (E)
13 (A) (B) (C) (D) (E)
14 (A) (B) (C) (D) (E)
15 (A) (B) (C) (D) (E)
16 (A) (B) (C) (D) (E)
17 (A) (B) (C) (D) (E)
18 (A) (B) (C) (D) (E)
19 (A) (B) (C) (D) (E)
20 (A) (B) (C) (D) (E)
21 (A) (B) (C) (D) (E)
22 (A) (B) (C) (D) (E)
23 (A) (B) (C) (D) (E)
24 (A) (B) (C) (D) (E)
25 (A) (B) (C) (D) (E)

Section 3 — Writing
30 minutes

1 (A) (B) (C) (D) (E)
2 (A) (B) (C) (D) (E)
3 (A) (B) (C) (D) (E)
4 (A) (B) (C) (D) (E)
5 (A) (B) (C) (D) (E)
6 (A) (B) (C) (D) (E)
7 (A) (B) (C) (D) (E)
8 (A) (B) (C) (D) (E)
9 (A) (B) (C) (D) (E)
10 (A) (B) (C) (D) (E)
11 (A) (B) (C) (D) (E)
12 (A) (B) (C) (D) (E)
13 (A) (B) (C) (D) (E)
14 (A) (B) (C) (D) (E)
15 (A) (B) (C) (D) (E)
16 (A) (B) (C) (D) (E)
17 (A) (B) (C) (D) (E)
18 (A) (B) (C) (D) (E)
19 (A) (B) (C) (D) (E)
20 (A) (B) (C) (D) (E)
21 (A) (B) (C) (D) (E)
22 (A) (B) (C) (D) (E)
23 (A) (B) (C) (D) (E)
24 (A) (B) (C) (D) (E)
25 (A) (B) (C) (D) (E)
26 (A) (B) (C) (D) (E)
27 (A) (B) (C) (D) (E)
28 (A) (B) (C) (D) (E)
29 (A) (B) (C) (D) (E)
30 (A) (B) (C) (D) (E)
31 (A) (B) (C) (D) (E)
32 (A) (B) (C) (D) (E)
33 (A) (B) (C) (D) (E)
34 (A) (B) (C) (D) (E)
35 (A) (B) (C) (D) (E)
36 (A) (B) (C) (D) (E)
37 (A) (B) (C) (D) (E)
38 (A) (B) (C) (D) (E)
39 (A) (B) (C) (D) (E)

Section 4 — Verbal
30 minutes

31 Ⓐ Ⓑ Ⓒ Ⓓ Ⓔ
32 Ⓐ Ⓑ Ⓒ Ⓓ Ⓔ
33 Ⓐ Ⓑ Ⓒ Ⓓ Ⓔ
34 Ⓐ Ⓑ Ⓒ Ⓓ Ⓔ
35 Ⓐ Ⓑ Ⓒ Ⓓ Ⓔ
36 Ⓐ Ⓑ Ⓒ Ⓓ Ⓔ
37 Ⓐ Ⓑ Ⓒ Ⓓ Ⓔ
38 Ⓐ Ⓑ Ⓒ Ⓓ Ⓔ
39 Ⓐ Ⓑ Ⓒ Ⓓ Ⓔ
40 Ⓐ Ⓑ Ⓒ Ⓓ Ⓔ
41 Ⓐ Ⓑ Ⓒ Ⓓ Ⓔ
42 Ⓐ Ⓑ Ⓒ Ⓓ Ⓔ
43 Ⓐ Ⓑ Ⓒ Ⓓ Ⓔ
44 Ⓐ Ⓑ Ⓒ Ⓓ Ⓔ
45 Ⓐ Ⓑ Ⓒ Ⓓ Ⓔ
46 Ⓐ Ⓑ Ⓒ Ⓓ Ⓔ
47 Ⓐ Ⓑ Ⓒ Ⓓ Ⓔ
48 Ⓐ Ⓑ Ⓒ Ⓓ Ⓔ
49 Ⓐ Ⓑ Ⓒ Ⓓ Ⓔ
50 Ⓐ Ⓑ Ⓒ Ⓓ Ⓔ
51 Ⓐ Ⓑ Ⓒ Ⓓ Ⓔ
52 Ⓐ Ⓑ Ⓒ Ⓓ Ⓔ
53 Ⓐ Ⓑ Ⓒ Ⓓ Ⓔ
54 Ⓐ Ⓑ Ⓒ Ⓓ Ⓔ
55 Ⓐ Ⓑ Ⓒ Ⓓ Ⓔ
56 Ⓐ Ⓑ Ⓒ Ⓓ Ⓔ
57 Ⓐ Ⓑ Ⓒ Ⓓ Ⓔ
58 Ⓐ Ⓑ Ⓒ Ⓓ Ⓔ
59 Ⓐ Ⓑ Ⓒ Ⓓ Ⓔ
60 Ⓐ Ⓑ Ⓒ Ⓓ Ⓔ

Section 5 — Math
30 minutes

26 Ⓐ Ⓑ Ⓒ Ⓓ Ⓔ
27 Ⓐ Ⓑ Ⓒ Ⓓ Ⓔ
28 Ⓐ Ⓑ Ⓒ Ⓓ Ⓔ
29 Ⓐ Ⓑ Ⓒ Ⓓ Ⓔ
30 Ⓐ Ⓑ Ⓒ Ⓓ Ⓔ
31 Ⓐ Ⓑ Ⓒ Ⓓ Ⓔ
32 Ⓐ Ⓑ Ⓒ Ⓓ Ⓔ
33 Ⓐ Ⓑ Ⓒ Ⓓ Ⓔ
34 Ⓐ Ⓑ Ⓒ Ⓓ Ⓔ
35 Ⓐ Ⓑ Ⓒ Ⓓ Ⓔ
36 Ⓐ Ⓑ Ⓒ Ⓓ Ⓔ
37 Ⓐ Ⓑ Ⓒ Ⓓ Ⓔ
39 Ⓐ Ⓑ Ⓒ Ⓓ Ⓔ
39 Ⓐ Ⓑ Ⓒ Ⓓ Ⓔ
40 Ⓐ Ⓑ Ⓒ Ⓓ Ⓔ

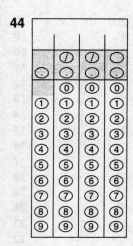

41 42 43 44 45

46 47 48 49 50

Answer Sheet

Use these Answer Sheets for additional practice.

Each mark should completely fill the appropriate space, and should be as dark as all other marks. Make all erasures complete. Traces of an erasure may be read as an answer. See pages vii and 27 for explanations of timing and number of questions.

Section 1 — Verbal
30 minutes

1 (A) (B) (C) (D) (E)
2 (A) (B) (C) (D) (E)
3 (A) (B) (C) (D) (E)
4 (A) (B) (C) (D) (E)
5 (A) (B) (C) (D) (E)
6 (A) (B) (C) (D) (E)
7 (A) (B) (C) (D) (E)
8 (A) (B) (C) (D) (E)
9 (A) (B) (C) (D) (E)
10 (A) (B) (C) (D) (E)
11 (A) (B) (C) (D) (E)
12 (A) (B) (C) (D) (E)
13 (A) (B) (C) (D) (E)
14 (A) (B) (C) (D) (E)
15 (A) (B) (C) (D) (E)
16 (A) (B) (C) (D) (E)
17 (A) (B) (C) (D) (E)
18 (A) (B) (C) (D) (E)
19 (A) (B) (C) (D) (E)
20 (A) (B) (C) (D) (E)
21 (A) (B) (C) (D) (E)
22 (A) (B) (C) (D) (E)
23 (A) (B) (C) (D) (E)
24 (A) (B) (C) (D) (E)
25 (A) (B) (C) (D) (E)
26 (A) (B) (C) (D) (E)
27 (A) (B) (C) (D) (E)
28 (A) (B) (C) (D) (E)
29 (A) (B) (C) (D) (E)
30 (A) (B) (C) (D) (E)

Section 2 — Math
30 minutes

1 (A) (B) (C) (D) (E)
2 (A) (B) (C) (D) (E)
3 (A) (B) (C) (D) (E)
4 (A) (B) (C) (D) (E)
5 (A) (B) (C) (D) (E)
6 (A) (B) (C) (D) (E)
7 (A) (B) (C) (D) (E)
8 (A) (B) (C) (D) (E)
9 (A) (B) (C) (D) (E)
10 (A) (B) (C) (D) (E)
11 (A) (B) (C) (D) (E)
12 (A) (B) (C) (D) (E)
13 (A) (B) (C) (D) (E)
14 (A) (B) (C) (D) (E)
15 (A) (B) (C) (D) (E)
16 (A) (B) (C) (D) (E)
17 (A) (B) (C) (D) (E)
18 (A) (B) (C) (D) (E)
19 (A) (B) (C) (D) (E)
20 (A) (B) (C) (D) (E)
21 (A) (B) (C) (D) (E)
22 (A) (B) (C) (D) (E)
23 (A) (B) (C) (D) (E)
24 (A) (B) (C) (D) (E)
25 (A) (B) (C) (D) (E)

Section 3 — Writing
30 minutes

1 (A) (B) (C) (D) (E)
2 (A) (B) (C) (D) (E)
3 (A) (B) (C) (D) (E)
4 (A) (B) (C) (D) (E)
5 (A) (B) (C) (D) (E)
6 (A) (B) (C) (D) (E)
7 (A) (B) (C) (D) (E)
8 (A) (B) (C) (D) (E)
9 (A) (B) (C) (D) (E)
10 (A) (B) (C) (D) (E)
11 (A) (B) (C) (D) (E)
12 (A) (B) (C) (D) (E)
13 (A) (B) (C) (D) (E)
14 (A) (B) (C) (D) (E)
15 (A) (B) (C) (D) (E)
16 (A) (B) (C) (D) (E)
17 (A) (B) (C) (D) (E)
18 (A) (B) (C) (D) (E)
19 (A) (B) (C) (D) (E)
20 (A) (B) (C) (D) (E)
21 (A) (B) (C) (D) (E)
22 (A) (B) (C) (D) (E)
23 (A) (B) (C) (D) (E)
24 (A) (B) (C) (D) (E)
25 (A) (B) (C) (D) (E)
26 (A) (B) (C) (D) (E)
27 (A) (B) (C) (D) (E)
28 (A) (B) (C) (D) (E)
29 (A) (B) (C) (D) (E)
30 (A) (B) (C) (D) (E)
31 (A) (B) (C) (D) (E)
32 (A) (B) (C) (D) (E)
33 (A) (B) (C) (D) (E)
34 (A) (B) (C) (D) (E)
35 (A) (B) (C) (D) (E)
36 (A) (B) (C) (D) (E)
37 (A) (B) (C) (D) (E)
38 (A) (B) (C) (D) (E)
39 (A) (B) (C) (D) (E)

Section 4 — Verbal
30 minutes

31 (A) (B) (C) (D) (E)
32 (A) (B) (C) (D) (E)
33 (A) (B) (C) (D) (E)
34 (A) (B) (C) (D) (E)
35 (A) (B) (C) (D) (E)
36 (A) (B) (C) (D) (E)
37 (A) (B) (C) (D) (E)
38 (A) (B) (C) (D) (E)
39 (A) (B) (C) (D) (E)
40 (A) (B) (C) (D) (E)
41 (A) (B) (C) (D) (E)
42 (A) (B) (C) (D) (E)
43 (A) (B) (C) (D) (E)
44 (A) (B) (C) (D) (E)
45 (A) (B) (C) (D) (E)
46 (A) (B) (C) (D) (E)
47 (A) (B) (C) (D) (E)
48 (A) (B) (C) (D) (E)
49 (A) (B) (C) (D) (E)
50 (A) (B) (C) (D) (E)
51 (A) (B) (C) (D) (E)
52 (A) (B) (C) (D) (E)
53 (A) (B) (C) (D) (E)
54 (A) (B) (C) (D) (E)
55 (A) (B) (C) (D) (E)
56 (A) (B) (C) (D) (E)
57 (A) (B) (C) (D) (E)
58 (A) (B) (C) (D) (E)
59 (A) (B) (C) (D) (E)
60 (A) (B) (C) (D) (E)

Section 5 — Math
30 minutes

26 (A) (B) (C) (D) (E)
27 (A) (B) (C) (D) (E)
28 (A) (B) (C) (D) (E)
29 (A) (B) (C) (D) (E)
30 (A) (B) (C) (D) (E)
31 (A) (B) (C) (D) (E)
32 (A) (B) (C) (D) (E)
33 (A) (B) (C) (D) (E)
34 (A) (B) (C) (D) (E)
35 (A) (B) (C) (D) (E)
36 (A) (B) (C) (D) (E)
37 (A) (B) (C) (D) (E)
39 (A) (B) (C) (D) (E)
39 (A) (B) (C) (D) (E)
40 (A) (B) (C) (D) (E)

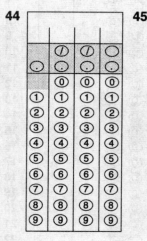

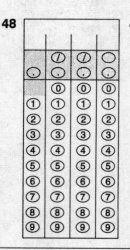

41 42 43 44 45 46 47 48 49 50

Answer Sheet

Use these Answer Sheets for additional practice.

Each mark should completely fill the appropriate space, and should be as dark as all other marks. Make all erasures complete. Traces of an erasure may be read as an answer. See pages vii and 27 for explanations of timing and number of questions.

Section 1 — Verbal
30 minutes

1 Ⓐ Ⓑ Ⓒ Ⓓ Ⓔ
2 Ⓐ Ⓑ Ⓒ Ⓓ Ⓔ
3 Ⓐ Ⓑ Ⓒ Ⓓ Ⓔ
4 Ⓐ Ⓑ Ⓒ Ⓓ Ⓔ
5 Ⓐ Ⓑ Ⓒ Ⓓ Ⓔ
6 Ⓐ Ⓑ Ⓒ Ⓓ Ⓔ
7 Ⓐ Ⓑ Ⓒ Ⓓ Ⓔ
8 Ⓐ Ⓑ Ⓒ Ⓓ Ⓔ
9 Ⓐ Ⓑ Ⓒ Ⓓ Ⓔ
10 Ⓐ Ⓑ Ⓒ Ⓓ Ⓔ
11 Ⓐ Ⓑ Ⓒ Ⓓ Ⓔ
12 Ⓐ Ⓑ Ⓒ Ⓓ Ⓔ
13 Ⓐ Ⓑ Ⓒ Ⓓ Ⓔ
14 Ⓐ Ⓑ Ⓒ Ⓓ Ⓔ
15 Ⓐ Ⓑ Ⓒ Ⓓ Ⓔ
16 Ⓐ Ⓑ Ⓒ Ⓓ Ⓔ
17 Ⓐ Ⓑ Ⓒ Ⓓ Ⓔ
18 Ⓐ Ⓑ Ⓒ Ⓓ Ⓔ
19 Ⓐ Ⓑ Ⓒ Ⓓ Ⓔ
20 Ⓐ Ⓑ Ⓒ Ⓓ Ⓔ
21 Ⓐ Ⓑ Ⓒ Ⓓ Ⓔ
22 Ⓐ Ⓑ Ⓒ Ⓓ Ⓔ
23 Ⓐ Ⓑ Ⓒ Ⓓ Ⓔ
24 Ⓐ Ⓑ Ⓒ Ⓓ Ⓔ
25 Ⓐ Ⓑ Ⓒ Ⓓ Ⓔ
26 Ⓐ Ⓑ Ⓒ Ⓓ Ⓔ
27 Ⓐ Ⓑ Ⓒ Ⓓ Ⓔ
28 Ⓐ Ⓑ Ⓒ Ⓓ Ⓔ
29 Ⓐ Ⓑ Ⓒ Ⓓ Ⓔ
30 Ⓐ Ⓑ Ⓒ Ⓓ Ⓔ

Section 2 — Math
30 minutes

1 Ⓐ Ⓑ Ⓒ Ⓓ Ⓔ
2 Ⓐ Ⓑ Ⓒ Ⓓ Ⓔ
3 Ⓐ Ⓑ Ⓒ Ⓓ Ⓔ
4 Ⓐ Ⓑ Ⓒ Ⓓ Ⓔ
5 Ⓐ Ⓑ Ⓒ Ⓓ Ⓔ
6 Ⓐ Ⓑ Ⓒ Ⓓ Ⓔ
7 Ⓐ Ⓑ Ⓒ Ⓓ Ⓔ
8 Ⓐ Ⓑ Ⓒ Ⓓ Ⓔ
9 Ⓐ Ⓑ Ⓒ Ⓓ Ⓔ
10 Ⓐ Ⓑ Ⓒ Ⓓ Ⓔ
11 Ⓐ Ⓑ Ⓒ Ⓓ Ⓔ
12 Ⓐ Ⓑ Ⓒ Ⓓ Ⓔ
13 Ⓐ Ⓑ Ⓒ Ⓓ Ⓔ
14 Ⓐ Ⓑ Ⓒ Ⓓ Ⓔ
15 Ⓐ Ⓑ Ⓒ Ⓓ Ⓔ
16 Ⓐ Ⓑ Ⓒ Ⓓ Ⓔ
17 Ⓐ Ⓑ Ⓒ Ⓓ Ⓔ
18 Ⓐ Ⓑ Ⓒ Ⓓ Ⓔ
19 Ⓐ Ⓑ Ⓒ Ⓓ Ⓔ
20 Ⓐ Ⓑ Ⓒ Ⓓ Ⓔ
21 Ⓐ Ⓑ Ⓒ Ⓓ Ⓔ
22 Ⓐ Ⓑ Ⓒ Ⓓ Ⓔ
23 Ⓐ Ⓑ Ⓒ Ⓓ Ⓔ
24 Ⓐ Ⓑ Ⓒ Ⓓ Ⓔ
25 Ⓐ Ⓑ Ⓒ Ⓓ Ⓔ

Section 3 — Writing
30 minutes

1 Ⓐ Ⓑ Ⓒ Ⓓ Ⓔ
2 Ⓐ Ⓑ Ⓒ Ⓓ Ⓔ
3 Ⓐ Ⓑ Ⓒ Ⓓ Ⓔ
4 Ⓐ Ⓑ Ⓒ Ⓓ Ⓔ
5 Ⓐ Ⓑ Ⓒ Ⓓ Ⓔ
6 Ⓐ Ⓑ Ⓒ Ⓓ Ⓔ
7 Ⓐ Ⓑ Ⓒ Ⓓ Ⓔ
8 Ⓐ Ⓑ Ⓒ Ⓓ Ⓔ
9 Ⓐ Ⓑ Ⓒ Ⓓ Ⓔ
10 Ⓐ Ⓑ Ⓒ Ⓓ Ⓔ
11 Ⓐ Ⓑ Ⓒ Ⓓ Ⓔ
12 Ⓐ Ⓑ Ⓒ Ⓓ Ⓔ
13 Ⓐ Ⓑ Ⓒ Ⓓ Ⓔ
14 Ⓐ Ⓑ Ⓒ Ⓓ Ⓔ
15 Ⓐ Ⓑ Ⓒ Ⓓ Ⓔ
16 Ⓐ Ⓑ Ⓒ Ⓓ Ⓔ
17 Ⓐ Ⓑ Ⓒ Ⓓ Ⓔ
18 Ⓐ Ⓑ Ⓒ Ⓓ Ⓔ
19 Ⓐ Ⓑ Ⓒ Ⓓ Ⓔ
20 Ⓐ Ⓑ Ⓒ Ⓓ Ⓔ
21 Ⓐ Ⓑ Ⓒ Ⓓ Ⓔ
22 Ⓐ Ⓑ Ⓒ Ⓓ Ⓔ
23 Ⓐ Ⓑ Ⓒ Ⓓ Ⓔ
24 Ⓐ Ⓑ Ⓒ Ⓓ Ⓔ
25 Ⓐ Ⓑ Ⓒ Ⓓ Ⓔ
26 Ⓐ Ⓑ Ⓒ Ⓓ Ⓔ
27 Ⓐ Ⓑ Ⓒ Ⓓ Ⓔ
28 Ⓐ Ⓑ Ⓒ Ⓓ Ⓔ
29 Ⓐ Ⓑ Ⓒ Ⓓ Ⓔ
30 Ⓐ Ⓑ Ⓒ Ⓓ Ⓔ
31 Ⓐ Ⓑ Ⓒ Ⓓ Ⓔ
32 Ⓐ Ⓑ Ⓒ Ⓓ Ⓔ
33 Ⓐ Ⓑ Ⓒ Ⓓ Ⓔ
34 Ⓐ Ⓑ Ⓒ Ⓓ Ⓔ
35 Ⓐ Ⓑ Ⓒ Ⓓ Ⓔ
36 Ⓐ Ⓑ Ⓒ Ⓓ Ⓔ
37 Ⓐ Ⓑ Ⓒ Ⓓ Ⓔ
38 Ⓐ Ⓑ Ⓒ Ⓓ Ⓔ
39 Ⓐ Ⓑ Ⓒ Ⓓ Ⓔ

Section 4 — Verbal
30 minutes

31 Ⓐ Ⓑ Ⓒ Ⓓ Ⓔ
32 Ⓐ Ⓑ Ⓒ Ⓓ Ⓔ
33 Ⓐ Ⓑ Ⓒ Ⓓ Ⓔ
34 Ⓐ Ⓑ Ⓒ Ⓓ Ⓔ
35 Ⓐ Ⓑ Ⓒ Ⓓ Ⓔ
36 Ⓐ Ⓑ Ⓒ Ⓓ Ⓔ
37 Ⓐ Ⓑ Ⓒ Ⓓ Ⓔ
38 Ⓐ Ⓑ Ⓒ Ⓓ Ⓔ
39 Ⓐ Ⓑ Ⓒ Ⓓ Ⓔ
40 Ⓐ Ⓑ Ⓒ Ⓓ Ⓔ
41 Ⓐ Ⓑ Ⓒ Ⓓ Ⓔ
42 Ⓐ Ⓑ Ⓒ Ⓓ Ⓔ
43 Ⓐ Ⓑ Ⓒ Ⓓ Ⓔ
44 Ⓐ Ⓑ Ⓒ Ⓓ Ⓔ
45 Ⓐ Ⓑ Ⓒ Ⓓ Ⓔ
46 Ⓐ Ⓑ Ⓒ Ⓓ Ⓔ
47 Ⓐ Ⓑ Ⓒ Ⓓ Ⓔ
48 Ⓐ Ⓑ Ⓒ Ⓓ Ⓔ
49 Ⓐ Ⓑ Ⓒ Ⓓ Ⓔ
50 Ⓐ Ⓑ Ⓒ Ⓓ Ⓔ
51 Ⓐ Ⓑ Ⓒ Ⓓ Ⓔ
52 Ⓐ Ⓑ Ⓒ Ⓓ Ⓔ
53 Ⓐ Ⓑ Ⓒ Ⓓ Ⓔ
54 Ⓐ Ⓑ Ⓒ Ⓓ Ⓔ
55 Ⓐ Ⓑ Ⓒ Ⓓ Ⓔ
56 Ⓐ Ⓑ Ⓒ Ⓓ Ⓔ
57 Ⓐ Ⓑ Ⓒ Ⓓ Ⓔ
58 Ⓐ Ⓑ Ⓒ Ⓓ Ⓔ
59 Ⓐ Ⓑ Ⓒ Ⓓ Ⓔ
60 Ⓐ Ⓑ Ⓒ Ⓓ Ⓔ

Section 5 — Math
30 minutes

26 Ⓐ Ⓑ Ⓒ Ⓓ Ⓔ
27 Ⓐ Ⓑ Ⓒ Ⓓ Ⓔ
28 Ⓐ Ⓑ Ⓒ Ⓓ Ⓔ
29 Ⓐ Ⓑ Ⓒ Ⓓ Ⓔ
30 Ⓐ Ⓑ Ⓒ Ⓓ Ⓔ
31 Ⓐ Ⓑ Ⓒ Ⓓ Ⓔ
32 Ⓐ Ⓑ Ⓒ Ⓓ Ⓔ
33 Ⓐ Ⓑ Ⓒ Ⓓ Ⓔ
34 Ⓐ Ⓑ Ⓒ Ⓓ Ⓔ
35 Ⓐ Ⓑ Ⓒ Ⓓ Ⓔ
36 Ⓐ Ⓑ Ⓒ Ⓓ Ⓔ
37 Ⓐ Ⓑ Ⓒ Ⓓ Ⓔ
39 Ⓐ Ⓑ Ⓒ Ⓓ Ⓔ
39 Ⓐ Ⓑ Ⓒ Ⓓ Ⓔ
40 Ⓐ Ⓑ Ⓒ Ⓓ Ⓔ

41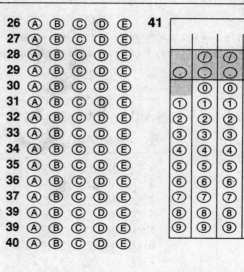

42

43

44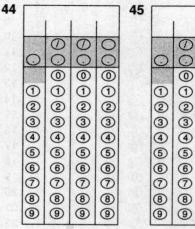

45

46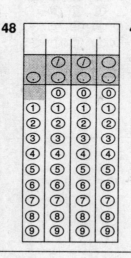

47

48

49

50